The Globalization of World Politics

THE GLOBALIZATION OF WORLD POLITICS

An introduction to international relations

Fourth edition

John Baylis • Steve Smith • Patricia Owens

OXFORD

UNIVERSITY PRESS

Great Clarendon Street, Oxford OX2 6DP

Oxford University Press is a department of the University of Oxford.
It furthers the University's objective of excellence in research, scholarship,
and education by publishing worldwide in

Oxford New York

Auckland Cape Town Dar es Salaam Hong Kong Karachi
Kuala Lumpur Madrid Melbourne Mexico City Nairobi
New Delhi Shanghai Taipei Toronto

With offices in

Argentina Austria Brazil Chile Czech Republic France Greece
Guatemala Hungary Italy Japan Poland Portugal Singapore
South Korea Switzerland Thailand Turkey Ukraine Vietnam

Oxford is a registered trade mark of Oxford University Press
in the UK and in certain other countries

Published in the United States
by Oxford University Press Inc., New York

First published 1997
Second edition 2001
Third edition 2005
Fourth edition 2008

British Library Cataloguing in Publication Data

Data available

Library of Congress Cataloging in Publication Data

The globalization of world politics : an introduction to international

relations / John Baylis, Steve Smith, Patricia Owens. — 4th ed.

p. cm.

ISBN 978–0–19–929777–1

1. International relations—Textbooks. 2. World politics—1989—Textbooks.

I. Baylis, John, 1946– II. Smith, Steve,1952–

III. Owens, Patricia, 1975– JZ1242.G58 2007

327—dc22 2007040813

Typeset by Laserwords Private Limited, Chennai, India
Printed in Spain
on acid-free paper by
Graficas Estella

ISBN 978–0–19–929777–1

1 3 5 7 9 10 8 6 4 2

Dedicated with love to Marion, Jeannie, and Jane

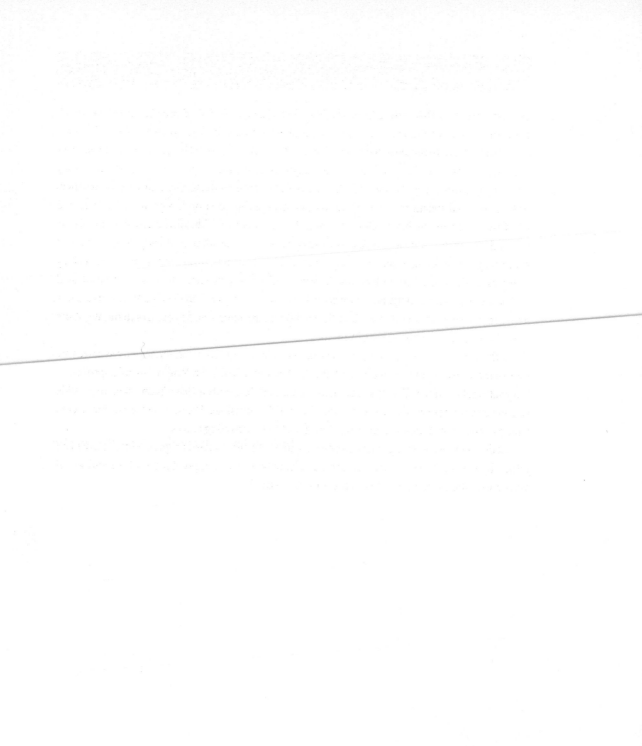

Preface

We have tried in this new edition of *The Globalization of World Politics* to follow much the same format as the previous three editions which have proved so successful. However, a number of improvements have been made. Oxford University Press commissioned over twenty reviews of the third edition, and we gained enormously from their comments. They told us what worked and what didn't. We have also been contacted by many of the teachers of International Relations around the world who use the book on a regular basis. Together, all of these comments have helped us identify a number of additional areas that should be covered. To make sure we didn't make the book even longer than it already was, we cut out some chapters that had appeared in the third edition, and also combined some of the history chapters. In their place we added new chapters on the changing character of war, international ethics, and human security. Based on reviewers' comments, we also decided to commission a new chapter on gender and move it to the section on Structures and Processes to highlight the role of gender in structuring world politics.

As the book has been taken up as a major text in more and more countries we have become increasingly aware of the danger of what might be described as an 'Anglo-Saxon' approach to international relations. For this reason, in the new edition, authors have been asked to provide as wide a range of examples from around the world as possible. We have also introduced case studies which focus, in particular, on Africa and the developing world.

Readers who have used previous editions will notice that the two original editors have been joined by Patricia Owens. Patricia had been heavily involved in previous editions and we all agreed that she should become a full editor of the book.

Acknowledgements

Once again we would like to thank all those who sent us or Oxford University Press comments on the strengths and weaknesses of the third edition. We hope that those who have gone to the trouble of contributing to the review process will see many of the changes they recommended reflected in the new edition. We would also like to thank our contributors for being so helpful in responding yet again to our detailed requests for revisions to the chapters that had appeared in the third volume. We would also like to thank those whose chapters appeared in the previous editions but which do not appear in the fourth edition. Thank you for your understanding.

However, our most sincere thanks must go to Sheena Chestnut, who has done a truly splendid job in helping us with the editorial work with this new edition. She has been untiring, extremely efficient, and conscientious in the work she has done. The editorial burden on her shoulders has been very heavy at times, especially as she has had to contend also with examinations at Oxford. However, she has never complained and always completed the tasks we have given her with great dedication. The book is significantly better as a result of her contribution. The editors would also like yet again to thank Ruth Anderson of Oxford University Press for her professionalism, support, and advice during the production of this new edition, and Sarah Bury for her excellent copy-editing.

John Baylis, Steve Smith, and Patricia Owens

This text is enriched with a range of learning tools to help you navigate the text material and reinforce your knowledge of International Relations. This guided tour shows you how to get the most out of your textbook package.

Reader's Guides

Reader's Guides at the beginning of every chapter set the scene for upcoming themes and issues to be discussed, and indicate the scope of coverage within each chapter topic.

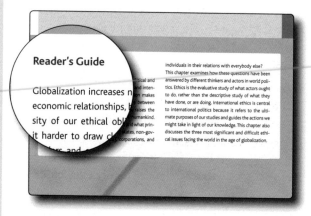

Reader's Guide

Globalization increases n... economic relationships, b... sity of our ethical obl... it harder to draw cl...

individuals in their relations with everybody else? This chapter examines how these questions have been answered by different thinkers and actors in world politics. Ethics is the evaluative study of what actors ought to do, rather than the descriptive study of what they have done, or are doing. International ethics is central to international politics because it refers to the ultimate purposes of our studies and guides the actions we might take in light of our knowledge. This chapter also discusses the three most significant and difficult ethical issues facing the world in the age of globalization.

Boxes

A number of topics benefit from further explanation or exploration in a way that does not disrupt the flow of the main text. Throughout the book boxes provide you with extra information on particular topics to complement your understanding of the main chapter text.

roles are to states' foreign policies and to the functioning of the global economy.

But making women visible does not explain why they are disproportionately situated in low-paid or nonremunerated occupations far from the halls of power. To explain this we must put on our gendered lenses and think abou...

Box 15.1 Gender-S...

'[A gender-sensitive lens] e... shaped by gendered concepts, ... Whenever we study a to... focuses our attention in pa... ing" what we look at, each ... reater detail or more ...

so often taken for granted in how the world is organized is, in fact, keeping in place certain social arrangements and institutional structures which contribute to the subordination of women and other disadvantaged groups.

To help them answer these questions IR feminists use a number of different theoretical approaches that build on feminist theory more generally (see also Ch.10). Let us look at some examples.

Liberal feminism

Liberal feminists document various aspects of women's subordination. They have investigated problems of refugee women, income inequalities between women and men, and the kinds of human rights violations incurred disproportionately by women, such as trafficking and rape in war. They look for women in the institutions and practices of global politics and observe how their presence (or lack thereof) affects and is affected by international policy-making. They ask what a world with more women in positions of power might look like. Liberal feminists believe that women's equality can be achieved

Case Study boxes demonstrate how political ideas, concepts, and issues manifest in the real world.

Case study: Is i...

tional law during the nineteenth century [Gong 1984]. According to this standard, non-Western polities were granted sovereign recognition only if they exhibited certain domestic political characteristics and only if they were willing and capable of participating in the prevailing diplomatic practices. The standard was heavily biased towards Western political and legal institutions as the accepted model. On the basis of the standard, European power divided the world's peoples into 'civilized', 'barbarian', and 'savage' societies, a division they used to justify various degrees of Western tutelage.

Many claim that Western bias still characterizes the international legal order. Cited here is the Anglo-European dominance of peak legal institutions, most notably the United Nations Security Council, and international human rights law, which is said to impose as set of Western values about the rights of the individual on non-Western societies where such ideas are alien. These biases are seen as coming together around the issue of humanitarian intervention. Western powers are accused of using their privileged position on the Security Council, and brandishing human rights norms, to intervene in the domestic politics of weak, developing countries.

All of these criticisms have veracity. However, the nature and role of international law in contemporary world politics is more complex than it at first appears. To begin with, at the heart of the modern international legal system lies a set of customary norms that uphold the legal equality of all sovereign states, as well as their rights to self-determination and non-intervention. Non-Western states have been the most vigorous proponents and defenders of these cardinal legal norms, and their survival as independent

From one perspective, international law is easily cast as a Western,

Key Points

Each main chapter section ends with a set of Key Points that summarize the most important arguments developed within that chapter topic.

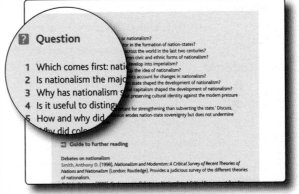

Questions

A set of carefully devised questions has been provided to help you assess your comprehension of core themes and may also be used as the basis of seminar discussion and coursework.

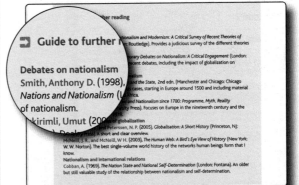

Further Reading

To take your learning further, reading lists have been provided as a guide to find out more about the issues raised within each chapter topic and to help you locate the key academic literature in the field.

Glossary Terms

Key terms appear in blue in the text and are defined in a glossary at the end of the book to aid you in exam revision.

www.oxfordtextbooks.co.uk/orc/baylis_smith4e/

The Online Resource Centre that accompanies this book provides students and instructors with ready-to-use teaching and learning materials.

For students

Case studies

Four case studies apply International Relations theories to the following topics: the 1999 Kosovo crisis, the 1990–91 Gulf War, the 2003 Iraq War, and China.

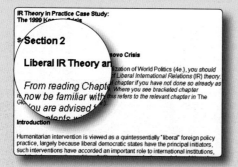

Video podcasts from the contributors

Listen to contributors from the book analysing current issues and extend and apply your knowledge to new situations.

News feeds

These feeds provide you with access to relevant articles from different news sites.

Links to OUP journal articles

These allow you to access the text of different OUP journal articles in the areas you are interested in.

Multiple choice questions

A bank of self-marking multiple choice questions has been provided for each chapter of the text. It gives instant feedback on your answers to help strengthen your knowledge.

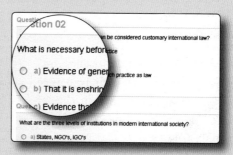

Flashcard glossary

A series of interactive flashcards containing key terms and concepts has been provided to test your understanding of terminology.

Web links

An annotated list of key web links allows you to easily research the topics that are of particular interest to you.

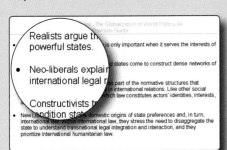

Revision guide

A checklist of the key points from each chapter.

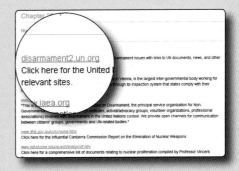

For lecturers

PowerPoint Slides

A suite of customizable PowerPoint slides has been included for use in lectures. Arranged by chapter, the slides may also be used as handouts in class.

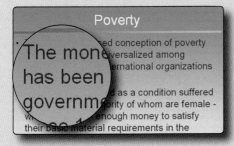

Question bank

A suite of short answer and essay questions allows you to test your students further and provides them with valuable exam practice.

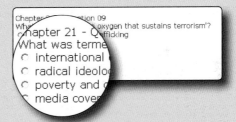

Figures and tables from the textbook

All figures and tables in the textbook are available to download electronically to assist preparation and help explain key concepts.

Test bank

Offers versatile testing tailored to the textbook and contains over 450 multiple choice and true/false questions. Downloadable to Virtual Learning Environments and also available in print format.

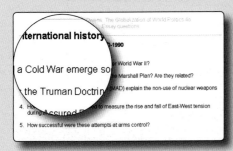

Brief contents

List of figures ⋯⋯⋯⋯⋯⋯⋯⋯⋯⋯⋯⋯ xxvii

List of boxes and case studies ⋯⋯⋯⋯⋯⋯⋯ xxviii

List of tables ⋯⋯⋯⋯⋯⋯⋯⋯⋯⋯⋯ xxxiii

About the contributors ⋯⋯⋯⋯⋯⋯⋯⋯ xxxiv

World map ⋯⋯⋯⋯⋯⋯⋯⋯⋯⋯⋯⋯ xl

Introduction ⋯⋯⋯⋯⋯⋯⋯⋯⋯⋯⋯⋯ 0
John Baylis, Steve Smith, and Patricia Owens

1 Globalization and global politics ⋯⋯⋯⋯⋯ 14
Anthony McGrew

Part One The historical context

2 The evolution of international society ⋯⋯⋯⋯ 36
David Armstrong

3 International history, 1900–90 ⋯⋯⋯⋯⋯⋯ 54
Len Scott

4 From the cold war to the war on terror ⋯⋯⋯ 70
Michael Cox

Part Two Theories of world politics

5 Realism ⋯⋯⋯⋯⋯⋯⋯⋯⋯⋯⋯⋯⋯ 90
Tim Dunne and Brian C. Schmidt

6 Liberalism ⋯⋯⋯⋯⋯⋯⋯⋯⋯⋯⋯⋯ 108
Tim Dunne

7 Contemporary mainstream approaches: neo-realism and neo-liberalism ⋯⋯⋯⋯ 124
Steven L. Lamy

8 Marxist theories of international relations ⋯⋯⋯ 142
Stephen Hobden and Richard Wyn Jones

9 Social Constructivism ⋯⋯⋯⋯⋯⋯⋯⋯ 160
Michael Barnett

10 Alternative approaches to international theory ⋯⋯ 174
Steve Smith and Patricia Owens

11 International ethics ⋯⋯⋯⋯⋯⋯⋯⋯⋯ 192
Richard Shapcott

Part Three Structures and processes

12 The changing character of war ⋯⋯⋯⋯⋯ 210
Mike Sheehan

13 International and global security ⋯⋯⋯⋯⋯ 226
John Baylis

14 **International political economy in an age of globalization** ·················242
    Ngaire Woods

15 **Gender in world politics** ·················262
    J. Ann Tickner

16 **International law** ·················278
    Christian Reus-Smit

17   **International regimes** ·················296
    Richard Little

18 **The United Nations** ·················312
    Paul Taylor and Devon Curtis

19 **Transnational actors and international organizations in global politics** ·················330
    Peter Willetts

Part Four International issues

20 **Environmental issues** ·················350
    John Vogler

21 **Terrorism and globalization** ·················370
    James D. Kiras

22 **Nuclear proliferation** ·················386
    Darryl Howlett

23 **Nationalism** ·················402
    John Breuilly

24 **Culture in world affairs** ·················418
    Simon Murden

25 **Regionalism in international affairs** ·················434
    Edward Best and Thomas Christiansen

26 **Global trade and finance** ·················450
    Jan Aart Scholte

27 **Poverty, development, and hunger** ·················468
    Caroline Thomas

28 **Human security** ·················490
    Amitav Acharya

29 **Human rights** ·················506
    Chris Brown

30 **Humanitarian intervention in world politics** ·················522
    Alex J. Bellamy and Nicholas J. Wheeler

Part Five Globalization in the future

31 **Globalization and the transformation of political community** ·······················542
    Andrew Linklater

32 **Globalization and the post-cold war order** ··560
    Ian Clark

Glossary ··577
References ···591
Index ···607

Detailed contents

List of figures ···xxvii
List of boxes and case studies ······························xxviii
List of tables ··xxxiii
About the contributors ·····································xxxiv
World map ···xl

Introduction ···0
From international politics to world politics   3
Theories of world politics   3
The four theories and globalization   6
Globalization and its precursors   8
Globalization: myth or reality?   10

1 Globalization and global politics ···············14
Introduction   16
Making sense of globalization   16
Conceptualizing globalization   18
Contemporary globalization   20
A world transformed: globalization and distorted global politics   23
From distorted global politics to cosmopolitan global politics?   29
Conclusion   32

Part One The historical context

2 The evolution of international society ············36
Introduction: the idea of international society   38
Ancient worlds   39
The Christian and Islamic orders   42
The emergence of the modern international society   44
The globalization of international society   48
Conclusion: problems of global international society 49

3 International history, 1900–90 ··························54
Introduction   56
Modern total war   56
End of empire   58
Cold war   60
Conclusion   67

4   **From the cold war to the war on terror** ·· 70

Introduction   72

The end of the cold war   72

Mapping the post-cold war era   74

From superpower to hyperpower—US primacy   75

Europe in the new world system   77

Russia: from Yeltsin to Putin   78

East Asia: primed for rivalry?   80

The haves and the have nots   81

The war on terror: from 9/11 to Iraq   83

Conclusion   86

Part Two   Theories of world politics

5   **Realism** ·· 90

Introduction: the timeless wisdom of Realism   92

One Realism, or many?   95

The essential Realism   100

Conclusion: Realism and the globalization of world politics   103

6   **Liberalism** ·· 108

Introduction   110

Core ideas in Liberal thinking on international relations   112

Liberalism and globalization   116

Conclusion   120

7   **Contemporary mainstream approaches: neo-realism and neo-liberalism** ·············· 124

Introduction   126

Neo-realism   127

Neo-liberalism   131

The neo-neo debate   133

Neo-liberals and neo-realists on globalization   136

Conclusion: narrowing the agenda of international relations   137

8   **Marxist theories of international relations** ································· 142

Introduction: the continuing relevance of Marxism   144

The essential elements of Marxist theories of world politics   145

World-system theory   147

Gramscianism   149

Critical theory   153

New Marxism   155

Conclusion: Marxist theories of international relations and globalization   157

9   **Social Constructivism** ·· 160

Introduction   162

The main Constructivist tenets   162

Constructivism and global change   168

Conclusion '   171

10 **Alternative approaches to international theory** ·······················174

Introduction   176

Explanatory/constitutive theories and foundational/anti-foundational theories   176

Historical sociology   179

Feminist theory   181

Post-modernism   185

Post-colonialism   187

Conclusion   190

11 **International ethics** ···192

Introduction   194

The ethical significance of boundaries: cosmopolitanism and its alternatives   194

Anti-cosmopolitanism: realism and pluralism   199

Global ethical issues   201

Conclusion   205

Part Three Structures and processes

12 **The changing character of war** ···210

Introduction   212

Definitions   213

The nature of war   214

The revolution in military affairs   217

Post-modern war   219

New wars   221

Conclusion   224

13 **International and global security** ···226

Introduction   228

What is meant by the concept of security?   229

The traditional approach to national security   230

The difficulties of cooperation between states   232

The opportunities for cooperation between states   232

Alternative views on international and global security   234

Critical security studies   235

Global society and international security   236

Conclusion: the continuing tensions between national, international, and global security 238

14 **International political economy in an age of globalization** ···········242

Introduction   244

The post-war world-economy   244

Traditional and new approaches to IPE   248

The globalization debate in IPE   252

International institutions in the globalizing world-economy   256

Conclusion   258

15 Gender in world politics   262

Introduction   264

Feminist theories   264

Feminists define gender   265

Putting a gender lens on global politics   266

Gendering security   268

Gender in the global economy   271

Using knowledge to inform policy practice   273

Conclusion   276

16 International law   278

Introduction: the paradox of international law   280

Order and institutions   280

The modern institution of international law   281

From international to supranational law?   286

The laws of war   288

Theoretical approaches to international law   289

Conclusion   293

17 International regimes   296

Introduction   298

The nature of regimes   300

Competing theories of regime formation   302

Conclusion   307

18 The United Nations   312

Introduction   314

A brief history of the United Nations and its principal organs   314

The United Nations and the maintenance of international peace and security   319

The United Nations and intervention within states   321

The United Nations and economic and social questions   324

The reform process in the economic and social arrangements of the United Nations   326

Conclusion   327

19 Transnational actors and international organizations in global politics   330

Introduction   332

Problems with the state-centric approach   332

Transnational companies as political actors   334

Non-legitimate groups and liberation movements as political actors   337

Non-governmental organizations as political actors   339

International organizations as structures of global politics   341

Conclusion: issues and policy systems in global politics   342

Part Four International issues

20 Environmental issues 350

Introduction 352

Environmental issues on the international agenda: a brief history 353

The functions of international environmental cooperation 356

Climate change 361

The environment and International Relations theory 365

Conclusion 366

21 Terrorism and globalization 370

Introduction 372

Definitions 372

Terrorism: from transnational to global phenomenon (1968–2001) 374

Terrorism: the impact of globalization 375

Globalization, technology, and terrorism 378

Combating terrorism 382

Conclusion 384

22 Nuclear proliferation 386

Introduction 388

Nature of nuclear weapons and their effects 389

Diffusion of nuclear and missile technology 391

Theorizing nuclear proliferation and non-proliferation 392

Evolution of global nuclear control and anti-proliferation measures 396

Conclusion 399

23 Nationalism 402

Introduction: concepts and debates 404

Nationalism, nation-states, and global politics in history 406

Nationalism, nation-states, and global politics today 412

Conclusion 414

24 Culture in world affairs 418

Introduction: culture in human affairs 420

The counter-revolutionaries of the global age 423

A counter-revolution at the civilization level?: the case of Islam 426

Islamic fundamentalism 427

Conclusion 431

25 Regionalism in international affairs 434

Introduction 436

Regional cooperation and regional integration 436

Regional cooperation in a global context 438

The process of European integration 444

Conclusion 447

26 Global trade and finance 450

Introduction 452

A globalizing economy 453

Global trade 457

Global finance 459

Continuity and change in economic globalization 462

Conclusion 466

27 Poverty, development, and hunger 468

Introduction 470

Poverty 471

Development 473

Hunger 482

Conclusion: looking to the future—globalization with a human face? 487

28 Human security 490

Introduction 492

What is human security? 492

Debates about human security 494

Dimensions of human security 496

Promoting human security 502

Conclusion 504

29 Human rights 506

Introduction 508

On rights in general 510

The liberal account of human rights 511

1948 and the modern agenda 513

Political and economic rights 514

Universalism challenged 516

Conclusion 519

30 Humanitarian intervention in world politics 522

Introduction 524

The case for humanitarian intervention 524

The case against humanitarian intervention 526

The 1990s: a golden era of humanitarian activism? 528

Humanitarian intervention and the war on terror 531

The responsibility to protect 535

Conclusion 538

Part Five Globalization in the future

31 **Globalization and the transformation of political community** ·················542

Introduction: what is a political community?   544

Nationalism and political community   545

Community and citizenship   547

The changing nature of political community   549

Beyond Realism?   553

Conclusion   556

32 **Globalization and the post-cold war order** ·················560

Introduction   562

A typology of order   563

The elements of contemporary order   564

Globalization and the post-Westphalian order?   567

Globalization and legitimacy   569

An international order of globalized states?   571

Conclusion   573

Glossary ·················577

References ·················591

Index ·················607

List of figures

1.1 The World Wide Web ···································· 25
1.2 The global governance complex ···················· 26
1.3 The disaggregated state···························· 29

8.1 The base–superstructure model ···················· 146
8.2 Interrelationships in the world-economy············ 148

10.1 International theory at the beginning of the twenty-first century ··· 178

18.1 The structure of the United Nations system············ 316

19.1 Who controls the United Kingdom subsidiary of a US TNC? ··· 336
19.2 The growth of NGOs at the UN···················· 339
19.3 The orthodox view of international relations ············ 344
19.4 The full range of international connections ············ 344

20.1 Map of world in proportion to carbon emissions············ 352
20.2 Greenhouse gas contributions to global warming············ 361

27.1 GDP per capita in the poorest and richest countries, 1960–2 and 2000–2 ··· 470
27.2 Millennium Development Goals: 2006 progress chart for selected goals··· 478
27.3 Global hunger map, 2006···························· 482
27.4 World population growth from 1800 with projections to 2050··· 483
27.5 Most populous countries, 2003, with projections to 2050 ··· 484

28.1 Conflicts by type, 1946–2005···························· 497
28.2 Conflict and underdevelopment: the vicious interaction ··· 499
28.3 Protection and development: the virtuous interaction ··· 500

32.1 Outside-in view of globalization ···················· 572
32.2 Inside-out view of globalization ···················· 572

List of boxes and case studies

Box 1.1   Definitions of globalization ·· 17

Case Study 1   Global production and the iPod ·· 19

Box 1.2   Globalization since 9/11 ·· 20

Box 1.3   The sceptical view of globalization ································· 21

Box 1.4   Patterns of contemporary globalization ······················· 21

Box 1.5   The engines of globalization ··· 22

Box 1.6   The three waves of globalization ····································· 22

Box 1.7   The Westphalian Constitution of world politics ··········· 23

Box 1.8   The post-Westphalian order ·· 24

Case Study 2   Security and violence in global politics ························· 27

Box 1.9   Cosmopolitan democracy ·· 30

Box 2.1   Bull on international society ·· 38

Box 2.2   Key dates ··· 40

Box 2.3   The Council of Constance ·· 45

Case Study   The Iranian Revolution 1979 ·· 49

Box 2.4   Robert Jackson on freedom and international society ····· 50

Box 2.5   Andrew Hurrell on the future of international society ····· 51

Case Study   The Cuban missile crisis ··· 63

Box 4.1   The end of an era ·· 73

Box 4.2   The gravity of globalization ·· 75

Box 4.3   The paradox of power ··· 76

Box 4.4   Europe's mid-life crisis? ·· 78

Box 4.5   A new cold war? ··· 79

Box 4.6   The China challenge ·· 81

Box 4.7   Poverty threats ·· 82

Box 4.8   End the crusade ··· 85

Case Study   The Iraq War and its origins ·· 85

Box 5.1   Realism and intra-state war ··· 94

Case Study   The Melian dialogue—realism and the preparation for war ·· 97

Box 5.2   Realism against wars: an unlikely alliance? ···················· 104

Box 6.1   Liberalism and the causes of war, determinants of peace ·· 111

Box 6.2   Immanuel Kant's 'Perpetual Peace: A Philosophical Sketch' ·· 112

Case Study   The 1990–1 Gulf War and collective security ················· 115

Box 6.3   George W. Bush and Liberalism in American foreign policy ·· 117

Box 6.4   Defending and extending the liberal zone of peace ········ 118

Case Study   'The underbelly of globalization': toxic waste dumping in the global South ··· 128

Box 7.1   Core assumptions of neo-realists ···································· 130

Box 7.2   The main features of the neo-realist/neo-liberal debate ·· 133

Box 7.3   Neo-liberalism and its current critics···136

Box 8.1   Indicators of world inequality··146
Case Study   The politics of neo-liberalism··152

Case Study   Social construction of refugees···164
Box 9.1   Alexander Wendt on the three cultures of anarchy································165
Box 9.2   Charli Carpenter on the effects of gender on the lives of
           individuals in war-torn societies··166
Box 9.3   Finnemore and Sikkink on the three stages of the life-cycle
           of norms···170

Box 10.1   Mann's IEMP model of power organization·······································180
Box 10.2   V. Spike Peterson on the global political economy and
           the sex/gender distinction··184
Box 10.3   Foucault's notion of genealogy···186
Box 10.4   Post-modern methodologies···187
Case Study   Edward Said on Orientalism··189

Box 11.1   Cosmopolitanism, realism, and pluralism···195
Box 11.2   The categorical imperative··197
Case Study 1   Ethics of global warming··198
Box 11.3   Rawls' *The Law of Peoples*··200
Box 11.4   The just war···201
Case Study 2   *Jus in bello*: saturation bombing··202
Box 11.5   Islamic just war tradition···202
Box 11.6   Peter Singer on distributive justice··203
Box 11.7   Rawls and the 'original position'··203
Box 11.8   Thomas Pogge on international order···204

Box 12.1   The obsolescence of war··212
Box 12.2   Thucydides on war··214
Case Study   The Iraq War, 2003–7··218
Box 12.3   Asymmetric warfare··218
Box 12.4   The revolution in military affairs: a cautionary note·····························219
Box 12.5   Globalization and war···221
Box 12.6   'Third tier' states··223

Box 13.1   Notions of 'security'··229
Box 13.2   Key definitions···230
Box 13.3   Democratic peace theory··233
Case Study   Insecurity in the post-cold war world: the case of the
           Democratic Republic of the Congo··238
Box 13.4   Observations on 9/11···240

Box 14.1   Planning the post-war economy and avoiding another
             Great Depression ·· 244
Box 14.2   The Bretton Woods institutions: the IMF and the World Bank ···························· 245
Box 14.3   The 'Bretton Woods system' and its breakdown ·················· 245
Box 14.4   The post-war trading system, the GATT, and the WHO ··········· 246
Box 14.5   Traditional perspectives on IPE ······························· 250
Box 14.6   Examples of new approaches to IPE ····························· 251
Box 14.7   Four aspects of globalization ································· 252
Box 14.8   The globalists ··· 253
Box 14.9   The sceptics ··· 254
Box 14.10   The Asian financial crisis ····································· 254
Case Study   The impact of globalization on different kinds of states ······· 255
Box 14.11   Anti-globalization protests against international organizations ········· 256

Box 15.1   Gender-sensitive lenses ·· 266
Box 15.2   Women leaders ·· 266
Box 15.3   Military prostitution as a security issue ····················· 269
Box 15.4   Challenging gender expectations: women workers organize ········· 272
Case Study 1 Microcredit: empowering women through investment ··············· 272
Box 15.5   Milestones in women's organizing ······························· 274
Box 15.6   Gender development index and gender mainstreaming ············· 274
Case Study 2 The self-employed women's movement ·························· 275

Box 16.1   Levels of international institutions ··························· 281
Box 16.2   Key constitutive legal treaties ······························· 282
Box 16.3   Features of the modern institution of international law ········· 285
Case Study   Is international law an expression of Western dominance? ········· 286

Box 17.1   Liberal Institutional v. Realist approaches to the analysis of regimes ··········· 298
Box 17.2   Defining regimes ··· 300
Box 17.3   The game of Prisoners' Dilemma ································· 304
Box 17.4   The Battle of the Sexes and Pareto's frontier ················· 306
Case Study   International whaling moratorium ······························· 308

Box 18.1   Selected Articles of the UN Charter ··························· 315
Box 18.2   The reform of the Security Council ····························· 317
Box 18.3   An agenda for peace ·· 320
Box 18.4   The UN Peacebuilding Commission ······························· 321
Case Study   The 2003 intervention in Iraq ·································· 323
Box 18.5   Selected documents related to the changing role of the
             United Nations system ·· 324
Box 18.6   The UN Conference on Environment and Development:
             the Earth Summit ··· 325

Box 19.1   Transnational corporations from developing countries ··········· 335
Case Study   The baby milk advocacy network ································· 343

Box 20.1	Chronology	354
Box 20.2	Sustainable development	355
Box 20.3	Trade and the environment	357
Box 20.4	The tragedy of the commons—local and global	359
Box 20.5	The Montreal Protocol and stratospheric ozone regime	360
Box 20.6	The Intergovernmental Panel on Climate Change	361
Box 20.7	The Kyoto Protocol	362
Case Study	Common but differentiated responsibilities?	363
Box 21.1	Types of terrorist group	372
Box 21.2	Legitimacy	373
Box 21.3	Al Qaeda Associated Movement (AQAM)	376
Case Study	Three generations of militant Islamic terrorists	379
Box 22.1	Waltz thesis	388
Box 22.2	Sagan's 'proliferation pessimism' argument	389
Box 22.3	Technology of nuclear weapons	390
Box 22.4	Compliance and non-compliance	394
Case Study 1	Democratic People's Republic of Korea (DPRK)	395
Case Study 2	United States–India nuclear cooperation agreement	397
Box 22.5	1995 NPT Review and Extension Conference	398
Box 22.6	Chronology	399
Box 23.1	The development of a world of nation-states	404
Box 23.2	Definitions of nation	405
Case Study	Interactions between nationalism and global politics: the cases of Germany and India	409
Box 24.1	Bhikhu Parekh on religion and the construction of identity	420
Box 24.2	The Western account of culture	421
Box 24.3	Francis Fukuyama on Islam in the world of universal liberalism	422
Box 24.4	Fundamentalism	424
Case Study	Schematic of the militant Islamic movement in the Afghan–Pakistan milieu (c. 2001)	429
Box 25.1	Dynamics of regionalism	437
Box 25.2	Around the world in regional organizations, 2006 (an illustrative and non-exhaustive list)	439
Case Study	Central America: a perpetual pursuit of union?	440
Box 26.1	Major public global governance agencies for trade and finance	452
Box 26.2	Some key events in global trade and finance	463
Case Study	Southern debt in global finance	464

Box 27.1   International Relations theory and the marginalization of
                priority issues for the Third World 471

Box 27.2   Development: a contested concept 473

Case Study 1   Competing ideas on development from the contemporary
                coffee sector 474

Case Study 2   Destruction of local agriculture, booming food imports,
                and rising malnutrition in Haiti 486

Box 28.1   A contested concept 493

Box 28.2   Trends in conflict 496

Box 28.3   Key facts about disease 499

Case Study   Human insecurity in South-East Asia 501

Box 29.1   The international protection of human rights: some key
                treaties, conventions, and declarations 508

Case Study 1   9/11, the global war on terror, and human rights 509

Box 29.2   Kinds of rights 511

Box 29.3   Sovereignty and the standards of civilization 512

Box 29.4   The feminist critique of human rights 516

Case Study 2   Islam, gender, and the cultural critique of human rights 517

Box 29.5   Asian values 518

Box 30.1   The Responsibility to Protect: principles for military
                intervention 525

Case Study   Iraq—a humanitarian intervention? 533

Box 30.2   Paragraphs 138 and 139 of the 2005 World Summit Outcome
                Document 536

Box 30.3   Recommendations of the High-Level Panel on Measures
                to Prevent War 537

Box 31.1   Some political theorists on political community 545

Box 31.2   Contrasting views about the scope of human sympathy 551

Box 31.3   Visions of new forms of community and citizenship 552

Case Study   Torture and the War on Terror 553

Box 32.1   Elements of discontinuity and continuity between cold war
                and post-cold war orders 562

Box 32.2   Elements of order 566

Box 32.3   Interpretations of globalization and the end of the cold war 568

Box 32.4   The debate about globalization and legitimacy 570

Case Study   The crisis of developing state legitimacy 571

List of tables

3.1   Second World War estimated casualties ···· 58
3.2   Principal acts of European decolonization, 1945–80 ···· 59
3.3   Cold war crises ···· 63
3.4   Revolutionary upheavals in the 'Third World', 1974–80 ···· 64
3.5   Principal nuclear weapons states: nuclear arsenals, 1945–90 ···· 66
3.6   Principal arms control and disarmament agreements ···· 66

5.1   A taxonomy of realisms ···· 96

14.1   The debate about institutions ···· 257

17.1   A typology of regimes ···· 301

19.1   The variety of political actors involved in different
          policy domains ···· 345

23.1   Debates on nationalism ···· 405

25.1   Important agreements in the history of the European Union ···· 445
25.2   Institutions of the EU ···· 446

26.1   Some indicators of contemporary economic globalization ···· 454

27.1   Mainstream and alternative conceptions of poverty,
          development, and hunger ···· 471
27.2   GDP growth in selected developing countries and regions,
          1960–2004 ···· 476
27.3   Per capita GDP growth in selected developing countries
          and regions, 1960–2004 ···· 477

28.1   Two conceptions of human security ···· 495

32.1   Typologies of order ···· 564

About the contributors

Amitav Acharya is Professor of International Relations at the University of Bristol. He has written widely on international and Asian security issues, including *Promoting Human Security: Ethical, Normative and Educational Frameworks in South East Asia* (United Nations Scientific, Cultural and Educational Organization, 2007).

David Armstrong is Professor of International Relations at Exeter University, having previously held posts at Birmingham and Durham Universities. His current research interests cover the historical development of international organization and international law. He is a Fellow of the Royal Historical Society and his books include *Revolution and World Order* (Clarendon Press, 1993), *The Rise of the International Organisation* (Macmillan, 1981), *Revolutionary Diplomacy* (California University Press, 1977), and *International Law and International Relations* (Cambridge University Press, 2007, forthcoming).

Michael Barnett is Stassen Professor of International Affairs at the Humphrey School of Public Affairs and Professor of Political Science at the University of Minnesota.

John Baylis is Professor of Politics and International Relations and Pro-Vice Chancellor at Swansea University. His PhD and D.Litt are from the University of Wales. He is the author of more than twenty books, the most recent of which are *Strategy in the Contemporary World: An Introduction to Strategic Studies* (2nd edn, with James Wirtz, Colin S. Gray, and Eliot Cohen, Oxford University Press, 2006) and *The United States and Europe: Beyond the Neo-Conservative Divide?* (edited with Jon Roper, Routledge, 2006).

Alex J. Bellamy is Professor of International Relations at the University of Queensland, Australia. He has written and edited eight books, the most recent of which is *Just Wars: From Cicero to Iraq* (Polity Press, 2006) and his articles have appeared in journals including *International Security, Ethics and International Affairs,* and the *Journal of Peace Research.* He is currently writing a book on the ethics of terrorism (Oxford University Press) and working on projects on the regionalization of peace operations (with Paul D. Williams and Sebastian Kaempf) and the 'responsibility to protect'.

Edward Best is Professor and Head of Unit at the European Institute of Public Administration (EIPA), Maastricht. He has worked in the regional security programme of the International Institute for Strategic Studies (IISS), publishing a book on *US Policy and Regional Security in Central America* (Gower/St Martins Press, 1987). He has been a consultant for the United Nations and the Inter-American Development Bank in Central America, for the European Commission in Latin America, and the Helsinki Commission in the Baltic Sea region. He now specializes in EU institutions and the political aspects of European integration as well as comparative regionalism and the management of regional organizations. He has co-edited two books on the EU—*Rethinking the European Union: IGC 2000 and Beyond* (EIPA, 2000) and *From Luxembourg to Lisbon and Beyond: Making the Employment Strategy Work* (EIPA, 2002)—and published numerous articles on the European Union and institutional arrangements for regional integration.

John Breuilly is Professor of Nationalism and Ethnicity at the London School of Economics. His major interests are in modern German and comparative European history and the historical study of nationalism. Recent publications include *Germany's Two Unifications: Anticipations, Experiences, Responses,* edited with Ronald Speirs (Palgrave, 2004) and 'Introduction' to Ernest Gellner, *Nations and Nationalism* (2nd edn, Blackwell, 2006).

Chris Brown is Professor of International Relations at the London School of Economics and Political Science, and the author of numerous books and papers, including *Sovereignty, Rights and Justice* (Polity Press, 2002) and *Understanding International Relations* (3rd edn, with Kirsten Ainley, Palgrave Macmillan, 2005).

Thomas Christiansen is Senior Lecturer at the European Institute for Public Administration in Maastricht, having previously worked as Director of the Jean Monnet Centre for European Studies at the University of Wales, Abersytwyth. He is also Professor at the College of Europe in Bruges as well as Executive Editor of the *Journal of European Integration.* He has published widely on different aspects of the institutional politics of the European Union. Among his publications are five edited volumes, including *Informal Governance of the European Union* (Edward Elgar, 2004), edited with Simona Piattoni, and *The Social Construction of Europe* (Sage, 2001), edited with Knud Erik Joergensen and Antje Wiener. *Constitutionalizing the European Union,* co-authored with Christine Reh, is forthcoming in the European Union Series at Palgrave Macmillan.

Ian Clark is Professor of International Politics at the University of Wales Aberystwyth. He is the author of standard works on globalization, such as *Globalization and Fragmentation* (Oxford University Press, 1997) and *Globalization and International Relations Theory* (Oxford University Press, 1999). His most recent book is *International Legitimacy and World Society* (Oxford University Press, 2007).

Michael Cox holds a Chair in International Relations at the London School of Economics. The author and editor of over a dozen books, including *E. H. Carr: A Critical Appraisal* (Palgrave, 2000), *A Farewell to Arms: Beyond the Good Friday Agreement* (2nd edn, Manchester University Press, 2006), *American Democracy Promotion* (Oxford University Press, 2000), *US Foreign Policy after the Cold War: Superpower Without a Mission?* (Pinter, 1995), and *The Interregnum: Controversies in World Politics, 1989–1999* (Cambridge University Press, 1999). His work has been translated into several languages, including Japanese, Chinese, Russian, Ukrainian, German, Italian, French, and Spanish. He is currently Chair of the European Consortium for Political Research, Director of the Cold War Studies Centre at the LSE, and Chair of the United States Discussion Group at Chatham House, London. He was Research Fellow at the Norwegian Nobel Institute in 2002 and 2007.

Devon Curtis is a Lecturer in the Department of Politics at the University of Cambridge, and a Fellow of Emmanuel College. Her main research interests and publications deal with power-sharing and governance arrangements following conflict, the 'transformation' of rebel movements to political parties in Africa, and security and development. Her field research has concentrated on the Great Lakes region of Africa. Previously, Curtis was a Post-doctoral Research Fellow at the Saltzman Institute of War and Peace Studies at Columbia University,

and a Pre-doctoral Fellow at the Center for International Security and Cooperation (CISAC) at Stanford University. She has also worked for the Canadian Government, the United Nations Staff College, and the Overseas Development Institute. Curtis received her PhD in International Relations from the London School of Economics in 2004.

Tim Dunne is Professor of International Relations, Head of the Department of Politics, and Deputy Head of the School of Humanities and Social Sciences, University of Exeter, UK. He is author of *Inventing International Society* (Macmillan, 1998) and is a former associate editor of the *Review of International Studies*. He has edited seven books, including *Worlds in Collision: Terror and the Future of Global Order* (with Ken Booth, Palgrave Macmillan, 2002), and *International Relations Theory* (with Milja Kurki, and Steve Smith, Oxford University Press, 2007).

Stephen Hobden is a Senior Lecturer in International Politics at the University of East London. His research and teaching interests include theories of large-scale social change, the politics of North–South relations, and the foreign policy of the United States.

Darryl Howlett is a Senior Lecturer in the Division of Politics and International Relations at the University of Southampton. His most recent publications include (with Jeffery S. Lantis) 'Strategic culture', in John Baylis, James Wirtz, Colin S. Gray, and Eliot Cohen (eds), *Strategy in the Contemporary World* (2nd edn, Oxford University Press, 2007) and 'Cyber security and the critical national infrastructure', in Paul Wilkinson (ed.), *Homeland Security in the UK* (Routledge, 2007).

James D. Kiras is an Assoicate Professor at the School of Advanced Air and Space Studies, Maxwell AFB, AL, where he directs the School's research programme and its course on irregular warfare. He received his PhD from the University of Reading in the UK in 2004 and has worked extensively in the defence policy and consulting fields. Dr Kiras is the author of *Special Operations and Strategy: From World War II to the War on Terrorism* (Routledge, 2006), as well as numerous book chapters and articles on special operations, insurgency, and suicide terrorism. He also serves as an Associate Senior Fellow of the Strategic Studies Division of the Joint Special Operations University, Hurlburt Field, Florida.

Steven L. Lamy is a Professor of International Relations at the School of International Relations at the University of Southern California. He was Director of the School from 2001 to 2006. His areas of research and teaching include international relations theory, foreign policy analysis and global governance and human security. He is currently chairing a research project that focuses on the impact of religion on international affairs.

Andrew Linklater is Woodrow Wilson Professor of International Politics at the University of Wales, Aberystwyth. His most recent book is *The English School of International Relations: A Contemporary Assessment,* co-authored with Hidemi Suganami (Cambridge University Press, 2006). Principal research interests include the control of violent and non-violent harm in international history.

Richard Little is Professor of International Politics at the University of Bristol. He is a former editor of the *Review of International Studies* and Chair of the British International

Studies Association. He is the co-author with Barry Buzan of *International Systems in World History* (Oxford University Press, 2000). His most recent book is *The Balance of Power in International Relations: Metaphors, Myths, and Models* (Cambridge University Press, 2007).

Anthony McGrew is Professor of International Relations and Head of the School of Social Sciences at Southampton University. He has written extensively on globalization and global governance. He is working on a project on new forms of global governance.

Simon Murden is a Senior Lecturer in Strategic Studies and International Affairs at Britannia Royal Naval College, Dartmouth. He was formerly a lecturer in international relations at Aberystwyth and Plymouth, specializing in the Middle East, politicized Islam, and globalization. He is the author of *Emergent Regional Powers and International Relations in the Gulf, 1988–91* (Ithaca Press, 1995) and *Islam, the Middle East and the New Global Hegemony* (Lynne Reinner, 2002). His current research interests focus on contemporary security issues and warfare, including on diffuse global networks and the utility of force.

Patricia Owens is Senior Lecturer in the Department of Politics at Queen Mary, University of London. She is author of *Between War and Politics: International Relations and the Thought of Hannah Arendt* (Oxford University Press, 2007) and *War and Security: An Introduction* (Polity Press, forthcoming). She has also written for *Review of International Studies*, *Millennium*, *Alternatives*, and *International Affairs*.

Christian Reus-Smit is Professor of International Politics and Head of the Department of International Relations in the Research School of Pacific and Asian Studies at the Australian National University. He is author of *American Power and World Order* (Polity Press, 2004) and *The Moral Purpose of the State* (Princeton University Press, 1999), co-author of *Theories of International Relations* (Palgrave, 2001, 2005), editor of *The Politics of International Law* (Cambridge University Press, 2004), and co-editor of *Resolving International Crises of Legitimacy* (Special Issue, *International Politics*, 2007), and *Between Sovereignty and Global Governance* (Macmillan, 1998).

Brian C. Schmidt is Associate Professor in the Department of Political Science at Carleton University, Canada. He is the author of *The Political Discourse of Anarchy: A Disciplinary History of International Relations* (SUNY, 1998) and *Imperialism and Internationalism in the Discipline of International Relations*, co-edited with David Long (SUNY, 2005).

Jan Aart Scholte is Professor in the Department of Politics and International Studies and Co-Director of the Centre for the Study of Globalisation and Regionalisation at the University of Warwick, UK. During 2007–10 he is also a Centennial Professor at the London School of Economics. His writings include *Globalization: A Critical Introduction* (2nd edn, Palgrave, 2005), *Civil Society and Global Democracy* (Palgrave, forthcoming), *Contesting Global Governance* (co-authored with Robert O'Brien, Anne-Marie Goetz, and Marc Williams, Cambridge University Press, 2000), *Civil Society and Global Finance* (co-edited with Albrecht Schnabel, Routledge, 2002), and *Encyclopedia of Globalization* (co-edited with Roland Robertson, Routledge, 2006). He is also on the current editorial team of *Global Governance*.

Len Scott is Professor of International Politics at the University of Wales, Aberystwyth. His recent publications include *Intelligence, Crises and Security: Prospects and Retrospects*, co-edited with R. Gerald Hughes (Routledge, 2007) and *Understanding Intelligence in the Twenty-First Century: Journeys in Shadows*, co-edited with Peter Jackson (Routledge, 2004).

Richard Shapcott is Senior Lecturer in International Relations at the University of Queensland, Australia. He is the author of *Justice, Community and Dialogue in International Relations* (Cambridge University Press, 2001) and is currently finalizing *A Critical Introduction to International Ethics* (Polity Press, forthcoming).

Michael Sheehan is Professor of International Relations at Swansea University. He is the author of *The Arms Race* (Martin Robertson, 1983), *The Economist Guide to Defence* (Economist, 1986), with James H. Wyllie, *Arms Control: Theory and Practice* (Blackwell, 1986), *A Bibliography of Arms Control Verification* (Dartmouth, 1990), with David Scrivener, *Balance of Power: History and Theory* (ed.) (Routledge, 1996), *New Dimensions of Security* (TAPRI, 1998), with Jouko Huru and Olli-Pekka Jalonen, *National and International Security* (ed.) (Ashgate, 2000), *Security: An Analytical Survey* (Lynne Rienner, 2005), and *The International Politics of Space* (Routledge, 2007).

Steve Smith is Vice-Chancellor of the University of Exeter. He has held Professorships of International Relations at the University of Wales, Aberystwyth and the University of East Anglia, and has also taught at the State University of New York (Albany), and Huddersfield Polytechnic. He was President of the International Studies Association for 2003–4, and was elected to be an Academician of the Social Sciences (AcSS) in 2000. He is the author or editor of thirteen books, including (with Martin Hollis) *Explaining and Understanding International Relations* (Oxford University Press, 1989) and (co-edited with Ken Booth and Marysia Zelewski) *International Theory: Positivism and Beyond* (Cambridge University Press, 1995), and of some 90 academic papers and chapters in major international journals and edited collections.

Paul Taylor is Emeritus Professor of International Relations, and, until July 2004, was Director of the European Institute, at the London School of Economics, where he specialized in international organization within the European Union and the United Nations system. Most recently he has published *International Organization in the Age of Globalization* (Continuum, 2003; paperback version, June 2005). He is a graduate of the University College of Wales, Aberystwyth, and of the London School of Economics, and is married with three children.

Caroline Thomas is Deputy Vice Chancellor and Professor of Global Politics at the University of Southampton. She specializes in North–South relations, and has published widely on the global politics of security, development, environment, and health.

J. Ann Tickner is Professor of International Relations at the University of Southern California. She was President of the International Studies Association for 2006–7. She is the author of *Gender in International Relations: Feminist Perspectives on Achieving Global Security* (Columbia University Press, 1992), *Gendering World Politics: Issues and Approaches in the Post-Cold War*

Era (Columbia University Press, 2001), as well as many articles and book chapters on feminist international theory and international security.

John Vogler is Professor of International Relations in the School of Politics, International Relations and Environment at Keele University, UK. His books include *The Global Commons: Environmental and Technological Governance* (John Wiley, 2000) and, with Charlotte Bretherton, *The European Union as a Global Actor* (Routledge, 2006). He has also edited with Mark Imber, *The Environment and International Relations* (Routledge,1996) and, with Alan Russell, *The International Politics of Biotechnology* (Manchester University Press, 2000).

Nicholas J. Wheeler is Professor in the Department of International Politics at the University of Wales, Aberystwyth. He is co-author of *The British Origins of Nuclear Strategy 1945–55* (Oxford University Press, 1989), co-editor with Tim Dunne of *Human Rights in Global Politics* (Cambridge University Press, 2000), and author of *Saving Strangers: Humanitarian Intervention in International Society* (Oxford University Press, 2000). He has written widely on humanitarian intervention and the Blair government's ethical foreign policy. His latest book with Ken Booth is *The Security Dilemma: Fear, Cooperation, and Trust in World Politics* (Palgrave Macmillan, 2007). He is Director of the David Davies Memorial Institute of International Studies, a Trustee of the Welsh Centre of International Affairs, and a member of the United Nations Association of the UK's Policy Advisory Committee.

Peter Willetts is Professor of Global Politics at City University, London. He has written extensively on international organizations, particularly on the Non-Aligned Movement. He was a pioneer in studying the impact of NGOs on global politics, editing two books on the subject, *Pressure Groups in the Global System* (Pinter, 1982) and *'The Conscience of the World': The Influence of Non-Governmental Organisations in the UN System* (Hurst, 1996).

Ngaire Woods is Director of the Global Economic Governance Programme at University College and the Department of Politics and International Relations at Oxford University. Her most recent book is *The Globalizers: the IMF, the World Bank and their borrowers* (Cornell University Press, 2006). She has previously published *The Political Economy of Globalization* (Macmillan, 2000), *Inequality, Globalization and World Politics,* with Andrew Hurrell (Oxford University Press, 1999), *Explaining International Relations since 1945* (Oxford University Press, 1986), and numerous articles on international institutions, globalization, and governance.

Richard Wyn Jones is a Professor at the Department of International Politics at the University of Wales, Aberystwyth. He has written extensively on critical security studies, nationalism, and Welsh politics. His most recent book is a study of the political thought of Plaid Cymru, the Welsh nationalist party (University of Wales Press, 2007).

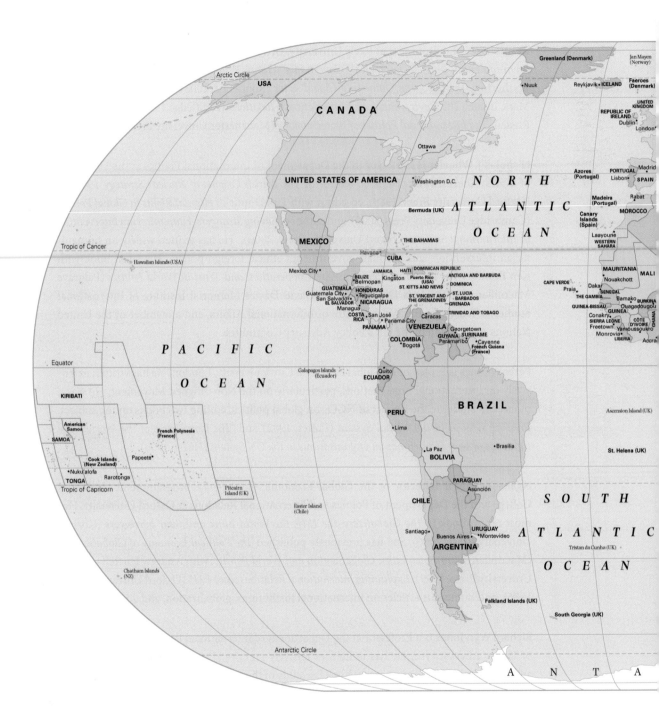

World Map

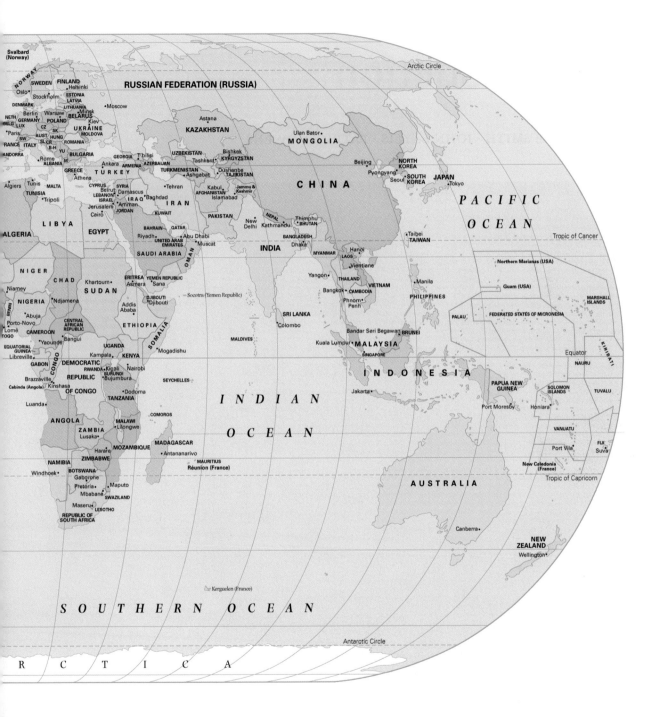

Svalbard
(Norway)

Arctic Circle

NORWAY
SWEDEN FINLAND
Oslo• •Helsinki
DENMARK •Stockholm ESTONIA
LATVIA
LITHUANIA
NETH BERLIN Warsaw Minsk BELARUS •Moscow
BELG GERMANY POLAND Kiev
•Paris LUX CZ SK UKRAINE
FRANCE AUST HUNG MOLDOVA
ITALY SW ROMANIA
ANDORRA Rome B-H YU BULGARIA
•Tunis ALBANIA GREECE GEORGIA •T'bilisi
Algiers• MALTA Athens Ankara ARMENIA AZERBAIJAN
TUNISIA •Tripoli TURKEY TURKMENISTAN
CYPRUS Beirut SYRIA Damascus
LEBANON Baghdad
Jerusalem ISRAEL Amman IRAQ
LIBYA Cairo• JORDAN KUWAIT
EGYPT BAHRAIN• QATAR
Riyadh• •Abu Dhabi
ALGERIA SAUDI ARABIA UNITED ARAB •Muscat
EMIRATES OMAN

RUSSIAN FEDERATION (RUSSIA)

KAZAKHSTAN

Astana•

Ulan Bator•
MONGOLIA

UZBEKISTAN Bishkek
Tashkent• KYRGYZSTAN
Ashgabat• Dushanbe
TAJIKISTAN
Tehran• Kabul• Jammu &
AFGHANISTAN Kashmir
Islamabad•
PAKISTAN New NEPAL Thimphu
Delhi• Kathmandu• •BHUTAN
INDIA BANGLADESH
Dhaka•

CHINA

Beijing• NORTH
Pyongyang• KOREA
Seoul• SOUTH JAPAN
KOREA •Tokyo

PACIFIC
OCEAN

Taibei•
TAIWAN

Tropic of Cancer

NIGER CHAD Khartoum•
Niamey•
NIGERIA Ndjamena•
BENIN SUDAN
Abuja• CENTRAL
Porto-Novo• AFRICAN ETHIOPIA
Lomé• CAMEROON REPUBLIC Addis
TOGO •Yaoundé Bangui• Ababa•
EQUATORIAL
GUINEA GABON UGANDA
Libreville• CONGO Kampala• KENYA
DEMOCRATIC RWANDA Kigali •Nairobi
Cabinda (Angola) REPUBLIC BURUNDI
Kinshasa• OF CONGO Bujumbura•
Luanda• •Dodoma
TANZANIA
ANGOLA
MALAWI
ZAMBIA Lilongwe•
Lusaka•
Harare• ZIMBABWE MOZAMBIQUE
NAMIBIA •Maputo
Windhoek• BOTSWANA Gaborone•
Pretoria•
Mbabane• SWAZILAND
Maseru• LESOTHO
REPUBLIC OF
SOUTH AFRICA

ERITREA YEMEN REPUBLIC
Asmara• •Sana
DJIBOUTI
•Djibouti
Socotra (Yemen Republic)

SOMALIA

Mogadishu•

SEYCHELLES

COMOROS

MADAGASCAR
•Antananarivo
MAURITIUS
Réunion (France)

MALDIVES

SRI LANKA
•Colombo

INDIAN

OCEAN

MYANMAR LAOS
Hanoi•
•Vientiane
Yangon• THAILAND VIETNAM
Bangkok• CAMBODIA •Manila
Phnom
Penh• PHILIPPINES

Bandar Seri Begawan •BRUNEI
Kuala Lumpur• MALAYSIA
SINGAPORE

INDONESIA

Jakarta•

Northern Marianas (USA)

Guam (USA)

FEDERATED STATES OF MICRONESIA

PALAU

MARSHALL
ISLANDS

KIRIBATI

NAURU

PAPUA NEW
GUINEA
Port Moresby•

SOLOMON
ISLANDS
Honiara•

TUVALU

Equator

VANUATU

Port Vila• FIJI
New Caledonia Suva•
(France)

AUSTRALIA

Canberra•

NEW
ZEALAND
Wellington•

Tropic of Capricorn

Kerguelen (France)

SOUTHERN   OCEAN

Antarctic Circle

R   C   T   I   C   A

Introduction

STEVE SMITH · JOHN BAYLIS · PATRICIA OWENS

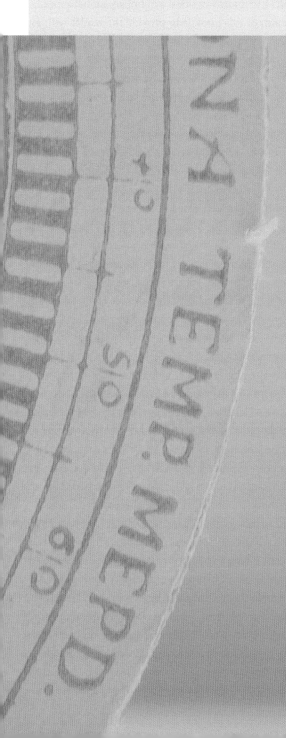

- From international politics to world politics ··· 3
- Theories of world politics ··· 3
- The four theories and globalization ··· 6
- Globalization and its precursors ··· 8
- Globalization: myth or reality? ·· 10

The events of **11 September 2001** (hereafter, 9/11), probably more than any other single event, brought home just how globalized the contemporary world is. The subsequent war in Afghanistan (2001–2) and the particularly controversial attack on Iraq in 2003, and the subsequent insurgency and civil war, are further clear examples of what it means to call the current era globalized—they involved international coalitions and transnational violent networks in conflicts that linked events in seemingly unrelated parts of the world. Let us open up some aspects of how these events illustrate globalization, using 9/11 as an example.

First, 9/11 was an event taking place in one country, the United States, but immediately observed throughout the world: the television pictures of the second plane crashing into the World Trade Center are probably the most widely seen images in television history. Thus 9/11 was a world event, which had far more of an effect than represented by the simple fact of the number of deaths involved (about 3,000 died in the four attacks that day; on an average day 30,000 children throughout the world die of malnutrition, though not often of course in front of the gaze of the television cameras). Second, the attacks were carried out by 19 individuals in the name of an until-then shadowy organization known as Al Qaeda. This organization was not a state or formal international body, but a loose coalition of committed men based, it is claimed, in over 50 countries. This was a truly globalized organization. Third, the attacks were coordinated by using some of the most powerful technologies of the globalized world, namely mobile phones, international bank accounts, and the Internet. Moreover, the key personnel travelled regularly between continents, using yet another symbol of globalization, mass air travel. Fourth, the reactions to the events throughout the world were intense, instantaneous, and very mixed: in some Arab and Muslim countries there was jubilation that the West generally, and the United States specifically, had been hit; in many other countries there was profound shock and an immediate empathy with the United States. Fifth, although the attacks were on buildings in the United States, these were not ordinary buildings; while the Pentagon is the symbol of the United States' military power, the World Trade Center was (as the name implies) an iconic symbol of the world financial network. Sixth, it is worth noting that although these were attacks on the United States, many individuals of other nationalities were killed; it is estimated that citizens from

about 90 countries were killed in the attacks on the World Trade Center. Finally, though there is a lot of disagreement over why Osama bin Laden ordered the attacks, the main reasons seem to have concerned events in yet other parts of the world: bin Laden himself cited the plight of the Palestinians and the continued support of the United States for the current Saudi regime, and the presence of their advisers on that country's (holy) soil. Therefore, though there are many indicators that the world has been becoming increasingly globalized over the last thirty years, 9/11 in many ways best symbolizes globalization.

The aim of this book is to provide the reader with an overview of world politics in this globalized world. Let us start, though, with a few words about the title of this book. The title is not accidental. First, we want to introduce you to world politics, as distinct from international politics or international relations. Second, many think that the contemporary, post-**cold war** world is distinctly different from previous periods because of the effects of globalization. We think that it is especially difficult to explain world politics in such an era because globalization is a particularly controversial term. There is considerable dispute over just what it means to talk of this being an era of globalization, and whether that means that the main features of world politics are any different from those of previous eras. In this Introduction we want to explain how we propose to deal with the concept of globalization and offer you some arguments in favour of seeing it as an important new **development** in world politics and also some arguments against such a view.

Before turning to look at globalization in order to set the scene for the chapters that follow, we want to do two things. We will first say something about the various terms used to describe **global politics**, and then we will spend some time looking at the main ways in which global politics has been explained. We need to do this because our aim in this Introduction is not to put forward one view of how to think about globalization, agreed by all the contributors to this volume. Rather we want to give the reader a context within which to read the chapters that follow and that means giving a variety of views on globalization and how to think about it. Our central concern is to point out that the main theoretical accounts of world politics all see globalization differently. Some treat it as nothing more than a temporary phase in human history, and one which does not mean that we need to fundamentally rethink how we understand world politics. Others see it as but the latest

manifestation of the growth of Western **capitalism** and modernization and some see it as representing a fundamental transformation of world politics, one that requires new ways of understanding. The different contributors to this book hold no one agreed view, and in fact there are representatives of all the responses just mentioned. Thus, for example, they would each have a different take on the events of 9/11. From what we have said so far you should note that there are three main aims of this book:

- To offer an overview of world politics in an era of globalization.
- To summarize the main theoretical approaches available to explain contemporary world politics.
- To provide the material necessary to answer the question of whether globalization marks a fundamental transformation in world politics.

From international politics to world politics

Why does the main title of this book refer to world politics rather than international politics or international relations? These are the traditional names used to describe the kinds of interactions and processes that are the concern of this book. Indeed, you could look at the table of contents of many other introductory books and find a similar listing of main topics dealt with, yet often these books would have either international relations or international politics as their main title. Furthermore, the discipline that studies these issues is nearly always called International Politics or International Relations. Our reason for choosing the phrase 'world politics' is that we think it is more inclusive than either of the alternative terms. It is meant to denote the fact that our interest is in the politics and political patterns in the world, and not only those between **nation-states** (as the term international politics implies). Thus, we are interested in relations between organizations that may or may not be states (such as, for example, multinational companies, terrorist groups, or human rights **non-governmental organizations** (NGOs); these are all known as **transnational actors**). Similarly, the term 'international relations' seems too exclusive. Of course, it does represent

a widening of our concern from simply the political relations between nation-states, but it still restricts our focus to **inter-national** relations, whereas we think that relations between, say, cities and other governments or **international organizations** can be equally important to what states do. So we prefer to characterize the relations we are interested in as those of world politics, with the important proviso that we do not want the reader to define politics too narrowly. You will see this issue arising time and time again in the chapters that follow, since many contributors want to define politics very widely. One obvious example concerns the relationship between politics and economics; there is clearly an overlap, and a lot of bargaining power goes to the person who can persuade others that the existing distribution of resources is 'simply' economic rather than a political issue. So, we want you to think about politics very broadly for the time being as several of the chapters will describe as political features of the contemporary world that you may not have previously thought of as such. Our focus is with the patterns of political relations, defined broadly, that characterize the contemporary world. Many will be between states, but many, perhaps most, will not.

Theories of world politics

The basic problem facing anyone who tries to understand contemporary world politics is that there is so much material to look at that it is difficult to know which things matter and which do not. Where on earth would you start if you wanted to explain the most important political processes?

How, for example, would you explain 9/11, or the 2003 war in Iraq? Why did Al Qaeda attack the United States? Why did President Bush and Prime Minister Tony Blair authorize the attack on Saddam Hussein's Iraq? As you will know, there are very different answers to questions such as

these and there seems no easy way of arriving at a definitive answer to them. Was the attack on Iraq motivated by a concern with human rights, with oil, with unfinished business, with **imperialism**, with the 'war against terrorism'? Whether they are aware of it or not, whenever individuals are faced with such a problem they have to resort to **theories.** A theory is not simply some grand formal model with hypotheses and assumptions. Rather **a theory is a kind of simplifying device that allows you to decide which facts matter and which do not.** A good analogy is with sunglasses with different coloured lenses; put on the red pair and the world looks red, put on the yellow pair and it looks yellow. The world is not any different, it just looks different. Well, so it is with theories. Shortly we are going to summarize the main theoretical views that have dominated the study of world politics, so you will get an idea of which 'colours' they paint world politics. But before we do so, please note that we do not think that theory is an option. It is not as if you can say that you do not want to bother with a theory, all you want to do is to look at the 'facts'. We believe that this is simply impossible, since the only way in which you can decide which of the millions of possible facts to look at is by adhering to some simplifying device which tells you which ones matter the most. We think of theory as such a simplifying device. Note also that you may well not be aware of your theory. It may just be the view of the world that you have inherited from family, peer group, or the media. It may just seem common sense to you and not at all anything complicated like a theory. But we fervently believe that all that is happening in such a case is that your theoretical assumptions are **implicit** rather than **explicit,** and we prefer to try to be as explicit as possible when it comes to thinking about world politics.

People have tried to make sense of world politics for centuries, and especially so since the separate academic discipline of International Politics was formed in 1919 when the Department of International Politics was set up at the University of Wales, Aberystwyth. Interestingly, the man who set up that department, a Welsh industrialist called David Davies, saw its purpose as being to help prevent war. By studying international politics scientifically, scholars could find the causes of the world's main political problems and put forward solutions to help politicians solve them. For the next twenty years, the discipline was marked by such a commitment to change the world. This is known as a **normative** position, with the task of academic study being one of making the world a better place. Its opponents characterized it as **Idealism**, in that it had a view of how the world ought to be and tried to assist events to turn out that way. In its place its opponents preferred an approach they called **Realism**, which, rather unsurprisingly, stressed seeing the world as it really is rather than how we would like it to be. And, the 'real' world as seen by Realists is not a very pleasant place; human beings are at best selfish and probably much worse. Notions such as the perfectibility of human beings and the possibility of an improvement of world politics seem far-fetched. This debate between Idealism and Realism has continued to the present day, but it is fair to say that Realism has tended to have the upper hand. This is mainly because it appears to accord more with common sense than does Idealism, especially when the media bombard us daily with images of how awful humans can be to one another. Having said this, we would like you to think about whether such a Realist view is as neutral as it is commonsensical. After all, if we teach world politics to generations of students and tell them that people are selfish, then doesn't that become common sense? And don't they, when they go off into the media or to work for government departments, or the military, or even when they talk to their children over the dinner table, simply repeat what they have been taught and, if in positions of power, act accordingly? We will leave you to think about this. For now, we would like to keep the issue open and simply point out that we are not convinced that Realism is as objective or non-normative as it is portrayed as being.

What is certainly true is that Realism has been the dominant way of explaining world politics in the last one hundred years. What we are now going to do is to summarize the main assumptions underlying Realism and then do the same for its three main rivals as theories of world politics, **Liberalism**, Marxism, and **Constructivism**. These theories will be discussed in much more detail in Part Two of this book, along with chapters dealing with some of the more recent alternative and normative approaches that seek to explain contemporary world politics. They will also be reflected in three of the other four parts that comprise the book. In Part One we look at the **historical** background to the contemporary world. In Part Three we will look at the main **structures** and processes of contemporary world politics. In Part Four we will deal with some of the main issues in the globalized world. So although we will not go into much depth now about these theories, we do need to give you a flavour of their main themes since we want, after summarizing them, to say something about how each might think about globalization.

Realism and world politics

For Realists the main actors on the world stage are **states**, which are legally sovereign actors. **Sovereignty** means that there is no actor above the state that can compel it to act in specific ways. Other actors, such as multinational corporations or international organizations, all have to work within the framework of inter-state relations. As for what propels states to act as they do, Realists see human nature as centrally important. For Realists, human nature is fixed, and crucially it is selfish. To think otherwise is to make a mistake, and it was such a mistake that the Realists accused the Idealists of making. As a result, world politics (or more accurately for Realists international politics) represents a struggle for **power** between states each trying to maximize their **national interests**. Such order as exists in world politics is the result of the workings of a mechanism known as the **balance of power**, whereby states act so as to prevent any one state dominating. Thus world politics is all about bargaining and alliances, with **diplomacy** a key mechanism for balancing various national interests. But finally, the most important tool available for implementing states' foreign policies is military force. Ultimately, since there is no sovereign body above the states that make up the international political system, world politics is a **self-help** system in which states must rely on their own military resources to achieve their ends. Often these ends can be achieved through **cooperation**, but the potential for conflict is ever present.

In recent years, an important variant of Realism, known as **Neo-realism**, has developed. This view stresses the importance of the **structure** of the international political system in affecting the behaviour of all states. Thus during the cold war there were two main powers dominating the **international system** and this led to certain **rules** of behaviour; now that the cold war has ended the structure of world politics is said to be moving towards **multipolarity** (after a phase of **unipolarity**) which for neo-realists will involve very different rules of the game.

Liberalism and world politics

Liberals have a different view of world politics, and like Realists, have a long tradition. Earlier we mentioned Idealism, and this was really one rather extreme version of Liberalism. There are many variants of Liberalism, but the main themes that run through Liberal thought are that

human beings are perfectible, that democracy is necessary for that perfectibility to develop, and that ideas matter. Behind all this lies a belief in **progress**. Accordingly, Liberals reject the Realist notion that war is the natural condition of world politics. They also question the idea that the state is the main actor on the world political stage although they do not deny that it is important. They see multinational corporations, transnational actors such as terrorist groups, and international organizations as central actors in some issue-areas of world politics. In those issue-areas in which the state acts, they tend to think of the state not as a unitary or united actor but as a set of bureaucracies, each with its own interests. Therefore there can be no such thing as a national interest, since it merely represents the result of whatever bureaucratic organizations dominate the domestic decision-making process. In relations between states, Liberals stress the possibilities for cooperation, and the key issue becomes devising international settings in which cooperation can be best achieved. The picture of world politics that results from the Liberal view is of a complex system of bargaining between many different types of actor. Military force is still important but the Liberal agenda is not as restricted as is the Realist one. Liberals see national interests in more than just military terms, and stress the importance of economic, environmental, and technological issues. Order in world politics emerges not from a balance of power but from the interactions between many layers of governing arrangements, comprising laws, agreed **norms**, **international regimes**, and institutional rules. Fundamentally, Liberals do not think that sovereignty is as important in practice as Realists think it is in theory. States may be legally sovereign, but in practice they have to negotiate with all sorts of other actor, with the result that their freedom to act as they might wish is seriously curtailed. **Interdependence** between states is a critically important feature of world politics.

Marxist theories and world politics

The third main theoretical position we want to mention, **Marxist theory,** is also known as **structuralism** or **world-system theory,** which immediately gives you clues as to its main assumptions. We want to point out that Marxist theory has been historically less influential than either Realism or Liberalism, and has less in common with either Realism or Liberalism than they do with each other. For Marxist theory, the most important feature

of world politics is that it takes place within a world capitalist economy. In this world-economy the most important actors are not states but classes, and the behaviour of all other actors is ultimately explicable by class forces. Thus states, multinational corporations, and even international organizations represent the dominant class interest in the world economic system. Marxist theorists differ over how much leeway actors such as states have, but all agree that the world-economy severely constrains the freedom of manoeuvre of states. Rather than world politics being an arena of conflict between national interests or an arena with many different issue-areas, Marxist theorists conceive world politics as the setting in which **class conflicts** are played out. As for order in world politics, Marxist theorists think of it primarily in economic rather than in military terms. The key feature of the international economy is the division of the world into core, semi-periphery, and periphery areas. Within the semi-periphery and the periphery there exist cores which are tied into the capitalist world-economy, while within even the core area there are peripheral economic areas. In all of this what matters is the dominance of the power not of states but of **international capitalism,** and it is these forces that ultimately determine the main political patterns in world politics. Sovereignty is not nearly as important for Marxist theorists as for Realists since it refers to political and legal matters, whereas the most important feature of world politics is the degree of economic autonomy, and here Marxist theorists see all states as having to play by the rules of the international capitalist economy.

Constructivism

Social Constructivism is a relatively new theory about world politics, one that developed in the late 1980s and is becoming increasingly influential since the mid-1990s.

The approach arose out of a set of events in world politics, notably the disintegration of the Soviet **empire**, as symbolized most notably by the fall of the Berlin Wall in 1989. This indicated that human agency had a much greater potential role in world politics than implied by Realism, Liberalism, and Marxism. But the theoretical underpinnings of the approach are much older, and relate to a series of social scientific and philosophical works that dispute the notion that the social world is external to the people that live in it, and is not easily changed. Realism, Liberalism, and Marxism, to different degrees, stress the regularities and 'certainties' of political life (though Liberalism is somewhat less adamant than the other two theories). By contrast, Constructivism argues that we make and re-make the social world and so there is much more of a role for human agency than other theories suggest. Moreover, Constructivists note that those who see the world as fixed underestimate the possibilities for human progress and for the betterment of the lives of people. In the words of one of the most influential Constructivist theorists, Alexander Wendt, even the self-help international system portrayed by Realists is something that we make and re-make: as he puts it, '**anarchy** is what states make of it' (Wendt 1992). Therefore, the world that Realists portray as 'natural' or 'given' is in fact far more open to change, and Constructivists think that self-help is only one possible response to the anarchical structure of world politics. Even more subversively, they think that not only is the structure of world politics amenable to change, but so are the identities and interests that the other theories take as given. In other words, Constructivists think that it is a fundamental mistake to think of world politics as something that we cannot change. The seemingly 'natural' structures, processes, identities, and interests of world politics could in fact be different from what they currently are, and implying otherwise is a political act.

The four theories and globalization

The first three of these theoretical perspectives, Realism, Liberalism, and Marxism, have tended to be the main theories that have been used to understand world politics, with Constructivism becoming increasingly influential since the mid-1990s. In the 1980s it became common to talk of there being an **inter-paradigm** debate between Realism, Liberalism, and Marxism; that is to say that the three theories (known as paradigms after the influential philosopher of natural science, Thomas Kuhn) were in competition and that the 'truth' about world politics lay

in the debate between them. At first sight each seems to be particularly good at explaining some aspects of world politics better than the others, and an obvious temptation would be to try to combine them into some overall account. But this is not the easy option it may seem. This is because the four theories are not so much different views of the same world, but are instead **four views of different worlds.** Let us explain this briefly.

While it is clear that each of the four theories focuses on different aspects of world politics (Realism on the power relations between states, Liberalism on a much wider set of interactions between states and **non-state actors,** Marxist theory on the patterns of the world-economy, and Constructivism on the ways in which we can develop different social structures and processes), each is saying more than this. Each view is claiming that it is picking out **the most important features** of world politics and that it offers a **better account** than do the rival theories. Thus, the four approaches are really in competition with one another; and while you can certainly choose between them it is not so easy to add bits from one to the others. For example, if you are a Marxist theorist, you think that state behaviour is ultimately determined by class forces: forces that the Realist does not think affect state behaviour. Similarly, Constructivism suggests that actors do not face a world that is fixed, and thus it is one that they can in principle change in direct contrast to the core beliefs of Realists and Marxists alike. In other words, these four theories are really versions of what world politics is like rather than partial pictures of it. They do not agree on what the 'it' is.

We do not think that any one of these theories has all the answers when it comes to explaining world politics in an era of globalization. In fact each sees globalization differently. We do not want to tell you which theory seems best, since the purpose of this book is to give you a variety of conceptual lenses through which you might want to look at globalization. All we will do is say a few words about how each theory might respond to globalization. We will then go on to say something about the rise of globalization and offer some ideas on its strengths and weaknesses as a description of contemporary world politics.

1 For **Realists,** globalization does not alter the most significant feature of world politics, namely the territorial division of the world into nation-states. While the increased interconnectedness between economies and societies might make them more dependent on one another, the same cannot be said about the states-system. Here, states retain sovereignty, and globalization does not render obsolete the struggle for political power between states. Nor does it undermine the importance of the threat of the use of force or the importance of the balance of power. Globalization may affect our social, economic, and cultural lives, but it does not transcend the international political system of states.

2 For **Liberals,** the picture looks very different. They tend to see globalization as the end product of a long-running transformation of world politics. For them, globalization fundamentally undermines Realist accounts of world politics since it shows that states are no longer such central actors as they once were. In their place are numerous actors, of differing importance according to the issue-area concerned. Liberals are particularly interested in the revolution in technology and communications represented by globalization. This increased interconnectedness between societies, which is economically and technologically led, results in a very different pattern of world political relations from that which has gone before. States are no longer sealed units, if ever they were, and as a result the world looks more like a cobweb of relations than like the state model of Realism or the class model of Marxist theory.

3 For **Marxist** theorists, globalization is a bit of a sham. It is nothing particularly new, and is really only the latest stage in the development of international capitalism. It does not mark a qualitative shift in world politics, nor does it render all our existing theories and concepts redundant. Above all, it is a Western-led phenomenon which basically simply furthers the development of international capitalism. Rather than make the world more alike, it further deepens the existing divide between the core, the semi-periphery, and the periphery.

4 For **Constructivist** theorists, globalization tends to be presented as an external force acting on states, which leaders often argue is a reality that they cannot challenge. This, Constructivists argue, is a very political act, since it underestimates the ability of leaders to challenge and shape globalization, and instead allows them to duck responsibility by blaming 'the way the world is'. Instead, Constructivists think that we can mould globalization in a variety of ways, notably because it offers us very real chances to create cross-national **social movements** aided by modern technological forms of communication such as the Internet.

By the end of the book we hope you will work out which of these theories (if any) best explains globalization (alternative theories are also discussed in this book which you might find even more compelling). We spend a lot of time in Part Two outlining these theories in more detail so as to give you much more of an idea of the main ideas involved. We will also introduce you to a set of other theories that many believe are crucial in explaining globalization, but which have not been the dominant theories in the discipline of International Relations. However, the central point we want to make here is to reinforce our comment earlier that theories do not portray 'the' truth. In other words, the theories we have mentioned will see globalization differently because they have **a prior** view of what is most important in world politics. Therefore the option is not available of simply answering the tempting question of which theory has the 'truest' or 'correct' view of globalization.

Globalization and its precursors

The focus of this book is globalization, and as we have already said our concern is with offering you an overview of world politics in a globalized era. **By globalization we simply mean the process of increasing interconnectedness between societies such that events in one part of the world more and more have effects on peoples and societies far away.** A globalized world is one in which political, economic, cultural, and social events become more and more interconnected, and also one in which they have more impact. In other words, societies are affected more and more extensively and more and more deeply by events of other societies. These events can conveniently be divided into three types, **social, economic, and political.** In each case, the world seems to be 'shrinking', and people are increasingly aware of this. The World Wide Web is but the most graphic example of this, since it allows you to sit at home and have instant communication with websites around the world. Electronic mail has also transformed communications in a way that the editors of this book would not have envisaged fifteen years ago. But these are only the most obvious examples. Others would include: worldwide television communications, global newspapers, international social movements such as Amnesty International or Greenpeace, global franchises such as McDonald's, Coca-Cola, and Pizza Hut, the global economy (go and look in your nearest supermarket and work out the number of countries' products represented there), and global risks such as pollution, global warming, and AIDS. There are, of course, many other examples, but you get the picture. It is this pattern of events that seems to have changed the nature of world politics from what it was just a few years ago. The important point to stress is that it is not just that the world has changed but that the changes are qualitative and not merely quantitative;

a strong case can be made that a 'new' world political system has emerged as a result of globalization.

Having said this, we want to point out that globalization is not some entirely new phenomenon in world history. Indeed, as we will note later on, many argue that it is merely a new name for a long-term feature. While we want to leave it to you to judge whether in its current manifestation it represents a new phase in world history or merely a continuation of processes that have been around for a long time, we do want to note that there have been several precursors to globalization. In other words, globalization bears a marked similarity to at least nine features of world politics discussed by writers before the contemporary period. We will now note these briefly.

First, globalization has many features in common with the **theory of modernization** (see Modelski 1972 and Morse 1976). According to these writers, industrialization brings into existence a whole new set of contacts between societies, and changes the political, economic, and social processes that characterized the pre-modernized world. Crucially, industrialization altered the nature of the state, both widening its responsibilities and weakening its control over outcomes. The result is that the old power-politics model of international relations becomes outmoded. Force becomes less usable, states have to negotiate with other actors to achieve their goals, and the very **identity** of the state as an actor is called into question. In many respects it seems that modernization is part of the globalization process, differing only in that it applied more to the developed world and involved nothing like as extensive a set of transactions.

Second, there are clear similarities with the arguments of influential writers such as Walt Rostow (1960), who argued that **economic growth** followed a pattern in all economies as they went through industrialization. Their

economies developed in the shadow of more 'developed' economies until they reached the stage where they were capable of self-sustained economic growth. What this has in common with globalization is that Rostow saw a clear pattern to economic development, one marked by stages which all economies would follow as they adopted capitalist policies. There was an automaticity to history that globalization theory also tends to rely on.

Third, there was the important literature emerging out of the Liberal paradigm discussed above. Specifically, there were very influential works on the nature of **economic interdependence** (Cooper 1968), the role of transnational actors (Keohane and Nye 1977), and the resulting cobweb model of world politics (Mansbach, Ferguson, and Lampert 1976). Much of this literature anticipates the main theoretical themes of globalization, although again it tends to be applied much more to the developed world than is the case with globalization.

Fourth, there are notable similarities between the picture of the world painted by globalization and that portrayed in Marshall McLuhan's (1964) influential work on the **global village**. According to McLuhan, advances in electronic communications resulted in a world where we could see in real time events that were occurring in distant parts of the world. For McLuhan, the main effects of this development were that time and space become compressed to such an extent that everything loses its traditional identity. As a result, the old groupings of political, economic, and social organization simply do not work any more. Without doubt, McLuhan's work significantly anticipates some of the main themes of globalization, although it should be noted that he was talking primarily about the communications revolution, whereas the globalization literature tends to be much more extensive.

Fifth, there are significant overlaps between some of the main themes of globalization and the work of writers such as John Burton (1972), who spoke of the emergence of a **world society**. According to Burton, the old **state system** was becoming outmoded, as increasingly significant interactions took place between non-state actors. It was Burton who coined the phrase the 'cobweb' model of world politics. The central message here was that the most important patterns in world politics were those created by trade, communications, language, ideology, etc., along with the more traditional focus on the political relations between states.

Sixth, in the 1960s, 1970s, and 1980s, there was the visionary work of those associated with the **World Order Models Project** (WOMP), which was an organization set up in 1968 to promote the development of alternatives to the inter-state system which would result in the elimination of war. What is most interesting about their many studies (see, for example, Mendlovitz (1975) and Falk (1975, 1995*b*) is that they focused on the questions of global government that today are central to much work going on under the name of globalization. For WOMPers (as they were known), the unit of analysis is the individual, and the level of analysis is the global. Interestingly, by the mid-1990s WOMP had become much wider in its focus, concentrating on the world's most vulnerable people and the environment.

Seventh, there are important parallels between some of the ideas of globalization and the thoughts of those who argued for the existence of an **international society**. Prominent among these was Hedley Bull (1977), who pointed to the development over the centuries of a set of agreed norms and common understandings between state leaders, such that they effectively formed a society rather than merely an international system. However, although Bull was perturbed by the emergence of what he called the 'new medievalism', in which a series of subnational and international organizations vied with the state for authority, he did not feel that the nation-state was about to be replaced by the development of a world society.

Eighth, globalization theory has several points in common with the infamous argument of Francis Fukuyama (1992) about the **end of history**. Fukuyama's main claim is that the power of the economic market is resulting in liberal democracy replacing all other types of government. Though he recognizes that there are other types of political **regime** to challenge liberal democracy, he does not think that any of the alternatives, such as communism, fascism, or **Islam**, will be able to deliver the economic goods in the way that liberal democracy can. In this sense there is a direction to history and that direction is towards the expansion of the economic market throughout the world.

Finally, there are very marked similarities between some of the political aspects of globalization and long-standing ideas of liberal progress. These have most recently been expressed in the **liberal peace theory** of writers such as Bruce Russett (1993) and Michael Doyle (1983a and 1983b), although they go back centuries to writers such as Immanuel Kant. The main idea is that liberal democracies do not fight one another, and although of course there can be dispute as to what is a liberal democracy, adherents to this view claim quite plausibly that there is no case

where two democracies have ever gone to war. The reason they claim this is that public accountability is so central in democratic systems that publics will not allow leaders easily to engage in wars with other democratic **nations**.

Again the main link with globalization is the assumption that there is progress to history, and that this is making it far more difficult to start wars.

Globalization: myth or reality?

Our final task in this Introduction is to offer you a summary of the main arguments for and against globalization as a distinct new phase in world politics. We do not expect you to decide where you stand on the issue at this stage, but we think that we have to give you some of the main arguments so that you can keep them in mind as you read the rest of this book. Because the arguments for globalization being an important new phase of world politics have been rehearsed above—and also because they are most effectively summarized in the chapter that follows—we will spend a little more time on the criticisms. The main arguments in favour of globalization comprising a new era of world politics are:

1 The pace of **economic transformation** is so great that it has created a new world politics. States are no longer closed units and they cannot control their economies. The world-economy is more interdependent than ever, with trade and finances ever expanding.

2 **Communications** have fundamentally revolutionized the way we deal with the rest of the world. We now live in a world where events in one location can be immediately observed on the other side of the world. Electronic communications alter our notions of the social groups we work with and live in.

3 There is now, more than ever before, a **global culture,** so that most urban areas resemble one another. Much of the urban world shares a common culture, much of it emanating from Hollywood.

4 The world is becoming more **homogeneous.** Differences between peoples are diminishing.

5 **Time and space seem to be collapsing.** Our old ideas of geographical space and of chronological time are undermined by the speed of modern communications and media.

6 There is emerging a **global polity,** with transnational social and political movements and the beginnings of a transfer of allegiance from the state to sub-state, transnational, and international bodies.

7 A **cosmopolitan culture** is developing. People are beginning to 'think globally and act locally'.

8 A **risk culture** is emerging with people realizing both that the main risks that face them are global (pollution and AIDS) and that states are unable to deal with the problems.

However, just as there are powerful reasons for seeing globalization as a new stage in world politics, often allied to the view that globalization is progressive, that is to say that it improves the lives of people, there are also arguments that suggest the opposite. Some of the main ones are given below.

1 One obvious objection to the globalization thesis is that it is merely a buzzword to denote the latest phase of capitalism. In a very powerful critique of globalization theory, Hirst and Thompson (1996) argue that one effect of the globalization thesis is that it makes it appear as if national governments are powerless in the face of global trends. This ends up paralyzing governmental attempts to subject global economic forces to control and regulation. Believing that most globalization theory lacks historical depth, they point out that it paints the current situation as **more unique than it is,** and also as more firmly entrenched than it might in fact be. Current trends may well be reversible. They conclude that the more extreme versions of globalization are 'a myth', and they support this claim with five main conclusions from their study of the contemporary world-economy (1996: 2–3): First, the present internationalized economy is not unique in history. In some respects they say it is less open than the international economy was between 1870 and 1914. Second, they find that 'genuinely' transnational companies are relatively rare; most are national companies trading internationally. There is no trend towards the development of international companies. Third, there is no shift of finance and capital from

the developed to the underdeveloped worlds. Direct investment is highly concentrated among the countries of the developed world. Fourth, the world-economy is not global, rather trade, investment, and financial flows are concentrated in and between three blocs—Europe, North America, and Japan. Finally, they argue that this group of three blocs could, if they coordinated policies, regulate global economic markets and forces. Note that Hirst and Thompson are only looking at economic theories of globalization, and many of the main accounts deal with factors such as communications and culture more than economics. Nonetheless, theirs is a very powerful critique of one of the main planks of the more extreme globalization thesis, with their central criticism that seeing the global economy as something beyond our control both misleads us and prevents us from developing policies to control the national economy. All too often we are told that our economy must obey 'the global market' . Hirst and Thompson believe that this is a myth.

2   Another obvious objection is that globalization is very **uneven in its effects.** At times it sounds very much like a Western theory applicable only to a small part of humankind. To pretend that even a small minority of the world's population can connect to the World Wide Web is clearly an exaggeration when in reality most people on the planet have probably never made a telephone call in their lives. In other words, globalization only applies to the developed world. In the rest of the world, there is nothing like the degree of globalization. We are in danger of overestimating the extent and the depth of globalization.

3   A related objection is that globalization may well be simply **the latest stage of Western imperialism.** It is the old modernization theory discussed above in a new guise. The forces that are being globalized are conveniently those found in the Western world. What about non-Western values? Where do they fit into this emerging global world? The worry is that they do not fit in at all, and what is being celebrated in globalization is the triumph of a Western worldview, at the expense of the worldviews of other cultures.

4   Critics have also noted that there are very considerable **losers** as the world becomes more globalized. This is because it represents the success of liberal capitalism in an economically divided world. Perhaps one outcome is that globalization allows the more efficient exploitation of less well-off nations, and all in the name of openness.

The technologies accompanying globalization are technologies that automatically benefit the richest economies in the world, and allow their interests to override local ones. So, not only is globalization imperialist, it is also exploitative.

5   We also need to make the straightforward point that not all globalized forces are necessarily **good ones.** Globalization makes it easier for drug cartels and terrorists to operate, and the World Wide Web's anarchy raises crucial questions of censorship and preventing access to certain kinds of material.

6   Turning to the so-called **global governance** aspects of globalization, the main worry here is about responsibility. To whom are the transnational social movements responsible and democratically accountable? If IBM or Shell becomes more and more powerful in the world, does this not raise the issue of how accountable it is to democratic control? David Held has made a strong case for the development of what he calls **cosmopolitan democracy** (1995), but this has clearly defined legal and democratic features. The worry is that most of the emerging powerful actors in a globalized world precisely are NOT accountable. This argument also applies to seemingly 'good' global actors such as Amnesty International and Greenpeace.

7   Finally, there seems to be a **paradox** at the heart of the globalization thesis. On the one hand, it is usually portrayed as the triumph of Western, market-led values. But how do we then explain the tremendous economic success that some national economies have had in the globalized world? Consider the so-called 'Tigers' of Asia, countries such as Singapore, Taiwan, Malaysia, and Korea, which have enjoyed some of the highest growth rates in the international economy, but subscribe to very different 'Asian' values. These nations emphatically reject Western values, and yet they have had enormous economic success. The paradox, then, is whether these countries can continue to modernize so successfully without adopting Western values. If they can, then what does this do to one of the main themes of globalization, namely the argument that globalization represents the spreading across the globe of a set of values? If these countries do continue to follow their own roads towards economic and social modernization, then we must anticipate future disputes between 'Western' and 'Asian' values over issues like human rights, **gender**, and religion.

We hope that these arguments for and against the dominant way of representing globalization will cause you to think deeply about the utility of the concept of globalization in explaining contemporary world politics. The chapters that follow do not take a common stance **for** or **against globalization.** We will end by posing some questions that we would like you to keep in mind as you read the remaining chapters:

- Is globalization a new phenomenon in world politics?
- Which theory discussed above best explains globalization?
- Is globalization a positive or a negative development?
- Is globalization merely the latest stage of capitalist development?
- Does globalization make the state obsolete?
- Does globalization make the world more or less democratic?
- Is globalization merely Western imperialism in a new guise?
- Does globalization make war more or less likely?
- In what ways is war a globalizing force in itself?

We hope that this Introduction and the chapters that follow help you to answer these questions, and that this book as a whole provides you with a good overview of the politics of the contemporary world. Whether or not you conclude that globalization is a new phase in world politics, and whether you think it is a positive or a negative development, we leave you to decide. But, returning to 9/11 and its aftermath, we think it important to conclude this chapter by stressing that globalization, be it a new form of world politics or merely a new name for an age-old set of features, clearly is a very complex phenomenon that is contradictory and difficult to comprehend. Just as the Internet is for most of us a liberating force, so was it the way in which those who planned the 9/11 attacks communicated. Similarly, television can bring live stories right into our living rooms so that we understand more about the world. But on 9/11 it was also a means of communicating a very specific message about the vulnerability of the United States, and ultimately a way of constructing the categories within which we reacted. Finally, maybe the most fundamental lesson of 9/11 is that not all people in the world share a view of globalization as a progressive force in world politics. Those who undertook the attacks were rejecting, in part, the globalization-as-Westernization project. Globalization is therefore not one thing. How we think about it will reflect not merely the theories we accept, but our own positions in this globalized world. In this sense, the ultimate paradox of 9/11 is that the answers to questions such as what it was, what it meant, how to respond to it, etc., may themselves be ultimately dependent on the social, cultural, economic, and political spaces we occupy in a globalized world. In other words, world politics suddenly becomes very personal: how does your economic position, your ethnicity, your gender, your culture, or your religion determine what globalization means to you?

⮑ Guide to further reading

There are several good introductory guides to globalization. A comprehensive discussion is found in D. Held *et al.* (1999), *Global Transformations* (Cambridge: Polity Press). See also D. Held and A. McGrew (eds) (2003), *The Global Transformations Reader*, 2nd edn (Cambridge: Polity Press). J. A. Scholte (1993), *International Relations of Social Change* (Buckingham: Open University Press) is an extremely clear and comprehensive introduction to the social relations aspects of globalization. His latest book (2000), *Globalization: A Critical Introduction* (London: Macmillan) offers an excellent overview. Also see Chamsy el-Ojeili and Patrick Hayden (2006), *Critical Theories of Globalization* (London: Palgrave Macmillan).

A. McGrew and P. Lewis (1992), *Global Politics* (Cambridge: Polity Press) is a good collection of essays about global politics and contains some very relevant chapters on the relationship between the three theories discussed above and globalization. R. Robertson (1992), *Globalization: Social Theory and Global Culture* (London: Sage) is a very widely cited survey of

the relations between globalization and global culture. J. N. Rosenau and E.-D. Czempiel (1992), *Governance without Government* (Cambridge: Cambridge University Press) is a good collection of essays dealing with the political aspects of globalization. J. N. Rosenau (1990), *Turbulence in World Politics* (Princeton, NJ: Princeton University Press), and J. A. Camilleri and J. Falk (1992), *The End of Sovereignty* (Aldershot: Edward Elgar) are both very good at looking at the main trends in world politics at the beginning of the 1990s. Cynthia Enloe (2007) *Globalization and Militarism: Feminists Make the Link* (Lanham, Md.: Rowman & Littlefield) is a good analysis from a leading feminist of the connections between globalization and various forms of violence.

Excellent critiques of the globalization thesis are David Held and Anthony McGrew (2002), *Globalization/Anti-globalization* (Cambridge: Polity Press), Barry Gills (ed.) (2002), *Globalization and the Politics of Resistance* (London: Palgrave Macmillan) and Barry K. Gills and William R. Thompson (eds) (2006), *Globalization and Global History* (London: Routledge), Joseph Stiglitz (2003), *Globalization and Its Discontents* (London: Penguin) and (2006) *Making Globalization Work* (New York: W. W. Norton), R. Falk (1999), *Predatory Globalization: A Critique* (Cambridge: Polity Press), L. Weiss (1998), *The Myth of the Powerless State* (Cambridge: Polity Press), P. Hirst and G. Thompson (1999), *Globalization in Question,* **2nd edn** (Cambridge: Polity Press), Tarak Barkawi (2006), *Globalization and War* (Oxford: Rowman & Littlefield), and Ray Kiely (2007) *The New Political Economy of Development: Globalization, Imperialism, Hegemony* (London: Palgrave Macmillan).

Mary Kaldor (2003) has written a powerful account of the relationship between globalization and international civil society in her *Global Civil Society: An Answer to War* (Cambridge: Polity Press). See also the series of yearbooks she and others have edited on global civil society, which is now in its fifth edition. The latest is Helmut Anheier, Mary Kaldor, and Marlies Glasius (eds), *Global Civil Society Yearbook 2006–7* (Oxford: Oxford University Press). For another very influential analysis of the relationship between globalization and governance see David Held and Anthony McGrew (2002), *Governing Globalization: Power, Authority and Global Governance* (Cambridge: Polity Press) and David Held *et al.* (2005), *Debating Globalization* (Cambridge: Polity Press).

Online Resource Centre

Visit the Online Resource Centre that accompanies this book to access more learning resources on this chapter topic at www.oxfordtextbooks.co.uk/uk/orc/baylis_smith4e/

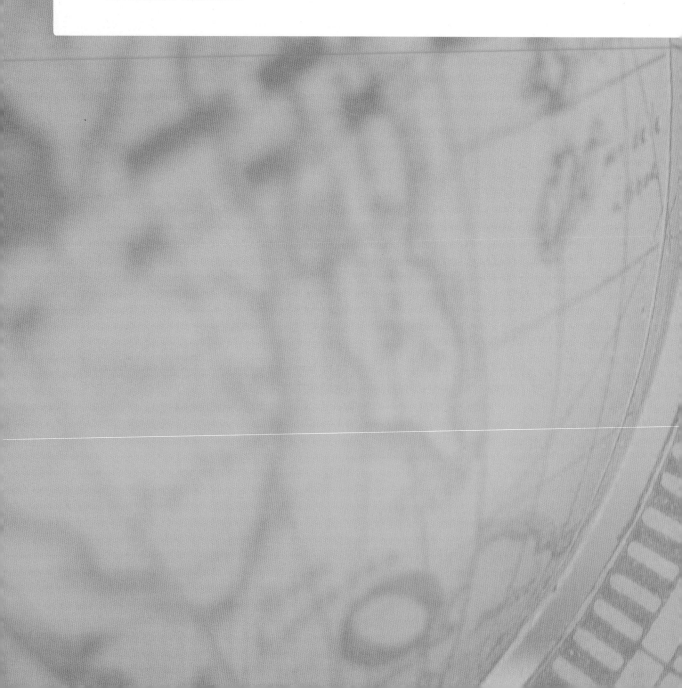

Chapter 1

Globalization and global politics

ANTHONY MCGREW

- Introduction ··· 16
- Making sense of globalization ·· 16
- Conceptualizing globalization ·· 18
- Contemporary globalization ·· 20
- A world transformed: globalization and distorted global politics ···························· 23
- From distorted global politics to cosmopolitan global politics? ····························· 29
- Conclusion ·· 32

Reader's Guide

This chapter offers an account of globalization and its consequences for world politics. It defines globalization as a historical process which involves the widening, deepening, speeding up and growing impact of worldwide interconnectedness. This process, however, is highly uneven such that far from bringing about a more cooperative world it generates powerful sources of friction, conflict, and fragmentation. It also has important consequences for the nation-state though it by no means, as many have argued or desired, prefigures its demise. Globalization is transforming world politics and this chapter explores some of those significant transformations. It concludes that a conceptual shift in our thinking is required to grasp fully the nature of these changes. This conceptual shift involves embracing the idea of global politics: the politics of an embryonic global society in which domestic and world politics, even if conceptually distinct, are practically inseparable. It also requires rethinking many of the traditional organizing assumptions and institutions of modern political life—from sovereignty to democracy—since in a globalized world power is no longer simply organized along national or territorial lines. The radically uneven distribution of power in today's world, however, makes for a distorted global politics in which the interests of the few more often than not take precedence over the interests of the majority of humankind. Whether a more just and democratic global politics can be fashioned out of the contemporary global condition is a matter of intense debate among theorists, practioners, and political activists alike. This chapter has three interrelated objectives: to elucidate and elaborate the concept of globalization; to examine and explore its implications for world politics; and to reflect upon the key normative issues it poses for the study of world politics.

Introduction

Globalization—simply the widening, deepening, and speeding up of worldwide interconnectedness—is a contentious issue in the study of world politics. Some—the **hyperglobalists**—argue that it is bringing about the demise of the sovereign **nation-state** as global forces undermine the ability of governments to control their own economies and societies (Ohmae 1995; Scholte 2000). Others—the **sceptics**—reject the idea of globalization as so much 'globaloney', and argue that states and geopolitics remain the principal forces shaping **world order** (Krasner 1999; Gilpin 2001). This chapter takes a rather different approach—a **transformationalist** perspective—arguing that both the hyperglobalists and sceptics alike exaggerate their arguments and thereby misconstrue the contemporary world order. By contrast, while the transformationalist perspective takes globalization seriously, it acknowledges that it is leading not so much to the demise of the sovereign state but to a globalization of politics: to the emergence of a conspicuously **global politics** in which the traditional distinction between domestic and international affairs is not terribly meaningful. Under these conditions 'politics everywhere, it would seem, are related to politics everywhere else' such that the orthodox approaches to

international relations—which are constructed upon this very distinction—provide at best only a partial insight into the forces shaping the contemporary world (Rosenau in Mansbach, Ferguson, and Lampert 1976: 22).

Since it is such a 'slippery' and misused concept it is hardly surprising that globalization should engender such intense debate. Accordingly, this chapter commences by elucidating the concept of globalization before exploring its implications for the study of world politics. The chapter is organized into three main sections: section one will address several interrelated questions, namely: What is globalization? How is it best conceptualized and defined? How is it manifest today, most especially given the events of **9/11**? Is it really all that new? Section two will discuss the ways in which globalization is contributing to the emergence of a distorted global politics which is highly skewed in favour of a global power elite and to the exclusion of the majority of humankind. Finally, section three will reflect upon the ethical challenges posed by the realities of this distorted global politics. It examines current thinking about the conditions, and prospects, for a more humane global politics which is both more inclusive of, and responsive to, those in greatest need in the global **community**.

Making sense of globalization

Over the last three decades the sheer scale and scope of global interconnectedness has become increasingly evident in every sphere from the economic to the cultural.

Worldwide economic **integration** has intensified as the expansion of global commerce, finance, and production links together the fate of **nations**, communities, and households across the world's major economic regions and beyond within an emerging global market economy. Crises in one region, whether the collapse of the Argentinean economy in 2002 or the East Asian recession of 1997, take their toll on jobs, production, savings, and investment many thousands of miles away, while a slowdown in the US economy is felt everywhere from Birmingham to Bangkok.

Every day over $1.88 trillion flows across the world's foreign exchange markets so that no government, even the most powerful, has the resources to resist sustained speculation against its currency and thereby the credibility of its economic policy (see Ch. 26). In 1992 the British government was forced to abandon its economic strategy and devalue the pound as it came under sustained attack from currency speculators.

Transnational corporations now account for between 25 and 33 per cent of world output, 70 per cent of world trade, and 80 per cent of international investment, while overseas production by these firms exceeds considerably the level of world exports, making them key players in the global economy controlling the

location and distribution of economic and technological resources.

New modes and infrastructures of global communication have made it possible to organize and mobilize like-minded people across the globe in virtual real time, as expressed in coordinated worldwide protests in early 2003 against military intervention in Iraq and the 45,000 international **non-governmental organizations** (NGOs), from Greenpeace to the Climate Action Network, not to mention the activities of transnational criminal and terrorist networks, from drugs cartels to Al Qaeda.

With a global communications infrastructure has also come the transnational spread of ideas, cultures, and information, from Madonna to Muhammad, both among like-minded peoples and between different cultural groups—reinforcing simultaneous tendencies towards both an expanded sense of global solidarity among the like-minded and difference, if not outright hostility, between different cultures, nations, and ethnic groupings.

People—with their cultures—are also on the move in their millions—whether legally or illegally—with global migration almost on a scale of the great nineteenth-century movements but transcending all continents, from south to north and east to west, while over 600 million tourists are on the move every year.

As globalization has proceeded so has the recognition of transnational problems requiring global regulation, from climate change to the proliferation of weapons of mass destruction. Dealing with these transnational issues has led to an explosive growth of transnational and global forms of rule-making and regulation. This is evident in both the expanding jurisdiction of established **international organizations**, such as the **International Monetary Fund** or the International Civil Aviation Organization, and the literally thousands of informal networks of **cooperation** between parallel government agencies in different countries, from the Financial Action Task Force (which brings together government experts on money-laundering from different countries) and the Dublin Group (which brings together drug enforcement agencies from the European Union, USA, and other countries).

With the recognition of global problems and global interconnectedness has come a growing awareness of

Box 1.1 Definitions of globalization

Globalization is variously defined in the literature as:

1 'The intensification of worldwide social relations which link distant localities in such a way that local happenings are shaped by events occurring many miles away and vice versa.'

(Giddens 1990: 21)

2 'The integration of the world-economy.'

(Gilpin 2001: 364)

3 'De-territorialization—or . . . the growth of supraterritorial relations between people.'

(Scholte 2000: 46)

4 'time–space compression.'

(Harvey 1989)

the multiple ways in which the **security** and prosperity of communities in different regions of the world is bound together. A single terrorist bombing in Bali has repercussions for public perceptions of security in **Europe** and the USA, while agricultural subsidies in the USA and the EU have significant consequences for the livelihoods of farmers in Africa, Latin America, and the Caribbean.

We inhabit a world in which the most distant events can rapidly, if not almost instantaneously, come to have very profound consequences for our individual and collective prosperity and perceptions of security. For those of a sceptical persuasion, however, this is far from a novel condition nor is it necessarily evidence of globalization if that term means something more than simply international **interdependence**, that is linkages between countries.

What, then, distinguishes the concept of globalization from notions of **internationalization** or interdependence? What, in other words, is globalization?

Key Points

- Over the last three decades the sheer scale and scope of global interconnectedness has become increasingly evident in every sphere from the economic to the cultural. Sceptics do not regard this as evidence of globalization if that term means something more than simply international interdependence, i.e. linkages between countries. The key issue becomes what we understand by the term 'globalization'.

Conceptualizing globalization

Initially, it might be helpful to think of globalization as a process characterized by:

- a *stretching* of social, political, and economic activities across political frontiers so that events, decisions, and activities in one region of the world come to have significance for individuals and communities in distant regions of the globe. Civil wars and conflict in the world's poorest regions, for instance, increase the flow of asylum seekers and illegal migrants into the world's affluent countries;

- the intensification, or the growing *magnitude*, of interconnectedness, in almost every sphere of social existence from the economic to the ecological, from the activities of Microsoft to the spread of harmful microbes, such as the SARS virus, from the intensification of world trade to the spread of weapons of mass destruction;

- the *accelerating pace* of global interactions and processes as the evolution of worldwide systems of transport and communication increases the rapidity or velocity with which ideas, news, goods, information, capital, and technology move around the world. Routine telephone banking transactions in the UK are dealt with by call centres in India in real time;

- the growing *extensity*, *intensity*, and *velocity* of global interactions is associated with a deepening enmeshment of the local and global in so far as local events may come to have global consequences and global events can have serious local consequences, creating a growing collective awareness or consciousness of the world as a shared social space, that is globality or **globalism**. This is expressed, among other ways, in the worldwide diffusion of the very idea of globalization itself as it becomes incorporated into the world's many languages, from Mandarin to Gaelic.

As this brief description suggests, there is more to the concept of globalization than simply interconnectedness. It implies that the cumulative scale, scope, velocity, and depth of contemporary interconnectedness is dissolving the significance of the borders and boundaries which separate the world into its some 193 constituent states or national economic and political spaces (Rosenau 1997). Rather than growing interdependence between discrete bounded national states, or internationalization as the sceptics refer to it, the concept of globalization seeks to capture the dramatic shift that is underway in the organization of human affairs: from a world of discrete but interdependent national states to the world as a shared social space. The concept of globalization therefore carries with it the implication of an unfolding process of structural change in the scale of human social and economic organization. Rather than social, economic, and political activities being organized primarily on a local or national scale today, they are also increasingly organized on a transnational or global scale. Globalization therefore denotes a significant shift in the scale of social organization, in every sphere from the economic to the security, transcending the world's major regions and continents.

Central to this structural change are contemporary informatics technologies and infrastructures of communication and transportation. These have greatly facilitated new forms and possibilities of virtual real-time worldwide organization and **coordination**, from the operations of multinational corporations to the worldwide mobilization and demonstrations of the anti-globalization movement. Although geography and distance still matter, it is nevertheless the case that globalization is synonymous with a process of **time–space compression**—literally a shrinking world—in which the sources of even very local developments, from unemployment to ethnic conflict, may be traced to distant conditions or decisions. In this respect globalization embodies a process of **deterritorialization**: as social, political, and economic activities are increasingly 'stretched' across the globe, they become in a significant sense no longer organized solely according to a strictly territorial logic. Terrorist and criminal networks, for instance, operate both locally and globally. National economic space, under conditions of globalization, is no longer coterminous with national territorial space since, for example, many of the UK's largest companies have their headquarters abroad while many domestic companies now outsource their production to China and East Asia among other locations. This is not to argue that **territory** and borders are now irrelevant, but rather to acknowledge that under conditions of globalization their *relative significance*, as constraints upon social action and the exercise of power, is declining. In an era of

Case Study 1 Global production and the iPod

Take just one component of the iPod nano, the central microchip provided by the U.S. company PortalPlayer. The core technology of the chip is licensed from British firm ARM and is modified by PortalPlayer's programmers in California, Washington State, and Hyderabad. PortalPlayer then works with microchip design companies in California that send the finished design to a 'foundry' in Taiwan (China) that produces 'wafers' (thin metal disks) imprinted with thousands of chips. The capital costs of these foundries can be more than $2.5 million. These wafers are then cut up into individual disks and sent elsewhere in Taiwan (China) where each one is tested. The chips are then encased in plastic and readied for assembly by Silicon-Ware in Taiwan (China) and Amkor in the Republic of Korea. The finished microchip is then warehoused in Hong Kong (China) before being transported to mainland China where the iPod is assembled.

Working conditions and wages in China are low relative to Western standards and levels. Many workers live in dormitories and work long hours. It is suggested that overtime is compulsory. Nevertheless, wages are higher than the average of the region in which the assembly plants are located and allow for substantial transfers to rural areas and hence contribute to declining rural povery. PortalPlayer was only established in 1999 but had revenues in excess of $225 million in 2005. PortalPlayer's chief executive officer has argued that the outsourcing to countries such as India and Taiwan (China) of 'non-critical aspects of your business' has been crucial to the development of the firm and its innovation: 'it allows you to become nimbler and spend R&D dollars on core strengths.'

Since 2003, soon after the iPod was launched, the share price of Apple, the company that produces and sells the iPod, has risen from just over $6 to over $60. Those who own shares in Apple have benefited from the globalization of the iPod.

Source: C. Joseph, 'The iPod's Incredible Journey',
Mail on Sunday, 15 July 2006; 'Meet the iPod's "Intel"'
Business Trends, 32(4) (April), 2006

(World Bank (2006), Global Economic Prospects 2007: Managing the Next Wave of Globalization (Washington, DC: World Bank): 118).

instantaneous real-time global communication and organization, the distinction between the domestic and the international, inside and outside the state breaks down. Territorial borders no longer demarcate the boundaries of national economic or political space.

A 'shrinking world' implies that sites of power and the subjects of power quite literally may be continents apart. Under these conditions the location of power cannot be disclosed simply by reference to local circumstances. As the War in Iraq (2003–) demonstrates, the key sites of global power, whether in Washington, the United Nations in New York, or London, are quite literally oceans apart from the local communities whose destiny they may determine. In this regard globalization involves the idea that power, whether economic, political, and cultural or military is increasingly organized and exercised at a distance. As such the concept of globalization denotes the **relative denationalization** of power in so far as, in an increasingly interconnected global system, power is organized and exercised on a transregional, transnational, or transcontinental basis while—see the discussion of political globalization—many other actors, from international organizations to criminal networks, exercise power within, across, and against states. States no longer have a monopoly of power resources whether economic, coercive, or political.

To summarize: globalization is a process which involves much more than simply growing connections or interdependence between states. It can be defined as:

> A historical process involving a fundamental shift or transformation in the spatial scale of human social organization that links distant communities and expands the reach of power relations across regions and continents.

Such a definition enables us to distinguish globalization from more spatially delimited processes such as **internationalization** and **regionalization**. Whereas internationalization refers to growing interdependence between states, the very idea of internationalization presumes that they remain discrete national units with clearly demarcated borders. By contrast, globalization refers to a

Box 1.2 Globalization since 9/11

'. . . 2004 was still a good one for globalization. International trade grew by a robust 9 percent, and trade became more central to most national economies. Trade in merchandise led the way, growing even faster than services. Many countries in the developing world shared in the profits as commodity prices soared, thanks to powerful demand from China. And it wasn't just steel, fuel, and concrete that headed east. So too did piles of mostly Western cash: Foreign investment in Asia jumped 45 percent from the previous year. Latin America also got a boost from foreign investors, who upped their ante in the region by 44 percent. Overall, foreign direct investment increased 9 percent, and most of that increase was due to investment in developing countries.'

(Foreign Policy, Nov. / Dec. 2006)

process in which the very distinction between the domestic and the external breaks down. Distance and time are collapsed, so that events many thousands of miles away can come to have almost immediate local consequences while the impacts of even more localized developments may be diffused rapidly around the globe. This is not to argue that distance and borders are now irrelevant. It is rather to acknowledge that, under conditions of globalization, their *relative significance*, as limits upon the exercise of power, is not quite so strong as it may have been in the past.

If globalization refers to transcontinental or transregional networks, flows, or interconnectedness, then regionalization can be conceived as the intensification of patterns of interconnectedness and integration among states which share common borders or are geographically proximate as in the European Union (see Ch.25). Accordingly, whereas flows of trade and finance between the world's three major economic blocs—North America, Asia Pacific, and Europe—constitute globalization, by contrast, such flows within these blocs are best described as regionalization.

Key Points

- Globalization is evident in the growing extensity, intensity, velocity, and deepening impact of worldwide interconnectedness.
- Globalization denotes a shift in the scale of social organization, the emergence of the world as a shared social space, the relative deterritorialization of social, economic, and political activity, and the relative denationalization of power.
- Globalization can be conceptualized as a fundamental shift or transformation in the spatial scale of human social organization that links distant communities and expands the reach of power relations across regions and continents.
- Globalization is to be distinguished from internationalization and regionalization.

Contemporary globalization

According to John Gray, the cataclysmic attacks on the United States on 11 September 2001 heralded a new epoch in world affairs, 'The era of globalization is over' (Naím 2002). States have reasserted their power and borders have been sealed, however imperfectly, in response to the perceived worldwide terrorist threat. Measured in terms of flows within the circuits of the world-economy, economic globalization undoubtedly stalled by comparison with the position at the turn of the century. This has been seized upon by those of a sceptical persuasion as confirmation of their argument (Hirst and Thompson 2003). Sceptics conclude that not only has globalization been highly exaggerated but it is a myth which has concealed the reality of a world which is less interdependent than it was in the nineteenth century and one which remains dominated by geopolitics (Hirst and Thompson

1999; Gilpin 2002). By contrast, for many of a more globalist persuasion, 9/11 and the climate of insecurity it has engendered are evidence of a pervasive 'clash of globalizations'. This is expressed in the form of a heightening confrontation between the globalization of Western modernity (i.e. ways of life) and the globalization of reactions against it. What is at issue here, at least in part, are differing (theoretical and historical) interpretations of globalization.

One of the problems of the sceptical argument is that it tends to conflate globalization solely with economic trends. It thus tends to overlook other evidence. Indeed, contemporary globalization is not a singular process: it operates within all aspects of social life from politics to production, culture to crime, and economics to education. It is implicated directly and indirectly in many

Box 1.3 The sceptical view of globalization

Sceptical accounts of globalization tend to dismiss its significance for the study of world politics. They do so on the grounds that:

1 By comparison with the period 1870 to 1914, the world is much less globalized economically, politically, and culturally.
2 Rather than globalization, the contemporary world is marked by intensifying geopolitics, regionalization, and internationalization.
3 The vast bulk of international economic and political activity is concentrated within the group of OECD states.
4 By comparison with the heyday of European global empires, the majority of the world's population and countries in the South are now much less integrated into the global system.

5 Geopolitics, state power, nationalism, and territorial boundaries are of growing, not less, importance in world politics.
6 Internationalization or regionalization are creatures of state policy not corporate actors or capitalist imperatives.
7 Globalization is at best a self-serving myth or ideology which reinforces Western and particularly US hegemony in world politics.

(Hirst and Thompson 1999, 2003; Hay 2000; Hoogvelt 2001; Gilpin 2002)

aspects of our daily lives, from the clothes we wear, the food we eat, the knowledge we accumulate, through to our individual and collective sense of security in an uncertain world. Evidence of globalization is all around us: universities are literally global institutions from the recruitment of students to the dissemination of academic research. To understand contemporary globalization therefore requires a mapping of the distinctive patterns of worldwide interconnectedness in all of the key sectors of social activity, from the economic and the political through to the military, the cultural, and the ecological.

As Box 1.4 illustrates, globalization is occurring, albeit with varying intensity and at a varying pace, in every domain of social activity. Of course it is more advanced in some domains than others. For instance, economic globalization is much more extensive and intensive than is cultural or mili-

tary globalization. To this extent contemporary globalization is highly uneven, with the result that in seeking to understand it we have to ask the prior question: the globalization of what? Contrary to the sceptics, it is crucial to recognize that globalization is a complex *multidimensional process*: patterns of economic globalization and cultural globalization are not identical. In this respect, to draw general conclusions about globalizing trends simply from one domain produces a false picture. As noted, in the aftermath of 9/11 the slowdown in economic globalization was heralded by sceptics as marking the end of globalization yet this ignored the accelerating pace of globalization in the military, technological, and cultural domains. Moreover, what is highly distinctive about contemporary globalization is the confluence of globalizing tendencies across all the key domains of social activity. Significantly, these tendencies have proved

Box 1.4 Patterns of contemporary globalization

Globalization, to varying degrees, is evident in all the principal sectors of social activity:

Economic: in the economic sphere, patterns of worldwide trade, finance, and production are creating global markets and, in the process, a single global capitalist economy—what Castells (2000) calls 'global informational capitalism'. Multinational corporations organize production and marketing on a global basis while the operation of global financial markets determines which countries get credit and upon what terms.

Military: in the military domain the global arms trade, the proliferation of weapons of mass destruction, the growth of transnational terrorism, the growing significance of transnational military corporations, and the discourse of global insecurity point to the existence of a global military order.

Legal: the expansion of transnational and international law from trade to human rights alongside the creation of new world legal

institutions such as the International Criminal Court is indicative of an emerging global legal order.

Ecological: a shared ecology involves shared environmental problems, from global warming to species protection, alongside the creation of multilateral responses and regimes of glbal environmental governance.

Cultural: involves a complex mix of homogenization and increased heterogeneity given the global diffusion of popular culture, global media corporations, communications networks, etc., simultaneously with the reassertion of nationalism, ethnicity, and difference. But few cultures are hermetically sealed off from cultural interaction.

Social: shifting patterns of migration from South to North and East to West have turned migration into a major global issue as movements come close to the record levels of the great nineteenth-century movements of people.

remarkably robust in the face of global instability and military conflicts.

If patterns of contemporary globalization are uneven, they are also highly *asymmetrical*. It is a common misconception of many sceptics that globalization implies universalism: that the 'global' in globalization implies that all regions or countries must be similarly enmeshed in worldwide processes. This is plainly not the case for it very markedly involves differential patterns of enmeshment, giving it what Castells calls its 'variable geometry' (Castells 2000). The rich OECD countries are much more globalized than many of the poorest sub-Saharan African states. Globalization is not uniformly experienced across all regions, countries, or even communities since it is inevitably a highly asymmetrical process. Even within OECD states and sub-Saharan African states many elites are in the vanguard of globalization while others find themselves excluded. As a highly asymmetrical process globalization exhibits a distinctive geography of inclusion and exclusion, resulting in clear winners and losers not just between countries but within and across them. For the most affluent it may very well entail a shrinking world—jet travel, global television and the World Wide Web—but for the largest slice of humanity it tends to be associated with a profound sense of disempowerment. Inequality is inscribed deeply in the very processes of contemporary globalization such that it is more accurately described as **asymmetrical globalization**.

Given such asymmetries it should not be surprising to learn that globalization does not prefigure the emergence of a global community or an ethic of global cooperation. On the contrary, as 9/11 tragically demonstrated, the more the world becomes a shared social space the greater the sense of division, difference, and conflict it creates. Asymmetrical globalization is principally perceived beyond the OECD core as Western globalization, provoking fears of a new **imperialism** and significant counter-reactions, from the protests of the anti-globalization movement to the actions of different cultural or national communities seeking to protect their indigenous culture and way of life. Rather than a more cooperative world order, contemporary globalization, in many respects, has exacerbated existing tensions and conflicts, generated new divisions and insecurities, creating a more unruly world. Globalization is a complex process embodying contradictory tendencies towards global integration and fragmentation, cooperation and conflict, order and disorder. This has been its history. Violence has always been central to globalization, whether in the form of the 'New Imperialism' of the 1890s or the current 'war on global terror'.

By comparison with previous periods, contemporary globalization combines a remarkable confluence of dense patterns of global interconnectedness, alongside their unprecedented **institutionalization** through new global and regional infrastructures of control and communication, from the World Trade Organization (WTO) to transnational corporations. In nearly all domains contemporary patterns of globalization have not only surpassed those of earlier epochs, but also displayed unparalleled qualitative differences—that is in terms of

---

Box 1.5 The engines of globalization

Explanations of globalization tend to focus on three interrelated factors, namely: technics (technological change and social organization); economics (markets and capitalism); and politics (power, interests, and institutions).

Technics is central to any account of globalization since it is a truism that without modern communications infrastructures, in particular, a global system or worldwide economy would not be possible.

Economics—crucial as technology is, so too is its specifically **economic** logic. Capitalism's insatiable requirement for new markets and profits lead inevitably to the globalization of economic activity.

Politics—shorthand here for ideas, interests, and power—constitutes the third logic of globalization. If technology provides the physical infrastructure of globalization, politics provides its normative infrastructure. Governments, such as those of the USA and the UK, have been critical actors in nurturing the process of globalization.

Box 1.6 The three waves of globalization

Globalization is not a novel phenomenon. Viewed as a secular historical process by which human civilizations have come to form a single world system, it has occurred in three distinct waves.

In the first wave, the age of discovery (1450–1850), globalization was decisively shaped by European expansion and conquest. The second wave (1850–1945) evidenced a major expansion in the spread and entrenchment of European empires.

By comparison, contemporary globalization (1960 on) marks a new epoch in human affairs. Just as the industrial revolution and the expansion of the West in the nineteenth century defined a new age in world history, so today the microchip and the satellite are icons of a globalized world order.

how globalization is organized and managed. The existence of new real-time global communications infrastructures, in which the world literally is transformed into a single social space, distinguishes very clearly contemporary globalization from that of the past. In these respects it is best described as a thick form of globalization or globalism (Held, McGrew *et al.* 1999; Keohane and Nye 2003).

As such it delineates the set of constraints and opportunities which confront governments and thereby conditions their freedom of action or autonomy, most especially in the economic realm. For instance, the unprecedented scale of global financial flows at over $1.88 trillion a day imposes a significant discipline on any government, even the most economically powerful, in its conduct of national economic policy. Thick globalization embodies a powerful systemic logic in so far as it structures the context in which states operate and thereby defines the parameters of state power. It therefore has significant consequences for how we understand world politics.

Key Points

- The contemporary phase of globalization has proved more robust in the aftermath of 9/11 than the sceptics recognize.
- Contemporary globalization is a multidimensional, uneven, and asymmetrical process.
- Contemporary globalization is best described as a thick form of globalization or globalism.

A world transformed: globalization and distorted global politics

Consider a political map of the world: its most striking feature is the division of the entire earth's surface into over 190 neatly defined territorial units, namely states. To a student of politics in the Middle Ages such a representation of the world, which gave primacy to borders and boundaries, would make little sense. Historically, borders are a relatively recent invention, as is the idea that states are sovereign, self-governing, territorially delimited political communities or polities. Although today a convenient fiction, this presumption remains central to orthodox state-centric conceptions of world politics as the pursuit of power and interests between sovereign states. Globalization, however, calls this state-centric conception of world politics into question. Taking globalization seriously therefore requires a conceptual shift in the way we think about world politics.

The Westphalian Constitution of world order

The Peace Treaties of Westphalia and Osnabruck (1648) established the legal basis of modern statehood and by implication the fundamental rules or constitution of modern world politics. Although Pope Innocent referred to the Westphalian settlement at the time as 'null, reprobate and devoid of meaning for all time', in the course of the subsequent four centuries it has formed the **normative structure** or constitution of the modern world order. At the heart of the Westphalian settlement was agreement among Europe's rulers to recognize each other's right to rule their own territories free from outside interference. This was codified over time in the doctrine of sovereign statehood. But it was only in the twentieth century, as global empires collapsed, that sovereign statehood and with it national **self-determination** finally acquired the status of universal organizing principles of world order. Contrary to Pope Innocent's desires, the Westphalian Constitution by then had come to colonize the entire planet.

Constitutions are important because they establish the location of legitimate political authority within a polity

---

Box 1.7 The Westphalian Constitution of world politics

1 **Territoriality**: humankind is organized principally into exclusive territorial (political) communities with fixed borders.
2 **Sovereignty**: within its borders the state or government has an entitlement to supreme, unqualified, and exclusive political and legal authority.
3 **Autonomy**: the principle of self-determination or self-governance constructs countries as autonomous containers of political, social, and economic activity in that fixed borders separate the domestic sphere from the world outside.

and the rules which inform the exercise and limits of political power. In codifying and legitimating the principle of sovereign statehood the Westphalian Constitution gave birth to the modern states-system. It welded together the idea of **territoriality** with the notion of legitimate sovereign rule. Westphalian sovereignty located supreme legal and political authority within territorially delimited states. Sovereignty involved the rightful entitlement to exclusive, unqualified, and supreme rule within a delimited territory. It was exclusive in so far as no ruler had the right to intervene in the sovereign affairs of other nations; unqualified in that within their territories rulers had complete authority over their subjects; and supreme in that there was no legal or political authority beyond the state. Of course for many, especially weak states, sovereignty—as the legitimate claim to rule—has not always translated into effective control within their territories. As Krasner recognizes, the Westphalian system has for many states been little more than a form of 'organized hypocrisy' (Krasner 1999). Nevertheless this never fundamentally compromised its **influence** upon the developmental trajectory of world politics. Although the UN Charter and the Universal Declaration of Human Rights modified aspects of the Westphalian Constitution, in qualifying aspects of **state sovereignty**, it remains the founding covenant of world politics. However, many argue that contemporary globalization presents a fundamental challenge to the Westphalian ideal of sovereign statehood and in so doing is transforming world order.

From (state-centric) geopolitics to (geocentric) global politics

As globalization has intensified over the last five decades, it has become increasingly difficult to maintain the popular fiction of the 'great divide': that is, treating political life as having two quite separate spheres of action, the domestic and the international, which operate according to different logics with different rules, actors, and agendas. There is a growing recognition that, as former President Clinton described it:

> the once bright line between domestic and foreign policy is blurring. If I could do anything to change the speech patterns of those of us in public life, I would like almost to stop hearing people talk about foreign policy and

---

> ### Box 1.8 The post-Westphalian order
>
> #### Territoriality
>
> Borders and territory still remain important, not least for administrative purposes. Under conditions of globalization, however, a new geography of political organization and political power is emerging which transcends territories and borders.
>
> #### State sovereignty
>
> The sovereign power and authority of national government—the entitlement of states to rule within their own territorial space—is being transformed but not necessarily eroded. Sovereignty today is increasingly understood as the shared exercise of public power and authority between national, regional, and global authorities.
>
> #### State autonomy
>
> In a more interdependent world, simply to achieve domestic objectives national governments are forced to engage in extensive multilateral collaboration and co-operation. But in becoming more embedded in systems of global and regional governance states confront a real dilemma: in return for more effective public policy and meeting their citizens' demands, whether in relation to the drugs trade or employment, their capacity for self-governance—that is state autonomy—is compromised.

domestic policy, and instead start discussing economic policy, security policy, environmental policy.

(quoted in Cusimano 2000: 6)

As the substantive issues of political life consistently ignore the artificial foreign/domestic divide, from the worldwide coordination of anti-globalization protests to national courts enforcing the rulings of the World Trade Organization, the Westphalian Constitution appears increasingly anachronistic. A post-Westphalian world order is emerging and with it a distinctive form of **global politics**.

To talk of global politics is to recognize that politics itself has been globalized and that as a consequence there is much more to the study of world politics than conflict and cooperation between states, even if this remains crucial. In other words, globalization challenges the one-dimensionality of orthodox accounts of world politics which conceive it purely in terms of geopolitics and the struggle for power between states. By contrast, the concept of global politics focuses our attention upon the global structures and processes of rule-making, problem-solving, and the maintenance of security and order in the world system (Brown 1992). It requires us to acknowledge the importance of states and geopolitics but not a priori to grant

them a privileged status in understanding and explaining contemporary world affairs. For under conditions of political globalization states are increasingly embedded in thickening and overlapping worldwide webs of: multilateral institutions and multilateral politics such as **NATO** and the World Bank; transnational associations and networks, from the International Chamber of Commerce to the World Muslim Congress; **global policy networks** of officials, corporate and non-governmental actors, dealing with global issues, such as the Global AIDS Fund and the Roll Back Malaria Initiative; and those formal and informal (transgovernmental) networks of government officials dealing with shared global problems, including the Basle Committee of central bankers and the Financial Action Task Force on money-laundering (Fig. 1.1).

Global politics directs our attention to the emergence of a fragile **global polity** within which 'interests are articulated and aggregated, decisions are made, values allocated and policies conducted through international or transnational political processes' (Ougaard 2004: 5). In other words, to how the global order is, or fails to be, governed.

Since the UN's creation in 1945 a vast nexus of global and regional institutions has evolved surrounded by a proliferation of non-governmental agencies and networks seeking to influence the governance of global affairs. While **world government** remains a fanciful idea, there does exist an evolving **global governance** complex—embracing states, international institutions, transnational networks and agencies (both public and private)—which functions, with variable effect, to promote, regulate, or intervene in, the common affairs of humanity (Fig. 1.2). Over the last five decades, its scope and impact have expanded dramatically with the result that its activities have become significantly politicized, as global protests against the WTO attest.

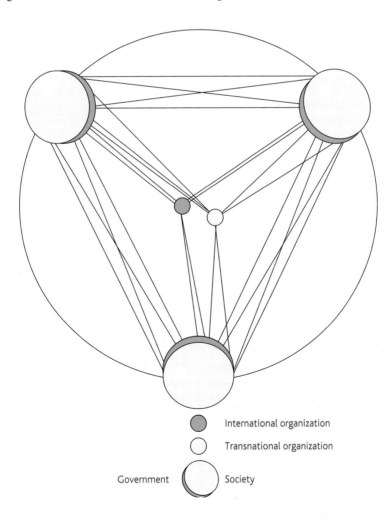

International organization

Transnational organization

Government   Society

Figure 1.1 The World Wide Web

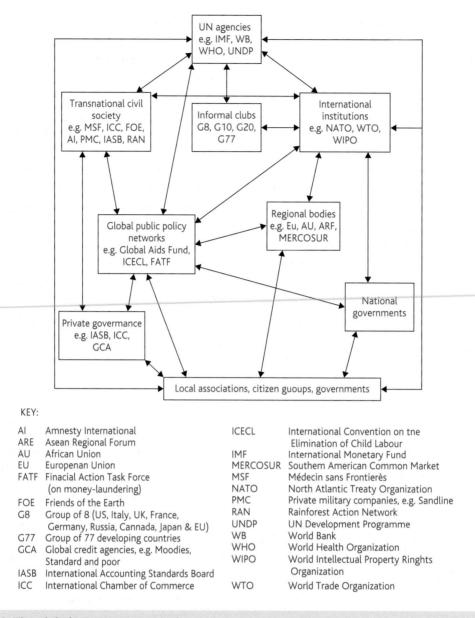

Figure 1.2 The global governance complex

This evolving global governance complex encompasses the multitude of formal and informal structures of political coordination among governments, inter-governmental and transnational agencies—public and private—designed to realize common purposes or collectively agreed goals through the making or implementing of global or transnational rules, and the regulation of transborder problems. A good illustration of this is the creation of international labour codes to protect vulnerable workers. The International Convention on the Elimination of Child Labour (ICECL), for instance, was the product of a complex politics involving public and private actors from trade unions, industrial associations, humanitarian groups, governments, legal experts, not forgetting officials and experts within the International Labour Organization (ILO).

Within this global governance complex private or non-governmental agencies have become increasingly influential in the formulation and implementation of global public policy. The International Accounting Standards Board establishes global accounting rules, while the major credit-rating agencies, such

as Moodys and Standard and Poor, determine the credit status of governments and corporations around the globe. This is a form of private global governance in which private organizations regulate, often in the shadow of global public authorities, aspects of global economic and social affairs. In those realms in which it has become highly significant, mainly the economic and the technological, this private global governance involves a relocation of authority from states and multilateral bodies to non-governmental organizations and private agencies.

Coextensive with the global governance complex is an embryonic **transnational civil society**. In recent decades a plethora of NGOs, transnational organizations (from the International Chamber of Commerce, international trade unions, and the Rainforest Network to the Catholic Church), advocacy networks (from the women's movement to Nazis on the net), and citizens' groups have come to play a significant role in mobilizing,

organizing, and exercising political power across national boundaries. This has been facilitated by the speed and ease of modern global communications and a growing awareness of common interests between groups in different countries and regions of the world. At the 2006 Ministerial Meeting of the WTO in Hong Kong, the representatives of environmental, corporate, and other interested parties outnumbered the formal representatives of government. Of course, not all the members of transnational civil society are either civil or representative; some seek to further dubious, reactionary, or even criminal causes while many lack effective accountability. Furthermore, there are considerable inequalities between the agencies of transnational **civil society** in terms of resources, influence and access to key centres of global decision-making. Multinational corporations, like Rupert Murdoch's News International, have much greater access to centres of power, and capacity to shape the global agenda, than does the Rainforest Action Network.

Case Study 2 Security and violence in global politics

Paradoxically, the same global infrastructures which make it possible to organize production on a worldwide basis can also be exploited to lethal effect. National security increasingly begins abroad, not at the border, since borders are as much carriers as barriers to transnational organized violence. This has become increasingly evident in relation to 'new wars' — complex irregular warfare in the global South. Inter-state war has been almost entirely supplanted by intra-state and trans-state conflict located in the global South, or on the perimeters of the West. These so-called 'new wars' are primarily located in weak states and rooted in identity politics, local conflicts, and rivalries. They involve complex irregular warfare between military, para-military, criminal, and private forces which rages through, but often around and across, state borders with little discrimina-

tion between civilians and combatants. The United Nations estimates, for instance, that thirty-five people die every hour across the globe as a consequence of irregular armed conflict. These 'new wars', whether in Bosnia, Darfur, or Venezuela, are curiously modern since they are sustained largely by the capacity of combatants to exploit global networks to provide finance, arms, *émigré* support, or aid as well as to facilitate profiteering, racketeering, and shadow economies, such as the diamond or drugs trade, which pays for arms and influence. Despite their apparently localized quality, 'new wars' are in fact a manifestation of the contemporary globalization of organized violence. Disorder in one part of the world (as in Darfur in 2006, or in Kosovo and Somalia in the 1990s) combines with global media coverage and the speed of travel to feed insecurity, creating overlapping global security complexes. These complexes bind together the security of societies across the North–South divide. They also highlight a major disjuncture between the distribution of formal military power and the distribution of effective coercive power in the world today. Al Qaeda, the Triads, private military companies, drug cartels, narco-terrorism, and the illicit global arms trade are all examples of the growth of informal organized violence or post-international violence. They pose, as Keohane starkly notes, a profound challenge since 'States no longer have a monopoly on the means of mass destruction: more people died in the attacks on the World Trade Center and the Pentagon than in the Japanese attack on Pearl Harbor in 1941'.

(Keohane 2002a: 284)

If global politics involves a diversity of actors and institutions it is also marked by a diversity of political concerns. The agenda of global politics is anchored to not just traditional geopolitical concerns but also to a proliferation of economic, social, cultural, and ecological questions. Pollution, drugs, human rights, and terrorism are among an increasing number of transnational policy issues which, because of globalization, transcend territorial borders and existing political jurisdictions, and thereby require international cooperation for their effective resolution. Politics today is marked by a proliferation of new types of 'boundary problem'. In the past, of course, nation-states principally resolved their differences over boundary matters by pursuing reasons of state backed by diplomatic initiatives and, ultimately, by coercive means. But this geopolitical logic appears singularly inadequate and inappropriate to resolve the many complex issues, from economic regulation to resource depletion and environmental degradation to chemical weapons proliferation, which engender—at seemingly ever greater speeds—an intermeshing of 'national fortunes'.

This is not to argue that the sovereign state is in decline. The sovereign power and authority of national government—the entitlement of states to rule within their own territorial space—is being transformed but by no means eroded. Locked into systems of global and regional governance, states now assert their sovereignty less in the form of a legal claim to supreme power than as a bargaining tool, in the context of transnational systems of rule-making, with other agencies and social forces. Sovereignty is bartered, shared, and divided among the agencies of public power at different levels from the local to the global. The Westphalian conception of sovereignty as an indivisible, territorially exclusive form of public power is being displaced by a new sovereignty regime, in which sovereignty is understood as the shared exercise of public power and authority. In this respect we are witnessing the emergence of a post-Westphalian world order.

Furthermore, far from globalization leading to 'the end of the state', it elicits a more activist state. This is because, in a world of global enmeshment, simply to achieve domestic objectives national governments are forced to engage in extensive multilateral **collaboration** and cooperation. But in becoming more embedded in frameworks of global and regional governance, states confront a real dilemma: in return for more effective public

policy and meeting their citizens' demands, their capacity for self-governance—that is, **state autonomy**—is compromised. Today, a difficult trade-off is posed between effective governance and self-governance. In this respect, the Westphalian image of the monolithic, unitary state is being displaced by the image of the **disaggregated state** in which its constituent agencies increasingly interact with their counterparts abroad, international agencies, and NGOs in the management of common and global affairs (Slaughter 2004) (Fig. 1.3).

Global politics is a term which acknowledges that the scale of political life has fundamentally altered: politics understood as that set of activities concerned primarily with the achievement of order and justice does not recognize territorial boundaries. It questions the utility of the distinction between the domestic and the foreign, inside and outside the **territorial state**, the national and the international since decisions and actions taken in one region impact upon the welfare of communities in distant parts of the globe, with the result that domestic politics is internationalized and world politics becomes domesticated. It acknowledges that power in the global system is not the sole preserve of states but is distributed (unevenly) among a diverse array of public and private actors and networks (from international agencies, through corporations to NGOs) with important consequences for who gets what, how, when, and where. It recognizes that political authority has been diffused not only upwards to supra-state bodies, such as the European Union, but also downwards to sub-state bodies, such as regional assemblies, and beyond the state to private agencies, such as the International Accounting Standards Board. It accepts that sovereignty remains a principal juridical attribute of states but concludes that it is increasingly divided and shared between local, national, regional, and global authorities. Finally, it affirms that, in an age of globalization, national polities no longer function as closed systems. On the contrary, it asserts that all politics—understood as the pursuit of order and justice—are played out in a global context.

However, as with globalization, inequality and exclusion are endemic features of contemporary global politics. There are many reasons for this but three factors in particular are crucial: first, enormous inequalities of power between states; second, global governance is shaped by an unwritten constitution that tends to privilege the interests

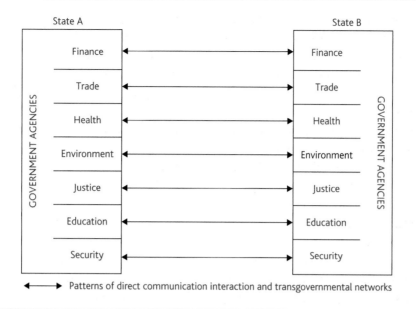

Figure 1.3 The disaggregated state

and agenda of global capitalism; third, the technocratic nature of much global decision-making, from health to security, tends to exclude many with a legitimate stake in the outcomes.

These three factors produce cumulative inequalities of power and exclusion—reflecting the inequalities of power between North and South—with the result that contemporary global politics is more accurately described as **distorted global politics**: 'distorted' in the sense that inevitably those states and groups with greater power resources and access to key sites of global decision-making tend to have the greatest control or influence over the agenda and outcomes of global politics. In short, global politics has few democratic qualities. This sits in tension with a world in which democracy is generally valued. Whether a more democratic global politics is imaginable and what it might look like is the concern of normative theorists and is the subject of the concluding section of this chapter.

Key Points

- Globalization is transforming but not burying the Westphalian ideal of sovereign statehood. It is producing the disaggregated state.
- Globalization requires a conceptual shift in our thinking about world politics from a primarily geopolitical perspective to the perspective of geocentric or global politics—the politics of worldwide social relations.
- Global politics is more accurately described as distorted global politics because it is afflicted by significant power asymmetries.

From distorted global politics to cosmopolition global politics?

Globalization, it can be argued, is associated with a double democratic deficit. On the one hand, it has compounded the tension between democracy as a territoriality rooted system of rule and the operation of global markets and transnational networks of corporate power. For if democratic governments are losing the capacity to manage transnational forces in accordance with the expressed preferences of their citizens, then the very essence of democracy, namely self-governance, is decidedly compromised. On the other hand, it is associated with the emergence of a distorted global politics in which power asymmetries and global institutions more often than not enhance the interests of global elites at the expense of the wider world community. Many of the agencies of global

Box 1.9 Cosmopolitan democracy

Guiding ethical principles/core values	Global social justice, democracy, universal human rights, human security, rule of law, transnational solidarity
Short-term measure	*Governance*
	• Reform of global governance: representative Security Council; establishment of Human Security Council (to coordinate global development policies); Global Civil Society Forum; strengthened systems of global accountability; enhancement of national and regional governance infrastructures and capacities; enhanced parliamentary scrutiny
	Economy
	• Regulating global markets: selective capital controls; regulation of offshore financial centres; voluntary codes of conduct for multinational corporations (MNCs)
	• Promoting development: abolition of debt for highly indebted poor countries (HIPCs); meeting UN aid targets of 0.7% GNP; fair trade rules; removal of EU and US subsidies of agriculture and textiles
	Security
	• Strengthening global humanitarian protection capacities; implementation of existing global poverty reduction and human development commitments and policies; strengthening of arms control and arms trade regulation
Long-term transformations	*Governance*
	• Double democratization (national to supra-state governance); enhanced global public goods provision; global citizenship
	Economy
	• Taming global markets; World Financial Authority; mandatory codes of conduct for MNCs; global tax mechanism; global competition authority
	• Market correcting: mandatory global labour and environmental standards; foreign investment codes and standards; redistributive and compensatory measures; commodity price and supply agreements
	• Market promoting: privileged market access for developing countries; convention on global labour mobility
	Security
	• Global social charter; permanent peacekeeping and humanitarian emergency forces; social exclusion and equity impact reviews of all global development measures
Institutional/political conditions	Activist states, global progressive coalition (involving key Western and developing states and civil society forces), strong multilateral Institutions, open regionalism, global civil society, redistributive regimes, regulation of global markets, transnational public sphere

civil society too are highly unrepresentative of the world's peoples. Distorted global politics, in other words, has weak democratic credentials. Arguably, redressing this double democratic deficit, alongside global **poverty** reduction, is the greatest ethical and political challenge of the twenty-first century.

Within the **normative theory** of world politics one particular approach speaks directly to the failings of distorted global politics, namely, **cosmopolitanism** (see Ch.11) (Held 2002; Moellendorf 2002). Cosmopolitanism presents a radical critique of distorted global politics for the manner in which it perpetuates global inequalities

and therefore global injustices. Realizing a more humane and just world order requires a reformed and more democratic system of global governance, which can at a minimum regulate global markets and prevent transnational harm to the most vulnerable. This might be termed the project of **cosmopolitan democracy** (Box 1.9).

Cosmopolitan democracy can be conceived as a basis for combining the democratization of global governance with the pursuit of global social justice (see Ch.31). It seeks to nurture and institutionalize some of the core values of social democracy—the rule of law, political equality, democratic governance, social justice, social solidarity, and economic efficiency—within global power systems. Cosmopolitan democracy seeks to reinvigorate democracy within states by extending democracy to relations between and across states. Only through such a double democratization will the double democratic deficit created by globalization be addressed. In effect, those global sites and transnational networks of power, which at present escape effective national democratic control, will be brought to account, so establishing the conditions befitting the realization of a more humane and democratic global politics. In the context of a deeply divided world, in which violence is endemic and might seeks to impose right, the prospects for its realization might currently appear somewhat remote. Yet its advocates argue that it is rooted in the actually existing conditions of global politics.

Cosmopolitanism builds upon the argument that globalization is bringing about a post-Westphalian order. As a result, the present world order combines, in an unstable mix, elements of both paradise and power: that is, of democratic principles and realpolitik (see Ch.5 and Ch.7). Thus the principles of self-determination, the rule of law, popular sovereignty, democratic legitimacy, the legal **equality of states**, and even redistribution (through aid) are embedded in global politics. So too are the ideas that might is right and that the **national interest** has primacy over all else. Globalization thereby has provoked major political reactions which in their more progressive manifestations have engendered a wider political debate about the democratic credentials of the existing

global governance complex. Regulating globalization in the public and global interest has become a paramount political issue across the world. Witness, for instance, the global campaign in 2005 to Make Poverty History. There is now increased political pressure on **G8** governments especially to bring good governance to global governance by making it more transparent, accountable, and legitimate. A broader global consensus appears to be emerging on the need for such reform, drawing political support from across the North–South divide and among diverse constituencies of transnational civil society. In short, distorted global politics gives expression to diverse democratic impulses and constituencies. However, it would be foolish to assume that such impulses and constituencies will triumph in the near future since arrayed against them are powerful global forces which resist the creation of a more cosmopolitan or humane global politics.

Arguably, distorted global politics embodies a historic struggle between the logic of power politics (statism) and the logic of cosmopolitanism, between power and paradise. Its future trajectory, however, remains wholly speculative. That it is so is a source of both intellectual despair and huge relief: despair since it reaffirms the limits of our current theories of world politics in so far as they offer scant guide to the future, relief because it confirms that the future remains to be made, even if, to paraphrase Marx, it is not within the conditions of our own choosing. Therefore globalization undoubtedly will remain a powerful force for global change, hopefully for the better but quite possibly for the worse.

Key Points

- Globalization creates a double democratic deficit in that it places limits on democracy within states and new mechanisms of global governance which lack democratic credentials.
- Global politics has engendered its own global political theory which draws upon cosmopolitan thinking.
- Cosmopolitanism offers an account of the desirability and feasibility of the democratization of global politics.
- Distorted global politics can be interpreted as expressing a contest between the forces of statism and cosmopolitanism in the conduct and management of world affairs.

Conclusion

This chapter has sought to elucidate the concept of globalization and identify its implications for the study of world politics. It has argued that globalization reconstructs the world as a shared social space. But it does so in a far from uniform manner: contemporary globalization is highly uneven—it varies in its intensity and extensity between different spheres of activity, and is highly asymmetrical—and it engenders a highly unequal geography of global inclusion and exclusion. In doing so it is as much a source of conflict and violence as of cooperation and harmony in world affairs.

In focusing upon the consequences of globalization for the study of international relations, this chapter has argued that it engenders a fundamental shift in the constitution of world politics. A post-Westphalian world order is in the making as sovereign statehood is transformed by the dynamics of globalization. A conceptual shift in our thinking is therefore required: from geopolitics (or inter-state politics) to global politics—the politics of state and **non-state actors** within a shared global social space. Global politics is imbued with deep inequalities of power such that in its current configuration it is more accurately described as distorted global politics: a politics of domination, contestation and competition between powerful states and transnational social forces. Cosmopolitan theory, it was noted, suggests that a more democratic form of global politics is both desirable and feasible. To this extent the trajectory of global politics will be shaped significantly by the struggle between the forces of statism and cosmopolitanism, or might is right versus right is might. The outcome of this contest will determine whether twenty-first-century global politics will be a politics of hope or of fear; in other words, whether a more humane and democratic global politics can be fashioned out of today's distorted global politics.

❓ Questions

1. Distinguish the concept of globalization from that of regionalization and internationalization.
2. What do you understand by the Westphalian Constitution of world order?
3. Why is global politics today more accurately described as distorted global politics?
4. Outline the principal causes of globalization.
5. Review the sceptical argument and critically evaluate it.
6. What are the principal characteristics of the post-Westphalian order?
7. Identify some of the key elements of political globalization.
8. What are the principal characteristics of contemporary globalization?
9. Distinguish the concept of global politics from that of geopolitics and inter-state politics.
10. Outline the main elements of cosmopolitan global politics.
11. Is the state being eclipsed by the forces of globalization and global governance?
12. Is state sovereignty being eroded or transformed? Explain your answer.

➜ Guide to further reading

Castells, M. (2000), (Oxford: Blackwells). This is a now contemporary classic account of the political economy of globalization which is comprehensive in its analysis of the new global informational capitalism.

Duffield, M. (2001), *Global Governance and the New Wars* (London: Zed). A very readable account of how globalization is leading to the fusion of the development and security agendas within the global governance complex.

Gilpin, R. (2001), *Global Political Economy* (Princeton, NJ: Princeton University Press). A more sceptical view of economic globalization which, although taking it seriously, conceives it as an expression of Americanization or American hegemony.

Held, D., and McGrew, A. (2007), *Globalization/Anti-Globalization: Beyond the Great Divide*, 2nd edn (Cambridge: Polity Press). A short introduction to all aspects of the current globalization debate and its implications for the study for world politics.

Hirst, P., and Thompson, G. (1999), *Globalization in Question*, 2nd edn (Cambridge: Polity Press). An excellent and sober critique of the hyperglobalist argument, which is thoroughly sceptical about the globalization thesis, viewing it as a return to the *belle époque* and heavily shaped by states.

Holton, R. (2005), *Making Globalization* (London: Palgrave). A comprehensive overview of globalization and its implications for the study of the social sciences written from a sociological perspective.

Kennedy, P., *et al.* (2002), *Global Trends and Global Governance* (London: Pluto Press). A good introduction to how globalization is reshaping world politics and the nature of global governance.

Robertson, R. (2003), *The Three Waves of Globalization: A History of Developing Global Consciousness* (London: Zed). A very good account of globalization as a long-term historical process driven by a combination of economic and political factors.

Scholte, J. A. (2005), *Globalization—A critical Introduction*, 2nd edn (Basingstoke: Macmillan). An excellent introduction to the globalization debate from its causes to its consequences for the global political economy from within a critical political economy perspective.

Online Resource Centre

 Visit the Online Resource Centre that accompanies this book to access more learning resources on this chapter topic at www.oxfordtextbooks.co.uk/uk/orc/baylis_smith4e/

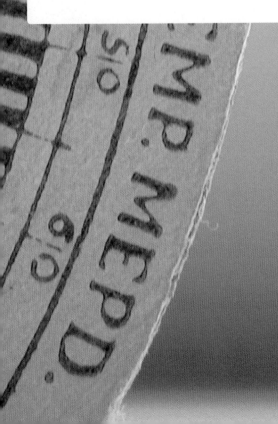

Part One
The historical context

In this part of the book, we want to provide you with a historical context within which to make sense of globalization. We have two main aims: **first**, we want to introduce you to the main aspects of international history and we will do this by giving you a more chronologically concentrated set of chapters. We start with an overview of international society from its origins in ancient Greece through to the beginning of the twenty-first century. We think that you need to have some basic understanding of the main developments in the history of world politics, as well as some kind of context for thinking about the contemporary period of world history. This is followed by a chapter that looks at the main themes of twentieth-century history until the end of the cold war. The final chapter of this section looks at developments within international history since 1990. We want these chapters to give you a lot of historical information which will be of interest in its own right, but our **second** aim is to draw to your attention the main themes of international history so that you can develop a deeper understanding of the issues, both theoretical and empirical, that are dealt with in the remaining four parts of this book. We think that an overview of international history gives you a context within which to begin thinking about globalization: is it a new phenomenon that fundamentally changes the main patterns of international history or are there precedents for it that make it seem less revolutionary?

Chapter 2

The evolution of international society

DAVID ARMSTRONG

- Introduction: the idea of international society ·· 38
- Ancient worlds ·· 39
- The Christian and Islamic orders ·· 42
- The emergence of the modern international society ······································ 44
- The globalization of international society ·· 48
- Conclusion: problems of global international society ···································· 49

Reader's Guide

This chapter discusses the idea of international society and some of its historical manifestations. 'International society' refers to the rules, institutions and shared practices that different groups of political communities have developed in the course of their interaction with each other. It has taken many forms over 5,000 years but today's international society is composed of interconnected but independent sovereign states. It faces a complex range of challenges in the era of globalization.

Introduction: the idea of international society

There are many different ways of characterizing the overall structure and pattern of relations among distinct political communities. At one hypothetical extreme we might imagine an unrestrained struggle of all against all, in which war, conquest, and the slaughter or enslavement of the defeated constituted the sole forms of contact between the communities. At the other extreme we might conceive a world government in which the individual societies retained distinctions based on such features as language, culture, or religion but their political and legal independence were no greater than that of the constituent parts of the USA. Between these extremes we find the many forms of interaction that have emerged in different times and places throughout world history. These range from **empires**, which can themselves be loosely or tightly organized, more or less centralized and relatively formal or informal, to **international systems** organized on the basis of the independence of individual units—or their **sovereignty**—with various kinds of **international hierarchical** orders in between.

In the broadest sense, the term **international society** may be applied to any of these modes of interaction that are governed to some degree by common rules and practices. However, the term has come to be applied more narrowly to a particular historical narrative and to a theoretical perspective derived, in part, from this historical narrative. The narrative concerns the emergence of the European **state system**, with its key principles of sovereignty and **non-intervention**, from the complex medieval order that preceded it. In one version of these events, the European states formed an association referred to as the 'family of nations' or the 'international society'. This was seen as founded both on their determination to safeguard their sovereign status and on a set of values, or a 'standard of civilization', that marked out the members of this inner circle from those outside. Within the club relations were to be governed by the principles of **sovereign equality** and non-intervention and the rules of **international law** (see Ch.16). Outside it, those societies deemed 'uncivilized' could be subject to various means of control or domination, ranging from the 'unequal treaties' which were used to carve out Western spheres of influence in China to outright colonization elsewhere.

The theoretical perspective that draws upon this experience as well as upon earlier ideas advanced by foundational figures in international law, notably **Grotius**, is known as the international society approach or the **English School** of International Relations, the most systematic and comprehensive presentation of whose ideas came from **Hedley Bull**. Like **Waltz** and the neo-realists (Ch.5 and Ch.7), Bull's starting point is that, as states accept no higher power than themselves, they exist in a condition of international **anarchy** (absence of government). Like Waltz, he sees this central facet of the overall international structure as an essential determinant of international relations. Unlike Waltz, who emphasizes the inevitability of power struggles that can only be constrained by a **balance of power**, he sees order in world politics as also potentially deriving from the existence of an international society. Historical examples of such international societies all had a common culture encompassing linguistic, ethical, religious, and artistic elements which assisted the degree of communication and mutual understanding that were required for common rules and institutions to emerge.

Both the English School and the much older historical narrative on which it draws have been attacked for helping to legitimize what was, in reality, an oppressive and exploitative colonial order. Although the notion of a Christian international society pre-dated Columbus, it was used in a more systematic way to justify the European seizure of land from the indigenous peoples of America and elsewhere (Keal 2003). Similarly, the idea of the 'standard of civilization' was employed to rationalize nineteenth-century imperialism and the unequal treatment of nations like China and the Ottoman Empire. Some

---

Box 2.1 Bull on international society

A society of states (or international society) exists when a group of states, conscious of certain common interests and common values, form a society in the sense that they conceive themselves to be bound by a common set of rules in their relations with one another, and share in the working of common institutions.

(Bull 1977: 13)

would argue that, from this perspective, the use today of terms like the international community merely masks the same old reality: one dominated by the great powers.

Such criticisms of the international society tradition may have much validity but it is also important to remain aware of the insights into world politics that a more nuanced and balanced understanding of international society can yield. The interactions among states and other international actors can only be fully comprehended if we can appreciate the larger context within which these interactions take place. There are, of course, many ways of conceptualizing this larger context, each of which gives rise to its own distinct perspective and findings. An emphasis on the world economic structure might interpret events in terms of the development of capitalism. A stress on the power relativities among states might see the world in terms of an ongoing struggle to contain attempts by one great power to achieve preponderance through a balance of power. An interpretation of world history in terms of the clash between different structures of ideas might perceive developments as part of an inevitable dialectic between modernity and reaction. Yet, while major transitions might have been driven by various deep-seated economic, power-political, or cultural factors, human agency has always played the key role in determining the underlying rules, norms, and institutions that shape the relations among international actors at any given time. The term 'international society' is, in essence, a shorthand way of depicting the overall structure constituted by such norms, rules, and institutions. In this sense, far from being a purely European invention, it has been present in different forms throughout world history.

> ## Key Points
>
> - 'International society' is any association of distinct political communities which accept some common values, rules, and institutions.
> - It is the central concept of the 'English School' of International Relations.
> - Although originally coined to refer to relations among European states, the term may be applied to many different sets of political arrangements among distinct political communities.

Ancient worlds

Contemporary international society comprises the norms, rules, established practices, and institutions governing the relations among sovereign states: communities occupying a defined territory within which they exercise juridical independence. Its essential principles, such as non-intervention and legal equality in international relations, reflect the common interest underpinning such an association, namely protecting and legitimizing sovereignty itself and excluding other contenders for legal authority within the state.

No early international society quite resembles this model, mainly because none has quite the unambiguous emphasis on sovereign equality: the equal status in international law of all states that characterizes contemporary international society. In some cases, such as Imperial China at its peak, one powerful state would only deal with others on the basis of an acknowledgement of its own superior standing. In some, other kinds of subordinate relationships prevailed. In others, such as early Islam and medieval Europe, different forms of **supranational** religious authority (the caliphate and the papacy) coexisted in a sometimes uneasy relationship with their secular, usually monarchical, counterparts. Medieval Europe was also marked by a complex mosaic of **subnational** and **transnational** entities, all of which claimed various entitlements and frequently possessed some independent military capacity. These included barons, dukes, bishops, chivalric orders like the Knights Templar and associations of trading cities, like the Hanseatic League.

The term 'international society' may, however, still be used in all of these cases since they all engaged in regular interaction that was, at least sometimes, non-violent and was also characterized by rules and shared values, or at least similar underlying normative assumptions. Such characteristics were in evidence even when the earliest communities began to settle in fixed territorial areas and consequently to develop more complex hierarchical social orders and more varied economies than their hunter-gatherer ancestors had enjoyed, as well as more comprehensive structures of religious beliefs (Buzan and

Box 2.2 Key dates

551–479 BCE	Life of Confucius	1789	French Revolution begins
490–480	Greeks victorious against Persia	1815	Napoleon defeated at Waterloo.
Circa 250	Kautilya writes Arthasastra		Commencement of Concert of Europe.
200	Idea of war crimes mentioned in Hindu code of Manu	1856	End of Crimean War. Ottoman Empire formally accepted as a member of the
146	Rome destroys Carthage, its great historical enemy		European international society
395 CE	Permanent division of Roman Empire	1863	Formation of the International Committee of the Red Cross in Geneva,
570–632	Life of Muhammad, founder of Islam		followed by the first Geneva Convention
1414–18	Council of Constance		on the laws of war in 1864
1453	Ottoman–Empire captures Constantinople	1919	Establishment of the League of Nations
1553	Ottoman-French Treaty against Habsburgs	1945	Establishment of the United Nations
		1948	United Nations Universal Declaration of Human Rights
1583–1645	Life of Grotius, 'father of international law'	1949	Four new Geneva Conventions
1648	Peace of Westphalia ends Thirty Years War	1960	UN General Assembly resolution condemns colonialism as a denial of fundamental human rights
1683	Defeat of Ottomans at Vienna	1979	Islamic Revolution in Iran
1713	Treaty of Utrecht formally recognizes balance of power as basis of order in European society of states	1989	Fall of Berlin Wall symbolizes end of the cold war
		2001	9/11 attack on United States
1776	American War of Independence begins	2003	Start of American-led war in Iraq

Little 2000). Territorial possession needed to be defined, defended, and, if possible, accepted by outside groups. Growing economic complexity and diversity gave rise to increasing trade relations with other communities, which in turn produced the need for mutual understanding and, ideally, rules about such issues as the rights of 'foreigners' to travel through or reside in other lands. As rulers extended their authority over ever-larger areas, so they were increasingly drawn to less violent (and therefore cheaper and safer) means of consolidating and legitimizing their positions. **Diplomatic envoys, treaties**, and careful definition of the rights and duties of lesser kings all played their part in such endeavours. Finally, as primitive religious beliefs evolved into comprehensive ideologies, embracing complex notions of right and wrong and divine reward and retribution, so did the relations among early societies acquire common normative assumptions. That, in turn, made it possible for agreements among these societies to include **sanctions** in the form of the threat of divine punishment for oath-breakers.

It is probable that some variant of these processes was apparent wherever tribes began to establish settled communities or city-states. In the ancient Middle East, the pattern from the third millennium BCE onwards was for the 'great kings' of Akkadia, Sumeria, Assyria, the Hittite Empire and Egypt to claim dominion over lesser lords—their vassals—who, in return for their allegiance, retained some freedom to form alliances and even have their own vassal states. Treaties between great kings and their vassals concerned matters such as borders, trade, grazing rights, inter-marriage, extradition, defence, and the rights and duties of citizens of one state visiting or residing in another. Treaties were accompanied by ceremonies and rituals and they generally contained clauses invoking divine sanctions upon treaty-breakers. They were often negotiated by diplomatic envoys, who did not, strictly speaking, enjoy the equivalent of diplomatic immunity characteristic of modern international society: they could be punished and held hostage and in several cases were actually killed. However, like ancient

treaties, the institution of diplomacy was invested with religious solemnity.

The fragmentary written evidence from this period offers tantalizing glimpses of the normative underpinnings of the relations among the major states. One post-war treaty between Egypt and the Hittites (c. 1300 BCE) pledged permanent alliance, freedom of commerce, and extradition of criminals, subject to the surprisingly humane provision that neither they nor their close relatives should be subjected to extreme punishment. However, the elements of international society that we can discern were almost certainly marginal aspects of a world in which the frequently brutal struggle for survival in economic conditions of bare subsistence constituted the central reality. As economic circumstances improved and settled communities became less vulnerable to marauding nomadic tribes who were outside and impervious to any conception of international rules, so more refined international systems began to appear. In the period from about 700 BCE to the beginnings of Roman domination in the first century BCE the three most notable examples of such systems were to be found in China, India, and Greece.

In all three cases, the countries were divided for much of the period into separate polities but, alongside often fierce competition and conflict, they also retained a sense of their cultural unity. In Greece, the city-states shared a common language and religion, together with institutions like the Olympic Games and the Delphic Oracle that were designed to emphasize this unity. All city-states placed a high value on their independence, which enabled them to unite against the threat of Persian hegemony.

Their common Greek identity did not prevent several bids at hegemony that were sometimes accompanied by brutal warfare. The most famous of these, the Peloponnesian War between Athens and Sparta (431–404 BCE), witnessed the notorious **Melian dialogue**, when Athens rebuffed a request from the island of Melos to remain neutral in the war. Melian appeals to justice, morality, and honour all fell on deaf ears. The Athenians stated bluntly: 'Let's not waste time with fine words which nobody will believe. You know as well as we do that the question of justice hardly ever comes into human affairs. The truth is that the powerful take what they can and the weak grant what they must' (also see Ch.5). When the Melians still refused, the Athenians, after a siege, killed all the men and enslaved all the women and children (Thucydides [1954] 1972).

This, of course, represents one of the most cold-blooded assertions of an ultra-realist view of international relations: only power counts, rules and morality play no part. Numerous similar occasions of ruthless conflict between Greek city-states caution against exaggerating the degree to which they constituted a highly developed international society. Nonetheless, other aspects of inter-city relations suggest that an authentic and well-established international society was also a genuine element in their affairs. First, there was a rudimentary institutional basis of international society in the form of the **Amphyctionic Council**, the use of **arbitration** to settle certain inter-city disputes and the '*proxenia*'. The Council was essentially a religious institution, whose concern was to provide some protection for shrines such as the Delphic Oracle and to enable Greeks to engage in religious rituals even during times of war. It also occasionally played a limited role in helping to bring war to an end. Resort to third-party arbitration to settle disputes was more common, especially in the case of territorial disputes where the land in question had a particular religious, strategic, or economic significance. The *proxenia* was essentially an ancient version of the modern institution of the consulate, in which a *proxenos* (lit: 'for the foreigner') was appointed to represent the interests of the foreign communities in the larger states.

Greek international society was also underpinned by shared moral understandings about rightful international conduct that were ultimately derived from religious norms. These concerned areas like diplomacy, the sanctity of treaties, entry into war and the treatment of enemy dead. Although violations in all these areas certainly occurred, there were also various forms of sanction, including incurring a reputation for unreliability or dishonesty and being punished following a subsequent arbitration.

Ancient India similarly had numerous religious norms that—in principle if not always in practice—applied to international relations. This was especially true of warfare, where India had a much wider and more complex set of norms than any of the other ancient societies. These ranged from conceptions of what constituted a **just war** through various rituals to be observed at the commencement of war to numerous prohibitions on certain forms of conduct during and after war. The concept of *dharma*, a multifaceted term signifying natural and eternal laws, provided the underlying moral foundation for these injunctions. Kautilya's *Arthasastra* (fourth century BCE) added a sophisticated set of maxims concerning the rules

to be followed by kings seeking to dominate the Indian state system. These present the necessity for humane conduct in war as a requirement of prudent statecraft rather than simply of morality. As with Greece and the earlier Near Eastern societies, treaties in India were regarded as having a sacred quality, although additional securities against the breaking of a treaty, such as hostages, were sometimes insisted on.

In the case of China during the five hundred years before its separate kingdoms were unified under the Chin dynasty in 221 BCE, international relations, as with India and Greece, took place in a context of cultural and intellectual richness and dynamism. This produced a complex range of contending schools of thought which, inevitably, touched upon questions of war and peace and other international issues. As with Greece and India, it is hard to determine with any precision the degree to which the principles of conduct elaborated by Confucius and other thinkers influenced the actual practice of the contending states. In the earlier 'Spring and Autumn' period (722–481 BCE) the frequent wars that characterized the constant struggle for hegemony were sometimes fought almost in a formalistic manner, with rules of chivalry strictly observed. During the later 'Warring States' period (403–221 BCE), however, great improvements in the techniques of warfare produced a fierce and brutal struggle for dominance that was eventually won by the Chin state. The new Imperial China was to last in different forms and with varying degrees of unity for more than 2000 years. It came to adopt the formal position that its civilization was so superior to all the others that relations with foreigners—'outer barbarians'—were only possible on the basis of an acknowledgement by the foreigners of China's higher status, including the payment of tribute to the emperor. In so far as the term 'international society' may be applied at all to this perspective, it needs to be formulated in very different ways from those revolving around the concept of a system of interacting, independent states. The Chinese identified themselves—at least in Confucian theory—essentially in cultural terms and saw their place in the world as at the centre of a culturally determined hierarchy.

Our final ancient society, Rome, was obliged during its Republican period to deal with rival powers, such as Carthage, on a basis of equality. Such relationships were based on similar principles relating to treaties and diplomacy to those found in Greece and India. Rome, however, developed a more extensive legal terminology than any other ancient society, and some of this was carried over into its international relations. Republican Rome often sought legal means of settling certain kinds of disputes with other states and also required various religious rituals to be gone through before a war could be declared just, and therefore legal. Rome also acknowledged a set of norms known as *ius gentium* (**law of nations**). As Rome's power grew from the first century BCE, its need to deal with other states on a basis of equality declined.

Key Points

- Elements of international society may be found from the time of the first organized human communities.
- Early forms of diplomacy and treaties existed in the ancient Middle East.
- Relations among the city-states of ancient Greece were characterized by more developed societal characteristics, such as arbitration.
- Ancient China, India, and Rome all had their own distinctive international societies.

The Christian and Islamic orders

Rome left a long shadow on Europe even after the formal division of the empire into eastern and western parts in 395 AD. Indeed the eastern, Byzantine Empire, with its capital at Constantinople (modern Istanbul), survived and even flourished for nearly a thousand years, although faced with constant pressure from the rising power of Islam, whose forces finally overthrew it in 1453.

Byzantium, which also became the centre of Orthodox Christianity, made up for its relative military weakness *vis-à-vis* the Islamic world by building up a highly effective intelligence network and using policies of divide and rule among its enemies, aided by the most organized and well-trained (if also the most duplicitous) diplomatic corps to have appeared in world politics up to that point.

In the West, the papacy long maintained its claim to have inherited Rome's **supranational** authority over the complex structure of **subnational, transnational,** and **national** entities that coexisted in medieval Europe. The Pope's role was usually conceptualized in terms of its 'authority' rather than 'power', and specific papal edicts were frequently ignored by secular rulers. Nonetheless, the Catholic Church was an important unifying element in medieval Europe's international society. The Church's comprehensive moral and ethical code touched upon international relations in several key respects. There were, for example, prohibitions against dealing with Muslim or other non-Christian states. In reality, neither the papal code nor the similar Islamic doctrine prevented either trade or alliance with non-believers, but it needed to be taken into account, if only because violations might need to be justified later. To back up its religious doctrines, the Church constructed an elaborate legal order, comprising a system of sanctions, the use of arbitration, formal legal hearings, and numerous specific rules called **canon law**. The Church laid down rules on the safe conduct of diplomats and on many aspects of treaties, including injunctions against their violation and the grounds on which they could be annulled. The Church's main sanction was the threat of excommunication but it could also order lesser punishments, such as fines or public penance. The structure as a whole was maintained by the priesthood: a 'massive international bureaucracy', in Martin Wight's words (1977: 22).

The Church also elaborated the most systematic doctrine to date of 'just war': the norms to be observed in embarking upon a war in the first place and in the actual conduct and conclusion of war. All of the ancient societies we considered in the last section formulated sets of moral and ethical principles relating to war. The specific problem confronting Augustine, Aquinas and other Christian thinkers was how to reconcile war—which might be necessary to defend Christian lands from their enemies—with fundamental Christian doctrines such as 'turning the other cheek' to enemies. Their attempted resolution of this conundrum, through requirements for war to have a just cause, use proportionate force, be declared by a proper authority, have a fair prospect of success and be waged with the right intention, were seldom, if ever, observed fully in practice. However, they entered the international discourse and stayed there to the present day. They also influenced later attempts to devise international conventions aimed at limiting the horrors of war.

The other great religion of this period, Islam, also had profound implications for international politics. First, the dramatic and rapid expansion of the Arab peoples in the century after the death of Muhammad in 632 across the Middle East and into Africa, Asia, and Europe created a dynamic new force that soon found itself at odds with both Roman and Byzantine Christianity. Second, Islam was originally conceived as creating a single unifying social identity for all Muslims—the *umma* or community of believers—that overrode other kinds of social identity, such as tribe, race, or state. In its early stages, the ideal of the *umma* was to some extent realized in practice through the institution of the caliphate (the successor to the governing role of Muhammad). The great schism between *sunni* and *shia* branches of the faith, together with the urge to independence of the numerous local leaders, brought an end to the caliphate as an effective central political institution, although the adoption of Islam by the nomadic Turks brought a new impetus. The Turks established the Ottoman Empire (1299–1922), which, at its peak, dominated much of southern Europe, the Middle East and North Africa. It did not suffer a major defeat in Europe until the battle of Vienna in 1683, after which it gradually declined in significance.

In early Islamic theory, the world was divided into the *dâr al-harb* (the abode of war) and the *dâr al-Islam* (the abode of Islam). A permanent state of war existed between the two abodes, although truces, lasting up to a maximum of ten years, were possible. Muslims were theoretically obliged to wage *jihad* (struggle by heart, words, hand, and sword) until the *dâr al-harb* had embraced Islam. The sole exception were the 'peoples of the book' (Christians and Jews, although the designation was sometimes pragmatically extended to other religions), who were permitted to continue their religions, albeit at the price of paying a poll tax and accepting fewer rights than Muslims. The periods of truce between the two abodes required treaties: once signed these were to be strictly observed by Muslims. Indeed, Islamic doctrine on honouring treaty commitments was rather stricter than its Catholic equivalent. Islam also laid down various moral principles to be observed in the course of war. Although, as with Christian just war ideas, these were frequently disregarded, there were occasions when military leaders (such as Saladin during the Crusades) attempted to observe them.

These doctrines were developed by Muslim jurists during Islam's initial, dramatic expansion. Inevitably, as

Islam's internal unity broke down and various nations successfully resisted the advance, the Islamic world had to accept the necessity of **peaceful coexistence** with unbelievers for rather longer than the ten-year truce. Close commercial links between the two 'abodes' developed and in some cases Christian rulers were allowed to set up settlements with some **extraterritorial** privileges in Muslim countries. The heads of these settlements were called 'consuls'. By the sixteenth century, the Ottoman Empire had also become an important player in the great power politics of Europe. In a noted treaty of 1535 between Sultan Sulayman and Francis I, King of France, the Ottomans lined up with one Christian king against the most powerful Christian force of the time, the Habsburg Empire.

Key Points

- Medieval Europe's international society was a complex mixture of supranational, transnational, national, and subnational structures
- The Catholic Church played a key role in elaborating the normative basis of medieval international society.
- Islam developed its own distinctive understanding of international society.

The emergence of the modern international society

As we have indicated, the contemporary international society is based upon a conception of the state as an independent actor that enjoys legal supremacy over all non-state actors (or that is sovereign). Logical corollaries of this essential facet include, first, the legal equality of all states, since any other system would be **hierarchical**, **hegemonial**, or **imperial**. The second corollary is the principle of non-intervention by outside forces (including other states) in the domestic affairs of states, since acknowledgement of a right by outsiders to intervene would implicitly give some other actor (such as the Pope) superior authority. The three central institutions of an international society based on these principles derive from its essential attributes. First, formal communication between states was carried on by diplomats who, because they stood for their sovereign masters, should have the same immunity from the laws of the land they were based in as their masters had. Second, rules given the status of international law could not be binding upon states without their consent. Third, given that order in international affairs could not be maintained—as it is in domestic societies—by a higher authority vested with adequate means of enforcement, such international order as was possible could only emerge from the ongoing struggle among states to prevent any of their number from achieving preponderance, or, more precisely, from the balance of power that such a struggle might produce. By the eighteenth century, the balance of power had come to be seen not just as a fortuitous occurrence in international relations but as a fundamental institution and even as part of international law.

These constituent ingredients of European international society took hundreds of years to take shape. The key development was the emergence of the modern state, which began with the assertion of monarchical power against other contenders such as the Pope or local barons. At the same time the power struggles among the royal houses as well as the external threat from the Ottomans pushed them constantly to refine what were to become the familiar tools of statecraft. These included, most crucially, the establishment of centralized and efficient military power; but three other elements were also of great importance: a professional diplomatic service; an ability to manipulate the balance of power; and the evolution of treaties from essentially interpersonal contracts between monarchs sanctioned by religion to agreements between states that had the status of 'law'.

It is impossible to allocate a precise date to any of these developments since, in reality, they were taking place in a random manner across Europe over centuries. The Byzantines, as we have seen, took diplomacy and intelligence gathering to a higher level. Even before the Italian Renaissance, Venice had learnt this new craft from its own interaction with Byzantium and issued the first set of formal rules relating to diplomacy in the thirteenth century. The jealous rivalry among the Italian city-states led them to set up the first system of **resident ambassadors** in order to keep a watchful eye on each other. The Italian states also engaged in a constant balance of power game, including frequent wars. Other European states absorbed Italian ideas about international relations so that permanent

Box 2.3 The Council of Constance

An important legal controversy that may be seen as anticipating modern doctrines of international society occurred at the Council of Constance (1414–18). One issue before the Council concerned Poland's alliance with the non-Christian state of Lithuania against the Teutonic Order, which had been authorized to spread Christianity by force. The alliance contradicted the prevailing doctrine that pagan communities had no legal rights and war against them was, therefore, justified. The Polish defence of their alliance argued that the question whether a community had rights under the law of nations depended entirely on whether they exercised effective jurisdiction over a given territory, not on their religious beliefs: a revolutionary doctrine at the time but one that gradually became established orthodoxy.

(Alexandrowicz, C. H. (1963), 'Paulus Vladimiri and the Development of the Doctrine of Coexistence of Christian and Non-Christian countries', British Yearbook of International Law, 441–48)

embassies, together with agreed rules about **diplomatic immunity** and other ambassadorial privileges, became an established part of European international society. Fourteenth-century Italy also saw an early statement of one of the key doctrines of the sovereignty principle: 'the king is emperor in his own kingdom'.

Three key developments from about the end of the fifteenth century played a crucial role in shaping the postmedieval European international society. First, the larger, more powerful states, such as France and the Habsburg Empire, were increasingly dominating some of the smaller states. Second, the Protestant Reformation of the sixteenth century dealt a devastating blow to the Catholic Church's claim to supreme authority, thus indirectly enhancing the counter-claim of state sovereignty. Finally, Columbus's voyage to the New World in 1492, followed by Vasco da Gama's discovery of a sea route to India in 1498 (thus enabling the dangerous and Muslim-controlled land route to be bypassed) had enormous consequences for European international relations. These included a new spatial awareness and interest in cartography, leading to a much stronger emphasis on territory and strictly defined boundaries.

Two parallel developments need to be borne in mind in evaluating the significance of all this for international society. The first is the struggle for power in Europe. Europe was to experience 450 more years of increasingly violent and widespread war, punctuated by Spanish, French and German bids at hegemony and by intermittent periods of peace before something resembling a final resolution of the tensions unleashed by these forces was

reached. History increasingly unfolded globally rather than regionally as the rest of the world was drawn into Europe's conflicts, first through colonization, then in the two world wars of the twentieth century, finally through the many consequences of decolonization. But the trend towards a uniform politico-legal entity, namely the sovereign state, was unstoppable, first in Europe and eventually in the rest of the world.

Second, there was an ongoing attempt further to develop the few ordering devices permitted by a society of sovereign states. The voyages of discovery gave a huge impetus both to the study of international law and to its use in treaties designed to clarify and define more precisely the various entitlements and responsibilities to which the age of discovery had given rise. In addition, the balance of power came to be increasingly recognized as the most effective instrument against would-be hegemonial powers, making its mastery one of the supreme objects of statecraft. Finally, several of the major wars were followed by systematic attempts to refine and improve upon such means of pursuing international order.

The first sixteenth-century writings on international law came mainly from Spanish jurists, such as Francisco de Vitoria (*c.* 1480–1546), who considered the thorny issue of whether the indigenous inhabitants of the Americas possessed any legal rights. Traditional Catholic theory denied them any such rights but Vitoria, though supporting the Spanish *conquista*, advanced a complex counter-argument, to the effect that the Indians did have some (albeit limited) rights under natural law. In doing so, however, he also went some way towards shifting the location of legitimate authority from the Pope to the emerging sovereign states. This argument, given the extreme inequality of power between the Indians and the Spanish, has been criticized more recently as advancing an early use of the sovereignty doctrine as a justification for imperial exploitation and oppression (Anghie 1996).

Later writings on international law attempted to define the rights and duties owed by sovereign states towards each other, the nature of the international society within which sovereign states existed, and the role of the balance of power in this international society, as well as setting down a host of specific rules relating to such matters as diplomacy, treaties, commerce, the law of the sea, and, most of all, war. Their works, especially those of Grotius and Vattel, were of considerable influence, being carefully scrutinized by, among others,

the governments of China and Japan in the nineteenth century, when they came under strong pressure from Europeans to grant what the Europeans were claiming as legal 'rights'—for example, to trade.

The Thirty Years War (1618–48) is often seen as Europe's last religious war but in fact it was not just a struggle for power but a conflict over legitimate authority among several different kinds of contenders. The Papacy was certainly one of these, but one of its chief supporters, the Habsburg Empire, stood for a kind of dynastic hegemony, while the Holy Roman Emperor was less concerned with his traditional religious dimension than with his continuing hold over the many German states, which, in their turn, stood for the new doctrine of sovereign independence. Holland's struggle (which had been proceeding ever since Philip II of Spain had declared a death sentence on all its inhabitants for heresy in 1568) may be regarded as an early example of a struggle to establish a state based on what was to become the dominating element of nationality.

The Peace of Westphalia (1648), which ended the Thirty Years War, is regarded by many as the key event ushering in the contemporary international system. The Peace established the right of the German states that constituted the Holy Roman Empire to conduct their own diplomatic relations: a very clear acknowledgement of their sovereignty. They were also formally stated to enjoy 'an exact and reciprocal Equality': the first formal acceptance of sovereign equality for a significant number of states. More generally, the Peace may be seen as encapsulating the very idea of a society of states. The participants very clearly and explicitly took over from the Papacy the right to confer international legitimacy upon individual rulers and states and to insist that states observe religious toleration in their internal policies (Armstrong 1993: 30–8). The balance of power was formally incorporated in the **Treaty of Utrecht** (1713), which ended the War of the Spanish Succession (1701–14), when a 'just equilibrium of power' was formally declared to be the 'best and most solid basis of mutual friendship and durable harmony'.

The period from 1648 to 1776 saw the international society that had been taking shape over the previous two hundred years come to fruition. Wars were frequent, if lacking the ideological intensity of the Thirty Years War. Some states, notably the Ottoman Empire, slowly declined; others, such as Britain and Russia, rose. Hundreds of mini-states still existed but it was the interaction among no more than ten key players that determined the course of events. Yet despite constant change and many wars, European writers from de Callière in 1716 to Heeren in 1809 were unanimous in their view that Europe in its entirety constituted a kind of 'republic' (Whyte 1919; Heeren 1971). Some pointed to religious and cultural similarities in seeking to explain this phenomenon, but the central elements that all were agreed on were a determination by all states to preserve their freedom, a mutual recognition of each other's right to an independent existence, and above all a reliance on the balance of power. Diplomacy and international law were seen as the other two key institutions of international society, so long as the latter was based clearly on state consent.

It should be noted that some scholars have disputed this interpretation of eigthteen-century international society. The French historian, Albert Sorel, dismissed the notion of an eigthteen-century 'Christian republic' as 'an august abstraction', arguing that ruthless self-interest was the only principle that mattered (Cobban and Hunt 1969). Indeed, even some, such as Edmund Burke, who believed that there was a true European international society, were appalled by the dismemberment of Poland from 1772 onwards, which Burke saw as a first move away from a system founded on 'treaties, alliances, common interest and public faith' towards a Hobbesian state of nature (Stanlis 1953). More recently, Stephen Krasner (1999) has argued more generally that sovereignty was never more than a legal fiction—or an 'organized hypocrisy'—that disguised the extent to which powerful states were able to pursue their own interests without hindrance. Such viewpoints, at the very least, caution against the more idealistic formulations of an international society whose foundation stone was undoubtedly the self-interest of its members.

The American and French revolutions were to have profound consequences for international society. In the case of the USA, these mainly stemmed from its emergence as a global superpower in the twentieth century. The consequences of the French Revolution were more immediate. First, the revolutionary insistence that sovereignty was vested in 'the nation' rather than the rulers—especially dynastic imperial rulers like the Habsburgs—gave a crucial impetus to the idea of 'national self-determination'. This was the principle that was increasingly to dominate international politics in the nineteenth and twentieth centuries and to endanger imperial systems that were

seen as denying the rights of **nations** (people defined by linguistic, ethnic, and cultural bonds) to become sovereign states themselves.

The second consequence of the French Revolution stemmed from the response to it of the main European powers. After the defeat of Napoleon, the leading states increasingly set themselves apart from the smaller ones as a kind of great powers' club. This system, known as the 'Concert of Europe', lasted until the First World War. It was characterized by regular meetings of the club that had the aims of maintaining the European balance of power drawn up at the end of the Napoleonic Wars and reaching collective decisions on various potentially divisive issues. The leading dynastic powers, Austria and Russia, wanted the Concert to give itself the formal right to intervene against any revolution. This was strongly resisted by Britain, which was the least threatened by revolution, on the grounds that such a move would violate the key principle of non-intervention. However, the Concert unquestionably marked a shift away from the free-for-all and highly decentralized system of eighteenth-century international society towards a more managed, hierarchical system. This affected all three of the key institutional underpinnings of the Westphalian international society: the balance of power, diplomacy, and international law. In 1814 the powers had already formally declared their intention to create a 'system of real and permanent balance of power in Europe', and in 1815 they carefully redrew the map of Europe to implement this system. The main diplomatic development was the greatly increased use of conferences to consider and sometimes settle matters of general interest. In a few technical areas, such as international postal services, telegraphy, and sanitation, permanent international organizations were set up. In international law, the powers sought to draft what Clark (1980: 91) terms 'a procedure of international legitimation of change', especially in the area of territorial change. There were attempts by the great powers collectively to guarantee various treaties, such as those defining the status of Switzerland, Belgium, and Luxembourg. A great many treaties laid down rules in various technical and economic areas as well as over a few humanitarian issues, notably slavery and the treatment of those wounded in war. It should be noted, however, that, while the Concert did help to bring some measure of peace and order to Europe, elsewhere it was one of the mechanisms whereby the European powers legitimized their increasing

domination of Asia and Africa. For example, the Congress of Berlin of 1885 helped to prevent a major war over rival claims in Africa but it also set out the rules governing 'new acts of occupation'. Pious sentiments about bringing the 'benefits of civilization' to Africa meant little.

The First World War brought an abrupt and permanent end to the Concert of Europe. New powers, notably the United States and Japan, had appeared and there were increasing demands for national liberation in India and other parts of the European empires. Moreover, existing smaller states were less willing to be dictated to by the great powers' club, as was apparent in the deliberations to set up the world's first multipurpose, universal international organization, the **League of Nations**, in 1919. This may be seen as the first comprehensive attempt to establish a formal organizational foundation for international society which would enshrine all of its key rules and norms.

If nineteenth-century Europe's international society had taken the form of a joint **hegemony** by the great powers' club, the League represented a significant departure from this in two important respects. First, in line with the belief of the highly influential American President, Woodrow Wilson, that the balance of power system itself had been a major cause of the war, the League was based on a new principle of **collective security** rather than a balance of power. The central notion here was that all states would agree in advance to unite against any act of aggression. This, it was hoped, would deter any potential aggressor. Second, League membership was worldwide, not merely European.

The League represented an ambitious attempt to construct a more highly organized *international society* capable of bringing order across a whole range of issues. The *international system*, however, remained one firmly based on the sovereignty principle and hence still reliant upon a balance of power among the major states. The reality of the post-war period was that one power, the United States, had refused to join the League and was pursuing a policy of non-involvement in European international relations. By the 1930s, four of the remaining powers, Germany, Italy, Japan, and Russia, all had governments characterized by extremist ideologies and expansionist tendencies that threatened the interests of other great powers, with only Britain and France committed to the status quo. In other words, there was a serious *imbalance* of power.

Key Points

- The main ingredients of contemporary international society are the principles of sovereignty and non-intervention and the institutions of diplomacy, the balance of power, and international law.
- These took centuries to develop, although the Peace of Westphalia (1648) was a key event in their establishment throughout Europe.

- The Napoleonic Wars were followed by a shift to a more managed, hierarchical, international society within Europe and an imperial structure in Europe's relations with much of the rest of the world.
- The League of Nations was an attempt to place international society on a more secure organizational foundation.

The globalization of international society

A significant cause of the League's weakness had been the refusal of the American Senate to ratify the post-war **Peace Treaty of Versailles** (including the League Covenant) and it was largely American determination not to make the same mistake in 1945 that led to a considerably stronger new version of the League in the shape of the United Nations (also see Ch.18). In practice, however, the UN was very seldom able to play the leading role envisioned for it in the post-war international society, largely because the **cold war** prevented agreement between the two most important members of the Security Council, the United States and the Soviet Union. Indeed, the cold war meant, effectively, the division of the world into two contending hegemonial international societies.

Although Soviet–American competition affected all aspects of world politics, the rough balance of power between the two superpowers did help to secure a degree of order, especially in Europe, where the military confrontation was greatest. There were also many relatively non-contentious areas where the two were able to agree to further development of international law. Elsewhere, decolonization brought about what amounted to the globalization of European international society as the newly free colonies unanimously opted for state sovereignty and for an international society based on the various corollaries of sovereignty that had emerged in European international society: mutual recognition, non-intervention,

diplomacy, and consensual international law. Successive leaders in the developing countries did attempt to promote alternatives, such as pan-Africanism, pan-Arabism and pan-Islam, but to no avail.

The collapse of the Soviet Union from 1989 completed the globalization of international society. Although in some respects resembling a traditional European empire, the Soviets had also stood for an alternative conception of international society: one based on the notion that the working classes of all countries enjoyed a solidarity that cut across state boundaries. This had enabled Moscow to call upon the loyalty of Communist parties round the world, as well as the services of sympathizers in the diplomatic and scientific establishments of several Western countries. After the 1979 Iranian Revolution, the Ayatollah Khomeini made a similar call on Muslims to see their religion rather than their state as the central focus of their loyalties.

Key Points

- The United Nations was intended to be a much improved League of Nations but the cold war prevented it from functioning as such.
- Decolonization led to the worldwide spread of the European model of international society.
- The collapse of the Soviet Union completed this process.

Case Study The Iranian Revolution 1979

Since 1941 Iran had been governed by Shah Mohammad Reza Pahlavi, who liked to portray himself as heir to the great Persian emperors. He allied himself closely to the United States and pursued modernization along Western lines but as his regime came increasingly to be seen as corrupt, brutal, and wasteful of its huge oil wealth, the USA was associated with his growing unpopularity. Opposition to his rule came from many groups, including liberals and leftists, but after the Iranian Revolution of 1979 the country was increasing dominated by conservative Muslim clerics, led by Ayatollah Khomeini, and declared itself an Islamic Republic.

Khomeini challenged not just American power but the prevailing conceptions of international society. He believed the problems of the Middle East and other Muslim countries to have been caused by their disregard of Islamic religious principles and called for the overthrow of 'the illegitimate political powers that now rule the entire Islamic world' and their replacement by religious governments. More generally, he argued that not only were earthly governments illegitimate, but the state itself and the concept of nationality were equally invalid. In opposition to the Westphalian division of the world into sovereign states, each defined by territorial boundaries ('the product of a deficient human mind'), Khomeini insisted that the only important social identity for Muslims was their membership of the community of believers, or umma.

If Khomeini had little time for the state itself, he had even less for the notion of a society of states with rules, norms of behaviour, and institutions to which Iran was supposed to adhere. For Khomeini, the correct approach to international relations, as to everything else, was determined by Islam: 'the relations between nations should be based on spiritual grounds'. These placed the transnational bonds of the umma above unnatural territorial boundaries that merely served to divide Muslims from each other. Relations with non-Muslim societies were also to be conducted according to traditional Islamic principles. As interpreted by Khomeini, these included, in the words of the Iranian constitution, support for 'the just struggle of the oppressed and deprived in every corner of the globe'. International institutions like the UN were merely part of the superpowers' structure of oppression, while international law should only be observed if it accorded with the Koran. Similarly, Khomeini supported the seizure of the American embassy in Tehran and the holding of many diplomats there hostage for more than a year.

Although Iran espouses the minority, Shia, branch of Islam, which is strongly opposed by many adherents of the majority, Sunni, branch, the Iranian Revolution, particularly its anti-American and Islamist aspects, had many admirers in the Muslim world and may be seen as a key event in the rise of radical Islamist movements around the world.

(Armstrong 1993: 188-97)

Conclusion: problems of global international society

As we have seen, in most earlier international societies some measure of independence coexisted with clear hegemonial or imperial elements. International society after the cold war was the first when sovereign equality was—in practice as well as theory—the central legal norm for the whole world. At the start of the new millennium, all 192 UN members had formally agreed to what Jackson terms a **global covenant** enshrining the core values of independence, non-intervention, and, generally, 'the sanctity, integrity and inviolability of all existing states, regardless of their level of development, form of government, political ideology, pattern of culture or any other domestic characteristic or condition' (Jackson and Owens 2001: 58). They had also agreed to severe constraints on

Box 2.4 Robert Jackson on freedom and international society

'[*The Global Covenant*] can be read as an extended essay on international freedom. Modern international society is a very important sphere of human freedom; it affords people the political latitude to live together within their own independent country, according to their own domestic ideas and beliefs, under a government made up of people drawn from their own ranks: international freedom based on state sovereignty.'

(Jackson 2000: vii)

their right to go to war and to promote respect for human rights for all. However, this conception of international society raises several major questions.

First, globalization itself is serving to dissolve traditional social identities as countless 'virtual communities' emerge and as the global financial markets limit states' freedom to control their own economic policies. Some argue that globalization is bringing in its wake a new cosmopolitan culture, in which the central norms revolve around the rights of individuals rather than states. They point to the growing importance of 'global civil society' in the form of non-governmental organizations like Amnesty or Greenpeace as a key aspect of this process (see Ch.19). Others use examples of 'humanitarian intervention' to argue that a more 'solidarist' international society is emerging in which a strict principle of non-intervention can be qualified in the event of serious humanitarian emergencies (Wheeler and Dunne 1998).

Second, the post-cold war order has produced an increasing number of *collapsed, failed* or *fragmenting* states, especially in Africa. Sovereign equality implies an ability not just to participate as an equal on the international stage but to maintain orderly government within the state. One consequence of the inability of some governments to perform these functions is a new set of serious security problems *within* rather than *between* states, with which international society—because of the principle of non-intervention—is poorly equipped to deal.

Third, American military power is currently greater than that of the next ten most powerful states combined. This has produced a situation without precedent in international history, which some term a 'unipolar moment'. Although China and a united Europe both have the potential eventually to balance American power, there is no realistic prospect of this happening in the next few decades. Since 9/11, the United States has, in both

rhetoric and action, shown a willingness to employ its power—unilaterally if necessary—to defend what it sees as its vital interest.

Fourth, earlier European international societies were underpinned by a common culture and shared values. Although all states have signed up to human rights norms and most declare their support of democracy, these are often interpreted very differently by different societies. Moreover, there is a growing tendency in developing states to see such values as part of a hypocritical Western strategy of imperialism. Radical Islamist movements have been at the forefront of this kind of resistance.

Fifth, two issues—the environment and severe poverty (Ch.20 and Ch.27)—are at the same time increasing in importance and difficult to accommodate within a sovereignty-based international society. Tackling global poverty might require sustained and far-reaching involvement by richer states in the poorer states' domestic affairs, together with constraints on economic freedom in the leading economies. Dealing with climate change—a problem that does not observe national boundaries—may need not just extensive international legislation but enforcement mechanisms that also severely curtail states' freedom.

All these issues revolve, in different ways, around two central questions: can an international society founded on the principle of sovereignty endure? And should it? English School theorists, like Bull, have always argued the need for international society to have a foundation of agreed ideas and values, which may mean much greater absorption of non-Western elements if it is to become genuinely universal. One possible future—that of a **clash of civilizations** (Huntington 1996)—starts from the assumption that Western and non-Western values are simply incompatible. What is envisaged here is essentially the existence of two or more distinct international societies in contention with each other, much as Christendom and Islam interacted in the Middle Ages. Another argues for a more assertive Westernism, including the imposition of Western values, if necessary: a return, in some respects, to the nineteenth century's international society, albeit with more altruistic intentions. A third emphasizes the need to develop 'globally institutionalized political processes by which norms and rules can be negotiated on the basis of dialogue and consent, rather than simply imposed by the most powerful' (Hurrell 2006: 213). In this formulation, sovereignty would remain the cornerstone of international society

Box 2.5 Andrew Hurrell on the future of international society

'All stable societies have to find some agreed process and procedure by which moral conflicts can be adjudicated and managed, if not resolved. Within world politics the challenge is still more daunting given the diversity and divisiveness of sentiments, attachments, languages, cultures and ways-of-living, combined with the massive inequalities of power, wealth and capacity. A global moral community in which claims about justice can both secure authority and be genuinely accessible to a broad swathe of humanity will be one that is built around some minimal notion of just process, that prioritizes institutions that embed procedural fairness, and that cultivates the shared political culture and the habits of argumentation and deliberation on which such institutions necessarily depend.'

(Hurrell 2006: 213)

they choose, including in their right to go to war. In the twentieth century the term came to be indelibly linked to the concept of national self-determination, bringing an end to the European powers' ability to insist on respect for all of their sovereign rights, while simultaneously denying these to their colonies. Peoples who have only won independence in the last few decades are unlikely to wish to relinquish it in favour of a more truly cosmopolitan order, so international society is likely to remain firmly based on the sovereignty principle. Whether such an international society will be able to deal with the new challenges it faces will depend on its capacity to evolve again as it has in the past.

but with more inclusive, responsive; and effective collective decision-making processes.

Sovereignty has always shown itself capable of evolving to meet different circumstances. Dynastic sovereignty gave way to popular sovereignty and states have accepted increasing limitations on their freedom to do as

Key Points

- Globalization poses serious problems for a sovereignty-based international society.
- These include the challenges emanating from new forms of community, failing states in Africa, American hyperpower, growing resistance to Western ideas, and global poverty and environmental issues.

? Questions

1 Discuss and evaluate Hedley Bull's concept of international society.
2 Compare and contrast medieval Christian and Islamic conceptions of international society.
3 Why has the balance of power been such a central institution of a society of sovereign states?
4 Critically evaluate the general view of the Peace of Westphalia as the founding moment of modern international society.
5 Was nineteenth-century European international society merely a means of legitimizing imperialism?
6 Why has an originally European society of states become the general norm around the world?
7 Why did the 1979 Iranian Revolution pose such a challenge to the accepted understanding of international society?
8 Can an international society of sovereign states resolve such problems as extreme poverty and climate change?

➡ Guide to further reading

Bellamy, A. J. (2005), *International Society and Its Critics* (Oxford: Oxford University Press). Useful recent collection of essays using several theoretical perspectives to look at the English School's contemporary relevance.

Bull, H. (2002), *The Anarchical Society: A Study of Order in World Politics* (Basingstoke: Palgrave). The third edition of this classic statement of the English School approach to international society, with valuable Forewords by Andrew Hurrell and Stanley Hoffmann.

Bull, H., and Watson, A. (eds) (1984), *The Expansion of International Society* (Oxford: Clarendon Press). Edited collection of essays (including five by Bull and Watson) on different aspects of the historical expansion of European international society to the rest of the world.

Buzan, B. (2004), *From International to World Society? English School Theory and the Social Structure of Globalisation* (Cambridge: Cambridge University Press). An important study that attempts to develop more rigorous conceptualizations of English School theory, particularly in the context of globalization.

Buzan, B., and Little, R. (2000), *International Systems in World History* (Oxford: Oxford University Press). A theoretically informed and wide-ranging discussion of the development of different kinds of international systems over five thousand years.

Clark, I. (2005), *Legitimacy in International Society* (Oxford: Oxford University Press). A historical and theoretical discussion of the notion of international legitimacy, conclusively demonstrating its centrality to the concept of an international society.

Jackson, R. (2000), *The Global Covenant: Human Conduct in a World of States* (Oxford: Oxford University Press). A richly textured re-examination of the underlying pluralist norms of classical international society theory in the contemporary world.

Keal, P. (2003), *European Conquest and the Rights of Indigenous Peoples: The Moral Backwardness of International Society* (Cambridge: Cambridge University Press). A challenging recent study of the contribution of international society to the destruction and dispossession of indigenous peoples.

Keene, E. *(2002), Beyond the Anarchical Society: Grotius, Colonialism and Order in World Politics* (Cambridge: Cambridge University Press). A valuable discussion of the dualistic nature of classical notions of international society: pluralistic toleration of difference alongside promotion of the 'standard of civilization'.

Little, R., and Williams, J. (eds) (2006), *The Anarchical Society in a Globalized World* (Basingstoke: Palgrave). A recent collection of essays considering Bull's classic work after thirty years.

Watson, A. (1992), *The Evolution of International Society* (London: Routledge). A general historical account of international society since the earliest times, with a particular focus on hegemony.

Online Resource Centre

 Visit the Online Resource Centre that accompanies this book to access more learning resources on this chapter topic at www.oxfordtextbooks.co.uk/uk/orc/baylis_smith4e/

Chapter 3

International history 1900–90

LEN SCOTT

- Introduction ·· 56
- Modern total war ·· 56
- End of empire ·· 58
- Cold war ·· 60
- Conclusion ··· 67

Reader's Guide

This chapter examines some of the principal developments in world politics from 1900 to 1990: the development of total war, the onset of the cold war, the advent of nuclear weapons, and the end of European imperialism. The dominance of, and conflict between, European states in the first half of the twentieth century was replaced as the key dynamic in world affairs by the confrontation betwixt the United States of America and the Union of Soviet Socialist Republics (USSR). The cold war encompassed ideological, political, and military interests of the two states (and their allies), and extended around the globe. How far, and in what ways, global conflict was promoted or prevented by the cold war are central questions. Similarly, how decolonization became entangled with East–West conflicts is central to understanding many struggles in the 'Third World'. Finally, how dangerous was the nuclear confrontation between East and West? The chapter explores the role of nuclear weapons in specific phases of the cold war, notably in *détente*, and then with the deterioration of Soviet–American relations in the 1980s.

Introduction

The First World War (also known as the Great War) began between European states on European battlefields, but extended across the globe. It was the first modern, industrialized **total war**, as the belligerents mobilized their populations and economies as well as their armies, and as they endured enormous casualties over many years. The Second World War was even more total in nature and global in scope, and helped bring about fundamental changes in world politics. Before 1939, **Europe** had been the arbiter of world affairs, when both the USSR and the USA remained, for different reasons, preoccupied with internal development at the expense of a significant global role. The Second World War brought the Soviets and the Americans militarily and politically deep into Europe, and helped transform their relations with each other. This transformation was soon reflected in their relations outside Europe, where various confrontations developed. Like the Second World War, the cold war had its origins in Europe, but quickly spread, with enormous consequences for countries and peoples around the world.

The Great War brought the demise of four European empires: Russian, German, Austro-Hungarian and Ottoman (in Turkey). After 1945, European power was in eclipse. The economic plight of the wartime belligerents, including those who emerged as victors, was increasingly apparent, as was growing realization of the military and economic potential of the USA and the USSR. Both emerged as 'superpowers', combining global political ambition with military capabilities that included weapons of mass destruction. European political, economic,

and military weakness contrasted with the appearance of Soviet strength and the growing Western perception of malign Soviet intent. The onset of the cold war in Europe marked the collapse of the wartime alliance between the UK, the USSR, and the USA. Whether this was inevitable after 1945 remains contentious. The most tangible legacy of the Second World War was the atomic bomb, built at enormous cost, and driven by fear that Nazi Germany might win this first nuclear arms race. After 1945, nuclear weapons posed unprecedented challenges to world politics and to the leaders responsible for conducting post-war diplomacy. The cold war provided context and pretext for the growth of nuclear arsenals that threatened the very existence of humankind, and which have continued (and continue to spread) beyond the end of the cold war and the East–West confrontation.

Since 1900 world politics has been transformed in a variety of ways, reflecting political, technological, and ideological developments, of which three are examined in this chapter: (1) the transition from European crises to modern, industrialized total war; (2) the end of empire and the withdrawal of European countries from their imperial acquisitions; and (3) the cold war: the political and military and nuclear confrontation between the United States and the Soviet Union. There have, of course, been other important changes, and indeed equally important continuities, which are explored in other chapters. Nevertheless, the three principal changes outlined above provide a framework for exploring events and trends that have shaped international politics and the world we now inhabit.

Modern total war

The origins of the Great War have long been debated. For the victorious allies, the question of how the First World War began became a question of how far the Germans and their allies should be held responsible. At Versailles, the victors imposed a statement of German war guilt in the final settlement, primarily to justify the reparations they demanded. Debates among historians about the war's origins focused on political, military and systemic factors.

Some suggested that responsibility for the war was diffuse, as its origins lay in complex dynamics of the respective alliances and their military imperatives. One of the more influential post-war interpretations, however, came from the West German historian, Fritz Fischer, who in his 1967 book, *Germany's Aims in the First World War*, argued that German aggression, motivated by the internal political needs of an autocratic elite, was responsible for the war.

However complex or contested the origins of the war were in retrospect, the motivations of those who fought were more explicable. The masses of the belligerent nations shared nationalist beliefs and patriotic values. As they marched off to fight, most thought war would be short, victorious, and in many cases, glorious. The reality of the European battlefield and the advent of trench warfare was otherwise. Defensive military technologies, symbolized by the machine gun, triumphed over the tactics and strategy of attrition, though by November 1918 the allied offensive finally achieved the rapid advances that helped bring an end to the fighting. It was total war in the sense that whole societies and economies were mobilized: men were conscripted into armies and women went to work in factories. The western and eastern fronts remained the crucibles of the fighting, though conflict spread to various parts of the globe, including when Japan went to war in 1914 as an ally of Britain. Most importantly, the United States entered the war in 1917 under President Woodrow Wilson, whose vision of international society, articulated in his **Fourteen Points**, was to drive the agenda of the Paris Peace Conference in 1919. The overthrow of the Tsar and the seizure of power by Lenin's Bolsheviks in November 1917 soon led Russia, now the USSR, to negotiate withdrawal from the war. Germany no long fought on two fronts, but soon faced a new threat as the resources of the USA were mobilized. With the failure of its last great military offensive in the west in 1918, and with an increasingly effective British naval blockade, Germany agreed to an armistice.

The **Peace Treaty of Versailles** failed to tackle what was for some the central problem of European security after 1870—a united and frustrated Germany—and precipitated German revanchism by creating new states and devising contested borders. For some scholars, 1914–45 represented a thirty-year war. Others saw the period 1919 to 1939 as a twenty-year crisis. Economic factors were also crucial. The effects of the Great Depression, triggered in part by the Wall Street Crash of 1929, weakened the forces of liberal-democracy in many areas and strengthened the appeal of communist, fascist, and Nazi parties. The effect on German society was particularly significant. All modernized states suffered mass unemployment, but in Germany, inflation was acute. Economic and political instability provided the ground in which support for the Nazis took root. By 1933, Adolf Hitler had achieved power, and the transformation of the German state began.

There remain debates about how far Hitler's ambitions were carefully thought through and how far he seized opportunities. A controversial analysis was provided by A. J. P. Taylor in his 1961 book, *Origins of the Second World War*, in which he argued that Hitler was no different from other German political leaders. What was different was the particular philosophy of Nazism and ideas of racial supremacy and imperial expansion. British and French attempts to negotiate with Hitler culminated in the Munich agreement of 1938. Hitler's territorial claims over the Sudetenland in Czechoslovakia were accepted as the price for peace, but within months Germany had seized the rest of Czechoslovakia and was preparing for war on Poland. Recent debates about **appeasement** have focused on whether there were realistic alternatives to negotiation, given the lack of military preparedness with which to confront Hitler.

By 1939, the defensive military technologies of the Great War gave way to armoured warfare and air power, as the German *blitzkrieg* brought speedy victories over Poland, and in the west. Hitler was also drawn into the Balkans in support of his Italian ally, Mussolini, and into North Africa. With the invasion of the Soviet Union in June 1941, the scale of fighting and scope of Hitler's aims were apparent. Massive early victories on the eastern front gave way to winter stalemate, and the mobilization of Soviet peoples and armies. German treatment of civilian populations and Soviet prisoners of war reflected Nazi ideas of racial supremacy, and resulted in the deaths of millions. German anti-Semitism and the development of concentration camps gained new momentum after a decision on the 'Final Solution of the Jewish Question' in 1942. The term **holocaust** entered the political lexicon of the twentieth century, as the Nazis attempted the genocide of the Jewish people and other minorities, such as the Roma, in Europe.

The rise and fall of Japan

After 1919, international attempts to provide collective security were pursued through the League of Nations. The US Senate prevented American participation in the league, however, and Japanese aggression against Manchuria in 1931, the Italian invasion of Abyssinia in 1935, and German involvement in the Spanish Civil War 1936–9 were met with ineffective international responses.

Hiroshima (6 August 1945): 70–80,000 'prompt'; 140,000 by end 1945; 200,000 by 1950
Nagasaki: (9 August 1945): 30–40,000 'prompt'; 70,000 by end 1945; 140,000 by 1950
Tokyo (9 March 1945): 100,000 +
Dresden (13–15 February 1945): 25–135,000
Coventry (14 November 1940): 568
Leningrad (siege 1941–4): 1,000,000 +

Table 3.1 Second World War estimated casualties

In 1868, Japan had emerged from several centuries of isolationism to pursue industrial and military modernization, and then imperial expansion. In 1937, China, already embroiled in civil war between communists and nationalists, was invaded by Japan. Tokyo's ambitions, however, could only be realized at the expense of European empires and American interests. President Roosevelt increasingly sought to engage the USA in the European war, against strong isolationist sentiments, and by 1941, German submarines and America warships were in an undeclared war. The imposition of American economic sanctions on Japan precipitated Japanese military preparations for a surprise attack on the US fleet at Pearl Harbor on 7 December 1941. When Germany and Italy declared war on America in support of their Japanese ally, Roosevelt decided to prioritize the European over the Pacific theatre. After a combined strategic bombing offensive with the British against German cities, the allies launched a 'second front' in France, for which the Soviets had been pressing.

Defeat of Germany in May 1945 came before the atomic bomb was ready. The destruction of the Japanese cities, Hiroshima and Nagasaki, remains a controversy. Aside from moral objections to attacking civilian populations, their destruction generated fierce debate, particularly among American historians, about why the bomb was dropped. Gar Alperovitz, in his 1965 book *Atomic Diplomacy*, argued that, as President Truman knew Japan was defeated, his real motive was to coerce Moscow in pursuit of post-war American interests in Europe and Asia. Such claims generated angry and dismissive responses from other historians. Ensuing scholarship has benefited from more historical evidence though debate persists over how far Truman dropped the bomb simply to end the war, and how far other factors, including coercion of the Soviet Union in post-war affairs, entered his calculations.

Key Points

- Debates about the origins of the First World War focus on whether responsibility should rest with the German government or whether war came because of more complex systemic factors.
- The Paris Peace settlement failed to address the central problems of European security, and in restructuring the European state system created new sources of grievance and instability.
- The rise of Hitler posed challenges that European political leaders lacked the ability and will to meet.
- The German attack on the Soviet Union extended the scope and barbarity of the war from short and limited campaigns to extended, large-scale, and barbaric confrontation, fought for total victory.
- The Japanese attack on Pearl Harbor brought America into the war in Europe and eventually led Germany into war on two fronts (again).
- Debate persists about whether the atomic bomb should have been used in 1945, and about the effect that this had on the cold war.

End of empire

The demise of imperialism in the twentieth century marked a fundamental change in world politics. It reflected, and contributed to, the decreasing importance of Europe as the arbiter of world affairs. The belief that national **self-determination** should be a guiding principle in international politics marked a transformation of attitudes and values. During the age of imperialism politi-cal status accrued to imperial powers. After 1945, imperialism became a term of opprobrium. Colonialism and the United Nations Charter were increasingly recognized as incompatible, though independence was often slow and sometimes marked by prolonged and armed struggle. The cold war often complicated and hindered the transition to independence. Various factors influenced the process

Country	Colonial state	Year of independence
India	Britain	1947
Pakistan	Britain	1947
Burma	Britain	1948
Sri Lanka	Britain	1948
Indonesia	Holland	1949
Ghana	Britain	1957
Malaya	Britain	1957
French African colonies*	France	1960
Zaïre	Britain	1960
Nigeria	Britain	1960
Sierra Leone	Britain	1961
Tanganyika	Britain	1961
Uganda	Britain	1962
Algeria	Britain	1962
Rwanda	Belgium	1962
Kenya	Britain	1963
Guinea-Bissau	Portugal	1974
Mozambique	Portugal	1975
Cape Verde	Portugal	1975
Sao Tome	Portugal	1975
Angola	Portugal	1975
Zimbabwe	Britain	1980

*including Cameroon, Central African Republic, Chad, Gabon, Ivory Coast, Madagascar, Mali, Mauritania, Niger, Senegal, and Upper Volta.

Table 3.2 Principal acts of European decolonization, 1945–80

of decolonization: the attitude of the colonial power; the ideology and strategy of the anti-imperialist forces; and the role of external powers. Political, economic, and military factors played various roles in shaping the transfer of power. Different imperial powers and newly emerging independent states had different experiences of withdrawal from empire.

Britain

In 1945, the British Empire extended across the globe. Between 1947 and 1980, 49 territories were granted independence. There was political disagreement within Britain over the UK's imperial role, but after 1945, a growing recognition of the justice of self-determination, combined with an understanding of the strength of nationalism, brought about a reappraisal of policy.

Withdrawal from India, the 'Jewel in the Crown' of the empire, in 1947 was the most dramatic. It paved the way for the creation of the world's largest democracy, though the creation of India and Pakistan led to intercommunal ethnic cleansing and hundreds of thousands of deaths. How far the ensuing hostility between India and Pakistan was avoidable and how far it reflected previous British efforts to divide and rule are issues for debate. What is clear is that Indian independence was largely an exception in the early post-war years, as successive British governments were reluctant to rush towards decolonization. End of empire in Africa came towards the end of the 1950s and early 1960s, symbolized by Prime Minister Harold Macmillan's speech in South Africa in February 1960 when he warned his hosts of the 'wind of change' blowing through their continent.

British withdrawal from Africa was relatively peaceful, save for conflicts with indigenous revolutionaries, notably in Kenya (1952–6) and Malaya (1948–60). From a European perspective, the British experience was more successful than the French. In Rhodesia/Zimbabwe, however, the transition to 'one person one vote' and black majority rule was prevented by a white minority prepared to disregard both the British government and world opinion. This minority was aided and abetted by the South African government. Under **apartheid**, after 1948, the South Africans engaged in what many saw as the internal equivalent of imperialism. South Africa also conducted more traditional imperialist practices in its occupation of Namibia. It also exercised an important influence in post-colonial/cold war struggles in Angola and Mozambique after the last European empire in Africa—that of Portugal—collapsed when the military dictatorship was overthrown in Lisbon.

France

The British experience of decolonization stood in contrast to that of the French. France had been occupied during the Second World War, and successive governments sought to preserve French international prestige by maintaining her imperial status. In Indo-China after 1945, Paris attempted to preserve colonial role, only withdrawing after prolonged guerrilla war and military defeat at the hands of Vietnamese revolutionary forces, the Viet Minh, led by Ho Chi Minh. In Africa, the picture was different.

The wind of change also blew through French Africa, and under President Charles de Gaulle, France withdrew from empire, while attempting to preserve its influence. In Algeria, however, the French refused to leave. Algeria was regarded by many French people to be part of France itself. The resulting war, from 1954 to 1962, led to up to 45,000 deaths, and France itself was brought to the edge of civil war.

Legacies and consequences: nationalism or communism?

The pattern of decolonization in Africa was thus diverse, reflecting attitudes of colonial powers, the nature of local nationalist or revolutionary movements, and in some cases the involvement of external states, including cold war protagonists. Tribal factors were also an ingredient in many cases. How far tribal divisions were created or exacerbated by the imperial powers is an important question in examining the political stability of the newly independent states. Equally important is how capable the new political leaderships in these societies were in tackling their political and economic problems.

In Asia, the relationship between nationalism and revolutionary Marxism was a potent force. In Malaya, the British defeated an insurgent communist movement (1948–60). In Indo-China (1946–54) the French failed to do likewise. For the Vietnamese, centuries of foreign oppression—Chinese, Japanese, and French—soon focused on a new imperialist adversary, the United States. For Washington, early reluctance to support European imperialism gave way to incremental and covert commitments, and, from 1965, open involvement with the newly-created state of South Vietnam. American leaders spoke of a domino theory, in which if one state fell to communism, the next would be at risk. Chinese and Soviet support provided additional cold

war contexts. Washington failed, however, to coordinate limited war objectives with an effective political strategy, and once victory was no longer possible, sought to disengage through 'peace with honor'. The *Tet* (Vietnamese New Year) offensive of the 'Viet Cong' guerrillas in 1968 marked a decisive moment, convincing many Americans that the war would not be won, though it was not until 1973 that American forces finally withdrew, two years before South Vietnam was defeated.

The global trend towards decolonization was a key development in the twentieth century, though one frequently offset by local circumstances. Yet, while imperialism withered, other forms of domination or **hegemony** took shape. The notion of hegemony has been used as criticism of the behaviour of the superpowers, most notably with Soviet hegemony in Eastern Europe, and American hegemony in Central America.

Key Points

- The First World War produced the collapse of four European empires (the Russian, German, Austro-Hungarian, and the Ottoman Empire in Turkey).
- Different European powers had different attitudes to decolonization after 1945: some, such as the British, decided to leave, while others sought to preserve their empires, in part (the French) or whole (the Portuguese).
- European powers adopted different attitudes to different regions/countries. For example, British withdrawal from Asia came much more quickly after 1945 than from Africa.
- The process of decolonization was relatively peaceful in many cases; it led to revolutionary wars in others (Algeria, Malaya, and Angola), whose scale and ferocity reflected the attitudes of the colonial power and the nationalist movements.
- The struggle for independence/national liberation became embroiled in cold war conflicts when the superpowers and/or their allies became involved, for example Vietnam.
- Whether decolonization was judged successful depends, in part, on whose perspective you adopt—that of the European power, the independence movement, or the people themselves.

Cold war

The rise of America as a world power after 1945 was of paramount importance in international politics. Its conflict with the Soviet Union provided one of the crucial dynamics in world affairs, and one that affected—directly or indirectly—every part of the globe. In the West, his-

torians have debated with vigour and acrimony who was responsible for the collapse of the wartime relationship between Moscow and Washington. The rise of the USSR as a global power after 1945 is equally crucial in this period. Relations between Moscow and its Eastern

European 'allies', with the People's Republic of China (PRC), and with revolutionary forces in the 'Third World', have been vital issues in world politics, as well as key factors in Soviet–American affairs.

Some historians date the origins of the cold war to the 'Russian revolution' of 1917, while most focus on events between 1945 and 1950. Whether the cold war was inevitable, whether it was the consequence of mistakes and misperceptions, or whether it reflected the response of courageous Western leaders to malign and aggressive Soviet intent, are central questions in debates about the origins and dynamics of the cold war. Hitherto, these debates have drawn from Western archives and sources, and reflect Western assumptions and perceptions. With the end of the cold war, greater evidence has emerged of Soviet motivations and understanding.

1945–53: Onset of the cold war

The onset of the cold war in Europe reflected failure to implement the principles agreed at the wartime conferences of Yalta and Potsdam. The future of Germany, and of various Central and Eastern European countries, notably Poland, were issues of growing tension between the former wartime allies. Reconciling principles of national self-determination with national security was a formidable task. In the West, there was growing feeling that Soviet policy towards Eastern Europe was guided not by historic concern with security but by ideological expansion. In March 1947, the Truman administration sought to justify limited aid to Turkey and Greece with rhetoric designed to arouse awareness of Soviet ambitions, and a declaration that America would support those threatened by Soviet subversion or expansion. The **Truman doctrine** and the associated policy of **containment** expressed the self-image of the United States as inherently defensive, and were underpinned by the Marshall Plan for European economic recovery, proclaimed in June 1947, which was essential to the economic rebuilding of Western Europe. In Eastern Europe, democratic socialist and other anti-communist forces were undermined and eliminated as Marxist-Leninist regimes, loyal to Moscow, were installed. The only exception was in Yugoslavia, where the Marxist leader, Marshal Tito, consolidated his position while maintaining independence from Moscow. Subsequently, Tito's

Yugoslavia was to play an important role in the 'Third World' Non-Aligned Movement.

The first major confrontation of the cold war took place over Berlin in 1948. The former German capital was left deep in the heart of the Soviet zone of occupation, and in June 1948 Stalin sought to resolve its status by severing road and rail communications. West Berlin's population and political autonomy were kept alive by a massive airlift. Stalin ended the blockade in May 1949. The crisis saw the deployment of American long-range bombers in Britain, officially described as 'atomic-capable', though none were actually armed with nuclear weapons. US military deployment was followed by political commitment enshrined in the **North Atlantic Treaty Organization** (NATO) treaty signed in April 1949. The key article of the treaty—that an attack on one member would be treated as an attack on all—accorded with the principle of collective self-defence enshrined in Article 51 of the UN Charter. In practice, the cornerstone of the alliance was the commitment of the USA to defend Western Europe. In reality, this soon meant the willingness of the United States to use nuclear weapons to deter Soviet 'aggression'. For the Soviet Union 'political encirclement' soon entailed a growing military, and specifically nuclear, threat.

While the origins of the cold war were in Europe, events and conflicts in Asia and elsewhere were also crucial. In 1949, the thirty-year-long Chinese civil war ended in victory for the communists under Mao Zedong. This had a major impact on Asian affairs and on perceptions in both Moscow and Washington. In June 1950, the North Korean attack on South Korea was interpreted as part of a general communist strategy, and a test case for American resolve, and the will of the United Nations to withstand aggression. The resulting American and UN commitment, followed in October 1950 by Chinese involvement, led to a war lasting three years, in which over 3 million people died before pre-war borders were restored. North and South Korea themselves remained locked in seemingly perpetual hostility, even after the end of the cold war.

Assessing the impact of the cold war on the Middle East is more difficult. The founding of the state of Israel in 1948 reflected the legacy of the Nazi genocide and the failure of British colonial policy. The complexities of politics, diplomacy, and armed conflict in the years immediately after 1945 cannot be readily understood through the prism of Soviet–American ideological or

geo-strategic conflict. Both the Soviet Union and the United States helped the creation of a Jewish state in previously Arab lands, though in the 1950s, Soviet foreign policy supported Arab nationalism. The pan-Arabism of the charismatic Egyptian leader, Gamal Abdel Nasser, embraced a form of socialism, but was far removed from Marxist-Leninism. The state of Israel was created by force, and owed its survival to a continuing capacity to defend itself against adversaries who did not recognize the legitimacy if its existence. Israel developed relations with the British and the French, culminating in their secret agreement to attack Egypt in 1956. Over time, a more crucial relationship developed with the United States, with whom a de facto strategic alliance emerged. Yet, Britain, France, and America also developed a complex of relationships with Arab states, reflecting historical, strategic and economic interests.

1953–69: Conflict, confrontation, and compromise

One consequence of the Korean War was the build-up of American forces in Western Europe, lest communist aggression in Asia distract from the real intent in Europe. The idea that communism was a monolithic political entity controlled from Moscow became an enduring American fixation, not shared in London and elsewhere. Western Europeans nevertheless depended on the USA for military security and this dependence deepened as the cold war confrontation in Europe was consolidated. The rearmament of the Federal Republic of Germany in 1954 precipitated the creation of the Warsaw Pact in 1955. The military build-up continued apace, with unprecedented concentrations of conventional and, moreover, nuclear forces. By the 1960s, there were some 7,000 nuclear weapons in Western Europe alone. NATO deployed nuclear weapons to offset Soviet conventional superiority, while Soviet 'theatre nuclear' forces in Europe compensated for overall American nuclear superiority.

The death of Stalin in 1953 portended significant consequences for the USSR at home and abroad. Stalin's eventual successor, Nikita Khrushchev, strove to modernize Soviet society, but helped unleash reformist forces in Eastern Europe. While Poland was controlled, the situation in Hungary threatened Soviet hegemony, and in 1956 the intervention of the Red Army brought bloodshed to the streets of Budapest and international condemnation on Moscow. Soviet intervention coincided with an attack on Egypt by Britain, France, and Israel, precipitated by Colonel Nasser's seizure of the Suez Canal. The British government's actions provoked fierce domestic and international criticism, and the most serious rift in the 'special relationship' between Britain and the United States. President Eisenhower was strongly opposed to his allies, and in the face of what were effectively US economic sanctions, the British abandoned the operation (and their support for the French and Israelis). International opprobrium at the Soviet action in Budapest was lessened and deflected by what many saw as the final spasms of European imperialism.

Khrushchev's policy towards the West mixed a search for political **coexistence** with the pursuit of ideological confrontation. Soviet support for movements of national liberation aroused fears in the West of a global communist challenge. American commitment to liberal democracy and national self-determination was often subordinated to cold war perspectives, as well as US economic and political interests. The cold war saw the growth of large permanent intelligence organizations, whose roles ranged from estimating intentions and capabilities of adversaries to covert intervention in the affairs of other states. Crises over Berlin in 1961 and Cuba in 1962 (see Case Study) marked the most dangerous moments of the cold war. In both, there was a risk of direct military confrontation and, certainly in October 1962, the possibility of nuclear war. How close the world came to Armageddon during the Cuban missile crisis and exactly why peace was preserved remain matters of debate among historians and surviving officials.

The events of 1962 were followed by a more stable period of coexistence and competition. Nuclear arsenals, nevertheless, continued to grow. Whether this is best characterized as an arms race, or whether internal political and bureaucratic pressures drove the growth of nuclear arsenals, are open to interpretation. For Washington, commitments to NATO allies also provided pressures and opportunities to develop and deploy shorter-range ('tactical' and 'theatre') nuclear weapons. The global nuclear dimension increased with the emergence of other nuclear weapon states: Britain in 1952, France in 1960, and China in 1964. Growing concern at the spread or proliferation of nuclear weapons led to the negotiation

Case Study   The Cuban missile crisis

In October 1962, the United States discovered that, contrary to private and public assurances, the Soviet leadership was secretly deploying nuclear missiles in Cuba. President Kennedy responded with a naval blockade of the island, and American nuclear forces moved to unprecedented states of alert. The superpowers stood 'eyeball to eyeball', and most historians believe this was the moment in the cold war when the risk of nuclear war was greatest. Evidence from Soviet archives and sources, together with Western records, suggest that as the crisis reached its climax on 26–28 October, both Kennedy and Khrushchev were increasingly anxious to reach a diplomatic settlement, including by political concessions. The United States possessed overwhelming nuclear superiority at this time, but both leaders recognized the risk of escalation to nuclear war would be a global, national, and personal disaster. Nevertheless, recent evidence suggests that the risk of inadvertent nuclear war—arising from a concatenation of misperception, the actions of subordinates, and organizational failure—was much greater than was realized by political leaders then or by historians later.

The diplomatic impasse was resolved six days after Kennedy announced the blockade, when Nikita Khrushchev undertook to withdraw the missiles in return for assurances that America would not invade Cuba. It has also now emerged that President Kennedy provided a secret undertaking to remove equivalent NATO nuclear missiles from Europe. While much of the literature has focused on the Soviet–American confrontation, greater attention has been given to the Cuban side. It is now clear that one of Khrushchev's primary objectives was to deter an American attack on Cuba that both Moscow and Havana anticipated. Fidel Castro's role has also received closer scrutiny. As the crisis reached its climax, he cabled Khrushchev, who interpreted the message as advocating a pre-emptive nuclear attack on the United States. Castro also later stated that he would have wanted to use the tactical nuclear weapons which (unbeknownst to the Americans) the Soviets had sent to fight an American invasion. Castro's message to Khrushchev reinforced the Soviet leader's determination to strike a deal with Kennedy, which he did without consulting the Cubans.

In the aftermath of the crisis, important progress was made towards negotiation of the Partial Test Ban Treaty in 1963, which banned the testing of nuclear weapons in the atmosphere. There was recognition that crises were to be avoided, and no further attempts were made by Moscow to coerce the West over Berlin. However, both sides continued the build-up of their nuclear arsenals.

of the Nuclear Non-Proliferation Treaty (NPT) in 1968, wherein states that had nuclear weapons committed themselves to halt the arms race, while those who did not promised not to develop them. Despite successes of the NPT, by 1990 several states had developed or were developing nuclear weapons, notably Israel, India, Pakistan, and apartheid South Africa.

1948–9	Berlin	USSR/USA/UK
1954–5	Taiwan straits	USA/PRC
1961	Berlin	USSR/USA/NATO
1962	Cuba	USSR/USA/Cuba
1973	Arab–Israeli war	Egypt/Israel/Syria/Jordan/ USA/USSR
1983	Exercise *Able Archer*	USSR/USA/NATO

Table 3.3 Cold war crises

1969–79: The rise and fall of *détente*

As America's commitment in Vietnam was deepening, Soviet–Chinese relations were deteriorating. Indeed, by 1969 the PRC and the USSR fought a minor border war over a territorial dispute. Despite (or because of) these tensions, the foundations for what became known as *détente* were laid between the USSR and USA, and for what became known as *rapprochement* between China and the United States. *Détente* in Europe had its origins in the *Ostpolitik* of the German Socialist Chancellor, Willy Brandt, and resulted in agreements that recognized the peculiar status of Berlin, and the sovereignty of East Germany. Soviet–American *détente* had its roots in mutual recognition of the need to avoid nuclear crises, and in the economic and military incentives in avoiding an unconstrained arms race. Both Washington and Moscow also looked towards Beijing when making their bilateral calculations.

Ethiopia	Overthrow of Haile Selassie	Sept. 1974
Cambodia	Khmer Rouge takes Phnom Penh	April 1975
Vietnam	North Vietnam/'Viet Cong' take Saigon	April 1975
Laos	Pathet Lao takes over state	May 1975
Guinea-Bissau	Independence from Portugal	Sept. 1974
Mozambique	Independence from Portugal	June 1975
Cape Verde	Independence from Portugal	June 1975
Sao Tome	Independence from Portugal	June 1975
Angola	Independence from Portugal	Nov. 1975
Afghanistan	Military coup in Afghanistan	April 1978
Iran	Ayatollah Khomeini installed in power	Feb. 1979
Grenada	New Jewel Movement takes power	March 1979
Nicaragua	Sandinistas take Managua	July 1979
Zimbabwe	Independence from Britain	April 1980

Source: Halliday F. (1986), *The Making of the Second Cold War* (London: Verso): 92.

Table 3.4 Revolutionary upheavals in the 'Third World', 1974–80

In the West, *détente* was associated with the political leadership of President Richard Nixon and his adviser Henry Kissinger, who were also instrumental in Sino–American *rapprochement*. This new phase in Soviet–American relations did not mark an end to political conflict, as each side pursued political goals, some of which were increasingly incompatible with the aspirations of the other superpower. Both sides supported friendly regimes and movements, and subverted adversaries. All this came as various political upheavals were taking place in the 'Third World' (see Table 3.4). The question of how far the superpowers could control their friends, and how far they were entangled by their commitments, was underlined in 1973 when the Arab–Israeli war embroiled both the USA and the USSR in what became a potentially dangerous confrontation. Getting the superpowers involved in the war—whether by design or serendipity—helped create the political conditions for Egyptian–Israeli *rapprochement*. Diplomatic and strategic relations were transformed as Egypt switched its allegiance from Moscow to Washington. In the short term, Egypt was isolated in the Arab world. For Israel, fear of a war of annihilation fought on two fronts was lifted. Yet continuing political violence and terrorism, and the enduring enmity between Israel and other Arab states, proved insurmountable obstacles to a more permanent regional settlement.

In Washington, Soviet support for revolutionary movements in the 'Third World' was seen as evidence of duplicity. Some Americans claim that Moscow's support for revolutionary forces in Ethiopia in 1975 killed *détente*. Others cite the Soviet role in Angola in 1978. Furthermore, the perception that the USSR was using arms control agreements to gain military advantage was linked to Soviet behaviour in the 'Third World'. Growing Soviet military superiority was reflected in growing Soviet influence, it was argued. Critics claimed the SALT (Strategic Arms Limitation Talks) process enabled the Soviets to deploy multiple independently targetable warheads on their large InterContinental Ballistic Missiles (ICBMs), threatening key American forces. America faced a 'window of vulnerability', it was claimed. The view from Moscow was different, reflecting different assumptions about the scope and purpose of *détente*, and the nature of nuclear deterrence. Other events were also seen to weaken American influence. The overthrow of the Shah of Iran in 1979 resulted in the loss of an important Western ally in the region, though the ensuing militant Islamic government was hostile to both superpowers.

December 1979 marked a point of transition in East–West affairs. NATO agreed to deploy land-based Cruise and Pershing II missiles in Europe if negotiations with the Soviets did not reduce what NATO saw as a serious imbalance. Later in the month, Soviet armed forces intervened in Afghanistan to support their revolutionary allies. The USSR was bitterly condemned in the West and in the 'Third World' for its actions, and soon became committed to a protracted and bloody struggle which many compared to the American war in Vietnam. In Washington, President Carter's image of the Soviet Union fundamentally changed. Nevertheless, Republicans increasingly used foreign and defence policy to attack the Carter presidency. Perceptions of American weakness abroad permeated domestic politics, and in 1980, Ronald Reagan was elected President. He was committed to a more confrontational approach with the Soviets on arms control, 'Third World' conflicts, and East–West relations in general.

1979–86: 'The second cold war'

In the West, critics of *détente* and arms control argued that the Soviets were acquiring nuclear superiority. Some suggested that the United States should pursue policies

and strategies based on the idea that victory in nuclear war was possible. The election of Ronald Reagan in 1980 was a watershed in Soviet–American relations. One issue that Reagan inherited, and which loomed large in the breakdown of relations between East and West, was nuclear missiles in Europe. NATO's decision to deploy land-based missiles capable of striking Soviet territory precipitated a period of great tension in relations between NATO and the USSR, and political friction within NATO. Reagan's own incautious public remarks reinforced perceptions that he was as ill-informed as he was dangerous in matters nuclear, though key arms policies were consistent with those of his predecessor, Jimmy Carter. On arms control, Reagan was disinterested in agreements that would freeze the status quo for the sake of getting agreement, and Soviet and American negotiators proved unable to make progress in talks on long-range and intermediate-range weapons. One particular idea had significant consequences for arms control and for Washington's relations with its allies and its adversaries. The Strategic Defense Initiative (SDI), quickly dubbed 'Star Wars', was a research programme designed to explore the feasibility of space-based defences against ballistic missiles. The Soviets appeared to take SDI very seriously, and claimed that Reagan's real purpose was to regain the nuclear monopoly of the 1950s. The technological advances claimed by SDI proponents did not materialize, however, and the programme was eventually reduced and marginalized.

The resulting period of tension and confrontation between the superpowers has been described as the **second cold war** and compared to the early period of confrontation and tension between 1946 and 1953. In Western Europe and the Soviet Union, there was real fear of nuclear war. Much of this was a reaction to the rhetoric and policies of the Reagan administration. American statements on nuclear weapons and military intervention in Grenada in 1983, and against Libya in 1986, were seen as evidence of a new belligerence. Reagan's policy towards Central America, and support for the rebel *Contras* in Nicaragua, were sources of controversy within the United States and internationally. In 1986, the International Court of Justice found the United States guilty of violating international law for the CIA's covert attacks on Nicaraguan harbours.

The Reagan administration's use of military power was nonetheless limited: rhetoric and perception were at variance with reality. Some operations ended in humiliating failure, notably in the Lebanon in 1983. Nevertheless, there is evidence that the Soviet leadership took very seriously the words (and deeds) of the Reagan administration and believed that Washington was planning a nuclear first strike. In 1983, Soviet air defences shot down a South Korean civilian airliner in Soviet airspace. The American reaction, and the imminent deployment of US nuclear missiles in Europe, created a climate of great tension in East–West relations. And in November 1983 Soviet intelligence misinterpreted a NATO training exercise (codenamed *Able Archer*) and led the Soviet leadership to believe that NATO was preparing to attack them. How close the world came to a serious nuclear confrontation in 1983 is not yet clear. Emerging evidence from Soviet sources suggests that the risk of inadvertent nuclear war in this period could have been significant.

Throughout the early 1980s, the Soviets were handicapped by a succession of ageing political leaders (Brezhnev, Andropov, and Chernenko), whose ill-health further inhibited Soviet responses to the American challenge and the American threat. This changed dramatically after Mikhail Gorbachev became President in 1985. Gorbachev's 'new thinking' in foreign policy, and his domestic reforms, created a revolution, both in the USSR's foreign relations and within Soviet society. At home *glasnost* (or openness) and *perestroika* (or restructuring) unleashed nationalist and other forces which, to Gorbachev's dismay, were to destroy the Union of Soviet Socialist Republics.

Gorbachev's aim in foreign policy was to transform relations with the United States and Western Europe. His domestic agenda was also a catalyst for change in Eastern Europe, though unlike Khrushchev, he was not prepared to react with force or coercion. When confronted with revolt in Eastern Europe, Gorbachev's foreign ministry invoked Frank Sinatra's song, 'I did it my way', to mark the end of the **Brezhnev doctrine** that had limited Eastern European sovereignty and political development. The **Sinatra doctrine** meant that Eastern Europeans were now allowed to 'do it their way'. Throughout Eastern Europe, Moscow-aligned regimes gave way to democracies, in what for the most part was a peaceful as well as speedy transition (see Ch.4). Most dramatically, Germany was united and East Germany (the German Democratic Republic) disappeared.

Gorbachev paved the way for agreements on nuclear and conventional forces that helped ease the tensions that had characterized the early 1980s. In 1987, he travelled

	1945	1950	1955	1960	1965	1970	1975	1980	1985	1990
USA	6	369	3,057	20,434	31,982	26,662	27,826	24,304	24,327	21,004
USSR	–	5	200	1,605	6,129	11,643	19,055	30,062	39,197	37,000
UK	–	–	10	30	310	280	350	350	300	300
France	–	–	–	–	32	36	188	250	360	505
PRC	–	–	–	–	5	75	185	280	425	430
Total	6	374	3,267	22,069	38,458	38,696	47,604	55,246	64,609	59,239

Source: Norris, R. S. and Kristensen, H. (2006), 'Nuclear notebook', *Bulletin of the Atomic Scientists*, 62(4) (July/Aug.): 66.

Table 3.5 Principal nuclear weapons states: nuclear arsenals, 1945–90

Treaty	Purpose of agreement	Signed	Parties
Geneva protocol	Chemical weapons: bans use	1925	100 +
Partial Test Ban Treaty	Bans atmospheric, underwater, outer-space nuclear tests	1963	100 +
Nuclear Non-Proliferation Treaty	Limits spread of nuclear weapons	1968	100 +
Biological Weapons Convention	Bans production/use	1972	80 +
SALT I Treaty	Limits strategic arms*	1972	USA/USSR
ABM Treaty	Limits anti-ballistic missiles	1972	USA/USSR
SALT II Treaty	Limits strategic arms*	1979	USA/USSR
INF Treaty	Bans two categories of land-based missiles	1987	USA/USSR
START 1 Treaty	Reduces strategic arms*	1990	USA/USSR

*Strategic arms are long-range weapons.

Source: adapted from Harvard Nuclear Study Group (1985), 'Arms Control and Disarmament: What Can and Can't be Done,' in F. Holroyd (ed.), *Thinking About Nuclear Weapons* (Buckinghan: Open University): 96.

Table 3.6 Principal arms control and disarmament agreements

to Washington to sign the Intermediate Nuclear Forces (INF) Treaty, banning intermediate-range nuclear missiles, including Cruise and Pershing II. This agreement was heralded as a triumph for the Soviet President, but NATO leaders, including Margaret Thatcher and Ronald Reagan, argued that it was vindication of the policies pursued by NATO since 1979. The INF Treaty was concluded more quickly than a new agreement on cutting strategic nuclear weapons, in part because of continuing Soviet opposition to SDI. And it was Reagan's successor, George Bush, who concluded a Strategic Arms Reductions Treaty (START) agreement that reduced long-range nuclear weapons (though only back to the level they had been in the early 1980s). Gorbachev used agreements on nuclear weapons as a means of building trust, and demonstrated the serious and radical nature of his purpose. However, despite similar radical agreements on conventional forces in Europe (culminating in the Paris agreement of 1990), the end of the cold war marked success in nuclear *arms control* rather than nuclear *disarmament*. The histories of the cold war and of the bomb are very closely connected, but while the cold war is now over, nuclear weapons are still very much in existence.

Key Points

- There are disagreements about when and why the cold war began, and who was responsible.
- Distinct phases can be seen in East–West relations, during which tension and the risk of direct confrontation grew and receded.
- Some civil and regional wars were intensified and prolonged by superpower involvement; others may have been prevented or shortened.
- The end of the cold war has not resulted in the abolition of nuclear weapons.

- Nuclear weapons were an important factor in the cold war. How far the arms race had a momentum of its own is a matter of debate.
- Agreements on limiting and controlling the growth of nuclear arsenals played an important role in Soviet–American (and East–West) relations.
- Various international crises occurred in which there was the risk of nuclear war. Judging how close we came to nuclear war at these times remains open to speculation.

Conclusion

The changes that took place in twentieth-century politics were enormous. Assessing their significance raises many complex issues about the nature of international history and international relations. How did war come in 1914? What accounts for the rise of Hitler? Who won the cold war, how, and with what consequences? These are questions that have generated robust debate and fierce controversy. Several points are emphasized in this conclusion concerning the relationship between the three aspects explored in the chapter (total war, end of empire, and cold war). However war came in 1914, the transformation of warfare into industrialized total war reflected a combination of technological, political, and social forces. Political leaders proved incapable of restoring peace and stability, and attempts to reconstruct the European state system after 1919 failed to address enduring problems and created new obstacles to a stable order. The rise of Nazi Germany brought a new conflagration and new methods of fighting and killing. The scale of carnage and suffering was unprecedented. Nazi ideas of racial supremacy brought brutality and mass murder across Europe and culminated in genocide against the Jews. One consequence was the creation of Israel in 1948, which helped set in motion conflicts and events that continue to have global repercussions. The rise of an aggressive military regime in Tokyo likewise portended protracted and brutal war across the Pacific.

The period of history since 1945 has witnessed the end of European empires constructed before, and in the early part of, the twentieth century, and has also witnessed the rise and fall of the cold war. The relationship between the

end of empire and cold war conflicts in the 'Third World' is a close, though complex, one. In some cases, the involvement of the superpowers helped bring about change. In others, direct superpower involvement resulted in escalation and prolongation of the conflict. Marxist ideology in various forms provided inspiration to many 'Third World' liberation movements, but provocation to the United States (and others). The example of Vietnam is most obvious in these respects, but in a range of anti-colonial struggles the cold war played a major part. Precisely how the cold war influenced decolonization is best assessed on a case-by-case basis. One key issue is how far the values and objectives of revolutionary leaders and their movements were nationalist rather than Marxist. It is claimed that both Ho Chi Minh in Vietnam and Fidel Castro in Cuba were primarily nationalists, who only turned to Moscow and to communism in the face of American and Western hostility. The divisions between the Soviet Union and the People's Republic of China also demonstrate the diverging trends within the practice of Marxism. In several instances, conflict between communists became as bitter as conflict between communists and capitalists. In other areas, notably the Middle East, Marxism faced the challenge of radical political ideas (pan-Arabism, revolutionary Islam) that held greater attraction for the peoples involved. The role of the superpowers was nevertheless apparent, even if their involvement was more complex and diffuse. In moments of crisis it was nevertheless significant.

Similarly, the relationship between the cold war and the history of nuclear weapons is a close, though problematic, one. Some historians contend that the use of atomic

weapons by the United States played a decisive part in the origins of the cold war. Others would see the paranoia generated by the threat of total annihilation as central to understanding Soviet defence and foreign policy: the unprecedented threat of devastation is crucial to understanding the mutual hostility and fear of leaders in the nuclear age. It is also argued that without nuclear weapons direct Soviet–American conflict would have been much more likely, and that had nuclear weapons not acted as a deterrent, then war in Europe would have been much more likely. On the other hand, there are those who contend that nuclear weapons played a limited role in East–West relations, and that their importance is exaggerated.

Nuclear weapons have been a focus for political agreement, and during *détente*, nuclear arms agreements acted as the currency of international politics. Yet how close we came to nuclear war in 1961 (Berlin), or 1962 (Cuba), or 1973 (Arab–Israeli war), or 1983 (Exercise *Able Archer*), and what lessons might be learned from these events, are crucial questions for historians and policy-makers alike. One central issue is how far cold war perspectives and the involvement of nuclear-armed superpowers imposed stability in regions where previous instability led to war and conflict. The cold war may have led to unprecedented concentrations of military and nuclear forces in Europe, but this was a period characterized by stability and great economic prosperity, certainly in the West.

Both the cold war and the age of empire are over, though across the globe their legacies, good and bad, seen and unseen, persist. The age of 'the bomb', and of other weapons of mass destruction (chemical and biological), continues. How far the clash of communist and liberal/capitalist ideologies helped facilitate or retard globalization is a matter for reflection. Despite the limitations of the human imagination, the global consequences of nuclear war remain all too real. The accident at the Soviet nuclear reactor at Chernobyl in 1986 showed that radioactivity knows no boundaries. In the 1980s, scientists suggested that if only a fraction of the world's nuclear weapons exploded over a fraction of the world's cities, it could bring an end to life itself in the northern hemisphere. While the threat of strategic nuclear war has receded, the global problem of nuclear weapons remains a common and urgent concern for humanity in the twenty-first century.

? Questions

1 How far was Germany responsible for the outbreak of war in 1914?
2 In what ways was the Versailles Treaty a contributory factor to European political instability in the period 1919–39?
3 Were there effective alternatives to the appeasement of Hitler?
4 Why were atomic bombs dropped on Hiroshima and Nagasaki?
5 Why did the United States become involved in wars in Asia after 1945? Illustrate your answer by reference to either the Korean or Vietnam wars.
6 Did *détente* succeed?
7 Why did France try to remain an imperial power in Indo-China and Algeria?
8 Were the British successful at decolonization after 1945?
9 Compare and contrast the end of empire in Africa with that in Asia after 1945.
10 What kept the peace in Europe after 1945?
11 How close did we come to nuclear war during either the Berlin crisis (1961) or the Cuban missile crisis (1962)?
12 What role did nuclear weapons play in Soviet–American relations during the 1980s?

⮑ Guide to further reading

Best, A., Hanhimäki, J. M., Maiolo, J. A., and Schulze, K. E. (2004), *International History of the Twentieth Century* (London: Routledge). A comprehensive and authoritative account of twentieth-century history.

Betts, R. (1998), *Decolonization* (London: Routledge). This book provides an introductory theoretical overview that examines the forces that drove decolonization, and explores interpretations of post-colonial legacies.

Chamberlain, M. E. (1999), *Decolonization: The Fall of the European Empires* (Oxford: Blackwell). An analysis of the end of British, French and smaller European empires on a region-by-region basis.

Halliday, F. (1986), *The Making of the Second Cold War*, 2nd edn (London: Verso). This book explores the phase in the cold war of Soviet–American antagonism, 1979–85, and places this within a broader thematic and critical analysis of the cold war.

Keylor, W. R. (2006), *The Twentieth Century World and Beyond: An International History since 1900* (Oxford: Oxford University Press). A comprehensive and balanced assessment of twentieth-century international history.

Mueller, J. (1990), *Retreat From Doomsday: The Obsolescence of Major War* (New York: Basic Books). A distinctive perspective on twentieth-century warfare and the importance (or otherwise) of nuclear weapons in international politics.

Newhouse, J. (1989), *The Nuclear Age* (London: Michael Joseph). An accomplished history of nuclear weapons that examines the technological and political aspects of the arms race, from Hiroshima to debates on nuclear strategy in the 1980s.

Young, J., and Kent. J. (2003), *International Relations since 1945* (Oxford: Oxford University Press). A comprehensive survey of the impact of the cold war on world politics since 1945, providing an analysis of war in the Middle East, the development of European integration, and the demise of the European empires in Africa and Asia.

Online Resource Centre

 Visit the Online Resource Centre that accompanies this book to access more learning resources on this chapter topic at www.oxfordtextbooks.co.uk/uk/orc/baylis_smith4e/

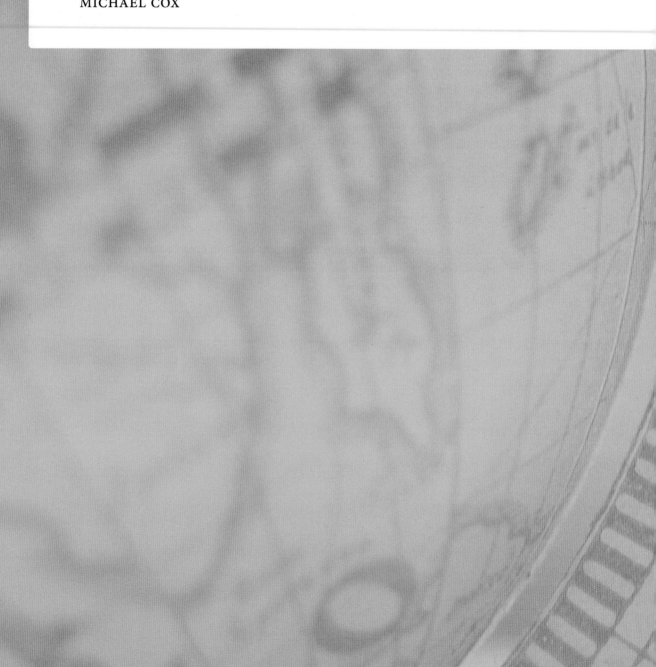

Chapter 4

From the cold war
to the war on terror

MICHAEL COX

- Introduction ·· 72
- The end of the cold war ·· 72
- Mapping the post-cold war era ·· 74
- From superpower to hyperpower—US primacy ·················· 75
- Europe in the new world system ······································ 77
- Russia: from Yeltsin to Putin ··· 78
- East Asia: primed for rivalry? ·· 80
- The haves and the have nots ··· 81
- The war on terror: from 9/11 to Iraq ································ 83
- Conclusion ·· 86

Reader's Guide

This chapter provides a broad overview of the period since 1989. The chapter is divided into three main sections. Section one begins with the unexpected end of the cold war itself. Section two goes on to discuss the main trends of the 1990s. The remainder of the chapter looks at September 11, the reasons for the war in Iraq, and the possible long-term consequences of both. Three broad theses will be advanced in this chapter. The first is that even if we speak of the world after 1989 as being 'post-cold war', we should never understate the extent to which this world was shaped by the way the cold war ended and the many problems and opportunities it left behind. The second relates to US primacy and notes that even though one of the more obvious structural features of the post-cold war international system has been a renewed US hegemony—what some in International Relations have defined as the 'unipolar moment'—this new position of strength has neither guaranteed international order nor is it likely to endure for ever. The third thesis is that new challenges to the status quo—and there are several, from terrorism, the spread of nuclear weapons, growing instability in the Middle East, and the rise of new economic powers in Asia—look unlikely to have a major impact on the underlying dynamics driving globalization. Thus we seem to confront a most interesting new period in the history of international politics, where, on the one hand, the world economy appears to be ever more successful and interdependent—as globalization theory might have predicted—but on the other hand, where international political relations are becoming increasingly uncertain.

Introduction

When major wars end they invariably pose enormous problems for those whose task it is to make the peace. This was true following the Napoleonic wars when the influential statesmen of the day sat down at the Congress of Vienna in an effort to construct a new European order after a twenty-year period of revolutionary turmoil. It was true once again following the even greater human catastrophe that was the First World War. And after the Second World War the major states convened yet again to settle the world in the wake of a conflict that left 50 million dead, millions displaced, and two of the most advanced countries in the world (Germany and Japan) in tatters. Great wars not only generate much suffering, however. They also create high expectations. Indeed, at the end of each major conflagration, many hoped that the world might be made anew, that global justice would prevail and peace would be secured for ever. Unfortunately, those who sat round the various high tables of international politics in 1815, 1919, and 1945 were driven by less lofty ambitions. Order, above all, was what tended to animate them, and to this end they devoted their often not inconsiderable talents to produce a desired diplomatic end that would both protect their interests and secure the **international system** from further disturbance and destruction.

So it was, once again, in 1989 when the last of the great 'wars' of the twentieth century—the **cold war**—finally wound down. As we shall see, the world it left behind was full of promise (especially for the victors) but full of potential risk as well. It was also one pregnant with the sources of further conflict. In fact, looking back now from the perspective of the post-**9/11** world, it would appear as if the years following the end of the cold war were but a mere interregnum, a resting-point between two ages, one defined by an ongoing struggle between two competing secular ideologies, and the other shaped by an emerging clash between two conceptions of **civilization** itself. How and why the promise of the end of the cold war concluded with a conflict between the modern West and radical Islamism is the subject of what follows.

The end of the cold war

The cold war divided the world for over forty years, threatened humanity with instant destruction, and led to the death of at least 25 million people, most of these occurring in that highly contested zone that came to be referred to during the cold war (though less after) as the **Third World**. Yet in spite of these dangers and costs, the cold war in its central core areas still managed to create a degree of stability that the world had not experienced since the early part of the twentieth century. For this reason many came to view the bipolar order after 1947 as something that was not merely the expression of a given international reality but something that was desirable and defensible too. Indeed, realists like Kenneth Waltz almost seemed to celebrate the **superpower** relationship on the grounds that a world in which there were two balancing powers limiting the actions of the other was likely to be a far more stable world than one in which there were several competing states.

If one feature of the cold war was its bipolar structure, another was its highly divided character born in the last analysis out of profoundly opposing views about the best way of organizing society. Yet for all its intensity the cold war was very much a managed conflict in which both sides recognized the limits of what they could and could not do. Certainly, policy-makers in East and West appeared to accept in private—if not in public—that their rival had legitimate security concerns that the other should recognize. The cold war was thus fought within the framework of a set of informal rules. This in part helps explain why it remained 'cold'. Indeed, how and why the cold war remained 'cold' has been the subject of much debate. Few, however, would dispute the fact that whatever else may have divided the two superpowers—ideology, economics, and the struggle for global influence—they were in full agreement about one thing: the overriding need to prevent a nuclear war that neither could win without destroying the world and

themselves. This in the end is why the superpowers acted with such caution for the greater part of the cold war era. In fact, given the very real fear of outright nuclear war, the shared aim of the two superpowers was not to destroy the other—though a few on both sides occasionally talked in such terms—but rather of containing its ambitions while avoiding anything that might lead to dangerous escalation (only once in 1962 did the two come close to a nuclear exchange). This, in turn, helps explain another important feature of the cold war: its stalemated and hence seemingly permanent character.

One can thus imagine the enormous shock waves produced by what happened in Eastern Europe in 1989. The world at the time was already undergoing dramatic changes, the result in the main of radical new policies introduced by Soviet leader Mikhail Gorbachev. Many of course hoped that Gorbachev's several reforms would make the world a safer and more humane place. Hardly anybody, though, seriously anticipated the collapse of communism and the coming down of the Berlin Wall. Moreover, few believed that this revolutionary process could be achieved peacefully. Such an eventuality had never been envisaged except by a few intellectual loners. Nor had policy-makers planned for it. It was all rather disturbing, and not just for those whose difficult job it was now to integrate former enemies back into the West. Academics too had to come to terms with changes they had not anticipated and a world they had not thought possible. At least two big questions now faced them.

One revolved around the problematic issue of prediction, or more precisely, why most of the experts failed to anticipate one of the most important events of the twentieth century. Here there was much shrugging of the proverbial shoulders but little by way of serious reflection other than to suggest that prediction was either impossible or that getting this mere 'data point' wrong proved

very little about their different theories. The other question focused on the issue of causation. This discussion produced a large and useful literature. It did not, however, arrive at a clear conclusion. Thus while most writers accepted that Gorbachev was critical to what happened to 1989 (not all international events it seemed could be reduced to structure), they could not agree as to his exact role. A few saw him as being far-sighted. Some though wondered whether he had ever intended to end the cold war at all. Nor did analysts come to any firm conclusion about the part played by Gorbachev's American counterpart, Ronald Reagan. To many Americans, Reagan's early tough policies towards what he termed 'the evil Empire' effectively consigned the USSR into the dustbin of history. Others, however, were less persuaded, arguing that other, more objective factors—long-term Soviet economic decline, East European debt to the West, and the attractive pull of Western capitalism on a moribund socialist system—played a much more important role in undermining communism.

Finally the end of the cold war generated a lively debate within the academic discipline of International Relations (IR). Indeed, the events of 1989 played a major role in shaping many of the discussions within the field during the 1990s, with an increasingly embattled group of realists continuing to stress the importance of material factors in compelling the USSR towards the negotiating table, and a rising generation of constructivists, many of whom had done their original research on the end of the cold war, insisting that the big transformation of the late 1980s was less the by-product of a change in the relative capabilities of either the USSR or the USA and more the result of Gorbachev's adoption of a set of ideas that undermined the logic of confrontation. In this way, a major discussion concerning one critical event in world politics helped to define the great debates that divided scholars of IR in the years thereafter.

Box 4.1 The end of an era

'Gorbachev may have earlier vowed that he would redefine the East–West relationship. In reality he did much more, and whether as a result of Soviet economic decline, a shift in ideas, imperial overstretch, or a simple failure to understand the consequences of his own actions, set off a series of chain reactions that did not just place the relationship on a new footing but brought it to an end for ever.'

(Michael Cox (2007), 'Hans J. Morgenthau, Realism and the Rise and Fall of the Cold War', in Michael C. Williams (ed.), Realism Reconsidered (Oxford: Oxford University Press): 166)

Key Points

- The cold war was a complex relationship that assumed competition but remained cold in large part because of the existence of nuclear weapons.
- Most experts assumed the cold war would continue and were surprised when it came to a peaceful conclusion.
- There is no academic consensus as to why the cold war came to an end when it did or why it did.
- The end of the cold war divided—and still divides—International Relations scholars into mainstream realists and ideas-oriented constructivists.

Mapping the post-cold war era

The end of the cold war therefore not only brought about a fundamental change in the structure of the international system but produced a series of divisions within the wider academic community. Naturally, many in the West celebrated the passing of an opposing economic system which they claimed had denied freedom and prosperity to millions. Indeed, the soon-to-be-famous liberal writer, Francis Fukuyama, interpreted the collapse of communism as marking the final end of one particular phase of history, when collectivism had posed a very real challenge to bourgeois society, and the beginning of another, where liberal principles would now be dominant. Others, though, were less sanguine about the future. Liberals may now be celebrating the collapse of the cold war system but, as John Mearsheimer pointed out in a much-discussed realist piece authored at the time, the passing of the old world was bound to pose a series of disturbing questions to which policy-makers may not have an easy answer. Western policy-makers appeared to agree judging by the caution and energy they now displayed. The tasks they confronted certainly seemed very great, ranging from the institutional one of devising new tasks for bodies such as **NATO**, the United Nations, and the **European Union**, to the more economic challenge of facilitating the transition in countries that had had little experience of running market democracies. Some even wondered whether or not the 'West' could survive in an environment where there was no longer a well-defined threat. Certainly, many questioned the need for high military spending, arguing that if the world was now becoming a safer and more integrated place what then was the purpose of spending billions on weapons that would no longer be required to fight enemies that did not exist in an international system that was rapidly becoming more united?

Globalization: a new international order?

If the cold war period was marked by a clear and sharp divide between opposing socioeconomic systems operating by radically different standards, then the post-cold war order could readily be characterized as one where states were compelled to play by a single set of rules within an increasingly competitive world economy. The term most frequently used to describe this new order was **globalization**, a notion that had barely been used before 1989, but now came be to employed ever more regularly to define an apparently new system of international relations. Globalization, however, seemed to mean different things to different theorists. Thus for one school it was assumed to be undermining borders and states—quite literally abolishing the Westphalian system. Others took a less cataclysmic view. Globalization, they agreed, was providing a different context within which international relations was now being played out. But it would be absurd to conclude that it was doing away with the state or destroying the underlying logic of **anarchy**. Some writers were even sceptical of whether there was anything especially novel about globalization. **Capitalism** after all had always been a global system. Since the sixteenth century **interdependence** had been one of its more obvious features. So why assume that there was very much new about the phenomenon simply because academics and publicists talked about it with greater frequency?

Such scepticism, however, did not prevent its many critics, and equally influential defenders, engaging in an extended and at times heated debate about the impact of globalization on global inequality, climate change and the more general distribution of **power** in the international system. Indeed, in one of the more heated exchanges between David Held (a social democratic critic) and Martin Wolf (a free market defender) it was almost as if the two combatants were talking about quite different things. It was all very confusing. It also made very little difference to what governments tended to say and do. Globalization, they insisted with increasing regularity, was a simple fact of economic life. There was no escaping its logic. The only thing one could do (using the oft-repeated words of President Clinton) was to 'compete not retreat'. Moreover, if one did not do so, the future for one's own people, and by implication one's state, was bleak. His ideological companion, Tony Blair, even appeared to use the menace of globalization as a means of attacking those in Europe who would defend old economic ways. In a world of global competition, Blair observed, there was really very little choice. Europe either had to reform or decline. There was no other way.

If globalization as a discourse (as much as a reality) served various political and economic purposes, it also raised a series of important questions for International Relations as a theoretical field. In fact, in many ways it helped recast a long-standing debate going back to Hans J. Morgenthau and continued afresh by that great iconoclast of International Relations, Susan Strange, about the precise relationship between politics and economics. Obviously, for realists like Morgenthau—and later Kenneth Waltz—globalization could not change the essence of how politics was conducted between states or the fact that international relations was bound to remain a primarily political activity. According to Strange (no apologist for globalization), this old-fashioned, statist approach simply missed the point, the most obvious one being that markets were fast becoming more important than states, and that until realists recognized this, it would remain ill-equipped to understand the modern world.

But if there was little meeting of minds among academics, there was little doubting the impact globalization was having on the world economy, and in particular on those three central core areas of it located in North America, Europe and East Asia. Here at least the theoretical debate about the novelty, existence, and the meaning of the phenomenon was being resolved as this very special triad of economic power (over 80 per cent of the world's total) experienced reasonable growth, increased economic interdependence, and massive wealth creation. No doubt the process created great national uncertainty as firms became ever more internationalized. There was also something

Box 4.2 The gravity of globalization

'Globalization is like gravity: there's no point denying its existence. Our job is to defy gravity and build a plane that flies. Our responsibility is to secure the benefits of globalization for all, to turn despair into hope and poverty into opportunity.'

(C.K. Prahalad (2007), 'The World for Sale', cited in Foreign Policy, May/June: 50)

distinctly unethical about an apparently unregulated economicprocess that literally made billions for the few (especially those in the financial sector) while generating insecurity for the many. However, this was a price well worth paying—or so its defenders inferred—if there was to be any semblance of economic progress. In a world where extreme competition ruled and money moved at the flick of a switch, there was only one thing worse than being part of this runaway system—and that was not being part of it

Key Points

- The term 'globalization' was rarely used before 1989 but became one of the most popular ways of defining international politics after the cold war.
- Though globalization is a much disputed term, analysts agree that it describes a one-world system where all actors have to play by the same economic rules.
- Globalization has become the master discourse of governments around the world.
- Globalization has produced many winners and a large number of losers, but there would appear to be no escaping its competitive logic.

From superpower to hyperpower—US primacy

If a one-world economy operating under the same set of highly competitive rules was at least one consequence of the end of the cold war, another was a major resurgence of American self-confidence in a new international system where it seemed to have no serious rival. This was not only a development that few had foretold (in the 1970s and 1980s many believed that the USA was in decline); it was one that many had thought impossible (most realists in fact believed that after the cold war the world would become genuinely **multipolar**). It was also a situation that many feared on the grounds that an America with

no obvious peer competitor would act more assertively and with less restraint. That aside, all of the most obvious indicators by the late 1990s—military, economic, and cultural—seemed to point to only one conclusion: that as a result of the Soviet collapse, followed in short order by the economic crisis in Japan and Europe's manifest failure in former Yugoslavia, the United States by the turn of the century had been transformed from a mere superpower (its designation hitherto) to what the French foreign minister Hubert Vedrine in 1998 termed a 'hyperpower'.

This new global conjuncture raised a series of important questions for both scholars of International Relations and US foreign policy-makers alike. The most central was how long could this position of primacy actually endure? There was no easy answer. Most realists, unsurprisingly, took it as read that other great powers would in time emerge to balance the United States. Others believed that because it enjoyed special advantage in nearly every sphere, the new US **hegemony** would last well into the twenty-first century. This in turn fed into a second debate concerning the exercise of US power under conditions of **unipolarity**. Liberals in general tended to advise restraint and the embedding of US power into international institutions as the most effective and acceptable way of it exercising global hegemony. Liberals also believed that the spread of democracy in an increasingly interdependent world economy would make the international system a safer place. Others of a more nationalist persuasion argued against such optimism and such constraint. The USA, they insisted, had the power. It had always used it wisely in the past. And there was no reason to suspect it would not use it wisely again in the future. Indeed, there was every reason for it to act alone when it deemed it necessary. The greater danger in fact was not an America that acted alone, but an America that did not lead.

This claim to unilateral privilege was linked to a particularly bleak view of the world that tended to be shared by many, though not all, US policy-makers. The cold war may have been over, they agreed: America might have emerged triumphant. But this was no reason to be complacent. To use a phrase often used at the time, although the 'dragon' in the form of the USSR might have been slain, there were still many 'vipers and snakes' lurking in the long grass. Among the three most dangerous and pernicious of these were various 'rogue states' (Iran, Iraq, North Korea, Libya, and Cuba), the constant threat of nuclear proliferation (made all the more likely because of the disintegration of the USSR and the unfolding nuclear arms race between Pakistan and India), and the threat of Islamic **terrorism** (all the more virulent now because of the fallout arising from the last great battlefield of the cold war in Afghanistan). Indeed, long before 9/11 the dangers posed by radical Islamism were very well known to US intelligence. The near destruction of the World Trade Center in 1993, the devastating bombings of the US embassies in Tanzania and Kenya five years later, and the audacious attacks on *USS Cole* in 2000 all pointed to a

Box 4.3 The paradox of power

'There is a paradox between the magnitude of American power and Washington's inability to use that power to always get what it wants in international politics ... hegemony is not omnipotence.'

(Christopher Layne (2006), 'Impotent Power', cited in The National Interest, Sep./Oct. 41–2)

new form of terrorism that could neither be deterred nor easily defeated by conventional means.

Yet in spite of these several threats, there was no clear indication that the United States was especially keen during the 1990s to project its power with any serious purpose. The United States may have possessed vast **capabilities**, and various American writers may have waxed lyrical about this new 'Rome on the Potomac'. But there appeared to be no real desire in a post-cold war environment of expending American blood and treasure in foreign adventures, a feeling that grew in intensity following the débâcle in Somalia in 1993 when the death of only 18 US soldiers created its own kind of 'Syndrome' that made any more US forays abroad extremely unlikely. The United States after the cold war was thus a most curious hegemon. On the one hand, its power seemed to be unrivalled (and was); on the other, it seemed to have very little idea about how to use this power other than to bomb the occasional 'rogue' when deemed necessary (as in former Yugoslavia), while supporting diplomatic solutions to most problems when needs be (as in the cases of the Middle East and North Korea). The end of the cold war and the disappearance of the Soviet threat may have rendered the international system more secure and the USA more powerful, but it also made the United States a very reluctant warrior. In a very important sense the United States during the 1990s remained a superpower without a mission.

Key Points

- Most experts did not anticipate—and some did not look forward to—the new American hegemony following the end of the cold war.
- In spite of the spread of democracy and globalization, most US policy-makers still viewed the world as a threatening and dangerous place during the 1990s.
- After the fiasco in Somalia the majority of Americans were reluctant to use US forces abroad.
- The United States after the cold war is best described as a 'superpower without a mission'.

Europe in the new world system

If for the United States the biggest post-cold war problem was how to develop a coherent global policy in a world where there was no single major threat to its interests, then for Europeans the main issue was how to manage the new enlarged space that had been created as a result of the events in 1989. Indeed, while more triumphant Americans would continue to proclaim that it was they who had actually won the cold war in Europe, it was Europeans who were the real beneficiaries of what had taken place in the late 1980s. There were sound reasons for thinking thus. A continent that had once been divided was now whole again. Germany had been peacefully united. The states of Eastern Europe had achieved one of the most important of international rights: the right of **self-determination**. The threat of serious war with potentially devastating consequences for Europe had been eliminated. Naturally, the transition from one order to another was not going to happen without certain costs being borne, most notably by those who would now have to face up to life under competitive capitalism. Nor was the collapse of communism in some countries an entirely bloodless affair, as events in former Yuogoslavia (1990–9) revealed only too tragically. That said, Europe—an enlarged Europe—still had much to look forward to.

But what kind of Europe would it be? To this there was more than one kind of answer, with some, especially the French, believing it should now develop its own specific European security arrangements (an optimism that soon foundered on the killing fields of Bosnia), and others that it should remain closely tied to the United States—a view most forcefully expressed by the new elites of Central Europe themselves. Europeans could not agree either about what kind of Europe they preferred. There were genuine federalists who sought an ever deeper Union that would fulfil the European dream while being able to balance the powerhouses of the United States and Japan. There were others who feared such a development and, marching under the traditional banner of **sovereignty**, managed to play the Eurosceptic card with some success among ordinary Europeans, who seemed more critical of the European project than the elites in Brussels themselves. Finally, Europeans divided over economics, with a clear line being drawn between *dirigistes,* who favoured

greater state involvement in the management of a specifically European social model, and free marketers—led by the British—who argued that under conditions of global competition such a protected system was simply not sustainable and that thoroughgoing economic reform was essential.

While many in 'old' Europe debated Europe's future, policy-makers themselves were confronted with the more concrete issue of how to bring the 'East' back into the 'West', a process that went under the general heading of enlargement. In terms of policy outcome, the strategy scored some notable successes. Indeed, by 2007 the European Union had grown to become 27 members, and NATO one less at 26. The two bodies also changed their club-like character in the process, much to the consternation of some older members who found the new entrants to be as much trouble as asset. In fact, according to critics, enlargement had proceeded so rapidly that the essential core meaning of both organizations had been lost. The EU, it was now argued by some, had been so keen to enlarge that it had lost the will to integrate. NATO meanwhile could no longer be regarded as a serious military organization with an integrated command structure. Still, it was difficult not to be impressed by the capacity of institutions that had helped shape part of Europe during the cold war being employed now in quite new roles to help manage the relatively successful (though never easy) transition from one kind of European order to another. For those realists who had earlier disparaged the part institutions might play in preventing anarchy in Europe, the important roles played by the EU and NATO seemed to prove that institutions were essential.

Institutions alone, though, did not provide a ready answer to what Europe ought or ought not be doing in a world system. Here again there was more than one European view. Hence several analysts continued to feel that Europe was bound to remain a largely 'civilian power', spreading its own values and acting as example, but should not become a serious military actor. Others took a more robust view. Europe's growing weight in the world-economy, they felt, its inability to act as a body in former Yugoslavia, not to mention the great capabilities gap that was rapidly opening up between itself and the

United States, all compelled Europe to think more seriously about hard power. The result was the birth of the European Security and Defence Policy in 1998, followed by a series of other moves that culminated with the publication of the *European Security Strategy* (*ESS*) in 2003 (EC 2003). Viewing security in broadly globalist terms, where open borders and disturbing events in far away places—especially poor ones—were bound to spew up their consequences on Europe's shores, Europe, it argued, was compelled by the logic of interdependence to engage seriously with international affairs. Isolationism or parochialism was no more an option for Europe as it was for the United States. However, unlike the United States, the document assumed these problems could only be tackled in association with others. Indeed, at several points, *ESS* even talked in decidedly English School terms of the need to maintain a 'well functioning international society' underpinned by 'functioning international institutions' and a system of **rules** (see Ch.2). Thus while insisting that a strong transatlantic relationship remained essential to order in the world, it was evident that how Europe hoped to achieve, that and how the United States would do so, would be quite different.

Significantly, the one question *ESS* did not try to address was Europe's future. Europe, it was generally recognized, remained what it had effectively been since the end of the Second World War: a work in progress. The problem was that nobody could quite agree when—if ever—this work would be completed, and where—if anywhere—would the European Union end? Some analysts remained remarkably upbeat. The EU's capacity in dealing with the consequences of the end of the cold war, the successful introduction of a single currency (the Euro), and its ability to bring in new members, all pointed to one obvious conclusion: that its future was assured. A few even speculated that the new twenty-first century would itself be European rather than American. Many, however, were more sceptical. After a decade-long period

---

Box 4.4 Europe's mid-life crisis?

'The future of the EU is hard to predict. Over the next decade it could undergo a bout of further integration; it could fall apart into opposing camps of those who would go forward or those who would go back; or perhaps most likely, it could just muddle through.'

(cited in The Economist, 17–23 March 2007, 'Special Report on the European Union', p. 20)

---

of expansion and experimentation, Europe, they felt, had reached a dead end, more divided than united over basic constitutional ends and facing several challenges—economic, cultural, and political—to which there seemed to be no easy answers. Indeed, according to some commentators, European leaders not only confronted older issues to which they had no ready-made solutions, they also faced a host of new ones (Turkish membership of the EU, how to integrate its 13 millions Muslim citizens, rising economic competition from China) to which they had no answer at all. As one seasoned observer of the European scene noted, Europe, by the beginning of the twenty-first century, may have been well aware of where it was coming from, but it had no blueprint for where it wanted to go to. In some ways, it had 'lost the plot'.

Key Points

- In spite of the break-up of former Yugoslavia, Europe benefited as much from the end of the cold war as the United States.
- Europeans after the cold war were divided over a series of key issues, most notably the degree of European integration, economic strategy, and the foreign policy aspirations of the European Union.
- The *European Security Strategy* of 2003 was one of the first serious efforts by the EU to think about its international role under conditions of globalization.
- Many issues face Europe, including Turkish membership of the EU, the position of Europe's Muslims, and China's economic challenge.

Russia: from Yeltsin to Putin

One of the many problems facing the new Europe after the cold war was how to define its relationship with post-communist Russia, a country confronting several degrees of stress after 1991 as it began to travel the road that would one day move it (hopefully) from what it had once been—a superpower with a planned economy and a formal Marxist ideology—to what it might one day become—democratic, liberal, and market-oriented. As even the most sanguine of Europeans accepted, none of this was ever going to be easy for a state that had had the

same system for nearly three quarters of a century. And so it proved during the 1990s, an especially painful decade during which Russia moved from being what it had once been before—a superpower that could effectively challenge the United States—to a declining power with diminishing economic and ideological assets. Nor was there much by way of economic compensation. On the contrary, as a result of its speedy adoption of Western-style privatization, Russia experienced something close to a 1930s-style depression, with industrial production plummeting, living standards falling, and whole regions once devoted to cold war military production experiencing free fall. President Boris Yeltsin's foreign policy meanwhile did little to reassure many Russians. Indeed, his decision to get close to Russia's old capitalist enemies gave the distinct impression that he was selling out to the West. This may have made him a hero outside Russia. However, to many ordinary Russians it seemed as if he (like his predecessor Gorbachev) was conceding everything and getting very little in return. Nationalists and old communists, of whom there were still a significant number, were especially scathing. Yeltsin and his team, they argued, had not only given away Russia's assets at knock-down prices to a new class of oligarchs, but he was also trying to turn Russia into a Western dependency. In short, he was not standing up for Russia's **national interest**.

Whether his successor Vladimir Putin had a clear vision for Russia when he took over the presidency matters less than the fact that having assumed office he began to stake out very different positions. These included a greater authoritarianism and nationalism at home, a much clearer recognition that the interests of Russia and those of the West would not always be one and the same, and what turned into a persistent drive to bring the Russian economy—and Russia's huge natural resources—back under state control. This did not lead to a turning back of the clock. What it did mean, though, was that the West could no longer regard Russia as for ever being what it had earlier hoped it would become: a 'strategic partner'. Certainly, it could no longer assume that Russia would for ever be in a state of almost irreversible decline. With almost unlimited supplies of oil and gas at its command, and with a leadership that look determined to defend Russia's interests, Russia no longer looked like the 'sick man' of Europe. Russia it seemed had turned yet another corner.

Still the West had less to fear now than it had during the cold war proper. Russia, after all, had nothing like the same resources as the old USSR. In the meantime, economic

Box 4.5 A new cold war?

'The West needs to calm down and take Russia for what it is: a major outside player that is neither an eternal foe nor an automatic friend.'

(Dmitri Trenin (2006), 'Russia Leaves the West',
Foreign Affairs, 85(4) July/Aug.: 95)

reform had made it dependent on the West (though some Western countries, like Germany, were dependent on it for their energy requirements). Furthermore, the official ideology did not in any way challenge Western institutions or values. The world had changed for ever since 1991. Nor was Russia the power it had once been during former Soviet times. Indeed, not only was it unable to prevent some of its former republics from either signing up to former enemy institutions like NATO, or moving more openly into the Western camp, by 2007 it was effectively 'encircled' by the three Baltic republics to the north-west, an increasingly pro-Western Ukraine to the south, and Georgia in the Caucasus. Adding to its potential woes was the fact that many of its more loyal, regional allies ran highly repressive and potentially unstable republics; meanwhile in Chechnya, it faced an insurgency which not only revealed deep weaknesses in the Russian military, but brought down Western opprobrium on its head—perhaps not to the point of causing a rupture, but certainly enough to sour relations and compel many in the United States (and a few in Europe) to conclude that while Russia may have changed in many positive way since the collapse of the USSR in 1991, at the end of the day it still remained historic Russia with an authoritarian outlook, a disregard for human rights, and an inclination towards empire. A new future may have beckoned, but the heavy hand of the past continued to influence relations between Russia and the West.

Key Points

- The first Russian President, Boris Yeltsin, sought a new partnership with the West but was often accused by his domestic enemies of not defending the Russian national interest.
- Vladimir Putin, his successor, has pursued more authoritarian policies at home, brought Russia's economic assets back under state control, and pursued a more nationalist foreign policy abroad.
- A new cold war between the West and Russia is unlikely because of the important economic and political changes that have occurred in Russia since the collapse of the USSR in 1991.

East Asia: primed for rivalry?

If history continues to play a crucial role in shaping modern Western images of post-Soviet Russia, then the past also plays a part in defining the international relations of East Asia—and a most bloody past it had been since the Second World War punctuated by several devastating wars (in China, Korea, and Vietnam), revolutionary insurgencies (in the Philippines, Malaya, and Indonesia), authoritarian rule (nearly everywhere), and revolutionary extremism (most tragically in Cambodia). The contrast with the post-war European experience could not have been more pronounced. In fact, scholars of International Relations have been much taken with the comparison, pointing out that whereas Europe managed to form a new liberal security community during the cold war, East Asia did not. In part this was the result of the formation of the EU and the creation of NATO (organizations of which there were no equivalent in Asia). But it was also because Germany managed to effect a serious reconciliation with its immediate neighbours while Japan (for largely internal reasons) did not. Nor did the end of the cold war do much to bring about a speedy resolution of these various issues. In fact, whereas the end of the cold war in Europe transformed the continent dramatically, this was much less true in East Asia where powerful communist parties continued to rule—in China, North Korea, and Vietnam—and at least two outstanding territorial disputes (one less important one between Japan and Russia, and a potentially far more dangerous one between China and Taiwan) continued to threaten the security of the region.

For all these reasons, one very influential American scholar, Aaron Friedberg, argued in an equally influential article in 1993 that, far from being 'primed for peace', East Asia was still ripe for new rivalries. Indeed, according to Aaron Friedberg, Europe's very bloody past between 1914 and 1945 could easily turn into Asia's future. This was not a view shared by every commentator, however. In fact, as events unfolded, this uncompromisingly tough-minded realist perspective came under sustained criticism. This did not deny the possibility of future disturbances; how could one argue otherwise given Korean division, North Korea's nuclear programme, and China's claim to Taiwan? But it did suggest that the region was not quite the powder keg painted by Friedberg. There were several reasons why.

The first and most important reason was the great economic success experienced by the region itself. The sources of this have been much debated, with some suggesting that the underlying reasons were cultural (Asian values), others that it was directly economic (cheap labour plus plentiful capital), and a few that it was the by-product of the application of a non-liberal model of development employing the strong state to drive through rapid economic development from above. Some have also argued that the United States played a crucial role by opening its market to East Asian goods while providing the region with critical security on the cheap. Whatever the cause or combination of causes, the simple fact remains that East Asia by the end of the twentieth century had become the third powerhouse in the global economy, accounting for nearly 25 per cent of world GDP.

Second, though many states in East Asia might have had powerful memories of past conflicts, these were beginning to be overridden in the 1990s by a growth in regional trade and investment. Indeed, though East Asia carried much historical baggage (some of this deliberately exploited by political elites in search of legitimacy), economic pressures and material self-interest appeared to be driving countries in the region together rather than apart. The process of East Asian economic integration may have been slow to develop (**ASEAN** was only formed in 1967). Nor was integration accompanied by the formation of anything like the European Union. However, once regionalism began to take off during the 1990s it showed no signs of slowing down.

A third reason for optimism lay with Japan. Here, in spite of an apparent inability to unambiguously apologize for past misdeed and atrocities—a failure that cost it dear in terms of soft power **influence** in the region—its policies could hardly be characterized as disturbing. On the contrary, having adopted its famous peace constitution in the 1950s and renounced the possibility of ever acquiring nuclear weapons (Japan was one the strongest upholders of the original Non-Proliferation Treaty), Japan demonstrated no interest at all in upsetting its suspicious neighbours by acting in anything other than a benign manner. Furthermore, by spreading its not inconsiderable largesse in the form of aid and large-scale investment, it went some of the way in fostering better international relations

in the region. Even its old rival China was a significant beneficiary, and by 2003 over 5,000 Japanese companies were operating on the Chinese mainland.

This leads us then to China itself. Much has been written about 'rising China', especially by realists who argue—in classical fashion—that when new powerful states emerge on to the international stage they are bound to disturb the peace. China may look benign now they agree. That, however, is not how things will look in a few years time—once it has risen. Again, though, there may be more cause for guarded optimism than pessimism, largely because China itself has adopted policies (both economic and military) whose purpose clearly is to reassure its neighbours that it can rise peacefully and thus effectively prove the realists wrong. It has also translated these reassuring words into concrete policies by supporting regional integration, exporting its not inconsiderable capital to other countries in East Asia, and working as a responsible rather than a spoiler inside regional multilateral institutions. Certainly, such policies are beginning bear fruit, with once sceptical neighbours—even possibly Japan—increasingly now viewing China as a benign instrument of development rather than threat.

In the end though, all strategic roads in China (and for East Asia as a whole) lead to the one state whose presence in the region remains critical: the United States of America. Though theoretically opposed to a unipolar world in which there is only one significant global player, the new Chinese leadership has pursued a most cautious policy towards the USA. No doubt some Americans will continue to be wary of a state run by the Communist Party whose human rights record can hardly be described as exemplary. However, so long as China continues to act in a cooperative fashion, of band-wagonning rather than balancing, there is every chance that relations will continue to prosper. But there is no guaranteeing the long-term outcome. With growth rates running at something like 10 per cent per annum, with its apparently insatiable demand for overseas raw materials, and enormous dol-

> **Box 4.6** The China challenge
>
> 'The task of creating more effective institutions to deal with short-term threats to regional stability is made all the more urgent because in the long run there is a very real structural transformation taking place that could alter the relatively benign constellation of factors currently at play: namely the rise of China.'
>
> *(Thomas Berger (2000), 'Set for Stability? Prospects for Conflict and Cooperation in East Asia', Review of International Studies, 26: 427–8)*

lar reserves at its disposal, China has already changed the terms of the debate about the future of international politics. For some time to come, it may well remain what one observer has called a 'colossus with a feet of clay', overly dependent on foreign investment and still militarily light years behind the United States. But even such a colossus presents a set of challenges that simply did not exist in the much simpler days of the cold war. Indeed, one of the great ironies of international history may be that China as a rising capitalist power playing by the rules of the market may turn out to be more of a problem for the West than China the communist power in those far-off days when it denounced the imperialists across the ocean and called upon Asians to drive the Yankees out of the region.

Key Points

- Compared to Europe after 1945, the international relations of East Asia during the cold war were highly volatile, marked by revolutions, wars, and insurgencies.
- The end of the cold war left many issues in its wake and led Aaron Friedberg (1993) to conclude that Asia was primed for further rivalry.
- Friedberg's thesis has been challenged as being too pessimistic: economic growth, regional integration, America's presence, and Japan's peaceful foreign policy continue to make the region less dangerous than he suggested.
- One of the big questions now facing the region and the United States is 'rising China'. Realists insist it will challenge the status quo. Others believe it can rise peacefully.

The haves and the have nots

Often the most significant facts about the international system are those sometimes least talked about by the discipline of International Relations—at least that used to be

the case during the cold war when most academics were almost completely fixated on the intentions and capabilities of the two superpowers. The world, from this point

of view, mattered not for its own sake, but in terms of the part it played in the larger drama involving its two principal actors, the United States and the USSR. Nowhere was this more true of course than in that vast sprawling undefined zone of formerly colonized countries known as the 'Third World', a vague and loose term conceived in the 1950s to denote a sense of popular solidarity among the poor married to the possibility of a different economic future outside the world market. Vague though it was, the term did at least have one advantage from the point of view of the two superpowers: of placing the less developed countries in their rightful place at the end of the political and economic queue. Not that the USSR and USA were entirely indifferent to the fate of the Third World. They fought their often bloody proxy wars there, sought whatever kind of allies they could muster (few progressive or democratic), and piled in their arms in a determined effort to outflank their main ideological rival in places as far apart as Cuba and Afghanistan, Vietnam and Angola.

The end of the cold war not only saw a rash of settlements in the Third World and the effective abandonment of many front-line states by their superpower backers (often with disastrous political and economic results for the countries in question), but something of an intellectual crisis as analysts tried to come to terms with what was happening. Some now wondered whether the term 'Third World' itself was of utility any longer in a world where there was no rivalry between the First capitalist world and the Second communist one. The whole idea in fact seemed to make no sense at all under conditions of globalization, where some previously underdeveloped countries were beginning to experience real development while others were busily signing up to new economic terms that were less concerned to defend the 'wretched of the earth' and more geared to attracting foreign investment. Moreover, what was the scientific status of a notion that put together continents as different as Africa and Latin America, countries as far apart economically as Tanzania and Argentina, and regions as dissimilar as the Middle East and Asia? Many analysts therefore drew the not unreasonable conclusion that the concept of the 'Third World' ought to be abandoned altogether.

Getting rid of the concept, however, did not alter the appalling material conditions under which the vast majority of the world's people continued to live. Recognizing

the reality of mass poverty however did not help analysts explain its existence nor create a consensus about how best to eradicate it. Here the more general debate about globalization and the more specific problem of underdevelopment intersected. For the opponents of globalization the only way of reducing **poverty** was either through less globalization or a much more regulated form of it. Supporters dismissed such fantasies. Globalization, they claimed, was here to stay. Indeed, the biggest problem facing the less developed countries was not getting drawn into the process but of remaining outside it. Here rapid economic growth in both China and India were deployed to make the case for globalization in the most spectacular fashion possible. For once, the facts did seem to tell a most credible story of once planned economic systems abandoning their old protectionist ways and successfully joining up to the world market. The results were spectacular with over 30 million Chinese being taken out of the poverty trap and a new wave of middle-class Indians emerging in a state that had once sneered at success. Naturally, this did not eliminate poverty nor inequality (quite the opposite). Nonetheless, in a relatively short space of time the two most populous countries in the world had shown to others what could be achieved by competing successfully in a global world-economy.

Still, the triumph of capitalism in some previously underdeveloped countries did not guarantee its success elsewhere. China and India may have made important economic leaps forward. However, the picture in other parts of the world was a much darker one, as the fate of sub-Saharan Africa during the 1990s most tragically demonstrated. Indeed, while millions in China and many in India may have been enjoying the benefits of globalization, the situation for billions around the globe remained dire. Thus half of the world's population—nearly 3 billion people—still continued to

Box 4.7 Poverty threats

'Since September 11, 2001, the US has launched a war on terrorism, but it has neglected the deeper causes of global instability. The nearly $500 billion that the US will spend this year on the military will never buy lasting peace if the US continues to spend only one-thirtieth of that, around $16 billion, to address the plight of the poorest in the world, whose societies are destabilized by extreme poverty.'

(Jeffrey D. Sachs (2005), 'The End of Poverty', Time Magazine, 6 March)

live on less than two dollars a day. The GDP of the 48 poorest nations in the world (a quarter of the world's countries) was less than the wealth of the world's three richest people combined. Of the 10.5 children under the age of five who died in 2006, over 98 per cent came from the less developed countries. Meanwhile, 790 million people remained chronically undernourished. Nor did things appear to be improving. In fact, whereas in 1960, 20 per cent of the world's people in the richest countries had 30 times the income of the poorest 20 per cent, by 2000 the figure had risen to nearly 75 times as much.

Of course it could be argued that while all of this constituted a human tragedy, in and of itself it did not represent a serious problem for the international system as such. This, though, is not how modern governments—especially those in the richer parts of the world—tended to view things. First, they recognized that with the gap growing between some parts of the world and others, it was inevitable that those from the less developed countries would do what they had always done before: namely make every effort to move to where they could at least eke out an existence of sorts. Second, poverty and inequality together bred insecurity, and insecurity fostered instabilities that would either force the more powerful countries

to 'do something' (by 2006 over 25 million peoples had been displaced within their own countries) or be compelled to deal with the results in the shape of refugees who turned up at their borders. Finally, so long as there was injustice (or at least the perception of such), there was always the risk that this would breed discontent. Political violence is no doubt the by-product of several factors, only one of which is material deprivation. Still, in a world where the 'haves' appeared to have so much and the 'have nots' so little, there was every chance that this would create a ready market for violent opposition. 'Blowback' against the powerful and the privileged—including those living in the United States—may not have been inevitable. Inequality, however, always made it more likely.

Key Points

- One of the defining areas of instability during the cold war was the Third World.
- With the end of the cold war the term 'Third World' has been challenged by many analysts.
- China and India are prime examples of countries where globalization has produced high levels of development.
- Inequality creates security challenges in the form of migration, refugees, and in certain instances, political violence directed against the more powerful West.

The war on terror: from 9/11 to Iraq

If the end of the cold war marked one of the great turning-points of the late twentieth century, September 11 was a reminder that the international order that had come into being as a result was not one that found ready acceptance everywhere. Bin Laden was no doubt motivated by far more than a distaste for globalization and American primacy. As his many would-be analysts have pointed out, his vision was one that pointed back to a golden age of Islam rather than forward to something modern. That said, his chosen method of attacking the United States using four planes, his use of video to communicate with followers, his employment of the global financial system to fund operations, and his primary goal of driving the United States out of the Middle East (whose

control by the West was essential to the continued working of the modern international economy) could hardly be described as mediaeval. US policy-makers certainly did not regard him as some odd throw back to earlier times. Indeed, the fact that he threatened to use the most modern and dangerous weapons—namely weapons of mass destruction—to achieve his objectives, made him a very modern threat, one though that could not be dealt with by the kind of traditional means developed during the cold war. As the Bush administration constantly reiterated, this new danger meant that old methods, such as containment and deterrence, were no longer relevant. If this was the beginning of a 'new' cold war, as some seemed to argue at the time, then it was one unlikely to be fought

using policies and methods learned between 1947 and 1989.

The very peculiar character of this new non-state threat led by a man whose various pronouncements owed more to holy texts than anything else, made it difficult for some in the West to understand the true character of radical Islamic terrorism. A few in fact believed that the threat was more existential than serious, more functionally useful for the United States in its quest for global pre-eminence than actually genuine. Furthermore, as the controversial war on terror unfolded—first in Afghanistan and then in other parts of the world—a few critics of a more radical persuasion began to wonder where the real danger actually lay. Indeed, as the United States began to flex its not inconsiderable military muscle and widened the war on terror to include Iraq, North Korea, and Iran, some began to turn their critical attention away from the original threat posed by radical Islamism towards the United States itself. In this way the original target of 9/11 was transformed from the early status of victim into the imperial source of most of the world's unfolding problems.

The various controversies surrounding the Bush administration's responses to international terrorism should not, however, obscure one simple fact: the impact that 9/11 was to have upon both the United States and US foreign policy more generally. Most obviously, the new threat environment provided the United States with a fixed point of reference around which to organize its international affairs; and organize it did, in the shape of building close relations with those many states—Russia, India, and China perhaps being the more important—that were now prepared to join it in waging a global war against terror. 9/11 also compelled the United States to act in a far more assertive fashion abroad. Indeed, some of Bush's more conservative supporters believed that one of the reasons for the attack on the USA in the first place was that it had not been assertive enough in the 1990s. Finally, in what some saw as a near revolution in US foreign policy, the Bush team seemed to abandon the defence of the status quo in the Middle East. 9/11, they argued, had changed the original formula whereby the United States turned a blind eye to autocratic regimes that existed in the region in exchange for cheap oil and stability. This was no longer enough, especially when it involved the USA doing deals with states like Saudi Arabia that produced the dangerous ideologies that had inspired those who had flown those planes on 9/11, or who directly or indirectly

had given (and were still giving) aid and comfort to terrorists around the world.

In this way the intellectual ground was prepared for the war against Iraq in 2003. The war, though, still remains something of a conundrum. After all, Iraq had not been involved in 9/11, the regime itself was secular, and it shared the same goal as the United States in at least one respect: of seeking to contain the geopolitical ambitions of Islamic Iran. For all these reasons, different analysts have identified rather different factors to explain the war, ranging from the ideological influence exercised by the 'neocons' on President Bush, America's close relationship with Israel, and America's desire to control Iraq's oil. No doubt all these things fed in to the final decision. However, one is still left with more questions than easy answers, with possibly the most credible answer being the less conspiratorial one that the United States went to war partly because it thought it would win fairly easily, partly because it got its intelligence wrong, and partly because it thought—rather unwisely—that building a new regime in Iraq would be just as easy as getting rid of the old one.

Whatever the original calculations made by those who planned this least realist of all modern wars, it is by now clear that this so-called 'war of choice' was a strategic blunder that has neither delivered stable democracy to Iraq nor inspired others in the region to undertake serious political reform. It has also had the doubly dangerous consequence of disturbing the whole of the Middle East, while making it possible for Iran to gain even greater influence in the region than it had before. In fact, by undermining the old regime in Iraq the United States has effectively created a vacuum into which an increasingly self-confident Iranian regime has marched. Finally, as result of its action in Iraq, the United States and its allies have provided radical Islamists around the world with a rallying point which they appear to have exploited with some skill. The bombings in London and Madrid were no doubt the result of many factors; however, few now believe they were entirely unconnected to what had been happening in the Middle East since 2003.

With or without Iraq, however, the West would still be confronted by a challenge in the form of violent radical Islam, one that not only feeds off Western blunders and policies (especially American ones in the Middle East), but a set of cultural values, state practices, and historical grievances that made it almost impossible to deal with effectively—without compromising what it meant to be

Box 4.8 End the crusade

'The debacle that is Iraq reaffirms the lesson that there is no such thing as a good crusade. This was true a thousand years ago when those European Christian knights tried to impose their faith and way of life on the holy Land – and is equally true today.... Divine missions and sensible foreign policy just don't go together.'

(Dimitri K. Simes (2007), 'End the Crusade', in The National Interest, 87 (Jan. – Feb.): 5)

part of the West. Herein, though, lay another problem: of how precisely to define this conflict. It was certainly not fashionable among some to characterize it as one between two different 'civilizations' (a term originally made popular by the American writer Samuel Huntington back in 1993). Nevertheless, there was something distinctly uncompromising about a conflict between those who on the one side supported democracy, pluralism, individualism, and a separation between state and church, and those on the other who preached intolerance and supported **theocracy** while calling for armed struggle and *jihad*

against the unbeliever. Not that these views were shared by all Muslims. Indeed, they were roundly condemned by the overwhelming majority. Still, as the antagonism unfolded, there seemed to be enough disaffected people in enough societies—including Western ones—to make this aggressive ideology an occasional but potent threat, and how the world in general, and the West in particular, chose to deal with it was likely to determine the shape of international relations for many years to come.

Key Points

- September 11 effectively brought the post-cold war era to an end and in the process transformed US foreign policy.
- The war to remove Saddam Hussein was sold as part of the war on terror; very few analysts, however, saw a connection between Iraq and 9/11.
- The reasons for going to war have been much disputed, though most people now believe it was a strategic error.
- The longer-term impact of the Bush doctrine could very easily weaken America's global position over the long term.

Case Study The Iraq War and its origins

Internationl relations as a field has always been concerned to understand the origins of wars. Long-term changes in the balance of power, fear of encirclement, imperial ambition—not to mention misperception and ideology—have all been employed at one time or another to explain why states engage in military action. The Iraq War presents a useful, and possibly difficult, test case for various theories of war origins. Several competing explanations have been advanced so far to explain the US decision to go to war against Iraq in 2003. These include, among others, the official argument that Iraq represented a serious and potentially rising threat to a critically important region; the more materialist thesis that the United States was determined to secure direct control of

Iraq's massive reserves of oil; and the popular claim that the war was the product of pressures arising from within the United States itself—here identified as being the Israel lobby, the ideologically inclined neo-conservatives, and their various supporters on the Christian right. The student of world politics, however, is still left with a number of unanswered questions. First, would the war have happened without the quite unexpected election of George W. Bush in late 2000? In other words, didn't the individual make a huge difference to the decision taken? Second, could Bush have then taken the United States to war without the profound shock created by the equally unexpected attack of 9/11? To this extent wasn't the war largely the by-product of fear and insecurity as much as anything else? Third, what role did British Prime Minister Tony Blair play? Indeed, was this a war made possible by an alliance with a middle-range power? Fourth, would it have been feasible at all if various American writers had not thought the United States so powerful that it could more or less do anything in the world? To what extent, in other words, did the notion of the 'unipolar moment' contribute to the final decision to go to war? Furthermore, were the intellectual grounds for the war not also laid by those during the post-cold war period who thought it wise to promote democracy and encouraged others to intervene into the internal affairs of sovereign states for humanitarian purposes? Finally, to what extent could one argue that the Iraq War was in the US national interest; and if it was, then why did so many realists oppose the war?

Conclusion

Thus, nearly twenty years after the end of a cold war that had produced such high hopes, the world seemed to be facing a more uncertain future. One should not exaggerate of course. In Europe, peace reigned. Great power war was not about to destroy the structure of the international system. The actual numbers being killed in wars around the world was on the decline. Globalization meanwhile continued to benefit more people than it disadvantaged. Still, in spite of these many obvious and positive features, the future contained many uncertainties, especially perhaps for the United States, a hegemon by any measure but one that fast seemed to be losing its capacity either to lead others or to solve the many challenges confronting it. It may be too soon to talk—as some are already beginning to—of the end of the American era, or (more dramatically) of the collapse of what some of late have been calling a 'new' American empire. It is certainly premature to predict somebody else's century replacing that of the United States. But only a few years after the collapse of its main ideological foe in the shape of the USSR, America no longer looked or sounded as self-confident as it once did when it appeared to be riding high during the glory days of the 1990s. Pundits have predicted the decline of the United States before—and been proved wrong. This time some believe they may be right. Perhaps another world order beckons?

? Questions

1 How have scholars of international relations attempted to explain the end of the cold war?
2 Why did liberal theorists assume the world would become a more stable place after the end of the cold war and why did realists disagree with them?
3 If the United States won the cold war, why did it have such problems defining a grand strategy for itself after 1989 and before 9/11?
4 Has globalization changed the basic character of world politics?
5 How successfully has Europe adapted to the challenges facing it since the end of the cold war?
6 Is the West facing a new cold war with post-communist Russia?
7 Has East Asia become ripe for rivalry?
8 Does poverty and inequality in the poorer countries threaten the security of the international system?
9 How has the war on terror changed international politics?
10 Why did the USA go to war against Iraq?
11 Has George W. Bush's foreign policy made the USA stronger or weaker?
12 Is the world a more or less dangerous place in the early part of the twenty-first century?

➡ Guide to further reading

Bisley, N. (2006), *Rethinking Globalization* (Basingstoke: Palgrave). The best single volume on the subject.
Booth, K., and Dunne, T. (eds) (2002), *Worlds in Collision* (Basingstoke: Palgrave). This is a collection of short, well-written essays on the world after 9/11.

Burstein, D. and de Keijzer, A. (1998), *Big Dragon: The Future of China* (New York: Simon & Schuster). In spite of the title, this is a relatively balanced account of China.

Cox, M., Booth, K., and Dunne, T. (eds) (1999), *The Interregnum: Controversies in World Politics, 1989–1999* (Cambridge: Cambridge University Press). A wide-ranging survey of most of the key issues facing the world after 1989.

Cox, M., Ikenberry, G. J., and Inoguchi, T. (eds) (2000), *American Democracy Promotion: Impulses, Strategies, and Impacts* (Oxford: Oxford University Press). This book looks at a critically important and neglected facet of US foreign policy.

Greider, W. (1997), *One World Ready or Not: The Manic Logic of Global Capitalism* (Harmondsworth: Penguin). A racy but highly readable account which argues that there is a fundamental instability at the heart of the new global economy.

Held, D. *et al*. (2005), *Debating Globalization* (Cambridge: Polity Press). A useful collection of opposing views.

Kaldor, M. (1999), *New and Old Wars: Organized Violence in a Global Era* (Cambridge: Polity Press). This book explains why millions have died in 'small' wars since the end of the cold war.

Kapstein, E., and Mastanduno, M. (eds) (1999), *Unipolar Politics: Realism and State Strategies after the Cold War* (New York: Columbia University Press). An empirically rooted attempt to show that the struggle for power between states did not stop when the cold war ended.

Leonard, M. (2005), *Why Europe will Run the 21st Century* (London: Fourth Estate). A now unfashionably optimistic perspective on the future of Europe.

Mann, J. (2004), *Rise of the Vulcans: The History of Bush's War Cabinet* (New York: Viking Press). An indispensable background on how the Bush administration viewed the world at large after 2001.

O'Meara, P., Mehlinger, H. D., and Krain, M. (eds) (2000), *Globalization and the Challenges of a New Century* (Bloomington, Ind.: Indiana University Press). This is a very useful collection of many well-known essays about global order and disorder.

Pillar, P. R. (2001), *Terrorism and U.S. Foreign Policy* (Washington, DC: Brookings Institution). A useful guide.

Ruthven, M. (2002), *A Fury for God: The Islamist Attack on America* (London: Granta Books). This is a fine analysis of the ideology of radical Islamism.

Sifry, M. L., and Cerf, C. (eds) (2003), *The Iraq Reader* (New York: Touchstone Books). The best collection on the debate to go to war.

Woodward, B. (2006), *State of Denial: Bush at War, Part III* (New York: Simon & Schuster). The most detailed insider account of the Bush team's decision to go to war with Iraq.

Online Resource Centre

 Visit the Online Resource Centre that accompanies this book to access more learning resources on this chapter topic at www.oxfordtextbooks.co.uk/uk/orc/baylis_smith4e/

Part Two
Theories of world politics

In this part of the book we introduce you to the main theories that try to explain world politics. We have two main aims: **first,** we want you to be able to grasp the main themes of the theories that have been most influential in explaining world politics. To this end, we have included in this section chapters on the four main theoretical perspectives on world politics: Realism, Liberalism, Marxism, and Constructivism. Of these, Realism has been by far the most influential theory but, as we mentioned in the Introduction, it has also attracted fierce criticism for being an ideology masquerading as an objective theory. Most of the history of International Relations theory has seen a dispute between Realism and its Liberal and Marxist rivals, with the debate between Realism and Liberalism being the most long-standing and well-developed. For this reason we have a chapter on contemporary mainstream debates between neo-realists and neo-liberals. This is followed by a chapter on the increasingly important approach of Social Constructivism. We then introduce you to other recent theoretical work in world politics, giving you an up-to-date survey of some alternative approaches to international

theory, namely historical sociology, feminism, post-modernism, and post-colonialism. Given the growing importance of explicitly normative approaches to world politics, we have decided to add a new chapter on this subject in this edition. So, by the end of this part we hope that you will be able to understand the main themes of the various theories and be able to assess their comparative strengths and weaknesses. Our **second** aim is to give you the overview of theory that you need to be able to assess the significance of globalization for our understanding of world politics. After reading these chapters on theory we hope that you will be in a better position to see how these theories of world politics might interpret globalization in different ways. We feel that you should then be able to decide for yourself both which interpretation you find most convincing and what kind of evidence you might find in the remaining sections of the book to enable you to be able to work out just how much globalization marks a new distinct stage in world politics, requiring new theories, or whether it is simply a fad or fashion which might alter the surface of world politics but not its main underlying features.

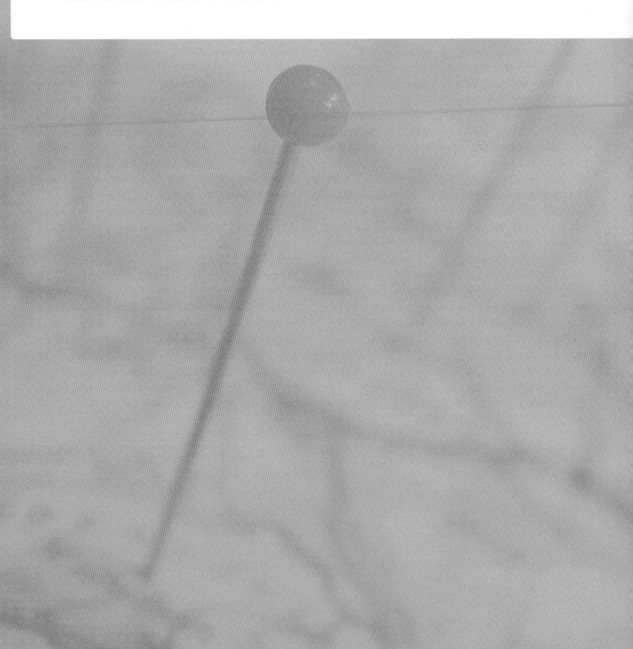

Chapter 5

Realism

TIM DUNNE · BRIAN C. SCHMIDT

- Introduction: the timeless wisdom of Realism ·· 92
- One Realism, or many? ·· 95
- The essential Realism ·· 100
- Conclusion: Realism and the globalization of world politics ·········· 103

Reader's Guide

Realism is the dominant theory of International Relations. Why? Because it provides the most powerful explanation for the state of war which is the regular condition of life in the international system. This is the bold claim made by realists in defence of their tradition, a claim which will be critically examined in this chapter. The second section will ask whether there is one Realism or a variety of Realisms. The argument presented below suggests that despite important differences, particularly between classical and structural realism, it is possible to identify a shared core set of assumptions and ideas. Section three outlines these common elements, which we identify as self-help, statism, and survival. In the final section, we return to the question how far Realism is relevant for explaining or understanding the globalization of world politics. Although there are many voices claiming that a new set of actors and forces are collectively challenging the Westphalian sovereign state system, realists are generally sceptical of these claims, arguing that the same basic patterns that have shaped international politics in the past remain just as relevant today.

Introduction: the timeless wisdom of Realism

The story of **Realism** most often begins with a mythical tale of the idealist or utopian writers of the inter-war period (1919–39). Writing in the aftermath of the First World War, the 'idealists', a term that realist writers have retrospectively imposed on the inter-war scholars, focused much of their attention on understanding the cause of war so as to find a remedy for its existence. Yet according to the realists, the inter-war scholars' approach was flawed in a number of respects. They, for example, ignored the role of power, overestimated the degree to which human beings were rational, mistakenly believed that **nation-states** shared a set of common interests, and were overly optimistic that humankind could overcome the scourge of war. The outbreak of the Second World War in 1939 confirmed, for the realists at least, the inadequacies of the idealists' approach to studying international politics.

A new approach, one based on the timeless insights of Realism, replaced the discredited idealist approach.[1] Histories of the academic field of International Relations describe a Great Debate that took place in the late 1930s and early 1940s between the inter-war idealists and a new generation of realist writers, which included E. H. Carr, Hans J. Morgenthau, Reinhold Niebuhr, and others, who all emphasized the ubiquity of power and the competitive nature of politics among **nations**. The standard account of the Great Debate is that the realists emerged victorious, and the rest of the International Relations story is, in many respects, a footnote to Realism.[2] It is important to note, however, that at its inception, there was a need for Realism to define itself against an alleged 'idealist' position. From 1939 to the present, leading theorists and policy-makers have continued to view the world through realist lenses. Realism taught American leaders to focus on interests rather than ideology, to seek peace through strength, and to recognize that great powers can coexist even if they have antithetical values and beliefs. The fact that Realism offers something of a 'manual' for maximizing the interests of the **state** in a hostile environment explains in part why it remains the dominant tradition in the study of world politics. This also helps to explain why alternative perspectives (see Ch.10) must of necessity engage with, and attempt to go beyond, Realism.

The theory of Realism that prevailed after the Second World War is often claimed to rest on an older, classical tradition of thought. Indeed, many contemporary realist writers often claim to be part of an ancient tradition of thought that includes such illustrious figures as Thucydides (*c*.460–406BC), Niccolo Machiavelli (1469–1527), Thomas Hobbes (1588–1679), and Jean-Jacques Rousseau (1712–78). The insights that these realists offered on the way in which state leaders should conduct themselves in the realm of international politics are often grouped under the doctrine of *raison d'état,* or **reason of state**. Together, writers associated with *raison d'état* are seen as providing a set of maxims to leaders on how to conduct their foreign affairs so as to ensure the **security** of the state.

According to the historian Friedrich Meinecke, *raison d'état* is the fundamental principle of international conduct, the State's First Law of Motion. It tells the statesman what he must do to preserve the health and strength of the State' (1957: 1). Most importantly, the state, which is identified as the key actor in international politics, must pursue power, and it is the duty of the statesperson to calculate rationally the most appropriate steps that should be taken so as to perpetuate the life of the state in a hostile and threatening environment. For realists of all stripes, the survival of the state can never be guaranteed, because the use of force culminating in war is a legitimate instrument of statecraft. As we will see, the assumption that the state is the principal actor, coupled with the view that the environment which states inhabit is a perilous place, helps to define the essential core of Realism. There is, however, one **issue** in particular that theorists associated with *raison d'état,* and classical realism more generally, were concerned with; that is, the role, if any, that morals and ethics occupy in international politics.

Realists are sceptical of the idea that universal moral **principles** exist and, therefore, warn state leaders against sacrificing their own self-interests in order to adhere to some indeterminate notion of 'ethical' conduct. Moreover, realists argue that the need for survival requires state leaders to distance themselves from traditional morality which attaches a positive value to caution, piety, and the greater good of humankind as a whole. Machiavelli argued that these principles were positively harmful if adhered to by state leaders. It was imperative that state leaders learned a different kind of morality which accorded not to traditional Christian virtues but to political necessity and

prudence. Proponents of *raison d'état* often speak of a **dual moral standard**: one moral standard for individual citizens living inside the state and a different standard for the state in its external relations with other states. Justification for the two moral standards stems from the fact that the condition of international politics often make it necessary for state leaders to act in a manner (for example, cheating, lying, killing) that would be entirely unacceptable for the individual. But before we reach the conclusion that Realism is completely immoral, it is important to add that proponents of *raison d'état* argue that the state itself represents a moral force, for it is the existence of the state that creates the possibility for an ethical **political community** to exist domestically. Preserving the life of the state and the ethical community it envelops becomes a moral duty of the statesperson. Thus it is not the case that realists are unethical, rather they find that sometimes 'it is kind to be cruel' (Desch 2003).

Although the advanced student might be able to detect some subtle differences, it is fair to say that there is a significant degree of continuity between classical realism and modern variants. Indeed, the three core elements that we identify with Realism—**statism, survival**, and **self-help**—are present in the work of a classical realist such as Thucydides and structural realists such as Kenneth Waltz.

Realism identifies the group as the fundamental unit of political analysis. When Thucydides and Machiavelli were writing, the basic unit was the *polis* or city-state, but since the Peace of Westphalia (1648) realists consider the sovereign state as the principle actor in international politics. This is often referred to as the state-centric assumption of Realism. Statism is the term given to the idea of the state as the legitimate representative of the collective will of the people. The legitimacy of the state is what enables it to exercise authority within its domestic borders. Yet outside the boundaries of the state, realists argue that a condition of **anarchy** exists. By anarchy what is most often meant is that international politics takes place in an arena that has no overarching central authority above the individual collection of sovereign states. Thus rather than necessarily denoting complete chaos and lawlessness, the concept of anarchy is used by realists to emphasize the point that the international realm is distinguished by the lack of a central authority.

Following from this, realists draw a sharp distinction between domestic and international politics. Thus while

Hans J. Morgenthau argues that 'international politics, like all politics, is a struggle for power,' he goes to great lengths to illustrate the qualitatively different result this struggle has on international politics as compared to domestic politics ([1948] 1955: 25). A prominent explanation that realists provide for this difference in behaviour relates to the different organizational **structure** of domestic and international politics. Realists argue that the basic structure of international politics is one of anarchy in that each of the independent sovereign states consider themselves to be their own highest authority and do not recognize a higher power above them. Conversely, domestic politics is often described as a hierarchical structure in which different political actors stand in various relations of super- and subordination.

It is largely on the basis of how realists depict the international environment that they conclude that the first priority for state leaders is to ensure the survival of their state. Under anarchy, the survival of the state cannot be guaranteed. Realists correctly assume that all states wish to perpetuate their existence. Looking back at history, however, realists note that the actions of some states resulted in other states losing their existence (for example, Poland has experienced this fate four times in the past three centuries). This is partly explained in light of the power differentials of states. Intuitively, states with more power stand a better chance of surviving than states with less power. **Power** is crucial to the realist lexicon and traditionally has been defined narrowly in military strategic terms. Yet irrespective of how much power a state may possess, the core **national interest** of all states must be survival. Like the pursuit of power, the promotion of the national interest is, according to realists, an iron law of necessity.

Self-help is the principle of action in an anarchical system where there is no global government. According to Realism, each state actor is responsible for ensuring its own well-being and survival. Realists do not believe it is prudent for a state to entrust its safety and survival on another actor or international institution, such as the United Nations. States, in short, should not depend on other states or **institutions** to ensure their own security. Unlike in domestic politics, there is no emergency number that states can dial when they are in mortal danger.

You may at this point be asking what options are available to states to ensure their own security. Consistent with the principle of self-help, if a state feels threatened,

it should seek to augment its own power **capabilities** by engaging, for example, in a military arms build-up. Yet this may prove to be insufficient for a number of smaller states who feel threatened by a much larger state. This brings us to one of the crucial mechanisms that realists throughout the ages have considered to be essential to preserving the liberty of states—the **balance of power**. Although various meanings have been attributed to the concept of the balance of power, the most common definition holds that if the survival of a state or a number of weaker states is threatened by a hegemonic state or coalition of stronger states, they should join forces, establish a formal alliance, and seek to preserve their own independence by checking the power of the opposing side. The mechanism of the balance of power seeks to ensure an equilibrium of power in which case no one state or coalition of states is in a position to dominate all the others. The **cold war** competition between the East and West, as institutionalized through the formal alliance system of the **Warsaw Pact** and the **North Atlantic Treaty Organization** (NATO), provides a prominent example of the balance of power mechanism in action.

The peaceful conclusion of the cold war caught many realists off guard. Given that many realists claim a scientific basis to their causal account of the world, it is not surprising that their inability to foresee the dynamics that led to the end of the bipolar cold war system sparked the publication of several powerful critiques of realist the-ory. Critics also maintained that realism was unable to provide a persuasive account of new **developments** such as regional **integration**, humanitarian intervention, the emergence of a **security community** in Western **Europe**, and the growing incidence of intra-state war wracking the global South. In addition, proponents of globalization argued that Realism's privileged actor, the state, was in decline relative to **non-state actors** such as transnational corporations and powerful regional institutions. Critics also contend that Realism is unable to explain the increasing incidence of intra-state wars plaguing the global South. As Box 5.1 discusses, Realists claim that their theory does indeed explain the incidence of intra-state conflicts. The cumulative weight of these criticisms led many to question the analytical and moral adequacy of realist thought.

By way of a response to the critics, it is worth reminding them that the death-knell of Realism has been sounded a number of times already, by the scientific approach in the 1960s and transnationalism in the 1970s, only to see the resurgence of a robust form of structural realism in the 1980s (commonly termed **neo-realism**). In this respect Realism shares with Conservatism (its ideological godfather) the recognition that a theory without the means to change is without the means of its own preservation. The question of Realism's resilience touches upon one of its central claims, namely, that it is the embodiment of laws of international politics that remain true across time

---

Box 5.1 Realism and intra-state war

Since the end of the cold war intra-state war (internal conflicts in one state) have become more prevalent than inter-state war. Since realists generally focus on the latter type of conflict, critics contend that Realism is irrelevant to the predicament of the global South that has been wracked by nationalist and ethnic wars. But this is not the case and realists have turned their attention to analyzing the causes of intra-state war and recommending solutions.

Structural realists maintain that when the sovereign authority of the state collapses, such as in Somalia and Haiti, internal wars happen for many of the same reasons that wars between states happen. In a fundamental sense, the dichotomy between domestic order and international disorder breaks down when the state loses the legitimate authority to rule. The resulting anarchy inside the state is analogous to the anarchy among states. In such a situation, realist theory contends that the different groups inside the state will vie for power in an attempt to gain a sense of security. Barry Posen (1993) has applied the key realist concept of the **security dilemma** to explain the political dynamics that result when different ethnic, religious, and cultural groups suddenly find themselves responsible for their own security. He argues that it is natural to expect that security will be their first priority and that they will seek the means to perpetuate their own existence. Yet just as in the case of states, one group's attempt to enhance its security will create uncertainty in the minds of rival groups, which will in turn seek to augment their own power. Realists argue that this revolving spiral of distrust and uncertainty leads to intense security competition and often to military conflict among the various independent groups who were earlier subject to the sovereign power of the state.

In addition to analyzing the cause of intra-state wars, realists have prescribed solutions. Unlike many liberal solutions to civil and ethnic wars that rest on power-sharing agreements and the creation of multi-ethnic states, realists have advocated separation or partition. For realists, anarchy can be eliminated by creating a central government. And while the creation of multi-ethnic states might be a noble endeavour, realists argue that they do not have a very good success rate. Ethnically, homogeneous states are held by realists to be more stable and less dependent on outside military occupation.

(history) and space (geopolitics). Thus while political conditions have changed since the end of the cold war, realists believe that the world continues to operate according to the logic of Realism.

The question whether Realism does embody 'timeless truths' about politics will be returned to in the conclusion of the chapter. In the following section we will begin to unravel Realism in order to reveal the way in which the tradition has evolved over the last twenty-five centuries. After considering the main tributaries that flow into the realist stream of thinking, the third section will establish a core set of realist principles to which all realists could subscribe.

Key Points

- Realism has been the dominant theory of world politics since the beginning of academic International Relations.
- Outside the academy, Realism has a much longer history in the work of classical political theorists such as Thucydides, Machiavelli, Hobbes, and Rousseau.
- The unifying theme around which all realist thinking converges is that states find themselves in the shadow of anarchy such that their security cannot be taken for granted.
- At the end of the millennium, Realism continues to attract academicians and inform policy-makers, although in the period since the end of the cold we have seen heightened criticism of realist assumptions.

One Realism, or many?

The intellectual exercise of articulating a unified theory of Realism has been criticized by writers who are both sympathetic and critical of the tradition (M. J. Smith 1986; Doyle 1997). The belief that there is not one Realism, but many, leads logically to a delineation of different types of Realism. A number of thematic classifications have been offered to differentiate Realism into a variety of distinct categories. The most simple distinction is a form of periodization that differentiates realism into three historical periods: classical realism (up to the twentieth century), which is frequently depicted as beginning with Thucydides' text on the Peloponnesian War between Athens and Sparta and incorporating the ideas of many of those included in the classic canon of Western political thought; modern realism (1939–79), which typically takes the so-called First Great Debate between the scholars of the inter-war period and a new wave of scholars who began to enter the field immediately before and after the Second World War as its point of departure; and structural or neo-realism (1979 onwards), which officially entered the picture following the publication of Kenneth Waltz's landmark text *Theory of International Politics* (1979). While these different periods suggest a neat historical sequence, they are problematic in so far as they close down the important question about divergence within each historical phase. Rather than opt for the neat but intellectually unsatisfactory system of historical periodization, we outline below our own representation of realisms that makes important

connections with existing categories deployed by other thinkers in the field. A summary of the varieties of Realism outlined below is contained in Table 5.1.

Classical Realism

The classical realist lineage begins with Thucydides' representation of power politics as a law of human behaviour. The drive for power and the will to dominate are held to be fundamental aspects of human nature. The behaviour of the state as a self-seeking egoist is understood to be merely a reflection of the characteristics of the people that comprise the state. It is human nature that explains why international politics is necessarily power politics. This reduction of Realism to a condition of human nature is one that frequently reappears in the leading works of the realist canon, most famously in the work of the high priest of post-war Realism, Hans J. Morgenthau. Classical realists argue that it is from the nature of man that the essential features of international politics, such as competition, fear, and war can be explained. Morgenthau notes, 'politics, like society in general, is governed by objective laws that have their roots in human nature' (Morgenthau [1948] 1955: 4). The important point for Morgenthau is, first, to recognize that these laws exist and, second, to devise the most appropriate policies that are consistent with the basic fact that human beings are flawed

Type of Realism	Key thinkers	Key texts	'Big idea'
Classical realism (Human nature)	Thucydides (c. 430–406 BC)	*The Peloponnesian War*	International politics is driven by an endless struggle for power which has its roots in human nature. Justice, law, and society have either no place or are circumscribed.
	Machiavelli (1532)	*The Prince*	Political realism recognizes that principles are subordinated to policies; the ultimate skill of the state leader is to accept, and adapt to, the changing power political configurations in world politics.
	Morgenthau (1948)	*Politics among Nations*	Politics is governed by laws that are created by human nature. The mechanism we use to understand international politics is through the concept of interests, defined in terms of power.
Structural realism (International system)	Rousseau (c. 1750)	*The State of War*	It is not human nature but the anarchical system which fosters fear, jealousy, suspicion, and insecurity.
	Waltz (1979)	*Theory of International Politics*	Anarchy leads to a logic of self-help in which states seek to maximize their security. The most stable distribution of power in the system is bipolarity.
	Mearsheimer (2001)	*Tragedy of Great Power Politics*	The anarchical, self-help system compels states to maximize their relative power position.
Neoclassical Realism	Zakaria (1998)	*From Wealth to Power*	The systemic account of world politics provided by structural realism is incomplete. It needs to be supplemented with better accounts of unit level variables such as how power is perceived, and how leadership is exercised.

Table 5.1 A taxonomy of realisms

creatures. For both Thucydides and Morgenthau, the essential continuity of the power-seeking behaviour of states is rooted in the biological drives of human beings.

Another distinguishing characteristic of classical realism is its adherents belief in the primordial character of power and ethics. Classical realism is fundamentally about the struggle for belonging, a struggle that is often violent. Patriotic virtue is required in order for communities to survive in this historic battle between good and evil, a virtue that long predates the emergence of **sovereignty**-based notions of community in the mid-seventeenth century. Classical realists therefore differ from contemporary realists in the sense that they engaged with moral philosophy and sought to reconstruct an understanding of virtue in light of practice and historical circumstance. Two classical realists who wrestled with the degree to which state leaders could be guided by ethical considerations were Thucydides and Machiavelli.

Thucydides was the historian of the Peloponnesian War, a conflict between two great powers in the ancient Greek world, Athens and Sparta. Thucydides' work has been admired by subsequent generations of realists for the insights he raised about many of the perennial issues of international politics. Thucydides' explanation of the underlying cause of the war was 'the growth of Athenian power and the fear which this caused in Sparta' (1.23). This is considered to be a classic example of the impact that the anarchical structure of international politics has on the behaviour of state actors. On this reading, Thucydides makes it clear that Sparta's national interest, like that of all states, was survival, and the changing distribution of power represented a direct threat to its existence. Sparta was, therefore, compelled by necessity to go to war in order to forestall being vanquished by Athens. Thucydides also makes it clear that Athens felt equally compelled to pursue power in order to preserve the **empire** it had acquired. The famous Athenian leader, Pericles, claimed to be acting on the basis of the most fundamental of human motivations: ambition, fear, and self-interest.

One of the significant episodes of the war between Athens and Sparta is known as the 'Melian dialogue' and represents a fascinating illustration of a number of

key realist principles. The Case Study reconstructs the dialogue between the Athenian leaders who arrived on the island of Melos to assert their right of conquest over the islanders and the response this provoked. In short, what the Athenians are asserting over the Melians is the logic of power politics. Because of their vastly superior military force, they are able to present a *fait accompli* to the Melians: either submit peacefully or be exterminated. The Melians for their part try to buck the logic of power politics, appealing in turn with arguments grounded in justice, God, and their allies the Spartans. As the dialogue makes clear, the Melians were forced to submit to the realist iron law that 'the strong do what they have the power to do and the weak accept what they have to accept'.

Later classical realists—notably Machiavelli and Morgenthau—would concur with Thucydides' suggestion that the logic of power politics has universal applicability. Instead of Athens and Melos, we could just as easily substitute the vulnerability of Machiavelli's beloved Florence to the expansionist policies of external great powers. In Morgenthau's era, there were many examples where the innate drive for more power and **territory** seemed to confirm the realist iron law: for example, Nazi Germany and Czechoslovakia in 1939, and the Soviet Union and Hungary in 1956. The seemingly endless cycle of war and conflict confirmed in the minds of twentieth-century classical realists the essentially aggressiveness impulses in human nature. For Morgenthau, 'the drives

Case Study The Melian dialogue—realism and the preparation for war

ATHENIANS. Then we on our side will use no fine phrases saying, for example, that we have a right to our empire because we defeated the Persians. . . . And we ask you on your side not to imagine that you will influence us by saying that you, though a colony of Sparta, have not joined Sparta in the war, or that you have never done us any harm . . . you know as well as we do that, when these matters are discussed by practical people, **the standard of justice depends on the equality of power to compel and that in fact the strong do what they have the power to do and the weak accept what they have to accept.**

MELIANS. Then in our view (since you force us to leave justice out of account and to confine ourselves to self-interest) . . . you should not destroy a principle that is to the general good of all men—namely, that in the case of all who fall into danger there should be such a thing as fair play and just dealing.

ATHENIANS. We do not want any trouble in bringing you into our empire, and we want you to be spared for the good both of yourselves and of ourselves.

MELIANS. And how could it be just as good for us to be the slaves as for you to be the masters?

ATHENIANS. You, by giving in, would save yourselves from disaster; we by not destroying you, would be able to profit from you.

MELIANS. So you do not agree to our being neutral, friends instead of enemies, but allies of neither side?

ATHENIANS. No . . . if we were on friendly terms with you, our subjects would regard that as a sign of weakness in us, whereas your hatred is evidence of our power. . . . So that **by conquering you we shall increase not only the size but the security of our empire.**

MELIANS. But do you think there is no security for you in what we suggest? For here again, since you will not let us mention justice, but tell us to give in to your interests, we, too, must tell you what our interests are and, if yours and ours happen to coincide, we must try to persuade you of the fact. Is it not certain that you will make enemies of all states who are at present neutral, when they see what is happening here and naturally conclude that in course of time you will attack them too? . . . Yet we know that in war, fortune sometimes makes the odds more level.

ATHENIANS. Hope, that comforter in danger!

MELIANS. We trust that the gods will give us fortune as good as yours, because we are standing for what is right against   what is wrong; and as for what we lack in power, we trust that it will be made up for by our alliance with the Spartans, who are bound, if for no other reason, then for honour's sake, and because we are their kinsman, to come to our help.

ATHENIANS. So far as the favour of the gods is concerned, we think we have as much right to that as you have. . . . Our opinion of the gods and our knowledge of men lead us to conclude that **it is a general and necessary law of nature to rule whatever one can.** This is not a law that we made ourselves, nor were we the first to act upon it when it was made. We found it already in existence, and we shall leave it to exist forever among those who come after us. We are merely acting in accordance with it, and we know that you or anybody else with the same power as ours would be acting in precisely the same way. And therefore, so far as the gods are concerned, we see no good reason why we should fear to be at a disadvantage. But with regard to your views about Sparta and

(continued) ▶

to live, to propagate, and to dominate are common to all men' (Morgenthau 1955: 30). How is a leader supposed to act in a world animated by such dark forces? The answer given by Machiavelli is that all obligations and treaties with other states must be disregarded if the security of the community is under threat. Moreover, imperial expansion is legitimate as it is a means of gaining greater security. Other classical realists, however, advocate a more temperate understanding of moral conduct. Mid-twentieth-century realists such as Butterfield, Carr, Morgenthau, and Wolfers believed that anarchy could be mitigated by wise leadership and the pursuit of the national interest in ways that are compatible with **international order**. Taking their lead from Thucydides, they recognized that acting purely on the basis of power and self-interest without any consideration of moral and ethical principles frequently results in self-defeating policies. After all, as Thucydides showed, Athens suffered an epic defeat while following the realist tenet of self-interest.

Structural Realism

Structural realists concur that international politics is essentially a struggle for power but they do not endorse the classical realist assumption that this is a result of human nature. Instead, structural realists attribute security competition and inter-state conflict to the lack of an overarching authority above states and the relative distribution of power in the international system. Waltz defined the structure of the international system in terms of three elements—organizing principle, differentiation of units, and distribution of capabilities. Waltz identifies two different organizing principles: anarchy, which corresponds to the decentralized realm of international politics, and hierarchy, which is the basis of domestic order. He argues that the units of the international system are functionally similar sovereign states, hence unit level variation is irrelevant in explaining international outcomes. It is the third tier, the distribution of capabilities across units, that is, according to Waltz, of fundamental importance to understanding crucial international outcomes. According to structural realists, the relative distribution of power in the international system is the key independent variable to understanding important international outcomes such as war and peace, alliance politics, and the balance of power. Structural realists are interested in providing a rank-ordering of states so as to be able to differentiate and count the number of great powers that exist at any particular point in time. The number of great powers, in turn, determines the structure of the international system. For example, during the cold war from 1945 to 1989 there were two great powers—the United States and the Soviet Union—that constituted the bipolar international system.

How does the international distribution of power impact the behaviour of states, particularly their power-seeking behaviour? In the most general sense, Waltz argues that states, especially the great powers, have to be sensitive to the capabilities of other states. The possibility that any state may use force to advance its interests results in all states being worried about their survival. According to Waltz, power is a means to the end of security. In a significant passage, Waltz writes 'because power is a possibly useful means, sensible statesmen try to have an appropriate amount of it'. He adds,

'in crucial situations, however, the ultimate concern of states is not for power but for security' (Waltz 1989: 40). In other words, rather than being power maximizers, states, according to Waltz, are security maximizers. Waltz argues that power maximization often proves to be dysfunctional because it triggers a counter-balancing coalition of states.

A different account of the power dynamics that operate in the **anarchic system** is provided by John Mearsheimer's theory of **offensive realism**, which is another variant of structural realism. While sharing many of the same basic assumptions with Waltz's structural realist theory, which is frequently termed **defensive realism**, Mearsheimer differs from Waltz when it comes to describing the behaviour of states. Most fundamentally, 'offensive realism parts company with defensive realism over the question of how much power states want' (Mearsheimer 2001: 21). According to Mearsheimer, the structure of the international system compels states to maximize their relative power position. Under anarchy, he agrees that self-help is the basic principle of action. Yet he also argues that not only do all states possess some offensive military capability, but there is a great deal of uncertainty about the intentions of other states. Consequently, Mearsheimer concludes that there are no satisfied or status quo states; rather, all states are continuously searching for opportunities to gain power at the expense of other states. Contrary to Waltz, Mearsheimer argues that states recognize that the best path to peace is to accumulate more power than anyone else. Indeed, the ideal position, although one that Mearsheimer argues is virtually impossible to achieve, is to be the global hegemon of the **international system**. Yet because Mearsheimer believes that global **hegemony** is impossible, he concludes that the world is condemned to perpetual great power competition.

Contemporary realist challenges to structural realism

While offensive realism makes an important contribution to realism, some contemporary realists are sceptical of the notion that the international distribution of power alone can explain the behaviour of states. Since the end of the cold war a group of scholars have attempted to move beyond the parsimonious

assumptions of structural realism and incorporated a number of additional factors located at the individual and domestic level into their explanation of international politics. While systemic factors are recognized to be an important influence on the behaviour of states, so are factors such as the perceptions of state leaders, state–society relationships, and the motivation of states. In attempting to build a bridge between structural and unit level factors (which many classical realists emphasized), this group of scholars has been characterized by Gideon Rose (1998) as 'neoclassical realists'. According to Stephen Walt, the causal logic of **neoclassical realism** 'places domestic politics as an intervening variable between the distribution of power and foreign policy behavior' (Walt 2002: 211).

One important intervening variable is leaders themselves, namely how they perceive the international distribution of power. There is no objective, independent reading of the distribution of power: rather, what matters is how state leaders derive an understanding of the distribution of power. While structural realists assume that all states have a similar set of interests, neoclassical realists such as Randall Schweller (1996) argue that historically this is not the case. He argues that with respect to Waltz, the assumption that all states have an interest in security results in neo-realism exhibiting a profoundly status quo basis. Schweller returns to the writings of realists such as Morgenthau and Kissinger to remind us of the key distinction that they made between status quo and revisionist states. Neoclassical realists would argue that the fact that Germany was a revisionist state in the 1930s and a status quo state since the end of the Second World War is of fundamental importance to understanding its role in the international system. Not only do states differ in terms of their interests, but they also differ in terms of their ability to extract and direct resources from the societies that they rule. Fareed Zakaria (1998) introduces the intervening variable of state strength into his theory of state-centred realism. State strength is defined as the ability of a state to mobilize and direct the resources at its disposal in the pursuit of particular interests. Neoclassical realists argue that different types of state possess different capacities to translate the various elements of national power into state power. Thus, contrary to Waltz, all states cannot be treated as 'like units'.

Given the varieties of Realism that exist, it is hardly surprising that the overall coherence of the realist tradition of inquiry has been questioned. The answer to the question of 'coherence' is, of course, contingent upon how strict the criteria are for judging the continuities which underpin a particular theory. Here it is perhaps a mistake to understand traditions as a single stream of thought, handed down in a neatly wrapped package from one generation of realists to another. Instead, it is preferable to think of living traditions like Realism as the embodiment of both continuities and conflicts. Despite the different strands running through the tradition, there is a sense in which all realists share a common set of propositions.

> ## Key Points
>
> - There is a lack of consensus in the literature as to whether we can meaningfully speak about Realism as a single coherent theory.
> - There are good reasons for delineating different types of Realism.
> - Structural realism divides into two camps: those who argue that states are security maximizers (defensive realism) and those who argue that states are power maximizers (offensive realism).
> - Neoclassical realists bring individual and unit variation back into the theory.

The essential Realism

The previous paragraphs have argued that Realism is a theoretical broad church, embracing a variety of authors and texts. Despite the numerous denominations, we argue that all realists subscribe to the following 'three Ss': statism, survival, self-help. Each of these elements is considered in more detail in the subsections below.

Statism

For realists, the state is the main actor and sovereignty is its distinguishing trait. The meaning of the sovereign state is inextricably bound up with the use of force. In terms of its internal dimension, to illustrate this relationship between violence and the state we need to look no further than Max Weber's famous definition of the state as 'the monopoly of the legitimate use of physical force within a given territory'(M. J. Smith 1986: 23).[3] Within this territorial space, **sovereignty** means that the state has supreme authority to make and enforce laws. This is the basis of the unwritten contract between individuals and the state. According to Hobbes, for example, we trade our liberty in return for a guarantee of security. Once security has been established, **civil society** can begin. But in the absence of security, there can be no art, no culture, no society. The first move, then, for the realist is to organize power domestically. Only after power has been organized, can community begin.

Realist international theory appears to operate according to the assumption that, domestically, the problem of order and security is solved. However, on the 'outside', in the relations among independent sovereign states, insecurities, dangers, and threats to the very existence of the state loom large. Realists largely explain this on the basis that the very condition for order and security—namely, the existence of a sovereign—is missing from the international realm.

Realists claim that in anarchy, states compete with other states for power and security. The nature of the competition is viewed in zero-sum terms; in other words, more for one actor means less for another. This competitive logic of power politics makes agreement on universal principles difficult, apart from the principle of non-intervention in the internal affairs of other sovereign states. But even this principle, designed to facilitate **coexistence**, is suspended by realists who argue that in practice non-intervention does not apply in relations between great powers and their 'near abroad'. As evidenced by the most recent behaviour of the United States in Afghanistan and Iraq, powerful states are able to overturn the non-intervention principle on the grounds of national security and international order.

Given that the first move of the state is to organize power domestically, and the second is to accumulate **power** internationally, it is self-evidently important to consider in more depth what realists mean by their ubiquitous fusion of politics with power. It is one thing to say that international politics is a struggle for power, but this merely begs the question of what realists mean by power. Morgenthau offers the following definition of power: 'man's control over the minds and actions of other men'

([1948] 1955: 26). There are two important points that realists make about the elusive concept of power. First, power is a relational concept; one does not exercise power in a vacuum, but in relation to another entity. Second, power is a relative concept; calculations need to be made not only about one's own power capabilities, but about the power that other state actors possess. Yet the task of accurately assessing the power of states is infinitely complex, and often is reduced to counting the number of troops, tanks, aircraft, and naval ships a country possesses in the belief that this translates in the ability to get other actors to do something they would not otherwise do.

There have been a number of criticisms made of how realists define and measure power, many of which are discussed in later chapters. Critics argue that Realism has been purchased at a discount precisely because its currency, power, has remained under-theorized and inconsistently used. Simply by asserting that states seek power provides no answer to crucial questions. Why do states struggle for power? Surely power is a means to an end rather than an end in itself? Is there not a difference between the mere possession of power and the ability to change the behaviour of others?

Structural realists have attempted to bring more conceptual clarity to bear on the meaning of power. Waltz tries to overcome the problem by shifting the focus from power to capabilities. He suggests that capabilities can be ranked according to their strength in the following areas: 'size of population and territory, resource endowment, economic capability, military strength, political stability and competence' (1979: 131). The difficulty here is that resource strength does not always lead to military victory. For example, in the 1967 Six Day War between Israel and Egypt, Jordan, and Syria, the distribution of resources clearly favoured the Arab coalition and yet the supposedly weaker side annihilated its enemies' forces and seized their territory. The definition of power as capabilities is even less successful at explaining the relative economic success of Japan over China. A more sophisticated understanding of power would focus on the ability of a state to control or influence its environment in situations that are not necessarily conflictual.

An additional weakness with the realist treatment of power concerns its exclusive focus upon state power. For realists, states are the only actors that really 'count'. Transnational corporations, **international organizations**, and ideologically driven terrorist **networks**, such as

Al Qaeda, rise and fall but the state is the one permanent feature in the landscape of modern global politics. Yet many today question the adequacy of the state-centric assumption of realism.

Survival

The second principle that unites realists is the assertion that, in international politics, the pre-eminent goal is survival. Although there is an ambiguity in the works of the realists as to whether the accumulation of power is an end in itself, one would think that there is no dissenting from the argument that the ultimate concern of states is for security. Survival is held to be a precondition for attaining all other goals, whether these involve conquest or merely independence. According to Waltz, 'beyond the survival motive, the aims of states may be endlessly varied' (1979: 91). Yet, as we mentioned in the previous section, a recent controversy among structural realists has arisen over the question of whether states are in fact principally security or power maximizers. Defensive realists such as Waltz argue that states have security as their principal interest and therefore only seek the requisite amount of power to ensure their own survival. According to this view, states are profoundly defensive actors and will not seek to gain greater amounts of power if that means jeopardizing their own security. Offensive realists such as Mearsheimer argue that the ultimate goal of all states is to achieve a hegemonic position in the international system. States, according to this view, always desire more power and are willing, if the opportunity arises, to alter the existing distribution of power even if such an action may jeopardize their own security. In terms of survival, defensive realists hold that the existence of status quo powers lessens the competition for power while offensive realists argue that the competition is always keen because revisionist states and aspiring hegemons are always willing to take risks with the aim of improving their position in the international system.

Niccolo Machiavelli tried to make a 'science' out of his reflections on the art of survival. His short and engaging book, *The Prince*, was written with the explicit intention of codifying a set of maxims that will enable leaders to maintain their hold on power. In important respects, we find two related Machiavellian themes recurring in the writings of modern realists, both of which derive from the idea that the realm of international politics requires different moral and political rules from those which apply

in domestic politics. The task of understanding the real nature of international politics, and the need to protect the state at all costs (even if this may mean the sacrifice of one's own citizens) places a heavy burden on the shoulders of state leaders. In the words of Henry Kissinger, the academic realist who became Secretary of State during the Nixon Presidency, 'a nation's survival is its first and ultimate responsibility; it cannot be compromised or put to risk' (1977: 204). Their guide must be an **ethic of responsibility**: the careful weighing up of consequences; the realization that individual acts of an immoral kind might have to be taken for the greater good. By way of an example, think of the ways in which governments frequently suspend the legal and political rights of 'suspected terrorists' in view of the threat they pose to **national security**. An ethic of responsibility is frequently used as a justification for breaking the laws of war, as in the case of the United States decision to drop nuclear bombs on Hiroshima and Nagasaki in 1945. The principal difficulty with the realist formulation of an 'ethics of responsibility' is that, while instructing leaders to consider the consequences of their actions, it does not provide a guide to how state leaders should weigh the consequences (M. J. Smith 1986: 51).

Not only does Realism provide an alternative moral code for state leaders, it suggests a wider objection to the whole enterprise of bringing ethics into international politics. Starting from the assumption that each state has its own particular values and beliefs, realists argue that the state is the supreme good and there can be no community beyond borders. This moral relativism has generated a substantial body of criticism, particularly from liberal theorists who endorse the notion of universal human rights. For a fuller discussion see Ch.6.

Self-help

Waltz's *Theory of International Politics* (1979) brought to the realist tradition a deeper understanding of the international system within which states coexist. Unlike many other realists, Waltz argued that international politics was not unique because of the regularity of war and conflict, since this was also familiar in domestic politics. The key difference between domestic and international orders lies in their structure. In the domestic polity, citizens do not have to defend themselves. In the international system, there is no higher authority to prevent and counter the use of force. Security can therefore only be realized through self-help. In an anarchic structure, 'self-help is necessarily the principle of action' (Waltz 1979: 111). But in the course of providing for one's own security, the state in question will automatically be fuelling the insecurity of other states.

The term given to this spiral of insecurity is the **security dilemma**. According to Wheeler and Booth, security dilemmas exist 'when the military preparations of one state create an unresolvable uncertainty in the mind of another as to whether those preparations are for "defensive" purposes only (to enhance its security in an uncertain world) or whether they are for offensive purposes (to change the status quo to its advantage)' (1992: 30). This scenario suggests that one state's quest for security is often another state's source of insecurity. States find it very difficult to trust one another and often view the intentions of others in a negative light. Thus the military preparations of one state are likely to be matched by neighbouring states. The irony is that at the end of the day, states often feel no more secure than before they undertook measures to enhance their own security.

In a self-help system, structural realists argue that the balance of power will emerge even in the absence of a conscious policy to maintain the balance (i.e. prudent statecraft). Waltz argues that balances of power result irrespective of the intentions of any particular state. In an anarchic system populated by states who seek to perpetuate themselves, alliances will be formed that seek to check and balance the power against threatening states. Classical realists, however, are more likely to emphasize the crucial role state leaders and diplomats play in maintaining the balance of power. In other words, the balance of power is not natural or inevitable, it must be constructed.

There is a lively debate among realists concerning the stability of the balance of power system. This is especially the case today in that many argue that the balance of power has been replaced by an unbalanced **unipolar** order. It is questionable whether other countries will actively attempt to balance against the United States as structural realism would predict. Whether it is the contrived balance of the Concert of Europe in the early nineteenth century, or the more fortuitous balance of the cold war, balances of power are broken—either through war or peaceful change—and new balances emerge. What the perennial collapsing of the balance of power demonstrates is that states are at best able to mitigate the worst consequences of the security dilemma but are not able to escape it. The reason for this terminal condition is the absence of trust in international relations.

Historically, realists have illustrated the lack of trust among states by reference to the parable of the 'stag hunt'. In *Man, the State and War*, Kenneth Waltz revisits Rousseau's parable:

> Assume that five men who have acquired a rudimentary ability to speak and to understand each other happen to come together at a time when all of them suffer from hunger. The hunger of each will be satisfied by the fifth part of a stag, so they 'agree' to cooperate in a project to trap one. But also the hunger of any one of them will be satisfied by a hare, so, as a hare comes within reach, one of them grabs it. The defector obtains the means of satisfying his hunger but in doing so permits the stag to escape. His immediate interest prevails over consideration for his fellows.
>
> *(1959: 167–8)*

Waltz argues that the metaphor of the stag hunt provides a basis for understanding the problem of coordinating the interests of the individual versus the interests of the common good, and the pay-off between short-term interests and long-term interests. In the self-help system of international politics, the logic of self-interest mitigates against the provision of collective goods, such as 'security' or 'free trade'. In the case of the latter, according to the theory of comparative advantage, all states would be wealthier in a world that allowed freedom of goods and services across borders. But individual states, or groups of states like the European Union, can increase their wealth by pursuing protectionist policies providing other states do not respond in kind. Of course the logical outcome is for the remaining states to become protectionist, international trade collapses, and a world recession reduces the wealth of each state. Thus the question is not whether all will be better off through **cooperation**, but rather who will likely gain more than another. It is because of this concern with **relative gains** issues that realists argue that cooperation is difficult to achieve in a self-help system (for a fuller discussion see Ch. 7).

Key Points

- **Statism** is the centrepiece of Realism. This involves two claims. First, for the theorist, the state is the pre-eminent actor and all other actors in world politics are of lesser significance. Second, state 'sovereignty' signifies the existence of an independent political community, one which has juridical authority over its territory.
  Key criticism: Statism is flawed both on empirical (challenges to state power from 'above' and 'below') and normative grounds (the inability of sovereign states to respond to collective global problems such as famine, environmental degradation, and human rights abuses).
- **Survival:** The primary objective of all states is survival; this is the supreme national interest to which all political leaders must adhere.
  Key criticism: Are there no limits to what actions a state can take in the name of necessity?
- **Self-help:** No other state or institution can be relied upon to guarantee your survival.
  Key criticism: Self-help is not an inevitable consequence of the absence of a world government; self-help is a logic that states have selected. Moreover, there are historical and contemporary examples where states have preferred collective security systems, or forms of regional security communities, in preference to self-help.

Conclusion: Realism and the globalization of world politics

The chapter opened by considering the often repeated realist claim that the pattern of international politics—wars interrupted for periods characterized by the preparation for future wars—have remained constant over the preceding twenty-five centuries. Realists have consistently held that the continuities in international relations are more important than the changes, but many find this to be increasingly problematic in the present age of globalization. But the importance of Realism has not been diminished by the dynamics of globalization. It is not clear that economic **interdependence** has made war less likely. The state continues to be the dominant unit in world politics. And globalization should not be seen as a process that is disconnected from the distribution of power in the international system. In this sense, this current phase of **globalization** is fundamentally tied to Westernization and, to be even more specific, Americanization.

Not surprisingly, leading realist thinkers have been quick to seize on the apparent convergence between our post-**9/11** experience and the cycle of violence predicted by the theory. There were, however, some apparent contradictions in the realist account of the conflict. To begin with, the attacks on the US homeland were committed

by a non-state actor. Had one of the significant norms of the Westphalian order become unhinged, namely, that war happens between sovereign states? Not only was the enemy a **global network** of Al Qaeda operatives, their goal was unconventional in that they did not seek to conquer territory but challenge by force the ideological supremacy of the West. Set against these anomalies, the leading states in the system were quick to identify the network with certain **territorial states**—the Taliban government of Afghanistan being the most immediate example, but also other pariah states who allegedly harboured terrorists. The United States was quick to link the overthrow of Saddam Hussein's Iraq with its global **war on terror**. Moreover, rather than identifying the terrorists as transnational criminals and using police enforcement methods to counter their threat, the USA and its allies defined them as enemies of the state who had to be targeted and defeated using conventional military means.

For realists such as John Gray and Kenneth Waltz, 9/11 was not the beginning of a new era in world politics so much as a case of 'business as usual' (see their essays in Booth and Dunne 2002). What matters most, argues Waltz, are the continuities in the structural imbalance of power in the system and the distribution of nuclear weapons. Crises are to be expected because the logic of self-help generates periodic crises. Their analysis is a stark rejoinder to the more idealist defenders of globalization who see a new pacific world order emerging out of the ashes of the previous order. According to realists, 9/11 was never going to trigger a new era in governance: the coalition of the willing that was forged in the immediate aftermath was, in Waltz's terms, 'a mile wide', but only

'an inch deep'. How prophetic those words have proven to be. The war against Iraq was executed by the USA with the UK being the only significant diplomatic and military ally. Not only did most states in the world oppose the war, leading American realists were public in their condemnation (see Box 5.2). Iraq, they argued, could have been deterred from threatening both the security of the United States and its neighbours in the Middle East. Furthermore, a costly military intervention followed by a lengthy occupation in the Middle East has weakened the USA's ability to contain the rising threat from China. In short, the Bush Presidency has not exercised power in a responsible and sensible manner.

Behind the rhetoric of universal values, the USA has used the war to justify a wide range of policy positions that strengthen its economic and military power while undermining various multilateral agreements on arms control, the environment, human rights, and trade.

Realists do not have to situate their theory of world politics in opposition to globalization *per se*; rather, what they offer is a very different conceptualization of the process. What is important about a realist view of globalization is the claim that rudimentary transnational governance is possible but at the same time it is entirely dependent on the distribution of power. Given the preponderance of power that the USA holds, it should not be a surprise that it has been one of the foremost proponents of globalization. The core values of globalization—liberalism, capitalism, and consumerism—are exactly those espoused by the United States. At a deeper cultural level, realists argue that modernity is not, as liberals hope, dissolving the boundaries of difference among the peo-

---

Box 5.2 Realism against wars: an unlikely alliance?

Realists are often portrayed as being advocates of an aggressive foreign policy. Such a representation has always lacked credibility. Hans Morgenthau opposed the US war against the North Vietnamese on the grounds that it defied a rational understanding of the national interest. He believed that US goals were not attainable 'without unreasonable moral liabilities and military risks' (M. J. Smith 1986: 158). The US-led war against Iraq in 2003 is the most recent example of Realism's council against the use of force. As the intense round of negotiations were underway in the Security Council, in the autumn of 2002, 34 leading realist thinkers co-signed an advert in the *New York Times* entitled 'War with Iraq is <u>Not</u> in America's National Interest' (original emphasis). John J. Mearsheimer and Stephen M. Walt developed this position further in early 2004. Why, they asked, had the USA given up on the policy of deterrence which proved to

be successful during the cold war? They end the article with a bold, and some might say prescient, conclusion:

'This war would be one the Bush administration chose to fight but did not have to fight. Even if such a war goes well and has positive long-range consequences, it will still have been unnecessary. And if it goes badly—whether in the form of high U.S. casualties, significant civilian deaths, a heightened risk of terrorism, or increased hatred of the United States in the Arab and Islamic world—then its architects will have even more to answer for.'

(Mearsheimer and Walt 2003: 59)

ples of the world. From classical realists such as Rousseau to structural realists such as Waltz, protagonists have argued that interdependence is as likely to breed 'mutual vulnerability' as peace and prosperity. And while questioning the extent to which the world has become any more interdependent in relative terms, realists insist that the state is not going to be eclipsed by global forces operating either below or above the nation-state. Nationalism, realists have continuously reminded us, remains a potent force in world politics.

There are good reasons for thinking that the twenty-first century will be a realist century. Despite efforts of federalists to rekindle the idealist flame, Europe continues to be as divided by different national interests as it is united by a common good. As Jacques Chirac put it in 2000, a 'united Europe of states' was much more likely than a 'United States of Europe'. Outside Europe and North America, many of the assumptions which underpinned the post-war international order, particularly those associated with human rights, are increasingly being seen as nothing more than a Western idea backed by economic dollars and military 'divisions'. If China continues its rate of economic growth, it will be more economically powerful than the USA by 2020 (Mearsheimer 1990: 398). By then, realism leads us to predict, that Western norms of individual rights and responsibilities will be under threat. Rather than transforming global politics in its own image, as Liberalism has sought to do in the twentieth century, the West may need to become more realist in order for its traditions and values to survive the twenty-first.

❓ Questions

1 How does the Melian dialogue represent key concepts such as self-interest, the balance of power, alliances, capabilities, empires, and justice?

2 Do you think there is one Real*ism*, or many?

3 Do you know more about international relations than an Athenian student during *The Peloponnesian War*?

4 Do realists confuse a *description* of war and conflict for an *explanation* of why it occurs?

5 Is Realism anything more than the ideology of powerful, satisfied states?

6 How would a realist explain the war on terrorism?

7 Will the West have to learn to be more realist, and not less, if its civilization is to survive in the twenty-first century?

8 What is at stake in the debate between defensive and offensive realism?

9 Is structural realism sufficient to account for the variation in the behaviour of states?

10 Can realism help us to understand the globalization of world politics?

➡ Guide to further reading

For a general survey of the realist tradition

Grieco, J. M. (1997), 'Realist International Theory and the Study of World Politics', in M. W. Doyle and G. J. Ikenberry (eds), *New Thinking in International Relations Theory* (Westview Press). A comprehensive critical appreciation of realist international theory.

Guzzini, S. (1998), *Realism in International Relations and International Political Economy* (London: Routledge). Provides an understanding of the evolution of the realist tradition.

Smith, M. J. (1986), *Realist Thought from Weber to Kissinger* (Baton Rouge: Louisiana State University Press. An excellent discussion of many of the seminal realist thinkers.

Walt, S. M. (2002), 'The Enduring Relevance of the Realist Tradition', in I. Katznelson and

H. V. Milner (eds), *Political Science: The State of the Discipline* (New York: W. W. Norton). A state-of-the-art exposition of the realist tradition.

Twentieth-century classical realism

Carr, E. H. (2001), *The Twenty Years' Crisis 1919–1939: An Introduction to the Study of International Relations* (London: Palgrave). An important critique of liberal idealism.

Morgenthau, H. J. (1946), *Scientific Man versus Power Politics* (Chicago: University of Chicago Press). A key statement of realist political philosophy.

——(1948), *Politics among Nations: The Struggle for Power and Peace* (New York: Alfred A. Knopf). A foundational text for the discipline of International Relations.

Structural realism

Baldwin, D. A. (1993), *Neorealism and Neoliberalism: The Contemporary Debate* (New York: Columbia University Press). This fine collection takes the debate further.

Keohane, R. (ed.) (1986), *Neorealism and its Critics* (New York: Columbia University Press). This collection of essays includes key chapters by Waltz, an interesting defence of Realism by Robert Gilpin, and powerful critiques by Richard Ashley, Robert Cox, and J. G. Ruggie.

Mearsheimer, J. (2001), *The Tragedy of Great Power Politics* (New York: W. W. Norton). This is the definitive account of offensive realism.

Waltz, K. (1979), *Theory of International Politics* (Reading, Mass.: Addison-Wesley). This the exemplar for structural realism.

Neoclassical realism

Rose, G. (1998), 'Neoclassical Realism and Theories of Foreign Policy', *World Politics*, 51: 144–72. An important review article that is credited with coining the term 'neoclassical realism'.

Schweller, R. L. (1996), 'Neorealism's Status-quo Bias: What Security Dilemma?', *Security Studies*, 5: 90–121. One of the leading neoclassical realist attempts to demonstrate the status quo bias of Waltz's version of structural realism.

Zakaria, F. (1998), *From Wealth to Power: The Unusual Origins of America's World Role* (Princeton, NJ: Princeton University Press). Puts forth his theory of state-centric realism.

Online Resource Centre

 Visit the Online Resource Centre that accompanies this book to access more learning resources on this chapter topic at www.oxfordtextbooks.co.uk/uk/orc/baylis_smith4e/

Notes

1 Realism, *realpolitik*, and *raison d'état* are broadly interchangeable. In this chapter, Realism with an upper case 'R' will be used to signify the general tradition. When discussing particular realists, or types of realism (such as historical realism), lower case 'r' will be used.

2 A number of critical histories of the field of International Relations have recently challenged the notion that the inter-war period was essentially 'idealist' in character. Both Peter Wilson (1998) and Brian C. Schmidt (1998) argue that it is simply a myth that an idealist paradigm dominated the study of international relations during the inter-war period of the field's history.

3 Weber is rightly regarded by Smith as the theorist who has shaped twentieth-century realist thought, principally because of his fusion of politics with power.

Chapter 6

Liberalism

TIM DUNNE

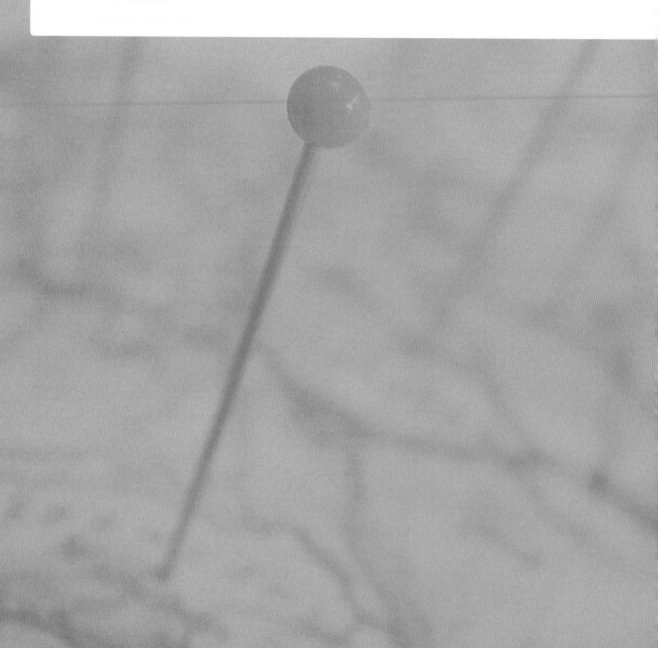

- Introduction ···110
- Core ideas in Liberal thinking on international relations ················112
- Liberalism and globalization ···116
- Conclusion ··120

Reader's Guide

The practice of international relations has not been accommodating to Liberalism. Whereas the domestic political realm in many states has witnessed an impressive degree of progress, with institutions providing for order *and* justice, the international realm in the era of the modern states-system has been characterized by a precarious order and the *absence* of justice. The introductory section of the chapter will address this dilemma before providing a definition of Liberalism and its component parts. Section two considers the core concepts of Liberalism, beginning with the visionary internationalism of the Enlightenment, through to the Idealism of the inter-war period, and the institutionalism which became dominant in the second half of the twentieth century. The third and final section considers Liberalism in an era of globalization: in particular, it contrasts a status quo reading of the liberal project with a radicalized version which seeks to promote and extend cosmopolitan values and institutions.

Introduction

Although **Realism** is regarded as the dominant theory of international relations, **Liberalism** has a strong claim to being the historic alternative. In the twentieth century, liberal thinking influenced policy-making elites and public opinion in a number of Western states after the First World War, an era often referred to in academic international relations as **Idealism**. There was a brief resurgence of liberal sentiment at the end of the Second World War with the birth of the United Nations, although this beacon of hope was soon extinguished by the return of **cold war** power politics. In the 1990s, Liberalism appeared resurgent as Western state leaders proclaimed a **New World Order** and intellectuals provided theoretical justifications for the inherent supremacy of their liberal ideas over all other competing ideologies. After **9/11**, the pendulum has once again swung towards the realist pole as the USA and its allies have sought to consolidate their power and punish those whom they define as terrorists and the states that provide them with shelter.

How do we explain the divergent fortunes of Liberalism in the domestic and international domains? While liberal values and institutions have become deeply embedded in Europe and North America, the same values and institutions lack legitimacy worldwide. To invoke the famous phrase of Stanley Hoffmann's, 'international affairs have been the nemesis of Liberalism'. 'The essence of Liberalism', Hoffmann continues, 'is self-restraint, moderation, compromise and peace' whereas 'the essence of international politics is exactly the opposite: troubled peace, at best, or the **state of war**' (Hoffmann 1987: 396). This explanation comes as no surprise to realists, who argue that there can be no progress, no law, and no justice, where there is no common power. Despite the weight of this realist argument, those who believe in the liberal project have not conceded defeat. Liberals argue that power politics itself is the product of ideas, and crucially, ideas can change. Therefore, even if the world has been inhospitable to Liberalism, this does not mean that it cannot be re-made in its image.

While the belief in the possibility of progress is one identifier of a liberal approach to politics (Clark 1989: 49–66), there are other general propositions that define the broad tradition of Liberalism. Perhaps the appropriate way to begin this discussion is with a four-dimensional definition (Doyle 1997: 207). First, all citizens are juridically equal and possess certain basic rights to education, access to a free press, and religious toleration. Second, the legislative assembly of the state possesses only the authority invested in it by the people, whose basic rights it is not permitted to abuse. Third, a key dimension of the liberty of the individual is the right to own property, including productive forces. Fourth, Liberalism contends that the most effective system of economic exchange is one that is largely market driven and not one that is subordinate to bureaucratic regulation and control, either domestically or internationally. When these propositions are taken together, we see a stark contrast between liberal values of **individualism**, tolerance, freedom, and constitutionalism, and conservatism, which places a higher value on order and authority and is willing to sacrifice the liberty of the individual for the stability of the **community**.

Although many writers have tended to view Liberalism as a theory of government, what is becoming increasingly apparent is the explicit connection between Liberalism as a political and economic theory and Liberalism as an international theory. Properly conceived, liberal thought on a global scale embodies a **domestic analogy** operating at multiple levels.[1] Like individuals, states have different characteristics—some are bellicose and war-prone, others are tolerant and peaceful: in short, the **identity** of the state determines its outward orientation. Liberals see a further parallel between individuals and sovereign states. Although the character of states may differ, all states are accorded certain 'natural' rights, such as the generalized right to non-intervention in their domestic affairs. On another level, the domestic analogy refers to the extension of ideas that originated inside liberal states to the international realm, such as the coordinating role played by institutions and the centrality of the rule of law to the idea of a just **order**. In a sense, the historical project of Liberalism is the domestication of the international.

Liberals concede that we have far to go before this goal has been reached. Historically, liberals have agreed with Realists that war is a recurring feature of the **anarchic states system**. But unlike realists, they do not identify **anarchy** as the cause of war. How, then, do liberals explain war? As Box 6.1 demonstrates, certain strands of Liberalism see the causes of war located in **imperialism**, others in

Box 6.1 Liberalism and the causes of war, determinants of peace

One of the most useful analytical tools for thinking about differences between individual thinkers or particular variations on a broad theme such as Liberalism is to differentiate between levels of analysis. For example, Kenneth Waltz's *Man, the State and War* (1959) examined the causes of conflict operating at the level of the individual, the state, and the international system itself. The table below turns Waltz on his head, as it were, in order to show how different liberal thinkers have provided competing explanations (across the three levels of analysis) for the causes of war and the determinants of peace.

'Images' of Liberalism	Public figure/period	Causes of conflict	Determinants of peace
First image (Human nature)	Richard Cobden (mid-19th century)	Interventions by governments domestically and internationally disturbing the natural order.	Individual liberty, free trade, prosperity, interdependence.
Second image (The state)	Woodrow Wilson (early 20th century)	Undemocratic nature of international politics, especially foreign policy and the balance of power.	National self-determination; open governments responsive to public opinion; collective security.
Third image (The structure of the system)	J. A. Hobson (early 20th century)	The balance of power system.	A world government, with powers to mediate and enforce decisions.

the failure of the **balance of power**, and still others in the problem of undemocratic **regimes**. And ought this to be remedied through **collective security**, commerce, or world government? While it can be productive to think about the various strands of liberal thought and their differing prescriptions (Doyle 1997: 205–300), given the limited space permitted to deal with a broad and complex tradition, the emphasis below will be on the core concepts of international Liberalism and the way in which these relate to the goals of order and justice on a global scale.[2]

At the end of the chapter, the discussion will return to a tension that lies in the heart of the liberal theory of politics. As can be seen from a critical appraisal of the four-fold definition presented above, Liberalism pulls in two directions: its commitment to freedom in the economic and social spheres leans in the direction of a minimalist role for governing institutions, while the democratic political culture required for basic freedoms to be safeguarded requires robust and interventionist institutions. This has variously been interpreted as a tension between different liberal goals, or more broadly as a sign of rival and incompatible conceptions of Liberalism. Should a liberal polity—no matter what the size or scale—preserve the right of individuals to retain property and privilege, or should Liberalism elevate equality over liberty so that resources are redistributed from the strong to the weak? When we are looking at politics on a global scale it is clear that inequalities are far greater while at the same time our institutional capacity to do something about them is that much less. As writers on **globalization** remind us, the intensification of global flows in trade, resources, and people has weakened the state's capacity to govern. Closing this gap requires nothing short of a radical reconfiguration of the relationship between **territoriality** and governance.

Key Points

- The liberal tradition in political thought goes back at least as far as the thinking of John Locke in the late seventeenth century. From then on, liberal ideas have profoundly shaped how we think about the relationship between government and citizens.
- Liberalism is a theory of both government within states and good governance between states and peoples worldwide. Unlike Realism, which regards the 'international' as an anarchic realm, Liberals seek to project values of order, liberty, justice, and toleration into international relations.
- The high-water mark of liberal thinking in international relations was reached in the inter-war period in the work of Idealists who believed that warfare was an unnecessary and outmoded way of settling disputes between states.

- Domestic and international institutions are required to protect and nurture these values. But note that these values and institutions allow for significant variations which accounts for the fact that there are heated debates within Liberalism.
- Liberals disagree on fundamental issues such as the causes of war and what kind of institutions are required to deliver liberal values in a decentralized, multicultural international system.
- An important cleavage within Liberalism, which has become more pronounced in our globalized world, is between those operating with a positive conception of Liberalism, who advocate interventionist foreign policies and stronger international institutions, and those who incline towards a negative conception, which places a priority on toleration and non-intervention.

Core ideas in Liberal thinking on international relations

Immanuel Kant and Jeremy Bentham were two of the leading liberals of the **Enlightenment**. Both were reacting to the barbarity of international relations, or what Kant graphically described as 'the lawless state of savagery', at a time when domestic politics was at the cusp of a new age of rights, **citizenship,** and constitutionalism. Their abhorrence of the lawless savagery led them individually to elaborate plans for 'perpetual peace'. Although written over two centuries ago, these manifestos contain the seeds of core liberal ideas, in particular the belief that reason could deliver freedom and justice in international relations. For Kant the imperative to achieve perpetual peace required the transformation of individual consciousness, republican constitutionalism, and a federal contract between states to abolish war (rather than to regulate it as earlier international lawyers had argued). This federation can be likened to a permanent peace treaty, rather than a 'superstate' actor or world government. The three components of Kant's hypothetical treaty for a permanent peace are outlined in Box 6.2.

Kant's claim that liberal states are pacific in their international relations with other liberal states was revived in the 1980s. In a much cited article, Michael Doyle argued that liberal states have created a 'separate peace' (1986: 1151). According to Doyle, there are two elements to the Kantian legacy: restraint among liberal states and 'international imprudence' in relations with non-liberal states. Although the empirical evidence seems to support the **democratic peace** thesis, it is important to bear in mind the limitations of the argument. In the first instance, for the theory to be compelling, believers in the thesis need to provide an explanation as to why war has become unthinkable between liberal states. Kant had argued that if the decision to use force was taken by the people, rather than by the prince, then the frequency of conflicts would be drastically reduced. But logically, this argument implies a lower frequency of conflicts between liberal and non-liberal states, and this has proven to be contrary to the historical evidence. An alternative explanation for the democratic peace thesis might be that liberal states tend to be wealthy, and therefore have less to gain (and more to lose) by engaging in conflicts than poorer authoritarian states. Perhaps the most convincing explanation of all is the simple fact that liberal states tend to be in relations of amity with other liberal states. War between Canada and the USA is unthinkable, perhaps not because of their liberal democratic constitutions, but because they are friends

---

Box 6.2 Immanuel Kant's 'Perpetual Peace: A Philosophical Sketch'

First Definitive Article: *The Civil Constitution of Every State shall be Republican*

'If, as is inevitably the case under this constitution, the consent of the citizens is required to decide whether or not war is to be declared, it is very natural that they will have great hesitation in embarking on so dangerous an enterprise. . . . But under a constitution where the subject is not a citizen, and which is therefore not republican, it is the simplest thing in the world to go to war. For the head of state is not a fellow citizen, but the owner of the state, and a war will not force him to make the slightest sacrifice so far as his banquets, hunts, pleasure palaces and court festivals are concerned.'

(Kant 1991: 99–102)

Second Definitive Article: *The Right of Nations shall be based on a Federation of Free States*

'Each nation, for the sake of its own security, can and ought to demand of the others that they should enter along with it into a constitution, similar to a civil one, within which the rights of each could be secured.....

But peace can neither be inaugurated nor secured without a general agreement between the nations; thus a particular kind of league, which we will call a pacific federation is required. It would be different from a peace treaty in that the latter terminates one war, whereas the former would seek to end all wars for good. . . . It can be shown that this idea of federalism, extending gradually to encompass all states and thus leading to perpetual peace, is practicable and has objective reality.'

(Kant 1991: 102–5)

Third Definitive Article: *Cosmopolitan Right shall be limited to Conditions of Universal Hospitality*

'The peoples of the earth have thus entered in varying degrees into a universal community, and it has developed to the point where a violation of rights in one part of the world is felt everywhere. The idea of a cosmopolitan right is therefore not fantastic and overstrained; it is a necessary complement to the unwritten code of political and international right, transforming it into a universal right of humanity.'

(Kant 1991: 105–8)

(Wendt 1999: 298–9) with a high degree of convergence in economic and political matters. Indeed, war between states with contrasting political and economic systems may also be unthinkable because they have a history of friendly relations. An example here is Mexico and Cuba, which maintain close bilateral relations despite their history of divergent economic ideologies.

Irrespective of the scholarly search for an answer to the reasons why liberal democratic states are more peaceful, it is important to note the political consequences of this hypothesis. In 1989 Francis Fukuyama wrote an article entitled '**The End of History**' which celebrated the triumph of Liberalism over all other ideologies, contending that liberal states were more stable internally and more peaceful in their international relations (Fukuyama 1989: 3–18). Other defenders of the democratic peace thesis were more circumspect. As Doyle recognized, liberal democracies are as aggressive as any other type of state in their relations with authoritarian regimes and stateless peoples (Doyle 1995b: 100). How, then, should states inside the liberal zone of peace conduct their relations with non-liberal regimes? How can the positive Kantian legacy of restraint triumph over the historical legacy of international imprudence on the part of liberal states? These are fascinating and timely questions which will be taken up in the final section of the chapter.

Two centuries after Kant first called for a 'pacific federation', the validity of the idea that democracies are more pacific continues to attract a great deal of scholarly interest. The claim has also found its way into the public discourse of Western states' foreign policy, appearing in speeches made by US presidents as diverse as Ronald Reagan, William Jefferson Clinton, and George W. Bush. Less crusading voices within the liberal tradition believe that a legal and institutional framework must be established that includes states with different cultures and traditions. Such a belief in the power of law to solve the problem of war was advocated by Jeremy Bentham at the end of the eighteenth century. 'Establish a common tribunal' and 'the necessity for war no longer follows from a difference of opinion' (Luard 1992: 416). Like many liberal thinkers after him, Bentham showed that federal states such as the German Diet, the American Confederation, and the Swiss League were able to transform their identity from one based on conflicting interests to a more peaceful federation. As Bentham famously argued, 'between the interests of nations there is nowhere any real conflict'.

Cobden's belief that **free trade** would create a more peaceful world order is a core idea of nineteenth-century Liberalism. Trade brings mutual gains to all the players, irrespective of their size or the nature of their economies. It is perhaps not surprising that it was in Britain that this argument found its most vocal supporters. The supposed universal value of free trade brought disproportionate gains to the hegemonic power. There was never an admission that free trade among countries at different stages of **development** would lead to relations of dominance and subservience.

The idea of a natural **harmony of interests** in international political and economic relations came under challenge in the early part of the twentieth century. The fact that Britain and Germany had highly interdependent economies before the Great War (1914–18) seemed to confirm the fatal flaw in the association of economic interdependence with peace. From the turn of the century, the contradictions within European civilization, of progress and exemplarism on the one hand and the harnessing of industrial power for military purposes on the other, could no longer be contained. Europe stumbled into a horrific war killing 15 million people. The war not only brought an end to three **empires** but also was a contributing factor to the Russian Revolution of 1917.

The First World War shifted liberal thinking towards a recognition that peace is not a natural condition but is one which must be constructed. In a powerful critique of the idea that peace and prosperity were part of a latent natural order, the publicist and author Leonard Woolf argued that peace and prosperity required 'consciously devised machinery' (Luard 1992: 465). But perhaps the most famous advocate of an international authority for the management of international relations was Woodrow Wilson. According to this US President, peace could only be secured with the creation of an **international organization** to regulate the international anarchy. Security could not be left to secret bilateral diplomatic deals and a blind faith in the balance of power. Just as peace had to be enforced in domestic society, the international domain had to have a system of regulation for coping with disputes and an international force which could be mobilized if non-violent conflict resolution failed. In this sense, more than any other strand of Liberalism, Idealism rests on the **domestic analogy** (Suganami 1989: 94–113).

In his famous 'Fourteen Points' speech, addressed to Congress in January 1918, Wilson argued that 'a general

association of nations must be formed' to preserve the coming peace—the League of Nations was to be that general association. For the League to be effective, it had to have the military power to deter aggression and, when necessary, to use a preponderance of power to enforce its will. This was the idea behind the **collective security** system which was central to the League of Nations. Collective security refers to an arrangement where 'each state in the system accepts that the security of one is the concern of all, and agrees to join in a collective response to aggression' (Roberts and Kingsbury 1993: 30). It can be contrasted with an alliance system of security, where a number of states join together usually as a response to a specific external threat (sometimes known as collective defence). In the case of the League of Nations, Article 16 of the League's Charter noted the obligation that, in the event of war, all member states must cease normal relations with the offending state, impose sanctions, and, if necessary, commit their armed forces to the disposal of the League Council should the use of force be required to restore the status quo.

The League's constitution also called for the **self-determination** of all nations, another founding characteristic of liberal idealist thinking on international relations. Going back to the mid-nineteenth century, self-determination movements in Greece, Hungary, and Italy received support among liberal powers and public opinion. Yet the default support for self-determination masked a host of practical and moral problems that were laid bare after Woodrow Wilson issued his proclamation. What would happen to newly created minorities who felt no allegiance to the self-determining state? Could a democratic process adequately deal with questions of identity—who was to decide what constituency was to participate in a ballot? And what if a newly self-determined state rejected liberal democratic norms?

The experience of the League of Nations was a disaster. While the moral rhetoric at the creation of the League was decidedly idealist, in practice states remained imprisoned by self-interest. There is no better example of this than the United States' decision not to join the institution it had created. With the Soviet Union outside the system for ideological reasons, the League of Nations quickly became a talking shop for the 'satisfied' powers. Hitler's decision in March 1936 to reoccupy the Rhineland, a designated demilitarized zone according to the terms of the Treaty of Versailles, effectively pulled the plug on the League's life-support system (it had been put on the 'critical' list following the Manchurian crisis in 1931 and the Ethiopian crisis in 1935).

According to the history of the discipline of International Relations, the collapse of the League of Nations dealt a fatal blow to Idealism. There is no doubt that the language of Liberalism after 1945 was more pragmatic; how could anyone living in the shadow of the Holocaust be optimistic? Yet familiar core ideas of Liberalism remained. Even in the early 1940s, there was recognition of the need to replace the League with another international institution with responsibility for international peace and security. Only this time, in the case of the United Nations there was an awareness among the framers of the Charter of the need for a consensus between the great powers in order for enforcement action to be taken, hence the veto system (Article 27 of the UN Charter), which allowed any of the five permanent members of the Security Council the power of veto. This revision constituted an important modification to the classical model of collective security (Roberts 1996: 315). With the ideological polarity of the cold war, the UN procedures for collective security were still-born (as either of the **superpowers** and their allies would veto any action proposed by the other).[3] It was not until the end of the cold war that a collective security system was put into operation, following the invasion of Kuwait by Iraq on 2 August 1990 (see Case Study).

An important argument advanced by liberals in the early post-war period concerned the state's inability to cope with modernization. David Mitrany (1943), a pioneer **integration** theorist, argued that transnational **cooperation** was required in order to resolve common problems. His core concept was ramification, meaning the likelihood that cooperation in one sector would lead governments to extend the range of **collaboration** across other sectors. As states become more embedded in an integration process, the 'cost' of withdrawing from cooperative ventures increases.

This argument about the positive benefits from transnational cooperation is one which informed a new generation of scholars (particularly in the USA) in the 1960s and 1970s. Their argument was not simply about the mutual gains from trade, but that other **transnational actors** were beginning to challenge the dominance of sovereign states. World politics, according to pluralists (as they are often referred to) was no longer an exclusive arena for states, as it had been for the first three hundred

Iraq had always argued that the sovereign state of Kuwait was an artificial creation of the imperial powers. When this political motive was allied to an economic imperative, caused primarily by the accumulated war debts following the eight-year war with Iran, the annexation of Kuwait seemed to be a solution to Iraq's problems. The Iraqi President, Saddam Hussein, also assumed that the West would not use force to defend Kuwait, a miscalculation which was fuelled by the memory of the support the West had given Iraq during the Iran–Iraq War (the so-called 'fundamentalism' of Iran was considered to be a graver threat to international order than the extreme nationalism of the Iraqi regime).

The invasion of Kuwait on 2 August 1990 led to a series of UN resolutions calling for Iraq to withdraw unconditionally. Economic sanctions were applied while the US-led coalition of international forces gathered in Saudi Arabia. Operation 'Desert Storm' crushed the Iraqi resistance in a matter of six weeks (16 January to 28 February 1991). The 1990–1 Gulf War had certainly revived the UN doctrine of collective security, although a number of doubts remained about the underlying motivations for the war and the way in which it was fought (for instance, the coalition of national armies was controlled by the USA rather than by a UN military command as envisaged in the Charter). President George H. Bush declared that the war was about more than one small country, it was about a 'big idea; a **new world order**'. The content of this new world order was 'peaceful settlement of disputes, solidarity against aggression, reduced and controlled arsenals, and just treatment of all peoples'.

years of the Westphalian states-system. In one of the central texts of this genre, Robert Keohane and Joseph Nye (1972) argued that the centrality of other actors, such as interest groups, **transnational corporations**, and **international non-governmental organizations** (INGOs), had to be taken into consideration. Here the overriding image of international relations is one of a cobweb of diverse actors linked through multiple channels of interaction.

Although the phenomenon of **transnationalism** was an important addition to the international relations theorists' vocabulary, it remained underdeveloped as a theoretical concept. Perhaps the most important contribution of **Pluralism** was its elaboration of **interdependence**. Due to the expansion of **capitalism** and the emergence of a global culture, Pluralists recognized a growing interconnectedness in which 'changes in one part of the system have direct and indirect consequences for the rest of the system' (Little 1996: 77). Absolute **state autonomy**, so keenly entrenched in the minds of state leaders, was being circumscribed by interdependence. Such a development brought with it enhanced potential for cooperation as well as increased levels of vulnerability.

In his 1979 work *Theory of International Politics*, the neo-realist Kenneth Waltz attacked the pluralist argument about the decline of the state. He argued that the degree of interdependence internationally was far lower than the constituent parts in a national political system. Moreover, the level of economic interdependence—especially between great powers—was less than that which existed in the early part of the twentieth century. Waltz concludes: 'if one is thinking of the international-political world, it is odd in the extreme that "interdependence" has become the word commonly used to describe it' (1979: 144). In the course of their engagement with Waltz and other neo-realists, early Pluralists modified their position. Neo-liberals,[4] as they came to be known, conceded that the core assumptions of **neo-realism** were indeed correct: the anarchic international structure, the centrality of states, and a rationalist approach to social scientific inquiry. Where they differed was apparent primarily in the argument that anarchy does not mean durable patterns of cooperation are impossible: the creation of **international regimes** matters here as they facilitate cooperation by sharing information, reinforcing **reciprocity**, and making defection from norms easier to punish (see Ch.17). Moreover, in what was to become the most important difference between neo-realists and neo-liberals (developed further in Ch.7), the latter argued that actors would enter into cooperative agreements if the gains were evenly shared. Neo-realists dispute this hypothesis: what matters is a question not so

much of mutual gains as of **relative gains**: in other words, a neo-realist state has to be sure that it has more to gain than its rivals from a particular bargain or regime.

There are two important arguments that set neo-liberalism apart from democratic peace Liberalism and the liberal idealists of the inter-war period. First, academic inquiry should be guided by a commitment to a scientific approach to theory building. Whatever deeply held personal values scholars maintain, their task must be to observe regularities, formulate hypotheses as to why that relationship holds, and subject these to critical scrutiny. This separation of fact and value puts

neo-liberals on the positivist side of the methodological divide. Second, writers such as Keohane are critical of the naïve assumption of nineteenth-century liberals that commerce breeds peace. A free-trade system, according to Keohane, provides incentives for cooperation but does not guarantee it. Here he is making an important distinction between cooperation and harmony. 'Co-operation is not automatic', Keohane argues, 'but requires planning and negotiation' (1986b: 11). In the following section we see how contemporary liberal thinking maintains that the institutions of world politics after 1945 successfully embedded all states into a cooperative order.

Key Points

- Early liberal thought on international relations took the view that the natural order had been corrupted by undemocratic state leaders and outdated policies such as the balance of power. Prescriptively, Enlightenment liberals believed that a latent cosmopolitan morality could be achieved through the exercise of reason and through the creation of constitutional states. In addition, the unfettered movement of people and goods could further facilitate more peaceful international relations.

- Although there are important continuities between Enlightenment liberal thought and twentieth-century ideas, such as the belief in the power of world public opinion to tame the interests of states,

liberal Idealism was more programmatic. For idealists, the freedom of states is part of the problem of international relations and not part of the solution. Two requirements follow from their diagnosis. The first is the need for explicitly normative thinking: how to promote peace and build a better world. Second, states must be part of an international organization, and be bound by its rules and norms.

- Central to Idealism was the formation of an international organization to facilitate peaceful change, disarmament, arbitration, and (where necessary) enforcement. The League of Nations was founded in 1920 but its collective security system failed to prevent the descent into world war in the 1930s.

Liberalism and globalization

When applying liberal ideas to international relations today, we find two clusters of responses to the problems and possibilities posed by globalization. Before outlining these, let us briefly return to the definition of Liberalism set out at greater length earlier, the four components being: juridical equality, democracy, liberty, and the free market. As we will see below, these same values can be pursued by very different political strategies.

The first alternative is that of the **Liberalism of privilege** (Richardson 1997: 18). According to this perspective, the problems of globalization need to be addressed by a combination of strong democratic states in the core of the international system, robust regimes, and open markets and institutions. For an example of the working out of such a strategy in practice, we need to look no further than the success of the liberal **hegemony** of the post-1945 era. The US writer, G. John Ikenberry, is an

articulate defender of this liberal order. In the aftermath of the Second World War, the USA took the opportunity to 'embed' certain fundamental liberal principles into the regulatory rules and institutions of international society. Most importantly, and contrary to Realist thinking, the USA chose to forsake short-run gains in return for a durable settlement that benefited all states. According to Ikenberry, the USA signalled the cooperative basis of its power in a number of ways. First, in common with liberal democratic principles, the USA was an example to other members of international society in so far as its political system is open and allows different voices to be heard. Foreign policy, like domestic policy, is closely scrutinized by the media, public opinion, and political committees and opposition parties. Second, the USA advocated a global free-trade regime in accordance with the idea that free trade brings benefits to all participants (it also has

Box 6.3 George W. Bush and Liberalism in American foreign policy

'The twentieth century ended with a single surviving model of human progress, based on non-negotiable demands of human dignity, the rule of law, limits on the power of the state, respect for women and private property and free speech and equal justice and religious tolerance. America cannot impose this vision—yet we can support and reward governments that make the right choices for their own people. In our development aid, in our diplomatic efforts, in our international broadcasting, and in our educational assistance, the United States will promote moderation and tolerance and human rights. And we defend the peace that makes all progress possible.

When it comes to the common rights and needs of men and women, there is no clash of civilizations. The requirements of freedom apply fully to Africa and Latin America and the entire Islamic world. The peoples of the Islamic nations want and deserve the same freedoms and opportunities as people in every nation. And their governments should listen to their hopes.'

(Excerpt from President George W. Bush, Graduation Speech at West Point, US Military Academy, New York, 1 June 2002. Available at: www.whitehouse.gov/news/releases)

the added advantage, from the hegemon's point of view, of being cheap to manage). Third, the USA appeared to its allies at least as a reluctant hegemon that would not seek to exploit its significant power-political advantage. Fourth, and most importantly, the USA created and participated in a range of important international institutions that constrained its actions. The Bretton Woods system of economic and financial accords and the **NATO** security alliance are the best examples of the highly institutionalized character of American power in the post-1945 period. Advocates of this liberal hegemonic order note wryly that it was so successful that allies were more worried about abandonment than domination.

The post-1945 system of regulatory regimes and institutions has been successful in part due to the fact that they exist. In other words, once one set of institutional arrangements becomes embedded it is very difficult for alternatives to make inroads. There are two implications that need to be teased out here. One is the narrow historical 'window' that exists for new institutional design; the other is the durability of existing institutions. 'In terms of American hegemony, this means that, short of a major war or a global economic collapse, it is very difficult to envisage the type of historical breakpoint needed to replace the existing order' (Ikenberry 1999: 137).

Let us accept for a moment that the **neo-liberal** argument is basically correct: the post-1945 **international order** has been successful and durable because US hegemony has been of a liberal character. The logic of this position is one of institutional conservatism. In order to respond effectively to global economic and security problems, there is no alternative to working within the existing institutional structure. This is a manifesto for managing an international order in which the Western states who paid the start-up costs of the institutions are now expe-

riencing significant returns on their institutional investment. At the other end of the spectrum, the current order is highly unresponsive to the needs of weaker states and peoples. According to the United Nations Development Programme, the resulting global inequality is 'grotesque'. One statistic is particularly graphic: the richest 20 per cent of the world's population holds three-quarters of the income, the poorest 20 per cent receive only 1.5 per cent.[5]

Given that Liberalism has produced such unequal gains for the West and the rest, it is not surprising that the hegemonic power has become obsessed with the question of preserving and extending its control of institutions, markets, and resources. When this hegemonic liberal order comes under challenge, as it did on 9/11, the response is uncompromising. It is noticeable in this respect that President George W. Bush mobilized the language of Liberalism against Al Qaeda, the Taliban, and also Iraq. He referred to the 2003 war against Iraq as 'freedom's war' and the term 'liberation' is frequently used by defenders of 'Operation Iraqi Freedom'.

Given the primacy of the neo-conservative ideology underpinning the Bush presidency, one needs to proceed with caution when advancing the claim that many liberal principles underpin contemporary American foreign policy. Nevertheless, the official discourse of US foreign policy overlaps in interesting ways with a number of liberal values and ideas (Rhodes 2003), as can be seen in Bush's speech at the West Point graduation ceremony in June 2002. A key opening theme in the speech is how force can be used for freedom: 'we fight, as we always fight, for a just peace'. Bush then goes on to locate this argument in historical context. Prior to the twenty-first century, great power competition manifested itself in war. Today, 'the Great Powers share common values' such as 'a deep commitment to human freedom'. In his State

of the Union address of 2004, he even declared that 'our aim is a democratic peace'. Box 6.3 further illustrates the connections between Liberalism, **democracy promotion**, and the Bush foreign policy.

The potential for Liberalism to embrace **imperialism** is a tendency that has a long history (Doyle 1986: 1151–69). We find in Machiavelli a number of arguments for the necessity for republics to expand. Liberty increases wealth and the concomitant drive for new markets; soldiers who are at the same time citizens are better fighters than slaves or mercenaries; and expansion is often the best means to promote a state's security. In this sense, contemporary US foreign policy is no different from the great expansionist republican states of the pre-modern period such as Athens and Rome. Few liberals today would openly advocate imperialism although the line between interventionist strategies to defend liberal values and privileges and imperialism is very finely drawn. Michael Doyle advocates a policy mix of forcible and non-forcible instruments that ought to be deployed in seeking regime change in illiberal parts of the world (see Box 6.4).

This strategy of preserving and extending liberal institutions is open to a number of criticisms. For the sake of simplicity, these will be gathered up into an alternative to the Liberalism of privilege that we will call **radical Liberalism**. An opening objection made by proponents of the latter concerns the understanding of Liberalism embodied in the neo-liberal defence of international institutions. The liberal character of those institutions is assumed rather than subjected to critical scrutiny. As a result, the incoherence of the purposes underpinning these institutions is often overlooked. The kind of economic **liberalization** advocated by Western financial institutions, particularly in economically impoverished countries, frequently comes into conflict with the norms of democracy and human rights. Three examples illustrate this dilemma. First, the more the West becomes involved in the organization of developing states' political and economic infrastructure, the less those states are able to be accountable to their domestic constituencies, thereby cutting through the link between the government and the people which is so central to modern liberal forms of representative democracy (Hurrell and Woods 1995: 463). Second, in order to qualify for Western aid and loans, states are often required to meet harsh economic criteria requiring cuts in many welfare programmes; the example of the poorest children in parts of Africa having to pay for primary school education (Booth and Dunne 1999: 310)—which is their right according to the Universal Declaration of Human Rights—is a stark reminder of the fact that economic liberty and political equality are frequently opposed. Third, the inflexible response of international financial institutions to various crises in the world-economy has contributed to a backlash against Liberalism per se. Richard Falk puts this dilemma starkly: there is, he argues, a tension between 'the ethical imperatives of the global neighbourhood and the dynamics of economic globalisation' (1995a: 573). Radical liberals argue that the hegemonic institutional order has fallen prey to the neo-liberal consensus which minimizes the role of the public sector in providing for welfare, and elevates the market as the appropriate mechanism

---

Box 6.4 Defending and extending the liberal zone of peace

As we have seen, advocates of the democratic peace thesis believe that liberal states act peacefully towards one another. Yet this empirical law does not tell liberal states how to behave towards non-liberal states. Should they try to convert them, thereby bringing them into the zone of peace, or should they pursue a more defensive strategy? The former has not been successful in the past, and in a world of many nuclear weapons states, crusading could be suicidal. For this reason, Michael Doyle suggests a dual-track approach.

- The first track is preserving the liberal community which means forging strong alliances with other like-minded states and defending itself against illiberal regimes. This may require liberal states to include in their foreign policy strategies like the balance of power in order to contain authoritarian states.
- The second track is more expansionist and aims to extend the liberal zone by a variety of economic and diplomatic instruments.

Doyle categorizes these in terms of 'inspiration' (hoping peoples living in non-democratic regimes will struggle for their liberty), 'instigation' (peace building and economic restructuring), and 'intervention' (legitimate if the majority of a polity is demonstrating widespread disaffection with their government and/or their basic rights are being systematically violated).

Doyle concludes with the warning that the march of Liberalism will not necessarily continue unabated. It is in our hands, he argues, whether the international system becomes more pacific and stable, or whether antagonisms deepen. We must be willing to pay the price—in institutional costs and development aid—to increase the prospects for a peaceful future. This might be cheap when compared with the alternative of dealing with hostile and unstable authoritarian states.

(Doyle 1999)

for allocating resources, investment, and employment opportunities.

A second line of critique pursued by radical liberals concerns not so much the contradictory outcomes but the illiberal nature of the regimes and institutions. To put the point bluntly, there is a massive **democratic deficit** at the global level. Issues of international peace and security are determined by only 15 members of international society, of whom only five can exercise a power of veto. In other words, it is hypothetically possible for up to 200 states in the world to believe that military action ought to be taken but such an action would contravene the UN Charter if one of the permanent members was to cast a veto. If we take the area of political economy, the power exerted by the West and its international financial institutions perpetuates structural inequality. A good example here is the issue of free trade, which the West has pushed in areas where it gains from an open policy (such as in manufactured goods and financial services) but resisted in areas that it stands to lose (agriculture and textiles). At a deeper level, radical liberals worry that *all* statist models of governance are undemocratic as elites are notoriously self-serving.

These sentiments underpin the approach to globalization taken by writers such as Danielle Archibugi, David Held, Mary Kaldor, and Jan Aart Scholte, among others, who believe that **global politics** must be democratized (Held and McGrew 2002). Held's argument is illustrative of the analytical and prescriptive character of radical Liberalism in an era of globalization. His diagnosis begins by revealing the inadequacies of the 'Westphalian order' (or the modern states-system which is conventionally dated from the middle of the seventeenth century). During the latter stages of this period, we have witnessed rapid democratization in a number of states, but this has not been accompanied by democratization of the **society of states** (Held 1993). This task is increasingly urgent given the current levels of interconnectedness, since 'national' governments are no longer in control of the forces which shape their citizens' lives (for example, the decision by one state to permit deforestation has environmental consequences for all states). After 1945, the UN Charter set limits to the **sovereignty** of states by recognizing the rights of individuals in a whole series of human rights conventions. But even if the UN had lived up to its Charter in the post-1945 period, it would still have left the building blocks of the Westphalian order largely intact, namely: the

hierarchy between great powers and the rest (symbolized by the permanent membership of the Security Council); massive inequalities of wealth between states; and a minimal role for **non-state actors** to **influence** decision-making in international relations.

In place of the Westphalian and UN models, Held outlines a **cosmopolitan model of democracy**. This requires, in the first instance, the creation of regional parliaments and the extension of the authority of such regional bodies (like the European Union) which are already in existence. Second, human rights conventions must be entrenched in national parliaments and monitored by a new International Court of Human Rights. Third, reform of the UN, or the replacement of it, with a genuinely democratic and accountable global parliament. Without appearing to be too sanguine about the prospects for the realization of the cosmopolitan model of democracy, Held is nevertheless adamant that if democracy is to thrive, it must penetrate the institutions and regimes which manage global politics.

Radical liberals place great importance on the civilizing capacity of global society. While the rule of law and the democratization of international institutions is a core component of the liberal project, it is also vital that citizens' **networks** are broadened and deepened to monitor and cajole these institutions. These groups form a linkage between individuals, states, and global institutions. It is easy to portray radical liberal thinking as 'utopian' but we should not forget the many achievements of global civil society so far. The evolution of international humanitarian law, and the extent to which these laws are complied with, is largely down to the millions of individuals who are active supporters of human rights groups like Amnesty International and Human Rights Watch (Falk 1995*b*: 164). Similarly, global protest movements have been responsible for the heightened sensitivity to environmental degradation everywhere.

This emphasis on what Richard Falk calls 'globalization from below' is an important antidote to neo-liberalism's somewhat status quo-oriented worldview. But just as imperialism can emerge from a complacent Liberalism of privilege, the danger for radical liberals is naïvety. How is it that global institutions can be reformed in such a way that the voices of ordinary people will be heard? And what if the views of 'peoples' rather than 'states' turn out to be similarly indifferent to global injustice? There is a sense in which radical liberal thought wants to turn back the

clock of globalization to an era in which local producers cooperated to produce socially responsible food in the day and wove baskets or watched street theatre in the evening. It is not clear that such an organic lifestyle is preferable to purchasing relatively inexpensive goods from a multinational supermarket outlet or finding entertainment on multichannel television. Perhaps the least plausible aspect of the radical liberal project is the injunction to reform global capitalism. Just how much of a civilizing effect is global civil society able to exert upon the juggernaut of capitalism? And can this movement bridge the globalization divide in which democratic institutions are territorially located while forces of production and destruction are global?

Key Points

- The victor states in the wartime alliance against Nazi Germany pushed for a new international institution to be created: the United Nations Charter was signed in June 1945 by 50 states in San Francisco. It represented a departure from the League in two important respects. Membership was near universal and the great powers were able to prevent any enforcement action from taking place which might be contrary to their interests.
- In the post-1945 period, liberals turned to international institutions to carry out a number of functions the state could not perform. This was the catalyst for integration theory in Europe and Pluralism in the United States. By the early 1970s Pluralism had mounted a significant challenge to Realism. It focused on new actors (trans-national corporations, non-governmental organizations) and new patterns of interaction (interdependence, integration).
- Neo-liberalism represents a more sophisticated theoretical challenge to contemporary Realism. Neo-liberals explain the durability of institutions despite significant changes in context. In their view, institutions exert a causal force on international relations, shaping state preferences and locking them into cooperative arrangements.
- Democratic peace Liberalism and neo-liberalism are the dominant strands in liberal thinking today.

Conclusion

The euphoria with which Liberals greeted the end of the cold war in 1989 has dissipated to a large extent by 9/11 and the **war on terror**. The pattern of conflict and insecurity that we have seen at the beginning of the twenty-first century suggests that liberal democracy remains at best an incomplete project. Images and narratives from countries in every continent—Afghanistan, Liberia, Chechnya, Columbia, Burundi, the Democratic Republic of Congo, Iraq, Myanmar, Zimbabwe, and so on—remind us that in many parts of the world, anti-liberal values of warlordism, torture, intolerance, and injustice are daily occurrences. Moreover, the reasons why these states have failed can to some extent be laid at the door of liberalism, particularly in terms of its promotion of often irreconcilable norms of sovereignty, democracy, national self-determination, and human rights (Hoffmann 1995–6: 169).

A deeper reason for the crisis in Liberalism is that it is bound up with an increasingly discredited Enlightenment view of the world. Contrary to the hopes of Bentham, Hume, Kant, Mill, and Paine, the application of reason and science to politics has not brought communities together. Indeed, it has arguably shown the fragmented nature of the **political community**, which is regularly expressed in terms of ethnic, linguistic, or religious differences. Critics of Liberalism argue that the universalizing mission of liberal values, such as democracy, capitalism, and secularism, undermines the traditions and practices of non-Western cultures (Gray 1995: 146). When it comes to doing inter-cultural politics, somehow Liberals just don't seem to take 'no' for an answer. The Marxist writer Immanuel Wallerstein has a nice way of expressing the dilemma over universalism. Liberals view it as 'a "gift" of the powerful to the weak' which places them in a double bind: 'to refuse the gift is to lose; to accept the gift is to lose' (in Brown 1999).

At the outset, the chapter pointed to a tension within Liberalism. The emphasis on personal liberty, unfettered trade, and the accumulation of property can lend itself to a society riven with inequality, suspicion, and rivalry. Pulling in the opposite direction, Liberalism contains within it a set of values that seek to provide for the conditions of a just society through democratic institutions and

welfare-oriented economies. Projecting this tension on to a global stage leads to two possibilities for Liberalism in an era of globalization. The neo-liberal variant is one where relatively weak institutions try to respond to the challenge of coordinating the behaviour of states in a decentralized international order. In this world economic growth is unevenly distributed. As a consequence, preventive military action remains an ever-present possibility in order to deal with chaos and violence produced by dispossessed communities and networks. The more progressive model, advocated by radical liberals, seeks to heighten regulation through the strengthening of international institutions. This is to be done by making institutions more democratic and accountable for the negative consequences of globalization. The charge of utopianism is one that is easy to make against this position and hard to refute. In so doing, liberals of a radical persuasion should invoke Kant's axiom that 'ought' must imply 'can'.

? Questions

1 Do you agree with Stanley Hoffmann that international affairs are 'inhospitable' to Liberalism?

2 What arguments might one draw upon to support or refute this proposition?

3 Was the language of international morality, used by liberal idealists in the inter-war period, a way of masking the interests of Britain and France in maintaining their dominance of the international system after the First World War?

4 Should liberal states promote their values abroad? Is force a legitimate instrument in securing this goal?

5 How much progress (if any) has there been in liberal thinking on international relations since Kant?

6 Are democratic peace theorists right, but for the wrong reasons?

7 Which strategy of dealing with globalization do you find more convincing: those who believe that states and institutions should maintain the current order or those who believe in reform driven by global civil society?

8 Is there a fundamental tension at the heart of Liberalism between liberty and democracy? If so, how is this tension played out in the international domain?

9 Are liberal values and institutions in the contemporary international system as deeply embedded as neo-liberals claim?

10 What liberal ideas, if any, have informed the George W. Bush administration's foreign policy?

→ Guide to further reading

Liberalism in International Relations

Brown, C., Nartin, T., and Rengger, N. (eds) (2002), *International Relations in Political Thought: Texts from the Ancient Greeks to the First World War* (Cambridge: Cambridge University Press). See especially the readings from classical liberal thought in sections 7, 8, and 9.

Doyle, M. (1997), *Ways of War and Peace* (New York: W. W. Norton). The best textbook on the principal theories of international relations. There are over 100 pages of analysis on Liberalism in the book. See also, in a shorter and modified form, his article: Doyle, M. (1986), 'Liberalism and World Politics', *American Political Science Review*, 80(4): 1151–69.

Hoffmann, S. (1987), *Janus and Minerva* (Boulder, Col.: Westview Press): 394–436. An excellent account of Liberalism and its troubled relationship to international relations.

Richardson, J. L. (1997), 'Contending Liberalisms: Past and Present', *European Journal of International Relations*, 3(1): 5–33. A thorough overview of Liberalism in political thought and in international relations. Parts of the argument in this chapter mirror Richardson's article.

Smith, M. J. (1992), 'Liberalism and International Reform', in T. Nardin and D. Mapel (eds), *Traditions of International Ethics* (Cambridge: Cambridge University Press): 201–24. A comprehensive

piece that draws out the premises of Liberalism and in particular the belief in international organization.

Walt, S. (1998), 'International Relations: One World, Many Theories', *Foreign Policy*, 110: 29–46. Not only does this contain a useful short overview of Liberalism, it highlights the imperfect application of liberal theory in practice.

Liberalism in American and British foreign policy

Cox, M., Ikenberry, G. J., and Inoguchi, T. (eds) (2000), *American Democracy Promotion: Impulses, Strategies and Impacts* (Oxford: Oxford University Press): 1–17. See especially the introduction which puts US democracy promotion in context.

——Booth, K., and Dunne, T. (eds) (1999), *The Interregnum: Controversies in World Politics 1989–1999* (Cambridge: Cambridge University Press). Contains a range of perspectives on the pattern of world power in the 1990s.

Held, D., and McGrew, A. (eds) (2002), *The Global Transformation Reader*, 2nd edn (Cambridge: Polity Press). A useful collection of essays with many contributors who represent radical Liberalism.

Paul, T. V., and Hall, J. A. (eds) (1999), *International Order and the Future of World Politics* (Cambridge: Cambridge University Press). See especially the essay on the role of liberal institutions by G. John Ikenberry, 'Liberal Hegemony and the Future of American Post-war Order', 123–45.

Rhodes, E. (2003), 'The Imperial Logic of Bush's Liberal Agenda', *Survival*, 45: 131–54. The article advances an important argument about the liberal values incorporated in the Republican presidency of George W. Bush.

Online Resource Centre

 Visit the Online Resource Centre that accompanies this book to access more learning resources on this chapter topic at www.oxfordtextbooks.co.uk/uk/orc/baylis_smith4e/

Notes

1 The term 'domestic analogy' was used by Hedley Bull and later developed by Hidemi Suganami.

2 Doyle classifies Liberalism into the following strands: liberal pacifism, liberal imperialism, and liberal internationalism (1986: 1151–69).

3 Between 1945 and 1990, there were 232 resolutions vetoed, between 1990 and April 2004 there were only 17 vetoed.

4 Many of the leading pluralists of the 1970s embraced neo-liberalism in the 1980s. Neo-liberalism is often referred to in the literature as neo-liberal institutionalism.

5 This is one statistic among many that throws the naïve optimism of some liberal internationalists into sharp relief. For a detailed empirical analysis of globalization and development, see the UN Human Development Report 2003, freely available on the web at: http://hdr.undp.org/reports/global/2005/pdf/HDR05_chapter_1.pdf. Statistic found on p.36.

Chapter 7

Contemporary mainstream approaches: neo-realism and neo-liberalism

STEVEN L. LAMY

- **Introduction** ⋯⋯⋯⋯⋯⋯⋯⋯⋯⋯⋯⋯⋯⋯⋯⋯⋯⋯ **126**
- **Neo-realism** ⋯⋯⋯⋯⋯⋯⋯⋯⋯⋯⋯⋯⋯⋯⋯⋯⋯ **127**
- **Neo-liberalism** ⋯⋯⋯⋯⋯⋯⋯⋯⋯⋯⋯⋯⋯⋯⋯⋯ **131**
- **The neo-neo debate** ⋯⋯⋯⋯⋯⋯⋯⋯⋯⋯⋯⋯⋯ **133**
- **Neo-liberals and neo-realists on globalization** ⋯⋯⋯⋯ **136**
- **Conclusion: narrowing the agenda of international relations** ⋯⋯⋯ **137**

Reader's Guide

This chapter reviews the core assumptions of neo-realism and neo-liberalism and explores the debate between these intellectual siblings that has dominated mainstream academic scholarship in international relations in the United States. Realism and neo-realism, and to some extent neo-liberalism, have also had a profound impact on US foreign policy. Neo-realists dominate the world of security studies and neo-liberals focus on political economy and more recently on issues like human rights and the environment. These theories do not offer starkly contrasting images of the world. Neo-realists state that they are concerned with issues of survival. They claim that neo-liberals are too optimistic about the possibilities for cooperation among states. Neo-liberals counter with claims that all states have mutual interests and can gain from cooperation. Both are normative theories of a sort, biased towards the state, the capitalist market, and the status quo. The processes of globalization have forced neo-realists and neo-liberals to consider similar issues and address new challenges to international order. In the introduction, I discuss the various versions of neo-liberalism and neo-realism and ask the reader to consider how theory shapes our image of the world. Each theory represents an attempt by scholars to offer a better explanation for the behaviour of states and describe the nature of international politics. Similarly, the more policy-relevant versions of these theories prescribe competing policy agendas. The next section reviews three versions of neo-realism: Waltz's structural Realism; Grieco's neo-realism or modern Realism, with its focus on absolute and relative gains; and what security scholars call offensive and defensive Realism or neo-realism. The third section of the chapter reviews the assumptions of neo-liberal and neo-liberal Institutionalist perspectives. The fourth section focuses on the 'neo-neo-debate'. This is a debate that many US scholars think is the most important intellectual issue in international relations today. Many other scholars see it as not much of a debate at all. It is a debate about refining common assumptions and about the future role and effectiveness of international institutions and the possibilities of cooperation. However, it is not a debate between mainstream and critical perspectives. It is a debate between 'rule-makers' and it leaves out the voices on the margins or the 'rule-takers'. In the fifth section of the chapter, I review how neo-realists and neo-liberal thinkers react to the processes of globalization. The chapter concludes with a suggestion that we are only seeing part of the world if we limit our studies to the neo perspectives and the neo-neo debate.

Introduction

The debate between neo-realists and neo-liberals has dominated mainstream international relations scholarship in the United States since the mid-1980s. Two of the major US journals in the field, *International Organization* and *International Security,* are dominated by articles that address the relative merits of each theory and its value in explaining the world of international politics. **Neo-realism** and neo-liberalism are the progeny of **Realism** and **Liberalism** respectively. They are more than theories; they are paradigms or conceptual frameworks that define a field of study, and define an agenda for research and policy-making. As previous chapters on Liberalism and Realism have suggested, there are many versions and interpretations of each paradigm or theory. Some Realists are more 'hard-line' on issues such as defence or participation in international agreements, while other Realists take more accommodating positions on these same issues. The previous chapter on Liberalism provides a useful description of the varieties of this theory, and this chapter will explore those that have the greatest impact on academic discourse in the United States and on the people who develop US foreign policy. This chapter will also show the considerable differences in how the scholarly and policy world define and use the labels neo-realism and neo-liberalism.

For most academics, neo-realism refers to Kenneth Waltz's *Theory of International Politics* (1979). Waltz's theory emphasizes the importance of the **structure** of the **international system** and its role as the primary determinant of **state** behaviour. Yet, most scholars and policymakers use neo-realism to describe a recent or updated version of Realism. Recently, in the area of security studies, some scholars use the terms **offensive** and **defensive realism** when discussing the current version of Realism; or neo-realism.

In the academic world, neo-liberal generally refers to neo-liberal Institutionalism or what is now called Institutional theory by those writing in this theoretical domain. However, in the policy world, neo-liberalism means something different. A neo-liberal foreign policy promotes free trade or open markets and Western democratic values and institutions. Most of the leading Western states have joined the US-led chorus, calling for the 'enlargement' of the **community** of democratic and capitalist **nation-states**. There is no other game in town, the financial and political institutions created after the Second World War have survived and these provide the foundation for current political and economic **power** arrangements.

In reality, neo-liberal foreign policies tend not to be as wedded to the ideals of **democratic peace**, free trade, and open borders. **National interests** take precedence over morality and universal ideals and, much to the dismay of traditional Realists, economic interests are given priority over geopolitical ones.

For students beginning their study of International Relations, these labels and contending definitions can be confusing and frustrating. Yet, as you have learned in your reading of previous chapters in this volume, understanding these perspectives and theories is the only way you can hope to understand and explain how leaders and citizens alike see the world and respond to issues and events. This understanding may be more important when discussing neo-realism and neo-liberalism because they represent dominant perspectives in the policy world and in the US academic community.

There are clear differences between neo-realism and neo-liberalism; however, these differences should not be exaggerated. Robert Keohane (in Baldwin 1993), a neo-liberal institutionalist, has stated that neo-liberal Institutionalism borrows equally from Realism and Liberalism. Both theories represent status-quo perspectives and are what Robert Cox calls problem-solving theories (see Ch.10). This means that both neo-realism and neo-liberalism address issues and problems that could disrupt the status quo, namely, the issues of **security**, conflict, and **cooperation**.

Neither theory advances prescriptions for major reform or radical transformation of the international system. Rather, they are **system maintainer** theories, meaning that adherents are generally satisfied with the current international system and its actors, values, and power arrangements. These theories address different sets of issues. In general, neo-realist theory focuses on issues of military security and war. Neo-liberal theorists focus on issues of cooperation, international political economy, and, most recently, the environment. For neo-liberal

Institutionalists, the core question for research is how to promote and support cooperation in an anarchic and competitive international system. For neo-realists, the core research question is how to survive in this system.

A review of the assumptions of each theory and an analysis of the contending positions in the so-called neos debate and a discussion of how neo-liberals and neo-realists react to the processes of **globalization** follows.

Key Points

- The neo-neo debate has been the dominant focus in international relations theory scholarship in the USA for the last 10–15 years.
- More than just theories, neo-realism and neo-liberalism represent paradigms or conceptual frameworks that shape individuals' images of the world and influence research priorities and policy debates and choices.
- There are several versions of neo-realism or neo-liberalism.
- Neo-liberalism in the academic world refers most often to neo-liberal Institutionalism. In the policy world, neo-liberalism is identified with the promotion of capitalism and Western democratic values and institutions.

- Rational choice approaches and game theory have been integrated into neo-realist and neo-liberal theory to explain policy choices and the behaviour of states in conflict and cooperative situations.
- Neo-realist and neo-liberal theories are status quo-oriented problem-solving theories. They share many assumptions about actors, values, issues, and power arrangements in the international system. Neo-realists and neo-liberals study different worlds. Neo-realists study security issues and are concerned with issues of power and survival. Neo-liberals study political economy and focus on cooperation and institutions.

Neo-realism

Kenneth Waltz's theory of **structural realism** is only one version of neo-realism. A second group of neo-realists, represented by the scholarly contributions of Joseph Grieco (1988*a* and 1988*b*), have integrated Waltz's ideas with the ideas of more traditional Realists, such as Hans Morgenthau, Raymond Aron, Stanley Hoffmann, and Robert Gilpin, to construct a contemporary or **modern realist** profile. A third version of neo-realism is found in security studies. Here scholars talk about offensive and defensive realists. These versions of neo-realism are briefly reviewed in the next few pages.

Structural realism

Waltz's neo-realism is distinctive from traditional or classical Realism in a number of ways. First, Realism is primarily an inductive theory. For example, Hans Morgenthau would explain international politics by looking at the actions and interactions of the states in the system. Thus, the decision by Pakistan and India to test nuclear weapons would be explained by looking at the influence of military leaders in both states and the long-standing differences compounded by their geographic proximity. All of these explanations are unit or bottom-up explanations.

Neo-realists, such as Waltz, do not deny the importance of unit-level explanations; however, they believe that the effects of structure must be considered. According to Waltz, structure is defined by the ordering principle of the international system, which is **anarchy**, and the distribution of **capabilities** across units, which are states. Waltz also assumes that there is no differentiation of function between different units.

The structure of the international system shapes all foreign policy choices. For a neo-realist, a better explanation for India and Pakistan's nuclear testing would be anarchy or the lack of a common power or central authority to enforce **rules** and maintain **order** in the system. In a competitive system, this condition creates a need for weapons to survive. Additionally, in an **anarchic system**, states with greater power tend to have greater influence.

A second difference between traditional Realists and Waltz's neo-realism is found in their view of power. To Realists, power is an end in itself. States use power to gain more power and thus increase their influence and ability to secure their national interests. Although traditional Realists recognize different elements of power (for example, economic resources and technology), military power is considered the most obvious element of a state's power. Waltz would not agree with those who say that military

force is not as essential as it once was as a tool of statecraft. As recent conflicts in Russia, Iraq, Sudan, Lebanon, and Sri Lanka suggest, many leaders still believe that they can resolve their differences with force.

For neo-realists, power is more than the accumulation of military resources and the ability to use this power to coerce and control other states in the system. Waltz and other neo-realists see power as the combined capabilities of a state. States are differentiated in the system by their power and not by their function. Power gives a state a place or position in the international system and that shapes the state's behaviour. During the **cold war**, the USA and the USSR were positioned as the only two **superpowers**. Neo-realists would say that such positioning explains the similarities in their behaviour. The distribution of power and any dramatic changes in that distribution of power help to explain the structure of

the international system. Specifically, states will seek to maintain their position or placement in the system. The end of the cold war and the disintegration of the Soviet empire upset the **balance of power** and, in the eyes of many neo-realists, increased uncertainty and instability in the international system. Waltz concurs with traditional Realists when he states that the central mechanism for order in the system is balance of power. The renewed emphasis on the importance of the United Nations and **NATO** and their interventions in crisis areas around the world may be indicative of the major powers' current search for order in the international system. Waltz would challenge neo-liberal Institutionalists who believe that we can manage the processes of globalization merely by building effective international institutions (see Case Study). He would argue that their effectiveness depends on the support of major powers.

Case Study 1 'The underbelly of globalization': toxic waste dumping in the global South

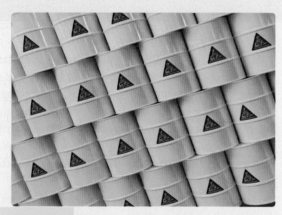

Families in several villages near Abidjan, Ivory Coast awoke one summer morning to a horrible smell of rotten eggs and many were suffering with burning eyes and nosebleeds. Eventually, ten people died, thousands sought medical care and children developed sores and blisters. The number of people seeking medical care overwhelmed the health care system in this region and demonstrations against the government led to arrests and the resignation of key political officials. This is the kind of political and human security problem that we will see more of as the industrialized North dumps its waste and worn out computers and cell phones on the poor South. What was the cause of this problem and are there not laws or treaties aimed at addressing these kinds of issues?

The source of this environmental and medical crisis was a 'stinking slick of black sludge' that had been illegally dumped in eighteen areas around Abidjan by tanker trucks hired by a local company with no experience in properly disposing of toxic materials. A Swiss oil and metals trading corporation that also leased the ship hired this local company. The *Probo Koala* had brought this

deadly mix to the Ivory Coast from Amsterdam. Trafigura, the global trading firm, planned on properly disposing the petrochemical wastes in Amsterdam. But once fumes overcame workers cleaning the ship in Amsterdam, the Dutch disposal company stopped the process, ordered an analysis of the wastes and alerted Dutch government authorities. An early analysis of the toxic waste showed concentrations of chemicals that could paralyze a person's nervous system and could kill. When the Amsterdam waste disposal company raised its price because of this danger, the *Probo Koala* was allowed to take back its waste and sailed for Estonia to pick up Russian oil products and then on to Western Africa.

Officials from Trafigura notified Ivorian officials that the ship was carrying toxic wastes but they were still allowed to land in Abidjan. Both company officials and the government of the Ivory Coast were well aware that there were no facilities in Abidjan for properly disposing of this waste. The Ivorian company, Tommy, hired tanker trucks that were loaded with the toxic wastes from the *Probo Koala*. During the night, the tankers dumped their loads in eighteen areas around the city of Abidjan.

The disposal and dumping of toxic wastes is a global problem. As environmental regulations in the North become more stringent, corporations move to the South for dumping. Wastes follow the path of least resistance—global corporations look for countries with weak laws and without the capacity or will to enforce any national or international laws aimed at regulating the waste disposal market. Who is responsible for this problem? How should it be managed? *Neoliberal Institutionalists* believe that we can establish regimes or governing arrangements to manage trade in toxic wastes and prevent illegal dumping. In fact, a previous dumping incident in Koko, Nigeria, was a catalyst for a conference and treaty to govern the transnational movement of toxic wastes. At the Basel convention in 1989, the global South wanted an absolute ban on all toxic waste trade and the global North

lobbied for a much weaker treaty. The first version of this treaty was ratified in 1992 and revisions in 1994 and 1998 have essentially banned the export of hazardous waste from North to South. Yet, enforcement depends on the cooperation of citizens, global corporations, and governments at all levels. At the time this was considered a victory for the poor and advocates for environmental justice and human security for all. Unfortunately, the Ivory Coast case shows how difficult it is to manage the processes of globalization and to control those individuals who place profits over the well-being of people.

(For more information: Basel Action Network, <www.ban.org>)

A third difference between Realism and Waltz's neo-realism is each one's view on how states react to the condition of anarchy. To Realists, anarchy is a condition of the system, and states react to it according to their size, location, domestic politics, and leadership qualities. In contrast, neo-realists suggest that anarchy defines the system. Further, all states are functionally similar units, meaning that they all experience the same constraints presented by anarchy and strive to maintain their position in the system. Neo-realists explain any differences in policy by differences in power or capabilities. Both Belgium and China recognize that one of the constraints of anarchy is the need for security to protect their national interests. Leaders in these countries may select different policy paths to achieve that security. A small country such as Belgium, with limited resources, responds to anarchy and the resulting **security dilemma** by joining alliances and taking an activist role in regional and international organizations, seeking to control the arms race. China, a major power and a large country, would most likely pursue a unilateral strategy of increasing military strength to protect and secure its interests.

Relative and absolute gains

Joseph Grieco (1988a) is one of several Realist/neo-realist scholars who focuses on the concepts of **relative** and **absolute gains**. Grieco claims that states are interested in increasing their power and influence (absolute gains) and, thus, will cooperate with other states or actors in the system to increase their capabilities. However, Grieco claims that states are also concerned with how much power and influence other states might achieve (relative gains) in any cooperative endeavour. This situation can be used to show a key difference between neo-liberals and neo-realists. Neo-liberals claim that cooperation does not work when states fail to follow the rules and 'cheat'

to secure their national interests. Neo-realists claim that there are two barriers to international cooperation: cheating and the relative gains of other actors. Further, when states fail to comply with rules that encourage cooperation, other states may abandon multilateral activity and act unilaterally.

The likelihood of states abandoning international cooperative efforts is increased if participants see other states gaining more from the arrangement. If states agree to a ban on the production and use of landmines, all of the signatories to the treaty will be concerned about compliance. Institutions will be established to enforce the treaty. Neo-realists argue that leaders must be vigilant for cheaters and must focus on those states that could gain a military advantage when this weapon system is removed. In some security situations, landmines may be the only effective deterrent against a neighbouring state with superior land forces. In this situation, the relative gains issue is one of survival. In a world of uncertainty and competition, the fundamental question, according to Grieco and others who share his view of neo-realism, is not whether all parties gain from the cooperation, but who will gain more if we cooperate?

Security studies and neo-realism

Recently, security studies scholars, primarily in the USA, have suggested a more nuanced version of a Realism that reflects their interests in understanding the nature of the security threats presented by the international system and the strategy options states must pursue to survive and prosper in the system. These two versions of neo-realism, offensive and defensive realism (many scholars in this area prefer to be called modern realists and not neo-realists), are more policy relevant than Waltz and Grieco's version of neo-realism and, thus, may be seen as more prescriptive than the other versions (Jervis 1999).

Box 7.1 Core assumptions of neo-realists

- States and other actors interact in an anarchic environment. This means that there is no central authority to enforce rules and norms or protect the interests of the larger global community.
- The structure of the system is a major determinant of actor behaviour.
- States are self-interest oriented, and an anarchic and competitive system pushes them to favour self-help over cooperative behaviour.

- States are rational actors, selecting strategies to maximize benefits and minimize losses.
- The most critical problem presented by anarchy is survival.
- States see all other states as potential enemies and threats to their national security. This distrust and fear creates a security dilemma, and this motivates the policies of most states.

Offensive neo-realists appear to accept most of Waltz's ideas and a good portion of the assumptions of traditional Realism. Defensive neo-realists suggest that our assumptions of relations with other states depend on whether they are friends or enemies. When dealing with friends such as the European Union, the assumptions governing US leaders are more akin to those promoted by neo-liberals. However, there is little difference between defensive and offensive neo-realists when they are dealing with expansionary or pariah states, or traditional enemies.

John Mearsheimer (1990, 1994/5), an offensive realist in security studies, suggests that relative power and not absolute power is most important to states. He would suggest that leaders of countries should pursue security policies that weaken their potential enemies and increase their power relative to all others. In this era of globalization, the incompatibility of states' goals and interests enhances the competitive nature of an anarchic system and makes conflict as inevitable as cooperation. Thus, talk of reducing military budgets at the end of the cold war was considered by offensive neo-realists to be pure folly. Leaders must always be prepared for an expansionary state that will challenge the global order. Moreover, if the major powers begin a campaign of disarmament and reduce their power relative to other states, they are simply inviting these expansionary states to attack.

John Mearsheimer and Stephen Walt (2003) were critical of the decision by George W. Bush to go to war in Iraq. They argue that the Bush administration 'inflated the threat' by misleading the world about Iraq's weapons of mass destruction and its links to terrorists who might attack the USA in the future.

More importantly for security neo-realists, this war was unnecessary because the **containment** of Iraq was working effectively and there was no 'compelling strategic rationale' for this war. The war with Iraq will cost the USA billions of dollars and it has already required

a tremendous commitment of US military forces. With Iraq, Afghanistan, and the global war on **terrorism**, the US military is over-extended. The unilateralism of the Bush administration concerns both offensive and defensive neo-realists because it hurts the absolute and relative power of the USA.

Defensive neo-realists Robert Jervis (1999) and Jack Snyder (1991) claim that most leaders understand that the costs of war clearly outweigh the benefits. The use of military force for conquest and expansion is a security strategy that most leaders reject in this age of **complex interdependence** and globalization. War remains a tool of statecraft for some; however, most wars are seen by citizens and leaders alike to be caused by irrational or dysfunctional forces within a society, such as excessive militarism or ethnonationalism.

Defensive neo-realists are often confused with neo-liberals. Although they have some sympathy for the neo-liberal argument that war can be avoided by creating security institutions (for example, alliances or arms control treaties) that diminish the security dilemma and provide mutual security for participating states, they do not see institutions as the most effective way to prevent all wars. Most believe that conflict is simply unavoidable in some situations. First, aggressive and expansionary states do exist and they challenge **world order** and, second, simply in pursuit of their national interests, some states may make conflict with others unavoidable.

Defensive neo-realists are more optimistic than are offensive neo-realists. However, they are considerably less optimistic than neo-liberals for several reasons (Jervis 1999). First, defensive neo-realists see conflict as unnecessary only in a subset of situations (for example, economic relations). Second, leaders can never be certain that an aggressive move by a state (for example, support for a revolutionary movement in a neighbouring state) is an expansionary action intended to challenge the existing order or

simply a preventive policy aimed at protecting their security. Third, defensive realists challenge the neo-liberal view that it is relatively easy to find areas where national interests might converge and become the basis for cooperation

and institution building. Although they recognize that areas of common or mutual interests exist, defensive neo-realists are concerned about non-compliance or cheating by states, especially in security policy areas.

Key Points

- Kenneth Waltz's structural realism has had a major impact on scholars in International Relations. Waltz claims that the structure of the international system is the key factor in shaping the behaviour of states. Waltz's neo-realism also expands our view of power and capabilities. However, he agrees with traditional Realists when he states that major powers still determine the nature of the international system.

- Structural realists minimize the importance of national attributes as determinants of a state's foreign policy behaviour. To these neo-realists, all states are functionally similar units, experiencing the same constraints presented by anarchy.

- Structural realists accept many assumptions of traditional Realism. They believe that force remains an important and effective tool of statecraft and balance of power is still the central mechanism for order in the system.

- Joseph Grieco represents a group of neo-realists or modern realists who are critical of neo-liberal Institutionalists who claim states are

mainly interested in absolute gains. Grieco claims that all states are interested in both absolute and relative gains. How gains are distributed is an important issue. Thus, there are two barriers to international cooperation: fear of those who might not follow the rules and the relative gains of others.

- Scholars in security studies present two versions of neo-realism or modern realism. Offensive neo-realists emphasize the importance of relative power. Like traditional Realists, they believe that conflict is inevitable in the international system and leaders must always be wary of expansionary powers. Defensive realists are often confused with neo-liberal Institutionalists. They recognize the costs of war and assume that it usually results from irrational forces in a society. However, they admit that expansionary states willing to use military force make it impossible to live in a world without weapons. Cooperation is possible, but it is more likely to succeed in relations with friendly states.

Neo-liberalism

As the previous chapter on Liberalism indicates, there are a number of versions of the theory and all have their progeny in contemporary neo-liberal debates. David Baldwin (1993) identified four varieties of Liberalism that influence contemporary international relations: commercial, republican, sociological, and Liberal Institutionalism.

The first, **commercial Liberalism,** advocates free trade and a market or capitalist economy as the way towards peace and prosperity. Today, this view is promoted by global financial institutions, most of the major trading states, and multinational corporations. The **Neoliberal orthodoxy** is championed by popular authors like Thomas Friedman (2005), and argues that free trade, private property rights and free markets will lead to a richer, more innovative, and more tolerant world. **Republican Liberalism** states that democratic states are more inclined to respect the rights of their citizens and are less likely to go to war with their democratic neighbours. In current scholarship, this view is presented as democratic peace theory. These two forms of Liberalism, commercial and

republican, have been combined to form the core foreign policy goals of many of the world's major powers.

In **sociological Liberalism,** the notion of community and the process of interdependence are important elements. As transnational activities increase, people in distant lands are linked and their governments become more interdependent. As a result, it becomes more difficult and more costly for states to act unilaterally and to avoid cooperation with neighbours. The cost of war or other deviant behaviour increases for all states and, eventually, a peaceful international community is built. Many of the assumptions of sociological Liberalism are represented in the current globalization literature dealing with popular culture and **civil society.**

Liberal Institutionalism or **neo-liberal Institutionalism** is considered by many scholars to present the most convincing challenge to Realist and neo-realist thinking. The roots of this version of neo-liberalism are found in the functional **integration** scholarship of the 1940s and the 1950s and regional integration studies of the 1960s. These

studies suggest that the way towards peace and prosperity is to have independent states pool their resources and even surrender some of their **sovereignty** to create integrated communities to promote economic growth or respond to regional problems (see Ch.25). The European Union is one such institution that began as regional community for encouraging multilateral cooperation in the production of coal and steel. Proponents of integration and community building were motivated to challenge dominant Realist thinking because of the experiences of the two world wars. Rooted in liberal thinking, integration theories promoted after the Second World War were less Idealistic and more pragmatic than the Liberal Internationalism that dominated policy debates after the First World War.

The third generation of liberal Institutional scholarship was the transnationalism and complex interdependence of the 1970s (Keohane and Nye 1972, 1977). Theorists in these camps presented arguments that suggested that the world had become more pluralistic in terms of actors involved in international interactions and that these actors had become more dependent on each other. Complex interdependence presented a world with four characteristics: (1) increasing linkages among states and **non-state actors**; (2) a new agenda of international issues with no distinction between low and high politics; (3) a recognition of multiple channels for interaction among actors across national boundaries; and (4) the decline of the efficacy of military force as a tool of statecraft. Complex interdependence scholars would suggest that globalization represents an increase in linkages and channels for interaction, as well as in the number of interconnections.

Neo-liberal Institutionalism or Institutional theory shares many of the assumptions of neo-realism. However, its adherents claim that neo-realists focus excessively on conflict and competition, and minimize the chances for cooperation even in an anarchic international system. Neo-liberal Institutionalists see 'institutions' as the mediator and the means to achieve cooperation among actors in the system. Currently, neo-liberal Institutionalists are focusing their research on issues of **global governance** and the creation and maintenance of institutions associated with managing the processes of globalization.

For neo-liberal Institutionalists, the focus on mutual interests extends beyond trade and **development** issues. With the end of the cold war, states were forced to address new security concerns like the threat of terrorism, the proliferation of **weapons of mass destruction**, and an increasing number of internal conflicts that threatened regional and global security. Graham Allison (2000) states that one of the consequences of the globalization of security concerns like terrorism, drug trafficking, and pandemics like HIV/AIDS is the realization that threats to any country's security cannot be addressed unilaterally. Successful responses to security threats require the creation of regional and global **regimes** that promote cooperation among states and the **coordination** of policy responses to these new security threats.

Robert Keohane (2002*b*) suggests that one result of the **9/11** terrorist attacks on the USA was the creation of a very broad coalition against terrorism, involving a large number of states and key global and regional institutions. Neo-liberals support cooperative **multilateralism** and are generally critical of the pre-emptive and unilateral use of force as is condoned in the 2002 Bush Doctrine. Most neo-liberals would believe that the US-led war with Iraq did more to undermine the legitimacy and influence of global and regional security institutions that operated so successfully in the first Gulf War (1990–1) and continue to work effectively in Afghanistan.

The core assumptions of neo-liberal Institutionalists include:

- States are key actors in international relations, but not the only significant actors. States are rational or instrumental actors, always seeking to maximize their interests in all issue-areas.
- In this competitive environment, states seek to maximize absolute gains through cooperation. Rational behaviour leads states to see value in cooperative behaviour. States are less concerned with gains or advantages achieved by other states in cooperative arrangements.
- The greatest obstacle to successful cooperation is non-compliance or cheating by states.
- Cooperation is never without problems, but states will shift **loyalty** and resources to institutions if these are seen as mutually beneficial and if they provide states with increasing opportunities to secure their international interests.

The neo-liberal institutional perspective is more relevant in issue-areas where states have mutual interests. For example, most world leaders believe that we will all benefit from an open trade system, and many support trade rules that protect the environment. Institutions have been

created to manage international behaviour in both areas. The neo-liberal view may have less relevance in areas in which states have no mutual interests. Thus, cooperation in military or national security areas, where someone's gain is perceived as someone else's loss (**a zero-sum perspective**), may be more difficult to achieve.

Key Points

- Contemporary neo-liberalism has been shaped by the assumptions of commercial, republican, sociological, and institutional Liberalism.
- Commercial and republican Liberalism provide the foundation for current neo-liberal thinking in Western governments. These countries promote free trade and democracy in their foreign policy programmes.
- Neo-liberal Institutionalism, the other side of the neo-neo debate, is rooted in the functional integration theoretical work of the 1950s and 1960s and the complex interdependence and transnational studies literature of the 1970s and 1980s.
- Neo-liberal Institutionalists see institutions as the mediator and the means to achieve cooperation in the international system.

Regimes and institutions help govern a competitive and anarchic international system and they encourage, and at times require, multilateralism and cooperation as a means of securing national interests.
- Neo-liberal Institutionalists recognize that cooperation may be harder to achieve in areas where leaders perceive they have no mutual interests.
- Neo-liberals believe that states cooperate to achieve absolute gains and the greatest obstacle to cooperation is 'cheating' or non-compliance by other states.

The neo-neo debate

By now it should be clear that the neos debate is not particularly contentious, nor is the intellectual difference between the two theories significant. As was suggested earlier in the chapter, neo-realists and neo-liberals share an epistemology; they focus on similar questions and agree on a number of assumptions about man, the state, and the international system. A summary of the major points of contention is presented in Box 7.2.

If anything, the current neo-liberal Institutionalist literature appears to try hard to prove that they are a part of the neo-realist/Realist family. As Robert Jervis (1999: 43) states, there is not much of a gap between the two theories.

Box 7.2 The main features of the neo-realist/neo-liberal debate

1 Both agree that the international system is anarchic. Neo-realists say that anarchy puts more constraints on foreign policy and that neo-liberals minimize the importance of survival as the goal of each state. Neo-liberals claim that neo-realists minimize the importance of international interdependence, globalization, and the regimes created to manage these interactions.

2 Neo-realists believe that international cooperation will not happen unless states make it happen. They feel that it is hard to achieve, difficult to maintain, and dependent on state power. Neo-liberals believe that cooperation is easy to achieve in areas where states have mutual interests.

3 Neo-liberals think that actors with common interests try to maximize absolute gains. Neo-realists claim that neo-liberals overlook the importance of relative gains. Neo-liberals want to maximize the total amount of gains for all parties involved, whereas the neo-realists believe that the fundamental goal of states in cooperative relationships is to prevent others from gaining more.

4 Neo-realists state that anarchy requires states to be preoccupied with relative power, security, and survival in a competitive international system. Neo-liberals are more concerned with economic welfare or international political economy issues and other non-military issue-areas such as international environmental concerns.

5 Neo-realists emphasize the capabilities (power) of state over the intentions and interests of states. Capabilities are essential for security and independence. Neo-realists claim that uncertainty about the intentions of other states forces states to focus on their capabilities. Neo-liberals emphasize intentions and preferences.

6 Neo-liberals see institutions and regimes as significant forces in international relations. Neo-realists state that neo-liberals exaggerate the impact of regimes and institutions on state behaviour. Neo-liberals claim that they facilitate cooperation, and neo-realists say that they do not mitigate the constraining effects of anarchy on cooperation.

(Adapted from Baldwin 1993: 4–8)

As evidence of this, he quotes Robert Keohane and Lisa Martin (1999: 3): 'for better or worse institutional theory is a half-sibling of neo-realism'.

The following reviews key aspects of this debate. With regard to anarchy, both theories share several assumptions. First, they agree that anarchy means that there is no common authority to enforce any rules or laws constraining the behaviour of states or other actors. Neo-liberal Institutionalists and neo-realists agree that anarchy encourages states to act unilaterally and to promote **self-help** behaviour. The condition of anarchy also makes cooperation more difficult to achieve. However, neo-realists tend to be more pessimistic and to see the world as much more competitive and conflictive. To most neo-realists, international relations is a struggle for survival, and in every interaction, there is a chance of a loss of power to a future competitor or enemy. For neo-liberal Institutionalists, international relations is competitive. However, the opportunities for cooperation in areas of mutual interest may mitigate the effects of anarchy.

Some scholars suggest that the real difference between the neos is that they study different worlds. The neo-liberal Institutionalists focus their scholarship on political economy, the environment, and human rights issues. Neo-liberals work in what we once called the low politics arena, issues related to human security and the good life. Their assumptions work better in these issue-areas.

Neo-realists tend to dominate the security studies area. They study issues of international security or what was once called the high politics issues. Many neo-realists assume that what distinguishes the study of international relations from political science is the emphasis on issues of survival.

For neo-liberal Institutionalists, foreign policy is now about managing complex interdependence and the various processes of globalization. It is also about responding to problems that threaten the economic well-being, if not the survival, of people around the world. Foreign policy leaders must find ways to manage financial markets so that the gap between rich and poor does not become insurmountable. These same leaders must find ways to deal with toxic waste dumping that threaten clean water supplies in developing states. The anodyne for neo-liberal Institutionalists is to create institutions to manage issue-areas where states have mutual interests. Creating, maintaining, and further empowering these institutions is the future of foreign policy for neo-liberal Institutionalists.

Neo-realists take a more state-centric view of foreign policy. They recognize international relations as a world of cooperation and conflict. However, close to their traditional Realist roots, neo-realists see foreign policy as dominated by issues of national security and survival. The most effective tool of statecraft is still force or the threat of force and, even in these times of globalization, states must continue to look after their own interests. All states, in the language of the neo-realists, are **egoistic value maximizers**.

Neo-realists accept the existence of institutions and regimes and recognize their role as tools or instruments of statecraft. From a neo-realist view, states work to establish these regimes and institutions if they serve their interests (absolute gain), and they continue to support these same regimes and institutions if the cooperative activities promoted by the institution do not unfairly advantage other states (relative gains). Neo-realists also would agree that institutions can shape the content and direction of foreign policy in certain issue-areas and when the issue at hand is not central to the security interests of a given state.

Neo-liberals agree that, once established, institutions can do more than shape or influence the foreign policy of states. Institutions can promote a foreign policy agenda by providing critical information and expertise. Institutions also may facilitate policy-making and encourage more cooperation at local, national, and international levels. They often serve as a catalyst for coalition building among state and non-state actors. Recent work on environmental institutions suggests that they can promote changes in national policies and actually encourage both national and international policies that address environmental problems (Haas, Keohane, and Levy 1993).

A major issue of contention in the debate is the notion that institutions have become significant in international relations. Further, they can make a difference by helping to resolve global and regional problems and encourage cooperation rather than conflict. Neo-liberal Institutionalists expect an increase in the number of institutions and an increase in cooperative behaviour. They predict that these institutions will have a greater role in managing the processes of globalization and that states will come to the point where they realize that acting unilaterally or limiting cooperative behaviour will not lead to the resolution or management of critical global problems. Ultimately, neo-liberal Institutionalists claim that the significance of these institutions as players in the game of international politics will increase substantially.

Neo-realists recognize that these institutions are likely to become more significant in areas of mutual interest, where national security interests are not at stake. However, the emphasis that states place on relative gains will limit the growth of institutions and will always make cooperation difficult. For neo-realists, the important question is not will we all gain from this cooperation, but who will gain more?

What is left out of the debate?

One could argue that the neo-neo debate leaves out a great number of issues. Perhaps with a purpose, it narrows the agenda of international relations. It is not a debate about some of the most critical questions like 'Why war?' or 'Why inequality in the international system?' Remember this is a debate that occurs within the mainstream of International Relations scholarship. Neo-realists and neo-liberal Institutionalists agree on the questions; they simply offer different responses. Some important issues are left out and assumptions about international politics may be overlooked. As a student of international relations, you should be able to identify the strengths and weaknesses of a theory. Let us consider three possible areas for discussion: the role of domestic politics, learning, and political globalization.

Both theories assume that states are value maximizers and that anarchy constrains the behaviour of states. But, what about domestic forces that might promote a more cooperative strategy to address moral or ethical issues? Neo-realist assumptions suggest a sameness in foreign policy that may not be true. How do we account for the

moral dimensions of foreign policy such as development assistance given to poor states which have no strategic or economic value to the donor? Or how do we explain domestic interests that promote isolationist policies in the USA at a time when system changes would suggest international activism might result in both absolute and relative gains? We may need to challenge Waltz and ask if the internal make-up of a state matters. All politics is now glocal (global and local) and neo-realists especially, but also neo-liberals, must pay attention to what goes on inside a state. Issues of political culture, **identity**, and domestic political games must be considered.

We must assume that leaders and citizens alike learn something from their experiences. The lessons of two world wars prompted Europeans to set aside issues of sovereignty and nationalism and build an economic community. Although some neo-liberal Institutionalists recognize the importance of learning, in general neither theory explores the possibility that states will learn and may shift from a traditional self-interest perspective to an emphasis on common interests. There may be a momentum to cooperation and institution building that both theories underestimate. Can we assume that institutions and cooperation have had some impact on conditions of anarchy?

Both neo-realists and neo-liberals neglect the fact the political activities may be shifting away from the state. A number of scholars have suggested that one of the most significant outcomes of globalization is the emergence of global or transnational political advocacy **networks** (Keck and Sikkink 1998). Institutions promoted primarily by these advocacy networks have had a major impact on human rights issues such as child labour and security.

Key Points

- The neo-neo debate is not a debate between two polar opposite worldviews. They share an epistemology, focus on similar questions, and agree on a number of assumptions about international politics. This is an intra-paradigm debate.
- Neo-liberal Institutionalists and neo-realists study different worlds of international politics. Neo-realists focus on security and military issues. Neo-liberal Institutionalists focus on political economy, environmental issues, and, lately, human rights issues.
- Neo-realists explain that all states must be concerned with the absolute and relative gains that result from international agreements and cooperative efforts. Neo-liberal Institutionalists are less concerned about relative gains and consider that all will benefit from absolute gains.
- Neo-realists are more cautious about cooperation and remind us that the world is still a competitive place where self-interest rules.

- Neo-liberal Institutionalists believe that states and other actors can be persuaded to cooperate if they are convinced that all states will comply with rules and cooperation will result in absolute gains.
- This debate does not discuss many important issues that challenge some of the core assumptions of each theory. For example, neo-realism cannot explain foreign policy behaviour that challenges the norm of national interest over human interests.
- Globalization has contributed to a shift in political activity away from the state. Transnational social movements have forced states to address critical international issues and in several situations that have supported the establishment of institutions that promote further cooperation, and fundamentally challenge the power of states.

Neo-liberals and neo-realists on globalization

As I suggested earlier in this chapter, most neo-realists do not think that globalization changes the game of international politics much at all. States might require more resources and expertise to maintain their sovereignty, but neo-realists think most evidence suggests that states are increasing their expenditures and their jurisdictions over a wide variety of areas. Ultimately, we still all look to the state to solve the problems we face, and the state still has a monopoly over the legal use of coercive power. Most neo-realists assume that conditions of anarchy and competition accentuate the concerns for absolute and relative gains. As Waltz suggested in a recent article on the topic, '[t]he terms of political, economic and military competition are set by the larger units of the international political system' (Waltz 2000: 53). Waltz recognizes that globalization presents new policy challenges for nation-states but he denies that the state is being pushed aside by new global actors. The state remains the primary force in international relations and has expanded its power to effectively manage the processes of globalization.

What neo-realists are most concerned with is the new security challenges presented by globalization. Two examples follow.

Neo-realists are concerned with the uneven nature of economic globalization. Inequality in the international sys-tem may be the greatest security threat in the future. People without food are inclined to seek change, and often that change will be violent. Economic globalization can also accentuate existing differences in societies, creating instability in strategic regions, thereby challenging world order.

Most neo-realists would claim that forces of globalization challenge sovereignty. However, states have not lost their authority and control. Yet, globalization has had a significant impact on domestic politics and the existing power structures. Transnational **social movements** (TSMOS) and global advocacy networks have successfully shifted many political issues away from the state. For example, some neo-realists are concerned that the power and security of the state are being undermined by political movements seeking to force states to make new rules that control the use of nuclear and conventional weapons. These movements deftly use the press, the Internet, and activist networks to challenge many of the core assumptions of the dominant Realist/neo-realist policy perspective. Realists and neo-realists tend to favour elitist models of decision-making, especially in security areas. Some neo-realists have expressed concern that globalization might contribute to an unwanted democratization of politics in critical security areas (see Ch.13). Their concern is that expertise will be overwhelmed by public emotions.

Box 7.3 Neo-liberalism and its current critics

Critical voices

'Free trade theorists claimed that the *rising tide will lift all boats, providing broad,* economic benefits to all levels of society. The evidence so far clearly shows that it lifts only yachts.'

(*Barker and Mander 1999: 4*)

After twenty years of carefully following international economic rules such as free trade, price deregulation, and privatization as promoted by the Neoliberal **Washington Consensus**, several Latin American countries have elected new governments that are more concerned about uneven economic growth and greater inequalities within their countries. Venezuela, Bolivia, and Ecuador have new leaders who are hostile to privatization schemes and who are not afraid of nationalizing foreign corporations to address much needed social programmes in their countries. Many of these 'socialist' governments are supported by native peoples or indigenous groups who are concerned with the foreign ownership of natural resources like coal, oil, and gas. Dani Rodrik (1997) argues that that globalization raises the mobility of capital, making it very difficult for governments to tax profit. Thus profits from

energy resources are not available for social programmes like health, education, and poverty reduction. The leader of this twenty-first-century socialist revolution is Hugo Chavez, the President of Venezuela. He is building a Latin American coalition to challenge US military and political hegemony and neo-liberal orthodoxy in the Latin American region and the world.

Neo-liberal defenders

The benefits of globalization are clear to neo-liberal free market advocates, and these advocates believe that those who fight against these processes suffer from globalphobia and neglect to appreciate key benefits of a global economy. First, the more global the economy, the more manufacturers or producers in a given country can take advantage of commodities, production processes, and markets in other countries. Second, globalization encourages the diffusion of knowledge and technology, which increases the opportunities for economic growth worldwide. Third, the rich countries and corporations in the global North have capital that they will lend to developing states for economic growth if these states accept the rules of the neo-liberal

economic system. Fourth and finally, if trade barriers are minimal and government takes a minor role in trying to manage their economy, the chances for government corruption and political interference are greatly reduced. Most neo-liberals have incredible faith in the market and believe that globalization will encourage further economic integration among public and private actors in the economy. Private forms of economic integration are increasing across the world. Banks, investment firms, and industries are merging, linking Europe with the USA, China with Africa, and Russia with Colorado. Neo-liberals predict that the globalization momentum will increase due to the declining costs of transportation, technology, and communications. Distance is disappearing.

(Adapted from Burtless et al. 1998)

Most of the discussion of globalization among neo-liberals falls into two categories: (1) a free market commercial neo-liberalism that dominates policy circles throughout the world; and (2) academic neo-liberal Institutionalism that promotes regimes and institutions as the most effective means of managing the globalization process.

The end of the cold war was the end of the Soviet experiment in command economics and it left capitalism and free market ideas with few challengers in international economic institutions and national governments. Free market neo-liberals believe that governments should not fight globalization or attempt to slow it down. These neo-liberals want minimal government interference in the national or global market. From this perspective, institutions should promote rules and norms that keep the market open and discourage states that attempt to interfere with market forces. Other more social democratic neo-liberals support institutions and regimes that manage the economic processes of globalization as a means to prevent the uneven flow of capital and other resources that might widen the gap between rich and poor states.

Recent demonstrations against global economic institutions in the USA and Europe suggest that there are many who feel that the market is anything but fair. People marching in the streets of London and Seattle called for global institutions that provide economic well-being for all and for reformed institutions that promote social justice, ecological balance, and human rights (see Box 7.3). The critics of economic globalization state that governments will have to extend their jurisdictions and intervene more extensively in the market to address these concerns, as well as open the market and all of its opportunities to those people now left out. Given the current neo-liberal thinking, this kind of radical change is unlikely.

Key Points

- Neo-realists think that states are still the principal actors in international politics. Globalization challenges some areas of state authority and control, but politics is still international.
- Neo-realists are concerned about new security challenges resulting from uneven globalization, namely, inequality and conflict.
- Globalization provides opportunities and resources for transnational social movements that challenge the authority of states in various policy areas. Neo-realists are not supportive of any movement that seeks to open critical security issues to public debate.
- Free market neo-liberals believe globalization is a positive force. Eventually, all states will benefit from the economic growth promoted by the forces of globalization. They believe that states should not fight globalization or attempt to control it with unwanted political interventions.
- Some neo-liberals believe that states should intervene to promote capitalism with a human face or a market that is more sensitive to the needs and interests of all the people. New institutions can be created and older ones reformed to prevent the uneven flow of capital, promote environmental sustainability, and protect the rights of citizens.

Conclusion: narrowing the agenda of international relations

Neo-realism and neo-liberal Institutionalism are status quo rationalist theories. They are theories firmly embraced by mainstream scholars and by key decision-makers in many countries. There are some differences between these theories, although these differences are minor compared to the issues that divide reflectivist and rationalist theories and critical and problem-solving theories (see Ch.10).

In scholarly communities, neo-realism generally represents an attempt to make Realism more theoretically rigorous. Waltz's emphasis on system structure and its impact on the behaviour of states leads one to conclude that international relations is not explained by looking inside the state. Neo-realists who reduce international politics to microeconomic rational choice or instrumental thinking also minimize the idiosyncratic attributes of individual decision-makers and the different cultural and historical factors that shape politics within a state. These more scientific and parsimonious versions of neo-realism offer researchers some powerful explanations of state behaviour. However, do these explanations offer a complete picture of a given event or a policy choice? Does neo-realist scholarship narrow the research agenda? Recently, neo-realist scholars were criticized for their inability to explain the end of the cold war and other major transformations in the international system. Neo-realists minimize the importance of culture, traditions, and identity—all factors that shaped the emergence of new communities that helped to transform the Soviet empire.

Contributions by neo-realists in security studies have had a significant impact on the policy community. Both defensive and offensive neo-realists claim that the world remains competitive and uncertain and the structure of the international system makes power politics the dominant policy paradigm. This fits with the interests and belief systems of most military strategists and foreign policy decision-makers in positions of power in the world today. This continues the Realist tradition that has dominated international politics for centuries and it suggests that the criticisms of the Realist/neo-realist tradition may be limited to the academic world. However, critical perspectives, inside and outside the academic world, are causing some Realists/neo-realists to re-examine their assumptions about how this world works. Certainly, defensive neo-realists represent a group of scholars and potential policy advisers who understand the importance of multilateralism and the need to build effective institutions to prevent arms races that might lead to war. There is some change, but the agenda remains state-centric and focused on military security issues.

Neo-liberalism, whether the policy variety or the academic neo-liberal Institutionalism, is a rejection of the more utopian or cosmopolitan versions of Liberalism. US foreign policy since the end of the cold war has involved a careful use of power to spread an American version of liberal democracy: peace through trade, investment, and commerce. In the last few years, US foreign policy has promoted business and markets over human rights, the environment, and social justice. Washington's brand of neo-liberalism has been endorsed by many of the world's major powers and smaller trading states. The dominant philosophy of statecraft has become a form of 'pragmatic meliorism' with markets and Western democratic institutions as the chosen means for improving our lives. Again, we see a narrowing of choices and a narrowing of the issues and ideas that define our study of international politics.

Neo-liberal Institutionalism, with its focus on cooperation, institutions, and regimes, may offer the broadest agenda of issues and ideas for scholars and policymakers. Neo-liberal Institutionalists are now asking if institutions matter in a variety of issue-areas. Scholars are asking important questions about the impact of **international regimes** and institutions on domestic politics and the ability of institutions to promote rules and norms that encourage environmental sustainability, human rights, and economic development. It is interesting that many neo-liberal Institutionalists in the USA find it necessary to emphasize their intellectual relationship with neo-realists and ignore their connections with the English School and more cosmopolitan versions of Liberalism (see Ch.6). The emphasis on the shared assumptions with neo-realism presents a further narrowing of the agenda of international politics. A neo-liberal institutional perspective that focuses on the nature of international society or community and the importance of institutions as promoters of norms and values may be more appropriate for understanding and explaining contemporary international politics.

Every theory leaves something out. No theories can claim to offer a picture of the world that is complete. No theory has exclusive claims to the truth. Theories in international politics offer insights into the behaviour of states. Realists and neo-realists give great insights into power, conflict, and the politics of survival. However, neo-realism does not help us understand the impact of economic interdependence on state behaviour or the potential effects of institutions and regimes on domestic politics. Here is where neo-liberal Institutionalism helps us construct a picture of international politics. Theories empower some actors and policy strategies and dismiss others. Neo-realism and neo-liberal Institutionalism are theories that address status quo issues and consider

questions about how to keep the system operating. These theories do not raise questions about the dominant belief system or the distribution of power, and how these may be connected to conditions of **poverty** and violence. As you continue your studies in international politics, be critical of the theories being presented. Which theories explain the most? Which theory helps you make sense of this world? What does your theory leave out? Who or what perspective does the theory empower? Who or what view of the world is left out?

? Questions

1 What are the similarities between traditional Realism and neo-realism?

2 What are the intellectual foundations of neo-liberal Institutionalism?

3 What assumptions about international politics are shared by neo-liberals and neo-realists? What are the significant differences between these two theories?

4 How do you react to those who say that the neo-neo debate is not much of a debate at all? Is this merely an academic debate or has this discussion had any influence on foreign policy?

5 Do you think globalization will have any impact on neo-realist and neo-liberal thinking? Is either theory useful in trying to explain and understand the globalization process?

6 What do defensive and offensive neo-realists believe? How important are their theories to military strategists?

7 What is the difference between relative and absolute gains? What role do these concepts play in neo-realist thinking? In neo-liberal thinking?

8 How might the proliferation of institutions in various policy areas influence the foreign policy process in major, middle-ranking, and small states? Do you think these institutions will mitigate the effects of anarchy as neo-liberals claim?

9 Why do you think neo-realism and neo-liberalism maintain such dominance in US International Relations scholarship?

10 If we study international politics as defined by neo-realists and neo-liberal Institutionalists, what are the issues and controversies we would focus on? What is left out of our study of international politics?

➔ Guide to further reading

General surveys with excellent coverage of the neo-realist and neo-liberal perspectives

Doyle, Michael (1997), *Ways of War and Peace* (New York: W. W. Norton). Discusses the antecedents to neo-realism and neo-liberalism. Excellent sections on Hobbes and structural Realism and varieties of Liberalism.

Halliday, F. (1994), *Rethinking International Relations* (Vancouver: University of British Columbia Press). Lively and honest analysis of the current theoretical debates.

Mandelbaum, M. (2002), *The Ideas that Conquered the World* (New York: Public Affairs). An excellent review of the core ideas of peace, democracy, and free market capitalism Liberalism is discussed as the sole surviving ideology as the cold war ended.

For the more advanced student of International Relations

Smith, S., Booth, K., and Zalewski, M. (eds) (1996), *International Relations Theory and Beyond* (Cambridge: Cambridge University Press). Excellent on critical theory and challenges to rationalist approaches.

For more information on the neo-liberal/neo-realist debate

Baldwin, D. (ed.) (1993), *Neo-realism and Neo-liberalism: The Contemporary Debate* (New York: Columbia University Press). Includes reflections on the debate section with articles by Grieco and Keohane.

Doyle, M., and Ikenberry, G. J. (eds) (1997), *New Thinking in International Relations Theory* (Boulder, Col.: Westview Press). The chapters by Grieco on Realism and world politics and Weber on institutions and change are very useful.

Kegley, C. (ed.) (1995), *Controversies in International Relations Theory: Realism and the Neoliberal Challenge* (New York: St Martins Press). The first part of the text includes excellent chapters by Waltz, Holsti, Doyle, and Grieco.

Security and neo-realism

Brown, M. E., Lynn-Jones, S. M., and Miller, S. E. (eds) (1995), *The Perils of Anarchy: Contemporary Realism and International Security* (Cambridge, Mass.: MIT Press). A collection of essays from *International Security*.

Mearsheimer, J. (2003), *The Tragedy of Great Power Politics* (New York: W. W. Norton). The author presents the basics of his offensive realist theory of world politics and uses historical evidence to support his position that all states seek to survive by maximizing their power.

——and Walt, S. (2003), 'An Unnecessary War', *Foreign Policy* (Jan.–Feb.): 51–9. The article raises several serious concerns about how the Bush administration distorted the facts to justify the war with Iraq.

Neo-liberalism and neo-liberal institutionalism

Allison, G. (2000), 'The Impact of Globalization on National and International Security', in J. S. Nye and J. D. Donahue (eds), *Governance in a Globalizing World* (Washington, DC: Brookings Institution Press): 72–85. A very useful survey.

Friedman, T. (2005), *The World is Flat: A Brief History of the Twenty-first Century* (New York: Farrar, Straus and Giroux). Friedman's latest popular book promoting the benefits of globalization and arguing for all of us to adjust to a new global environment.

Haas, P., Keohane, R., and Levy, M. (eds) (1993), *Institutions for the Earth* (Cambridge, Mass.: MIT Press). An excellent collection of case studies asking if institutions have any impact on international, regional, and domestic environmental policies.

Nye, J., and Donahue, J. (eds) (2000), *Governance in a Globalizing World* (Washington, DC: Brookings Institution Press). Explores the meaning of globalization, its impact on nation-states, and how globalization might be managed to solve global problems and serve the interests of humankind.

Rodrick, D. (1997), *Has Globalization Gone Too Far?* (Washington, DC: Institute for International Economics). Rodrick offers some interesting arguments for more control of the global markets and other economic forces.

Yergin, D., and Stanislaw, J. (2002), *The Commanding Heights: The Battle for the World Economy* (New York: Touchstone). A basic review of the global economy that covers every region in the world. It has been developed as a very accessible television series.

Online Resource Centre

 Visit the Online Resource Centre that accompanies this book to access more learning resources on this chapter topic at www.oxfordtextbooks.co.uk/uk/orc/baylis_smith4e/

Chapter 8

Marxist theories of international relations

STEPHEN HOBDEN · RICHARD WYN JONES

- Introduction: the continuing relevance of Marxism ··· 144
- The essential elements of Marxist theories of world politics ······························· 145
- World-system theory ··· 147
- Gramscianism ··· 149
- Critical theory ·· 153
- New Marxism ·· 155
- Conclusion: Marxist theories of international relations and globalization ············· 157

Reader's Guide

This chapter will introduce, outline, and assess the Marxist contribution to the study of International Relations. Having identified a number of core features common to Marxist approaches, the chapter discusses four strands within contemporary Marxism which make particularly significant contributions to our understanding of world politics: world-system theory; Gramscianism; critical theory; and New Marxism. The chapter argues that no analysis of globalization is complete without an input from Marxist theory. Indeed, Marx was arguably the *first* theorist of globalization, and from the perspective of Marxism, the features often pointed to as evidence of globalization are hardly novel, but are rather the modern manifestations of long-term tendencies within the development of capitalism.

Introduction: the continuing relevance of Marxism

With the end of the **cold war** and the global triumph of 'free market' capitalism, it became commonplace to assume that the ideas of Marx, and his numerous disciples, could be safely consigned to the dustbin of history. The 'great experiment' had failed. While Communist parties retained **power** in China, Vietnam, and Cuba, they did not now constitute a threat to the **hegemony** of the global capitalist system. Rather, in order to try to retain power, these parties were themselves being forced to submit to the apparently unassailable logic of 'the market' by aping many of the central features of contemporary capitalist societies. One of the key lessons of the twentieth century, therefore, would appear to be that Marxist thought leads only to a historical dead end. The future is liberal and capitalist.

Yet despite this, Marx and Marxist thought more generally refuse to go away. The end of the Soviet experiment and the apparent lack of a credible alternative to capitalism may have led to a crisis in Marxism, but two decades later there appears to be something of a renaissance. There are probably two reasons why this renaissance is occurring, and why Marxists walk with a renewed spring in their step.

First, for many Marxists the communist experiment in the Soviet Union had become a major embarrassment. In the decades immediately after the October Revolution, most had felt an allegiance to the Soviet Union as the first 'Workers' State'. Subsequently, however, this **loyalty** had been stretched beyond breaking point by the depravities of Stalinism, and by Soviet behaviour in its post-Second World War satellites in Eastern Europe. What was sometimes termed 'actually existing socialism' was plainly not the communist utopia that many dreamed of and that Marx had apparently promised. Some Marxists were openly critical of the Soviet Union. Others just kept quiet and hoped that the situation, and the human rights record, would improve.

The break-up of the Soviet bloc has, in a sense, wiped the slate clean. This event reopened the possibility of being able to argue in favour of Marx's ideas without having to defend the actions of governments that justify their behaviour with reference to them. Moreover, the disappearance of the Soviet Union has encouraged an appreciation of

Marx's work less encumbered by the baggage of Marxism-Leninism as a state ideology. The significance of this is underlined when it is realized that many of the concepts and practices that are often taken as being axiomatic of Marxism do not in fact figure in Marx's writings: these include the 'vanguard party', 'democratic centralism', and the centrally directed 'command economy'.

Second, and perhaps more importantly, Marx's social theory still retains formidable analytical purchase on the world we inhabit. The vast bulk of his theoretical efforts consisted of a painstaking analysis of **capitalism** as a mode of production and the basic elements of his account have not been bettered. Indeed, with the ever-increasing penetration of the market mechanism into all aspects of life, it is arguable that Marx's forensic examination of both the extraordinary dynamism and the inherent contradictions of capitalism are even more relevant now than in his own time. A particular strength of Marx's work is his analysis of crisis. Liberal accounts of capitalism suggest that free markets will move towards equilibrium and will be inherently stable. Our day-to-day lived experience suggests otherwise. The 1987 stock-market crash and the Asian financial crisis of the late 1990s demonstrate that global capitalism continues to be rocked by massive convulsions which have enormous implications for the lives of individuals around the globe. On Marx's account, such convulsions, and their baleful human consequences, are an inherent and inescapable part of the very system itself.

Compared to **Realism** and **Liberalism** (see Ch.5, Ch.6 and Ch.7), Marxist thought presents a rather unfamiliar view of international relations. While the former portray world politics in ways which resonate with those presented in the foreign news pages of our newspapers and magazines, Marxist theories aim to expose a deeper, underlying—indeed hidden—truth. This is that the familiar events of world politics—wars, treaties, international aid operations, etc.—all occur within structures which have an enormous **influence** on those events. These are the structures of a global capitalist system. Any attempt to understand world politics must be based on a broader understanding of the processes which operate within global capitalism.

In addition to presenting an unfamiliar view of world politics, Marxist theories are also discomfiting, for they

argue that the effects of global capitalism are to ensure that the powerful and wealthy continue to prosper at the expense of the powerless and the poor. We are all aware that there is gross inequality in the world. Statistics concerning the human costs of **poverty** are truly numbing in their awfulness (the issue of global poverty is further discussed in Ch.27). Marxist theorists argue that the relative prosperity of the few is dependent on the destitution of the many. In Marx's own words, 'Accumulation of wealth at one pole is, therefore, at the same time accumulation of misery, agony of toil, slavery, ignorance, brutality at the opposite pole'.

In the next section we will outline some of the central features of the Marxist approach—or historical **materialism** as it is often known. Following on from this, subsequent sections will explore some of the most important strands in contemporary Marx-inspired thinking about world politics. We should note, however, that given the richness and variety of Marxist thinking about world politics, the account that follows is inevitably destined to be partial and to some extent arbitrary. Our aim in the following is to provide a route map that we hope will encourage readers themselves to explore further the work of Marx and of those who have built on the foundations he laid.

Key Points

- Marx's work retains its relevance despite the collapse of Communist Party rule in the former Soviet Union.
- Of particular importance is Marx's analysis of capitalism, which has yet to be bettered.
- Marxist analyses of international relations aim to reveal the hidden workings of global capitalism. These hidden workings provide the context in which international events occur.

The essential elements of Marxist theories of world politics

In his inaugural address to the Working Men's International Association in London in 1864, Karl Marx told his audience that history had 'taught the working classes the duty to master [for] themselves the mysteries of international politics'. However, despite the fact that Marx himself wrote copiously about international affairs, most of this writing was journalistic in character. He did not incorporate the international dimension into his theoretical mapping of the contours of capitalism. This 'omission' should perhaps not surprise us. The sheer scale of the theoretical enterprise in which he was engaged, as well as the nature of his own methodology, inevitably meant that Marx's work would be contingent and unfinished.

Marx was an enormously prolific writer and his ideas developed and changed over time. Hence, it is not surprising that his legacy has been open to numerous interpretations. In addition, real-world developments have also led to the revision of his ideas in the light of experience. A variety of schools of thought have emerged, which claim Marx as a direct inspiration, or whose work can be linked to Marx's legacy. This chapter will focus on four strands of contemporary Marxist thought that have all made major contributions to thinking about world politics. Before we discuss what is distinctive about these approaches, it is important that we examine the essential elements of commonality that lie between them.

First, all the theorists discussed in this chapter share with Marx the view that the social world should be analyzed as a **totality.** The academic division of the social world into different areas of inquiry—history, philosophy, economics, political science, sociology, international relations, etc.—is both arbitrary and unhelpful. None can be understood without knowledge of the others: the social world had to be studied as a whole. Given the scale and complexity of the social world, this entreaty clearly makes great demands of the analyst. Nonetheless, for Marxist theorists, the disciplinary boundaries that characterize the contemporary social sciences need to be transcended if we are to generate a proper understanding of the dynamics of world politics.

Another key element of Marxist thought, which serves further to underline this concern with interconnection and context, is the **materialist conception of history.** The central contention here is that processes of historical change are ultimately a reflection of the economic development of society. That is, economic development

is effectively the motor of history. The central dynamic that Marx identifies is tension between the **means of production** and **relations of production** that together form the **economic base** of a given society. As the means of production develop, for example through technological advancement, previous relations of production become outmoded, and indeed become fetters restricting the most effective utilization of the new productive capacity. This in turn leads to a process of social change whereby relations of production are transformed in order to better accommodate the new configuration of means. Developments in the economic base act as a catalyst for the broader transformation of society as a whole. This is because, as Marx argues in the Preface to his *Contribution to the Critique of Political Economy*, 'the mode of production of material life conditions the social, political and intellectual life process in general'. Thus the legal, political, and cultural **institutions** and practices of a given society reflect and reinforce—in a more or less mediated form—the pattern of power and control in the economy. It follows logically, therefore, that change in the economic base ultimately leads to change in the 'legal and political **superstructure**'. (For a diagrammatical representation of the **base–superstructure model** see Fig. 8.1.)

Class plays a key role in Marxist analysis. In contrast to Liberals, who believe that there is an essential harmony of interest between various social groups, Marxists hold that society is systematically prone to class conflict. Indeed, in the *Communist Manifesto*, which Marx co-authored with Engels, it is argued that 'the history of all hitherto existing societies is the history of class struggle' (Marx and Engels 1967). In capitalist society, the main axis of conflict is between the bourgeoisie (the capitalist) and the proletariat (the workers).

Despite his commitment to rigorous scholarship, Marx did not think it either possible or desirable for the analyst to remain a detached or neutral observer of this

---

Box 8.1 Indicators of world inequality

- More than 1.2 billion people live on less than US$1 per day.
- In 1990 the average American was 38 times richer than the average Tanzanian. By 2005 this had risen to 61 times richer.
- More than 1.1 billion people lack access to clean water.
- Average incomes in more than 50 developing countries are now at a lower level than they were in 1990. In 21 countries a larger proportion of the people are hungry. In 14 countries a higher proportion of children are dying before reaching the age of 5, and in 34 countries life expectancy has decreased.
- Tariffs on manufactured goods from the developing world are four times higher than those on manufactured goods from other OECD countries.
- One-sixth of the world's adults are illiterate (two-thirds of the world's illiterates are women).
- In the developed world subsidies to agricultural producers are six times higher than overseas development aid.
- More than 10 million children die every year from easily preventable diseases.
- A child born in Zambia today is less likely to live past the age of 30 than a child born in 1840 in England.
- In Africa only one child in three completes primary education.
- In sub-Saharan Africa a woman is 100 times more likely to die in childbirth than women in high-income OECD countries.
- African countries pay out US$40 million every day on debt repayment.

(Sources: World Bank, United Nations Development Programme, Jubilee Research)

---

great clash between capital and labour. He argued that 'philosophers have only interpreted the world in various ways; the point, however, is to change it'. Marx was committed to the cause of **emancipation**. He was not interested in developing an understanding of the dynamics of capitalist society simply for the sake of it. Rather, he expected such an understanding to make it easier to overthrow the prevailing order and replace it with a communist society—a society in which wage labour and private property are abolished and social relations transformed.

It is important to emphasize that the essential elements of Marxist thought, all too briefly discussed in this section, are also essentially contested. That is, they are subject to much discussion and disagreement even among those contemporary writers who have been influenced by Marxist writings. There is disagreement as to how these ideas and concepts should be interpreted and how they should be put into operation. Analysts also differ over which elements of Marxist thought are most relevant, which have been proven to be mistaken, and which should now be considered as outmoded or in

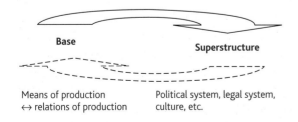

Base   Superstructure

Means of production   Political system, legal system,
↔ relations of production   culture, etc.

Figure 8.1 The base–superstructure model

need of radical overhaul. Moreover, there are substantial differences between them in terms of their attitudes to the legacy of Marx's ideas. The work of the New Marxists draws far more directly on Marx's original ideas than does the work of the critical theorists. Indeed, the latter would probably be more comfortable being viewed as post-Marxists than as straightforward Marxists. But even for them, as the very term post-Marxism suggests, the ideas of Marx remain a basic point of departure.

Key Points

- Marx himself provided little in terms of a theoretical analysis of international relations.
- His ideas have been interpreted and appropriated in a number of different and contradictory ways, resulting in a number of competing schools of Marxism.
- Underlying these different schools are several common elements that can be traced back to Marx's writings.

World-system theory

The origins of world-system theory

The origins of world-system theory can be traced back to the first systematic attempt to apply the ideas of Marx to the international sphere, that is, to the critique of **imperialism** advanced by a number of thinkers at the start of the twentieth century (see Brewer 1990). The most well-known and influential work to emerge from this debate is the pamphlet written by Lenin, and published in 1917, called *Imperialism, the Highest Stage of Capitalism*. Lenin accepted much of Marx's basic thesis, but argued that the character of capitalism had changed since Marx published the first volume of *Capital* in 1867 (Marx 1992). Capitalism had entered a new stage—its highest and final stage—with the development of **monopoly capitalism**. Under monopoly capitalism, a two-tier structure had developed within the world-economy with a dominant **core** exploiting a less-developed **periphery.** With the development of a core and periphery, there was no longer an automatic **harmony of interests** between all workers. The bourgeoisie in the core countries could use profits derived from exploiting the periphery to improve the lot of their own proletariat. In other words, the capitalists of the core could pacify their own working class through the further exploitation of the periphery.

Lenin's views were developed by the Latin American Dependency School, the writers of which developed the notion of core and periphery in greater depth. In particular, Raul Prebisch argued that countries in the periphery were suffering as a result of what he called 'the declining terms of trade'. He suggested that the price of manufactured goods increased more rapidly than that of raw materials. So, for example, year by year it requires more tons of coffee to pay for a refrigerator. As a result of their reliance on primary goods, countries of the periphery become poorer relative to the core. These arguments were developed further by writers such as André Gunder Frank and Henrique Fernando Cardoso. It is from the framework developed by such writers that contemporary world-system theory emerged.

The key features of Wallerstein's world-system theory

In order to outline the key features of world-system theory, we shall concentrate on the work of perhaps its most prominent protagonist, Immanuel Wallerstein. For Wallerstein, history has been marked by the rise and demise of a series of world-systems. The modern world-system emerged in Europe at around the turn of the sixteenth century. It subsequently expanded to encompass the entire globe. The driving force behind this seemingly relentless process of expansion and incorporation has been capitalism, defined by Wallerstein as 'a system of production for sale in a market for profit and appropriation of this profit on the basis of individual or collective ownership' (1979: 66). Within the context of this system, all the institutions of the social world are continually being created and re-created. Furthermore, and crucially, it is not only the elements within the system which change. The system itself is historically bounded. It had a beginning, has a middle, and will have an end.

In terms of the geography of the modern world-system, in addition to a core–periphery distinction, Wallerstein

added an intermediate **semi-periphery**. According to Wallerstein, the semi-peripheral zone has an intermediate role within the world-system displaying certain features characteristic of the core and others characteristic of the periphery. Although dominated by core economic interests, the semi-periphery has its own relatively vibrant indigenously owned industrial base (see Fig. 8.2). Because of this hybrid nature, the semi-periphery plays important economic and political roles within the modern world-system. In particular, it provides a source of labour that counteracts any upward pressure on wages in the core and also provides a new home for those industries that can no longer function profitably in the core (for example, car assembly and textiles). The semi-periphery also plays a vital role in stabilizing the political structure of the world-system.

According to world-system theorists, the three zones of the world-economy are linked together in an exploitative relationship in which wealth is drained away from the periphery to the centre. As a consequence, the relative positions of the zones become ever more deeply entrenched: the rich get richer while the poor become poorer.

Together, the core, semi-periphery, and periphery make up the geographic dimension of the world-economy. However, described in isolation they provide a rather static portrayal of the world-system. In order to understand the dynamics of their interaction over time we must turn our attention to the **temporal** dimensions of Wallerstein's description of the world-economy. These are cyclical rhythms, secular trends, contradictions, and crisis. It is these, when combined with the spatial dimensions, which determine the historical trajectory of the system.

The first temporal dimension, **cyclical rhythms**, is concerned with the tendency of the capitalist world-economy to go through recurrent periods of expansion and subsequent contraction, or more colloquially, boom and bust. Whatever the underlying processes responsible for these waves of growth and depression, it is important to note that each cycle does not simply return the system to the point from which it started. Rather, if we plot the end point of each wave we discover the **secular trends** within the system. Secular trends refer to the long-term growth or contraction of the world-economy. The third temporal feature of the world-system is **contradictions**. These arise because of 'constraints imposed by systemic structures which make one set of behavior optimal for actors in the short run and a different, even opposite, set of behavior optimal for the same actors in the middle run' (Wallerstein 1991a: 261). For Wallerstein, one of the central contradictions is 'under-consumption'. This refers to the situation where it is in the interests of capitalists to have well-paid workers so that they can consume the items that they produce. It is also in their interest to reduce wage levels in order to increase profitability. In practice it is not possible to fulfil both of these aims. The pressure of the capitalist system means that, to remain profitable, capitalist seek to reduce wages—though this also reduces consumption. Contradictions in the world-economy arise from the fact that the structure of the system can mean that apparently sensible actions by individuals can, in combination or over time, result in very different—and possibly unwelcome—outcomes from the ones originally intended.

In the context of the world-system, Wallerstein reserves the term 'crisis' to refer to a very specific temporal occurrence. Crisis constitutes a unique set of circumstances that can only be manifested once in the lifetime of a world-system. It occurs when the contradictions, secular trends, and cyclical rhythms combine in such a way as to mean that the system cannot continue to reproduce itself. Thus, a crisis within a particular world-system heralds its end and replacement by another system.

Controversially, Wallerstein argues that the end of the cold war, rather than marking a triumph for Liberalism,

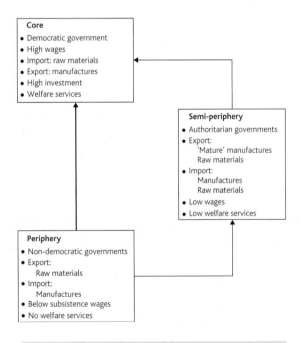

Figure 8.2 Interrelationships in the world-economy

indicates its imminent demise (Wallerstein 1995). This has sparked a crisis in the current world-system that will involve its demise and replacement by another system. Such a period of crisis is also a time of opportunity. When a system is operating smoothly, behaviour is very much determined by its structure. In a time of crisis, however, actors have far greater agency to determine the character of the replacement structure. Much of Wallerstein's recent work has been an attempt to develop a political programme to promote a new world-system that is more equitable and just than the current one (Wallerstein 1998, 1999, 2006). Even more contentious, particularly in the light of recent discussion of an 'imperial United States', is his claim that the American power is in rapid decline, and that its recent military adventures are a confirmation of such a decline (Wallerstein 2003, 2004). From this perspective, to focus on **globalization** is to miss out on what is truly novel about the contemporary era. Indeed, for Wallerstein, current globalization discourse represents a 'gigantic misreading of current reality' (Wallerstein 2003: 45). Those phenomena evoked by 'globalization' are manifestations of a world-system that emerged in **Europe** during the sixteenth century to incorporate the entire globe; a world-system now in terminal decline.

Recent developments in world-system theory

Various writers have built on the framework established by Wallerstein (Denemark *et al.* 2000). Christopher Chase-Dunn, for example, lays much more emphasis on the role of the inter-state system than Wallerstein. He argues that the capitalist mode of production has a single logic in which both politico-military and exploitative economic relations play key roles. In a sense he attempts to bridge the gap between Wallerstein's work and that of the New Marxists (discussed below), by placing much more of an emphasis on production in the world-economy and how this influences its development and future trajectory (see Chase-Dunn 1998).

André Gunder Frank (one of the most significant Dependency School writers) has launched a significant critique of Wallerstein's work, and of Western social theory in general. He argues not only that the world-system is far older than suggested by Wallerstein (Frank and Gills 1996), it is also an offshoot of a system that originated in Asia (Frank 1998). His work builds on that of Janet Abu-Lughod. She has challenged Wallerstein's account of the emergence of the modern world-system in the sixteenth century, arguing that, during the medieval period, Europe was a peripheral area to a world-economy centred on the Middle East (Abu-Lughold 1989). Frank argues that the source of the capitalist world-economy was not in Europe; rather, the rise of Europe occurred within the context of an existing world-system. Hence social theory, including Marxism, which tries to examine 'Western exceptionalism', is making the mistake of looking for the causes of that rise to dominance in the wrong place, Europe, rather than within the wider, global context in which it occurred.

Key Points

- World-system theory can be seen as a direct development of Lenin's work on imperialism and the Latin American Dependency School.
- Immanuel Wallerstein and his work on the modern world-system makes a key contribution to this school.
- Wallerstein's work has been developed by a number of other writers who have built on his initial foundational work.

Gramscianism

In this section we discuss the strand of Marxist theory that has emerged from the work of the Italian Marxist Antonio Gramsci. Gramsci's work has become particularly influential in the study of International Political Economy, where a neo-Gramscian or 'Italian' school is flourishing. Here we will discuss Gramsci's legacy, and the work of Robert W. Cox, a contemporary theorist who has been instrumental in introducing his work to an International Relations audience.

Antonio Gramsci (1891–1937) was a Sardinian and one of the founding members of the Italian Communist Party. He was jailed in 1926 for his political activities, and

spent the remainder of his life in prison. Although he is regarded by many as the most creative Marxist thinker of the twentieth century, he produced no single, integrated theoretical treatise. Rather, his intellectual legacy has been transmitted primarily through his remarkable *Prison Notebooks* (Gramsci 1971). The key question which animated Gramsci's theoretical work was why had it proven to be so difficult to promote revolution in Western Europe? Marx, after all, had predicted that revolution, and the **transition** to socialism, would occur first in the most advanced capitalist societies. But, in the event, it was the Bolsheviks of comparatively backward Russia that had made the first 'breakthrough', while all the subsequent efforts by putative revolutionaries in Western and Central Europe to emulate their success had ended in failure. The history of the early twentieth century seemed to suggest, therefore, that there was a flaw in classic Marxist analysis. But where had they gone wrong?

Gramsci's answer revolves around his use of the concept of **hegemony.** For Gramsci, hegemony reflects his conceptualization of power. He develops Machiavelli's view of power as a centaur, half beast, half man: a mixture of coercion and consent. In understanding how the prevailing order was maintained, Marxists had concentrated almost exclusively on the coercive practices and **capabilities** of the state. On this understanding, it was simply coercion, or the fear of coercion, that kept the exploited and alienated majority in society from rising up and overthrowing the system that was the cause of their suffering. Gramsci recognized that while this characterization may have held true in less developed societies, such as pre-revolutionary Russia, it was not the case in the more developed countries of the West. Here the system was also maintained through consent.

Consent, on Gramsci's reading, is created and re-created by the hegemony of the ruling class in society. It is this hegemony that allows the moral, political, and cultural values of the dominant group to become widely dispersed throughout society and to be accepted by subordinate groups and classes as their own. This takes place through the institutions of **civil society:** the **network** of institutions and practices that enjoy some autonomy from the state, and through which groups and individuals organize, represent, and express themselves to each other and to the state (for example, the media, the education system, churches, voluntary organizations, etc.).

Several important implications flow from this analysis. The first is that Marxist theory needs to take superstructural phenomena seriously, because while the structure of society may ultimately be a reflection of social relations of production in the economic base, the nature of relations in the superstructure are of great relevance in determining how susceptible that society is to change and transformation. Gramsci used the term **historic bloc** to describe the mutually reinforcing and reciprocal relationships between the socioeconomic relations (base) and political and cultural practices (superstructure) that *together* underpin a given order. For Gramsci and Gramscians, to reduce analysis to the narrow consideration of economic relationships, on the one hand, or solely to politics and ideas on the other, is deeply mistaken. It is the interaction that matters.

Another crucial implication is for political practice. If the hegemony of the ruling class is a key element in the perpetuation of its dominance, then society can only be transformed if that hegemonic position is successfully challenged. This entails a **counter-hegemonic** struggle in civil society, in which the prevailing hegemony is undermined, allowing an alternative historic bloc to be constructed.

Gramsci's writing reflects a particular time and a particular, and in many ways unique, set of circumstances. This has led several writers to question the broader applicability of his ideas (see Burnham 1991; Germain and Kenny 1998). But the most important test, of course, is how useful ideas and concepts derived from Gramsci's work prove to be when they are removed from their original context and applied to other **issues** and problems? It is to this that we now turn our attention.

Robert Cox—the analysis of 'world order'

The person who has done most to introduce Gramsci to the study of world politics is the Canadian scholar Robert W. Cox. He has developed a Gramscian approach that involves both a critique of prevailing theories of International Relations and International Political Economy, and the development of an alternative framework for the analysis of world politics.

To explain Cox's ideas we would like to begin by discussing one particular sentence in his seminal 1981 article

'Social Forces, States, and World Orders: Beyond International Relations Theory'. The sentence, which has become one of the most often-quoted lines in all of contemporary International Relations theory, reads as follows: 'Theory is always *for* some one, and *for* some purpose' (1981: 128). It expresses a worldview that follows logically from the Gramscian, and broader Marxist position, that has been explored in this chapter. If ideas and values are (ultimately) a reflection of a particular set of social relations, and are transformed as those relations are themselves transformed, then this suggests that all knowledge (of the social world at least) must reflect a certain context, a certain time, a certain space. Knowledge, in other words, cannot be objective and timeless in the sense that some contemporary Realists, for example, would like to claim.

One key implication of this is that there can be no simple separation between facts and values. Whether consciously or not, all theorists inevitably bring their values to bear on their analysis. This leads Cox to suggest that we need to look closely at those theories, those ideas, those analyses that claim to be objective or value-free, and ask who or what is it for, and what purpose does it serve? He subjects Realism, and in particular its contemporary variant **neo-realism,** to thoroughgoing critique in these grounds. According to Cox, these theories are for—or serve the interests of—those who prosper under the prevailing order, that is the inhabitants of the developed states, and in particular the ruling elites. Their purpose, whether consciously or not, is to reinforce and legitimate the status quo. They do this by making the current configuration of International Relations appear natural and immutable. When Realists (falsely) claim to be describing the world as it is, as it has been, and as it always will be, what they are in fact doing is reinforcing the ruling hegemony in the current world order.

Cox contrasts **problem-solving theory,** that is theory which accepts the parameters of the present order, and thus helps legitimate an unjust and deeply iniquitous system, with **critical theory.** Critical theory attempts to challenge the prevailing order by seeking out, analyzing, and, where possible, assisting social processes that can potentially lead to emancipatory change.

One way in which theory can contribute to these emancipatory goals is by developing a theoretical understanding of world orders that grasps both the sources of stability in a given system, and also the dynamics of processes of transformation. In this context, Cox draws upon Gramsci's notion of hegemony and transposes it to the international realm, arguing that hegemony is as important for maintaining stability and continuity here as it is at the domestic level. According to Cox, successive dominant powers in the international system have shaped a world order that suits their interests, and have done so not only as a result of their coercive capabilities, but also because they have managed to generate broad consent for that order even among those who are disadvantaged by it.

For the two hegemons that Cox analyzes (the United Kingdom and the United States) the ruling, hegemonic idea has been 'free trade'. The claim that this system benefits everybody has been so widely accepted that it has attained 'commonsense' status. Yet the reality is that while 'free trade' is very much in the interests of the hegemon (which, as the most efficient producer in the global economy, can produce goods which are competitive in all markets, so long as they have access to them), its benefits for peripheral states and regions are far less apparent. Indeed, many would argue that 'free trade' is a hindrance to their economic and social development. The degree to which a state can successfully produce and reproduce its hegemony is an indication of the extent of its power. The success of the United States in gaining worldwide acceptance for neo-liberalism suggests just how dominant the current hegemon has become (see Case Study).

But despite the dominance of the present world order, Cox does not expect it to remain unchallenged. Rather, he maintains Marx's view that capitalism is an inherently unstable system, riven by inescapable contradictions. Inevitable economic crises will act as a catalyst for the emergence of counter-hegemonic movements. The success of such movements is, however, far from assured. In this sense, thinkers like Cox face the future on the basis of a dictum popularized by Gramsci, that is, combining 'pessimism of the intellect' with 'optimism of the will'.

Recent Gramscian writing

More recent Gramsican writing, including notable contributions by Mark Rupert (1995, 2000; Rupert and Solomon, 2005) and W. I. Robinson (1996, 2004), continue

Case Study   The politics of neo-liberalism

A very good example of the hegemonic power of the United States, many Marxists would argue, is the success that it has had in getting neo-liberal policies accepted as the norm throughout the world. The set of policies most closely associated with the neo-liberal project (in particular reduction of state spending, currency devaluation, privatization, and the promotion of free markets) are, revealingly, known as the **Washington Consensus**. Many would argue that these are 'commonsense' policies and that those Third World countries that have adopted them have merely realized that such economic policies best reflect their interests. However, Marxists would argue that an analysis of the self-interest of the hegemon, and the use of coercive power, provide a more convincing explanation of why such policies have been adopted.

The adoption of neo-liberal policies by Third World countries has had a number of implications. Spending on health and education has been reduced, they have been forced to rely more on the export of raw materials, and their markets have been saturated with manufactured goods from the industrialized world. It does not take a conspiracy theorist to suggest that these neo-liberal policies are in the interests of capitalists in the developed world. There are three main areas where the adoption of neo-liberal policies in the Third World is in the direct interest of the developed world. First there is the area of free trade. We need not enter into arguments about the benefits of free trade, but it is clear that it will always be in the interest of the hegemon to promote free trade—this is because, assuming it is the most efficient producer, its goods will be the cheapest anywhere in the world. It is only if countries put up barriers to trade, to protect their own production,

that the hegemon's products will be more expensive than theirs. Second, there is the area of raw materials. If Third World countries are going to compete in a free trade situation the usual result is that they become more reliant on the export of raw materials (because their industrial products cannot compete in a free trade situation with those of the developed world). Again this is in the interest of the hegemon, as increases in the supply of raw material exports mean that the price falls. Additionally where Third World countries have devalued their currency as part of a neo-liberal package the price of their exported raw materials goes down. Finally, when Third World governments have privatized industries, investors from North America and Europe have frequently been able to snap up airlines, telecommunications companies, and oil industries at bargain prices. Duncan Green (1995) gives an eloquent description of the impacts of neo-liberalism on Latin American counties.

If neo-liberal policies appear to have such negative results for Third World countries why have they been so widely adopted? This is where the coercive element comes in. Through the 1970s and 1980s and continuing to today there has been a major debt crisis between the Third World and the West. This debt crisis came about primarily as a result of excessive and unwise lending by Western banks. Third World countries were unable to pay off the interest on these debts, let alone the debt itself. They turned to the major global financial institutions such as the International Monetary Fund for assistance. Although the IMF is a part of the United Nations it is heavily controlled by Western countries, in particular the United States. For example, the United States has 18 per cent of the votes, while Mozambique has only 0.07 per cent. In total the 10 most industrialized countries have over 50 per cent of the votes. For Third World countries, the price of getting assistance was that they would implement neo-liberal policies. Only once these were implemented, and only on condition that the policies were maintained, would the IMF agree to provide aid to continue with debt repayment.

Hence Marxists would argue that a deeper analysis of the adoption of neo-liberal policies is required. Such an analysis would suggest that the global acceptance of neo-liberalism is very much in the interests of the developed world and has involved a large degree of coercion. That such policies seem 'natural' and 'commonsense' is an indication of the hegemonic power of the United States.

to display this characteristically Gramscian combination of pessimism and optimism—in their case, a search for plausible alternative futures within a capitalist system that both regard as increasingly globalized—as well as a central focus on the question of hegemony. Robinson's most recent work (2004) posits the formation of a transnational capitalist class and traces the emergence of a

'transnational state', existing alongside more traditional 'nation-states', a state-form that the author considers increasingly anachronistic. Indeed, on Robinson's reading, and in contrast with Cox's analysis of earlier periods, in the twenty-first century it is increasingly this transnational capitalist class, rather than any particular **nation-state,** that wields hegemonic power.

Key Points

- Drawing upon the work of Antonio Gramsci for inspiration, writers within an 'Italian' school of International Relations have made a considerable contribution to thinking about world politics.
- Gramsci shifted the focus of Marxist analysis more towards superstructural phenomena. In particular, he explored the processes by which consent for a particular social and poitical system was produced and reproduced and through the operation of hegemony.

Hegemony allows the ideas and ideologies of the ruling stratum to become widely dispersed, and widely accepted, throughout society.
- Thihkers such as Robert W.Cox have attempted to 'internationalize' Gramsci's thought by transposing several of his key concepts, most notably hegemony, to the global context.

Critical theory

There are, without doubt, many overlaps between critical theory and Gramscian approaches to the study of world politics. As we saw in the previous section, Robert W. Cox refers to his own Gramsci-influenced approach as critical theory. Moreover, both Gramscianism and critical theory have their roots in Western Europe of the 1920s and 1930s—a place and a time in which Marxism was forced to come to terms not only with the failure of a series of attempted revolutionary uprisings, but also with the rise of fascism. Nevertheless, there are differences between them. Contemporary critical theory and Gramscian thoughts about International Relations draw upon the ideas of different thinkers, with differing intellectual concerns. In addition, there is a clear difference in focus between the two strands, with those influenced by Gramsci tending to be much more concerned with issues relating to the subfield of international political economy than critical theorists. Critical theorists, on the other hand, have involved themselves with questions concerning **international society**, international ethics, and **security**. In this section we introduce critical theory and the thought of one of its main proponents in the field of International Relations, Andrew Linklater. In addition, we will briefly introduce Critical Security Studies, an approach to the study of security that draws on both critical theory and Gramscian influences.

Critical theory developed out of the work of the **Frankfurt School**. This was an extraordinarily talented group of thinkers who began to work with each other in the 1920s and 1930s. As left-wing German Jews, the members of the school were forced into exile by the Nazis' rise to power in the early 1930s, and much of their most creative work was produced in the United States. The leading lights of the first generation of the Frankfurt School included **Max Horkheimer**, **Theodor Adorno**, and **Herbert Marcuse**. A subsequent generation has taken up the legacy of these thinkers and developed it in important and innovative ways. The best known is **Jürgen Habermas**, who is regarded by many as the most influential of all contemporary social theorists. Given the vast scope of critical theory writing, we can do no more here than introduce some of the key features.

The first point to note is that their intellectual concerns are rather different from those of most other Marxists in that they have not been much interested in the further development of analysis of the economic base of society. They have instead concentrated on questions relating to culture, bureaucracy, the social basis and nature of authoritarianism, the structure of the family, and on exploring such concepts as reason and **rationality** as well as theories of knowledge. Frankfurt School theorists have been particularly innovative in terms of their analysis of the role of the media, and what they have famously termed the 'culture industry'. In other words, in classical Marxist terms, the focus of critical theory is almost entirely superstructural.

Another key feature is that critical theorists have been highly dubious as to whether the proletariat in contemporary society does in fact embody the potential for emancipatory transformation in the way that Marx had believed. Rather, with the rise of mass culture and the increasing commodification of every element of social life, Frankfurt School thinkers have argued that the working class has simply been absorbed by the system and no longer represents a threat to it. This, to use Marcuse's famous phrase, is a **one-dimensional** society to which the vast majority simply cannot begin to conceive an alternative.

Finally, critical theorists have made some of their most important contributions through their explorations of the meaning of **emancipation**. Emancipation, as we have seen, is a key concern of Marxist thinkers, but the meaning that they give to the term is often very unclear and deeply ambiguous. Moreover, the historical record is unfortunately replete with examples of unspeakably barbaric behaviour being justified in the name of emancipation, of which imperialism and Stalinism are but two. Traditionally, Marxists have equated emancipation with the process of humanity gaining ever greater mastery over nature through the development of ever more sophisticated technology, and its use for the benefit of all. But early critical theorists argued that humanity's increased domination over nature had been bought at too high a price, claiming that the kind of mind-set that is required for conquering nature slips all too easily into the domination of other human beings. In contrast, they argued that emancipation had to be conceived in terms of a **reconciliation with nature**—an evocative if admittedly vague vision. By contrast, Habermas's understanding of emancipation, is more concerned with communication than with our relationship with the natural world. Setting aside the various twists and turns of his argument, Habermas's central political point is that the route to emancipation lies through **radical democracy**. That is, it is through a system in which the widest possible participation is encouraged not only in word (as is the case in many Western democracies) but also in deed, by actively identifying barriers to participation—be they social, economic, or cultural—and overcoming them. For Habermas and his many followers, participation is not to be confined within the borders of a particular sovereign state. Rights and obligations extend beyond state frontiers. This, of course, leads him directly to the concerns of International Relations, and it is striking that Habermas's recent writings have begun to focus on the international realm. However, thus far, the most systematic attempt to think through some of the key issues in world politics from a recognizably Habermasian perspective has been made by **Andrew Linklater**.

Andrew Linklater has used some of the key **principles** and precepts developed in Habermas's work in order to argue that emancipation in the realm of international relations should be understood in terms of the expansion of the moral boundaries of a **political community** (see Ch.31). In other words, he equates emancipation with a process in which the borders of the sovereign state lose their ethical and moral significance. At present, state borders denote the furthest extent of our sense of duty and obligation, or at best, the point where our sense of duty and obligation is radically transformed, only proceeding further in a very attenuated form. For critical theorists, this situation is simply indefensible. The goal is therefore to move towards a situation in which citizens share the same duties and obligations towards non-citizens as they do towards their fellow citizens.

To arrive at such a situation would, of course, entail a wholesale transformation of the present institutions of governance. But an important element of the critical theory method is to identify—and, if possible, nurture—tendencies that exist within the present conjuncture that point in the direction of emancipation. On this basis, Linklater identifies the development of the European Union as representing a progressive or emancipatory tendency in contemporary world politics. If true, this suggests that an important part of the international system is entering an era in which the sovereign state, which has for so long claimed an exclusive hold on its citizens, is beginning to lose some of its pre-eminence. Given the notorious pessimism of the thinkers of the Frankfurt School, the guarded optimism of Linklater in this context is indeed striking.

Critical Security Studies

Critical Security Studies (CSS) is the name given to a trend in the study of security issues that has gained prominence in recent years (in particular through the work of Keith Krause and Mike Williams (1997), Ken Booth (1991, 2004) and Richard Wyn Jones (1995, 1999). CSS combines influences from Gramscianism and critical theory with aspects of peace research and the so-called 'alternative defence thinking'. In contrast to much mainstream security thinking (in the West at least), CSS refuses to accept the state as the 'natural' object of analysis, arguing that, for much of the world's population, states are part of the security problem rather than a provider of security. Instead, proponents of CSS tend to argue that it is beholden on security analysts to place individual human beings at the centre of their analysis. Like Linklater, they regard their work as supporting and nurturing emancipatory tendencies, for it is only through emancipation that security can ultimately be assured.

Key Points

- Critical theory has its roots in the work of the Frankfurt School.
- Habermas has argued that emancipatory potential lies in the realm of communication and that radical democracy is the way in which that potential can be unlocked.

- Andrew Linklater has developed on critical theory themes to argue in favour of the expansion of the moral boundaries of the political community and has pointed to the European Union as an example of a post-Westphalian institution of governance.

New Marxism

In this section we examine the work of writers who derive their ideas more directly from Marx's own writings. These New Marxists have returned to the fundamental tenets of Marxist thought and sought to reappropriate ideas that they regard as having been neglected or somehow misinterpreted by subsequent generations. On this basis they have sought both to criticize other developments within Marxism, and to make their own original theoretical contributions to the understanding of contemporary trends. In this section we will introduce the work of two writers associated with this strand of Marxist thought: Justin Rosenberg and Benno Teschke, who have used key elements of Marx's writings to critique other theoretical approaches to International Relations and globalization theory.

Justin Rosenberg—capitalism and global social relations

The focus of Rosenberg's analysis is the character of the international system and its relationship to the changing character of social relations. His starting point is a critique of Realist International Relations theory. In particular, Rosenberg challenges Realism's claim to provide an ahistorical, essentially timeless account of international relations by analyses of the differences in the character of international relations between the Greek and Italian city-states. A touchstone of Realist theory is the similarity between these two historical cases. Rosenberg, however, describes the alleged resemblances between these two eras as a 'gigantic optical illusion'. Instead, his analysis suggests that the character of the international system in each period was completely different. In addition, he charges that attempts to provide an explanation

of historical outcomes during these periods, working purely from the inter-state level, is not feasible (as, for example, in Realist accounts of the Peloponnesian War). Finally, Rosenberg argues that Realist attempts to portray international systems as autonomous, entirely political realms founder because in the Greek and Italian examples this external autonomy was based on the character of internal—and in each case different—sets of social relations.

As an alternative, Rosenberg argues for the development of a theory of international relations that is sensitive to the changing character of world politics. This theory must also recognize that international relations are part of a broader pattern of social relations. His starting point is Marx's observation (Rosenberg 1994: 51) that:

> It is always the direct relationship of the owners of the conditions of production to the direct producers . . . which reveals the innermost secret, the hidden basis of the entire social structure, and with it the political form of the relation of sovereignty and dependence, in short, the corresponding specific form of the state.

In other words, the character of the relations of production permeate the whole of society—right up to, *and including,* relations between states. The form of the state will be different under different modes of production, and as a result the characteristics of inter-state relations will also vary. Hence if we want to understand the way that international relations operate in any particular era, our starting point has to be an examination of the mode of production, and in particular the relations of production.

In his more recent work Rosenberg has turned his critical attention to 'globalization theory' (Rosenberg 2000, 2006). He argues that globalization is a descriptive

category denoting 'the geographical extension of social processes'. That such social processes have become a global phenomenon is beyond dispute, and a 'theory of globalization' is needed to explain what and why this is happening. Such a theory, for Rosenberg, should be rooted in classical social theory. But instead of this, a body of 'globalization theory' has emerged premised on the claim that the supposed compression of time and space that typifies globalization requires a whole new social theory in order to explain contemporary developments. But on Rosenberg's reading, this body of theory has produced little in terms of explaining the processes. Moreover, the events of the early twenty-first century were not those predicted by globalization theory. As a result, Globalization theory is best understood as a product of changes that occurred in the last years of the twentieth century, and in particular the political and economic vacuum created by the collapse of the Soviet Union, rather than an adequate explanation of them. A proper explanation, rooted in classical social theory, would examine the underlying social relations which have led to the capitalist system becoming dominant throughout the globe.

Benno Teschke—social property relations

In a major contribution to the Marxist literature on international relations, Benno Teschke (2003) provides not only a critique of existing international relations theory, but also, through the concept of social property relations, a means of analyzing changes in the constitution and practices of actors in the international system. Teschke's work can be seen as building on Rosenberg's observation that social relations provide the starting point for an analysis of international relations, in particular through presenting an analysis of how system transformation occurs, and describing the major transitions of the past millennium.

A social property approach examines the way in which class relations, forms of exploitation, and control of the means of production have changed in different historical epochs. Teschke argues that such an approach is 'applicable to all geopolitical orders' (2003: 47). A major claim of his analysis is that rather than one major change between the feudal and modern international system, there have been two major transformations—between feudal and early modern (dominated by absolutist monarchies) and between early modern and modern (capitalist states). Both these periods of change were gradual periods of transformation during which the international system comprised more than one type of actor: during the former transition a mixture of feudal and absolutist states; during the latter absolutist and capitalist states.

The practice of international relations was different during each of these three periods, reflecting the character of social property relations dominant in each epoch. Such an analysis leads to the claim that the significance of the **Treaty of Westphalia,** seen by most international relations theorists as the major transition to modernity, has been overstated. Instead, Westphalia constitutes the point at which absolutist rather than capitalist states became the key actors of the international system. The modern international system only started to emerge with the appearance of the first capitalist state (Britain). This capitalist state form reflected the development of capitalist property relations. Since the seventeenth century, the capitalist state has become the prominent state form. As a result, the practices of international relations have changed, reflecting, Teschke argues, developments in the character of social property relations.

Key Points

- New Marxism is characterized by a direct (re)appropriation of the concepts and categories developed by Marx.
- Rosenberg uses Marx's ideas to criticize Realist theories of international relations, and globalization theory. He seeks to develop an alternative approach which understands historical change in world politics as a reflection of transformations in the prevailing relations of production.
- For Benno Teschke, the study of social property relations provides the means for analyzing the key elements of international relations, and the transitions between one international system and another.

Conclusion: Marxist theories of international relations and globalization

As outlined in the first chapter of this book, globalization is the name given to the process whereby social transactions of all kinds increasingly take place without account for national or state boundaries, with the result that the world has become 'one relatively borderless social sphere'. The particular trends pointed to as typifying globalization include: the growing **integration** of national economies; a growing awareness of ecological interdependence; the proliferation of companies, **social movements**, and intergovernmental agencies operating on a global scale; and a communications revolution which has aided the development of a global consciousness.

Marxist theorists would certainly not seek to deny that these developments are taking place, nor would they deny their importance, but they would reject any notion that they are somehow novel. Rather, in the words of Chase-Dunn, they are 'continuations of trends that have long accompanied the expansion of capitalism' (1994: 97). Marx and Engels were clearly aware not only of the global scope of capitalism, but also of its potential for social transformation. In a particularly prescient section of the *Communist Manifesto* (Marx and Engels 1967: 83–4), for example, they argue that:

> The bourgeoisie has through its exploitation of the world market given a cosmopolitan character to production and consumption in every country. . . . All old-established national industries have been destroyed or are daily being destroyed. They are dislodged by new industries, whose introduction becomes a life and death question for all civilized nations, by industries that no longer work up indigenous raw material, but raw material drawn from the remotest zones; industries whose products are consumed, not only at home, but in every quarter of the globe. . . .

According to Marxist theorists, the globe has long been dominated by a single integrated economic and political entity—a global capitalist system—which has gradually incorporated all of humanity within its grasp. Within this system, all elements have always been interrelated and interdependent. 'National economies' have long

been integrated to such an extent that their very nature has been dependent on their position within a capitalist world-economy. The only thing 'new' is an increased awareness of these linkages. Similarly, ecological processes have always ignored state boundaries, even if it is only recently that growing environmental degradation has finally allowed this fact to permeate into public consciousness.

The growth of multinational corporations certainly does not signify any major change in the structure of the modern capitalist system. Rather, they form part of a long-term trend towards the further integration of the global economy. Neither is international contact between those movements which oppose the prevailing political and economic order a new development. In fact, as even the most cursory examination of the historical record will amply attest, such movements, be they socialist, nationalist, or ecological in character, have always drawn inspiration from, and forged links with, similar groups in other countries. Finally, the much-vaunted communications revolution is the latest manifestation of a long-term trend.

While the intensity of cross-border flows may be increasing, this does not necessarily signify the fundamental change in the nature of world politics proclaimed by so many of those who argue that we have entered an era of globalization. Marxist theorists insist that the only way to discover how significant contemporary developments really are is to view them in the context of the deeper structural processes at work. When this is done, we may well discover indications that important changes are afoot. Many Marxists, for example, regard the delegitimation of the sovereign state as a very important contemporary development. However, the essential first step in generating any understanding of those trends regarded as evidence of globalization must be to map out the contours of global capitalism itself. If we fail to do so, we will inevitably fail to gauge the real significance of the changes that are occurring.

Another danger of adopting an ahistoric and uncritical attitude to globalization is that it can blind us to the way in which reference to globalization is increasingly becoming part of the ideological armoury of elites within the contemporary world. 'Globalization' is now regularly cited as a reason to promote measures to reduce workers' rights and lessen other constraints on business. Such ideological justifications for policies which favour the interests of business can only be countered through a broader understanding of the relationship between the political and economic structures of capitalism. As we have seen, the understanding proffered by the Marxist theorists suggests that there is nothing natural or inevitable about a world order based on a global market. Rather than accept the inevitability of the present order, the task facing us is to lay the foundations for a new way of organizing society—a global society which is more just and more humane than our own.

? Questions

1 How would you account for the continuing vitality of Marxist thought?
2 How did Lenin's approach to international relations differ from that of Marx?
3 How useful is Wallerstein's notion of a semi-periphery?
4 Assess Warren's criticisms of world-system theory.
5 Evaluate Rosenberg's critique of globalization theory.
6 In what ways does Gramsci's notion of hegemony differ from that employed by Realist International Relations writers?
7 How has Linklater developed critical theory for an International Relations audience?
8 How do Marxist theorists view the notion of 'globalization'?
9 What do you regard as the main contribution of Marxist theory to our understanding of world politics?
10 How useful is the notion of emancipation used by critical theorists?
11 Do you agree with Cox's distinction between 'problem-solving theory' and 'critical theory'?
12 Assess Wallerstein's claim that the power of the United States is in decline.

⤷ Guide to further reading

Marx, K., and Engels, F. (1848), *The Communist Manifesto* (London: Bookmarks). An ideal introduction to Marx's thinking.

Morton, A. (2007), *Unravelling Gramsci: Hegemony and Passive Revolution in the Global Political Economy* (London: Pluto Press). A discussion of the contemporary relevance of Gramsci.

Teschke, B. (2003), *The Myth of 1648: Class, Geopolitics and the Making of Modern International Relations* (London: Verso). A powerful alternative reading of the development of International Relations.

Wallerstein, I. (1974, 1980, 1989), *The Modern World-System* (San Diego, Cal.: Academic Press). The most complete account of the world-system approach to the study of International Relations.

Wyn Jones, R. (1999), *Security, Strategy and Critical Theory* (Boulder, Col.: Lynne Rienner). The first three chapters provide an introduction to some of the key intellectual concerns of the Frankfurt School while the remainder outline Critical Security Studies.

Online Resource Centre

 Visit the Online Resource Centre that accompanies this book to access more learning resources on this chapter topic at www.oxfordtextbooks.co.uk/uk/orc/baylis_smith4e/

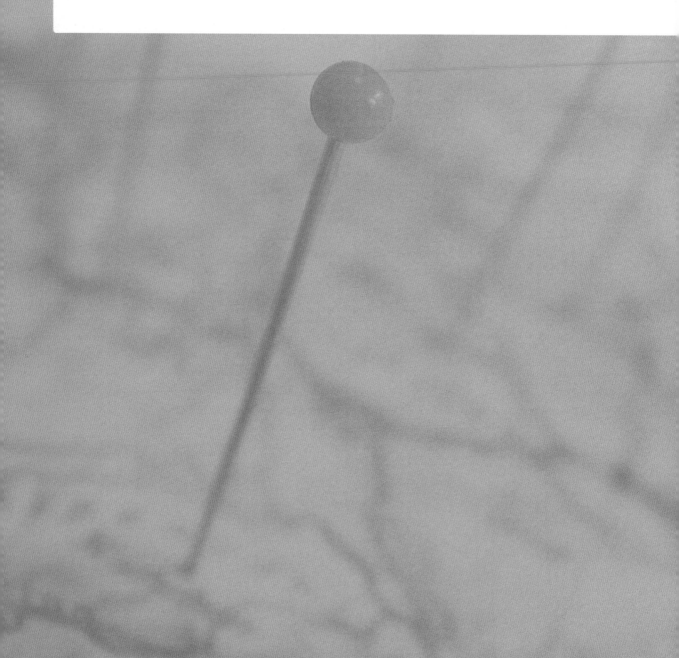

Chapter 9

Social Constructivism

MICHAEL BARNETT

- Introduction ·· 162
- The main Constructivist tenets ·· 162
- Constructivism and global change ·· 168
- Conclusion ··· 171

Reader's Guide

This chapter provides an overview of Constructivist approaches to international relations theory. Constructivismm's antecedents are located in the 1980s and in a series of critical reactions to mainstream international relations theory in the United States, namely neo-realism and neo-liberal Institutionalism. These theories emphasized the distribution of power and the unwavering pursuit by states of power and wealth, and minimized the power of ideas. Constructivism countered by highlighting how ideas define and can transform the organization of world politics, shape the identities and interests of states, and determine what counts as legitimate action. Although initially given a cold reception, Constructivism quickly gained credibility and popularity in the 1990s due to the end of the cold war, the enduring insights of sociological and critical theory, and the ability to generate novel accounts of world politics. Although there are important differences among Constructivists, they share several commitments that generate a distinctive approach for understanding how the world is made and re-made through human action.

Introduction

Constructivism rose very quickly from rather humble beginnings to become one of the leading schools in International Relations. Now Constructivism is widely recognized for its ability to capture important features of global politics and is viewed as an important theory of international relations. Although there are various versions of Constructivism, they share a common concern with how ideas define the international **structure**; how this structure shapes the identities, interests, and foreign policies of states; and how **state** and **non-state actors** reproduce that structure—and at times transform it. The concern with the making and re-making of world politics underscores Constructivism's strong interest in global change. Although Constructivism has investigated various features of global change, in this chapter I will focus on two: the convergence by states around similar ways for organizing their domestic and international life; and how **norms** become internationalized and institutionalized, that is, globally accepted to the point that they constrain what states and non-state actors do and influence their ideas of what is legitimate behaviour. Constructivist arguments thus help us understand some elementary features of the globalization of world politics.

The main Constructivist tenets

Before proceeding to identify Constructivism's tenets, two caveats are in order. Constructivism is a social theory and not a substantive theory of international politics. Social theory is broadly concerned with how to conceptualize the relationship between agents and structures; for instance, how should we think about relationship between states and the structure of international politics? Substantive theory offers specific claims and hypotheses about patterns in world politics; for instance, how do we explain why democratic states tend not to wage war on one another? In this way Constructivism is best compared to **rational choice**. Rational choice is social theory that offers a framework for understanding how actors operate with fixed preferences which they attempt to maximize under a set of constraints. It makes no claims about the content of those preferences; they could be wealth or religious salvation. Nor does it assume anything about the content of these constraints; they could be guns or ideas. Rational choice offers no claims about the actual patterns of world politics. For instance, neo-realism and neo-liberalism subscribe to rational choice, but they arrive at rival claims about patterns of conflict and **cooperation** in world politics because they make different assumptions about the effects of **anarchy**. Like rational choice, Constructivism is a social theory that is broadly concerned with the relationship between agents and structures, but it is not a substantive theory. Constructivists, for instance, have different arguments regarding the rise of sovereignty and the impact of human rights norms on states. In order to generate substantive claims, scholars must delineate who are the principal actors, what are their interests and capacities, and what is the content of the **normative structures**.

Also, there are many different types of Constructivism. Some draw from the insights of James March, John Meyer, and organizational theory, and others from Michel Foucault and discourse analysis. Some prioritize agents and others structures. Some focus on inter-state politics and others transnationalism. There are differences over the possibility of social science. Different empirical puzzles drive different approaches. These fault-lines have spawned a proliferating number of labels. Neoclassical. Modernist. Post-modern. Naturalistic. Thick. Thin. Linguistic. Narrative. Weak. Strong. Systemic. Holistic. This development should not be surprising. All schools have internal rivalries.

Still, there is unity within such diversity. 'Constructivism is about human consciousness and its role in international life' (Ruggie 1998: 856). This focus on human consciousness suggests a commitment to Idealism and holism, which, according to Wendt (1999), represent the core of Constructivism. **Idealism** demands

that we take seriously the role of ideas in world politics. The world is defined by material and ideational forces. But these ideas are not akin to beliefs or psychological states that reside inside our heads. Instead, these ideas are social. Our mental maps are shaped by collectively held ideas such as knowledge, symbols, language, and rules. Idealism does not reject material reality but instead observes that the meaning and construction of that material reality is dependent on ideas and interpretation. The **balance of power** does not objectively exist out there waiting to be discovered; instead states debate what is the balance of power, what is its meaning, and how they should respond. Constructivism also accepts some form of **holism** or structuralism. The world is irreducibly social and cannot be decomposed to the properties of already existing actors. The emphasis on holism does not deny agency but instead recognizes that agents have some autonomy and their interactions help to construct, reproduce, and transform those structures. Although the structure of the cold war seemingly locked the United States and the Soviet Union into a fight to the death, leaders on both sides creatively transformed their relations and, with it, the very structure of global politics.

This commitment to idealism and holism has important implications for how we think about and study world politics. But in order to appreciate its insights requires that we learn more about its conceptual vocabulary, and in order to demonstrate the value of learning this 'second language' I will contrast Constructivism's vocabulary with that of rational choice. The core observation is the **social construction of reality.** This has a number of related elements. One is the emphasis on the socially constructed nature of actors and their identities and interests. Actors are not born outside and prior to society, as individualism claims. Instead, actors are produced and created by their cultural environment. Nurture, not nature. For instance, what makes an Arab state an *Arab* state is not the fact that the populations speak Arabic but rather that there are rules associated with Arabism that shape the Arab states' identity, interests, and foreign policies that are deemed legitimate and illegitimate. Another element is how knowledge, that is symbols, rules, concepts, and categories, shapes how individuals construct and interpret their world. Reality does not exist out there waiting to be discovered; instead, historically-produced and culturally-bound knowledge enables individuals to construct and give meaning to reality.

This constructed reality frequently appears to us an objective reality, which relates to the concept of **social facts.** There are those things whose existence is dependent on human agreement and those things whose existence is not. Brute facts, such as rocks, flowers, gravity, and oceans, exist independent of human agreement and will continue to exist even if humans disappear or deny their existence. Social facts are dependent on human agreement and are taken for granted. Money, refugees, terrorism, human rights, and sovereignty are social facts. Their existence depends on human agreement, they will only exist so long as that agreement exists, and their existence shapes how we categorize the world and what we do.

The social construction of reality also shapes what is viewed as legitimate action. Do we only choose the most efficient action? Do the ends justify the means? Or, is certain action just unacceptable? The earlier distinction between constitutive and regulative rules parallels the conceptual distinction between the **logic of consequences** and the **logic of appropriateness.** The logic of consequences attributes action to the anticipated costs and benefits, mindful that other actors are doing just the same. The logic of appropriateness, however, highlights how actors are rule-following, worrying about whether their actions are legitimate. The two logics are not necessarily distinct or competing. What is viewed as appropriate and legitimate can affect the possible costs of different actions; the more illegitimate a possible course of action appears to be, the higher the potential cost for those who proceed on their own. The United States' decision to go into Iraq without the blessing of the Security Council meant that other states viewed the USA's actions as illegitimate, were less willing to support it, and thus raised the costs to the United States when it went ahead.

By emphasizing the social construction of reality we also are questioning what is frequently taken for granted. This points to several issues. One is a concern with the origins of those social constructs that now appear to us as natural and are now part of our social vocabulary. Sovereignty did not always exist; it was a product of historical forces and human interactions that generated new distinctions regarding where political authority resided. The category of **weapons of mass destruction** is a modern invention. Although individuals have been forced to flee their homes ever since Adam and Eve were exiled from Eden, the political and legal category of 'refugees' is only a century old (see Case Study). To understand the

Case Study   Social construction of refugees

Who is a refugee, why does this category matter, and how has it changed? There are many ways to categorize people who leave their homes, including migrants, temporary workers, displaced peoples, and refugees. Prior to the twentieth century refugee as a legal category did not exist, and it was not until the First World War that states recognized peoples as refugees and gave them rights. Who was a refugee? Although many were displaced by the First World War, Western states limited their compassion to Russians who were fleeing the Bolsheviks (it was easier to accuse a rival state of persecuting its people); only they were entitled to assistance from states and the new refugee agency, the High Commissioner for Refugees. However, the High Commissioner took his mandate and the category and began to apply it to others in Europe who also had fled their country and needed assistance. Although states frequently permitted him to expand into other regions and provide more assistance, states also pushed back and refused to give international recognition or assistance to many

in need—most notably when Jews were fleeing Nazi Germany After the Second World War and as a consequence of mass displacement, states re-examined who could be called a refugee and what assistance they could receive. Because Western states were worried about having obligations to millions of people around the world, they defined a refugee as an individual 'outside the country of his origin owing to a well-founded fear of persecution' as a consequence of events that occurred in Europe before 1951. In other words, their definition excluded those outside Europe who were displaced because of war or natural disasters because of events after 1951. Objecting to this arbitrary definition that excluded so many, the new refugee agency, the United Nations High Commissioner for Refugees, working with aid agencies and permissive states, seized on events outside Europe and argued that there was no principled reason to deny to them what was given to Europeans. Over time the political meaning of refugee came to include anyone who was forced to flee their home and crossed an international order, and eventually states changed the international legal meaning to reflect the new political realities. Now, in the contemporary era, we are likely to call someone a refugee if he is forced to flee his home because of man-made circumstances and do not worry if he has crossed an international border. To capture the idea of those who flee but are still in their homeland, we use the term 'internally displaced peoples'. One reason why states wanted to differentiate 'statutory' refugees from internally-displaced peoples is because they have little interest in extending their international legal obligations to millions of people and do not want to become too involved in the domestic affairs of states. Still, the concept of refugees has expanded impressively over the last 100 years, and the result is that there are millions of peoples who are now entitled to forms of assistance that are a matter of life and death.

origins of these concepts requires attention to the interplay between existing ideas and institutions, the political calculations by leaders who had ulterior motives, and morally minded actors who were attempting to improve humanity. Also of concern are alternative pathways. Although history is path-dependent, there are contingencies, historical accidents, the conjunction of material and ideational forces, and human intervention that can force history to change course. The events of **11 September 2001** and the response by the Bush administration arguably transformed the direction of world politics. This interest in possible and counter-factual worlds works against historical determinism. Alexander Wendt's (1992) claim that 'anarchy is what states make of it' calls attention to how different beliefs and practices will generate divergent patterns and organization of world politics (see Box 9.1). A world of Mahtma Gandhis will be very different from a world of Osama bin Ladens.

Constructivists also examine how actors make their activities meaningful. Following Max Weber's (1949: 81) insight that 'we are cultural beings with the capacity and the will to take a deliberate attitude toward the world and to lend it *significance*', Constructivists attempt to recover the **meanings** that actors give to their practices and the objects that they construct. These derive not from private beliefs but rather from culture. In contrast to the Rationalist presumption that culture, at most, constrains action, Constructivists argue that culture informs the meanings that people give to their action. Sometimes Constructivists have presumed that such meanings derive from a hardened culture. But because culture is fractured and because society is comprised of different interpretations of what is meaningful activity, scholars need to consider these cultural fault-lines and treat the fixing of meanings as an accomplishment that is at the essence of politics. Some of the most important debates

Box 9.1 Alexander Wendt on the three cultures of anarchy

'[T]he deep structure of anarchy [is] cultural or ideational rather than material. . . . [O]nce understood this way, we can see that the logic of anarchy can vary. . . . [D]ifferent cultures of anarchy are based on different kinds of roles in terms of which states represent Self and Other. [T]here are three roles, enemy, rival, and friend . . . that are constituted by, and constitute, three distinct macro-level cultures of international politics, Hobbesian, Lockean, and Kantian, respectively. These cultures have different rules of engagement, interaction logics, and systemic tendencies. . . . The logic of the Hobbesian anarchy is well known: "the war of all against all . . ." This is the true self-help system . . . where actors cannot count on each other for help of even to observe basic-self-restraint. . . . Survival depends solely on military power. . . . Security is deeply competitive, a zero-sum affair. . . . Even if what states really want is security rather than power their collective beliefs force them to *act* as if they are power-seeking. . . . The Lockean culture has a different logic . . . because it is based on a different role structure, rivalry rather than enmity. . . . Like enemies, rivals are constituted by representations about Self and Other with respect to Violence, but these representations are less threatening: unlike enemies, rivals expect each other to act as if they recognize their sovereignty, their "life and liberty", as a *right*, and therefore not to try to conquer or dominate them. . . . Unlike friends, however, the recognition among rivals does not extend to the right to be free from violence in disputes. The Kantian culture is based on a role structure of friendship. . . within which states expect each other to observe two simple rules: (1) disputes will be settled without war or the threat of war (the rule of non-violence); and (2) they will fight as a team if the security of any one is threatened by a third party.'

(Wendt 1999: 43, 279, 251, 298–9)

in world politics are about how to define particular activities. **Development**, human rights, security, humanitarian intervention, **sovereignty** are all important orienting concepts that can have any number of meanings. States and non-state actors have rival interpretations of the meanings of these concepts and will fight to try to have collectively accepted their preferred meaning.

The very fact that these meanings are fixed through politics and that once these meanings are fixed they have consequences for the ability of people to determine their fates suggests an alternative way of thinking about **power**. Most international relations theorists treat power as the ability of one state to compel another state to do what it otherwise would not and tend to focus on the material technologies, such as military firepower and economic statecraft, which have this persuasive effect. Constructivists have offered two important additions to this view of power. The forces of power go beyond material, they also can be ideational. Consider the issue of **legitimacy.** States, including great powers, crave legitimacy, the belief that they are acting according to and pursuing the values of the broader international community. There is a direct relationship between their legitimacy and the costs with a course of action: the greater the legitimacy the easier time they will have convincing others to cooperate with their policies, the lesser the legitimacy the more costly the action. This means, then, that even great powers will frequently feel the need to alter their policies in order to be viewed as legitimate—or bear the consequences. Further evidence of the constraining

power of legitimacy is offered by the tactic of 'naming and shaming' by human rights activists. If states did not care about the reputation and the perception that they were acting in a manner that was consistent with prevailing international standards, then such a tactic would have little visible impact; it is only because law-breaking governments want to be perceived as acting in a manner that is consistent with international norms that they can be taunted into changing their conduct.

Moreover, the effects of power go beyond the ability to change behaviour. Power also includes how knowledge, the fixing of meanings, and the construction of identities allocate differential rewards and capacities. If development is defined as *per capita* income, then some actors, namely states, and some activities, namely industrialization, are privileged. However, if development is defined as basic needs, then other actors, namely peasants and women, gain voice, and other activities, namely small-scale agricultural initiatives and cottage industries, are visible. International humanitarian law tends to assume that 'combatants' are men and 'civilians' are women, children, and the elderly. Consequently, as Box 9.2 relates, men and women might be differentially protected by the laws of war.

Although there is tremendous debate among Constructivists over whether and how they are committed to social science, there is some common ground. To begin, they reject the unity of science thesis, that is, that the methods of the natural sciences are appropriate for understanding the social world. Instead, they argue that

Box 9.2 Charli Carpenter on the effects of gender on the lives of individuals in war-torn societies

'International agencies mandated with the protection of war-affected civilians generally aim to provide protection in a neutral manner, but when necessary they prioritize the protection of the "especially vulnerable." According to professional standards recently articulated by the International Committee for the Red Cross "special attention by organizations for specific groups should be determined on the basis of an assessment of their needs and vulnerability as well as the risks to which they are exposed". If adult men are most likely to lose their lives directly as a result of the fall of a besieged town, one would expect that, given these standards, such agencies would emphasize protection of civilian men in areas under siege by armed forces. Nonetheless, in places where civilians have been evacuated from besieged areas in an effort to save lives, it is typically women, children, and the elderly who have composed the evacuee population. . . . While in principle all civilians are to be protected on the basis of their actions and social roles, in practice only certain categories of population (women, elderly, sick, and disabled) are presumed to be civilians regardless of context. . . . Thus . . . gender is encoded within the parameters of the immunity norm: while in principle the "innocent civilian" may include other groups, such as adult men, the presumption that women and children are innocents, whereas adult men may not be means that "women and children" signifies "civilian" in a way that "unarmed adult male" does not. . . . Similarly, gender beliefs are embedded in . . . the concept of "especially vulnerable populations." . . . In this context it never would have occurred to protection agencies to evacuate men and boys first, even if they had had the chance.'

(Carpenter 2003: 662, 671, 673–4)

the objects of the natural world and the social world are different in one crucial respect: in the social world the subject knows herself through reflection upon her actions as a subject not simply of experience but of intentional action as well. Humans reflect on their experiences and use these experiences to inform their reasons for their behaviour. Atoms do not. What necessitates a human science, therefore, is the need to understand how individuals give significance and meaning to their actions. Only then will we be able to explain human action. Consequently, the human sciences require methods that can capture the interpretations that actors bring to their activities. Max Weber, a founding figure of this approach, advocated that scholars employ *vershten* to recreate how people understand and interpret the world. To do so, scholars need to exhibit empathy, to locate the practice within the collectivity so that one knows how this practice or activity counts, and to unify these individual experiences into objectively, though time-bound, explanations (Ruggie 1998: 860).

Most Constructivists remain committed to causality and explanation, but insist on a definition of causality and explanation that is slightly different from conventional usage. A highly popular view of causality is that independent and dependent variables are unrelated and that a cause exists when the movement of one variable precedes and is responsible for the movement of another variable. Constructivists, though, add that structures can have a causal impact because they make possible certain kinds of behaviour and thus generate certain tendencies in the international system. Sovereignty does not cause states to behave one particular way; instead, it produces them and invests them with certain capacities that make possible certain kinds of behaviours. Being a sovereign state, after all, means that states have certain rights and privileges that other actors in world politics do not. States are permitted to use violence (though within defined limits) while non-state actors that use violence are, by definition, terrorists. Knowing something about the structure, therefore, does important causal work. Constructivists also are committed to explanatory theory, but reject the idea that explanation requires the discovery of timeless laws. In fact, it is virtually impossible to find such laws in international politics. The reason for their absence is not because of some odd characteristic of international politics. Instead, this elusiveness exists for all the human sciences. As Karl Popper observed, the search for timeless laws in the human sciences will be forever elusive because of the ability of humans to accumulate knowledge of their activities, to reflect on their practices and acquire new knowledge, and to change their practices as a consequence. Accordingly, Constructivists reject the search for laws in favour of contingent generalizations (Price and Reus-Smit 1998).

Constructivists use a variety of methods. They adopt ethnographic and interpretive techniques in order to recreate the meanings that actors bring to their practices and how these practices relate to social worlds. They employ large-n quantitative studies in order to demonstrate the emergence of a world culture that spreads specific practices, values, and models. They use genealogical methods to identify the contingent factors that produced the

categories of world politics that are subsequently taken for granted. They utilize structured, focused comparisons in order better to understand the conditions under which norms diffuse from one context to another. They even use computer simulations to model the emergent properties of world politics.

Throughout, though, Constructivists have attempted to interpret evidence as it relates to alternative explanations. Although they have largely positioned their claims against neo-realism and neo-liberal Institutionalism, they have clarified the differences by contrasting Constructivism with rational choice. The presumption, then, is that these are rival social theories. In many ways, they are. Rational choice treats actors as pre-social; Constructivism as social. Rational choice treats interests as fixed; Constructivism as constructed by the environment and interactions. Rational choice holds that the only effect of the environment is to constrain and regulate the actions of already constituted actors; Constructivism adds that it also can construct the actors' identities and interests. Rational choice uses the logic of consequences to understand behaviour; Constructivism adds the logic of appropriateness.

Given that rationalists and constructivists adopt such different frameworks for thinking about world politics, some scholars argue that these social theories are incommensurable, that is, they cannot be combined or reconciled because they contain opposing assumptions and capture different features of reality. Consequently, the only kind of possible relationship is some form of pluralism and any attempt at a grand synthesis, the mother of all social theories, will produce either a theoretic mutant or theoretical **imperialism**. For much the same reason, other scholars ridicule a gladiatorial, winner-take-all, competition.

Other scholars look for points of connection and evaluate the relative strengths of each approach in order to see when they might be combined to enrich our understanding of the world. One possibility is strategic social construction (Finnemore and Sikkink 1998). Actors attempt to change the norms that subsequently guide and constitute state identities and interests. Human rights activists, for instance, try to encourage compliance with human rights norms not only by naming and shaming those who violate these norms, but also by encouraging states to identify with these norms because it is the right thing to do. Another possibility is to consider the relationship between the normative structure and strategic behaviour. Some use Constructivism to identify how identity shapes the state's interests and then turn to rational choice for understanding strategic behaviour. In this view, the American identity shapes **national interests**, and then the structure of the **international system** informs its strategies for pursuing those interests. Yet some scholars go further and argue that the cultural context shapes not only identities and interests of actors but also the very strategies they can use as they pursue their interests. In other words, while 'game' metaphors are most closely associated with **game theory** and rational choice, some Constructivists also argue that the normative structure shapes important features of the game, including the identity of the players and the strategies that are appropriate. Not all is fair in love, war, or any other social endeavour. For decades Arab nationalism shaped the identities and interests of Arab states, contained norms that guided how Arab leaders could play the game of Arab politics, and encouraged Arab leaders to draw from the symbols of Arab politics to try to manoeuvre around their Arab rivals and further their own interests. How Arab leaders played out their regional games was structured by the norms of Arab politics. They had very intense rivalries, and as they vied for prestige and status they frequently accused each other of being a traitor to the Arab nation or harming the cause of Arabism. But rarely did they use military force. Until the late 1970s the idea of relations with Israel was a virtual 'taboo', violated by Egyptian Anwar Sadat's trip to Jerusalem in 1977 and separate peace treaty in 1979. Arab states did not respond through military action but rather by evicting Egypt from the Arab League, and then Sadat paid the ultimate price for his heresy when he was assassinated in 1981.

In general, these examples of the connections between Constructivism and rational choice remind us that we should be open to and utilize as many approaches as possible as we try to enrich our understanding of how the world works.

Key Points

- Constructivists are concerned with human consciousness, treat ideas as structural factors, consider the dynamic relationship between ideas and material forces as a consequence of how actors interpret their material reality, and are interested in how agents produce structures and how structures produce agents.
- Knowledge shapes how actors interpret and construct their social reality.
- The normative structure shapes the identity and interests of actors such as states.
- Social facts such as sovereignty and human rights exist because of human agreement, while brute facts such as mountains are independent of such agreements.
- Social rules are regulative, regulating already existing activities, and constitutive, making possible and defining those very activities.

- Social construction denaturalizes what is taken for granted, asks questions about the origins of what is now accepted as a fact of life and considers the alternative pathways that might have produced and can produce alternative worlds.
- Power can be understood not only as the ability of one actor to get another actor to do what she would not do otherwise but also as the production of identities and interests that limit the ability of actors to control their fate.
- Although the meanings that actors bring to their activities are shaped by the underlying culture, meanings are not always fixed and the fixing of meaning is a central feature of politics.
- Although Constructivism and rational choice are generally viewed as competing approaches, at times they can be combined to deepen our understanding of global politics.

Constructivism and global change

Constructivism's focus on how the world hangs together, how normative structures construct the identities and interests of actors, and how actors are rule-following, might seem ideal for explaining why things stay the same but useless for explaining why things change. This is hardly true. Constructivism claims that what exists need not have and need not—inviting us to think of alternative worlds and the conditions that make them more or less possible. Indeed, Constructivism scolded neo-realism and neo-liberal Institutionalism for their failure to explain contemporary global transformations. The Peace of Westphalia helped to establish sovereignty and the norm of non-interference, but in recent decades various processes have worked against the principle of non-interference and suggested how state sovereignty is conditional on how states treat their populations. **World orders** are created and sustained not only by great power preferences but also by changing understandings of what constitutes a legitimate **international order**. Until the Second World War the idea of a world organized around **empires** was hardly illegitimate; now it is. One of the today's most pressing and impressive issues concerning global change is the **end of history** and the apparent homogenization of world politics—that is, the tendency of states to organize their domestic and international lives in similar ways and the growing acceptance of certain international norms for defining the good life and how to get there. Below I

explore two concepts that figure centrally in such discussions: diffusion and the **internationalization** and **institutionalization of norms**.

A central theme in any discussion of global change is diffusion. Stories about **diffusion** concern how particular models, practices, norms, strategies, or beliefs spread within a population. Constructivists have highlighted two important issues. One is **institutional isomorphism**, which observes that those organizations that share the same environment will, over time, resemble each other. In other words, if once there was a diversity of models within the population, over time that diversity yields to conformity and convergence around a single model. There used to be various ways to organize state structures, economic activity, free trade agreements, and on and on. But now the world is organized around the **nation-state**, states favour democratic forms of governance and market economies, and most international organizations now have a multilateral form. It is possible that the reason for this convergence is because states now realize that some institutions are just superior to others. An additional possibility is that states are looking alike because they want acceptance, legitimacy, and status. For instance, one explanation for the recent wave of democratization and elections is that states now accept that democratic elections are a more efficient and superior way to organize politics; it also could be, though, that lots of states have

decided to turn democratic and run elections not because they were persuaded that it would be more efficient but rather because they wanted to be viewed as part of the 'modern world' and receive the benefits associated with being a legitimate state.

How do things diffuse? Why are they accepted in new places? One factor is coercion. Colonialism and great power imposition figured centrally in the spread of capitalism. Another factor is strategic competition. Heated rivals are likely to adopt similar weapons systems in order to try to stay even on the military battlefield. States will also adopt similar ideas and organizations for at least four other reasons. Formal and informal pressures can cause states to adopt similar ideas because doing so will bring them needed resources. States want resources and in order to attract these resources they will adopt and reform their institutions in order to signal to various communities that they are part of the club and are utilizing 'modern' techniques. In other words, they value these new institutions not because they truly believe that they are superior, but rather because they are symbols that will attract resources. Eastern European countries seeking entry into the European Union adopted various reforms not only because they believe that they are superior but also because they are the price of admission.

Also, during periods of uncertainty when states are unsure of how to address existing challenges, they are likely to adopt those models that are perceived as successful or legitimate. Political candidates in newly democratizing countries reorganize their party and campaign organizations in order to increase their prospects of electoral victory. Towards that end, they draw from those models of success, largely from the American context, not necessarily because they have evidence that the American campaign model is truly better, but rather because it appears modern, sophisticated, and superior. Furthermore, frequently states adopt particular models because of their symbolic standing. Many **Third World** governments have acquired very expensive weapons systems that have very little military value because they convey to others that they are sophisticates and are a part of the 'club'. Iran's nuclear ambitions might owe to its desire for regional dominance, but it also could be that it wants to own this ultimate status symbol. Finally, professional associations and expert communities also diffuse organizational models. Most associations have established techniques, codes of conduct, and methodologies for determining how to confront challenges in their area of expertise. They learn these techniques through informal interactions and in formal settings such as in universities. Once these standards are established, they become the 'industry standard' and the accepted way of addressing problems in an area. Part of the job of professional associations and expert **networks** is to communicate these standards to others; doing so makes them agents of diffusion. Economists, lawyers, military officials, arms control experts, and others diffuse practices, standards, and models through networks and associations. If the American way of campaigning is becoming increasingly accepted around the world it is in part due to a new class of professional campaign consultants that have converged around a set of accepted techniques and are ready to peddle their wares to willing customers.

Discussions of diffusion also draw attention to the internationalization of norms. Norms are standards of appropriate behaviour for actors with a given identity. Norms of humanitarianism, **citizenship**, military intervention, human rights, trade, arms control, and the environment not only regulate what states do, they also can be connected to their identities and thus expressive of how they define themselves and their interests. Norms not only constrain behaviour because actors are worried about the costs of doing so; they also constrain behaviour because they are connected to a sense of self. 'Civilized' states are expected to avoid settling their difference through violence not because war might not pay but rather because it violates how 'civilized' states are expected to act. Human rights activists aspire to reduce human rights are violations not only by 'naming and shaming' those who violate these rights, but also by persuading potential violators that human rights are tied to their identity as a modern, responsible state. The domestic debates on the USA's treatment of 'enemy combatants' concerned not only whether torture worked, but also whether it is a legitimate practice for civilized states.

These expectations of what constitutes proper behaviour can diffuse across the population to the point that they are taken for granted. Norms, therefore, do not simply erupt but rather evolve through a political process. A central issue, therefore, is the internationalization and institutionalization of norms, or what is now called the **life cycle of norms** (see Box 9.3). Although many international norms have a taken-for-granted quality, they have to come from somewhere and their path to acceptance is

Box 9.3 Finnemore and Sikkink on the three stages of the life-cycle of norms

Norm emergence

This stage is typified by persuasion by norm entrepreneurs [who] attempt to convince a critical mass of states . . . to embrace new norms. 'Norm entrepreneurs call attention to issues or even "create" issues by using language that names, interprets, and dramatizes them.' Norm entrepreneurs attempt to establish 'frames . . . that resonate with broader public understandings and are adopted as new ways of talking about and understanding issues'. Norm entrepreneurs need a launching pad to promote their norms, and will frequently work from non-governmental organizations and with international organizations and states. 'In most cases for an emergent norm to reach a threshold and move toward the second stage, it must become institutionalized in specific sets of international rules and organizations. . . . After norm entrepreneurs have persuaded a critical mass of states to become norm leaders and adopt new norms . . . the norm reaches a critical threshold or tipping point.'

Norm cascade

'The second stage is characterized more by a dynamic of imitation as the norm leaders attempt to socialize other states to become norm followers. The exact motivation for this second stage, where the norm "cascades" through the rest of the population (in this case, states), may vary, but . . . a combination of pressure for conformity, desire to enhance international legitimation, and the desire of state leaders to enhance their self-esteem facilitate norm cascades.' These processes can be likened to socialization. 'To the degree that states and state elites fashion a political self or identity in relationship to the international community the concept of socialization suggests that the cumulative effect of many countries in a region adopting new norms' is akin to peer pressure.

Norm internalization

The third stage is 'norm internalization. . . . Norms acquire a taken-for-granted quality and are no longer a matter of . . . debate' and thus are automatically honoured. 'For example, few people today discuss whether women should be allowed to vote, whether slavery is useful, or whether medical personnel should be granted immunity during war.'

(Adapted from Finnemore and Sikkink 1998: 894–905)

nearly always rough and rocky. Although most states now recognize that prisoners of war have certain rights and cannot be subjected to summary executions on the battlefield, this was not always the case. These rights originated with the emergence of international humanitarian law in the late nineteenth century, and then slowly spread and became increasingly accepted over the next several decades in response to considerable debate regarding how to minimize the horrors of war. Now most states accept that prisoners of war have rights, even if those rights are not fully observed. Several decades ago many scholars and jurists objected to the very idea of humanitarian intervention because it violated sovereignty's principle of interference and allowed great powers to try to become sheep in wolf's clothing. Over the last fifteen years, though, there is a growing acceptance of **humanitarian intervention** and a **responsibility to protect**—when states are unable or unwilling to protect their citizens, then the international community inherits that responsibility. This revolutionary concept emerged through fits and starts and in response to tragedies such as Rwanda, and was propelled by various states and humanitarian organizations.

Among the various consequences of institutional isomorphism and the internationalization of norms, three are noteworthy. There used to be a myriad of ways to organize human activities, but that diversity has slowly but impressively yielded to conformity. Yet just because states look alike does not mean that they act alike. After all, many states gravitate towards particular models not because they really think that the model is better but in order to improve their legitimacy. These states, then, can be expected to act in ways that are inconsistent with the expectations of the model. For instance, if governments are adopting democratic forms of governance and elections solely for symbolic reasons, then we should expect the presence of democratic institutions to exist alongside authoritarian and illiberal practices. There also is a deepening sense of an 'international community'. The internationalization of norms suggests that actors are increasingly accepting standards of behaviour because they are connected to a sense of self that is tied to the international community. These norms, in other words, are bound up with the values of the international community. To the extent that these values are sh+ared, then it becomes possible to speak of an international community. A third consequence is **socialization,** the process by which states and their societies take on the identities and interests of the dominant peer group in international society. Diffusion rarely goes from the Third World to the West; instead, it travels from the West to the Third World.

The international society of states began as a European society and then expanded outward; the internationalization of this society and its norms shaped the identities and foreign policy practices of new members. In other words, the convergence on similar models, the internationalization of norms, and the possible emergence of an international community should not be mistaken for a world without power and hierarchy. In general, the Constructivist concern with international diffusion and the internationalization of norms touches centrally on global change because of the interest in a world in motion and transformation.

Key Points

- The recognition that the world is socially constructed means that Constructivists can investigate global change and transformation.
- A key issue in any study of global change is diffusion, captured by the concern with institutional isomorphism and the life-cycle of norms.
- Although diffusion sometimes occurs because of the view that the model is superior, frequently actors adopt a model either because of external pressures or its symbolic legitimacy.
- Institutional isomorphism and the internationalization of norms raise issues of growing homogeneity in world politics, a deepening international community, and socialization processes.

Conclusion

This chapter surveyed the global-historical, intellectual, and disciplinary forces that made Constructivism a particularly attractive way for thinking about international politics. It invites students to imagine the continuities and transformations of international politics. It explores why the world is organized in the way it is, considers the different factors that shape the durable forms of world politics, and seeks alternative worlds. In doing so, it challenges received wisdoms and opens up new lines of inquiry. Although many in the discipline treated as strange the claim that ideas can shape how the world works, in fact what is strange is a view of a world devoid of ideas. After all, is it even possible to imagine such a world? What would it look like? Is it even possible to imagine a world driven only by materialist forces? What would it look like?

Constructivism challenged the discipline's mainstream on its own terms and on issues that were at the heart of its research agenda. Its success has sometimes led to the false impression that Constructivism is a substantive theory and not the social theory that it is. As such, it is much more and much less than meets they eye. It is much less because it is not properly a theory that can be viewed as a rival to many of the theories in this volume. It offers no predictions about enduring regularities or tendencies in world politics. Instead, it suggests how to investigate them. Consequently, it is much more than meets the eye because it offers alternative ways of thinking about a range of concepts and issues, including power, alliance formation, war termination and military intervention, the liberal peace, and international organizations.

What of the future of Constructivism? It depends on which version of Constructivism we are discussing. Constructivists generally accept certain commitments, including Idealism, holism, and an interest in the relationship between agents and structures. They also accept certain basic claims, such as the social construction of reality, the existence and importance of social facts, the constitution of actors' identities, interests, and subjectivities, and the importance of recovering the meaning actors give to their activities. But they also exhibit tremendous differences. Although sometimes these disagreements can appear to derive from academic posturing, the search for status, and the narcissism of minor differences, in fact there also can be much at stake, as suggested in Ch.10. These differences will exist as long as Constructivism exists. This is healthy because it will guard against complacency and enrich our understanding of the world.

❓ Questions

1 What were the silences of neo-realism and neo-liberal Institutionalism?

2 How did International Relations scholars use critical and sociological theory to address important issues overlooked by neo-realism and neo-liberal Institutionalism?

3 What is the core of Constructivism?

4 Do you find Constructivism a useful approach for thinking about world politics?

5 Do you agree that we should try to understand how actors make meaningful their behaviour in world politics? Or is it enough to examine behaviour?

6 How are meanings fixed in world politics?

7 Do you think that Constructivism adds richness and complexity at the expense of our desire to understand patterns in world politics?

8 What sort of relationship can exist between rational choice and Constructivism?

9 What do you think are the core issues for the study of global change and how does Constructivism help you address those issues? Alternatively, how does a Constructivist framework help you identify new issues that you had not previously considered?

10 What sorts of question are opened up by thinking about socialization in world politics?

11 How does the concept of diffusion help you understand why and how the world has changed?

➲ Guide to further reading

Adler, E. (2003), 'Constructivism', in W. Carlneas, B. Simmons, and T. Risse (eds), *Handbook of International Relations* (Thousand Oaks, Cal.: Sage). A terrific overview of the origins and fundamentals of Constructivism and its relationship to existing theories of international politics.

Barnett, M. (1998), *Dialogues in Arab Politics: Negotiations in Regional Order* (New York: Columbia University Press). Examines how Arab leaders played the game of Arab politics and, in doing so, transformed the very nature of Arab politics. An example of how Constructivists might think about how strategic action is shaped by a normative structure.

Carpenter, C. (2003), ' "Women and Children First": Gender, Norms, and Humanitarian Evacuation in the Balkans 1991–1995', *International Organization*, 57(4) (Fall): 661–94.

Fearon, J., and Wendt, A. (2003), 'Rationalism vs. Constructivism', in W. Carlneas, B. Simmons, and T. Risse (eds), *Handbook of International Relations* (Thousand Oaks, Cal.: Sage). A very useful exposition of how rational choice and Constructivism overlap, written by two of the leading proponents of each approach in international relations.

Finnemore, M., and Sikkink, K. (1999), 'International Norms and Political Change', in P. Katzenstein *et al.* (eds), *Explorations and Controversies in World Politics* (Cambridge, Mass.: MIT Press).

—— ——(2001), 'Taking Stock: The Constructivist Research Program in International Relations and Comparative Politics', *Annual Review of Political Science*, 4: 391–416. A highly insightful account of Constructivism's insights and future directions of research.

Hollis, M., and Smith, S. (1990), *Explaining and Understanding International Relations* (New York: Oxford University Press). Explains in an exceptionally clear fashion the contrast between a conception of world politics driven by self-interested action and a conception informed by rules and interpretative methods.

Katzenstein, P. (ed.) (1996), *The Culture of National Security* (New York: Columbia University Press). An edited collection that clearly identified why we need to examine how identities and norms shape state interests, and explored those claims in a range of critical security areas.

Wendt, A. (1999), *A Social Theory of International Politics* (Cambridge: Cambridge University Press). The seminal text that explains the central elements and dissects the important controversies of Constructivism.

Online Resource Centre

 Visit the Online Resource Centre that accompanies this book to access more learning resources on this chapter topic at www.oxfordtextbooks.co.uk/uk/orc/baylis_smith4e/

Chapter 10

Alternative approaches to international theory

STEVE SMITH · PATRICIA OWENS

- Introduction ··· 176
- Explanatory/constitutive theories and foundational/anti-foundational theories ············· 176
- Historical sociology ·· 179
- Feminist theory ··· 181
- Post-modernism ·· 185
- Post-colonialism ·· 187
- Conclusion ·· 190

Reader's Guide

Following from the preceding five chapters, which very broadly might be described as the new 'mainstream' theories of international relations, this chapter outlines other important contributions to thinking about world politics. The main theories dealt with are: historical sociology, feminist theory, post-modernism, and post-colonialism. The chapter begins by establishing some important preliminary distinctions between theories that are explanatory and foundationalist (like Realism, Liberalism, and most of all Marxism) and those that are constitutive and non-foundationalist. Explanatory/foundationalist theories are termed rationalist. Constitutive/non-foundationalist theories have developed in two broad versions, one is known as Social Constructivism (dealt with in Ch. 9) and the other group is termed for convenience here 'alternative' approaches. The latter theories are the main concern of this chapter. Although both Social Constructivism and these alternative approaches reject the main assumptions of rationalist theories and see theories as constituting the social world, the alternative approaches are more critical of the mainstream and move beyond it in more far-reaching ways.

Introduction

The previous five chapters have given you overviews of the four most dominant theories of international relations (Realism, Liberalism, Marxism, and Constructivism) and the contemporary debate between the two leading mainstream theories, **neo-realism** and **neo-liberalism**. With the exception of Social Constructivism, which is relatively new, these approaches have governed the discipline for the last fifty years, and the debate between their adherents has defined the areas of disagreement in international theory. The **inter-paradigm debate** between Realism, Liberalism, and Marxism has been extremely influential, with generations of students told that the debate between the various elements effectively exhausts the kinds of questions that can be asked about international relations. However, the inter-paradigm debate by no means covers the range of issues that any contemporary theory of world politics needs to deal with. Instead, this 'debate' ends up being a rather conservative political move because it gives the impression of open-mindedness and intellectual pluralism whereas, in fact, Realism has tended to dominate. Indeed, one factor supporting the dominance of Realism has been that it seems to portray the world as commonsensically understood. Thus alternative views can be dismissed as **value-laden**, to be negatively compared with the so-called **objectivity** of Realism.

In the last decade or so this picture has changed dramatically in two ways. First, there has been a major debate between neo-realism and neo-liberalism (see Ch.7), known as the **neo-neo** debate. The second change has been the appearance of a range of new approaches developed to understand world politics. In part this reflects a changing world. The end of the **cold war** system signifi-cantly reduced the creditability of Realism, especially in its neo-realist guise where the stability of the bipolar system was seen as a continuing feature of world politics. As that **bipolarity** dramatically disappeared, so too did the explanatory power of the theory that most relied on it. But this was not by any means the only reason for the rise of new approaches. There are three other obvious reasons. First, Realism's dominance was called into question by a resurgence of its historical main competitor, Liberalism, in the form of neo-liberal Institutionalism, as discussed in Ch. 7, with this debate now comprising the mainstream of the discipline. Second, there were other changes under way in world politics that made the **development** of new approaches important, such as the kinds of features discussed under the heading **globalization**. Whatever the explanatory power of Realism, it did not seem very good at dealing with issues such as the rise of **non-state actors**, identity politics, transnational **social movements**, and information technology. In short, new approaches were needed to explain these features of world politics, even if Realism still claimed to be good at dealing with power politics. Third, there were major developments under way in other academic disciplines in the social sciences, but also in the philosophy of social science, that attacked the underlying methodological (i.e. how to undertake study) assumption of Realism, a position known as **positivism** (discussed below). In its place a whole host of alternative ways of thinking about the social sciences were being proposed, and International Relations simply caught up. Since then, a series of alternative approaches have been proposed as more relevant to world politics in the twenty-first century.

Explanatory/constitutive theories and foundational/anti-foundational theories

In order to understand the current situation with regard to international theory it is important to introduce two distinctions. The terms can be a little unsettling, but they are merely convenient words for discussing fairly straightforward ideas. The first distinction is between **explanatory** and **constitutive theory**. An explanatory theory is one that sees the world as something external to our theories of it. In contrast, a constitutive theory is one

that thinks our theories actually help construct the world. This is actually a distinction adopted in both scientific and non-scientific disciplines. But a moments thought should make you realize why it is more appealing in the non-scientific world. In a very obvious way our theories about the world shape how we act, and thereby make those theories become self-confirming. For example, if we think that individuals are naturally aggressive, then we are likely to adopt a different posture towards them than if we think they are naturally peaceful. However, you should not regard this claim as self-evidently true, since it assumes that our ability to think and reason makes us able to determine our choices (i.e. that we have free will rather than having our 'choices' determined behind our backs). What if our human nature is such that we desire certain things 'naturally', and that our language and seemingly 'free choices' are simply our rationalizations for our needs? This is only the opening stage of a very complex but fascinating debate about what it is to be human (Hollis and Smith 1990). However, the upshot, whichever position you eventually adopt, is that there is a genuine debate between those theories that think of the social world as like the natural world, and those theories that see our language and concepts as helping create that reality. Theories claiming the natural and the social worlds are the same are known as **naturalist**.

In International Relations, the more structural Realist and Structuralist theories dealt with in Ch. 5 and Ch. 7 tend to be explanatory theories, which see the task of theory as being to report on a world that is external to our theories. Their concern is to uncover **regularities** in human behaviour and thereby explain the social world in much the same way as a natural scientist might explain the physical world. By contrast, nearly all the approaches developed in the last fifteen years or so tend to be constitutive theories, and interestingly the same is true of some Liberal thought. Here theory is not external to the things it is trying to explain, and instead may construct how we think about the world. Or, to put it another way, our theories define what we see as the external world. Thus the very concepts we use to think about the world help to make that world what it is. (Think about the concepts that matter in your own life, such as love, happiness, wealth, status, etc.).

The **foundational/anti-foundational** distinction refers to the simple-sounding issue of whether our beliefs about the world can be tested or evaluated against any neutral or objective procedures. This is a distinction central to the branch of the philosophy of social science known as **epistemology** (the study of how we can claim to know something). A foundationalist position is one that thinks that all truth claims (about some feature of the world) can be judged true or false. An anti-foundationalist thinks that truth claims cannot be so judged since there are never neutral grounds for so doing. Instead, each theory will define what counts as the facts and so there will be no neutral position available to determine between rival claims. Think, for example, of a Marxist and a Liberal arguing about the 'true' state of the economy, or a feminist and an Islamic Fundamentalist discussing the 'true' status of women. Foundationalists look for what are termed **metatheoretical** (or above any particular theory) grounds for choosing between truth claims. In contrast, anti-foundationalists think that there are no such positions available, and that believing there to be some is itself simply a reflection of an adherence to a particular view of epistemology.

In many senses most of the new approaches to international theory discussed later are much less wedded to foundationalism than were the traditional theories that comprised the inter-paradigm debate. Thus, **post-modernism**, **post-colonialism**, and some **feminist theory** would tend towards anti-foundationalism. However, the **neo-neo debate**, some **historical sociology**, and some **critical theory** would tend towards foundationalism. Interestingly, **Social Constructivism** wishes to portray itself as occupying the middle ground (see Ch.9). On the whole, and as a rough guide, explanatory theories tend to be foundational while constitutive theories tend to be anti-foundational. The point at this stage is not to construct some checklist, nor to get you thinking yet about the differences. Rather, we want to draw your attention to the role that these assumptions about the nature of knowledge have on the theories that we are going to discuss. The central point at this stage is that the two distinctions mentioned in this section were never really discussed in the literature of International Relations until very recently. The last fifteen years has seen these underlying assumptions brought more into the open and the most important effect of this has been to undermine Realism's claim to be delivering *the* truth.

The distinctions between explanatory and constitutive theories and between foundational and anti-foundational theories have been brought into the open because of a massively important reversal in the way in which social scientists have thought about their ways of constructing

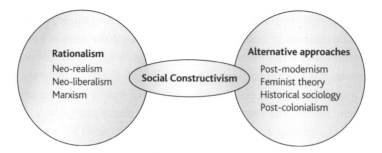

Figure 10.1 International theory at the beginning of the twenty-first century

knowledge. Until the late 1980s, most social scientists in International Relations tended to be **positivists**. But since then positivism has been under attack. Positivism is best defined as a view of how to create knowledge that relies on four main assumptions. The first is a belief in the unity of science, that is that roughly the same methodologies apply in both the scientific and non-scientific worlds. Second, there is a distinction between facts and values, with facts being neutral between theories. Third, that the social world, like the natural one, has regularities, and that these can be 'discovered' by our theories in much the same way as a scientist does in looking for the regularities in nature. Finally, that the way to determine the truth of statements is by appeal to these neutral facts; this is known as an empiricist epistemology.

It is the rejection of these assumptions that has characterized the debate in international theory in the last twenty years or so. Yosef Lapid (1989) has termed this 'a post-positivist era'. In simple terms, traditional international theory was dominated by the four kinds of positivistic assumptions noted above. Since the late 1980s, the new approaches that have emerged have tended to question these same assumptions. The resulting map of international theory at the beginning of the twenty-first century has three main features. First, the continuing dominance of the three theories that together made up the inter-paradigm debate. This can be termed the **rationalist** position, and is epitomized by the neo-neo debate. Second, the emergence of non-positivistic theories, which together can be termed alternative approaches, and epitomized by much critical theory (discussed in Ch.8), historical sociology, much feminist work, post-modernism, and post-colonialism, to be discussed below. And third, the development of an approach that tries to speak to both rationalist and alternative approaches known as Social Constructivism. Figure 10.1 illustrates the resulting configuration of the theories today.

Note that this is a very rough representation of how the various theories can be categorized. It is misleading in some respects since, as the previous five chapters have shown, there are quite different versions of the main theories and some of these are less rationalistic than others. Moreover, critical theory can seem like quite a radical departure from the mainstream. Similarly, some of the approaches classified as 'alternative' in this chapter are markedly less so than others. For example, work in historical sociology often adopts similar theoretical methods to rationalist approaches, though this is not always the case. Because historical sociology tends to reject the central unit of rationalism in IR, the state, and is compatible with much post-positivism we discuss it in this chapter. In other words, the classifications are broadly illustrative of the theoretical landscape, and are best considered a useful starting point for thinking about the differences between theories. As you learn more about them you will see how rough and ready a picture this is, but it is as good a categorization as any other.

Key Points

- Theories can be distinguished according to whether they are explanatory or constitutive and whether they are foundational or anti-foundational. As a rough guide, explanatory theories tend to be foundational and constitutive theories tend to be anti-foundational.
- The three main theories comprising the inter-paradigm debate were based on a set of positivist assumptions.
- Since the late 1980s there has been a rejection of positivism.
- The current theoretical situation is one in which there are three main positions: first, rationalist theories that are essentially the latest versions of the Realist and Liberal theories; second, alternative theories that are post-positivist; and third, Social Constructivist theories that try to bridge the gap.
- Alternative approaches at once differ considerably from one another, and at the same time overlap in some important ways. One thing that they do share is a rejection of the core assumptions of rationalist theories.

Historical sociology

Just as critical theory (see Ch.8) questions the state and refuses to see it as some kind of given in world politics, so does historical sociology. Indeed, the main theme of this field is the way in which societies develop through history. It is concerned with the underlying **structures** that shape the **institutions** and organizations into which human society is arranged, including violence, economy, and **gender** (Hall 1992; Skocpol 1992). Historical sociology has a long history. The first wave, which was a response to the great events of the eighteenth century—the American and French revolutions, the processes of industrialization, and **nation** building—ran until the 1920s (D. Smith 1991). The second wave has been of particular interest to international theory, because the key writers, Michael Mann (1986, 1993), Theda Skocpol (1979, 1984), Immanuel Wallerstein (1974, 1984), Charles Tilly (1981, 1990), John Hall (1985, 1994), and Martin Shaw (1984, 2003) have all to various degrees focused their sociological analyses on the relationship between the domestic and the international (Hobden 1998). Tilly has neatly summarized this interest with the statement that 'states made war but war made the state'. In short, the central feature of historical sociology has been an interest in how the structures that we take for granted (as 'natural') are the products of a set of complex social processes.

Thus, whereas neo-realism takes the state as a given, historical sociology asks how specific kinds of states have been produced by the various forces at work in domestic and international societies. Historical sociologists show just how complex the state is as an organization, thereby undermining the rather simple view of the state found in neo-realism. They also fundamentally undermine the notion that a state is a state is a state through time and across the world. States differ—they are not functionally similar as neo-realism portrays them. Furthermore, historical sociologists show that there can be no simple distinction between international and domestic societies. They are inevitably interlinked. There is no such thing as an **international system**, as suggested by Waltz, which is self-contained and thereby able to exert decisive influence on the behaviour of states. Finally, historical sociology shows that international and domestic forces create the state, and that the international is itself a determinant of the nature of the state (Shaw 2000; Hobden and Hobson 2002). This claim, of course, looks particularly relevant to the debate on globalization, since one of its dominant themes is that the international economic system places demands on states such that only certain kinds of states can prosper.

Charles Tilly's work is particularly interesting because it is a clear example of the complexity of the state as an entity. In his 1990 book, *Coercion, Capital and European States, AD 900–1990*, Tilly poses the following question: 'What accounts for the great variation over time and space in the kinds of states that have prevailed in **Europe** since AD 990, and why did European states eventually converge on different variants of the national state?' (1990: 5). The answer he gives is that the national state eventually dominated because of its role in fighting wars. Distinguishing between capital-intensive and coercion-intensive **regimes** (or economic power-based and military power-based systems), Tilly notes that three types of state resulted from the combinations of these forms of power: tribute-making **empires**, systems of fragmented **sovereignty** (city-states), and national states. These states were the result of the different class structures that resulted from the concentrations of capital and coercion. Broadly speaking, coercion-intensive regimes had fewer cities and more agricultural class systems than did capital-intensive systems, which led to the development of classes representing commercial and trading interests. Where capital accumulation was high relative to the ability of the state to coerce its citizens, city-states developed. On the other hand, where there was coercion but not capital accumulation, then tribute-making empires developed. As Dennis Smith notes (1991: 83), each of these is a form of indirect rule, requiring the ruler to rely on the **cooperation** of relatively autonomous local powers. But with the rise in the scale of war, the result was that national states started to acquire a decisive advantage over the other kinds of state organizations. This was because national states could afford large armies and could respond to the demands of the classes representing both agricultural and commercial interests.

Through about a 350-year period starting around 1500, national states became the norm, as they were the

only states that could afford the military means to fight the kind of large-scale wars that were occurring. States, in other words, became transformed by war. Tilly notes that the three types of state noted above all converged on one version of the state, so now that is seen as the norm. Yet, in contrast to neo-realism, Tilly notes that the state has not been of one form throughout its history. His work shows how different types of state have existed, all with different combinations of class structures and modes of operating. And, crucially, it is **war** that explains the convergence of these types of state into the national state form. War plays this central role because it is through preparing for war that states gain their powers as they have to build up an infrastructure of taxation, supply, and administration (McNeill 1982). The national state thus acquires more and more power over its population by its involvement in war, and therefore could dominate other state forms because they were more efficient than either tribute-gathering empires or city-states in this process.

The second example of historical sociology is the work of Michael Mann. Mann is involved in a four-volume study of the sources of social power dealing with the whole of human history. The first two volumes appeared in 1986 and 1993 and deal with the period up to 1914. This is an enormously ambitious project, aimed at show-ing just how states have taken the forms that they have. In other words, Mann studies the ways in which the various forms of power have combined in specific historical circumstances. He makes a major contribution to our thinking of how states have come into existence and about how they have related to the international political system. In this sense, his work is similar to that of Tilly, but the major innovation of Mann's work is that he has developed a sophisticated account of the forms of power that combine to form certain types of state. This is his IEMP model (Ideological, Economic, Military, and Political forms of power). This argument is summarized in Box 10.1 to give you an idea of its potential to shed light on how the state has taken the form that it has throughout history. It should make you think that the version of the state presented by neo-realism is very simple, but note also that there is some overlap between the focus of neo-realism on war and the focus of historical sociology on how states, classes, and war interact.

Historical sociology is a method and focus of research. It is possible, therefore, to be both a historical sociologist and a realist, and a critical theorist, and a feminist concerned with how gender and patriarchy have shaped states and societies (Miller 1998). It is also possible to be a postmodern historical sociologist; for example, Foucault's

---

Box 10.1 Mann's IEMP model of power organization

Mann differentiates between three aspects of power:

1 Between distributive power and collective power, where distributive power is the power of *a* over *b* (for *a* to acquire more distributive power, *b* must lose some), and collective power is the joint power of actors (where *a* and *b* can cooperate to exploit nature or another actor, *c*).
2 Power may be extensive or intensive. Extensive power can organize large numbers of people over far-flung territories. Intensive power mobilizes a high level of commitment from participants.
3 Power may be authoritative or diffused. Authoritative power comprises willed commands by an actor and conscious obedience by subordinates. It is found most typically in military and political power organizations. Diffused power is not directly commanded; it spreads in a relatively spontaneous, unconscious, and decentred way. People are constrained to act in different ways but not by command of any particular person or organization. Diffused power is found most typically in ideological and economic power organizations.

Mann argues that the most effective exercise of power combines all three elements. He argues that there are four sources of social power, which together may determine the overall structure of societies. The four are:

1 Ideological power derives from the human need to find ultimate meaning in life, to share norms and values, and to participate in aesthetic and ritual practices. Control over ideology brings general social power.
2 Economic power derives from the need to extract, transform, distribute, and consume the resources of nature. It is peculiarly powerful because it combines intensive cooperation with extensive circuits of distribution, exchange, and consumption. This provides a stable blend of intensive and extensive power and normally of authoritative and diffused power.
3 Military power is the social organization of physical force. It derives from the necessity of organized defence and the utility of aggression. Military power has both intensive and extensive aspects, and it can also organize people over large areas. Those who monopolize it can wield a degree of general social power.
4 Political power derives from the usefulness of territorial and centralized regulation. Political power means state power. It is essentially authoritative, commanded, and willed from a centre.

The struggle to control ideological, economic, military, and political power organizations provides the central drama of social development. Societies are structured primarily by entwined ideological, economic, military, and political power.

(Mann 1993: 6–10)

method of **genealogy** (see Box 10.3) has much in common with the concerns of the field (Dean 1994; Kendall and Wickham 1999; for a similar discussion of Hannah Arendt, see Owens 2007). Though Foucault is most famously a 'post-modern' theorist, there is no contradiction between drawing on his understanding of power and knowledge (discussed later) and approaching questions such as the organization of violence historically (Drake 2001).

Key Points

- Historical sociology has a long history. Its central focus is with how societies develop the forms that they do. It is basically a study of the interactions between states, classes, capitalism, and war.
- Charles Tilly looks at how the three main kinds of state forms that existed at the end of the Middle Ages eventually converged on one form, namely the national state. He argues that the decisive reason was the ability of the national state to fight wars.

- Michael Mann has developed a powerful model of the sources of state power, known as the IEMP model.
- The concerns of historical sociology are compatible with a number of the other approaches surveyed in this chapter including feminism and post-modernism.

Feminist theory

Chapter 15 details some of the main varieties of gender issues in world politics. Here we offer an overview of five main types of feminist theory, which have become common since the mid-1980s. These are liberal, socialist/Marxist, standpoint, post-modern, and post-colonial. Although this section is titled 'feminist theory', it is both a deliberate and misleading heading. It is deliberate in that it focuses on the socially constructed roles that 'women' occupy in world politics. It is misleading because this question has to be understood in the context of the construction of differences between women and men and contingent understandings of masculinity and **femininity**. In other words, the focus could more accurately be on 'gender' rather than on 'women' because the very categories of 'women' and 'men', and the concepts of masculinity and femininity, are highly contested in much feminist research. Similarly, the distinctions of liberal/socialist, etc., are slightly misleading for as you will discover below these categories do not exactly correspond to the diverse work of feminist scholars, especially in contemporary work in which elements from each 'type' are often integrated.

The term 'gender' usually refers to the social construction of difference between 'men' and 'women'. Some of the theories covered in this section assume natural and biological (e.g. sex) differences between men and women. Some of the approaches do not. What all of the most interesting work in this field does, however, is analyze how gender both affects world politics and is an effect of world politics; in other words, how different concepts (such as the state or sovereignty) are gendered and, in turn, how this gendering of concepts can have differential consequences for 'men' and 'women' (Steans 1998). It is important to note that feminists have always been interested in how understandings of gender affect men's lives as well as women. Indeed, there is also a field of research known as **men's studies** that models itself after, and was made possible by the emergence of, 'women's studies' (see Brittan 1989; Seidler 1989; Connell 1995; Carver 1996; for a feminist discussion see Zalewski and Parpart 1998).

Feminist theory in international relations originally developed in work on the politics of development and in peace research. But by the late 1980s a first wave of **feminism**, **liberal feminism**, was more forcefully posing the question of 'where are the women in world politics?' The meaning of 'liberal' in this context is decidedly NOT the same as the meaning of the term in Ch.6. In the context of feminism, the term starts from the notion that the key units of society are individuals, that these individuals are biologically determined as either men or women, and that these individuals possess specific rights and are equal. Thus, one strong argument of liberal feminism is that all rights should be granted to women equally with men. Here we can see how the **state** is gendered in that rights, such as voting rights, right to possess property, etc., were

predicated solely on the experiences and expectations of men—and, typically, a certain ethnic/racial class of men. Thus, taking women seriously made a difference to the standard view of world politics. Liberal feminists look at the ways in which women are excluded from power and prevented from playing a full part in political activity. They examine how women have been restricted to roles critically important for the functioning of things (such as reproductive economies) but that are not usually deemed to be important for theories of world politics.

To ask 'where are the women?' was at the time quite a radical political act, precisely because women were absent from the canonical texts of international relations, and thus appeared invisible. Writers such as **Cynthia Enloe** (1989, 1993, 2000) began from the premise that if we simply started to ask 'where are the women?' we would be able to see their presence and importance to world politics, as well as the ways in which their exclusion from world politics was presumed a 'natural' consequence of their biological or natural roles. After all, it was not that women were actually absent from world politics. Indeed, they played absolutely central roles, either as cheap factory labour, as prostitutes around military bases, or as the wives of diplomats. The point is that the conventional picture painted by traditional international theory both ignored these contributions and, if recognized, designated them as less important than the actions of states-'men'. Enloe demonstrated just how critically important were the activities of women to the functioning of the international economic and political systems. She illustrated exactly how crucial women and the conventional arrangements of 'women's and men's work' were to the continued functioning of international politics. Most specifically, Enloe documented how the concepts and practice of militarization influenced the lives and choices of men and women around the world. 'Militarization', she writes, 'is a step-by-step process by which a person or a thing gradually comes to be controlled by the military or comes to depend for its well-being on militaristic ideas' (2000: 3; also see Elshtain 1987; Elshtain and Tobias 1990). Enloe is an example of a scholar who begins from a liberal premise, that is that women and men should have equal rights and responsibilities in world politics, but draws upon socialist feminism to analyze the role of economic structures and standpoint feminism to highlight the unique and particular contributions of women.

A second strand of feminist theory is **socialist/Marxist feminism**, with its insistence on the role of material and primarily economic forces in determining the lives of women (see Ch.8). This approach is also sometimes known as materialist feminism (Hennessy and Ingraham 1997). For Marxist feminism, the cause of women's inequality is to be found in the capitalist system; overthrowing **capitalism** is the necessary route for the achievement of the equal treatment of women (Sargent 1981). Socialist feminism, noting that the oppression of women occurred in pre-capitalist societies, and continues in socialist societies, differs from Marxist feminism in that it introduces a second central material cause in determining women's unequal treatment, namely the patriarchal system of male dominance (Braun 1987; Gottlieb 1989). For Marxist feminists, then, capitalism is the primary oppressor, for socialist feminists it is capitalism plus patriarchy. For socialist/Marxist feminists the focus of a theory of world politics would be on the patterns by which the world capitalist system and the patriarchal system of power lead to women being systematically disadvantaged compared to men. The approach, therefore, has much in common with **post-colonial feminism**, which is discussed below; both are especially insightful when it comes to looking at the nature of the world-economy and its differential advantages and disadvantages that apply to women. But post-colonial feminism criticizes socialist/Marxist feminism for presuming the 'sameness' of patriarchy throughout the world and across time; rather than seeing the ways in which patriarchy both falsely presumes a universal experience of male domination and obscures the intersections of oppression of both men and women of colour.

The third version of feminist theory is **standpoint feminism** (Zalewski 1993a; Hartsock 1998). This variant emerged out of socialist feminism and the idea of a particular class system. The goal was to try to think about how women as a class might be able to 'envision' or see politics from a perspective denied to those who benefited from the subordination of women. Radical feminism was premised upon the unique qualities and individuality of women. Drawing upon socialist feminist interpretations of structure, standpoint feminism began to identify how the subordination of women, as a particular class, by virtue of their sex rather than economic standing (although the two were related) possessed a unqiue perspective— or standpoint—on world politics as a result of their subordination. This first insight was later developed to consider also how the knowledge, concepts, and categories of world politics were predicated upon a norm of

masculine behaviour and masculine experiences, and therefore represented not a universal standard—but a highly specific, particular standard. Standpoint feminists argue that seeing the world from the standpoint of women radically alters our understanding of that world. Standpoint feminism has undergone dramatic changes since its first articulation to incorporate the critiques of women of colour, who argued that, like socialism, it presumed that class **identity** (or in this case, sex identity) was the primary affiliation of all women and, accordingly, the single source of their oppression. The standpoint position also runs the risk of essentializing and fixing the views and nature of women, by saying that *this* is how women see the world (Gioseffi 2003). Nonetheless despite these dangers, standpoint feminism has been very influential in showing just how male-dominated the main theories of world politics are—in part because it is grounded in a simple premise. In an important early essay, for example, **J. Ann Tickner** (1988) reformulated the famous 'Six principles of political realism' developed by the 'godfather' of Realism, Hans Morgenthau. Tickner showed how the seemingly 'objective' **rules** of Morgenthau in fact reflect male values and definitions of reality, rather than female ones. As a riposte, Tickner reformulated these same rules taking women's (as opposed to men's) experiences as the starting point.

The fourth version is **post-modern feminism**, which develops the work of post-structuralism (especially that of Foucault and Derrida) to analyze specifically the concept of gender. Therefore, it might help to read the following in conjunction with the section on post-modernism below. Essentially, post-modern feminism criticizes the basic distinction between **sex** and 'gender' that earlier feminist theories found so useful in thinking about the roles/lives of men and women in world politics and in analyzing the gendered concepts of world politics itself. This distinction between sex and gender was useful because it allowed feminists to argue that the position of women and men in the world was not natural, but highly contingent and dependent upon the meaning given to biological differences. Yet, while extremely useful, the acceptance of the sex–gender distinction retained the binary opposition of male–female, and presumed that while gender was constructed, sex was wholly natural. However, as a number of scholars demonstrated, what we understood sex to be, what biological differences were, was heavily influenced by our understanding of gender—that is, that sex was

as constructed as gender (Fausto-Sterling 1992, 2000; Haraway 1989, 1991; Fox-Keller 1985; Longino 1990). Thus, as Helen M. Kinsella argues:

> it is an increasingly difficult position to defend that sex is prior to gender. The more one searches for the brute reality of sex, the more one finds that is gendered—that is, that the understanding of sex as a fact is itself a 'cultural conceit' (Haraway 1991: 197). In other words, this understanding of sex and sex difference is paradigmatic for a way of thinking about difference—as binary, as complementary, as given in nature. What are obscured, then, is the relations of power and politics which produce, distinguish, and regulate these concepts of 'gender' and of 'sex'.
>
> *(2003: 295)*

This does not mean that our biological bodies or 'the determination of sex' is not important. Rather it suggests that 'understanding this process leads to questions concerning how sex and gender operate to create the reality through which bodies materialize as sexed, as sexualized …as objects of knowledge and subjects of power' (Kinsella 2003: 296; also see Kinsella 2005a, 2005b, 2006).

In questioning the sex–gender distinction, in arguing that sex is not the origin of gender but an effect of gender, post-modern feminists introduced the concept 'gender performativity' (Butler 1990). Performativity is itself a tricky concept, and one that is easily misunderstood. However, a good place to begin is thinking about an act that is repeatable, yet alterable, and an act or a production that can only make sense within a larger social construct of agreed-upon **norms**. To think about gender performativity is to think about gender as not given or rooted in sex, but as something that is enacted and produced in social relations. In Judith Butler's famous phrase 'gender is a doing'. This is still a difficult concept in feminist theory, and it is highly contested as well. Nonetheless, the concept of gender performativity opens the sex–gender distinction to analysis while, simultaneously, displacing the subject of 'woman' from the centre of feminist theorizing and introducing the question of identity. For, rather than presuming women are the subjects of feminism, Butler asks how subjects are produced. To try to understand this process in world politics is to ask, to put it simply, how world politics produces certain kinds of 'soldiers', certain kinds of 'workers', certain kinds of 'states' that are not simply men or women, male or female, but complexly positioned states that seem, to us, completely natural.

Box 10.2 V. Spike Peterson on the global political economy and the sex/gender distinction

In her book on the global political economy, feminist V. Spike Peterson focuses upon two roughly simultaneous occurrences—the 'explosive growth in financial markets that shape business decision-making and flexible work arrangements' and the 'dramatic growth in informal and flexible work arrangements that shapes income generation and family well being'. She notes that 'informalization reaps higher profits for capital, depresses formal wages, disciplines all workers and through the isolation of informalized workers impedes collective resistance' while 'flexibilization *feminizes* the workforce: an increasing number of jobs require few skills and the most desirable workers are those deemed to be unorganized, docile, but reliable [and] available for part time and temporary work and willing to accept low wages'. Taken together, Spike Peterson argues, these developments render 'women, the poor, migrants, and recent immigrants the prototypical workers of the informal economy and arguably the future of all but elite workers worldwide'.

'It is here that the distinction between (positivist) sex and (constructivist) gender is crucial. In contrast to positivist notions of sex (as a biologically natural binary of male–female) gender is a systematic social construction that dichotomizes....As a social construct, gender is not "given" but learned (and therefore mutable). Most significantly, gender is not simply a trait of individuals, but an institutionalized structural feature of social life. . . . In short, gender is not simply an empirical category (referring to embodied men and women) but an analytical one, such that all social life is gendered.... [Gender] structures divisions of power and authority, which determine whose voices and experiences dominate culturally and coercively . . . and it structures divisions of labor which determine what counts as work, who does what kind of work and how different kinds of work are valued.'

(V. Spike Peterson 2003: 1, 111, 31, original italics)

The final form of feminism to mention is **post-colonial** feminism. It might help to read the following in conjunction with the discussion of post-colonialism in this chapter. Post-colonial feminists work at the intersection of class, race, and gender on a global scale, and especially analyzes the gendered effects of transnational culture and the unequal division of labour in the global political economy. From this perspective, it is not good enough to simply demand (as liberal feminists do) that men and women should have equal rights in a Western-style democracy. Such a move ignores the way in which poor women of colour in the global South remain subordinated by the global economic system; a system that liberal feminists were slow to challenge in a systematic way. In other words, the concerns and interests of feminists in the West and those in the rest of the world may not, therefore, so easily fit. Post-colonial feminists are also critical of Western, privileged academic intellectuals (men and women) who claim to be able to 'speak for' the oppressed, a form of cultural **imperialism** with important material effects. Perhaps the most influential post-colonial feminist scholar in this vein

is Gayatri Spivak, who combines Marxism, feminism, and deconstruction (discussed below) to interpret imperialism, past and present, and ongoing struggles for decolonization. In an influential essay 'Can the Subaltern Speak?', Spivak (1988) acknowledged the ambiguity of her own position in a privileged Western university and argued that elite scholars should be wary of homogenizing the 'subaltern' and try to speak *for* them in their 'true' voice (what she calls a form of 'epistemic violence'). The concept of the subaltern is discussed below, but it essentially refers to subordinated groups and in this instance to underprivileged women in the global South. In not recognizing the **heterogeneity** of experience and opinion of these diverse women, seemingly benevolent and well-meaning academics are at once patronizing in their desire to redeem them and unwittingly complicit in new forms of colonialism. Some post-modernists have also been criticized along similar lines for being too Western-centric and gender-blind. The combination of colonialism and **patriarchy** has made it doubly difficult for the resistance and agency of the subaltern to be heard and recognized.

Key Points

- Liberal feminism looks at the roles women play in world politics and asks why they are marginalized.
- Marxist/socialist feminists focus on the international capitalist system and patriarchy.
- Standpoint feminists want to correct the male dominance of our knowledge of the world.

- Post-modernist feminists are concerned with gender as opposed to the position of women as such. They look into the ways in which masculinity and femininity get constructed.
- Post-colonial feminists work at the intersection of gender, race, and class on a global scale.

Post-modernism

Post-modernism has been a particularly influential theoretical development throughout the social sciences in the last twenty-five years. It reached international theory in the mid-1980s, but can only be said to have really arrived in the past fifteen years. Nonetheless, it is probably as popular a theoretical approach as any discussed in this chapter and overlaps with a number of them. Part of the difficulty, however, is precisely defining post-modernism. This is in addition to the fact, of course, that there are substantial theoretical differences within its various strands. One useful definition is by Jean-François Lyotard: 'Simplifying to the extreme, I define post-modern as incredulity towards metanarratives' (1984: xxiv). Incredulity simply means scepticism; 'metanarrative' means any theory that asserts it has clear foundations for making knowledge claims and involves a **foundational** epistemology. Post-modernism is essentially concerned with **deconstructing** and distrusting any account of human life that claims to have direct access to 'the truth'. Thus, Marxism (including critical theory), Freudian psychoanalysis, and standpoint feminisms are all suspect from a post-modern perspective because they claim to have uncovered some fundamental truth about the world.

Three central themes in post-modern work are briefly discussed in this section: the **power–knowledge** relationship, the performative nature of identity, and various textual strategies used by post-modern thinkers. Work on the power–knowledge relationship has been most influenced by **Michel Foucault** (1977, 1978, 1984, 1994). (Note, however, that this relationship is also a key concern of **critical theory** (see Ch.8).) Foucault was opposed to the notion dominant in **rationalist** theories and **positivism** that knowledge is immune from the workings of power. Instead, Foucault argued that power in fact **produces knowledge.** All power requires knowledge and all knowledge relies on and reinforces existing power relations. Thus, there is no such thing as 'truth' existing outside power. To paraphrase Foucault, how can history have a truth if truth has a history? Truth is not something external to social settings but is instead part of them.

Accordingly, post-modernists look at what power relations are supported by 'truths' and knowledge practices.

Post-modern international theorists have used this insight to examine the 'truths' of international relations theory to see how the concepts and knowledge claims that dominate the discipline in fact are highly contingent on specific power relations. Three recent examples on the concept of sovereignty in the history and theory of international politics are by Cynthia Weber (1995), Jens Bartelson (1995), and Jenny Edkins *et al.* (1999). In each book, the concept of sovereignty is revealed to be both historically variable despite the attempts of mainstream scholars to imbue it artificially with a fixed meaning, and is itself caught up in the practice of sovereignty by producing the discourse about it.

How do post-modernists study history in the light of this relationship between power and knowledge? Foucault's approach is known as **genealogy**, which is to undertake a 'history of the present' and turn what we accept as natural into a question. Box 10.3 reproduces Richard Ashley's (1987) summary of this. The central message of genealogy is that various **regimes of truth** merely reflect the ways in which, through history, both power and truth develop together in a mutually sustaining relationship. The way to uncover the workings of power is to undertake a **detailed historical analysis** of how the practices and statements about the social world are only 'true' within specific **discourses.** Accordingly, post-modernism is concerned with how some discourses, and therefore some truths, dominate others in very concrete ways (see, for example, Edwards 1996). It is for this reason that post-modernists are opposed to metanarratives, since they imply that there are conditions for establishing the truth or falsity of knowledge claims that are not the product of any discourse, and thereby not the product of power.

A second theme is how post-modernists view identity not as a fixed 'thing' but as a **performative** site (you may wish to refer back to the discussion of post-modern feminism in the previous section). One way to approach this is to make a comparison with how identity is understood in mainstream Constructivism (see Ch.9). David Campbell has summarized the approach to identity by a leading Constructivist, Alexander Wendt:

Box 10.3 Foucault's notion of genealogy

'First, adopting a genealogical attitude involves a radical shift in one's analytical focus. It involves a shift away from an interest in uncovering the structures of history and towards an interest in understanding the movement and clashes of historical practices that would impose or resist structure.... [W]ith this shift ... social enquiry is increasingly disposed to find its focus in the posing of "how" questions, not "what" questions. How ... are structures of history produced, differentiated, reified, and transformed? How ... are fields of practice prised open, bounded and secured? How ... are regions of silence established?

Second, having refused any notion of universal truth or deep identities transcending differences, a genealogical attitude is disposed to comprehend all history, including the production of order, in terms of the endless power political clash of multiple wills. Only a single drama is ever staged in this non-place, the endlessly repeated play of dominations. Practices ... are to be understood to contain their own strategies, their own political technologies ... for the disciplining of plural historical practices in the production of historical modes of domination.

Third, a genealogical attitude disposes one to be especially attentive to the historical emergence, bounding, conquest, and administration of social spaces ... one might think, for example, of divisions of territory and populations among nation states ... one might also think of the separation of spheres of politics and economics, the distinction between high and low politics, the differentiation of public and private spaces, the line of demarcation between domestic and international, the disciplinary division between science and philosophy, the boundary between the social and the natural, or the separation of the normal and legitimate from the abnormal and criminal ... a genealogical

posture entails a readiness to approach a field of practice historically, as an historically emergent and always contested product of multiple practices ... as such, a field of practice ... is seen as a field of clashes, a battlefield ... one is supposed to look for the strategies, techniques, and rituals of power by which multiple themes, concepts, narratives, and practices are excluded, silenced, dispersed, recombined, or given new or reverse emphases, thereby to privilege some elements over others, impose boundaries, and discipline practice in a manner producing just this normalised division of practical space.

Fourth, what goes for the production and disciplining of social space goes also for the production and disciplining of subjects. From a genealogical standpoint there are no subjects, no fully formed identical egos, having an existence prior to practice and then implicated in power political struggles. Like fields of practice, subjects emerge in history ... as such, the subject is itself a site of political power contest and ceaselessly so.

Fifth, a genealogical posture does not sustain an interest in those noble enterprises—such as philosophy, religion, positive social science, or the utopian political crusade—that would embark on searches for the hidden essences, the universal truths, the profound insights into the secret identity that transcends difference ... from a genealogical standpoint ... they are instead resituated right on the surface of political life. They are seen as political practice intimately engaged in the interpretation, production, and normalisation of modes of imposed order, modes of domination. They are seen as means by which practices are disciplined and domination advances in history.'

(Ashley 1987: 409–11)

---

identity is said to come in two basic forms, one of which is 'those [deemed] intrinsic to an actor ...'. As an instance of this, [Wendt] claims that 'being democratic . . . is an intrinsic feature of the U.S. state relative to the structure of the international system.' It is not difficult to appreciate that a position that regards certain identities as 'intrinsic,' and includes among the[m] highly contestable concepts such as 'democracy', is reductionist in its representation of politics.

(1998: 279)

Campbell is suggesting that in mainstream Constructivism identity is regarded as a kind of object or substance that can be observed and measured. But for post-modernists, identity ought to be conceived as having 'no ontological status apart from the various acts which constitute its reality' (Campbell 1992: 9). In contrast, stressing the performative make-up of identity and the constitutive

nature of **political agency** reveals culture as 'a relational site for the politics of identity, rather than a substantive phenomen[on] in its own right' (Campbell 1998: 221; also see Campbell 1992, 1993). On this view, while appropriating some of the labels and terms of post-modernism, Constructivism does not really challenge the dominant discourse about identity.

A third post-modern theme concerns **textual strategies**. The main claim is that, following **Jacques Derrida** (1976), the very way in which we construct the social world is textual. For Derrida, the world is constituted like a text in the sense that interpreting the world reflects the concepts and structures of language, what he terms textual interplay. Derrida has two main ways of exposing these textual interplays, **deconstruction** and **double reading**. Deconstruction is based on the idea that seemingly stable and natural concepts and relations within language are in fact artificial constructs. They are arranged hierarchically

Box 10.4 Post-modern methodologies

In her book on discourse analysis and the Bosnian war, Lene Hansen directly challenges the assumption that post-modern and post-structuralist writing is not very good at empirical research and is vague as to its methodological choice.

'Many of the methodological questions that poststructuralist discourse analysis confronts are those that face all academic work: what should be the focus of analysis?, how should a research design be built around it?, and how is a body of material and data selected that facilitates a qualitatively and quantitatively reliable answer? Poststructuralism's focus on discourses as articulated in written and spoken text calls ... for particular attention to the methodology of reading (how identities are identified within foreign policy texts and how should the relationship between opposing discourses be studied?) and the methodology of textual selection (which forums and types of texts should be chosen and how many should be included?).'

(Hansen 2006: 2)

in the case of opposites in language where one term is always privileged over the other. Therefore, deconstruction is a way of showing how all theories and discourses rely on artificial stabilities produced by the use of seemingly objective and natural oppositions (such as public/private, good/bad, male/female, civilized/barbaric, right/wrong). Double reading is Derrida's way of showing how these stabilizations operate by subjecting the text to two readings. The first is a repetition of the dominant reading to show how it achieves its coherence. The second is to point out the internal tensions within a text that result from the use of seemingly natural stabilizations. The aim is not to come to a 'correct' or even 'one' reading of a text, but instead to show how there is always more than one reading.

In international theory, Richard Ashley (1988) has performed exactly such a double reading of the concept of anarchy by first providing a reading of anarchy according to the traditional IR literature. He then undertook a second reading showing how the seemingly natural opposition between anarchy and sovereignty in the first reading is in fact a false opposition. By disrupting the first reading, Ashley shows just how arbitrary is the 'truth' of the traditional assumptions made about anarchy and the kind of logic of state action that it requires. In a similar move, R. B. J. Walker (1993) looked at the construction of the tradition of Realism and shows how this is only possible by ignoring the major nuances and complexities within the thought of the key thinkers of this tradition, such as Machiavelli and Hobbes (also see Williams 2005, 2007). Post-modernism is taking apart the very concepts and methods of our thinking. It helps us think about the conditions under which we are able to theorize about world politics and for many is the most appropriate theory for a globalized world.

Key Points

- Lyotard defines post-modernism as incredulity towards meta-narratives, meaning that it denies the possibility of foundations for establishing the truth of statements existing outside of discourse.
- Foucault focuses on the power–knowledge relationship and sees the two as mutually constituted. It implies that there can be no truth outside of regimes of truth. How can history have a truth if truth has a history?
- Derrida argues that the world is like a text in that has to be interpreted. He looks at how texts are constructed, and proposes two main tools to enable us to see how arbitrary the seemingly 'natural' oppositions of language actually are. These are deconstruction and double reading.

Post-colonialism

Post-colonialism has been an important approach in cultural studies, literary theory, and anthropology for some time now, and has a long and distinguished pedigree. Founding texts arguably date back as far as the first oral histories and journals of freed African slaves in the United States (Gates 1987) and the political writing of W. E. B. DuBois, the leading African-American intellectual of his generation ([1903] 1993). Despite such ancestry, post-colonial scholarship has only recently begun to make an impact in the discipline of IR. This might seem especially odd given that the diverse subject matter of post-colonialism is intimately connected to the structure and processes of world politics—the transnational flows of peoples and identity constructions, issues of nation and nationalism, the effects of **cultural chauvinism**, how culture makes **imperialism** possible, and the cultures of

diasporas, to name just a few. A diaspora is the voluntary or forcible movement of peoples from their homelands into new regions.

Despite this overlap of subject mater, post-colonial approaches have been largely ignored in IR given its **state-centrism** and **positivism**. But this is now changing, not least because old disciplinary boundaries are breaking down, and since the attacks of 11 September 2001 scholars in International Relations are beginning to understand how the histories of the West and the global South have always been intertwined (Barkawi 2004, 2006). Post-colonialism, given its interdisciplinary origins, has made a significant contribution to the destruction of these disciplinary boundaries. And as a result, IR scholars have begun to see the world in new 'post-colonial' ways (Barkawi and Laffey 2006), also making use of both traditional and non-traditional sources for understanding the world such as literature, poetry, and film (Holden and Ruppel 2003).

As with the other approaches surveyed in this chapter, there is no one satisfactory definition of post-colonialism. For a start, the prefix 'post' might seem to imply the end of colonial practices. This would be a mistake. **Colonialism** is 'the political control, physical occupation, and domination of people over another people and their land for purposes of extraction and settlement to benefit the occupiers' (Crawford 2002: 131). In many ways, of course, this **juridical** practice of controlling territory and peoples has ended. And a number of post-colonial scholars have looked at how this major transformation altered the politics and society of both the metropole (e.g. Britain) and the former colony (e.g. India) (Hall 2002). But much post-colonial scholarship also highlights the important degree of **continuity** and **persistence** of colonial forms of power in contemporary world politics. For example, the level of economic and military control of Western interests in the global South is in many ways actually greater now than it was under direct control—a form of 'neo'-**colonialism** (Grovogui 1996; Duffield 2001). So although the era of formal colonial imposition by force of arms is apparently over (with the exception of the US occupation of Iraq in 2003–4), an important starting point for post-colonial scholarship is the issue of vast inequality on a global scale, the forms of power that make this systematic inequality possible, and the continued domination of **subaltern** peoples. The term 'subaltern' was originally used by **Gramsci** to describe the classes dominated under **hegemony** (see Ch.8). More recently, feminist post-colonial scholars such as **Gayatri Spivak** (1987, 1988, 1998) have used it to describe poor rural women in the global South. Spivak's work was briefly discussed in the feminist theory section above, but note again how she writes at the intersection of three literatures, **Marxism**, feminism, and post-modernism.

In fact, for many, the 'post' is actually more indicative of the **post-positivist** assumptions of the field. Most post-colonial scholars reject the assumptions of the explanatory and foundational theories described earlier in this chapter because they obscure how identities are not fixed and essential but are produced through essentially social processes and practices. 'The representation of [cultural] difference', Homi K. Bhabha writes, 'must not be hastily read as the reflection of pre-given ethnic or cultural traits . . . . The social articulation of difference . . . . is a complex, ongoing negotiation that seeks to authorize **cultural hybridities** that emerge in moments of historical transformation' (1994: 2). Hybridity is the idea that the identities of the colonized and colonizers are constantly in flux and mutually constituted. This is missed in positivist IR scholarship. Indeed, positivist assumptions, post-colonial writers claim, are not neutral in terms of race, gender, and class but have helped secure the domination of the Western world over the global South (Doty 1996). For example, in his influential book *Orientalism*, Edward Said argued that knowledge and material power could not be separated; Western culture (literally in the form of novels, etc.) was fundamentally entwined with imperialism and specifically the domination of the Islamic world of the Middle East (1979, 1993). Orientalism, for Said, refers to the hegemonic ways of representing 'the East' and its people from the beginning of 'Western' civilization. These **representations** have been absolutely crucial to the success of the economic and military domination of the West over the East and the construction of identities (be it race, class, or gender) in both.

Thus, an important claim of post-colonialism is that global hierarchies of subordination and control, past and present, are made possible through the social construction of racial, gendered, and class differences (Spivak 1987, 1998; Bhabha 1990). As other chapters in this volume suggest, International Relations has been slightly more comfortable with issues of class (Chs 8, 14, 27) and

'Unlike the Americans, the French and British . . . have had a long tradition of what I shall be calling Orientalism, a way of coming to terms with the Orient that is based on the Orient's special place in European Western Experience. The Orient is not only adjacent to Europe; it is also the place of Europe's greatest and richest and oldest colonies, the source of its civilizations and languages, its cultural contestant, and one of its deepest and most recurring images of the Other. In addition, the Orient has helped to define Europe (or the West) as its contrasting image, idea, personality, experience. Yet none of this Orient is merely imaginative. The Orient is an integral part of European material civilization and culture. Orientalism expresses and represents that part culturally even ideologically as a mode of discourse with supporting institutions, vocabulary, scholarship, imagery, doctrines, even colonial bureaucracies and colonial styles.'

(Said 1979:1)

gender (Ch.15). But the issue of race has been almost entirely ignored. This is even though race and **racism** continue to shape the contemporary theory and practice of world politics in far-reaching ways (Doty 1993; Castles 2000; Vitalis 2000; Persaud 2002). As an international institution, racism has historically been part of the emergence of humanitarian norms sanctioning obligations as a kind of colonial mission. But racism may also help explain the lack of 'humanitarian' action by the West in the 1994 Rwanda genocide. It has been an important factor in garnering support for the increased militarization of Western **immigration policies** (Simon 1998). And the unprecedented increase in US prison growth in recent years, which has overwhelmingly relied on racist assumptions about crime and conviction rates, is intimately connected to structural adjustments in the domestic economy associated with globalization (Gilmore 1998/9). In 1903, W. E. B. DuBois famously argued that the problem of the twentieth century would be the problem of the 'colour-line'. How will transnational racism continue to shape the twenty-first century?

It is absolutely crucial to bear in mind that for post-colonial scholars imperial and other forms of power really operate at the **intersection of gender**, **race**, and **class**. Consider, for example, how it is possible for nations in the West to perceive of themselves as **civilized** and their enemies as **barbaric**. As a way to justify imperial rule in India the British employed both racist and sexist assumptions in pointing to the 'uncivilized' way woman were being treated by Indian men. The enlightened (white) British males would bring civilization to (dark) India at the same time as they exploited the country economically. The issue at stake, however, was not so much the freedom of women in either Victorian Britain or India, as effective strategies of imperial rule (Metcalf 1997).

Post-colonial scholars do not only focus on issues of domination, though this surely is important. For example, Franz Fanon used **psychoanalytical** theory to suggest how colonialism and Western stereotypes warped the psyche of colonized subjects (1967*a*). But post-colonial scholars also look at how forms of power have been resisted in both violent and non-violent ways. Antonio Gramsci argued that even though powerful ideologies (hegemony) subordinated some classes of people there would always be counter-hegemonies of **resistance** (see Ch.8). In *The Wretched of the Earth* (1967*b*), Fanon, who was a revolutionary during the Algerian independence struggles against France, identified what he saw as the inherent violence in struggles for decolonization. But resistance has also taken more peaceful forms, with some arguing that post-colonial scholarship itself is an example of effective dissidence (Chowdhry and Nair 2002). Post-colonial scholars, therefore, also investigate the multiple and diverse forms of resistance to colonizing ideologies and offer strategies of empowerment and not only critique.

Key Points

- Given the state-centrism and positivism of IR, post-colonial approaches have been largely ignored until recently as old disciplinary boundaries are breaking down.
- Post-colonialism essentially focuses on the persistence of colonial forms of power in contemporary world politics, especially how the social construction of racial, gendered, and class differences uphold relations of power and subordination.
- Racism, in particular, continues to operate in both obvious and sometimes subtle ways in contemporary world politics but this is not captured in traditional approaches to international theory.
- Post-colonial research seeks to offer positive resources for resistance to imperial and other forms of power and not just critique.

Conclusion

This chapter has summarized the main alternative accounts of world politics to the dominant rationalist mainstream of international theory. The rationalist perspective, and particularly the **neo-neo synthesis**, as discussed in Ch.7, dominates the literature in the discipline of International Relations. That is the theoretical debate you will find in most of the journals, particularly in the USA. It focuses on the kinds of international political relations that concern many Western governments, particularly the debate about the future **security** structure of the international system and economic foreign policy. But do you think that it is wide enough a perspective to capture what are to you the most important features of world politics? You might think that we need theories that define the political realm rather more widely, to take in identity, ethnicity, and culture. You might also think that the alternative theoretical perspectives outlined here are actually even better than rationalist accounts for thinking about security and economics.

Alternative theories obviously differ enormously with regard to what they are 'alternative' about. They are really very different, but they were put together in one category because they all reject the central concerns of rationalism. Of course, these alternative theories do not cohere to one theoretical position in the way that the rationalist theories do. In some important ways, if you are a liberal feminist, then you do not necessarily agree with post-modernism. In short, some theories gathered under 'alternative' have a set of mutually exclusive assumptions and there is

no easy way to see the theories being combined. Some combinations are possible (a feminist post-modernism, or a critical historical sociology), but the one thing that is clearly correct is that the whole lot cannot be added together to form one theoretical agenda in the way that the neo-neo debate serves on the rationalist side. Moreover, some of these alternative theories do not have the same idea of how to construct knowledge as the rationalists, and therefore often reject the notion of coming up with testable hypotheses to compare with those provided by the rationalist position (see Keohane 1989a). This means that the prospect of a rationalist-post-modern debate, for example, is very low. The two sides simply see world politics in very different ways. You have to decide which side (or which subdivision) you think explains world politics most effectively.

There is no one theory of world politics that is right simply because it deals with the truth. What you should take from the theoretical positions outlined here is scepticism any time a theorist tells you that they are dealing with 'reality' or with 'how the world really is'. This is where the values of the theorist can be smuggled in through the back door. World politics is very complex and there are a variety of theories that try to account for different parts of that complexity. You should work out which theories both explain best the things you are concerned with and also offer you the chance to reflect on their own assumptions. One thing is for sure: there are enough theories to choose between and they paint very different pictures of world politics.

❓ Questions

1 Why do the post-positivist theories reject positivism?
2 What does it mean to say that the main difference between theories is whether they are explanatory or constitutive?
3 What is at stake in the debate between foundational and anti-foundational theories?
4 Why have alternative theoretical approaches to Realism become more popular in recent years?
5 What are the main implications of historical sociology for the study of world politics?
6 Which variant of feminist theory, or any combination of them, seems to capture most accurately the way 'gender makes the world go around' (Enloe)?

7 What might adopting a genealogical approach to the history of the present do for our understanding of world politics?

8 Why has International Relations ignored issues concerning race for so long? What does post-colonialism have to say on the subject?

9 What is it about some of the theories outlined in the chapter that makes them incompatible with others and why are some theories often used together?

10 Which of the main alternatives discussed in this chapter do you think offers the best account of world politics? Why?

Guide to further reading

Historical sociology

Hobden, S., and Hobson, J. M. (2002), *Historical Sociology of International Relations* (Cambridge: Cambridge University Press). An excellent survey of opinion on the connections between the two fields.

Mann, M. (1986, 1993), *The Sources of Social Power,* vols 1 and 2 (Cambridge: Cambridge University Press). Two monumental texts of historical sociology.

Feminist theory

Enloe, C. (1989), *Bananas, Beaches and Bases: Making Feminist Sense of International Politics* (London: Pandora). This was the classic text charting the way forward for feminist IR.

Post-modernism

Campbell, D. (1998), *Writing Security: United States Foreign Policy and the Politics of Identity,* rev. edn (Manchester: Manchester University Press). This important book shows how the identity of the United States is constructed through perceptions of danger in foreign policy discourse.

Walker, R. J. B. (1993), *Inside/Outside: International Relations as Political Theory* (Cambridge: Cambridge University Press). An important early contribution to post-modern IR theory, which challenged some of the central categories of the discipline.

Post-colonialism

Chowdhry, G. and Nair, S. (eds) (2002), *Power, Post-colonialism and International Relations: Reading Race, Gender and Class* (London: Routledge). An edited volume looking at how the intersection of race, class, and gender structure much of world politics.

Said, E. (1979), *Orientalism* (New York: Vintage). A seminal post-colonial text showing how colonial literary and artistic texts create the 'other' with devastating material consequences.

Gilroy, P. (1993), *The Black Atlantic: Modernity and Double Consciousness* (Cambridge, Mass.: Harvard University Press). A look at the unique racial and cultural identity of those black people forced to move from their native countries to the West and how Europeans were also affected by this cultural exchange.

Online Resource Centre

 Visit the Online Resource Centre that accompanies this book to access more learning resources on this chapter topic at www.oxfordtextbooks.co.uk/uk/orc/baylis_smith4e/

International ethics

RICHARD SHAPCOTT

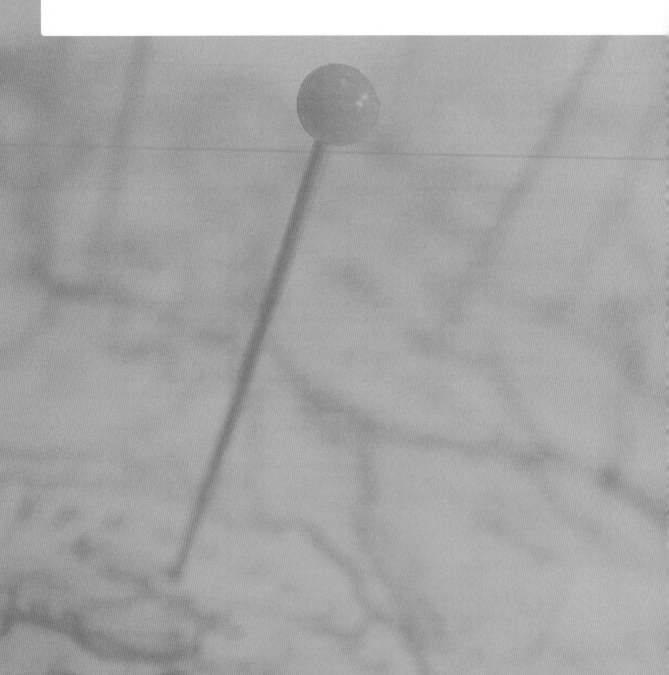

Introduction

According to the *Oxford English Dictionary* the field of ethics is 'The science of morals; the department of study concerned with the principles of human duty'. Ever since human beings gathered into social groups they have been confronted by the issue of how to treat outsiders. Most communities have drawn significant moral distinctions between insiders and outsiders, applying different standards accordingly. It is also the case that many communities, and individuals, have not made these distinctions into an absolute moral standard and have offered hospitality, aid, and charity to strangers with whom they come into contact. International ethics is the study of the nature of duties across community boundaries. It is the study of how members of 'bounded' communities, mostly nation-states, ought to treat 'outsiders' and 'strangers' and of whether it is right to make such a distinction. Two questions therefore lie at the heart of international ethics as field of study. The first is whether outsiders ought to be treated according to the same principles that insiders are (in other words, ought outsiders to be treated as moral equals?). The second question refers to how this can be done.

International ethics asks how it is possible to treat others as equals in a world characterized by two conditions: the existence of international anarchy and moral pluralism. The first of these is often seen as a practical challenge because anarchy makes it harder to get things done and reinforces self-interested, rather than altruistic, tendencies of individuals and states. The second presents both a practical and an ethical challenge. Not only is it harder to get things done when there is no agreement, but deciding which ethics should apply, and whether there are any universal rules is itself an ethical problem.

The advent of globalization provokes a re-examination of these challenges and prompts us to ask whether human beings ought to be considered, first, as one single moral community with some rules that apply to all (**cosmopolitanism**); second, as a collection of separate communities each with their own standards and no common morality (**realism**), or, third, as a collection of separate communities with some minimally shared standards (**pluralism**). Most thinkers on international ethics can be situated somewhere on the spectrum covered by these three positions and discussion of them forms the first part of this chapter.

The ethical significance of boundaries: cosmopolitanism and its alternatives

Most academic debate on international ethical issues draws from Western traditions of moral theory. In particular **deontological** and **consequentialist** ethics, and especially **Kantianism** and **utilitarianism** have been important. Deontology refers to the nature of human duty or obligation. Deontological approaches spell out rules that are always right for everyone to follow, in contrast to rules that might produce a good outcome for an individual, or their society. For deontologists, rules ought to be followed because they are right in themselves and not because of the consequences they may produce. Kantian approaches emphasize rules that are right because they can be, in principle, agreed upon by everyone (universalizability) and are the most important traditions of deontological ethics in the international sphere.

In contrast, consequentialist accounts judge actions by their desirability of their outcomes. Realism (see Ch.5), for instance, judges a statesperson's actions as right or wrong depending on whether they serve the **state**'s interests. Utilitarianism on the other hand, judges acts by their expected outcomes in terms of human welfare and the 'greatest good of the greatest number'. These ethical theories provide different ways of assessing action and deciding what is in fact ethical.

While understanding these distinctions is important, what matters more in international ethics are the conclusions they draw about the ethical significance of national borders. A more relevant distinction exists between **cosmopolitan**, or **universalist**, positions and anti-cosmopolitan, sometimes referred to as communitarianism or

particularism Cosmopolitans, including deontologists and utilitarians, argue that morality itself is universal: that a truly moral rule or code will be applicable to everyone. National borders are therefore 'morally irrelevant'. In contrast, anti-cosmopolitans argue that national boundaries provide important ethical constraints. They tend to fall into two different streams: realism and pluralism. Realism (see Ch.5) claims that the facts of international **anarchy** and **sovereignty** mean that the only viable ethics are those of self-interest and survival. Pluralism argues that anarchy does not prevent states from agreeing to a minimal core of standards for **coexistence**. Both realism and pluralism begin from the premise that morality is 'local' to particular cultures, times, and places. Because ethics are local, our morality is derived from, and only has meaning in, the specific—what Michael Walzer calls 'thick'—culture to which we belong. Different cultures have their own ethics and it is impossible to claim, as cosmopolitans do, access to one single account of morality. Therefore they reject the idea of a single universal morality as a cultural product with no global legitimacy. Realists and pluralists claim that cosmopolitanism is both impossible (impractical) and undesirable because of the international state of nature, and because profound cultural pluralism means

there is a lack of agreement about whose ethics should apply universally.

Cosmopolitanism, realism, and pluralism are reflected in current practices of states and other actors. For instance, since the end of the Second World War many international actors have used the universalist vocabulary of human rights to claim that there are cosmopolitan standards of treatment that all people can claim and that all states recognize. In other words, human rights should 'trump' states' sovereign rights and the international community has a responsibility to uphold them, by armed intervention if necessary. In contrast, others have claimed that threats to national security require states to do 'unthinkable' things, like torture or carpet bombing (see Case Study 2) which override conventional ethics. Alternatively, it also argued that because there is no real agreement on comprehensive standards, it is indefensible to enforce human rights laws against those, like certain Asian or African states, who do not share the cultural assumptions underpinning these laws. In this view it is the responsibility of individual states, and not the international community, to define and uphold human rights. Thus while it is true that a common apparently universal language of human rights exists, there is no clear agreement about what this entails.

Box 11.1 Cosmopolitanism, realism, and pluralism

Cosmopolitanism

'We should recognize humanity wherever it occurs, and give its fundamental ingredients, reason and moral capacity, our first allegiance.'
(Martha Nussbaum 1996: 7)

Liberal cosmopolitanism: 'First, individualism, ultimate units are human beings, or persons. . . . Second, universality: the status of ultimate unit of concern attaches to every living human being equally, not merely to some subset. . . . Third, generality . . . person are the ultimate unit of concern for everyone—not only for their compatriots, fellow religionists, or such like.'
(Thomas Pogge 1994: 9)

'The key point is that it is wrong to promote the interest of our own society or our own personal advantage by exporting suffering to others, colluding in their suffering, or benefiting from the ways in which others exploit the weakness of the vulnerable.'
(Andrew Linklater 2002: 145)

Communitarianism

'Humanity, has members but no memory, so it has no history and no culture, no customary practices, no familiar life-ways, no festivals, no shared understanding of social goods.'
(Michael Walzer 1994a: 8)

'Justice is rooted in the distinct understanding of places honours, jobs, things of all sorts, that constitute a shared way of life. To override those understandings is (always) to act unjustly.'
(Michael Walzer 1983: 314)

Realism

'The appeal to moral principles in the international sphere has no concrete universal meaning . . . that could provide rational guidance for political action, . . . it will be nothing but the reflection of the moral preconceptions of a particular nation . . .'

'. . . a foreign policy guided by universal moral principles . . . is under contemporary conditions . . . a policy of national suicide.'
(Hans Morgenthau 1952: 10)

Pluralism

'. . . a world of diversity in which the variety of national cultures finds expression in different sets of citizenship rights, and different schemes of social justice, in each community.'
(David Miller 2002: 976)

Globalization brings these different ethical positions into greater relief and, for many, provides the strongest reason for applying universal standards. Because globalization increases interconnections between communities, it also increases the varieties of ways in which communities can harm each other, either intentionally or not. For instance, globalization makes it harder to ignore the impact of day-to-day actions, such as driving a car or buying new clothes, on the global environment and in the global economy. The more intense governance of the global economy also raises ethical issues of fairness associated with the rules of international institutional structures. Globalization exacerbates and intensifies these ethical dilemmas by increasing the effects that different communities and individuals have on each other. It especially allows for a far greater awareness of the suffering, of 'distant strangers'. Under these conditions, the ethical framework associated with Westphalian sovereignty—which gives only minor moral significance to the suffering of outsiders—seems less adequate. In a globalized world, communities are challenged to develop new principles or refine old ones to govern these interactions. However, the lack of any single standard of fairness and justice between states makes this task more difficult because it raises the question of whose principles should apply. Therefore in a world that is being globalized, one ethical challenge is to ask 'Is it possible to define some principles that everyone might be able to agree upon?'

Cosmopolitanism

Even though our world may be characterized by high levels of **interdependence**, we still tend to live morally 'constrained' lives, in which national borders have significant ethical status. Cosmopolitans, however, argue that despite this division of humanity into separate historically constituted communities, it remains possible to identify with, and have a moral concern for, humanity. Cosmopolitanism refers to the idea that humanity is to be treated as a single moral community that has moral priority over our national (or subnational) communities.

The first part of the cosmopolitan claim is that there are no good reasons for ruling any person out of ethical consideration. The second dimension of cosmopolitan thought is the attempt to define exactly what obligations and rules ought to govern the universal community. The attempt to give inclusion substantive content is usually associated with deontological and Kantian thought in

particular. Deontologists argue that not only should we consider outsiders as morally equal, but also that, as a consequence, we are morally obliged to do certain things and refrain from others.

One of the common arguments of cosmopolitanism is that treating everyone as equal requires 'impartial consideration of the claims of each person' (Beitz 1992: 125). Impartiality arguments are usually deployed in terms of defending the idea of global distributive justice. Because there are no morally significant differences between people as people, everyone's interests should be judged from a disinterested position. Impartiality requires that particular affiliations, like national identity, must be assessed from the position of the good of the whole—because they are not in themselves necessarily just or defensible. Most cosmopolitans agree that national membership and the borders between nations are defensible only in so far as they serve individuals' needs, by providing them with a sense of belonging, identity, and stability that is necessary to be a fully functioning human being. This has led some to argue that national favouritism, or 'compatriot priority', can be defended from an impartial position. In other words, impartiality does not necessarily lead to a cosmopolitan account of global justice (Goodin 1988). However, cosmopolitans still maintain that our fundamental moral claims derive from our status as human beings and therefore national loyalties have at best a derivative moral status.

Kant and cosmopolitanism

Long before the existence of modern states and telecommunications, the Stoic philosopher Diogenes claimed he was a 'citizen of the world'. However, in modern times, the source of greatest inspiration for cosmopolitanism was the German **Enlightenment** philosopher Immanuel Kant. For Kant, the most important philosophical and political problem facing humankind was the eradication of war and the realization of a universal community governed by a rational cosmopolitan law. The central concept of Kant's thought, and the lynchpin upon which his project for a perpetual peace (see Ch.6) between states rested, is the principle of the **categorical imperative** (CI).

Specifically, one should: 'Act only on that maxim through which you can at the same time will that it shall become a universal law' (Kant, quoted in Linklater 1990a: 100). This means that to act morally, a rational

person must act upon a principle which anybody could wish everybody else to obey towards everybody else. For Kant, the most important expression of this imperative was that principle that humans should be treated as ends in themselves: 'Act in such a way that you always treat humanity, whether in your own person or in the person of any other, never simply as a means, but always at the same time as an end' (Kant, quoted in Linklater 1990*a*: 101). The effect of the CI is to grant every individual equal moral standing in relation to each other. Most Kantian thought focuses on the nature of the obligations that accompany the belief in human equality and freedom. This principle directly and indirectly underpins much of contemporary international ethics, especially discussions about global justice. However, the more basic argument is that treating people as ends in themselves requires that we must think universally. Restricting moral concern to members of one's own state or nation renders any belief in equality incomplete.

Kantian thought has given rise to a number of different approaches. A common distinction is made between moral and institutional cosmopolitanism, where the first refers to the acts required of individuals, and the second to the rules that govern societies. Cosmopolitan duties to recognize individual equality apply to individuals, as well as to the global institutional/legal order.

Box 11.2 The categorical imperative

The categorical imperative states that for a rational being to act morally, it must act according to universal laws. Specifically one should: 'Act only on that maxim through which you can at the same time will that it shall become a universal law' (quoted in Linklater 1990*a*: 100). This means that to act morally, a rational person must act upon a principle which anybody could wish everybody else to obey towards everybody else. For Kant, the most important expression of this imperative was that principle that humans should be treated as ends in themselves: 'Act in such a way that you always treat humanity, whether in your own person or in the person of any other, never simply as a means, but always at the same time as an end' (quoted in Linklater 1990*a*: 101). An example is slavery, because slaves are humans who are reduced to the status of the property of others. They have no rights and their interests are not taken into account in regard to decisions which affect them. Warfare between states is likewise another violation, because it reduces both citizens and non-citizens alike to means of achieving (the states') ends. For Kant, this is a moral law that results from the nature of reason itself, but also from human nature, understood as both self-interested and reasonable, that is our capacity to be 'rational devils'.

In sum, the major tasks of cosmopolitanism are to defend moral universalism, to explore what it might mean to follow the CI in a world divided into separate states, and to develop an account of an alternative political order based on Kant's work (see Ch.1 and Ch.31). Most discussion of international ethics refers to the dilemmas states and other actors face in seeking to decide, interpret, and act according to these obligations in their policies.

Cosmopolitanism is often charged with requiring either a world state or the wholesale rejection of national loyalties. Cosmopolitans, however, claim that universal principles can be institutionalized in a number of ways that fall short of a global state, while still recognizing the significance of national identity. Two examples of this are the principles of humanitarianism and 'do no harm'.

Humanitarianism and harm

The most common way in which cosmopolitan obligations are discussed is in terms of either positive or negative duties. Positive duties are duties to act, to do something often expressed as humanitarian obligations. Humanitarianism involves an obligation to those who are in dire need or suffering unnecessarily, wherever they may be and regardless of the cause of their suffering. This includes aid to the victims of famine and natural disasters, but also those who suffer during wartime such as non-combatants and soldiers retired from the field. These are not charity provisions but moral duties which it would be not only bad but morally *wrong* to ignore. The idea of a positive duty underlies the recent UN Report on the international **responsibility to protect** (see Ch.30), which spells out the responsibilities of states to uphold human rights within their own borders and abroad. The responsibility to protect argument also emphasizes that states' rights are dependent on their fulfilling this duty.

Negative duties are duties to stop doing something, usually duties to avoid unnecessarily harming others. States have traditionally recognized a negative duty of non-intervention that requires them to refrain from certain actions. Problems arise in the discussion of negative duties because they rely upon a fairly clear line of causation: if a state is harming another one, then it should cease doing so. However, it is not always clear who is harming who and how. Sometimes the effects of our actions are diffuse, or more than one party may be engaged in

a harmful practice, as in the case of global warming (see Case Study 1).

In the public eye, positive duties, such as aid to victims of tsunamis or ethnic cleansing, take a higher profile and demand more attention, but in academic contexts at least as much attention is given to negative duties, and in particular duties not to harm others.

Positive duties can give rise to negative duties and, more controversially, vice versa. The positive duty to recognize human rights might give rise to a negative duty to cease certain practices. However, whereas a negative duty to cease harming implies only a cessation of action, some argue that there is also a positive duty to prevent other harms occurring, as well as duties of compensation or redress.

Andrew Linklater argues that cosmopolitan duties to do no harm generally fall into three categories. First, bilateral relationships: what 'we' do to 'them' and vice versa.

Second, third-party relationships: what they do to each other. Third, global relationships: what we all do to each other (Linklater 2002, 2005). Examples of the *first* are cases where one community 'exports' damaging practices, goods, or by-products to another. In this case states have a duty to consider the negative effects they have on each other, as well as a duty to prevent and punish harmful actions of **non-state actors** and individuals for whom they are directly responsible. For instance, some states have laws which punish citizens who engage in 'sex tourism' abroad. It means that states should not pursue their own national advantage without considering the harm this may cause others. An example of the *second* is when a state is involved in harming either members of its own community or its neighbour's, such as in cases of genocide. Third-party states and the **international community** also have duties to prevent, stop, or punish the perpetrators of these harms.

Case Study 1 Ethics of global warming

If there is one item on the international agenda that raises truly global ethical questions it is the case of global warming (GW) because it potentially affects every person on the planet. The environment of the planet earth, and the atmosphere in particular, are considered commons (see Ch.19) because they are shared by all. The ethics of the global commons are explicitly cosmopolitan in the sense that they refer to the earth's environment as a single biological community that creates a human community of interdependence. This ethics emphasizes that national gains or advantages need to be sacrificed or moderated if the environmental problems are to be solved and the 'tragedy of the commons' is to be avoided.

GW is a good example of both positive and negative duties. At face value it seems reasonably clear that there are negative duties of those countries who have contributed most to GW, and who will do so in the future, to cease doing so. Most people would agree that we should all take responsibility for harming someone else, especially if we have benefited from it. In the case of GW this would mean that there is a proportionate responsibility on behalf of the advanced industrial countries, especially the USA, Europe, and Canada, to reduce their greenhouse emissions (GHE) and to take financial responsibility for the harms that their past and future emissions will cause others. There are also positive duties on behalf of the richer states to aid those with the least capacity to adjust to the costs involved in GW. This is regardless of the rich countries' role in causing the problem. That is, there are positive duties to aid the poorest states and populations, who will be disproportionately affected and who have done the least to contribute to GW. We can think, for instance, of counties like Bangladesh, mostly at or below sea level, or pacific island states, which are barely industrialized but which are likely to be the first to disappear. It seems clear that on both positive and negative

grounds there is a responsibility to help for those who can. In addition, there is also a positive duty that is arguably generated by the negative duty. If we have harmed someone we ought help them overcome the harm we have caused them, especially if they are unable to do so unassisted. That is, there is not only a negative duty to cease or reduce GHE, but also a positive duty to redress the damage done. This is an issue of redistributive justice; a duty to aid those most affected by one's harms.

These arguments are buttressed by further points regarding the capacity of rich states to pay and by the two different types of cost that are likely to be faced by all countries. One is the cost of reducing GHE and the other is the cost of dealing with the likely impacts of rising sea levels and other environmental consequences. Poorer countries are at a disadvantage in both regards. This issue is of course complicated by the fact that the production of GHE is so central to economic growth, especially in industrializing countries. Any attempt to curtail their output implies a restriction on the prospects for economic growth in those countries that perhaps need it most. Indeed, there is even an argument that the 'people in the developing world need to increase their emissions in order to attain a minimally decent standard of living for themselves and their families' (Singer and Gregg 2004: 57). The overall cost to rich states of addressing GW are proportionally lower than for poor states. Because they are richer they can afford more. In addition, the costs that might be incurred by the rich states are likely to be of a qualitatively different nature. For rich states, dealing with climate change might only impact upon the *luxury* or non-necessary end of their quality of life, such as whether or not they can afford to drive large cars or have air conditioning, whereas for poor states reducing emissions will more likely impact upon the basic necessities of life and survival.

The *third* relationship refers to practices or harms to which many communities contribute, often in different proportions such as in the case of global warming (see Case Study 1). States have a negative duty not to export harms to the world as a whole and a positive duty to contribute to the resolution of issues arising from such harms.

This account of global cosmopolitan duties emphasizes both individual and institutional obligations without claiming either the need for a world state or denying national identity. A cosmopolitan commitment to avoiding harm involves only the idea that one's national identity and well-being should not come at the expense of outsiders. Obligations to friends, neighbours, and fellow countrymen must be balanced with obligations to strangers and to humanity.

Key Points

- Globalization lends support for cosmopolitan ethical theory.
- Cosmopolitanism advances the idea of a universal human community in which everybody is treated as equal.
- The most important cosmopolitan thinker is Immanuel Kant.
- Cosmopolitanism has both moral and political meaning.

- Cosmopolitanism does not require a world state.
- Cosmopolitans emphasize both positive and negative duties, usually expressed in terms of responsibilities not to harm and responsibilities to provide humanitarian assistance or hospitality.

Anti-cosmopolitanism: realism and pluralism

While cosmopolitanism in one form or another tends to predominate academic debate on international ethics, anti-cosmopolitan arguments tend to be more persuasive in the practices of states. Anti-cosmopolitans also provide powerful criticism of some of the assumptions and blindspots of cosmopolitan thought. They also help us to understand why cosmopolitanism has only limited applicability in the contemporary international order.

Realist ethics

For realists, the facts of anarchy and statehood mean that the only viable ethics are those of self-interest. Many people have characterized realist ethics as Machiavellian at worst and amoral at best. Realist ethics seem to contradict universal ethics such as human rights. But realists, such as Hans Morgenthau and George F. Kennan, often argue that underlying this toughness is a different, more pragmatic, morality. The statesperson's duty is to ensure the survival of their state in the uncertain conditions of international anarchy. To do otherwise would be to risk the lives and interests of their own people. Thus **self-help** is a moral duty and not just a practical necessity. Realists therefore advise states to focus on material and strategic outcomes rather than the morality,

conventionally understood, of their actions. For instance, a realist like Henry Kissinger may advise bombing a neutral state, such as Laos, if it will serve the military goals of defeating the enemy, North Vietnam. Alternatively, it may also involve having friendly relations and support for governments with poor human rights records, such as Chile under the military rule of Augusto Pinochet, or arguably Pakistan today, in order to secure an advantage against a military foe, such as the USSR or Al Qaeda. While the critics say this can slip into opportunism, justifying almost any actions on ethical grounds, realists maintain that statespeople have a duty to their own people first and that ignoring these realities in the name of some Kantian ideal would be a dereliction of that duty (Morgenthau 1948).

Many realists proclaim such self-interested ethics as virtuous and agree with E. H. Carr's (1939) scepticism towards those individuals and states who claim to be acting in the name of universal morality. Thus contemporary realists, like John Mearsheimer, are sceptical about US President George W. Bush's aims of spreading democracy in the Middle East and the claim in the National Security Strategy of the USA (NSS 2001: 5) that 'American values are universal values'. Realists believe that such statements are usually either a cynical mask or a self-interested delusion. In reality, there are no such universal values, and even

if there were, anarchy would prevent states from acting in accordance with them.

More importantly, realists are vulnerable to the observation that not every choice that states face is between survival and destruction, rather than, say, advantage or disadvantage. It does not stand to reason that seeking advantage allows the statesperson to opt out of conventional morality in the same way that survival might. It is a limitation of most realist writers that they simply favour the **national interest** over the interests of outsiders. In other words, realists display a preference for the status quo, the states-system and **nationalism**, which is not fully defensible. This favouritism reminds us that realism is as much prescriptive and normative as it is descriptive and explanatory.

Pluralist ethics of coexistence

The other main expression of communitarian assumptions is pluralism. Because communitarians value community and diversity, they recognize that the many ways in which individuals are formed in different cultures is a good thing in itself. Therefore, they argue that the best ethics is one which preserves diversity over homogeneity. Pluralism recognizes that states have different ethics but can agree upon a framework whereby they tolerate each other, do not impose their own views upon others, and agree on certain, limited, harm principles. These duties are best expressed through an ethic of tolerance and coexistence between **political communities**. States have different ethics but can agree upon a framework, sometimes likened to an egg-box, whereby they tolerate and do not impose their own views upon each other. This allows them to feel reasonably secure and to go about their business in relative peace. In this view, sovereignty is an ethical principle which allows states and the different cultures they harbour to exist alongside each other.

For pluralists, we have greater and more specific duties to our 'own kind' than we do to outsiders. Any duties to humanity are at best attenuated and mediated by states. Pluralism is distinguished from **solidarism,** which argues that states have duties to act against other states when basic human values are denied by practices like genocide. Pluralists resist attempts to develop a more solidarist world in which **humanitarian intervention**, for instance, is institutionalized. 'The general function of international society is to separate and cushion, not to act' (Vincent 1986: 123).

Pluralists are sceptical about the use of human rights in diplomacy as it gives some states the opportunity to deny others their sovereignty (Bull 1977; Jackson 2000). Likewise, pluralists do not believe in universal distributive justice, either as a practical possibility or as a moral good in itself, because it requires the imposition of a specific, usually liberal, account of justice upon other cultures. They see the imposition of any specific values or ethics upon others as a harmful thing both for that community and for **international order** as a whole (Walzer 1994a; Jackson 2000; Miller 2002). The primary ethical responsibility of the statesperson is to maintain order and peace between states, not develop a global account of justice.

The most developed account of a pluralist ethics is John Rawls' *The Law of Peoples* (1999). According to Rawls, liberal states have no cosmopolitan duties to globalize their own conception of distributive justice. Instead, societies are to be understood as if they have only minimal impact upon each other. For Rawls, the conditions required for global distributive justice are not present. Therefore, the best that can be hoped for is a 'law of peoples', which covers rules of self-determination, just war, mutual recognition (sovereignty), non-intervention, and mutual aid.

However, pluralists invoke a universal principle that it is wrong for people to impose harm upon others. More importantly, cosmopolitans ask whether 'eggbox' ethics is enough under conditions of globalization. Cosmopolitans argue that a strict ethics of coexistence is simply out of date and can actually be harmful when the scope for intercommunity harm has increased exponentially.

Box 11.3 Rawls' *The Law of Peoples*

1 People are free and independent, and their freedom and independence are to be respected by other peoples
2 Peoples are to observe treaties and undertakings
3 Peoples are to observe a duty of non-intervention
4 Peoples have the right of self-defense but no right to instigate war for reasons other than self-defense
5 Peoples are to honour human rights
6 People are to observe certain specified restrictions in the conduct of war
7 Peoples have a duty to assist other people living under unfavourable conditions that prevent their having a just or decent political and social regime (Mutual Aid)

(Rawls 1999)

Key Points

- Realism and pluralism are the two most common objections to cosmopolitan ethics and the possibility of moral universalism.
- Realists argue that necessity demands a statist ethics, restricting moral obligations to the nation-state.
- Pluralism is an 'ethics of coexistence' based on sovereignty.

Global ethical issues

The following sections discuss two important international ethical issues, one new and the other older, that are exacerbated under conditions of globalization. The just war tradition has provided one of the most enduring sets of ethical standards for states and their servants in their conduct with outsiders. In contrast, the topic of global distributive justice has only been taken seriously in the last forty years or so. Both issues highlight the nature of the ethical challenges that face states in a world in which the effects of their actions are capable of being globalized.

Just war tradition

The just war tradition (JWT) (often erroneously referred to as just war theory) is a set of guidelines for determining and judging whether and when a state may have recourse to war and how it may fight that war. The JWT is concerned with applying moral limits to states' recourse to war and to limiting harms that states can commit against other states, military forces, and civilians. It consists of two parts: the *jus ad bellum* (or justice of war) and the *jus in bello* (the justice in war). Where *jus ad bellum* refers to the occasion of going to war, *jus in bello* refers to the means, the weapons, and tactics employed by the military in warfare (see Box 11.4 and Case Study 2).

The aim of JWT is not a just world. Nor is the idea of just war (JW) to be confused with holy wars or crusading, which are wars designed to spread a particular faith or political system. The JWT aims only to limit wars by restricting the types of justification that are acceptable. The European JWT has its origins in the works of Christian theologians and especially St Augustine. Just

---

Box 11.4 The just war

Jus ad bellum

- Just cause: this usually means self-defence or defence of a third party.
- Right authority: only states can wage legitimate war. Criminals, corporations, and individuals are illegitimate.
- Right intention: the state leader must be attempting to address an injustice or an aggression, rather than seeking glory, expansion, or loot.
- Last resort: the leaders must have exhausted all other reasonable avenues of resolution or have no choice because of imminent attack.
- Reasonable hope of success: states should not begin wars they cannot reasonably expect to win.
- Restoration of peace: it is just to wage a war if the purpose is to restore the peace or return the situation to the status quo.
- Proportionality of means and ends: the means of war, including the war itself, must be proportionate to the ends being sought. States must use minimal force in order to achieve their objectives. It is not justifiable to completely destroy enemy forces or their civilian populations in order to remove them from your territory.

Jus in bello

- Proportionality of means: states must use minimal, or proportionate, force and weaponry. Thus it is not justifiable to completely destroy the enemy's forces if you can use enough force to merely defeat them. For example, a state should not use a nuclear weapon when a conventional one might do.
- Non-combatant immunity: states should not directly target non-combatants, including soldiers retired from the field, or civilians and civilian infrastructure not required for the war effort. Non-combatant immunity is central to just war theory, 'since without it that theory loses much of its coherence. How can a theory that claims to regard wars as an instrument of justice countenance the injustice involved in the systematic suppression of the rights of non-combatants?' (Coates 1997: 263).
- The law of double effect: actions may incur non-combatant losses if these are unintended (but foreseeable) consequences. For example, civilians living adjacent to an arms factory. However, the real issue is whether deaths can really be unintended if they are foreseeable. The dilemma facing just war theorists is whether to be responsible for those deaths in the same way as intended deaths.

Case Study 2 *Jus in bello*: saturation bombing

One example which illustrates many of the issues of *jus in bello* is the use of 'saturation' or 'area' city bombing during the Second World War. During the war, both the allied and axis powers targeted each other's cities with large-scale bombing raids. In pursuance of their war against Hitler, the British targeted massive bombing runs against Germany, destroying many cities and killing hundreds of thousands of civilians. The most famous of these was the bombing of the German city of Dresden. Dresden was especially controversial because it had no military significance at all. In the firestorm that was created by the allies, at least 100,000 people died. Likewise, the Americans, during the closing stages of the war against Japan, repeatedly bombed Tokyo and other major Japanese cities, in raids that targeted cities rather than military sites. The main argument used to defend these clear breaches of the discrimination principle was that it was necessary to break the will of the people to continue fighting. Other arguments were that it was not possible to discriminate between civilians and non-civilians any longer because of the advent of 'total war'. Others claimed that the war against Hitler was a 'supreme emergency' where the survival of Britain was at stake. In most of these arguments, except the first, strategists refer to the doctrine of double effect: the death of civilians was foreseeable but unintentional.

However, British military planners had developed the tactic of saturation bombing before the war began, as part of an overall strategic plan. In addition, the campaigns lasted well beyond the immediate danger to Britain's survival that existed during the battle of Britain. So it is clear that civilian deaths were both anticipated and planned as part of a war fighting strategy. On these grounds, most authors now agree that this practice constituted a fundamental violation of just war principles.

war thinking is also important in Islam and is often incorrectly associated entirely with the idea of *jihad*.

JWT has both cosmopolitan and pluralist elements. Broadly speaking the *jus ad bellum* tradition is generally associated with pluralism, or what Michael Walzer calls the legalist tradition. In this view what is acceptable or unacceptable are rules about and for states, concerning what states owe each other. The rules it lays down refer to times when it is legitimate for states to wage war. The justifications for war are given not to God or humanity, but to other states. The only acceptable justifications are the defence of individual state sovereignty and, arguably, the defence of the principle of a society of states itself.

We can compare this with the more cosmopolitan elements of *jus in bello*, which refer explicitly to civilians and to what is owed to them in terms of harm minimization. The *jus in bello* principle informs, and has been codified in, international humanitarian law, such as the Geneva Conventions, as well as a number of other treaties limiting the use and deployment of certain weapons, including chemical weapons, landmines, and **weapons of mass destruction** (WMD). The ultimate referent is humanity and the rules about proportionality, noncombatant immunity, and discrimination all refer to the rights of individuals to be exempt from harm.

From the position of the realist, the JWT provides unjustifiable limits upon statecraft. International politics is the realm of necessity and in warfare any means must be used to achieve the end of the state. Necessity overrides ethics when it is a matter of state survival or when military forces are at risk. The state must judge for itself when it is most prudent to wage war and what is necessary for victory. From the position of the pacifist, the core doctrine of the JWT only encourages war by providing the tools to justify it. For pacifists and other critics, not only is killing always wrong, the just war tradition is unethical because it provides war with a veneer of legitimacy.

Box 11.5 Islamic just war tradition

The ethics of war are central to Islam. The prophet Muhammad himself led troops into battle in the name of Islam. It is clear from both the Koran and the teachings (*hadith*) of Muhammad that at (limited) times it is incumbent upon Muslims to wage war. For this reason it is often said that while Islam's ultimate purpose is to bring peace through universal submission to Allah, there is no 'pacifist' tradition within Islam. At times some Muslim authorities have argued that there is a duty to spread the realm of Islam through war, as happened in the centuries after Muhammad's death, with the establishment of the caliphate. Others, the majority, argue that the Koran sanctions war only in self-defence. Fundamentalist groups like Al Qaeda use this to justify their campaigns against the USA and its allies, both in the USA and in Iraq and Afghanistan. However, most Islamic authorities reject both Al Qaeda's interpretation of 'defence' and its strategy of attacking civilian targets outside the 'occupied' or threatened territory of the 'Dar al Islam' as illegitimate interpretations. Most interpreters argue that there are Islamic equivalents of the just cause clause, right authority, right intent, and some *jus in bello* clauses, including civilian immunity.

Global justice, poverty and starvation

The globalizing of the world-economy, especially since the Second World War, has undoubtedly given rise to large global inequalities. It has also been responsible for

an increase in the number and proportion of the human population suffering from absolute **poverty** and starvation (see Ch.27). At the same time, cosmopolitans like Pogge point out that globalization also means there is now the capacity to end global poverty, relatively quickly and cheaply. Globalization raises the issue of universal distributive justice and the nature of the moral duties owed to the world's poor by the world's rich. The existence of both significant inequality and of massive hunger and starvation raises the question of whose responsibility it is either to decrease inequality or to end absolute starvation, especially in the presence of extreme wealth.

The Singer solution

According to Peter Singer, 'globalization means that we should value equality between societies, and at the global level as much as we value political equality within one society' (2002: 190). Singer argues that an impartial and universalist (and utilitarian) conception of morality requires that those who can help, ought to, regardless of any causal relationship with poverty. He argues that 'if it is in our power to prevent something bad from happening, without thereby sacrificing anything of comparable moral importance we ought, morally, to do it' (1985: 231). People in affluent countries, and in affluent sections of poor countries, are morally obligated to help those who are in danger of losing their lives from poverty-related causes.

In order to justify this claim Singer asks us to consider the following situation: 'if I am walking past a water pond and see a child drowning in it, I ought to wade in and pull the child out. This will mean getting my clothes muddy, but this is insignificant, while the death of the child would presumably be a very bad thing' (1985: 231).

Persistent global hunger and dire poverty presents us with the same moral choice. If we think it wrong to let a child die for fear of muddying our trousers, then we ought also think it is wrong to let a child, or millions of other people, die from hunger and poverty when it is in our capacity to prevent it without incurring a significant loss. Therefore we, who are able to help, have a positive duty to aid those in need.

According to Singer and Peter Unger, people in well-off countries ought to give all the money left over after paying for necessities to alleviate third-world poverty. This is a moral duty and not an issue of charity, that is, we ought to consider ourselves to be doing something *wrong* if we do not help. In Kantian terms, we are not treating the world's poor as ends in themselves, because we are in effect placing less value on their lives than our own material pleasure.

Liberal institutional cosmopolitanism

Liberal institutional cosmopolitans, like Charles Beitz, Darrel Moellendorf, and Thomas Pogge, argue that global interdependence generates a duty to create a globally just institutional scheme. For Beitz and Moellendorf, John Rawls' substantive account of justice can provide the criteria for justice globally.

Rawls (1971) argued that justice begins with the 'basic structure' of society, by which he meant 'the way in which the major social institutions distribute fundamental rights and duties and determine the division of

---

Box 11.7 Rawls and the 'original position'

Rawls' social contract is the result of an experiment in which members of a closed society have been told they must design its basic rules. The catch is, no individual can know where they may end up within this society. They may be wealthy, poor, black, white, male, female, talented, intelligent, etc. All they know about themselves is that they have a capacity to conceive of 'the good', to think rationally about ends, and possess certain basic physical needs. Rawls describes this as decision-making behind 'a veil of ignorance'. Rawls thinks rational contractors constrained like this would choose a society in which each person would have 'an equal right to the most extensive scheme of equal basic liberties compatible with a similar scheme of liberties for others' (1971: 60). He also thinks there would be a form of equality of outcome, as well as opportunity. This he refers to as the difference principle, where inequality is unjust except in so far as it is a necessary means to improving the position of the worst-off members of society. For the international realm, a second contracting session takes place between the representatives of peoples. The conclusion of this round is a contract that resembles the traditional rules of international society: self-determination, just war, mutual recognition, and non-intervention. In other words, rules of coexistence, not justice. Cosmopolitan interpreters of Rawls reject this conclusion and the necessity of the second contracting session.

Box 11.6 Peter Singer on distributive justice

'Each one of us with wealth surplus to his or her essential needs should be giving most of it to help people suffering from poverty so dire as to be life-threatening. That's right: I'm saying that you shouldn't buy that new car, take that cruise, redecorate the house or get that pricey new suit. After all, a $1,000 suit could save five children's lives.'

(Singer 1999)

advantages from social cooperation' (Rawls 1971: 7). To be just, society must have just basic assumptions about who has rights, or equal moral standing, and duties, and who benefits materially from the production of goods and services. Rawls' theory of justice is both a procedural account of justice and a substantive one, concerned with distribution of wealth and advantage. Rawls, as noted above, rejected the possibility of global distributive justice modelled on his theory. However, most Rawlsians argue that Rawls' conclusions do not follow from his own premises.

Cosmopolitans concerned with global justice are predominantly, but not exclusively, concerned with the basic structure of global society. That is, with the ways in which the rules of global order distribute rights, duties, and the benefits of social cooperation. The basic structure of international order should be governed by cosmopolitan principles focused on the inequalities between individuals rather than states. What ultimately matters is how poor or badly off someone is in the world, not just in their own country.

Thus, while Beitz and Moellendorf have some differences over the exact mechanisms for addressing inequalities, they nonetheless agree with Thomas Pogge's claim that the difference principle that 'the terms of international cooperation . . . should . . . be designed so that the social inequalities . . . tend to optimize the worst representative individual share' (Pogge 1989: 251) should apply globally. In practice, this comes down to a claim that the global original position might entail the redistribution of wealth to counter natural resources inequality and some compensation 'for the uneven distribution of natural resources or to rectify past injustices . . . and a portion of the global product actually attributable to global (as opposed to domestic) social cooperation should be redistributed' (Beitz 1979: 169).

Pogge's solution

Unlike Singer and Beitz, Thomas Pogge emphasizes the **causal** relationship between the wealth of the rich and the poverty of the poor. Pogge argues that the rules of the system and basic structure of international society actively damage or disadvantage certain sectors of the economy, thus directly contradicting Rawlsian principles of justice. The rich have a duty to help the poor because the international order, which they largely created, is a major cause of world poverty. Indeed, Pogge argues that the rich countries are collectively responsible for about 18 million deaths from poverty annually.

Most importantly, Pogge argues that our negative duties not to harm others give rise to positive duties to aid them. Therefore, we who gain most from the current order have an obligation to change the order and to change it in such a way that the most needy benefit. The structure of international trade and economic interdependence should ensure that, despite an unequal distribution of material resources worldwide, no one should be unable to meet their basic requirements, nor should they suffer disproportionately from the lack of material resources. Finally, pluralist objections do not cancel out this obligation: 'There is an injustice in the economic scheme, which it would be wrong for more affluent participants to perpetuate. And that is so quite independently of whether we and the starving are united by a communal bond' (Pogge 1994: 97).

Box 11.8 Thomas Pogge on international order

'The affluent countries and their citizens, continue to impose a global economic order under which millions avoidably die each year from poverty-related causes. We would regard it as a grave injustice, if such an economic order were imposed within a national society.'

(Pogge 2001b: 44)

Key Points

- There are two components of the just war tradition: *jus ad bellum* and *jus in bello*.
- Just war is different from holy war.
- The just war tradition contains elements of cosmopolitanism and communitarianism.

- Discussions of global justice are dominated by utilitarian and Rawlsian theories.
- It is not always agreed that inequality is itself a moral problem.
- Cosmopolitans argue that there is a responsibility of the rich to help the poor stemming from positive and negative duties.

Conclusion

This chapter outlined some of the main approaches to international ethics and some of the most important ethical issues that characterize globalization. Ethical issues confront all actors in the international realm and especially states which have a large capacity to aid or harm others. The biggest challenge facing states and other actors extends from the existence of moral pluralism and political anarchy in the international realm. These challenges make our decisions harder and our reasoning more complex, but they do not remove our obligations to outsiders. In the context of globalization, cosmopolitanism challenges realists and pluralists on two grounds. First, they ask is it possible any longer to defend not acting to help others when we can without harming ourselves? Second, and more problematically, they ask is it possible any longer to resist the duty to create a world in which unnecessary suffering is minimized and the equality of everyone is realized in political institutions? Most thinkers on international ethics therefore reject either a thoroughgoing realism or a strict pluralism. Instead, for most writers, given the scope of interdependence occurring under globalization, the question is not whether, but *how* to be ethical in the international realm.

Cosmopolitanism, perhaps more so than ever before in human history, is present in both the words and deeds of many states, international institutions, and individuals, inlcuding the Universal Declaration of Human Rights (UDHR) and the International Criminal Court (ICC). A cosmopolitan commitment to prevent unnecessary harm is present in the Geneva Conventions and the treaties banning the use of anti-personnel landmines. The presence of a global **civil society** made of individuals and **non-governmental organizations** (NGOs), which calls states to account for their action or inaction on pressing issues such as global poverty (e.g. the 'Make Poverty History' campaign, led by Bob Geldof and Bono), is testament to the cosmopolitan idea of world citizenship. Many of these actors work upon the belief that all humans ought to be treated equally. They invoke basic conceptions of what humans are due as humans, including basic rights to food, shelter, and freedom from unnecessary suffering.

While there are elements of cosmopolitanism present in the international order, most state practice and most people continue to give priority to their fellow nationals. State practice continues to favour insiders over outsiders, especially in relation to issues like global warming where core activities are put into question. The advent of the **war on terror** has exacerbated this tension in recent years. Fearing for their **security**, states have focused their attention on security issues to the detriment of human rights issues in particular. Likewise, the failure of the Doha round of **World Trade Organization** negotiations in July 2006 was evidence of the inability of states to address effectively the concerns of the poorest states and to cease harming them through maintaining unfair trade rules. While even basic ethical obligations remain unfulfilled for many people, the cosmopolitan ethics underpinning this agreement also raise the possibility of more advanced duties. While disagreement remains, there is nonetheless significant agreement about basic rights, freedom from poverty and starvation, and the idea that national boundaries should not prevent us from treating all others with respect.

❓ Questions

1 What is the core idea of cosmopolitanism?

2 What are the ethical implications of globalization?

3 What are the main objections to cosmopolitanism?

4 How ethically significant should national borders be considered?

5 In what ways does globalization challenge communitarian ethics?

6 Are principles of justice universal?

7 Is there a responsibility of the rich countries to end global poverty?

8 Are positive or negative duties more helpful in addressing global and international ethical issues?

Guide to further reading

Beitz, C. (1979), *Political Theory and International Relations* (Princeton, NJ: Princeton University Press). The first cosmopolitan reading of John Rawl's *Theory of Justice* (1971).

Dower, N. (1998), *World Ethics: The New Agenda* (Edinburgh: Edinburgh University Press). A useful overview of the ethical agenda under globalization.

Hashmi, S. H. (ed.), (2002), *Islamic Political Ethics: Civil Society, Pluralism, and Conflict* (Princeton, NJ: Princeton University Press). An insightful collection of essays exploring the domestic and international ethics of Islam.

Hayden, P. (2005), *Cosmopolitan Global Politics* (Aldershot: Ashgate). A systematic cosmopolitan treatment of the ethical and political issues surrounding globalization.

Hoffmann, S. (1981), *Duties Beyond Borders* (Syracuse, NY: Syracuse University Press). A 'liberal realist' take on the possibilities of international ethics.

Moellendorf, D. (2002), *Cosmopolitan Justice* (Boulder, Col.: Westview Press). A more recent application of a Rawlsian approach.

Nardin, T. and Mapel, D. (eds) (1992), *Traditions of International Ethics* (Cambridge: Cambridge University Press). The most comprehensive account of the ways in which people have thought about international ethics.

Pogge, T. (2002), *World Poverty and Human Rights: Cosmopolitan Responsibilities and Reforms* (Cambridge: Polity Press). Develops the most detailed and rigorous argument in favour of cosmopolitan principles of distributive justice based on negative obligations generated by rich countries' complicity in global poverty.

Rawls, J. (1999), *The Law of Peoples* (Cambridge, Mass.: Harvard University Press). Rawls' own contribution to international ethics develops something like an ethics of coexistence between 'reasonable peoples'.

Singer, P. (2002), *One World: The Ethics of Globalisation* (Melbourne: Text Publishing). The most important utilitarian argument in favour of positive duties to redistribute wealth from rich to the poor. It also examines the ethics of global trade and global warming.

Walzer, M. (1994), *Thick and Thin: Moral Argument at Home and Abroad* (Notre Dame, Ind.: University of Notre Dame Press). A controversial 'communitarian' account, defending cultural difference and the limiting of human rights.

—— (2000), *Just and Unjust Wars: A Moral Argument with Historical Illustrations* (New York: Basic Books). A classic philosophical and historical study on the just war tradition and ethics of war more generally.

Online Resource Centre

 Visit the Online Resource Centre that accompanies this book to access more learning resources on this chapter topic at www.oxfordtextbooks.co.uk/uk/orc/baylis_smith4e/

- Introduction ··· 194
- The ethical significance of boundaries: cosmopolitanism and its alternatives ················ 194
- Anti-cosmopolitarism: realism and pluralism ·· 199
- Global ethical issues ·· 201
- Conclusion ·· 205

Reader's Guide

Globalization increases not only human political and economic relationships, but also the scope and intensity of our ethical obligations. Globalization makes it harder to draw clear ethical distinctions between insiders and outsiders and, consequently, raises the idea of a cosmopolitan community of humankind. How then should we think about ethics and what principles ought to guide the policies of states, non-governmental organizations (NGOs), corporations, and individuals in their relations with everybody else?

This chapter examines how these questions have been answered by different thinkers and actors in world politics. Ethics is the evaluative study of what actors ought to do, rather than the descriptive study of what they have done, or are doing. International ethics is central to international politics because it refers to the ultimate purposes of our studies and guides the actions we might take in light of our knowledge. This chapter also discusses the three most significant and difficult ethical issues facing the world in the age of globalization.

Part Three
Structures and processes

In this part of the book we want to introduce you to the main underlying structures and processes in contemporary world politics. There is obviously going to be some overlap between this part and the next, since the division between structures and processes, and international issues is largely one of perspective. For us, the difference is that by structures and processes we mean relatively stable features of world politics that are more enduring and constant than are the issues dealt with in the next part. Again, we have two aims in this part: **first,** we want you to get a good overview of some of the most important structures and processes in world politics at the beginning of the twenty-first century. We have therefore chosen a series of ways of thinking about world politics that draw attention to these underlying features. Again, note that we realize that what is a structure and what is a process is largely a matter of debate, but it may help to say that together these provide the setting in which the issues dealt with in the next part of the book have to be played out. All of the features examined in this part of the book will be important for the resolution of the issues we deal with in the next part, since they comprise both the main structures of world politics that these issues have to face and the main processes that will determine their fate. Our **second** aim is that these structures and processes will help you to think about globalization by forcing you to ask again whether or not it is a qualitatively different form of world politics than hitherto. Does globalization require or represent an overthrow of the structures and processes that have been central in world politics to date?

Chapter 12

The changing character of war

MICHAEL SHEEHAN

- Introduction...212
- Definitions...213
- The nature of war 214
- The revolution in military affairs 217
- Post-modern war 219
- New wars...221
- Conclusion..224

Reader's Guide

War has been one of the key institutions of the practice of international relations, and has always been a central focus of the study of international relations. In the post-cold war period many observers have suggested that the nature of war is undergoing fundamental changes, or even that in some parts of the world at least, it has become obsolete. With the advance of economic interdependence through globalization, and the spread of democracy, some groups of states seem to have formed security communities where war between them is no longer a possibility.

Elsewhere, however, war has continued to exist, and to take a number of different forms. For some countries, such as the United States, the use of advanced technology to achieve dramatic victories against conventional armies has led to suggestions that a **revolution in military affairs** is under way. Other parts of the world, however, have been characterized by warfare in which non-state actors have been prominent, the military technology employed has been relatively unsophisticated, and atrocities have been commonplace. Such new wars, it is argued by many, are a direct result of the process of globalization.

Introduction

The British strategic thinker Basil Liddell Hart once wrote that 'if you want peace, understand war', while the revolutionary Marxist Leon Trotsky declared confidently that 'you may not be interested in war, but war is interested in you'. This advice remains appropriate in the contemporary world. Around 14,400 wars have occurred throughout recorded history, claiming the lives of some 3.5 billion people. Since 1815 there have been between 224 and 559 wars, depending on the definition of war that is used (Mingst 2004: 198). War has not disappeared as a form of social behaviour and shows no signs of doing so, though it is not necessarily an inevitable form of human behaviour and seems to have become effectively extinct in some parts of the world. Since the end of the cold war, the annual number of wars, the number of battle deaths, and the number of war-related massacres have all declined sharply compared with the cold war period. Between 1989 and 1992 nearly one hundred wars came to an end, and in terms of battle deaths, the 1990s were the least violent decade since the end of the Second World War (University of British Columbia, Human Security Center 2005: 17). Despite the overall decline in the incidence of war, however, in many regions it is very much present and is displaying some novel features in comparison to those typical of the cold war period.

Box 12.1 The obsolescence of war

A striking feature of war in some parts of the contemporary world is its absence. The North Atlantic region has been described as a **security community**, a group of states for whom war has disappeared as a means of resolving disputes between each other, though they may continue to use war against opponents outside the security community. One common characteristic of these states is that they are all democracies, and it has been suggested that while democracies will go to war, they are not prepared to fight against a fellow democracy. The assumption of this **democratic peace** argument is that where groups of democracies inhabit a region, war will become extinct in that region, and that as democracy spreads throughout the world, war will decline. However, there is a danger that some wars will occur as democracies attempt to overthrow non-democratic regimes to spread the 'democratic zone of peace', so that wars will be fought in the name of peace. In addition, for some observers, even non-democracies will be averse to fighting wars when both they and their great power rivals are armed with nuclear weapons.

In the contemporary world there are powerful pressures producing changes to national economies and societies. Some of these can be seen to reflect the impact of **globalization**, others are the result of the broader effects of **post-modernity**, but their cumulative effect has been to bring about significant political and social changes, which have in turn been reflected in changed perceptions of the nature of threats coming from the external environment. This in turn has influenced beliefs regarding the utility of force as an instrument of policy, and the forms and functions of war. In the past two centuries, the 'modern' era of history, war has traditionally been seen as a brutal form of politics, a way in which **states** sought to resolve certain issues in international relations, and an outcome of their willingness to amass military power for defence and deterrence, and to project it in support of their foreign and defence policies. The two 'world wars' of the twentieth century typified this approach to the instrumentality of war. In the post-cold war period, the kinds of threats that have driven the accumulation of military power in the developed world have not taken the form of traditional state-to-state military rivalry, but have been a response to rather more amorphous and less predictable threats such as **terrorism**, **insurgencies**, and internal crises in other countries that seem to demand the projection of military force to resolve them.

For some observers, the current era has seen a major evolution in the structure of international relations, with the dramatic political changes that followed the end of the cold war and the dissolution of the Soviet Union. Changes in the **international system** on this scale are not common in history, and when they occur can be expected to have a major impact on the mechanisms by which the international system is governed. At the same time, and partly as a result of the evolution of the international environment, changes are also occurring in the domestic attributes of many of the states that make up the international system. There has, for example, been a notable increase in the number of democratic political systems, but in the same period many other states have disintegrated into civil wars and insurgency. The identity of the key players in international relations has also changed since the end of the cold war. The world has become temporarily subject to the hegemonic control of a single state,

the United States, so that the processes of globalization and **Americanization**, have become synonymous for many, who have responded with fierce cultural and political resistance.

The influential nineteenth-century strategist Carl von Clausewitz argued that the fundamental nature of war is immutable. The characteristics or **form** of war typical in any particular age might change, but the essential **nature** of war could not. For Clausewitz, the novel characteristics of war were not the result of new inventions, but of new ideas and social conditions. It would not be surprising, therefore, to see that the processes of post-modernity and globalization, of an international system characterized by constant and even accelerating change, should be marked by changes in the forms of warfare being waged in the system. Evolution in the characteristic form of warfare might be expected from the changing perceptions of threat in the post-cold war era. If, indeed, wars are taking distinctive and perhaps novel forms in the post-cold war world, this is a reflection of broader changes in the international system, rather than war being the primary agent of those changes. Wars are a socially constructed form of large-scale human group behaviour, and must be understood within the wider contexts of their political and cultural environments.

In an era of unprecedented communications technologies, new fields of warfare have emerged. **Non-state actors** in the post-cold war period have moved to transform both cyberspace and the global media into crucial battlegrounds, alongside terrestrial military and terrorist operations, so that war is now fought on a number of different planes of reality simultaneously, and reality itself is subverted in the cause of war through sophisticated strategies of informational and electronic deception. The battlefield of the past has now become the **battlespace**, and it is three-dimensional in the sense of including airpower and the use of space **satellites**, and in some senses is non-dimensional in that it also embraces cyberspace and communications wavebands.

At the same time, the tangible capacity for war-making has also been developing. Military technology with enormous destructive capacity is becoming available to more and more states. This is important not just because the technology to produce and deliver **weapons of mass destruction** is spreading, but because highly advanced 'conventional' military technology is becoming more widely available. One of the effects of the end of the cold war was that there was a massive process of disarmament by the former cold war enemies. This surplus weaponry flooded on to the global arms market, much of it highly advanced equipment being sold off comparatively cheaply.

Key Points

- War has been a central feature of human history.
- Since the end of the cold war both the frequency and lethality of war has shown a sharp decline.
- War between the great powers in particular has become much more unlikely than in previous eras.
- Changes in the international system may be changing the character of war.

Definitions

Because war is a fluid concept, it has generated a large number of sometimes contradictory definitions. Many of these are so general as to not be particularly helpful in understanding it. Some have seen it as any form of armed and organized physical conflict, while for Quincy Wright war was 'a violent contact of distinct but similar entities' (quoted in Freedman 1994: 69). General descriptions of this sort are not particularly helpful in understanding contemporary war, the first because it is insufficiently specific and could equally describe gang warfare, the latter because it makes an unreasonable assumption about the nature of the combatants. Violent crime is an important aspect of global human insecurity, killing more people each year than war and terrorism combined, but it is not war. More useful is Clausewitz's statement that it is 'an act of force intended to compel our opponents to fulfil our will', and 'a continuation of political intercourse with a mixture of other means'. In Clausewitz's work, the meaning is clarified in context by the assumption that the reader understands that he is talking about large-scale military confrontations between the representatives of states. *Webster's Dictionary* reinforces this position by

defining war as 'a state of usually open and declared armed hostile conflict between states or nations'. Unfortunately, in the current era, that is not something that can simply be assumed, because non-state groups have become prominent actors in contemporary warfare. A more useful definition in this sense is Hedley Bull's. It is 'organised violence carried on by political units against each other' (Bull 1977: 184). Bull goes on to insist that violence is not war unless it is both carried out by a political unit, and directed against another political unit.

It is possible to argue that war is simply any form of armed violence between groups of people, but it is valid to ask what sorts of goals are involved and how much violence is required for an armed clash to be called a 'war'. Is a clash between two street gangs in which several people are killed, really the same phenomenon as a military conflict between two or more states in which millions

are deliberately killed? Choosing a particular threshold can also seem arbitrary, as with the influential Singer and Small definition which requires a war to involve at least 1,000 battle deaths per year. By this token the **1982 Falklands/Malvinas War** between Argentina and the United Kingdom would barely qualify, though few would argue that that conflict was not a war. Some sense of scale is clearly needed, but perhaps Quincy Wright's less specific formulation is still reasonable, that war is 'a conflict among political groups, especially sovereign states, carried on by armed forces of considerable magnitude, for a considerable period of time' (Wright 1968: 453).

Key Points

- War in the contemporary era is not always easy to define.
- War is a brutal form of politics.

The nature of war

If, as some have argued, war has indeed taken on new forms in the post-cold war era, or perhaps has even seen an evolution in its essential nature, then it is necessary to compare these recent examples with traditional forms and interpretations of war in order to determine what, if anything, has changed and what are simply contemporary manifestations of an ancient phenomenon. This is not as straightforward an exercise as might at first appear. War is a form of organized human violence, and when conducted by states using significant quantities of personnel, materiel, and firepower, it is comparatively easy to recognize. But at the lower end of the spectrum of violence it begins to overlap with other forms of conflict, such as **terrorism**,

Box 12.2 Thucydides on war

In some ways wars have changed little over the ages. 2,500 years ago the Greek historian Thucydides observed:

'War is an evil, is something we all know, and it would be pointless to go on cataloguing all the disadvantages involved in it. No one is forced into war by ignorance, nor, if he thinks he will gain by it, is he kept out of it by fear. The fact is that one side thinks that the profits to be won outweigh the risks to be incurred, and the other side is ready to face danger rather than accept an immediate loss.'

(Thucydides [1954] 1972: Book IV)

insurgency, and criminal violence, and clear distinctions and definitions become harder to maintain. War always involves violence, but not all violence can be described as war. Violence is a necessary, but not a sufficient, requirement for a conflict to be defined as a war.

Wars are fought for reasons. The Western understanding of war, following Clausewitz, sees it as instrumental, a means to an end. Wars in this perspective are not random violence; they reflect a conscious decision to engage in them for a rational political purpose. They are rationalized by those who initiate them by appeal to belief and value systems.

War is a form of social and political behaviour. This was one of the central arguments of Clausewitz. It remains true at the start of the twenty-first century, but only if we operate with a broad and flexible understanding of what constitutes politics. As our understanding of politics, and the forms it can take, has evolved in the post-modern era, we should expect the same to be true of the character of war since that is itself a form of politics.

The political nature of war has been evolving in recent decades under the impact of globalization, which has increasingly eroded the economic, political, and cultural **autonomy** of the state. Contemporary warfare takes place in a local context, but it is also played out in wider fields

and influenced by **non-governmental organizations**, **intergovernmental organizations**, regional and global media, and users of the Internet. In many ways, contemporary wars are partly fought on television, and the **media** therefore have a powerful role in providing a framework of understanding for the viewers of the conflict. One effect of the constant coverage of international violence by the global media may be to gradually weaken the legal, moral, and political constraints against the use of force by making it appear routine, and thereby reverse the moral questioning of war that was a feature of the second half of the twentieth century. The advent of such 'war fatigue' might make recourse to war appear a normal feature of international relations.

War is an extremely paradoxical activity. Human beings have the capacity for intense violence, but are also capable of complex **cooperation**. In one sense, war is very clearly 'made up of acts of enmity rather than co-operation, of imposition rather than negotiation, of summary killing rather than due process, of destruction rather than creation' (Francis 2004: 42). Or as Robert A. Heinlein put it (in Porter 1994: xiii), 'the army is a permanent organisation for the destruction of life and property'. Yet in another sense, war is clearly a profoundly social activity, an example of humanity's 'enormous capacity for friendly co-operation' (Bigelow 1969: 3). Michel Foucault called the institution of war 'the military dimension of society' (1996: 415). This is because the conduct of war requires a society to cooperate in performing complex tasks on a large scale. Societies can fight wars because they are able to cooperate at the internal level. On the other hand, they feel themselves compelled to fight other societies because they often find it difficult to cooperate at the external level. The very act of fighting outsiders may make it easier to cooperate internally. Unless a war is highly unpopular domestically, there is a sense in which a state at war is also a state at peace.

War is both highly organized and a highly *organizing* phenomenon. In the words of the sociologist Charles Tilly (1975: 42), 'war made the state, and the state made war'. The machinery of the state derived historically from the organizational demands of warfare, and modern states owe their origins and development to a large degree to the effects of earlier wars. The modern state was born during the renaissance, a time of unprecedented violence. The intensity of armed conflict during this period triggered an early revolution in military affairs, in which the size of armies, their associated firepower, and the costs of warfare all increased dramatically. The need to survive in such a competitive and violent era favoured larger, more centralized political units that were able to control extensive tracts of territory, master complex military technologies, and mobilize the immense human resources required for success in battle.

The high point of this evolution was the Thirty Years War, which racked Europe from 1618 to 1648. By the end of that conflict **Europe** was entering a new phase of historical development, **modernity**, which would come to dominate international history for the next three hundred years before giving way to **post-modernity** in the late twentieth century. Modernity had many features and, as Clausewitz noted, each age has its own dominant characteristic form of war, which reflects the era in which it occurs, though there will also be other forms reflecting cultural and geographical realities. There was therefore a form of warfare that was typical of modernity.

The period of modernity was characterized by the rise of **nationalism** and increasingly centralized and bureaucratic states with rapidly rising populations, by the scientific and industrial revolutions, and by the growth of secular ideologies with messianic visions and an intolerance of opposing **metanarratives** and, broad overarching ideologies, such as Marxism. The warfare that was characteristic of the period reflected the forces of modernity, and its enormous transformational effects. States mobilized mass armies through centralized bureaucracies and the power of nationalism. They armed and equipped them with the products of industrialization and expected their populations to sacrifice themselves for the state, and to show no mercy to the opposing population that was being called upon to make the same self-sacrifice for its own motherland. The result was industrialized warfare on a massive scale, in which civilian populations as much as enemy soldiers were seen as legitimate targets, a process that culminated in the **nuclear** attacks on Japan in 1945.

At the same time, another feature of warfare during the modern period was that, at least in the conflicts between the developed states, it was governed by **rules**. An entire body of international law was developed to constrain and regulate the use of violence in wartime. Quincy Wright argues that war always involves a legal relationship which distinguishes it from mere fighting, even organized fighting. It is 'a condition of time in which special rules permitting and regulating violence between governments

prevails' (Wright 1965: 2). This is an important feature distinguishing war from other forms of violence. It is a particular *kind* of relationship between politically motivated groups. Wright insists, therefore, that war cannot be said to be occurring when the antagonists do not recognize each other as participants, but see the opponent simply as an obstacle to the achievement of certain goals, as a geographical barrier might be.

The intensity of war often unleashes or accelerates numerous forces for change, transforming industry, society, and government in ways that are fundamental and permanent. By weakening or destroying traditional structures, or by compelling internal reforms, war may create conditions conducive to social change and political modernization. The requirement to defeat the opponent's forces may lead to advances in **technologies** such as transportation, food manufacture and storage, communications, and so on, that have applications well beyond the military sphere. It was in this sense that, for the ancient Greek thinker Heraclitus, war was 'the father of all and the king of all'.

Historically, during the period of modernity, the conduct of war compelled governments to centralize power in order to mobilize the resources necessary for victory. Bureaucracies and tax burdens increased in size to support the war effort. But the strains involved in preparing for and engaging in war can also lead to the weakening or **disintegration** of the state, as happened with South Vietnam in 1975 and to some extent the Soviet Union in 1991.

Nevertheless, war, both in terms of preparation for it and its actual conduct, may be a powerful catalyst for change, but technological or even political modernization does not necessarily imply moral progress. Evolution in war, including its contemporary forms, may involve change that is morally problematic, as indeed is the case with the forces of globalization more generally. War is a profound **agent of historical change**, but it is not the fundamental driving force of history. There are a wide variety of factors that can contribute to the outbreak of war, such as nationalism, class conflict, human nature, and so on. These are the main drivers of change rather than war itself. War is not something imposed by an outside force.

The willingness to go to war comes from within states and societies.

For many analysts of war, war's **nature,** as the use of organized violence in pursuit of political goals, always remains the same, and is unaltered even by radical changes in political forms, in the motives leading to conflict, or technological advances (Gray 1999*b*: 169). For Colin Gray, if war's nature were to change, it would become something else, so he, like Clausewitz, insists that all wars have the same political nature, one fundamentally based on the idea that war is a **political act**, the use of force for conscious political ends.

For Clausewitz and Gray, there is an important distinction between the **nature** and the **character** of war. The former refers to the constant, universal, and inherent qualities that ultimately define war throughout the ages, such as violence, chance, and uncertainty. The latter relates to the impermanent, circumstantial, and adaptive features that war develops and that account for the different periods of warfare throughout history, each displaying attributes determined by socio-political and historical preconditions, while also influencing those conditions. Clausewitz also distinguished between the **objective** and **subjective** nature of war, the former comprising of the elements common to all wars and the latter consisting of those features that make each war unique.

A number of questions follow from this survey of war in relation to its contemporary and future forms. Does the current era have a dominant form of war and if so what is it? In what ways are the processes associated with globalization changing contemporary warfare? In what ways are the characteristics of post-modernity being reflected in contemporary modes of warfare? Does the prevailing ethical basis of warfare reflect early or late modernity, or is it recognizably new?

Key Points

- Contemporary warfare is being influenced by globalization.
- War requires highly organized societies.
- War can be a powerful catalyst for change.
- The nature of war remains constant, but its form reflects the particular era and environment in which it occurs.

The revolution in military affairs

Although many observers have suggested that the character of war is changing significantly, their reasons for coming to this conclusion are often quite different. One school of thought focuses on the so-called revolution in military affairs (RMA). The concept of the revolution in military affairs became popular after the dramatic American victory in the **1991 Gulf War**. The manner in which superior technology and doctrine appeared to give the United States an almost effortless victory suggested that future conflicts would be decided by the possession of technological advantages such as advanced guided weapons and space satellites. However, the subsequent popularity of the RMA concept has not produced a clear consensus on what exactly the RMA is or what its implications might be. Although analysts agree that RMAs involve a radical change or some form of discontinuity in the history of warfare, there is disagreement regarding how and when these changes or discontinuities take place, or what causes them.

The former US Secretary of Defense, William Cohen, defined an RMA as 'when a nation's military seizes an opportunity to transform its strategy, military doctrine, training, education, organization, equipment, operations and tactics to achieve decisive military results in fundamentally new ways' (quoted in Gray 2002: 1).

RMA proponents argue that recent breakthroughs and likely future advances in military technology mean that military operations will be conducted with such speed, precision, and selective destruction that the whole character of war will change and this will profoundly affect the way that military/political affairs are conducted in the next few decades. Most of the RMA literature focuses on the implications of developments in **technology**. In the conflicts in Kuwait (1991), Serbia (1999), and Iraq (2003), American technology proved vastly superior to that of its opponent. In particular, computing and space technology allowed the US forces to acquire information about the enemy to a degree never before seen in warfare, and allowed precision targeting of weapon systems. Advanced communications allowed generals to exercise

detailed and instant control over the developing battle and to respond quickly to developments. The speed, power, and accuracy of the weapons employed allowed them to be carefully targeted so as to destroy vital objectives without inflicting unnecessary casualties on civilian populations, though absolute precision and reliability proved impossible to achieve. Opponents lacking counters to these technologies found themselves helpless in the face of overwhelming American superiority. However, the RMA emphasis on military technology and **tactics**, while understandable, risks producing an oversimplistic picture of what is an extremely complex phenomenon, in which non-technological factors can play a crucial part in the outcome.

In addition, most of the literature and debate on the RMA has been American and has tended to take for granted the dominance conferred by technological superiority. The current RMA is based upon a particularly Western concept of war fighting and may well only be of utility in certain well-defined situations. There has been far less discussion of how the opponents of a technologically advanced state might use unconventional or **asymmetric** responses to fight effectively against a more technologically sophisticated opponent. Asymmetry works both ways. Asymmetric conflicts since 1990 have been fought by US-led 'coalitions of the willing' against Iraq (1991 and 2003), Yugoslavia, and Afghanistan. Because of the extreme superiority in combat power of the coalition, the battle phases of these asymmetric conflicts have been fairly brief and have produced relatively few combat deaths compared to the cold war period. However, in the post-conventional insurgency phases in Iraq and Afghanistan, the asymmetry has produced guerrilla-style conflict against the technological superiority of the coalition forces.

A skilful opponent will always seek to capitalize on its strengths while minimizing those of the enemy. In any war, the outcome will be largely determined by the relative power of the combatants, which will influence the methods they use to fight the war. Some combatants may not even be trying to defeat the enemy armed forces as such,

Case Study   The Iraq War, 2003–7

On 20 March 2003, US-led coalition forces invaded Iraq with the objective of locating and disarming suspected Iraqi weapons of mass destruction. The coalition forces conducted a swift and overwhelmingly successful campaign, leading to the capture of Baghdad and the collapse and surrender of the Iraqi armed forces. President George W. Bush declared the official end of major combat operations on the 2 May 2003. While casualties during this conventional phase of fighting were historically low for a major modern war, the fighting quickly evolved into an insurgency in which guerrilla and terrorist attacks on the coalition forces and Iraqi civilian population were the norm. By the spring of 2007 the coalition had suffered around 3,500 deaths and 24,000 wounded. Estimates of total Iraqi war-related deaths ranged from conservative estimates of 60,000 to a maximum figure of 650,000.

The Iraq War illustrates a number of the themes that have been prominent in discussions of the possible future development of war. The rapid coalition victory saw the Iraqi armed forces shattered by the technological superiority of the advanced weapons and information systems of the United States forces, suggesting that a revolution in military affairs was underway.

The doctrine employed by the American forces was also vital. The allied success was the result not just of technological superiority, but also of a superior manoeuvre-oriented operational doctrine. The swift and comparatively bloodless victory for the American-led forces reinforced the view that in the post-cold war strategic environment, there were few inhibitions on the use of force by the United States. With the trauma of Vietnam laid to rest, war had become swift, decisive, and affordable for the United States, and the end of the cold war removed the threat of regional conflict escalating into a nuclear conflict with another superpower.

A central feature of the conflict was the American dominance of information warfare, both in the military sense of the ability to use satellite systems for reconnaissance, communications, and weapons targeting, and in the post-modern sense of the manipulation of the civilian communications and global media images of the war to produce an international understanding of the fighting that reflected what the US administration wished the watching world to perceive.

However, the conflict did not end with the surrender of the regular Iraqi forces, confirming, in turn, some of the arguments of the proponents of the 'post-modern' and 'new' wars theses. The ability to operate using complex informal military networks allowed the insurgency to conduct effective asymmetric warfare, despite the overwhelming superiority of the US military technology. In addition, the insurgents were able to use the global media to manipulate perceptions of the character and implications of the strategy of terrorism and destabilization. The techniques used by the insurgents were brutal, ruthless and targeted against the civilian population, in a campaign supported by outside forces and finance, and sustained by an overtly identity-based campaign, again reflecting features of the post-modern and 'new wars' conceptions.

but simply to manipulate violence in order to demoralize the opponent and lead them to make concessions. RMA authors also tend to work within a Westphalian state-centric model that overemphasizes the traditional state-to-state confrontation, and may not be particularly relevant in the intra-state insurgency warfare that has been prevalent since 1991.

The conflict in Iraq from 2003 onwards (see Case Study), raised major questions about the pattern of warfare likely after the RMA. Who are the most likely future opponents of states capable of adopting the RMA technologies? Does the RMA influence all forms of war or simply large-scale, conventional inter-state war? What about urban warfare or nuclear weapons? What is the likely response of opponents such as terrorists, insurgents, and armed forces unable to acquire RMA technology themselves?

Box 12.3 Asymmetric warfare

Asymmetric warfare exists 'when two combatants are so different in their characters, and in their areas of comparative strategic advantage, that a confrontation between them comes to turn on one side's ability to force the other side to fight on their own terms.... The strategies that the weak have consistently adopted against the strong often involve targeting the enemy's domestic political base as much as his forward military capabilities. Essentially such strategies involve inflicting pain over time without suffering unbearable retaliation in return.'

(L. Freedman (1998), 'Britain and the Revolution in Military Affairs', Defense Analysis, 14: 58)

The danger in the emphasis on technological aspects that is central to the RMA literature is that it can lead to an underestimation of the political and social dimensions of

war. The outcomes of wars are influenced by a wide range of factors in addition to technology, and in most parts of the contemporary world, the current and potential wars are not being influenced by the RMA technology which is possessed by only a handful of states. However, some conflicts are being influenced by elements of the RMA, such as specific technologies. The **conventional warfare** between India and Pakistan in the late 1990s involved highly advanced weapon systems and the use by India of satellite technology.

The increasing importance of information in warfare may be a validation of Clausewitz's argument that the form of war reflects the culture and technologies of the age. Alvin and Heidi Toffler (1993) argue that the way a society makes war reflects the way it makes wealth. Starting with the very invention of agriculture, every revolution in the system for creating wealth triggered a corresponding revolution in the system for making war. Therefore, to the extent that a new 'information economy' is emerging, this will bring with it a parallel revolution in warfare. In the Information Age, information is the central resource for wealth production and power, and the RMA is the inevitable outgrowth of basic changes in the form of economic production.

The proposition that military revolutions are the product of deep social, political, and economic changes connects organized political violence and society. What exactly that relationship is, however, is still debatable, with some seeing the RMA as the result of dramatic changes in technology and society generally since the 1980s, and others seeing the technological advances as the result of the state's need to maximize its military capabilities in the late cold war and post-cold war periods. Cause and effect are not easy to distinguish.

A major part of the appeal of the RMA concept in Western societies is that it suggests the possibility of using so-called **smart weapons** to achieve a quick, clean victory in war. The RMA technologies allow the battlefield to be controlled in a way that was not possible in previous eras,

---

Box 12.4 The revolution in military affairs: a cautionary note

Benjamin Lambeth warns that, "a revolution in military affairs" cannot be spawned merely by platforms, munitions, information systems and hardware equities. These necessary but insufficient preconditions must be supported by an important set of intangibles that have determined war results since the days of Alexander the Great—namely, clarity of goals backed by proficiency and boldness in execution. In the so-called "RMA debate", too much attention has been devoted to technological magic at the expense of the organisational, conceptual and other human imputs needed to convert the magic from lifeless hardware into combat outcomes.'

(B. S. Lambeth (1997), 'The Technology Revolution in Air Warfare', Survival, 39: 75)

---

so that the tempo of battle can be orchestrated and wars won without massive loss of life. To the extent that such an RMA is occurring, for the foreseeable future it is very much an American-led RMA, and reflects American understandings of how and why military affairs are conducted. The American approach has been to attempt to win wars quickly by applying overwhelming force, and to use the industrial and technological strength of the United States to minimize casualties. Yet the reality of war is that it is never clean or bloodless. Even in the age of smart weapons and space technology, war remains a brutal and bloody undertaking where political objectives are achieved through the infliction of human suffering on a major scale.

Key Points

- Dramatic technological advances mean that a revolution in military affairs may be underway.
- Few states currently possess such technology.
- The 'information age' is increasingly reflected in 'information warfare'.
- Opponents with little or no access to RMA technology are likely to use 'asymmetric warfare' to fight the war on their own terms.

Post-modern war

If war is a reflection of its age, as Clausewitz argued, then contemporary warfare should reflect key aspects of post-modernity. A number of authors have suggested that this is in fact the case, that the world is undergoing a dramatic

evolution into post-modernity and that this will inevitably lead to a radical redefinition of war itself.

Global society is moving from the modern to the post-modern age. This is a process that has been underway

for several decades and is the result of a wide range of economic, cultural, social, and political changes that are altering the meaning of the 'state' and the **nation**. It has been marked by a shift from production to information as a core output of advanced economies. As this happens, it will affect the character of war. In some parts of the world the state is deliberately transferring functions, including military functions, to private authorities and businesses. In other areas, these functions are being seized from the state by other political actors. At the same time, globalization has weakened the 'national' forms of **identity** that have dominated international relations in the past two centuries, and reinvigorated earlier forms of political identity and organization, such as religious, ethnic, and clan loyalties.

The greatly increased role of the media is one feature of this evolution. The media have become far more important in terms of shaping or even constructing understandings of particular wars. Media warfare has made war more transparent. Each side now goes to great lengths to manipulate media images of the conflict, and journalists have effectively been transformed from observers into active participants, facing most of the same dangers as the soldiers and helping to shape the course of the war through their reporting. This reflects a broader change. Just as 'modernity' and its wars were based on the mode of production, so 'post-modernity' and its wars reflect the mode of information.

Another post-modern development has been the increasing 'outsourcing' of war. Over the past decade more and more states have contracted out key military services to private corporations. Privatized Military Firms (PMFs) sell a wide range of war-related services to states, overwhelmingly in the logistical and security roles rather than direct combat. Hundreds of PMFs have operated in more than 50 countries since the end of the cold war. The growth of PMFs reflect a broader global trend towards the privatization of public assets. Through the provision of training and equipment, PMFs have influenced the outcomes of several recent wars, including those in Angola, Croatia, Ethiopia, and Sierra Leone. PMFs played a significant role in the 2003 US-led invasion of Iraq.

For some authors in the late 1990s, the possibility of casualty-free or **virtual war** seemed to be becoming a possibility. Democracies in recent decades have shown a reluctance to tolerate heavy military casualties, which can undermine public support for the war-effort. From the **NATO** perspective, the 1999 war against Yugoslavia over Kosovo appeared to be just such a conflict, a 'virtual' war in which the NATO forces attempted to employ their technological superiority in such a way as to reduce the risk of casualties to the absolute minimum. The increasing importance of information warfare and the need to dominate cyberspace and the airwaves also encourages the idea that war might become 'virtual' and lose its traditional connection to the clear and deliberate use of deadly force.

For the Kosovan and Serbian victims of ethnic violence on the ground and the Serbian victims of allied air attacks, the war was anything but 'virtual'. As Freedman points out in relation to the temptations of the RMA, the new technologies do not 'offer the prospect of a virtual war by creating a situation in which only information matters so that there is never any point in fighting about anything other than information. ... War is not a virtual thing, played out on screens, but intensely physical. That is why it tends to violence and destruction' (Freedman 1998: 78). War's very nature involves the use of violence.

Predictions of 'virtual war' seemed particularly utopian in the wake of the carnage in Iraq that followed the American-led invasion and the subsequent insurgency in 2003. There has been a trend in the past fifteen years towards forms of warfare that are notably savage at the smaller-scale level, and where the cumulative death toll has been extremely high. This has been a feature of some of the conflicts in Africa, for example, notably in Rwanda, Liberia, and Sierra Leone. Edward Luttwak has suggested that the world has entered a new age of post-heroic warfare 'easily started and fought without restraint' (Luttwak 1995: 110). Many other observers have also suggested that the wars since 1990 have been particularly barbaric, that they have been driven by irrationality and that they represent the expression of primordial hatreds that had been suppressed during the cold war and that re-emerged in the 1990s. The result was that wars seemed to be accompanied by an unprecedented level of ferocity or outright brutality.

In one important sense this is not particularly a feature of post-modern, or post-cold war conflicts. Modern war was more brutal and indiscriminate, and produced far greater casualties lists than has post-modern war to date, as the attacks on cities such as London, Hamburg, Dresden, Hiroshima, and Nagasaki during the Second World War clearly show. The twentieth century saw the advent of **total war**, which involved the complete

mobilization of the human, economic, and military resources of the state in the pursuit of victory, and which recognized few if any moral restraints in terms of who could be targeted if their destruction would bring victory closer. The effects of the industrial revolution, along with the advent of popular democracy and modern bureaucracy, had combined to 'nationalize' war to involve the whole of society. Raymond Aron (1954: 19) called this **hyperbolic war**, where the growing scale and intensity of war is driven by the pressure of industrial and technological advances.

The brutality and ethnic-cleansing characteristic of many contemporary wars are not only not historically novel, but they are in many ways a variant of the same totalizing mentality that dominated Western war-fighting during the era of modernity. In modern Western interstate war, as Foucault noted, wars 'are waged on behalf of the existence of everyone; entire populations are mobilised for the purpose of wholesale slaughter in the name of life necessity; massacres have become vital' (Foucault 1990: 137). Martin Shaw (2003: 23) uses the term 'degenerate wars' to capture the continuity of contemporary wars with the genocidal total wars of the twentieth century.

The conduct of war in some areas has seemed particularly barbaric because the combatants do not conform to the internationally accepted rules of war. But such conflicts may still be adhering to the rules of a local value-system. In the Liberian civil war, for example, animist religious beliefs lay behind many of the rituals involved in the killing. Much of the alleged 'motiveless' violence in recent conflicts has in fact been used to gain military advantage, rather than simply to inflict suffering upon the civilian population gratuitously or for economic gain. Most of the conflicts in the past decade have been fought by poorly trained, lightly armed forces. While often conducted with great brutality, these conflicts kill far fewer people than was true of the major conventional conflicts of the cold war period.

Box 12.5 Globalization and war

'The impact of globalisation is visible in many of the new wars. The global presence in these wars can include international reporters, mercenary troops and military advisers, diaspora volunteers as well as a veritable "army" of international agencies ranging from non-governmental organisations (NGO's) like Oxfam, Save the Children, Médicin sans Frontières, Human Rights Watch and the International Red Cross, to international institutions like the United Nations High Commissioner for Refugees (UNHCR), the European Union (EU), the United Nations Children's Fund (UNICEF), the Organisation for Security and Cooperation in Europe (OSCE), the Organisation for African Unity (OAU) and the United Nations itself, including peacekeeping troops.'

(Kaldor 1999: 4)

The political nature of war is nevertheless being affected by globalization. Globalization has increasingly eroded the economic, political, and cultural autonomy of the state in recent decades. As complex transnational **networks** develop and increase, and flows of people, knowledge, and money become the pattern, wars have an increasingly global impact. Contemporary wars may be localized, but they invariably involve a wide range of international networks of actors such as non-governmental organizations, the media, foreign military forces, and **diplomats**.

Key Points

- Most recent conflicts have been characterized by the kind of ferocity that was typical of 'modern' war, but overall casualty levels have been much lower.
- The post-modern age has seen warfare take numerous, varied forms.
- 'Virtual war', with few casualties, is an attractive option, but is extremely difficult and probably impossible to achieve in practice.

New wars

Mary Kaldor has suggested that a category of **new wars** has emerged since the mid-1980s. The driving force behind these new wars is globalization, 'a contradictory process involving both integration and fragmentation, homogenization and diversification, globalization and localization' (Kaldor 1999: 3). These conflicts are typically based around the disintegration of states and subsequent struggles for control of the state by opposing

groups, who are simultaneously attempting to impose their own definition of the national identity of the state and its population. Just as earlier wars were linked to the emergence and creation of states, the new wars are related to the disintegration and collapse of states, and much of the pressure on such states has come from the effects of globalization on the international system. In the past decade, 95 per cent of armed conflicts have taken place within states rather than between them. The new wars occur in situations where the economy of the state is performing extremely poorly, or even collapsing, so that the tax revenues and power of the state decline dramatically, producing an increase in corruption and criminality. As the state loses control, access to weapons and the ability to resort to violence is increasingly privatized and paramilitary groups proliferate, organized crime grows, and political legitimacy collapses. One of the effects of these developments is that the traditional distinction between the 'soldier' and the 'civilian' become blurred or disappear altogether.

For Kaldor, a significant feature of these conflicts is the combatants' focus on questions of **identity**, which she sees as being a result of the pressures produced by globalization. In the post-modern world there has been a breakdown of traditional cleavages based on class and ideology, and a greater emphasis on identity and culture. To the extent that war is a continuation of politics, therefore, war has become increasingly driven by questions of culture and identity. A major cause of the wars since 1990 has been the demands of various groups for national **self-determination**. Questions of 'identity' in a broader sense have also underpinned recent wars. It can be argued that Islamic fundamentalists are not fighting for control of territory or political power in the traditional Westphalian sense, but in order to defend or expand a particular cultural autonomy against the globalizing pressures of Westernization and secularism.

The relationship between identity and war is also shifting in terms of the **gender** and age of the combatants. The 'feminization' of war has grown as women have come to play increasingly visible and important roles, from auxiliaries in the late modern period, to direct front-line roles in the post-modern period, from uniformed military personnel to female suicide bombers. **Children** have also become more visible as participants rather than non-combatants in war. Helen Brocklehurst has drawn attention to the meaning and implications

of the increasing visibility of children as victims of war at many different levels. Child soldiers can be found on every continent, but have been particularly prevalent in recent African conflicts. In the civil war in Sierra Leone, nearly 70 per cent of the combatants were under the age of 18. Children fight in around three-quarters of today's armed conflicts, and may make up 10 per cent of current armed combatants (Brocklehurst 2007: 373). Nearly one-third of the militaries that use child soldiers include girls in their ranks.

Mark Duffield argues that the non-state dimension of much contemporary warfare is striking and that describing such conflicts as 'internal' or 'intra-state' is misleading since the combatants often are not attempting to impose a political authority in the traditional sense. The use of **statist** terminology is therefore too limiting, leading him to propose the alternative terminology of **post-modern conflict** (Duffield 1998: 76), although the use of the term in this way is also rather constraining. Sub-state threats do not trigger the full mobilization of the state's military and other resources in the way that an inter-state threat would. Because they often blur political and military threats, they are more difficult to counter within the traditional state-to-state strategic approach.

The assumption that 'war' is something that takes place between states is based on an acceptance of the 'Westphalian' **state system** as the **norm**. This was the case during the 'modern' period of history, from the mid-eighteenth century till the late twentieth century. This was the period when the 'state system' was most clearly defined, and historically there is a powerful linkage between the nature of the existing 'international' system, and the prevailing mode of warfare. Inter-state warfare in the modern era was therefore typical of that particular historical period. War was an armed conflict between opposing states, fought by uniformed, organized bodies of men. They were regulated by formal acts, including declarations of war, laws of neutrality, and peace treaties. As the state system evolves in response to post-modernity and globalization, typical forms of warfare can be expected to evolve also. Thus it is not surprising that commentators should speak of 'post-Westphalian war'. The sub-state features of many wars are prominent, as they are increasingly fought by militias, paramilitaries, warlord armies, criminal gangs, private security firms, and tribal groupings, so that the Westphalian state's monopoly of violence is increasingly challenged both from outside and

inside. This has been notable in conflicts such as those in the **Democratic Republic of Congo**, **Sudan** and **Bosnia**. 'Paramilitaries' include armed police, border guards, internal security forces, riot squads, militias, and privatized armies. They are usually more heavily armed than police forces, but less well equipped than regular soldiers. Because of this they can be quickly raised, equipped, and trained, making them particularly prominent in recent conflicts. The growth of paramilitaries is one of the most notable features of the global conflict scene.

The relationship of terrorism campaigns to war is also important. The **war on terror** can be seen simply as a metaphor for an intense national commitment against Al Qaeda, but it can also be seen as a recognition that a long-duration military–terrorist campaign and the counter-measures taken by the target group are a form of warfare in the sense that Clausewitz described—a violent form of politics.

These complex interrelationships of non-traditional actors are not limited to insurgents or criminal gangs. Because of the prevalence of **humanitarian interventions** and the belief that economic development acts as a deterrent to war, aid organizations, UN agencies, armed forces, and private security firms are increasingly networked in areas such as the Balkans, Africa, and the Middle East. The causes of internal conflict are often related to poverty and underdevelopment, so that issues of **poverty**, stability, **development**, and peace have become increasingly seen as being linked in an overall pattern of insecurity. This has meant a greater willingness by developed states to see war as in many ways an issue of underdevelopment and political insecurity, and the presence of such social and economic insecurity as being in itself a justification for **wars of intervention**.

Many of the features of the new wars are not new in the sense that they have been common in earlier periods of history—ethnic and religious wars, for example, or conflicts conducted with great brutality. **Looting** and plunder have been a feature of most wars in history. Low-intensity conflicts have in fact been the most common form of armed conflict since the late 1950s. However, it can be argued that the initiators of the new wars have been empowered by the new conditions produced by globalization, which have weakened states and created parallel economies and privatized protection. These new wars are made possible by the inability of many governments to successfully exercise many of the functions associated with the traditional Westphalian state. Such conflicts will typically occur in **failed states**, countries where the government has lost control of significant parts of the national territory and lacks the resources to re-impose control. Steven Metz has termed the countries falling into this category as the **third tier** states of the global political system.

This weakness of the state produces a significant difference in the economic support for the 'new wars' compared to their 'modern' predecessors. The new globalized economy is quite different from the centralized economies that were typical during the Second World War. The new war economies are decentralized and highly reliant on external assets. Participation in the war by the general population is usually low. Unemployment is generally high, providing a source of recruits seeking an income. The fighting units therefore finance themselves through plunder and the black market, or through external assistance, not through state taxation as in the 'old' wars. Criminal activities such as **hostage-taking**, trafficking of weapons, drugs, and people, and money-laundering are also used to support the war effort. Where foreign aid is

---

Box 12. 6 'Third tier' states

Steven Metz groups the world's states into three 'tiers' for the purpose of predicting likely future forms of conflict. Those of the first tier are the states which have effective functioning economies and political systems, and exhibit high degrees of internal stability and external law-abiding behaviour. The democracies of the North Atlantic region are typical of this group. Second-tier states exhibit periodic instability, and may have areas within their territory where the government does not exercise internal **sovereignty**. However, the state is not in danger of collapse. Third-tier states are marked by crisis. There are considerable areas where the central government has lost control and non-governmental armed forces are operating. In such areas, the 'warlords' or other groupings neither exercise full control over the areas they dominate, nor contribute to the stability of the country as a whole, which is therefore essentially ungovernable. War in such areas will typically 'involve substate groups fighting for the personal glory of the leader, or wealth, resources, land, ethnic security or even revenge for real or perceived past injustices'. Such conflicts may involve groups representing different ethnic or communal groupings and 'the fighting will usually be undertaken with low-technology weapons but fought with such intensity that the casualty rates may be higher than in conventional warfare, especially among civilians caught up in the fighting'.

(Craig Snyder and J. Johan Malik (1999), 'Developments in Modern Warfare', in C. Snyder (ed.), Contemporary Security and Strategy (London: Macmillan): 204)

reaching the conflict zone, theft or extortion of the aid will also fund the fighting. Globalization also means that the combatants do not produce their own weaponry, as was typical in 'modern' war, but acquire it directly or indirectly through intermediaries on the global arms market, or through the disintegration of the state structures as in **Moldova** and **Chechnya**.

For some observers, the economic rationale, rather than politics, is what drives the new wars, so that war has become a continuation of **economics** by other means. It is the pursuit of personal wealth rather than political power that is the motivation of the combatants. In some conflicts, therefore, war has become the end rather than the means.

Key Points

- 'New wars', following state collapse, are often conflicts over identity as much as territory.
- The new wars in fact follow a pattern of warfare that has been typical since the late 1950s.
- Such conflicts typically occur in countries where development is lacking and there is significant economic insecurity.

Conclusion

The end of the cold war has not significantly altered the dominant patterns of war that have been in place for the past fifty years. The 'new' forms of conflict are for the most part not new as such, but have received more Western attention since the end of the cold war. While they are often characterized by great brutality, the absence of heavy weaponry and superpower support means that casualty levels are markedly lower than during the cold war. RMA technologies have dramatic potential, but have so far had little impact outside US operations. While war is less common and less deadly than in the 1945–92 period, it remains a brutal and inhumane form of politics.

? Questions

1 To what extent is globalization a cause of war?

2 In what ways are wars examples of cooperative behaviour?

3 Why do some authors believe that war between the current great powers is highly unlikely?

4 What is the distinction between the *nature* and the *character* (or form) of war?

5 To what extent is a 'revolution in military affairs' taking place?

6 What is 'asymmetric warfare'?

7 How important is gender in understanding war?

8 What do you understand by the term, the 'new wars'?

9 What is the relationship between children and contemporary war?

10 Has war become more brutal since the end of the cold war?

↪ Guide to further reading

Biddle, S. (2004), *Military Power: Explaining Victory and Defeat in Modern Battle* (Princeton, NJ: Princeton University Press). An interesting and stimulating study of warfare since 1900, analysing the techniques and technologies which have aided the offence and defence to achieve victory in modern wars.

Blank, S. J. (1996), 'Preparing for the Next War: Reflections on the Revolution in Military Affairs', *Strategic Review*, 24: 17–25. An analysis of the post-1990 revolution in military affairs, which

argues cogently that in order to benefit from the technological advantages in the RMA, states must embrace necessary organizational and doctrinal changes.

Brocklehurst, H. (2006), *Whose Afraid of Children? Children, Conflict and International Relations* (Aldershot: Ashgate). A ground-breaking study of the place of children in modern warfare, exploring their roles as warriors, as victims, and as witnesses. The book raises searching questions about the meaning of 'childhood' and 'child' in the light of contemporary conflict.

Cohen, E. A. (2004), 'Change and Transformation in Military Affairs', *The Journal of Strategic Studies,* 27(3): 395–407. An engaging article in which the author argues that the changes in the structures of military forces and the nature of battle mean that there has been fundamental change in the character of war in the past two decades.

Coker, C. (2001), *Humane Warfare* (London: Routledge). A challenging book which argues that the horrors of mid-twentieth-century warfare has led Western democracies to seek to fight 'humane wars' characterized by minimal civilian and military casualties on both sides.

Duyvestyn, I., and Angstrom, J. (eds) (2005), *Rethinking the Nature of War* (London: Frank Cass). A collection of excellent essays debating the changing nature of war in the post-cold war era.

Gray, C. S. (2002), *Strategy for Chaos: Revolutions in Military Affairs and the Evidence of History* (London: Frank Cass). A very good introduction to the RMA debates with useful historical case studies of earlier RMAs.

Ignatieff, M. (1997), *The Warriors Honor: Ethnic War and the Modern Conscience* (New York: Henry Holt). An examination of the motivations of 'moral interventionists' such as aid workers, journalists, and peacekeepers, and those of the ethnic warriors with whom they engage in postmodern war zones.

Kaldor, M. (1999), *New and Old Wars: Organised Violence in a Global Era* (Cambridge: Polity, Press). Kaldor argues that key features of the conflicts waged since 1990 allow them to be termed 'new wars'. Sadly, the long history of warfare demonstrates that there is little that is genuinely novel about such conflicts.

Record, J. (2004), *Dark Victory: America's Second War Against Iraq* (Washington, DC: US Naval Institute Press). This is a study of the 2003 war against Iraq, which sees it as a long-delayed completion of business begun in 1990–1. Although it does not deal with the insurgency phase of the war, Record strongly advocated a comprehensize programme for post-war reconstruction as a key to long-term success.

Van Creveld, M. (1991), *The Transformation of War* (New York: Free Press). An analysis that is particularly strong in bringing out the socio-economic demands of modern warfare.

von Clausewitz, C. (1989), *On War*, edited and translated by Michael Howard and Peter Paret (Princeton, NJ: Princeton University Press). Clausewitz remains essential reading for the serious student of war.

Online Resource Centre

 Visit the Online Resource Centre that accompanies this book to access more learning resources on this chapter topic at www.oxfordtextbooks.co.uk/uk/orc/baylis_smith4e/

Chapter 13

International and global security

JOHN BAYLIS

- Introduction 228
- What is meant by the concept of security? 229
- The traditional approach to national security 230
- The difficulties of cooperation between states 232
- The opportunities for cooperation between states 232
- Alternative views on international and global security 234
- Critical security studies 235
- Global society and international security 236
- Conclusion: the continuing tensions between national, international,
  and global security 238

Reader's Guide

This chapter focuses on the effects of the end of the cold war on global security. In particular, it looks at the question of whether international relations, especially in an era of increasing globalization, is likely to be as violent in the future as it has been in the past. It begins by looking at disagreements that exist about the causes of war and whether violence is always likely to be with us. We then turn to traditional/classical Realist and more contemporary neo-realist perspectives on international security, before turning to alternative approaches. The chapter ends by considering the continuing tension between national and international security and suggests that, despite the important changes associated with the processes of globalization, it remains too early to make a definitive judgement about whether a fundamentally different paradigm of international politics is emerging, or whether it is possible for such a transformation to occur.

Introduction

Students of international politics deal with some of the most profound questions it is possible to consider. Among the most important of these is whether international security is possible to achieve in the kind of world in which we live. For much of the intellectual history of the subject, a debate has raged about the causes of war. For some writers, especially historians, the causes of war are unique to each case. Other writers believe that it is possible to provide a wider, more generalized explanation. Some analysts, for example, see the causes lying in human nature, others in the outcome of the internal organization of states, and yet others in international **anarchy**. In a major work on the causes of war, Kenneth Waltz considers what he calls the three 'images' of war (man, the **state** and the **international system**) in terms of what thinkers have said about the origins of conflict throughout the history of Western civilization (Waltz 1954). Waltz himself puts particular emphasis on the nature of international anarchy ('wars occur because there is nothing to stop them from occurring'), but he also recognizes that a comprehensive explanation requires an understanding of all three. In his words: 'The third image describes the framework of world politics, but without the first and second images there can be no knowledge of the forces that determine policy, the first and second images describe the forces in world politics, but without the third image it is impossible to assess their importance or predict their results' (Waltz 1954: 238).

In this ongoing debate, as Waltz points out, there is a fundamental difference between political philosophers over whether conflict can be transcended or mitigated. In particular, there has been a difference between Realist and Idealist thinkers, who have been respectively pessimistic and optimistic in their response to this central question in the international politics field (see Ch.5). In the post-First World War period, **Idealism** claimed widespread support as the League of Nations seemed to offer some hope for greater **international order**. In contrast, during the **cold war** which developed after 1945, **Realism** became the dominant school of thought. War and violent conflict were seen as perennial features of inter-state relations stretching back through human history. With the end of the cold war, however, the debate began again. For some, the end of the intense ideological confrontation between East and West was a major turning point in international history, ushering in a new paradigm in which inter-state violence would gradually become a thing of the past and new cosmopolitan values would bring greater **cooperation** between individuals and human collectivities of various kinds (including states) (see Ch.31). This reflected more optimistic views about the development of a peaceful global society. For others, however, Realism remained the best approach to thinking about international **security**. In their view, very little of substance had changed as a result of the events of 1989. The end of the cold war initially brought a new, more cooperative era between the superpowers into existence. But this more harmonious phase in international relations was only temporary. With the first Gulf War (1990–1) and then the **9/11** attacks it became increasingly clear that states and **non-state actors** (including international terrorist groups) continued to view force as an effective way to achieve their objectives.

This chapter focuses on this debate, highlighting the different strands of thinking within these two optimistic and pessimistic schools of thought. Before this can be done, however, it is necessary to consider what is meant by 'security' and to probe the relationship between **national security** and **international security**. Attention will then shift to traditional ways of thinking about national security and the influence which these ideas have had on contemporary thinking. This will be followed by a survey of alternative ideas and approaches which have emerged in the literature in recent years. The conclusion will then provide an assessment of these ideas before returning to the central question of whether or not greater international security is more, or less, likely in the new century.

What is meant by the concept of security?

Most writers agree that security is a 'contested concept'. There is a consensus that it implies freedom from threats to core values (for both individuals and groups) but there is a major disagreement about whether the main focus of inquiry should be on 'individual', 'national', or 'international' security. For much of the cold war period, most writing on the subject was dominated by the idea of **national** security, which was largely defined in militarized terms. The main area of interest for both academics and statespeople tended to be on the military **capabilities** that their own states should develop to deal with the threats that faced them. More recently, however, this idea of security has been criticized for being **ethnocentric** (culturally biased) and too narrowly defined. Instead, a number of contemporary writers have argued for an expanded conception of security outward from the limits of parochial national security to include a range of other considerations. Barry Buzan, in his study *People, States and Fear* (1983), argued for a view of security which includes political, economic, societal, environmental as well as military aspects and which is also defined in broader international terms. Buzan's work raises interesting and important questions about whether national and international security considerations can be compatible and whether states, given the nature of the international system, are capable of thinking in more cooperative international and global terms.

This focus on the tension between national and international security is not accepted by all writers on security. There are those who argue that the emphasis on the state and inter-state relations ignores the fundamental changes which have been taking place in world politics especially in the aftermath of the cold war. For some, the dual processes of **integration** and fragmentation which characterize the contemporary world mean that much more attention should be given to 'societal security'. According to this view, growing integration in regions like **Europe** is undermining the classical political order based on **nation-states**, leaving nations exposed within larger political frameworks (like the **European Union**) (see Ch.25). At the same time, the fragmentation of various states, like the Soviet Union and Yugoslavia, has created new problems of boundaries, minorities, and organizing ideologies which are causing increasing regional instability (Waever *et al.* 1993: 196). This has led to the argument that ethno-national groups, rather than states, should become the centre of attention for security analysts.

At the same time, there are other commentators who argue that the stress on national and international security is less appropriate because of the emergence of an embryonic global society in the post-cold war era. Like the 'societal security' theorists, they point to the fragmentation of the nation-state but they argue that more attention should be given, not to society at the ethno-national level, but to global society. These writers argue that one of the most important contemporary trends is the broad process of **globalization** which is taking place. They accept that this process brings new risks and dangers. These include the risks associated with such things as international **terrorism**, a breakdown of the global monetary system, global warming, and the dangers of nuclear accidents. These threats to security, on a planetary level, are viewed as being largely outside the control of nation-states. Only the development of a global **community**, they believe, can deal with this adequately.

Box 13.1 Notions of 'security'

'A nation is secure to the extent to which it is not in danger of having to sacrifice core values if it wishes to avoid war, and is able, if challenged, to maintain them by victory in such a war.'

(Walter Lippmann)

'Security, in any objective sense, measures the absence of threats to acquired values and in a subjective sense, the absence of fear that such values will be attacked.'

(Arnold Wolfers)

'In the case of security, the discussion is about the pursuit of freedom from threat. When this discussion is in the context of the international system, security is about the ability of states and societies to maintain their independent identity and their functional integrity.'

(Barry Buzan)

'Stable security can only be achieved by people and groups if they do not deprive others of it; this can be achieved if security is conceived as a process of emancipation.'

(Wheeler and Booth)

At the same time, there are other writers on globalization who stress the transformation of the state (rather than its demise) and the new security agenda in the early years of the new century. In the aftermath of what has become known as '9/11' in September 2001 and the new era of violence which followed it, Jonathan Friedman argued that we are living in a world 'where polarization, both vertical and horizontal, both class and ethnic, has become rampant, and where violence has become more globalized and fragmented at the same time, and is no longer a question of wars between states but of sub-state conflicts, globally networked and financed, in which states have become one actor, increasingly privatized, amongst others' (Friedman 2003: ix). For many of those who feel like this, the post-September 11 era is a new and extremely dangerous period in world history. Whether the world is so different today from in the past is a matter of much contemporary discussion. In order to consider this issue we need to begin by looking at the way 'security' has been traditionally conceived.

Key Points

- Security is a 'contested concept'.
- The meaning of security has been broadened to include political, economic, societal, environmental, and military aspects.
- Differing arguments exist about the tension between national and international security.
- Different views have also emerged about the significance of 9/11 for the future of international security.

The traditional approach to national security

As Chapter 2 has shown, from the **Treaty of Westphalia** in 1648 onwards states have been regarded as by far the most powerful actors in the international system. They have been 'the universal standard of political legitimacy' with no higher authority to regulate their relations with each other. This has meant that security has been seen as the priority obligation of state governments. They have taken the view that there is no alternative but to seek their own protection in what has been described as a **self-help** world.

In the historical debate about how best to achieve national security, writers like Hobbes, Machiavelli, and Rousseau tended to paint a rather pessimistic picture of the implications of **state sovereignty**. The international system was viewed as a rather brutal arena in which states would seek to achieve their own security at the expense of their neighbours. Inter-state relations were seen as a struggle for power as states constantly attempted to take advantage of each other. According to this view, **permanent peace** was unlikely to be achieved. All that states could do was to try to balance the power of other states to prevent any one from achieving overall **hegemony**. This was a view which was shared by writers like E. H. Carr and

Box 13.2 Key definitions

'A **security community** is a group of people which has become "integrated". By integration we mean the attainment, within a territory, of a "sense of community" and of institutions and practices strong enough and widespread enough to assure . . . dependable expectations of "peaceful change" among its population. By a "sense of community" we mean a belief . . . that common social problems must and can be resolved by processes of "peaceful change".'
(Karl Deutsch)

'**Security regimes** occur when a group of states co-operate to manage their disputes and avoid war by seeking to mute the security dilemma both by their own actions and by their assumptions about the behaviour of others.'
(Robert Jervis)

'A **security complex** involves a group of states whose primary security concerns link together sufficiently closely that their national securities cannot realistically be considered apart from one another.'
(Barry Buzan)

'Acceptance of **common security** as the organizing principle for efforts to reduce the risk of war, limit arms, and move towards disarmament, means, in principle, that co-operation will replace confrontation in resolving conflicts of interest. This is not to say that differences among nations should be expected to disappear. . . . The task is only to ensure that these conflicts do not come to be expressed in acts of war, or in preparations for war. It means that nations must come to understand that the maintenance of world peace must be given a higher priority than the assertion of their own ideological or political positions.'
(Palme Report 1992)

Hans Morgenthau, who developed what became known as the realist (or 'classical' realist) school of thought in the aftermath of the Second World War. More recent attempts to up-date these ideas can be seen in the works of Alastair J. H. Murray (1997), Thomas Christensen (1996), Randall Schweller (1998), William Wohlforth (1993), and Fareed Zakaria (1998). Their work is sometimes referred to as **neoclassical realism** (see Ch.5). Alastair J. H. Murray, and Anatol Lieven and John Hulsman have also developed what has become known as **ethical realism**. According to Lieven and Hulsman:

> Ethical realism ... embodies a strong sense of the fundamentally tragic nature of the human condition. Its vision is not purely tragic, however, because it also believes in the ability of men and nations to transcend in spirit their circumstances and to strive toward the good, though never fully to achieve it. In this, ethical realism differs from much of the 'traditional' or 'classical' realism, whose exponents also have a tragic sense but too often ignore both, moral factors and the possibility of domestic progress, and believe that in the end, states, and the relative power of states, are the only really important imperatives on the international scene.
>
> *(Lieven and Hulsman 2006: 58)*

The realist pessimistic view of international relations is shared by other contemporary writers like Kenneth Waltz and John Mearsheimer. The pessimism of these **neo-realists** rests on a number of key assumptions they make about the way the international system works (see Ch.5).

Key neo-realist assumptions

- The international system is **anarchic.** They do not mean by this that it is necessarily chaotic. Rather, anarchy implies that there is no central authority capable of controlling state behaviour.
- States claiming sovereignty will inevitably develop **offensive military capabilities** to defend themselves and extend their power. As such they are potentially dangerous to each other.
- **Uncertainty,** leading to **a lack of trust,** is inherent in the international system. States can never be sure of the intentions of their neighbours and, therefore, they must always be on their guard.
- States will want to maintain their independence and sovereignty, and, as a result, **survival** will be the most basic driving force influencing their behaviour.
- Although states are rational, there will always be **room for miscalculation.** In a world of imperfect information, potential antagonists will always have an incentive to misrepresent their own capabilities to keep their opponents guessing. This may lead to mistakes about 'real' state interests.

Taken together, neo-realists argue that these assumptions produce a tendency for states to act aggressively towards each other.

According to this view, national security, or insecurity, is largely the result of the **structure** of the international system (this is why these writers are sometimes called 'structural realists'). The structure of anarchy is seen as being highly durable. The implication of this is that international politics in the future is likely to be as violent as international politics in the past. In an important article entitled 'Back to the Future' written in 1990, John Mearsheimer argued that the end of the cold war was likely to usher in a return to the traditional multilateral **balance of power** politics of the past in which extreme nationalism and ethnic rivalries would lead to widespread **instability** and **conflict**. Mearsheimer viewed the cold war as a period of peace and stability brought about by the bipolar structure of power which prevailed. With the collapse of this system, he argued that there would be a return to the kind of great power rivalries which had blighted international relations since the seventeenth century.

For neo-realist writers like Mearsheimer, international politics may not be characterized by constant wars but there is nevertheless a relentless security competition which takes place, with war, like rain, always a possibility. It is accepted that cooperation among states can and does occur, but such cooperation has its limits. It is 'constrained by the dominating logic of security competition, which no amount of co-operation can eliminate' (Mearsheimer 1994/5: 9). Genuine long-lasting peace, or a world where states do not compete for power, therefore, is very unlikely to be achieved. For neo-realists the contemporary unipolar structure of power, with US pre-eminence, is likely to give way to a new international structure, with the rise of states like China.

Key Points

- Debates about security have traditionally focused on the role of the state in international relations.
- Realists and neo-realists emphasize the perennial problem of insecurity.
- The 'security dilemma' is seen by some writers as the essential source of conflict between states.

The difficulties of cooperation between states

For most contemporary neo-realist writers there is little prospect of a significant change in the nature of security in the post-cold war world. Pointing to the Gulf War in 1991, the violent disintegration of the former Yugoslavia and parts of the former Soviet Union, continuing violence in the Middle East, and the Iraq War in 2003, it is argued that we continue to live in a world of mistrust and constant security competition. Cooperation between states occurs, but it is difficult to achieve and even more difficult to sustain. There are two main factors, it is suggested, which continue to make cooperation difficult, even after the changes of 1989. The first is the prospect of cheating; the second is the concern which states have about what are called **relative gains.**

The problem of cheating

Writers like Waltz and Mearsheimer do not deny that states often cooperate or that in the post-cold war era there are even greater opportunities than in the past for states to work together. They argue, however, that there are distinct limits to this cooperation because states have always been, and remain, fearful that others will cheat on any agreements reached and attempt to gain advantages over them. This risk is regarded as being particularly important, given the nature of modern military technology which can bring about very rapid shifts in the balance of power between states. 'Such a development', Mearsheimer has argued, 'could create a window of opportunity for the cheating side to inflict a decisive defeat on the victim state' (1994/5: 20). States realize that this is the case and although they join alliances and sign arms control agreements, they remain cautious and aware of the need to provide for their own national security in the last resort.

The problem of relative gains

Cooperation is also inhibited, according to many neo-realist writers, because states tend to be concerned with 'relative gains', rather than **absolute gains**. Instead of being interested in cooperation because it will benefit both partners, states always have to be aware of how much they are gaining compared with the state they are cooperating with. Because all states will be attempting to maximize their gains in a competitive, mistrustful, and uncertain international environment, cooperation will always be very difficult to achieve and hard to maintain.

Such a view of the problems of cooperation in the post-cold war world is not, however, shared by all writers. There is a wide body of opinion among scholars (and politicians) that the neo-realist view of international relations should be modified or even replaced. Opposition to neo-realism takes a wide variety of different forms. To illustrate alternative ways of thinking about contemporary international security, a number of different approaches will be considered. Despite the differences which exist between writers in these fields many of them share a common view that greater international security in the future is possible.

Key Points

- Trust is often difficult between states, according to realists and neo-realists, because of the problem of cheating.
- Realists and neo-realists also point out the problem of 'relative gains' whereby states compare their gains with those of other states when making their decisions about security.

The opportunities for cooperation between states

Liberal Institutionalism

One of the main characteristics of the neo-realist approach to international security is the belief that international institutions do not have a very important part to play in the prevention of war. Institutions are seen as being the product of state interests and the constraints which are imposed by the international system itself. It is these

interests and constraints which shape the decisions on whether to cooperate or compete rather than the institutions to which they belong.

Such views have been challenged by both statespeople and a number of international relations specialists, particularly following the end of the cold war. The British Foreign Secretary Douglas Hurd, for example, made the case in June 1992 that institutions themselves had played, and continued to play, a crucial role in **enhancing security**, particularly in Europe. He argued that the West had developed 'a set of international institutions which have proved their worth for one set of problems'. He went on to argue that the great challenge of the post-cold war era was to adapt these institutions to deal with the new circumstances which prevailed (Hurd, quoted in Mearsheimer 1994/5).

This view reflected a belief, widely shared among Western statespeople, that a framework of complementary, mutually reinforcing institutions—the EU, **NATO**, WEU (Western European Union), and the Organization for Security and Co-operation in Europe (OSCE)—could be developed to promote a more durable and stable European security system for the post-cold war era. It is a view which is also shared by a distinctive group of academic writers which developed since the 1980s and early 1990s. These writers share a conviction that the developing pattern of **institutionalized cooperation** between states opens up unprecedented opportunities to achieve greater international security in the years ahead. Although the past may have been characterized by constant wars and conflict, important changes are taking place in international relations at the beginning of the twenty-first century which creates the opportunity to dampen down the traditional security competition between states.

This approach, known as **Liberal Institutionalism**, operates largely within the Realist framework, but argues that international institutions are much more important in helping to achieve cooperation and stability than 'structural realists' realize (see Ch.7). According to Keohane and Martin (1995: 42), 'institutions can provide information, reduce transaction costs, make commitments more credible, establish focal points for coordination and, in general, facilitate the operation of reciprocity'. Supporters of these ideas point to the importance of European economic and political institutions in overcoming the traditional hostility of European states. They also point to the developments within the European Union and NATO in the post-cold war era to demonstrate that by investing major resources states themselves clearly believe in the importance of institutions.

As such, it is suggested that in a world constrained by state power and divergent interests, international institutions operating on the basis of reciprocity at least will be a component of any lasting peace. In other words, international institutions themselves are unlikely to eradicate war from the international system but they can play a part in helping to achieve greater cooperation between states. This was reflected in Prime Minister Margaret Thatcher's call in 1990 to 'bring the new democracies of Eastern Europe into closer association with the institutions of Western Europe'. Despite some scepticism about the European Community, she argued that the EC had reconciled antagonisms within Western Europe in the post-Second World War period and it could be used to overcome divisions between East and West in Europe in the post-cold war period. This has been very much at the heart of the campaign to expand the EU in the early years of this century (see Ch.25).

Box 13.3 Democratic peace theory

Another 'liberal' approach to international security has gathered momentum in the post-cold war world. This centres on the argument that democratic states tend not to fight other democratic states. Democracy, therefore, is seen as a major source of peace (see Ch.8). As with 'Liberal Institutionalism', this is a notion which has received wide support in Western political and academic circles. In his State of the Union Address in 1994 President Bill Clinton went out of his way to point to the absence of war between democracies as a justification for American policies of promoting a process of democratization. Support for this view can be seen in the Western policy of promoting democracy in Eastern and Central Europe following the end of the cold war and opening up the possibility of these states joining the European Union.

Democratic peace theory has been largely associated with the writings of Michael Doyle (1995a) and Bruce Russett (1995). In the same way that contemporary Realists have been influenced by the work of Hobbes, Rousseau, and Machiavelli, Doyle points to the importance of the insights contained in Immanuel Kant's 1795 essay, *Perpetual Peace*. Doyle contends that democratic representation, an ideological commitment to human rights, and transnational interdependence provide an explanation for the 'peace-prone' tendencies of democratic states (1995a: 180–4). Equally, the absence of these attributes, he argues, provides a reason why non-democratic states tend to be 'war-prone'. Without these domestic values and restraints the logic of power replaces the liberal logic of accommodation.

Key Points

- Neo-realists reject the significance of international institutions in helping many to achieve peace and security.
- Contemporary politicians and academics, who write under the label of Liberal Institutionalism see institutions as an important mechanism for achieving international security.

- Liberal Institutionalists accept many of the assumptions of Realism about the continuing importance of military power in international relations, but argue that institutions can provide a framework for cooperation which can help to overcome the dangers of security competition between states.

Alternative views on international and global security

'Constructivist' theory

The notion that international relations are not only affected by power politics but also by ideas is also shared by writers who describe themselves as 'Constructivist' theorists. According to this view, the fundamental structures of international politics are **social** rather than strictly **material**. This leads Social Constructivists to argue that changes in the nature of social interaction between states can bring a fundamental shift towards greater international security (see Ch.9).

At one level, many Constructivists, like Alexander Wendt, share a number of the major realist assumptions about international politics. For example, some accept that states are the key referent in the study of international politics and international security; that international politics is anarchic; that states often have offensive capabilities; that states cannot be absolutely certain of the intentions of other states; that states have a fundamental wish to survive; and that states attempt to behave rationally. Some, such as Wendt, also see themselves as structuralists; that is to say they believe that the interests of individual states are in an important sense constructed by the structure of the international system.

However, Constructivists think about international politics in a very different way from neo-realists. The latter tend to view structure as being made up only of a distribution of material capabilities. On the other hand, Constructivists view structure as the product of social relationships. Social structures are made possible by **shared knowledge, material resources** and **practices**. This means that social structures are defined, in part, by shared understandings, expectations, or knowledge. As an example of this, Wendt argues that the security dilemma is a social structure composed of **inter-subjective understandings** in which states are so distrustful that they make worst-case assumptions about each other's intentions, and, as a result, define their interests in 'self-help' terms. In contrast, a security community is a rather different social structure, composed of shared knowledge in which states trust one another to resolve disputes without war.

The emphasis on the structure of shared knowledge is important in Constructivist thinking. Social structures include material things, like tanks and economic resources, but these only acquire **meaning** through the shared knowledge in which they are embedded. The idea of power politics, or *realpolitik*, has meaning to the extent that states accept the idea as a basic rule of international politics. According to Social Constructivist writers, power politics is an idea which does affect the way states behave, but it does not describe all inter-state behaviour. States are also influenced by other ideas and **norms**, such as the rule of law and the importance of institutional cooperation and restraint. In his study, 'Anarchy is What States Make of It' (1992), Wendt argued that security dilemmas and wars can be seen, in part, as the outcome of self-fulfilling prophecies. The 'logic of reciprocity' means that states acquire a shared knowledge about the meaning of power and act accordingly. Equally, he argues, policies of reassurance can also help to bring about a structure of shared knowledge which can help to move states towards a more peaceful security community (see Wendt 1999).

Although Constructivists argue that security dilemmas are not acts of God, they differ over whether they can be escaped. For some, the fact that structures are socially constructed does not necessarily mean that they can be changed. This is reflected in Wendt's comment that 'sometimes social structures so constrain action

that transformative strategies are impossible' (1995: 80). Many Constructivist writers, however, are more optimistic. They point to the changes in ideas introduced by Gorbachev during the second half of the 1980s, which led to a shared knowledge about the end of the cold war. Once both sides accepted the cold war was over, it really was over. According to this view, understanding the crucial role of social structure is important in developing policies and processes of interaction which will lead towards cooperation rather than conflict. For the optimists, there is sufficient 'slack' in the international system which allows states to pursue policies of peaceful social change rather than engage in a perpetual competitive struggle for power. If there are opportunities for promoting social change, most Constructivists believe it would be irresponsible not to pursue such policies.

Key Points

- Constructivist thinkers base their ideas on two main assumptions: (1) that the fundamental structures of international politics are socially constructed; and (2) that changing the way we think about international relations can help to bring about greater international security.
- Some Constructivist thinkers accept many of the assumptions of neo-realism, but they reject the view that 'structure' consists only of material capabilities. They stress the importance of social structure defined in terms of shared knowledge and practices as well as material capabilities.
- Constructivists argue that material things acquire meaning only through the structure of shared knowledge in which they are embedded.
- The power politics and *realpolitik* practices emphasized by Realists are seen as derived from shared knowledge which can be self-fulfilling.

Critical security studies

Despite the differences between Constructivists and Realists about the relationship between ideas and material factors, they tend to agree on the central role of the state in debates about international security. There are other theorists, however, who believe that the state has been given too much prominence. Keith Krause and Michael C. Williams have defined critical security studies in the following terms: 'Contemporary debates over the nature of security often float on a sea of unvoiced assumptions and deeper theoretical issues concerning to what and to whom the term *security* refers. . . . What most contributions to the debate thus share are two inter-related concerns: what security is and how we study it' (1997: 34). What they also share is a wish to de-emphasize the role of the state and the need to re-conceptualize security in a different way. Critical security studies, however, includes a number of different approaches. These include critical theory, 'feminist' approaches and 'post-modernist' approaches (see Ch.10 and Ch.14). Given that these are discussed in other chapters they are dealt with briefly here.

Robert Cox draws a distinction between **problem-solving theories** and **critical theories**. Problem-solving theorists work within the prevailing system. They take the existing social and political relations and institutions as starting points for analysis and then see how the problems rising from these can be solved and ameliorated. In contrast, critical theorists focus their attention on the way these existing relationships and institutions emerged and what might be done to change them (see Ch.8). For critical security theorists, states should not be the centre of analysis because they are not only extremely diverse in character but they are also often part of the problem of insecurity in the international system. They can be providers of security, but they can also be a source of threat to their own people. According to this view, therefore, attention should be focused on the individual rather than the state (see Ch.28).

Feminist writers also challenge the traditional emphasis on the central role of the state in studies of international security. While there are significant differences between feminist theorists, all share the view that works on international politics in general, and international security in particular, have been written from a 'masculine' point of view (see Ch.10 and Ch.14). In her work, Ann Tickner (1992: 191) argues that women have 'seldom been recognized by the security literature' despite the fact that conflicts affect women, as much, if not more, than men. The vast majority of casualties and refugees in war are women and children and, as the recent war in Bosnia confirms, the rape of women is often used as a tool of war.

In a major feminist study of security, *Bananas, Beaches and Bases* (1989), Cynthia Enloe points to the patriarchal structure of privilege and control at all levels which, in her view, effectively legitimizes all forms of violence. Like Tickner, she highlights the traditional exclusion of women from international relations, suggesting 'that they are in fact crucial to it in practice and that nowhere is the state more gendered in the sense of how power is dispersed than in the security apparatus' (Terriff *et al.* 1999: 91). She also challenges the concept of 'national security', arguing that the use of such terms is often designed to preserve the prevailing male-dominated **order** rather than protect the state from external attack.

Feminist writers argue that if **gender** is brought more explicitly into the study of security, not only will new issues and alternative perspectives be added to the security agenda, but the result will be a fundamentally different view of the nature of international security. According to Jill Steans, 'Rethinking security involves thinking about militarism and patriarchy, mal-development and environmental degradation. It involves thinking about the relationship between poverty, debt and population growth. It involves thinking about resources and how they are distributed' (Steans 1998; see also Smith 1999: 72–101).

Recent years have seen the emergence of **post-modernist** approaches to international relations which has produced a somewhat distinctive perspective towards international security (see Ch.10). Post-modernist writers share the view that ideas, discourse, and 'the logic of interpretation' are crucial in understanding international politics and security. Like other writers who adopt a 'critical' approach, post-modernists see 'Realism' as one of the central problems of international insecurity. This is because Realism is a **discourse of power and rule** which has been dominant in international politics in the past and which has encouraged security competition between states. Power politics is seen as an image of the world that encourages behaviour that helps bring about war. As such, the attempt to balance power is itself part of the very behaviour that leads to war. According to this view, alliances do not produce peace, but lead to war. The aim, for many post-modernists, therefore, is to replace the discourse of Realism or power with a different discourse and alternative interpretations of threats to 'national security'. The idea is that once the 'software' program of Realism that people carry around in their heads has been replaced by a new 'software' program based on cooperative norms, individuals, states, and regions will learn to work with each other and global politics will become more peaceful.

Key Points

- Critical security theorists argue that too much emphasis is given by most approaches to the state.
- Some critical security theorists wish to shift the main referent to the individual and suggest that 'emancipation' is the key to greater domestic and international security.
- Feminist writers argue that gender tends to be left out of the literature on international security, despite the impact of war on women.
- Feminist writers also argue that bringing gender issues back in will result in a reconceptualization of the study of international security.
- Post-modernists try to reconceptualize the debate about global security by looking at new questions which have been ignored by traditional approaches.
- There is a belief among post-modernist writers that the nature of international politics can be changed by altering the way we think and talk about security.

Global society and international security

The opportunity to pursue changes in the international system is shared by scholars who point to new trends that are already taking place in world politics. In the past, the state has been the centre of thinking about international relations. This state-centric view, however, is now increasingly challenged. Writers from the **global society** school of thought argue that at the beginning of the twenty-first century the process of globalization (which has been developing for centuries) has accelerated to the point where the clear outlines of a global society are now evident. The emergence of a global economic system, global communications, and the elements of a global culture have helped to provide a wide network of social relationships which **transcend state frontiers** and encompass people all over the world. This has led to the growing obsolescence of territorial wars between the great powers.

At the same time, so the argument goes, new risks associated with the environment, **poverty**, and **weapons of mass destruction** are facing humanity, just at a time when the nation-state is in crisis.

Supporters of the 'global society' school accept that globalization is an uneven and contradictory process. The end of the cold war has been characterized not only by an increasing global awareness and the creation of a range of global social movements, but also by the fragmentation of nation-states. This has been most obvious among the former communist states, especially the Soviet Union, Yugoslavia, and Czechoslovakia. The result of this 'fracture of statehood' has been a movement away from conflicts between the great powers to new forms of insecurity caused by nationalistic, ethnic, and religious rivalries within states and across state boundaries. This has been reflected in the brutal civil wars that have been fought in Bosnia, Russia, Somalia, Rwanda, Yemen, and Kosovo during the 1990s. Mary Kaldor (1999) has described these conflicts as **new wars**, which can only be understood in the context of globalization. The intensification of interconnectedness, she argues, 'has meant that ideological and/or territorial cleavages of an earlier era have increasingly been supplanted by an emerging political cleavage between . . . cosmopolitanism, based on inclusive, multicultural values and the politics of particularist identities' (Kaldor 1999: 6). The cleavage between those who are part of the global processes and those who are excluded give rise to wars which are characterized by 'population expulsion through various means such as mass killing, forcible resettlement, as well as a range of political, psychological and economic techniques of intimidation' (Kaldor 1999: 8).

Such conflicts pose a critical problem for the international community of whether to intervene in the domestic affairs of sovereign states to safeguard minority rights and individual human rights (see Ch.28 and Ch.29). This dilemma, according to global society theorists, reflects the historic transformation of human society which is taking place at the beginning of the twenty-first century. Although states continue to limp along, many global theorists argue that it is now increasingly necessary to think of the security of individuals and of groups within the emergent global society.

Not all writers on globalization, however, agree with this view. There are those who argue that while the state is being transformed (both from within and without) by the processes of globalization, it remains a key referent in the contemporary debate about security. This is one of the central arguments in Ian Clark's study of *Globalization and International Relations Theory* (1999). Clark argues that: 'What globalization can bring to bear on the topic of security is an awareness of widespread systemic developments without any resulting need to downplay the role of the state, or assume its obsolescence' (1999: 125). What is interesting for Clark is the way that security is being reshaped by globalization and the changes that this is creating for the security agenda of states. In particular, as states become less able to provide what they have traditionally provided, he argues that domestic bargains about what citizens are prepared to sacrifice for the state are being renegotiated. This is reflected in the type of security activities in which states are prepared to engage, and in the extent to which they are prepared to pursue them unilaterally. According to this view of globalization, states are not withering away but are being transformed as they struggle to deal with the range of new challenges (including those of security) that face them (see Ch.32).

Key Points

- Supporters of the 'global society school' argue that the end of the twentieth century witnessed an accelerating process of globalization.
- Globalization can be seen in the fields of economic development, communications, and culture. Global social movements are also a response to new risks associated with the environment, poverty, and weapons of mass destruction.
- The 'fracture of statehood' is giving rise to new kinds of conflict within states rather than between states which the state system cannot deal with. This has helped encourage an emerging politics of global responsibility.
- There are disputes about whether globalization will contribute to the weakening of the state or simply to its transformation, and over whether a global society can be created which will usher in a new period of peace and security.

Case Study Insecurity in the post-cold war world: the case of the Democratic Republic of the Congo

Events in the Democratic Republic of the Congo (DRC) since the end of the cold war provide a good illustration of the complexities of contemporary conflict and the dangers of providing simple explanations of why wars occur. Between 1996 and 2006 in this 'forgotten war' (sometimes called 'Africa's World War') nearly 4 million people lost their lives as a result of ethnic strife, civil war, and foreign intervention, as well as starvation and disease. The key events are as follows:

In 1996 the conflict and genocide in neighbouring Rwanda (in which 800,000 people died) spilled over into the Congo (named Zaïre at the time). Rwandan Hutu forces, who fled after a Tutsi-led government came to power, set up bases in the eastern part of the country to launch attacks on Rwanda. This resulted in Rwandan forces invading the Congo with the aim of ousting the existing government of Mobutu Sese-Soko and putting its own government under Laurent-Désiré Kabila in power. This was achieved in May 1997. Kabila soon fell out with his backers in August 1998, however, and Rwanda and Uganda inspired a rebellion designed to overthrow him. This led to further intervention, this time by Zimbabwe, Angola, Namibia, Chad, and Sudan, in support of the Kabila government. Although a ceasefire was signed in 1999,

fighting continued in the eastern part of the country. In January 2001 Kabila was assassinated and replaced by his son, Joseph Kabila. Fighting continued until 2003, partly due to ethnic divisions (the DRC is a country of 250 ethnic groups and 242 different languages), but also because of the continuing occupation of foreign troops (often engaged in illegal mining of minerals and diamonds). These foreign troops often formed alliances with local militias to fight their enemies on DRC soil. Negotiations designed to broker a peace agreement eventually led to the Pretoria Accord in April 2003. As a result, some of the foreign troops left but hostilities and massacres continued, especially in the east of the country, as rival militias backed by Rwanda and Uganda continued to fight and plunder the resources of the DRC.

On 18 July 2003, the Transitional Government was set up as a result of what was known as the Global and All-inclusive Agreement. The Agreement required parties to help reunify the country, disarm, and integrate the warring parties and hold elections. Continued instability, however, meant that the elections did not take place until July 2006, and even after these elections, the peace remained very fragile.

This conflict in the DRC highlights the utility of a broader definition of 'security' and the importance of new ideas relating to 'human' and 'societal' security. It also illustrates the relative shift from interstate wars to intra-state conflicts, involving ethnic militias, in what are sometimes called 'failed states'. Nevertheless, the war also highlights the continuing importance of conflict across state boundaries and traditional, regional balance-of-power rivalries.

Conclusion: the continuing tensions between national, international, and global security

At the centre of the contemporary debate about global and international security dealt with above is the issue of continuity and change. This involves questions about how the past is to be interpreted and whether international politics is in fact undergoing a dramatic change as a result of the processes of globalization, especially after 9/11. There is no doubt that national security is being challenged by the forces of globalization, some of which have a positive effect, bringing states into greater contact with each other. As Bretherton and Ponton have argued, the intensification of global connectedness associated with economic globalization, ecological interdependence, and the threats posed by weapons of mass destruction, means that

'co-operation between states is more than ever necessary' (1996: 100–1). It has also been argued that the increased need for interdependence caused by globalization will help 'to facilitate dialogue at the elite level between states, providing significant gains for global security' (Lawler 1995: 56–7). At the same time, however, globalization also appears to be having negative effects on international security. It is often associated with fragmentation, rapid social change, increased economic inequality, and challenges to cultural identity which contribute to conflicts within, and between, states. This ambivalent effect of globalization, in turn, reinforces the search for national security, unilateralism, and pre-emptive strategies, and at the

same time often leads other less powerful states to seek greater multilateral and global solutions as they are less able to provide security for their citizens.

In the early years of the twenty-first century, therefore, despite important changes which are taking place in world politics, the traditional **ambiguity** about international security remains. In some ways the world is a much safer place to live in as a result of the end of the cold war and the removal of nuclear confrontation as a central element in East–West relations. It can be argued that some of the processes of globalization and the generally cooperative effects of international institutions have played an important part in dampening down the competitive aspects of the security dilemma between states. These trends, however, are offset to a significant extent as the continuing turmoil in the Middle East, the wars in Afghanistan and Iraq, and the subsequent **war on terror**, demonstrate. It is evident that military force continues to be an important arbiter of disputes both between and particularly within states, as well as a weapon used by terrorist movements who reject the status quo. This was reflected especially in the ongoing conflict in Dafur, the war in the Lebanon in 2006, and the violence in Iraq from 2003 onwards. Also, conventional arms races continue in different regions of the world. Nuclear, chemical, and biological weapons still provide a powerful influence on the security calculations of many states, crazy and ambitious politicians remain at the head of some governments, and cultural differences, as well as diverse values and the tensions inherent in globalization itself, prevent the emergence of global agreement on a wide range of important issues. Water resources and energy also remain a potential source of conflict in the years ahead. In an age of increasing globalization, individual and societal insecurity are increasingly evident as the forces of fragmentation and integration destabilize traditional identities and thereby complicate relationships within and between states.

As a result, it remains much too soon to conclude that a paradigmatic shift towards a more peaceful world is taking place in international politics and global security in the aftermath of the cold war, or indeed that such a permanent shift is possible. The empirical historical evidence as well as contemporary events suggests caution. Periods of more cooperative inter-state (and inter-group) relations have often in the past led to a false dawn and an unwarranted euphoria that 'perpetual peace' was about to break out. The structure of the international system, particular kinds

of political system, and human nature provide important constraints on the way that individuals, states, or international institutions behave. So does the predominance of Realist attitudes towards international and global security among many of the world's political leaders.

The end of the cold war has certainly brought **new patterns of international security and insecurity**. The major confrontations of the previous fifty years gave way initially to a period of cooperative security (albeit of a tentative nature) between the cold war great power antagonists. The expansion of NATO and the EU opened up the possibility of the development of a major new security community in Europe. The spread of democracy appeared to be the basis of a dynamic new emerging international order. At the same time, however, with the discipline of the cold war gone, new security problems associated with clashes over identity (as in the former Yugoslavia), the search for regional dominance (as with the Gulf War in the early 1990s), and the disintegration of **failed states** (especially in Africa) all helped to undermine the prospects for a more peaceful world. The international system was increasingly unipolar, with America leading 'coalitions of the willing' in a number of campaigns to bring about a Western-inspired international order. The aim of bringing Western democracy to areas like the Middle East, however, has itself been a source of conflict. Nuclear proliferation is an increasing problem and US pre-eminence seems likely to be challenged in the years ahead by the rise of powers like China.

This is not to argue that there is no room for peaceful change or that new ideas and discourses about international relations are unimportant in helping to shape choices that have to be made. Opportunities to develop greater international and global security will always exist. In a world of continuing diversity, mistrust, and uncertainly, however, it is likely that the search for a more cooperative global society is likely to remain in conflict with the powerful pressures which exist for states, and other political communities, to look after what they perceive to be their own sectional, national, or regional security against threats from without and within. This seems particularly apparent given the level of violence which has occurred since September 11. Whether and how greater international and global security can be achieved, still remains, as Herbert Butterfield once argued, 'the hardest nut of all' for students and practitioners of international politics to crack. This is what makes the study of global security such a fascinating and important activity.

Box 13.4 Observations on 9/11

'... global security was changed dramatically by the events of 11 September 2001. The definition of security has ... once again been narrowed. The concern is very much national security in a globalized world, in which direct attacks are now, as they were during the Cold War, seen as the primary and most imminent challenge ... [I]ssues such as the promotion of democratization, respect for human rights, and problems with environmental degredation appear, at least for the moment, to have been put on the back-burner.'

(Stubbs 2002: 178–9)

'If "the post-Cold War security bubble finally burst" on September 11, what also shattered along with it was a series of cosy assumptions about the world within which we happen to live—one of the most influential of which was that under conditions of globalization the propensity for international conflict would more likely diminish than increase. As the terrorist attacks on New York and Washington revealed only too graphically, globalization not only appeared to have many determined enemies as well-meaning friends, but enemies of a quite novel (and undeterrable) character. What it also revealed—again to the discomfort of those who assumed the world was becoming a better, safer place—was that the worst sometimes happens.'

(Michael Cox, in Booth and Dunne 2002: 152)

? Questions

1 Why is security a 'contested concept'?

2 Why do traditional realist writers focus on national security?

3 What do neo-realist writers mean by 'structure'?

4 Why do wars occur?

5 Why do states find it difficult to cooperate?

6 Do you find Liberal Institutionalism convincing?

7 Why might democratic states be more peaceful?

8 What is distinctive about Constructivist views of international security?

9 How do 'critical security' theory, 'feminist' views and post-modernist views about international security differ from those of 'neo-realists'?

10 Has increasing globalization brought more or less global security?

11 Is the tension between national and global security resolvable?

12 Has international security changed since 9/11?

→ Guide to further reading

Kenneth N. Waltz's study *Man, the State and War* (New York: Columbia University Press, 1954) is one of the best sources for the study of the causes of war, and see also J. C. Garnett, 'The Causes of War and the Conditions of Peace', in J. Baylis, J. Wirtz, E. Cohen, and C. S. Gray (eds), *Strategy in the Contemporary World,* 2nd edn (Oxford: Oxford University Press, 2006).

B. Buzan's *People, States and Fear* (London: Harvester, 1983) provides an excellent starting point for the study of national and international security. The book is written largely from a neo-realist perspective.

Michael Joseph Smith, *Realist Thought from Weber to Kissinger* (Baton Rouge: Louisiana State University Press, 1986) covers the development of what has been described as classical Realism and discusses some of the major thinkers in the field. For neo-classical approaches see Thomas Christensen, *Useful Adversaries: Grand Strategy, Domestic Mobilization and Sino-American Conflict, 1947–1958,* (Princeton, NJ: Princeton University Press, 1996); Randall Schweller, *Deadly Imbalances: Tripolarity and Hitler's Strategy of World Conquest* (New York: Columbia University Press, 1998); William Wohlforth, *The Elusive Balance: Power and Perceptions during the Cold War*

(Ithaca, NY: Cornell University Press, 1993); and Fareed Zakaria, *From Wealth to Power* (Princeton, NJ: Princeton University Press, 1998). For an interesting account of 'ethical realism', see Alastair J. H. Murray, *Reconstructing Realism: Between Power Politics and Cosmopolitan Ethics* (Edinburgh: Keele University Press, 1997) and Anatol Lieven and John Hulsman, *Ethical Realism: A View of America's Role in the World* (New York: Pantheon Books, 2006).

Alexander Wendt's article, 'Anarchy is What States Make of It: The Social Construction of Power Politics', in *International Organization*, 46(2) (1992), gives a very useful analysis of the Constructivist perspective. See also Alexander Wendt, *Social Theory of International Politics* (Cambridge: Cambridge University Press, 1999).

Ole Waever, Barry Buzan, Morten Kelstrup, and Pierre Lemaitre, *Identity, Migration and the New Security Agenda in Europe* (London: Pinter, 1993) provides an original perspective for studying the kind of non-state aspects of security which have affected Europe in the post-cold war period. Very useful discussions about the changing nature of security can be found in C. Bretherton and G. Ponton (eds), *Global Politics: An Introduction* (Oxford, Blackwell, 1996); T. Terriff, S. Croft, L. James, and P. Morgan, *Security Studies Today* (Cambridge: Polity Press, 1999); K. Krause and M. C. Williams (eds), *Critical Security Studies: Concepts and Cases* (London: UCL Press, 1997); S. Lawson (ed.), *The New Agenda for Global Security: Cooperating for Peace and Beyond* (St Leonards: Allen and Unwin, 1995); R. D. Kaplan, *The Coming Anarchy: Shattering the Dreams of the Post-Cold War* (New York: Random House, 2000); K. Booth and T. Dunne, *Worlds in Collision: Terror and the Future of Global Order* (London: Palgrave, 2002); and I. Clark, *Globalization and International Relations Theory* (Oxford: Oxford University Press, 1999).

For a discussion of different theoretical approaches to security and some of the contemporary debates about security studies, see Alan Collins (ed.), *Contemporary Security Studies* (Oxford: Oxford University Press, 2006) and Steve Smith, 'The Increasing Insecurity of Security Studies: Conceptualising Security in the Last Twenty years', *Contemporary Security Policy*, 20(3) (Dec. 1999). See also Richard Stubbs, 'The Many Faces of Asian Security', *Contemporary Southeast Asia*, 24(1) (April 2002), and J. Ann Tickner, *Gender in International Relations: Feminist Perspectives on Achieving Global Security* (New York: Columbia University Press, 1992).

The best guide to the use of the Internet on the subject of international security is William M. Arkin, *The Internet and Strategic Studies* (Baltimore, Md.: The Center for Strategic Education, the Paul Nitze School of Advanced International Studies, Johns Hopkins University, 1998).

Online Resource Centre

 Visit the Online Resource Centre that accompanies this book to access more learning resources on this chapter topic at www.oxfordtextbooks.co.uk/uk/orc/baylis_smith4e/

Chapter 14

International political economy in an age of globalization

NGAIRE WOODS

- Introduction ·· 244
- The post-war world-economy ·· 244
- Traditional and new approaches to IPE ······································· 248
- The globalization debate in IPE ··· 252
- International institutions in the globalizing world-economy ·············· 256
- Conclusion ·· 258

Reader's Guide

This chapter examines what drives actors and explains events in the international economy. The first section outlines the history of the post-war economy. The history helps to explain why and how international political economy (IPE) has become so central to the study of international relations. Amid the many actors, processes, and events in the recent history of the world-economy, it is not obvious where one might begin to analyze IPE. This task is made easier by three traditional approaches which outline for us specific actors, processes, and levels of analysis. These are the liberal, mercantilist, and Marxist traditions. More recently, IPE has become divided by an argument about the uses (and abuses) of 'rational choice' analysis. What 'rational choice' means and the argument about how it should be used are both explored. These perspectives and tools for studying IPE are then applied to help us to make sense of globalization and its impact on the world-economy. What is globalization? Is it diminishing the role of states in the world-economy? What explains the very different kinds of impact globalization has on different kinds of states? Globalization poses new challenges for all states (and other actors) in the world-economy. It is often assumed that international institutions and organizations will manage these challenges. In the final section of the chapter we return to the theories of IPE in order to answer the question: what role can we expect institutions to play in managing globalization?

Introduction

International political economy (IPE) is about the interplay of economics and politics in world affairs. The core question of IPE is: what drives and explains events in the world-economy? For some people, this comes down to a battle of `states versus markets'. However, this is misleading. The `markets' of the world economy are not like local street bazaars in which all items can be openly and competitively traded and exchanged. Equally, politicians cannot rule the global economy much as they might like to. World markets and countries, local firms, and multinational corporations which trade and invest within them are all shaped by layers of **rules**, **norms**, laws, organizations, and even habits. Political scientists like to call all these features of the system **institutions**. International political economy tries to explain what creates and perpetuates institutions and what impact institutions have on the world-economy.

Since the 1970s, IPE has continued to advance as a core subject of international relations. As will be discussed below, **globalization** and its causes and effects on **states**, and international cooperation and institutions

have become defining features of international relations. Furthermore, the end of the cold war ended many of the geo-strategic aspirations and influence the West had enjoyed. The challenge of integrating the former Eastern bloc countries into the world system was soon defined primarily as one of economic transformation and integration. Equally, an explosion of tribal, religious, and ethnic conflict on the edges of **Europe** (in the former Yugoslavia) as well as in Africa (such as in Rwanda), in Asia (such as in Indonesia), and in the Middle East forced analysts more closely to examine the links between **poverty**, economic stagnation, and the indebtedness of countries on the one hand, and intra-state conflict on the other. Finally, the end of the cold war thrust international institutions into the limelight. The United Nations, the **International Monetary Fund** (IMF), the World Bank, and the newly created **World Trade Organization** (WTO) all became an important focus of study and attention, providing further grist to the mill of IPE scholars concerned with examining the causes, determinants, and impact of international institutions and cooperation among states in economic affairs.

The post-war world-economy

The institutions and framework of the world-economy have their roots in the planning for a new economic order which took place during the last phase of the Second World War. In 1944, policy-makers gathered at **Bretton Woods** in the United States to consider how to resolve two very serious problems. First, they needed to ensure that the **Great Depression** of the 1930s would not happen

again. In other words, they had to find ways to ensure a stable global monetary system and an open world trading system (see Box 14.1). Second, they needed to rebuild the war-torn economies of Europe.

At Bretton Woods three institutions were planned in order to promote a **new world economic order** (see Boxes 14.2 and 14.4). The International Monetary Fund

---

Box 14.1 Planning the post-war economy and avoiding another Great Depression

The Great Depression had been greatly exacerbated, if not caused, by 'beggar thy neighbour' economic policies. In the late 1920s and 1930s, governments all over the world tried to protect themselves from economic crisis by putting up trade barriers and devaluing their currencies. Each country believed that by doing this they would somehow manage to keep their economy afloat while all around them neighbouring economies sank. The Great Depression demonstrated that this did not work. At the end of the Second World War,

the challenge was to create a system which would prevent this, in particular by ensuring:
- a stable exchange rate system;
- a reserve asset or unit of account (such as the gold standard);
- international capital flows could be controlled;
- the availability of short-term loans to countries facing a temporary balance of payments crisis;
- rules to keep economies open to trade.

Box 14.2 The Bretton Woods institutions: the IMF and the World Bank

Both the International Monetary Fund and the World Bank were established in 1946 after wartime negotiations held at Bretton Woods in the United States with headquarters (opposite one another) in Washington, DC. The **IMF** was created to promote international monetary cooperation and resolve the inter-war economic problems (see Box 14.1), although several of these functions ended when the Bretton Woods system broke down in 1971 (see Box 14.3). The IMF now has a membership of 185 countries, each of whom contributes a quota of resources to the organization (proportionate to the size of their economy), which also determines their percentage of voting rights and the amount of resources to which they can have automatic access. Since the 1980s, the IMF has become an institution offering financial and technical assistance to developing and transitional economies. The terms on which countries receive assistance include the government having to commit to undertake specific `conditions' or policy reforms, called **conditionality** (see www.imf.org).

What we now call the **World Bank** started out as the International Bank for Reconstruction and Development (IBRD), an agency to foster reconstruction in war-torn Europe as well as development in the rest of the world. It has since become the world's largest source of development assistance, providing nearly $16 billion in loans annually to eligible member countries, through the IBRD, the International Development Association (IDA), the International Finance Corporation (IFC), and the Multilateral Guarantee Agency (MIGA). As with the IMF, the World Bank requires members to whom it lends to undertake specific reforms within their economy. Most recently, this has included requiring borrowing governments to demonstrate their commitment to reducing poverty within their countries. With the exception of IDA (which is funded by donations), the World Bank's resources come from its issue of bonds in the capital markets. These bonds are backed up by guarantees provided by the governments who belong to the institution (see www.worldbank.org).

was created to ensure a stable exchange rate regime and the provision of emergency assistance to countries facing a temporary crisis in their balance of payments regime. The International Bank for Reconstruction and Development (IBRD and later called the World Bank) was created to facilitate private investment and reconstruction in Europe. The Bank was also charged with assisting **development** in other countries, a mandate which later became the main reason for its existence. Finally,

the **General Agreement on Trade and Tariffs** (GATT) was signed in 1947 and became a forum for negotiations on trade **liberalization**.

The 1944 plans for the world-economy, however, were soon postponed when in 1945 the United States made its first priority the **containment** of the Soviet Union. Fearing the rise of communism in war-ravaged Europe, the United States took a far more direct role than planned in reconstructing Europe and managing the world-economy.

Box 14.3 The 'Bretton Woods system' and its breakdown

What was the 'Bretton Woods system'?

At the Bretton Woods Conference in 1944 it was agreed that all countries' currencies would be fixed at a certain value. They became fixed to the dollar, and the US government promised to convert all dollars to gold at $35 per ounce. In other words, exchange rates were anchored to a dollar–gold standard. In the Bretton Woods system, any country wanting to change the value of its currency had to apply to the IMF for permission. The result was very stable and unchanging exchange rates.

What was the 'breakdown' of the system?

In August 1971 the US government announced that it was suspending the convertibility of the dollar to gold at $35 per ounce. This removed gold from the dollar–gold standard and paved the way for major currencies to 'float' instead of staying at fixed values. The United States also announced in August 1971 that it was adding a 10 per cent surcharge on import duties (to improve trade balance by curtailing imports which were flooding into the USA, and to try to stem the outflow of dollars to the rest of the world), hence also

turning back the Bretton Woods ideal of maintaining open trade in times of economic difficulty.

Was this a sign of declining US hegemony?

Over a decade after the breakdown of the Bretton Woods system, leading academics debated whether the change reflected a loss in US power, or was indeed an exercise of its power. For some, the breakdown of the system was an exercise of US leadership: the US hegemon smashed the BW system in order to increase its own freedom of economic and political action (Gowa 1983). Others argued that the USA had lost its capacity to maintain the system, but explained that a regime could nevertheless survive without the hegemon (Keohane 1984). At the heart of the debate was a disagreement about whether cooperation in the international political economy depends upon one state being both capable and willing to set and enforce the rules of the game, with powers to abrogate and adjust those same rules. This debate about the nature of cooperation continues today in competing explanations of international institutions (see last section of this chapter).

The USA announced the **Marshall Plan** in 1947, which directed massive financial aid to Europe and permitted the USA to set conditions on it. The planned gold standard was replaced by the **dollar standard** which the United States managed directly, backing the dollar with gold. Unsurprisingly, by the time the IMF, the World Bank, and the GATT began to function in the 1950s, they were distinctly **Western bloc organizations** which depended heavily on the United States.

US support for the Bretton Woods system began to change when weaknesses emerged in the US economy. After 1965 the USA widened its costly military involvement in Vietnam, and also started to spend more money on public education and urban redevelopment programmes in the United States (President Johnson's 'Great Society' programmes), and all this without raising taxes. The damage was dramatic. As prices rose within the US economy, the **competitiveness** of US goods and services in the world-economy dropped. Likewise, confidence in the US dollar plummeted. Firms and countries turned away from the dollar and the US capacity to back its currency with gold was brought into question. Meanwhile, other countries in the world-economy were enhancing their position. European allies were benefiting from the growing and deepening economic **integration** in Europe. By the late 1960s, the development of the European Economic Community (EEC) provided a springboard for European policy-makers to diverge from US positions, such as over **NATO**, military exercises, and support for the gold standard. In Asia, the phenomenal success of **export-led growth** in Japan and in newly industrializing

countries such as South Korea and Taiwan created a new challenge to US trade competitiveness, and a new agenda for trade negotiations.

Facing these pressures, the United States changed the rules of the international monetary system in 1971. The government announced that it would no longer convert dollars to gold at $35 per ounce, and that it was imposing a 10 per cent surcharge on import duties (to improve its trade balance by curtailing imports which were flooding into the USA, and to try to stem the outflow of dollars to the rest of the world). These actions broke the Bretton Woods system. This was not the only change in the world-economy in the 1970s.

In the 1970s, the period of high growth enjoyed after the Second World War came to an abrupt end, leaving very high inflation. Further compounding the problem, the first oil crisis in 1973 plunged the world-economy into **stagflation** (a combination of economic stagnation or low growth and high inflation). In the monetary system, the role of the IMF collapsed when the Bretton Woods system broke down in 1971 and the major industrialized countries failed to find a way to coordinate their exchange rate policies within the IMF framework. Instead, the major currencies floated and industrialized countries began to discuss monetary issues among themselves in groups such as the **Group of Seven** (comprising the United States, Japan, Germany, the United Kingdom, France, Italy, and Canada), which first met in 1975.

In the trading system, **cooperation** had steadily grown in negotiations under the auspices of the GATT (see Box 14.4). However, in the 1970s, the gains which had been

---

Box 14.4 The post-war trading system, the GATT, and the WTO

The General Agreement on Trade and Tariffs (GATT) was an interim agreement signed in 1947 in the expectation that it would be superseded by an international trade organization. A permanent trade organization was not created until 1994, and so for four decades the interim GATT continued to exist as an arrangement among 'contracting parties' backed up by a very small secretariat based in Geneva and a minuscule budget. In essence, the GATT was a forum for trade negotiations, with numerous rounds of talks culminating in the very successful Kennedy Round of 1962–7, where breakthroughs were made in the reduction of trade barriers among industrialized countries. However, when protectionism flourished in the 1970s, the GATT proved powerless to restrain powerful members such as the United States and European countries from restricting trade (e.g. the Multifiber Arrangement 1974 restricting textile imports)

and abusing the many exceptions and safeguards written into the agreement. The GATT also functioned as a forum for dispute settlement (i.e. upholding trade rules). However, it was both slow and impotent in this regard, constrained by the need for consensus on any decision regarding disputes. The GATT was replaced by the World Trade Organization (WTO) as a result of agreements forged in the last round of GATT talks, the Uruguay Round (1986–94). Established on 1 January 1995, the WTO's functions include: administering WTO trade agreements; being a forum for trade negotiations; handling trade disputes; monitoring national trade policies; supplying technical assistance and training for developing countries; and cooperating with other international organizations. It is located in Geneva with a secretariat staff of 500 (see www.wto.org).

made in reducing tariff barriers, especially among industrialized countries, were reversed by policies of **new protectionism.** As each country grappled with stagflation, many introduced new forms of barriers (or 'non-tariff barriers'), in particular to keep out the new competitive imports from successful developing countries. An egregious example of the new protectionism was the Multifiber Arrangement of 1973 which placed restrictions on all textile and apparel imports from developing countries, blatantly violating the GATT principle of **non-discrimination.**

The new protectionism in industrialized countries further fuelled the anger of developing countries who in the 1970s launched a concerted campaign in the United Nations General Assembly for a **New International Economic Order** (NIEO). The determination of develo-ping countries to alter the rules of the game was further bolstered by the success of OPEC oil-producing developing countries in raising oil prices in 1973. The agenda of the NIEO covered trade, aid, investment, the international monetary and financial system, and institutional reform. Developing countries sought better representation in international economic institutions, a fairer trading system, more aid, the regulation of foreign investment, the protection of economic **sovereignty**, and reforms to ensure a more stable and equitable financial and monetary system.

A kind of **summit diplomacy** which also took place in the 1970s was that between **North** (the industrialized countries) and **South** (developing countries). These negotiations were underpinned by a different kind of thinking and scholarship about IPE. The developing countries' push for reform of the international economic system reflected **dependency theory** and structuralist theories of international economic relations which highlighted negative aspects of **interdependence.** In particular, these theorists were concerned to identify aspects of the international economy and institutions which impeded the possibilities of development in the South. Their central concern was to answer why so many countries within the world-economy remained underdeveloped, in spite of the promises of modernization and global growth. The most sympathetic official 'Northern' answer to these concerns was voiced in the **Brandt Report** in 1980, the findings of a group of high-level policy-makers who had been asked to examine how and why the international community should respond to the challenges of interdependence and development.

The NIEO campaign was unsuccessful for several reasons. The United Nations General Assembly (UNGA) was an obvious institution for developing countries to choose in making their case since, unlike the IMF or World Bank, it offers every country one vote. However the UNGA had no power to implement the agenda of the developing countries. Furthermore, although many industrialized countries were sympathetic to the developing countries' case in the 1970s, these governments did not act on the agenda in the 1970s and by the 1980s a new set of governments with a distinctly less sympathetic ideology had come to power in the United States, the United Kingdom, and Western Germany.

The 1980s opened with a shift in US economic policy. In 1979 the US Federal Reserve dramatically raised interest rates. This action was taken to stem inflation by contracting economic activity in the United States. However, the reverberations in the rest of the world-economy were immediate and extensive. During the 1960s and 1970s US and European policies had facilitated the rapid growth of **global capital markets** and financial flows. In the 1970s these flows were further buoyed by the investments of oil producers who needed to find outlets for the vast profits made from the oil price rise of 1973. The money found its way to governments in developing countries who were offered loans at knock-down prices. The rise in interest rates in 1979 was an abrupt wake-up call to both borrowers and creditors (many of whom were US-based banks), who suddenly realized that many of the loans could not be repaid. The IMF was immediately called in to prevent any developing country defaulting on these loans, since it was feared that such a default would causes a global financial crisis.

The **debt crisis** meant that the IMF's role in the world-economy became largely that of ensuring that indebted countries undertook 'structural adjustment' in their economies. **Structural adjustment** meant immediate measures to reduce inflation, government expenditure, and the role of the government in the economy, including trade liberalization, privatization, and **deregulation.** These 'neo-liberal' policies were in marked contrast to the Keynesian analysis which had prevailed until the 1980s, during the decades of growth in the world-economy. **Keynesians** (named after economist John Maynard Keynes) believe that governments should play an active and interventionist role in the economy in order to ensure both growth and equity. By contrast, the new 'neo-liberalism' sought to roll back the

state and the role of government, leaving decisions about allocation, production, and distribution in the economy to the market. By the late 1980s the term **Washington Consensus** was being used, sometimes pejoratively, to imply that these policies were mainly a reflection of US interests.

The 1990s brought the end of the cold war and the challenge of how to integrate Central and Eastern European countries and the former Soviet Union into the global economy. The IMF and World Bank became deeply involved but the Washington Consensus was not broad enough for the purpose. Both institutions began to embrace a broader and deeper view of conditionality aimed at promoting 'good governance' in member countries. But many thought conditionality had gone too far when, in the wake of the East Asian financial crisis in 1997, the IMF imposed far-reaching and overly draconian conditions on countries such as Korea. The impact would be felt in subsequent years as the IMF's lending role waned in most emerging market economies. Over this time, the World Bank sought to broaden its appeal through enhanced relations with governments as well as with **non-governmental organizations** (NGOs). Its legitimacy seemed less tarnished. At the same time, the newly established World Trade Organization began operations in 1995, opening up a new forum within which a broad range of international issues would be negotiated, including not just traditional trade issues but such things as **intellectual property rights**, trade-related investment measures, and food safety standards.

In the first decade of the twenty-first century, a shift in global economic power was emerging. In September 2003, during global trade negotiations in Mexico, a group of 20 countries including Brazil, South Africa, India, and China, resisted the powerful United States and European Union and refused to engage unless some of their terms were heeded. In the IMF and World Bank in 2006 a shift in voting power was conceded in favour of China, Mexico,

Turkey, and Korea. Yet few believed this would be enough fully to engage these countries in the institutions. Several emerging countries—with China in the lead—became donors in their own right. As world energy consumption grew, so too did the power of countries supplying energy resources. In Venezuela, this led to a rhetoric of renewed Third Worldism not seen since the 1970s. Meanwhile, across most industrialized countries, calls for greater efforts to reduce climate-changing emissions became ever stronger. For scholars of international relations, the twenty-first century brought serious questions about how international institutions might assist not only in managing new challenges in the global economy, but equally in managing a shift in power among the states which make up—and make work—the existing institutions.

Key Points

- Immediately after the Second World War international institutions were created to facilitate cooperation in the world-economy.
- The onset of the cold war postponed the operation of these institutions, as the United States stepped in directly to manage the reconstruction of Europe and the international monetary system based on the dollar.
- The Bretton Woods system of managed exchange rates and capital flows operated until its breakdown in 1971 when the USA announced it would no longer convert the dollar to gold.
- The 1970s were marked by a lack of international economic cooperation among the industrialized countries, which floated their exchange rates and indulged in new forms of trade protectionism.
- Developing countries' dissatisfaction with the international system came to a head in the 1970s when they pushed unsuccessfully for a new international economic order.
- Trade negotiations were broadened to include many new areas but this led to later resistance from emerging economies.
- In 2007 a power shift became more obvious in the global economy, with emerging economies such as China and India playing a more prominent role in negotiations in trade, finance, and development assistance.

Traditional and new approaches to IPE

Traditional approaches to IPE: liberal, mercantilist, and Marxian

There are several competing explanations for the nature of the institutions and system described above. A slightly old-fashioned way to describe the competing approaches

to IPE is to divide the subject into liberal, mercantilist, and Marxist traditions. These labels still usefully describe different economic traditions, each of which has a particular moral and analytical slant on global economic relations.

The liberal tradition

The liberal tradition is the **free market** one in which the role of voluntary exchange and markets is emphasized both as efficient and as morally desirable. The assumption is that free trade and the free movement of capital will ensure that investment flows to where it is most profitable to invest (hence, for example, flowing into underdeveloped areas where maximal gains might be made). Free trade is crucial for it permits countries to benefit from their comparative advantages. In other words, each country can exploit its own natural advantages, resources, and endowments and gain from specialization. The economy is oiled by freely exchangeable currencies and open markets which create a global system of prices which, like an **invisible hand**, ensures an efficient and equitable distribution of goods and services across the world-economy. Order in the global economy is a fairly minimal one. The optimal role of governments and institutions is to ensure the smooth and relatively unfettered operation of markets. It is assumed that governments face a wide range of choices in the world system and likewise *vis-à-vis* their own societies and populations. This means that governments which fail to pursue 'good' economic policies do so because decision-makers are either too corrupt or too ignorant of the correct economic choices they might make.

The mercantilist tradition

The mercantilist tradition stands in stark contrast to the liberal one. Mercantilists share the presumptions of **Realists** in international relations. They do not focus on individual policy-makers and their policy choices but rather assume that the world-economy is an arena of **competition among states** seeking to maximize relative strength and power. Simply put, the **international system** is like a jungle in which each state has to do what it can to survive. For this reason, the aim of every state must be to maximize its wealth and independence. States will seek to do this by ensuring their self-sufficiency in key strategic industries and commodities, and by using trade protectionism (tariffs and other limits on exports and imports), subsidies, and selective investments in the domestic economy. Obviously, within this system some states have more power and capability than others. The most powerful states define the rules and limits of the system: through **hegemony**, alliances, and **balances of power**. Indeed, stability and order will only be achieved

where one state can play the role of hegemon, or in other words, is willing and able to create, maintain, and enforce basic rules. Amid this, the economic policies of any one government will always be subservient to its quest to secure the external and internal sovereignty of the state.

The Marxian tradition

The Marxian tradition also sees the world-economy as an arena of competition, but not among states. **Capitalism** is the driving force in the world-economy. Using Marx's language, this means that world-economic relations are best conceived as a **class struggle** between the 'oppressor and the oppressed'. The oppressors or capitalists are those who own the **means of production** (trade and industry). The oppressed are the working class. The struggle between the two arises because capitalists seek to increase their profits and this requires them to exploit ever more harshly the working class. In international relations this description of 'class relations' within a capitalist system has been applied to describe relations between the **core** (industrialized countries) and **periphery** (developing countries), and the unequal exchange which occurs between the two. **Dependency theorists** (who have focused mainly on Latin America) describe the ways classes and groups in the 'core' link to the 'periphery'. Underdevelopment and poverty in so many countries is explained as the result of economic, social, and political structures within countries which have been deeply influenced by their international economic relations. The global capitalist order within which these societies have emerged is, after all, a global capitalist order which reflects the interests of those who own the means of production.

It becomes clear in contrasting these traditions of thinking about international economic relations that each focuses on different actors and driving forces in the world-economy, and that each has a different conception of what 'order' means and what is necessary to achieve it. Comparing the different traditions also highlights three different **levels of analysis:** the structure of the international system (be that international capitalism or the configuration of power among states in the system), the nature of a particular government or competition within its institutions, and the role of interest groups and societal forces within a country. At each of these levels of analysis we need to ask: what drives the actors concerned and therefore how might we explain their preferences, actions,

Box 14.5 Traditional perspectives on IPE

Liberal	Mercantilist	Marxist
The world-economy has the potential to be a seamless global market place in which free trade and the free movement of capital shape the policies of governments and economic actors. Order would be achieved by the 'invisible hand' of competition in the global market place.	As an arena of inter-state competition, the world-economy is one in which states seek to maximize their wealth and independence *vis-à-vis* other states. Order is achieved only where there is a **balance of power** or hegemony.	The world-economy is best described as an arena of capitalist competition in which classes (capitalists and workers) and social groups are in constant conflict. Capitalists (and the states they are based in) are driven by the search for profits, and order is achieved only where they succeed in exacting the submission of all others.

and the outcomes which result? In answering this question we enter into more methodological preoccupations which today divide the study of IPE.

New approaches to IPE

International political economy is divided by the different normative concerns and analytical questions which are highlighted by the traditions outlined above. Equally, the discipline is now subject to a lively **methodological debate** about how scholars might best explain policies and outcomes in IPE. In essence, this debate is about whether you can assume what states' (and other actors') preferences and interests are. If you can, then rational choice (or 'neo-utilitarian') approaches to IPE make sense. However, if you open up the question as to why and how states and other actors come to have particular preferences, then you are pushed towards approaches now often labelled 'Social Constructivism' (see Ch.9).

Political economy: the application of rational choice to groups within the state

In the United States, the study of IPE has become dominated by a 'rational choice' or neo-utilitarian approach. This borrows economic concepts to explain politics. Instead of exploring the ideas, personalities, ideologies, or historical

traditions which lie behind policies and institutions, rational choice focuses on the **incentive structure** faced by those making decisions. It is assumed that actors' interests and preferences are known or fixed and that actors can make strategic choices as to how best to promote their interests. The term 'rational choice' is a useful one to describe this approach since it proposes that even though a particular policy may seem stupid or wrong, it may well have been rational. 'Rational' in this sense means that for the actor or group concerned, this was the optimal choice given the specific incentives and institutional constraints and opportunities that existed at the time (see Ch.7).

Rational choice has been applied to interest groups and their influence on IPE in what has been called a **political economy approach**. This approach has its roots in explanations of trade policy which focus on interest groups. More recent applications have attempted to explain why countries adapt in particular ways to changes in the world-economy. The analysis proceeds on the assumption that governments and their policies are important but that the policies and preferences of governments reflect the actions of specific interest groups within the economy. These groups may emerge along class or sectoral lines. Indeed, the assumptions of rational choice are applied to explain how particular groups within the economy emerge and what their goals and policy preferences are. Furthermore, rational choice provides a framework for understanding the coalitions into which these groups enter and their interactions with other institutions. For example, in explaining developing country responses to the debt crisis of the 1980s, a political economy approach starts out by examining the effect of **economic shocks** such as high interest rates and structural adjustment on interest groups. By demonstrating that the power of some interests (such as those working in the export sector) has increased and the power of others (such as those working in industries relying on diminishing state subsidies) has diminished, the approach proffers an explanation for radical shifts in government policies.

Institutionalism: the application of rational choice to states

A different application of rational choice lies in the **institutionalist approach** to IPE (about which more is said in the last section). This approach applies the assumptions of rational choice to states in their interaction with other states. Drawing on theories of **delegation**

Box 14.6 Examples of new approaches to IPE

Institutionalist

Institutionalists regard the world economy as an arena of inter-state cooperation. They see the core actors as governments and the institutions to whom they delegate power, and the key driving forces as rational choice at the level of the state motivated by the potential gains from cooperation. For institutionalists, the key condition for order is the existence of international institutions which permit cooperation to continue.

Political economy

For political economists, the world-economy is characterized by competition among vested interests within different kinds of states, and the core actors are interest groups formed within the domestic economies of the states. The key driving force is rational choice at the level of groups within the domestic economy responding to changes in the international economy. Political economists are not concerned with theorizing about the conditions necessary for international order.

Neo-Gramscians

Neo-Gramscians see the world-economy as an over-arching structure of knowledge, ideas, and institutions which reflects the interests of dominant actors and within which competition takes place. They regard the structure of the system itself as vital in understanding the identities and preferences of the actors. The key driving force of the system is capitalist competition, which is constrained by the need of the powerful to gain the consent of the less powerful. Dominance by one state is an insufficient condition for international order. Hegemony requires control over the structures of knowledge and ideas as well.

and agency, it offers an explanation as to why institutions exist and for what purposes. The core assumption is that states create international institutions and delegate power to them in order to maximize utility within the constraints of world markets and world politics. Frequently, this comes down to the need to resolve collective-action problems. For example, states realize that they cannot achieve their goals in areas such as trade or environment unless all other states also embark upon a particular course of action. Hence, institutions are created to ensure that there is no defection or free-riding, and the collective goal is achieved.

Social Constructivism

In contrast to rational choice analysis, other approaches to international political economy assume that policies within the world-economy are affected by **historical** and **sociological factors**. Much more attention is paid to the ways in which actors formulate preferences, as well as to the processes by which decisions are made and implemented. In other words, rather than assuming that a state or decision-maker's preferences reflect rational choices within given constraints and opportunities, analysts in a broader tradition of IPE, examine the beliefs, roles, traditions, ideologies, and patterns of **influence** which shape preferences, behaviour, and outcomes.

Interests, actions, and behaviour in the world-economy are conceived as taking place within a structure of ideas, culture, and knowledge. We cannot simply assume that the preferences of actors within the system reflect objectively definable competing 'interests'. Rather, the way actors understand their own preferences will depend heavily upon prevailing beliefs and patterns of thinking in the world-economy, many of which are embodied in institutions. The question this poses is: whose interests and ideas are embodied in the rules and norms of the system?

For some the answer to the question 'in whose interest' lies in **hegemony**. The dominant power within the system will achieve goals not just through coercion but equally by ensuring the consent of other actors within the system. This means that dominant powers will promulgate institutions, ideologies, and ideas, all of which help to persuade other actors that their best interests converge with those of the dominant power. For example, neo-Gramscians interpret the dominance of neo-liberalism since the 1980s as a reflection of US interests in the global economy, successfully projected through structures of knowledge (it became the dominant paradigm in top research universities), through institutions (such as the IMF, which became forceful proponents of neo-liberal policy prescriptions), and through broader cultural beliefs and understandings (the very language of 'free' market contrasting with restricted or repressive regimes).

New approaches to IPE highlight a powerful debate within the subject about whether we should treat states' interests and preferences as given or fixed. We return to this question in the final section of this chapter. There we will examine why states form institutions and what role such institutions might play in managing globalization. First, though, we need to establish what is globalization in the world-economy and what are its implications.

Key Points

- Rational choice explains outcomes in IPE as the result of actors' choices, which are assumed always to be rationally power or utility maximizing within given particular incentives and institutional constraints.
- Institutionalists apply rational choice to states in their interactions with other states in order to explain international cooperation in economic affairs.

- Constructivist approaches pay more attention to how governments, states, and other actors construct their preferences, highlighting the role of identities, beliefs, traditions, and values in this process.
- Neo-Gramscians highlight that actors define and pursue their interests within a structure of ideas, culture, and knowledge which itself is shaped by hegemonic powers.

The globalization debate in IPE

The nature and impact of globalization is the subject of profound debate within IPE (as within other areas of international relations discussed in this book). The term globalization is used to refer to at least four different sets of forces or processes in the world-economy. **Internationalization** describes the increase in economic transactions across borders which has been taking place since the turn of the century but which some argue has undergone a quantitative leap in recent decades. The **technological revolution** is a second aspect of globalization, describing the effect of new electronic communication which permits firms and other actors to operate globally with much less regard for location, distance, and borders. One effect of the technological revolution is to speed up **deterritorialization** or the extent to which territorial distances, borders, and places influence the way people collectively identify themselves and act, and seek political voice or recognition. Finally, **liberalization** describes the policies undertaken by states which have made a new global economy possible. This includes both the rules and institutions created by powerful states to facilitate a new scale of transnational economic activity in certain sectors (but by no means all) of the world-economy. It also includes the policies of smaller and less powerful states in the system, which, by liberalizing trade, investment, and production, have integrated into the world-economy.

In IPE several competing claims are made about globalization. For example, while some scholars argue that globalization is nothing new, others posit that globalization is dramatically diminishing the role of the state (see Ch.1). Still others claim that globalization is exacerbating inequalities and giving rise to a more unequal and unjust

Box 14.7 Four aspects of globalization

- **Internationalization** describes the increase in transactions among states reflected in flows of trade, investment, and capital (see the argument that these flows have not increased as much as is claimed: UNDP 1997). The processes of internationalization have been facilitated and are shaped by inter-state agreements on trade, investment, and capital, as well as by domestic policies permitting the private sector to transact abroad.
- The **technological revolution** refers to the way modern communications (Internet, satellite communications, high-tech computers), made possible by technological advances, have made distance and location less important factors not just for government (including at local and regional levels) but equally in the calculations of other actors, such as firms' investment decisions or in the activities of **social movements**.

- **Deterritorialization** is accelerated by the technological revolution and refers to the diminuition of influence of territorial places, distances, and boundaries over the way people collectively identify themselves or seek political recognition. This permits an expansion of global civil society but equally an expansion of global criminal or terrorist networks.
- **Liberalization** describes government policies which reduce the role of the state in the economy, such as through the dismantling of trade tariffs and barriers, the deregulation and opening of the financial sector to foreign investors, and the privatization of state enterprises.

world. To make sense of these different arguments, and the evidence adduced to support them, it is worth thinking about the approaches to IPE covered in previous sections, for they help to identify key differences in emphasis which give rise to conflicting interpretations of globalization. For example, sceptics who deny that globalization is transforming world politics tend to focus on the 'internationalization' element of globalization (see Box 14.7). They can then draw upon evidence which throws into doubt whether the number of transactions taking place among states has indeed risen (UNDP 1997), and make the argument that there is 'nothing new' in the growing interdependence of states. By contrast, **liberal enthusiasts** of globalization focus on technological innovation and the non-political 'objective' forces which are shrinking the world-economy. They argue that this is creating a less political, more efficient, more unified world order. Those who focus on deterritorialization highlight that there is also a negative side to globalization. Just as technological innovation permits a more active global civil society, so too it permits the growth of an uncivil one. Terrorist **networks** and the growth of transnational crime grow easily and are harder to combat in an era of globalization. This puts an important caveat on a final argument about globalization—one which prioritizes the role powerful states play in shaping the process. Focusing on liberalization, several analysts highlight the role of powerful states in setting the rules of the new globalized international economy, and their increasing influence over less powerful states. Yet this has two faces. On the one hand, powerful states find it relatively easy to set down rules with little or no consultation with less powerful states. This is as true in the global economy as it has been in recent years in the US (and selected allies) **war against terrorism** and invasions of Afghanistan and Iraq. Yet in the latter case, the subsequent challenge of pacifying weakened states through military occupation highlights how difficult it is even for the most powerful states to control other countries.

Is globalization diminishing the role of the state in the world economy?

The globalists

'A global economy is emerging' claim those who depict a world in which multinational trade, production, invest-

ment, and financing moves in and out of countries ever more easily. The 'globalists' tell us that, as a result, governments and **states are losing** their capacity to **control** economic interactions. This is partly because the quantity and rapidity of flows make it more difficult for governments to regulate trade, investment, or capital. Equally important is the fact that firms and investors can more easily take their business elsewhere. This puts new constraints on governments trying to retain and encourage investment. The argument here is that **footloose modern businesses** will simply exit from a country if a government does not pursue liberalizing policies which foster corporate profitability and flexibility. For this reason, governments are under pressure to reduce taxes and to cut back state expenditure on health, education, pensions, and so forth. When it comes to regulating international business, governments are permitting investors themselves to set the rules and these private actors are doing so though new private international networks and self-regulatory agencies. In sum, states are losing power in a global economic order in which state borders and governments are less influential. This eventuality is, of course, embraced by those interpreting it from a 'liberal' (see Box 14.5) starting point.

Box 14.8 The globalists

'The nation state has become an unnatural, even dysfunctional, unit for organizing human activity and managing economic endeavour in a borderless world. It represents no genuine, shared community of economic interest; it defines no meaningful flows of economic activity.'

(Ohmae 1990: 24)

The sceptics

Countering the 'global economy' view are a variety of sceptics who highlight flaws in the argument and the evidence proposed by those who argue that the state is losing power. The proposition that states are under pressure to cut taxes and reduce expenditure is attacked by scholars who examine data of industrialized countries and demonstrate that the evidence does not back up this claim. Nor does the evidence suggest that multinational enterprises (MNEs) relocate investment to areas where there are lower wages and lower taxes. Rather, contemporary research

Box 14.9 The sceptics

'The closer we looked the shallower and more unfounded became the claims of the more radical globalists. In particular, we began to be disturbed by three facts: first, the absence of a commonly accepted model of the new global economy and how it differs from previous sates of the international economy; second . . . the tendency casually to cite examples of internationalization of sectors and processes as if they were evidence of the growth of an economy dominated by autonomous global market forces; and third, the lack of historical depth, the tendency to portray current changes as both unique and without precedent and firmly set to persist long into the future.'

(Hirst and Thompson 1996: 2)

into actual patterns of MNE investment discloses that in the new knowledge-intensive economy, factors such as the availability of skilled and semi-skilled labour, good infrastructure, and proximity to market are crucial ingredients to choices of location. The conclusion drawn from this evidence is that the **role of states is not eroding**. To the contrary, states and government still have a very important and substantial role to play in a successful economy.

New constraints on states

While sceptics knock holes in some of the arguments about the erosion of state **power** in the face of global multinational enterprises, other aspects of globalization do constrain all states. In particular, the fact that billions of dollars can flood in—or out—of a country overnight sets a new constraint on monetary policy and opens up **new vulnerabilities** in the financial sectors of all countries. In other words, governments have to be very careful in managing interest rates and **managing or floating exchange rates**. Equally, they need robust domestic banking and financial systems to weather the onslaught or recession of a tidal wave of capital. The punishment for poor policy is instantaneous and devastating. Furthermore, as the **Asian financial crisis** of 1997 (see Box 14.10) showed, it is not only the culprit country who bears the punishment. The financial crisis in Asia highlighted the potential vulnerability of all countries to massive inflows and outflows of capital. It also underlined that some states suffer the impact of globalization more than others.

Box 14.10 The Asian financial crisis

In 1997 a financial crisis spread rapidly throughout Asia. It began in March of that year when difficulties in Thailand's financial institutions sparked a tremendous outflow of capital from the country. As capital fled, the Thai currency was weakened, forcing the government to float (after which the currency depreciated by 15–20 per cent). Within weeks, the crisis in Thailand spread to Indonesia, Malaysia, and the Philippines in what the IMF referred to as a 'currency meltdown'. By the end of 1997 Thailand, Indonesia, and Korea had all been forced to turn to the IMF to negotiate access to funds in return for agreement to abide by tough conditions, setting out reforms they had to promise to undertake within their economies. Meanwhile, the Malaysian government undertook its own policies of adjustment and imposed capital controls in order to stem the damaging effects of capital mobility. Scholars are still debating the relative advantages and disadvantages of these strategies. A vigorous debate has focused in particular on whether the IMF was right to impose tough conditions, with some arguing that in so doing it exacerbated a deep recession in the region.

The debate about the IMF's intervention in the Asian financial crisis

The IMF applied heavy conditions to the Asian countries on the grounds that the causes of the crisis were 'mainly domestic': 'these countries became victims of their own success' which 'led domestic and foreign investors to underestimate the countries' economic weaknesses'. 'The fundamental policy shortcomings' of policy-makers in these countries included permitting a 'build-up of overheating pressures', 'pegged exchange regimes', and 'weak management and poor control of risks, lax enforcement of prudential rules and inadequate supervision' in the financial system.

(IMF, World Economic Outlook, 1998: 3)

Critics argued that the IMF applied the wrong policies: 'The particular set of models that the IMF uses have been inappropriate in many situations, e.g. in the crisis in East Asia, it is clear that their forecasts concerning the countries affected by the crisis were badly misguided.'

(Joseph Stiglitz, in Christopher Gilbert and David Vines (eds) (2000), The World Bank: Policies and Structure (Cambridge: Cambridge University Press)

And that the IMF had no right to impose these kinds of conditions: 'The legitimate political institutions of the country should determine the nation's economic structure and the nature of its institutions. A nation's desperate need for short-term financial help does not give the IMF the moral right to substitute its technical judgements for the outcomes of the nation's political process.'

(Feldstein 1998: 24)

Case Study The impact of globalization on different kinds of states

The Asian crisis highlights that states have different capacities to respond to globalization. Even though all states in the region were affected by the crisis, their responses suggested that some enjoyed more choice or 'sovereignty' than others. Indonesia, Thailand and Korea turned to the IMF for assistance conditional on a raft of policies mostly defined in Washington, DC. Meanwhile Malaysia formulated its own policies of adjustment and imposed policies such as capital controls, which were greatly disapproved of in Washington, DC. Although globalists and sceptics treat all states as equal in their arguments about globalization, it is worth questioning this.

One way to think about the impact of globalization is to distinguish between **strong states** and **weak states**. At the extreme end, strong states are those which shape the rules and institutions which have made a global economy possible: we have already seen the way US policies shaped the creation, implementation, and breakdown of the Bretton Woods system. A more general description of strong states is that they can control—to some degree—the nature and speed of their integration into the world-economy. Into this category we might place not only relatively strong industrialized countries, but also developing countries such as Brazil, Malaysia, China, Iraq, and Iran. In all of these cases,

globalization is having a powerful effect, as is evidenced by the restructuring of national and private industries in industrialized countries, the past decade of economic liberalization in Brazil, and in a radically different way, through international coercive interventions in Iraq. Yet at the same time, in each of these countries there are **high protective barriers** in important sectors of the economy, and serious debate about capital controls and the regulation of international capital. The capacity of these countries to control their integration into the world-economy is doubtless related to their size, resources, geostrategic advantages, and economic strength. However, interestingly, it seems also to be related to their national ideology and the domestic power of the state. One thing that all 'strong states' have in common is that they guard with equal ferocity their independence in economic policy, foreign policy, human rights, and security issues.

'Weak states', by contrast, suffer from a lack of choice in their international economic relations. They have little or no influence in the creation and enforcement of rules in the system, and they have exercised little control over their own integration into the world-economy. For example, in the aftermath of the debt crisis of the 1980s, many 'weak states' opened up their economies, liberalized, and deregulated, more as a result of coercive liberalization than of democratic policy choice. In the 1990s, this continued with what an international economist called **forced harmonization**, whereby, for instance, in the case of trade negotiations on intellectual property, developing countries were coerced into an agreement which transfers `billions of dollars' worth of monopoly profits from poor countries to rich countries under the guise of protecting the property rights of inventors' (Rodrik 1999).

Distinguishing among states according to their capacity to shape and respond to globalization is vital in analyzing the impact on IPE. The example of the international financial system demonstrates that some states, in particular the United States, are rule-makers in the world economy, while less powerful states are rule-takers.

Key Points

- Globalization poses some new constraints for all states, including the most powerful. In particular, the emergence of global capital markets means that all governments have to be cautious in their choice of exchange rate and interest rate policies.
- On other issues of economic policy, wealthier and more powerful countries are less constrained by globalization than is portrayed by the

globalists. This is because the firms and investors whom governments are keen to attract are not solely concerned with levels of taxation and wages. They are equally concerned with factors such as the skills of the workforce, the provision of infrastructure, and proximity to markets.
- At the international level the more powerful states in the system get to set (and enforce) many of the rules of the new global economy.

International institutions in the globalizing world-economy

We have seen that globalization is increasing interdependence among states, it is also increased global interconnectedness, and the capacity of some states to influence others. The **Asian financial crisis** exhibited all three of these changes. The countries of Asia had 'liberalized' into global capital markets (with much encouragement from the United States and other industrialized countries) and soon became recipients of large inflows of short-term capital. As soon as confidence in Thailand faltered, reactions were instantaneously transmitted to investors (through the new communications networks). The subsequent débâcle of 1997 demonstrated how quickly, easily, and devastatingly a financial crisis in one country can spill over into others.

The management of the Asian financial crisis led some policy-makers to call for stronger, more effective international institutions, including a capacity to ensure better information and monitoring, deeper cooperation, and regulation in the world-economy. At the same time, however, others argued that the crisis revealed the problems and flaws of existing international institutions and the bias or interests which they reflect (see Box 14.10). These positions echo a larger debate in IPE about the nature and impact of institutions in the world economy. This debate is important in helping us to determine what role international institutions might play in managing the new problems and challenges arising from globalization.

Competing accounts of institutions echo the differences in approaches to IPE already discussed. Institutionalists (or neo-liberal Institutionalists (see Ch.7)) tell us that states will create institutions in order better to achieve gains through policy **coordination** and cooperation. However, several preconditions are necessary for this to occur. Under certain conditions, Institutionalists argue that states will agree to be bound by certain rules, norms, or decisions of **international organizations**. This does not mean that the most powerful states in the system will always obey the rules. Rather, institutions affect international politics because they open up new reasons to cooperate, they permit states to define their interests in a more cooperative way, they foster negotiations among states as well as compliance with mutually agreed rules and standards.

The Institutionalist account offers reasons for a certain kind of optimism about the role international institutions will play in managing globalization. Institutions will smooth over many gaps and failures in the operation of markets, and serve to ensure that states make genuinely rational and optimizing decisions to cooperate. Globalization will be managed by existing institutions and organizations and, indeed, new institutions will probably also emerge. Globalization managed in this way will ensure that the world-economy moves more towards the **liberal** model (see Box 14.5) and that both strong and weak states benefit. Although there have been

---

Box 14.11 Anti-globalization protests against international organizations

Many believed the invasion of Iraq would cause the anti-globalization protests to abate:

'The anti-globalization movement, a loose-knit network of activists focused on reforming international financial institutions, surged in popularity after thousands shut down a World Trade Organization summit in Seattle in 1999, but it has struggled recently to retain its momentum and numbers. The Bush administration's war on terrorism since the attacks of Sept. 11, 2001, has been the focus of most U.S. grass-roots organizing and street protests.'

(*Washington Post, 14, April 2003*)

However, at the WTO Ministerial Conference in Montreal, July 2003 (the day before):

'Several downtown blocks will be closed to traffic, office employees going to work will be funnelled through special corridors and the local police have called in reinforcements from the provincial force. With

26 trade ministers coming to Montreal on Monday for a meeting of the World Trade Organization, police are gearing up for the presence of demonstrators, who are talking of shutting down the event and recreating the success of the massive marches that disrupted past gatherings in Seattle and Quebec City.'

(*Canada's Globe & Mail, 26 July 2003*)

And at the G8 Summit in Evian, June 2003:

'Several hundred black-hooded protesters blocked roads and trashed shops in the Lake Geneva area early on the weekend as heads of the world's leading industrial democracies gathered for their annual G8 summit. French and Swiss riot police fired teargas to contain the anti-capitalist crowds kept in two towns kilometres (miles) away from the lakeside spa of Evian where U.S. President George W. Bush was due around noon (1000 GMT) to meet leaders who opposed the Iraq war.'

(*Reuters News Service, 3 June 2003*)

many protests about international organizations (see Box 14.11), these are the result of people misunderstanding the advantages of free trade and free movements of capital in the world-economy.

Realists (and neo-realists in particular) disagree with institutionalists (see Ch.5 and Ch.7). Realists reject the idea that institutions emerge primarily as a solution to universal problems or market failures. They argue that international institutions and organizations will always reflect the interests of dominant states within the system. When these states wish to coordinate policies with others, they will create institutions. Once created, however, these institutions will not (as the Institutionalists argue) transform the way states define and pursue their interests. Institutions will be effective only for as long as they do not diminish the power of dominant states *vis-à-vis* other states.

Let us consider what this means in practice. Take a state deciding whether to sign up to a new trade agreement or support the decision of an international organization. The Institutionalists argue that policy-makers will consider the **absolute gains** to be made from the agreement, including the potential longer-term gains, such as advancing a more stable and credible system of rules. The neo-realists, by contrast, argue that policy-makers will primarily be concerned with **relative gains**. In other words, they will ask, 'do we gain more from this than other states?' (rather than 'do we gain from this?'). If other states stand to gain more, then the advantages of signing up are outweighed by the fact that the power of the state will be diminished *vis-à-vis* other states (see Ch.7).

For Realists, cooperation and institutions are heavily constrained by underlying calculations about power. Having signed an agreement or created an international organization, a powerful state will not necessarily be bound by it. Indeed, if it got in the way of the state's interests (defined in Realist terms), a powerful state will simply sweep the institution aside. The implications for globalization and its impact on weak states are rather grim. International institutions, including organizations such as the IMF, the World Bank, the WTO, the G8 and the EU, will manage globalization but in the interests of their most powerful members. Institutions will only accommodate the needs and interests of weaker states where in so doing they do not diminish the dominant position of powerful states. From a Realist perspective, it follows that anti-globalization protesters are right to argue that the international institutions do not work for the interests of poor and developing countries. However, the Realists are equally certain that such protests will have little impact.

This interpretation of international institutions is rebutted not only by Institutionalists, but by those who delve into the ways ideas, beliefs, and interactions shape the behaviour of states. In an earlier section, we explored the **neo-Gramscian approach,** let us now introduce the broader Constructivist approach which has been mentioned in other chapters of this book.

	Institutionalist (or 'neo-liberal Institutionalist')	Realist (or 'neo-realist')	Constructivist
Under what conditions will states create international institutions?	For mutual gains (rationally calculated by states).	Only where relative position *vis-à-vis* other states is not adversely affected.	Institutions arise as a reflection of the identities and interests of states and groups which are themselves forged through interaction.
What impact do institutions have on international relations?	Expand the possible gains to be made from cooperation.	Facilitate the coordination of policies and actions but only in so far as this does not alter the balance of power among states.	Reinforce particular patterns of interaction, and reflect new ones.
The implications for globalization	Institutions can manage globalization to ensure a transition to a more 'Liberal' economy (see Box 14.5).	Institutions will 'manage' globalization in the interests of dominant and powerful states.	Changing patterns of interaction and discourse will be reflected in institutional responses to globalization.

Table 14.1 The debate about institutions

Constructivists reject the idea that institutions reflect the 'rational' calculations of states either within inter-state competition (Realists) or as part of a calculation of longer-term economic advantage and benefits from cooperation (Institutionalists). In fact, what Constructivists reject is the idea that states' interests are objectively definable and fixed. Instead, they argue that any one state's interests are affected by its **identity** as a state and that both its interests and identity are influenced by a **social structure of interactions, normative ideas**, and beliefs. If we cannot assume that states have a particular identity or interest prior to their interactions, then the Institutionalists are wrong to assume that institutions emerge as rational responses to the needs of markets, trade, finance, and the like. Equally, the Realists are wrong to assume that institutions can only be reflections of power politics. To quote Constructivist Alex Wendt, 'anarchy is what states make of it' (1992). In other words, identities and interests are more fluid and changing than Realists permit. Through their interactions and discourse, states change and these changes can reflect in institutions.

Constructivism and the neo-Gramscian approach highlight actors and processes involved in globalization which are neglected in Realist and Institutionalist accounts, and have important ramifications for institutions. For example, the protesters against the WTO, the IMF, and the World Bank can be construed as part of an ongoing dialogue which affects states in several ways. The international attention to these issues places them on the agenda of international meetings and organizations. It also puts pressures on political leaders and encourages interest groups and pressures to form within the state. As a result, the beliefs, ideas, and conceptions of interest in international relations change and this can shift the attention, nature, and functions of international institutions. On this view, globalization is not just a process affecting and managed by states. **Several other actors** are involved, both within and across societies, including international institutions, which play a dynamic role. The governance or management of globalization is shaped by a mixture of interests, beliefs, and values about how the world works and how it ought to be. The existing institutions doubtless reflect the interests of powerful states. However, these interests are the products of the way states interact and are subject to reinterpretation and change.

Key Points

- Institutionalists argue that international institutions will play an important and positive role in ensuring that globalization results in widely spread benefits in the world-economy.
- Realists and neo-realists reject the institutionalist argument on the grounds that it does not account for the unwillingness of states ever to sacrifice power relative to other states.

- Constructivists pay more attention to how governments, states, and other actors construct their preferences, highlighting the role that state identities, dominant beliefs, and ongoing debates and contestation plays in this process.

Conclusion

Globalization increases the challenges faced by all actors in the world-economy: states, firms, **transnational actors**, and international organizations. Strong states are trying to shape institutions to manage financial crises, powerful NGOs, and globalizing firms. Weak states are trying to survive increasingly precarious and changeable economic circumstances. Common to all states is the search for greater stability and predictability, although governments disagree over how and where this should be achieved. One layer of governance this chapter has not examined is that of regional organizations and institutions (see Ch.25). The fact that in recent years virtually every state in the world has joined at least one regional trade grouping underscores the search for new ways to manage globalization. At the same time, **regionalism** highlights the scepticism of many states about international institutions, and their fears that institutions are too dominated by powerful states, or unlikely to constrain them. The result is an emerging multi-layered governance in the world-economy. At each level (international, regional, and state) the

core issues debated in this chapter arise. These include: whose interests are served by the institution? What forces are shaping it? Who has access to it? Whose values does it reflect? Globalization casts a spotlight on these arrangements since the transformations occurring in the world-economy are being powerfully shaped by them.

❓ Questions

1 In what ways did the Bretton Woods framework for the post-war economy try to avoid the economic problems of the inter-war years?

2 What was the 'breakdown in the Bretton Woods system'?

3 Did a loss of US hegemony cause the breakdown of the Bretton Woods system?

4 Are there any issues on which mercantilists agree with liberals?

5 What is different about the Marxian and mercantilist depictions of power in the international economy?

6 Does rational choice theory explain more about outcomes than actors' preferences?

7 In what way do neo-Gramscians invoke structure in their explanation of IPE?

8 Why do sceptics doubt that globalization is transforming IPE?

9 What vulnerabilities faced by states in the globalizing economy did the Asian financial crisis demonstrate?

10 How can we explain the different impact globalization has on different states?

11 How and why do institutionalists argue that institutions change the behaviour of states?

12 For whom might the realist account of institutions and globalization be cheerful reading?

➲ Guide to further reading

Frieden, J., and Lake, D. A. , (eds) (2000), *International Political Economy: Perspectives on Global Power and Wealth* (New York: St Martin's Press). Introduces core texts from each approach to international political economy with very useful editors' introductions.

Grieco, J. M., and Ikenberry, G. J. (2003), *State Power and World Markets: The International Political Economy* (New York: W. W. Norton & Company). An over-arching text with an underlying realist view of the world-economy.

Held, D., McGrew, A., Goldblatt, D., and Perrator, J. (1999), *Global Transformations: Politics, Economics and Culture* (Cambridge: Polity Press). A useful resource book on the empirical evidence of globalization in all aspects of international relations.

Helleiner, E. (1994), *States and the Reemergence of Global Finance: From Bretton Woods to the 1990s* (Ithaca, NY: Cornell University Press). An excellent account of the ways in which the policies of states have shaped the emergence of the international financial system.

Katzenstein, P., Keohane, R., and Krasner, S. (1998), 'International Organization and the State of World Politics', *International Organization*, 52(4): 645–85. A useful review article of key developments in the study of international relations and international political economy.

Oatley, T., and Silver, M. (2003), *International Political Economy: Interests and Institutions in the Global Economy* (Harlow: Pearson). An excellent example of the public or rational choice approach to international political economy.

Palan, R. (ed.) (2000), *Global Political Economy: Contemporary Theories* (London: Routledge). A good sampling of European approaches and theories of international political economy.

Rodrik, D. (1999), *The New Global Economy and Developing Countries: Making Openness Work* (Washington, DC: Overseas Development Council). A good critical analysis of the advantages and disadvantages of globalization for developing countries.

Woods, N. (2006), *The Globalizers: The IMF, the World Bank, and their Borrowers* (Ithaca, NY: Cornell University Press). A useful overview on the roles, evolution, and politics of the IMF and World Bank and their relations with developing countries.

Online Resource Centre

 Visit the Online Resource Centre that accompanies this book to access more learning resources on this chapter topic at www.oxfordtextbooks.co.uk/uk/orc/baylis_smith4e/

Chapter 15

Gender in world politics

J. ANN TICKNER[1]

- Introduction 264
- Feminist theories 264
- Feminists define gender 265
- Putting a gender lens on global politics 266
- Gendering security 268
- Gender in the global economy 271
- Using knowledge to inform policy practice 273
- Conclusion 276

Reader's Guide

This chapter introduces you to the way in which gender helps to structure world politics. It does so using feminist perspectives on international relations. It begins with an overview of feminist theories more generally and offers a feminist definition of gender. Feminists define gender as an unequal structural relationship of power. Building on a variety of the IR theoretical perspectives discussed in Part Two of this book, IR feminists use gender, defined in this way, to help them understand why women are disadvantaged relative to men in all societies. The chapter focuses on feminist perspectives on security and the global economy. It examines the masculinity of war and national security, suggesting that states' national security policies are often legitimated in terms of masculine characteristics. This helps us understand why women have been so underrepresented in powerful positions in the international policy world and in militaries. Feminists consider the security of individuals to be as important as the security of states. We will see how gendered economic structures of inequality, associated with a global gendered division of labour, can help us explain why the majority of the world's poor are women. The chapter concludes by outlining some policy practices that are helping to lessen gender inequality.

Introduction

Feminist perspectives entered the international relations discipline at the end of the 1980s, at about the same time as the end of the **cold war**. This was not a coincidence. During the previous forty years, the conflict between the United States and the Soviet Union had dominated the agenda of international relations (see Ch.3). The decade after the end of the cold war (1989–2000) was one of relative peace between the major powers (see Ch.4). Many new issues appeared on the international relations' agenda. More attention was paid to economic relations. There were lively debates between proponents of economic globalization and those who claimed that it was not helping to decrease world poverty. The meaning of security was expanded to include human as well as state security (see Ch.28). International relations began to pay more attention to ethno-national conflicts and to the high number of civilians killed or injured in these conflicts (see Ch.13). More attention was also paid to **international organizations**, **social movements**, and **non-state actors** (see Ch.19). As the globalization theme of this book makes clear, international politics is about much more than inter-state relations.

This broad set of issues seems the most compatible with feminist approaches. Feminists are not satisfied with framing international politics solely in terms of inter-state politics. While women have always been players in international politics, their participation has more often taken place in non-governmental settings such as social movements rather than in inter-state policy-making. Women also participate in international politics as diplomats' wives, as nannies going abroad to find work to support their families, and as sex workers trafficked across international boundaries. Women's voices have rarely been heard in the halls of state power or in the leadership of militaries. Nevertheless, women are deeply impacted by decisions that their leaders make. Civilian casualties constitute about 90 per cent of the casualties in today's wars, and women and children make up the majority of these casualties. Women are the majority of the world's poorest population. Economic policies, constructed in distant centres of power, affect how resources are distributed in local communities. Broader global frameworks are more suited to investigating these issues.

Before investigating how gender is at work in these global issues, let us begin with a brief introduction to feminist theory and a definition of what feminists mean by the term **gender**.

Feminist theories

Feminism as an academic discipline grew out of the feminist movement of the 1960s and 1970s—a movement dedicated to achieving political, social, and economic equality for women. Many feminists link constructing knowledge to political practice. This form of knowledge-building is called **emancipatory knowledge**. It means producing knowledge that can help inform practices to improve women's lives. The most important goal for feminist theory is to explain women's subordination, which exists to varying degrees in all societies, and to seek ways to end it. However, feminists disagree on why women are subordinate and thus, how to overcome it.

There are many different types of feminist theory. They all give us different reasons for women's subordination. They include liberal, Marxist, socialist, post-colonial, and post-modern (see Ch.10). Liberal feminists believe that removing legal obstacles can overcome women's subordination. However, all the other approaches—which we will call post-liberal—see deeply rooted structures of **patriarchy** in all societies, which cannot be overcome by legal remedies alone. Marxist and socialist feminists look for explanations for women's subordination in the labour market that offers greater rewards and prestige for paid work in the public sphere than for unpaid work in the household. (Women do most of the unpaid work, even when they work for wages, thus imposing what feminists call a **double burden**.) Post-colonial and post-modern feminists believe that we cannot generalize about all women. Women experience subordination differently because they are differently placed in and among

societies depending on their class and race, as well as their gender. All these post-liberal feminist theo- ries use gender as an important category of analysis.

Key Points

- Feminism is a movement dedicated to achieving political, social, and economic equality for women.
- The goal of feminist theory is to explain why women are subordinated. Feminists believe that we cannot separate knowledge from political practice and that feminist knowledge should help improve women's lives.

- There are a variety of feminist theories, such as liberal, Marxist, socialist, post-modern, and post-colonial. Each gives us different explanations for women's subordination.

Feminists define gender

In everyday usage, gender denotes the biological sex of individuals. However, feminists define gender differently—as a set of socially and culturally constructed characteristics that vary across time and place (see Ch.10). When we think of characteristics such as **power**, autonomy, **rationality**, and public, we associate them with masculinity or what it means to be a 'real man'. Opposite characteristics, such as weakness, dependence/connection, emotionality, and private, are associated with femininity. There have been studies that show that both women and men assign a more positive value to masculine characteristics. These definitions of **masculinity** and **femininity** are relational, which means that they depend on each other for their meaning. In other words, what it means to be a 'real man' is not to display 'womanly' weaknesses. Since these characteristics are social constructions, not biological ones, it is quite possible for women, particularly those in powerful positions like US Secretary of State Condoleezza Rice or British Prime Minister Margaret Thatcher, appear to many to act like 'real men'. In fact, certain feminists have argued that such behaviour is necessary for both women and men to succeed in the tough world of international policy-making (Cohn 1993: 230–1, 237–8).

Sometimes gender is thought to be synonymous with women. But feminists believe that gender is as much about men and masculinity as it is about women. Since, at the top level, international politics is a masculine world, it is particularly important to pay attention to various forms of masculinity that are often used to legitimate states' foreign and military policies. For example, characteristics such as power, autonomy, and rationality, which we have identified as masculine, are characteristics that are most valued in states' foreign policies.

But gender is about more than personal characteristics. Since, as we have seen, gender characteristics are generally unequal—meaning that people of both sexes ascribe more positive value to the masculine ones—gender is also a structure of meaning that signifies power relationships. If gender characteristics denote inequality, gender becomes a mechanism for the unequal distribution of social benefits and costs. Therefore, gender is crucial for analyzing global politics and economics, particularly with respect to issues of inequality, insecurity, and social justice. Feminists believe we need to make unequal gender structures visible in order to move beyond them.

We have shown that gender is an analytical tool not just a descriptive category. Now that we have examined feminist theory and defined gender, let us look at how International Relations (IR) feminists use gender as a category of analysis.

Key Points

- Feminists define gender as distinct from sex. Gender is a set of socially constructed characteristics that define what we mean by masculinity and femininity. It is possible for women to display masculine characteristics and vice versa.
- Gender is a system of social hierarchy in which masculine characteristics are more valued than feminine ones.
- Gender is a structure that signifies unequal power relationships between women and men.

Putting a gender lens on global politics

IR feminists use gender analysis to help them answer questions about global politics. V. Spike Peterson and Anne Sisson Runyan call this putting on our **gender-sensitive lenses**. Let us see what kind of questions we might ask when we put on our gender-sensitive lenses.

Some feminist questions

Less than 10 per cent of the world's heads of state are women and most of the world's military personnel are men. In order to understand the lack of women in high places we might begin by asking 'where are the women?'. Cynthia Enloe (1989: 8) suggests that we need to look in unconventional places, not normally considered within the boundaries of global politics, to answer this question. She asks us to consider whether women's roles, as secretaries, clerical workers, domestic servants, and diplomats' wives, are relevant to the business of international politics. She shows us how vital women in these various roles are to states' foreign policies and to the functioning of the global economy.

But making women visible does not explain why they are disproportionately situated in low-paid or non-remunerated occupations far from the halls of power. To explain this we must put on our gendered lenses and think about women's places within gendered global structures and processes that constrain their security and their economic opportunities. We might want to ask some further

---

Box 15.2 Women leaders

World percentage of women in parliaments (2006): 17%

Percentage of women in Upper House or Senate (2006): 15.9%

Percentage of women in Single House or Lower House of parliament (2006): 17.2%

Percentage of women in the world's top business executive positions (*c.* 2000): between 1% and 3%

---

questions. How are the types of power necessary to keep unequal gender structures in place perpetuated? Does it make any difference to states' policy practices that their foreign and security policies are often legitimated through appeals to various types of masculinity? Does it make a difference that it is predominantly men who fight wars? Answering these questions may help us to see that what is so often taken for granted in how the world is organized is, in fact, keeping in place certain social arrangements and institutional structures which contribute to the subordination of women and other disadvantaged groups.

To help them answer these questions IR feminists use a number of different theoretical approaches that build on feminist theory more generally (see also Ch.10). Let us look at some examples.

Liberal feminism

Liberal feminists document various aspects of women's subordination. They have investigated problems of refugee women, income inequalities between women and men, and the kinds of human rights violations incurred disproportionately by women, such as trafficking and rape in war. They look for women in the institutions and practices of global politics and observe how their presence (or lack thereof) affects and is affected by international policy-making. They ask what a world with more women in positions of power might look like. Liberal feminists believe that women's equality can be achieved by removing legal and other obstacles that have denied them the same rights and opportunities as men.

Box 15.1 Gender-sensitive lenses

'[A gender-sensitive lens] enables us to "see" how the world is shaped by gendered concepts, practices, and institutions . . .

Whenever we study a topic, we do so through a lens that focuses our attention in particular ways. By filtering or "ordering" what we look at, each lens enables us to see some things in greater detail or more accurately or in better relation to certain other things.

. . . [D]ifferent [theoretical perspectives] act as lenses and shape our assumptions about who the significant actors are, . . . what their attributes are, . . . how social processes are categorized, . . . and what outcomes are desirable . . .'

(Peterson and Runyan 1999: 1–2)

Many IR feminists disagree with liberal feminism. As we noted earlier, post-liberal feminists emphasize that gender inequalities continue to exist in societies that have long since achieved formal legal equality. They suggest that we must look more deeply at gender hierarchies in order to explain these inequalities. Post-liberal feminists draw on, but go beyond, a variety of IR approaches discussed in Part Two, such as Marxism, Social Constructivism and post-modernism. What is unique to these feminist approaches is that they use gender as a category of analysis. Let us look at some examples of each.

Feminist critical theory

Feminist critical theory has roots in Gramscian Marxism (see Ch.8). It explores both the ideational and material manifestations of gendered **identities** and gendered power in global politics. Sandra Whitworth is a feminist critical theorist. In her book, *Feminism and International Relations* (1994), she claims that understanding gender depends only in part on the material conditions of women and men in particular circumstances. She suggests that gender is also constituted by the meaning given to that reality—in other words, *ideas* that men and women have about their relationships to one another. Whitworth examines the different ways gender was understood over time in the International Planned Parenthood Federation (IPPF) and the International Labour Organization (ILO). She shows that changes in the meaning of gender had differing effects on these institutions' population policies at various times in their history.

Feminist Social Constructivism

Feminist **Constructivism** builds on Social Constructivism (see Ch.9). Feminist constructivists study the processes whereby ideas about gender influence global politics as well as the ways that global politics shape ideas about gender. Elisabeth Prügl is a feminist constructivist. Her book, *The Global Construction of Gender* (1999), uses feminist Constructivism to analyze the treatment of home-based work in international law. Since most home-based workers are women, the debate about regulating this type of employment is an important one for feminists. Low wages and poor working conditions are often justified on

the grounds that home-based work is not 'real work' since it takes place in the private reproductive sphere of the household rather than in the more valued public sphere of waged-based production. Prügl shows how ideas about femininity have contributed to the international community's debates about institutionalizing these home-based workers' rights, a debate that finally culminated in the passage of the ILO's Homework Convention in 1996 (see Case Study 2 below).

Feminist post-modernism

Post-modernists focus on meaning as it is codified in language (see Ch.10). They claim that we understand reality through our use of language. They are particularly concerned with the relationship between knowledge and power—meaning that those who construct meaning and create knowledge gain a great deal of power by so doing. Feminist post-modernists point out that men have generally been seen as the knowers and that what has counted as knowledge has generally been based on men's lives in the public sphere. Women have generally not been seen as knowers or as the subjects of knowledge.

Charlotte Hooper's book *Manly States* (2001) is an example of post-modern textual analysis. Hooper claims that we cannot understand international relations unless we understand the implications of the fact that it is conducted mostly by men. She asks how might international relations shape men as much as men shape international relations. Hooper sets about answering this question through an analysis of masculinity, together with a textual analysis of *The Economist*, a prestigious British weekly newspaper that covers business and politics. She concludes that *The Economist* is saturated with signifiers of masculinity and that gendered messages are encoded in the newspaper regardless of the intentions of its publishers or authors. This is one example of how gender politics pervades our understanding of world politics.

Post-colonial feminism

Post-colonialists focus on colonial relations of domination and subordination, established under European **imperialism** in the eighteenth and nineteenth centuries (see

Ch.10). Post-colonialists claim that these dominance relationships still persist and that they are built into the way Western knowledge portrays people and countries in the South today. Post-colonial feminism makes similar claims about the way Western feminism has constructed knowledge about non-Western women. Just as feminists have criticized Western knowledge for being knowledge constructed mainly from men's lives, post-colonial feminists see similar problems arising from feminist knowledge that is based largely on the experiences of relatively privileged Western women. Chandra Mohanty (1988) suggests that women's subordinations must be addressed within their own cultural context, rather than through some universal understanding of women's needs. She criticizes Western feminists' portrayal of **Third World** women as poor, undereducated, victimized, and lacking in agency.

We have examined some writings of IR feminists who have put on their gender lenses in order to understand why women are disadvantaged relative to men and what difference this makes to global politics. Let us now look through our gendered lenses at two important realms of global politics—security and economic globalization.

Key Points

- IR feminists use gender-sensitive lenses to help them answer questions about why women often play subordinate roles in global politics. IR feminists build on other IR theories, such as liberalism, critical theory, Constructivism, post-modernism, and post-colonialism. They go beyond them by introducing gender as a category of analysis.
- Liberal feminists believe women's equality can be achieved by removing legal obstacles that deny women the same opportunities as men.
- Post-liberal feminists disagree with liberal feminists. They claim that we must look more deeply at unequal gendered structures in order to understand women's subordination.
- Feminist critical theory examines how both ideas and material structures shape people's lives. IR feminist critical theorists show how changes in the meaning of gender have changed the practices of international organizations over time.

- Feminist constructivists show us the various ways in which ideas about gender shape and are shaped by global politics. Elisabeth Prügl shows us how these ideas shaped the framing of international legal conventions.
- Post-modern feminists are concerned with the link between knowledge and power. They suggest that men have generally been seen as knowers and as subjects of knowledge. This influences how we see global politics.
- Post-colonial feminists criticize Western feminists for basing feminist knowledge on Western women's lives and for portraying Third World women as lacking in agency. They suggest that women's subordination must be differentially understood in terms of race, class, and geographical location, and that all women should be seen as agents rather than victims.

Gendering security

Challenging the myth of protection

We often think of men as protectors and women and children as people who need protection. One of the stories that has been told throughout history is that men fight wars to protect women and children. The high number of civilian casualties in contemporary wars, about 90 per cent of total casualties, suggests that we should be questioning this story. A large proportion of these casualties are women and children. Women and children constitute the majority of the world's refugee population.[2] When women, often acting as heads of households, are forced into refugee camps, their vulnerability, and that of their children, increases. In wartime, women are particularly subject to rape and prostitution (see Box 15.3). Rape is not just an accident of war but often a systematic military strategy. It is estimated that 20,000 to 35,000 women were raped during the war in Bosnia and Herzegovina. In Bosnia, rape was associated with a policy of ethnic cleansing. The strategy included forced pregnancies to make Bosnia a Serbian state by implanting Serbian babies in Bosnian Muslim mothers (Pettman 1996: 101).

These stories about women in conflict situations severely challenge the **protection myth**. Yet, such myths have been important in upholding the legitimacy of war. Using our gender lenses to look at the effects of war on

Box 15.3 Military prostitution as a security issue

Around many army bases, women are kidnapped and sold into prostitution. Katharine Moon has written an account of military prostitution around US military bases in South Korea in the 1970s. As part of an attempt to provide a more hospitable environment for American troops, the South Korean government undertook a policy of policing sexual health and work conduct of prostitutes. Moon's account shows us how military prostitution interacted with US–Korean security policies at the highest level. In the name of national security, the Korean state promoted policies that exploited these women's lives. Stories like Moon's shed light on the lives of women in places not normally considered relevant to global politics. By linking their experiences to wider processes, they show how national security can translate into personal insecurity for certain individuals.

(Adapted from Moon 1997)

women helps us to gain a better understanding of the unequal **gender relations**, such as the protector/protected relationship, that legitimate military activities and hide some of the negative effects of war on civilians. Let us now look more deeply at how these gendered constructions can help us understand national and international **security**.

Gendering war

Gender lenses help us see the association between war and masculinity. Militaries work hard to turn men into soldiers who must go into combat. Military training depends on the denigration of anything considered feminine—to act like a soldier is not to be 'womanly'. This image of a soldier is related to the protection myth—the soldier as a just warrior, self-sacrificially protecting women, children, and other vulnerable people. The idea that young men fight wars to protect these vulnerable groups who cannot be expected to protect themselves has been an important motivator for the recruitment of military forces. It has also helped sustain support for war by both women and men. In wartime, the just warrior, who displays heroic masculine characteristics, is often contrasted with an enemy who is portrayed as dangerous often through the use of feminized and sometimes racialized characteristics. This serves as further support for the need for protection. For example, the US-led war in Afghanistan was partially justified as a heroic intervention on behalf of presumably helpless Afghani women. The Taliban response was also shaped by gendered justifications of protecting 'their' women from outside influence. Both sides in the conflict further justified their positions through the use of feminized imagery of the other (Tickner 2002).

These images of the masculinity of war depend on rendering women's role in war invisible, or as the patriotic and supportive mother, wife, or daughter. Even in exceptional circumstances, such as in the Second World War when women took over factory jobs vacated by men who went off to war, women were expected to return to traditional roles when the war was over. But now that women are being accepted into the armed forces of certain states in ever-larger numbers, the picture is more complicated. The presence of women in militaries stirs deep currents, particularly with respect to women in combat. Placing women in combat is in strong tension with our culturally embedded view of what it means to be a warrior and who the people in need of protection actually are. In certain cases, it has been strongly resisted by the military itself, with claims of its negative effect on combat readiness. It is a controversial issue for feminists. Most feminists believe that equality dictates that women should be allowed to serve in militaries. However, some feminists believe that women should reject fighting in men's wars.

It is interesting to note the degree to which the importance of militarized masculinity varies over time and place and how these variations affect international policy-making. During the 1990s, a time of relative peace—at least in the North—we were becoming more accustomed to less militarized models of masculinity. Global businessmen conquering the world with briefcases rather than bullets became our new heroes. Bill Gates, the chairman of Microsoft Corporation, a bourgeois hero who looks distinctly unwarriorlike amasses dollars rather than weapons. And, in 1992, Bill Clinton was elected President of the United States after having refused to serve in the Vietnam War.

In the United States, these softer images of masculinity ended abruptly on **11 September 2001**. Post-**9/11**, militarized masculinity came back in vogue. After the attacks on the World Trade Center, firefighters and police officers in New York became the new male heroes. Women disappeared from television news broadcasts as male experts briefed Americans about 'America's New War'. However, this new form of warfare, the **war on terror** as it was called, came with multiple gendered images. Americans saw

new enemies in the form of young Muslim men, who were subjected to ethnic, as well as gender profiling under the excuse that the USA was 'at war'. Militarized masculinity influenced the 2004 US presidential campaign where both Republican George W. Bush and Democrat John Kerry emphasized their military or National Guard service as qualifications for the office of President. Clearly, this puts female candidates for high office in the United States at a disadvantage. While the 2006 mid-term elections saw Congresswomen Nancy Pelosi become the first woman House Majority Leader, only one out of the Democratic Party's top 11 women candidates to the US House of Representatives in the 2006 election was successful. Nine out of 11 of their male counterparts won. Many of them emphasized their toughness and ability to stand up to security threats during their campaigns.[3] These trends suggest that in times of war US voters, women and men alike, show greater support for leaders who demonstrate a more obviously militarized masculinity.

We have seen that, in spite of the myth of protection, civilians are not being protected in today's wars. We have also seen that, in certain cases, such as military prostitution camps, individuals' security may be sacrificed to national security. Qualifications for leadership positions in foreign policy are often tied up with what it means to be a 'real man'. This may help us understand why there are relatively few women in these top positions and in militaries. Let us conclude this section by thinking how we might redefine security using our gender lenses.

Feminist definitions of security

Since, as we have seen, **national security** can be in tension with individual security, feminists prefer to define security broadly—as the diminution of all forms of violence, including physical, economic, and ecological. They suggest that we think about security from the bottom up instead of the top down, meaning that we start with the security of individual or **community** rather than with that of the **state** or the **international system**. This allows us to examine critically the role of states as adequate security providers. In certain states torn by conflict, the more the government is preoccupied with national security, the less its citizens, especially women, experience physical security. While state violence is a particular problem in certain states, many states formally at peace sustain huge military

budgets at the same time as social spending, on which women depend more than men, is being cut.

We have seen how the security-seeking behaviour of states is legitimated by its association with certain types of masculinity. This narrows the range of permissible ways for states to act and may actually decrease the likelihood of achieving a peaceful solution to a conflict. Conciliatory gestures are often seen as weak and not in the **national interest**. This can also contribute to the perceived inauthenticity of women's voices in matters of policy-making.

We have also seen how most war casualties today are civilians—often women and children. But it is important not to see women only as victims. If we are to define security more broadly, we must begin to see women, as well as men, as security providers. As civilian war casualties increase, women's responsibilities rise. When men go off to fight, women are left behind as mothers, family providers, and caregivers. Instead of a warrior patriot, we might begin to think about a citizen defender as a definition of a security provider that could include us all, civilians and soldiers alike. It could also provide a less militarized notion of security.

As we said at the beginning of this section, feminist definitions of security also include economic security. Let us now turn to an examination of economic security as well as some broader issues of gender in the global economy.

Key Points

- Traditional stories about war portray men as protectors and women and children as being protected. In today's wars, women and children are being killed and injured in large numbers. This challenges the myth of protection.
- War is associated with masculinity. Our image of a soldier is a heroic male. This image is being challenged by an increasing number of women in militaries around the world. There is a debate among policy-makers and in militaries, and even among some feminists, as to whether women should fight in military combat.
- Militarized masculinity is popular when states are preoccupied with national security threats. This has larger consequences. Conciliatory options in policy-making tend to get discounted. It makes it difficult for women's voices to be seen as legitimate, particularly in matters of security policy.
- Feminists define security broadly to include the diminution of all forms of violence, physical, economic, and ecological. The national security of states, defined in masculine terms that emphasize military strength, can cause a trade-off with the physical and economic security of individuals.

Gender in the global economy

There are enormous differences in the socioeconomic status of women, depending on their race, class, nationality, and geographic location. Nevertheless, women are disproportionately located at the bottom of the socioeconomic scale in all societies. Three-fifths of the world's one billion poorest people are women and girls (United Nations Development Programme 2006*b*: 20). On average, women earn two-thirds of men's earnings[4] even though they work longer hours, many of which are spent in unremunerated reproductive and caring tasks. Even when women do rise to the top, they almost always earn less than men.

We cannot explain the disproportionate numbers of women in marginal under-rewarded economic activities by attributing them to legal restrictions and economic barriers alone. Women do not do as well as men in societies where legal restrictions on employment and earnings have long since been removed. Putting on our gender lenses we might ask to what extent these disturbing figures are attributable to unequal gendered structures in the global economy? Feminists call these structures the **gendered division of labour**.

The historical foundations of the gendered division of labour

We can trace the origins of the contemporary gendered division of labour back to seventeenth-century **Europe**. At that time, definitions of male and female were becoming polarized in ways that were suited to the growing division between work and home required by early **capitalism**. Industrialization and the increase in waged labour, largely performed by men, shifted work from home to factory. The term **housewife**, which began to be used to describe women's work in the private domestic sphere, reinforced the gender dimensions of this split. Gendered constructs, such as **breadwinner** and 'housewife' have been central to modern Western definitions of masculinity, femininity, and capitalism. Even though many women do work outside the home for wages, the association of women with domestic roles, such as housewife and caregiver, has become institutionalized and even naturalized. This means

that it is seen as **natural** for women to do the domestic work. Putting the burden of household labour on women decreases their autonomy and economic security.

As a result of these role expectations, when women do enter the workforce, they are disproportionately represented in the caring professions, such as nursing, social services, and primary education, or in **light industry** (performed with light machinery). Women choose these occupations not on the basis of market rationality and profit maximization alone, but also because of values and expectations about mothers and caregivers that are emphasized in the socialization of young girls. Occupations that are disproportionately populated by women tend to be the most poorly paid. Assumptions about appropriate gender roles mean that women are often characterized as supplemental wage earners to the male head of household. But estimates suggest that one-third of all households worldwide are headed by women, a fact frequently obscured by role expectations that derive from the notion of male breadwinners and female housewives.

Consequences of the gendered division of labour

Gender expectations about appropriate roles for women contribute to low wages and double burdens. Women's cheap labour is particularly predominant in textiles and electronics. These industries favour hiring young unmarried women who can achieve a high level of productivity at low wages. Frequently, they are fired if they get married or pregnant. Because of expectations associated with traditional gender roles, there is a belief that women possess 'nimble fingers', have patience for tedious jobs, and are 'naturally' good sewers. When women are seen as naturally good at these tasks, it means that these kinds of work are not seen as skilled and are remunerated accordingly. Moreover, political activity does not go with female respectability. Employers hire women on the assumption that they will provide a 'docile' labour force unlikely to organize for better conditions.

Gender expectations about suitable roles for women enter into another global labour issue, that of home-based

Box 15.4 Challenging gender expectations: women workers organize

In the early 1980s, US athletic shoe manufacturers sought to increase profits by subcontracting to male entrepreneurs setting up factories in South Korea and Taiwan where labour costs were low. The companies took advantage of a political climate that suppressed labour rights and played on women's cultural socialization to work hard for low wages in order to serve their country, their husbands, and their fathers. Defying their docile reputation, South Korean women began to organize labour unions and fight for their rights to unionize, to better working conditions, and to fair wages. As women's efforts were successful, the shoe companies withdrew their contracts and renegotiated with companies in China, Indonesia, and Thailand. In these new locations, companies were able to maintain higher profit margins by exploiting women workers who had fewer rights and thus were more acquiescent. This story shows us how companies take advantage of cultural expectations about women in order to increase profits. Now, women are organizing across borders, trying to overcome the employment insecurities fostered by mobile companies.

(Adapted from Enloe 2004)

work. As companies have moved towards a more **flexible labour** force (less benefits and job security) in all parts of the world, cost-saving has included hiring home-based workers who are easily hired and fired. Exempt from any national labour standards which may exist in the worker's home country, home-based workers are generally paid lower wages than factory workers and are not paid at all when there is no work. Since women, often of necessity, prefer work that more easily accommodates family responsibilities, home-based workers are predominantly women. The gendered division of labour that defines women as housewives, a category with expectations that labour is free, legitimizes wages at below subsistence levels (Prügl 1999: 198).

Even when women do enter the workforce, they continue to suffer from a double burden. This means that, in addition to their paid work, women usually carry most of the responsibility for household labour. We are accustomed to think that women are not 'working' when they engage in household labour. In actual fact, such tasks are crucial for reproducing and caring for those who perform waged work. However, these tasks often constrain women's opportunities for paid work and the narrow definition of work, as work in the waged economy, tends to render invisible many of the contributions women *do* make to the global economy.

The gendered division of labour also affects women's work in agriculture, a role that is significant, particularly in many parts of Africa. While women do undertake cash crop production, frequently they work as unpaid family labour in small units that produce independently or on contract. Consequently, men are more likely to gain access to money, new skills, and technology. When agricultural production moves into the monetarized economy, women tend to get left behind in the **subsistence** (not for wages) sector, producing for family needs.

Case Study 1 Microcredit: empowering women through investment

In 1976, a Bangladeshi economist, Muhammad Yunus, founded the Grameen Bank. The Bank is a lending programme that provides its largely female clientele with small loans for business investment. These small loans, which are called microcredit, are directed towards women because women have a better record for investment and repayment than men. Women are more likely to invest the loans rather than spend it on themselves and they are more likely to repay. Loan repayment rates fluctuate between 96 per cent and 100 per cent. Loans directed towards women are also seen as a method of empowerment that gives women access to resources, economic security, and higher status in the household. Up to 5 per cent of borrowers per year rise out of poverty. Borrowers also increase the educational and nutritional standards within their families.

In Bangladesh in 2006, Grameen Bank reported 6.83 million borrowers in 73,609 villages, 97 per cent of whom were women. In addition to financing small enterprises, home-building and education, the Bank encourages women's empowerment through fostering entrepreneurialism and encouraging family planning. Borrowers now own 94 per cent of the Bank, with the other 6 per cent owned by the government. The Bank earns a profit, and since

1995, has been self-sufficient. Since the 1970s, the microcredit lending model has been replicated in 40 countries. Organizations participating in the microcredit model number in the thousands, and the Grameen Bank and its founder were jointly awarded the 2006 Nobel Peace Prize.

Microcredit is widely publicized as a successful model for development *and* the empowerment of women. To a large extent this has proved to be correct. However, there are critics who argue that gender-based money lending can actually reinforce gendered social hierarchies. Critics suggest that, while women get access to *micro* credit, men continue to dominate the *real* credit market. And, while women are the actual borrowers, in certain cases, men retain control.

In this section we have seen how women are disadvantaged relative to men by the gendered division of labour. Women's relative lack of economic opportunities are not caused by market forces alone but by processes which result from gendered expectations about the kinds of work for which women are believed to be best suited. Nevertheless, when women do work for wages it undermines the legitimacy of men's domination that occurs because of men's traditional role as family providers. For women, having a job can be better than no work at all and extra cash significantly enhances the income of poor families. It also increases women's financial independence.

We can see that it is difficult to generalize about the gender consequences of economic globalization.

Nevertheless, the claim that we live in a world characterized by gendered boundaries of economic inequality is undisputed. The global economy operates not only according to market forces but also according to gendered divisions of labour that value women's work less than men's. In addition, much of women's non-monetarized labour contributes to the global economy, but remains invisible. In our earlier discussion of security, we saw how masculine values influence states' national security policy and how this can be detrimental to women's political opportunities. When we discussed feminist theory, we saw that one of the goals of feminism is to produce knowledge that can help improve women's lives. Let us now look at some of the improvements that are being made by, and on behalf of, women throughout the world.

Key Points

- In every society, women are disadvantaged relative to men in terms of material well-being. We need to put on our gender lenses to explain why. This gender-sensitive perspective helps us see how women's relative disadvantage is due to the gendered division of labour.
- The gendered division of labour dates back to seventeenth-century Europe and the subsequent separation of paid work in the public sphere from unpaid work in the private sphere. The role distinction between workers in the public and private spheres has an effect on the kind of work that women do in the public sphere.
- Women are disproportionately clustered in low-paying jobs in garment industries and services. Home-based workers are predominantly women also. Women do more subsistence agriculture than men and men more often work with advanced agricultural technologies.
- In addition to paid work, women perform most of the reproductive and caring labour in the private sphere. This is known as the double burden. The double burden constrains women's choices in the public sphere. When it is not paid, household labour is invisible in economic analyses.
- We must not overgeneralize about the negative effects of the gendered division of labour. When women have more opportunities for waged work, this is empowering. However, women often perform the same tasks for lower wages than men.

Using knowledge to inform policy practice

Now that we understand how structures of gender inequality contribute to women's subordination, let us examine some of the efforts women are making to diminish the negative effects of these gendered structures in both the political and economic realms. Many of the improvements in women's lives can be attributed to women themselves working in **non-governmental organizations** (NGOs) and in social movements. Frequently, their actions are

informed by feminist emancipatory knowledge. (It may be helpful for you to refer back to the earlier discussion about emancipatory knowledge.)

The United Nations (UN) held its first official conference on women in Mexico City in 1975. This conference launched the UN Decade for Women (1976–85). It was the first in a series of official intergovernmental women's conferences, sponsored by the UN. It is largely due to women organizing worldwide that the UN has put women's issues on its agenda. At the beginning of the UN Decade, women from the North took the lead in organizing. Economic issues having to do with employment and wages took precedence. By the end of the Decade, women from the South began to organize around the impact of the economic crisis of the 1970s caused by high prices for food and oil on the international market and a downturn in the global economy. Their work led to the establishment of a network of Southern women known as Development Alternatives with Women for a New Era (DAWN). DAWN is not only engaged in political advocacy. Using feminist knowledge, it also publishes analyses of the impact of global economic policy on Southern countries, focusing on Southern women.

Parallel NGO conferences have been held at each of the official UN Conferences on Women. Attendance at these conferences increased from 5,000 in Mexico City in 1975 to an estimated 25,000 in Beijing in 1995 (Jaquette 2003: 336). Pressure from women's groups was important in getting the United Nations to disaggregate its data, such as its quality of life indicators, by sex. The availability of data is important in getting issues on policy agendas. Adoption of the Gender Development Index (GDI) by the UN Human Development Programme in 1995 was an important step in helping to formulate policies to improve women's well-being. Another important step towards gender equality was the adoption by the UN and other international **intergovernmental organizations** of a policy called gender mainstreaming. Gender mainstreaming requires organizations that adopt it to evaluate the gendered effects of all aspects of their institutional decision-making (see Box 15.6).

In 1996, the International Labour Organization adopted a convention that set international standards for the type of home-based work we discussed earlier. Pressure for adoption began with the organizing and lobbying efforts of the Self-Employed Women's Association (SEWA), a trade union based in India composed of women engaged in small-scale trade and home-based work (see Case Study 2).

Box 15.5   Milestones in women's organizing

1975	First United Nations World Conference on Women, Mexico City, Mexico
1976–85	UN Decade for Women
1979	The Convention on the Elimination of All Forms of Discrimination against Women (CEDAW) adopted by the UN General Assembly
1980	Second UN World Conference on Women, Copenhagen, Denmark
1985	UN World Conference to Review and Appraise the Achievements of the UN Decade for Women, Nairobi, Kenya
1995	Fourth UN World Conference on Women, Beijing, China
1996	Gender mainstreaming adopted as official UN policy by the UN General Assembly
2000	Women 2000: Gender Equality, Development and Peace for the 21st Century, also known as 'Beijing+5'. Held at UN headquarters, New York, USA
2005	Review and Appraisal of the 1995 World Conference on Women in Beijing and Beijing+5, Commission on the Status of Women (CSW), 49th Session, United Nations, New York, USA

Box 15.6   Gender development index and gender mainstreaming

The Gender Development Index (GDI) measures states' development using the Human Development Index (HDI) indicators: literacy, life expectancy, school enrolment, and income disaggregated by gender, to illustrate a state's development, adjusted for degrees of gender inequality. This index takes as its central assumption that the larger the degree of gender inequality, the more this has a negative effect on states' quality of development. The GDI also shows that states high on the HDI may have high degrees of gender inequality.

Gender mainstreaming was established as a global strategy for achieving gender equality in the 1995 Beijing Platform for Action ratified by all UN member states. It has been adopted as the official policy of the United Nations, the European Union, the Organization of American States and a number of other governmental and intergovernmental organizations. Gender mainstreaming prescribes the review and revision of policy processes in all sectors of government, with an eye towards eliminating gender-based disparities in policy formulation and implementation.

(True 2003)

Case Study 2 The self-employed women's movement

The Self-Employed Women's Association (SEWA) is a women's labour union founded in 1972 in the city of Ahmedabad, India. It has grown into a community-based movement organizing self-employed women in 13 Indian states into labour unions, a lending cooperative, education, and other community-based empowerment initiatives. It has also advocated for and achieved policy changes in national and international forums.

SEWA was founded by labour organizer Ela Bhatt as a response to the large number of women workers in the informal market who were not recognized as workers by the state or by society. Over 90 per cent of working Indian women were and are employed in the informal sector. These self-employed and home-based workers are especially susceptible to exploitation by contractors and middlemen, job insecurity, and police harassment. SEWA women began to organize themselves in order to achieve recognition and establish their rights and protections as workers. For example, women banded together to stop police extortion of vegetable vendors in Ahmedabad.

The movement expanded to include broader empowerment initiatives. In 1974, SEWA instituted a member-funded and -directed microcredit bank that gives poor women access to capital and at the same time managerial and organizational experience. The SEWA Bank is member-owned and -directed, in keeping with the grass-roots strategy of the movement.

As the SEWA Bank expanded and SEWA success grew, the movement extended its influence further into the policy realm and into organizing in rural areas. In 1986, SEWA succeeded in instituting a national commission to analyze and advise on issues of self-employed women. At the international level, SEWA was instrumental in getting the International Labour Organization to adopt home-based work as a policy issue in 1991, and in contributing to a global alliance of home-based workers called the HomeNet Organization in 1994. In 1996, this resulted in the ILO Homework Convention, legislation designed to protect home-based workers' rights.

SEWA, faithful to the movement's philosophy of using member-driven strategies, developed contextually specific objectives for poor women in rural areas. For example, when SEWA organizers in rural regions encountered opposition from employers, SEWA focused on increasing work opportunities through cooperative enterprises in order to increase women's employment alternatives. These agricultural and crafts cooperatives give women more access to and control over resources. Liberal feminists often cite SEWA as an example of successfully integrating women into the market economy. Post-colonial feminists cite it as an example of local voices speaking for themselves and achieving culturally and contextually specific empowerment.

The work of women's caucuses at various UN conferences has resulted in feminist agendas based on some of the ideas we have discussed. Women's activism has challenged the hierarchical political **structures**, evident at intergovernmental UN conferences, and NGO forums have practised forms of participatory democracy and moved feminist ideas into the policy mainstream of various international organizations. Women in NGOs and social movements, informed by feminist knowledge, are playing an important role in pressuring international organizations and national governments to adopt policies that will further women's equality.

Key Points

- Much of the success in moving towards gender equality is due to women's organizing in NGOs and social movements. These organizations have been able to get women's issues on the policy agendas of the United Nations and other intergovernmental organizations.
- Feminists believe that feminist knowledge should be useful for improving women's lives. Many feminist social movements are informed by feminist emancipatory knowledge.
- The United Nations has begun to disaggregate its data by sex. This was an important step in getting women's issues on its

agenda. Data are vital for identifying problems and lobbying for change. The adoption of the Gender Development Index has helped us to see where problems are most acute and to track evidence of improvement.
- Gender mainstreaming is a policy that evaluates legislation in terms of whether it is likely to increase or decrease gender equality. It has been adopted by a number of intergovernmental organizations, such as the United Nations, and by some national governments.

Conclusion

Using a number of different feminist approaches, this chapter has introduced you to some of the ways gender structures world politics. We began by situating IR feminist approaches in feminist theory more generally and by offering a feminist definition of gender. IR feminists have drawn on a variety of feminist theories to help them understand why women have not been visible in global politics and why women are economically disadvantaged relative to men in all societies. They also examine broader questions about how gender shapes and is shaped by global politics. When we are sensitive to gender as a category of analysis, we can see how characteristics we associate with masculinity are particularly valued in global politics, especially in matters of national security. Feminists define security more broadly—not just in terms of the security of the state, but also in terms of the physical and economic security of individuals. Evidence suggests that women as a group suffer certain economic insecurities by virtue of being women. To explain this, IR feminists point to a gendered division of labour. Differing expectations about what is meant by women's and men's work lead to problems when women end up in lower-paying jobs and with a larger share of unremunerated work in the household.

We have seen that IR feminism can tell us some new things about global policy-making and about the workings of the global economy that other approaches do not. This does not mean that feminism can tell us *everything* we need to know about global politics. However, it *is* important to note that since all global actors have a gender identity, gender is present in all global processes. For this reason, it is hard to separate feminist approaches from other IR approaches in the same way that we can separate **Realism** from **Liberalism** or from Marxism. We have seen that IR feminism is grounded in different IR theoretical approaches, such as Liberalism, Constructivism and post-modernism. One further question we might think about is how our gender-sensitive lenses might help us to see these other approaches in new ways.

❓ Questions

1 Feminists define gender as a social construction. What does this mean? What kinds of questions does IR feminism try to answer using gender as a category of analysis?

2 Women's participation at the highest levels of international and national policy-making has been extremely limited. Do you think this is important for understanding global politics?

3 Do you think women's roles, as diplomats' and soldiers' wives, domestic servants, sex workers, homemakers, and home-based workers, are relevant to the business of international politics? If so, how?

4 Why is the myth that wars are fought to protect women and children problematic from a feminist perspective? What would be a feminist approach to understanding state violence?

5 Does women's participation in military combat undermine or reinforce militarized masculinity? Consider how different feminist perspectives would answer this question

6 How do feminists define security? Why do some of them believe that national security may undermine personal security? Do you agree or disagree with this claim?

7 How and why does the gendered division of labour contribute to women's subordination relative to men? How does it contribute to men's relative success?

8 Do you see potential for feminist activism/feminist IR to change conventional masculinist practices of international relations?

9 Can men be feminists? Why or why not?

10 Since feminist approaches draw from different IR perspectives, does feminism belong in one chapter of this book? How might gender-sensitive lenses see theories in other chapters?

Guide to further reading

Ackerly, B. A., Stern, M., and True, J. (eds) (2006), *Feminist Methodologies for International Relations* (Cambridge: Cambridge University Press). A good introduction to feminist methods and methodologies for IR feminist scholarship.

Enloe, C. (2004), *The Curious Feminist: Searching for Women in a New Age of Empire* (Berkeley: University of California Press). A collection of essays exploring the unrecognized ways that women participate in international politics, including security, war, and the global political economy.

Marchand, M. H., and Runyan, A. S. (eds) (2000), *Gender and Global Restructuring: Sightings, Sites, and Resistances* (New York: Routledge). This book addresses gender in the global economy, going beyond conventional approaches to globalization to reveal the complexities of global restructuring based on economic and social disparities.

Peterson, V. S., and Runyan, A. S. (1999), *Global Gender Issues*, 2nd edn (Boulder, Col.: Westview Press). A useful introduction to the subject matter of feminist IR. The authors apply 'gender-sensitive lenses' to global politics.

Tickner, J. A. (2001), *Gendering World Politics: Issues and Approaches in the Post-Cold War Era* (New York: Columbia University Press). A survey and synthesis of feminist scholarship in the major subfields of International Relations, and a set of visions for the future of feminist IR.

Online Resource Centre

Visit the Online Resource Centre that accompanies this book to access more learning resources on this chapter topic at www.oxfordtextbooks.co.uk/uk/orc/baylis_smith4e/

Notes

1 I should like to thank Angela McCracken for her valuable research assistance for this chapter and in Case Study 1.

2 Females make up approximately half of the world's total displaced persons population. Children under age 18 make up 44 per cent of the total population, with 12 per cent of those under the age of 5. (United Nations High Commissioner for Refugees (2006), *Measuring Protection by Numbers 2005*. Available online at: http://www.unhcr.org/publ/PUBL/4579701b2.pdf.).

3 This phenomenon was reported in Lizza, R. (2007), 'The Invasion of the Alpha Male Democrat', *New York Times*, 7 January.

4 This worldwide average was approximated. See ILO (n.d.), 'Facts on Women at Work', available online at: www.ilo.org/public/english/region/eurpro/budapest/download/womenwork.pdf.

Chapter 16

International law

CHRISTIAN REUS-SMIT

- Introduction: the paradox of international law ··· 280
- Order and institutions ·· 280
- The modern institution of international law ··· 281
- From international to supranational law? ·· 286
- The laws of war ··· 288
- Theoretical approaches to international law ·· 289
- Conclusion ··· 293

Reader's Guide

This chapter introduces students to the practice of modern international law and to debates surrounding its nature and efficacy. It begins by exploring the reasons why international societies construct institutions, and why different sorts of institutions have emerged in different historical contexts. It then considers the nature and origins of the modern institution of international law, its close connection with the practice of multilateralism, and the recent cosmopolitanization of the global legal order. After a brief discussion of the laws of war, we conclude with a survey of different theoretical approaches to international law.

Introduction: the paradox of international law

As students of international relations, our default position is to assume that **international law** matters little to the cut and thrust of international politics. The **power** and interests of **states** are what matters, and law is either a servant of the powerful or an irrelevant curiosity. Widespread as this scepticism is, it is confounded by much state behaviour. If international law doesn't matter, why do states and other actors devote so much effort to negotiating new legal regimes and augmenting existing ones? Why does so much international debate revolve around the legality of state behaviour, around the applicability of legal rules, and around the legal obligations incumbent on states? And why is compliance with international law so high, even by domestic standards?

This chapter introduces students to the practice of modern international law and to debates surrounding its nature and efficacy. It is written primarily for students of international politics, but should also be of interest to law students curious about the political foundations of international law. Our starting point is the idea that international law is best understood as a core international **institution**, a set of **norms**, **rules**, and practices created by states and other actors to facilitate diverse social goals, from **order** and **coexistence** to justice and human development. It is, however, an institution with distinctive historical roots, and understanding these roots is essential to grasping its unique institutional features.

Order and institutions

Realists portray international relations as a struggle for power, a realm in which states are 'continuously preparing for, actively involved in, or recovering from organised violence in the form of war' (Morgenthau 1985: 52). While war has certainly been a recurrent feature of international life, it is a crude and deeply dysfunctional way for states to ensure their **security** or realize their interests. Because of this, states have devoted as much, if not more, effort to liberating themselves from the condition of war than to embroiling themselves in violent conflict. Creating some modicum of **international order** has been an abiding common interest of most states, most of the time (Bull 1977: 8).

To achieve international order, states have created international institutions. People often confuse institutions and organizations, incorrectly using the two terms interchangeably. International institutions are commonly defined as complexes of norms, rules, and practices that 'prescribe behavioral roles, constrain activity, and shape expectations' (Keohane 1989a: 3). **International organizations**, like the United Nations, are physical entities that have staff, head offices, and letterheads. International institutions can exist without any organizational **structure**—the 1997 Ottawa Convention banning landmines

is an institution, but there is no landmines head office. Many institutions have organizational dimensions, though. The World Trade Organization (formerly the General Agreement on Tariffs and Trade) is an institution with a very strong organizational structure. While institutions can exist without an organizational dimension, international organizations cannot exist without an institutional framework, as their very existence presupposes a prior set of norms, rules, and principles that empower them to act and which they are charged to uphold. If states had never negotiated the Charter of the United Nations, the organization simply could not exist, let alone function.

In modern **international society**, states have created three levels of institutions. There are deep **constitutional** institutions, such as the principle of **sovereignty**, which define the terms of legitimate statehood. Without the institution of sovereignty, the world of independent states, and the international politics it engenders, would simply not exist. States have also created **fundamental** institutions, like international law and **multilateralism**, which provide the basic rules and practices that shape how states solve **cooperation** and **coordination** problems. These are the institutional norms, techniques, and structures that states and other actors invoke and employ

Box 16.1 Levels of international institutions

Constitutional institutions

Constitutional institutions comprise the primary rules and norms of international society, without which society among sovereign states could not exist. The most commonly recognized of these is the norm of sovereignty, which holds that within the state, power and authority are centralized and hierarchical, and outside the state no higher authority exists. The norm of sovereignty is supported by a range of auxiliary norms, such as the right to self-determination and the norm of non-intervention.

Fundamental institutions

Fundamental institutions rest on the foundation provided by constitutional institutions. They represent the basic norms and practices that sovereign states employ to facilitate coexistence and cooperation under conditions of international anarchy. They are the rudimentary practices states reach for when seeking to collaborate or coordinate their behaviour. Fundamental institutions have varied from one historical system of states to another, but in the modern international system the fundamental institutional practices of contractual international law and multilateralism have been the most important.

Issue-specific institutions or 'regimes'

Issue-specific institutions or 'regimes' are the most visible or palpable of all international institutions. They are the sets of rules, norms, and **decision-making procedures** that states formulate to define who constitute legitimate actors and what constitutes legitimate action in a given domain of international life. Examples of regimes are the Nuclear Non-Proliferation Treaty, the Framework Convention on Global Climate Change, the Ottawa Convention on Anti-Personnel Landmines, and the International Covenant on Civil and Political Rights. Importantly, issue-specific institutions or regimes are concrete enactments in specific issue-areas of fundamental institutional practices, such as international law and multilateralism.

---

when they have common ends they want to achieve or clashing interests they want to contain. Lastly, states have developed **issue-specific** institutions or **regimes**, such as the Nuclear Non-Proliferation Treaty (NPT), which enact fundamental institutional practices in particular realms of inter-state relations. The NPT is a concrete expression of the practices of international law and multilateralism in the field of arms control.

We are concerned here with the middle strata of fundamental institutions. 'Fundamental institutions are the elementary rules of practice that states formulate to solve the coordination and **collaboration** problems associated with coexistence under **anarchy**' (Reus-Smit 1999: 14). In modern international society, a range of such institutions exist, including international law, multilateralism, bilateralism, **diplomacy**, and management by the great powers. Since the middle of the nineteenth century, however, the first two of these have provided the basic framework for international cooperation and the pursuit of order.

Key Points

- States have strong incentives to free themselves from the insecurities of international anarchy.
- States face common coordination and collaboration problems, yet cooperation remains difficult under anarchy.
- To facilitate cooperation, states create international institutions, of which three levels exist in modern international society: constitutional institutions, fundamental institutions, and issue-specific institutions or 'regimes'.
- We are concerned with fundamental institutions, of which international law is one of the most important.

The modern institution of international law

Historical roots

The contemporary international legal system is a historical artefact. Not in the sense of being irrelevant to present circumstances, but in the sense of being deeply structured by the social and political conditions of modernity. Like most present-day institutions, it bears the imprint of the revolutions in social thought and practice that from

the eighteenth century onwards transformed the political landscape of Europe and then much of the world. Great thinkers such as Hugo Grotius (1583–1645) and Emerich de Vattel (1714–67) are often cast as the 'fathers' of international law, and the Treaties of Augsburg (1555), Westphalia (1648), and Utrecht (1713) are seen as landmarks in the development of international public law. Yet despite the importance of these historical figures and moments, the modern international legal system acquired many of its distinctive characteristics as late as the nineteenth century.

The present international system has its roots in **Europe**, and prior to the nineteenth century the vast majority of European states were monarchies. The kings and queens who ruled these states justified their power by appealing to the doctrine of divine right, to the idea that monarchs were ordained with authority directly from God (Bodin 1967: 40). At this time law was generally understood as the command of a legitimate superior—humanity in general, including monarchs, was subject to God's law and **natural law**, both of which embodied the command of God. The subjects of particular states were also ruled by municipal law, which was the command of monarchs, who stood above such law. These ideas about divinity, authority, and law had a profound **influence** on early international law. Derived from the law of nature, international law was understood as a set of divinely ordained principles of state conduct, accessible to all endowed with right reason. European monarchs were obliged to observe international law not because they had reached a contractual agreement with one another, or at least not primarily, but because of fealty to God (Grotius 1925: 121).

In the late eighteenth and early nineteenth centuries, the legitimacy of the absolutist state was challenged by

---

Box 16.2 Key constitutive legal treaties

Over the past five centuries, the nature and scope of international society has been conditioned by a series of international legal instruments that have defined the nature of legitimate statehood, the scope of sovereign authority, and the bounds of rightful state action, international and domestic. Some of the more important of these are as follows:

The Treaties of Westphalia, 1648

The Treaties of Osnabruck and Munster, which together form the 'Peace of Westphalia', ended the Thirty Years War and were crucial in delimiting the political rights and authority of European monarchs. Among other things, the Treaties granted monarchs rights to maintain standing armies, build fortifications, and levy taxes.

The Treaties of Utrecht, 1713

The Treaties of Utrecht, which brought an end to the Wars of Spanish Succession, consolidated the move to territorial sovereignty in Europe. The Treaties of Westphalia did little to define the territorial scope of sovereign rights, the geographical domain over which such rights could extend. By establishing that fixed territorial boundaries, rather than the reach of family ties, should define the reach of sovereign authority, the Treaties of Utrecht were crucial in establishing the present link between sovereign authority and territorial boundaries.

The Treaty of Paris, 1814

The Treaty of Paris ended the Napoleonic Wars and paved the way for the Congress of Vienna (1814–15). The Congress of Vienna, in turn, defined the nature of the post-Napoleonic War settlement, and ultimately led to the **Concert** of Europe. The Concert has often been credited with successfully limiting great power warfare for a good part of the nineteenth century, but it is also noteworthy as an institution for upholding monarchical authority and combating liberal and nationalist movements in Europe.

The Peace Treaty of Versailles, 1919

The Treaty of Versailles formally ended the First World War (1914–18). The Treaty established the League of Nations, specified the rights and obligations of the victorious and defeated powers (including the notorious regime of reparations on Germany), and created the 'Mandatories' system under which 'advanced nations' were given legal tutelage over colonial peoples.

The Charter of the United Nations, 1945

The Charter of the United Nations is the legal regime that created the United Nations as the world's only 'supranational' organization. The Charter defines the structure of the United Nations, the powers of its constitutive agencies, and the rights and obligations of sovereign states party to the Charter. Among other things, the Charter is the key legal document limiting the use of force to instances of self-defence and collective peace enforcement endorsed by the United Nations Security Council.

The Declaration on Granting Independence to Colonial Countries and Peoples, 1960

Though not a legally binding document, General Assembly Resolution 1514 (XV) signalled the normative delegitimation of European colonialism, and was critical in establishing the right to self-determination which in turn facilitated the wholesale decolonization of the European **empires**.

the principles of **Liberalism** and **nationalism**. By the second half of the nineteenth century, European states underwent dramatic internal transformations, as the principles of constitutionalism and popular sovereignty weakened monarchs' authority, empowered parliamentary institutions, and extended the franchise. With this transformation came a new conception of law—law as reciprocal accord. Law was deemed legitimate to the extent that it was authored by those subject to the law, or their representatives, and it applied equally to all citizens in all like circumstances. Once this ideal was firmly established within the major European states, it started to filter into relations between states, leading to the rise of contractual international law, or what is often termed 'positive' law. International law was now seen as the product of negotiations between sovereign states, not the command of God, and states were obliged to observe such law, not because of fealty, but because they had entered into reciprocally binding agreements with other states—because international law represents the 'mutual *will* of the nations concerned' (Von Martens 1795: 47–8).

Conditioned by these historical forces, the modern institution of international law has developed four distinctive characteristics: a multilateral form of legislation; a consent-based form of legal obligation; a peculiar language of reasoning and argument; and a strong discourse of institutional autonomy.

Multilateral legislation

If we define legislation broadly, as the formulation and enactment of legally binding norms or rules, then the legislation of international law takes place formally and informally. New norms and rules evolve constantly through the informal arguments, social learning, and repeated practices of states and **non-state actors**. For instance, there is now considerable debate about whether new legal norms are evolving to qualify **state sovereignty** and permit **humanitarian intervention**. If such norms are evolving, these processes are far from complete. If they do consolidate, however, it will have been less the result of formal legal codification than persistent normative debate and the reinterpretation of existing legal norms. Informal processes such as these are crucially important, as they are one of the principal means by which customary norms of

international law evolve. Customary norms are a special category of international law; they have such high normative standing in the community of states that they are considered binding upon all states irrespective of whether they have consented. Many of the rules governing territorial jurisdiction, freedom of the seas, and the diplomatic immunities of states are customary, and most of these evolved through informal processes (Byers 1999: 3).

In addition to these informal modes of law-making, states have also developed more formal methods of legislation, the most distinctive being the practice of multilateralism. Prior to the Napoleonic Wars, multilateralism was a relatively marginal institutional practice. States certainly engaged in cooperative practices involving three or more states, but these were often aggregations of bilateral arrangements (such as the Peaces of Westphalia and Utrecht), and were seldom based on reciprocally binding rules of conduct (a mark of true multilateralism (Ruggie 1993)). It was only in the nineteenth century, as Liberalism began transforming the internal constitutions of leading European powers, that multilateralism became the preferred mode of international legislation. If law was legitimate only if those subject to it authored it, and only if it applied equally to all subjects in all like circumstances, then an international means of legislation had to be found that could meet such standards. It was in this context that multilateralism rose to prominence. New ideas of international law are thus deeply entwined with the rise of multilateralism, and it is not surprising that the nineteenth and twentieth centuries saw a dramatic proliferation of multilateral treaties.

Consent and legal obligation

Grotius wrote that states are obliged to obey the law of nations—along with the laws of nature and God—'even though they have made no promise' (1925: 121). Fealty to God was the ultimate root of all legal obligations in the Age of Absolutism, and consent constituted a secondary, if still important, source of obligation. This contrasts dramatically with the situation today, in which consent is treated as the primary source of international legal obligation (Henkin 1995: 27). This emphasis on consent is integral to much contemporary discourse on international law. Leaders of states will often use the fact of their consent, or the lack of such, to display their sovereign

rights. And critics use evidence of state consent to criticize governments for failing to live up to their obligations under international law.

The status of consent as the principal source of modern international legal obligation is complicated, however, by two things. To begin with, we have already noted that states are, in reality, bound by rules to which they have not formally consented, principally those of **customary international law**. In determining whether a norm constitutes customary law, scholars and jurists look for general observance of the norm and *opinio juris,* the recognition by states that they are observing the norm because it constitutes law (Price 2004: 107). Both of these are thought to be indicators of tacit consent, but as critics of Liberalism have long argued, tacit consent is not the same as actual consent, and extrapolating tacit consent from norm-consistent behaviour is fraught with difficulties. Second, the idea that consent is the principal source of international legal obligation is philosophically highly problematic (Reus-Smit 2003). As the celebrated legal theorist H. L. A. Hart observed, consent can only be obligating if there exists a prior rule that specifies that promises to observe legal rules are binding. But because this rule would be what gives consent its normative standing, consent cannot be the source of that prior rule's obligatory force (1994: 225).

Language and practice of justification

In addition to its distinctive forms of legislation and legal obligation, the modern institution of international law is characterized by a peculiar language and practice of justification. If we consider the role that international law plays in global life, we see that it operates as more than a pristine set of rules calmly and logically applied to clear-cut situations by authoritative juridical interpreters. International law is alive in the central political debates of international society; it structures arguments about right and wrong, about the bounds of legitimate action, about authority and membership, and about the full spectrum of international issues, from the management of fisheries to the use of force. On close inspection, though, we see that this argument and debate takes a distinctive form.

First, international legal argument is rhetorical. It is tempting to believe that legal argument is strictly logical, that it is concerned with the straightforward, objective application of a rule to a situation. But this ignores the central and inevitable role that interpretation plays in determining which rules apply, their meaning, and the nature of the case at hand. In reality, legal argument appears as rhetorical as it is logical. As Friedrich Kratochwil argues:

> Legal arguments deal with the finding and interpretation of the applicable norms and procedures, and with the presentation of the relevant facts and their evaluations. Both questions turn on the issue of whether a particular interpretation of a fact-pattern is acceptable rather than 'true'; consequently strict logic plays a minor role in this process of finding the law.
>
> *(1989: 42)*

Second, international legal argument is analogical; it is concerned 'to establish similarities among different cases or objects in the face of (striking) dissimilarities' (Kratochwil 1989: 223). International actors reason with analogies in three different ways. They use them to interpret a given rule (rule A was interpreted in a particular way, and given the logic applied, rule B should be interpreted the same way). They draw similarities between one class of action and another to claim that the former is, or is not, rule-governed (case C was rule-governed, and given the similarities with case D, case D should be rule-governed as well). And they invoke analogies to establish the status of one rule with reference to other rules (rule E has customary status, and since the same levels of assent and dissent are evident in the case of rule F, rule F should be accorded customary status as well).

The discourse of institutional autonomy

The final distinctive characteristic of the modern institution of international law is its strong discourse of institutional autonomy. As students of international relations, we are accustomed to think of politics and law as separate social domains, as realms of human action with distinct logics and practices. One of the most interesting insights of recent studies is that political actors regularly speak and act as if at some point in a negotiation, at some stage in a crisis, action moved from the political to the legal realm, a realm in which different types of argument and practice

Box 16.3 Features of the modern institution of international law

Multilateral legislation

The principal mechanism modern states employ to 'legislate' international law is multilateral diplomacy, which is commonly defined as cooperation between three or more states based on, or with a view to formulating, reciprocally binding rules of conduct.

Consent and legal obligation

It is a norm of the modern international legal system that states are obliged to observe legal rules because they have consented to those rules. A state that has not consented to the rules of a particular legal treaty is not bound by those rules. The only exception to this concerns rules of customary international law, and even then implied or tacit consent plays an important role in the determination of which rules have customary status.

Language and practice of justification

Modern international law is characterized by a distinctive form or argument, justification, or reasoning. As accompanying text explains, this practice is both rhetorical and analogical.

The discourse of institutional autonomy

In many historical periods, and in many social and cultural settings, the political and legal realms have been entwined. For instance, the Absolutist conception of sovereignty bound the two realms together in the figure of the sovereign. In the modern era, by contrast, the political and legal realms are thought to be radically different, with their own logics and institutional settings. Domestically, this informs ideas about the constitutional separation of powers; internationally, it has encouraged the view that international politics and law are separate spheres of social action. This has not only affected how the academic disciplines of international relations and law have evolved, but also how state practice has evolved.

---

prevail. In the political realm, claims of self-interest and barely veiled coercive practices are considered legitimate if distasteful, but in the legal realm legal reasoning and argument become the legitimate form of action. Compare, for instance, US strategies on Iraq within the confines of the UN Security Council in 2003, where Washington's arguments were constrained by available legal justifications, with its practices outside the Council, where its claims were more self-interested and its practices more openly coercive.

Two things should be noted about this discourse of institutional autonomy. First, imagining the political and legal realms as separate and distinct is a modern phenomenon. In the age of absolute monarchies in Europe, politics and law were joined in the figure of the sovereign. One of the features of modern, particularly liberal, thought is the idea that political and legal powers need to be separated by quarantining politics to the executive and legislative realms, and legal interpretation and application to the judicial realm. This is what lies behind the modern constitutional idea of a 'separation of powers'. Second, imagining separate political and legal realms in international relations contributes to international order, and is thus politically functional for states. Perception of a legal realm, recognition that a spectrum of issues,

practices, and processes are governed by legal rules and procedures, and mutual understanding that certain forms of action are empowered or foreclosed within the legal realm, brings a certain discipline, structure, and predictability to international relations that would be missing in conditions of pure anarchy.

Key Points

- Modern international law is a historical artefact, a product of the revolutions in thought and practice that transformed the governance of European states after the French Revolution (1789).
- Prior to the French Revolution, in the 'Age of Absolutism', law was understood principally as the command of a legitimate superior, and international law was seen as a command of God, derived from natural law. In the modern period law has come to be seen as something contracted between legal subjects, or their representatives, and international law has been seen as the expression of the mutual will of nations.
- Because of its historical roots, the modern institution of international law has a number of distinctive characteristics, informed largely by the values of political Liberalism.
- The most distinctive characteristics of the modern institution of international law are its multilateral form of legislation, its consent-based form of legal obligation, its language and practice of justification, and its discourse of institutional autonomy.

Case Study Is international law an expression of Western dominance?

From one perspective, international law is easily cast as a Western, even imperial institution. As we have seen, its roots lie in the European intellectual movements of the sixteenth and seventeenth centuries. Ideas propagated at that time not only drew on ideas of natural law, which could be traced back to ancient Greek and Roman thought; they also drew a clear distinction between international laws that were appropriate among Christian peoples and those that should govern how Christians related to peoples in the Muslim world, the Americas, and later Asia. The former were based on assumptions of the inherent equality of Christian peoples, the latter on the inherent superiority of Christians over non-Christians.

Further evidence of this Western bias can be found in the 'standard of civilization' that European powers codified in interna-

tional law during the nineteenth century (Gong 1984). According to this standard, non-Western polities were granted sovereign recognition only if they exhibited certain domestic political characteristics and only if they were willing and capable of participating in the prevailing diplomatic practices. The standard was heavily biased towards Western political and legal institutions as the accepted model. On the basis of the standard, European power divided the world's peoples into 'civilized', 'barbarian', and 'savage' societies, a division they used to justify various degrees of Western tutelage.

Many claim that Western bias still characterizes the international legal order. Cited here is the Anglo-European dominance of peak legal institutions, most notably the United Nations Security Council, and international human rights law, which is said to impose a set of Western values about the rights of the individual on non-Western societies where such ideas are alien. These biases are seen as coming together around the issue of humanitarian intervention. Western powers are accused of using their privileged position on the Security Council, and of brandishing human rights norms, to intervene in the domestic politics of weak, developing countries.

All of these criticisms have veracity. However, the nature and role of international law in contemporary world politics is more complex than it at first appears. To begin with, at the heart of the modern international legal system lies a set of customary norms that uphold the legal equality of all sovereign states, as well as their rights to self-determination and non-intervention. Non-Western states have been the most vigorous proponents and defenders of these cardinal legal norms, and their survival as independent political entities depends on the continued salience of such principles. Second, non-Western peoples were more centrally involved in the development of the international human rights regime than is commonly acknowledged. The Universal Declaration of Human Rights was the product of a deliberate and systematic process of intercultural dialogue, a dialogue involving representatives of all of the world's major cultures (Glendon 2002). And the International Covenant on Civil and Political Rights, which is often portrayed as a reflection of Western values, was shaped in critical ways by newly independent post-colonial states (Reus-Smit 2001a). What is more, international human rights law has been an important resource in the struggles of many subject peoples against repressive governments and against institutions such as colonialism.

From international to supranational law?

So long as international law was designed primarily to facilitate international order—to protect the negative liberties of sovereign states—it remained a relatively circumscribed, if essential, institution. This was apparent in four characteristics of international law, at least until developments of the last three decades. First,

states were the primary *subjects* of international law, the principal bearers of rights and obligations. 'The classic view has been that international law applies only to states' (Higgins 1994: 40). The 1933 Montevideo Convention on the Rights and Duties of States establishes the 'state as a person of international law', defines what constitutes a

state, and lays down the principal rights and obligations enjoyed by states (Weston *et al.* 1990: 12). Second, and related to the above, states were the primary *agents* of international law, the only actors empowered to formulate, enact, and enforce international law. International law was thus viewed as an artefact of state practice, not the legislation of a **community** of humankind. Third, international law was concerned with the regulation of **inter-state** relations. How states interacted with one another fell within the purview of international law, how they operated within their territorial boundaries was not, a distinction enshrined in the twin international norms of **self-determination** and non-intervention. Finally, the scope of international law was confined—or attempted to be confined—to questions of order not justice. The principal objective of international law was the maintenance of peace and stability based on mutual respect for each state's territorial integrity and domestic jurisdiction; issues of distributive justice and the protection of basic human rights lay outside its brief.

In recent decades states have sought to move beyond the simple pursuit of international order towards the ambitious yet amorphous objective of **global governance**, and international law has begun to change in fascinating ways. First, although states are 'still at the heart of the international legal system' (Higgins 1994: 39), individuals, groups, and organizations are increasingly becoming recognized subjects of international law. The development of an expansive body of international human rights law, supported by evolving mechanisms of enforcement, has given individuals, as well as some collectivities, such as minority groups or indigenous peoples, clear rights under international law. And recent moves to hold individuals criminally responsible for violations of those rights—evident in the war crimes tribunals for Rwanda and the former Yugoslavia, the creation of a new International Criminal Court, and the arrest in London of Augusto Pinochet, the former Chilean dictator, for crimes against humanity—indicate the clear obligations individuals bear to observe basic human rights. Second, non-state actors are becoming important agents in the international legal process. While such actors cannot formally enact international law, and their practices do not contribute to the development of customary international law, they often play a crucial role in shaping the normative environment in which states are moved to codify specific legal rules, in providing information to national governments that encourages the redefinition of state interests and the convergence of policies across different states, and, finally, in actually drafting international treaties and conventions. This last role was first seen in how the International Committee of the Red Cross drafted the 1864 Geneva Convention (Finnemore 1996*b*: 69–88), and more recently in the role that non-state actors played in the development of the Ottawa Convention on Anti-Personnel Landmines (Price 1998) and in the creation of the International Criminal Court.

Third, international law is increasingly concerned with global, not merely international, regulation. Where the principles of self-determination and non-intervention once erected a fundamental boundary between the international and domestic legal realms, this boundary is now being breached by the development of international rules that regulate how states should behave within their territories. Notable here is international trade law, the growing corpus of international environmental law, as well as the previously mentioned body of international human rights law. The penetration of these laws through the boundaries of the sovereign state is facilitated by the growing tendency of national courts to draw on precepts of international law in their rulings. Finally, the rules, norms, and principles of international law are no longer confined to maintaining international order, narrowly defined. Not only does the development of international humanitarian law indicate a broadening of international law to address questions of global justice, but recent decisions by the United Nations Security Council, which warrant international interventions in places like East Timor, have seen gross violations of human rights by sovereign states treated as threats to international peace and security, thus legitimating action under Chapter 7 of the UN Charter. In doing so, the Security Council implies that international order is dependent upon the maintenance of at least minimum standards of global justice.

Because of these changes, it has been suggested that international law may be gradually transforming into a system of supranational law. Once states are no longer the only subjects and agents of international law, once international law is involved in global regulation, and once its scope has been extended to encompass issues of justice as well as order, it has broken the bounds of both its initial intent and original practice. While these changes have not yet prompted the rewriting of international legal texts, and both international lawyers and international relations scholars are responding

cautiously, current developments have injected new excitement and energy into the field of international law, which many previously regarded as moribund, and have caused international relations scholars to look afresh at the role of legal norms in shaping world politics, something often dismissed as idealism.

Key Points

- So long as international law was designed to facilitate international order, it was circumscribed in key ways: states were the principle subjects and agents of international law; international law was concerned with the regulation of inter-state relations; and the scope of international law was confined to questions of order.
- The quest for global governance is pushing international law into new areas, raising questions about whether international law is transforming into a form of supranational law.
- Individuals, and to some extent collectivities, are gradually acquiring rights and responsibilities under international law,

establishing their status as both subjects and agents under international law.
- Non-governmental actors are becoming increasingly important in the development and codification of international legal norms.
- International law is increasingly affecting domestic legal regimes and practices, and the rules of the international legal system are no longer confined to issues of order. As international humanitarian law evolves, issues of global justice are permeating the international legal order.

The laws of war

International law governing the use of force is rightly considered the core of the modern international legal system. Traditionally, such law has divided into two types: ***jus ad bellum***, the law governing when states may use force or wage war, and ***jus in bello***, the law governing the conduct of war once launched. Two things should be noted about these dimensions of the laws of war. First, from their earliest articulations, they have always been entwined. For instance, Grotius's three-volume *The Law of War and Peace* devoted one volume to *jus ad bellum* and one to *jus in bello*. Second, the content of *jus ad bellum* and *jus in bello* has undergone significant change, with what were once cardinal norms being, in some cases, completely reversed. The laws of war have thus been an evolving project, responding over time to the profound social and technological changes that have transformed the international system over the last five centuries.

The most dramatic change has occurred in the central precepts of *jus ad bellum*. Early writings on just war stressed the importance of just cause, the idea that waging war was justified, morally as well as legally, if a state was responding to an unwarranted attack or seeking reparations for damages. This was greatly complicated, however, by norms that appeared to cut in the opposite direction. For instance, it was widely believed that sovereign rights could be secured through conquest. In others words, if a ruler succeeded in establishing control over a territory and

its people, he or she was the sovereign authority. During the nineteenth century, the idea that just cause established just war gave way to the much more permissive notion that war was justified if it served a state's vital national interests, interests which the state itself had the sole right to define. This was the heyday of the principle that the right to wage war was a fundamental sovereign right, a privilege that defined the very essence of sovereignty. The dire consequences of this principle were evident in the First and Second World Wars, and after 1945 the scope of legally justifiable war was dramatically circumscribed. The Charter of the United Nations confines the legitimate use of force to two situations: the use of force in self-defence (Chapter 7, Article 51), which remained an unqualified sovereign right, and the use of force as part of a Security Council sanctioned peace enforcement action (Chapter 7, Article 42).

Parallel to these changes, the precepts of *jus in bello* have evolved as well. Here the trend has been less one of radical change in core principles than a gradual expansion of the scope of international legal constraints on permissible conduct in war. Three areas of constraint are particularly noteworthy. The first relates to the kind of weaponry that is legally permitted. The Hague Conferences of 1899 and 1907 were landmark in this regard, establishing conventions prohibiting the use of expanding bullets, the dropping of bombs from balloons, and the use

of projectiles that diffused gases. Since then legally binding treaties have come into force proscribing a range of weaponry, including the use and deployment of landmines and the manufacture and use of chemical weapons. The second area of constraint relates to how military combatants must be treated. Of central importance here are the four Geneva Conventions of 1864, 1949, 1929, and 1949 respectively, along with their three additional protocols of 1977 (the first two) and 2005 (the third). The third area concerns the treatment of non-combatants, for which the Geneva Conventions were also crucially important. The deliberate targeting of non-combatants has long been proscribed, but in recent years attempts have been made to tighten these proscriptions further. Worth

noting here is the successful move to codify rape in war as an international crime.

The evolution of the laws of war is one of the clearest examples of the aforementioned shift from international to supranational law. This is particularly apparent in the development since the end of the **cold war** of, first, the international criminal tribunals for the former Yugoslavia and Rwanda (ICTY and ICTR) and, second, the International Criminal Court (ICC). The last of these is the most ambitious international judicial experiment since the end of the Second World War, established to prosecute the crimes of genocide, crimes against humanity, war crimes, and the crime of aggression (as yet undefined by the Court).

Key Points

- Placing limits on the legitimate use of force is one of the key challenges of the international community, and the laws of war have evolved to meet this challenge.
- The laws of war have traditionally been divided into those governing when the use of force is legitimate, *jus ad bellum*, and how war may be conducted, *jus in bello*.
- Laws governing when war is legally permitted have changed dramatically over the history of the international system, the

most notable difference being between the nineteenth-century view that to wage war was a sovereign right to the post-1945 view that war was only justified in self-defence or as part of a UN mandated international peace enforcement action.
- Laws governing how war may be conducted divide, broadly, into three categories: those governing weaponry, combatants, and non-combatants.

Theoretical approaches to international law

Like most aspects of international relations, several theoretical perspectives have been formulated to explain the nature, function, and salience of international law. What follows is a brief survey of the most prominent theoretical perspectives on international law, focusing on those approaches that together constitute the principal axes of contemporary debate.

Realism

Realists are great sceptics about international law, and they are deeply hostile to the Liberal-Idealist notion of 'peace through law'. George Kennan, the renowned Realist diplomat-scholar, argued that this 'undoubtedly represents in part an attempt to transpose the Anglo-Saxon concept of individual law into the international field and

to make it applicable to governments as it is applicable here at home to individuals' (1996: 102). The absence of a central authority to legislate, adjudicate, and enforce international law leads Realists to doubt whether international law is really law at all. At best, Morgenthau claimed, it is a form of 'primitive law', akin to that of 'preliterate societies, such as the Australian aborigines and the Yurok of northern California' (1985: 295). For Realists, international legal obligation is weak at best. Within the state, citizens are obliged to obey the law because sanctions exist to punish illegal behaviour. Yet sanctions are few in international relations, and enforcement mechanisms are rudimentary. To speak of states having strong international legal obligations is thus nonsensical for Realists.

Although this perspective on international law has many adherents, it is not without its weaknesses. To

begin with, Realists struggle to explain the growth of the immensely complex and dense international legal order in which international politics now takes place. Legal regimes govern everything from telecommunications and fisheries, arms control and world trade, to human rights and trafficking in endangered species, and as noted earlier compliance with these regimes is high. Furthermore, there is a trend to ever more 'legalized' regimes, as rules become more precise, obligations become clearer, and third-party adjudication spreads (Abbott *et al.* 2000). Second, Realists have trouble explaining how international law comes to constrain strong states. If their perspective were correct, we would expect powerful states to violate international law with impunity. But more often than not we see these states going to considerable lengths to confine their actions within the bounds of prevailing law (Wheeler 2004*b*), and when they do act outside the law, and without the international community's endorsement, they seek to justify their actions as consistent with prevailing law, and if they fail to do this persuasively they often pay high costs to their reputation and perceived legitimacy. Third, Realists ignore the way in which materially weak state and non-state actors have used international law to achieve advantageous outcomes, even in the face of opposition from powerful states. Washington's failure to get its way in the negotiations that created the International Criminal Court is a good example of this phenomenon (Wippman 2004).

Neo-liberal Institutionalism

Until recently, neo-liberals shied away from directly discussing international law, even though their concept of 'regimes' bore a close affinity (see Ch.6 and Ch.7). This was partly because much of their inspiration came from economic theory rather than law, and partly because in the Realist-dominated field of cold war international relations it was less provocative to speak the language of regimes and institutions than that of international law. Since the end of the cold war, however, neo-liberals have been at the forefront of calls for a more productive dialogue between international relations and international law. Not surprisingly, though, their understanding of this dialogue, and the initiatives they have taken to foster it, have been heavily influenced by their rationalist theoretical commitments (see Ch.9 and Ch.10 for criticisms).

States are treated as rational egoists, law is seen as an intervening variable between the goals of states and political outcomes, and law is seen as a regulatory institution, not a constitutive one that conditions states' identities and interests (see Goldstein *et al.* 2000).

By accepting the logic of anarchy and the self-interested nature of states, and then showing that international law matters, neo-liberals contribute much to our understanding of the strategic sources of such law. The perspective is not without it weaknesses, though. To begin with, it is strongest in areas where states have clear self-interests, such as trade or security. But it is of declining value when it comes to explaining the development and functioning of international law in areas that stretch or contradict the self-interests of states. Second, neo-liberals struggle to explain the origins of the modern institution of international law itself. In different historical systems, states have developed different sorts of institutions to facilitate cooperation and coexistence—we have already seen the institutional differences between the absolutist and modern systems. Yet neo-liberals have few theoretical resources to account for variations in basic institutional practices. Third, because neo-liberals explicitly bracket preference formation, they have little to say about the way in which international law can constitute the identities and interests of states. Prominent thinkers, such as Robert Keohane, note how regimes can 'prescribe behavioural roles' (1989*a*: 3), but how international law might do this is left unexplored.

Constructivism

As explained in Chapter 9, Constructivists argue that normative and ideational structures are as, if not more, important than material structures; they hold that understanding how actors' identities shape their interests and strategies is essential to understanding their behaviour; and they believe that social structures are only sustained through routinized human practices. These ideas provide clear openings for the study of international law, and it is not surprising that Constructivists have found considerable common ground with legal theorists. By broadening our understanding of politics to include issues of identity and purpose as well as strategy, by treating rules, norms, and ideas as constitutive, not just constraining, and by stressing the importance of discourse,

communication, and socialization in framing actors' behaviour, Constructivists offer resources for understanding the politics of international law lacking in Realist and neo-liberal thought.

But like its theoretical counterparts, **Constructivism** also has its limitations. Most importantly, for our purposes, the Constructivist account of international law is under-specified and underdeveloped. This is evident principally in Constructivist arguments about the difference between social and legal norms. Constructivists tend to speak of norms in general, and they often slide, almost unconsciously, between different categories of norms—social, legal, political, or moral. For many theoretical purposes this is relatively unproblematic, but it inhibits the development of a coherent Constructivist account of the nature and functioning of international law. This is not to suggest that Constructivists have neglected entirely the difference, and relationship, between social and legal norms. They have so far failed, however, to develop a common position on this. Some Constructivists wonder whether there is any meaningful distinction (Finnemore 2000), others strongly emphasize the differences, arguing that legal norms are more codified and powerful (Katzenstein 1996), and still others deny categorical differences but stress the styles of reasoning that attend each type of norm (Kratochwil 1989; Reus-Smit 2004). Until Constructivists overcome this ambiguity they will struggle to provide a systematic or compelling account of the social role of law in international life.

The New Liberalism

The 'New Liberalism' in international relations (which draws on strands of liberal thought discussed in Ch.6 and Ch.7) seeks to reformulate Liberalism as a positive social scientific paradigm, in a 'nonideological and nonutopian form appropriate to empirical social science' (Moravcsik 1997: 513). The theory rests on three core assumptions. The first holds that the 'fundamental actors in international politics are individuals and private groups, who are on average rational and risk-averse' (1997: 516). The second proposes that '[s]tates (or other political institutions) represent some subset of domestic society, on the basis of whose interests state officials define state preferences and act purposively in world politics' (1997: 518). The third and final assumption is that, in

the arena of international relations, the 'configuration of interdependent state preferences determines state behavior' (1997: 520). In sum, the New Liberalism is a 'second image' theory that gives analytical priority to the domestic sources of international relations.

Building on Moravcsik's three core assumptions, Anne-Marie Slaughter has proposed a three-tiered conception of international law. It is important to note, however, that her departure from the idea of the state as a unitary actor is more radical than Moravcsik's. Where he simply emphasizes the primacy of individuals and private groups, the most prominent of which shape state preferences, Slaughter disaggregates the state itself, stressing the transnational linkages between the executive, legislative, administrative, and judicial parts of different states. Her three tiers of international law thus consist of the following: the voluntary law of individuals and groups in transnational society; the law of transnational governmental institutions; and the law of inter-state relations (Slaughter 1995). The influence of liberal thought on Slaughter's theory does not stop at the schematic level, though. Because liberal theory stresses the primacy of individuals and private groups in shaping political and legal outcomes, the traditional ordering of international law, which privileges the international public law of inter-state relations, is turned on its head, with law that directly regulates individuals and groups (the first two tiers) taking precedence. Furthermore, within international public law, law that most directly affects individual–state relations is given priority, thus placing human rights law at the 'core' of international law (Slaughter 2000).

The explanatory merits of this perspective on international law are evident in Slaughter's insightful writings on the European Court of Justice (Mattli and Slaughter 1995, 1998), but it too has significant limitations. In the first instance, because the New Liberalism is founded on the same rationalist assumptions about social action as neo-liberalism, it is similarly handicapped. In particular, it has little to say about how law, domestic or international, might constitute actors' identities and interests (Reus-Smit 2001a: 584). Second, while New Liberals gain analytical advantage from their focus on domestic politics, they are disadvantaged by their relative neglect of international-level politics, processes, and structures. The question of how the politics of international law feeds back to condition the domestic politics of states (as well as their foreign policies) is left unanswered. Finally,

Moravcsik's quest for a 'nonideological' and 'nonutopian' liberal social science of international relations handicaps Slaughter's attempt to develop a liberal theory of international law. Like all international lawyers, Slaughter wants a theory to be prescriptive as well as descriptive, to be capable of sustaining recommendations for normative change as well as empirical explanations. But because Moravscik has tried to strip Liberalism of its normative content, Slaughter lacks the theoretical or philosophical resources on which to make her desired prescriptions for legal change (Reus-Smit 2001a: 585–9).

Critical legal studies

To this point we have considered a number of theories bearing the mark of political Liberalism. During the 1980s a body of critical international legal theory emerged to challenge the inherent Liberalism of modern international legal thought and practice. Often termed 'critical legal studies' or the 'New Stream', its proponents argue that Liberalism is stultifying international legal theory, pushing it between the equally barren extremes of 'apology'—the rationalization of established sovereign order—and 'utopia'—the naïve imagining that international law can civilize the world of states (Koskenniemi 1989). Their critique of Liberalism in international law incorporates four propositions (see Purvis 1991). First, they argue that the underlying logic of Liberalism in international law is incoherent. Such Liberalism denies that there can be any objective values beyond the particularistic values of individual states, and yet it imagines that international conflicts can be resolved on the basis of objective and neutral rules. Second, critical legal scholars claim that international legal thought operates within a confined intellectual structure. The twin pillars of this structure are liberal ideology and public international legal argument. The former works to naturalize the sovereign order, to place beyond critical reflection the principles of sovereignty and sovereign equality. The latter confines legitimate legal argument within certain confines. '[T]raditional international legal argument', Nigel Purvis contends,

'must be understood as a recurring self-referential search for origins, authority, and coherence' (1991: 105). Third, critical legal scholars challenge the purported determinacy of international legal rules. Legal positivism holds that a rule has a singular and objective meaning—hence the idea of 'finding the law'. For the critics, this is patently false: 'any international legal doctrine can justify multiple and competing outcomes in any legal debate' (Purvis 1991: 108). Finally, critical legal scholars argue that the authority of international law can only ever be self-validating; it is only through its own internal rituals that it can attain the legitimacy needed to attract state compliance and engagement (Purvis 1991: 109–13).

At first glance these criticisms appear devastating, but ironically critical international legal studies suffer from some of the same deficiencies as more traditional perspectives. To begin with, the argument that international law is inherently indeterminate bears a striking similarity to the Realist claim that the powerful can always bend the law to their will. The difficulty with this position is, though, that law does not in practice appear completely indeterminate; states certainly offer rival interpretations of the same rules, but not all interpretations are equally plausible, and through processes of argument (and possibly adjudication) states generally work their way to a socially acceptable determination of a rule's meaning and implications. Another deficiency concerns critical legal scholars' blindness to the emancipatory potential of contemporary international law. It is undoubtedly true that traditional public international law has served to sustain the sovereign order and many of its pathologies, but this very same system, informed by its liberal underpinnings, has been a resource for positive international social change. The development of the international human rights regime is the ongoing product and feature of the modern liberal international legal order, and without this regime many of the world's weakest and most vulnerable people would have no institutional resources against their rulers' excesses. In emphasizing the conservative face of the liberal order, critical legal scholars neglect its more emancipatory face.

Key Points

- Realists argue that international law is only important when it serves the interests of powerful states.
- Neo-liberals explain how self-interested states come to construct dense networks of international legal regimes.
- Constructivists treat international law as part of the normative structures that condition state and non-state agency in international relations. Like other social norms, they emphasize the way in which law constitutes actors' identities, interests, and strategies.

- New Liberals emphasize the domestic origins of state preferences and, in turn, international law. Within international law, they stress the need to disaggregate the state to understand transnational legal integration and interaction, and they prioritize international humanitarian law.
- Critical legal studies concentrates on the way in which the inherent Liberalism of international law seriously curtails its radical potential.

Conclusion

This chapter opened by noting the 'paradox' of international law, the fact that while scholars often downplay the value and efficacy of international law, sovereign states devote enormous amounts of time and energy to constructing ever more elaborate legal regimes. We then considered the role that institutions play in facilitating coexistence and cooperation among states, and how the modern institution of international law arose historically. It was argued that international law was both functional to the needs of an increasingly complex international system, but also deeply grounded in ideas about legitimate rule that accompanied the rise of political Liberalism. After considering trends that may be transforming the international law into a form of supranational, or transnational law, we concluded by surveying the principal theories about the nature and efficacy of international law, each of which presents a different set of viewpoints on the 'paradox' of international law.

? **Questions**

1 Can you think of other factors, in addition to the ones listed in the chapter, which contributed to the rise of modern international law in the last two centuries?

2 Is the 'paradox of international law' really a paradox?

3 Do you find the argument that states create institutions to sustain international order persuasive?

4 Can you think of other distinctive characteristics of the modern institution of international law not raised in the chapter?

5 Which of the theories of international law surveyed do you find most persuasive, and why?

6 If you were asked to predict the future of international law, how would you use the theories surveyed to construct an answer?

7 What do you think are the strengths and weaknesses of the international legal system?

8 What evidence do you see that international law is transforming into a form of supranational law?

9 What are the implications of the rise of supranational law for the sovereignty of states?

10 How should we think about the relationship between international law and justice and ethics in international relations?

⤵ Guide to further reading

Barker, J. Craig (2000), *International Law and International Relations* (London: Continuum). A good survey on the relationship between international law and international relations.

Byers, Michael (2000), *The Role of Law in International Politics* (Oxford: Oxford University Press). An excellent collection of advanced essays on the politics of international law.

Cassese, Antonio (2001), *International Law* (Oxford: Oxford University Press). An excellent international legal text by a leading scholar and jurist.

Goldsmith, Jack L., and Posner, Eric A. (2006), *The Limits of International Law* (New York: Oxford University Press). A vigorous critique of the institution of international law and its capacity to produce substantial goods for international society.

Higgins, Rosalyn (1994), *Problems and Process: International Law and How We Use It* (Oxford: Oxford University Press). A very good introduction to international law by a justice of the International Court of Justice.

Lynch, Cecelia, and Loriaux, Michael (eds) (2000), *Law and Moral Action in World Politics* (Minneapolis: Univeristy of Minnesota Press). A good collection of essays on the relationship between international law and ethics.

Kratochwil, Friedrich (1989), *Rules, Norms, and Decisions* (Cambridge: Cambridge University Press). The most sustained and advanced Constructivist work on international legal reasoning.

Reus-Smit, Christian (ed.) (2004), *The Politics of International Law* (Cambridge: Cambridge University Press). An edited collection that presents a Constructivist perspective on international law, illustrated by a range of contemporary case studies.

Von Glahn, Gerhard (1995), *Law Among Nations: An Introduction to Public International Law,* 7th edn (New York: Addison-Wesley). A traditional, yet comprehensive introduction to international law by a political scientist.

Online Resource Centre

 Visit the Online Resource Centre that accompanies this book to access more learning resources on this chapter topic at www.oxfordtextbooks.co.uk/uk/orc/baylis_smith4e/

Chapter 17

International regimes

RICHARD LITTLE

- Introduction ···298
- The nature of regimes ···300
- Competing theories of regime formation ·······································302
- Conclusion ···307

Reader's Guide

Liberal Institutionalists and Realists are engaged in a major debate about the role played by regimes—delineated areas of rule-governed activity—in the international system. Both schools acknowledge that although the international system is anarchic (without a ruler) in structure, it has never been anomic (without rules). Interest in regimes surfaced in the 1970s along with concern about the ability of the United States to sustain the economic regimes formed after the Second World War. What are the essential features of regimes? There is no straightforward answer to this question, and the chapter uses a definition, typology, and examples to reveal their complex character. Under what circumstances do regimes come into existence? This question forms the nub of the debate. Although Liberal Institutionalists and Realists use very similar tools of analysis—drawing on microeconomics and game theory—they arrive at very different conclusions. Are the conclusions compatible? The question remains contested.

Introduction

An important dimension of **globalization** has been the establishment of worldwide **regimes**—rule-governed activity within the **international system**. Although international rules predate the emergence of the modern **state**, it was during the twentieth century that regimes became a global phenomenon, with states enmeshed in increasingly complex sets of rules and **institutions** which regulated international relations around the world. There is now no area of international intercourse devoid of regimes, where states are not circumscribed by the existence of mutually accepted sets of rules. Indeed, many regimes are so firmly embedded in the system that they are almost taken for granted. Most people do not consider it at all surprising, for example, that we can put a letter in a post-box, and be confident that it will be delivered anywhere in the world from the Antarctic to Zimbabwe, or that we can get on an aeroplane and expect to fly unmolested to our destination at any point across the globe. Only when something goes drastically wrong, as, for example, in 1983, when the Soviet Defence Forces shot down the civilian South Korean airliner KAL 007, killing all 269 persons on board, is our attention drawn to the fact that international relations are, in practice, extensively regulated by complex regimes negotiated and policed by states. International **terrorism** is, as a consequence, particularly disturbing because terrorists do not consider themselves bound by regimes.

It may seem unremarkable, at first sight, that states have established regimes to ensure that mail gets delivered anywhere in the world and that aircraft can fly safely from one country to another. The advantages of such regimes appear so obvious that it would be more remarkable if such regimes had not been put in place. However, the existence of these regimes becomes rather more surprising when it is acknowledged how much controversy can surround the formation of regimes, how contentious established regimes can prove to be, and how frequently attempts to form regimes can fail. It is because the use of regimes to promote everything from arms control to the enhancement of global economic welfare seems to be so self-evidently beneficial, that the difficulty of securing regimes requires some explanation. Sadly, there is no agreed answer. Although few doubt that regimes are an important feature of the contemporary international system, as

this chapter aims to demonstrate, theorists in the field of international relations are deeply divided about how and why regimes are formed and maintained.

From the 1970s onwards a series of global **developments,** to be discussed below, have encouraged theorists in International Relations to focus on the rapid expansion of regimes in the international system. The new breed of regime theorists has spawned an enormous literature (Levy *et al.* 1995), with increasingly complex and diverse research now being conducted across the globe (Rittberger 1993).

It is argued in this chapter that regime theorists are located within two broad schools of thought: **Realism** and **Liberalism** (see Ch.5 and Ch.6). Although Hasenclever, Mayer, and Rittberger (1997; Hasenclever 2000) see this division as an oversimplification, it does allow us to trace the broad parameters of the debate precipitated by the attempts to understand regimes. The chapter also aims to illustrate that in the attempt to accommodate the growth of regimes, both Realists and Liberals have had to extend their frames of reference.

Realists are often sceptical of or uninterested in **international law**, and yet they have developed an important position on regimes. At the same time, regime theorists in the liberal camp, identified as Liberal Institutionalists, have accepted key assumptions made by neo-realists, and these, along with their social science credentials, move them beyond the established liberal tradition (see Ch.7). But despite the shared theoretical assumptions, Liberal Institutionalists and Realists adhere to very different assessments of regimes (see Box 17.1). Liberal Institionalists focus on the way that regimes allow states to overcome the obstacles to **collaboration** imposed by the

---

Box 17.1 Liberal Institutional v. Realist approaches to the analysis of regimes

Common assumptions

1 States operate in an anarchic international system.
2 States are rational and unitary actors.
3 States are the units responsible for establishing regimes.
4 Regimes are established on the basis of cooperation in the international system.
5 Regimes promote international order.

continues

Box 17.1 continued

Liberal Institutionalists	**Realists**

Liberal Institutionalists

1 Regimes enable states to collaborate.
2 Regimes promote the common good.
3 Regimes flourish best when promoted and maintained by a benign hegemon.
4 Regimes promote globalization and a liberal world order.

Realists

1 Regimes enable states to coordinate.
2 Regimes generate differential benefits for states.
3 Power is the central feature of regime formation and survival.
4 The nature of world order depends on the underlying principles and norms of regimes.

anarchic structure of the international system. Realists, by contrast, are interested in the way that states use their **power capabilities** in situations requiring **coordination** to **influence** the nature of regimes and the way that the costs and benefits derived from regime formation are divided up. Collaboration and coordination are seen to constitute different approaches to **cooperation**.

Although there are important differences between these two schools of thought, there are also important similarities (see Ch.7). In particular, both consider regimes to be the product of rational self-interested actors. As a consequence, they approach the establishment of rules from a very different perspective to Social Constructivists, who assume that the existence of rules can help to shape how actors define their **identity** and interests and demonstrate that they share a common view of the world (see Ch.9 and Ch.15). Although the literature on regimes is still dominated by rationalists, critics of this perspective are now starting to focus on regimes that are more difficult to explain from a rationalist perspective, such as the international protection of minority rights (Cronin 2003).

Why did IR theorists focus on regime formation in the 1970s? One factor was the growing awareness that, outside of the Soviet sphere, the United States had played the role of **hegemon** after the Second World War. The term derives from the Greek, meaning leader, and the United States could play this role because of its preponderance of power in the international system. During this era, the United States, because of its hegemonic position, had been able to establish and maintain a complex array of economic regimes in the West. These regimes played a vital role in the growing prosperity after the Second World War. By the 1970s, however, partly because of the economic success in **Europe** and Japan, and partly because of the disastrous policy in Vietnam, the capacity of the United States to maintain its hegemonic status was in doubt. It is unsurprising that an interest in regimes coincided with this development.

Liberal Institutionalists and Realists reacted to this development in very different ways. Liberal Institutionalists were concerned because while the need for regimes was becoming increasingly urgent, they believed that the loss of hegemonic status by the United States made it increasingly difficult to establish these regimes. Realists argued, by contrast, that if the United States did lose its hegemonic status, then with the shift in the **balance of power** the liberal **principles** governing these regimes established by the United States would be challenged by **Third World** states wanting new regimes established on the basis of different **norms** and principles. Although their analysis pointed in different directions, both Liberal Institutionalists and Realists acknowledged the need for a more sophisticated theoretical understanding of regimes.

Since the end of the **cold war**, the United States has become more hegemonic than in the past. But there is now growing concern that the United States is pursuing an increasingly exceptionalist foreign policy and is failing to support new **international regimes**. For example, President Bush withdrew President Clinton's support for the Kyoto Protocol to the UN Framework Convention on Climate Change, which was ratified or acceded to by over 120 states in 2004. The key question now, therefore, is whether regimes can be successful without US support.

Key Points

- Regimes represent an important feature of globalization.
- There is a growing number of global regimes being formed.
- The term regimes, and social science approaches to them, are recent but fit into a long-standing tradition of thought about international law.
- The onset of *détente*, the loss of hegemonic status by the USA, and the growing awareness of environmental problems sensitized social scientists to the need for a theory of regimes.
- Liberal Institutionalists and Realists have developed competing approaches to the analysis of regimes.

The nature of regimes

Before presenting the theoretical approaches developed by the Liberal Institutionalists and the Realists, this section discusses in more detail their conceptualization of an international regime and then uses some of the major areas of world politics now regulated by regimes, to illustrate the concept.

Conceptualizing regimes

Although it may be helpful in the first instance to think of regimes as rule-governed behaviour, a more complex conceptualization has been developed by theorists working in the field of international relations. This conceptualization is captured by a definition and typology of regimes.

Defining regimes

There are many definitions of a regime, but the one formulated in the early 1980s by Stephen Krasner remains the standard formulation and it very effectively encapsulates the complexity of the phenomenon (see Box 17.2). Krasner's definition reveals that a regime is more than a set of rules; it presupposes quite a high level of **institutionalization**. Indeed, regime theorists have been criticized for doing no more than introducing new terminology to characterize the familiar idea of an **international organization**. Regime theorists acknowledge that international organizations can be embraced by regime theory, but they insist that their approach encompasses much more. Reus-Smit's (Ch.16) distinction between institutions and organizations establishes the same point. The parameters of a regime can be illustrated by means of a typology.

Classifying regimes

One simple but useful classification establishes a typology of regimes along two dimensions (Levy *et al.* 1995). The vertical dimension highlights the formality of a regime (see Table 17.1). A regime can be associated with a highly formalized agreement or even the emergence of

---

Box 17.2 Defining regimes

Regimes are identified by Krasner (1983: 2) as 'sets of implicit or explicit principles, norms, rules, and decision-making procedures around which actors' expectations converge in a given area of international relations'.

An example of a regime

This is a complex definition and it needs to be unpacked. Krasner has done this, by drawing on the **General Agreement on Tariffs and Trade** (GATT) for illustrative purposes. The GATT was initially an agreement drawn up in 1947 and reflected the belief of its signatories that it was necessary to establish an organization which would be responsible for the regulation of international trade. In fact, it proved impossible to establish such an organization at that time, and the GATT acted as a substitute. It was given a secretariat and a general director responsible for carrying out the preparatory work for a series of conferences where the signatories of the GATT met and reached agreements intended to foster international trade. In 1994, after the Uruguay Round of negotiations, it was agreed that it was now time to move beyond the GATT and establish a formal World Trade Organization, as originally intended. Krasner was writing before this development took place, but it does not affect the utility of the GATT as an illustration of what is meant by a regime.

The four defining elements of a regime

1 **Principles** are represented by coherent bodies of theoretical statements about how the world works. The GATT operated on the basis of liberal principles which assert that global welfare will be maximized by free trade.

2 **Norms** specify general standards of behaviour, and identify the rights and obligations of states. So, in the case of the GATT, the basic norm is that tariffs and non-tariff barriers should be reduced and eventually eliminated. Together, norms and principles define the essential character of a regime and these cannot be changed without transforming the nature of the regime.

3 **Rules** operate at a lower level of generality than principles and norms, and they are often designed to reconcile conflicts which may exist between the principles and norms. Third World states, for example, wanted rules which differentiated between developed and underdeveloped countries.

4 **Decision-making procedures** identify specific prescriptions for behaviour, the system of voting, for example, which will regularly change as a regime is consolidated and extended. The rules and procedures governing the GATT, for example, underwent substantial modification during its history. Indeed, the purpose of the successive conferences was to change the rules and decision-making procedures.

(Krasner 1985: 4–5)

Convergence of expectations		Formality
Low	High	
No regimes	Tacit regimes	Low
Dead-letter regimes	Full-blown regimes	High

Source: Adapted from Levy *et al.* (1995).

Table 17.1 A typology of regimes

an international organization. But, at the other extreme, a regime can come into existence in the absence of any formal agreements. Historically, informal agreements between states have been established on the basis of precedence. The horizontal axis then focuses on the extent to which states expect or anticipate that their behaviour will be constrained by their accession to an implicit or explicit set of agreements.

If there are no formal agreements, and no convergence in the expectation that rules will be adhered to, then it is clear that there is **no regime** in existence. On the other hand, even in the absence of formal rules, there can be an expectation that informal rules will be observed, suggesting the existence of a **tacit regime**. By contrast, it is also possible to identify situations where formal rules have been brought into existence without any expectation that they will be observed, indicating the existence of a **dead-letter regime**. Finally, there are **full-blown regimes**, where there is a high expectation that formal rules will be observed (see Table 17.1). Examples of these different types of regimes will be given in the next section.

Globalization and international regimes

As we move into the twenty-first century it becomes increasingly clear that not every aspect of the globalization of world politics is beneficial. Technology makes it possible to see and talk to people on the other side of the globe and to fill the supermarkets—at least those in the wealthy sectors of the global economy—with increasingly exotic commodities from all round the world. But it has also made it possible to build weapons with the potential to wreak global devastation and to pollute the atmosphere irreversibly. It is becoming increasingly apparent that if we are all to benefit rather than suffer from globalization, it is essential to manage the process. No one thinks that this task will be easy; pessimists doubt that it is even possible. Regime theorists, on the other hand, see grounds for

optimism. They believe that **survival** depends upon our capacity to regulate global activity by means of regimes; and, as we demonstrate in this section, although not in any comprehensive fashion, the evidence indicates that states can establish regimes across a wide range of activities.

Security regimes

Although **security regimes** are primarily a twentieth-century phenomenon, permitting states to escape from the security dilemma (see Ch.13), it is possible to identify earlier examples. The Concert of Europe, for instance, constitutes a regime formed by the conservative states of post-Napoleonic Europe to counter future revolution and conflict. At the same time, on the other side of the Atlantic, the British and Americans established the Rush–Bagot agreement in 1817 to demilitarize the Great Lakes. But whereas the tacit regional regime in Europe began to decay soon after it was formed, the full-blown bilateral regime in North America became steadily stronger until, eventually, the long border between Canada and the United States was permanently demilitarized.

Regular attempts to establish full-blown security regimes, however, only started to proliferate during the twentieth century, particularly after the onset of the cold war. But the effectiveness of these regimes has often been questioned. Jervis (1983b), for example, argues that some of the major regimes, such as SALT 1 (1972) and SALT 2 (1979), designed to bring the arms race between the United States and the Soviet Union under control, were effectively dead-letter regimes. Despite the prolonged negotiations and detailed agreements, there was no evidence that they brought the arms race under control, because neither **superpower** expected the other to desist from developing new weapons technology. Nevertheless, arms control agreements can establish fragile security regimes and, for example, the Partial Test Ban Agreement of 1963 has undoubtedly encouraged a prohibition of atmospheric testing.

Environmental regimes

As scientists have become increasingly aware of the damage being done to the global environment, so the importance attached to environmental regimes has steadily risen (see Ch.20). Oil pollution, global warming, and damage to the ozone layer are the issues that have

attracted most public attention, but regimes have been established in a wide range of areas in the attempt to protect the global environment. For example, international conventions to save endangered plant and animal species can be traced back to the 1970s, and a comprehensive Convention on Biological Diversity came into force in December 1993. There have also been attempts since the mid-1980s to regulate the international movement of hazardous waste material, with the Basle Convention establishing a complete ban in March 1993 on the shipping of hazardous waste from countries in the developed world to countries in the underdeveloped world.

Economic regimes

It is often argued that the regimes in the economic arena are more firmly entrenched than those in any other. As already noted, however, the international economy could not function in the absence of the infrastructure provided by the communication regimes. The two sets of regimes are inextricably interlinked. Indeed, over the last decade, as the regimes governing the international economy have become ever more firmly established, the underlying liberal principles governing these regimes have started to impinge on the communication regimes. This development is reflected in the growing attempts to open postal services, telecommunications, and national airlines to greater competition. This development is leading to a modification of the basic principle underlying these regimes which in the past has always favoured state control over the rules regulating these activities (Zacher, with Sutton 1996).

It is not possible to provide even a brief survey of the complex economic regimes established in the era after the Second World War. But it is worth noting that they reflect the determined effort made by the United States, in particular, to consolidate a set of regimes built upon liberal principles. In particular, the United States wished to establish a trading regime established on free trade principles and, as we have seen, the GATT, now the **World Trade Organization** (WTO), was established to achieve this goal. At the same time, however, the United States also recognized that trade requires stable domestic economies and a stable monetary system to flourish. A range of international organizations, such as the **International Monetary Fund** and the International Bank of Reconstruction and Development, was established after 1945 to promote an environment where trade could flourish. Although there were fears that the economic regimes established by the United States would collapse as weaknesses in its own economy became apparent in the late 1960s, the economic regimes brought into existence after 1945 have proved to be surprisingly resilient (but see Ch.14).

Key Points

- Regime theory is an attempt initiated in the 1970s by social scientists to account for the existence of rule-governed behaviour in the anarchic international system.
- Regimes have been defined by principles, norms, rules; and decision-making procedures.
- Regimes can be classified in terms of the formality of the underlying agreements and the degree of expectation that the agreements will be observed. Full-blown, tacit, and dead-letter regimes can be identified.
- Regimes now help to regulate international relations in many spheres of activity.

Competing theories of regime formation

Both Liberal Institutionalists and Realists acknowledge that regimes are an important feature of contemporary international relations and they also start from the same theoretical premise that a regime represents the response of rational actors operating within the anarchic structure of the international system (see Ch.7). But despite this common starting point, Realists and Liberal Institutionalists develop very different theoretical assessments of regimes.

The Liberal Institutional approach

For Liberal Institutionalists regimes help to overcome the problem of **anarchy**. They draw on theoretical ideas

developed outside international relations to explain why anarchy inhibits collaboration and how to promote regime formation.

Impediments to regime formation

To explain why anarchy impedes regime formation, Liberal Institutionalists turn to **microeconomics** and **game theory**. Microeconomists study economic units operating under the conditions of perfect competition found, in theory, within the market-place, and Liberal Institutionalists then draw an analogy between the economic market and the international system because both are constituted by anarchic structures. For microeconomists, the absence of centralized institutions constitutes an important asset of the market-place. Unrestrained by external interference, rational economic units pursue competitive and self-interested strategies that result in goods being bought and sold at what microeconomic theory demonstrates is the optimum price.

This benign image of the economic market might seem to generate very little insight for Liberal Institutionalists. But the microeconomic approach becomes more relevant when attention is turned to the concept of **market failure**. Although microeconomists insist that an unrestrained market provides the most effective mechanism for the production of economic goods, it is accepted that the market is not effective when it comes to the production of **public goods** like roads and hospitals, and, indeed, there are circumstances when unrestrained competition produce **public bads**, the obvious example being pollution. Microeconomists argue that the underprovision of public goods or the proliferation of public bads occur because sometimes economic actors need to collaborate rather than compete. The principal mechanism to promote collaboration, often only accepted with reluctance, takes the form of state intervention. The state can, when necessary, intervene into the market place and require economic actors to collaborate. So, for example, if rivers have become polluted as the result of industrial waste, the state can pass legislation that requires all the economic actors involved to produce alternative outlets for the industrial waste. Here, the anarchic structure of the market gives way to the hierarchical structure of the state.

Within the international system, of course, no global equivalent of the state exists to enact legislation compelling sovereign states to subscribe to a common policy.

As a consequence, the widespread evidence of global problems persisting because of sovereign states failing to collaborate is unsurprising Global pollution, resource depletion, arms races, and trade barriers are all evidence of market failure—where states have preferred to compete rather than to collaborate. Nevertheless, the existence of regimes indicates that collaboration is certainly possible within the anarchic arena. Anarchy does not preclude collaboration; it simply makes it difficult to achieve and game theory helps to explain why.

Game theorists are mathematicians interested in non-zero sum games that focus on the strategic interaction between rational actors who can pursue either competitive or collaborative strategies. The interaction produces a much more complex situation than is found in the purely competitive market setting. Liberal Institutionalists, while generally avoiding the mathematics, have drawn on some of the conceptual apparatus developed by game theorists in order to enhance their theoretical appreciation of why anarchy inhibits collaboration. Theory building requires a distillation of the essential elements of the situation under scrutiny and game theory is particularly parsimonious. It focuses on the interaction between two actors, each with only two possible strategies—one cooperative and the other competitive—and so strategic interaction involves four possible outcomes. On the basis of this very simple conceptual apparatus it becomes possible to model a wide range of social situations. By stripping away the detail, it becomes easier to understand the underlying dynamics of the situation. So, for example, it is argued that all instances of market failure can be modelled by the game known as **Prisoners' Dilemma** (see Box 17. 3).

The logic associated with the Prisoners' Dilemma is seen by Liberal Institutionalists to account for why a wide range of irrational outcomes in the international arena can be explained in rational terms. It explains why states have persisted in overfishing the seas, in polluting the atmosphere, in selling arms to undesirable regimes, and in promoting policies that inhibit trade. All represent cases of market failure, with states choosing to pursue competitive rather than collaborative strategies. They fail to pursue collaborative strategies because they expect the other members of the **anarchic system** to pursue competitive strategies. It would be irrational for one state to require its fishing industry to observe a fishing quota, for example, if it is believed that the fishing industries in other states are intending to disregard the quota. As a consequence,

Box 17.3 The game of Prisoners' Dilemma

The Prisoners' Dilemma scenario

The governor of a prison once had two prisoners whom he could not hang without a voluntary confession of at least one. Accordingly, he summoned one prisoner and offered him his freedom and a sum of money if he would confess at least a day before the second prisoner did so, so that an indictment could be prepared and so that the second prisoner could be hanged. If the latter should confess at least a day before him, however, the first prisoner was told, then the prisoner would be freed and rewarded and he would be hanged. 'And what if we both should confess on the same day, your Excellency?', asked the first prisoner. 'Then you each will keep your life but will get ten years in prison.' 'And if neither of us should confess, your Excellency?' 'Then both of you will be set free—without any reward, of course. But will you bet your neck that your fellow prisoner—that crook—will not hurry to confess and pocket the reward? Now go back to your solitary cell and think about your answer until tomorrow.' The second prisoner in his interview was told the same, and each man spent the night alone considering his dilemma (Deutsch 1968: 120).

The two actors are confronted with two possible strategies, generating a situation with four possible outcomes. Being rational, the prisoners can place these outcomes on a preference ranking. The matrix below reveals the preference rankings for the two prisoners. Both prisoners will pursue the strategy which will optimize their position in the light of the strategies available to the other prisoner. To avoid being hanged, both prisoners will confess and end up in prison for ten years, thereby demonstrating how individual **rationality** leads to collective irrationality. The sub-optimal outcome could

only be avoided if the two prisoners possessed a mechanism which allowed them to collaborate.

		A	
		Silent	Confess*
B	Silent	3, 3‡	4, 1
	Confess*	1, 4	2, 2†

In this figure, cell numerals refer to ordinally ranked preferences: 4 = best, 1 = worst. The first number in each cell refers to A's preference and the second number refers to B's preference.

Key

* Dominant strategy: both players have dominant rather than contingent strategies. A strategy becomes dominant if it is preferable to the alternative strategy no matter which strategy the other player adopts.

† Denotes an equilibrium outcome.

‡ A Pareto optimal outcome: Vilfredo Pareto (1848–1923) was an Italian sociologist and economist who developed a criterion for identifying when an exchange between two parties has reached its most efficient or optimum point. He argued, in essence, that the point is reached when one party is better off and the other party is no worse off than before the exchange took place. An implication of this optimum is discussed later.

states avoid a Pareto optimal outcome and are driven by rational calculation to pursue a strategy which, through strategic interaction, leads to a sub-optimal outcome.

If the Prisoners' Dilemma game does accurately map this situation, however, then it not only explains why anarchy inhibits collaboration, but also indicates that states acknowledge the advantages of collaboration. They are only inhibited from moving to collaborative strategies by their expectation that other states will defect. The Prisoners' Dilemma demonstrates the importance of identifying a mechanism that will convince all the actors that there is no danger of defection. Liberal Institutionalists believe that the establishment of regimes provides evidence that mechanisms of this kind must exist.

The facilitation of regime formation

Liberal Institutionalists have followed two different routes in their attempt to explain the emergence of regimes. First, they have drawn on the work of microeconomists, who have insisted that state intervention is not the only mech-

anism available to produce public goods. It is suggested that if there is a dominant or hegemonic actor operating within the market, then that actor may well be prepared to sustain the cost of producing a public good (Olson 1965). Liberal Institutionalists have had no difficulty extending this line of argument to the international arena. During the course of the nineteenth century, for example, a regime was established which outlawed the international traffic of slaves. States agreed to observe the humanitarian principle underpinning this regime because they expected other states to do so. The expectation emerged because it was recognized that Great Britain intended to police the regime and possessed the naval capacity to do so. The regime was consolidated, therefore, because of Britain's hegemonic status within the international system.

As already indicated, it is widely accepted that the economic regimes established after the Second World War owe their existence to the presence of the United States as a hegemonic power. But when Liberal Institutionalists examined the consequences of hegemonic decline, they concluded that established regimes would persist.

Although the Prisoners' Dilemma indicated that market failures occur because in an anarchic system there is an expectation that states will compete rather than collaborate, once states have moved away from the sub-optimum outcome resulting from mutually competitive strategies, then there is no incentive to defect from the mutually collaborative strategies and return to the sub-optimum outcome. Even in the absence of a hegemon, therefore, Liberal Institutionalists argue that established regimes will survive (Keohane 1984).

A second route explored by the Liberal Institutionalists reinforces this conclusion. It is argued that if the Prisoners' Dilemma is only played once, then the game exaggerates the difficulty of generating collaboration. It is more realistic, however, to see the game being played repeatedly. The **shadow of the future** then looms over the players, affecting their strategic calculations. Because the game will be played on future occasions, it becomes worthwhile taking a risk and pursuing a collaborative strategy in order to produce the optimum outcome. If all states can be persuaded to do the same, then there will be little incentive to defect in the future, because if one state defects, then, 'tit for tat', all the others will follow. The major mechanism for establishing and maintaining a regime is not then the existence of a hegemon, but the principle of **reciprocity**. Liberal Institutionalists have increasingly come to focus on factors that will strengthen reciprocity within the system. Inspection and surveillance facilities become very important for ensuing that states are operating within the parameters of a regime. The establishment of satellite surveillance, for example, was a significant factor in encouraging the United States and the Soviet Union to reach arms control agreements. Attention has also been drawn to the importance of scientific knowledge. States are unwilling to restrict their activities on the basis of speculation and respond much more effectively when scientists start to agree about the significance of their findings. With states becoming ever more open and the constant expansion in scientific understanding, so the international environment will become increasingly 'information rich'. It is this trend, Liberal Institutionalists argue, that will do most to facilitate regime building in the future (Keohane 1984).

The Realist approach

Unsurprisingly, Realists contest the Liberal Institutional approach. First, they attack the comparison drawn between a hegemon providing public goods in the international system and the state dealing with domestic cases of market failure. Second, Realists deny that regimes emerge as the result of states endeavouring to overcome the pressure to compete under conditions of anarchy. Regimes form, Realists argue, in situations when uncoordinated strategies interact to produce sub-optimum outcomes.

Power and regimes

Despite being aware in the 1970s and 1980s that the hegemonic status of the United States was being questioned, Realists did not conclude that this development might lead to an anomic world. Instead, they focused on Third World demands for a new set of principles and norms to underpin the regimes associated with the world-economy. Existing regimes were seen to work against the interests of Third World states, opening them up to unfair competition and malign economic forces. Realists took the case presented by the Third World seriously, but argued that the principles and norms demanded by the Third World would only come into operation if the balance of power moved against the West (Tucker 1977; Krasner 1985). This assessment runs directly counter to the Liberal Institutionalist image of the United States as a benign benefactor, underwriting a set of regimes which allowed the members of the anarchic international system to escape from a sub-optimum outcome and into a position of Pareto optimality. Instead, the United States was a hegemon that used its power to sustain a regime that promoted its own long-term interests. Liberal Institutionalists ignore the contested status of liberal norms and principles.

From the Realist perspective, therefore, the United States helped to ensure that regimes were underpinned by a particular set of principles and norms. But a full appreciation of the Realist's position also requires the recognition that a hegemon can effectively veto the formation of a regime. For example, in 1972, when the United States launched its first remote-sensing satellite, the event caused concern among a large range of countries. These satellites have the capacity to gather important and sensitive commercial and strategic data about countries all around the world. Not only can the satellites identify where military equipment is located, but they can also identify the size of a crop yield and the location of minerals. There were several attempts to establish a regime which would limit the right of states to acquire data without the permission

of the state under surveillance (Brown *et al.* 1977). Many states have considered that they would benefit from such a regime. But because the balance of power was tilted in favour of states that possessed these satellites and they were clear that such a regime would not work to their benefit they vetoed the proposed regime.

Regimes and coordination

The Realist account of regimes, however, must also explain why states adhere to the principles and norms underlying a regime that they oppose. In accounting for this phenomenon, Realists, like Liberal Institutionalists, resort to game theory. They argue that states wishing to form a regime confront the problem of coordination, as illustrated by the **Battle of the Sexes** (see Box 17.4), not collaboration, as illustrated by the Prisoners' Dilemma. Here the problem is not associated with the danger of defection to a competitive strategy, but the possibility of failing to coordinate strategies, with the consequence that a mutually desired goal is unintentionally missed.

Coordination problems are very familiar to strategic thinkers. Schelling (1960) illustrates the problem with the example of a couple getting separated in a department store. Both wish to get back together again, but there is a danger that they will wait for each other in different places; situations of this kind generate a coordination problem.

In the absence of communication, solving coordination problems can be difficult, even impossible. But with the aid of communication, a solution can be very straightforward and uncontroversial. For example, while communication between an aircraft and an air traffic control centre can occur in any mutually agreed language, it is obviously unacceptable for the pilot and the air traffic controller not to be able to speak a common language. Under the rules of the International Civil Aviation Organization, every international pilot and some personnel in every air traffic control centre must be able to speak English. This is a highly stable equilibrium and the rule undoubtedly contributes to air safety. But it is only one of a large body of rules which form the regime that regulates international civil aviation. It has major training implications and it is not an issue that can be constantly renegotiated. It needs to be embodied in a stable regime that all the involved parties can treat as a constant.

The decision to choose English under these circumstances may have been relatively uncontroversial, but it does not follow that a common aversion to certain outcomes (a pilot speaking only German and the air traffic controller speaking only Japanese) will necessarily generate a common interest in a particular outcome (everyone speaking English). And this is the main lesson to be learned from the Battle of the Sexes game—there can be more than one outcome reflecting a Pareto optimum.

Box 17.4 The Battle of the Sexes and Pareto's frontier

The Battle of the Sexes

The scenario of this game envisages a couple who have just fallen in love and decide to go on holiday together. The problem is that one wants to go hiking in the mountains and the other wants to visit art galleries and museums in the city. But both much prefer to be with their partner than to go on holiday alone. When mapped on to a matrix, two stable equilibriums emerge from the scenario.

		A (male)	
		Holiday in city	Holiday in mountains
B (female)	Holiday in city	4, 3*	1, 2
	Holiday in mountains	2, 1	3, 4*

In this figure, cell numerals refer to ordinally ranked preferences: 4 = best, 1 = worst. The first number in each cell refers to A's preference and the second number refers to B's preference.
* Denotes an equilibrium outcome and a Pareto optimal strategy.

The Pareto frontier

Wishing to reach a compromise, the couple might decide to split their week's holiday, spending time in the city and in the mountains. Since the two extreme positions represent a Pareto optimum, so too must all the possible combinations and these can be mapped to form a Pareto frontier.

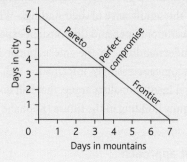

Indeed, there can be many positions that represent a Pareto optimum and they can then be located on what is referred to as the Pareto frontier (see Box 17.4). So in the context of civil aviation, every spoken language can be located on the frontier because, in principle, any language could be chosen, provided that everyone spoke it. And the use of any common language is preferable to the alternative that would arise in the event of a failure to coordinate and identify a common language.

Realists argue that this line of analysis helps us to understand why states might conform to a regime while wishing to change the underlying principles. The explanation is that the states are already operating on the Pareto frontier. They observe the regime because they are operating in a coordination situation, and a failure to coordinate will move them into a less advantageous situation. The French can rail against the use of English in the civil aviation context, but they have no alternative but to persist with the policy. The same argument applies to Third World states; they wish to trade with the West, while preferring to do so on more advantageous terms. The application of new trade principles would represent another point on the Pareto frontier. But, as yet, because the balance of power continues to favour the West, there are few signs of new economic principles emerging that are more favourable to the Third World.

The situation is somewhat different in the area of communication regimes. All forms of electronic communication use electromagnetic waves that are emitted along an electromagnetic spectrum. Coordination here is essential, because interference occurs if more than one user adopts the same frequency of the spectrum at the same time over the same area. It is not possible, therefore, for states to operate on a unilateral basis, and the establishment of a regime was essential. Moreover, because the electromagnetic spectrum is a limited resource, principles and rules for partitioning the resource had to be determined. In the first instance, states agreed that the spectrum should be allocated on the basis of need. But by 1980 this principle had resulted in the Soviet Union and the United States claiming half of the available frequencies and 90 per cent of the spectrum was allocated to provide benefits for 10 per cent of the world's population (Krasner 1985). It is unsurprising to find this outcome being challenged by developing states, which argued that part of the spectrum should be reserved for future use. More surprisingly, this new principle has been accepted. But Realists argue that this is not the result of altruism on the part of the developed world. It is a consequence of the fact that developing states can interfere with the signals of neighbouring countries. This gave them access to a power lever, which they otherwise would not have possessed (Krasner 1991).

Key Points

- The market is used by Liberal Institutionalists as an analogy for the anarchic international system.
- In a market/international setting, public goods get underproduced and public bads get overproduced.
- Liberal Institutionalists draw on the Prisoners' Dilemma game to account for the structural impediments to regime formation.
- A hegemon, 'the shadow of the future', and an information-rich environment promote collaboration and an escape route from Prisoners' Dilemmas.
- Realists argue that Liberal Institutionalists ignore the importance of power when examining regimes.
- Realists draw on the Battle of the Sexes to illuminate the nature of coordination and its link to power in an anarchic setting.

Conclusion

Although Liberal Institutionalists and Realists acknowledge that regimes are an important feature of the international system, and draw on similar tools of analysis, they reach very different conclusions about the circumstances in which regimes emerge. For Liberal Institutionalists, regimes arises because there is always a danger in the anarchic international system that competitive strategies will trump cooperative strategies. By contrast, Realists link the emergence of regimes to situations where there is a mutual desire to cooperate, but where anarchy generates a problem of coordination.

The implications of power for the two approaches also diverge. For Liberal Institutionalists, power may be used by a hegemon to pressure other states to collaborate and conform to a regime. But it is also acknowledged that states can establish and maintain regimes in the absence

of hegemonic power. Collaborative strategies are pursued and maintained because of the 'shadow of the future'—a mutual recognition that if any state defects from a regime, it will result in mass defection on a 'tit for tat' basis and states moving from an optimum to a sub-optimum outcome. For Realists, on the other hand, power is seen to play a crucial role, not as a threat to discipline states caught defecting from a collaborative agreement, but in the bargaining process—to determine the shape of a regime around which all states will coordinate their actions.

Stein (1983), who introduced the distinction between collaborative and coordination games into the regime literature, never assumed, however, that they represented mutually incompatible approaches to regime formation. In practice, the two games discussed in this chapter that capture the distinction simply distil different aspects of the complex processes associated with regime forma-

tion. The case study on the international whaling moratorium illustrates the complexity that surrounds regime analysis.

In the first instance, the 15 major whaling nations established the regime because they acknowledged the need to regulate the whaling industry. The Prisoner's Dilemma game helps us to understand the kind problems that they wished to overcome. These problems revolved around the uncertainty about what the other states were going to do. Once they agreed to collaborate, establishing quotas proved to be relatively straightforward because they recognized that if they went over their quota, then the regime would collapse.

With the passage of time, however, problems arose not because of difficulties associated with policing the regime, but because differences emerged amongst the members about the fundamental goal of the regime. Initially, the

Case Study   International whaling moratorium

In 1986, the International Whaling Commission (IWC) established a total moratorium on commercial whaling that remains in place today. The IWC is an international regulatory body established in 1946 by the 15 major whaling nations that agreed, on a voluntary basis, to establish and maintain a whaling regime. Commercial whaling was, as a consequence, regulated by quotas for the next four decades. But by the 1970s there were growing concerns among environmentalists that many species of whales could soon become extinct.

The 1986 moratorium was controversial from the start, however, because the IWC was, by then, split into pro-whaling and anti-whaling camps. On the one hand, some long-established whaling nations, such as Britain and the United States, were now no longer interested in maintaining whaling fleets. At the same time, powerful environmental lobbies, like Greenpeace, had raised the spectre of species extinction and promoted the image of whale hunting as barbaric. On the other hand, in states like Norway, Iceland, and

Japan, whaling was portrayed as integral to national identity as well as crucial to the way of life of aboriginal peoples.

As the IWC fractured, however, new states were joining, often siding with the United States in the anti-whaling camp, thereby shifting the balance of power against pro-whalers and the anti-whalers eventually secured the necessary three-quarters majority in favour of a moratorium; it passed on a 25 to 7 vote with five abstentions. Unsurprisingly, states in the pro-whaling camp have never accepted the need for a moratorium, questioning the validity of the scientific evidence and insisting on the viability of quotas. Nevertheless, only Iceland withdrew from the IWC, in 1992, although it was permitted to rejoin in 2002, despite its reservation to the moratorium.

Japan has spearheaded the resistance to the moratorium, making the most of the exemptions on scientific and aboriginal whaling. In 2007, for example, Japan planned to catch 1,300 whales for scientific research (more than was caught in the final year of commercial whaling). The whales are subsequently sold for commercial use. The research reveals that there is now no need for a moratorium and that the growing population of whales consumes five times more fish than humans—scientific evidence that anti-whalers vigorously dispute (see Heazle 2006).

But Japan is now the major aid donor in the world and some of its aid recipients, with no historical interest in whaling have been encouraged to join the IWC; new members include states from West Africa and Central America, as well as micro-states in the Pacific and the Caribbean. As membership, mainly from the Third World, has steadily increased to over 70 states, so the balance of power has tipped once again in favour of the pro-whalers. In 2006, a IWC vote calling for an end to the moratorium was passed by 33 to 32 votes, not enough to overturn the moratorium, but enough to destabilize the whaling regime.

International Whaling Commission (IWC) members all agreed that the goal was to eliminate the danger of harvesting too many whales each year. But by the 1970s, this goal began to be questioned by environmentalists who believed that there was no satisfactory justification for continuing to catch whales because there are more efficient and humane ways of feeding people. Because of these competing positions, the issue has now become highly politicized and the difficulty of maintaining the regime at this juncture is much more effectively captured by the Battle of the Sexes game: one camp wants a regime that ensures that whaling is effectively regulated and the other camp wants a regime that outlaws whaling.

The whaling moratorium came into force, at least in part, because of the hegemonic status of the United States. New members with no vested interest in whaling chose to vote with the United States, thereby bolstering the anti-whaling camp. But ever since the moratorium came into force, Japan has endeavoured to challenge the US-backed policy, thereby risking US resentment and indeed international opprobrium as well as prolonging a dispute that has become the source of escalating bitterness. The unremitting determination of Japan to overturn the moratorium is often considered surprising because the consumption of whale meat by the Japanese has plummeted and is no longer a significant element in their diet. But opposition to the moratorium has become an issue of principle and there is an unwillingness to bow to pressures that from the Japanese perspective are not validated by science and are dictated primarily by emotion.

Third world states with no established interests in whaling have been the unexpected beneficiaries of the dispute as Japan, unwilling to withdraw from the whaling regime, has drawn on its influence on Third World states in an attempt to wrestle control from the anti-whaling camp. Because of the continuing hegemonic influence of the United States, the Japanese are unlikely to overturn the moratorium (McNeill 2006), but the stalemate that emerged in 2006 is sufficient to threaten the survival of the regime. None of the key actors wishes to see this happen and the Battle of the Sexes game predicts that a compromise formula will be sought and eventually found.

❓ Questions

1 What are the defining elements of a regime?
2 Is a regime the same as an organization?
3 Why did the study of international regimes develop in the 1970s?
4 What characteristic features do the Realist and Liberal Institutionalist approaches to regime analysis share?
5 How has microeconomics influenced the Liberal Institutionalist approach to regimes?
6 What are the main implications of strategic interaction
7 What are the implications of the Prisoners' Dilemma game for regime analysis?
8 What major mechanisms do Liberal Institutionalists advance to promote regime formation?
9 How does the Realist approach to regime analysis differ from the Liberal Institutional approach?
10 What does the Battle of the Sexes game tell us about the role of power in regime formation?
11 What does operating at the Pareto frontier mean in the context of regime theory?
12 Are Realist and Liberal Institutionalist approaches to regime analysis compatible?

➡ Guide to further reading

Brown, S. *et al.* (1997), *Regimes for the Ocean, Outer Space and the Weather* (Washington, DC: Brookings Institution). An early attempt to examine areas which need to be regulated by regimes.

Cronin, B. (2003), *Institutions for the Common Good: International Protection Regimes in International Society* (Cambridge: Cambridge University Press). An important counter to rationalist-based accounts of regimes.

Gruber, L. (2000), *Ruling the World: Power Politics and the Rise of Supranational Institutions* (Princeton, NJ: Princeton University Press). Associates great powers in supranational institutions with go-it-alone power that requires other states to follow suit.

Hasenclever, A., Mayer, P., and Rittberger, V. (1997), *Theories of International Regimes* (Cambridge: Cambridge University Press). Argues that in addition to Realism that focuses on power, and neo-liberalism that focuses on interests, cognitivism, focusing on ideas, now forms a third school of thought in the regime literature.

Keohane, R. O. (1984), *After Hegemony: Cooperation and Discord in the World Political Economy* (Princeton, NJ: Princeton University Press). One of the most influential Liberal Institutional texts on the theory underlying regime formation.

—— and Nye, J. S. (1977), *Power and Interdependence* (Boston: Little Brown). Examines the role of regimes in an interdependent world, advancing four models to account for regime change.

Krasner, S. D. (ed.) (1983), *International Regimes* (Ithaca, NY: Cornell University Press). A seminal text setting out the main theoretical issues.

—— (1985), *Structural Conflict: The Third World against Global Liberalism* (Berkeley: University of California Press). This is one of the major Realist texts. It explores North–South disputes over regimes.

Oye, K. A. (ed.) (1986), *Cooperation under Anarchy* (Princeton, NJ: Princeton University Press). An influential set of theoretical essays on how cooperation takes place under anarchic conditions.

Rittberger, V. (ed.) (1993), *Regime Theory and International Relations* (Oxford: Clarendon Press). This important book examines regime theory from European and American perspectives.

Zacher, M. W., with Sutton, B. A. (1996), *Governing Global Networks: International Regimes for Transportation and Communications* (Cambridge: Cambridge University Press). A Liberal Institutional account of regimes, arguing that they are based on mutual interests, and not the dictates of the most powerful states.

Online Resource Centre

 Visit the Online Resource Centre that accompanies this book to access more learning resources on this chapter topic at www.oxfordtextbooks.co.uk/uk/orc/baylis_smith4e/

Chapter 18

The United Nations

PAUL TAYLOR · DEVON CURTIS

- Introduction ··· 314
- A brief history of the United Nations and its principal organs ·· 314
- The United Nations and the maintenance of international peace and security ··············· 319
- The United Nations and intervention within states ··· 321
- The United Nations and economic and social questions ·· 324
- The reform process in the economic and social arrangements of the United Nations ····· 326
- Conclusion ··· 327

Reader's Guide

This chapter focuses on the development of the United Nations (UN) and the changes and challenges that it has faced since its establishment in 1945. The UN is a grouping of states, and is therefore premised on the notion that states are the primary units in the international system. The institutions of the United Nations reflect an uneasy hybrid between traditions of great power consensus and traditions of universalism that stress the equality of states. Furthermore, while the UN was established as a grouping of sovereign states, the chapter argues that United Nations institutions have taken on an increasing range of functions, and have become much more involved within states. Justice for individuals is increasingly seen as a concomitant of international order. Serious deficiencies in human rights, or in economic welfare, can lead to international tensions. This development has led to challenges to traditional views about intervention within states. It has also led to the expansion of UN institutions to address an increased number of economic and social questions, and the search for better ways to coordinate these activities.

Introduction

The United Nations (UN) is made up of a group of international **institutions**, which include the central system located in New York, the **Specialized Agencies**, such as the World Health Organization (WHO) and the International Labour Organization (ILO), and the **Programmes and Funds**, such as the United Nations Children's Fund (UNICEF) and the United Nations Development Programme (UNDP). When created more than half a century ago in the aftermath of the Second World War, the United Nations reflected the hope for a just and peaceful global **community**. It is the only global institution with the legitimacy that derives from universal membership, and a mandate that encompasses **security**, economic and social development, the protection of human rights, and the protection of the environment. Yet the UN was created by **states** for states and the relationship between **state sovereignty** and the protection of the needs and interests of people has not been fully resolved. Questions about the meaning of **sovereignty** and the limits of UN action have remained key **issues**. Since the founding of the UN, there has been an expansion of UN activities to address conditions within states,

an improvement in UN capacity in its economic and social work, and an increased tendency to accord the UN a moral status. Threats to global security addressed by the UN now include inter-state conflict, threats by **non-state actors**, as well as political, economic, and social conditions within states. Despite the growth in UN activities, however, there are some questions about the relevance and effectiveness of the UN. The failure by the USA and the UK to get clear UN Security Council authorization for the war in Iraq in 2003 led to well-publicized criticism of the UN and a crisis in international relations. Yet the troubled aftermath of the invasion and persistent questions about the legitimacy of a war that was not sanctioned by the UN show that the UN has acquired important moral status in **international society**.

After describing the main organs of the UN, this chapter will look at the changing role of the UN in addressing matters of peace and security, and then matters of economic and social development. It will focus on how the UN's role has evolved in response to changes in the global political context, and on some of the problems that it still faces.

A brief history of the United Nations and its principal organs

The United Nations was established on 24 October 1945 by 51 countries, as a result of initiatives taken by the governments of the states that had led the war against Germany and Japan. By 2006, 192 countries were members of the United Nations, nearly every state in the world. When joining, member states agreed to accept the obligations of the **United Nations Charter**, an international treaty that set out basic principles of international relations. According to the Charter, the UN had four purposes: to maintain international peace and security; to develop friendly relations among nations; to cooperate in solving international problems and in promoting respect for human rights; and to be a centre for harmonizing the actions of nations. At the UN, all the member states—large and small, rich and poor, with differing political views and social systems—had a voice and a vote in this process.

Interestingly, while the United Nations was clearly created as a grouping of states, the Charter referred to the needs and interests of peoples as well as those of states (see Box 18.1).

In many ways, the United Nations was set up to correct the problems of its predecessor, the **League of Nations**. The League of Nations had been established after the First World War, and was intended to make future wars impossible, but a major problem was the League's lack of effective **power**. There was no clear division of responsibility between the main executive committee (the League Council) and the League Assembly, which included all member states. Both the League Assembly and the League Council could only make recommendations, not binding resolutions, and these recommendations had to be unanimous. Any government was free to reject any

Box 18.1 Selected Articles of the UN Charter

The UN Charter contains references to both the rights of states and the rights of people.

The Preamble of the UN Charter asserts that 'We the peoples of the United Nations [are] determined [...] to reaffirm faith in fundamental human rights, in the dignity and worth of the human person, in the equal rights of men and women and of nations large and small'.

Article 1(2) states that the purpose of the UN is to develop 'friendly relations among nations based on respect for the principle of equal rights and self-determination of peoples and to take other appropriate measures to strengthen universal peace'.

Article 2(7) states that 'Nothing contained in the present Charter shall authorize the United Nations to intervene in matters which are essentially within the domestic jurisdiction of any state'.

Chapter VI deals with the 'Pacific Settlement of Disputes'.

Article 33 states that 'The parties to any dispute, the continuance of which is likely to endanger the maintenance of international peace and security, shall, first of all, seek a solution by negotiation, enquiry, mediation, conciliation, arbitration, judicial settlement, resort to regional agencies or arrangements, or other peaceful means of their own choice'.

Chapter VII deals with 'Action with Respect to Threats to the Peace, Breaches of the Peace, and Acts of Aggression'.

Article 42 states that the Security Council 'may take such action by air, sea, or land forces as may be necessary to maintain or restore international peace and security'. The Security Council has sometimes authorized member states to use 'all necessary means', and this has been accepted as a legitimate application of Chapter VII powers.

Article 99 authorizes the Secretary-General to 'bring to the attention of the Security Council any matter which in his opinion may threaten the maintenance of international peace and security'.

---

recommendation. Furthermore, in the League, there was no mechanism for coordinating military or economic actions against miscreant states, which further contributed to the League's weakness. Key states, such as the United States, were not members of the League. By the Second World War, the League had already failed to address a number of acts of aggression.

The **structure** of the United Nations was intended to avoid some of the problems faced by the League of Nations. The United Nations has six main organs: the Security Council, the General Assembly, the Secretariat, the Economic and Social Council, the Trusteeship Council, and the International Court of Justice (see Fig. 18.1).

The Security Council

In contrast to the League of Nations, the United Nations recognized great power prerogatives in the Security Council. The UN Security Council was given the main responsibility for maintaining international peace and security. It was made up initially of 11 states, and then, after 1965, of 15 states. It includes five permanent members, namely the USA, Britain, France, Russia (previously the Soviet Union), and China, as well as ten non-permanent members. Unlike the League, the decisions of the Security Council are binding, and must only be passed by a majority of nine out of the 15 members, as well as each of the five permanent members. These five permanent members therefore have **veto power** over all Security Council decisions. The convention emerged that abstention by a permanent member is not regarded as a veto.

The five permanent members of the Security Council were seen as the major powers when the UN was founded, and they were granted a veto on the view that if the great powers were not given a privileged position, the UN would not work. This view stems from Realist theory. Indeed, this tension between the recognition of power politics through the Security Council veto, and the universal ideals underlying the United Nations, is a defining feature of the organization. There have been widespread and frequent calls for the reform of the Security Council, but this is very difficult (see Box 18.2).

When the Security Council considers a threat to international peace, it first explores ways to settle the dispute peacefully under the terms of **Chapter VI** of the UN Charter (see Box 18.1). It may suggest **principles** for a settlement or may suggest mediation. In the event of fighting, the Security Council tries to secure a ceasefire. It may send a **peacekeeping** mission to help the parties maintain the truce and to keep opposing forces apart (see the discussion of peacekeeping below). The Council can also take measures to enforce its decisions under **Chapter VII** of the Charter. It can, for instance, impose economic sanctions or order an arms embargo. On rare occasions, the Security Council has authorized member states to use **all necessary means**, including collective military action, to see that its decisions are carried out.

The United Nations System

Principal Organs

| Trusteeship Council | Security Council | General Assembly | Economic and Social Council | International Court of Justice | Secretariat |

Trusteeship Council

Subsidiary Bodies

Military Staff Committee
Standing Committee and ad hoc bodies
International Criminal Tribunal for the former Yugoslavia (ICTY)
International Criminal Tribunal for Rwanda (ICTR)

Security Council

Subsidiary Bodies

UN Monitoring, Verification and Inspection Commission (Iraq) (UNMOVIC)
United Nations Compensation Commission
Peacekeeping Operations and Missions

General Assembly

Subsidiary Bodies

Main committees
Human Rights Council
Other sessional committees
Standing committees and ad hoc bodies
Other subsidiary organs

Advisory Subsidiary Body

United Nations kkv Commission

Programmes and Funds

UNCTAD United Nations Conference on Trade and Development
ITC International Trade Centre (UNCTAD/WTO)
UNDCP[1] United Nations Drug Control Programme
UNEP United Nations Environment Programme
UNICEF United Nations Children's Fund
UNDP United Nations Development Programme
UNIFEM United Nations Development Fund for Women
UNV United Nations Volunteers
UNCDF United Nations Capital Development Fund
UNFPA United Nations Population Fund
UNHCR Office of the United Nations High Commissioner for Refugees
WFP World Food Programme
UNRWA[2] United Nations Relief and Works Agency for Palestine Refugees in the Near East
UN-HABITAT United Nations Human Settlements Programme

Research and Training Institutes

UNICRI United Nations Interregional Crime and Justice Research Institute
UNITAR United Nations Institute for Training and Research
UNRISD United Nations Research Institute for Social Development
UNIDIR[2] United Nations Institute for Disarmament Research
INSTRAW International Research and Training Institute for the Advancement of Women

Other UN Entities

OHCHR Office of the United Nations High Commissioner for Human Rights
UNOPS United Nations Office for Project Services
UNU United Nations University
UNSSC United Nations System Staff College
UNAIDS Joint United Nations Programme on HIV/AIDS

Other UN Trust Funds[7]

UNIFIP United Nations Fund for International Partnerships
UNDEF United Nations Democracy Fund

Economic and Social Council

Functional Commissions

Commissions on:
Narcotic Drugs
Crime Prevention and Criminal Justice
Science and Technology for Development
Sustainable Development
Status of Women
Population and Development
Commission for Social Development
Statistical Commission

Regional Commissions

Economic Commission for Africa (ECA)
Economic Commission for Europe (ECE)
Economic Commission for Latin America and the Caribbean (ECLAC)
Economic and Social Commission for Asia and the Pacific (ESCAP)
Economic and Social Commission for Western Asia (ESCWA)

Other Bodies

Permanent Forum on Indigenous Issues (PFII)
United Nations Forum on Forests
Sessional and standing committees
Expert, ad hoc and related bodies

Related Organizations

WTO World Trade Organization
IAEA[4] International Atomic Energy Agency
CTBTO Prep.Com[5] PrepCom for the Nuclear-Test-Ban-Treaty Organization
OPCW[5] Organization for the Prohibition of Chemical Weapons

International Court of Justice

Specialized Agencies[6]

ILO International Labour Organization
FAO Food and Agriculture Organization of the United Nations
UNESCO United Nations Educational, Scientific and Cultural Organization
WHO World Health Organization

World Bank Group

IBRD International Bank for Reconstruction and Development
IDA International Development Association
IFC International Finance Corporation
MIGA Multilateral Investment Guarantee Agency
ICSID International Centre for Settlement of Investment Disputes

IMF International Monetary Fund
ICAO International Civil Aviation Organization
IMO International Maritime Organization
ITU International Telecommunication Union
UPU Universal Postal Union
WMO World Meteorological Organization
WIPO World Intellectual Property Organization
IFAD International Fund for Agricultural Development
UNIDO United Nations Industrial Development Organization
UNWTO World Tourism Organization

Secretariat

Departments and Offices

OSG[3] Office of the Secretary-General
OIOS Office of Internal Oversight Services
OLA Office of Legal Affairs
DPA Department of Political Affairs
DDA Department for Disarmament Affairs
DPKO Department of Peacekeeping Operations
OCHA Office for the Coordination of Humanitarian Affairs
DESA Department of Economic and Social Affairs
DGACM Department for General Assembly and Conference Management
DPI Department of Public Information
DM Department of Management
OHRLLS Office of the High Representative for the Least Developed Countries, Landlocked Developing Countries and Small Island Developing States
DSS Department of Safety and Security
UNODC United Nations Office on Drugs and Crime

UNOG UN Office at Geneva
UNOV UN Office at Vienna
UNON UN Office at Nairobi

Published by the United Nations
Department of Public Information
06-39572—August 2006—10,000—DPI/2431

NOTES: Solid lines from a Principal Organ indicate a direct reporting relationship; dashes indicate a non-subsidiary relationship.

1 The UN Drug Control Programme is part of the UN Office on Drugs and Crime
2 UNRWA and UNIDIR report only to the GA
3 The United Nations Ethics Office and the United Nations Ombudsman's Office report directly to the Secretary-General
4 IAEA reports to the Security Council and the General Assembly (GA)
5 The CTBTO Prep.Com and OPCW report to the GA
6 Specialized agencies are autonomous organizations working with the UN and each other through the coordinating machinery of the ECOSOC at the intergovernmental level, and through the Chief Executives Board for coordination (CEB) at the inter-secretariat level
7 UNIFIP is an autonomous trust fund operating under the leadership of the United Nations Deputy Secretary-General. UNDEF's advisory board recommends funding proposals for approval by the Secretary-General.

Source: Reproduced by permission of the United Nations Department of Public Information (see www.un.org/aboutun/chart.pdf).

Figure 18.1 The structure of the United Nations system

Box 18.2 The reform of the Security Council

Since the Security Council is the main executive body within the United Nations with primary responsibility for maintaining international peace and security, it is not surprising that many discussions of UN reform have focused on the Security Council.

The founders of the UN deliberately established a universal General Assembly and a restricted Security Council that required unanimity among the great powers. Granting permanent seats and the right to a veto to the great powers of the time, the United States, the Soviet Union (now Russia), France, the United Kingdom, and China, was an essential feature of the deal.

The composition and decision-making procedures of the Security Council were increasingly challenged as membership of the United Nations grew, particularly after decolonization. Yet the only significant reform of the Security Council occurred in 1965, when the Council was enlarged from 11 to 15 members and the required majority from seven to nine votes. Nonetheless, the veto power of the permanent five (P–5) members was left intact.

The Security Council does not reflect today's distribution of military or economic power, and does not reflect a geographic balance. Germany and Japan have made strong cases for permanent membership. Developing countries have demanded more representation on the Security Council, with countries such as South Africa, India, Egypt, Brazil, and Nigeria making particular claims. However, it has proved to be impossible to reach agreement on new permanent members. Should the European Union be represented instead of Great Britain, France, and Germany individually? How would Pakistan feel about India's candidacy? How would South Africa feel about a Nigerian seat? What about representation by an Islamic country? These issues are not easy to resolve. Likewise, it is very unlikely that the P–5 countries will relinquish their veto.

Nonetheless, while large-scale reform has proved impossible, there have been changes in Security Council working procedures that have made it more transparent and accountable.

The Council also makes recommendations to the General Assembly on the appointment of a new Secretary-General and on the admission of new members to the UN.

The General Assembly

The recognition of power politics through veto power in the Security Council can be contrasted with the universalist principles underlying the other organs of the United Nations. All UN member states are represented in the General Assembly—a 'parliament of nations'—which meets to consider the world's most pressing problems. Each member state has one vote. A two-thirds majority in the General Assembly is required for decisions on key issues such as international peace and security, the admission of new members, and the UN budget. A simple majority is required for other matters. However, the decisions reached by the General Assembly only have the status of recommendations, rather than binding decisions. One of the few exceptions is the General Assembly's Fifth Committee, which makes decisions on the budget that are binding on members.

The General Assembly can consider any matter within the scope of the UN Charter. There were 156 items on the agenda of the sixty-first session of the General Assembly (2006–7), including topics such as globalization, the role of diamonds in fuelling conflict, international **cooperation** in the peaceful uses of outer space, peacekeeping operations, sustainable development, and international migration. Since General Assembly resolutions are non-binding, they cannot force action by any state, but its recommendations are important indications of world opinion and represent the moral authority of the community of nations.

The Secretariat

The Secretariat carries out the substantive and administrative work of the United Nations as directed by the General Assembly, the Security Council, and the other organs. It is led by the Secretary-General, who provides overall administrative guidance. In December 2006, Ban Ki-Moon from South Korea was sworn in as the eighth Secretary-General. The Secretariat consists of departments and offices with a total staff of 8,900 under the regular budget, and a nearly equal number under special funding.

On the recommendation of the other bodies, the Secretariat also carries out a number of research functions and some quasi-management functions. Yet the role of the Secretariat remains primarily bureaucratic and it lacks the political power and the right of initiative of, for instance, the Commission of the European Union. The one exception to this is the power of the Secretary-General under Article 99 of the Charter, to bring situations that are likely to lead to a breakdown of

international peace and security to the attention of the Security Council. This Article, which may appear innocuous at first, was the legal basis for the remarkable expansion of the diplomatic role of the Secretary-General, compared with its League predecessor. Due to this, the Secretary-General is empowered to become involved in a large range of areas that can be loosely interpreted as threats to peace, including economic and social problems, and humanitarian crises.

The Economic and Social Council

The Economic and Social Council (ECOSOC), under the overall authority of the General Assembly, is intended to coordinate the economic and social work of the United Nations and the UN family of organizations. It also consults with **non-governmental organizations** (NGOs), thereby maintaining a vital link between the United Nations and **civil society**. ECOSOC's subsidiary bodies include: Functional Commissions, such as the Commission on the Status of Women; Regional Commissions, such as the Economic Commission for Africa; and other bodies (see Fig. 18.1).

Along with the Secretariat and the General Assembly, ECOSOC is responsible for overseeing the activities of a large number of other institutions known as the United Nations system. This includes the Specialized Agencies and the Programmes and Funds (see Fig. 18.1). The Specialized Agencies, such as the World Health Organization (WHO) and the International Labour Organization (ILO), have their own constitutions, regularly assessed budgets, executive heads, and assemblies of state representatives. They are self-contained constitutionally, financially, and politically, and not subject to the management of the central system.

The Programmes and Funds are much closer to the central system in the sense that their management arrangements are subject to direct General Assembly supervision, can be modified by Assembly resolution, and are largely funded on a voluntary basis. Since the establishment of the United Nations in 1945, a number of new issues have come on to the international agenda, such as the rights and interests of women, climate change, resource depletion, population growth, **terrorism**, and the spread of HIV/AIDS. Frequently, those issues led to a new organization in the Programmes and Funds. Examples of Programmes and Funds include the United Nations Development Programme (UNDP), and the United Nations Children's Fund (UNICEF).

Whereas the League of Nations attributed responsibility for economic and social questions to the League Assembly, the Charter of the United Nations established ECOSOC to oversee economic and social institutions. This change was a consequence of thinking in more **functionalist** terms. Organizations were set up to deal with specific economic and social problems. However, ECOSOC was not given the necessary management powers. It can only issue recommendations and receive reports from the Specialized Agencies. In consequence, the UN's economic and social organizations have continuously searched for better ways of achieving effective management (see discussion of the reform process below).

The Trusteeship Council

When the United Nations was created, the Trusteeship Council was established to provide international supervision for 11 Trust Territories administered by seven member states and to ensure that adequate steps were taken to prepare the territories for self-government or independence. By 1994, all Trust Territories had attained self-government or independence, either as separate states or by joining neighbouring independent countries. The last to do so was the Trust **Territory** of the Pacific Islands, Palau, which had been previously administered by the United States. Its work completed, the Trusteeship Council now consists of the five permanent members of the Security Council. It has amended its **rules** of procedure to allow it to meet when necessary.

The International Court of Justice

The International Court of Justice is the main judicial organ of the UN. Consisting of 15 judges elected jointly by the General Assembly and the Security Council, the Court decides disputes between countries. Participation by states in a proceeding is voluntary, but if a state agrees to participate, it is obligated to comply with the Court's decision. The Court also provides advisory opinions to other UN organs and Specialized Agencies upon request.

Key Points

- The United Nations was established to preserve peace between states after the Second World War.
- In a number of ways, the institutions of the United Nations reflected lessons learned from its predecessor, the League of Nations.
- The institutions and mechanisms of the United Nations reflect both the demands of great power politics (i.e. Security Council veto) and

universalism. They also reflect demands to address the needs and interests of people, as well as the needs and interest of states. The tensions between these various demands are a key feature of UN development.

The United Nations and the maintenance of international peace and security

The performance of the United Nations in questions of peace and security has been shaped by the global political context. Clearly, there have been changes in international society since the UN was founded in 1945 that have had an impact on the UN system. The **cold war** between the United States and the Soviet Union hampered the functioning of the UN Security Council, since the veto could be used whenever the major interests of the United States or Soviet Union were threatened. From 1945 to 1990, 193 substantive vetoes were invoked in the Security Council, compared to only 19 substantive vetoes from 1990 to 2007. Furthermore, while the UN Charter provided for a standing army to be set up by agreement between the Security Council and consenting states, the East–West cold war rivalry made this impossible to implement. The end result was that the UN Security Council could not function in the way in which the UN founders had expected.

Since member states could not agree upon the arrangements laid out in Chapter VII of the Charter, especially with regard to setting up a UN army, there followed a series of improvizations to address matters of peace and security. First, a procedure was established under which the Security Council agreed to a mandate for an agent to act on its behalf. This occurred in the Korean conflict in 1950, and the Gulf War in 1990, when action was undertaken principally by the United States and its allies.

Second, there have been many instances of classical peacekeeping. No reference to peacekeeping exists in the UN Charter, but classical peacekeeping mandates and mechanisms are based on Chapter VI of the UN Charter. Classical peacekeeping involves the establishment of a

UN force under UN command to be placed between the parties to a dispute after a ceasefire. Such a force only uses its weapons in self-defence, is established with the consent of the host state, and does not include forces from the major powers. This mechanism was first used in 1956, when a UN force was sent to Egypt to facilitate the exodus of the British and French forces from the Suez canal area, and then to stand between Egyptian and Israeli forces. Since the Suez crisis, there have been a number of classical peacekeeping missions, for instance, monitoring the Green Line in Cyprus, and in the Golan Heights.

Third, there has been a new kind of peacekeeping, sometimes called multidimensional peacekeeping or **peace enforcement**, which emerged after the end of the cold war. These missions are more likely to use force to achieve humanitarian ends. The new peacekeeping mandates are sometimes based on Chapter VII of the UN Charter. Such forces have been used when order has collapsed within states, and therefore address civil wars as well as international conflict. A key problem has been that the peacekeepers have found it increasingly difficult to maintain a neutral position and have been targeted by belligerents. Examples include the intervention in Somalia in the early 1990s and intervention in the former Yugoslavia in the mid-1990s.

UN peacekeeping went through a rapid expansion in the early 1990s. In 1994, UN peacekeeping operations involved nearly 80,000 military personnel around the world, seven times the figure for 1990 (Pugh 2001: 115). In early 2007, the total number of peacekeeping personnel (military and police) in the UN's 15 ongoing peacekeeping operations was just over 82,000.

Increased attention to conditions within states

The new peacekeeping was the product of a greater preparedness to intervene within states. This challenged the traditional belief that diplomats should ignore the internal affairs of states in order to preserve international stability. An increasing number of people believed that the international community, working through the UN, should address individual political and civil rights, as well as the right to basic provisions like food, water, health care, and accommodation. Under this view, violations of individuals' rights were a major cause of disturbances in relations between states: a lack of internal justice risked international disorder. The UN reinforced this new perception that pursuing justice for individuals, or ensuring **human security**, was an aspect of **national interest**.

In some states, contributions to activities such as peacekeeping were defended in terms of national interest. Indeed, states like Canada could justify their contributions to peacekeeping as a 'moral' course of action, but it was also in their national interest since Canada gained status in the international community through such contributions. The Japanese also responded to moral pressure founded in national interest when they contributed substantially to defraying the cost of British involvement in the 1990–1 Gulf War. This act can be explained in terms of the synthesis of morality and interest. For some states, reputation in the United Nations had become an important national good.

These actions reflected an increasing concern with questions of justice for individuals and conditions within states. Yet in the past, the United Nations had helped promote the traditional view of the primacy of **international order** between states over justice for individuals, so the new focus on individual rights was a significant change. What accounts for this change?

First, the international environment had changed. The cold war stand-off between the East and the West had meant that member states did not want to question the conditions of the sovereignty of states. Jean Kirkpatrick's (1979) notorious essay, which recommended tolerating abhorrent dictatorships in Latin America in order to fight communism, was a reasonable report of the situation at that time: unsavoury right-wing **regimes** in Latin America were tolerated because they were anti-Soviet, and interfering in the other's sphere risked escalation of conflict (Forsythe 1988: 259–60).

Second, the process of decolonization had privileged statehood over justice. The UN reflected the claims of colonies to become states, and had elevated the right to statehood above any tests of viability, such as the existence of a nation, adequate economic performance, defensibility, or a prospect for achieving justice for citizens. This unconditional right to independence was enunciated in the General Assembly Declaration on the Granting of Independence to Colonial Countries and Peoples in 1960. There emerged a convention that the claims of elites in the putative states could be a sufficient indication of popular enthusiasm, even when the elites were crooks and the claims misleading.

Charles Beitz was one of the first to question this when he concluded that statehood should not be unconditional: attention had to be given to the situation of individuals after independence (Beitz 1979). Michael Waltzer and Terry Nardin produced arguments leading to similar conclusions: states were conditional entities in that their right to exist should be dependent on a criterion of performance with regard to the interests of their citizens (Walzer

---

Box 18.3 An agenda for peace

In the early 1990s after the end of the cold war, the UN agenda for peace and security expanded quickly. Then Secretary-General Boutros Boutros-Ghali outlined the more ambitious role for the UN in his seminal report, *An Agenda for Peace* (1992). The report described interconnected roles for the UN to maintain peace and security in the post-cold war context. These included:

- **Preventive diplomacy:** involving confidence-building measures, fact-finding, and preventive deployment of UN authorized forces.
- **Peacemaking:** designed to bring hostile parties to agreement, essentially through peaceful means. However, when all peaceful means have failed, **peace enforcement** authorized under Chapter VII of the Charter may be necessary. Peace enforcement may occur without the consent of the parties.
- **Peacekeeping:** the deployment of a UN presence in the field with the consent of all parties (this refers to classical peacekeeping).
- **Post-conflict peacebuilding:** to develop the social, political, and economic infrastructure to prevent further violence and to consolidate peace.

Box 18.4 The UN Peacebuilding Commission

The UN Peacebuilding Commission was established in December 2005 as an advisory subsidiary body of the General Assembly and the Security Council. It was first proposed by the Secretary-General's High Level Panel on Threats, Challenges and Change in December 2004, and again in the Secretary-General's Report *In Larger Freedom* in March 2005 (UN 2005). Existing mechanisms at the UN were thought to be insufficient in responding to the particular needs of countries emerging from conflict. Many countries, such as Liberia, Haiti, and Somalia in the 1990s, had signed peace agreements and hosted UN peacekeeping missions, but reverted to violent conflict. The Peacebuilding Commission aims to provide targeted support to countries in the volatile post-conflict phase to prevent the recurrence of conflict. It will propose integrated strategies and priorities for post-conflict recovery, in order to improve coordination among the myriad of actors involved in post-conflict activities. The establishment of the Peacebuilding Commission is indicative of a growing trend at the UN to coordinate security and development programming.

The organizational committee of the Peacebuilding Commission is made up of 31 member states, and the first session was held in June 2006. The Peacebuilding Support Fund, with a target of $250 million, is designed to support the activities of the Commission. There are also country-specific meetings to look at the post-conflict strategies, priorities, and programming for specific countries. The first two countries considered by the Peacebuilding Commission are Sierra Leone and Burundi.

1977; Nardin 1983). Such writings helped alter the moral content of **diplomacy**.

The new relationship between **order** and **justice** was, therefore, a product of particular circumstances. After the cold war, it was felt that threats to international peace and security did not only emanate from aggression between states. Rather, global peace was also threatened by civil conflict (including refugee flows and regional instability), humanitarian emergencies, violations of global standards of human rights, and other conditions such as **poverty** and inequality. In 1992, then Secretary-General Boutros Boutros-Ghali outlined a new ambitious UN agenda for peace and security in a report called *An Agenda for Peace* (see Box 18.3). More recently, other types of non-state-based threat, such as terrorism and the proliferation of small arms and **weapons of mass destruction**, have an increasingly prominent place on the UN security agenda. Partly due to the terrorist attacks in the USA in 2001 as well as the impasse reached in the UN Security Council over Iraq in 2003, then Secretary-General Kofi Annan named a high-level panel to examine the major threats and challenges to global peace. The 2004 final report emphasized the interconnected nature of security threats, and presented development, security, and human rights as mutually reinforcing. Many of the report's recommendations were not implemented, but some were, notably the establishment of a new UN Peacebuilding Commission (see Box 18.4).

Key Points

- The cold war and the decolonization process had discouraged more active involvement by the United Nations within states.
- After the cold war, it became more difficult for states and diplomats to accept that what happened within states was of no concern to outsiders.
- It became more common for governments to see active membership in the United Nations as serving their national interest as well as being morally right.
- By the mid-1990s the UN had become involved in maintaining international peace and security by resisting aggression between states, by attempting to resolve disputes within states (civil wars), and by focusing on conditions within states, including economic, social, and political conditions.

The United Nations and intervention within states

As issues of peace and **security** were increasingly understood to include **human security** and justice, the UN was expected to take on a stronger role in maintaining standards for individuals within states. A difficulty with carrying out the new tasks was that it seemed to run against the doctrine of non-intervention. **Intervention** was traditionally defined as a deliberate incursion into a state without its consent by some outside agency, in

order to change the functioning, policies, and goals of its government and achieve effects that favour the intervening agency (Vincent 1974) (see Ch. 30).

At the founding of the UN, **sovereignty** was regarded as central to the system of states. States were equal members of international society, and were equal with regard to **international law**. Sovereignty also implied that states recognized no higher authority than themselves, and that there was no superior jurisdiction. The governments of states had exclusive jurisdiction within their own frontiers, a principle which was enshrined in Article 2(7) of the United Nations Charter. Intervention in the traditional sense was in opposition to the principles of international society, and it could only be tolerated as an exception to the rule.

In earlier periods, however, states had intervened in each other's business and thought that they had a right to do so. The United States refused to accept any curtailment of their right to intervene in the internal affairs of other states in their hemisphere until 1933, when they conceded the point at the seventh International Conference of American States. The US position was very similar to the **Brezhnev doctrine** of the 1970s, which held that the Soviet Union had the right to intervene in the member states of the socialist commonwealth to protect the principles of socialism.

Much earlier, the British had insisted on the abolition of slavery in their relations with other states. They stopped ships on the high seas, and imposed the abolition of slavery as a condition in treaties (Bethell 1970). There were also occasions when states tried to bind other states to respect certain principles in their internal affairs. A number of states in Eastern **Europe**, such as Hungary and Bulgaria, were bound to respect the rights of minorities within their frontiers based on agreements made at the Berlin Conference of 1878 by the great powers. In practice, then, intervention was a common feature of international politics, sometimes for good cause.

By the 1990s, some people believed that there should be a return to this earlier period where intervention was justified, but it was felt that a wider range of instruments should be used to protect generally accepted standards. They insisted on a key role for the United Nations in granting a licence to intervene. It was pointed out that the UN Charter did not assert merely the rights of states, but also the rights of peoples: statehood could be interpreted as being conditional upon respect for such rights. There was

ample evidence in the UN Charter to justify the view that extreme transgressions of human rights could be a justification for intervention by the international community.

The major pronouncements of the UN General Assembly on humanitarian assistance referred to the primary responsibility of states for dealing with complex crises within their frontiers. A 1991 General Assembly resolution implied some relaxation of this principle when it held that 'The sovereignty, territorial integrity and national unity of States must be fully respected in accordance with the Charter of the United Nations. In this context, humanitarian assistance should be provided with the consent of the affected country and in principle on the basis of an appeal by the affected country' (A/RES/46/182). The use of the phrase 'in principle', and the term 'should', implied that there could be occasions where intervention was necessary even when consent in the target state was not possible. In the Outcome Document of the 2005 World Summit, the General Assembly said that if national authorities are 'manifestly failing to protect their populations from genocide, war crimes, ethnic cleansing and crimes against humanity' and if peaceful means are inadequate, the international community could take collective action through the UN Security Council according to Chapter VII of the Charter (A/RES/60/1, para. 138 and 139). This document echoes recommendations from the *Responsibility to Protect*, the 2001 final report of the International Commission on Intervention and State Sovereignty (see Ch.30).

Yet the number of occasions where a UN resolution justified intervention due to gross infringements of the rights of individuals has remained limited. The justification of intervention in Kosovo represented a break from the past in that it included a clear humanitarian element. Kosovo was arguably the first occasion in which international forces were used in defiance of a sovereign state in order to protect humanitarian standards. NATO launched the air campaign in March 1999 in Kosovo against the Republic of Yugoslavia without a mandate from the Security Council, since Russia had declared that it would veto such action. Nonetheless, NATO states noted that by intervening to stop ethnic cleansing and crimes against humanity in Kosovo they were acting in accordance with the principles of the UN Charter.

The Iraq War in 2003 was questionably another case, although the legality of intervention under existing Security Council resolutions is contested, especially in

Case Study The 2003 intervention in Iraq

In March 2003, a US-led coalition launched a highly controversial war in Iraq, which removed Saddam Hussein from power. The justification for war stressed Iraq's possession of weapons of mass destruction, in defiance of earlier UN resolutions. Unlike in Kosovo, the gross violation of human rights was not given as a main justification for the invasion until later. Yet the failure to find weapons of mass destruction in Iraq as well as the ongoing civil war, have fuelled the claims of critics that the war was unjustified.

There was no agreement over whether the UN Security Council authorized military action in Iraq. American and British diplomats pointed to UN Security Council Resolution 687 of 1991, which required the destruction of Iraqi weapons of mass destruction under UN supervision, and UN Security Council Resolution 1441 of 2002 which threatened 'serious consequences' if this were not done. Yet efforts to reach a Security Council resolution in the winter of 2003 that would clearly authorize the use of force against Iraq were unsuccessful. France and Russia threatened to veto a second Security Council resolution authorizing force.

The credibility of the UN was damaged by the failure to agree on a second Security Council resolution, and by the decision of the US and British administrations, along with a small number of allies, to use force against Iraq without clear UN authorization. There are fears of an increased tendency for the USA to act without UN authorization. The Bush administration's National Security Strategy of September 2002 states that '[W]e will be prepared to act apart when our interests and unique responsibilities require' (NSS 2002: 31).

Nonetheless, the aftermath of the invasion and the continued difficulties in establishing security in Iraq highlight the need for international cooperation. The UN enhances the legitimacy of military action, and can also help share in global risks, burdens, and strategies for rebuilding.

view of the failure to obtain a second UN Security Council resolution to give an explicit mandate for the action (see Case Study). The US action against Afghanistan in 2001 is an exceptional case in which the UN Security Council acknowledged the right of a state which had been attacked—referring to the events of **11 September 2001** in the United States—to respond in its own defence.

Arguably, earlier instances of intervention did not explicitly breach sovereignty. The 1991 Security Council resolution sanctioning intervention in Iraq (S/Res/688) at the end of the Gulf War did not breach Iraqi sovereignty in so far as its implementation depended on Saddam Hussein's consent. The 1992 Security Council resolution (S/Res/733) that first sanctioned UN involvement in Somalia was based on a request by Somalia. A later resolution for Somalia (S/Res/794) authorizing the United States to intervene did not mention the consent of Somali authorities, but by that time a central Somali government did not exist.

The difficulty in relaxing the principle of non-intervention should not be underestimated. For instance, the UN has been reluctant to send peacekeepers to Darfur without the consent of the Sudanese government. Some fear a slippery slope whereby a relaxation of the non-intervention principle by the UN will lead to military action by individual states without UN approval. It could be argued that the action against Iraq in 2003 illustrates the danger (see Case Study). There are significant numbers of non-UN actors, including regional organizations, involved in peace operations, and several countries are suspicious of what appears to be the granting of a licence to intervene in their affairs.

In summary, an increasing readiness by the UN to intervene within states in order to promote internal justice for individuals would indicate a movement towards **global governance** and away from unconditional sovereignty. There have been some signs of movement in this direction, but principles of state sovereignty and non-intervention remain important. There is no clear consensus on these points. There is still some support for the view that Article 2(7) of the UN Charter should be interpreted strictly: that there can be no intervention within a state without the express consent of the government of that state. Others believe that intervention within a country to promote human rights is only justifiable on the basis of a threat to international peace and security. Evidence

Box 18.5 Selected documents related to the changing role of the United Nations system

Development of the economic and social organizations

A/32/197, Dec. 1977. The first major General Assembly resolution on reform of the economic and social organizations.

A/48/162, Dec. 1993. A major step towards reform of the economic and social organization of the United Nations, especially ECOSOC.

Development of the UN's role in maintaining international peace and security

SC Res. 678, Nov. 1990, sanctioned the use of force against Saddam Hussein.

SC Res. 816, Apr. 1993, enforced the no-fly zone over Bosnia in that it permitted NATO war planes to intercept Bosnian Serb planes in the zones.

SC Res. 1160, 1199, and 1203 contained arguments relevant to the action on Kosovo. SC Res. 1244 contained the agreement at the end of the bombing.

Development of humanitarian action through the UN

SC Res. 688, Apr. 1991, sanctioned intervention at the end of the Gulf War to protect the Kurds in northern Iraq.

SC Res. 733, Jan. 1992, sanctioned UN involvement in Somalia. **A/46/182, Apr. 1992,** is the major document on the development of the machinery for humanitarian assistance.

SC Res. 794, Dec. 1992, sanctioned American intervention in Somalia under Chapter VII of the UN Charter. The government of Somalia had ceased to exist in the eyes of the member states of the Security Council.

SC Res. 1441, Nov. 2002, resolution on Iraq which threatened serious consequences if Saddam Hussein failed to reveal his weapons of mass destruction to the team of UN inspectors.

---

of a threat to international peace and security could be the appearance of significant numbers of refugees, or the judgement that other states might intervene militarily. Some Liberals argue that this condition is flexible enough to justify intervention to defend human rights whenever possible.

Overall, then, the UN's record on the maintenance of international peace and security has been mixed. On the one hand, there has been a stronger assertion of the responsibility of international society, represented by the United Nations, for gross offences against populations. Nonetheless, the practice has been patchy. Intimations of a new **world order** in the aftermath of the Gulf War in 1991 quickly gave way to despondency with what were

seen as failures in Somalia, Rwanda, other parts of Africa, and the former Yugoslavia, and increasing disagreement about the proper role of the UN in Kosovo and Iraq. Compared to the enthusiasm about the potential for the UN in the early 1990s, the debates and disagreements at the time of the war in Iraq in 2003 were striking.

Key Points

- New justifications for intervention in states were being considered by the 1990s.
- Most operations of the United Nations were justified in the traditional way: as a response to a threat to international peace and security.

The United Nations and economic and social questions

As described above, there has been an increased tendency to view threats to peace and security in terms of traditional threats such as aggression between states, but also civil conflict within states, threats emanating from non-state actors, and threats relating to economic and social conditions within states. This view believes that conditions within states, including human rights, justice, development, and equality have a bearing on global peace. The more integrated global context has meant that economic and social problems in one part of the world may impact other areas. Furthermore, promoting social

and economic development is an important UN goal in itself. The preamble of the UN Charter talks of promoting 'social progress and better standards of life in larger freedom', and the need to 'employ international machinery for the promotion of the economic and social advancement of all peoples'.

The number of institutions within the UN system that address economic and social issues has significantly increased since the founding of the UN. Nonetheless, the main contributor states have been giving less and less to economic and social institutions. By the mid-1990s, there

Box 18.6 The UN Conference on Environment and Development: the Earth Summit

The UN Conference on Environment and Development (Earth Summit) held in 1992 in **Rio de Janeiro** was unprecedented for a UN conference in both its size and its scope of concerns. Representatives of 172 countries, as well as 2,400 NGOs, discussed ways to help reach the goal of sustainable development.

The Rio Earth Summit was held twenty years after the first UN Conference on the Human Environment in Stockholm. That 1972 Conference had stimulated the creation of national environmental ministries around the world, and established the United Nations Environment Programme (UNEP).

The central concern of the Rio Earth Summit was the need for broad-based, environmentally sustainable development. As a result of the Summit, 108 governments adopted three major agreements concerned with changing the traditional approach to development. These agreements included: the Rio Declaration on Environment and Development (a series of principles defining the rights and responsi-

bilities of states), the Statement of Forest Principles, and **Agenda 21** (a comprehensive programme of action to attain sustainable development on a global scale). In addition, the UN Framework Convention on Climate Change and the Convention on Biological Diversity were signed by many governments.

The **UN Commission on Sustainable Development** was formed after the 1992 Earth Summit to ensure follow-up and to report on the implementation of Earth Summit agreements at the local, national, regional, and international levels. A five-year review of Earth Summit progress took place in New York in 1997 and a ten-year review at the **World Summit on Sustainable Development** held in Johannesburg in 2002. There were significant divisions at the Johannesburg Summit. The conference was thought to be too large and the outcome was generally seen as disappointing. Nonetheless, by 2002 it was clear that environmental questions were prominent issues on the UN agenda.

was a crippling financial crisis in the regular Assessed Budget for the UN, and in the budget for peacekeeping operations. This was only mitigated when the United States agreed, under certain conditions, to repay what it owed the UN and when it returned to full funding in December 2002.

Paradoxically, despite the shortage of funds, the UN has acquired skills and resources with regard to key economic and social problems. During the 1990s, a number of new issues were brought on to the international agenda. Several **Global Conferences** were convened to discuss pressing problems, such as environmental issues at a conference in Rio de Janeiro (1992), human rights at a conference in Vienna (1993), population questions at a conference in Cairo (1994), and women's issues at a conference in Beijing (1995). These conferences each spawned a Commission to carry forward the programme. Such conferences represented a growing sense of **interdependence** and the **globalization** of human concerns. They also stimulated a renewed interest in translating broad socioeconomic concerns into more specific manageable programmes (see Box 18.6). Follow-up conferences were held ten years later to take stock of progress.

In 2000, the UN convened a Millennium Summit, where heads of state committed themselves to a series of measurable goals and targets, known as the Millennium Development Goals (MDGs). These goals, to be achieved by 2015, include reducing by half the number of people living on less than a dollar a day, achieving universal primary education, and reversing the spread of HIV/AIDS and malaria (A/55/L.2). Since 2000, the UN has been integrating the MDGs into all aspects of its work at the country level, but progress on reaching the MDGs has been very uneven.

Key Points

- The number of institutions within the UN system that address economic and social issues has significantly increased. Several Programmes and Funds were created in response to Global Conferences.
- Despite a shortage of funds and coordination problems, the UN has done important work in key economic and social areas.
- The Millennium Development Goals have focused attention on measurable socioeconomic targets and have further integrated the work of the UN at the country level, but progress towards reaching the goals has been uneven.

The reform process in the economic and social arrangements of the United Nations

In the mid- to late 1990s, alongside growing UN involvement in development issues, the UN economic and social arrangements underwent reform at two levels: first, reforms concerned with operations in the country (field) level; and second, reforms at the general or headquarters level.

Country level

The continuing complaints of NGOs about poor UN performance in the field served as a powerful stimulus for reform. A key feature of the reforms at the country (field) level was the adoption of Country Strategy Notes. These were statements about the overall development process tailored to the specific needs of individual countries. They were written on the basis of discussions between the Specialized Agencies, Programmes and Funds, donors, and the host country, and described the plans of the various institutions and donors in a particular country. The merit of the Country Strategy Notes is that they clearly set out targets, roles, and priorities.

Another reform at the country level was the strengthening of the Resident Coordinator, usually an employee of the United Nations Development Programme (UNDP). He or she became the responsible officer at the country level, and was provided with more training to fulfil this role. Field-level officers were also given enhanced authority, so that they could make decisions about the redeployment of funds within a programme without referring to headquarters. There was also an effort to introduce improved communication facilities and information-sharing. The activities of the various UN organizations were brought together in single locations or 'UN houses', which facilitated inter-agency communication and collegiality. The new country-level approach was called an Integrated Programmes approach. The adoption of the Millennium Development Goals framework has also helped country field staff achieve a more coherent approach to development. This can be contrasted to earlier arrangements whereby the various agencies would work separately on distinct projects, often in ignorance of each other's presence in the same country.

Headquarters level

If the UN role in economic and social affairs at the country level was to be effective, reform was also required at the headquarters level. The United Nations family of economic and social organizations has always been a polyc... Historically, there was no organization or ...... the system that was capable of managing the ..... of economic and social activities under the UN umbrella. Reform efforts in the 1990s focused on the reorganization and rationalization of the Economic and Social Council (ECOSOC).

In the UN Charter, the powers given to the General Assembly and ECOSOC were modest. ECOSOC could only issue recommendations and receive reports. By contrast, UN reform in the mid- to late 1990s allowed ECOSOC to become more assertive and to take a leading role in the coordination of the UN system. ECOSOC was to ensure that General Assembly policies were appropriately implemented on a system-wide basis. ECOSOC was given the power to take final decisions on the activities of its subsidiary bodies and on other matters relating to system-wide coordination in economic, social, and related fields (A/50/227, para. 37).

One of ECOSOC's responsibilities was to review common themes in the work of the nine Functional Commissions, such as the Commission on Narcotic Drugs, the Commission on Sustainable Development, and the Commission on the Status of Women (see Fig. 18.1). The reform effort aimed to eliminate duplication and overlap in the work of the Functional Commissions. ECOSOC would integrate the work of its Functional Commissions and provide input to the General Assembly, which was responsible for establishing the broader economic and social policy framework. The Boards of the

Programmes and Funds were also reformed to enhance their day-to-day management.

Overall, economic and social reorganization meant that the two poles of the system were better coordinated: the pole where intentions are defined through global conferences and agendas, and the pole where programmes are implemented. Programmes at the field level were better integrated and field officers were given enhanced discretion. The reform of ECOSOC sharpened its capacity to shape broad agreements into cross-sectoral programmes with well-defined objectives. At the same time, ECOSOC acquired greater capacity to act as a conduit through which the results of field-level monitoring could be conveyed upwards to the Functional Commissions. These new processes had the effect of strengthening the **norms** of a multilateral system.

Key Points

- In the mid- to late 1990s under the leadership of then Secretary-General Kofi Annan, the UN embarked on an overarching reform effort.
- Reform of the economic and social arrangements of the UN aimed at improving coordination, eliminating duplication, and clarifying spheres of responsibility.
- These efforts strengthened the norms of the multilateral system.

Conclusion

Changes in the role of the UN reflect the changes in perceptions of international society and the nature of sovereign states. Over the past sixty years, the rules governing the **international system** have become increasingly numerous and specific, covering a large range of the activities of relations between states. Concerns have expanded to include not only the protection of the rights of states, but also the rights of individuals. Yet obtaining the agreement of governments to principles of individual rights is only a first step in building a more orderly and just world. It is also necessary to have consistent and reliable instruments to trigger action when standards are breached.

The United Nations Security Council is the instrument that comes closest to meeting these aims. Despite the flaws of the Security Council, it is striking that even the largest states prefer to get authorization from the United Nations Security Council for any action they propose. In Kosovo, the states that participated in the NATO intervention wanted to demonstrate that they were acting according to the UN Charter and the relevant Security Council resolutions. In Iraq, the US and UK governments invested considerable diplomatic energy in getting a second Security Council resolution in support of military action. The effort failed, but nevertheless it was attempted.

Participation in the United Nations gives governments status in the international system. Membership and success in the UN has come to be regarded as legitimizing **state autonomy.** Hence holding office, taking the initiative, providing personnel, and policing norms are seen to have value because they add to the self-esteem as well as to power of the state. The UN has become the essential club for states.

The capacity of the UN in its economic and social work, its development work, and its management of peacekeeping and post-conflict reconstruction has expanded since the 1990s. Nonetheless, the predominance of United States military power, the possibility that the USA will act again without clear UN authorization, the heightened concern over terrorism and weapons of mass destruction, the inability to respond effectively to the crisis in Darfur, and the pervasiveness of inequality and injustice across the world, signal that further changes and adaptations within the UN system will be necessary.

❓ Questions

1   How does the United Nations try to maintain international order?
2   Why have more states decided to support the work of the United Nations?
3   What are some of the barriers to UN Security Council reform?
4   Does increased UN activity undermine the sovereignty of states?
5   How far have traditional restraints with regard to intervention within states been relaxed?
6   How have definitions of threats to peace and security changed in the post-cold war period?
7   How has UN peacekeeping evolved?
8   Has reform of the economic and social arrangements of the UN been effective?
9   Why was there greater opposition to developing the international accountability of states during the cold war?
10   What lessons about the present role and future of the UN might be drawn from the experience of the war in Iraq?

⤵ Guide to further reading

Archer, C. (2001), *International Organisations*, 3rd edn (London: Routledge). A succinct survey of the range of international institutions and their main purposes.

Berdal, M., and Economides, S. (eds) (2007), *United Nations Interventionism, 1991–2004* (Cambridge: Cambridge University Press). Includes case studies of eight UN operations, and discusses the impact of the 'new interventionism' on international order.

Claude, I. L. Jr. (1971, 1984), *Swords into Plowshares: The Progress and Problems of International Organization*, 4th edn (New York: Random House). A classic text on the history of international institutions, particularly concerned with their role in war and peace. Useful for the history of the UN.

Dodds, F. (ed.) (1997), *The Way Forward: Beyond Agenda 21* (London: Earthscan). An account of the involvement of the UN system in the issues raised in the Functional Commissions, such as social development, the status of women, and environmental protection.

Karns, M., and Mingst, K. (2004), *International Organizations: The Politics and Processes of Global Governance* (Boulder, Col.: Lynne Rienner). A comprehensive overview of the main actors and processes of global governance.

Malone, D. (ed.) (2004), *The UN Security Council: From the Cold War to the 21st Century* (Boulder, Col.: Lynne Rienner). Discusses the history of the UN Security Council and major UN operations.

Roberts, A., and Kingsbury, B. (eds) (1993), *United Nations, Divided World: The UN's Roles in International Relations*, 2nd edn (Oxford: Clarendon Press). An important collection of readings by practitioners and academics.

Taylor, P., and Groom, A. J. R. (eds) (2000), *The United Nations at the Millennium* (London: Continuum). A detailed account of the institutions of the central UN system.

Thakur, R. (2006), *The United Nations, Peace and Security* (Cambridge: Cambridge University Press). Discusses the changing role of the UN peace operations.

Online Resource Centre

 Visit the Online Resource Centre that accompanies this book to access more learning resources on this chapter topic at www.oxfordtextbooks.co.uk/uk/orc/baylis_smith4e/

Chapter 19

Transnational actors and international organizations in global politics

PETER WILLETTS

- **Introduction** ···332
- **Problems with the state-centric approach**·······································332
- **Transnational companies as political actors**·································334
- **Non-legitimate groups and liberation movements as political actors** ·······················337
- **Non-governmental organizations as political actors**··················339
- **International organizations as structures of global politics**··········341
- **Conclusion: issues and policy systems in global politics** ·············342

Reader's Guide

The subject of International Relations originally covered simply the relations between states. Economic bodies and social groups, such as banks, industrial companies, students, environmentalists, and women's organizations, were given secondary status as non-state actors. This two-tier approach has been challenged, particularly by the effects of globalization. First, ambiguities in the meaning given to 'a state', and its mismatch with the contemporary world, result in it not being a useful concept. Greater clarity is obtained by analyzing inter-governmental and inter-society relations, with no presumption that one sector is more important than the other. Second, we can recognize governments are losing sovereignty when faced with the economic activities of transnational companies and the violent threat from criminals, terrorists, and guerrillas. Third, non-governmental organizations (NGOs) engage in such a web of global relations, including participation in diplomacy, that governments have lost their political independence. We conclude that events in any area of global policy-making have to be understood in terms of complex systems, containing governments, companies, and NGOs interacting in a variety of international organizations.

Introduction

In **diplomacy**, **international law**, journalism, and academic analysis, it is widely assumed that international relations consist of the relations between coherent units called **states**. This chapter will argue that better understanding of political change is obtained by analyzing the relations between governments and many other actors from each country. **Global politics** also includes companies and **non-governmental organizations** (NGOs). Thus the five main categories of political actors in the global system are:

- nearly 200 governments in the global system, including 192 members of the UN;
- 77,200 **transnational companies** (TNCs), such as Vodaphone, Ford, Shell, Microsoft, or Nestlé, with these parent companies having just over 773,000 foreign affiliates;
- more than 10,000 single-country non-governmental organizations, such as Population Concern (UK), or the Sierra Club (USA), which have significant transnational activities;
- 246 **intergovernmental organizations** (IGOs), such as the UN, **NATO**, the European Union, or the International Coffee Organization; and
- 7,300 international non-governmental organizations (INGOs), such as Amnesty International, the Baptist World Alliance or the International Chamber of Shipping, plus a similar number of less well-established international caucuses and **networks** of NGOs.

All these actors play a regular part in global politics and each government interacts with a diverse range of **non-state actors**. Sometimes guerrilla groups challenge the authority of particular governments. In addition, even though they are considered not to be legitimate participants in the system, terrorists and other criminal gangs have an impact, often minor, but sometimes in a major way. Very many more companies and NGOs only operate in a single country, but have the potential to expand into other countries.[1]

Nobody can deny the number of these organizations and the range of their activities. The controversial questions are whether the non-state world has significance in its own right and whether it makes any difference to the analysis of inter-state relations. It is possible to *define* international relations as covering the relations between states. This is known as the state-centric approach, or **Realism**. Then it is only a tautology (true by definition) to say that non-state actors are of secondary importance. A more open-ended approach, known as **Pluralism**, is based on the assumption that all types of actor can affect political outcomes. The very words, **non-state actors**, imply that states are dominant and other actors are secondary. An alternative phrase, **transnational actors**, has been coined by academics in order to assert forcefully that international relations are not limited to governments and other actors operate across country boundaries.

It is an unacceptable analytical bias to decide, before research starts, that only states have any **influence**. Until the evidence indicates otherwise, we must assume that governments also interact with NGOs, companies, and **international organizations**. This chapter will first consider how assumptions made about 'states' inhibit analysis of transnational actors and international organizations. Then the nature of the different types of actor will be outlined. Finally, the case will be argued for always considering the activities of a diverse range of political actors.

Problems with the state-centric approach

The great advantage of the state-centric approach is that the bewildering complexity of world politics is reduced to the relative simplicity of the interactions of less than 200 supposedly similar units. However, there are *four* major

problems that suggest the benefits of simplification have been gained at the cost of the picture being distorted and blurred.

Ambiguity between different meanings of a 'state'

Writers who refer to the **state** often fail to use the term consistently and lack intellectual rigour by merging three concepts. The state as a legal person is a highly abstract fiction. This is easily confused with the concrete concept of a **country**, with a distinct political system of people sharing common values. Then there is a very dissimilar concept of a state as the apparatus of **government**. Unfortunately, no standard method exists to handle the ambiguity. From now on, this chapter will use the word 'state' to indicate the abstract legal concept, while country and government will be used to analyze political behaviour.

Within traditional International Relations scholarship, **civil society** is understood to be *part of the state*, whereas for philosophers and sociologists, focusing on the state as government, civil society is *separate from the state*. Thus, in international law or when the state means the whole country, there is very little room to acknowledge the existence of distinct transnational actors. Alternatively, when the state means the government and does not encompass civil society, we can investigate both intergovernmental relations and the inter-society relations of transnational actors.

The lack of similarity between countries

The second problem is that giving all 'states' the same legal status implies they are all essentially the same type of unit, when in fact they are not remotely similar. Orthodox analysis does acknowledge differences in size between the **superpowers** and middle and small **powers**. Nevertheless this does not suggest that at the end of the **cold war** the United States economy was twice the size of the Soviet Union's economy, nor that at the start of this century the US economy was eight times China's, 64 times Saudi Arabia's, more than 1,400 times Ethiopia's, and over 100,000 times greater than Kiribati's. In terms of population, the divergences are even greater. The small island countries of the Caribbean and the Pacific with populations measured in tens of thousands are not comparable entities to ordinary small countries, let alone China or India: they are truly 'micro-states'. Alternatively, comparing the governments of the world reveals a diverse range of democracies, feudal regimes, ethnic oligarchies, economic oligarchies, populist regimes, theocracies, military dictatorships, and idiosyncratic combinations. The only thing that the countries have in common is the general recognition of their right to have their own government. They are legally equal and politically very different.

The consequence of admitting the differences in size is to make it obvious that the largest transnational actors are considerably larger than many of the countries. In 2004, the 50 largest transnational industrial companies, by sales, each had annual revenues greater than the GNP of 133 members of the United Nations. Using people as the measure, many NGOs, particularly trade unions, churches, and campaigning groups in the fields of human rights, women's rights, and the environment, have their membership measured in millions, whereas 42 of the 192 countries in the UN have populations of less than 1 million, of which twelve are less than 100,000.[2] There is also great variation in the complexity and diversity of the economies and the societies of different countries and hence the extent to which they are each involved in transnational relations.

State systems and international systems

Third, there is an underlying analytical inconsistency in supposing 'states' are located in an **anarchic international system**. Whether it means a legal entity, a country, or a government, the 'state' is seen as a coherent unit, acting with common purpose and existing as something more than the sum of its parts (the individual people). At the same time, most advocates of the state-centric approach deny the possibility of such collective entities existing at the global level. The phrase the **international system** is denied its full technical meaning of a collectivity in which the component elements (the individual 'states') lose some of their independence. No philosophical argument has been put forward to explain this inconsistency in the assumptions made about the different levels of analysis. By exaggerating the coherence of 'states' and downplaying the coherence of global politics, both

transnational relations and intergovernmental relations are underestimated.

The difference between state and nation

Fourth, there is a behavioural assumption that politics within 'states' is significantly different from politics between 'states'. This is based on the idea that people's loyalty to their **nation** is more intense than other loyalties. Clearly, it cannot be denied that **nationalism** and national **identity** invoke powerful emotions for most people, but various caveats must be made about their political relevance. Communal identities form a hierarchy from the local through the nation to wider groupings. Thus, both local communities and intergovernmental bodies, such as the European Community, can also make claims on a person's loyalty.

There has been a long-standing linguistic conjuring trick whereby national loyalty is made to appear as if it is focused on the **nation-state**. Both inter*national* relations and trans*national* relations cover relations across 'state' boundaries, although logically the words refer to relations between national groups, such as the Scots and the Welsh.

In the real world, only a few countries, such as Iceland, Poland, and Japan, can make a reasonable claim that their people are from a single nation and in all such cases there are significant numbers of the national group resident in other countries, often in the USA. Most countries are multinational and many national groups are present in several countries. Thus national loyalty is actually quite different from loyalty to a country.

Key Points

- The concept of the 'state' has three very different meanings: a legal person, a political community, and a government.
- The countries and governments around the world may be equal in law, but have few political similarities. Many governments control less resources than many transnational actors.
- It cannot be assumed that all country-based political systems are more coherent than global systems, particularly as national loyalties do not match country boundaries.
- By abandoning the language of 'states' and 'non-state' actors, we can admit the possibility of theorizing about many types of actors in global politics. By distinguishing government from society and nation from country, we can ask whether private groups, companies, and national minorities in each country engage in transnational relations

Transnational companies as political actors

All companies that import or export are engaging in transnational economic activities. If they lobby foreign governments about trade, they become transnational political actors. However, they are not known as **transnational companies** (TNCs) until they have branches or subsidiaries outside their home country. The first companies to expand in this way were in agriculture, mining, or oil, operating in the European **empires**. Now they occur in all economic sectors, while industrialized countries that never had empires and most developing countries have seen some of their companies expand transnationally. In 2004, among the 100 TNCs with the highest

levels of assets outside their home country, 53 were from eleven Western European countries, 25 from the USA, four with dual headquarters in Western countries, nine from Japan, three from Canada, one from Australia and one each from China, Malaya, Singapore, Hong Kong, and South Korea. Only developed countries, East and South-East Asia, a few Latin American countries, India, and South Africa host large TNCs. Nevertheless, there are now transnational companies based in as many as 138 countries—35 from developed countries and 103 from transition and developing countries, including 31 African countries.[3]

Box 19.1 Transnational corporations from developing countries

The classical image of a TNC is a large company from the USA that has expanded production and sales overseas, dominating a global market and exploiting cheap labour in developing countries. In contrast to this, in the twenty-first century, TNCs from developing countries have become increasingly important.

- More than one-quarter of all TNCs now have their headquarters in developing countries.
- The top 100 developing country TNCs are from 14 countries: China, Hong Kong, Taiwan, India, Malaysia, Singapore, Korea, the Philippines, Thailand, Brazil, Mexico, Venezuela, South Africa, and Egypt. However, the total foreign assets of all these companies in 2004 are less than those of one US company, General Electric, the world's biggest TNC.
- Most developing country TNCs are small, but some are becoming major players in particular industries, such as cars, electronics, steel, and container shipping. The Chinese TNC, Lenovo, now owns the IBM PC brand, while the Indian TNC, Tata, has taken over Corus,

the major European steel manufacturer.
- Developing country TNCs are more likely to invest in neighbouring countries, but they are increasingly investing in the developed world as well. They own more than 500 affiliates in the USA and a similar number in Britain.
- In the USA, opposition in Congress to developing country TNCs has been strong enough to block a Chinese take-over of the US oil company, UNOCAL, and to force Dubai Ports World to divest itself of six US ports.

Two examples illustrate this new world of successful developing country TNCs: Marcopolo, a Brazilian company, manufactures buses in several South American countries and sells them in more than 80 countries; and Hikma Pharmaceuticals, a Jordanian company, manufactures in two other Arab countries and in Portugal, having strong sales in West Asia and North Africa, along with recent expansion in Europe and the USA.

(Source: World Investment Report 2006 (UNCTAD 2006b))

Financial flows and loss of sovereignty

The consequences of the extensive transnationalization of major companies are profound. It is no longer possible to regard each country as having its own separate economy. Two of the most fundamental attributes of **sovereignty**—control over the currency and control over foreign trade—have been substantially diminished. The two factors combined mean governments have lost control of financial flows. In the case of the currency, the successive crises in the 1980s and the 1990s for the dollar, the pound, the French franc, and the yen established that even the governments with the greatest financial resources are helpless against the transnational banks and other speculators.

The effects of trade on finance are less obvious. When goods move physically across frontiers, it is usually seen as being trade between the relevant countries, but it may also be **intra-firm trade**. As the logic of intra-firm trade is quite different from inter-country trade, governments cannot have clear expectations of the effects of their financial and fiscal policies on TNCs. A company may respond to higher tax rates by changing its **transfer prices** to reduce its tax bill. Several other motives might induce a company to distort transfer prices, including evasion of controls on the cross-border movements of profits or capital.

Triangulation of trade and loss of sovereignty

Governments have great difficulty regulating international transactions. Even the US administration was unable to prevent its citizens visiting communist Cuba during the cold war. It may be possible to prevent the *direct* import or export of goods. However, there is no guaranteed method of preventing *indirect* trade from one country to another. This is known as **triangulation**. Only if a UN Security Council resolution obliges all the countries of the world to impose sanctions is there a reasonable prospect of a determined government preventing TNCs from evading sanctions. However, in such a situation, sovereignty over the relevant trade then lies with the Security Council and not with the individual governments.

Regulatory arbitrage and loss of sovereignty

It is difficult for governments to regulate the commercial activities of companies within their country, because companies may choose to engage in **regulatory arbitrage**. If a company objects to one government's policy, it may threaten to limit or close down its local production and increase production in another country. The government that imposes the least demanding health, safety, welfare, or environmental standards will offer

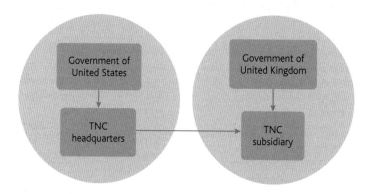

Figure 19.1 Who controls the United Kingdom subsidiary of a US TNC?

competitive advantages to less socially responsible companies. There is also a strong global trend towards the reduction of corporation taxes. It thus becomes difficult for any government to set high standards and maintain taxes. In the case of banking, the political dangers inherent in the risks of a bank collapsing through imprudent or criminal behaviour are so great that the major governments have set common capital standards, under the Basle Committee **rules**. Whatever control is achieved does not represent the successful exercise of sovereignty over companies: it is the partial surrender of sovereignty to an intergovernmental body.

Extraterritoriality and sovereignty

In addition, transnational companies generate clashes of sovereignty between different governments. Let us consider the example of a company that has its headquarters in the United States and a subsidiary company that it owns in the United Kingdom. Three lines of authority exist. The United States government can control the main company and the United Kingdom government can control the subsidiary. Each process would be the standard exercise of a government's sovereignty over its internal affairs. In addition, both governments would accept that the TNC can, within certain limits, control its own policies on purchasing, production, and sales. Under normal circumstances these three lines of authority can be exercised simultaneously and in harmony. However, when the US government decisions cover the global operations of the TNC, there is a clash of sovereignty. Does the subsidiary obey the UK government or the orders of the US government issued via its headquarters? This problem of **extraterritoriality** is inherent in the structure of all TNCs.

As a matter of routine policy implementation, clashes now have to be resolved between different decisions in different jurisdictions on competition policy, mergers and acquisitions, accounting procedures, and anti-corruption measures. Will US accounting standards apply to European companies because some of their operations are in the USA? Can the directors of parent TNCs be prosecuted for the payment of bribes by their overseas branches? The long-term trend is for such questions to be resolved by global standardization of domestic policy. For example, the **OECD** has developed a Convention on Combating Bribery of Foreign Public Officials in International Business Transactions.

From domestic deregulation to global re-regulation

For most companies most of the time, their interests will be in accord with the government's policy of increasing employment and promoting economic growth. Conflicts will arise over the regulation of markets to avoid the risks of **market failures** or externalization of social and environmental costs of production. Domestic deregulation and **globalization** of economic activity mean regulation is now occurring at the global level rather than within individual countries.. Three factors involving TNCs push

towards the globalization of politics. First, governments can only reassert control by acting collectively. Second, consumer pressures are leading to global codes of conduct being accepted by companies and implemented in **collaboration** with NGOs. A third push is for global companies to submit to social and environmental auditing.

These factors are coming together in the collaboration between governments, NGOs, and the UN Secretariat to recruit the major TNCs as voluntary partners in a Global Compact to implement ten principles of corporate social responsibility on human rights, labour standards, the environment, and anti-corruption.

Key Points

- The ability of TNCs to change transfer prices means that they can evade taxation or government controls on their international financial transactions.
- The ability of TNCs to use triangulation means individual governments cannot control their country's international trade.
- The ability of TNCs to move production from one country to another means individual governments are constrained in regulating and taxing companies.

- The structure of authority over TNCs generates the potential for intense conflict between governments, when the legal authority of one government has extraterritorial impact on the sovereignty of another government.
- In some areas of economic policy, governments have lost sovereignty and regulation now has to be exercised at the global level rather than by governments acting independently.

Non-legitimate groups and liberation movements as political actors

A variety of groups engage in violent and/or criminal behaviour on a transnational basis. A distinction can be made between activity that is considered criminal around the world, such as theft, fraud, personal violence, piracy, or drug trafficking, and activity that is claimed by those undertaking it to have legitimate political motives. In reality, the distinction may sometimes be blurred, for example when criminals claim political motives or political groups are responsible for acts such as terrorism, torture, or involving children in violence. For all governments, neither criminal activity nor political violence can be legitimate within their own jurisdiction and generally not in other countries.

Transnational criminals and their political impact

Politically, the most important criminal industries are illicit trading in arms and in drugs. As travel has increased, trafficking in people has become easier and has increased significantly in recent years. There is a new slave trade, mainly for sexual exploitation of young women. TNCs are most concerned to prevent trade in counterfeit goods and theft of intellectual property, particularly of music,

films, and computer software. The same four sovereignty problems arise with tackling criminals as with regulating TNCs. First, criminal financial flows can be massive and money-laundering threatens the integrity of banking and other financial institutions. Second, criminal trade has been so extensively diversified through triangulation that no government can confidently claim that their country is not a transit route for drugs or arms. Third, as with regulatory arbitrage by TNCs, police action may displace well-organized gangs to another country, rather than stop their activities. Fourth, illicit drugs and money-laundering involve questions of extraterritorial jurisdiction. However, in contrast to the regulation of TNCs, transnational police activities involve high levels of **cooperation**.

Terrorists, guerrillas, and national liberation movements

Political violence is most common when broadly-based nationalist movements or ethnic minorities reject the legitimacy of a government. These groups are often called **terrorists** to express disapproval, **guerrillas** by those who are more neutral, or **national liberation**

movements by their supporters. In the past, nationalists were usually able to obtain some external support. Now, because of widespread revulsion against political violence, national groups and ethnic minorities are subject to pressure to negotiate instead of fighting. Political violence is more likely to be legitimate when a group has widespread support; when political channels have been closed to them; when the target government is exceptionally oppressive; and when the violence is limited to 'military targets'. Groups that fail to match these four characteristics only obtain very limited transnational support. When Palestinian groups first used terrorist methods, the Palestine Liberation Organization (PLO) gained attention, but not support. When **terrorism** stopped in the mid-1970s, they achieved membership of the Arab League, along with observer status at the UN. However, suicide bombing, targeted at civilians, by some Palestinians during the second *intifada* greatly reduced the Palestinian Authority's legitimacy.

Since **11 September 2001**, the political balance has changed substantially. The scale of the destruction wrought by Al Qaeda organizing 19 hijackers simultaneously taking control of four passenger aircraft and using these as weapons against New York and Washington did much to delegitimize *all* groups who use violence for political purposes. Historically, terrorism has mainly been an instrument of internal conflict within a single society, but Al Qaeda suddenly presented the world with a new threat of a transnational **global network**. Within a few years they staged attacks in Kenya, Tanzania, Yemen, Saudi Arabia, the USA, Tunisia, Indonesia, Turkey, and Spain. Despite this, contemporary terrorism is not a single phenomenon. The Basque, Palestinian, Kashmiri, Tamil, and Chechnya disputes clearly have roots that are totally independent of each other and have little or no connection to Al Qaeda. There are different transnational processes for different conflicts generating terrorism. Even Al Qaeda itself is a disparate coalition of anti-American fundamentalist groups rather than a coherent disciplined organization.

Extensive political violence used by governments against their citizens was commonplace and immune from diplomatic criticism, as recently as the 1970s. Because of a widespread desire to end the impunity of individual government leaders, soldiers, and officials responsible for the horrors of large-scale political violence at the end of the twentieth century, a revolution has occurred in international law. First, temporary tribunals were established to cover atrocities in Yugoslavia and Rwanda. Then a new permanent International Criminal Court (ICC) was created in July 2002 to prosecute those who commit genocide, war crimes, or crimes against humanity. The ICC is a modification of the inter-state system because it was created by political campaigning of human rights NGOs, because bitter opposition from the sole 'superpower' was defeated, and because the sovereign responsibility to prosecute criminals has been assumed by a global court. In September 2005, the United Nations went further, replacing **state sovereignty** with a collective **responsibility to protect**, when national authorities are manifestly failing (General Assembly Resolution 60/1).

The significance of criminals, terrorists, and guerrillas

Before September 2001, analysis of transnational criminals and guerrillas did not present a challenge to orthodox state-centric theory. Criminals seemed to be marginal because they are not legitimate and are excluded from normal international transactions. The violent groups that gained military, political, and diplomatic status on a transnational basis could be presented as nationalist groups, aspiring to gain their place in the inter-state system. Such arguments ignore the way globalization has changed the nature of sovereignty and the processes of government. The operations of criminals and other non-legitimate groups have become more complex, spread over a wider geographical area, and increased in scale because the improvements in communications have made it so much easier to transfer people, money, weapons, and ideas on a transnational basis. Government attempts to control such activities have become correspondingly more difficult. The legal concept of sovereignty may nominally still exist, but political practice has become significantly different. Now virtually every government feels it has to mobilize external support, to exercise 'domestic jurisdiction' over criminals. Defeat of Al Qaeda will not be achieved by military counter-terrorism, but by global political change that delegitimizes **fundamentalism** and violence. Oppressive action by governments is subject to extensive review under global human rights mechanisms and, in some situations, may be subject to prosecution at the ICC.

Key Points

- Effective action against transnational criminals by individual governments is difficult for the same reasons as control of TNCs is difficult.
- Groups using violence to achieve political goals generally do not achieve legitimacy, but in exceptional circumstances they may be recognized as national liberation movements and take part in diplomacy.
- The transnational activities of criminals and guerrillas shift problems of the domestic policy of countries into the realm of

global politics.
- Terrorism may be particular to individual countries, have transnational aspects or be carried out by groups in a transnational network, but it is not a single political force.
- Governments cannot act as independent sovereign actors in response to terrorism nor in using violence themselves.

Non-governmental organizations as political actors

The politics of an individual country cannot be understood without knowing what groups lobby the government and what debate there has been in the media. Similarly, international diplomacy does not operate on some separate planet, cut off from global civil society.

Because diplomats like to claim that they are pursuing **the national interest** of a united society, they will not admit to relations with interest groups or pressure groups and they use the bland title, non-governmental organizations or simply NGOs.

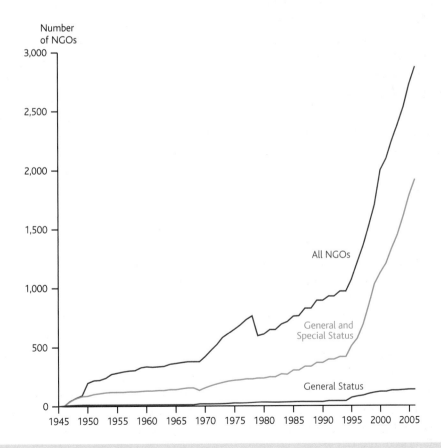

Figure 19.2 The growth of NGOs at the UN

Consultative status at the UN for NGOs

As a result of pressure, primarily from American groups, the United Nations Charter contains Article 71, providing for the Economic and Social Council (ECOSOC) to consult with NGOs. In 1950, the Council formally codified its practice, in a statute for NGOs. It recognized *three categories* of groups: (1) a small number of high-status NGOs, concerned with most of the Council's work; (2) specialist NGOs, concerned with a few fields of activity and having a high reputation in those fields; and (3) a Roster of other NGOs that are expected to make occasional contributions to the Council.[4] Since then the term NGO has, for diplomats, been synonymous with a group that is eligible for ECOSOC consultative status.

The UN definition of an acceptable NGO

The ECOSOC statute and the way it has been applied embodies six principles:

1 An NGO should support the aims and the work of the UN. However, it is very rare that objections are made to the political purposes of NGOs.
2 Officially, an NGO should be a representative body, with identifiable headquarters, and officers who are responsible to a democratic policy-making conference. In practice, many highly prestigious NGOs, particularly development and environment NGOs, are not membership organizations.
3 An NGO cannot be a profit-making body. Individual companies cannot gain consultative status, but trade federations of commercial interests are recognized as NGOs.
4 An NGO cannot use or advocate violence.
5 An NGO must respect the norm of 'non-interference in the internal affairs of states'. This means an NGO cannot be a political party, but parties can, like companies, form international federations. Also, NGOs concerned with human rights should not restrict their activities to a particular group, nationality, or country.
6 An international NGO is one that is not established by intergovernmental agreement.

Many NGO activists believe the UN should be more restrictive and only accept groups that are 'true' NGOs, contributing to 'progressive' **social movements**. Environmentalists are often upset that business federations are accepted and the whole NGO community at the UN agonized over the National Rifle Association being admitted to the Roster in November 1996.

Globalization and the expansion of NGOs

The creation of a complex global economy has had effects way beyond the international trade in goods and services. Most companies, in each distinct area of activity, have formed organizations to facilitate communication, to harmonize standards, and to manage adaptation to complex change. Equally, the employees have found they face common problems in different countries and so trade unions and professional bodies have developed their own transnational links. Any form of **international regime** to formulate policy for an industry, whether it is non-governmental or intergovernmental, will encourage the strengthening of the global links among the NGOs concerned with its activities.

For most of the twentieth century, any individual could travel in person or communicate in writing to most parts of the world. The technical revolution in recent years lies in the increased density, the increased speed, and the reduced cost of communication. The political revolution lies in these changes bringing rapid global communication within the capabilities of most people. This includes even the poor, if they band together to fund a representative to articulate their case or gain access to the news media. Changes in communications constitute a fundamental change in the structure of world politics. Governments have lost sovereignty over the transnational relations of their citizens. They may attempt to monitor or control trans-boundary communications, but closing the border is no longer technologically possible.

The shift of NGOs from the local to the global

One effect of the globalization of communication is to make it physically and financially feasible for small groups of people to establish and to maintain cooperation, even though they may be based thousands of miles apart from each other. Thus it is very easy for NGOs to operate transnationally, but not all NGOs make this choice. They vary

from local organizations solely operating in one small town to large global bureaucracies with a presence in most countries.

When NGOs cooperate transnationally, they may use one of four different types of **structure**. In the past, a formal joint organization, known as an INGO (an international NGO) was usually established, with a permanent headquarters, a secretariat, and a regular programme of meetings. With the advent of the Internet it is now just as likely that a looser **network** will be formed, often with a single NGO providing the technical support for e-mail communications and a joint website. The most famous networks, such as Jubilee 2000, the Coalition for an International Criminal Court, and the International Campaign to Ban Land Mines, have united around a single policy domain, brought together hundreds of NGOs from all around the world, and achieved major policy changes against the opposition of leading governments. These are known as advocacy networks. At the meetings of intergovernmental organizations, NGOs may combine in a caucus. This is a temporary network formed solely for the purpose of lobbying on the agenda items at the particular meeting. Finally, there are governance networks, formed by NGOs to maintain and enhance the participation rights of NGOs in intergovernmental meetings. They differ from advocacy networks and caucuses in not having common political goals, other than their common interest in being allowed access to the policy-making process.

Key Points

- Most transnational actors can expect to gain recognition as NGOs by the UN, provided they are not individual companies, criminals, or violent groups and they do not exist solely to oppose an individual government.
- The ECOSOC statute provides an authoritative statement that NGOs have a legitimate place in intergovernmental diplomacy.
- The creation of a global economy leads to the globalization of unions, commercial bodies, the professions, and scientists in international NGOs, which participate in the relevant international regimes.
- Governments can no longer control the flow of information across the borders of their country.
- Improved communications make it more likely that NGOs will operate transnationally and make it very simple and cheap for them to do so.
- NGOs from each country may combine in four ways: as international NGOs, as advocacy networks, as caucuses, and as governance networks.

International organizations as structures of global politics

International organizations provide the focus for global politics. The new physical infrastructure of global communications makes it easier for them to operate. In addition, when the sessions of the organizations take place, they become distinct structures for political communication. Face-to-face meetings produce different outcomes from telephone or written communications. Multilateral discussion produces different outcomes from interactions in networks of bilateral communications.

International organizations as systems

It was argued earlier that it is inconsistent to see 'states' as coherent entities, while asserting that **anarchy** exists at the global level. We can be consistent by accepting the existence of systems at all levels of world politics. In the modern world, human groups are never so coherent that they are independent, closed systems (perhaps excepting monastic orders). Equally, once distinct organizational processes are established, they are never so open that the boundaries become insignificant. Thus international organizations of all types transcend country boundaries and have a major impact on the governmental actors and transnational actors composing them.

For a system to exist, there must be a sufficient density of interactions, involving each of its elements, at a sufficient intensity to result both in the emergence of properties for the system as a whole and in some consistent effect on the behaviour of the elements. Generally, international organizations will have founding documents defining their goals, rules of procedure constraining the modes of behaviour, secretariats committed to the status and identity of the organization (or at least committed to

their own careers), past decisions that provide norms for future policy, and interaction processes that socialize new participants. All these features at the systemic level will be part of the explanation of the behaviour of the members and thus the political outcomes will not be determined solely by the initial goals of the members. The statement that international organizations form systems is a statement that they are politically significant and that global politics cannot be reduced to 'inter-state' relations.

Normally a sharp distinction is made between intergovernmental organizations and international non-governmental organizations. This conveys the impression that inter-state diplomacy and transnational relations are separate from each other. In practice, governments do not rigidly maintain the separation. There is an overlapping pattern of relations in another category of international organizations, **hybrid INGOs**, in which governments work with NGOs. Among the most important hybrids are the International Red Cross, the World Conservation Union (IUCN), the International Council of Scientific Unions, the International Air Transport Association, and other economic bodies combining companies and governments.

In order to be regarded as a hybrid, the organization must admit as full members *both* NGOs, parties, or companies *and* governments or governmental agencies. Both types of member must have full rights of participation in policy-making, including the right to vote on the final decisions. When the principle of formal equality of NGOs and governments is acknowledged by both sides in such a manner, the assumption that governments can dominate must be totally abandoned.

Key Points

- International organizations are structures for political communication. They are systems that constrain the behaviour of their members.
- Governments form intergovernmental organizations and transnational actors form international non-governmental organizations. In addition, governments and transnational actors accord each other equal status by jointly creating hybrid international NGOs.
- International organizations are more than the collective will of their members. They have a distinct impact upon other global actors.

Conclusion: issues and policy systems in global politics

State-centric writers accommodate transnational activity by distinguishing the high politics of peace and security, taking place in military alliances and UN diplomacy, from the low politics of other policy questions, debated in specialist UN bodies, other IGOs, and INGOs. Then, by asserting it is more important to analyse peace and war, actors in low politics are defined out of the analysis. In practice it is not so simple. Scientists, the Red Cross, religious groups, and other NGOs are involved in arms control negotiations; economic events may be treated as crises; social policy can concern matters of life and death; and heads of government do at times make the environment a top priority. It is useful to analyze global politics in terms of a variety of dimensions describing each **policy domain** and the actors within it, but the different dimensions do not correlate. A single high/low classification does not work.

The move from a state-centric to a Pluralist model depends on rejecting a static unidimensional concept of power. Actors enter a political process possessing resources and seeking particular goals. However, contrary to the Realist view, **capabilities** alone do not determine influence. Explaining outcomes requires examining whether the resources of actors are relevant to the goals being pursued, describing the degree of divergence between the goals of the different actors, and analyzing how they are changed by the interaction processes.

Governments are usually characterized as having legal authority and control over military capabilities and economic resources. They may also have high status, possess specialist information, have access to communications and be able to articulate widely shared values in support of their goals, but all these latter four capabilities can also be attributes of transnational actors and international organizations. In the process of political debate something else is crucial. It is the ability to communicate in a manner that commands the attention and respect of other actors. While this is enhanced by possession of sta-

Case Study The baby milk advocacy network

The prototype for global campaigning by NGOs has been the International Baby Foods Action Network, which challenges the marketing of dried milk powder by the major food and pharmaceutical TNCs. In the early 1970s, medical staff in developing countries gradually became aware that the death rate for babies was rising because of decreased breast feeding. If the family was poor and used insufficient milk powder, the baby was undernourished. If the water or the bottle was not sterile, the baby developed gastric diseases. Bottle feeding today causes around one and a half million deaths a year.

The question was first taken up by the *New Internationalist* magazine and War on Want (WoW) in Britain in 1973-4. A Swiss NGO, the Third World Action Group (AgDW), then published a revised translation of WoW's report, under the title 'Nestlé Kills Babies'. When Nestlé sued for libel, AgDW mobilized groups from around the world to supply evidence for their defence. The Swiss Court found AgDW guilty in December 1976 on one of Nestlé's four original counts, on the technical basis that Nestlé was only indirectly responsible for the deaths.

The question moved to the USA, when religious groups involved in Latin America fought another court case against

Bristol-Meyers. Increased awareness led to a new group, the Infant Formula Action Coalition, organizing a boycott of Nestlé's products that spread to many countries. In the hope of diffusing the increasing pressure, the International Council of Infant Food Industries accepted a proposal by Senator Kennedy for the World Health Organization (WHO) and UNICEF to hold a meeting on infant feeding in October 1979. Rather than depoliticizing the question, the companies found they were facing demands to limit their marketing. The meeting also taught a group of NGOs how much they could benefit from working together with a common political strategy. They decided to continue to cooperate by forming IBFAN, as a global advocacy network.

The new network was able to mobilize a diverse coalition of medical professionals, religious groups, development activists, women's groups, community organizations, consumer lobbies, and the boycott campaigners. Against intense opposition from the TNCs and the US administration, IBFAN succeeded in achieving the adoption of an International Code of Marketing of Breast-Milk Substitutes, by WHO's Assembly in May 1981. The key provisions of the Code were that 'there should be no advertising or other form of promotion to the general public' nor any provision of free samples to mothers.

As of 2004, 27 countries had implemented the Code by means of a comprehensive law, another 33 countries had implemented many, but not all, provisions as law, and a further 58 countries had weak legal provisions or voluntary policies. IBFAN's work continues along two tracks: it monitors and reports violations of the Code by companies, including in countries where marketing is now illegal; and it also seeks to upgrade the law in countries that are only partially implementing the Code.

(This account is based upon A. Chetley (1986), The Politics of Baby Foods (London: Pinter) and information on www.ibfan.org, the IBFAN website)

tus and resources, in practice—when making speeches, during interviews for the news media, in negotiations or when lobbying—the ability to communicate is a personal attribute of the speaker. Some presidents and prime ministers fail to command respect, while some NGO activists are inspiring and cannot be ignored. If power is seen solely in military terms, governments are expected to be dominant. If power is seen solely in economic terms, TNCs are expected to be dominant. However, if power includes possession of status, information, and communication skills, then it is possible for NGOs and international organizations to mobilize support for their values and to exercise

influence over governments. Most real-world situations will see a mix of different capabilities being brought to bear upon the policy debate.

The types of authority, status, resources, information, and skills that are relevant to political success are issue-specific. (They vary from one **issue** to another.) Thus which actors will have the ability to exercise influence varies according to the issues invoked by a policy problem. Table 19.1 illustrates the point that there is not a single international system of nearly 200 'states', but a variety of policy domains, each involving their own distinct actors. Governments have a special role, linking

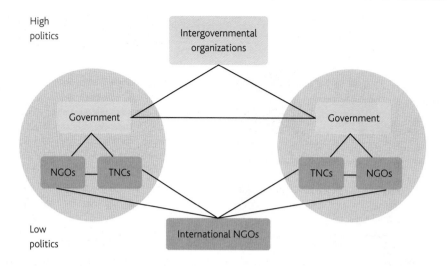

Figure 19.3 The orthodox view of international relations

the different domains, because membership of the UN obliges governments to form policy and vote on most issues. In practice, they are less centralized and cohesive than it appears in the UN, because different departments of government handle the different policy questions. The transnational actors and international organizations generally are more specialist and involved in a limited range of policy questions. Amnesty International rarely has significance in environmental politics and Greenpeace rarely is concerned with human rights, but each is central to its own domain. Being a specialist generates high status, provides command over information, and enhances communication skills. These capabilities enable a challenge to be made to the governments that control military

and economic resources.

Within both domestic and global politics, civil society is the source of change. Companies usually initiate economic change and NGOs are usually the source of new ideas for political action. At any one point in time, economics and politics may seem to be relatively stable and under governmental control. Under the exceptional circumstances of war or under exceptional leadership, governments can generate change. However, NGOs generally provide the dynamics of politics. The European empires were dismembered by nationalist movements, with support from lawyers, journalists, unions, and the churches. Democracy and human rights have been extended by women's groups, ethnic minorities, and dissident groups.

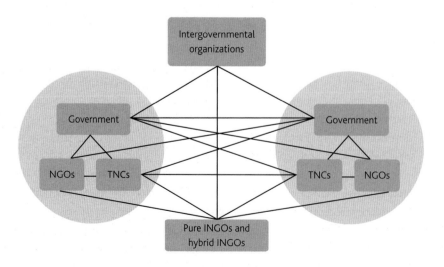

Figure 19.4 The full range of international connections

	Apartheid in South Africa	Human rights	Population planning	Environment
Main governments involved	South Africa, UK, USA versus African governments	Democratic versus authoritarian governments	All types of governments	Those who feel threatened by problems versus those who do not
Transnational companies	Wide range, but especially mining and oil	Any working with oppressive governments	Medical, pharmaceutical, and food	Mainly industrial, energy, and transport
Guerrillas	ANC, PAC, and SWAPO	Any taking hostages	Any in control of territory	Generally not concerned
Grass roots NGOs	Anti-Apartheid Movement	Human rights groups and the oppressed	Religious, women's, and health groups	Friends of the Earth, WWF, Greenpeace, etc.
UN inter-governmental policy forum	Committee Against Apartheid and Security Council	Human Rights Council	Commission on Population and Development	Commission on Sustainable Development
UN Secretariat	Centre Against Apartheid	Office . . . for Human Rights	UNICEF, UN Population Fund	UNDP, UNEP
Other IGOs	Organization of African Unity	Council of Europe, OAS, and AU	WHO, World Bank	World Bank
International NGOs	Many involved, with a secondary concern	Amnesty International and others	International Planned Parenthood Federation	Environment Liaison Centre International and other networks
Hybrid INGOs	Those concerned with trade	ILO	None	World Conservation Union (IUCN)

Table 19.1 The variety of political actors involved in different policy domains

The environment has moved up the agenda in response to grassroots anger at the loss of natural beauty, protests against threats to health, and warnings from scientists about ecosystems being at risk of collapse. The right to have access to family planning has been established as a global **norm**. In some countries, notably the USA, this initially required women to go to jail to challenge repressive laws, but since 1953 the International Planned Parenthood Federation has grown to become the world's second largest NGO, even operating in virtually all Catholic and Islamic countries. The start of the cold war was not simply the formation of military alliances: it was a political struggle of communism as a transnational movement against the transnational appeal of democracy, the Catholic Church, and nationalism. The arms race and the process of *détente* included conflict between arms manufacturers and peace movements, with scientists being crucial to both sides. The end of the cold war was driven by economic failure within communist countries and the political failure in response to demands from unions, human rights dissidents, the churches, and environmentalists. The response to refugee crises has been dominated by the media, the UN, and NGOs. The

shift from seeing development as increasing a country's GNP to meeting ordinary people's basic needs and using resources in a sustainable manner was driven by development NGOs and the environmental movement. The international relations of the twentieth century have all occurred within complex, pluralist political systems.

Key Points

- The high politics/low politics distinction is used to marginalize transnational actors. It is invalid because politics does not reduce to these two categories.
- A simple concept of power will not explain outcomes. Military and economic resources are not the only capabilities: communication facilities, information, authority, and status are also important political assets. In addition, skills in mobilizing support will contribute to influence over policy.
- Different policy domains contain different actors, depending upon the salience of the issues being debated.
- TNCs gain influence through the control of economic resources. NGOs gain influence through possessing information, gaining high status and communicating effectively. TNCs and NGOs have been the main source of economic and political change in global politics.

❓ Questions

1 Outline three meanings of the concept of a 'state' and explain the implications of each for the study of transnational actors.

2 What are the different types of transnational actor? Give examples of each type.

3 What is a nation? How does the concept differ from that of a state?

4 How do transnational companies affect the sovereignty of governments?

5 What measures could you use to compare the size of countries, TNCs, NGOs, and international organizations? Are countries always larger than transnational actors?

6 What types of NGO are, and what types are not, eligible to obtain consultative status with the Economic and Social Council of the United Nations?

7 Explain the expansion in the number of NGOs engaging in transnational activities.

8 What is a hybrid international NGO?

9 How is it possible for NGOs to exercise influence in global politics? (Note: this question can be answered both in theoretical terms and in practical empirical terms).

10 Explain the difference between analyzing international relations as a single international system and as the global politics of many different policy domains.

➡ Guide to further reading

Case study materials

Edwards, M., and Gaventa, J. (2001), *Global Citizen Action: Lessons and Challenges* (Boulder, Col.: Lynne Rienner). Focuses on broadly-based campaigning networks, with six case studies on civil society interaction with the international financial institutions and seven case studies on environment, human rights, and development campaigns.

Keck, M. E., and Sikkink, K. (1998), *Activists Beyond Borders: Advocacy Networks in International Politics* (Ithaca, NY: Cornell University Press). A major contribution to the literature on the nature of modern transnational advocacy networks, with case studies on Latin America, the environment, and violence against women.

Risse-Kappen, T. (ed.) (1995), *Bringing Transnational Relations Back In* (Cambridge: Cambridge University Press). Provides a set of six case studies around the theme that transnational influence depends upon the structures of governance for an issue-area at both the domestic level and in international institutions.

Weiss, T. G., and Gordenker, L. (eds) (1996), *NGOs, the UN and Global Governance* (Boulder, Col.: Lynne Rienner). Six studies of NGO activity and three chapters addressing cross-cutting themes, set within a Pluralist approach.

Willetts, P. (ed.) (1982), *Pressure Groups in the Global System: The Transnational Relations of Issue-Orientated Non-Governmental Organizations* (London: Pinter). In reaction against the omission of non-economic groups by Keohane and Nye, examines how pressure groups move from single-country to global activity.

—— (ed.) (1996), '*The Conscience of the World': The Influence of Non-Governmental Organizations in the UN System* (London: Hurst and Co.). Defines what is an NGO, gives the history of the League

and the UN consultative arrangements and offers seven case studies of the influence of NGOs in the UN system.

Theoretical debate

Rosenau, J. N. (1980), *The Study of Global Interdependence: Essays on the Transnationalisation of World Affairs* (London: Pinter). A fruitful source of theoretical ideas for a Pluralist approach. Viotti, P. R., and Kauppi, M. V. (1998), *International Relations Theory: Realism, Pluralism, Globalism*, 3rd edn (New York: Macmillan). Gives excellent focus on the fundamentals of the theoretical debate. Willetts, P. (1990), 'Transactions, Networks and Systems', in A. J. R. Groom and P. Taylor (eds), *Frameworks for International Co-operation* (London: Pinter), Ch.17. More detailed coverage of the development of International Relations theory on transnational and intergovernmental relations. See also the editors' chapters in the case study books.

UN materials

Kaul, I., *et al.* (1993), *Human Development Report* (New York: Oxford University Press). An official UN annual report, which in this edition concentrates on the contribution made by NGOs to development.

UNCTAD, Division on Transnational Corporations and Investments (1991–), *World Investment Report* (New York: UN). An official UN annual report, which assesses the scale of TNC participation in global production, investment, and trade.

Online Resource Centre

 Visit the Online Resource Centre that accompanies this book to access more learning resources on this chapter topic at www.oxfordtextbooks.co.uk/uk/orc/baylis_smith4e/

Notes

1 Data on transnational corporations is given in annual reports from the United Nations. The figures quoted come from *World Investment Report 2006* (UNCTAD 2006b: 270–73 and 280–4). The numbers of different types of transnational and international organization are from the *Yearbook of International Organizations 2005–2006*, Vol. 5, p. 7 (Munich: K. G. Saur, 2006).

2 The *World Investment Report 2006* lists the 100 largest non-financial TNCs, ranked by foreign assets: of these 50 had global sales of $40 billion or more in 2004. Data for each country on GNP and population is given in the *World Development Indicators, 2006* (Washington, DC: World Bank, 2006).

3 *World Investment Report 2006*, Annex tables A.I.6 and A.I.11.

4 ECOSOC Resolution 288(X)B Arrangements for Consultation with Non Governmental Organizations was passed in February 1950. It was amended and replaced by Resolution 1296(XLIV) in May 1968 and again by Resolution 1996/31 in July 1996.

- Turba...
Kara-
Kum
...rkmenische
SSR   Mar
...n Aschchabad
Kuschka
...rud   Meschhed   Herat   Ma...
Chorasan
Heri Rud
...AFGHANI...
Birdschand   Hilmend   Gha...
Wüste   Ferah
Kandahar
...Lut   ...mun-i-
Helmand   Cham...
Wüste   Rudbar

Part Four
International issues

In this part of the book we want to give you a wide-ranging overview of the main issues in contemporary world politics. The previous three parts have been designed to give you a comprehensive foundation for the study of contemporary international issues. As with the other sections, this one also has two aims: **first**, we want to give you an understanding of some of the more important pressing problems which appear every day in the media headlines and which, directly and indirectly, affect the lives of each of us. These issues are the stuff of globalization, and they take a number of different forms. Some, like the environment and nuclear proliferation, pose dangers of global catastrophe. Others, like nationalism, cultural differences, and humanitarian intervention, together with regionalism and integration, raise important questions and dilemmas about the twin processes of fragmentation and unification which characterize the world in which we live. Yet other issues, such as terrorism, global trade and finance, human rights, human security, poverty, development, and hunger, are fundamentally intertwined with globalization. Our **second** aim, of course, is that by providing overviews of these issues we are posing questions about the nature of globalization. Is it new? Is it beneficial? Is it unavoidable? Does it serve specific interests? Does it make it more or less easy to deal with the problems covered in these chapters? The picture that emerges from these chapters is that the process of globalization is a highly complex one, with major disagreements existing about its significance and its impact. Some contributors see opportunities for greater cooperation because of globalization while others see dangers of increased levels of conflict at the beginning of the twenty-first century. What do you think?

Chapter 20

Environmental issues

JOHN VOGLER

- Introduction 352
- Environmental issues on the international agenda: a brief history 353
- The functions of international environmental cooperation 356
- Climate change 361
- The environment and International Relations theory 365
- Conclusion 366

Reader's Guide

As environmental problems transcend national boundaries they come to be a feature of international politics. This chapter indicates that environmental issues have become increasingly prominent on the international agenda over the last fifty years assisted by the effects of globalization. It shows how this has prompted attempts to arrange cooperation between states and surveys the form and function of such activity with reference to some of the main international environmental regimes. Because climate change has become a problem of such enormous significance, a separate section is devoted to the efforts to create an international climate regime. This is followed by a brief consideration of how some of the theoretical parts of this book relate to international environmental politics.

Introduction

Although humankind as a whole now appears to be living well above Earth's carrying capacity, the **ecological footprints** of individual states vary to an extraordinary extent. See, for example, the unusual map of the world (Fig. 20.1), where the size of countries is proportionate to their carbon emissions. Indeed, if everyone were to enjoy the current lifestyle of the developed countries, more than three additional planets would be required.

This situation is rendered all the more unsustainable by the process of **globalization**, even though the precise relationship between environmental degradation and the over-use of resources, on the one hand, and globalization, on the other, is complex and sometimes contradictory. Globalization has stimulated the relocation of industry, population movement away from the land, and ever-rising levels of consumption, along with associated emissions of effluents and waste gases. While often generating greater income for poorer countries exporting basic goods to developed country markets, ever freer trade can also have adverse environmental consequences, by disrupting local ecologies and livelihoods.

On the other hand, there is little evidence that globalization has stimulated a 'race to the bottom' in environmental standards, and it has even been argued that increasing levels of affluence have brought about local environmental improvements, just as birth rates tend fall as populations become wealthier. Economists claim that globalization's opening up of markets can increase efficiency and reduce pollution, provided that the environmental and social damage associated with production of a good is properly factored into its market price. Similarly, globalization has promoted the sharing of knowledge and the influential presence of **non-governmental organizations (NGOs)** in global environmental politics. Whatever the ecological balance sheet of globalization, the resources upon which human beings depend for survival, such as fresh water, a clean atmosphere, and a stable climate, are now under serious threat.

Global problems may need global solutions and pose a fundamental requirement for **global environmental governance**, yet local or regional action remains a vital aspect of responses to many problems; one of the

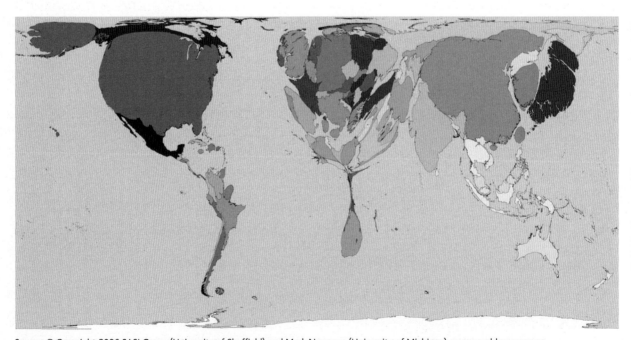

Source: © Copyright 2006 SASI Group (University of Sheffield) and Mark Newman (University of Michigan). www.worldmapper.org.

Figure 20.1 Map of world in proportion to carbon emissions

defining characteristics of environmental politics is the awareness of such interconnections and of the need to 'think globally—act locally'. NGOs have been very active in this respect, as shown in Chapter 19 of this book.

Despite the global dimensions of environmental change, an effective response still has to depend upon a fragmented international political system of over 190 sovereign **states**. Global environmental governance consequently involves bringing to bear inter-state relations, **international law**, and **international organizations** in addressing shared environmental problems. Using the term 'governance'—as distinct from government—implies that regulation and control have to be exercised in the absence of central government, delivering the kinds of service that a world government would provide if it were

to exist. You should refer to Chapter 17 for the essential concepts employed in **regime** analysis, which is commonly applied in the study of international governance.

Key Points

- The current use and degradation of the Earth's resources is unsustainable and closely connected in sometimes contradictory ways to the processes of globalization.
- There are vast inequalities between rich and poor in their use of the Earth's resources and the ecological shadow or footprint that they impose on it.
- The response at the international level is to attempt to provide global environmental governance. In a system of sovereign states this involves international cooperation.

Environmental issues on the international agenda: a brief history

Before the era of globalization there were two traditional environmental concerns: conservation of natural resources and the damage caused by pollution. Pollution, like wildlife, does not respect international boundaries and action to mitigate or conserve them sometimes had to involve more than one state. There were also numerous, mostly unsuccessful, attempts to regulate exploitation of maritime resources lying beyond national jurisdiction, including several multilateral fisheries commissions. The 1946 International Convention for the Regulation of Whaling and its International Whaling Commission (IWC) offer an interesting move away from the original goal of conserving the whaling industry by regulating catches, towards the preservation of the Great Whales *per se* through declaring an international moratorium on whaling. This shift still generates bitter confrontation between NGOs, most IWC members, and the small number of nations—Japan, Norway, and Iceland—that wish to resume commercial whaling.

Post-Second World War global economic recovery brought with it evidence of damaging pollution of the atmosphere, of watercourses, and of the sea, notably the Mediterranean, leading to international agreements in the 1950s and 1960s covering such matters as discharges

from oil tankers. This worthy activity was, though, hardly the stuff of great power politics. Such 'apolitical' matters were the domain of new United Nations **Specialized Agencies**, like the Food and Agriculture Organization, but were hardly central to diplomacy at the UN General Assembly (UNGA) in New York. This neglect was reflected in academic writing at the time, as exemplified by Hans J. Morgenthau's famous text, *Politics among Nations* (1955), which mentions the natural environment only as a fixed contextual factor or a constituent of national power.

However, the salience of environmental issues grew in the 1960s, and in 1968 the UNGA accepted a Swedish proposal for what became the 1972 UN Conference on the Human Environment (UNCHE) 'to focus governments' attention and public opinion on the importance and urgency of the question'. This Conference led to the creation of the United Nations Environment Programme (UNEP) and the establishment of environment departments by many governments. Yet it was already clear that for the countries of the South, constituting the majority in the UNGA, environmental questions could not be separated from their demands for development, aid, and the restructuring of international economic relations. This was the political context surrounding the emergence

Box 20.1 Chronology

1946	International Convention for the Regulation of Whaling
1955	UK Clean Air Act to combat 'smog' in British cities
1958	International Convention for the Prevention of Pollution of the Sea by Oil
1959	Antarctic Treaty
1962	Rachel Carson publishes *Silent Spring*
1967	*Torrey Canyon* oil tanker disaster
1969	Greenpeace founded
1971	At the Founex Meeting in Switzerland, Southern experts formulated a link between environment and development
1972	United Nations Conference on the Human Environment (UNCHE) in Stockholm,
	Establishment of the United Nations Environment Programme (UNEP)
1973	MARPOL Convention on oil pollution from ships
	Convention on International Trade in Endangered Species (CITES)
1979	Long Range Transboundary Air Pollution Convention (LRTAP)
1980	Convention on the Conservation of Antarctic Marine Living Resources
1982	UN Law of the Sea Convention (enters into force in 1994)
1984	Bhopal chemical plant disaster
1985	Vienna Convention for the Protection of the Ozone Layer. The Antarctic 'ozone hole' confirmed
1986	Chernobyl nuclear disaster
1987	Brundtland Commission Report
	Montreal Protocol on Substances that Deplete the Ozone Layer
1988	Establishment of the Intergovernmental Panel on Climate Change (IPCC)
1989	Basel Convention on the Transboundary Movement of Hazardous Wastes
1991	Madrid Protocol (to the Antarctic Treaty) on Environmental Protection
1992	United Nations Conference on Environment and Development (UNCED) held at Rio de Janeiro. Publication of the Rio Declaration and *Agenda 21*. United Nations Conventions on Climate Change (UNFCCC) and Biological Diversity (CBD) both signed. Establishment of the Commission on Sustainable Development (CSD)
1995	World Trade Organization (WTO) founded
1997	Kyoto Protocol to the UNFCCC
1998	Rotterdam Convention on Hazardous Chemicals and Pesticides
	Aarhus Convention on Access to Information, Public Participation in Decision-making and Access to Justice in Environmental Matters
2000	Cartagena Protocol on Biosafety
	Millennium Development Goals set out
2001	US President Bush revokes signature of the Kyoto Protocol
2002	World Summit on Sustainable Development (WSSD), Johannesburg. Johannesburg Plan of Implementation
2005	Entry into force of the Kyoto Protocol and introduction of the first international emissions trading system by the European Union
2006	International discussions commenced on the climate change regime after 2012
2007	Fourth Assessment Report of the IPCC
2008	First Commitment Period of Kyoto begins

of the concept of **sustainable development** (also see Ch.27) but before this was formulated by the Brundtland Commission in 1987, the environment had been pushed to the periphery of the international agenda by the global economic downturn of the 1970s and then the onset of the second cold war (see Ch.3).

Environmental degradation continued nonetheless. Awareness of new forms of transnational pollution, such as 'acid rain', joined existing concerns over point-source pollution (when the pollutant comes from a definite source), followed by a dawning scientific realization that some environmental problems—the thinning of the stratospheric ozone layer and the possibility of climate change—were truly global in scale. The attendant popular concern over such issues and the relaxation of East–West tension created the opportunity for a second great UN conference, for which the connection between environment and development had been explicitly drawn through the Brundtland Commission's notion of sustainable development. Though subject to many subsequent interpretations, its political essence is an accommodation between the environmental concerns of developed states and the development demands of the South, without which there could have been no Earth Summit and no Rio process.

The 1992 UN Conference on Environment and Development (UNCED) or 'Earth Summit' was the largest international conference so far held, raising the profile of the environment as an international issue while

Box 20.2 Sustainable development

Over 50 separate definitions of sustainable development have been counted. Its classic statement was provided by the 1987 Brundtland Commission Report:

> Sustainable development is development that meets the needs of the present without compromising the ability of future generations to meet their own needs. *(Brundtland et al. 1987: 43)*

Behind it lay an explicit recognition of limitations to future growth which were social, technological, and environmental. In addressing them, emphasis was placed upon needs, and the highest priority was given to those needs experienced by the world's poor. Central to the concept was the idea of fairness between generations as well as between the rich and poor currently inhabiting the planet.

By the time of the 2002 World Summit the concept had been subtly altered:

> ... to ensure a balance between economic development, social development and environmental protection as interdependent and mutually reinforcing components of sustainable development. *(UNGA, A/57/532/add.1, 12 December 2002)*

Ensuring environmental sustainability, by integrating sustainable development principles into national decision-making, was the seventh of eight UN Millennium Development Goals agreed in 2000.

---

concluding several significant documents and agreements, such as *Agenda 21* and international conventions on climate change and the preservation of biodiversity. The event's underlying politics were captured in its title—a conference on 'environment and development'—where the most serious arguments concerned aid pledges to finance the environmental improvements under discussion. A process was created at the UN to review the implementation of the Rio agreements, including meetings of the new Commission on Sustainable Development (CSD) and a Special Session of the UNGA in 1997.

On UNCED's tenth anniversary in 2002, the World Summit on Sustainable Development (WSSD) was held in Johannesburg. The change of wording indicated how conceptions of environment and development had shifted since the 1970s. Now discussion was embedded in recognition of the importance of globalization and of the dire state of the African continent. **Poverty** eradication was clearly emphasized, along with practical progress in providing clean water, sanitation, and agricultural improvements. One controversial element was the role to be played in such provision by private–public sector partnerships.

While the UN conferences marked the stages by which the environment entered the international political mainstream, they also reflected underlying changes in the scope and perception of environmental problems. As scientific understanding expanded, it was becoming a commonplace, by the 1980s, to speak in terms of global environmental change, as most graphically represented by the discovery of the 'ozone hole' and the creeping realization that human activities might be dangerously altering the global climate itself.

Alongside actual environmental degradation and advances in scientific knowledge, the international politics of the environment has responded to the issue-attention cycle in developed countries, peaking at certain moments and then declining. The causes are complex and during the 1960s reflected the counter-cultural and radical movements of the time along with wider public reactions to a series of trends and events. The most totemic of these was Rachel Carson's hugely influential book *Silent Spring* (1962), which powerfully conjoined the conservationist and anti-pollution agendas by highlighting the damage inflicted upon bird-life by industrial pesticides like DDT. Well-publicized environmental disasters, such as the 1959 mercury poisoning at Minimata in Japan and the 1967 wreck of the *Torrey Canyon* oil tanker close to Cornish beaches, fed public concern. The failure of established political parties to embrace these issues effectively encouraged the birth of several new high-profile NGOs—Friends of the Earth, Greenpeace, and the World Wildlife Fund for Nature—alongside more established pressure groups such as the US Sierra Club and the British Royal Society for the Protection of Birds. The interest in environmental action at the international level and, indeed, most of the NGOs exerting pressure to this end were an almost exclusively developed world phenomenon. Public attention then receded until the ending of the second cold war coincided with a new concern over global environmental problems, providing the political impetus for the 1992 Earth Summit. Interest waned again during the ensuing decade, although by 2005–6 public alarm over the impact of climate change again propelled environmental issues up the political agenda. The demand was, of course, for international action and governance, but what exactly did this mean? The next section attempts to answer this question by reviewing the functions of international environmental cooperation.

Key Points

- In the late nineteenth and early twentieth century international environmental politics was strictly limited, but from around 1960 its scope expanded as environmental problems acquired a transnational and then a global dimension.
- The process was reflected in and stimulated by the three great UN conferences of 1972, 1992, and 2002, whose most important role

was to make the connection between the international environmental and development agendas, as expressed in the important concept of sustainable development.
- International environmental politics reflected the issue-attention cycle in developed countries and relied heavily on increasing scientific knowledge.

The functions of international environmental cooperation

International **cooperation** establishes governance regimes to regulate transboundary environmental problems and sustain the global commons. Regimes encompass more than formal agreements between states, although these are very important (see Ch.17). Moreover, there are other functions and consequences of international cooperation beyond regime formation.

The pursuit of **power**, status, and wealth are rarely absent from international deliberations. This is often neglected in discussions of international environmental cooperation, even though many of the great international gatherings and even some of the more mundane ones clearly reflect struggles for national and organizational advantage. Organizations seek to maintain their financial and staff resources as well as their place within the UN system. UNEP, for example, despite extensive debates over granting it the higher and more autonomous status of a UN Specialized Agency, remains a mere programme. Some suspect that much of the activity at international environmental meetings is simply to issue declarations convincing domestic publics that something is being done, even if environmental conditions continue to deteriorate.

Transboundary trade and pollution control

When animals, fish, water, or pollution cross national frontiers the need for international cooperation arises and the regulation of transboundary environmental problems is the most long-established function of international cooperation, reflected in hundreds of multilateral, regional, and bilateral agreements providing for joint efforts to manage resources and control pollution.

An important example is provided by the 1979 Convention on Long-Range Transboundary Air Pollution (LRTAP) and its various protocols. They responded to the growing problem of acidification and so-called 'acid rain' by providing mechanisms to study atmospheric pollution problems in Europe and North America and securing commitments by the states involved to control and reduce their emissions. Another set of multilateral environmental agreements (MEAs) regulates the transboundary movement of hazardous wastes and chemicals in the interests of protecting human health and the environment, and requires that when hazardous chemicals and pesticides are traded, the government from whose territory the exports originate shall obtain the 'prior informed consent' of the importing country.

Controlling, taxing, and even promoting trade has always been one of the more important functions of the state, and trade restrictions can also be used as an instrument for nature conservation. The 1973 Convention on International Trade in Endangered Species (CITES) does this by attempting to monitor, control, or prohibit international trade in species (or products derived from them) whose continued survival might be put at risk by the effects of such trade. Species at risk are 'listed' in three appendices to the Convention; some 600 animal and 300 plant species currently enjoy the highest level of protection (a trade ban) through listing on Appendix I, though decisions on the 'up-listing' and 'downlisting' of species are sometimes controversial, as in the case of the African Elephant.

The use of trade penalties and restrictions by MEAs has been a vexed issue when the objective of environmental protection has come into conflict with the rules of the GATT/World Trade Organization (WTO) trade regime

(see Ch.14). Such a problem arose when the international community attempted to address the controversial question of the new biotechnology and genetically modified organisms (GMOs). There was much resistance to the claims of biotechnology corporations that had made huge investments in developing GMO seed, pharmaceutical, and food products, and argued that these innovations had positive environmental and development potential (through reducing pesticide use and increasing crop yields). European publics, supermarkets, and some developing countries were very wary of GMO technologies on safety and other grounds, leading to pressure for controls on their transboundary movement and the negotiation of the Biosafety Protocol to the Convention on Biological Diversity (CBD) that had been agreed at Rio in 1992. The resulting Cartagena Protocol was signed in 2000 and establishes an advanced informed agreement procedure between governments to be applied when GMOs are transferred across frontiers for ultimate release into the environment. The criteria to guide decisions on blocking imports reflected a precautionary approach rather than insistence on conclusive scientific evidence of harmfulness. Much of the argument in negotiating the Cartagena Protocol concerned the relationship of these new environmental rules to the requirements of the trade regime and arose from the concern of the USA and other potential GMO exporters that the Protocol would permit a disguised form of trade protectionism. Whether the WTO trade rules should take precedence over the emerging biosafety rules was debated at length until the parties agreed to avoid the issue by providing that the two sets of rules should be 'mutually supportive'.

Norm creation

The development of international environmental law and associated **norms** of acceptable behaviour has been both rapid and innovative over the last thirty years. Some of the norms mentioned above are in the form of quite technical policy concepts that have been widely disseminated and adopted as a result of international discussion. The **precautionary principle** has gained increasing but not uncritical currency. Originally coined by German policy-makers, it states that where there is a likelihood of environmental damage, banning an activity should not require full and definitive scientific proof. As we saw in the example of GMOs, the latter has tended to be the requirement in trade law (and indeed in UK environmental policy before European Community doctrines on precaution took hold). The norm of 'prior informed consent' has also been promoted alongside that of the 'polluter pays'. In the longer term, one of the key effects of the climate change regime (dealt with in detail below) may well be the dissemination of new approaches to pollution control such as emissions trading and joint implementation.

The UN Earth Summits were important in establishing environmental norms. The 1972 Stockholm Conference produced its 'Principle 21', which combines **sovereignty** over national resources with state responsibility for external pollution. This should not be confused with *Agenda 21*, issued by the 1992 Rio Earth Summit, a complex 40-chapter document of some 400 pages that took two years to negotiate in UNCED's Preparatory Committee. *Agenda 21* was frequently derided, not least because of its non-binding

---

Box 20.3 Trade and the environment

The issue of the relationship between trade and environmental degradation is much broader than disputes over the relationship between the World Trade Organization (WTO) and particular multilateral environmental agreements (MEAs). Globalization is partly shaped by the efforts of the GATT/WTO to open up protected markets and expand world trade. Many green activists argue that trade itself damages the environment by destroying local sustainable agriculture and by encouraging the environmentally damaging long-range transport of goods. The rearrangement of patterns of production and consumption has indeed been one of the hallmarks of globalization. Liberal economists and apologists for the WTO claim that if the 'externalities', such as the pollution caused, can be factored into the price of a product, then trade can be beneficial to the environment through allowing the most efficient allocation of resources. In this view, using trade restrictions as a weapon to promote good environmental behaviour would be unacceptable and, indeed, the rules of the WTO allow only very limited restrictions to trade on environmental grounds (GATT XXg) and certainly not on the basis of 'process and production methods'. A number of trade dispute cases have largely confirmed that import controls cannot be used to promote more sustainable or ethical production abroad, including the famous 1991 GATT Tuna–Dolphin case which upheld Mexican and EC complaints against US measures blocking imports of tuna caught with the methods that kill dolphins as by-catch. Developing country governments remain resistant to green trade restrictions as a disguised form of protection for developed world markets.

character, but this internationally agreed compendium of environmental 'best practice' subsequently had a wide impact and remains a point of reference. For example, many local authorities have produced their own 'local Agenda 21s'. Under the Aarhus Convention (1998), North American and European governments agreed to guarantee to their publics a number of environmental rights, including the right to obtain environmental information held by governments, to participate in policy decisions, and to have access to judicial processes.

Capacity building

Although not a specific norm of the type dealt with above, **sustainable development** provides a normative framework reflecting an underlying deal between developed and developing worlds. Frequent North–South arguments since Rio about the levels of aid and technology transfer that would allow developing countries to achieve sustainable development have seen many disappointments and unfulfilled pledges. In 1991, UNEP, UNDP, and the World Bank created the Global Environmental Facility (GEF) as an international mechanism specifically for funding environmental projects in developing countries. In 2003–6 it attracted donations of around US\$3 billion. Most environmental conventions now aim at **capacity building** through arrangements for the transfer of funds, technology, and expertise, because most of their member states simply lack the resources to participate fully in international agreements. The stratospheric ozone and climate change regimes aim to build capacity and could not exist in their current form without providing for this function.

Scientific understanding

International environmental cooperation relies upon shared scientific understanding, as reflected in the form of some important contemporary environmental regimes. An initial **framework convention** will signal concern and establish mechanisms for developing and sharing new scientific data, thereby providing the basis for taking action in a **control protocol**. Generating and sharing scientific information has long been a function of international cooperation in such public bodies as the World Meteorological Organization (WMO) and myriad academic organizations such as the International Council for the Exploration of the Seas (ICES) and the International Union for the Conservation of Nature

(IUCN). Disseminating scientific information on an international basis makes sense but it needs funding from governments because, except in areas like pharmaceutical research, the private sector has no incentive to do the work. International environmental regimes usually have standing scientific committees and subsidiary bodies to support their work. Perhaps the greatest international effort to generate new and authoritative scientific knowledge has been in the area of climate change, through the Intergovernmental Panel on Climate Change (IPCC) (see Box 20.6 below).

Governing the commons

The global commons are usually understood as areas and resources that are not under sovereign jurisdiction—they are not owned by anybody. The high seas and the deep ocean floor come within this category (beyond the 200-mile exclusive economic zone), as does Antarctica (based upon the 1959 Antarctic Treaty.) Outer space is another highly important common, its use being vital to modern telecommunications, broadcasting, navigation, and surveillance. Finally, there is the global atmosphere.

The commons all have an environmental dimension, as resources but also as 'sinks' for waste products that have been increasingly degraded. The fish and whale stocks of the high seas have been relentlessly over-exploited to the point where some species have been wiped out and long-term protein sources for human beings are imperilled. The ocean environment has been polluted by land-based effluent and oil and other discharges from ships. It has been a struggle to maintain the unique wilderness of the Antarctic in the face of increasing pressure from human beings and even outer space now faces an environmental problem in the form of increasing amounts of orbital debris left by decades of satellite launches. Similarly, the global atmosphere has been degraded in a number of highly threatening ways, through damage to the stratospheric ozone layer and, most importantly, by the enhanced greenhouse effect now firmly associated with changes to the Earth's climate. This is often characterized as a 'tragedy of the commons'. Where there is unrestricted access to a resource owned by no one, there will be an incentive for individuals to grab as much as they can and, if the resource is finite, there will come a time when it is ruined by over-exploitation as the short-term interests of individual users overwhelm the longer-run collective interest in sustaining the resource.

Box 20.4 The tragedy of the commons—local and global

Many writers, including Garrett Hardin (1968), who coined the term 'tragedy of the commons', have observed an inherent conflict between individual and collective interest and **rationality** in the use of property that is held in common. Hardin argued that individual actions in exploiting an `open access` resource will often bring collective disaster as the pasture, fish stock (common pool), or river (common sink) concerned suffers ecological collapse through over-exploitation. Of course, no problem will be perceived if the 'carrying capacity' of the common is sufficient for all to take as much as they require, but this is rarely now the case due to the intensity of modern exploitation and production practices, and recent scientific advances have sharpened humankind's appreciation of the full extent of the damage imposed on the Earth's ecosystems. Hardin's solution to the dilemma—enclosure of the commons through privatization or nationalization—has only limited applicability in the case of the global commons, for two main reasons: it is physically or politically impossible to enclose them; and there is no central world government to regulate their use.

Within the jurisdiction of governments it may be possible to solve the problem by turning the common into private property or nationalizing it, but for the global commons such a solution is, by definition, unavailable. Therefore the function of international cooperation in this context is the very necessary one of providing a substitute for **world government**, to ensure that global commons are not misused and subject to tragic collapse. This has been done through creating regimes for the governance of the global commons, which have enjoyed varying degrees of effectiveness. Many of the functions discussed above can be found in the global commons regimes, but their central contribution is a framework of rules to ensure mutual agreement between users about acceptable standards of behaviour and levels of exploitation, consistent with sustaining the ecology of the commons.

Enforcement poses difficult challenges due to the incentives for users to 'free ride' on these arrangements by taking more than a fair share, or refusing to be bound by the collective arrangements. This can potentially destroy regimes because other parties will then see no reason to restrain themselves either. In local commons regimes, inquisitive neighbours might deter rule-breaking and a similar role at the international level can be performed by NGOs. However, it is very difficult to enforce compliance with an agreement on the part of sovereign states, even when they have undertaken to comply—a fundamental difficulty for international law and hardly unique to environmental regimes (see Ch.16). Mechanisms have been developed to cope with this problem but how effective they, and the environmental regimes to which they apply, can be is hard to judge, as this involves determining the extent to which governments are in legal and technical **compliance** with their international obligations. Moreover, it also involves estimating the extent to which

state behaviour has actually been changed as a result of the international regime concerned. Naturally, the ultimate and most demanding test of the effectiveness of global commons regimes is whether or not the resources or ecologies concerned are sustained or even improved.

Some of the first and least successful global commons regimes were the various fisheries commissions for the Atlantic and elsewhere, which sought agreement on limiting catches in order to preserve stocks. Pollution from ships has been controlled by MARPOL (an international marine environmental convertion—short for marine pollution) and there is a patchwork of other treaties to manage such issues as the dumping of radioactive waste at sea. For the Antarctic, a remarkably well developed set of rules designed to preserve the ecological integrity of this last great wilderness has been devised within the framework of the 1959 Treaty. The Antarctic regime is a rather exclusive club: the Treaty's 'Consultative Parties' include the states that had originally claimed sovereignty over parts of the area while new members of the club have to demonstrate their involvement in scientific research on the frozen continent. There is a comprehensive agreement on conserving the marine ecosystem around the continent and in the late 1980s preparations for regulated minerals mining were defeated and replaced by a new Protocol on Environmental Protection including a 50-year mining ban. The success of a restricted group of countries in governing this crucial laboratory for understanding global environmental change, with only a minimal level of formal organization, demonstrates what can be achieved by international action.

Antarctic science was crucial to the discovery of a problem which resulted in what is perhaps the best example of effective international action to govern the commons. In 1985, a British Antarctic Survey balloon provided definitive evidence of serious thinning of the stratospheric ozone layer. A diminishing ozone layer is

Box 20.5 The Montreal Protocol and stratospheric ozone regime

The consequences of the thinning of stratospheric ozone layer include excessive exposure to UV/B radiation resulting in increased rates of skin cancer for human beings and damage to immune systems. Stratospheric ozone depletion arose from a previously unsuspected source—artificial chemicals containing fluorine, chlorine, and bromine which were involved in chemical reaction with ozone molecules at high altitudes. Most significant were the CFCs (chlorofluorocarbons), which had been developed in the 1920s as 'safe' inert industrial gases and which had been blithely produced and used over the next fifty years for a whole variety of purposes from refrigeration to air-conditioning and as propellants for hair spray. There was no universal agreement on the dangers posed by these chemicals and production and use continued—except, significantly, where the US Congress decided to ban some non-essential uses. This meant that the US chemical industry found itself under a costly obligation to find alternatives. As evidence on the problem began to mount, UNEP acted to convene an international conference in Vienna. It produced a 'framework convention'—the 1985 Vienna Convention on substances that deplete the stratospheric ozone layer—agreeing that international action might be required and that the parties should continue to communicate and develop and exchange scientific findings. These proved to be very persuasive, particularly with the added public impetus provided by the dramatic discovery of the Antarctic 'ozone hole'.

Within two years the Montreal Protocol was negotiated. In it the parties agreed to a regime under which the production and trading of CFCs and other ozone depleting substances would be progressively

phased out. The developed countries achieved this for CFCs by 1996 and Meetings of the Parties (**MoP**) have continued to work on the elimination of other substances since that time. There was some initial resistance from European chemical producers, but the US side had a real incentive to ensure international agreement because otherwise its chemical industry would remain at a commercial disadvantage. The other problem faced by the negotiators involved the developing countries, which themselves were manufacturing CFC products. As the Indian delegate put it, it was the developed countries' mess and their responsibility to clear it up! Why should developing countries be forced to change over to higher cost CFC alternatives? There were two responses to this. The first was an article in the Protocol giving the developing countries a period of grace. The second was a fund, set up in 1990, to finance the provision of alternative non-CFC technologies for the developing world.

Illegal production and smuggling of CFCs was evident in the 1990s. This tested the monitoring and compliance systems of the Protocol (which included a possible use of trade sanctions against offenders). Nonetheless, the regime has generally proved to be effective and has continually widened the scope of its activities to deal with further classes of ozone-depleting chemicals. The damage to the ozone layer will not be repaired until the latter part of the twenty-first century, given the long atmospheric lifetimes of the chemicals involved. However, human behaviour has been significantly altered to the extent that the scientific subsidiary body of the Montreal Protocol has been able to report a measurable reduction in the atmospheric concentration of CFCs.

---

a global problem *par excellence,* because it protects the Earth and its inhabitants from the damaging effects of the sun's UV/B radiation. A framework convention was signed about the issue in 1985, followed in 1987 by its Montreal Protocol, imposing international controls over ozone-depleting chemicals. The further evolution of the ozone layer regime offers the paramount example of how international cooperation can achieve an effective solu-

tion to a global environmental problem. The problem's causes were isolated, international support was mobilized, compensatory action was taken to ensure that developing countries participated, and a set of rules and procedures were developed which proved to be effective, at least in reducing the concentration of the offending chemicals in the atmosphere, if not yet fully restoring the stratospheric ozone layer.

Key Points

- International environmental meetings serve several political objectives alongside environmental aims.
- A key function of international cooperation is transboundary regulation but attempts at environmental action may conflict with the rules of the world trade regime.

- International action is needed to promote environmental norms, develop scientific understanding, and assist the participation of developing countries.
- International cooperation is necessary to provide governance regimes for the global commons.

Climate change

Unlike the ozone layer problem, climate change and the enhanced greenhouse effect had long been debated among scientists, but only in the late 1980s did sufficient international consensus emerge to stimulate action. There were still serious disagreements over the likelihood that human-induced changes in mean temperatures were altering the global climate system. The greenhouse effect is essential to life on Earth. Greenhouse gases (ghgs) in the atmosphere (see Fig. 20.2) insulate the Earth's surface by trapping solar radiation. Before the industrial revolution, carbon dioxide concentrations in the atmosphere were around 280 parts per million, and have since grown exponentially (to a 2005 figure of 379 ppm) due to burning of fossil fuels and reductions in some of the 'sinks' for carbon dioxide—notably forests. Methane emissions have also risen with the growth of agriculture (IPCC 2007: 11). The best predictions of the IPCC are that, if nothing is done to curb intensive fossil fuel emissions, there will be a likely rise in mean temperatures of the order of 2.4–6.4°C by 2099. The exact consequences of this are difficult to predict on the basis of current climate modelling but sea level rises and turbulent weather are generally expected. According to the EU, to avoid climate catastrophe, it would be necessary to hold temperature increases below 2°C by keeping atmospheric CO_2 concentrations below 550 ppm. In the first decade of the twenty-first century unusual weather patterns, storm events, and the melting of polar ice sheets have added a dimension of public concern to the fears expressed by the scientific community.

As a commons problem, climate change is on a quite different scale from anything that the international system has previously encountered. Climate change is really not a 'normal' international environmental problem—it

---

Box 20.6 The Intergovernmental Panel on Climate Change

Set up in 1988 under the auspices of the World Meteorological Organization (WMO) and UNEP, the Intergovernmental Panel on Climate Charge (IPCC) brings together the majority of the world's climate change scientists in three working groups: on climate science, impacts, and economic and social dimensions. They have produced assessment reports in 1990, 1995, and 2001, which are regarded as the authoritative scientific statements on climate change. The reports are carefully and cautiously drafted with the involvement of government representatives and represent a consensus view.

The Fourth Assessment Report, published in February 2007, concluded that 'warming of the climate system is unequivocal, as is now evident from observations of increases in global average air and ocean temperatures, widespread melting of snow and ice and rising global sea level' (IPCC 2007: 4). Most of the temperature increase 'is *very likely* due to the observed increase in anthropogenic greenhouse gas concentrations' (*ibid*.: 8, original italics). The use of words is significant here for the IPCC defines *'very likely'* as being more than 90 per cent certain. This represents a change from the previous report which had only estimated that human activity was *'likely'* or more than 66 per cent certain to be responsible for temperature increases.

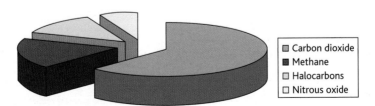

Legend:
■ Carbon dioxide
■ Methane
□ Halocarbons
□ Nitrous oxide

Source: IPCC 2007, 'Radiative Forcing Components': 16.

Figure 20.2 Greenhouse gas contributions to global warming

threatens huge changes in living conditions and challenges existing patterns of energy use and security. There is almost no dimension of international relations that it does not actually or potentially affect and it has already become the subject of 'high politics', discussed at **G8** summits and in high-level meetings between political leaders. Indeed, the UK Foreign Secretary stated in 2006 that climate change and climate security must now be a priority for foreign policy.

One way of examining the dimensions of the problem and the steps taken at the international level to respond to the threat is to make a comparison to the stratospheric ozone problem discussed in the previous section. There are, of course, some similarities. CFCs are in themselves greenhouse gases and the international legal texts on climate change make it clear that controlling them is the responsibility of the Montreal Protocol. The experience with stratospheric ozone and other recent conventions has clearly influenced efforts to build a climate change regime, as shown at the very start of climate discussions, when the same approach of a framework convention followed by protocols was adopted.

The UN Framework Convention on Climate Change (UNFCCC) was signed at the Rio Earth Summit in 1992. It envisaged the reduction of greenhouse gas emissions and their removal by sinks, hoping that a start could be made by including a commitment from the developed nations to cut their emissions back to 1990 levels by 2000. In a US election year this proved to be impossible and the parties had to be content with a non-binding declaration that an attempt would be made. There was a binding commitment, however, for parties to draw up national inventories of sources and sinks. As this included the developing nations, many of whom were ill-equipped to fulfil this obligation, there was also funding for capacity building. Most importantly, the convention locked the parties into holding a continuing series of annual conferences—the **CoPs**—to consider possible actions and review the adequacy of existing commitments, supported by regular meetings of the subsidiary scientific and implementation bodies. By the second CoP in Kyoto in 1997, the parties agreed a 'control' measure—the Kyoto Protocol involving emissions reductions be developed countries facilitated by 'flexibility mechanisms'.

The problem faced by the framers of the Kyoto Protocol was vastly more complex and demanding than that which their counterparts at Montreal had confronted so successfully in 1987. Instead of controlling a single set of industrial gases for which substitutes were available, reducing greenhouse gas emissions would involve energy, transport, and agriculture—the fundamentals of life in modern societies. Whether this must involve real sacrifices in living standards and 'impossible' political choices is a tough question for governments, although there are potential economic benefits from cutting emissions through the development of alternative energy technologies.

A second key difference from the ozone regime experience was that, despite a quite unprecedented international scientific effort in support of the IPCC to

---

Box 20.7 The Kyoto Protocol

The 1997 Kyoto Protocol to the UN Framework Convention on Climate Change commits the developed countries to make an average of a 5.2 per cent cut in their greenhouse gas emissions from a 1990 baseline. Within this, different national targets were negotiated: for example, 7 per cent for the United States and 8 per cent for the European Union (EU). These were to be achieved by the first commitment period—2008–12.

The Kyoto mechanisms

In order to provide flexible ways of achieving these targets, three mechanisms were also agreed:

1 **Emissions Trading**. This envisages a system where a market in rights to pollute is created. For example, efficient power plants can sell their permits to emit carbon dioxide to others and a long-term reduction in the number of permits available will mean that the price of carbon rises, alternative power sources become more competitive, and the overall amount of carbon dioxide emitted is reduced.

2 **Joint Implementation (JI)**. Under this mechanism a developed country can receive credits against its own emissions reduction target by financing projects in another developed country. The argument is that a given amount of money is best spent where it can achieve the greatest reduction in world emissions of greenhouse gases. Countries with very efficient power plants will have an incentive to use this scheme.

3 **The Clean Development Mechanism (CDM)**. Applies the same principle to relations between developed and developing countries. This has already stimulated a good deal of interest in China and elsewhere because it is a source of new funds and technology transfer.

establish the causes and consequences of warming, there was no scientific consensus of the kind that had promoted agreement on CFCs. There was scientific disagreement over the significance of human activities and projections of future change (which has since narrowed dramatically). There were those who had an economic interest in denying or misrepresenting the science, including fossil fuel interests and producers such as Saudi Arabia. At the other end of the spectrum, the Alliance of Small Island States, some of whose members' territory would simply disappear under projected sea level rises, were desperately concerned that these projections be taken seriously.

There is a further problem in that, even though the effects of climate change are not fully understood, there is enough evidence for some nations to calculate that there might be benefits to them from climatic alterations. Regions of Russia, for example, might become more temperate with rises in mean temperature and more suitable for agricultural production (although one could equally well argue the extremely damaging effects of melting permafrost in Siberia). One generalization that could be made with certainty is that it is the developing nations, with limited infrastructure and major populations located at sea level, which are most vulnerable. In recognition of this and on the understanding that a certain level of warming is now inevitable, international attention has begun to shift towards the problem of adaptation to the inevitable effects of climate change as well as mitigation of its causes. Once again, the comparative simplicity of the stratospheric ozone problem is evident—the effects of ozone depletion were spread across the globe and affected North Europeans as well as those living in the southern hemisphere.

At the heart of the international politics of climate change as a global environmental problem is the structural divide between North and South (see Ch.8 and Ch.26). For the Montreal Protocol there was a solution available at an acceptable price, delivered through the Multilateral Ozone Fund. Once again, climate change is different. One of the most significant **principles** set out in the UNFCCC was that of **common but differentiated responsibilities**. That is to say that while climate change was the 'common concern' of all, it had been produced as a consequence of the development of the old industrialized nations and it was their responsibility to take the lead in cutting emissions.

Case Study Common but differentiated responsibilities?

A key principle of the climate change regime, written into the 1992 UNFCCC, was the notion of 'common but differentiated responsibilities'. This, in effect, meant that although all nations had to accept responsibility for the world's changing climate, it was developed nations that were immediately responsible because they had benefited from the industrialization which was generally regarded as the source of the excess carbon dioxide emissions that had caused mean temperature increases (refer back to Fig. 20.1).

Consider the relationship between national carbon dioxide emissions and share of global population. The USA emits around 25 per cent of the global total but has only 4.5 per cent of global population. The Chinese figures are 14 per cent and over 20 per cent of the world's population while the 35 least developed nations emit under 1 per cent and account for over 10 per cent of the world's population.

Accordingly, the developed countries were listed in Annex I of the Convention and it was agreed that they, rather than developing countries, would have to lead the way in making emissions reductions.

This approach was followed in the Kyoto Protocol, where only developed country parties are committed to make reductions. Even before the Protocol was agreed, the US Senate passed the Byrd–Hagel Resolution making it clear that it would not ratify any agreement where developing nations, who were now economic competitors of the United States, did not also have to make emissions reductions.

(continued) ▶

(continued)

The future of the climate change regime

In 2004 the International Energy Agency published projections that underlined how globalization was radically changing the pattern of energy-related carbon dioxide emissions. It estimated that emissions would rise by 62 per cent by 2030 but, most significantly, that at some point in the 2020s developing world emissions would overtake those of the developed OECD countries.

It therefore became clear that to have any chance of success the future climate change regime would have to include emissions reductions by countries such as China and India, but that they in turn would not even consider this if the United States remained outside the Kyoto system. The fundamental question is upon what basis should countries be asked to reduce their emissions? The most radical and equitable answer would be to give each individual a fixed carbon allowance, probably allowing rich people to maintain something of their lifestyle by buying the allowances of the poor. A more likely alternative is to find ways of creating and then raising a global carbon price such that utilizing alternatives to fossil fuel becomes an economically attractive development path.

The achievement at Kyoto was to bind most of the developed nations to a set of emissions cuts that varied (see Box 20.7). This achieved at least part of the objectives of the European Union, but it was soon seen to be wholly inadequate in terms of the projected scale of the global warming problem. In return, the European Union accepted the US proposal for the Kyoto mechanisms and has since become their enthusiastic champion. However, none of the detail of what was to become a highly complex and innovative agreement had been worked out. It was to take a series of difficult CoPs to achieve this, to write the rules for the operation of the Protocol, and, above all, to meet the demanding requirements for its **ratification** and entry into force. These were that 55 parties had to ratify the agreement and that these parties must also produce over 55 per cent of global emissions. It was very evident that the United States would not ratify Kyoto and the administration of George W. Bush actually denounced US signature of the Protocol, claiming it to be 'fatally flawed' and that the emissions cuts required would be impossibly damaging to the US economy. Australia also refused to ratify, thus making it essential that Russia and Japan should ratify alongside the European Union. Much of the burden of ensuring that Kyoto eventually entered into force fell upon the EU and tested the diplomatic capabilities of this new type of international actor and its component member states in what became a direct contest with the US government. The EU also pioneered the world's first international emissions trading system which commenced operation at the beginning of 2005. This was in the hope that it would not only help to achieve the EU's Kyoto target of an 8 per cent reduction in emissions by 2012, but that it would also encourage other countries to join the scheme.

The climate regime has been afflicted by the 'free rider' problem. If some countries join together and agree to make cuts which are costly, then others who do not can enjoy the environmental benefits of such action without paying. Thus, proceeding without the USA has been very difficult, not only because it produces around one-quarter of global carbon dioxide emissions, but also because its failure to be involved affects the willingness of others to participate and particularly the fast developing economies of the South. There is some hope that the Kyoto targets may be achieved by 2012, but even that is uncertain. The Bush administration has resolutely opposed Kyoto and from its entry into force in 2005, discussions have been proceeding as to how a new regime might be constructed that involves all of the main industrialized and industrializing countries in a collective scheme to make significant cuts in their greenhouse gas emissions, but also to work together to adapt to the effects of climate change that are already becoming evident. There is probably no more urgent or important task for international cooperation.

Key Points

- Climate change, because of its all-embracing nature and its roots in essential human activities, poses an enormous challenge for international cooperation.
- A limited start has been made with the Kyoto regime but this is undermined by the absence of the United States. Much more radical arrangements will be required in the period after 2012 and these will have to involve the major developing world economies.

The environment and International Relations theory

The academic study of the international relations of the environment has naturally tried to understand the circumstances under which potentially effective international cooperation can occur. The preceding discussion of climate change shows that this question remains important. Most scholars have used the concept of regime as explained in Chapter 17. Note, for instance, how the defining characteristics of regimes—principles, norms, **rules** and **decision-making procedures**—can be applied to the environmental cases mentioned in this chapter (also see Ch.9). Those who try to explain the record of environmental regimes tend to adopt a liberal institutionalist stance, stressing as a key motivating factor the joint gains arising from cooperative solutions to the problem of providing public goods such as a clean atmosphere (see Ch.6 and Ch.7). One important addition to the regime literature, made by scholars of environmental politics, reflects the importance of scientific knowledge and the roles of NGOs in this area. Whereas orthodox regime approaches assume that behaviour is based upon the pursuit of power or interest, students of international environmental cooperation have noted the independent role played by changes in knowledge (particularly scientific understanding). This cognitive approach is reflected in studies of the ways in which transnationally organized groups of scientists and policy-makers—often referred to as **epistemic communities**—have influenced the development of environmental regimes (see Ch.9).

Liberal Institutionalist analysis of regime creation may still be the predominant IR approach to global environmental change, but it is not the only one. It makes the important, but often unspoken, assumption that the problem to be solved is how to obtain global governance in a fragmented system of sovereign states. Marxist and Gramscian writers would reject this formulation (see Ch.8). For them, the **state system** is part of the problem rather than the solution, and the proper object of study is the way in which global **capitalism** reproduces relationships that are profoundly damaging to the environment. The global spread of neo-liberal policies accelerates those features of globalization—consumerism, the relocation of production to the South, and the thoughtless squandering of resources—driving the global ecological crisis (see Ch.27). Proponents of this view also highlight the incapacity of the state to do anything other than assist such processes. It follows that the international cooperation efforts described here, at worst legitimize this state of affairs and at best provide some marginal improvements to the devastation wrought by global capitalism. For example, they would point to how free market concepts are now routinely embedded in discussions of sustainable development and how the WTO rules tend to subordinate attempts to provide environmental regulation of GMOs. This argument is part of a broader debate among political theorists concerning whether the state can ever be 'greened'. The opposing view would be that within any time frame that is relevant to coping with a threat of the immediacy and magnitude of climate change, the state and international cooperation remain the only plausible mechanisms for providing the necessary global governance and we shall simply have to make the best we can with existing state and international organizational structures.

The other theoretical connection that must be made is to the pre-eminent concern of orthodox IR—**security** (see Ch.13). This link can be thought of in two ways. First, it is argued that environmental change contributes to the incidence of both internal conflict and even inter-state war, even though the causal connections are complex and involve many factors. It is already evident that desertification and the degradation of other vital resources are intimately bound up with cycles of poverty, destitution, and war in Africa. However, if we consider such predicted consequences of climate change as mass migrations of populations across international boundaries and acute scarcity of water and other resources, the outlines of potential future conflicts come into sharper focus (see Ch.26 and Ch.27).

The link between environmental change and armed conflict is essentially an extension of traditional thinking about security, defined in terms of collective violence and attacks upon the state. A more intriguing question is whether we should now redefine the idea of security to

encompass environmental threats as well as those stemming from **terrorism** and war (see Ch.12). As the public becomes more sharply aware of the full magnitude of the climate problem, political discourse begins to 'securitize' the environment, that is, to characterize the environment as a security problem. Because governments usually prioritize security matters, people wishing to mobilize political attention and resources, and encourage potentially painful societal adaptation, will be tempted to stretch traditional definitions of security.

Key Points

- The environment has been a growth area for IR scholars interested in identifying the conditions under which effective international cooperation can emerge.
- Scholars differ in the importance that they attach to various kinds of explanatory factors in their analyses of international environmental regime-building activities—crude calculations of the power and interests of key actors such as states, cognitive factors such as shared scientific knowledge, the impact of non-governmental actors, and even the extent to which the system of states is itself part of the problem.
- IR scholars are also interested in the extent to which the environment in general and particular environmental problems are now being seen as security issues in academic, political, and popular discourse, and whether this securitization of the environment is something to be welcomed.

Conclusion

This chapter has shown, briefly, how environmental issues have moved from the margins to an increasingly central place on the international agenda. Climate change is now widely perceived to be at least the equal of any other issue and arguably the most important faced by humankind. The rise to prominence of environmental issues is intimately associated with globalization due to the strain that this places on the Earth's carrying capacity in terms consumption levels, resource depletion, and rising greenhouse gas emissions. Globalization has also facilitated the growth of transnational green politics and interventions by NGOs to raise public awareness, influence international conferences, and even monitor the implementation of agreements by states.

At every stage, two distinctive aspects of international environmental politics have played a central role. The first is the complex relationship between scientific understanding of the biosphere, politics, and policy, as exemplified by the interplay between the IPCC and the actions of governments building the climate regime. The second is the connection between environment and development, which has been expressed in the shifting meanings given to the concept of sustainable development and whose acknowledgement has been a precondition for international action on a whole range of environmental issues. Nowhere is this more evident than in debates about the future direction of the climate regime.

The international response to environmental change has been in the form of attempts to arrange global environmental governance through extensive cooperation between governments. This chapter has attempted to provide some insight into the range and functions of such regime-creating activities, which provide a basis upon which the international community is attempting to grapple with the climate problem. The academic community has generally followed this enterprise by concentrating upon the question of how regimes may be formed and sustained. More critical theorists will take a different view of the meaning of international cooperation (see Ch.8 and Ch.10). Furthermore, the challenges posed to international theory by the global environmental predicament will undoubtedly involve the need to think through the connections between security, climate change, and globalization.

❓ Questions

1 What are the possible connections, both negative and positive, between globalization and environmental change?

2 Why did environmental issues appear on the international agenda and what were the key turning points?

3 Summarize the consequences of the 1972 UNCHE and the 1992 UNCED.

4 How would you interpret the meaning of sustainable development?

5 How can regime concepts be applied to the study of international environmental cooperation (also see Ch.17)?

6 Can international trade and environmental protection ever be compatible?

7 Why did the framework convention/control protocol prove useful in the cases of stratospheric ozone depletion and climate change?

8 Analyze the development implications of three of the regimes mentioned in the chapter.

9 How does the 'tragedy of the commons' analogy help to illustrate the need for governance of the global commons?

10 Describe the 'free rider' problem in relation to the climate change regime.

11 Can 'common but differentiated responsibilities' continue to be relevant to the future climate change regime?

12 Consider the possible security implications of the climate predictions made by IPCC.

➔ Guide to further reading

Barnett, J. (2001), *The Meaning of Environmental Security: Ecological Politics and Policy in the New Security Era* (London: Zed Books). This lively and critical book is for readers who wish to explore the growing connections between environmental and security issues.

Barry, J., and Eckersley, R. (eds) (2005), *The State and the Global Ecological Crisis* (Cambridge, Mass.: MIT Press). A provocative set of essays on the continuing relevance of the state, long forsaken by green activists, but still the fundamental unit of global environmental governance.

Birnie, P., and Boyle, A., (2002), *International Law and the Environment* (Oxford: Oxford University Press). An invaluable source of detailed information on formal aspects of international environmental cooperation.

Brenton, T. (1994), *The Greening of Machiavelli: The Evolution of International Environmental Politics* (London: Earthscan). A diplomatic participant's account of the international politics of the environment up to and including the Rio Earth Summit.

Dauvergne, P. (ed.) (2005), *Handbook of Global Environmental Politics* (Cheltenham: Edward Elgar). This very extensive collection of 30 essays covering states governance and security, capitalism, trade and corporations, civil societies, knowledge and ethics will provide the reader with a more 'advanced' view of current concerns and controversies in the field.

de Sombre, B. (2006), *Global Environmental Institutions* (Abingdon: Routledge). Provides a concise introduction within a series on global governance.

Dryzek, J. (1997), *The Politics of the Earth: Environmental Discourses* (Oxford: Oxford University Press). Still extremely useful as a guide to thinking through the different approaches that are applied to the problems of environmental politics and sustainable development.

Elliott, L. (2004), *The Global Politics of the Environment* (Basingstoke: Palgrave). This comprehensive and up-to-date text provides detailed and wide-ranging coverage of the field and of the key international agreements.

Lipschutz, R. D. (2004), *Global Environmental Politics: Power Perspectives and Practice* (Washington, DC: CQ Press). Makes innovative and critical connections between global environmental politics and a broad array of relevant political thought and practice.

Paterson, M. (2001), *Understanding Global Environmental Politics: Domination, Accumulation, Resistance* (Basingstoke: Palgrave). As the title suggests, this book provides an alternative critical view of global environmental politics, investigating such problems as the political economy of car use.

Vogler, J. (2000), *The Global Commons: Environmental and Technological Governance* (Chichester: John Wiley). Uses regime analysis to compare and account for the various international arrangements for the ocean, Antarctic, space, and atmospheric commons.

Online Resource Centre

 Visit the Online Resource Centre that accompanies this book to access more learning resources on this chapter topic at www.oxfordtextbooks.co.uk/uk/orc/baylis_smith4e/

Chapter 21

Terrorism and globalization

JAMES D. KIRAS

- Introduction ···372
- Definitions ··372
- Terrorism: from transnational to global phenomenon (1968–2001) ·······················374
- Terrorism: the impact of globalization ··············375
- Globalization, technology, and terrorism ·············378
- Combating terrorism ···································382
- Conclusion ···384

Reader's Guide

Globalization has contributed to the growth of terrorism from a regional phenomenon into a global one. Precisely how it has contributed, however, is hard to determine. The difficulty lies in the complex nature of terrorism and disagreements on what constitutes globalization. Global terrorism has been explained in cultural, economic, and religious terms linked to globalization. Such terms are necessary, but ultimately are not sufficient to explain the relationship. Technology associated with globalization has enabled terrorist groups to conduct operations that are deadlier, more distributed, and more difficult to combat than they were in the past. Technological advantage, however, is not one-sided, and states can use technology to diminish the global impact of terrorism.

Introduction

The relationship between **terrorism** and **globalization** is difficult to describe accurately. Each phenomenon is complicated in its own right and defies simple characterization. It is inaccurate to suggest that globalization is responsible for terrorism, but technologies associated with globalization have been exploited by terrorists. In particular, technologies have improved the ability of terrorist groups to work together, share information, and reach out to previously unavailable audiences. Technology, how-ever, cannot change the character of the terrorist message or the nature of the struggle. Terrorism is a weapon of the weak conducted by a minority of individuals who promote an extremist ideology—it often fails to create political change. The global community is not powerless in the face of such violence. In order to succeed, the global community must utilize the resources at its disposal collaboratively to diminish support for terrorism and demonstrate the illegitimacy of terrorist messages and aspirations.

Definitions

Terrorism and globalization share at least one thing in common—both are complex phenomena open to subjective interpretation. Definitions of terrorism vary widely but all start from a common point of departure. Terrorism is characterized, first and foremost, by the use of violence. This tactic of violence takes many forms and often indiscriminately targets non-combatants. The purpose for which violence is used, and its root causes, is where most of the disagreements about terrorism begin. Historically, the term 'terrorism' described **state** violence against citizens during the French Revolution. Over the past half-century, however, terrorism has come to mean the use of violence by small groups to achieve political change. Terrorism differs from criminal violence in its degree of political legitimacy. Those sympathetic to terrorist causes suggest that violence is the only remaining option that can draw attention to the plight of the aggrieved. Such causes have included ideological, ethnic, and religious exclusion or persecution.

Defining terrorism can be difficult as groups often espouse multiple grievances and compete with one another for resources and support. In addition, the relative importance of these grievances within groups can change over time. Those targeted by terrorists are less inclined to see any justification, much less legitimacy, behind attacks that are designed to spread fear by killing and maiming civilians. As a result, the term 'terrorist' has a pejorative value that is useful in delegitimizing those who commit such acts.

Reaching consensus on what constitutes terrorism is difficult. The legitimacy of terrorist means and methods is the foremost reason for disagreement. Some view ter-

---

Box 21.1 Types of terrorist groups

Audrey Kurth Cronin has outlined different types of terrorist groups and their historical importance in the following way:

'There are four types of terrorist organizations currently operating around the world, categorized mainly by their source of motivation: left-wing terrorists, right-wing terrorists, ethnonationalist/separatist terrorists, and religious or 'sacred' terrorists. All four types have enjoyed periods of relative prominence in the modern era, with left-wing terrorism intertwined with the Communist movement, right-wing terrorism drawing its inspiration from Fascism, and the bulk of ethnonationalist/separatist terrorism accompanying the wave of decolonization especially in the immediate post-World War II years. Currently, "sacred" terrorism is becoming more significant . . . . Of course, these categories are not perfect, as many groups have a mix of motivating ideologies some ethnonationalist groups, for example, have religious characteristics or agendas—but usually one ideology or motivation dominates.'

(Cronin 2002/3: 39)

Box 21.2 Legitimacy

Martha Crenshaw provides an analytic, albeit subjective approach to determine the legitimacy of terrorist acts of violence:

'The value of the normative approach (to terrorism) is that it confronts squarely a critical problem in the analysis of terrorism, and indeed any form of political violence: the issue of legitimacy. Terrorists of the left deny the legitimacy of the state and claim that the use of violence against it is morally justified. Terrorists of the right deny the legitimacy of the opposition and hold that the violence in the service of order is sanctioned by the values of the status quo ... the need for scholarly objectivity and abstraction does not excuse use from the obligation to judge the morality of the use of force, whether by the state or against.'

She adds that morality can be judged in two ways:

... 'morality of the ends and the morality of the means. First, are the goals of the terrorists democratic or nondemocratic? That is, is their aim to create or perpetuate a regime of privilege and inequality, to deny liberty to other people, or to further the ends of justice, freedom, and equality ... Terrorism must not, as the terrorists can foresee, result in *worse* injustice than the condition the terrorists oppose .. The morality of the means of terrorism is also open to judgment. The targets of terrorism are morally significant; witness the difference between material objects and human casualties.'

(Crenshaw 1983: 2–4)

rorist acts as legitimate only if they meet the criteria associated with the 'just war' tradition. These criteria, which apply to all applications of force, have been expanded to include a just cause, proportional use of violence, and the use of force as a last resort. Realists suggest that the political violence used by terrorist groups is illegitimate on the basis that states alone have a **monopoly on the legitimate use of physical force.**

Yet even with the use of violence by states, there is disagreement on what constitutes the legitimate application of armed force. For example, during the 1980s Libya sponsored terrorist acts as an indirect method of attacking the United States, France, and the United Kingdom. Those states, in turn, condemned Libyan sponsorship as contravening international **norms** and responded with sanctions, international court cases, and occasional uses of force. Disagreement associated with the invasion of Iraq in 2003, led by the United States, relates to interpretations over whether or not the conditions for 'just war' were met prior to commencement of military operations. Some suggest that the conditions were not met, and that actions by the coalition should be considered as an 'act of terrorism' conducted by states. Leaders in the United States and the United Kingdom dismiss the charge on the basis that a greater evil was removed. Violating international norms in the pursuit of terrorists runs the risk of playing into perceptions that the state itself is a terrorist threat. Critics suggest that US policy towards terrorist detainees and 'extraordinary renditions' damages the nation's credibility as a global champion for individual rights and freedoms.

As with other forms of irregular warfare, terrorism is designed to achieve political change for the purposes of obtaining power in order to right a perceived wrong. Terrorism, however, is the weakest form of irregular warfare with which to alter the political landscape. The reason for this weakness is that terrorist groups rarely possess the broader support of the population that characterizes insurgency and revolution. Terrorist groups often lack broader support for their objectives because their goals for change are based on radical ideas that do not have widespread appeal. In order to influence change, terrorists must provoke drastic responses that act as a catalyst for change or weaken their opponent's moral resolve. In a few cases, terrorist acts have achieved relatively rapid change. The bombings in Madrid in 2004, for example, influenced the outcome of elections in Spain in a dramatic fashion and anecdotal evidence suggests that the attack was designed with just such a purpose in mind. Many terrorist leaders hope that their actions will lead to disproportionate reactions by a state that in turn disaffects public or international opinion and increases support for their cause. Some suggest, for example, that Al Qaeda goaded the United States into invading and 'occupying' Iraq, which has bolstered terrorist recruiting. Terrorist campaigns, however, often take years or decades to achieve meaningful results and the amount and nature of force used can be problematic. Terrorist groups

risk fading into obscurity if they do not cow the public or conduct newsworthy attacks. However, as the recent violence in Iraq suggests, attacks by terrorists that are so horrific, such as publicized beheadings, puts support for terrorist causes at risk. Therefore terrorism is defined here as 'the use of violence by sub-state groups to inspire fear, by attacking civilians and/or symbolic targets, for purposes such as drawing widespread attention to a grievance, provoking a severe response, or wearing down their opponent's moral resolve, to effect political change'.

As with definitions of terrorism, there is general agreement on at least one aspect of globalization. Technologies allow the transfer of goods, services, and information almost anywhere quickly and efficiently. In the case of information, the transfer can be secure and is nearly instantaneous. The extent of social, cultural, and political change brought on by globalization, including increasing interconnectedness and homogeneity in the **international system**, remain the subject of much disagreement and debate, as other chapters in this volume have outlined. These disagreements, in turn, influence discussion of the extent to which globalization has contributed to the rise of modern terrorism. There is little doubt that the tech-

nologies associated with globalization have been used to improve the effectiveness and reach of terrorist groups. The relationship between globalization and terrorism is best understood as the next step in the evolution of political violence since terrorism became a transnational phenomenon in the 1960s. In order to understand the changes perceived in terrorism globally, it is useful to understand the evolution of terrorism from a transnational to a global phenomenon.

Key Points

- Agreement on what constitutes terrorism continues to be difficult given the range of potential acts involving violence.
- Terrorism, or acts of violence by sub-state groups, has been separated from criminal acts on the basis of the purpose for which violence is applied, namely political change.
- Terrorist groups succeed when their motivations or grievances are perceived to be legitimate by a wider audience. Disproportionate or heavy-handed responses by states to acts of terrorism serve to legitimize terrorist groups.
- The definition of globalization, as with terrorism, is open to subjective interpretation but the technologies associated with globalization have improved terrorist capabilities.

Terrorism: from transnational to global phenomenon (1968–2001)

Historically, terrorists have used readily available means to permit small numbers of individuals to spread fear as widely as possible. In the late nineteenth and early twentieth century, anarchists relied upon revolvers and dynamite. Yet terrorists and acts of terrorism rarely had an impact beyond national borders. Three factors led to the birth of transnational terrorism in 1968: the expansion of commercial air travel, the availability of televised news coverage, and broad political and ideological interests among extremists that intersected around a common cause. As a result, terrorism grew from a local to a transnational threat. Air travel gave terrorists unprecedented mobility. For example, the Japanese Red Army trained in one country and attacked in another, such as the 1972 Lod Airport massacre in Israel. Air travel appealed to terrorists for other reasons. Airport security measures, including passport control, were almost non-existent when terrorists began hijacking airlines. These **skyjackings** suited terrorist purposes well. Hijacked airlines

offered a degree of mobility, and therefore **security**, for the terrorists involved. States also acquiesced to terrorist demands, which encouraged further incidents. The success of this tactic spurred other terrorist groups, as well as criminals and political refugees, to follow suit. As a result, incidents of hijacking skyrocketed from five in 1966 to 94 in 1969. Shared political ideologies stimulated **cooperation** and limited exchanges between groups as diverse as the Irish Republican Army (IRA) and the Basque separatist Euzkadi Ta Askatasuna (ETA). Besides sharing techniques and technical experience, groups demanded the release of imprisoned 'fellow revolutionaries' in different countries, giving the impression of a coordinated **global terrorist network**. The reality was that groups formed relationships of convenience, based around weapons, capabilities, and money, to advance local political objectives.

Televised news coverage also played a role in expanding the audience who could witness the **theatre of terrorism**

in their own homes. Individuals who had never heard of 'the plight of the Palestinians' became notionally aware of the issue after incidents such as the live coverage of the hostage taking conducted by Black September during the 1972 Munich Olympics. Although media coverage was termed **the oxygen that sustains terrorism**, terrorists discovered that reporters and audiences lost interest in repeat performances over time. In order to sustain viewer interest and compete for coverage, terrorist groups undertook increasingly spectacular attacks, such as the seizure of Organization of Petroleum Exporting Countries (OPEC) delegates by 'Carlos the Jackal' in Austria in December 1975. Terrorism experts speculated that terrorist leaders understood that horrific, mass casualty attacks might cross a **threshold of violence.** This may explain why few terrorist groups attempted to acquire or use **weapons of mass destruction**, including nuclear, chemical, and biological weapons.

The Iranian 'Islamic Revolution' of 1979 was a watershed event in transnational terrorism. Although Israeli interests remained primary targets for attack, due to continued sympathy for the Palestinian cause, a number of groups began to target citizens and other symbols of the United States. The **decade of terrorism** (1980–90), included incidents such as suicide bombings (Lebanon, 1983) and hijackings (TWA Flight 847, 1985). During this decade three disturbing trends emerged: fewer attacks that were more deadly and indiscriminate; the increasing sophistication of attacks; and a greater willingness to perform suicide attacks.

Transnational Marxist-Leninist groups discovered that their source of support disappeared at the end of the **cold war**. In addition, state law enforcement and paramilitary forces were increasingly effective in **combating terrorism**. Other terrorist groups discovered that transnational attacks were counter-productive in achieving local aims. For example, ETA and the IRA sought negotiations but still used terrorist attacks as a bargaining ploy and to remain visible domestically. Although Marxist-Leninist, transnational terrorism was decreasing in scale and intensity, militant Islamic terrorism, symbolized by the group Al Qaeda and enabled by globalization, was growing into a global phenomenon.

Key Points

- The majority of transnational terrorist attacks from 1979 onwards targeted American citizens and symbols.
- Trends in terrorism since 1968 include greater casualties, increasing sophistication, and suicide attacks.
- Transnational Marxist-Leninist groups have replaced by global militant Islamic terrorist groups.

Terrorism: the impact of globalization

Al Qaeda, or 'The Base', received global recognition as a result of its attacks conducted in New York and Washington on **11 September 2001**. But what exactly is Al Qaeda? Is it a global terrorist group that threatens Western civilization and values, a sub-state financial and resource provider to like-minded terrorist groups, or merely the purveyors of an extremist set of beliefs that justifies political violence to fulfil militant Islamic myths? Experts continue to debate what Al Qaeda is, what it represents, and the actual threat that it poses. Part of the reason for the disagreement stems from the fact that Al Qaeda, as the standard bearer for militant Islam, has evolved considerably since the invasion of Afghanistan. Immediately after **9/11**, Al Qaeda was depicted as the centre of a global nexus of terrorism connected to almost all terrorist groups. More recently, however, Al Qaeda has appeared less as a group and more as a global movement that markets and exploits its own form of militant Islam in a loose **network** of 'franchised' cells and groups. Regardless of how one views Al Qaeda, one cannot dispute the influence and appeal of its message across national boundaries. Efforts to explain the vitality of global terrorism in general—and Al Qaeda in particular—focus on three areas linked to aspects of globalization: culture, economics, and religion.

Cultural explanations

Culture is one way to explain why militant Islam's call for armed struggle has been successful in underdeveloped countries. In particular, violence is the only method to preserve traditions and values against a cultural tsunami of Western products and **materialism**. Once sought after

Box 21.3 Al Qaeda Associated Movement (AQAM)

In early 2006, the Office of the Chairman of the Joint Chiefs of Staff in the Pentagon released the *National Military Strategic Plan for the War on Terrorism*, which characterizes the fluid nature of the militant Islamic terrorism:

'There is no monolithic enemy network with a single set of goals and objectives. The nature of the threat is more complicated. In the GWOT [global war on terror], the primary enemy is a transnational movement of extremist organizations, networks, and individuals— and their state and non-state supporters—which have in common that they exploit Islam and use terrorism for ideological ends. The Al

Qa'ida Associated Movement (AQAM), comprised of Al Qa'ida and affiliated extremists, is the most dangerous present manifestation of such extremism . . . . The [Al Qaeda network's] adaptation or evolution resulted in the creation of an extremist 'movement,' referred to by intelligence analysts as AQAM, extending extremism and terrorist tactics well beyond the original organization. This adaptation has resulted in decentralizing control in the network and franchising its extremist efforts within the movement.'

(National Military Strategic Plan for the War on Terrorism (Unclassified), p. 13)

as an entry method to economic prosperity, Western secular, materialist values are increasingly rejected by those seeking to regain or preserve their own unique cultural identity. The social changes associated with globalization and the spread of free market **capitalism** appear to overwhelm the identity or values of groups who perceive themselves as the losers in the new international system. In an attempt to preserve their threatened identity and values, groups actively distinguish themselves from despised 'others'. At the local level, this cultural friction may translate into conflicts divided along religious or ethnic lines to safeguard **identity**.

According to one explanation, however, the number of distinct civilizations is limited globally. They include Western, Confucian, Japanese, Islamic, Hindu, Slavic-Orthodox, and Latin American (Huntington 1993: 25). Geography and relative cultural stability limits abrasion between some of the civilizations. Where individuals perceive their own civilization to be weak, insecure, or stagnant, and interaction is high between weak and strong civilizations, conflict may be inevitable. Samuel Huntington suggests that a major **fault-line** exists between the liberal Western civilization and an Islamic one 'humiliated and resentful of the West's military presence in the Persian Gulf, the West's overwhelming military dominance, and . . . [unable] to shape their own destiny' (1993: 32).

Critics of Huntington suggest, among other things, that he ascribes a degree of homogeneity within the Islamic world that simply does not exist (also see Ch.24). Theologically and socially, the Islamic 'civilization' contains a number of deep fault-lines that impede the cooperation required to challenge the West. The extremely bloody sectarian violence between Sunni and

Shi'a in Iraq is only one example of these very real fissures. Militant Islamic calls to kill non-combatants and fellow Muslims represent another internal fault-line. Non-believers fall into the categories of infidels (those of different religion) and apostates (those Muslims who do not share their interpretation of the Koran). As a result, Osama bin Laden's unequivocal sanction to Abu Musab al-Zarqawi to kill Muslim Shi'a in Iraq in 2005 calls into question the morality of the means, and therefore the legitimacy of bin Laden and militant Islam as the champions of Muslim values among the wider and moderate Islamic community.

Economic explanations

Not everyone agrees that defence of culture or identity is the primary motivation for globalized terrorist violence. Others see economic aspects as the crucial motivating factor in the use of violence to effect political change. Although globalization provides access to a world market for goods and services, the net result has also been perceived as a form of Western economic **imperialism**. The United States and the post-industrial states of Western Europe form the global North or economic 'core' which dominates international economic institutions such as the **World Bank**, sets exchange rates, and determines fiscal policies. The actions and policies can be unfavourable to the underdeveloped countries, or global South, that comprise the **periphery** or **gap**. Political decisions by the leaders of underdeveloped countries to deregulate or privatize industries to be competitive globally may lead to significant social and economic upheaval. The citizenry may shift loyalties to illegal activities such as terrorism if the state breaks its social contract with them (Junaid 2005: 143–4).

Wealth is also linked to personal security and violence. With little possible opportunity to obtain wealth locally, individuals will leave to pursue opportunities elsewhere. The result is emigration and/or the rapid growth of burgeoning urban centres that act as regional hubs for the flow of global resources. Movement, however, is no guarantee that individual aspirations will be realized. In that case, individuals may turn to violence for criminal (i.e. personal gain) or political (i.e. to change the existing political system through insurgency or terrorism) reasons. Paradoxically, rising standards of living and greater access to educational opportunities associated with globalization may lead to increased expectations. If those expectations are unrealized, individuals can turn to extreme political views and action against 'the system' that denies them the opportunity to realize their ambitions. A prominent study suggests that a sense of alienation and lack of opportunity among some Muslim males is a contributing factor for their decision to turn to violence globally (Sageman 2004: 95–6).

Other views offer a broader explanation. In particular, the writings of revolutionary Franz Fanon provide insights in the use of political violence to right economic wrongs (Onwudiwe 2001: 52–6). In the 1960s, Fanon suggested that the end of colonialism would not end conflict between the West and the oppressed. This struggle would be replaced by another until the economic and power imbalances were removed (Fanon 1990: 74). Terrorist violence is motivated by inequalities of the global economy. Therefore terrorist attacks against the World Trade Center in 1993 and 2001 were not reactions against the policies of the United States *per se*, but rather a blow against an icon of global capitalism. Statements by fringe groups, including neo-Nazis, anarchists, and the 'New, New Left', are additional evidence that globalization might be a stimulus for political violence (Rabasa, Chalk, *et al.* 2006: 86-93).

The explanation that recent terrorist violence is a reaction to economic globalization is flawed for a number of reasons. These reasons include the personal wealth and social upbringing of a number of members of global terrorist groups as well as trends in regional patterns of terrorist recruitment. Many former leaders and members of transnational terrorist groups, including the German Red Army Faction and the Italian Red Brigades, came from respectable families. The same holds true for a number of modern-day anti-globalization anarchists. Within militant Islamic groups, most of their leaders and senior operatives attended graduate schools around the globe in fields as diverse as engineering and theology, and were neither poor nor downtrodden (Sageman 2004: 73-4).

The links between terrorism and **poverty** also varies considerably between regions. Many militant Islamic terrorists in Europe have employment rates and salaries that are close to EU averages for their age group (Bakker 2006: 41, 52). One might expect that the poorest region globally would account for a high percentage of terrorists but this is not the case. Despite conditions that favour the outbreak of terrorist violence in sub-Saharan Africa against economic imperialism and global capitalism, the region has not proved a breeding ground for terrorism.

Religion and 'new' terrorism

In the decade prior to September 11, a number of scholars and experts perceived that fundamental changes were taking place in the character of terrorism. The use of violence for political purposes, to change state ideology or the representation of ethnic minority groups, had failed in its purpose and a new trend was emerging (see Ch.12). **Postmodern** or **'new' terrorism** was conducted for different reasons altogether. Motivated by promises of rewards in the afterlife, some terrorists are driven by religious reasons to kill as many of the non-believers and unfaithful as possible (Laqueur 1996: 32–3). Although suicide tactics had been observed in Lebanon as early as 1983, militant Islam had previously been viewed as a state-sponsored, regional phenomenon (Wright 1986: 19–21).

New terrorism, which some authors use to explain the global *jihad*, is seen as a reaction to the perceived oppression of Muslims worldwide and the spiritual bankruptcy of the West. As globalization spreads and societies become increasingly interconnected, Muslims have a choice: accept Western beliefs to better integrate or preserve their spiritual purity by rebelling. Believers in the global *jihad* view the rulers of 'Islamic' countries such as Pakistan, Saudi Arabia, or Iraq as apostates who have compromised their values in the pursuit and maintenance of secular, state-based **power**. The only possible response is to fight against such influences through *jihad*. *Jihad* is understood by most Islamic scholars and imams to mean the internal struggle for purity spiritually, although it has also been interpreted historically as a method to establish the basis for just war. Extremists who espouse militant Islam, including Osama bin Laden and Ayman al-Zawahiri, understand *jihad* in a different

way. For the *jihadi* terrorist, there can be no compromise with either infidels or apostates.

The difference in value structures between secular and religious terrorists makes the responses to the latter difficult. Religious terrorists will kill themselves and others to secure rewards in the afterlife. Differences in value **structures** make the **deterrence** of religious terrorism difficult if not impossible, as secular states cannot credibly threaten materially that which terrorists value spiritually. Secular terrorism has had as its goal the pursuit of power in order to correct flaws within society but retain the overarching system. Religious terrorists, in contrast, do not seek to modify but rather replace the normative structure of society (Cronin 2002/3: 41).

The use of religion, as a reaction to and an explanation for the phenomenon of global terrorism, contains some of the same incongruities as those focused on cultural and economic aspects. For Western observers, religious reasons appear to explain how individual terrorists are convinced to take their own lives and kill others. Personal motivations can include promises of financial rewards for family members, achieving fame within a community, taking revenge for some grievance, or simply achieving a form of self-actualizing. Yet few religious terrorist leaders, planners, and coordinators martyr themselves. Religion provides terrorist groups with a crucial advantage: the mandate and sanction of

the divine to commit otherwise illegal or immoral acts. There is a substantial difference between religious motivation as the single driving factor for individuals to commit acts of terrorism and the ultimate purpose for which violence is being used. Scholars disagree on the ultimate political purpose of religiously-inspired suicide violence. Such purposes can include competing with other terrorist groups for popular support in a process of 'outbidding' (Bloom 2005: 77–9) or for self-determination, to convince foreign occupiers to withdraw their forces (Pape 2005: 45–6). A common theme among *jihadi* statements is another political purpose: overthrowing apostate regimes and assuming political power. Political power, in turn, is necessary to impose the militant Islamic form of Sharia law within a state and restore the just and pure society of the caliphate.

Key Points

- Cultural, economic, and religious aspects provide necessary, but insufficient explanations for globalized terrorist violence individually.
- The current wave of terrorist violence uses religion as a motivator and to provide the justification to kill non-combatants.
- The ultimate purpose for modern militant Islamic violence is applied is obtaining political power in order to conduct political, social, economic, and religious reform according to Sharia law.

Globalization, technology, and terrorism

Few challenge the point that terrorism has become much more pervasive worldwide due to the processes and technologies of globalization. The technological advances associated with globalization have improved the **capabilities** of terrorist groups to plan and conduct operations with far more devastation and **coordination** than their predecessors could have imagined. In particular, technologies have improved the capability of groups and cells in the following areas: proselytizing, coordination, security, mobility, and lethality.

Proselytizing

Terrorist groups have traditionally sought sympathy and support within national boundaries or in neighboring

countries as a means to sustain their efforts. Sustaining terrorist causes has traditionally been more difficult as terrorist messages, goals, and grievances tend to be extreme, and therefore less appealing, than those of insurgents. For example, land reform, government corruption, or foreign occupation motivates larger numbers of individuals to support or join insurgencies, whereas the radical political ideology espoused by groups such as the Japanese Red Army and the Weather Underground had little appeal in largely prosperous and stable democratic societies. States traditionally have had an advantage in their ability to control information flows and use their resources to win the **battle of hearts and minds** against terrorist groups. Terrorist leaders understand how the Internet has changed this dynamic: 'we are in a battle, and

Case Study Three generations of militant Islamic terrorists

The first generation of militant Islamic terrorists who were closely affiliated with Al Qaeda shared a number of common traits. A significant number fought in Afghanistan against the Soviet Union and aligned with Osama bin Laden as a result of an intellectual split that occurred in 1994. Bin Laden believed it was necessary to fight next against the 'far' enemy, the United States (and by extension, the West) which was responsible for a number of perceived injustices against Islam. Others continued to advocate the overthrow of 'near' enemies who ruled over secular Islamic states. In preparation for the fight against the 'far' enemy, bin Laden moved to Afghanistan in 1998 and established numerous training camps, research facilities, and a support bureaucracy. One of those who migrated to Afghanistan at this time was Mustafa Setmariam Nasar.

Nasar is better known as 'Abu Musab al-Suri' or 'The Syrian'. He shares a number of traits with first-generation jihadists,

including experience against the Soviets in Afghanistan and supporting local jihadist groups in Algeria and elsewhere. Prior to 11 September 2001, Nasar was suspected of running training camps in Afghanistan and Pakistan for Osama bin Laden. Like a number of members of this cohort, Nasar is well educated and this is apparent in his writings. His works include the 1,600-page tract and detailed training manual entitled 'Global Islamic Resistance Call'. In addition, Nasar videotaped a number of his lectures based upon it. US actions succeeded in removing or dispersing first-generation leaders and Nasar himself as a second-generation link to future jihadists by transferring his knowledge and skills to them. Both the manual and the videos continue to be circulated online despite Nasar's capture in Pakistan sometime in late 2005/early 2006.

Younis Tsouli represents another generation of militant Islamic terrorism with different skills from his predecessors. His identity was unknown to authorities until just before his arrest. The same cannot be said for Tsouli's virtual persona, 'Irhabi 007' ('Terrorist 007'). Irhabi 007 achieved notoriety in jihadist discussion forums for his technical acumen for hacking websites, circumventing online surveillance techniques, and posting militant Islamic training and propaganda videos. Law enforcement officials suspected that Irhabi 007 was in the United States as he hosted *jihadi* websites and hid other material on servers based there. Cooperation between British and American officials led to Tsouli's eventual discovery and arrest at a flat in West London in late 2005. His reputation in online jihadist circles was built in just over a year.

that more than half of this battle is taking place in the battlefield of the media. And that we are in a media battle in a race for the hearts and minds of our Umma' (Office of the Director of National Intelligence 2005: 10).

The continued expansion of the number of Internet service providers, especially in states with relaxed or ambivalent content policies or laws, combined with capable and cheap computers, software, peripherals, and wireless technologies, has **empowered** individuals and groups with the ability to post tracts on or send messages throughout the World Wide Web. One form of empowerment is the virtual presence that individuals have. Although prominent *jihadi* terrorists' physical presence can be removed through imprisonment or death, their virtual presence and influence is immortalized on the World Wide Web, as the case of Mustafa Setmariam Nasar suggests (see Case Study).

Another form of empowerment for terrorist groups brought on by globalization is the volume, range, and

sophistication of propaganda materials. Terrorist groups were once limited to mimeographed manifestos and typed communiqués. Terrorist supporters and sympathizers now build their own websites. An early example was a website sympathetic to the Tupac Amaru Revolutionary Movement. This website posted the group's communiqués and videos during the seizure of the Japanese embassy in Lima in 1997. Webmasters sympathetic to terrorist groups also control the content and connotation of the material posted on their websites. The website of the Liberation Tigers of Tamil Eelam, for example, posts items that cast the group as an internationally 'accepted' organization committed to conflict resolution. Messages, files, and polemics can be dispatched to almost anywhere on the globe via the Internet or text messaging almost instantaneously.

For the purposes of spreading messages to the widest possible audience for those without Internet or text messaging capabilities, and where speed of communication

is not a requirement or a possibility for security reasons, terrorists need not rely exclusively on virtual methods. Any computer of modest capabilities can be used by members of terrorist groups and their sympathizers to create propaganda leaflets and posters at very low cost in large quantities. Whereas offset printing machines and photocopiers are difficult to move, a laptop computer and printer can be packed in a suitcase, increasing the mobility of the terrorist cell generating the material and making them more difficult to locate.

Terrorist groups in Chechnya and the Middle East have also made increasing use of video cameras to record the preparations for and results of attacks, including successful roadside bombings and the downing of helicopters. With the right software and a little knowledge, individuals or small groups can download or obtain digital footage and music and produce videos that appeal to specific groups. Video footage is useful in inspiring potential recruits and seeking donations by support elements within the organization. For example, videos of sniper and other attacks against coalition forces in Iraq, produced by Al-Furquan and As-Sahab, have been distributed by terrorist recruiters. The competition between global news outlets ensures that the images of successful and/or dramatic attacks reach the widest audience possible. These outlets have a ready source of material via sites such as press-release.blogosphere.com. Its front page lists statements and videos (some as large as 300Mb) from groups such as Ansar al-Sunna, the Islamic State of Iraq, and Al-Qaeda Organization in the Islamic Maghreb.

Coordination

During the era of transnational terrorism, groups planned and conducted individual attacks or mounted multiple attacks from a single staging base. The technologies associated with globalization have enabled terrorist cells and groups to mount coordinated attacks in different countries. Indeed, a hallmark of militant Islamic groups is their ability to conduct multiple attacks in different locations. The simultaneous bombings of the US embassies in Kenya and Tanzania in 1998 are one example. Other examples include the synchronized detonation of ten of 13 bombs on packed commuter trains in Madrid in March 2004 and three of the four July 2005 London Underground bombings.

The technologies associated with globalization, including commercially available handheld radios and phones, have allowed terrorist cell member and groups to operate independently at substantial distances from one another and network together. The Global System for Mobile Communications (GSM) standard, for example, ensures that any compliant phone will work anywhere in the world where a GSM network has been established. E-mail and cell phone contact among geographically separated group members allows them to conduct their attacks in separate locations or converge on a specific target area. For example, the 9/11 hijackers utilized cheap and readily available pre-paid phone cards to communicate between cell leaders and senior leadership and, according to at least one press account, coordinated final attack authorization prior to the jets taking off from different locations.

Terrorist groups under pressure from aggressive counter-measures have utilized technologies and other innovations to maintain their activities tactically and strategically. On a tactical level, IRA and Al Qaeda in Iraq bomb manufacturers have demonstrated the ability to respond rapidly to electronic counter-measures. At the strategic level, Al Qaeda has continued to evolve despite losing their sanctuary and training camps in Afghanistan since December 2001. Instead of a hierarchical organization with fixed training bases, what has developed in its stead is a virtual global militant Islamic 'community of practice' characterized by individuals exchanging information and discussing the best ways to coordinate and conduct attacks. Some Western analysts have labelled the current decentralized version of global terrorism as **Al Qaeda 2.0**, which is neither centrally planned nor controlled. Cells form around individuals sympathetic to militant Islamic goals accessible via webcast or online *jihadi* discussion forums. At present, law enforcement officials believe that there are more than 5,000 active militant Islamic discussion sites along the lines of the now-defunct Muntada al-Ansar al-Islami. The watchword for such violence can be thought of as a variation on the activist motto **think globally, act locally** which reinforces the perception of militant Islam's global depth, power, and reach.

Security

Terrorist cells without adequate security precautions are vulnerable to discovery and detection. Translations of

captured Al Qaeda manuals, for example, demonstrate the high value its writers place on security, including surveillance and counter-surveillance techniques. The technological enablers of globalization assist terrorist cells and leaders in preserving security in a number of ways, including distributing elements in a coordinated network, remaining mobile (see below), and utilizing clandestine and/or encrypted communications.

The security of terrorist organizations has historically been preserved by limiting communication and information exchanges between cells. This ensures that if one cell is compromised, its members only know each other's identities and not those of other cells. Therefore the damage done to the organization is minimized. Security is even more important to clandestine cells operating on their own without central direction. The use of specific codes and ciphers, known only to a few individuals, is one way of preserving the security of an organization. Although code and ciphers inevitably have been broken, and information obtained through interrogation, such activities take time. During that time, terrorist groups adjust their location and operating methods in an attempt to stay ahead of counter-terrorist forces. Technological advancements, including faster processing speeds and software developments, now mean that those sympathetic to terrorist causes can contribute to the cause virtually through servers located hundreds or thousands of miles away.

Terrorist groups have been able to leverage technological developments designed to shield a user's identity from unauthorized commercial or private exploitation (Gunaratna 2002: 35). Concerns about infringements on civil liberties and privacy during the early years of the Internet led to the development of 64 and 128-bit encryption freeware that is extremely costly and time-consuming to crack. In addition, access to hardware such as cell phones, personal data assistants, and computers can be restricted via the use of passwords. The use of Internet protocol address generators, anonymity protection programs, and rerouted communications, as well as private chat rooms where password-protected or encrypted files can be shared, also provide a degree of security. Within the virtual jihadist community, youth sympathetic to the militant Islamic cause, post information in discussion groups on ways to circumvent electronic surveillance through awareness of phishing and mobile phone monitoring techniques and the use of electronic 'dead letters'—saving draft messages in shared third-party email accounts, such as Hotmail, without sending anything that could be intercepted.

Mobility

The reduced size and increased capabilities of personal electronics also gives terrorists mobility advantages. Mobility has always been a crucial consideration for terrorists and insurgents alike, given the superior resources that states have been able to bring to bear against them. In open societies that have well-developed infrastructures, terrorists have been able to move rapidly within and between borders, and this complicates efforts to track them. The globalization of commerce has also improved terrorist mobility. The expansion in the volume of air travel and goods that pass through ports has increased exponentially through globalization. Between states, measures have been taken to ease the flow of goods, services, and ideas in a less restrictive fashion to improve efficiency and lower costs. One example is the European Schengen Agreement, in which border security measures between EU member states have been relaxed to speed deliveries. Market demands for efficiencies of supply, manufacture, delivery, and cost has complicated efforts of states to prevent members of terrorist groups from exploiting gaps in security measures designed to deter or prevent illicit activities. Additional mobility also allows terrorist groups to transfer expertise, as the arrest of three members of the IRA suspected of training counterparts in the Fuerzas Armadas Revolucionarias de Columbia (FARC) in Bogota in August 2001 appears to demonstrate.

The use of air travel by terrorists prior to September 11 has been well documented. Mohammed Atta, for example, travelled extensively between Egypt, Germany, and the Middle East beforehand. In this respect, the latest generation of terrorists resembles their transnational predecessors in exploiting travel methods for attacks. Terrorist use of transportation need not necessarily be overt in nature, as the volume of goods transported in support of a globalized economy is staggering and difficult to monitor effectively. For example, customs officials cannot inspect all of the vehicles or containers passing through border points or ports. To illustrate the scale of the problem, the United States receives 10 million containers per year and one port, Los Angeles, processes the equivalent of 12,000 twenty-foot containers daily. Western government officials fear that terrorist groups will use containers as

a convenient and cheap means to ship weapons of mass destruction. Incidents in Italy in 2001 and Israel in 2004 confirm that terrorist groups are aware of the convenience and cheapness of globalized shipping to improve their mobility.

Lethality

Globalization has undoubtedly had a troubling influence on terrorism, but the one element that concerns counter-terrorism experts and practitioners the most is future catastrophic attacks using weapons of mass destruction. During the transnational era, terrorists could obtain advanced weapons to conduct more lethal attacks, including rudimentary radiological (more commonly know as **dirty bombs**), biological, or chemical weapons, but they largely did not. Few tried to acquire them and fewer still, including the Weather Underground, threatened their use. The precise reasons why terrorists did not acquire and use such weapons during this era are unclear. Experts speculated, however, that terrorist leaders understood that the more lethal their attacks were, the greater the likelihood that a state or the international community would focus their entire efforts on hunting them down and eradicating them.

Since the end of the cold war, however, some terrorist leaders have expressed both the desire and will to use weapons of mass destruction. Evidence recovered in Afghanistan in 2001 outlined plans by Al Qaeda to produce and test biological and chemical weapons. In addition, a raid on a suspected Al Qaeda flat in London in 2004 revealed quantities of the toxin ricin. Militant Islamic statements have mentioned, and one *fatwa* supports, the use of any means, including weapons of mass destruction, to kill as many infidels and apostates as possible. Globalized media, ironically, may have played a role in shaping terrorist plans. Al Qaeda leaders are alleged to have conjured up mass casualty attacks as a result of spectacular special effects contained in Hollywood blockbuster movies.

In the absence of weapons of mass destruction, globalization has facilitated access to weapons, resources, and proficiency required to conduct smaller, but more lethal attacks. Terrorist groups from Chechnya to Sri Lanka have shared their expertise in the manufacturing of lethal bombs triggered by increasingly sophisticated and globally available remote control devices. Within Iraq since 2003, terrorist groups have been able to obtain the knowledge and resources required to build sophisticated **improvised explosive devices** (IEDs). Such IEDs range in scale and complexity. The United States, for example, claims that Iran supports terrorist violence in Iraq through the supply of specific IED technology. State sponsorship, however, may no longer be necessary in a globalized world. Digital videos suggests that terrorists are already conducting **distance learning** through a **virtual *jihad* academy** in which prospective terrorists study everything from conducting ambush attacks to making and using IEDs, in order to increase their effectiveness and lethality.

> ### Key Points
>
> - Elements of globalization that permit the rapid exchange of ideas and goods can also be leveraged and exploited by terrorist groups.
> - The technologies associated with globalization allow terrorists to operate in a highly distributed global 'network' that shares information and allows small cells to conduct highly coordinated, lethal attacks.
> - Globalization may allow some terrorist groups to acquire, manufacture, and use weapons of mass of destruction in order to conduct catastrophic attacks.

Combating terrorism

States plagued by transnational terrorism responded individually and collectively to combat the phenomenon during the cold war. These responses ranged in scope and effectiveness and included passing anti-terrorism laws, taking preventative security measures at airports, and creating special operations counter-terrorism forces such as the West German Grenzschutzgruppe–9 (GSG–9). Successful rescues in Entebbe (1976), Mogadishu (1977), and Prince's Gate, London (1980) demonstrated that national counter-terrorism forces could respond effectively both domestically and abroad. A normative approach to tackling the problem, founded on the

principles of **international law** and collective action, was less successful. Attempts to define and proscribe transnational terrorism in the United Nations bogged down in the General Assembly over semantics but other cooperative initiatives were successfully implemented. These included the conventions adopted through the International Civil Aviation Organization (ICAO) to improve information sharing and legal cooperation, such as the Hague Convention for the Suppression of Unlawful Seizure of Aircraft (1970). Another collective response to improve information sharing and collaborative action was the creation of the Public Safety and Terrorism Sub-Directorate within Interpol in 1985. However, most initiatives and responses throughout this decade were largely unilateral, regional, or *ad hoc* in nature.

State leaders disagree on how best to deal with the current form of global terrorist violence. Much of the controversy relates to the nature of the threat and approach that should be taken to deal with it. Some national leaders view the form of militant Islam as an intractable problem in which there can be no negotiation. The leaders of the United States, Great Britain, and Australia suggest that all states should cooperate in a global **war on terror** to deal with the threat. The stakes in **The Long War** consist of the preservation of basic freedoms and a way of life. In order to defeat terrorism, individual states have a responsibility to protect civilian populations while dealing with terrorist cells, supporters, and sympathizers within their own borders. Given the global, elusive, and adaptive character of the militant Islamic threat, the best approach for dealing with global terrorism is to pool resources together in a **coalition of the willing**, in which forces from the global North are seeking to improve the capabilities of specific partner states in the global South. The end result will be the development of a **Global Counter-terrorism Network** (GCTN) of states able to detect, track, and eliminate terrorist threats while non-military efforts address the root causes of terrorism.

Other national leaders are less comfortable with the concept of 'war' against terrorism. In their view, actions by the military can only lead to terrorist reprisals, or worse—the return of terrorism to its original connotation, the sanctioned use of terror by the state to repress its own citizenry. In their eyes, terrorism is a crime that is best dealt with through law enforcement methods. By dealing with terrorism as a police problem, states uphold the rule of law, maintain the high moral ground, preserve democratic principles, and prevent the establishment

of martial law. Military force should only be used in extreme circumstances and even then its use may have negative consequences. Terrorism is best dealt with inside state borders and through cooperative international law enforcement efforts to arrest suspects and provide them with due process. The law enforcement approach to terrorism must balance taking enough measures against terrorist groups without crossing over into the realm of ' "political justice," where the rules and rights enshrined in the principle of due process are either willfully misinterpreted or completely disregarded' (Chalk 1996: 98). To do little against domestic or global terrorism, in the name of upholding the rule of law, risks offering terrorist groups a sanctuary and the security of rights and laws.

The virtual opinion of a number of **non-governmental organizations** (NGOs), members of blogs, and webmasters has also been critical of the 'war' on terrorism. Those suspicious of the motives of the political elite of the United States range widely in their opinions. Conspiracy theorists online suggest that the war in Iraq, Afghanistan, and elsewhere is the first stage in the establishment of an Orwellian system that is constantly in conflict with the terrorist 'other' to justify continued violation of personal privacy. More objective communities of practice and NGOs, such as Human Rights Watch, routinely provide monitoring and online reporting of suspected government human rights and civil liberties abuses. One example is the persistent attention paid to the status of terrorist detainees held in US custody at **Guantanamo Bay**.

Although disagreements still exist over how best to deal with terrorism philosophically, pragmatically the largest problems reside in locating terrorists and isolating them from their means of support. Locating and identifying terrorists is a tedious and time-consuming process that requires collecting, assessing, and analyzing information collected from a range of sources. Information technologies associated with globalization have been useful in assisting this process. Such technologies allow identification of terrorist patterns before and after attacks, with systems capable of performing calculations measured in the trillions per second (floating point operations, or flops). Terrorist finances and organizations are evaluated through link analysis to construct a more comprehensive picture of the how terrorist elements interact. In addition, huge volumes of information can be reduced and exchanged electronically between departments, agencies, and other

governments, or made available on secure servers whose capacities are measured in terabytes. Discovering terrorist cells, however, has much to do with luck and pursuing non-technical leads. States bureaucracies can impede or negate technical and resources advantages over terrorist groups.

In order to deal with global terrorism, the international community must address its most problematic modern aspects: the appeal of messages that inspire terrorists to commit horrific acts of violence. Killing or capturing individuals does little to halt the spread of extremist viewpoints that occur under the guise of discussion and education. In the case of Islam, for example, radical mullahs and imams twist the tenets of the religion into a doctrine of action and hatred, where spiritual achievement occurs through destruction rather than personal enlightenment. In other words, suicide attacks offer the promise of private goods (spiritual reward) rather than public good (positive contributions to the community over a lifetime). Precisely how the processes and technologies of globalization can assist in delegitimizing the pedagogy that incites terrorists will remain one of the most vexing challenges for the international community for years to come.

Key Points

- States, individually and collectively, have political, military, legal, economic, and technologies advantages in the struggle against terrorist groups.
- Differences between states over the nature and scope of the current terrorist threat, and the most appropriate responses to combat it, reflect subjective characterizations based on national biases and experiences.

Conclusion

Terrorism remains a complex phenomenon in which violence is used to obtain political power to redress grievances that may have become more acute through the process of globalization. Globalization has improved the technical capabilities of terrorists and given them global reach, but has not altered the fundamental fact that terrorism represents the extreme views of a minority of the global population. In other words, globalization has changed the scope of terrorism but not its nature. The benefits that globalization provides terrorists is neither one-sided nor absolute. The same technologies and processes also enable more effective means of states to combat them. Global terrorists can only succeed through popular uprising or the psychological or physical collapse of their state-based adversary. Neither outcome is likely given the limitations of terrorist messages and capabilities. Terrorist and counter-terrorist campaigns are characterized by prolonged struggle to maintain advantages in legitimacy domestically and internationally. The challenge for the global community will be in utilizing its advantages to win the war of ideas that motivates and sustains those responsible for the current wave of terrorist violence.

❓ Questions

1 Why is linking terrorism with globalization so difficult to do theoretically?
2 When did terrorism become a truly global phenomenon and what enabled it to do so?
3 In what ways are the technologies and processes associated with globalization more beneficial to states or terrorists?
4 Given that terrorism has been both a transnational and a global phenomenon, why has it not been more successful in effecting change?
5 Of all of the factors that motivate terrorists, is any one more important than others and if so, why?
6 What has changed in terrorism over the past half-century and have any factors remained the same? If so, what are they and why have they remained constant?

7   What is the role that technology plays in terrorism and will it change how terrorists operate in the future? If so, how?

8   What are the dilemmas that terrorist groups face with respect to weapons of mass destruction?

9   What is the primary challenge that individual states and the international community as a whole face in confronting terrorism?

10   How can globalization be useful in diminishing the underlying causes of terrorism?

Guide to further reading

Ganor, B. (2005), *The Counter-Terrorism Puzzle: A Guide for Decision Makers* (New Brunswick, NJ: Transaction). Emphasizes the dilemmas and practical difficulties associated with various counter-terrorism policy options.

Hoffman, B. (2006), *Inside Terrorism*, revised and expanded edition (New York: Columbia University Press). The best single-volume work on the development of terrorism, its evolution over time, and current and future prospects for defeating it.

Juergensmeyer, M. (2000), *Terror in the Mind of God: The Global Rise of Religious Violence* (Berkeley, Cal.: University of California Press). Highlights similarities between religious leaders across faiths and sects at how they justify killing non-combatants.

Office of the Chairman of the Joint Chiefs of Staff (2006), *National Military Strategic Plan for the War on Terrorism* (Washington, DC: The Pentagon). The unclassified version of this document is available for downloading at: www.strategicstudiesinstitute.army.mil/pdffiles/gwot.pdf.

Rabasa, A., Chalk, P., *et al.* (2006), *Beyond al-Qaeda. Part 1: The Global Jihadist Movement and Part 2: The Outer Rings of the Terrorist Universe* (Santa Monica, Cal. :RAND). This two-part report provides a comprehensive survey of current militant Islamic terrorist groups, the impact of Iraq on the global *jihad*, and the linkages between terrorism and organized crime. Available for downloading at: www.rand.org/pubs/monographs/2006/RAND_MG429.pdf (Part 1) and www.rand.org/pubs/monographs/2006/RAND_MG430.pdf (Part 2).

Roy, O. (2004), *Globalized Islam: The Search for the New Ummah* (New York: Columbia University Press). A provocative work that challenges many of the assumptions about and explanations for the rise of militant Islam.

Sageman, M. (2004), *Understanding Terror Networks* (Philadelphia, Penn. : University of Pennsylvania Press). Analyzes Al Qaeda members based on information gathered from open sources that arrives at thought-provoking conclusions about the formation of the militant global *jihad* network.

Schmid, A. P., Jongman, A. J., *et al.* (1988), *Political Terrorism: A New Guide to Actors, Authors, Concepts, Data Bases, Theories, and Literature* (New Brunswick, NJ: Transaction Books). A still useful, if at times overwhelming reference work that highlights the problems associated with defining and studying terrorism.

Online Resource Centre

 Visit the Online Resource Centre that accompanies this book to access more learning resources on this chapter topic at www.oxfordtextbooks.co.uk/uk/orc/baylis_smith4e/

Chapter 22

Nuclear proliferation

DARRYL HOWLETT

- Introduction···388
- Nature of nuclear weapons and their effects························389
- Diffusion of nuclear and missile technology·······················391
- Theorizing nuclear proliferation and non-proliferation········392
- Evolution of global nuclear control and anti-proliferation measures·····396
- Conclusion···399

Reader's Guide

This chapter identifies those factors that have made nuclear proliferation a global phenomenon since 1945. Over this period the nature of nuclear weapons has transformed military and political relationships, while the global diffusion of nuclear and ballistic missile technology has meant that more actors are in a position both to acquire a nuclear capability and deliver it over longer distances. This chapter also reveals the complexities associated with the globalization of the nuclear proliferation issue and some of the theoretical aspects related to it. There are difficulties in determining the motivations driving nuclear weapons acquisition and the capabilities that might be constructed once it has occurred. This complexity has been made more acute as a result of novel proliferation concerns in the last twenty years. As a result, non-proliferation efforts have focused on measures that: raise the costs of nuclear acquisition; develop standards of nuclear and missile behaviour; and create the conditions allowing for reductions in nuclear stockpiles to occur in a safe and secure manner. A debate has also emerged about whether the international treaty approach, or what traditionally has been termed the nuclear non-proliferation regime, is sufficient to contain proliferation dynamics. Against this background there has been renewed interest in nuclear power generation to deal with future energy demand and in response to global environmental change.

Introduction

The issue of nuclear proliferation represents one of the more marked illustrations of the **globalization** of world politics. Although only five **states** (China, France, Russia (Soviet Union), United Kingdom and United States) are acknowledged by the Treaty on the Non-Proliferation of Nuclear Weapons (NPT) as possessing nuclear weapons, others have the capability to construct nuclear devices. This was emphasized in May 1998 when India and Pakistan, previously regarded as 'threshold' or near-nuclear states, demonstrated their respective capabilities by conducting a series of nuclear tests followed by ballistic missile launches. These events highlighted another aspect of nuclear globalization: the potential emergence of a regionally differentiated world. While some regions have moved from a situation where nuclear weapons once had a high profile in strategic thinking to one where these weapons have assumed lower significance, other regions may be moving in the opposite direction. In Latin America, South-East Asia, Africa, and Central Asia the trend has been towards developing the region as a **Nuclear Weapon Free Zone** (NWFZ). In other regions, such as South Asia and possibly elsewhere, the trend appears to be towards a higher profile for nuclear capabilities. What is unclear is the impact that **nuclearization** (meaning nuclear weapons acquisition) in some regions will have on those moving towards **denuclearization** (meaning a process of removing nuclear weapons).

Many of the factors that have made nuclear proliferation an important issue have been under way for several decades. Knowledge of the enormous destructive effects of nuclear weapons dates back to the bombings of the Japanese cities Hiroshima and Nagasaki at the end of the Second World War. Similarly, the fire that destroyed a reactor at Chernobyl in the former Soviet Union in 1986 revealed the devastating effects of accidents at operating nuclear power plants.

Developments stemming from the dissolution of the Soviet Union have also raised novel problems. This is the only case where a previously acknowledged **nuclear weapon state** (NWS) has been subjected to political disintegration. At the time there was little understanding of what the nuclear consequences would be from such a tumultuous state implosion and only in hindsight can we judge its full significance. That it was a period of unprecedented nuclear transformation requiring long-term **cooperation** between previously hostile states is not in doubt. Less obvious is the observation that this period of **transition** was facilitated by the foresight of policymakers from both sides of the former **cold war** divide and by the framework of arms control and disarmament agreements then in place. Ensuring nuclear stability during this period might therefore have been more difficult had it not been for policies such as the **Co-operative Threat Reduction Programme** and agreements like the multilateral NPT and bilateral **Strategic Arms Reduction Treaties** (START), signed initially between the USA and the Soviet Union (and later between the USA and Russia). One debate that has sparked diverging responses is a thesis asserting that the gradual spread of nuclear weapons to additional states is to be welcomed rather than feared. The thesis is based on the proposition that just as nuclear **deterrence** maintained stability during the cold war, so can it induce similar stabilizing effects on other conflict situations. This argument is challenged by those who hold that more will be worse not better, and that measures to stem nuclear proliferation represent the best way forward (Sagan and Waltz 1995 and 2003).

The responses to nuclear proliferation encompass unilateral, bilateral, regional, and global measures that collectively have been termed the nuclear non-proliferation

---

Box 22.1 Waltz thesis

1 Nuclear weapons have spread rather than proliferated because these weapons have proliferated only vertically as the Nuclear Weapon States have increased their arsenals.

2 Nuclear weapons have spread horizontally to other states only slowly. This slowness is fortunate as rapid changes in international conditions can be unsettling.

3 The gradual spread of nuclear weapons is better than either no spread or rapid spread.

4 New nuclear states will feel the constraints that nuclear weapons impose and this will induce a sense of responsibility on the part of their possessors and a strong element of caution on their use.

5 The likelihood of war decreases as deterrent and defensive capabilities increase; nuclear weapons, responsibly used, make wars hard to start.

(Sagan and Waltz 1995)

Box 22.2 Sagan's 'proliferation pessimism' argument

1 Professional military organizations, because of common biases, inflexible routines, and parochial interests, display organizational behaviours that are likely to lead to deterrence failures and deliberate or accidental war.

2 Because future nuclear-armed states are likely to have military-run or weak civilian governments, they will lack the positive constraining mechanisms of civilian control while military biases may serve to encourage nuclear weapons use, especially during a crisis.

(Sagan and Waltz 1995)

regime (see Ch.16 and Ch.17). Advocates of this regime argue it is these measures (including treaties like the NPT, export controls, international safeguards, nuclear supplier agreements, and other standard setting arrangements) that have constrained nuclear acquisition. Conversely, there have been several criticisms of this regime and even some long-term supporters acknowledge it is in 'need of intensive care' (Ogilvie-White and Simpson 2003). Among the criticisms of the nuclear non-proliferation regime are that it: is a product of a bygone **first nuclear age** (1945–90) and is not suited to the demands of the potentially more dangerous **second nuclear age** (1990–); is unable to alleviate the security dilemma that many states confront and, hence, does not address the security motivation driving nuclear weapons acquisition; and is a discriminatory arrangement because the NPT only requires that the five NWS pursue nuclear disarmament in good faith (under its Article VI) while all other parties (designated as **Non-Nuclear Weapon States** (NNWS)) must forgo the acquisition of nuclear weapons. Thus, there has always been a tension between whether the NPT is primarily a

non-proliferation measure for preventing additional nuclear armed states emerging or a means for achieving nuclear disarmament. This aspect was in evidence during discussion at the NPT Conference in 1995 when the Treaty was extended indefinitely after an initial twenty-five years in operation (under Article X). It also featured at the NPT Review Conference in 2000 when the five NWS reiterated their commitment to the goal of nuclear weapons elimination. During these dialogues emphasis was placed on the need for all parties to improve transparency in their nuclear operations and for additional measures to enhance verification and compliance.

More recently, a debate has emerged concerning the worth of the nuclear non-proliferation regime as an instrument of global nuclear policy. It is being addressed in a manner that has not been seen since the 1960s and 1970s, and against an international backdrop that differs radically from that time. At its heart are **issues** relating to the future global **security** environment, including the likely proliferation challenges of the coming decades and whether the treaty-based approach (centred around the nuclear non-proliferation regime) needs to be supplemented with additional arrangements or supplanted altogether with a new response involving a mix of measures depending on the circumstances and the actors involved (Ayson 2001; Bohlen 2003; Bracken 2003 and 2004; Allison 2004; Feinstein and Slaughter 2004). Additionally, there is the question of what impact the so-called 'renaissance in nuclear power generation' will have on the NPT, and on energy and environmental discussions generally. The outcome of this debate will consequently set the tone for what some envisage as the basis for global nuclear governance in the twenty-first century.

Nature of nuclear weapons and their effects

Technical basis of nuclear weapons

Unless a nuclear weapon or the materials required for its manufacture can be obtained 'off the shelf' as a result of purchase or theft, the usual route for any state or **non-state actor** seeking nuclear weapons would be via the acquisition of the necessary technological infrastructure.

The latter include a range of nuclear, conventional, computational, and electronic technologies. It also requires individuals with key scientific skills.

Nuclear reactors and nuclear weapons differ in their management of the nuclear chain reaction and the energy produced. Whereas in a reactor energy output is achieved through a sustained and regulated process, in a nuclear

Box 22.3 Technology of nuclear weapons

Separate processes are required to obtain the two fissile materials needed to construct a nuclear weapon. Uranium is found in nature and comprises 99.3% uranium 238 (U–238) and 0.7% uranium 235 (U–235). The U–235 has the same chemical properties as the U–238 but has a different atomic weight. It is the latter isotopic form that is used in a nuclear weapon. To produce the weapon, the amount of U–235 in a quantity of natural uranium is increased to weapons grade by a process called enrichment so that eventually it becomes 90%+ of the sample. Once a sufficient quantity of weapons grade U–235 has been accumulated to achieve a critical mass, defined by the International Atomic Energy Agency (IAEA) as 25 kilograms—although the amount could be smaller—then there is enough fissile material to construct one nuclear weapon.

Plutonium does not occur naturally: it is one of the end products of the irradiation of natural or only very slightly enriched (2–3%) uranium in a nuclear reactor. Plutonium 239 (Pu–239) is the result of a controlled nuclear reaction process. Because the two are chemically different, it is possible to separate plutonium and uranium through a process known as reprocessing. The figure of 6 to 8 kilograms is usually the quantity quoted for one weapon although this varies with the design.

weapon the objective is to attain a large explosive yield by creating a critical mass of nuclear material as a result of an uncontrolled and rapid chain reaction (Gardner 1994: 6–7). Nuclear weapons consequently derive their explosive energy from techniques designed either to split the atoms rapidly, thus creating a chain reaction (so-called fission weapons), or by using fission weapons as a primary initiator to compress and heat hydrogen atoms so they combine or fuse (so-called thermonuclear or fusion weapons). Energy production in a nuclear reactor involves a means for regulating the chain reaction, a moderator that surrounds the fissile core for maintaining the chain reaction, and a means for removing the heat produced from the reactor core by the chain reaction, which can also provide the steam to drive turbines and generate electricity.

Nuclear weapons effects

The effects of nuclear weapons are considerable. Because of this the United Nations Commission for Conventional Armaments in 1948 introduced a new category of **weapons of mass destruction** (WMD) to distinguish nuclear weapons from conventional forms. More recently, another concept known as **CBRN** (referring to chemical, biological, radiological, and nuclear capabilities) has appeared and some analysts have also argued that the term WMD should be unravelled because each of the weapons types has different effects, with nuclear weapons being the true WMD (Panofsky 1998).

A nuclear weapon produces its energy in three distinct forms: **blast**; **heat or thermal radiation**; and **nuclear radiation**. Experience of nuclear testing has also indicated another feature of a nuclear weapons explosion, the phenomenon known as electro-magnetic pulse (EMP). This can cause acute disruption to electronic equipment (Grace 1994: 1).

Extensive damage to human populations may result from a nuclear weapons detonation. Awareness of these effects stems from the two weapons dropped on Hiroshima and Nagasaki at the end of the Second World War, which remains the only time nuclear weapons have been used. What is also known is that the weapons that destroyed these Japanese cities were relatively small in comparison to the destructive forces generated by later testing of thermonuclear weapons (see Ch.3). The largest weapon of this kind known to have been tested was estimated to be a 50-megaton device (i.e. 50 million tonnes of TNT) produced by the Soviet Union in 1961. One trend in recent years has been a movement away from nuclear weapons with large explosive potential towards designs with lower yields.

Key Points

- Nuclear weapon production requires a broad-based technological infrastructure and individuals with key skills.
- Nuclear reactors and nuclear weapons differ in their management of the chain reaction, and in the nature of the energy produced.
- In 1948, the United Nations introduced the category known as WMD.
- A new category has appeared known as CBRN.
- Nuclear weapons produce energy in three forms—blast, heat and nuclear radiation—and the phenomenon known as EMP.
- Nuclear weapons were used at the end of the Second World War and have not been used in conflict since.
- The testing of thermonuclear weapons indicated the greater explosive capacity of this type of weapon, although the trend has been towards weapon designs with lower yields.

Diffusion of nuclear and missile technology

Diffusion of nuclear technology

Since 1945 nuclear technology for civil and military uses has disseminated on a global scale. Immediately after the Second World War only the United States possessed the capability to manufacture a nuclear weapon. By 1964 four other states had crossed the nuclear weapons threshold, an event traditionally understood as the testing of a nuclear explosive device (Soviet Union (1949), United Kingdom (1952), France (1960), and China (1964)).

Complications for the definition of a NWS contained in the NPT were raised by the detonation of nuclear devices by India and Pakistan in 1998. Neither state was party to the NPT so they were not in breach of any international legal obligation. Yet, India and Pakistan's move from a presumed 'threshold' position to demonstrating an overt nuclear weapons capability not only questioned the NPT's definition of a NWS, but also raised the issue of whether other states that had signed the Treaty might follow this path.

There are also concerns about the future of nuclear supply arrangements and the role of transnational non-state **networks**. At the inter-state level there has been a structural change in the civil nuclear trading market since 1945. After the Second World War the United States was the pre-eminent nuclear supplier. By the 1970s this position was challenged, first by France and Germany, and then by Japan. Today, with several nuclear suppliers, coupled with the possibility that transnational networks operating outside established controls may exist (such as the one discovered in 2004), there is the prospect that the acquisition of at least rudimentary nuclear capabilities has become easier. In response, efforts have been underway to strengthen supplier guidelines while the United Nations has made it mandatory, via Security Council Resolution 1540, for states to pass and enforce domestic legislation that criminalizes those individuals or networks engaged in transnational WMD-related activities (Bosch and Van Ham 2007).

Nuclear delivery

During the 1950s nuclear weapons required large aircraft designed to carry these weapons to their target. Thereafter, as the technology developed for manufacturing ballistic missiles and for nuclear ordnance that was compact enough to be carried by these missiles, so the possibility increased that more states would seek to deliver nuclear weapons by this means.

Ballistic missiles consequently represent the most sophisticated method of nuclear delivery and were once restricted to a few states. But just as the diffusion of nuclear technology is a global phenomenon, so has the capability to deploy a ballistic missile become more commonplace. Should these missiles be linked to the delivery of nuclear ordnance then more states will have the capacity to hit targets over longer distances and, by implication, also widen their potential for strategic engagement. It is this aspect that brought to the fore once more the debate over the merits of deploying defences against ballistic missiles.

The debate entered a new phase when the US Congress passed the National Missile Defense (NMD) Act in 1999. This Act proposed that the United States should develop the technical means to counter a possible small-scale ballistic missile attack on the US mainland. The announcement generated a range of reactions within the United States and elsewhere. The overall programme cost and technical feasibility became central elements of the US domestic debate, for, unlike the 1983 Strategic Defence Initiative, which intended to use a range of technologies including nuclear explosions to intercept incoming missiles, the new Ballistic Missile Defense (BMD) system has been developed primarily using kinetic energy. This means the intention is to hit an incoming missile with another defensive missile during its flight path. Such a system inevitably requires considerable early warning and computational capabilities, and a missile that is fast and manoeuvrable enough to hit a target potentially travelling at 7 kilometres per second. International reaction to US missile defence proposals met with concerns in Russia and China about the impact on stability if the ABM Treaty was eroded, while in **Europe** similar reservations were expressed.

The United States eventually moved forward with a testing programme for missile interceptors, withdrew from the ABM Treaty, negotiated a new agreement with Russia known as the **Strategic Offensive Reductions Treaty** (SORT), and began initial BMD deployments. Japan and Israel have also decided to deploy missile defences

while a debate has emerged in Europe over the proposed stationing of US BMD in Poland, the Czech Republic, and possibly elsewhere. Russia has responded negatively to the latter proposal because of concerns about the effects on stability in the region and its implications for arms control agreements. One consideration in this context is that START 1 expires in 2009 and SORT in 2012, and thus the existing rules governing US–Russian strategic arms will no longer apply unless a new agreement can be forged.

Key Points

- The nature of nuclear weapons and the dissemination of the capabilities to manufacture them around the world since 1945 makes nuclear proliferation a good illustration of the globalization of world politics.
- The end of the cold war and the dissolution of the former Soviet Union generated new problems.
- Greater attention has been paid to theoretical aspects.
- A debate has emerged over the merits of the further proliferation/spread of nuclear weapons.
- Because of new proliferation challenges generated by what some analysts call the 'second nuclear age', a debate has begun over whether the nuclear non-proliferation regime should be supplemented or supplanted by a new more flexible approach to the problems of global nuclear governance.
- A major element of the nuclear proliferation process is the acquisition of the technologies to produce fissile materials to construct either a fission (nuclear) or fusion (thermonuclear) weapon.

- The effects of nuclear weapons are considerable and are manifest in the form of blast, heat, and nuclear radiation.
- Since 1945, the spread of nuclear technology for civil and military purposes has meant that states beyond the five which possess nuclear weapons now have the capacity to produce nuclear devices at relatively short notice, if they have not already done so.
- Over the same period the structure of the civil nuclear trading market has also changed, leading to proliferation concerns because there are more nuclear suppliers around.
- There has also been a diffusion of ballistic missile and space-launch technology since 1945.
- A debate over the merits of deploying defensive systems to counter ballistic missiles has emerged and the ABM Treaty agreed in 1972 between the United States and the former Soviet Union is no longer in force.

Theorizing nuclear proliferation and non-proliferation

Conceptual issues

One question that has provoked interest is what constitutes nuclear proliferation: does it refer to a single decision to acquire a nuclear weapon or is it part of a process that may stretch over several years and consequently no one identifiable decision can be located? Research on what has been referred to as 'the proliferation puzzle' has thus embraced several conceptual issues (Meyer 1984; Davis and Frankel 1993; Lavoy 1995; Ogilvie-White 1996; Hymans 2006). Similarly, while much literature endorses the propositions derived from political **Realism**, which asserts that in an anarchic international environment states will seek nuclear weapons to enhance their security, insights from other theoretical positions have become more commonplace (see chapters in Part Two). This has generated questions concerning what the 'level of analysis' should be in studying nuclear proliferation. Should the focus be on the individual, the organization, the cultural group, the state, the **international system**, or some combination of these?

The argument has also been advanced that **norms, taboos**, and **epistemic communities** have played an important role in the nuclear context (Adler 1992; Price and Tannenwald 1996). One viewpoint sees international norms as increasingly significant both as constraints on nuclear behaviour and in setting appropriate standards among a range of actors. Similarly, in fostering nuclear non-proliferation dialogues some analysts stress the role played by culture and **identity** factors (Krause and Williams 1997). Scholars have also drawn attention to **non-governmental organizations** (NGOs) and epistemic communities, referring to groups of individuals often from different disciplines and countries which operate as conduits for ideas on non-proliferation.

Another issue with enduring resonance concerns the question of what can explain nuclear 'non-use' since 1945. This debate started early in the nuclear calendar as authors like Bernard Brodie argued that nuclear weapons were useful only in their non-use (Brodie 1946; Gray 1996). Over the years the main explanation of non-use

has centred on the notion of nuclear deterrence: states have been deterred from using nuclear weapons because of concerns of retaliation in kind by adversaries.

In looking to alternative accounts of non-use, some have focused more on the nature of the weapon and the impact this has on normative judgements. Nina Tannenwald has challenged those arguments that rely on rational cost–benefit analysis relating to **power, capabilities** and interests by exploring other non-material aspects, such as the constraining **influence** of what is termed the 'nuclear taboo' (Tannenwald 1999). In identifying such a taboo, Barry Buzan and Eric Herring define it as 'a strategic cultural prohibition against the use of nuclear weapons … an assumption that nuclear weapons should not be used rather than a conscious cost–benefit calculation' (1998: 165).

Nuclear motivations

Traditional analysis of the motivations for nuclear proliferation has focused at the state and inter-state levels. For much of the post-Second World War period the pattern of nuclear weapon acquisition established by the five NWS was considered to be the one most likely to be followed by any future proliferating state. Analysis of the motivational aspect consequently addressed the strategic, political, and prestige rationales that led these states to seek nuclear weapons. The **strategic motivation** focused on the role that nuclear weapons played in the Second World War and its immediate aftermath when initially they were seen as war-fighting or war-winning weapons. Later, attention shifted to the role that nuclear weapons played in deterrence, leading to the assumption that one of the principal motivations for acquisition was the deterrence of other nuclear weapons-capable states. Similarly, the **political and prestige benefits** that nuclear weapons conferred on those states with the wherewithal to manufacture them were also deemed significant. Nuclear weapons were seen as the most modern form of weaponry and their custodians were automatically afforded a seat at the 'top table of international affairs'.

Inherent in traditional analyses was a form of technological determinism, that once a state acquired the necessary infrastructure it would then develop nuclear weapons. Supporting this assumption was the view that these states would also follow the same path as the five NWS. Thus, it could be predicted that any new nuclear state would pursue a dedicated military nuclear programme, conduct an overt nuclear test, produce a stockpile of weapons, and finally acquire an effective means for delivering the weapons to their target. While this explanation of the process is still relevant, over time analyses of the dynamics of nuclear proliferation have become more complex.

It is now more difficult to explain nuclear proliferation by focusing on a single variable. Analysts have argued that it is necessary to consider a range of factors that may influence nuclear weapons acquisition. These may include: traditional technological factors, the availability of nuclear technology, and a cadre of trained nuclear scientists who encourage acquisition; domestic politics, imperatives within a political party, or the domestic political situation may propel a state towards nuclear weapons; diplomatic bargaining, that acquisition of a nuclear capability can be used to influence or bargain with both perceived allies and enemies; and non-intervention, that a nuclear capability can deter or prevent intervention by other states.

Other features of the 'proliferation puzzle' that need to be understood are the instances of nuclear restraint—why some states abandon the nuclear weapons option—and nuclear reversal—why some states relinquish their nuclear capabilities (Campbell, Einhorn, and Reiss 2004). Factors having a bearing here are: there may have been a change in strategic circumstances, such as the forging of an alliance with a NWS; technical difficulties in the construction of the nuclear weapon may have been encountered; or a perception emerges that the acquisition of such weapons would increase vulnerabilities. Developments since 1945 have thus questioned the technological determinist argument.

Further complexity is added when attention is focused at the **sub-state** or **transnational actor** level as the motivations of non-state actors may be different from those associated with states. In much traditional thinking, only states were considered to have the wherewithal to acquire nuclear capabilities. Nuclear commerce was conducted on a state-to-state basis and it was states that entered into international arms control and disarmament treaties. Today, states are no longer the sole focus of attention as non-state actors have also featured.

Studies conducted during the 1970s and 1980s on **nuclear terrorism** indicated that there were risks

associated with particular groups acquiring a nuclear device or threatening to attack nuclear installations. One study by the International Task Force on Prevention of Nuclear Terrorism concluded that it was possible for a terrorist group to build a crude nuclear device provided it had sufficient quantities of chemical high-explosives and weapons-usable fissile materials. More significantly, it was felt that such a group would be more interested in generating social disruption by making a credible nuclear threat rather than actually detonating a nuclear device and causing mass killing and destruction (Leventhal and Alexander 1987). More recent occurrences have served to alter this latter judgement.

Events in the mid-1990s, such as the first bombing of the World Trade Center in New York in 1993 and the attack against the US Government building in Oklahoma in April 1995, revealed the extent of damage and loss of life that could be caused. While both instances involved traditional methods of inflicting damage, the use of nerve agents (chemical weapons) in an underground train network in central Tokyo in March 1995 to cause both death and widespread panic has been viewed as representing a quantum change in methods. These concerns have intensified since the tragic events of **11 September 2001** when the World Trade Center this time was destroyed by a coordinated attack using civilian aircraft loaded with aviation fuel as the method of destruction. The attack not only produced mass casualties, it also changed the assumption about terrorist use of CBRN capabilities (Wilkinson 2003).

Nuclear capabilities and intentions

Paralleling the problems of analyzing the motivational aspect are those associated with determining whether a state or terrorist group actually possesses a radiological or nuclear capability. The case of South Africa indicates the difficulties in this area. On 24 March 1993 the then President F. W. de Klerk announced that South Africa had produced six nuclear devices prior to 1989 but had dismantled them before signing the NPT. While this announcement confirmed what many previously speculated—that South Africa possessed a nuclear capability during the 1980s—it also suggested that a state did not

need to test a nuclear device to be in possession of a nuclear stockpile. Additionally, there are currently other industrialized states with large nuclear power programmes that could be used to produce quantities of fissile materials for military purposes if a decision was taken to do so. The main barrier to nuclear weapon acquisition in such cases may therefore be political not technological.

The situations in the Democratic People's Republic of Korea (DPRK), Iran, and Iraq have raised important issues concerning capabilities and intentions. These instances reveal the difficulties in obtaining consensus in international forums on how to respond to **non-compliance** and the problems associated with verifying treaty compliance in situations where special inspection or nuclear development arrangements are agreed. In the case of Iraq, a special inspection arrangement known as UNSCOM (United Nations Special Committee) was established following the 1991 Gulf War to oversee the dismantlement of the WMD programme that had come to light as a result of the conflict. By the late 1990s problems were encountered over access to particular sites and UNSCOM inspectors were withdrawn. Disagreements also surfaced among the five Permanent Members of the United Nations Security Council concerning how to implement the UN resolutions that had been passed in connection with Iraq since 1991. These had not been resolved at the time of the intervention in Iraq that occurred in 2003 and subsequent inspections in Iraq were unable to find evidence of significant undeclared WMD.

Box 22.4 Compliance and non-compliance

Compliance with international treaty obligations has been a perennial issue in the nuclear proliferation context. It has raised complex questions related to both the nature of any violation of agreements and the type of response to it. Violations may be only minor and relate to misinterpretation of procedures: conversely, they may be major and linked to breaches of specific treaty obligations. The type of response could therefore vary depending on how the violation is judged and, as a consequence, may involve a spectrum from a procedural warning issued through an international organization like the IAEA or more stringent measures such as special inspection arrangements, sanctions, and the use of force. The issue of compliance is therefore likely to receive continuing attention in the years ahead as it is not just responses to states that will be the subject of attention but responses to non-state actors as well.

Case Study 1   Democratic People's Republic of Korea (DPRK)

Following the attention that focused on the DPRK between 1991 and 1993, when there were fears that the country was pursuing an undeclared nuclear programme, a special nuclear arrangement was instituted in 1994. Known as the 'Agreed Framework', it provided the DPRK with Light-Water Reactors and fuel supplies in exchange for that country's agreement that it would not produce nuclear weapons. Thereafter the Agreed Framework experienced problems, prompting continued uncertainty surrounding the DPRK's nuclear intentions. The situation was exacerbated in August 1998 when the DPRK tested a missile whose trajectory took it over the territory of Japan. Tensions were heightened when the DPRK stated in January 2003 that it had withdrawn from the NPT and would continue its nuclear programme. Concomitantly, efforts began to find an appropriate response, including several rounds of a forum known as the six-party talks involving China, Japan, Russia, Republic of Korea, DPRK, and the United States. On 19 September 2005, at the fourth round of these talks, the parties agreed a Joint Statement aimed at the denuclearization of the DPRK and the Korean Peninsula. The Statement included a plan of coordinated steps linking denuclearization with cooperation in economic and energy development in accordance with the principle of 'commitment for commitment'. But subsequent meetings produced little progress. Pessimism that the plan would never get implemented grew following the announcement by the DPRK in early October 2006 that it had tested a nuclear weapon. The test resulted in the Security Council imposing sanctions on the DPRK and a flurry of diplomatic activity by the other five participants in the talks to find a response. A potentially significant breakthrough was achieved on 15 February 2007 following concerted negotiations. The DPRK accepted a package, based on the terms of the 2005 Statement, that it would begin a process to shut down, seal, and eventually disable the Yongbyon nuclear complex in return for energy and humanitarian aid. Recent developments thus provide a mixed picture for the future of the DPRK's nuclear programme: on the one hand, past activities signal the pursuit of a nuclear capability; on the other, attempts are underway to provide a basis for the denuclearization of the DPRK and the Korean Peninsula.

The complexity associated with compliance has similarly featured in connection with Iran. The country became the subject of attention from the International Atomic Energy Agency (IAEA) over delays in signing an Additional Protocol to Iran's safeguards agreement that requires increased transparency on the part of a NNWS in respect of its nuclear programme. Although Iran later did sign the Protocol, speculation was fuelled because the IAEA discovered facilities capable of enriching uranium that had not been declared to it. In an effort to find a solution, a dialogue between Iran and the so-called EU–3 (France, Germany, and the United Kingdom) began in October 2003. While an agreement was reached between the parties in Paris in November 2004, the situation was not resolved and by 2006 the UN Security Council passed resolutions, under Chapter VII of the UN Charter, requiring Iran to comply with its international obligations concerning the nuclear programme.

Key Points

- The characterization of motivations for acquiring nuclear weapons has become more complex.
- There are difficulties in determining whether nuclear proliferation has occurred.
- A number of states have the potential to manufacture nuclear weapons if they wanted, and a few embarked on military nuclear programmes before abandoning them.
- The role of non-state actors has added a further dimension to the nuclear proliferation issue.
- There is an ongoing task of ensuring the safety and security of nuclear materials around the world.
- The complexity surrounding compliance with international obligations has been a feature of debate since the early 1990s.

Evolution of global nuclear control and anti-proliferation measures

Early efforts to control nuclear weapons, 1945–70

Global efforts to constrain nuclear weapons acquisition began soon after 1945. In January 1946 the UN General Assembly passed a resolution establishing the UN Atomic Energy Commission (UNAEC). The remit of the UNAEC was to make proposals for the elimination of nuclear weapons and the use of nuclear energy for peaceful purposes under **international control.** Due to disagreements between the United States and the Soviet Union these proposals were never implemented.

The issue of international atomic energy control was revisited following President Eisenhower's **Atoms for Peace** speech on 8 December 1953. It was stressed that Eisenhower's proposal was not a disarmament plan but an initiative to open the benefits of atomic energy to the world community. Negotiations to implement 'Atoms for Peace' culminated in the establishment of the IAEA on 29 July 1957, although it was not until the mid-1960s that this organization was able to implement a comprehensive monitoring system (or **safeguards**) to ensure that materials in the nuclear energy programmes were not diverted for military use.

In the late 1950s negotiations also began on a Comprehensive Test Ban Treaty (CTBT). These occurred in the context of a Soviet Union–United Kingdom–United States moratorium on nuclear testing (1958–61), and calls for the three NWSs to engage in nuclear disarmament. The negotiations did not result in an agreement, largely because the three states were unable to overcome differences concerning **verification**: namely, the provisions for a system that could provide assurance of detection of violation, especially for underground testing. However, in 1963 the three states did agree the Partial Test Ban Treaty (PTBT). This prohibited nuclear testing in the atmosphere, in outer space, and underwater, and meant that future testing by parties to the Treaty had to be conducted underground.

Measures to prevent the nuclearization of specific environments and geographical areas have also been agreed (Goldblat 2002). The first NWFZ applied to a populated region is the Treaty for the Prohibition of Nuclear Weapons in Latin America (the Tlatelolco Treaty), which was opened for signature in 1967. Between 1958 and 1968 the issues posed by more states acquiring nuclear weapons received international attention. In 1961 the UN General Assembly adopted the **Irish Resolution**, which called for limitations to prevent additional states from acquiring nuclear weapons and for all states to refrain from transfer or acquisition of such weapons. A breakthrough in the negotiation of a non-proliferation treaty came as a result of Resolution 2028, adopted by the UN General Assembly in 1965, and the tabling of a joint US–Soviet draft on 11 March 1968. Following further amendments, the latter draft was passed by the UN General Assembly on 12 June 1968, opened for signature on 1 July 1968, and the NPT formerly entered into force on 5 March 1970 (Shaker 1980).

Anti-proliferation efforts since 1970

Since 1970 anti-proliferation measures have continued to evolve. In March 1971 the IAEA negotiated its INFCIRC/153 safeguards document, which provides a model for all safeguards negotiated with parties to the NPT. Additional arrangements have been established for the conduct of international nuclear trade. In 1971 the Zangger Committee adopted guidelines or a 'trigger list' pursuant to the NPT allowing for IAEA safeguards to be applied on nuclear transfers, especially those involving the equipment or material for the processing, use, or production of special fissionable materials. But following the global expansion of nuclear power programmes, the increasing trade with non-NPT parties, and what India referred to as a 'peaceful' nuclear explosion it conducted in 1974, some nuclear suppliers decided that further export guidelines were necessary. Formed in 1975, the Nuclear Suppliers Group (NSG) agreed that additional conditions should be attached to sensitive nuclear exports like reprocessing and uranium enrichment plants.

At the First United Nations Special Session on Disarmament (UNSSOD–1) in 1978, China, France, Soviet Union, United Kingdom, and United States all issued unilateral statements on so-called negative security assurances on the use or threat of use of nuclear weapons

Case Study 2 United States–India nuclear cooperation agreement

On 18 July 2005 the United States and India signed a cooperation agreement on civil nuclear energy. Previously, the United States had imposed restrictions on nuclear and other technology transfers to India. India, for its part, had remained a non-party to the NPT and developed a civil and military nuclear capability. The 2005 agreement would allow India to acquire technology from the United States and for US companies to construct nuclear reactors in India and provide fuel for its civil nuclear programme. In return for this technology India agreed to: grant the IAEA access to its civil nuclear facilities (but military ones remain excluded); sign an Additional Protocol with the IAEA to allow for more intrusive safeguards inspections; continue the moratorium on nuclear testing; improve the security arrangements for its nuclear forces; and support nuclear non-proliferation measures. The agreement has met with a mixed reception domestically in the two countries and internationally. Proponents of the agreement consider it will allow for closer collaboration in areas such as nuclear power production and non-proliferation as well as other aspects of mutual security interest. Opponents argue that it: allows India to continue developing its nuclear forces because the military facilities are not covered; allows India the possibility of diverting nuclear materials from the civil to the military programme once US transfers have begun; could weaken the NPT by undermining Article 1; sends the wrong non-proliferation message by granting concessions to those states seeking nuclear weapons. In India, critics consider the agreement allows the United States too much oversight of its nuclear programme and economic future, and that it will be detrimental to India's long-term security.

---

against NNWSs. These assurances embraced specific qualifications related to each state's nuclear doctrine and security arrangements, but only China's was unconditional. China stated that it would not be first to use nuclear weapons and undertook not to threaten to use nuclear weapons against any NNWS.

In 1987, seven missile technology exporters established identical export guidelines to cover the sale of nuclear-capable ballistic or cruise missiles. Known as the **Missile Technology Control Regime** (MTCR), this supply arrangement seeks 'to limit the risks of nuclear proliferation by controlling transfers of technology which could make a contribution to nuclear weapons delivery systems other than manned aircraft' (Karp 1995). Membership of the MTCR has expanded to include many of the major missile producers and the guidelines now embrace missile systems capable of carrying chemical and biological payloads. Over time concerns have been expressed about the long-term viability of the MTCR. While these acknowledge that the arrangement has fulfilled its initial purpose in slowing down missile proliferation, there are calls for new measures. Missile defences are one means for dealing with the problem, but other suggestions include global or regional ballistic test notification centres and multilateral arms limitation measures for missiles with certain ranges. Also in 2002 a new initiative, known as

The Hague Code of Conduct, was launched (Smith 2002). As the name implies, the Code seeks to develop standards of appropriate behaviour in the transfer of missiles and missile parts.

At the time of the 1995 NPT Extension Conference, expectations were high that the documents adopted by consensus then would provide the foundation for strengthening the Treaty. Events afterwards indicated that this assessment was premature as differences surfaced between the parties over how these documents should be interpreted. Similarly, in 1995, expectations were high that a CTBT would soon be agreed and implemented, but again this proved premature. Although a CTBT was opened for signature in 1996, it has not entered into force. This will only occur once a group of 44 states (including the five NWSs and states such as India, Pakistan, and the DPRK) have signed and ratified the Treaty. This has meant that the success or otherwise of the CTBT is dependent on developments in several states. Significantly, also, not everyone agrees that this Treaty is a worthwhile measure. Proponents claim that the restriction on nuclear testing will limit both **vertical** and **horizontal proliferation**. Critics of a CTBT argue that any such testing prohibition is unverifiable and will therefore be unable to constrain proliferation.

Box 22.5 1995 NPT Review and Extension Conference

On 11 May 1995 the NPT Review and Extension Conference extended the NPT indefinitely without a vote. This extension decision was adopted in conjunction with two other documents and a resolution which established a set of principles and objectives for nuclear non-proliferation and disarmament; outlined new procedures for strengthening the Treaty review process; and called for the establishment of a Middle East zone free of nuclear weapons and other weapons of mass destruction within the context of the Middle East peace process. However, the parties were unable to agree a consolidated text on the review of the Treaty and, as in 1980 and 1990, the Conference concluded on 12 May without a final declaration. Even then, the outcome of the 1995 NPT Conference was hailed a success. This was because the Treaty became permanent, new measures were established to strengthen future NPT review conferences, and a plan of action for non-proliferation and disarmament was outlined.

Problems have similarly been encountered over attempts to negotiate a Fissile Material Cut-off Treaty (FMCT). One issue has been whether the FMCT should prevent future production of **fissile materials** only or deal with this aspect in conjunction with an agreement to remove existing stockpiles. The verification provisions of any such treaty have also been the subject of differing proposals. One feature of this debate that inevitably will demand innovative thinking is how, as safely and cost effectively as possible, any excess fissile material can be disposed of, given the large quantities involved.

The document tabled at the 1995 Conference by the Arab states party to the NPT, known as the Resolution on the Middle East, calls on all states in the region to accede to the NPT. The debate over this resolution has highlighted the problems associated with the attempt to ensure universal adherence to the Treaty. For although signatories to the NPT have increased to the point where 188 states are now party, Israel, India, and Pakistan have remained non-signatories while the DPRK withdrew in 2003. The question is therefore how, if at all, the Treaty can be made universal?

It is against this background that the events in South Asia have significance. The nuclear tests by India and Pakistan provoked an array of commentary on the consequences for anti-proliferation efforts and future stability in the region. The South Asian tests, combined with the difficulties encountered over other Treaty aspects, such as non-compliance, suggested that the globalization of the nuclear proliferation issue was entering a new phase. Whereas the early to mid-1990s had witnessed a period of relative optimism that anti-proliferation efforts were being strengthened and that nuclear weapons were becoming marginalized, the latter part of the decade gave way to an alternative observation of the future. A view emerged that a 'second nuclear age' was already upon us and that there were greater risks associated with this age than those experienced during the 'first nuclear age' between 1945 and 1990 (Gray 1999*a*; Baylis and O'Neill 2000).

In response to this situation, new initiatives were devised. One strategy that began during this period is **counter-proliferation**, which emphasizes the use of measures such as ballistic missile defences and a more proactive stance to prevent nuclear proliferation. Another concept known as **anti-proliferation** also emerged, and this was deemed to incorporate 'the traditional nonproliferation agenda as well as new elements responding to the political and military implications of the proliferation process itself' (Roberts 1993: 140).

Thus, as the turn of the millennium dawned the context of nuclear proliferation was undergoing change. Developments thereafter would add a greater sense of urgency to find a way forward that would be responsive to the complexities of the globalization of the nuclear proliferation issue in the twenty-first century. This generated measures like the **Proliferation Security Initiative** (PSI), established originally by 11 states in June 2003 and now involves 15 with 60 other states participating on an *ad hoc* basis. The PSI is designed as a means for the interdiction of trafficking in WMD, delivery systems, and related materials. There have also been calls for a reappraisal of the prospects for creating new multilateral nuclear fuel centres (an idea that has been around for several decades). Regional safeguards organizations, such as the one established in the European Union (known as EURATOM), have similarly been the subject of attention as possible models for facilitating greater regional oversight of nuclear energy developments.

Key Points

- Nuclear control and anti-proliferation measures have been evolving since 1945.
- The IAEA has established a global safeguards system.
- Attempts to implement a CTBT and negotiate a FMCT have stalled following a period of renewed impetus after 1995.
- A number of NWFZs have been negotiated.
- The NPT now has 188 parties, although India, Israel, and Pakistan remain non-signatories.
- In 1987 the MTCR began operating and The Hague Code of Conduct was introduced in 2002.

- NPT Review Conferences have been held every five years since 1970.
- Since 1995, the NPT has encountered several challenges related to new incidences of nuclear testing, attempts to achieve universality, disposal of fissile material, compliance, and verification.
- It has been suggested that a 'second nuclear age' has emerged.
- New measures have been implemented in response to the continuing globalization of the nuclear proliferation issue.

Conclusion

At the heart of the current debate are thus complex issues related to the future global security environment. They include questions such as: what are likely to be the main proliferation challenges of the coming decade? what would happen if the NPT weakens irreparably over time? and what the implications are of the renewed interest in nuclear power generation in the context of the debate over global warming? One response to these questions could be to develop the initiatives already underway into a comprehensive approach for long-term global nuclear governance, though ensuring it remains situated on the original treaty-based foundations. The NPT is now an old treaty with many limitations, but it also provides an international legal framework that allows for collective actions to address pressing global security issues. Such an approach might encompass: attempts to resolve disputes and build trust and confidence at the bilateral and regional levels; the strengthening of international norms; innovation in areas such as compliance, verification, safeguards, intelligence, and fissile and radiological material production, security and disposal; the involvement of non-parties to the NPT; ongoing efforts aimed at nuclear disarmament; and continuing commitment by all parties to the Treaty's objectives.

Box 22.6 Chronology

1945	United States detonates the world's first nuclear weapon.	1961	United Nations General Assembly adopts the 'Irish Resolution' calling for measures to limit the spread of nuclear weapons to additional states.
1946/7	United States and the Soviet Union submit plans for the international control of atomic energy to the newly formed United Nations Atomic Energy Commission (UNAEC).	1963	Partial Test Ban Treaty (PTBT) entered into force.
		1964	China becomes the fifth state to test a nuclear weapon.
1949	Soviet Union tests its first nuclear weapon.	1967	Treaty for the Prohibition of Nuclear Weapons in Latin America (the Tlatelolco Treaty) was opened for signature.
1952	United Kingdom tests its first nuclear weapon.		
1953	President Eisenhower of the United States introduces his 'Atoms for Peace' proposal to the United Nations General Assembly.	1968	Treaty on the Non-Proliferation of Nuclear Weapons (the NPT) opened for signature.
		1969	Tlatelolco Treaty entered into force.
1957	International Atomic Energy Agency (IAEA) inaugurated.	1970	NPT entered into force.
1958	European Atomic Energy Community (EURATOM) begins its operation within the European Community.	1971	IAEA concludes the INFCIRC (Information Circular)/153 Safeguards Agreement and the Zangger Committee also adopted a set of nuclear export guidelines pursuant to the NPT.
1960	France becomes the fourth state to test a nuclear weapon.		

(continued) ▶

Box 22.6 (continued)

1972	Anti-Ballistic Missile (ABM) Treaty is signed between the United States and the Soviet Union.
1974	India detonates a nuclear explosive device declared to be for peaceful purposes and the Nuclear Suppliers Group (NSG) is formed.
1975	First Review Conference of the NPT is held in Geneva, and by the end of the year 97 states had become party to the Treaty.
1978	First United Nations Special Session on Disarmament (UNSSOD-1) provides the forum for the five Nuclear Weapon States to issue unilateral statements on negative security assurances.
1980	Second NPT Review Conference is held in Geneva.
1983	United States announces its Strategic Defence Initiative (SDI).
1985	Third NPT Review Conference is held in Geneva.
1987	Missile Technology Control Regime (MTCR) is established.
1990	Fourth NPT Review Conference is held in Geneva.
1991	A United Nations Special Committee (UNSCOM) is established to oversee the dismantling of Iraq's undeclared nuclear weapons programme. The United States announces its Safety, Security, Dismantlement (SSD) Programme following the dissolution of the Soviet Union.
1993	South Africa announces that it had produced six nuclear devices up until 1989 and then dismantled them prior to signing the NPT. The Democratic People's Republic of Korea (DPRK) announced its intention to withdraw from the NPT following allegations concerning its nuclear programme.

1995	Review and Extension Conference of the NPT is held in New York and the then 179 parties decide to extend the NPT indefinitely and also establish a new Treaty Review Process and a set of principles and objectives for non-proliferation and disarmament.
1996	The Comprehensive Test Ban Treaty (CTBT) is opened for signature.
1997	First Preparatory Committee (PrepCom) for the new NPT Treaty Review Process convenes in Geneva.
1998	India and Pakistan conduct a series of nuclear and missile tests.
1999	United States announces its National Missile Defense (NMD) Act.
2000	Sixth NPT Review Conference is held in New York for the now 188 parties to the Treaty. The five Nuclear Weapon States reiterate the undertaking 'to accomplish the total elimination of their nuclear arsenals'.
2002	Cuba becomes the 189th party to the NPT and The Hague Code of Conduct for missile technology transfers is initiated.
2003	The issue of non-compliance and responses to it become the focus of attention as the DPRK announces its 'withdrawal' from the NPT and intervention occurs in Iraq.
2004	A transnational non-state nuclear supply network is discovered and Libya agrees unconditionally to dismantle its weapons of mass destruction infrastructure in compliance with international agreements and the United Nations Security Council passes Resolution 1540.
2005	Seventh NPT Review Conference is held in New York.
2006	DPRK announces that it has tested a nuclear weapon.

❓ Questions

1 What properties make nuclear weapons different from conventional forms?

2 What are the implications of the global diffusion of nuclear and long-range delivery vehicle technology?

3 What role do norms, taboos, and epistemic communities play in the context of nuclear proliferation?

4 How have the motivations for acquiring nuclear weapons changed since 1945?

5 In what ways has it become more difficult to determine whether nuclear proliferation has actually occurred?

6 Does the non-state actor represent a new nuclear proliferation challenge?

7 What nuclear proliferation concerns have stemmed from the dissolution of the Soviet Union?

8 What are the main arguments for and against the proliferation/spread of nuclear weapons?

9 Were the early efforts to control nuclear weapons doomed to failure?

10 What initiatives are needed to ensure global nuclear governance for the twenty-first century?

Guide to further reading

Theoretical aspects

Buzan, Barry, and Herring, Eric (1998), *The Arms Dynamic in World Politics* (London: Lynne Rienner). This text covers theoretical and empirical aspects associated with the arms dynamic in the context of nuclear weapons.

Campbell, Kurt M., Einhorn, Robert J., and Reiss, Mitchell B. (2004), *The Nuclear Tipping Point: Why States Reconsider Their Nuclear Choices* (Washington, DC: Brookings Institute Press). This volume explores the factors that lead states to reconsider their nuclear options.

Hymans, Jacques E. (2006), *The Psychology of Nuclear Proliferation* (Cambridge: Cambridge University Press). Using four case studies, the author draws on materials from the humanities, social sciences, and natural sciences to analyze nuclear decision-making in the states chosen for study.

Sagan, Scott D., and Waltz, Kenneth N. (1995), *The Spread of Nuclear Weapons. A Debate* (New York and London: W. W. Norton, and 2nd edn 2003). This book juxtaposes the contrasting arguments of the two authors concerning the spread of nuclear weapons.

On nuclear use and non-use

Herring, Eric (ed.) (2000), *Preventing the Use of Weapons of Mass Destruction* (special issue), *Journal of Strategic Studies*, 23(1) (March). The contributors to this volume concentrate on the issues associated with preventing the use of WMD.

Lavoy, Peter R., Sagan, Scott, and Wirtz, James J. (eds) (2000), *Planning the Unthinkable: How New Powers Will Use Nuclear, Biological and Chemical Weapons* (Ithaca, NY: Cornell University Press). The authors compare how military threats, strategic cultures, and organizations shape the way leaders intend to employ WMD.

Historical context and background

Walker, William (2004), *Weapons of Mass Destruction and International Order*, Adelphi Paper 370 (Oxford: Oxford University Press for the International Institute for Strategic Studies). This IISS Paper addresses the 'problem of order' associated with weapons of mass destruction by drawing on historical evidence and ideas.

Non-proliferation/anti-proliferation measures

Bosch, Olivia, and Van Ham, Peter (eds) (2007), *Global Non-Proliferation and Counter-Terrorism* (Washington, DC: Brookings Institute Press). This volume assesses the impact of UN Security Resolution 1540.

Dhanapala, Jayantha, with Rydell, R. (2005), *Multilateral Diplomacy and the NPT: An Insider's Account* (Geneva: United Nations Institute for Disarmament Research). This book provides an analysis of the multilateral diplomacy surrounding the 1995 NPT Review and Extension Conference and is written by two authors who were closely involved in the negotiating process (one of which was the President of that Conference).

Simpson, John, and Howlett, Darryl (eds) (1995), *The Future of the Non-Proliferation Treaty* (New York: St Martin's Press). This explores the background issues associated with the NPT in the lead up to the 1995 Review and Extension Conference.

Alternative nuclear futures

Baylis, John, and O'Neill, Robert (eds) (2000), *Alternative Nuclear Futures* (Oxford: Oxford University Press). This edited volume provides an overview of the different positions related to the nuclear future.

 Visit the Online Resource Centre that accompanies this book to access more learning resources on this chapter topic at www.oxfordtextbooks.co.uk/uk/orc/baylis_smith4e/

Chapter 23

Nationalism

JOHN BREUILLY

- Introduction: concepts and debates ···404
- Nationalism, nation-states, and global politics in history·······································406
- Nationalism, nation-states, and global politics today··412
- Conclusion···414

Reader's Guide

In this chapter I consider the relationship between nationalism and global politics. I question the conventional view that nationalism brought about a world order of nation-states and that this world order has subsequently come under threat from globalization. Instead, I argue that global politics and nationalism accompany one another and the most important task is to understand their interactions over time. I begin by looking at how nationalism has been defined and explained. I then outline how global politics and nationalism have developed together in distinct phases since 1750. The key connection between the two is the nation-state, the main power container of the modern world. However, the nation-state and relations between nation–states also change in each phase. Only with this historical perspective can we understand current relationships between global politics and nationalism.

Introduction: concepts and debates

A standard view of the relationship between nationalism, **nation-states**, and **global politics** might go something like this. (1) There developed in Europe from about mid-seventeenth century an order of sovereign, **territorial states** (the 'Westphalian system') (see Ch.2.). (2) The rise of nationalism from the late eighteenth century nationalized this state order, later extending beyond **Europe** until the whole world was organized as a series of nation-states (see Box 23.1). International relations were relations between nation-states. (3) **Globalization** undermines this political order. It undermines 'state' by eroding sovereign territorial **power**. It undermines 'nation' by creating competing identities. Before considering propositions (2) and (3), I will outline key concepts and debates concerning nationalism and nation-state.

I define **nationalism** as the idea that the world is divided into nations which provide the overriding focus of political **identity** and **loyalty** which in turn demands national **self-determination**. Let us take three key words in this definition. Nationalists think of the **nation** in different ways. The same group can be claimed by competing nationalists. (Turkish nationalists claim Kurds in Turkey as Turkish, a view Kurdish nationalists reject.) Defining nation is more difficult than defining nationalism. Some writers stress certain objective features; others its subjective, imagined character; yet others are sceptical about using the term at all. Box 23.2 provides examples of these three views. By **overriding**, I mean that many people

think the world is divided into nations but not that nations demand supreme loyalty. **Self-determination** usually means independent statehood. However, nationalists might settle for something less, such as autonomy within a federal state.

Nationalism can be considered as **ideology**, as **politics**, as **sentiments**. Definitions of nationalism usually frame it as ideology, a political worldview. However, we might ignore this ideology unless it becomes significant. This can happen if nationalism shapes people's sense of identity: **nationalism as sentiments**. It can happen if nationalism is taken up by movements able to form nation-states: **nationalism as politics.**

Each aspect of nationalism can be divided into types. Here are some examples. Ideology can be **civic** and **ethnic**. **Civic nationalism** is commitment to a state and its values. State membership determines nationality, as in the multi-ethnic immigrant society of the USA. **Ethnic nationalism** is commitment to a group of (imagined) common descent. Nation precedes state, as in ethno-national states formed in modern Europe. There are problems with this distinction. Every nationalism invokes culture and values and these change, often quickly. Cultural factors like religion and language cannot easily be assigned to the ethnic or civic category. There is a danger of moralizing the distinction (civic good; ethnic bad). Nevertheless, the distinction is important.

Nationalist sentiments can be of the **elite** or the **masses**. Some nationalist ideas only appeal to a small stratum of the population whereas others have popular resonance. In terms of politics, nationalism can be state-strengthening and state-subverting. **State-strengthening** nationalism accepts an existing state as broadly legitimate but seeks to strengthen it, internally by 'purifying' the nation and reforming government, externally by reclaiming 'national' territory and extending power. **State-subverting** nationalism aims to create a new state, usually by separation from a larger state, sometimes by unifying smaller states.

The relationship of nationalism to global politics varies with these types. Mass-nationalism, using ethnic ideas to subvert an existing state, is very different from elite-nationalism, using civic ideas to strengthen an existing state.

It is generally agreed that nationalism is modern. Explanations of its origins and growth revolve round four

---

Box 23.1 The development of a world of nation-states

Date	Rough number of nation(al) states*
1500	2 (England, France)
1800	6 (Britain, France, Holland, USA, Spain, Portugal)
1900	30 (including Belgium, Germany, Italy, Serbia, Romania, Greece, Brazil, Argentina, Japan, Canada)
1923	45 members of the League of Nations
1945	51 states established the United Nations
1950	60 members of UN
1960	99 members of UN
1970	127 members of UN
2006	192 members of UN

*Before 1923 this is an estimate based on historical judgement. Thereafter it is based on membership of the League of Nations and the United Nations.

Box 23.2 Definitions of nation

'[The nation] . . . is an imagined political community—imagined as both inherently limited and sovereign. . . . It is imagined because the members of even the smallest nation will never know most of their fellow-members, meet them, or even hear of them, yet in the minds of each lives the image of their communion. . . . The nation is imagined as *limited* because even the largest of them encompassing perhaps a billion living human beings, has finite, if elastic boundaries, beyond which lie other nations. . . . It is imagined as sovereign because the concept was born in an age in which Enlightenment and Revolution were destroying the legitimacy of the divinely-ordained, hierarchical dynastic realm.'

(Benedict Anderson 1991, p 5–6)

'. . . let us define it [the nation] at the outset as a large social group integrated not by one but by a combination of several kinds of objective relationships (economic, political, linguistic, cultural, religious, geographical, historical), and their subjective reflection in collective consciousness. Many of these ties could be mutually substitutable—some playing a particularly important role in one nation-building process, and no more than a subsidiary part in others. But among them, three stand out as irreplaceable: (1) a "memory" of some common past, treated as a "destiny" of the group—or at least of its core constituents; (2) a density of linguistic or cultural ties enabling a higher degree of social communication within the group than beyond it; (3) a conception of the equality of all members of the group organized as a civil society.'

(Miroslav Hroch 1996, esp. p 79)

'Neither objective nor subjective definitions are thus satisfactory, and both are misleading. In any case, agnosticism is the best initial posture of a student in this field, and so this book assumes no *a priori* definition of what constitutes a nation. As an initial working assumption any sufficiently large body of people whose members regard themselves as members of a "nation", will be treated as such. However, whether such a body of people does so regard itself cannot be established simply by consulting writers or political spokesmen of organizations claiming the status of "nation" for it. The appearance of a group of spokesmen for some "national idea" is not insignificant, but the word "nation" is today used so widely and imprecisely that the use of the vocabulary of nationalism today may mean very little indeed.'

(Eric Hobsbawm 1990)

key questions: (1) Does nationalism depend upon the prior existence of nations? (2) Are nations modern or do they extend far back in time? (3) Should we privilege culture, or economics, or politics in our explanations? And (4) What is the role played by internal factors (such as a shared culture) in relation to external factors (such as threats or support from powerful states) in shaping nationalism? Table 23.1 summarizes positions in this debate.

There is also some confusion over the usage of 'nation' and 'state'. The leading **international organization** is the United Nations. The term 'Nations' actually means 'States'.

In many states, cultural diversity is so great as to render implausible any claim that these are ethno-national states. In many states, the lack of democracy renders implausible any claim that these are civic-national states. What then does the term nation-state mean? I do not think it worth trying to identify how 'national' states are both because the criteria are so fuzzy, and also because it means accepting the basic nationalist assumption. Instead, I will treat as nation-states states which claim to be national, however nation is defined, and are not confronted by powerful state-subverting opposition and are accepted by the international community.

Priority (Nation or Nationalism)	Dating (pre-modern/ modern)	Type (ideology, politics, sentiment)	Key factor (culture, economy, politics)	Theory (short name)	Theorist (example)
Nation	Modern	Sentiment	Culture (belief as identity)	Primordialism	Walker Connor
Nation	Pre-modern (ethnie)	Sentiment	Culture (myths and memories)	Ethno-symbolism	Anthony Smith
Nation	Pre-modern	Sentiment	Culture (beliefs as creeds)	Perennnialism	Adrian Hastings
Nationalism	Modern	Sentiment	Economy (industry)	Modernism	Ernest Gellner
Nationalism	Modern	Sentiment	Culture (communication)	Modernism	Benedict Anderson
Nationalism	Modern	Ideology	Culture (intellectuals)	Modernism	Elie Kedourie
Nationalism	Modern	Politics	Politics (elites)	Modernism	Paul Brass, Charles Tilly

Table 23.1 Debates on nationalism

Nationalism, nation-states, and global politics in history

We start with the historical relationship between nationalism and the global spread of nation-states. Worldwide connections between human beings can be traced back at least to 1500 when the Americas were brought into contact with Eurasia and Africa. Some historians claim to trace nationalism and nation-states back at least that far. However, it is generally agreed that nationalism became significant from around 1750, also a time when one can identify the first significant conflict between nation-states deploying nationalism and which took on a global dimension.

Anglo-French rivalry, c. 1750–1815

Global power

In Europe and beyond, France and Britain deployed land and sea forces against each other. They used others as proxies in at least three continents (Europe, India, and North America). Both states sought to control global trading in mass commodities (cotton, tobacco, sugar) which were superimposed upon older **networks** of luxury trade. Europeans explained and justified their power as due to greater civilizational achievements than the rest of the world, which was seen as consisting of primitive cultures and decaying civilizations.

Global conflict and nationalism

The dominant form of nationalism was **state-strengthening**, **civic**, and **elite.** Within France and Britain, there

were demands for the removal of privilege and to make government accountable to the 'nation'. This 'civic nation' was based on the interests of an expanding middle class which was itself shaped by globalization. The conflict between Britain and France provided public opinion in each state with a clear enemy. The conflict hit France harder than Britain and precipitated revolution. From that revolution came the declaration that the state existed for the nation. Revolutionary France, when it embarked on war in Europe, appealed to other nations to rise up against their governments. Those governments deployed nationalist rhetoric in reply.

Nationalism, nation-state formation, and international relations

Nationalism became significant in British and French politics but remained mainly just an intellectual idea elsewhere in Europe. Rebellion in the Americas freed territories from Spanish and British control, and elites used the language of civic national independence. The defeat of Napoleon left Britain the major world power.

Pax Britannica, c. 1815–1914

Global power

States in Europe and America were preoccupied with regional affairs. Elsewhere, Britain exerted global power. Apart from **diplomacy** to coopt or divide opponents,

Britain relied upon naval supremacy. Instead of combining coercive and economic power in traditional imperial form, Britain proclaimed their separation. She abolished tariffs, ceased monopolizing overseas trade and shipping, and tied major currencies to the price of gold. This was linked to industrialization accompanied by transformations in communications (telegraph) and transportation (steam power). All this enabled huge increases in long-distance migration.

Britain attributed its success to Christianity, parliamentary institutions, and free trade. However, the indirect, coordinating nature of British power meant these could not be directly imposed. Within Europe, the Americas, and Asia, wars in the 1860s were won by modernizing states which then turned their attention outwards, challenging British **hegemony**. Close links between technology and power led to state intervention; the belief that power depended upon control of overseas resources fuelled the rise of imperialist conflict.

Global conflict and nationalism

Nationalism initially imitated the civic forms projected by France and Britain, partly because success breeds imitation, partly because nationalists aimed at support from France and Britain. These nationalists ignored 'non-historic' nationalities (Romanians, Slavs) insisting that they must assimilate into 'high-culture' nations. This stimulated counter-nationalism which stressed folk culture, popular religion, and spoken language. These had little initial success.

Beyond Europe there was little stimulus to nationalism, given the indirect nature of British power which was not yet projected in nationalist forms. There were reactions against Christianity and secular modernity. Such values could be accepted (e.g. Christian conversion) or rejected. Most important were combinations, for example the 'codification' of Hinduism in India which rejected Christianity but conferred 'Christian' features upon Hindu beliefs (see India Case Study below).

As the contradictions of British-led globalization grew, this generated new forms of nationalism. Imperialist conflict promoted popular state-strengthening nationalism. These combined with race ideas which replaced civilizational and religious claims to superiority. Although mainly projected on to the non-European world, these were also used within Europe, as in modern anti-semitism. The tightening of direct control in empires, justified in race and nationalist terms, stimulated counter-nationalisms.

Nationalism, nation-state formation, and international relations

The success of state-strengthening, elite, civic nationalism was linked to war using modern technology and organization. Nationalism became central in the new nation-states. Its liberal values were abandoned as elites confronted problems of state-building, economic development, and imperialist expansion. Ethnic, state-subverting nationalism had limited success against declining multinational states. Support from powerful states like Russia was more important than the intrinsic strength of nationalist movements. Powerful nation-states challenged British hegemony. Britain responded in like fashion. The world increasingly divided into formal and controlled spheres of **influence** after 1880. International relations were dominated by arms races based on new technology and formal alliances. Politicians appealed to public opinion and **national interests**. They then found themselves trapped by the nationalist sentiments they had helped create.

Implications for global politics

British hegemony was justified in cosmopolitan and free trade terms. Liberal nationalism developed in modernizing societies outside British zones of influence. Industrialized war enabled liberal nationalists to form new nation-states. These states established a new model. The state ruled with a bureaucratic apparatus, in conjunction with a dynamic industrial sector, over demarcated **territory**. Armed with nationalist ideas, it penetrated society in new ways: mass education and media, tariff protection, and subsidies. It projected its aggressive nationalism abroad in pursuit of **empire**. As political conflict globalized, it nationalized. Imperial powers aimed at new forms of control over other parts of the world. There was a contradiction between civilizational justifications and the reality of subordination and exploitation accompanied by race ideas. Counter-nationalism rejected imperial power. Making rejection effective became possible when global political conflict turned into world war.

The era of world war, c. 1914–45

Global power

Initially Eurocentric, the First World War became global (see Ch.3). In 1917 the USA entered the war. State control over population and economy increased massively. Although the inter-war period saw military dismantling and reduced state intervention, the Second World War was even more global, and state intervention more extensive. Radio communication and air power, large-scale economic assistance, and military **coordination** gave this war a transnational character. Military globalization was accompanied by economic de-globalization. Free trade and fixed exchange rates disappeared. Voluntary international migration decreased. Attempts to return to 'normality' in the 1920s were blown off course by the **Great Depression**. New technologies (radio, film and television, air travel, and automobiles) expanded massively. They were brought under state control, especially during war. Rather than undermining nationalism, these global processes became components of state-strengthening nationalism.

Global conflict and nationalism

In both wars the Western Allies proclaimed their cause as liberal democracy, not narrow nationalism, though liberal democracy was organized in the form of civic nation-states. However, their alliance with Russia compromised that claim; as did their failure to universalize liberal democracy after victory. Germany expressed clear-cut ethnic nationalism in 1914. Her Ottoman and Habsburg allies went to war to block state-subverting, ethno-nationalism. Victory for the Allies meant victory for the liberal democratic **principle** of 'national self-determination' embodied in Woodrow Wilson's **Fourteen Points**, but the beneficiaries were the ethno-nationalist opponents of the defeated empires. Each state had governments ruling in the name of the dominant nation which regarded minorities with suspicion. Nationalists representing minorities looked to their 'own' national state for support and invoked minority rights provisions in the peace treaties. Such nationalism was inward-looking. The USA turned inward. After a brief phase of stressing a world socialist mission, the USSR also turned inwards.

However, one distinct form of nationalism—fascism—was not insular. Fascists hated communism and **Liberalism**, while rejecting old conservative elite politics. Fascists saw the nation as a supra-individual, classless collective requiring a strong state, mass mobilization, and a genius leader to assert itself in the world. The First World War gave nationalism a statist and militarist character on which fascists built. With economic depression and loss of faith in liberal democracy, fascism gained popularity. Fascist ideology was imperialist but profoundly anti-universalist. The fascist vision was of huge power blocs, each organized as a master nation/race ruling over inferior slave classes.

In the colonial world, military mobilization and attempts at economic development increased subordination and exploitation. World war made clear the divisions and fragilities of existing power structures. This promoted nationalist dreams of gaining independence, justified in liberal democratic or socialist terms.

Nationalism, nation-state formation, and international relations

Nationalism alone could not form nation-states. More important was the destruction of multinational states through war. The doctrine of national self-determination was applied after 1918 to the defeated powers, and only within Europe. International relations were transformed with the League of Nations. But the defeated powers were denied membership, and the US Senate voted against joining. The League was led by France and Britain and seen as an instrument of their interests. The League did much in pioneering concepts of **international law** and administration but failed in its ambitious objectives of creating a new peaceful **order**.

International relations became more violent and expressed in terms of competing ideologies. In each state there were strong disputes and politics were no longer monopolized by small elites. Communist and fascist ideologies justified extreme policies which assumed that sheer willpower could overcome 'reality'. Fascism and communism did not envisage a global order of nation-states but super-empires led by dominant races/nations or classes. Communist states eventually recognized limits which helped them survive this era. The Third Reich

Case Study Interactions between nationalism and global politics: the cases of Germany and India

These two cases have been selected to show how the changing interactions between nationalism and global politics considered above in general terms play out in particular ways. In both cases one can connect the emergence of nationalism and its changing forms to changing phases in the nature of global politics. In both cases the key connecting factor is state formation—whether the imperial state as in India or the nation-state as in Germany. Nationalism itself is so diverse as to resist understanding but makes more sense when placed within this global context.

Germany

In 1750 the German lands were fragmented and its major powers—Austria and Prussia—increasingly weak in relation to Britain, France, and Russia. The wars (1740–8, 1756–63) between Austria and Prussia were also part of the Anglo-French conflict. These two states lost heavily in wars against Napoleon up to 1809. Intellectuals took up romantic and ethnic ideas of nationalism but eventual recovery had more to do with a broad alliance against France which formed after Napoleon's setbacks in Russia in 1812. After 1815 Britain was concerned that the major European powers balanced each other, leaving her free in the wider world. This included an Austria–Prussia balance in Germany. The major nationalist challenge took a liberal, constitutional form, influenced by Britain and France, but it could never develop a popular and unified appeal and was opposed by the main states. The key shift came when liberal nationalism shifted to a state-strengthening position in support of Prussia. Early industrialization, especially in transportation (railways), communication (telegraph), and manufacturing (coal, iron, steel), had an unexpected military consequence which enabled Prussia to gain dramatic and swift victories over Austria in 1866 and France in 1870–1.

Continued rapid industrialization in Germany, mass emigration of Germans to America, and concern to challenge British hegemony led to the growth of a more populist, illiberal, and imperialist nationalism. A key moment was when Germany began building a modern battleship fleet, seen as a direct threat by Britain.

That stimulated popular nationalism in Britain and alliances with Russia and France, leading to world war. German defeat spawned an extreme ethnic nationalism which, compounded by the Great Depression, brought Hitler to power. Nazism pursued race empire in Europe, and at least parity with what Hitler envisaged would be the only other two world powers in the world, the British Empire and the USA.

It required a global coalition to defeat Germany, Italy, and Japan. The result was a *de facto* partition of Germany, dividing with the cold war into a western and a communist state. Ethnic nationalism was rejected in the name of liberalism and socialism. (The third German state—Austria—declared itself neutral and not even German!) New generations in each state came to identify with that state rather than the German nation. German reunificaiton appears to contradict the rejection of nationalism. Really, however, reunification was part of the 'triumph of the West'. There was no powerful nationalist demand for unity in advance of the event itself. The collapse of communism took everyone by surprise. However, for East Germans, unification offered a fast track into the European Union and Western affluence. West Germany's liberal democratic commitment to unity with less fortunate brethren made it impossible to refuse or delay unification. Indeed, one could see reunification as the first step towards the expansion of the European Union eastwards rather than a revival of nationalism.

India

Before 1750 India was enmeshed in global ties. The Mughal Empire was linked to Islamic, imperial, and long-distance trading networks which spread eastwards into China, through Asia Minor and the Middle East, into north and west Africa and, through connections with European powers, to the Americas and South-East Asia, even north Australia. The British East India Company and others like them built on the existing trading and political networks, and introduced new features, such as plantation production of tobacco, tea, coffee, opium, and cotton. There was little attempt to impose European culture or religion, or to impose direct rule. Britain and France fought for influence and by 1815 Britain had

(continued) ▶

(continued)

prevailed. The following period was one of free trade and informal empire. The East India Company ruled but under public scrutiny. Christian pressures increased. Reactions against Christianization promoted the codification and indigenization of Hinduism. This broad, anti-British sentiment culminated in the Indian Mutiny of 1857 and, after its repression, the imposition of formal imperial rule. This, along with the increased exploitation of India in rivalry with other imperialist challenges, promoted nationalist ideas. The Indian National Congress, elite, civic, and at first state-strengthening, was founded in 1885. By 1914 the British had responded with communal electorates and local councils which classed Hindu and Muslim as political identities.

World war brought home to many Indians that they were part of a system of global conflict. Mass-based nationalism emerged in the 1920s. Depression intensified mass discontent while the Congress party penetrated and came to control the devolved provincial government. Britain, confronted by opponents in every part of the world, made concessions. By 1939 independence appeared

just a matter of time. But with war Britain tightened control, imprisoned nationalist leaders, and courted Muslim politicians. British collapse against Japan increased nationalist expectations. Britain could not resist these once war finished but the speed of decolonization and the legacy of the wartime policies meant this took the form of partition rather than one post-colonial state.

Independent India tried to detach itself from cold war polarization by acting as leader of the non-aligned states. Congress pursued a civic territorial nationalism with much success but has been confronted by vibrant religious resistance to secularism, culminating in Hindu and Sikh nationalist challenges. Pakistan, set up as a secular but Islamic state, was unable to keep control of East Pakistan and has found Islamism increasingly important in West Pakistan.

With the end of the cold war and the latest era of globalization, India has begun to exhibit spectacular economic growth rates. The old model of India as part of the 'Third World' clearly does not work.

---

pursued an escalating and ultimately self-destructive radicalism (see Case Study on Germany).

In the colonial world the concern was to survive murderous conflict between the major powers. Nationalists sought to exploit these conflicts but imperial states kept control unless defeated in war. Conflict created opportunities. Nationalism could become entrenched, strong, and popular (see India case study).

Implications for global politics

World war demanded global political strategies and undermined **state sovereignty**. It reversed earlier economic globalization. Liberal democracy was threatened, reactive, and defensive, confronted by communism and fascism. In 1941 the fascist world vision seemed close to realization. Those who initially thought the fascist powers offered ways of throwing off existing imperial rule discovered it meant exchanging one master for a worse one. Nationalism could only succeed if old imperial power was dismantled but not replaced by new fascist power. How did this come about? In 1941–2 the USA moved out of post-1918 isolationism into world war. Its leaders were compelled to think about the war in global and integrated terms. Within two years, military victory looked likely. Global strategy turned to plotting the shape of a post-war world. Nationalism and nation-states figured centrally.

The era of cold war, 1945–90

Global power

The major shapers of the post-war era were the USA and the USSR (see Ch.2). Stalin regarded Soviet expansion as providing a defensive bulwark rather than a stepping-stone to global domination. Yet that expansion, plus Communist victory in China, made communism appear a global threat. Communist power was organized as conventional territorial rule, albeit with novel institutions and ideologies. The USA envisioned hegemony differently. Sole control of nuclear weapons initially made it possible to envisage power as coordinating rather than direct (except in occupied Japan and Germany). The foundations were laid of a liberal global order based on national **sovereignty** with low tariffs, managed exchange rates, and extensive reconstruction. The first wave of decolonization in 1947–9 presaged the worldwide extension of this order.

However, the USSR soon acquired nuclear weapons and credible missile delivery systems. This intensified mutual perception of threat and made military capacity literally global. The USA retreated from its anti-imperialist stance. The nuclear umbrella handed initiatives to local states which presented themselves as valued clients of one or other **superpower**. Each had its own sphere of power. Contested zones in the Middle East, South-East Asia, and Africa were where nationalism could flourish. US

hegemony contributed to economic and cultural globalization, in such forms as mass media and consumption. US aid, private investment, low tariffs, stable exchange rates, and cheap energy produced high growth rates and integration between developed regions of the 'free world'. This world consisted of an ever-increasing number of nation-states as the decolonization process resumed from the late 1950s.

Global politics and nationalism

In Europe the focus was on stabilizing nation-states within a supranational framework (see Ch.25). Ethnic homogenization rendered ethno-nationalism redundant and made civic nationalism easily acceptable. This ideology could accommodate US doctrines of free markets and national sovereignty. The USSR accorded formal sovereignty to its European satellites. Beyond Europe, colonial nationalists demanded territorial independence, a principle enshrined in UN **conventions** and declarations. For those who equated ethno-nationalism with nationalism, this signalled the end of nationalism. Yet independent states with poorly integrated political institutions, economies, and cultures confronted major problems. The dominant principle was that of (nation)-state sovereignty. The United Nations made no provision for minority rights, which were seen as threatening state sovereignty and encouraging ethno-nationalism. Nation-states were highly unequal and mostly located in one or other superpower bloc but the political order was presented as one of sovereign nation-states.

Nationalism, nation-state formation, and international relations

The United Nations included from the outset the two major powers. The defeated powers became members. Decolonization increased membership sharply. The principle of state sovereignty was accommodated to decolonization. Anti-colonial nationalism was usually focused on gaining international legitimacy rather than violently achieving liberation. This, along with continued economic dependency, helps explain post-colonial problems like military coups, corruption, and ethnic politics: national solidarity had not been forged in the struggle for independence. These problems generated new forms of nationalism; some demanding separation, others reforms to create 'real' independence. Nationalist opposition could precipitate state collapse. However, the bipolar order and sacrosanct principle of state sovereignty prevented state collapse turning into new states. The system preferred dysfunctional states.

Implications for global politics

The nation-state was reasserted and globalized but in civic rather than ethnic form. States were legitimized by non-national values (democracy, communism), contained within blocs dominated by the USA or USSR, their sovereignty, even their 'stateness', often a fiction. Civic, state-supporting nationalism dominated. Both the USSR and USA recognized ethnic diversity but contained within the framework of state sovereignty and civic national identity. State-subverting nationalism used civic language and demanded only devolution. Ethno-nationalism, secessionism, and irredentism would only re-emerge when the **cold war** ended.

I have gone quickly through a complex history but it is the only way to grasp the relationship between nationalism and global politics. There is no simple relationship between nationalism and global politics. There is no linear direction to the history, such as the rise of nationalism and then the challenge of globalization. There are patterns and I have suggested what some of these are, but I leave it to you to decide if the historical record supports these suggestions. There is constantly changing interaction in which nationalism, nation-state, and global politics each take on different and related forms. With each phase, the number of nation-states increases. The ideology of nationalism becomes the principal way of justifying the existence of particular states. It combines the democratic principle (nation = people), the claim to sovereignty (national self-determination), and a sense of distinct identity. It is flexible enough to accommodate different social and political arrangements.

Nationalism is a chameleon-like idea which can adapt to the changes in the global political order, matching its claims to the changing ways in which states interact. It mirrors, with its argument that the world is divided into distinct nations with particular territories, the formation of a world divided into sovereign states with sharply demarcated territories.

The chapter has not tried to write about 'nationalism in general': I do not think there is such a thing. If one accepts this view, it suggests that one should look at the contemporary relationship between global politics and nationalism as yet another set of different interactions. Our awareness of the history alerts us to what is new in these interactions.

Key Points

- There is no simple sequence leading either from nationalism to nation-state formation to changes in the global political order or the other way round.
- There is no single, dominant form of nationalism. Instead it can take ethnic, civic, and other forms, be elite or popular, strengthen or subvert existing states.
- The best place to start is with the central political actors. These are the most important state or states in each historical phase.
- The political ideology of states matters most because they have the most power and others tend to respond to their power and ideologies. At the start of our history global conflict is shifting power to extensive middle classes in Britain and France, and the national idea justifies demands for reforms which challenge 'top-down' ideals of power based on religion, monarchy, and privilege.
- Once the process is in motion it develops its own momentum. British victory over France popularizes its liberal, constitutionalist nationalism which is taken up in imitative form by elites elswhere. These elites are able, especially when linked to modernizing states like Prussia, Japan, and the North in the American Civil War, to form powerful nation-states.
- Those nation-states generate new forms of nationalism. Subordinate nationalities react against new state nationalism. These states take up illiberal, imperialist nationalism to challenge British hegemony. Such imperialist nationalism provokes colonial societies to develop counter-nationalism.
- State-subverting nationalism usually cannot on its own defeat imperial powers. Also important is that those powers are weakened in global conflict with each other.
- Therefore the ability of state-subverting nationalism to form nation-states is based on a combination of its own social base and political organization, the power and policy of the state it confronts, and a favourable international situation.

Nationalism, nation-states, and global politics today

Forms of global politics

The collapse of the USSR led to a new wave of nation-state formations. Beyond Europe the removal of the cold war freeze permitted the emergence of state-subverting nationalism. The end of managed exchange rates and deregulation of financial markets undermined state power. At the same time, the regional concentration of economic development has permitted supra-state coordination in certain regions, most notably Europe. While capital, goods, and information move freely and quickly across the world, the same does not apply to labour, especially that of unskilled people in poor countries. The digital information revolution, which has expanded massively the speed and capacity for information storage and processing, opens up the prospects of global culture, whether envisaged as homogenized culture for the masses or as a vast plurality of niche cultures, including diaspora national ones. All this opens up opportunities for new forms of nationalism.

Global politics and nationalism

At a political level the key point is that the cold war labelling and preservation of a particular set of states as civic nation-states was undermined. This enabled the rapid emergence of new forms of nationalism which were not bound to the existing state system.

First, there was state-subverting ethno-nationalism in the former Soviet Union and Yugoslavia. To counter this, the international community and the new Russian government rapidly conceded new state formations—thus turning state-subverting into state-strengthening nationalism. Furthermore, these new states were recognized as civic, territorial entities based on the federal republics of the former states. However, unlike earlier decolonization, these republics were officially based on ethnic identities. That led to conflict over ethnic minorities within the new states. This has remained fairly low-key so far as Russian speakers in the new non-Russian states are concerned, but it led to war and violent ethnic cleansing in parts of former Yugoslavia. The combination of intra-state conflict based on ethnic nationality, the lack of international support for state sovereignty but also for intervention could in some **failed states** lead to vicious ethno-nationalist violence. Rwanda was a case in point.

Second, there have been reactions against this resurgence of ethno-nationalism. One important change from the cold war phase is the increased resort to external intervention into state affairs, involving the United Nations, regional political-military organizations like **NATO**, individual states, and **non-governmental**

organizations (NGOs). The justifications for these interventions are universalist—human rights, the promotion of democracy—rather than the protection of minorities. That, in turn, conditions the development of nationalism. Noting that the international community disapproves of ethno-nationalism, whether practised by the state against minorities or by minorities to subvert the state, nationalism presents itself instead as a movement for human rights, including cultural recognition, and asks for constitutional change such as devolution rather than independent statehood.

Nationalism, nation-state formation, and international relations

In the first unstable phase after 1990 there was a rapid emergence of ethno-nationalism and new nation-state formations. However, after that phase, the international community, above all the USA, has reacted against ethno-nationalism and state break-up, while at the same time enabling new forms of intervention into the internal affairs of weaker states. Nationalism has adapted accordingly and come to focus less on the classical demand for 'one state, one ethno-nation'. Instead, nationalism frequently combines sub-state and transnational connections, for example in the ways the European Union is seen to promote regional autonomy within and across individual states.

Nationalist politics is frequently re-presented as ethnic politics but now demanding cultural recognition and affirmative action rather than political independence. Arguably, the nation-state is ceasing to be the overwhelmingly important power-container of earlier phases of global politics. This can produce one kind of state-strengthening nationalism designed to resist the weakening of the nation-state. Here one can think of the rise of radical right nationalism, particularly concerned with the control of immigration.

Yet the very erosion of nation-state power can also promote the shift of nationalism away from either state-strengthening or state-subversion to other kinds of politics. That kind of politics can also take up connections to transnational or global political actors other than states, such as diaspora organizations. Whether we should continue to call these politics based on ethnic or culturally defined groups nationalism is a matter of debate.

The impact on global politics

The rapid emergence of new kinds of nationalism, the formation of new nation-states, and the violent conflicts with which this was sometimes associated, have altered patterns of global politics. They have stimulated new interventions by a variety of state and **non-state actors**. These interventions have been justified in universalist terms: human rights, democracy (see Ch.29). This is new: in the era of world wars the justification was (ethno-national) minority rights and in the cold war period the principle of state sovereignty blocked intervention. All these interventions appear to undermine nation-states—culturally, politically, economically, and militarily. Obviously the impact is varied; it is greatest for the weakest states. Above all, nationalism is not the same as nation-state. It is precisely when nation-states are most threatened that nationalism, as a reaction against that, can be strongest. At the same time, the very globalization of politics can stimulate new forms of sub- and transnational politics, including that of nationalism.

Key Points

- The sacrosanct principle of state sovereignty was weakened with the end of the cold war, new nation-state formation, and new economic and cultural forms of globalization.
- This provoked a first wave of state-subverting ethno-nationalisms which could lead to violence and ethnic cleansing.
- However, international recognition for new states as civic, territorial entities, along with new forms of intervention and pressure, put pressure on nationalism to move away from this ethnic and state-subverting character.

- There is a state-strengthening nationalism which focuses on the threats globalization pose to the nation-state. This nationalism can paradoxically get stronger the more the nation-state is weakened.
- However, perhaps more important is the shift of nationalism away from a state focus towards concerns with devolution, cultural recognition, and transnational linkages. Nationalism, once again, is showing how adaptive it is to changes in the nature of global politics.

Conclusion

Global politics has a history preceding the rise of nationalism and the formation of nation-states. Roughly, one can divide the history of global politics into its pre-history (to *c.* 1500) when there were widespread but not worldwide political networks, its pre-national stage (*c.* 1500–1750) when such networks were worldwide but states were not yet nation-states and nationalism had not yet developed as a significant political force, and the modern period (1750 to the present) when global politics, nationalism, and the nation-state interacted with each other.

The general trend in the various historical phases from 1750 to the end of the cold war has been an increase in the number of nation-states, and—by around 1970—the acceptance, in ordinary experience but also in international politics and law, that national identity and the nation-state provide the basis of the global political order. However, it is debatable how far this can be attributed to what one might call 'the rise of nationalism'. Nationalism reflected developments in the global political order as much as it caused them. The key connecting elements between nationalism and the global political order were the formation of nation-states and their relations with each other. Furthermore, the type of nation-state and structure of international relations itself changed from one phase to the next, changes which were accompanied by changes in nationalism. Obviously there is an 'internal' history to nationalism, based on pre-existing sentiments and senses of identity, on struggles between social groups for power, and on changes in the way states function and relate to their societies. However, studies of nationalism tend to focus overwhelmingly on this internal history and neglect the way nationalism is shaped by—as well as shapes—the changing forms of global politics. In this chapter I have tried to focus on this aspect of the subject.

In the contemporary stage of the interaction between global politics and nationalism there remains one superpower and speeded up forms of globalization based on open economies and new technologies of movement and communication. The unfreezing of international relations has allowed many diverse and conflicting forms of nationalism to take shape. Some of these seek to subvert and others to strengthen existing nation-states in ways which are similar to historical forms of nationalism. Thus

nationalists who stress protection against immigration or the imposition of cultural homogeneity on citizens follow in the footsteps of earlier types of ethnic nationalism. Nationalists who demand expansion in the name of claiming 'national' territory do the same. So do nationalists who try to lead secessions from existing states. The language used may change, with separatist movements stressing human rights and democracy perhaps rather than ethnic identity, as that fits better the current global political situation, but the politics is similar. There may also be more in the way of such movements, given the weakening of the commitment to the principle of state sovereignty.

More interestingly, the ways in which nation-state sovereignty is being eroded can help generate novel forms of nationalism. In other chapters in this book it has been suggested that one should think of globalization as transforming rather than either destroying or leaving untouched nation-state sovereignty. The nation-state becomes more an enabling institution in a web of international, transnational, and global networks. If this is the case, I suggest it will generate new kinds of nationalism. Some of these will see their purpose as to resist this transformation of the nation-state, for example by opposing supranational agreements on free population movement or the development of multilateral military institutions. Some of these will see it as their purpose to exploit these transformations in the nation-state, for example by arguing for devolution and multiculturalism, for connections between the 'same' nationality groups across state boundaries. New kinds of diaspora nationalism are emerging, using the new technologies of communications to maintain links. Notions like a 'Europe of the regions' can also underpin new kinds of national movements. What the historical perspective suggests as the most important change is that nationalism is shifting away from a focus on the independent nation-state towards other kinds of political or cultural objectives. Indeed, it is often not even calling itself nationalism. No sooner do we think we have tied down the subject, than it transmutes into something else. It is only by putting it into its precise historical or contemporary context that we can grasp these transmutations.

Writers on nationalism have constantly anticipated that it is about to come to an end. The first secular creeds

of modernity—liberalism and socialism—assumed that global ties would create a cosmopolitan world, whether based on free trade **capitalism** or classless communism. 'Narrow' nationalism had no place in such a globalized world. What these ideas failed to grasp was that the major power-container for managing the new global processes would be the territorial, sovereign state. This state used new technology to create superior military power, guided economic development, and increasingly shaped its population through mass schooling and control over the patterns of their interactions, and finally by providing many of the social services earlier associated with families and small communities. At the same time, the formation of a mobile, participatory society swept aside legitimations for state authority based on privilege, heredity, and religion.

Nationalism provides the new legitimation for such states. It matched the development of the sovereign state ruling over the demarcated territory with the idea that the world was divided into diverse and distinct nations. It put the nation as source of authority in place of privilege and religion. It also proved capable of generating emotional solidarity that appealed to large-scale societies made up of diverse people who were strangers to each other. This was something that liberalism and socialism had not been able to achieve on their own.

Why nationalism has managed to achieve this is a matter of fierce debate. At one extreme, nationalism is seen as an expression of a pre-existing and strong sense of solidarity (nations, ethnies, races). Only on such an existing solidarity, these writers argue, is it possible to create the modern bonds of nationalism. At the other extreme, nationalism is seen as something manipulated by modern political elites in order to secure power in the state. The second view can fit well with the view of international relations as relations between states which act fairly rationally on the basis of clear interests and calculations. The first view, by contrast, tends to see honour and emotions as playing an important part in international relations and making them unstable.

My own view is somewhat different. I have argued that nationalism is a political idea and practice which mirrors the emergence of the new order of sovereign, territorial states and which alters its character as that order goes through different historical phases. Where there are shared values, nationalism will exploit these as expressions of national identity (e.g. making Hinduism 'Indian'), but this only works effectively in the context of modern

state-formation and global political conflict. These and other approaches can be combined in a great variety of arguments so I doubt the debate will ever be settled.

As nation-states espousing nationalist values—for whatever reason they have come into existence—extended their domination through the world, above all in the form of imperialist-nationalist conflict, those living in the areas brought under their domain were in turn compelled to use the nationalist idea. The nationalist idea is derivative in the sense that there is a constant imitation of the basic claims about the existence of nations and their right to have their own states. However, nationalism takes distinctive customs, histories, values, and ways of life to justify these basic claims, so it always looks very different in one place compared to another. (This is why it is pointless to argue, for example, that nationalism is opposed to religion or is combined with religion, or replaces religion. It does all three, depending on whether a 'nationalizing' of religion serves the political purposes of nationalism.) It is this that gives some plausibility to the self-perception of each nationalism that it is unique and that it is its unique national qualities that account for the appeal and strength of nationalism.

Nevertheless, one nationalism on closer inspection looks very like another. Furthermore, despite the capacity of nationalists to form organizations and even generate popular support, generally speaking state-subverting nationalism also required a favourable international situation which weakened the resistance of the state it opposed in order to succeed. This international situation also conditioned whether nationalism presented itself in ethnic or civic forms, as that was as much about gaining support from powerful external states as it was about mobilizing popular support for the nationalist movement.

In the most recent phase of globalization, the nation-state as the basis of the global political order has been called into question. But whatever we might think will happen to the nation-state, that is an issue distinct from nationalism. State-strengthening nationalism might well mobilize around the defence of a threatened nation-state. State-subverting nationalism might well exploit the new preparedness of the USA and international bodies to intervene in the affairs of states in order to demand support for claims to separate statehood. But beyond this, nationalism may well also take on new forms in which the sovereign nation-state is no longer central but rather what matters are demands such as devolution or cultural

recognition, which actually weaken the concept of state sovereignty. Having established itself as such a powerful idea, sentiment, and politics, nationalism is likely to adapt to new global political patterns just as it has done constantly over more than two centuries. Where it may once have matched the formation of a global political order founded on the sovereign nation-state, it may well adapt to a new political order in which the sovereign nation-state is less central. Certainly it is too early to write the obituary of nationalism.

❓ Question

1 Which comes first: nations or nationalism?

2 Is nationalism the major factor in the formation of nation-states?

3 Why has nationalism spread across the world in the last two centuries?

4 Is it useful to distinguish between civic and ethnic forms of nationalism?

5 How and why did nationalism develop into imperialism?

6 Why did colonial peoples take up the idea of nationalism?

7 How can changes in global politics account for changes in nationalism?

8 How has the rise of the modern state shaped the development of nationalism?

9 How has the formation of global capitalism shaped the development of nationalism?

10 Is nationalism ultimately about preserving cultural identity against the modern pressure towards homogenization?

11 'Nationalism is more important for strengthening than subverting the state.' Discuss.

12 'Contemporary globalization erodes nation-state sovereignty but does not undermine nationalism.' Discuss.

➡ Guide to further reading

Debates on nationalism

Smith, Anthony D. (1998), *Nationalism and Modernism: A Critical Survey of Recent Theories of Nations and Nationalism* (London: Routledge). Provides a judicious survey of the different theories of nationalism.

Ozkirimli, Umut (2005), *Contemporary Debates on Nationalism: A Critical Engagement* (London: Palgrave). Deals with a number of recent debates, including the impact of globalization on nationalism.

Broad historical studies of nationalism

Breuilly, John (1993), *Nationalism and the State,* 2nd edn (Manchester and Chicago: Chicago University Press). Compares various cases, starting in Europe around 1500 and including material from twentieth-century Asia and Africa.

Hobsbawm, Eric (1990), *Nations and Nationalism since 1780: Programme, Myth, Reality* (Cambridge: Cambridge University Press). Focuses on Europe in the nineteenth century and the world more broadly after 1918.

Broad historical studies of globalization

Osterhammel, J., and Peterssen, N. P. (2005), *Globalisation: A Short History* (Princeton, NJ: Princeton University Press). A short and clear overview.

Princeton McNeill, J. R., and McNeill, W. H. (2003), *The Human Web: A Bird's Eye View of History* (New York: W. W. Norton). The best single-volume world history of the networks human beings form that I know.

Nationalism and international relations

Cobban, A. (1969), *The Nation State and National Self-Determination* (London: Fontana). An older but still valuable study of the relationship between nationalism and self-determination.
Mayall, J. (1990), *Nationalism and International Society* (Cambridge: Cambridge University Press). The principal general study of the subject.
Moore, M. (ed.) (1998), *National Self-Determination and Secession* (Oxford: Oxford University Press). An account of the issue of secession.

Nationalism and globalization

So far as I know there are no general studies concerned solely with this subject. However, recent handbooks and general studies devote chapters to the relationship between globalization and nationalism. Among these are: **Spencer, P., and Wollman, H.** (2002), *Nationalism: A Critical Introduction* (Edinburgh: Edinburgh University Press); **Delanty, G., and Kumar, K.** (eds) (2006), *The Sage Handbook of Nations and Nationalism* (London: Sage), especially the chapters in Part 2, 'Nations and Nationalism in a Global Age'; **Hutchinson, J.** (2004), *Nations as Zones of Conflict* (London: Sage), especially Chapter 5, 'Nationalism and the Clash of Civilisations'; **Day, G., and Thompson, A.** (2004), *Theorizing Nationalism* (London: Palgrave), Chapter 9, 'The "Challenge of Globalization": Between Nationalism and Globalism'; **Guibernau, M.** (2001), 'Globalisation and nationalism', in **Guibernau, M., and Hutchinson, J.** (eds), *Understanding Nationalism* (Cambridge: Polity Press).

Online Resource Centre

Visit the Online Resource Centre that accompanies this book to access more learning resources on this chapter topic at www.oxfordtextbooks.co.uk/uk/orc/baylis_smith4e/

Chapter 24

Culture in world affairs

SIMON MURDEN

- Introduction: culture in human affairs ···420
- The counter-revolutionaries of the global age ·····················423
- A counter-revolution at the civilizational level?: the case of Islam ·····426
- Islamic fundamentalism ···427
- Conclusion ··431

Reader's Guide

The human experience is one of cultures. Culture and cultural differences have been at the heart of human behaviour throughout history. Indeed, as the twentieth century drew to a close, the salience of cultural explanations in international relations appeared to be heightened by the tremendous reorganization of world politics which followed the end of the cold war and the release of a new wave of globalization. A step-change in humanity's connectedness brought different cultures into closer contact, and challenged traditional patterns of culture and social order across the world. The new era of globalization forced the pace at which all peoples were meshing their cultural values with the imperatives of the global economic system and its ideological software. The West was the dominant ideological and cultural force in late-twentieth-century globalization, and while Western-inspired culture appeared to be making the world more alike, the era also exhibited evolving patterns of cultural synthesis and, increasingly, new flows of cultural reciprocity. The pressures for change were great and so were the frictions produced. Different cultural groups clashed at a local level, but there was also a broader tension between global and local forces. New cultural suspicions contributed to new frontiers of international security.

: culture in human affairs

human beings form communities, a **culture** comes into existence. Cultures may be constructed on a number of levels: in village or city locations, or across family, clan, ethnic, national, religious, and other **networks**. All communities produce a linguistic, literary, and artistic genre, as well as beliefs and practices that characterize social life and indicate how society should be run. Culture transcends ideology, and is about the substance of **identity** for individuals in a society. An **awareness of a common language, ethnicity, history, religion, and landscape represent the building blocks of culture**. Few cultures are completely insular or unchanging but, to be recognizable, totems of identity must enjoy some consensus and persistence within the **community**. Societies also define internal and external boundaries by inducing individuals and communities to believe in the value of their culture and the importance of its distinctiveness. Cultures almost always embody ideas and practices that support patterns of domination or **hegemony** within and between societies.

Cultures refer to a variety of totems and boundaries, but religious affiliation has historically been among the most powerful of **influences**. Religions transmit values about the existence of god/gods, and how such knowledge must shape human life. The model established by religious doctrines gives most worshippers and worshipping societies a moral core, a community spirit, and a guide to social stability. While some religions—Judaism, Hinduism, and Sikhism—define a limited community and have little appeal to outsiders, other religions—Christianity and **Islam**—offer universal values to the community of humankind. When claims are made in societies about 'cultural authenticity', they are most often made about

religious totems, and by those priests, mullahs, and gurus that claim to be qualified to transmit them.

The rational and scientific foundations of Western modernity have challenged all religious faiths since the eighteenth century. The Western **Enlightenment** gradually allowed individuals to challenge god and its worldly government with questions and doubt. However, religion has retained a grip on the mind of humanity to this day; a fact that events in the late twentieth century appeared to confirm. The Islamic revival from the 1970s was one of the great phenomena of the twentieth century. In India, the secular foundations of the political system have been challenged by the rise of the Hindu revivalist, Bharatiya Janata Party (BJP). In China, the relaxation of Communist totalitarianism allowed an explosion of local superstitions, most notably the Falun Gong movement, a cult inspired by a Chinese guru based in the United States. Across South-East Asia, Islamic, Christian, and Buddhist revivalism was evident, as was increasing inter-communal conflict. In Russia and Eastern Europe, Orthodox and other Christian sects retook a public space in former communist societies.

Culture is clearly important to human beings, then, but using it as an analytical tool can be problematic. Culture is such a multifaceted concept that it may only be possible to apply in rather vague and intuitive ways. Deciding what culture is and isolating its influence is the key problem. Cultures can never really be described in their entirety, partly because they are too complex and dynamic. In practice, seeing through the cultural maze requires the identification of cultural totems and some generalization about them: the images, meanings, **norms**, values, stories, and practices that seem particularly significant in

---

Box 24.1 Bhikhu Parekh on religion and the construction of identity

Outlining why religion matters so much to the construction of individual identity and culture in many societies, Bhikhu Parekh observed:

'However unworldly its orientation might be, every religion has a moral core, and an inescapable political dimension. If I am expected to be "my brother's keeper" or to "love my neighbour" or be an integral part of the umma (the

universal Islamic community), or if I believe that everyone is created by God, it deeply matters to me how others live and are treated by their fellow humans and the state . . . . Religious people sincerely wish to live out their beliefs and do not see this as an exclusively private or even personal matter.'

(Parekh 1997a: 5)

determining what political or social life looks like. Describing patterns of belonging and exclusion by undertaking some degree of generalization can be a fraught kind of study. Few thinkers on culture can have escaped being accused of too much generalization or of some biased and malign motive. Cultural analysis often produces deep disagreements. Yet, thinking about culture is worthwhile. It is difficult to look at the world and not see culture. Culture can help us understand why humans act in the way they do, and what similarities and differences exist among them. Indeed, understanding the role of culture in world politics has been given added relevance by the quantitative and qualitative revolution in human connectedness and the corresponding acceleration of cultural syntheses which has taken place since the development of a new era of **globalization** in the late twentieth century.

Culture writ large: the civilization

The broadest construction of cultural identity is the **civilization**. In the eighteenth and nineteenth centuries, the European notion of civilization was linked to social and intellectual accomplishment. The supposed superiority of European civilization, with its Greek and Roman heritage and its modernity expressed in the **nation-state** and science, was implicit in the term. Defining those outside civilization—**the Other**—made the idea more meaningful, and shaped the way in which areas and peoples of the world were regarded. Within **Europe**, 'civilized' rules were applicable. Outside they were not. As Europeans built their world **empires**, they imposed their culture by force. Only by the mid-twentieth century did European beliefs about their cultural superiority begin to change, although the idea that the West represented a model of progress continued. Civilization was redefined as a descriptive term to categorize the broadest groups of people that were able to identify with a sufficiently coherent set of aesthetic, philosophic, historic, and social traditions.

Civilizations represent coherent traditions, but are dynamic over time and place. For instance, medieval Christendom drew on ancient and eastern civilizations for many of its philosophical and technological advances; subsequently, Christendom was remoulded into a European civilization based around the nation-state and, finally, was expanded and adapted in North America, and eventually redesignated as Western civilization.

The process embodied both physical and conceptual reformulation, with theocratic, monarchial, and nationalist values superseded by the liberal ideal of human rights, **democracy**, and free markets. What is important to understand about the rise of the liberal ideal as the definitive marker of Western civilization was that, even for its principal promoters in Britain and the United States, it emerged from a long process of **meshing** and disentangling with quite contradictory ideas and practices. In the nineteenth and twentieth centuries, Britons and Americans meshed their **Liberalism** with a concept of civilization that claimed cultural and racial superiority over non-Europeans. Liberalism ran alongside the contradictions of imperial conquest, racial enslavement, and colonial rule. In the second half of the twentieth century—with the signing of the Atlantic Charter in 1941 being an important moment of future intentions—the most outrageous contradictions in Anglo-American Liberalism were ironed out, and the liberal ideal became synonymous with what it was to be Western.

Today, a number of distinct cultural formations clearly exist, notably the Western, Islamic, Indian, and Chinese. Other peoples are not so easily pigeonholed, either because they are not united around sufficiently distinct or powerful cultural totems, or because they are torn between different civilizations; in this respect, the location of peoples in South America, Africa, and Russia is problematic. However, no civilization is completely distinct from the influence of others and all have been particularly affected by the influence of the West.

Box 24.2 The Western account of culture

'There is the whole corpus of cultural and philosophical knowledge which provides the underpinning for the "Western cultural account".... Primarily this account emphasises the possibility of individual and social progress through the application of universal **rationality** and empirical science, goals which involve the mastery of nature for human ends. Then there is the status of the individual human being, who is at the ontological centre of the Western idea of modernity. The significance of the individual is reflected in debates about the sources of moral and political authority in the conceptions of free will versus determinism, and in accounts seeking to explain the dynamism of market societies by reference to the purposive behaviour of rational consumers

(Axford 1995: 2)

The significance of cultures today

During the **cold war**, cultural differences ostensibly took a back seat to the global geopolitical struggle between the United States and Soviet Union. Differences were defined in ideological and economic terms, and superimposed upon world politics regardless of cultural characteristics. Both **superpowers** offered their model to the world for imitation, and alignment to one of the two great blocs defined the 'Other'.

The end of the cold war saw a radical reshaping of world politics, with the triumph of the West reinforced by a revolution in the technology of communications. A new age of globalized **capitalism** was in the making. Cultural analysis was central in a number of seminal texts that appeared to explain what was happening in the post-cold war world, especially Francis Fukuyama's *End of History* (1992), Samuel Huntington's *Clash of Civilizations* (1996) and Benjamin Barber's *Jihad vs McWorld* (1996). Above all, culture offered a way of understanding the similarities and differences of the new age, where a new globalizing cosmopolitan culture met a world of many cultures, and where existing communities and cultures were in closer contact with each other.

The **power** of global capitalism and its consumer culture looked immense. The United States, and its European and Japanese allies, initially dominated the emerging pattern of global hegemony. John Agnew and Stewart Corbridge perceived that a new 'deterritorialized' geopolitical order—**the hegemony of 'transnational liberalism'**—was emerging, and commented that 'a new ideology of the market (and of market access) [was] being embedded in and reproduced by a powerful constituency of liberal states, international **institutions**, and what might be called the "circuits of capital" themselves' (Agnew and Corbridge 1995: 166). Much of the world was brought into the world market economy and indoctrinated with its values. In most of the developing world, state-centred socialism was abandoned, and engagement with the West sought. Francis Fukuyama certainly thought that the great debates about how societies should be run were basically over. What Fukuyama termed the **liberal idea**—the combination of liberal democracy and the market—had drawn a finishing line in the history of political and social **development** (Fukuyama 1992: 45). The liberal idea was the best that anybody was going to get. Other forms of political and social organization had been superseded.

The degree of cultural penetration embodied in the new hegemony was profound. A wave of democratization passed through much of the world. Just as significant was the influence of what Benjamin Barber called McWorld: the inescapable experience of consumer icons, such as Coca Cola, McDonald's, Disney, Nike, and Sony, and the ubiquitous landscape of shopping malls, cinemas, sports stadiums, and branded restaurants. Beside the phenomenon of cultural 'crowding out', liberal reformism also drove the transformation of non-Western societies by drawing women and young people into a world of wage-earning work and consumption. Traditional socioeconomic hegemonies were liable to be blown apart as men and women were encouraged to count value in terms of money, consumption, and entertainment rather than in terms of duty, community, and piety. 'Economic man' was disinclined to care about the socio-cultural being if that contradicted the imperatives of the market. The cultural impact of the new wave of globalization was

---

Box 24.3 Francis Fukuyama on Islam in the world of universal liberalism

For Francis Fukuyama, the end of the cold war had left the 'liberal idea'—liberal democracy and market capitalism—as humankind's universal project. To Fukuyama, it seemed that there was 'no ideology with pretensions to universality that [was] in a position to challenge liberal-democracy, and no universal principle of legitimacy other than the sovereignty of the people'. Fukuyama could only see localized resistance to the liberal idea, notably in the form of Islam. Fukuyama perceived that:

'The appeal of Islam [was] potentially universal, reaching out to all men as men.... And Islam has indeed defeated liberal democracy in many parts of the Islamic world, posing a grave threat to liberal practices even in countries where it has not achieved political power directly.... Despite the power demonstrated by Islam in its current revival, however, it remains the case that this religion has virtually no appeal outside those areas that were culturally Islamic to begin with. The days of Islam's cultural conquests, it would seem, are over. It can win back lapsed adherents, but has no resonance for the young people of Berlin, Tokyo, or Moscow. And while nearly a billion are culturally Islamic—one-fifth of the world's population—they cannot challenge liberal-democracy on its own territory on the level of ideas. Indeed, the Islamic world would seem more vulnerable to liberal ideas in the long run than the reverse.'

(Fukuyama 1992: 45–6)

felt worldwide, including in the West itself, although the discontinuities were much greater for non-Westerners.

The multiculturalism of globalization

As the new era of globalization unfolded in the 1990s, Western culture was undoubtedly the predominant stream, but the development of globalizing cosmopolitan culture drew on many influences and it would become increasingly multicultural. The never-ending quest of global and local capitalists to entertain and sell did much to further cultural synthesis, most obviously in the realms of dress, art, film, television, and food. One only has to think of the output of Disney to see how the stories and images of local cultures are absorbed into a globalized mainstream. Elsewhere, Western-originated images and aspirations are mediated to the Middle East and Asian continent through India's Bollywood film industry. Chinese, Indian, and French culinary culture coexists with McDonald's and Kentucky Fried Chicken almost everywhere on Earth. By the early twenty-first century, it seemed likely that the rising giants of China and India would begin exerting a much more sustained cultural influence across the world. The international production and marketing of the Chinese-inspired motion pictures, *Crouching Tiger Hidden Dragon* (2000), *Hero* (2002) and *House of Flying Daggers* (2004), for instance, looked like an important cultural moment for China and the world.

Globalization did create a cosmopolitan consumer culture which was apt to make different parts of the world more alike, but humanity was not about to become identical. Local ethnic and religious cultures survive alongside globalized culture and, as people and ideas increasingly flow around the world, they exist in closer proximity to other cultures. The arenas for cultural mixing were the world's great cities—London, Paris, Berlin, Moscow, New York, Los Angeles, Sydney, and others—and living in such places required embracing tolerance and multiculturalism, or it meant an urban nightmare of inter-communal suspicion and conflict. Today, Muslims, Christians, Jews, Hindus, Sikhs, Buddhists, and pagans from all races and sects do live side by side in varying degrees of conflict and **cooperation**. The consequences of cultural proximity are complex. Multicultural settings create multiple identities, and so challenge the totems of existing cultures as well as the interests of some of those within them. Above all, multiculturalism tends to undermine patriarchal culture. The uplifting of women in the West was the most significant social phenomeno of the twentieth century, and one that multiculturalism and globalization promises to extend everywhere.

Key Points

- Culture defines the identity of individuals in a society. A culture is composed of the customs, norms, and genres that inform social life. Religion remains a key influence.
- Civilization is the broadest form of cultural identity, and represents a level of identity that may spread across nations and states.
- Cultural groups often define themselves by representing different cultures as alien, or as the 'Other'.

- The West has been the dominant civilization in the modern age, and all other civilizations have had to deal with its influence, whether welcome or not.
- The end of the cold war heightened the significance of cultural identity. The hegemony of the West and of its liberal-capitalism challenged the culture and social order of most societies. Globalization also fostered multicultural landscapes across the world.

The counter-revolutionaries of the global age

As globalized modernity challenged all societies, the forces of reaction gathered everywhere, although this was especially notable in the non-Western world. The West was widely stereotyped for its arrogance, irresponsible **individualism**, and permissive sexual practices, and its liberal-capitalism denounced as exploitative and morally bankrupt. In the absence of a global-level theory of resistance, the opposition to liberalizing globalization was largely parochial and led by cultural conservatives, a fact reflected in the religious core of much of it. Across the world, societies clung to the familiar by remembering religion and associated values, for not everyone wishes the

freedom to question, to doubt, and to be troubled. As ever, religion helped humans deal with uncertainty and fear, clarifying the purpose of human life and regulating the behaviour of individuals, families, and groups in worldly society. If religious doctrines were not taken on wholesale, then they were often translated into backward-looking moral prescriptions about such things as the role of women, the education of youth, the nature of personal responsibility, the punishment of deviancy, and the definition of the outsider. Wherever religious values made ground, it was clear that they could not be kept out of politics.

Popular culture was at the forefront of the cultural counter-revolution. In Saudi Arabia and Iran, the Islamic **regimes** sought to exclude news, films, music videos, and the world's rising tide of pornography by banning satellite television and restricting access to the Internet. It was a battle that was difficult to win. The place of women in society, and especially the issue of veiling (the *hijab*), was the key totem for Islamists who sought to bolster the institutions of traditional culture and social control. In Asia, a debate about the importance of 'Asian values' also got underway, with the state-business elite turning the 'liberal idea' on its head, and arguing that individualism and **Pluralism** actually negated economic success. 'Asian values' in Malaysia and Singapore meant illiberal legislation to control the aspirations and behaviour of youth. Even in the United States, revivalist Christians who railed against the secular **state**, 'Hollywood social values', abortion, the teaching of evolution, and the putative **cosmopolitanism** of contemporary America were a force to be reckoned with; the contemporary Christian mission was to imbue America's capitalism with older notions of community and morality.

Religious revivalism sometimes took the form of extreme literalism, often termed **fundamentalism**. The roots of fundamentalism varied. Messianic preachers continued to find audiences around the world. More significantly, fundamentalism often stemmed from a wider angst that existing society was being overrun in some way. Many fundamentalist groups were born in opposition to the perceived evils of modernity's secularism, pluralism, social atomization, and moral emptiness. Claiming the legitimacy of God, fundamentalists could formulate interpretations of their faith that allowed for political and social violence, and sometimes even looked forward to some apocalyptic final vision.

Fundamentalists often sought to 'purify' society in the most extreme ways. Thus, just as the Marxist-inspired revolutionaries of the 1950s and 1960s disappeared, a new breed of religious militants became a principal cause of sub-state **terrorism** in the world. Islamic fundamentalism led a new wave of violence. In Algeria and Egypt, Islamists proved themselves to God by committing the most terrible acts of brutality. In India, fundamentalist Muslim and Sikh secessionists fought pitched battles with the Indian Army, while Hindu extremists responded with force. Extremism could also be found in Christianity. In the United States, the Waco siege and the Oklahoma bombing were the most spectacular manifestations of violent paranoia. Eastern religion produced the Aum Shindri Kyo sect in the 1990s, a group that sought to commit mass murder on the Tokyo underground with the use of Sarin nerve gas. Where fundamentalists did find a credible voice, the prospects for meshing global and local cultures smoothly was much reduced.

A clash of civilizations?

The significance of culture following the cold war was reflected in a debate led by Harvard professor, Samuel Huntington. In an article entitled 'The Clash of Civilizations' (*Foreign Affairs*, 1993) and in a subsequent book (1996), Huntington offered a new paradigm of world politics in which the principal patterns of conflict and cooperation were shaped by culture and, ultimately, by civilization. Huntington suggested that the civilizations that would determine the future of international politics were the 'Western, Confucian, Japanese, Islamic, Hindu, Slavic-Orthodox, Latin American, and possibly African' (Huntington 1993: 25).

Box 24.4 Fundamentalism

'Fundamentalism is more than a political protest against the West or the prevailing establishment. It also reflects deep-seated fear of modern institutions and has paranoid visions of demonic enemies everywhere. It is alarming that so many people in so many different parts are so pessimistic about the world that they can only find hope in fantasies of apocalyptic catastrophe. Fundamentalism shows a growing sense of grievance, resentment, displacement, disorientation, and anomie that any humane, enlightened government must attempt to address.'

(Armstrong 1997: 17)

For Huntington, the clash of civilizations was a historic development. The history of the **international system** had been essentially about the struggles between monarchs, **nations**, and ideologies within Western civilization. The end of the cold war inaugurated a new era, where non-Westerners were no longer the hapless recipients of Western power, but now counted among the movers of history. The rise of civilizational politics intersected four long-run processes at play in the international system.

1 The relative decline of the West.
2 The rise of the Asian economy and its associated 'cultural affirmation', with China poised to become the greatest power in human history.
3 A population explosion in the Muslim world, and the associated resurgence of Islam.
4 The impact of globalization, including the extraordinary expansion of transnational flows of commerce, information, and people.

The coincidence of these factors was forging a new **international order.**

Underpinning the new politics were cultural revivals on a grand scale. The world was becoming a smaller place, and this was raising human consciousness about cultural differences. Global economic changes had also weakened local loyalties. With Western-originated ideas widely seen to have failed, communities sought to recreate some rooted past. Socialism and **nationalism** gave way to 'Islamization, Hinduization, and Russianization'. The 'liberal idea' may have been presented as a new universal by the West, but its individualism, secularism, pluralism, democracy, and human rights had only superficial resonance in Islamic, Sinic, Hindu, Buddhist, and Orthodox cultures. In reality, the differences between civilizations ran deep: they were about man and God, man and woman, the individual and the state, and notions of rights, authority, obligation, and justice. Culture was about the basic perceptions of life that had been constructed over centuries.

For Huntington, culture worked at the level of motivation. States remained key actors, but civilizational politics became real when states and peoples identified with each other's cultural concerns or rallied around the 'core state' of a civilization. The Orthodox, Hindu, Sinic, and Japanese civilizations were clearly centred on powerful unitary states. The West had a closely linked core that included the United States, Britain, France, and Germany. Islam was without a clear core state, and for this reason experienced much more intra-civilizational conflict as a number of contenders—Turkey, Iran, Iraq, Egypt, Saudi Arabia—competed for influence. The fact that Islam was divided did not refute the idea that a pan-Islamic consciousness existed.

Cultural conflict could be found at a 'micro' and a 'macro' level. At the 'micro-level', groups from different civilizations were prone to conflict across local 'fault-lines', and by means of a 'kin-country syndrome' were liable to bring in their wider brethren. Huntington observed that Islam had particularly 'bloody borders', a situation that would continue until Muslim population growth slowed in the second or third decade of the twenty-first century. At the 'macro-level', a more general competition was evident, with the principal division between the 'West' and, to varying degrees, the 'Rest'. According to Huntington, the West's dominance was most contested by the two most dynamic non-Western civilizations, the Sinic and Islamic. Resistance to the West was most evident over **issues** such as arms control and the promotion of Western political values, which were regarded as a form of neo-**imperialism.**

Huntington's thesis was highly contentious, with critics pointing to conceptual and empirical problems (Murden 1999). The treatment of culture was brief, and the conclusions very pessimistic. Huntington failed to tell the stories of interaction and synthesis that have always gone on between civilizations. Having lost the Soviet Union as its Other, some thought Huntington was needlessly constructing new enemies for the West, and that the *Clash of Civilizations* could become a self-fulfilling prophecy. Much of the criticism was based on caricature, but some reflected the difficulty of trying to use culture to analyze world politics. Unpacking the myriad of factors that cause conflicts with such an all-encompassing tool as the notion of civilization is problematic. Where Huntington could really be criticized, though, was in his downplaying of the power of global economics and its culture. Huntington failed to recognize the extent to which traditional cultures are penetrated by global-level society and markets, and how the belligerency of even the keenest of civilizational warriors is usually tempered

by the imperatives of the market and the international system.

Notwithstanding the problems with his proposed paradigm, Huntington initiated an important discussion about human motivations following the cold war, and about the emerging patterns of international conflict and cooperation. The civilization may be not a particularly coherent unit, but that did not mean that underlying cultural preferences do not exert specific and general influences. The *Clash of Civilizations* may not have told the whole story of what was happening in the post-cold war world, but it told part of it.

> ### Key Points
>
> - The new wave of globalization has met local resistance in some places from those seeking to preserve their cultures from unbridled change. Religious revivalism has been a global phenomenon since the 1970s.
> - Religious fundamentalism has become the most important cause of domestic and international terrorism in many parts of the world.
> - As the cold war came to an end, a discourse was led by Samuel Huntington which suggested that a 'Clash of Civilizations' was about to become the principal cause of international conflict.

A counter-revolution at the civilizational level?: the case of Islam

In much of the post-cold war debate about culture in world politics, Islam came into the frame. Parts of the Muslim world seemed troubled by modernity, and appeared to be a particular source of conflict. Many Islamic activists were locked in conflict against adjoining civilizations and secular states across the Balkans, West and East Africa, the Middle East, the Caucasus, Central Asia, India, Indonesia, and the Philippines, with their efforts to promulgate Islamic law a particularly explosive issue. An Islamic militancy that emphasized the corrupt character of Western modernity had also been clear factor in world politics since the Iranian revolution of 1978–9.

Islamic culture in the modern age

The Islamic world represents an example *par excellence* of the experience of almost all non-Western societies in the modern age. Islamic peoples have had to deal with the geopolitical and cultural hegemony of the West since the eighteenth century. The collapse of the Ottoman Empire at the end of the First World War heralded a new era in which the secular, nationalist, and authoritarian state became the dominant form of political organization. Modernizers in the Muslim world argued that Islam was the cause of backwardness and decline, and that modernization required the imitation of Western forms of

culture and organization. In Mustafa Kemal's Turkey, the Ottoman Caliphate was abolished in 1924, and Western forms of law, script, and dress enforced. Women were forcibly unveiled. A similar model was adopted in Iran and the Arab world, although the attack on Islam was never quite so thoroughly pursued. Islam was divided by Turkish, Iranian, and Arab nationalisms.

Secular nationalism was to be a failure in the Middle East. In some places, notably Syria and Iraq, the state was hijacked by minority groups. The forces of Arab nationalism also foundered on their demonstrable inability to take on Israel, with the Six Day War of June 1967 being a shattering blow. Jerusalem was lost. The June War was a turning point, and although the idea of an Arab nation retained an appeal, a new force was stirring: that force was revivalist Islam. Economic failure deepened the crisis. Rapid population growth and rural–urban migration meant that urban life was characterized by poor housing, strained services, and widespread underemployment. The young urban poor had little hope of a better life. In the 1950s and 1960s, secular elites had at least appealed to the masses with socialism and nationalism, but after the *infitah* (opening) model was initiated in Anwar Sadat's Egypt in the 1970s, the interests, values, and lifestyles of the elites turned towards the West. The elites essentially abandoned the masses, leaving Islam as the voice of opposition not only to the ruling regimes, but also to the cultural penetration that came with *infitah*. A deeper malaise

within Islamic societies also drove the revival. According to Sohail Hashemi:

> The Islamic revival [was] a complex mix of elements both unique to the Muslim world and shared with other post-colonial societies. The Islamic challenge is trivialized if explained as merely resentment of the power and wealth of the West. It derives its vitality and its appeal from a much more elemental factor: the widespread conviction that Islamic history has gone horribly astray, and that Muslim realities for centuries have been widely divergent from Islamic ethics. The fact today that Muslim countries are characterized by some of the most notoriously authoritarian regimes provides a powerful internal dynamic to the use of Islam as a revolutionary force. The fact that Muslim countries range in economic prosperity from the fabulously wealthy to the hopelessly impoverished provides a second powerful internal dynamic to the upsurge of religiously based calls for social justice.
>
> *(Hashemi 1996: 17)*

The Islamic revival that began in the Middle East would eventually spread across the entire Muslim world. The conservative Islamic monarchies of the Gulf promoted missionary (*da'wa*) activities, but the Islamic revival was really a mass movement born in the crisis of modernization. Many young Muslims, especially those in the urban poor and lower middle class, turned to Islam as a culture that gave the forgotten and the hopeless self-worth.

Key Points

- The impact of the West has been the principal issue facing Islamic civilization since the eighteenth century. Muslim modernizers sought to imitate the West, but the performance of the secular state disappointed many in much of the Middle East.
- A crisis of modernization exists in many Muslim societies. Poor economic performance has left large umbers of the urban population poor and frustrated.
- Islam remains a powerful influence in the Muslim world. When secular states faltered, Islam was there to fill the vacuum of leadership.

Islamic fundamentalism

The Islamic revival had many manifestations, but it was a new militant politics that had the most dramatic effects. Sayyid Qutb in Egypt (d. 1966), Abu al-Ala al-Mawdudi in Pakistan (d. 1979), and Ruhollah Khomeini in Iran (d. 1989) led a militant Islamic discourse that struck a chord across the Muslim world. Most militants advocated a return to the basic texts of Islam—thus, the term **Islamic fundamentalists**—and the implementation of an Islamic state through Islamic law (the *sharia*). The militants spoke of striving for the faith in the language of *jihad* (Holy struggle) and martyrdom.

Militant Islam stood in opposition to Western-led modernity. Liberalism and Islam do represent two different systems for understanding, appreciating, and behaving in the world. Liberalism is a vision of economic liberation, individual choice, and the removal of social restraints. Islam may be able to absorb some liberal references, but, ultimately, it is a vision of submission to God, the believer community, and a certain kind of social **order**. Islamic societies tend to frown on the idea of individual consciousness and choice. In the post-Enlightenment West, the idea of a better future has been a central one. In militant Islam, Muslims look forward to a better past. The perfect Islamic polity was established in the first years of Islam, and its eternal **principles** recorded in the Koran and other early scripts. The Koran and *sharia* represented the perfect constitution, in which **sovereignty** resided in God, not in human beings. Many Islamists recognized the validity of consultation (*shura*), but the idea of popular democracy was alien. For some militants, certain Islamic injunctions—such as a criminal law that conducts public executions as well as amputations, and the archaic regulation of women and non-Muslims—were totems of an authentic Islamic community and could not be reformed.

The Muslim Brotherhood (*Ikhwan al-Muslimin*)—an organization originally founded in Egypt by Hasan al-Banna in 1928, and spread to Syria, Palestine, Jordan, and North Africa—organized the Islamic revival. Muslim Brotherhoods were both political organizations and benevolent social foundations. Much of the time, Muslim Brotherhoods focused on supporting Muslims

in their communities, but on occasions members turned to politics and even to violence. In Egypt, the Muslim Brotherhood led a violent protest against the secular-socialist state led by Gamal Abdul Nasser. Sayyid Qutb, executed by Nasser's regime in 1966, became the icon of Sunni Muslim radicalism. Qutb argued that Islam was subject to a modern state of *jahiliyya*, a term referring to the condition of ignorance that existed before the Prophet Mohammed's time. Refusing to accept the idea or legitimacy of the state or nation, Qutb denounced Nasser as an infidel; it was a Muslim's duty to wage a *jihad* against such corruption.

Shia Muslims were moving in a separate but similar direction to militant Sunnis in the 1960s and 1970s. The driving force of Shia revivalism was Grand Ayatollah Ruhollah Khomeini. Khomeini proposed a state dominated by religious scholars in which both **political and religious** primacy was vested in a supreme religious figure or council; the new system was termed the *velayet-e faqih* (the guardianship of the jurisconsult. The most senior Islamic expert would have the last word in ruling the state; it was a position that Khomeini was to fill himself. The Iranian Revolution that followed in 1978–9 would be about entrenching the *velayet-e faqih* in power, a process that was to take a number of years, and require the elimination of the Shia clergy's partners in the rebellion against the Shah's regime.

The Iranian Revolution itself provided great impetus to the Islamic revival. While Iran's Revolution was of limited theological significance to Sunni radicals, it was an example to emulate. A populist Islamic movement had overthrown a powerful secular state; what had seemed impossible had been done, and the language of *jihad* and martyrdom vindicated. In fact, Islamic revolution was not about to sweep across the Arab world, but during the 1970s and 1980s a crescendo of Islamic protest shook the Middle East. Most Islamic violence was directed at Muslim societies themselves. While most Islamic revivalists broadly agreed over ends—an Islamic state and *sharia* law—they did differ over means. The most militant wanted a revolution, but most were reluctant to engage in all-out war. Mainstream Islamists sought to conduct a dialogue over gradually extending their values. For Muslim governments, keeping the mainstream away from the extremists was the central dynamic of politics. In Jordan, the Muslim Brotherhood was brought into a democratization process quite successfully. In Egypt, the state struggled to keep the Muslim Brotherhood and violent secret societies apart, but eventually ground the Islamists down. In Algeria, the army took decisions that brought mainstream and militants together in agreement over means, and produced a savage civil war. For the time being, the Islamic militants had met their match in the Middle Eastern state.

11 September 2001 and its aftermath

By the early 1990s, the Islamic revival appeared to have peaked. The grand dreams of some militants about seizing the state could not be realized. Instead, some puritanical preachers now hoped to revive Islam from the grassroots first. The threat to the Middle Eastern state receded, but the result was chronic social violence as these grassroots Islamists sought to take back the streets. However, just as the Islamic revival seemed blocked, the new wave of globalization which followed the end of the cold war as well as the Gulf War of 1991 gave it new life; the coincidence of socio-cultural pressures with real geopolitical grievances primed what happened next. Following Iraq's defeat in 1991, the United States created a security regime across the Middle East, which included the garrisoning of US forces in Saudi Arabia. The presence of infidel troops in the land of the two Holy Cities of Mecca and Medina was so outrageous to a body of Islamic opinion that it galvanized a new phenomenon: a cadre of wealthy and well educated Islamists–Osama bin Laden was the doyen—who had the ideas, the money, and the contacts to forge a new global alliance of militants, dedicated to fighting the 'invasions' of the West and its version of modernity. From a refuge in Afghanistan and Pakistan, what was to become known as the Al Qaeda organization offered ideological, training, and financial support to various kinds of Islamic militants everywhere. Drawing on religious references to *jihad* and martyrdom, the organization fostered the cult of the suicide bomber—an innovation in Sunni Islam—not simply as an act of nihilism, but as the ultimate expression of the worship of God. Attacks on US interests in Saudi Arabia and East Africa in the latter 1990s were but a prelude to the colossal events which took place at the World Trade Center in New York and the Pentagon in Washington on **11 September 2001**.

Case Study Schematic of the militant Islamic movement
in the Afghan–Pakistan milieu (*c.* 2001)

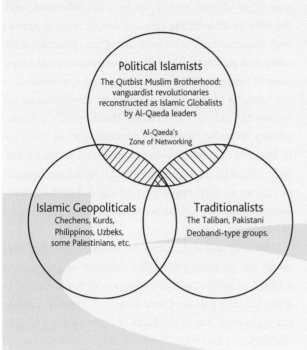

Political Islamists
The Qutbist Muslim Brotherhood:
vanguardist revolutionaries
reconstructed as Islamic Globalists
by Al-Qaeda leaders

Al-Qaeda's
Zone of Networking

Islamic Geopoliticals
Chechens, Kurds,
Philippinos, Uzbeks,
some Palestinians, etc.

Traditionalists
The Taliban, Pakistani
Deobandi-type groups.

Al Qaeda leaders declared a global-level counter-revolution against the USA and its allies while residing in Afghanistan in the mid-late 1990s. However, it is important to understand that few Islamic militants in the Afghan–Pakistan milieu aspired in reality to overthrow the West and the entire world order. The concerns of the vast majority of Islamic militants were far more parochial. What made Al Qaeda significant in the Afghan–Pakistan milieu was that it was able to position itself at the intersection between what can be seen as the three constellations of emphasis/interest in the contemporary Islamic movement: the globalists (global counter-revolutionaries), the geopoliticals (those harnessing Islam in local geopolitical conflicts), and the traditionalists. Above all, Al Qaeda exploited the grievances stemming from older geopolitical conflicts for its own global-level objectives; it was where non-Muslim foreign powers, such as the USA, Serbia, Israel, Russia, India, Australia, and the Philippines, affronted Muslims in their homelands which enabled Al Qaeda to network among other kinds of Islamic activist. Thus, it is arguable that Al Qaeda could not be seen as a manifestation of some vast ideological struggle between liberal modernity and a coherent movement of Islamic rejectionists. Rather, Al Qaeda's real centre of gravity lay in older geopolitical conflicts which could, in principle, be resolved.

The attacks of **9/11** not only led to the so-called global **war on terrorism**, but also to developments in the discourse about civilization. The US administration of George W. Bush steered its definition of civilization back towards an association with a standard of good. Of course, this standard of good was formed around an essentially American vision of freedom and democracy. The conceptual guru of this universal civilization was Fukuyama, not Huntington. The world was to be divided into two civilizations—not six or seven—described as the civilized and the uncivilized. The uncivilized were led by the so-called **axis of evil**, composed of the states of Iraq, Iran, and North Korea. Thus, in the months after 9/11, most Western leaders were keen to emphasize that the West had no fundamental quarrel with Islam itself, but only with the uncivilized stragglers of modernity, or, as Fukuyama termed them, Islamo-fascists. Of course, the new alignment of America's strategic interests with a new mission to civilize would eventually lead to the conquest of Iraq in 2003, although Fukuyama himself would later reject the viability of the vast socio-cultural experiment that this represented. Indeed, it was soon evident that Iraqis were having some trouble in meshing their cultural

inclinations with the interests of the United States and the culture of Liberalism.

In the meantime, one of the consequences of 9/11 and its aftermath was that borders began to go back up. In the West, there was a new wave of alarm which fed into existing angst about an Islamic fifth-column within Western societies as well as more general concerns about the influx of immigrants and asylum seekers. The nature of multicultural society itself was questioned, with some Western leaders—notably in the United Kingdom—beginning to argue that a stable multicultural society required a bit less tolerance of difference and a bit more integration by minority communities. New security laws made the West a less liberal place. For those who believed that the struggle between liberal democracy and Islamo-fascism eventually would be resolved in the favour of the West, the tightening of borders and the rolling-back of liberal values was a temporary expedient. Once the particular emergency was defeated, the new restrictions could be eased.

Other Western thinkers wondered whether cultural conflict was endemic to the world of liberalizing globalization. Benjamin Barber perceived that the real problem

lay in global capitalism's assault on local societies, which created the conditions of alienation, despair, and chaos. For Barber, what he termed, 'McWorld and Jihad' existed in a 'parasitic dialetic'. What was needed was a new civic-democratic approach to manage globalized interdependency better; one that did not simply spread the worst features of globalization—organized crime, consumerism, and immorality—but gave local peoples more time and space to adapt (Barber 2002*b*: 262) Reflecting some of the themes developed by Huntington, the British thinker, Roger Scruton, took an even more pessimistic view. For Scruton, Western civilization had developed in a way that embodied the seeds of its own destruction. Cosmopolitan Liberalism was not only devoid of any deeply-held values or sense of community, but it was now also weakening the territorial jurisdictions which made Western-style democracy possible. Scruton urged that the nation-state be bolstered and some of the free-flowing exchanges of globalization controlled in order to preserve the territorialized existence of the Western societies as well as reduce the numbers of people in a state of flux from becoming lost, disillusioned, and vengeful (Scruton 2002: 159–60).

The future of Islam in the global age

The events of 9/11 and its aftermath set back the march of liberalizing globalization. Yet, while it was easy to emphasize the compatibility problems and conflicts between the Western and Islamic worlds, Muslim countries could not escape the realities of practical politics and economics. Even Islamists have had to be pragmatic whether in opposition or power.

The case of Iran is illuminating. The Revolution of 1978–9 promoted a missionary Islam that sought to oppose the 'forces of corruption on earth', especially the United States. The Islamic Republic neglected the realities of power, but the costs were unsustainable and by the mid-1980s, the Revolution had produced its 'pragmatists'. Fences were mended, and while the Islamic Republic continued to speak up for Muslim rights everywhere, it was less prone to act on this mission. The death of Ayatollah Khomeini in 1989 led to further reorganization. The Presidencies of Hashemi Rafsanjani and Mohammad Khatami speeded change, with attempts to reform politics, economy, and society. The reformers realized that an Islamic insularity was not tenable in the global age.

The young, women, and the middle class wanted more freedom, although there was a powerful conservative establishment determined to stop them having it. The process of change would not be straightforward, with the reformists suffering ups and downs in their sparing with the conservative incumbents of the theocratic institutions of the state. The fairness of parliamentary elections in February 2004, for instance, was undermined by the banning of hundreds of reformist candidates by the unelected Council of Guardians. The election of a revolutionary revivalist, Mahmoud Ahmadinejad, as President in June 2005 was also a significant setback for those with more liberal inclinations. The struggle to define the future of Iranian society would be prolonged, but the Islamic Republic still held out the potential for becoming a model of Islamic adaptation.

The inescapable dilemma for Islamists was that they could not promote their values without engaging with a world of politics and economics which was bound to affect the very nature of the Islamic community. Finding the 'right path' was at the heart of contemporary Islamic discourse. By the 1990s, the breeze of reform also appeared to be growing in the Arab world, with the Islamic idea of *shura* (consultation) acting as a touchstone for political and social reform. Morocco, Jordan, and most of the Gulf States referred to *shura* when they introduced limited forms of representative assembly. Even among the ranks of Islamic fundamentalists, there was recognition that many ordinary Muslims wanted a voice. The struggle for the body and soul of Arab societies would also be lengthy, and it was difficult to imagine that Muslim democracy would resemble Western democracy anytime soon. The forces of globalization may demand a degree of conformity from all those engaged with it, but that does not mean that all traditional cultures will be tamed in the same way.

Beyond the debates about the form of the Muslim state, the future of Islam stood to be influenced from the sub-state level. The Islamic community sustains a vast network of transnational contacts and **non-governmental organizations** (NGOs) which has been multiplied by the advent of the Internet. Islam has an enormous presence in cyber space. While the cyberspace activities of violent Islamic groups are well known, the vast bulk of Islam-online is benign, with much of its content limited to trying to influence the politics and culture of the Muslim societies. Conservative forces have a substantial presence but

cyberspace is also a forum for reformists, notably from the Muslim community in the West who have more freedom to articulate innovative ideas about adapting Islam to the contemporary world.

Muslim peoples have met liberalizing globalization with infinitely various combinations of imitation, resistance, and synthesis. Thus, for all the talk about civilizational conflict in the post-cold war world, Islam's influence on international relations remains diffuse: its influence on Muslim states and their international organizations is often overmatched by countervailing forces. Islamic civilization has no rallying point. While some Islamic militants are doing their best to rally the brethren, their grandiose dreams of a transnational Islamic revolution seem destined to be disappointed. Ultimately, and short of another aberration on the scale of 9/11, the likes of Al Qaeda represent only a limited threat to Muslim states, Western states, and the international order. Islam is most influential as a social ideology among Muslims, and that

is the realm in which it exerts its diffuse but considerable effect in the world. The sum of these Islamic social effects is important. Islam is a brake on the capacity of liberalizing globalization to transform Muslim societies, and it does limit the extent to which Muslim societies can absorb the norms of Western-style politics and economics.

Key Points

- Islam militants have embraced a cultural conflict with the West. In the 1980s, the Iranian Revolution led militant Islamists against the West. In the 1990s, the Sunni Islamists of the Al Qaeda network took up the torch.
- Islamic movements are suspicious of the global, but the pressures to be pragmatic are strong. The Iranian Revolution is a good example of how political and economic realities can force compromise on Islamists.
- Islam does not have a common voice. Muslims meet the forces of globalization in different ways. Muslim societies will continue to change in the twenty-first century.

Conclusion

The new wave of globalization that emerged in the late twentieth century brought an unknown level of intercultural interaction. The speed at which most cultures were evolving seemed to increase significantly. At the same time, there was a growing awareness that existing cultural identities were under threat, although whether this was translating itself into a reorganization of world politics in the way suggested by Samuel Huntington was another matter. What is clear, though, is that the globalization stressed societies and produced belligerent forms of cultural revivalism. A revival of religions was one of the most important manifestations of social and cultural insecurity: religion appeared to offer fixed cultural totems, even

if it did not. While most societies adapted to the momentous changes brought by globalization, violent resistance accompanied cultural revivalism. Religious fundamentalism was the most significant form of resistance, and although it was unlikely that these fundamentalists could stop the march of liberalizing globalization, the aggregate level of **anarchy** they created and the West's response to it, especially after the 11 September attacks, did begin to slow its progress. Localized cultural rearguard actions would continue to be fought well into the twenty-first century, but the imaginings of cultural authenticity were not only those of the parochial backwater, but were an impossible dream in the age of globalization.

❓ Questions

1 What is culture?

2 How useful is the concept of culture when thinking about human societies and international relations?

3 How does religion influence cultural identity, and why has religion remained such a powerful influence in the world?

4 Why did Samuel Huntington argue that differences between civilizations would become the principal cause of international conflict after the end of the cold war?

5 Is the 'Clash of Civilizations' credible as a paradigm for understanding world politics after the cold war? Are the alternative visions more plausible?

6 How many civilizations exist in the contemporary world? Does it matter?

7 How have Middle Eastern peoples responded to the pre-eminence of the West in the modern world?

8 Can the doctrines of Islamic revivalism forge an alternative model of modernity?

9 How have the 11 September 2001 attacks on the United States changed the debate about culture and globalization? Will any changes be lasting?

10 Human societies appear increasingly multicultural. Can such a world be stable?

➔ Guide to further reading

Agnew, John, and Corbridge, Stuart (1995), *Mastering Space: Hegemony, Territory, and International Political Economy* (London: Routledge). A study on hegemony and cultural discourse since the nineteenth century, which argues that globalization has created a 'deterritorialized' global hegemony.

Axford, Barrie (1995), *The Global System: Economics, Politics and Culture* (Cambridge: Polity Press). A study of Western modernity, and how it has been extended across the world.

Barber, Benjamin (1996), *Jihad vs McWorld* (New York: Ballantine Books). An eloquent account of global culture and capitalism, and ways that it challenges local social systems and identities.

Booth, Ken, and Dunne, Tim (eds) (2002), *Worlds in Collision: Terror and the Future of Global Order* (Basingstoke: Palgrave Macmillan). An edited volume reflecting on many aspects of world politics following the 11 September 2001 attacks, including chapters by Fukuyama, Der Derian, Chomsky, Cox, Barber, Halliday, and Waltz.

Fukuyama, Francis (1992), *The End of History and the Last Man* (London: Penguin Books). The book that explained the power of the liberal idea, and proclaimed that the history of political development was now at an end.

——(2004), *State Building: Governance and World Order in the Twenty-first Century* (London: Profile Books). Fukuyama's second thoughts about the progress of the liberal idea. Fukuyama is now concerned that many developing states are too weak and divided to take on Liberalism without a prolonged period of state-building. Entrenching the rule of law first is more important than instituting liberal political, social, and economic freedoms.

Huntington, Samuel (1996), *The Clash of Civilizations and the Remaking of the World Order* (New York: Touchstone). The follow-up to his Foreign Affairs article (1993) that argued that civilizational references were becoming the driving force of international affairs.

Scruton, Roger (2002), *The West and the Rest: Globalization and the Terrorist Threat* (London: Continuum). An opinion piece that reflects some of the anxieties about globalization within the West following 11 September 2001. It argues that civilizations are different and that all have been damaged by liberal globalization, including the West.

Online Resource Centre

 Visit the Online Resource Centre that accompanies this book to access more learning resources on this chapter topic at www.oxfordtextbooks.co.uk/uk/orc/baylis_smith4e/

Chapter 25

Regionalism in international affairs

EDWARD BEST · THOMAS CHRISTIANSEN

- Introduction··436
- Regional cooperation and regional integration··········436
- Regional cooperation in a global context··············438
- The process of European integration··················444
- Conclusion··447

Reader's Guide

This chapter provides an overview of the different regional arrangements that have emerged around the globe over the past fifty years. Having clarified the various concepts and definitions that are being used in this respect, the chapter outlines the main driving forces that explain the rise of regionalism in recent decades. The chapter then looks at the developments that have occurred in this regard in the Americas, in Africa, in Asia, and in the European Union, highlighting both the similarities and the differences between the various regional arrangements. The chapter argues that there is a global trend towards the establishment of regional mechanisms of cooperation and integration, and that there is no contradiction between globalization and regionalism—by contrast, regional arrangements are one way in which states in different parts of the world respond to the challenges of globalization.

Introduction

Regionalism has become a pervasive feature of international affairs. According to the **World Trade Organization** (WTO), by July 2005 only one WTO member—Mongolia—was not party to any regional trade agreement, and a total of 330 such agreements had been notified. Regional **peacekeeping** forces have become active in some parts of the world. Regionalism has in the last decades become one of the forces challenging the traditional centrality of **states** in international relations.

That challenge comes from two directions. The word 'region' and its derivatives denote one distinguishable part of some larger geographical area. Yet they are used in different ways. On the one hand, regions are **territories** within a state, occasionally crossing state borders. On the other, regions are particular areas of the world, covering a number of different sovereign states. The issues raised for international relations have some elements in common. This chapter, however, looks only at regionalism in the international context: the range of special relationships between neighbouring countries which represent more than normal diplomatic relations but in which the component parts retain legal personality under **international law**.

The first section presents some basic concepts, dimensions, and debates. The second places regional **cooperation** in a global context and, without pretending to be exhaustive, reviews the main developments in the Americas, Africa, and Asia. The final section looks at the European Union (EU), where **integration** has, so far uniquely, gone beyond a regional organization to produce a new form of regional governance.

Regional cooperation and regional integration

Regionalism has various dimensions, and terms need to be clarified. The term **regionalization** is often used to refer to 'the growth of societal integration within a region and [. . .] the often undirected processes of social and economic interaction' (Hurrell 1995: 39). Such processes produce **interdependence** and may also constitute deepening perceptions of common interests and identity, including self-awareness as a region. Yet the very nature and membership of regions may be contested, and there are very different forms of interaction between the various dimensions and dynamics of regionalism. Regional agreements cover different mixtures of economic, social, political, and **security** concerns; and there are different forms of interaction between 'regionalization' and the various ways in which states may promote regional cohesion. In some cases, state-led actions have been responsible for an increase in 'real' interaction. In others, the development of ties has been more one of 'market-led integration'.

When considering the different kinds of arrangements which may be agreed between countries, a distinction is often made between 'cooperation' and 'integration'. Regional cooperation has various forms. **Functional cooperation** refers to limited arrangements which are agreed between states in order to work together in particular areas, for example, in transport, energy, or health. Economic cooperation refers to agreements which foresee some degree of commercial preferentialism, but with no harmonization of domestic rules nor any obligation for common action in international affairs. Political cooperation entails mutual support and commitment regarding the implementation of certain values and practices within the countries. Cooperation in foreign and security policy means that governments systematically inform and consult each other, try to adopt common positions in **international organizations**, and may even implement joint actions elsewhere. There are no necessary connections between these different areas of cooperation. And none of this has any consequence for the international status of participating countries beyond normal obligations under international law.

Formal **regional integration** refers to processes by which states go beyond the removal of obstacles to interaction between their countries and create a regional space subject to some distinct common rules. With regard to economic integration, several degrees of ambition are usually distinguished: free trade area, customs union, common market, economic and monetary union. From a customs union 'up', in addition to removing barriers to trade between themselves, the countries must not only adopt

some measures of positive integration (i.e. harmonization of **rules**), but also must act with a single voice internationally, at the very least in tariff policy. Such processes may lead to a new level of governance above the **nation-states**, although this does not mean creation of a new 'super-state'.

While this distinction does involve some clear and fundamental choices, it should be treated with caution. Cooperation and integration are not mutually exclusive general approaches for regional governance so much as options which may be pursued for different sectors and dimensions of regional relations. All regional systems, including the EU today, contain a mixture of both.

The formal institutional arrangements of a regional system cannot be assumed to be a measure of the real depth or dynamics of a regional integration process. If regional goals are complex and long-term (e.g. to create a full common market), states may set up 'commitment institutions' in order to increase the prospects of effective compliance over time (Mattli 1999). States thus accept some pooling of **sovereignty** (i.e. the renunciation of autonomous action and/or the veto), delegation of powers to supranational bodies, and/or of 'legalization' (Moravscik 1998; Abbott *et al.* 2000). This has mainly been the case in **Europe**. The institutional **structure** of the European Community, however, has often been imitated elsewhere. In some cases, formally supranational bodies exist with little real connection with national or transnational life. Conversely, strong formal commitments may not be required to achieve important results in certain fields in certain conditions: the Nordic countries, for example, established both a Passport Union and Common Labour Market in the 1950s without any supranational arrangements (Best 2006).

Why do states decide to pursue regional integration, and what dynamics may explain the evolution of such regional arrangements? A first theme historically has been the 'management of independence': that is, the need for newly-independent states to settle down in their relations (1) between themselves, (2) with the former colonial power, and (3) with other, often rival, powers. This may be summarized as the process of consolidating international **identity** and 'actorhood': how do sets of societies want to participate in international affairs? Federal union has been the result in some cases. In others, regional organizations of one sort or another have been an important instrument for managing this often conflictual process.

A second set of issues may be grouped as the 'management of **interdependence**'. This partly refers to economic and social interaction—whether the adoption of state-led integration schemes intended to increase such interaction or of measures to ensure stability where there is market-led integration—but also to **issues** of peace and security. Regional organizations can foster 'security communities' (i.e. transnational communities in which peoples have dependable expectations of peaceful change) by promoting cooperation, establishing **norms** of behaviour, and serving as sites of socialization and learning (Adler and Barnett 1998b).

A third theme may be summed up as the 'management of **internationalization**', that is, the interrelationship between regional arrangements and the rest of the world. The debate about the implications of regionalism for multilateral processes of liberalization was termed the 'building-blocks-or-stumbling-blocks' question by Bhagwati (1991). Proponents of regionalism as building blocks argue that: (1) such arrangements promote internal and international dynamics that enhance the prospects for **multilateralism**; (2) regionalism can have important demonstration effects in accustoming actors to the effects of liberalization; (3) increased numbers of regional arrangements can weaken opposition to multilateral liberalization because each successive arrangement reduces the value of the margin of preference; (4) regional agreements are often more to do with strategic or political alliances than trade liberalization; and (5) regionalism has more positive than negative political effects.

Opponents of regionalism have been concerned that: (1) the net result of preferential agreements may be trade diversion; (2) there may be 'attention diversion', with participating countries losing interest in the multilateral system, or simply an absorption of available negotiating resources; (3) competing arrangements may lock in incompatible regulatory structures and standards; (4) the creation of

---

Box 25.1 Dynamics of regionalism

Management of independence	Settling down by newly-independent states in their relations between themselves, with the former colonial power, and with other powers
Management of interdependence	Regional mechanisms to guarantee peace and security; responses to 'regionalization'; promotion of cooperation and/or state-led integration
Management of internationalization	Regional negotiations in the multilateral system; regional/UN peacekeeping; regional responses to globalization

multiple legal frameworks and dispute settlement mechanisms may weaken discipline and efficiency; and (5) regionalism may contribute to international frictions between competing blocs (Bergsten 1997; World Bank 2005).

The historical context in which this tension plays itself out has changed considerably. In the first wave of post-war regionalism, notably in Latin America, this largely took the form of state-led efforts to reduce dependency on exports of primary commodities and to achieve industrialization through import substitution, with widespread suspicion of foreign direct investment.

The 'New Regionalism' taking place since the late 1980s has been more a response to new forms of globalization, as well as taking place in a more multipolar world after the end of the **cold war**. Various common features could be seen in the 1990s. Regional arrangements tended to be more open than before in terms of economic integration, as well as more comprehensive in scope. The new **open regionalism**, indeed, seemed to lose some of the very defining characteristics of regionalism, forming part of 'a global structural transformation in which **non-state actors** are active and manifest themselves at several levels of the global system [and] can therefore not be understood only from the point of view of the single region' (Hettne 1999: 7–8).

Yet regionalism may also be seen as one of the few instruments which are available to states to try to manage the effects of **globalization**. If individual states no longer have the effective capacity to regulate in the face of uncontrolled movements of capital, then regionalism may be seen as a means to regain some control over global market forces—and to counter the more negative social consequences of globalization. The debate is far from over.

Key Points

- Regionalism has various dimensions and takes different forms across the world.
- Some regional integration processes are more state-led, others more market-led.
- There is a basic difference between cooperation arrangements and integration processes, but both approaches may be followed within a regional system.

Regional cooperation in a global context

Regionalism in the Americas

The American continent has been characterized by multiple, and often competing, levels of regionalism. The basic tensions date back to independence. The former British colonies in North America eventually settled down into two international actors: one federal union, the United States of America, in 1865, and one confederation, Canada, in 1867. Portuguese Brazil ended up as a federal republic in 1889. In former Spanish territories, in contrast, efforts at union failed. Two short-lived federal republics were formed: the Federal Republic of Greater Colombia (1819–31) and the Federal Republic of Central America (1823–39). Unity of Spanish America was the dream of Simon Bolívar, who in 1826 convened the Congress of Panama, proposing a 'Treaty of Union, League, and Perpetual Confederation' with a common military, a mutual defence pact, and a supranational parliamentary assembly. Bolívar's vision was not anti-American, but he preferred not to include the USA. And like the federal republics, it soon succumbed to civil wars and rivalries between governing *caudillos*.

Latin American regionalism has thus played itself out against the background of the conflictual consolidation of current states, in which national sovereignty became a dominant feature of actorhood, and a love–hate relationship with the USA. There has been partial acceptance of a continental identity as 'America', but also a widespread perception of an identity as 'Latin America', often in opposition to the USA.

Hemispheric regionalism began with the first Pan-American Conference in Washington in 1889–90. Nine such conferences took place, leading in the 1930s and 1940s, following decades of US interventionism, to several agreements on peace and security. The Pan-American Union became the Organization of American States (OAS) in 1948. An Inter-American System grew up, including the Inter-American Development Bank and the Inter-American Court of Human Rights. During the cold war, however, it was seen with suspicion in much of the Americas as an instrument of US foreign policy.

The US policy on regional agreements changed in the later 1980s. It began in 1986 to negotiate a free-trade

Box 25.2 Around the world in regional organizations, 2006 (an illustrative and non-exhaustive list)

AMERICAS	Organization of American States	OAS
	North American Free Trade Agreement	NAFTA
	Central American Integration System	SICA
	Central American Common Market	CACM
	Caribbean Community	CARICOM
	Andean Community [of Nations]	CAN
	Common Market of the South	MERCOSUR
	South American Community of Nations	
	Latin American Integration Association	LAIA
AFRICA	African Union	AU
	Arab Maghreb Union	UMA
	Community of Sahel-Saharan States	CEN-SAD
	Economic Community of West African States	ECOWAS
	West African Economic and Monetary Union	WAEMU
	Central African Monetary and Economic Community	CEMAC
	Economic Community of the Great Lakes Countries	CEPGL
	Economic Community of Central African States	ECCAS
	East African Community	EAC
	Common Market for Eastern and Southern Africa	COMESA
	Intergovernmental Authority for Development	IGAD
	Southern African Customs Union	SACU
	Southern African Development Community	SADC
ASIA	Gulf Cooperation Council	GCC
	Association of South-East Asian Nations	ASEAN
	ASEAN Regional Forum	ARF
	South Asian Association for Regional Cooperation	SAARC
	Shanghai Cooperation Organization	SCO
	Economic Cooperation Organization	ECO
ASIA-PACIFIC	Asia Pacific Economic Cooperation	APEC
	Pacific Economic Cooperation Council	PECC
	Pacific Islands Forum	
EURASIA	Commonwealth of Independent States	CIS
	Eurasian Economic Community	EAEC
	Black Sea Economic Cooperation	BSEC
EUROPE	European Union	EU
	Council of Europe	CoE
	Nordic Council/Council of Ministers	
	Benelux Economic Union	Benelux
	Visegrad Group	V4
EURO-ATLANTIC	North Atlantic Treaty Organization	NATO
	Organization for Security and Cooperation in Europe	OSCE

Case Study   Central America: a perpetual pursuit of union?

Central America can seem to present a paradox. The observer sees a number of small countries, with a common history, a relatively high degree of common identity, and apparently everything to gain from integration, but which have consistently failed, so far, to achieve the ambitious regional goals they proclaim.

Following independence, the Captaincy-General of Guatemala became the Federal Republic of Central America (1823–39), before splitting into Guatemala, El Salvador, Honduras, Nicaragua, and Costa Rica. Restoration of this Union has been a constant theme in integrationist discourse. Yet Central America was more a collection of communities than a clearly defined overarching entity, local elites elsewhere resisted leadership by Guatemala, and Costa Rica early on showed a tendency to isolationism. Nationalism grew, unionism was undermined by conflict, and outside involvement was often unhelpful. A powerful mythology of union thus coexisted with various sources of division.

A first Central American Peace Conference in Washington, convened in 1907 to help end local conflicts, led to a short-lived Central American Court of Justice (1908–18). The Organization of Central American States (ODECA) was created in 1951. The first organizations of functional cooperation emerged around this time. Some 25 such bodies now exist, covering everything from water to electrical energy, creating a complex web of regional interactions. Formal economic integration began in 1960, with the Central American Common Market (CACM). Intra-regional trade grew, but the system entered crisis at the end of 1960s. Efforts at reform in the 1970s were overtaken by political crisis and conflicts. In the 1980s, integration became associated with the Central American peace process. In this context of confidence-building, a Central American Parliament was created as a forum for regional dialogue. In 1991, with conflicts in El Salvador and Nicaragua ended, the cold war over, and a new wave of regional integration across the world, a new period began with the Central American Integration System (SICA). This aimed to provide a global approach to integration, with four sub-systems—political, economic, social, and cultural.

The institutional system is concentrated around the Presidential summits. The Central American Parliament is directly elected but has no powers. It does not include Costa Rica. As of 2006, only El Salvador, Honduras, and Nicaragua participated in the Central American Court of Justice. There have been repeated discussions of institutional reform. By 2005, intra-regional trade represented around 27 per cent of exports and 12 per cent of imports. Most goods originating in Central American countries enjoy free circulation. The same levels of external tariff were being applied for 95 per cent of goods. General negotiations for a Central American customs union began in 2004. The future is being shaped also by international agreements. The Central American countries signed a free trade agreement with the USA in 2004, modelled on NAFTA, and also began in 2006 to negotiate an association agreement with the European Union including a free-trade agreement.

The pursuit of union continues.

---

agreement with Canada. Negotiations then began between the United States, Canada, and Mexico, leading to the establishment in 1994 of the North American Free Trade Agreement (NAFTA). This is broader in scope than most such agreements. Agriculture is covered, and the treaty was accompanied by supplementary agreements on labour and the environment, although there are no supranational elements. A first 'Summit of the Americas was held in Miami in 1994, with the aim of achieving a Free Trade Area of the Americas (FTAA) as well as deepening cooperation in drugs, corruption, **terrorism**, hemispheric security, **sustainable development**, and the environment. By the fourth summit in Argentina in 2005, however, the political context of Inter-Americanism had significantly changed.

Latin American regionalism in the post-war decades was shaped by the model of state-led, import-substituting industrialization. In order to overcome dependence on exports of primary commodities, a combination of protection and planning would make it possible to reduce manufactured imports. Regional integration was a response to the limitations of this approach at the national level. This first wave produced the Central American Common Market (CACM, 1960), the Latin American Free Trade Association (LAFTA, 1961) and the Andean Pact (1969), all of which had limited success.

A wave of 'new regionalism' began in the 1980s and took off in the 1990s. The Central American Integration System (SICA) was created in 1991. The Common Market of the South (MERCOSUR) was created in 1991 by Argentina and Brazil, together with Paraguay and Uruguay. A common market was proclaimed in 1994, although there remain exceptions. MERCOSUR has not adopted a supranational institutional system but there have been important political dimensions. In the early phases this included mutual

support for the consolidation of **democracy** and the ending of rivalry between Argentina and Brazil.

In 1990, the Andean Presidents also re-launched their integration process. A Common External Tariff was announced in 1994. The group was renamed the Andean Community of Nations (CAN) in 1997, with the aim of consolidating a common market by 2005. The institutional system is modelled on the European Community, with elements of formal **supranationalism**: Andean norms are to be directly applicable and to enjoy primacy over national law, and they are monitored by common institutions including a Court of Justice.

The 'New' forms of integration in the Americas were seen as fundamentally different, part of broad-based structural reforms aimed at locking in commitments in a context of unilateral and multilateral liberalization. It also seemed that there might be a new convergence of hemispheric and Latin American initiatives.

Yet developments in the 2000s have brought this into question. Proposals to bring together Andean integration and MERCOSUR around a continental project began in the 1990s. They accelerated in 2000 with the adoption of the South American Regional Integration Initiative, supporting major projects in transport, energy, and communications. 'South American summits' were held in 2000 and 2002. The creation of a 'South American Community of Nations' was announced in 2004. In 2005 CAN and MERCOSUR mutually recognized the associate membership of each other's member countries. In 2006, Venezuela, under President Chávez, left the Andean Community and joined MERCOSUR. Bolivia applied at the beginning of 2007 and Ecuador seemed likely to follow. The expanded MERCOSUR at the heart of this new South American Community of Nations has raised a strong question mark over the future of the Free Trade Area of the Americas.

Regionalism in Africa

Contemporary regionalism in Africa emerged with the politics of anti-colonialism but often on the basis of pre-existing colonial arrangements. French West Africa was a Federation between 1904 and 1958, and a common currency known as the CFA franc was created in 1945. After several organizational transformations, Benin, Burkina Faso, Côte d'Ivoire, Guinea-Bissau, Mali, Niger, Senegal, and Togo have become members of the present West African Economic and Monetary Union (WAEMU).

In Central Africa, a monetary union guaranteed by France and a formal customs union were created in 1964. This was transformed into the Economic and Monetary Community of Central Africa (CEMAC) which fully took over in 1999. This is a monetary union using the CFA franc (now pegged to the Euro) with a common monetary policy, and is formally a customs union, aiming to create a single market by 2014.

The Southern African Customs Union (SACU) was originally created in 1910. An agreement was signed in 1969 with the independent countries of Botswana, Lesotho, Swaziland, and Namibia. This has included a common external tariff and a revenue-sharing mechanism, as well as a Common Monetary Area (except for Botswana) with currencies pegged to the South African rand. A new treaty came into force in 2004.

Colonial Kenya and Uganda formed a customs union in 1917, which Tanzania (then Tanganyika) joined in 1927. After independence, cooperation continued under the East African Common Services Organization. An East African Community was created in 1967 but collapsed in 1977 as a result of political differences. Following efforts at re-integration in the 1990s, the present East Africa Community (EAC) was established in 2000. A customs union formally came into effect in 2005.

In the 1970s and 1980s, a variety of other regional organizations emerged, often cutting across the previous arrangements. With Nigerian leadership, the Economic Community of West African States (ECOWAS) was created in 1975 between the francophone countries which are also members of WAEMU, and the anglophone countries of West Africa. A Preferential Trade Area cutting across eastern and southern Africa was created in 1981. This was succeeded in 1994 by the Common Market for Eastern and Southern Africa (COMESA), which in 2006 had 19 member states stretching from Libya to Madagascar. In 1983, the French Central African countries, together with the members of the Economic Community of the Great Lakes Countries, created in 1976, and São Tomé and Principe, created the Economic Community of Central African States (ECCAS). Finally, straddling the continent from Senegal to Eritrea is the Community of Sahel-Saharan States (CEN-SAD) established in 1998.

Some organizations had particular political aspects to their foundation. The aim of the Frontline States to reduce dependence on apartheid South Africa

prompted the creation in 1980 of the Southern African Development Coordination Conference (SADCC). This was transformed into the Southern African Development Community (SADC) in 1992, of which post-apartheid South Africa became a member.

Others have started with a particular special mandate which was then extended. The Intergovernmental Authority on Development (IGAD) in East Africa was founded in 1986 with a narrow mandate to deal with drought and desertification, but did little in view of tensions between its members and as a result of the situation in Somalia. In 1996 it was given a broader mandate covering conflict prevention and management.

Sub-regional cultural identity has played a particular role, for example, in the case of the Arab Maghreb Union (AMU), which came into being in 1989.

The first stage of pan-African organization was primarily political in nature. The Organization of African Unity (OAU), created in 1963, was dedicated to the ending of colonialism and political liberation. The continental agenda has subsequently broadened. The 1991 Treaty of Abuja, coming into force in 1994, established the African Economic Community (AEC). In 2002, the OAU and AEC became the African Union (AU), formally modelled on the European Union.

There was also a move towards continental **coordination** of the multiple regional arrangements which had grown up, with a 1997 protocol formalizing relations between the AEC and 14 Regional Economic Communities (RECs)—that is, the various organizations mentioned above. The RECs have had some success in functional cooperation. However, they suffer from various institutional weaknesses which have been exacerbated by the multiplicity of arrangements, prompting recent initiatives for a 'rationalization'. Moreover, the factors necessary for deep integration remain elusive. There is little complementarity across economies. There are few strong regional focal points. Integration has a limited domestic constituency, in the sense of pressure from business interests or **civil society**. And there remains a general unwillingness to consider sharing sovereignty (Economic Commission for Africa and African Union 2006).

There has been a certain evolution in this respect, reflected in the New Partnership for Africa's Development (NEPAD) adopted in 2001, which includes an African Peer Review Mechanism (APRM). In addition, regional organizations have become active in conflict management. The best known is the ECOWAS Monitoring Group (ECOMOG), created in 1990 to intervene in Liberia. It also acted in Sierra Leone and Guinea-Bissau in the 1990s, before being given a formal basis in 1999. Since then, it has acted in Côte d'Ivoire in 2002 and Liberia in 2003. An AU Peace and Security Council was created in 2003, the AU deployed a Peace Mission in Burundi (AMIB) in 2003, and a Peace Mission in the Sudan (AMIS) in 2004.

Regionalism in Asia

Regionalism in Asia has followed quite different patterns. South-East Asia is not a region with a clear historical identity. The very term 'South-East Asia' seems to have come to prominence internationally to describe the areas south of China that were occupied by Japan in the Second World War. The first post-war organizations, notably the 1954 South-East Asian Treaty Organization (SEATO), were US-backed bodies made up of an international range of interested powers. Malaya, the Philippines, and Indonesia briefly formed the Association of South-East Asia (ASA, 1961) and MAPHILINDO (1963) as a means to promote regional solidarity. These were interrupted by intra-regional conflict, notably over the future of Borneo. As elsewhere, Britain had looked to federation as a means to ease its withdrawal from colonial territories. The Federation of Malaya, created in 1948, formed a new Federation of Malaysia in 1963, together with Singapore (until 1965), Sarawak, and British North Borneo (Sabah). A period of 'Confrontation' ensued between Malaysia and Indonesia, while the Philippines claimed Sabah. The Confrontation ended in 1966.

The establishment of the Association of South-East Asian Nations (**ASEAN**) in 1967 between Indonesia, Malaysia, Philippines, Singapore, and Thailand was thus motivated less by a sense of common identity than by a realization that failure to prevent conflicts within the region would invite external intervention, which would in turn exacerbate intra-regional tensions. No supranational elements were foreseen. Regional cooperation was to be built by an 'ASEAN Way' based on consultation, consensual decision-making, and flexibility. Rather than starting with ambitious political commitments, ASEAN would proceed by small, informal, and voluntary steps, which could eventually become more binding and institutionalized.

Although economic cooperation was foreseen, the evolution of ASEAN was driven by political and security concerns. The first new step was taken amid the regional uncertainties following the fall of Saigon in the Vietnam War, and the communist victories in Laos and Cambodia in 1975. ASEAN leaders held their first summit in 1976, signing the Declaration of ASEAN Concord and the Treaty of Amity and Cooperation in South-East Asia, which reaffirmed the **principles** of mutual respect, non-interference, and peaceful settlement of differences. The next turning point came at the beginning of the 1990s as ASEAN sought to affirm its identity and centrality. On the security front, in the context of the withdrawal of Vietnam from Cambodia and the end of the cold war, a succession of proposals culminated in the creation of the ASEAN Regional Forum (ARF). This came into effect in 1994, with the aim of pursuing confidence-building measures, preventive diplomacy, and eventually conflict resolution. Other steps were taken in response to the creation of the Asia Pacific Economic Cooperation (APEC).

APEC had been formed in 1989 on the principle of 'open regionalism'. It was not to involve any discrimination *vis-à-vis* other countries. Nor did it reflect any distinctive regional identity so much as 'the desire of the "non-Asian states" of the region to consolidate links with the "open market-oriented economies" of East Asia' (Higgott 1995: 377). In response, Malaysia under Dr Mahathir—one of the key defenders of 'Asian values' in Asian regionalism—proposed an 'East Asian Economic Caucus' excluding Australia, Canada, New Zealand, and the USA. The United States put pressure on Japan and South Korea not to participate. At the same time, it was agreed in 1992 to establish an ASEAN Free Trade Area (AFTA). The Asian financial crisis of 1997–98 provided a renewed impetus for regional cooperation and also led to a new format of cooperation with China, Japan, and South Korea as 'ASEAN plus Three' (APT), seen by some as the realization of the idea underlying the East Asian Economic Caucus.

In 2003, the member states agreed to create an ASEAN Security Community, an ASEAN Economic Community, and an ASEAN Socio-cultural Community by 2020. The Economic Community is a 'Free Trade Area–plus', aiming at a single market but with no common external tariff, and restricted flows of labour. While not pursuing supranationalism, it was agreed to strengthen ASEAN's institutional arrangements. A new formal dispute settlement mechanism was created, and the role of the Secretariat was reinforced, together with a Development Fund and increased institutional involvement of the business sector. The development gap between old and new members (Vietnam, Myanmar/Burma, Laos, and Cambodia) also prompted new efforts to promote solidarity, through the Initiative for ASEAN Integration and the Economic Cooperation Strategy.

Asian regionalism in the mid-2000s is thus evolving on two planes. On the one hand, ASEAN is moving towards some institutional deepening as a means to preserve its own position. The 'strengthening of ASEAN integration through the accelerated establishment of an ASEAN Community' by 2015, which was agreed at the January 2007 summit, was explicitly intended to 'reinforce ASEAN's centrality and role as the driving force in charting the evolving regional architecture' (ASEAN 2007). On the other hand, regional agreements reflect the continuing competition between the major powers. A comprehensive economic cooperation agreement between ASEAN and China was signed in 2002, and China (with Malaysia) promoted an East Asia Summit in 2005, bringing together the APT countries and (at the insistence of Japan, Singapore, and Indonesia) Australia and New Zealand, as well as India—but not the USA. A Framework Agreement on Comprehensive Economic Cooperation between ASEAN and India was signed in 2003. Japan made a series of proposals for an East Asian Community (including Australia and New Zealand) in 2002 and, in 2006, an East Asian Free Trade Area, with an offer to provide major funding for a Comprehensive Economic Partnership in East Asia.

Eurasia and the post-Soviet states

A complex and shifting pattern of regional agreements has resulted from the efforts of the former components of the Soviet Union to settle down in a zone of cooperation and competition between Russian, Chinese, and EU influence. The Commonwealth of Independent States (CIS) was created in 1991 among all of the former Soviet republics except the three Baltic states and Georgia (which then joined and then left). A CIS Customs Union was proclaimed in 1995 between Russia, Belarus, and Kazakhstan. A Collective Security Treaty was signed in 1992. In 2002 this became the Collective Security Treaty Organization (CSTO), comprising Russia, Belarus, Armenia, Kazakhstan, Kyrgyzstan, and Tajikistan.

A Central Asian Commonwealth composed of all five Central Asian republics was created in 1991. A series of formations with different memberships and names produced two bodies which merged in 2006 as the Eurasian Economic Community, bringing together Central Asian Republics (other than Turkmenistan) with Russia and Belarus. The shifting patterns of these sub-regional organizations reflect not only evolving relations between newly-independent states and Russia, the former dominant power. They must also be understood against the background of rivalries between Russia and China, as well as partially-shared concerns between those two powers as to the role of the USA (with its military presence in the context of operations in Afghanistan, and apparent aspirations to balance Russian and Chinese influence in 'Greater Central Asia').

The 'Shanghai Five' mechanism was created by China, Russia, Kazakhstan, Kyrgystan, and Tajikistan in 1996. This was transformed in 2002 (with the participation of Uzbekistan) into the Shanghai Cooperation Organization (SCO), with Iran, Mongolia, India, and Pakistan as observers. It promotes confidence-building actions, and various forms of cooperation, including collaboration to counter terrorism, drug trafficking, money-laundering, and weapons smuggling. The Economic Cooperation Organization (ECO), revived by Iran, Pakistan, and Turkey in 1985, was joined by the Central Asian republics as well as Afghanistan in 1992.

In the area of Ukraine and the Caucasus, the evolution of sub-regional agreements has had more to do with support for the consolidation of democracy, as well as management of local conflicts, in the context of a certain rivalry for influence between Russia and the European Union. The GUAM Organization for Democracy and Economic Development was set up in 1997 as a forum for cooperation without Russia, and was consolidated with a new Charter in 2006. It brings together Georgia, Ukraine, Azerbaijan, and Moldova. The Community of Democratic Choice was created in Kiev in December 2005 with the stated objective of promoting 'democracy, human rights, and the rule of law'. Its members are Georgia, Macedonia, Moldova, Ukraine, as well as five EU member states—the three Baltic states, Romania and Slovenia—with observer status for Azerbaijan, and four other EU member states (Bulgaria, the Czech Republic, Hungary, and Poland) as well as the EU as such, the United States and the Organization for Security and Cooperation in Europe (OSCE). Finally, the 1992 Black Sea Economic Cooperation (BSEC) links Armenia, Azerbaijan, Georgia, Russia, and the Ukraine to Turkey, as well as Albania, Bulgaria, Greece, Moldova, Romania, Serbia, and Montenegro.

Key Points

- Regionalism can be seen as one level in an emerging system of global governance, but the relationship between regionalism and multilateralism is debated in regard to both economic liberalization and international security.
- Regionalist experiences in each continent have followed different patterns which reflect their different historical and cultural contexts.
- The earlier waves of regionalism arose in a context of post-colonial restructuring, economic protectionism, or regional security concerns. A new wave of 'open regionalism' began around 1990 with the end of the cold war and the surge in globalization.

The process of European integration

In Europe, regionalism after 1945 has taken the form of a gradual process of integration leading to the emergence of the European Union. It was initially a purely West European creation between the 'original Six' member states born out of the desire for reconciliation between France and Germany in a context of ambitious federalist plans. Yet the process has taken the form of a progressive construction of an institutional architecture, a legal framework, and a wide range of policies, which in 2007 encompassed 27 European states.

The European Coal and Steel Community was created in 1951 (in force in 1952), followed by the European Economic Community and the European Atomic Energy Community in 1957 (in force in 1958). These treaties involved a conferral of Community competence in various areas—the supranational management of coal and steel,

the creation and regulation of an internal market, and common policies in trade, competition, agriculture, and transport. Since then, powers have been extended to include new legislative competences in some fields such as the environment. Since the 1992 Treaty on European Union (the Maastricht Treaty, in force in 1993) the integration process has also involved the adoption both of stronger forms of unification, notably monetary union, as well as other forms of cooperation such as non-binding coordination in economic and employment policy, or more intergovernmental cooperation in foreign and security policy.

From very limited beginnings, both in terms of membership and in terms of scope, the EU has therefore gradually developed to become an important political and economic actor whose presence has a significant impact, both internationally and domestically. This gradual process of European integration has taken place at various levels. The first is the signature and reform of the basic treaties. These are the result of **Intergovernmental Conferences** (IGCs), where representatives of national governments negotiate the legal framework within which the EU institutions operate. Such treaty changes require ratification in each country and are the `grand bargains' in the evolution of the EU.

Within this framework, the institutions have been given considerable powers to adopt decisions and manage policies, although the dynamics of decision-making differ significantly across different arenas. There are important differences between the more integrated areas of economic regulation on the one hand, and the more 'intergovern-

mental' pillars of foreign policy and police or judicial cooperation in criminal matters on the other. In some areas, a country may have to accept decisions which are 'imposed' on it by the (qualified) majority of member states. In other areas, it may be able to block decisions.

To understand the integration process, one needs to take account of the role played by both member states *and* supranational institutions. Moreover, member states are not just represented by national governments, since a host of state, **non-state**, and **transnational actors** participate in the processes of domestic preference formation or direct representation of interests in Brussels. The relative openness of the European policy process means that political groups or economic interests will try to influence EU decision-making if they feel that their position is not sufficiently represented by national governments. That is one reason why the EU is increasingly seen as a system of multilevel governance, involving a plurality of actors on different territorial levels: supranational, national, and sub-state.

The complexity of the EU institutional machinery, together with continuous change over time, has spawned a lively debate among integration theorists (Rosamond 2000; Wiener and Diez 2004). Some approaches are applications of more general theories of international relations: the literature on both **Realism** and interdependence has contributed to theorizing integration. Other scholars have regarded the European Union as sui generis—in a category of its own—and therefore in need of the development of dedicated theories of integration. The most prominent among these has been neo-functionalism, which sought to

Year	Treaty	Main subjects
1951	Paris Treaty	Regulation of coal and steel production in the member states, creation of supranational institutions
1957	Rome Treaties	European Economic Community—creation of a customs union (removal of all intra-union duties and creation of a common customs tariff); plans for a common market and common policies Euratom—cooperation in atomic energy.
1986	Single European Act	Removal of all non-tariff barriers to the movement of persons, goods, services, and capital (the '1992 programme'); foreign policy cooperation included in the treaty provisions
1992	Maastricht Treaty	Creation of the European Union, encompassing the European Community and two parallel pillars for Common Foreign and Security Policy (CFSP) and justice and home affairs; economic and monetary union (the euro)
1997	Amsterdam Treaty	Various institutional reforms, High Representative for CFSP, provisions for enhanced cooperation
2001	Nice Treaty	Reform of Commission and Council (voting weights), expansion of majority voting
2004	Constitutional Treaty (signed but not ratified)	Simplification of the treaties, incorporation of the European Charter of Fundamental Rights, creation of the post of President of the Council and EU Foreign Minister.

Table 25.1 Important agreements in the history of the European Union

EU institution	Responsibilities	Location
European Commission	Initiating, administering, and overseeing the implementation of EU policies and legislation	Brussels and Luxembourg
European Parliament (EP)	Directly elected representatives of EU citizens, scrutinizing the operation of the other institutions, and, in certain areas, sharing with the Council the power to determine EU legislation	Strasbourg (plenary sessions); Brussels (MEP offices, committee meetings and some plenary sessions); Luxembourg (administration)
Council of Ministers	Representing the views of national governments and determining, in many areas jointly with the EP, the ultimate shape of EU legislation	Brussels (some meetings in Luxembourg)
European Council	Regular summits of the Heads of State or Government and the President of the Commission, setting the EU's broad agenda and a forum of last resort to find agreement on divisive issues (NB: different from the Council of Europe)	Brussels
European Court of Justice	The EU's highest court, supported by a Court of First Instance. Main competences include actions for annulment of Community acts, infringement procedures against member states for failing to comply with obligations and preliminary rulings on the validity or interpretation of EC law on request from national courts	Luxembourg
European Central Bank	Central bank responsible for setting the interest rates and controlling the money supply of the single European currency, the euro	Frankfurt am Main
Court of Auditors	The EU's audit office, responsible for auditing the revenues and the expenditure under the EU budget	Luxembourg

Table 25.2 Institutions of the EU

explain the evolution of integration in terms of 'spillover' from one sector to another as resources and loyalties of elites were transferred to the European level. More recently, as aspects of EU politics have come to resemble the domestic politics of states, scholars have turned to approaches drawn from comparative politics.

However, it has been the exchange between 'supranational' and 'intergovernmental' approaches which has had the greatest impact on the study of European integration. **Supranational approaches** regard the emergence of supranational institutions in Europe as a distinct feature and turn these into the main object of analysis. Here, the politics above the level of states are regarded as the most significant, and consequently the political actors and institutions at the European level receive most attention. **Intergovernmentalist approaches**, on the other hand, continue to regard states as the most important aspect of the integration process and consequently concentrate on the study of politics *between* and *within* states (see Box 25.1). But whatever one's theoretical preferences,

most scholars would agree that no analysis of the EU is complete without studying both the operation and evolution of the central institutions and the input from political actors in the member states. More recently, debate in EU studies has also centred on a wider fault-line in the social sciences: the difference between **rationalist and constructivist approaches.** Constructivists have challenged the implicit rationalism of much integration research until the 1990s (see Ch.9). Their critique focused on the tendency of rationalist studies to privilege decision-making over agenda-setting, and outcomes over process. The Social Constructivist research agenda instead concentrates on the framing of issues *before* decisions about them are made, and therefore emphasizes the role of ideas, discourses, and social interaction in shaping interests (Christiansen, Jørgensen, and Wiener 2001).

The prospect of an ever *wider* European Union has raised serious questions about the nature and direction of the integration process. The 2004 enlargement has generally been seen as a qualitative leap for the EU. Concerns

that the enlarged Union, if not reformed substantially, would find it difficult to take decisions and maintain a reliable legal framework led to several attempts to reform the treaties. The most wide-ranging proposals, and the most significant step-change in the language of integration, came with the Treaty establishing a Constitution for Europe which EU Heads of State or Government signed in 2004. The very fact that the EU should discuss something referred to in the media as a 'European Constitution' is a sign of how far it has developed from its modest beginnings. However, the time may still not be right for such a project. The Constitutional Treaty was rejected in referendums in France and the Netherlands, raising serious doubts not only about this attempt at institutional reform, but also about ambitions for a formal constitutionalization more generally. In 2007, with intergovernmental negotiations about a revised 'Reform Treaty', the EU seems likely to continue along the established path of a succession of gradual developments rather than big leaps.

> ### Key Points
>
> - The process of integration in post-war Europe was launched in the context of long debates about the creation of a federal system, but ultimately the choice was made in favour of a gradual path towards an 'ever closer union'.
> - Integration has proceeded by conferring competence for many economic sectors to supranational institutions which can take decisions that are binding on the member states.
> - Over time, more politically sensitive areas, such as monetary policy or internal and external security, have also become the domain of the European Union.
> - Successive reforms of the EU treaties have sought to maintain and enhance the legitimacy and efficiency of a Union that had grown, by 2007, to twenty-seven member states, the latest stage being the debate over a formal 'European constitution'.

Conclusion

We can conclude this overview of the development of mechanisms of regional cooperation and integration with three brief observations. First, regionalism is a truly global phenomenon. It is not the case that the entire world is engulfed in a single process of globalization, or that the world is being divided along simple ideological or civilizational fault-lines. Rather, different parts of the globe are looking for different ways to accommodate themselves within the globalized **world order**, and regional arrangements are one important way of doing so. There is thus no paradox, and even less a contradiction, between regionalism and globalization. Instead, regionalism is one aspect of the process of globalization, and developments in one region inform and indeed feed into developments in others. Second, within the global trend of regionalism there are important differences in the types of organization that are being set up, ranging from rather loose and non-binding agreements to the complex institutional architecture set up by the European Union, depending on the scope and depth with which members are seeking to address issues of transnational governance. And third, there is no single or simple path of regionalism. The ways in which different regional mechanisms develop are contingent upon a multitude of factors, both internal and external to the region. Both the driving forces for more regional integration and cooperation and the obstacles which may limit those aspirations vary across the different continents. Regionalism as a global phenomenon may be here to stay, but so are the differences between the kinds of regional arrangements that are being developed in different parts of the globe.

> ### Key Points
>
> - The creation of regional governance structures is not a contradiction to globalization but the expression of local attempts to accommodate and respond to the challenges of globalization.
> - Despite the observation of a global trend towards greater regionalism, important differences remain between the depth and the scope of regional institutions that develop in different parts of the globe.
> - Regional cooperation and integration are not linear processes but depend on the varying contingencies that provide opportunities and limits in different regional contexts.

❓ Questions

1 What have been the driving forces behind processes of regional integration and cooperation?

2 What is the relative weight of economic and political factors in explaining the emergence of regional institutions?

3 What are the dynamics behind the 'new regionalism'?

4 What impact have processes of regional integration and cooperation had on the Westphalian state?

5 Compare and contrast European integration with the process of regional cooperation in at least one other continent.

6 What are the main differences between supranationalist and intergovernmentalist approaches to the study of the European Union?

7 How important has the legal dimension been to the evolution of the European Union?

8 What role do the supranational institutions play in the European policy process?

➡ Guide to further reading

Christiansen, T., Jørgensen, K. E., and Wiener, A. (eds) (2001), *The Social Construction of Europe* (London: Sage). Provides a discussion of different aspects of European integration applying insights from Social Constructivism, and also includes debates with critics of this approach.

De Lombaerde, P. (ed.) (2006), *Assessment and Measurement of Regional Integration* (London and New York: Routledge). An informative and innovative collection which considers from different perspectives the challenge of evaluating the actual impact of regional arrangements.

Farrell, M., Hettne, B., and Van Langenhove, L. (eds) (2005), *Global Politics of Regionalism: Theory and Practice* (London and Ann Arbor, Mich.: Pluto Press). A good overview of theoretical questions and key issues in regionalism, as well as the particular approaches followed in individual regions.

Fawcett, L., and Hurrell, A. (1995), *Regionalism in World Politics* (Oxford: Oxford University Press). Covers various forms of regional cooperation in different parts of the globe, looking at both the conceptual and empirical issues arising from the revival of regionalism.

Hix, S. (2005), *The Political System of the European Union* (Basingstoke: Macmillan). This advanced textbook approaches the subject from a comparative politics angle, looking in detail at the executive, legislative, and judicial politics as well as at developments in various policy areas.

Laffan, B., O'Donnell, R., and Smith, M. (1999), *Europe's Experimental Union* (London: Routledge). This co-authored volume puts the study of European integration into the context of world politics and the international political economy.

Moravcsik, A. (1998), *The Choice for Europe: Social Purpose and State Power from Messina to Maastricht* (Ithaca, NY: Cornell University Press). This important text approaches the study of European integration from an intergovernmental angle. It provides an in-depth analysis of the key decisions in the history of the EU.

Wallace, H., Wallace, W., and Pollack, M. (eds) (2005), *Policy-making in the European Union* (Oxford: Oxford University Press). This is a wide-ranging textbook that covers all major policies and also examines ways of studying the institutional setting and the dynamics of governance in the EU.

Wiener, A., and Diez, T. (2004), *European Integration Theory* (Oxford: Oxford University Press). A comprehensive and topical reader bringing together the most important contributions to the theoretical debates in the study of European integration.

World Bank (2005), *Global Economic Prospects 2005: Trade, Regionalism and Development* (Washington, DC: World Bank). A thorough discussion of regionalism from an economic perspective, looking both at the rationales and the results of regional arrangements around the world, as well as their implications for multilateralism.

Online Resource Centre

 Visit the Online Resource Centre that accompanies this book to access more learning resources on this chapter topic at www.oxfordtextbooks.co.uk/uk/orc/baylis_smith4e/

Chapter 26

Global trade and finance

JAN AART SCHOLTE

- Introduction ··· 452
- A globalizing economy ··· 453
- Global trade ··· 457
- Global finance ·· 459
- Continuity and change in economic globalization ················· 462
- Conclusion ·· 466

Reader's Guide

This chapter explores various economic aspects of contemporary globalization. It begins by distinguishing three general conceptions of economic globalization and highlights the third, geographical notion of increasing transborder production, markets, and investment. This global dimension of contemporary world commerce is then described in more detail under the headings of global trade and global finance. A fourth section of the chapter counters exaggerated claims about economic globalization by emphasizing some qualifications about its nature and extent. Finally, globalization of commerce is linked to several major problems of injustice and insecurity in contemporary world politics.

Introduction

The **globalization** of world politics involves, among other things, a globalization of economics. As Ngaire Woods has emphasized elsewhere (Ch.14), politics and economics are inseparable within social relations. Economics does not explain everything, but no account of world politics (and hence no analysis of globalization as a key issue of contemporary world history) is adequate if it does not explore the economic dimension.

Countless discussions of globalization have highlighted its economic aspects. For example, Milton Friedman, a Nobel Prize-winning economist, remarks that it has become possible 'to produce a product anywhere, using resources from anywhere, by a company located anywhere, to be sold anywhere' (cited in Naisbitt 1994: 19). A senior researcher with American Express has described global financial **integration** of recent decades as marking 'the end of geography' (O'Brien 1992). **Global governance** bodies like the **Bank for International Settlements** (BIS), the **Group of Eight** (G8), the **International Monetary Fund** (IMF), the **Organization of Economic Co-operation and Development** (OECD), the **United Nations Conference on Trade and Development** (UNCTAD),

---

Box 26.1 Major public global governance agencies for trade and finance

BIS　Bank for International Settlements. Established in 1930 with headquarters in Basle. Membership (2007) of 55 shareholding central banks, although many other public financial institutions also use BIS facilities. Promotes cooperation among central banks and provides various services for global financial operations. For example, the Basle Committee on Banking Supervision, formed through the BIS in 1974, has spearheaded efforts at multilateral regulation of global banking.

G8　Group of Eight. Established in 1975 as the G5 (France, Germany, Japan, the UK, and the USA); subsequently expanded as the G7 to include Canada and Italy, and since 1998 as the G8 to include the Russian Federation. The G8 conducts semi-formal collaboration on world economic problems. Government leaders meet in annual G8 Summits, while finance ministers and/or their leading officials periodically hold other consultations.

GATT　General Agreement on Tariffs and Trade. Established in 1947 with offices in Geneva. Membership had reached 122 states when it was absorbed into the WTO in 1995. The GATT coordinated eight 'rounds' of multilateral negotiations to reduce state restrictions on cross-border merchandise trade.

IMF　International Monetary Fund. Established in 1945 with headquarters in Washington, DC. Membership (2007) of 185 states. The IMF monitors short-term cross-border payments and foreign exchange positions. When a country develops chronic imbalances in its external accounts, the IMF supports corrective policy reforms, often called 'structural adjustment programmes'. Since 1978 the IMF has undertaken comprehensive surveillance both of the economic performance of individual member states and of the world economy as a whole. The IMF also provides extensive technical assistance. In recent years the Fund has pursued various initiatives to promote efficiency and stability in global financial markets.

IOSCO　International Organization of Securities Commissions. Established in 1983 with headquarters in Montreal; secretariat now in Madrid. Membership (2007) of 192 official securities regulators and (non-voting) trade associations and other agencies. IOSCO aims to promote high standards of regulation in stock and bond markets, to establish effective surveillance of transborder securities transactions, and to foster collaboration between securities markets in the detection and punishment of offences.

OECD　Organization of Economic Co-operation and Development. Founded in 1962 with headquarters in Paris. Membership (2007) of 30 states with advanced industrial economies and further relationships with some 70 other states. Provides a forum for multilateral intergovernmental consultations on pretty well all policy issues except military affairs. OECD measures have especially addressed environmental questions, taxation, and transborder corporations. At regular intervals the OECD Secretariat produces an assessment of the macroeconomic performance of each member, including suggestions for policy changes.

UNCTAD　United Nations Conference on Trade and Development. Established in 1964 with offices in Geneva. Membership (2007) of 192 states. UNCTAD monitors the effects of world trade and investment on economic development, especially in the South. It provided a key forum in the 1970s for discussions of a New International Economic Order.

WBG　World Bank Group. A collection of five agencies, the first established in 1945, with head offices in Washington, DC. The WBG promotes development in medium- and low-income countries with project loans, structural adjustment programmes, and various advisory services.

WTO　World Trade Organization. Established in 1995 with headquarters in Geneva. Membership (2007) of 150 states. The WTO is a permanent instititution to replace the provisional GATT. It has a wider agenda, covering services, intellectual property, and investment issues as well as merchandise trade. The WTO also has greater powers of enforcement through its Dispute Settlement Mechanism. The organization's Trade Policy Review Body conducts surveillance of members' commercial measures.

the **World Bank Group** (WBG), and the **World Trade Organization** (WTO) have all put economic globalization high on their agendas (see Box 26.1). Usually these official circles have endorsed and encouraged the trend, as have most national governments. Meanwhile many **social movements** have focused their critiques of globalization on economic aspects of the process. Their analyses have depicted contemporary globalization of trade and finance as a major cause of higher unemployment, a general decline in working standards, increased inequality, greater **poverty** for some (see Ch.27), recurrent financial crises, and large-scale environmental degradation (see Ch.20).

In their different ways, all of these assessments agree that economic globalization is a key development of contemporary history. True, the scale and impact of the trend are often exaggerated. However, it is just as wrong to argue, as some sceptics have done, that claims about a new globalizing economy rest on nothing but hype and myth. Instead, as in the case of most historical developments, economic globalization involves an intricate interplay of changes and continuities.

A globalizing economy

One key reason for disagreements over the extent and significance of economic globalization relates to the contrasting definitions that different analysts have applied to notions of globality. What, more precisely, is 'global' about the global economy? The following paragraphs distinguish three contrasting ways that the globalization of trade and finance has been broadly conceived, namely, in terms of: (1) the crossing of borders; (2) the opening of borders; and (3) the transcendence of borders. Although the three conceptions overlap to some extent, they involve important differences of emphasis. Most arguments concerning economic globalization have pitted sceptics, who adopt the first perspective, against enthusiasts, who apply the second notion. However, the third conception of globality offers a more distinctive and revealing approach. Later sections of the present chapter therefore develop that alternative notion in relation to trade and finance.

Cross-border transactions

Scepticism about the significance of contemporary economic globalization has often arisen when analysts have conceived the process in terms of **increased cross-border movements** between countries of people, goods, money, investments, messages, and ideas. From this perspective, globalization is seen as equivalent to **internationalization**. No significant distinction is drawn between global companies and international companies, between global trade and international trade, between global money and international money, between global finance and international finance.

When conceived in this way, economic globalization is nothing particularly new. Commerce between different territorial-political units has transpired for centuries and in some cases even millennia. Ancient Babylon and the Roman Empire knew forms of long-distance lending and trade, for example. Shipments between Arabia and China via South and South-East Asia occurred with fair regularity more than a thousand years ago. Certain coins circulated widely around maritime South-East Asia in a prototypical 'international monetary regime' of the tenth century. Long-distance monies of the pre-modern Mediterranean world included the Byzantine *solidus* from the fifth century onwards and the Muslim *dinar* from the eighth to the thirteenth centuries. Banks based in Italian city-states maintained (temporary) offices along long-distance trade routes as early as the twelfth century. The Hanseatic League in the fourteenth century and companies based in Amsterdam, Copenhagen, London, and Paris in the seventeenth century operated overseas trading posts. The first brokerage houses with cross-border operations appeared in the eighteenth century with Amsterdam-based Hope & Co. and London-based Barings.

Indeed, on certain (though far from all) measures, cross-border economic activity reached similar levels in the late nineteenth century as it did a hundred years later. Relative to world population of the time, the magnitude of permanent migration was in fact considerably greater than today. When measured in relation to world output,

cross-border investment in production facilities stood at roughly the same level on the eve of the First World War as it did in the early 1990s. International markets in loans and securities also flourished during the heyday of the **gold–sterling standard** between 1870 and 1914. Under this regime the British pound, fixed to a certain value in gold, served as a global currency and thereby greatly facilitated cross-border payments. Again citing proportional (rather than aggregate) statistics, several researchers (for example, Zevin 1992) have argued that these years witnessed larger capital flows between countries than in the late twentieth century. Meanwhile the volume of international trade grew at some 3.4 per cent per annum in the period 1870–1913, until its value was equivalent to 33 per cent of world output (Barraclough 1984: 256; Hirst and Thompson 1999: 21). By this particular calculation, cross-border trade was greater at the beginning than at the end of the twentieth century.

For the sceptics, then, the contemporary globalizing economy is nothing new. In their eyes, recent decades have merely experienced a phase of increased cross-border trade and finance, much as occurred a hundred years before. Moreover, they note, just as growth of international **interdependence** in the late nineteenth century was substantially reversed with a forty-year wave of **protectionism** after 1914, so economic globalization of the present-day may prove to be temporary. Governments can block cross-border flows if they wish, say the sceptics, and **national interest** may well dictate that states once more tighten restrictions on international trade, travel, foreign exchange, and capital movements. Contemporary economic globalization gives little

evidence, say these doubters, of an impending demise of the **state**, a weakening of national loyalties, and an end of war. Thus, for example, sceptics regularly point out that most so-called 'global' companies: (a) still conduct the majority of their business in their country of origin; (b) retain a strong national character and allegiances; and (c) remain heavily dependent on states for the success of their enterprises.

Open-border transactions

In contrast to the sceptics, enthusiasts for contemporary globalization of trade and finance generally define these developments as part of the long-term evolution towards a global society. In this second conception, globalization entails not an extension of internationalization, but the progressive removal of official restrictions on transfers of resources between countries. In the resultant world of **open borders,** global companies replace international companies, global trade replaces international trade, global money replaces international money, and global finance replaces international finance. From this perspective, globalization is a function of **liberalization**, that is, the degree to which articles, communications, financial instruments, fixed assets, and people can circulate throughout the world economy free from state-imposed controls. Whereas sceptics generally back up their arguments of historical repetition with proportional data, globalists usually substantiate their claims of historical change with aggregate statistics, many of which do indeed appear quite staggering (see Table 26.1).

Measure (worldwide figures)	Earlier level	Recent level
Foreign direct investment	$68 (1960)	$10,672 (2005)
Exports	$629 (1960)	$10,159 (2005)
Official foreign exchange reserves	$100 (1970)	$5,028 (2006)
Daily turnover on foreign exchange markets	$100 (1979)	$1,880 (2004)
Bank deposits by non-residents	$20 (1964)	$7,876 (1995)
Cross-border loan announcements	$9 (1972)	$1,465 (2000)
Cross-border bond issues	$1 (1960)	$1,157 (1999)
Euroequity issues	Initiated 1984	$50 (1995)
Cross-border share dealing	$10 (1980)	$120 (1994)
Daily turnover of financial derivatives contracts	Small before 1980	$1,162 (1995)

Sources: BIS, IMF, OECD, UNCTAD, WTO.

Table 26.1 Some indicators of contemporary economic globalization ($US billion)

Globalists regard the forty-year interlude of protectionism (*c.* 1910–50) as a temporary detour from a longer historical trend towards the construction of a single integrated world economy. In their eyes, the tightening of border controls in the first half of the twentieth-century was a major cause of economic depressions, authoritarian **regimes**, and international conflicts such as the world wars. In contrast, the emergent open world economy (so runs the globalist promise) will yield prosperity, liberty, **democracy**, and peace for all humanity. From this perspective—which is often termed neo-liberalism—contemporary economic globalization continues the universalizing project of modernity launched several centuries ago.

Recent history has indeed witnessed considerable opening of borders in the world economy. For one thing, a succession of inter-state accords through the **General Agreement on Tariffs and Trade** (GATT) has since 1948 brought major reductions in customs duties, quotas, and other measures that previously inhibited cross-border movements of merchandise. Average tariffs on manufactures in countries of the North fell from over 40 per cent in the 1930s to less than 4 per cent by 1999. Following the Uruguay Round of multilateral trade negotiations (1986–94), the GATT was subsumed within the new World Trade Organization. This successor agency has greater competences both to enforce existing trade agreements and to pursue new avenues of liberalization, for example, in respect of shipping, telecommunications, and investment flows. Meanwhile, as indicated in Chapter 25, regional frameworks in most areas of the world have (to varying degrees) removed official restrictions on trade between participating countries. Encouraged by such liberalization, cross-border trade expanded between 1950 and 1994 at an annual rate of just over 6 per cent: thus almost twice as fast as in the late nineteenth century. Total international trade multiplied fourteen-fold in real terms over this period, while expansion of trade in manufactures was even greater, with a twenty-six-fold increase (WTO 1995).

Borders have also opened considerably to money flows since 1950. A **gold–dollar standard** became fully operational through the IMF in 1959. Under this regime major currencies—and especially the United States dollar—could circulate worldwide (though not in communist-ruled countries) and be converted to local monies at an official **fixed exchange rate**. The gold–dollar standard thereby broadly recreated the situation that prevailed under the gold–sterling standard in the late nineteenth century. Contrary to many expectations, the US government's termination of dollar–gold convertibility on demand in 1971 did not trigger new restrictions on cross-border payments. Instead, a regime of **floating exchange rates** developed: *de facto* from 1973 and formalized through the IMF in 1976. Moreover, from the mid-1970s onwards most states reduced or eliminated restrictions on the import and export of national currencies. In these circumstances the average volume of daily transactions on the world's wholesale foreign exchange markets burgeoned from $15 billion in 1973 to $1,900 billion in 2004.

Alongside the liberalization of trade and money movements between countries, recent decades have also witnessed the widespread opening of borders to investment flows. These movements involve both direct investments (i.e. fixed assets like research facilities and factories) and portfolio investments (i.e. liquid assets like loans, bonds, and shares).

Apart from a spate of expropriations in the South during the 1970s (many of them subsequently reversed), states have generally welcomed **foreign direct investment** (FDI) into their jurisdictions in contemporary history. Indeed, many governments have actively lured externally based business by lowering corporate tax rates, reducing restrictions on the repatriation of profits, relaxing labour and environmental standards, and so on. Since 1960 there has been a proliferation of what are variously called 'international', 'multinational', 'transnational', or 'global' corporations (hence the frequently encountered abbreviations **MNC** and **TNC**). The number of such companies grew from 3,500 in 1960 to 64,000 in 2005. The aggregate stock of FDI worldwide increased in tandem from $68 billion in 1960 to $10,672 billion in 2005, as compared with only $14 billion in 1914 (UNCTAD 1996: ix, 4; UNCTAD 2006*b*). In this world of more open borders, various globalists have described MNCs as 'footloose' and 'stateless'.

Substantial liberalization has also occurred since the 1970s in respect of cross-border portfolio investments. For example, many a state now permits non-residents to hold bank accounts within its jurisdiction. Other **deregulation** has removed legal restrictions on ownership and trading of stocks and bonds by non-resident investors. Further legislation has reduced controls on participation in a country's financial markets by externally based banks, brokers, and fund managers. As a result of such deregulation (e.g. the City of London's so-called 'Big Bang' in

1986), financial institutions from all over the world have converged on **global cities** like Hong Kong, New York, Paris, and Tokyo. Levels of cross-border banking and securities business have risen markedly since the 1960s in tandem with such liberalization, as several statistics in Table 26.1 indicate. Corresponding indicators for the period between 1870 and 1914 come nowhere close to these aggregate figures.

In sum, legal obstructions to economic transactions between countries have greatly diminished worldwide in contemporary history. At the same time, cross-border flows of merchandise, services, money, and investments have reached unprecedented levels, at least in aggregate terms. To this extent, enthusiasts for globalization as liberalization can argue against the sceptics that borders have opened more than ever. That said, significant official restrictions on cross-border economic activity persist. They include countless trade restrictions and continuing **capital controls** in many countries. While states have on the whole welcomed FDI, there is as yet no multilateral regime to liberalize investment flows comparable to the GATT/WTO in respect of trade or the IMF in respect of money. (Negotiations for a **Multilateral Agreement on Investment** were abandoned at the end of 1998, although states have concluded hundreds of liberalizing bilateral investment treaties.) In addition, while many governments have loosened visa and travel restrictions in recent times, **immigration controls** are on the whole as tight as ever. Indeed, many have recently been reinforced. To this extent sceptics have grounds to affirm that international borders remain very much in place and can be opened or closed as states choose to do.

Transborder transactions

As mentioned earlier, most debates concerning economic globalization have unfolded between sceptics, who regard the current situation as a limited and reversible expansion of cross-border transactions, and globalists, who see an inexorable trend towards an open world economy. However, these two most common positions do not exhaust the possible interpretations. Indeed, neither of these conventional perspectives requires a distinct concept of 'globalization'. Both views resurrect arguments that were elaborated using other vocabulary long before the word 'globalization' entered widespread circulation in the 1990s.

In a third conception, globalization refers to processes whereby social relations acquire relatively distanceless and borderless qualities, so that human lives are increasingly played out in the world as a single place. In this usage, 'globalization' refers to a transformation of geography that occurs when a host of social conditions become less tied to territorial spaces (see Ch.1).

On these lines, a globalizing economy is one in which patterns of production, exchange, and consumption become increasingly de-linked from a geography of territorial distances and territorial borders. 'Global' economic activity extends across widely dispersed terrestrial locations at the same time and moves between locations scattered across the planet, often in effectively no time. While the patterns of 'international' economic interdependence are strongly influenced by territorial distances and national state divisions, patterns of 'global' trade and finance often have little correspondence to distance and state boundaries. With air travel, satellite links, telecommunications, transworld organizations, global consciousness (i.e. a mind-set that conceives of the planet as a single place) and more, much contemporary economic activity transcends borders. In this third sense globalization involves the growth of a **transborder** (as opposed to cross-border or open-border) economy.

This rise of **supraterritoriality** is reflected *inter alia* in increased transactions between countries. However, the geographical character of these **transplanetary** (as opposed to long-distance) movements is different from the territorial framework that has traditionally defined international interdependence. This qualitative shift means that contemporary statistics on international trade, money, and investment can only be crudely compared with figures relating to earlier times. Hence the issue is not so much the amount of trade between countries, but the way that much of this commerce forms part of transborder production processes and global marketing **networks**. The problem is not only the quantity of money that moves between countries, but also the instantaneity with which most funds are transferred. The question is not simply the number of international securities deals so much as the emergence of stock and bond issues that involve participants from multiple countries at the same time. In short, if one accepts this third conception of globalization, then both the sceptics and the enthusiasts are largely missing the crucial point of historical change.

Key Points

- The 'globalization' of economic activity can be understood in several different ways.
- Sceptical interpretations emphasize that current levels of cross-border trade, money movements, and investment flows are neither new nor as great as some claim.
- Globalist interpretations argue that large-scale relaxations of border controls have taken international economic activity to unprecedented levels.
- Geographical conceptions of globalization highlight the proliferation of economic transactions in which territorial distance and borders present limited if any constraint.

Global trade

The distinctiveness of transborder, supraterritorial economic relations should become clearer with illustrations. Examples concerning global trade are given in the present section. Others regarding global finance are discussed in the next section. In each case, it is seen that their significance relates mainly to contemporary history (although the phenomena in question made some earlier appearances).

Transborder production

Transborder production arises when a single process is spread across widely dispersed locations both within and between countries. Global **coordination** links research centres, design units, procurement offices, materials processing installations, fabrication plants, finishing points, assembly lines, quality control operations, advertising and marketing bureaux, data-processing offices, after-sales services, and so on.

Transborder production can be contrasted with territorially-centred production. In the latter instance, all stages of a given production process—from initial research to after-sales service—occur within the same local or national unit. In global production, however, the stages are dispersed across different and often widely scattered countries. Each of the various links in the transborder chain specializes in one or several functions, thereby creating economies of scale and/or exploiting cost differentials between locations. Through **global sourcing**, the company draws materials, components, machinery, finance, and services from anywhere in the world. Territorial distance and borders figure only secondarily, if at all, in determining the sites. Indeed, a firm may relocate certain stages of production several times in short succession in search of profit maximization.

What have been described as **global factories** were unknown before the 1940s. They did not gain major prominence until the 1960s and have mainly spread since the 1970s. Transborder production has developed mainly in the manufacture of textiles, garments, motor vehicles, leather goods, sports articles, toys, optical products, consumer electronics, semiconductors, aeroplanes, and construction equipment.

With the growth of global production, a large proportion of purportedly 'international' transfers of goods and services have entailed **intra-firm trade** within transborder companies. When the intermediate inputs and finished goods pass from one country to another they are officially counted as 'international' commerce; yet they primarily involve movements within a global company rather than between national economies. Conventional statistics do not measure intra-firm transfers, but estimates of the share of such exchanges in total cross-border trade have ranged from 25 to over 40 per cent.

Much (though far from all) transborder production has taken advantage of what are variously called special economic zones (SEZs), export processing zones (EPZs), or free production zones (FPZs). Within these enclaves the ruling national or provincial government exempts assembly plants and other facilities for transborder production from the usual import and export duties. The authorities may also grant other tax reductions, subsidies, and waivers of certain labour and environmental

regulations. The first such zone was established in 1954 in Ireland, but most were created after 1970, mainly in Asia, the Caribbean, and the so-called *maquiladora* areas along the Mexican frontier with the USA. Several thousand EPZs are now in place across more than 100 countries. Among other things, these manufacturing centres have been distinguished by their frequent heavy reliance on female labour.

Transborder products

Much of the output of both transborder and country-based production has acquired a planet-spanning market in the contemporary globalizing economy. Hence a considerable proportion of 'international' trade now involves the distribution and sale of **global goods**, often under a transworld brand name. Consumers dispersed across many corners of the planet purchase the same articles at the same time. The country location of a potential customer for, say, a Xerox photocopier, a Britney Spears CD, or Kellogg's corn flakes is of secondary importance. Design, packaging, and advertising determine the market far more than territorial distances and borders.

Like other aspects of globalization, supraterritorial markets have a longer history than many contemporary observers appreciate. For example, Campbell Soup and Heinz began to become household names at widely dispersed locations across the world in the mid-1880s, following the introduction of automatic canning. From the outset, Henry Ford regarded his first automobile, the Model T, as a world car. Coca-Cola was bottled in 27 countries and sold in 78 by 1929 (Pendergrast 1993: 174). On the whole, however, the numbers of goods, customers, and countries involved in these earlier global markets were relatively small.

In contrast, global goods pervade the contemporary world economy. They encompass a host of packaged foods, bottled beverages, tobacco products, designer clothes, household articles, music recordings, audiovisual productions, printed publications, interactive communications, office and hospital equipment, armaments, transport vehicles, and travel services. In all of these sectors and more, global products inject a touch of the familiar almost wherever on earth a person might visit. The countless examples include Nescafé (sold in 200 varieties worldwide), Heineken beer (drunk in over 170 countries), Kiwi shoe polish (applied in almost 200 countries), Nokia mobile phones (used in more than 130 countries), Thomas Cook tourist bureaux (available in 140 countries), American International Group insurance policies (offered in more than 130 countries), television programmes by Globo of Brazil (distributed in 128 countries), and the *Financial Times* newspaper (printed in 19 cities across the globe). Covering smokers in 170 lands, 'Marlboro Country' is a distinctly global place.

Today many shops are mainly stocked with transborder articles. Moreover, since the 1970s a number of **retail chains** have gone global. Examples include Italy-based Benetton, Japan-based 7-Eleven, Sweden-based IKEA, UK-based Body Shop, and US-based Toys 'Я' Us. Owing largely to the various 'megabrands' and transborder stores, shopping centres of the twenty-first century are in good part global emporia.

Other supraterritorial markets have developed since the 1990s through **electronic commerce**. Today's global consumer can—equipped with a credit card and telephone, television, or Internet links—shop across the planet from home. Mail-order outlets and telesales units have undergone exponential growth, while e-commerce on the World Wide Web has expanded hugely.

Through transborder production and transworld products, global trade has become an integral part of everyday life for a notable proportion of the world's firms and consumers. Indeed, these developments could help to explain why the recessions of contemporary history have not, in spite of frequently expressed fears of 'trade wars', provoked a wave of protectionism. In previous prolonged periods of commercial instability and economic hardship (e.g. during the 1870s–90s and 1920s–30s) most states responded by imposing major protectionist restrictions on cross-border trade. Reactions to contemporary recession have been more complicated (see Milner 1988). While many territorial interests have pressed for protectionism, global commercial interests have generally resisted it. Thus many transborder companies actively promoted the Uruguay Round and have, on the whole, vigorously supported the WTO.

Global finance

Finance has attracted some of the greatest attention in contemporary debates on globalization, especially following a string of crises in Latin America (1994–5), Asia (1997–8), Russia (1998), Brazil (1999), and Argentina (2001–2). The rise of supraterritoriality has affected both the forms that money takes and the ways that it is deployed in banking, securities, derivatives, and (although not detailed below) insurance markets. As international, cross-border activities, such dealings have quite a long history. However, as commerce that unfolds through telephone and computer networks that make the world a single place, global finance has experienced its greatest growth since the 1980s.

Transplanetary money

The development of global production and the growth of global markets have each encouraged—and been facilitated by—the spread of global monies. It was noted earlier that the fixed and later floating exchange regimes operated through the IMF have allowed a number of 'national' currencies to enter transworld use. As familiar 'bureau de change' signs indicate, today retail outlets in scores of countries deal in multiple currencies on demand.

No national denomination has been more global in this context than the US dollar. About as many dollars circulate outside as inside the USA. Indeed, in certain financial crises, this global money has displaced the locally issued currency in the everyday life of a national economy. Such 'dollarization' has occurred in parts of Latin America and Eastern Europe. Since the 1970s the German Mark (now superseded by a regional money in the shape of the euro), Japanese yen, Swiss franc, and other major currencies have also acquired a substantial global character. Hence huge stocks of notionally 'national' money are now used in countless transactions that never touch the 'home' soil.

Foreign exchange dealing has become a thoroughly supraterritorial business. This round-the-clock, round-the-world market has no central meeting place. Many of the deals have nothing directly to do with the countries where the currencies involved are initially issued or eventually spent. The trading itself has also taken place without distance. Transactions are generally concluded over the telephone and confirmed by telex or e-mail between buyers and sellers across whatever distance. Meanwhile shifts in exchange rates are flashed instantaneously and simultaneously on video monitors across the main dealing rooms worldwide.

Transborder money also takes other forms besides certain national currencies. Gold has already circulated across the planet for several centuries, although it moves cumbersomely through territorial space rather than instantly through telecommunication lines. A newer and more fully supraterritorial denomination is the **Special Drawing Right** (SDR), issued through the IMF since 1969. SDRs reside only in computer memories and not in wallets for everyday transactions.

Meanwhile other supraterritorial money has entered daily use in plastic form. For example, many bank cards can extract local currency from automated teller machines (**ATMs**) worldwide. In addition, several types of **smart card** (e.g. Mondex) can simultaneously hold several currencies as digital cash on a microchip. Certain **credit cards** like Visa and MasterCard are accepted at several million venues the world over to make purchases in whatever local denomination.

In sum, contemporary globalization has—through the spread of transborder currencies, distinctly supraterritorial denominations, digital purses, and global credit and

debit cards—significantly altered the shape of money. No longer is money restricted to the national-state-territorial form that prevailed from the nineteenth to the middle of the twentieth century.

Transplanetary banking

Globalization has touched banking mainly in terms of: (a) the growth of transborder deposits; (b) the advent of transborder bank lending; (c) the expansion of transborder branch networks; and (d) the emergence of instantaneous transworld interbank fund transfers.

So-called **eurocurrency** deposits are bank assets denominated in a national money different from the official currency in the country where the funds are held. For instance, euroyen are 'Japanese' yen deposited in, say, Canada. Eurocurrency accounts first appeared in the 1950s, but mainly expanded after 1970, especially with the flood of so-called **petrodollars** that followed major rises of oil prices in 1973–4 and 1979–80. Eurocurrencies are supraterritorial: they do not attach neatly to any country's money supply; nor are they systematically regulated by the national central bank that issued them.

Globalization has also entered the lending side of banking. Credit creation from eurocurrency deposits first occurred in 1957, when 'American' dollars were borrowed through the 'British' office of a 'Soviet' bank. However, euroloans mainly proliferated after 1973 following the petrodollar deluge. Today it is common for a loan to be issued in one country, denominated in the currency of a second country (or perhaps a basket of currencies of several countries), for a borrower in a third country, by a bank or syndicate of banks in fourth and more countries.

Global banking takes place not only at age-old sites of world finance like London, New York, Tokyo, and Zurich, but also through multiple **offshore finance centres**. Much like EPZs in respect of manufacturing, offshore financial arrangements offer investors low levels of taxation and regulation. Although a few offshore finance centres, including Luxembourg and Jersey, pre-date the Second World War, most have emerged since 1960 and are now found in over 40 jurisdictions. For example, less than thirty years after passing relevant legislation in 1967, the Cayman Islands hosted over 500 offshore banks, with total deposits of $442 billion (Roberts 1994; BIS 1996: 7).

The supraterritorial character of much contemporary banking also lies in the instantaneity of **interbank fund transfers**. Electronic messages have largely replaced territorial transfers by cheque or draft—and cost far less. The largest conduit for such movements is the Society for Worldwide Interbank Financial Telecommunications (SWIFT). Launched in 1977, SWIFT interconnected 8,100 financial institutions in 207 countries by 2007, carrying an average of 12.3 million payments per day.

Transplanetary securities

Globalization has altered not only banking, but also the shape of securities markets. First, some of the bonds and stocks themselves have become relatively detached from territorial space. Second, many investor portfolios have acquired a transborder character. Third, electronic interlinkage of trading sites has created conditions of anywhere/anytime securities dealing.

In regard to the first point, contemporary globalization has seen the emergence of several major securities instruments with a transborder character. These bonds and equities involve issuers, currencies, brokers, and/or exchanges across multiple countries at the same time. For example, a so-called **eurobond** is denominated in a currency that is alien to a substantial proportion of the parties involved: the borrower who issues it; the underwriters who distribute it; the investors who hold it; and/or the exchange(s) that list it. This transborder financial instrument is thereby different from a **foreign bond**, which is handled in one country for an external borrower. Cross-border bonds of the latter type have existed for several hundred years, but eurobonds first appeared in 1963. In that year the state highways authority in Italy issued bonds denominated in US dollars through managers in Belgium, Britain, Germany, and the Netherlands, with subsequent quotation on the London Stock Exchange.

On a similar pattern, a **euroequity** issue involves a transborder syndicate of brokers selling a new share release for simultaneous listing on stock exchanges in several countries. This supraterritorial process contrasts with an international offer, where a company based in one country issues **equity** in a second country. Like foreign bonds, international share quotations have existed almost as long as stock markets themselves. However, the first transborder equity issue occurred in 1984, when 15 per cent of a privatization of British Telecommunications was offered on exchanges in Japan, North America, and Switzerland concurrently with the majority share release

in the UK. Transworld placements of new shares have occurred less frequently than eurobond issues. However, it has become quite common for major transborder firms to list their equity on different stock exchanges across several time zones, particularly in Asia, **Europe**, and North America.

Not only various securities instruments, but also many **investor portfolios** have acquired a transborder character in the context of contemporary financial globalization. Thus, for example, an investor in one country may leave assets with a fund manager in a second country who in turn places those sums on markets in a collection of third countries. In other words, even when individual securities have a territorial character, they can be combined in a supraterritorial investment package. Indeed, a number of pension funds, insurance companies, and unit trusts have created explicitly designated 'global funds' whose component securities are drawn from multiple corners of the world. Many transborder institutional investors have furthermore registered offshore for tax and other cost advantages. For example, the Africa Emerging Markets Fund has its investments in Africa, its listing in Ireland, and its management office in the USA. As of 1995, Luxembourg hosted some $350 billion in offshore investment funds, largely outside the regulatory reach of the managers' home governments.

Finally, securities markets have gone global through the growing supraterritorial character of many exchanges since the 1970s. The open-outcry trading floors of old have largely given way to electronic transactions by telephone and computer networks. These telecommunications provide the infrastructure for distanceless deals (so-called **remote trading**), in which the brokers can, in principle, be located anywhere on Earth. Most major investment banks (Daiwa Securities, Dresdner Kleinwort, Merrill Lynch, etc.) now coordinate offices across several time zones in round-the-clock, round-the-world trading of bonds and shares. The first computerized order-routing system became operational in 1976, connecting brokers across the USA instantly to the trading floor of the New York Stock Exchange. Similar developments have, since 1996, begun to link brokers anywhere in the European Union directly to its main exchanges. For its part, the wholly computer-based National Association of Securities Dealers Automated Quotation system (Nasdaq) has, since its launch in 1971, had no central meeting place at all. This transborder cyberspatial network has become the world's largest stock market, listing around 3,200 companies

with a combined market capitalization of over $4.1 trillion and annual trading of 580 billion shares as of 2006. Meanwhile, beginning with the Toronto and American Stock Exchanges in 1985, a number of securities markets have established electronic links to enable transborder dealing between them. This extensive growth of supraterritoriality in the securities markets helps to explain why, for example, the Wall Street crash of October 1987 triggered transworld reverberations within hours.

Much like global banking, transborder securities trading is mainly conducted through computerized clearing systems. The equivalents of SWIFT are the Euroclear network, established in 1968, and Cedel (now renamed Clearstream), launched in 1971. Euroclear alone handled a turnover of over €350 trillion in 2005.

Transplanetary derivatives

A fourth area of finance suffused with globalization is the **derivatives** industry. A derivative product is a contract, the value of which depends on (hence is 'derived' from) the price of some underlying asset (e.g. a raw material or an equity) or a particular reference rate (e.g. an interest level or stock-market index). Derivatives connected to 'tangible' assets like raw minerals and land date from the middle of the nineteenth century, while derivatives based on financial indicators have proliferated since their introduction in 1972.

Derivatives contracts take two principal forms. The first type, called **futures** or **forwards,** oblige a buyer and seller to complete a transaction at a predetermined time in the future at a price agreed upon today. The second main type, called **options**, give parties a right (without obligation) to buy or sell at a specified price for a stipulated period of time up to the contract's expiry date. Other kinds of derivatives include 'swaps', 'warrants', and further—seemingly ever more obscure—financial instruments.

Additional technical details and the various rationales relating to derivatives need not detain us here. It suffices for present purposes to emphasize the magnitude of this financial industry. Public derivatives exchanges have proliferated worldwide since 1982 along with even larger over-the-counter (OTC) markets. By 1995 the volume of trading on world derivatives markets totalled some $1.2 trillion per day. The notional value of outstanding OTC financial derivatives contracts alone reached $370 trillion in mid-2006 (BIS 1996: 27; BIS 2006).

Like banking and securities, much derivatives business has become relatively distanceless and borderless. For example, a number of the contracts relate to supraterritorial indicators, such as the world price of copper, the interest rate on euroswiss franc deposits, and so on. In addition, much derivatives trading is undertaken through global securities houses and transworld telecommunications links. A number of derivatives instruments are traded simultaneously on several exchanges in a round-the-world, round-the-clock market. For example, contracts related to three-month eurodollar interest rates have been traded concurrently on Euronext.liffe (a pan-European derivatives exchange), the New York Futures Exchange (NYFE), the Sydney Futures Exchange (SFE), and the Singapore Exchange (SGX).

Owing to these tight global interconnections, major losses in the derivatives markets can have immediate worldwide repercussions. For example, deficits of $1.3 billion accumulated by the Singapore-based futures trader Nick Leeson triggered a transborder collapse of the venerable Barings investment bank in 1995. A succession of similarly huge losses in other quarters has caused some to worry that global derivatives trading could undermine the world financial system as a whole, although the sector has been more stable since 2000.

> ### Key Points
>
> - Globalization has changed forms of money with the spread of transborder currencies, distinctly supraterritorial denominations, digital cash, and global credit cards.
> - Globalization has reshaped banking with the growth of supraterritorial deposits, loans, branch networks, and fund transfers.
> - Securities markets have gained a global dimension through the development of transborder bonds and stocks, transworld portfolios, and electronic round-the-world trading.
> - Globalization has likewise affected the instruments and modes of trading on derivatives markets.

Continuity and change in economic globalization

Having now reviewed the development of a supraterritorial dimension in the contemporary world economy (summarized chronologically in Box 26.2), and emphasized its significance, it is necessary also to recognize continuities alongside these changes. One can appreciate the importance of globalization without slipping into **globalism**. Four main points are highlighted in this respect below: (1) the unevenness with which the globalization of trade and finance has spread; (2) the continuing importance of **territoriality** in the contemporary globalizing economy; (3) the continuing key place of the state amid these changes; and (4) the continuing significance of national attachments and cultural diversity more generally in the present era of economic globalization.

Irregular incidence

Globalization has not been experienced everywhere and by everyone to the same extent. In general, transborder trade and finance have developed furthest: (a) in East Asia, North America, and Western Europe; (b) in urban areas relative to rural districts; and (c) in wealthier and professional circles. On the other hand, few people and places are today completely untouched by economic globalization.

Supraterritorial trade and finance have transpired disproportionately in the so-called **North,** and then most especially in its **cities.** For instance, although McDonald's fast food is dished up in 30,000 establishments across 119 countries, the vast majority of these meals are consumed in a handful of those lands. In contrast to currencies issued in the North, the national denominations of countries in Africa have had scarcely any mutual convertibility. Thus far three-quarters and more of foreign direct investment, credit card transactions, stock-market capitalization, derivatives trade, and transborder loans flowed within the North.

This marginalization of the South is far from complete, however. For instance, certain products originating in the South have figured significantly in global markets (e.g. wines from Chile and package holidays in the Caribbean). Electronic banking has even reached parts of rural China. A number of offshore finance centres and

Box 26.2 Some key events in global trade and finance

1929	Institution of the first offshore finance arrangements (in Luxembourg)	1974	Formation of Basle Committee on Banking Supervision following the collapse of two banks heavily involved in foreign exchange dealing
1944	Bretton Woods Conference drafts constitutions of the IMF and the World Bank	1974	US government relaxes foreign exchange controls (other states follow in later years)
1954	Establishment of the first export processing zone (in Ireland)	1976	IMF meeting in Jamaica formalizes the regime of floating exchange rates
1954	Launch of the 'Marlboro cowboy' as a global commercial icon	1977	Inauguration of the SWIFT system of electronic interbank fund transfers worldwide
1955	First McDonald's restaurant opened (operating in 119 countries 50 years later)	1982	Mexico's threatened default on global loans triggers Third World debt crisis
1957	Issuance of the first eurocurrency loan	1983	Formation of the International Organization of Securities Commissions
1959	Gold–dollar standard enters into full operation	1984	First transborder equity issue (by British Telecommunications)
1963	Issuance of the first eurobond	1985	First transborder electronic link between stock exchanges
1965	Start of the *maquiladora* programme in Mexico	1987	Stock-market crash on Wall Street reverberates worldwide within hours
1968	Launch of Euroclear computerized transworld settlement of securities deals	1994	Conclusion of the Uruguay Round of the GATT
1969	Introduction of the Special Drawing Right	1995	Inauguration of the World Trade Organization
1971	Establishment of the first wholly electronic stock exchange (Nasdaq)	1995	Leeson Affair highlights the volatility of global derivatives markets
1972	Launch of markets in financial derivatives, starting with currency futures	1997–2002	Crises in Asia, Russia, Brazil, and Argentina raise concerns about underregulated global finance
1973	Quadrupling of oil prices floods euromarkets with petrodollars	2003	Doha Development Round of multilateral trade talks stalls and bilateral trade agreements increase

large sums of transborder bank debt are found in the South (see Case Study). Global portfolios have figured strongly in the development of new securities markets in major cities of Africa, Asia, Eastern Europe, and Latin America since the mid-1980s. SGX and the São Paulo-based Bolsa de Mercadorias & Futuros (BM&F) have played a part in the burgeoning derivatives markets of recent decades.

Indeed, involvement in global trade and finance is often as much a function of **class** as the North–South divide. The vast majority of the world's population—including many in the North—have lacked the means to purchase most global products. Likewise, placing investments in global financial markets depends on wealth, the distribution of which does not always follow a North–South pattern. For example, substantial petrodollars have been owned by elites in the oil-exporting countries of Africa, Latin America, and the Middle East.

Space limitations do not permit full elaboration of the point here, but transborder markets and investments can be shown to have contributed significantly to **growing wealth gaps** within countries as well as between North

Case Study Southern debt in global finance

The global character of much contemporary finance is well illustrated by the struggles that many middle- and low-income countries have had with large transborder debts. The problems developed in the 1970s, when the surge in oil prices generated huge export earnings of so-called 'petrodollars' that were largely placed in bank deposits. The banks in turn needed to lend the money, but demand for loans in the OECD countries was low at the time owing to recession. So, instead large bank loans went to countries of the South (in some cases partly to help pay for the increased cost of oil imports). Often the lenders were insufficiently careful in extending these credits, and often the borrowers were reckless in spending the money. Starting with Mexico in August 1982, a string of borrowing governments in the South defaulted on their transborder loans.

The initial response to this situation of unsustainable debts was to implement short-term emergency rescue packages for each country as it ran into crisis. Payments were rescheduled, and additional loans were provided to cover unpaid interest charges. This piecemeal approach only tended to make things worse. From 1987 onwards a series of comprehensive plans for Third World debt relief were promoted. During the following decade unsustainable commercial bank loans were gradually written off or converted into long-term bonds. Many bilateral loans from Northern governments to Southern borrowers were also cancelled. However, in the mid-1990s major problems persisted in regard to debts owed by low-income countries to multilateral lenders such as the IMF and the World Bank. A much-touted Highly Indebted Poor Countries (HIPC) initiative launched in 1996 and recast in 1999 has brought slow and limited returns. In 2005, the G8 Summit in Gleneagles agreed to write off the debts of 18 HIPCs to the multilateral agencies.

Throughout these twenty years, programmes of debt relief for low-income countries have received major support from global citizen campaigns. Activists formed a first Debt Crisis Network in the mid-1980s. Regional coalitions such as the European Network on Debt and Development emerged in the early 1990s. These efforts coalesced and broadened in the global Jubilee 2000 campaign of the late 1990s which, among other things, assembled 70,000 people in a 'human chain' around the G8 Summit in Birmingham, UK in 1998. Most commentators agree that these global citizen mobilizations significantly increased, improved, and accelerated programmes of debt relief.

and South (Scholte 2005: Ch.10). For example, the global mobility of capital, in particular to low-wage production sites and offshore finance centres, has encouraged many states to reduce upper-tax brackets and to downgrade some social welfare provisions. Such steps have contributed to growing inequality across much of the contemporary world. Increasingly, poverty has become connected as much to supraterritorial class, **gender** and race structures as to country of domicile (see further Ch.14 and Ch.27).

The persistence of territory

Yet the transcendence of territorial space in the contemporary world economy must not be overestimated. True, evidence presented earlier in this chapter suggests that distance and borders have often lost the determining influence on economic geography that they once had. However, this is not to say that territoriality has lost all significance in the contemporary organization of production, exchange, and consumption.

On the contrary, after several decades of accelerated globalization a great deal of commercial activity still has only a secondary if any supraterritorial dimension. For example, although transborder manufacturing through global factories has affected a significant proportion of certain industries, most processes have remained contained within one country. Even many globally distributed products (Boeing jets, Ceylon teas) are prepared within a single country.

Many types of money, too, have remained restricted to a national or local domain. Likewise, the great bulk of retail banking has stayed territorial, as clients deal with their local branch offices. In spite of substantial growth since the 1980s, transborder share dealing remains a small fraction of total equity trading. Moreover, a large majority of turnover on most stock exchanges continues to involve shares of firms headquartered in the same country.

Nor has most global commercial activity been wholly divorced from territorial geography. For example, local circumstances have strongly influenced corporate decisions regarding the location of transborder production facilities. In the foreign exchange markets, dealers have mainly been clustered in half a dozen cities, even if their transactions are largely cyberspatial and can have immediate consequences anywhere in the world. It remains rare for a transborder company to issue a large proportion of its stock outside its country of origin.

Hence the importance of globalization is that it has ended the monopoly of territoriality in defining the spatial character of the world economy. The trend has by no means eliminated territoriality. The global dimension of contemporary world commerce has grown alongside, and in complex relations with, its territorial aspects. Globalization has been reconfiguring geography (alongside concurrent processes of **regionalization** and localization) rather than obliterating **territory**.

The survival of the state

Similarly, globalization has repositioned the (territorial) state rather than signalled its demise. The expansion of transborder trade and finance has made claims of **Westphalian sovereign statehood** obsolete, but the significance of states themselves remains. Through both unilateral decisions and multilaterally coordinated policies, states have done much to facilitate economic globalization and influence its course.

As already mentioned, states have encouraged the globalization of commerce *inter alia* through various policies of liberalization and the creation of special economic zones and offshore finance centres. At the same time, some governments have also slowed globalization within their jurisdiction by retaining certain restrictions on transborder activity. However, most states have sooner or later responded to strong pressures to liberalize. In any case, governments have often lacked effective means fully to enforce their territorially bound controls on globally mobile capital. Only in respect of immigration restrictions have states largely sustained their borders against economic globalization, and even then substantial traffic in unregistered migrants occurs.

Yet states are by no means powerless in the face of economic globalization. Even the common claim that global finance lies beyond the state requires qualification. After all, governments and central banks continue to exert major influence on money supplies and interest rates, even if they no longer monopolize money creation and lack tight control over the euromarkets. Likewise, particularly through cooperative action, states can significantly shift exchange rates, even if they have lost the capacity to fix the conversion ratios and are sometimes overridden by currency dealers. Governments have also pursued collective regulation of transborder banking to some effect via the Basle Committee on Banking Supervision, set up through the BIS in 1974. The survival of offshore finance centres, too, depends to a considerable extent on the goodwill of governments, both the host regime and external authorities. Recent years have seen increased intergovernmental consultations, particularly through the OECD, to obtain tighter official oversight of offshore finance. Similarly, national regulators of securities markets have collaborated since 1984 through the International Organization of Securities Commissions (IOSCO).

In short, there is little sign that global commerce and the state are antithetical. On the contrary, the two have shown considerable mutual dependence. States have provided much of the regulatory framework for global trade and finance, albeit that they have shared these competences with other regulatory agencies.

The continuance of cultural diversity

Much evidence also confounds the common presumption that economic globalization is effecting **cultural homogenization** and a rise of cosmopolitan orientations over national **identities**. The growth of transborder production, the proliferation of global products, the multiplication of supraterritorial monies, and the expansion of transworld financial flows have shown little sign of heralding an end of cultural difference in the world economy.

True, global trade and finance are moved by much more than national loyalties. Consumers have repeatedly ignored exhortations to 'buy British' and the like in favour of global products. Shareholders and managers have rarely put national sentiments ahead of the profit margin. For example, the global media magnate Rupert Murdoch happily traded Australian for US **citizenship** in 1985 when it suited his commercial purposes. Foreign exchange dealers readily desert their national currency in order to reap financial gain.

However, in other respects national identities and solidarities have survived—and sometimes thrived—in the contemporary globalizing economy. Most transborder companies have retained a readily recognized national affiliation. Most firms involved in global trade and finance have kept a mononational board of directors, and the operations of many of these enterprises continue to reflect a national style of business practice connected with the country of origin. Different national **conventions** have persisted in global finance as well. For instance, since equities have traditionally held a smaller place in German finance, globalization in that country has mainly involved banks and the bond markets.

Cultural diversity has also persisted in transborder marketing. Local peculiarities have often affected the way that a global product is sold and used in different places. Advertising has often been adjusted to local tastes to be more effective.

In sum, then, like globalization in general, its economic dimension has not had universal scope. Nor has the rise of global trade and finance marked the end of territorial space, the demise of the state, or full-scale cultural homogenization. However, recognition of these qualifications does not entail a rejection of notions of globalization, on the lines of the sceptics noted earlier. After discounting for exaggeration and *non sequiturs*, the growth of globality remains a highly significant **development** in the contemporary world economy.

Key Points

- Global trade and finance have spread unevenly between different regions and different circles of people.
- Transborder commerce has to date often widened material inequalities within and between countries.
- Territorial geography continues to be important in the contemporary globalizing economy.
- Although now lacking Westphalian sovereign powers, states still exercise significant influence in global trade and finance.
- While economic globalization has weakened cultural diversity and national attachments in some respects, it has promoted them in others.

Conclusion

This chapter has shown that, among other things, the globalization of world politics is a deeply economic affair. The growth of global trade and finance has deeply shaped—and been shaped by—the general developments described in Chapter 1. Economic globalization has affected different places and persons to different extents, and it has far from eliminated older core structures of world politics: territory, state, and **nation**. However, these developments have already shifted many contours of geography, governance, and **community**; and economic globalization seems likely to unfold further still in the future.

The preceding pages have only touched on the wide-ranging and deeply significant questions of global trade and finance. In particular, this discussion has but hinted at the substantial problems of **human security**, social justice, and democracy that contemporary economic globalization has raised. The next chapter by Caroline Thomas addresses a number of these matters at greater length.

❓ Questions

1 Distinguish different conceptions of economic globalization.

2 To what extent is economic globalization new to contemporary history?

3 How does transborder production differ from territorial production?

4 How has globalization been manifested in changed forms of money?

5 What makes financial dealings in the euromarkets 'supraterritorial'?

6 What is an offshore financial centre?

7 To what extent has contemporary economic globalization marked 'the end of geography'?

8 How has globalization of trade and finance affected state capacities for economic regulation?

9 Discuss the impact of global products on cultural diversity.

10 To what extent can it be said that global capital carries no national flag?

11 Assess the relationship between globalization and income inequality.

12 In what ways might global commerce be reshaped to promote greater distributive justice?

Guide to further reading

Dunning, J. H. (ed.) (2004), *Making Globalization Good: Moral Challenges of Global Capitalism* (Oxford: Oxford University Press). Essays exploring ways to make global markets environmentally sustainable and socially equitable.

Held, D. *et al.* (1999), *Global Transformations: Politics, Economics and Culture* (Cambridge: Polity Press). Excellent on indicators and repercussions of economic globalization.

Hirst, P., and Thompson, G. (1999), *Globalization in Question: The International Economy and the Possibilities of Governance*, 2nd edn (Cambridge: Polity Press). A critique of 'globalist' presumptions that economic globalization is new, irreversible, and wholly beyond state control.

Hocking, B., and McGuire, S. (eds) (2004), *Trade Politics*, 2nd edn (London: Routledge). Covers the main issues of, and perspectives on, global trade.

O'Brien, R., and Williams, M. (2004), *Global Political Economy: Evolution and Dynamics* (Basingstoke: Palgrave Macmillan). A thorough overview of the history and current challenges of global production and exchange.

Peterson, V. S., and Runyan, A. S. (1999), *Global Gender Issues*, 2nd edn (Boulder, Col.: Westview Press). A critical examination of the impacts of globalization on, *inter alia*, women's employment and the feminization of
poverty.

Porter, T. (2005), *Globalization and Finance* (Cambridge: Polity Press). A thorough analysis of global finance and its governance.

Scholte, J. A. (2005), *Globalization: A Critical Introduction*, 2nd edn (Basingstoke: Palgrave Macmillan). Elaborates the arguments presented in this chapter, including the implications of economic globalization for human security, social justice, and democracy.

Stubbs, R., and Underhill, G. R. D. (eds) (2006), *Political Economy and the Changing Global Order*, 3rd edn (Basingstoke: Palgrave). A textbook in International Political Economy with much concerning global trade and finance.

UNDP (1990–), *Human Development Report* (New York: Oxford University Press). This annual publication of the United Nations Development Programme includes much on the welfare consequences of economic globalization. See especially the 1999 edition.

Online Resource Centre

 Visit the Online Resource Centre that accompanies this book to access more learning resources on this chapter topic at www.oxfordtextbooks.co.uk/uk/orc/baylis_smith4e/

Chapter 27

Poverty, development, and hunger

CAROLINE THOMAS

- Introduction ·· 470
- Poverty ·· 471
- Development ··· 473
- Hunger ··· 482
- Conclusion: looking to the future—globalization with a human face? ··········· 487

Reader's Guide

This chapter explores and illustrates the contested nature of a number of important concepts in International Relations. It examines the orthodox mainstream understanding of poverty, development, and hunger, and contrasts this with a critical alternative approach. Consideration is given to how successful the development orthodoxy has been in incorporating and thereby neutralizing the concerns of the critical alternative. The chapter then closes with an assessment of the likelihood of a globalization with a human face in the twenty-first century.

Introduction

Since 1945 we have witnessed over sixty years of unprecedented official development policies and impressive global economic growth. Yet global polarization is increasing, with the economic gap between rich and poor **states** and people growing (see Fig. 27.1). Box 27.1 shows that as a discipline International Relations has been slow to engage with these **issues**.

Poverty, hunger, and disease remain widespread, and women and girls continue to comprise the majority of the world's poorest people. Moreover, this general situation is not confined to that part of the world that we have traditionally termed the 'South' or the **Third World**. Particularly since the 1980s and 1990s, the worldwide promotion of neo-liberal economic policies (the so-called **Washington Consensus**) by **global governance** institutions has been accompanied by increasing inequalities within and between states. During this period, the Second World countries of the former Eastern bloc have been incorporated into the Third World grouping of states, and millions of people previously cushioned by the state have been thrown into **poverty** with the **transition** to market economies. In the developed world, rising social inequalities characterized the social landscape of the 1980s and 1990s. Within the Third World countries, the adverse

impact of **globalization** has been felt acutely, as countries have been forced to adopt free market policies as a condition of debt rescheduling and in the hope of attracting new investment to spur **development**. Gendered outcomes of these neo-liberal economic policies have been noted, though the global picture is very mixed, with other factors such as class, race, and ethnicity contributing to local outcomes (Buvinic 1997: 39).

The enormity of the current challenges was recognized by the UN in 2000 with the acceptance of the **Millennium Development Goals** (www.undp.org). These set time-limited, quantifiable targets across eight areas, ranging from poverty to health, **gender**, education, environment, and development. The first goal was the eradication of extreme poverty and hunger, with the target of halving the proportion of people living on less than a dollar a day by 2015.

The attempts of the majority of governments, **intergovernmental organizations**, and **non-governmental organizations** (NGOs) since 1945 to address global hunger and poverty can be categorized into two very broad types, depending on the explanations they provide for the existence of these problems and the respective solutions that they prescribe. These can be identified as the dominant

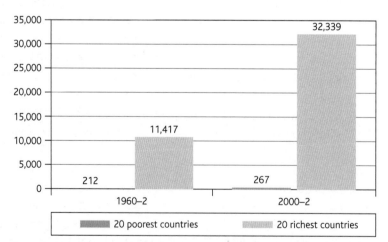

Source: Reprinted from World Commission on Social Dimensions of Globalisation (2004): 37. (*Original data source*: Based on a sample of 94 countries and territories with continuous time-series data from 1960 to 2002, as available from World Bank, *World Developement Indicators* 2003.)

Figure. 27.1 GDP per capita in the poorest and richest countries, 1960–2 and 2000–2 (in constant 1995 US$, simple averages)

Box 27.1 International Relations theory and the marginalization of priority issues for the Third World

- Traditionally, the discipline focused on issues relating to inter-state conflict, and regarded security and development as separate areas.
- Mainstream Realist and Liberal scholars neglected the challenges presented to human well-being by the existence of global underdevelopment.
- Dependency theorists were interested in persistent and deepening inequality and relations between North and South, but they received little attention in the discipline.
- During the 1990s, debate flourished, and several subfields developed or emerged which touched on matters of poverty, development, and hunger, albeit tangentially (e.g. global environmental politics, gender, international political economy).
- More significant in the 1990s in raising within the discipline the concerns of the majority of humanity and states, were the

contributions from post-colonial theorists, Marxist theorists (Hardt and Negri), scholars adopting a **human security** approach (Nef, Thomas), and the few concerned directly with development (Saurin, Weber).
- At the beginning of the twenty-first century, the discipline is better placed to engage with the interrelated issues of poverty, development, and hunger.
- And therefore to influence the diplomatic world, where interest in these issues is increasing, spurred on by fears of terrorist threats and recognition of the uneven impact of globalization.

(Thomas and Wilkin 2004)

mainstream or **orthodox approach**, which provides and values a particular body of developmental knowledge, and a **critical alternative approach**, which incorporates other more marginalized understandings of the development challenge and process (see Table 27.1). Most of this chapter will be devoted to an examination of the differences between these two approaches in relationship

to the three related topics of poverty, development, and hunger, with particular emphasis being placed upon the topic of development. The chapter concludes with an assessment of whether the desperate conditions in which so many of the world's citizens find themselves today are likely to improve. Again, two contrasting approaches are outlined.

	Poverty	Development	Hunger
Mainstream approach	Unfulfilled material needs	Linear path—traditional to modern	Not enough food to go around everyone
Critical alternative approach	Unfulfilled material and non-material needs	Diverse paths, locally driven	There is enough food, the problem is distribution and entitlement

Table 27.1 Mainstream and alternative conceptions of poverty, development, and hunger

Poverty

Different conceptions of poverty underpin the mainstream and alternative views of development. There is basic agreement on the material aspect of poverty, such as lack of food, clean water, and sanitation, but disagreement on the importance of non-material aspects. Also, key differences emerge in regard to how material needs should be met, and hence about the goal of development.

Most governments, **international organizations** citizens in the West, and many elsewhere adhere to the orthodox

conception of poverty. This refers to a situation where people do not have the money to buy adequate food or satisfy other basic needs, and are often classified as un- or underemployed. This mainstream understanding of poverty based on money has arisen as a result of the globalization of Western culture and the attendant expansion of the market. Thus a community which provides for itself outside monetized cash transactions and wage labour, such as a hunter-gatherer pygmy group, is regarded as poor.

Since 1945, this meaning of poverty has been almost universalized. Poverty is seen as an economic condition dependent on cash transactions in the market-place for its eradication. These transactions in turn are dependent on development defined as economic growth. An economic yardstick is used to measure and to judge all societies.

Poverty has widely been regarded as characterizing the Third World, and it has a gendered face. An approach has developed whereby it is seen as incumbent upon the developed countries to 'help' the Third World eradicate 'poverty', and increasingly to address female poverty. James Wolfensohn, Managing Director of the World Bank, declared in February 2000 that 'The World Bank is committed to making gender equality central to its fight against poverty' (cited in World Bank 2000). The solution advocated to overcome global poverty is the further **integration** of the global economy (Thomas 2000) and of women into this process (Pearson 2000; Weber 2002). Increasingly, however, as globalization has intensified, poverty defined in such economic terms has come to characterize significant sectors of population in advanced developed countries such as the USA (see Bello 1994).

Critical, alternative views of poverty exist in other cultures where the emphasis is not simply on money, but on spiritual values, community ties, and availability of common resources. In traditional subsistence methods, a common strategy for **survival** is provision for oneself and one's family via **community**-regulated access to common water, land, and fodder. The autonomy characteristic of such methods may be highly valued by those who have traditionally practised them. Indeed, some such methods have been sustained over thousands of years. For many people in the developing world the ability to provide for oneself and one's family may be preferable to dependence on an unpredictable market and/or an unreliable government.

Critical views on poverty have emanated from within Western society also. For example, it has been asserted that our emphasis on monetary values has led to the creation of 'a system of production that ravishes nature and a society that mutilates man' (Schumacher 1973).

Some global **institutions** have been important in promoting a conception of poverty that extends beyond material indicators. The work of the United Nations Development Programme (UNDP) since the early 1990s is significant here for distinguishing between income poverty (a material condition) and human poverty (encompassing human dignity, agency, opportunity, and choices).

The issue of poverty and the challenge of poverty alleviation moved up the global political agenda at the close of the twentieth century, as evidenced in the UN's first Millennium Development Goals cited earlier. While World Bank figures for the 1990s showed a global improvement in reducing the number of people living on less than a dollar a day (its orthodox measurement of extreme poverty), the picture was uneven: in sub-Saharan Africa the situation deteriorated, and elsewhere, such as the Russian Federation, the Commonwealth of Independent States, Latin America and the Caribbean, and some Middle Eastern states, the picture remains bleak. Most of the global improvement resulted from trends in China and India, and even there, deep pockets of poverty remain.

Having considered the orthodox and critical alternative views of poverty, we will now turn to an examination of the important topic of development. This examination will be conducted in three main parts. The first part will start by examining the orthodox view of development and

---

Key Points

- The monetary-based conception of poverty has been almost universalized among governments and international organizations since 1945.
- Poverty is interpreted as a condition suffered by people—the majority of whom are female—who do not earn enough money to satisfy their basic material requirements in the market-place.
- Developed countries have regarded poverty as being something external to them and a defining feature of the Third World. This view has provided justification for the former to help 'develop' the latter by promoting their further integration into the global market.

- However, such poverty is increasingly endured by significant sectors of the population in the North, as well as the Third World, hence rendering traditional categories less useful.
- A critical alternative view of poverty places more emphasis on lack of access to community-regulated common resources, community ties, and spiritual values.
- Poverty moved up the global political agenda at the start of the twenty-first century.

will then proceed to an assessment of its effect on post-war development in the Third World. The second part will examine the critical alternative view of development and its application to subjects such as empowerment and democracy. In the third part consideration will be given to the ways in which the orthodox approach to development has responded to some of the criticisms made of it by the critical alternative approach.

Development

When we consider the topic of **development** it is important to realize that all conceptions of development necessarily reflect a particular set of social and political values. Indeed, it is true to say that 'Development can be conceived only within an ideological framework' (Roberts 1984: 7).

Since the Second World War the dominant understanding, favoured by the majority of governments and multilateral agencies, has seen development as synonymous with economic growth within the context of a free market international economy. Economic growth is identified as necessary for combating poverty, defined as the inability of people to meet their basic material needs through cash transactions. This is seen in the influential reports of the World Bank, where countries are categorized according to their income. Those countries that have the lower national incomes per head of population are regarded as being less developed than those with higher incomes, and they are perceived as being in need of increased integration into the global market-place.

An alternative view of development has, however, emerged from a few governments, UN agencies, grass-roots movements, NGOs, and some academics. Their concerns have centred broadly on entitlement and distribution. Poverty is identified as the inability to provide for the material needs of oneself and one's family by subsistence or cash transactions, and by the absence of an environment conducive to human well-being broadly conceived in spiritual and community terms. These voices of opposition are growing significantly louder, as ideas polarize following the apparent universal triumph of economic **liberalism**. The language of opposition is changing to incorporate matters of **democracy** such as political empowerment, participation, meaningful **self-determination** for the majority, protection of the commons, and an emphasis on pro-poor growth. The fundamental differences between the orthodox and the alternative views of development are summarized in Box 27.2,

Box 27.2 Development: a contested concept

The orthodox view

Poverty: a situation suffered by people who do not have the *money to buy food* and satisfy other basic *material needs*.

Purpose: transformation of traditional subsistence economies defined as 'backward' into industrial, commodified economies defined as 'modern'. Production of surplus. Individuals sell their labour for money, rather than producing to meet their family's needs.

Core ideas and assumptions: the possibility of unlimited economic growth in a free-market system. Economies would reach a 'take-off' point and thereafter wealth would trickle down to those at the bottom. Superiority of the 'Western' model and knowledge. Belief that the process would ultimately benefit everyone. Domination, exploitation of nature.

Measurement: economic growth; Gross Domestic Product (GDP) per capita: industrialization, including of agriculture.

Process: top-down; reliance on 'expert knowledge', usually Western and definitely external; large capital investments in large projects; advanced technology; expansion of the private sphere.

The alternative view

Poverty: a situation suffered by people who are not able to meet their *material and non-material needs* through their own effort.

Purpose: creation of human well-being through sustainable societies in social, cultural, political, and economic terms.

Core ideas and assumptions: sufficiency. The inherent value of nature, cultural diversity, and the community-controlled commons (water, land, air, forest). Human activity in balance with nature. Self-reliance. Democratic inclusion, participation, for example, voice for marginalized groups, such as women, indigenous groups. Local control.

Measurement: fulfilment of basic material and non-material human needs of everyone; condition of the natural environment. Political empowerment of marginalized.

Process: bottom-up; participatory; reliance on appropriate (often local) knowledge and technology; small investments in small-scale projects; protection of the commons.

and supplemented by Case Study 1 illustrating competing ideas on development from the contemporary coffee sector. In the following two sections we will examine how the orthodox view of development has been applied at a global level and assess what measure of success it has achieved.

Case Study 1 Competing ideas on development from the contemporary coffee sector

Contemporary debate on the coffee sector provides a graphic example of competing ideas and values concerning development, and has relevance far beyond coffee. The impact of commodity price volatility and a long-term decline in terms of trade of primary products has profound effects on livelihoods of millions of rural householders in the poorest countries. In the case of coffee, about 25 million small farmers depend directly on coffee production in over 50 countries. During the 1980s, export production increased in poor countries, fuelled significantly by policy advice from the World Bank and International Monetary Fund (IMF) that hard currency earnings had to be boosted though increased commodity exports to pay off spiralling Third World debt. Oversupply since the early 1980s has resulted in a decline of about 70 per cent in nominal coffee prices, with prices reaching a thirty-year low in 2001. The impact on livelihoods of smallholder peasant farmers and plantation workers has been devastating. At the eleventh World Coffee Conference in Salvador da Bahia in September 2005, 12 groups representing peasant farmers and workers launched an alternative approach to coffee production, in the Salvador declaration:

'For a truly sustainable coffee sector, all who take part in coffee production must share its wealth: small-scale producers, permanent and seasonal rural workers, industry and retail workers.

Many say that the solutions to the crisis are only associated with methods of production, including increased investment in substitutes for local coffee varieties, use of toxic fertilisers and pesticides, and mechanization—all aimed at greater productivity. This vision . . . allows for the consolidation of production and marketing by a small group of companies that do not practise social responsibility but make decisions that impact millions of people while they reap the lion's share of the benefits of the trade. This vision is not sustainable. . . .'

Real sustainability of the coffee sector should not be viewed through an economic lens alone but must include ethical and political perspectives.

From an ethical perspective, the citizenship rights of people who participate in wealth generation must be guaranteed. Those rights are: stability of prices; recognition of efforts to protect the rural landscape and biological diversity by improving cultivation, harvest, and post harvesting practices; and recognition of the basic rights of rural workers, including the fundamental rights of association and collective bargaining, particularly for seasonal rural workers . . .

From a political perspective, . . . governments (must) agree to and implement public policies that guarantee the rights of coffee producers and rural workers. It should be possible to develop a sustainable model based on food security and sovereignty.

In conclusion, we expect the World Coffee Conference to acknowledge . . . the issue of sustainability from the perspective of all actors involved in the coffee chain and sanction space for direct representation by small-scale farmers and rural workers organisations . . . (and) seek to establish the basis for fair trade between nations.

(Oxfam et al. 2006: 11–12)

Economic liberalism and the post-1945 international economic order: sixty years of orthodox development

During the Second World War there was a strong belief among the allied powers that the protectionist trade policies of the 1930s had contributed significantly to the outbreak of the war. Plans were drawn up by the USA and the UK for the creation of a stable post-war **international order** with the United Nations (UN), its affiliates the **International Monetary Fund** (IMF) and the **World Bank Group**, plus the **General Agreement on Tariffs and Trade** (GATT), providing the institutional bases. The latter three provided the foundations of a liberal international economic **order** based on the pursuit of free trade, but allowing an appropriate role for state intervention in the market in support of **national security** and national and global stability (Rapley 1996). This has been called **embedded liberalism**. The **decision-making procedures** of these international economic institutions favoured a small group of developed Western states. Their relationship with the UN, which in the General Assembly has

more democratic procedures, has not always been an easy one.

In the early post-war years, reconstruction of previously developed states took priority over assisting developing states. This reconstruction process really took off in the context of the **cold war**, with the transfer of huge sums of money from the United States to **Europe** in the form of bilateral aid from the Marshall Plan of 1947. In the 1950s and 1960s as decolonization progressed, the focus of the World Bank and the UN system generally shifted to the perceived needs of developing countries. The USA was heavily involved as the most important funder of the World Bank and the UN, and also in a bilateral capacity.

There was a widespread belief in the developed Western countries, among the managers of the major multilateral institutions, and throughout the UN system, that Third World states were economically backward and needed to be 'developed'. This process would require intervention in their economies. This attitude was widely shared by Western-educated elites in those countries. In the context of independence movements, the development imperative came to be shared by many citizens in the Third World. The underlying assumption was that the Western lifestyle and mode of economic organization were superior and should be universally aspired to.

The cold war provided a context in which there was a competition between the West and the Eastern bloc to win allies in the 'Third World'. The USA believed that the path of liberal economic growth would result in development, and that development would result in hostility to socialist ideals. The USSR, by contrast, attempted to sell its economic system as the most rapid means for the newly independent states to achieve industrialization and development. The process of industrialization underpinned conceptions of development in both East and West, but whereas in the capitalist sphere the market was to be the engine of growth, in the socialist sphere central planning by the state was the preferred method.

The majority of Third World states were born into and accepted a place within the Western, capitalist orbit, while a few, either by choice or lack of options, ended up in the socialist camp. Yet in the early post-war and post-colonial decades all states—whether in the West, East, or Third World—favoured an important role for the state in development. Many Third World countries pursued a strategy of import substitution industrialization in order to try to break out of their dependent position in

the world-economy as peripheral producers of primary commodities for the core developed countries.

This approach, which recognized the important role of the state in development, suffered a major setback in the early 1980s. The developing countries had borrowed heavily in the 1970s in response to the rise in oil prices. The rich countries' strategy for dealing with the second oil price hike in 1979 resulted in massive rises in interest rates and steep falls in commodity prices in the early 1980s. The developing countries were unable to repay spiralling debts. Mexico threatened to default in 1982. The Group of Seven (G7) leading developed Western countries decided to deal with the debt problem on a country-by-country basis, with the goal of avoiding the collapse of the international banking system by ensuring continued repayment of debt. In this regard, the IMF and the World Bank pursued a vigorous policy of **structural adjustment lending** throughout the developing world. In applying this policy, the Fund and Bank worked together in an unprecedented fashion to encourage developing countries to pursue market-oriented strategies based on rolling back the power of the state and opening Third World economies to foreign investment. Exports were promoted so that these countries would earn the foreign exchange necessary to keep up with their debt repayments.

With the ending of the cold war and the collapse of the Eastern bloc after 1989, this **neo-liberal economic and political philosophy** came to dominate development thinking across the globe. The championing of unadulterated liberal economic values played an important role in accelerating the globalization process. This represented an important ideological shift. The 'embedded liberalism' of the early post-war decades gave way to the unadulterated neoclassical economic policies which favoured a minimalist state and an enhanced role for the market: the so-called **Washington Consensus**. The belief was that global welfare would be maximized by the **liberalization** of trade, finance, and investment, and by the restructuring of national economies to provide an enabling environment for capital. Such policies would also ensure the repayment of debt. The former Eastern bloc countries were now seen to be in transition from centrally planned to market economies, and throughout the Third World the state was rolled back and the market given the role of major engine of growth and associated development. This approach was presented as common sense, with the attendant idea that 'There is No Alternative' or TINA (Thomas 2000). It

informed the strategies of the IMF and World Bank, and importantly through the Uruguay Round of trade discussions carried out under the auspices of GATT, it shaped the **World Trade Organization** (WTO).

By the end of the 1990s the G7 (later the **G8**) and associated international financial institutions were championing a slightly modified version of the neo-liberal economic orthodoxy, labelled the **post-Washington Consensus**, which stressed pro-poor growth and poverty reduction based on continued domestic policy reform and growth through trade liberalization. Henceforth, locally owned national poverty reduction strategy (PRS) papers would be the focus for funding (Cammack 2002). These papers quickly became the litmus test for funding from an increasingly integrated line-up of global financial institutions and donors.

The achievements of the post-1945 international economic order

There has been an explosive widening of the gap between the rich and the poor since 1945 compared with previous history, and more particularly in the 1990s (Adams 1993: vii; Thomas 2000). Nevertheless, there have been major gains for developing countries since 1945 as measured by the orthodox criteria of economic growth, GDP per capita, and industrialization. The rates of total and per capita growth for developing countries in the period 1960–2004 are shown in Tables 27.2 and 27.3. A striking feature of both is the marked **regional diversity**. The East Asian experience has been generally positive throughout this period, the African experience not so. China has been strong since the early 1980s, and India has fared better since the late 1980s.

In the 1990s, the picture was far from positive. The UNDP reports that: 'no fewer than 100 countries—all developing or in transition—have experienced serious economic decline over the past three decades. As a result, per capita income in these 100 countries is lower than it was 10, 20, even 30 years ago' (UNDP 1998: 37). Moreover, the 1990s saw 21 countries experience decade-long declines in social and economic indicators, compared with only four in the 1980s (UNDP 2003). Financial crises spread across the globe and indicated marked reversals in Mexico, the East Asian states, Brazil, and Russia. The African continent looked increasingly excluded from any economic benefits of globalization, and

Region/country	1960–5	1965–70	1970–5	1975–80	1980–5	1985–90	1990–5	1995–200	2000–4
Africa	5.4	4.9	4.4	3.8	2.2	2.6	1.1	3.4	3.9
Sub-Saharan Africa, excl. South Africa	3.9	3.9	3.9	1.9	1.7	3.2	1.5	3.7	4.2
Latin America	4.6	5.8	6.6	5.1	0.5	1.8	3.6	2.8	1.5
East-Asia	5.0	7.5	6.8	7.6	7.1	8.2	8.8	4.9	6.2
China	2.1	5.3	5.1	6.1	11.0	7.8	12.9	8.5	9.4
First-tier NIEs	8.0	9.8	8.3	9.0	7.1	9.1	7.3	4.2	3.8
South Asia	4.5	4.9	2.3	3.6	5.3	5.9	5.0	5.3	5.7
India	4.2	4.9	2.4	3.0	5.3	6.6	5.3	5.8	6.1
Developing countries	4.8	6.0	6.4	5.1	2.9	5.4	5.4	4.1	4.4

Source: UNCTAD secretarial calculations, based on World Bank, *World Development Indicators*, various issues United Nations Statisitcs Division (UNSd) *National Accounts Main Aggregates* Database; and Taiwan Province of China, *MacroEconomics* Database

Note: Calculations are based on GDP in constant 1995 dollars.
Source: UNCTAD (2006a: 46).

Table 27.2 GDP growth in selected developing countries and regions, 1960–2004 (average annual percentage change)

Region/country	1960–5	1965–70	1970–5	1975–80	1980–5	1985–90	1990–5	1995–200	2000–4
Africa	2.8	2.2	1.6	0.9	0.7	-0.2	-1.5	1.0	1.6
Sub-Saharan Africa, excl. South Africa	1.3	1.2	1.1	-1.0	-1.2	0.2	-1.3	1.1	1.8
Latin America	1.7	3.1	4.0	2.7	-1.6	-0.2	1.9	1.2	0.1
East-Asia	3.0	4.7	4.4	5.9	5.4	6.4	7.5	3.8	5.3
China	0.3	2.6	2.8	4.6	9.5	6.1	11.7	7.5	8.7
First-tier NIEs	5.0	7.2	6.1	7.1	5.5	8.0	6.1	3.2	3.2
South Asia	2.2	2.5	0.0	1.4	2.9	3.6	2.8	3.3	4.0
India	1.9	2.5	0.1	0.9	3.1	4.4	3.3	4.0	4.5
Developing countries	2.5	3.4	3.9	2.9	0.7	2.2	3.5	2.4	2.9

Source: UNCTAD secretariat calculations, based on World Bank, *World Development Indicators*, various issues UNSD, *Population* Database and *National Accounts Main Aggregates* Database; and Taiwan Province of China, *MacroEconomics* Database

Source: UNCTAD (2006a: 47).

Table 27.3 Per capita GDP growth in selected developing countries and regions, 1960–2004 (average annual percentage change)

33 countries there ended the 1990s more heavily indebted than they had been two decades earlier (Easterly 2002). By the end of the century, not a single former Second or Third World country had joined the ranks of the First World in a solid sense. Significant growth occurred in a handful of countries such as China, India, and Mexico—the 'new globalizers'—but the benefits were not well distributed within those countries. Despite significant improvements in global social indicators such as adult literacy, access to safe water, and infant mortality rates, global deprivation continues. This is illustrated vividly in Fig. 27.2.

Having outlined the broad development achievements of the post-war international economic order, we will now evaluate these from two different development perspectives: a mainstream orthodox view and a critical alternative view.

The development achievement of the post-war international economic order: orthodox and alternative evaluations

The orthodox liberal assessment of the past sixty years of development suggests that states which have integrated most deeply into the global economy through trade liberalization have grown the fastest, and it praises these 'new globalizers'. It acknowledges that neo-liberal economic policy has resulted in greater inequalities within and between states, but regards inequality positively as a spur to competition and the entrepreneurial spirit.

It was clear at least from the late 1970s that 'trickle-down' (the idea that overall economic growth as measured by increases in the GDP would automatically bring benefits for the poorer classes) had not worked. Despite impressive rates of growth in GDP per capita enjoyed by developing countries, this success was not reflected in their societies at large, and while a minority became substantially wealthier, the mass of the population saw no significant change. The even greater polarization in wealth evident in recent decades is not regarded as a problem, so long as the social and political discontent which inequality engenders is not so extensive as potentially to de-rail implementation of the liberalization project itself. This discontent will be alleviated by the development of national PRSs, which it is claimed put countries and their peoples in the driving seat of development policy, thus empowering the local community and ensuring a better distribution of benefits.

Advocates of a critical alternative approach emphasize the pattern of distribution of gains within global society

Goals and Targets	Africa		Asia				Oceania	Latin America & Caribbean	Commonwealth of Independent States	
	Northern	Sub-Saharan	Eastern	South-Eastern	Southern	Western			Europe	Asia
GOAL 1 | Eradicate extreme poverty and hunger										
Reduce extreme poverty by half	low poverty	very high poverty	moderate poverty	moderate poverty	very high poverty	low poverty	---	moderate poverty	low poverty	low poverty
Reduce hunger by half	very low hunger	very high hunger	moderate hunger	moderate hunger	very high hunger	moderate hunger	moderate hunger	moderate hunger	very low hunger	high hunger
GOAL 2 | Achieve universal primary education										
Universal primary schooling	high enrolment	low enrolment	high enrolment	high enrolment	high enrolment	moderate enrolment	moderate enrolment	high enrolment	high enrolment	high enrolment
GOAL 3 | Promote gender equality and empower women										
Equal girls' enrolment in primary school	close to parity	almost close to parity	parity	parity	close to parity	almost close to parity	close to parity	parity	parity	parity
Women's share of paid employment	low share	medium share	high share	medium share	low share	low share	medium share	high share	high share	high share
Women's equal representation in national parliaments	very low representation	low representation	moderate representation	low representation	low representation	very low representation	very low representation	moderate representation	low representation	low representation
GOAL 4 | Reduce child mortality										
Reduce mortality of under-five-year-olds by two thirds	moderate mortality	very high mortality	moderate mortality	moderate mortality	high mortality	moderate mortality	high mortality	moderate mortality	low mortality	high mortality
Measles immunization	high coverage	low coverage	moderate coverage	moderate coverage	low coverage	moderate coverage	very low coverage	high coverage	high coverage	high coverage
GOAL 5 | Improve maternal health										
Reduce maternal mortality by three quarters*	moderate mortality	very high mortality	low mortality	high mortality	very high mortality	moderate mortality	high mortality	moderate mortality	low mortality	low mortality
GOAL 6 | Combat HIV/AIDS, malaria and other diseases										
Halt and reverse spread of HIV/AIDS	---	very high prevalence	low prevalence	moderate prevalence	moderate prevalence	---	moderate prevalence	moderate prevalence	high prevalence	low prevalence
Halt and reverse spread of malaria*	low risk	high risk	moderate risk	moderate risk	moderate risk	low risk	low risk	moderate risk	low risk	low risk
Halt and reverse spread of tuberculosis	low mortality	high mortality	moderate mortality	moderate mortality	moderate mortality	low mortality	moderate mortality	low mortality	moderate mortality	moderate mortality

Country experiences in each region may differ significantly from the regional average. For the regional groupings and country data, see mdgs.un.org.

Sources: United Nations, based on data and estimates provided by: Food and Agriculture Organization; Inter-Parliamentary Union; International Labour Organization; International Telecommunication Unit; UNESCO; UNICEF; World Health Organization; UNAIDS; UN-Habitat; World Bank—based on statistics available June 2006.
Compiled by: Statistics Division, UN DESA. Photo credit: Adam Rogers/UNCDF.

The progress chart operates on two levels. The words in each box tell what the current rate of compliance with each target is. The colours show the trend, towards meeting the target by 2015 or not. See legend below:

- Target already met or very close to being met.
- Target is expected to be met by 2015 if prevailing trends persist, or the problem that this target is designed to address is not a serious concern in the region.
- Target is not expected to be met by 2015, if prevailing trends persist.
- No progress, or a deterioration or reversal.
- Insufficient data.

* The available data for maternal mortality and malaria do not allow a trend analysis. Progress in the chart has been assessed by the responsible agencies on the basis of proxy indicators.
** The current assessment for forests is based on new methodology and therefore not comparable with previous assessments.

Source: Adapted from http://milleniumindicators.un.org/unsd/mdg/Resources/Static/Products/Progress2006/MDGProgressChart2006.pdf

Figure 27.2 Millennium Development Goals: 2006 progress chart for selected goals

and within individual states, rather than growth. They believe that the economic liberalism which underpins the process of globalization has resulted, and continues to result, in increasing economic differentiation between and within countries, and that this is problematic. Moreover, they note that this trend has been evident over the very period when key global actors have been committed to promoting development worldwide, and indeed when there were fairly continuous world economic growth rates and positive rates of GDP growth per capita, at least until 1990 (Brown and Kane 1995).

The increasing gap between rich and poor was regarded as inevitable, and undesirable, by dependency theorists such as André Gunder Frank (1967). Writing in the 1960s and 1970s, they stressed how the periphery, or Third World, was actively underdeveloped by activities which promoted the growth in wealth of the core Western countries, and of elites in the periphery (see Case Study 1).

At the beginning of the twenty-first century, exponents of a critical alternative—in contrast to their orthodox colleagues—question the value of national PRSs, arguing that while a new focus on issues such as health and education is important, the more fundamental issue of discussion of possible links between Washington-Consensus policies and poverty creation is ignored.

The orthodox and alternative evaluations are based on different values and they are measuring different things. Glyn Roberts' words are pertinent: 'GNP growth statistics might mean a good deal to an economist or to a maharajah, but they do not tell us a thing about the quality of life in a Third World fishing village' (Roberts 1984: 6).

A critical alternative view of development

Since the early 1970s, there have been numerous efforts to stimulate debate about development and to highlight its contested nature. Critical alternative ideas have been put forward that we can synthesize into an alternative approach. These have originated with various NGOs,

grassroots development organizations, individuals, UN organizations, and private foundations. Disparate **social movements** not directly related to the development agenda have contributed to the flourishing of the alternative viewpoints: for example, the women's movement, the peace movement, movements for democracy, and green movements (Thomas 2000). Noteworthy was the publication in 1975 by the Dag Hammarskjöld Foundation of *What Now? Another Development?* This alternative conception of development (see Ekins 1992: 99) argued that the **process of development** should be:

- need-oriented (material and non-material);
- endogenous (coming from within a society);
- self-reliant (in terms of human, natural, and cultural resources);
- ecologically sound; and
- based on structural transformations (of economy, society, gender, power relations).

Since then, various NGOs, such as the World Development Movement, have campaigned for a form of development that takes aspects of this alternative approach on board. Grassroots movements have often grown up around specific issues, such as dams (Narmada in India) or access to common resources (the rubber tappers of the Brazilian Amazon; the Chipko movement, which began as a women's movement to secure trees in the Himalayas). Such campaigns received a great impetus in the 1980s with the growth of the green movement worldwide. The two-year preparatory process before the UN Conference on Environment and Development (UNCED) in Rio, in June 1992, gave indigenous groups, women, children, and other previously voiceless groups a chance to express their views. This momentum has continued, and it has become the norm to hold alternative NGO forums, parallel to all major UN conferences. Also, the World Social Forum meets annually.

Democracy, empowerment, and development

Democracy is at the heart of the alternative conception of development. Grassroots movements are playing an important role in challenging entrenched structures of power in formal democratic societies. In the face of increasing globalization, with the further erosion of local community control over daily life and the further extension of the power of the market and **transnational corporations**, people are standing up for their rights as they define them. They are making a case for local control and local empowerment as the heart of development. They are protecting what they identify as the immediate source of their survival—water, forest, and land. They are rejecting the dominant agenda of private and public (government-controlled) spheres and setting an alternative one. Examples include the Chiapas uprising in Mexico, and Indian peasant protests against foreign-owned seed factories. Protests at the annual meetings of the WTO, and also the IMF and World Bank, have become routine since the late 1990s, and are indicative of an increasingly widespread discontent with the process of globalization and with the distribution of its benefits. Such protests symbolize the struggle for substantive democracy which communities across the world are working for. In this context, development is about facilitating a community's participation and lead role in deciding what sort of development is appropriate for it; it is not about assuming the desirability of the Western model and its associated values. This alternative conception of development therefore values diversity above universality, and is based on a different conception of rights.

The Alternative Declaration produced by the NGO Forum at the Copenhagen Summit enshrined **principles** of community participation, empowerment, **equity**, self-reliance, and sustainability. The role of women and youth was singled out. The Declaration rejects the economic liberalism accepted by governments of North and South, seeing it as a path to aggravation rather than alleviation of the global social crisis. It called for the immediate cancellation of all debt, improved terms of trade, transparency and accountability of the IMF and World Bank, and the regulation of multinationals. An alternative view of democracy was central to its conception of development. Similar ideas emanated from the parallel NGO forums, which accompanied all the UN global conferences in the 1990s.

For some commentators, national PRSs offer the opportunity—albeit as yet unrealized—for greater community participation in development policy-making in the South. If all parties operate in the spirit which was intended, the PRS process could enhance representation and voice for states and peoples in the South, and it offers the best hope available for expanding national ownership of economic policy.

Now that we have looked at the critical alternative view of development, we will look at the way in which the orthodox view has attempted to respond to the criticisms of the alternative view.

The orthodoxy incorporates criticisms

In the mainstream debate, the focus has shifted from growth to sustainable development. The concept was championed in the late 1980s by the influential Brundtland Commission (officially entitled the World Commission on Environment and Development—see Brundtland *et al.* 1987), and supported in the 1990s by a series of UN global conferences. Central to the concept of **sustainable development** is the idea that the pursuit of development by the present generation should not be at the expense of future generations. In other words, it stressed inter-generational equity as well as intra-generational equity. The importance of maintaining the environmental resource base was highlighted, and with this comes the idea that there are natural limits to growth. The Brundtland Report made clear, however, that further growth was essential; but it needed to be made environment-friendly. The Report did not address the belief, widespread among a sector of the NGO community, that the emphasis on growth had caused the environmental crisis in the first place. The World Bank accepted the concerns of the Report to some degree. When faced with an NGO spotlight on the adverse environmental implications of its projects, the Bank moved to introduce more rigorous environmental assessments of its funding activities. Similarly, concerning gender, when faced with critical NGO voices, the World Bank eventually in 1994 came up with its Operational Policy 4.20 on gender. The latter aimed to 'reduce gender disparities and enhance women particularly in the economic development of their countries by integrating gender considerations in its country assistance programmes' (www.worldbank.org).

With the United Nations Conference on the Environment and Development (UNCED—sometimes referred to as the Rio Summit) in June 1992, the idea that the environment and development were inextricably interlinked was taken further. However, what came out of the official inter-state process was legitimation of market-based development policies to further sustainable

development, with self-regulation for transnational corporations. Official output from Rio, such as Agenda 21, however, recognized the huge importance of the sub-state level for addressing sustainability issues, and supported the involvement of marginalized groups. But while the groups had a role in the preparatory process, they have not been given an official role in the follow-up to UNCED. At the alternative summit, where the largest selection of non-governmental views ever expressed was aired, the viability of this strategy was challenged. For example, the possibility of structural adjustment policies being made environment-friendly was seriously questioned.

The process of incorporation has continued ever since. This is seen most recently in the language of poverty reduction being incorporated into World Bank and IMF policies: 'growth with equity' and 'pro-poor growth' are the buzzwords, yet underlying macroeconomic policy remains unchanged. An examination of the contribution of the development orthodoxy to increasing global inequality is not on the agenda. The gendered outcomes of macroeconomic policies are largely ignored. Despite promises of new funding at the UN Monterrey Conference on Financing for Development in 2002, new transfers of finance from developed to developing countries have been slow in coming, and all eyes are fixed now on the new promises made by the G8 at their Summit in 2006. In addition to new finance, that Summit saw commitments to write off $40 billion of debt owed by the Heavily Indebted Poor Countries (HIPCs). However, the commitment was not implemented with immediate effect and didn't cover all needy countries. The North–South agenda has changed little in the years since the Rio Summit, when sustainable development hit the headlines.

It is important to note that some parts of the UN family have been genuinely responsive to criticisms of mainstream development. The UNDP is noteworthy for its advocacy of the measurement of development based on life expectancy, adult literacy, and average local purchasing power—the Human Development Index (HDI). The HDI results in a very different assessment of countries' achievements than does the traditional measurement of development based on per capita GDP (Thomas *et al.* 1994: 22). For example, China, Sri Lanka, Poland, and Cuba fare much better under HDI assessments than they do under more orthodox assessments, while Saudi Arabia and Kuwait fare much worse.

An appraisal of the responses of the orthodox approach to its critics

During 2000, a series of official '+ 5' mini-conferences were held, such as Rio + 5, Copenhagen + 5, and Beijing + 5, to assess progress in specific areas since the major UN conferences five years earlier. The assessments suggested that the international community had fallen short in its efforts to operationalize conference action plans and to mainstream these concerns in **global politics**. For example, a critical reading of Beijing suggests that the conference represented a continuation of the attempts of the 1970s and 1980s to integrate women into prevailing development practice (so-called 'WID'), in other words to increase their economic opportunities within the existing economic system. This stands in contrast to an attempt fundamentally to alter the social and economic power of women relative to men, which would require a transformation in prevailing development practice via the promotion of a gender and development ('GAD') approach. The World Bank's own assessment of its mainstreaming of gender, undertaken by the Social Development Task Force in 1996, concluded that gender concerns are not incorporated systematically into projects and are regarded by many as 'add-ons'.

Voices of criticism are growing in number and range. Even among supporters of the mainstream approach, voices of disquiet are heard as increasingly the maldistribution of the benefits of economic liberalism are seen to have been a threat to local, national, regional, and even global order. Moreover, the social protest which accompanies economic globalization is regarded by some as a potential obstacle to the neo-liberal project. Thus supporters of globalization are keen to temper its most unpopular effects by modification of neo-liberal policies. Small but nevertheless important changes are taking place. For example, the World Bank has guidelines on the treatment of indigenous peoples, resettlement, the environmental impact of its projects, gender, and on disclosure of information. It is implementing social safety nets when pursuing structural adjustment policies, and it is promoting microcredit as a way to empower women. With the IMF, it developed a Heavily Indebted Poor Country (HIPC) Initiative to reduce the debt burden of the poorest states. What is important, however, is whether these guidelines and concerns really inform policy, and whether these new policies and facilities result in practical outcomes that impact on the fundamental causes of poverty.

The Bank has admitted that such changes have been incorporated largely due to the efforts of NGOs which have monitored its work closely and undertaken vigorous international campaigns to change the way the Bank funds projects, and to change its general operational processes. These campaigns continue, with the Bretton Woods Campaign, the Fifty Years is Enough, Jubilee 2000, and, most recently, the Make Poverty History Campaign being particularly significant in calling for open, transparent, and accountable decision-making by global economic institutions, for local involvement in project planning and implementation, and for debt write-off. In addition to the NGO pressure for change, pressure is building within the institutional champions of the neo-liberal development orthodoxy.

There is a tremendously long way to go in terms of gaining credence for the core values of the alternative model of development in the corridors of power, nationally and internationally. Nevertheless, the alternative view, marginal though it is, has had some noteworthy successes in modifying orthodox development. These may not be insignificant for those whose destinies have up till now been largely determined by the attempted universal application of a selective set of local, essentially Western, values.

We have now concluded our examination of the topic of development from the orthodox and alternative approaches and will turn our attention to the topic of hunger.

Key Points

- Development is a contested concept.
- The orthodox or mainstream approach and the alternative approach reflect very different values.
- Development policies over the last sixty years have been dominated by the mainstream approach—embedded liberalism and, more recently neo-liberalism—with a focus on growth.
- The last two decades of the twentieth century saw the flourishing of alternative conceptions of development based on equity, participation, empowerment, sustainability, etc., with input especially from NGOs and grassroots movements and some parts of the UN.
- The mainstream approach has been modified slightly and has incorporated the language of its critics (e.g. pro-poor growth).

Hunger

In addressing the topic of global hunger, it is necessary to face the paradox that while 'the production of food to meet the needs of a burgeoning population has been one of the outstanding global achievements of the post-war period' (ICPF 1994: 104, 106), there were nevertheless in 2006 around 852 million malnourished people in around 80 countries, and at least 40,000 die every day from hunger-related causes. The current depth of hunger across different world regions is shown Fig. 27.3. While famines may be exceptional phenomena, hunger is ongoing. Why is this so?

Broadly speaking there are two schools of thought with regard to hunger: the orthodox, nature-focused approach which identifies the problem largely as one of overpopulation, and the entitlement, society-focused approach, which sees the problem more in terms of distribution. Let us consider each of these two approaches in turn.

The orthodox, nature-focused explanation of hunger

The orthodox explanation of hunger, first mapped out in its essentials by Thomas Robert Malthus in his *Essay on the Principle of Population in* 1798, focuses on the relationship between human population growth and the food supply. It asserts that population growth naturally outstrips the growth in food production, so that a decrease in the per capita availability of food is inevitable, until eventually a point is reached at which starvation, or some other disaster, drastically reduces the human population to a level which can be sustained by the available food supply. This approach therefore places great stress on human overpopulation as being the cause of the problem, and seeks for ways to reduce the fertility of the human

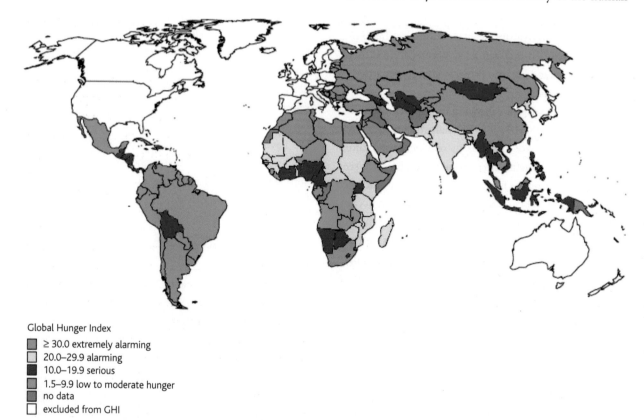

Global Hunger Index

- ≥ 30.0 extremely alarming
- 20.0–29.9 alarming
- 10.0–19.9 serious
- 1.5–9.9 low to moderate hunger
- no data
- excluded from GHI

Source: Wiesmann, Doris (2006). *2006 Global Hunger Index: A Basis for Cross-Country Comparisons*, Issue Brief 47 (Washington, DC: International Food Policy Research Institute). Reproduced with permission from the International Food Policy Research Institute, www.ifpri.org. The brief from which this map comes can be found online at http://www.ifpri.org/pubs/ib/ib47.pdf.

Figure 27.3 Global hunger map, 2006

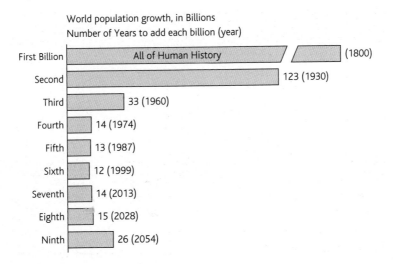

Figure 27.4 World population growth from 1800 with projections to 2050

Source: First and second billion: Population Reference Bureau. Third through ninth billion: United Nations, *World Population Prospects: The 1998 Revision* (medium scenario). See www.prb.org, last accessed 25 June 2007.

race, or rather, that part of the human race which seems to breed faster than the rest—the poor of the 'Third World'. Recent supporters of this approach, such as Paul Ehrlich and Denis and Donella Meadows (1972), argue that there are natural limits to population growth—principally that of the carrying capacity of the land—and that when these limits are exceeded disaster is inevitable.

The available data on the growth of the global human population indicate that it has quintupled since the early 1800s, and is expected to grow from six billion in 1999 to ten billion in 2050. Over 50 per cent of this increase is expected to occur in seven countries: Bangladesh, Brazil, China, India, Indonesia, Nigeria, and Pakistan. Figure 27.4 provides data on world population growth from 1800, with projections through to 2050, and shows that the rate of world population growth is set to increase over the coming decades. Figure 27.5 focuses on the most populous countries—almost all of which are located in the Third World—and only 11 of them account for over half of the world's population. It is figures such as these that have convinced many adherents of the orthodox approach to hunger that it is essential that Third World countries adhere to strict family-planning policies which one way or another limit their population growth rates. Indeed, in the case of the World Bank, most women-related efforts until very recently were in the area of family planning.

The entitlement, society-focused explanation of hunger

Critics of the orthodox approach to hunger and its associated implications argue that it is too simplistic in its analysis and ignores the vital factor of food distribution. They point out that it fails to account for the paradox we observed at the beginning of this discussion on hunger: that despite the enormous increase in food production per capita that has occurred over the post-war period (largely due to the development of high-yielding seeds and industrial agricultural techniques), little impact has been made on the huge numbers of people in the world who experience chronic hunger. For example, the UN Food and Agriculture Organization (FAO) estimates that although there is enough grain alone to provide everyone in the world with 3,600 calories a day (i.e. 1,200 more than the UN's recommended minimum daily intake), there are still over 800 million hungry people.

Furthermore, critics note that the Third World, where the majority of malnourished people are found, produces much of the world's food, while those who consume most of it are located in the Western world. Meat consumption tends to rise with household wealth, and a third of the world's grain is used to fatten animals. A worrying recent trend is the use of corn produced in the USA to produce

Most populous countries, 2003

Rank	Country	Population (millions)
1	China	1,289
2	India	1,069
3	United States	292
4	Indonesia	220
5	Brazil	176
6	Pakistan	149
7	Bangladesh	147
8	Russia	146
9	Nigeria	134
10	Japan	128

Most populous countries, 2050

Rank	Country	Population (millions)
1	India	1,628
2	China	1,394
3	United States	422
4	Pakistan	349
5	Indonesia	316
6	Nigeria	307
7	Bangladesh	255
8	Brazil	221
9	Congo, Dem. Rep. of	181
10	Ethiopia	173

Source: www.prb.org, last accessed 25 June 2007.

Figure. 27.5 Most populous countries, 2003, with projections to 2050

green fuel, thus reducing what is available to feed the hungry overseas. Such evidence leads opponents of the orthodox approach to argue that we need to look much more closely at the social, political, and economic factors that determine how food is distributed and why access to food is achieved by some and denied to others.

A convincing alternative to the orthodox explanation of hunger was set forward in Amartya Sen's pioneering book, *Poverty and Famines: An Essay on Entitlement and Deprivation*, which was first published in 1981. From the results of his empirical research work on the causes of famines, Sen concluded that hunger is due to people not having enough to eat, rather than there not being enough to eat. He discovered that famines have frequently occurred when there has been no significant reduction in the level of per capita food availability and, furthermore, that some famines have occurred during years of peak food availability. For example, the Bangladesh famine of 1974 occurred in a year of peak food availability, yet because floods wiped out the normal employment opportunities of rural labourers, the latter were left with no money to purchase the food which was readily available, and many of them starved.

Therefore, what determines whether a person starves or eats is not so much the amount of food available to them, but whether or not they can establish an entitlement to that food. For example, if there is plenty of food available in the shops, but a family does not have the money to

purchase that food, and does not have the means of growing their own food, then they are likely to starve. The key issue is not therefore per capita food availability, but the distribution of food as determined by the ability of people to establish entitlements to food. With the globalization of the market, and the associated curtailing of subsistence agriculture, the predominant method of establishing an entitlement to food has become that of the exercise of purchasing power, and consequently it is those without purchasing power who will go hungry amid a world of plenty (Sen 1981, 1983).

Sen's focus on entitlement enables him to identify two groups who are particularly at risk of losing their access to food: landless rural labourers—such as in South Asia and Latin America—and pastoralists—such as in sub-Saharan Africa. The landless rural labourers are especially at risk because no arrangements are in place to protect their access to food. In the traditional peasant economy there is some **security** of land ownership, and therefore rural labourers have the possibility of growing their own food. However, this possibility is lost in the early stages of the transition to capitalist agriculture, when the labourers are obliged to sell their land and join the wage-based economy. Unlike in the developed countries of the West, no social security arrangements are in place to ensure that their access to food is maintained. In this context, it is important to note that the IMF/World Bank austerity policies of the 1980s ensured that any little welfare

arrangements that were previously enjoyed by vulnerable groups in developing countries were largely removed, and therefore these policies directly contributed to a higher risk of hunger in the Third World.

Building upon the work of Sen, the researcher Susan George in *The Hunger Machine* (Bennett and George 1987: 1–10) details how different groups of people experience unequal levels of access to food. She identifies six factors which are important in determining who goes hungry: (1) the North–South divide between developed and developing countries; (2) national policies on how wealth is shared; (3) the rural–urban bias; (4) social class; (5) gender; and (6) age. In addition, one could add to the list two other very important, and often neglected, factors determining hunger—that of race and disability. Consequently, people are more likely to experience hunger if they are disabled rather than able-bodied, black rather than white, a child rather than an adult, poor rather than wealthy, a rural dweller rather than a town dweller, and an inhabitant of a developing country rather than a developed country.

Globalization and hunger

It is possible to explain the contemporary occurrence of hunger by reference to the process of globalization. Globalization means that events occurring in one part of the globe can affect, and be affected by, events occurring in other, distant parts of the globe. Often, as individuals, we remain unaware of our role in this process and its ramifications. When we drink a cup of tea or coffee, or eat imported fruit and vegetables, in the developed countries, we tend not to reflect on the changes experienced at the site of production of these cash crops in the developing world. However, it is possible to look at the effect of the establishment of a global, as opposed to a local, national, or regional system of food production. This has been done by David Goodman and Michael Redclift in their book, *Refashioning Nature: Food, Ecology and Culture* (1991), and the closing part of this discussion on hunger is largely based on their findings.

Since 1945, a global food regime has been established, and as we enter the twenty-first century we are witnessing an increasingly global organization of food provision and of access to food, with transnational corporations playing the major role. This has been based on the incorporation of local systems of food production into a global system of food production. In other words, local subsistence producers, who traditionally have produced to meet the needs of their family and community, may now be involved in cash-crop production for a distant market. Alternatively, they may have left the land and become involved in the process of industrialization. The most important actor in the development and expansion of this global food regime has been the USA, which, at the end of the Second World War, was producing large food surpluses. These surpluses became cheap food exports and initially were welcomed by the war-ravaged countries of Europe. They were also welcomed by many developing countries, for the model of development prevalent then depended on the creation of a pool of cheap wage labour to serve the industrialization process. Hence, in order to encourage people off the land and away from subsistence production, the incentive to produce for oneself and one's family had to be removed. Cheap imported food provided this incentive, while the resulting low prices paid for domestic subsistence crops made them unattractive to grow; indeed, for those who continued to produce for the local market, such as in Sudan, the consequence has been the production of food at a loss (Bennett and George 1987: 78). Not surprisingly, therefore, the production of subsistence crops in the developing world for local consumption has drastically declined in the post-war period.

The post-war, US-dominated, global food regime has therefore had a number of unforeseen consequences. First, the domestic production of food staples in developing countries was disrupted. Second, consumer preferences in the importing countries changed in line with the cheap imports, and export markets for American-produced food were created. Effectively, a dependence on food aid was created (Goodman and Redclift 1991: 123). Third, there has been a stress on cash-crop production. The result has been the drive towards export-oriented, large-scale, intensively mechanized agriculture in the South. Technical progress resulted in the 'Green Revolution', with massively increased yields being produced from high-yield seeds and industrialized agricultural practices. This has in some respects been an important achievement. However, the cost has been millions of peasants thrown off the land because their labour was no longer required, the greater concentration of land in a smaller number of hands, and environmental damage from pesticides, fertilizers, and inappropriate irrigation techniques.

With its per capita income of $556, Haiti is the poorest country in the Western hemisphere. Two-thirds of people live in rural areas; 80 per cent are poor. Nearly half the population consumes less than 75 per cent of the recommended intake of food energy. Rice is a major staple of the diet, and mainly produced by small farmers. Twenty per cent of people depend on rice cultivation for their livelihoods, and the sector has a major economic spin-off, with thousands of agricultural labourers, traders, and millers earning their living from it.

In recent years Haiti has undergone rapid trade liberalization, and is now one of the most open economies in the world. Liberalization of the rice market started in the 1980s, but the final stroke came in 1994–5 when, under pressure from the international community (notably the IMF and the USA), the tariff on rice was cut from 35 per cent to 3 per cent.

Rice producers reported that prices fell by 50 per cent during 1986–7, after the first wave of liberalization. In 1995, local production fell by 27 per cent. Rice imports increased by 30 times between 1985 and 1999 as a result of the market slump. Food aid in rice surged from zero in 1994 to 16,000 tonnes in 1999. Most rice imports are of subsidized US rice.

These trends have severely undermined the livelihoods of more than 50,000 rice-farming families and led to a rural exodus. While cheap imports initially benefited poor consumers, in recent years these benefits have vanished . . . the FAO says that overall malnutrition has increased since the start of the trade liberalization, affecting 48 per cent of the population in 1979–81, and 62 per cent in 1996–8. Almost half of Haiti's food needs are now met by imports.

(Oxfam 2003: 10)

Since the early 1980s, the reform of national economies via SAPs has given a further boost to the undermining of the national organization of agriculture, and a further fillip to the activities of agribusiness. Also the aggressive pursuit of unilateralist trade policies by the USA, such as the invocation of free trade to legitimize prising open the Korean agricultural market, has added to this. Global trade liberalization since the early 1980s, and especially the Uruguay Round's Agreement on Agriculture (the original text of which was drafted by the multinational Cargill's Vice President Dan Amstutz—Oxfam 2003: 23), are further eroding local food security and throwing peasant producers and their families off the land. The Haitian example portrayed in Case Study Box 27.6 is repeated cross the developing world; for example, the crisis facing Niger, 2005-6 has been called a 'free market

famine' (Mousseau and Mittal: 2006: 1). This has fuelled resentment in the South about the global rules governing agriculture. For example, in India disputes over intellectual property rights in regard to high-yielding crop seeds have resulted in violent protest by peasant farmers at foreign-owned seed factories. In the North, NGOs have campaigned against the double standards operated by their governments in expecting Southern countries to liberalize their food markets while Northern economies continue to be protected and while Northern agriculture is heavily subsidized.

We have now concluded our discussion of the three topics of poverty, development, and hunger, and in the last part of this chapter we will assess the likelihood of globalization with a more human face.

Key Points

- In recent decades global food production has burgeoned, but paradoxically hunger and malnourishment remain widespread.
- The orthodox explanation for the continued existence of hunger is that population growth outstrips food production.
- An alternative explanation for the continuation of hunger focuses on lack of access or entitlement to available food. Access and

entitlement are affected by factors such as the North–South global divide, particular national policies, rural–urban divides, class, gender, and race.
- Globalization can simultaneously contribute to increased food production and increased hunger.

Conclusion: looking to the future—globalization with a human face?

It is clear when we consider the competing conceptions of poverty, development, and hunger explored above that there is no consensus on definitions, causes, or solutions.

We are faced with an awesome development challenge. Early indications suggest that the UN Millennium Development Goal (MDG) targets will not be met. Most gains are being made in very few countries like China and India, and even within those states there remain deep pockets of poverty. Beyond, the picture is less encouraging. If sub-Saharan Africa continues on its current course, it will take another 150 years to reach the MDG target of halving poverty, and the hunger situation continues to worsen there (UNDP 2003).

The orthodox model of development is being held up for closer scrutiny, as we become more aware of the risks as well as the opportunities which globalization and the Washington Consensus bring in their wake. The key question is: can globalization develop a human face?

Opinions differ. For Michel Camdessus, speaking as Head of the IMF, it is clear that a new reformist paradigm of development is already emerging which entails the 'progressive humanization of basic economic concepts' (Camdessus 2000). However, more critical voices see in the reforms under way a complete failure to tackle fundamental issues of redistribution, which require valuing an economic system only if it works for people and the planet.

The current development orthodoxy is following the reformist pathway. History will reveal whether this pathway bears the seeds of its own destruction by delivering too little, too late to too few people. As students of International Relations it is imperative that we bring these issues in from the margins of our discipline and pursue them as central to our study.

❓ Questions

1 What does poverty mean?

2 Explain the orthodox approach to development and outline the criteria by which it measures development.

3 Assess the critical alternative model of development.

4 How effectively has the orthodox model of development neutralized the critical, alternative view?

5 Compare and contrast the orthodox and alternative explanations of hunger.

6 What are the pros and cons of the global food regime established since the Second World War?

7 Account for the increasing gap between rich and poor states and people after fifty years of official development policies.

8 Critically explore the gendered nature of poverty.

9 Is the recent World Bank focus on poverty reduction evidence of a change of direction by the Bank?

10 Which development pathway—the reformist or the alternative—do you regard as the more likely to contribute to global peace in the twenty-first century?

11 Are national poverty reduction strategies contributing to national ownership of development policies in the Third World?

12 Why has the discipline of International Relations been slow to engage with issues of poverty and development?

➜ Guide to further reading

General

Adams, N. B. (1993), *Worlds Apart: The North–South Divide and the International System* (London: Zed). Presents a broad economic and political history of the North–South divide, and focuses on the role of the international economic system. This book provides an effective introduction to the politics of North–South economic relations over the past half-century.

Kiely, R. (2006), *The New Political Economy of Development: Globalization, Imperialism and Hegemony* (Basingstoke: Palgrave Macmillan). An important new text which examines development in a historic and political-economic context. This is a book for ambitious students who want to take their understanding of development to a deeper level.

Rapley, J. (1996), *Understanding Development* (Boulder, Col.: Lynne Rienner). Analyzes the theory and practice of development in the Third World since the Second World War in a straightforward, succinct manner. It provides the reader with a firm grasp of changing development policies at the international level and their take-up over time in different states.

Thomas, C. (2000), *Global Governance, Development and Human Security* (London: Pluto). Examines the global development policies pursued by global governance institutions, especially the IMF and the World Bank, in the 1980s and 1990s. It assesses the impact of these policies on human security, and analyzes different paths towards the achievement of human security for the twenty-first century.

Development

Rahnema, M., with Bawtree, V. (eds) (1997), *The Post Development Reader* (Dhaka: University Press, and London: Zed). Challenges the reader to think critically about the nature of development and assumptions about meanings. This is an extremely stimulating interdisciplinary reader.

Hunger

Dreze, J., Sen, A., Hussain, A. (eds) (1995), The *Political Economy of Hunger* (Oxford: Clarendon Press). An excellent collection on the political economy of hunger.

Sen, A. (1981), *Poverty and Famines* (Oxford: Clarendon Press). Provides a ground-breaking analysis of the causes of hunger which incorporates detailed studies of a number of famines and convincingly challenges the orthodox view of the causes of hunger.

Wiesmann, D. (2006), *Global Hunger Index 2006: A Basis for Cross-country Comparisons*, Issue Brief 47 (Washington, DC: International Food Policy Research Institute). The Global Hunger Index (GHI), published by the International Food Policy Research Institute, was developed in 2006 to increase attention on the hunger problem and to mobilize the political will to address it.

Online Resource Centre

 Visit the Online Resource Centre that accompanies this book to access more learning resources on this chapter topic at www.oxfordtextbooks.co.uk/uk/orc/baylis_smith4e/

Chapter 28

Human security

AMITAV ACHARYA[1]

- Introduction ···492
- What is human security? ·····························492
- Debates about human security ·····················494
- Dimensions of human security ·····················496
- Promoting human security ·······························502
- Conclusion ···504

Reader's Guide

This chapter examines the origins of the concept of human security, debates surrounding its definition and scope, some of the threats to human security in the world today, and international efforts to promote human security. It proceeds in four parts. The section, 'What is human security?', traces the origin and evolution of the concept, and examines competing definitions offered by scholars and policy-makers. The next section reviews debates and controversies about human security, especially over the analytic and policy relevance of the notion, and the broad and narrow meanings of the concept ('freedom from fear' versus 'freedom from want'). The third section examines some of the threats to human security today. While the concept of human security encompasses a wide range of threats, due to lack of space, this section will focus on the trends in armed conflicts as well as the interrelationship between conflict and other non-violent threats to human security, such as poverty, disease, and environmental degradation. The final section analyzes the international community's efforts to promote human security and concludes by identifying the major challenges to promoting the notion of human security today.

Introduction

The concept of **human security** represents a powerful, but controversial, attempt by sections of the academic and policy community to redefine and broaden the meaning of **security**. Traditionally, security meant protection of the **sovereignty** and territorial integrity of **states** from external military threats. This was the essence of the concept of **national security**, which dominated security analysis and policy-making during the cold war period. In the 1970s and 1980s, academic literature on security, responding to the Middle East oil crisis and the growing awareness of worldwide environmental degradation, began to think of security in broader, non-military terms. Yet, the state remained the object of security, or the entity that is to be protected. The concept of human security challenges the state-centric notion of security by focusing on the individual as the main referent object of security.

Human security is about security for the people, rather than of states or governments. As such, it has generated much debate. Critics wonder whether such an approach would widen the boundaries of security studies too much, and whether 'securitizing' the individual is the best way to address the challenges facing the international community from the forces of **globalization**. On the other side, advocates of human security find the concept to be an important step forward in highlighting the dangers to human safety and survival posed by **poverty**, disease, environmental stress, human rights abuses, as well as armed conflict. These disagreements notwithstanding, the concept of human security captures a growing realization that, in an era of rapid globalization, security must encompass a broader range of concerns and challenges than simply defending the state from external military attack.

What is human security?

The origin of the concept of human security can be traced to the publication of the *Human Development Report* of 1994, issued by the United Nations Development Programme (UNDP 1994). The Report defined the scope of human security to include seven areas:

- Economic security—an assured basic income for individuals, usually from productive and remunerative work, or, in the last resort, from some publicly financed safety net.
- Food security—ensuring that all people at all times have both physical and economic access to basic food.
- Health security—guaranteeing a minimum protection from diseases and unhealthy lifestyles.
- Environmental security—protecting people from the short- and long-term ravages of nature, man-made threats in nature, and deterioration of the natural environment.
- Personal security—protecting people from physical violence, whether from the state or external states, from violent individuals and sub-state factors, from domestic abuse, and from predatory adults.

- Community security—protecting people from the loss of traditional relationships and values, and from sectarian and ethnic violence.
- Political security—ensuring that people live in a society that honours their basic human rights and ensuring the freedom of individuals and groups from government attempts to exercise control over ideas and information.

Unlike many other efforts to redefine security where political scientists played a major role, human security was the handiwork of a group of development economists, such as the late Pakistani economist Mahabub ul Haq, who conceptualized the UNDP's *Human Development Report*. They were increasingly dissatisfied with the orthodox notion of development, which viewed it as a function of economic growth. Instead, they proposed a concept of **human development** which focuses on building human **capabilities** to confront and overcome poverty, illiteracy, diseases, discrimination, restrictions on political freedom, and the threat of violent conflict: 'Individual freedoms and rights matter a great deal, but people are restricted in what

Box 28.1 A contested concept

'Human security can be said to have two main aspects. It means, first, safety from such chronic threats as hunger, disease and repression. And second, it means protection from sudden and hurtful disruptions in the patterns of daily life – whether in homes, in jobs or in communities. Such threats can exist at all levels of national income and development.'

(UNDP 1994)

'Human security is not a concern with weapons. It is a concern with human dignity. In the last analysis, it is a child who did not die, a disease that did not spread, an ethnic tension that did not explode, a dissident who was not silenced, a human spirit that was not crushed'.

(Mahbub ul Haq 1995)

'For Canada, human security means from pervasive threats to people's rights, safety or lives. ... Through its foreign policy, Canada has chosen to focus its human security agenda on promoting safety for people by protecting them from threats of violence.'

(Department of Foreign Affairs and International Trade (Canada) 2000)

'the concept of human security had better be confined to freedom from fear of *man-made* physical violence, also referred to as direct, personal violence. A broader understanding of human security as freedom from structural violence will undermine the clarity of the notion and make it difficult to develop priorities and devise effective policy responses.'

(Sverre Lodgaard 2000)

'Human security may be defined as the preservation and protection of the life and dignity of individual human beings. Japan holds the view, as do many other countries, that human security can be ensured only when the individual is confident of a life free of fear and free of want.'

(Japanese Foreign Ministry Official, 2000, http://www.mofa.go.jp/ policy/human_secu/speech0006.html)

'Human security can no longer be understood in purely military terms. Rather, it must encompass economic development, social justice, environmental protection, democratization, disarmament, and respect for human rights and the rule of law. ... Moreover, these pillars are interrelated; progress in one area generates progress in another.'

(Kofi Annan 2001)

'The objective of human security is to safeguard the "vital core of all human lives in ways that enhance human freedoms and human fulfilment"'.

(UN Commission on Human Security 2003)

they can do with that freedom if they are poor, ill, illiterate, discriminated against, threatened by violent conflict or denied a political voice . . .' (UNDP 2005: 18–19).

Closely related to the attempt to create a broader paradigm for development was the growing concern about of the negative impact of defence spending on development, or the so-called 'guns versus butter' dilemma. As a global study headed by Inga Thorsson of Sweden concluded, 'the arms race and development are in a competitive relationship' (Roche 1986: 8). Drawing upon this study, a UN-sponsored International Conference on the Relationship between Disarmament and Development in 1986 in Paris sought 'to enlarge world understanding that human security demands more resources for development and fewer for arms'.

The move towards human security was also advanced by the work of several international commissions. They offered a broader view of security which looked beyond the cold war emphasis on East–West military competition. Foremost among them was the Report of the Palme Commission of 1982, which proposed the doctrine of 'common security'. The Report stressed that: 'In the Third World countries, as in all our countries, security requires economic progress as well as freedom from military fear' (Palme Commission 1982: xii). In 1987, the Report of the World Commission on Environment and Development (also known as the Brundtland Commission) highlighted the linkage between environmental degradation and conflict: 'The real sources of insecurity encompass unsustainable development, and its effects can become intertwined with traditional forms of conflict in a manner that can extend and deepen the latter' (Brundtland *et al.* 1987: 230)

Along with attempts to broaden the notion of security to include non-military threats, there was also a growing emphasis on the individual as the central object of security. The Palme Commission's notion of **common security** became the conceptual basis of the Conference on Security and Cooperation in Europe (CSCE). The CSCE made East–West security **cooperation** conditional upon the improvement of the human rights situation in the former Soviet bloc. The North–South Roundtable on the 'Economics of Peace', held in Costa Rica in 1990, called for a shift from 'an almost exclusive concern with military security … to a broader concern for overall security of individuals from social violence, economic distress and environmental degradation' (Jolly and Ray 2006: 3).

In the post-cold war era, the importance given to people's security has grown in salience. One reason for this is the rising incidence of civil wars and intra-state conflicts involving huge loss of life, ethnic cleansing, displacement of people within and across borders, and disease outbreaks. Traditional national security approaches have not been sufficiently sensitive towards conflicts that arise over cultural, ethnic, and religious differences, as

happened in Eastern Europe, Africa, and Central Asia in the post-cold war era (Tow and Trood 2000). Another reason is the spread of democratization and the post-cold war emphasis on human rights and **humanitarian intervention**. The latter involves the principle that the international community is justified in intervening in the internal affairs of states accused of gross violation of human rights. This has led to the realization that while the concept of national security has not been rendered irrelevant, it no longer sufficiently accounts for the kinds of danger that threaten the societies, states, and the international community. The notion of human security has also been brought to the fore by the crises induced by accelerating globalization. For example, the widespread poverty, unemployment, and social dislocation caused by the Asian financial crisis 1997 underscored the vulnerability of people to the effects of economic globalization (Acharya 2004).

Key Points

- The concept of human security represents both a vertical and horizontal expansion (or deepening and widening) of the traditional notion of national security, defined as protection of state sovereignty and territorial integrity from external military threats.
- In its broader sense, human security is distinguished by three elements: (1) its focus on the individual/people as the referent object of security; (2) its multidimensional nature; (3) its universal or global scope, applying to states and societies of the North as well as the South.
- The concept of human security has been influenced by four developments: (1) the rejection of economic growth as the main indicator of development and the accompanying notion of 'human development' as empowerment of people; (2) the rising incidence of internal conflicts; (3) the impact of globalization in spreading transnational dangers such as terrorism and pandemics; and (4) the post-cold war emphasis on human rights and humanitarian intervention.

Debates about human security

Debates over human security fall into two categories. First, believers and sceptics of the concept disagree over whether human security is a new or necessary notion and what are the costs and benefits of adopting it as an intellectual tool or a policy framework. Second, there have been debates over the scope of the concept, mainly among the believers themselves.

For critics of human security, the concept is too broad to be analytically meaningful or useful as a tool of policymaking. Roland Paris has argued: 'Existing definitions of human security tend to be extraordinarily expansive and vague, encompassing everything from physical security to psychological well-being, which provides policymakers with little guidance in the prioritization of competing policy goals and academics little sense of what, exactly, is to be studied' (Paris 2001: 88).

Another criticism is that such a concept might cause more harm than good: 'Speaking loudly about human security but carrying a Band-Aid only gives false hopes to both the victims of oppression and the international community' (Khong 2001: 3). The definition of human security is seen to be too moralistic compared to the traditional understanding of security, and hence unattainable and unrealistic (Tow and Trood 2000: 14).

A third and perhaps most powerful criticism of human security is that it neglects the role of the state as a provider of security. Buzan argues that states are a 'necessary condition for individual security because without the state it is not clear what other agency is to act on behalf of individuals' (Buzan 2001: 589). This criticism has been echoed my others, especially scholars with a realist orientation.

Advocates of human security have never totally discounted the importance of the state as a guarantor of human security. As the Report of the Commission on Human Security (UN Commission on Human Security 2003) acknowledges, 'Human security complements state security'. Nor do they claim that human and traditional security concerns are always antithetical. Weak states are often incapable of protecting the safety and dignity of their citizens. But whether traditional state security and human security conflict with each other depends very much on the nature of the regime that presides over the state. In many countries, human security as security for the people can

	Freedom from want	Freedom from fear
Original proponents	Development economists, Mahabub ul Haq, Amartya Sen	Western governments (Canada, Norway)
Main stimulus	Dissatisfaction over orthodox growth-oriented development models; guns versus butter concerns	End of the cold war; rise of complex emergencies, ethnic strife, state failure, humanitarian intervention
Type of threats addressed	Non-military and non-traditional security concerns: poverty, environmental degradation, disease, etc.	Armed conflicts, violence against individuals
Main policy goal	Promoting human development, defined as 'building human capabilities—the range of things that people can do, and what they can be. . . . The most basic capabilities for human development are leading a long and healthy life, being educated and having adequate resources for a decent standard of living . . . [and] social and political participation in society'. These capabilities are undermined by poverty, disease and ill-health, illiteracy, discrimination, threat of violent conflict, and denial of political and civil liberties. *(UNDP 2005: 18–19)*	Protecting people in conflict zones; reducing the human costs of conflict through a ban on landmines and child soldiers; protecting human rights; developing peace-building mechanisms.

Table 28.1 Two conceptions of human security

and does get threatened by the actions of their own governments. Hence, while the 'state remains the fundamental purveyor of security . . . it often fails to fulfil its security obligations—and at times has even become a source of threat to its own people' (Mack 2004: 366). At the very least, from a human security perspective, the state cannot be regarded as the sole source of protection for the individuals. (Mack 2004: 366).

Another major debate about human security has occurred over the scope of the concept: whether it should be primarily about 'freedom from fear' or 'freedom from want'. The former view, initially articulated by the former Canadian External Affairs Minister, Lloyd Axworthy, focuses on reducing the human costs of violent conflicts through measures such as a ban on landmines, using women and children in armed conflict, child soldiers, child labour, and small arms proliferation, the formation of an International Criminal Court, and promulgating human rights and international humanitarian law (Department of Foreign Affairs and International Trade (Canada) 1999; *The Ottawa Citizen*, 28 May 1998: A18). From this perspective, the UN Charter, the Universal Declaration of Human Rights, and the Geneva Conventions are the 'core elements' of the doctrine of human security. The latter view, advocated by Japan (Director-General of the Foreign Ministry of Japan 2000), is closer to the original UNDP formulation. It stresses the ability of individuals and societies to be free from a broad range of non-military threats, such as poverty, disease, and environmental degradation (see Table 28.1).

But the differences between the two conceptions of human security can be overstated, since both regard the individual as the referent object of security, and both acknowledge the role of globalization and the changing nature of armed conflict in creating new threats to human security. Moreover, both perspectives stress safety from violence as a key objective of human security, and both call for a rethinking of **state sovereignty** as a necessary part of promoting human security. (Hubert 2004: 351). There is considerable overlap between the two conceptions: '[D]evelopment . . .[is] a necessary condition for [human] security, just as security is a necessary condition for [human] development' (University of British Columbia, Human Security Center (hereafter *Human Security Report*) 2005: 155). Seeking freedom from fear without addressing freedom from want would amount to addressing symptoms without the cause. As the following section shows, while the deaths caused by armed conflicts have declined, other challenges to the safety and well-being of the individual have remained, and in some cases escalated.

Key Points

- The concept of human security has been criticized: (1) for being too broad to be analytically meaningful or to serve as the basis for policy-making; (2) for creating false expectations about assistance to victims of violence which the international community cannot deliver; and (3) for ignoring the role of the state in providing security to the people.
- Even among its advocates differences exist as to whether human security is about 'freedom from fear' or 'freedom from want'. The former stresses protecting people from violent conflicts through measures such as a ban on landmines and child soldiers. For the latter, human security is a broader notion involving the reduction of threats to the well-being of people, such as poverty and disease.
- Ultimately, however, both sides agree that human security is about security of the individuals rather than states, and that protecting people requires going beyond traditional principles of state sovereignty.

Dimensions of human security

A pioneering report released by the Human Security Center at the University of British Columbia (2005) points to several significant trends in armed conflicts around the world (see Box 28.2 for some of the Report's main findings).

What explains the downward trend in armed conflicts around the world?[2] The report lists several factors: growing democratization (the underlying assumption here being that democracies tend to be better at peaceful resolution of conflicts); rising economic **interdependence** (which increases the costs of conflict); the declining economic utility of war owing to the fact that resources can be more easily bought in the international market-place than acquired through force; the growth in the number of international **institutions** that can mediate in conflicts; the impact of international **norms** against violence, such as human sacrifice, witch-burning, slavery, duelling, war crimes, and genocide; the end of colonialism; and the end of the cold war. A specific reason identified by the Report is the dramatic increase in the UN's role in areas such as preventive **diplomacy** and **peacemaking** activities, **post-conflict peacebuilding**, the willingness of the UN Security Council to use military action to enforce peace agreements, the deterrent effects of war crime trials by the International Criminal Court (ICC) and other tribunals, and the greater resort to reconciliation and addressing the root causes of conflict. The 80 per cent decline in the most deadly civil conflicts since the early 1990s, argued the Report, is due to the dramatic growth of international efforts at preventive diplomacy, peacemaking, and peacebuilding (*Human Security Report* 2005: Part V).

Yet, the picture is not entirely positive. The decline in armed conflicts reported by the *Human Security Report* is from 1991 onwards. The number of armed conflicts had actually increased between 1960 and 1990–1, especially intra-state conflicts (which jumped from twelve in 1960

Box 28.2   Trends in conflict

- A 40% drop in armed conflicts in the world since 1991. (This counts only conflicts with at least 25 battle-related deaths where one of the parties was a state.)
- An 80% decline in the number of genocide and 'politicides'* between the high point in 1988 and 2001.
- A 70% decline in the number of international crises between 1981 and 2001.
- A 45% decrease in the number of refugees between 1992 and 2003. The number of internally displaced persons has increased, although accurate information is hard to obtain.

- A 98% decline in the average number of battle deaths per conflict per year. In 1950, an average armed conflict killed 38,000 people. In 2002, the figure was 600.**

(Source: University of British Columbia, Human Security Center (2005))

* The term 'politicide' describes policies that seek to destroy groups because of their political beliefs rather than religion or ethnicity (the latter being captured by the term 'genocide').

** Most of the battle deaths in the cold war period were accounted for by the Korean and Vietnam Wars. If these are excluded, the drop in battle deaths will be less dramatic.

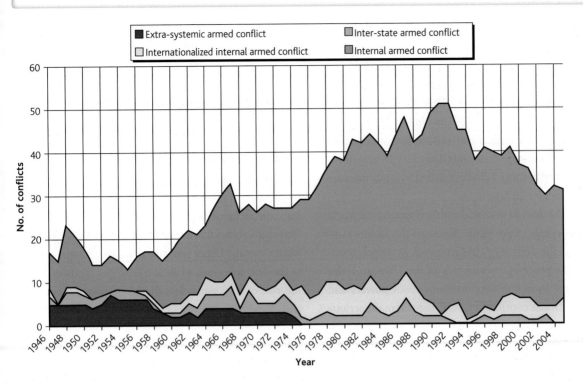

Legend:
- Extra-systemic armed conflict
- Inter-state armed conflict
- Internationalized internal armed conflict
- Internal armed conflict

Source: Uppsala Conflict Data Project (UCDP), Uppsala University, http://www.pcr.uu.se/research/UCDP/graphs/type/_year.gif, last accessed 25 June 2007.

Figure 28.1 Conflicts by type, 1946–2005

to 49 in 1991). And there are still 121 active armed conflicts during the 1989–2005 period (some of them started before 1989).[3] As Figure 28.1 shows, armed conflicts are now on the same level as during the 1970s, and markedly higher than during the 1950s and early 1960s.

And there are some horrific costs associated with these conflicts. For example, deaths directly or indirectly attributed to the conflict in the Democratic Republic of the Congo since 1998 have surpassed casualties sustained by Britain in the First World War and Second World War combined. The conflict in Sudan's Darfur region has displaced nearly 2 million people. (UNDP 2005: 12). In Iraq, a team of American and Iraqi epidemiologists estimates that Iraq's mortality rate has more than doubled since the US invasion: from 5.5 deaths per 1,000 people in the year before the invasion to 13.3 deaths per 1,000 people per year in the post-invasion period. In all, some 655,000 more people have died in Iraq since the invasion in March 2003 than would have died if the invasion had not occurred (Brown 2006: A12).

The share of civilian casualties in armed conflict has increased since the Second World War. Civilians accounted for 10 per cent of the victims during the First World War and 50 per cent of the victims during the Second World War. They constitute between 80 and 85 per cent of the victims of more recent wars. Many of these victims are children, women, the sick, and the elderly (*Gendering Human Security* 2001: 18). Although death tolls from organized campaigns against civilians have declined in recent years, the number of such campaigns increased by 55 per cent between 1989 and 2005 (Univeristy of British Columbia, Human Security Center 2006: 3).

International terrorist incidents and the number of fatalities increased worldwide between 2002 and 2005. Most of the increases were associated with the war in Iraq, where the number of fatalities grew from about 1,700 in 2004 to approximately 3,400 in 2005 (National Counterterrorism Center 2005). Excluding Iraq, however, terrorist action killed fewer people worldwide in 2005—1,500 as opposed to 3,000 in 2004 (National Counterterrorism Center 2005).

Furthermore, some of the most serious issues of human security in armed conflicts still need to be overcome, such as child soldiers and landmines. According to one study,

75 per cent of the armed conflicts today involve child soldiers (*Human Security Report* 2005: 35). Landmines and
unexploded ordnance cause between 15,000 and 20,000
new casualties each year (United States Campaign to Ban
Land Mines, date accessed 3 February 2007). Despite the
justified optimism generated by the Ottawa Treaty (to be
discussed later), there remain 80 million live mines unde-
tected—someone steps on a landmine every 28 minutes—
and 80 per cent of those killed or injured by landmines are
civilians (Koehler 2007).

Finally, the decline in armed conflicts around the world
is not necessarily irreversible. Some of the factors contributing to the decline of conflicts, such as democratization and the peace operations role of the UN, can suffer
setbacks due to lack of support from major **powers** and
the international community. And there remain serious
possible threats to international peace and security which
can cause widespread casualties, such as a conflict in the
Korean peninsula, and war between China and Taiwan.

Battle deaths are not itself an adequate indicator of
threats to human security posed by armed conflict. Many
armed conflicts have indirect consequences on human life
and well-being. Wars are a major source of economic disruption, disease, and ecological destruction, which in turn
undermine human development and thus create a vicious
cycle of conflict and underdevelopment. As the *Human
Development Report* (UNDP 2005: 12) puts it: 'Conflict
undermines nutrition and public health, destroys education systems, devastates livelihoods and retards prospects
for economic growth.' It found that out of the 52 countries that are reversing or stagnating in their attempts to
reduce child mortality, 30 have experienced conflict since
1990. A British government *White Paper* on International
Development notes:

> Violent conflict reverses economic growth, causes hunger,
> destroys roads, schools and clinics, and forces people to
> flee across borders. . . . Women and girls are particularly
> vulnerable because they suffer sexual violence and
> exploitation. And violent conflict and insecurity can spill
> over into neighbouring countries and provide cover for
> terrorists or organised criminal groups.
>
> *(Department for International Development 2006: 45)*

Wars also damage the environment, as happened
with the US use of Agent Orange defoliant during the
Vietnam War or Saddam Hussein's burning of Kuwaiti
oil wells in the 1990–1 Gulf War, leading to massive air
and land pollution. Similar links can be made between

conflict and the outbreak of disease: '[W]ar-exacerbated
disease and malnutrition kill far more people than missile, bombs and bullets' (*Human Security Report* 2005: 7).
Disease accounts for most of the 3.9 million people who
have died in the conflict in the Democratic Republic of
Congo (UNDP 2005: 45).

Just as wars and violent conflict have indirect consequences in causing economic disruption, ecological
damage, and disease, levels of poverty and environmental
degradation contribute to conflict and hence must be taken
into consideration in human security research (see Ch.27).
One study shows that a country at US$250 GDP per capita
has an average 15 per cent risk of experiencing a civil war
in the next five years, while at a GDP per capita of $5,000,
the risk of civil war is less than 1 per cent (Humphreys
and Varshney 2004: 9; Department for International
Development 2005: 8). While no direct link can be established between poverty and terrorism, terrorists often
'exploit poverty and exclusion in order to tap into popular discontent—taking advantage of fragile states such as
Somalia, or undemocratic regimes such as in Afghanistan
in the 1990s, to plan violence' (UNDP 2005: 47).

Environmental degradation, which is often linked to
poverty, is another source of conflict (Homer-Dixon 1991,
1994). Analysts have identified competition for scarce
resources as a source of possible conflict between Israel
and its Arab neighbours, India and Pakistan, Turkey and
Syria, Egypt and Ethiopia (Rice 2006: 78). The world's
poorer countries, where families often see the need for
more children to compensate for a high infant mortality
rate and to raise their income potential, account for a significant proportion of the growth in the world's population,
which has doubled between 1950 and 1998 (Rice 2006: 80).
Population growth, in turn, contributes to resource scarcity
and environmental stress, often resulting in conflict. For
example, South Asia, one of the poorest and most heavily populated regions of the globe, faces intensified competition and the possibility of conflict over scarce water
resources. Examples include the Indo-Pakistan dispute
over the Wular Barrage, the Indo-Bangladesh water dispute over the Farakka Barrage, and the Indo-Nepal dispute
over the Mahakali River Treaty (Power and Interest News
Report 2006). The potential for political upheaval or war
as a consequence of environmental problems is evident in
a host of poor regions around the world, including North
Africa, the sub-Saharan Sahel region of Africa (including Ethiopia, Sudan, Somalia, Mali, Niger, and Chad),

Box 28.3 Key facts about disease

Those who take a broad definition of **human security** look not only at threats to the survival and safety of the individual from violent conflict, but also from such non-violent factors as disease, environmental degradation, and natural disasters. Below are some of the key trends in disease.

- The world has seen the appearance of at least 30 new infectious diseases, including avian flu, HIV/AIDS, Severe Acute Respiratory Syndrome, Hepatitis C, and West Nile virus, in the past three decades. Twenty diseases previously detected have re-emerged with new drug-resistant strains. *(Rice 2006: 79)*
- AIDS is the leading cause of death in Africa and the fourth leading cause of death worldwide. Around 40 million people worldwide are infected with HIV, 95% of whom live in developing countries. In 2004, approximately 5 million people were newly infected with the virus. HIV/AIDS killed more than 20 million people worldwide, and 3.1 million people died of AIDS-related causes in 2004. It is estimated that per capita growth in half of the countries in sub-Saharan Africa is falling by 0.5–1.2% each year as a direct result of AIDS. By 2010, per capita GDP in some of the hardest-hit countries may drop by 8% and per capita consumption may fall even farther (The Global Fund to Fight AIDS, Tuberculosis and Malaria, http://

www.theglobalfund.org/en/about/aids/).
- Malaria causes about 350–500 million infections in humans and approximately 1–3 million deaths annually (Breman 2001: 1–11)—this would translate as about one death every 30 seconds (Greenwood *et al.* 2005: 1487–98). The majority, which amounts to 85–90% of malaria fatalities, occurs in sub-Saharan Africa. The economic impact of malaria has been estimated to cost Africa US$12 billion every year. *(World Health Organization n.d.)*
- Annually, 8 million people become ill with tuberculosis, and 2 million people die from the disease worldwide (Center, for Disease Control 2005). Presently, tuberculosis is the world's greatest infectious killer of women of reproductive age and the leading cause of death among people with HIV/AIDS. *(PR Newswire Europe 2002)*
- The outbreaks of highly pathogenic H5N1 avian influenza that began in South-East Asia in mid-2003 and have now spread to parts of Europe are the largest and most severe on record. To date, nine Asian countries have reported outbreaks (listed in order of reporting): the Republic of Korea, Vietnam, Japan, Thailand, Cambodia, the Lao People's Democratic Republic, Indonesia, China, and Malaysia. *(World Health Organization 2006)*

---

the island nations of the western Pacific Ocean, the Ganges River basin (principally north-eastern India and Bangladesh), and some parts of Central and South America (Petzold-Bradley, Carius, and Vincze 2001). Darfur illustrates the linkage between poverty, environmental degradation, and conflict. Traditional inter-communal conflict in Darfur over scarcity of resources and land deteriorated as a result of desertification and a shortage of rainfall. In the 1970s and 1980s, droughts in northern parts of Darfur sent its nomadic population to migrate southwards in search of water and herding grounds, and brought them into conflict with the local tribes (Environmental Degradation and Conflict in Darfur 2004).

Natural disasters can also affect the course of conflicts by either exacerbating or mitigating them. The December 2004 Indian Ocean tsunami changed the course of two separatist conflicts: Aceh in Indonesia and Tamil separatism in Sri Lanka. In Aceh, where the government announced a ceasefire to permit relief work, improved prospects for reconciliation followed. In contrast, the conflict in Sri Lanka, where relief supplies did not reach rebel-held territory, saw an escalation of violence.

From the foregoing discussion, we can establish a conceptual link between the broader and narrower understandings of human security (see Figs 28.2 and 28.3).

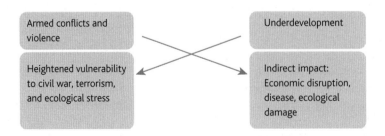

Figure 28.2 Conflict and underdevelopment: the vicious interaction

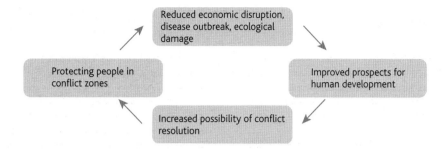

Figure 28.3 Protection and development: the virtuous interaction

Women, conflict, and human security

The relationship between gender and human security has multiple dimensions. The United Nations Inter-Agency Committee on Women and Gender Equality notes five aspects: (1) violence against women and girls; (2) gender inequalities in control over resources; (3) gender inequalities in power and decision-making; (4) women's human rights; and (5) women (and men) as actors, not victims (United Nations Inter-Agency Committee on Women and Gender Equality 1999: 1). Recent conflicts have shown women as victims of rape, torture, and sexual slavery. For example, between 250,000 and 500,000 women were raped during the 1994 genocide in Rwanda. Such atrocities against women are now recognized as a crime against humanity (Rehn and Sirleaf 2002: 9).

War-affected areas often see a sharp increase in domestic violence directed at women and a growth in the number of women trafficked to become forced laboures or sex workers. Women and children comprise 73 per cent of an average population, but account for 80 per cent of the refugees in the world today, and perhaps a larger percentage as internally displaced persons. Another important aspect of the gender dimension of human security is the role of women as actors in conflicts. This involves considering the participation of women in combat. In the Eritrean war of independence, women made up 25–30 per cent of combatants. A similar proportion of women are fighting with the Tamil Tigers. Women play an even larger role in support functions, such as logistics, staff, and intelligence services in a conflict. It has been noted that women become targets of rape and sexual violence because they serve as a social and cultural symbol. Hence violence against them may be undertaken as a deliberate strategy by parties to a conflict with a view to undermine the social fabric of their opponents. Similarly, securing women's participation in combat may be motivated by a desire among the parties to a conflict to increase the legitimacy of their cause. It signifies 'a broad social consensus and solidarity, both to their own population and to the outside world' (*Gendering Human Security* 2001: 18).

In recent years, there has been a growing awareness of the need to secure the greater participation of women in international peace operations. The UN Department of Peacekeeping Operations noted in a 2000 report that:

> Women's presence [in peacekeeping missions] improves access and support for local women; it makes male peacekeepers more reflective and responsible; and it broadens the repertoire of skills and styles available within the mission, often with the effect of reducing conflict and confrontation. Gender mainstreaming is not just fair, it is beneficial.
>
> *(cited in Rehn and Sirleaf 2002: 63)*

In 2000, the UN Security Council passed a resolution (Security Council Resolution 1325) mandating a review of the impact of armed conflict on women and the role of women in peace operations and conflict resolution. The review was released in 2002, entitled *Women, Peace and Security* (UN 2002). In his introduction to the report, UN Secretary General Kofi Annan noted that that 'women still form a minority of those who participate in peace and security negotiations, and receive less attention than men in post-conflict agreements, disarmament and reconstruction' (UN 2002: ix). There is still a long way to go before the international community can fully realize the benefits of greater participation by women in UN peace operations and conflict resolution activities.

Key Points

• There has been a noticeable decline in the number of armed conflicts and battle deaths caused by conflicts. Factors contributing to this trend include rising economic interdependence among nations, the end of colonialism and the cold war, and the growing role of international institutions and the international community in peace operations.

• But the outlook is not all rosy. The world has experienced horrific acts of violence and genocide in recent years in places like Congo, and new forms of violence may emerge. The growing number of weak or failing states, such as Iraq, Afghanistan, Burma, Nepal, Bangladesh, and Pakistan pose a growing threat to human security.

• There is an interactive relationship between armed conflict and non-violent threats to human security such as poverty and disease. Wars and internal conflicts can lead to impoverishment, disease outbreaks, and environmental destruction. Conversely, poverty, inequality, and environmental degradation can lead to weakening and even collapse of states. Human security research should look not just at the direct and indirect consequences of conflict, but also the range of socioeconomic, political, and ecological factors that contribute to conflict. Such an understanding of human security opens the way for reconciling the two conceptions of human security as freedom from fear and freedom from want.

• Women feature in armed conflicts both as victims and actors (in combat and support roles). Rape and other forms of sexual violence against them increasingly feature as an instrument of war and are now recognized as crimes against humanity. The international community is seeking ways to increase the participation of women in UN peace operations and conflict resolution functions.

Case Study Human insecurity in South-East Asia

Whether going by its narrow (freedom from fear) or broad (freedom from want) conception, South-East Asia faces some of the most critical challenges to human insecurity in the world. The region, comprising Vietnam, Laos, Cambodia, Burma (Myanmar), Indonesia, Malaysia, Thailand, Philippines, Brunei, and Singapore, has witnessed some of the worst violence of the twentieth century. The Khmer Rouge regime in Cambodia killed about 1.7 million (a quarter of the Cambodian population) during its brutal rule between 1975 and 1979 (Yale University Cambodian Genocide Program). In Indonesia, anti-Communist riots in the mid-1960s, which accompanied the transition from President Sukarno to President Suharto, claimed about 400,000 lives (Schwarz 1999: 20). The US war in Vietnam produced 250,000 South Vietnamese, 1.1 million North Vietnamese, and 60,000 American casualties (Olson 1988). Ethnic and separatist movements in East Timor and Aceh have claimed 200,000 and more than 2,000 lives, respectively (Wessel and Wimhofer 2001). And while there are no proper collated figures for ethnic separatism in Myanmar—usually low-scale, random casualties and conflicts—600,000 internally displaced persons from these conflicts have been recorded (US Department of State 2003).

The region has been free of major conflict since the fighting in Cambodia (1979–91) ended. But internal conflicts in Southern Thailand, Southern Philippines, and Myanmar pose a serious challenge to human security. Military rule, which accounted for some of the worst human rights violations in the region, continues in Myanmar, has returned in Thailand, and remains a possibility in Philippines.

South-East Asia also faces other threats to human security. Absolute poverty levels have declined, but the prevalence of underweight children under 5 years of age in South-East Asia is third highest in the World (28%), after sub-Saharan Africa (30%), and South Asia (47%). In Asia, national HIV infection levels are highest in South-East Asia. The outbreaks of highly pathogenic H5N1 avian influenza, which began in South-East Asia in mid-2003 and have now spread to parts of Europe, are the largest and most severe on record.

South-East Asia has also experienced a range of transnational threats in recent years. These include the Asian economic crisis of 1997, described by the World Bank as 'the biggest setback for poverty reduction in East Asia for several decades' (Ching 1999). Other challenges include the recurring haze problem (1997, 2006) from forest fires in Indonesia, the Severe Acute Respiratory Syndrome (SARS) outbreak in 2003, and the Indian Ocean Tsunami that devastated coastal areas in Indonesia, Thailand, and other South-East Asian nations in December 2004 and killed at least 200,000 people in Asia, with Indonesia suffering 128,000 dead and 37,000 missing.

Conceptually, South-East Asia shows a link between underdevelopment and conflict. Its poorest areas—Indonesia, Cambodia, Myanmar, and the southern regions of Thailand and Philippines—have been especially prone to conflict. Economic development has led to relative stability in Singapore and Malaysia.

(Acharya 2007)

Promoting human security

The role of the international community

Because of the broad and contested nature of the idea of human security, it is difficult to evaluate policies undertaken by the international community that can be specifically regarded as human security measures. But the most important multilateral actions include the International Criminal Court (ICC) and the Anti-Personnel Land Mines Treaty. The ICC was established on 1 July 2002 with its headquarters in The Hague, the Netherlands, although its proceedings may take place anywhere. It is a permanent institution with 'the power to exercise its jurisdiction over persons for the most serious crimes of international concern' (Rome Statute, Article 1). These crimes include genocide, crimes against humanity, war crimes, and the crime of aggression, although the Court would not exercise its jurisdiction over the crime of aggression until such time as the state parties agree on a definition of the crime and set out the conditions under which it may be prosecuted. The ICC is a 'court of last resort'. It is 'complementary to national criminal jurisdictions', meaning that it can only exercise its jurisdiction when national courts are unwilling or unable to investigate or prosecute such crimes (Rome Statute, Article 1). The Court can only prosecute crimes that were committed on or after 1 July 2002, the date its founding treaty entered into force. Since its establishment, the ICC has been involved in the prosecution of some high-profile war criminals in the former Yugoslavia, Liberia, and Congo, including the former President of Yugoslavia, Slobodan Milošević (whose trial ended without a verdict after he was found dead in his cell in March 2006), and former Liberian President Charles Taylor.

The Convention on the Prohibition of the Use, Stockpiling, Production, and Transfer of Anti-Personnel Mines and on their Destruction, signed in Ottawa on 3–4 December 1997, bans the development, production, acquisition, stockpiling, transfer, and use of anti-personnel mines (Ottawa Treaty, Article 1, General Obligations, 1997). It also obliges signatories to destroy existing stockpiles. Among the countries which have yet to sign the treaty are the People's Republic of China, the Russian Federation, and the United States.

The surge in UN **peacekeeping** and peacebuilding operations has contributed to the decline in conflict and enhanced prospects for human security. The number of UN peacekeeping operations increased three-fold between the first forty years of the UN's founding and the twenty years since—from 13 to 47 missions (United Nations Peacekeeping website, UN n.d.). More recently, a UN Peacebuilding Commission was inaugurated in 2006. Its goal is to assist in post-conflict recovery and reconstruction, including institution-building and sustainable development, in countries emerging from conflict. The UN has also been centre-stage in promoting the idea of humanitarian intervention, a central policy element of human security (see Ch.30; see also International Commission on Intervention and State Sovereignty 2001). The concept of humanitarian intervention was endorsed by the report of the UN Secretary-General's High-Level Panel on Threats, Challenges and Change, *A More Secure World* (2004: 66, 106), the subsequent report by the Secretary-General, entitled *In Larger Freedom* (UN March 2005), and finally by the UN Summit in September 2005.

UN **Specialized Agencies** play a crucial role in promoting human security. For example, the UN Development Programme and the World Health Organization (WHO) have been at the forefront of fighting poverty and disease respectively. Other UN agencies, such as the United Nations High Commissioner for Refugees (UNHCR), United Nations Children's Fund (UNICEF), and United Nations Development Fund for Women (UNIFEM), have played a central role in getting particular issues, such as refugees and the rights of children and women, on to the agenda for discussion, and in providing a platform for advocacy and action (MacFarlane and Khong 2006).

Non-governmental organizations contribute to human security in a number of ways: as a source of information and early warning about conflicts, providing a channel for relief operations, often being the first to do so in areas of conflict or natural disaster, and supporting government or UN-sponsored peacebuilding and rehabilitation missions. NGOs also play a central role in promoting sustainable development. A leading NGO with a human security mission is the International Committee of the Red Cross (ICRC). Established in Geneva, it has a unique

authority based on the international humanitarian law of the Geneva Conventions to protect the lives and dignity of victims of war and internal violence, including the war-wounded, prisoners, refugees, civilians, and other non-combatants, and to provide them with assistance. Other NGOs include Médicine Sans Frontières), (emergency medical assistance), Save the Children (protection of children), and Amnesty International (human rights).

Challenges to human security promotion

Yet, whether viewed as freedom from fear or freedom from want, the concept of human security has not replaced national security. The *Human Development Report* of 2005 estimates that the rich nations of the world provide $10 to the military budget for every $1 they spend on aid. Moreover, the current global spending on HIV/AIDS, 'a disease that claims 3 million lives a year, represents three day's worth of military spending' (UNDP 2005: 8).

Why the continued importance of national/state security over human security? For developing countries, state sovereignty and territorial integrity take precedence over security of the individual. Many countries in the developing world are artificial **nation-states**, whose boundaries were drawn arbitrarily by the colonial powers without regard for the actual ethnic composition or historical linkages between peoples. State responses to ethnic separatist movements (now conflated with terrorism), which are partly rooted in people's rejection of colonial-imposed boundaries, have been accompanied by the most egregious violations of human security by governments. Moreover, many **Third World** states, as well as China, remain under authoritarian rule. Human security is stymied by the lack of political space for alternatives to state ideologies and restrictions on civil liberties imposed by authoritarian **regimes** to ensure their own survival, rather than providing security for the their citizens.

In the developed as well as developing world, one of the most powerful challenges to human security has come from the **war on terror** led by the United States in response to the **9/11** attacks. These have revived the traditional emphasis of states on national security (Suhrke 2004: 365). Although terrorists target innocent civilians and thus threaten human security, governments have used the war on terror to impose restrictions on, and commit violations of, civil liberties. The US decision to put Saddam Hussein on trial in an Iraqi court rather than the ICC illustrates the continued US defiance of a key policy instrument of human security, even though it focuses on the more Western-oriented conception of 'freedom from fear'. The US questioning of the applicability of the Geneva Conventions, the abandoning of its commitments on the issue of torture in the context of war in Iraq, and Russia's flouting of a wide range of its international commitments (including the laws of war, CSCE (Conference on Security and Cooperation in Europe) and OCSE (Organization for Security and Cooperation) Conference on security and cooperation in Europe commitments, as well as international and regional **conventions** on torture) in the context of its war in Chechnya have further undermined the agenda of human security.

Key Points

- The most important multilateral actions to date to promote human security include the International Criminal Court and the Anti-Personnel Land Mines Treaty.
- UN agencies such as the UNHCR, UNICEF, and UNIFEM have been crucial in addressing human security issues such as refugees and the rights of children.
- Canada and Japan are two of the leading countries which have made human security a major part of their foreign policy agenda. Their approach, however, shows the contrast between the 'freedom from fear' and 'freedom from want' conceptions of human security respectively.
- Non-governmental organizations promote human security by acting as a source of information and early warning about conflicts, providing a channel for relief operations, supporting government or UN-sponsored peacebuilding and rehabilitation missions, and promoting sustainable development.
- The September 11 attacks on the United States and the 'war on terror' have revived the traditional state-centric approach to national security at the expense of civil liberties and human security.

Conclusion

The concept of human security reflects a number of developments that have incrementally challenged the traditional view of security as the protection of states from military attack. What initially began as a rejection of orthodox notions of economic growth in favour of a broader notion of human development has been reinforced by new security threats such as genocides in the Balkans and Africa, the Asian financial meltdown of 1997, and the threat of global pandemics. The concept of human security represents an ongoing effort to put the individual at the centre of national and global security concerns while expanding our understanding of the range of challenges that can threaten individual saftey and well-being to encompass both armed conflict as well as social, economic, and ecological forces. To be sure, human security has a long way to go before being universally accepted as a conceptual framework or as a policy tool for national governments and the international community. The linkages between armed conflict, poverty, disease, and environmental stress are poorly understood and need clarification and elaboration. Nonetheless, there can be little doubt that threats to human security, whether understood as freedom from fear or freedom from want, are real world challenges which cannot be wished away or dismissed because of a lack of agreement over the concept and meaning of human security. Notwithstanding debates about the utility and scope of human security, there is increasing acceptance that the traditional notion of security, focusing on state sovereignty, would no longer suffice and that the international community must develop new responses to ensure the protection of people from transnational dangers in an era of globalization. The challenge for the international community is to find ways of promoting human security as a means of addressing a growing range of complex transnational dangers which have a much more destructive impact on the lives of people than conventional military threats to states.

? Questions

1. What is human security? How is it different from the concept of national security?
2. Is redefining the concept of security to focus on the individual useful analytically and for policy formulation?
3. Describe the main difference between the two conceptions of human security: 'freedom from fear' and 'freedom from want'. Are the two understandings irreconcilable?
4. Some studies show that the incidence of armed conflict in the world is in long-term decline. What are the rreasons for this trend?
5. How do you link health with human security?
6. How are poverty and conflict interconnected?
7. What are the various ways in which the international community is engaged in promoting human security?
8. What are the main areas of progress in the promotion of human security by the international community?
9. What are the obstacles to human security promotion by the international community?
10. Why do we need to give special consideration to the suffering of women in conflict zones?

⤳ Guide to Further Reading

Acharya, A. (2001), 'Human Security: East Versus West', *International Journal*, 56(3): 442–60. Examines the debate between two conceptions of human security: 'freedom from fear' and 'freedom from want', with particular reference to Asia.

Burgess, P., and Taylor, O. (eds) (2004), 'What is Human Security?', *Security Dialogue*, 35 (September): 345–87. A round-table among scholars working on the area of human security who offer perspectives on the meaning, utility, and limitations of the concept.

Commission on Human Security (2003), *Human Security Now: Protecting and Empowering People* (New York: United Nations). This report, from a commission proposed by Japan and headed by Sadako Ogata of Japan and Amartya Sen of India, offers a broad conception and overview of human security, its meaning, and the challenges facing it, and recommends steps to promote human security.

Gough, I. (2004), *Insecurity and Welfare Regimes in Asia, Africa and Latin America: Social Policy in Development Contexts* (Cambridge: Cambridge University Press.) A comparative study of social and economic welfare approaches to addressing human security challenges in the developing world.

Haq, M. (1995), *Reflections on Human Development* (Oxford: Oxford University Press). The book by the late Pakistani development economist, who played a pioneering role in the Human Development Report, outlines his thinking on human development and human security.

United Nations Development Programme (1995), *Human Development Report 1994* (Oxford: Oxford University Press). The original souwrce of the idea of human security.

Online Resource Centre

 Visit the Online Resource Centre that accompanies this book to access more learning resources on this chapter topic at www.oxfordtextbooks.co.uk/uk/orc/baylis_smith4e/

Notes

1 The author would like to thank Brian Job, Andrew Mack, and Peter Wallensteen for their comments on an earlier draft of this chapter.

2 For an earlier account of conflicts in the Third World which anticipated this decline, see Acharya (1993) and Acharya (1997)

3 This estimate is from the Uppsala Conflict Data Project (UCDP), Uppsala University. The author is grateful to Peter Wallensteen and Lotta Harbom of the UCDP for drawing this to his attention.

Chapter 29

Human rights

CHRIS BROWN

- Introduction ···508
- On rights in general ··510
- The liberal account of human rights ···511
- 1948 and the modern agenda ···513
- Political and economic rights ··514
- Universalism challenged ···516
- Conclusion ··519

Reader's Guide

Over the last sixty years the growth of an international human rights regime based on the idea that human rights should be internationally protected has been striking, and seems a prime example of globalization. However, the record of compliance with human rights law is patchy, and states seem unwilling to give international action in support of human rights a high priority. Moreover, there are serious conceptual problems involved in widening the notion of 'rights' to incorporate economic and collective rights. The Western origin of the doctrine of rights has also come to be seen as problematic in the post-colonial era. Recent developments, such as the establishment of an International Criminal Court, have re-animated the human rights regime, but the consequences of the global war on terror have been less positive, with core political rights coming under question in many Western states.

Introduction

On the face of it, human rights are an ideal focus for a consideration of processes of **globalization**. Whereas it was once the case that rights were almost always associated with domestic legal and political systems, in the last sixty years a complex network of international law and practice (the 'international human rights regime') has grown up around the idea that individuals possess rights simply by virtue of being human, of sharing in a **common humanity**. The purpose of this chapter is to explain how this came about, but also, and in particular, to examine the many problems associated with the idea of universal human rights. This introduction will set the scene; the next section will examine some basic **issues** raised by rights language; the liberal position on human rights will then be examined, followed by discussion of the politics of international human rights protection as this has developed since 1945.

Many cultures and civilizations have developed ideas about the intrinsic worth and dignity of human beings, but the notion that humans are 'rights-bearers' is specifically European. Medieval in origin, this notion was embodied in the positive law of a few countries in the early modern era. By the late eighteenth century the slow process of broadening the idea of the 'rights of man' by recognizing the rights of women, and, via campaigns against the slave trade, those of non-Europeans, began. These preliminary moves set the scene for the globalization processes of the post-1945 era. Here we have seen a number of

global and regional treaties and declarations concerning human rights, and the emergence of **non-governmental organizations** (NGOs) such as Amnesty International dedicated to their enforcement. Moreover, governments, such as that of the United States, and **intergovernmental organizations** (INGOs), such as the **International Monetary Fund** and the Commonwealth, have increasingly (and controversially) seen it as part of their remit to promote human rights.

All of this amounts to an impressive body of international law and diplomatic practice, which has led to a further broadening and deepening of the idea of rights, often (although somewhat inaccurately) conceptualized in terms of three generations. Early statements concentrated on **first-generation** (political) rights such as freedom of speech and assembly and 'the right to take part in the government of his (*sic*) country, directly or through freely chosen representatives' (**Universal Declaration, Article 21**). But the same declaration also recognized **second-generation** rights to the 'economic, social and cultural rights indispensable for his dignity and the free development of his personality' (Article 22) and these economic and social rights feature very largely in later UN documents, especially, of course, the **International Covenant on Economic, Social and Cultural Rights.** Both first- and second-generation rights are, in essence, possessed by individuals. **Third-generation** rights build on this collective dimension and concern the rights of 'peoples'; for example, under the **Banjul Charter**

Box 29.1 The international protection of human rights: some key treaties, conventions, and declarations

1948	The Universal Declaration of Human Rights (United Nations General Assembly)	1979	The American Convention on Human Rights
1948	The Convention on the Prevention and Punishment of the Crime of Genocide	1979	The International Convention on the Elimination of Discrimination Against Women (CEDAW)
1950	The European Convention for the Protection of Human Rights and Fundamental Freedoms	1981	The African Charter on Human and Peoples' Rights (the Banjul Charter)
1965	The International Convention on the Elimination of All Forms of Racial Discrimination	1984	The Convention against Torture and Other Cruel, Inhuman or Degrading Treatment or Punishment
1966	The International Covenant on Civil and Political Rights and the International Covenant on Economic, Social and Cultural Rights	1984	The Convention on the Rights of the Child
		1989	The Declaration of Principles of Indigenous Rights
		1993	The Vienna Declaration and Action Programme

In the 1990s most of the interesting debates about human rights concerned either cultural issues, or the status of 'economic rights'. The general assumption was that classical political rights, such as the right to a fair trial or the right not to be tortured, were firmly established in people's minds more or less everywhere, and were seriously violated only in peripheral states. 9/11 and the global war on terror (GWOT) changed all that. The murder of 3,000 innocent civilians was, of course, itself a major human rights violation, but the reaction of the USA and other vulnerable states to the terrorist threat has been almost equally problematic. The USA has created an internment camp at Guantanamo Bay intended to be beyond the reach of the Supreme Court, has interned there hundreds of people without trial, and has redefined torture to exclude inter-

rogation techniques such as 'waterboarding' (simulated drowning) which, when practised by the Gestapo, were certainly regarded as such. The reaction of Western European states has been rather less dramatic but still controversial, as with attempts by the British government to introduce extended periods of detention without charge. A free pass has been issued to regimes with poor human rights records but who are on the right side of the GWOT, such as Pakistan. The US policy of moving prisoners to these jurisdictions ('extraordinary rendition') is clearly designed to allow for easier violations of human rights. Indeed, Harvard Professor Alan Dershowitz has called for the introduction of 'torture warrants' as a way of regularizing and controlling the practice (Dershowitz 2003). Such extreme positions are now being modified. The US Supreme Court has asserted its jurisdiction over Guantanamo Bay, and insisted on proper trials for those held there—partly, it should be said, at the urging of lawyers from the US Navy's Judge Advocate General's Department—while the latest set of US Army Field Regulations specifically outlaw violent methods of interrogation. Still, the problems to which these steps were intended to be a solution remain. Can human rights be regarded as absolutes to be upheld in all circumstances, as is usually argued by their promoters, or are some (minor) violations to be seen as the 'lesser evil' in the face of an existential threat, as Michael Ignatieff has argued (Ignatieff 2005)? It is striking that, within the West, popular opinion has almost always taken the latter view, a significant finding, since, ultimately, the strength of the human rights regime, domestically and internationally, rests on popular support.

(see Box 29.1) peoples have the right to 'freely dispose of their wealth and natural resources' (**Article 21(1)**), while the individual has a duty 'to serve his natural community by placing his physical and intellectual abilities at its service' and to 'preserve and strengthen positive African cultural values in his relations with other members of the society. . .' (Article 29(2) and (7)).

This international human rights regime provides a mixed and varied menu of items for discussion. There are legal issues concerning the ratification of these treaties, the interpretation of particular clauses, and so on. These legal issues lead into politico-legal questions such as the vexed issue of **compliance**. This in turn raises foreign policy issues, such as whether it is either practicable or prudent to make compliance with human rights law a touchstone of one's foreign relations. Clearly, there are straightforward political and moral issues here concerning the trade-off between particular values—is it worth risking a trading contract in order to make a point about a violation of human rights? The political problems posed by US trade policy towards the People's Republic

of China since 1989 illustrate the difficulties here. Again, should foreign aid to poor countries be made dependent on the establishment of effective human rights? Realists who privilege the **national interest**, and communitarian political philosophies, which assert the right of communities to determine their own forms of **rule**, inevitably clash with the cosmopolitan universalism of the international human rights regime (see Ch.31). Finally, there are philosophical questions that cannot be avoided even by an account of human rights that tries to keep both feet firmly planted on the ground. For example, are first-, second-, and third-generation rights compatible with each other? Indeed, are second- or third-generation 'rights', rights at all?

Each of these dimensions of human rights is worthy of discussion but nowadays the latter, political and philosophical, issues are increasingly coming to the fore. This is because of a general change of atmosphere after the end of the **cold war**. Until comparatively recently, few objected to the notion that human rights are universal; the content of human rights declarations and **conventions** was regarded

by practical people as being rather less problematic than the issue of compliance. The key human rights problem was seen as one of forcing states to adhere to reasonably uncontroversial standards of behaviour.

Post-cold war, this problem has not gone away but some progress has been made and there is a spreading consensus that at least extreme human rights violations are a matter for the international community. As against this, the association of human rights with **democracy promotion** and the dilemmas posed by the post-**9/11 war on terror** may damage this consensus (see Case Study 1).

In any event, this marginal but significant progress has been accompanied by the emergence of another set of issues putting in question the universality of human rights. Clearly one of the (third-generation) rights of a 'people' must be to be different from other people and could

such difference be achieved other than at the expense of universal standards? In any event, does not the alleged universality of human rights hide the actual privileging of an essentially Western notion of politics, as is suggested by, among others, advocates of 'Asian values'? Moreover, the 'masculinist' assumptions of human rights language have already been noted, and feminists have been critical of articles in the various Declarations and Covenants which assume traditional **gender** roles. These new issues challenge, indeed reverse, the normal assumption of a process of globalization. The development of rights thinking from local and national to global and universal is usually seen as the great, albeit incomplete, achievement of the human rights movement—but a return to a more limited conception of basic rights may be the only way the regime can, in fact, survive.

Key Points

- The international human rights regime is an established feature of contemporary world society, and a good example of the processes of globalization.
- Modern thinking distinguishes between three generations of rights: first, broadly political; second, economic and social; third, the rights of peoples.

- One major set of contemporary problems concerns compliance with human rights standards, especially in the context of the war on terror.
- More recently, the universal status of human rights has come to be challenged by critics who stress the Western, masculine, intolerant nature of this universalism.

On rights in general

As we can no longer take the idea of rights for granted, we must now ask some fundamental questions: What kinds of rights might there be? Do rights necessarily imply **duties**? The standard legal answer to the first two questions is to distinguish different kinds of 'rights', some of which involve 'duties'. These same categories can be used in a wider political and moral context.

On what **foundations** do rights rest? The answer in legal terms must be that they rest within a legal system, but what kind of legal system? Here we must return and re-examine the starting point of this chapter—the theory and practice of medieval European politics. The theory of rights in the Middle Ages rested on the idea of **natural law**. Natural law theorists differed on many issues, but the central proposition is clear. Universal moral standards exist upon which the rights that individuals have are founded and there is a general duty to adhere to these

standards (Finnis 1980). The most important feature of this position is that it is not limited in application to any particular legal system, **community**, **state**, race, creed, or civilization. Here is to be found the origin of much of the rhetoric of universal human rights.

Natural law provided the theory but in the rougher world of medieval political practice, rights had rather different connotations. Here a right was a concession one extracted from a nominal superior, probably by force. The **Magna Carta** (1215) is a case in point. The Barons of England obliged King John to grant to them and their heirs in perpetuity a series of liberties which are, for the most part, very specific and related to particular grievances. The Great Charter as a whole was based on the important principle that the subjects of the King owe him duty only if he meets their claims. This is clearly a political bargain or contract.

Box 29.2 Kinds of rights

A standard analysis here, deriving from the American jurist Wesley Hofeld (see Jones 1994 for a modern version) distinguishes four kinds of rights. **Claim-rights** are the most basic rights—the only true rights, Hofeld believed. The classic example of a claimright is a right generated by a contract and accompanied by correlative duties. **Liberty-rights** occur when I have the right to do something in the sense that I have no obligation *not* to do it—for example, I may dress as I please. Here there is no correlative duty, except perhaps the duty to let me do as I choose. Sometimes a right involves the exercise of a power. For example, to have the right to vote means to be empowered to vote, to be enfranchised. Finally, a right sometimes means an **immunity-right**, the essence of which is that others are disbarred from making claims under certain circumstances, for example, to be legally insane, or under age, is to be immune from criminal prosecution. Hofeld holds that only claim-rights are truly 'rights'.

There is no necessary incompatibility between the rights established by political bargaining between monarch and subjects and the rights entailed by natural law, but it should not be forgotten that these two sources of the notion of rights are actually based not simply on different, but on opposed principles. Whereas rights based on **natural law** are derived from reason and the notion of human flourishing and are universal in time and space, **charter rights** simply describe in legal terms the result of a political bargain or contract and, by definition, are limited to the parties to the bargain, and thus restricted in time and space.

Key Points

- We need to establish the status of rights—what a right is, what kind of rights people have, whether rights imply duties, and why?
- The distinction between rights as claims, liberties, powers, and immunities helps to clarify these questions.
- The origin of thinking about rights can be traced to the doctrine of natural law and the political practice of extracting charters of liberties.
- Natural law generates universal rights and duties, while a charter confers local and particular liberties. A potential conflict exists between these two sources of the idea of rights.

The liberal account of human rights

The complex language of medieval thinking on rights carried over into the modern period. Political philosophers such as **Hugo Grotius, Thomas Hobbes, and John Locke** continued to use notions of natural law, albeit in radically different ways from their predecessors. Political activists such as the Parliamentarians in the English Civil War drew on the rights and privileges they believed to have been granted to their forebears to sustain their notion of themselves as **free-born Englishmen**. Gradually, a synthesis emerged which can be termed the **Liberal Account of Rights**. This position is made up of two basic components:

1 Human beings possess rights to life, liberty, the secure possession of property, the exercise of freedom of speech, and so on which are **inalienable**—cannot be traded away—and **unconditional**—the only acceptable reason for constraining any one individual is to protect the rights of another.

2 The primary function of government is to protect these rights. Political **institutions** are to be judged on their performance of this function, and political obligation rests on their success in this. In short, political life is based on a kind of implicit or explicit **contract** between people and government.

From a philosophical and conceptual point of view, this position is easy to denigrate as a mish-mash of half-digested medieval ideas. As **G. W. F. Hegel** and many subsequent communitarian thinkers have pointed out, it assumes that individual rights, indeed individuals, predate society—and yet it is difficult to see how one could exist as an individual without being part of a society. For **Jeremy Bentham** the function of government was to promote the general good (which he called utility) and the idea that individuals might have the right to undermine this seemed to him madness, especially since no one could tell him where these rights came from; the whole

idea was 'nonsense upon stilts'. **Karl Marx**, on the other hand, and many subsequent radicals, pointed to the way in which the liberal position stresses property rights to the advantage of the rich and powerful. All these points raise compelling questions, but they underestimate the powerful **rhetorical** appeal of the liberal position. Most people are less likely to be worried about the conceptual inadequacies associated with the liberal position on human rights than they are to be attracted by the obvious benefits of living in a political system based on or influenced by it.

One of the uncertain features of the liberal position is the extent to which the rights it generates are considered to be universal. For example, the French Revolutionary **Declaration of the Rights of Man and of the Citizen** clearly, by its very title, is intended to be of universal scope, but even here the universalism of Article 1 'Men are born and remain free and equal in respect of rights' is soon followed by Article 3 'The nation is essentially the source of all sovereignty . . .'; and when Revolutionary and Napoleonic France moved to bring the Rights of Man to the rest of **Europe**, the end result looked to most contemporaries remarkably like a French **empire**. The liberal position, while universal in principle, is particularistic in application and state boundaries are more or less taken for granted.

The humanitarianism and international standard-setting of the nineteenth and twentieth centuries brought these issues to the fore. The Congress of Vienna of 1815 saw the great powers accept an obligation to end the slave trade, which was finally abolished by the **Brussels Convention** of 1890, while slavery itself was formally outlawed by the **Slavery Convention** of 1926. The **Hague Conventions** of 1907 and the **Geneva Conventions** of 1926 were designed to introduce humanitarian considerations into the conduct of war. The International Labour Office,

formed in 1901, and its successor the International Labour Organization, attempted to set standards in the workplace via measures such as the **Convention Concerning Forced or Compulsory Labour** of 1930.

However, although these and other subsequent measures taken together do provide a quite elaborate framework for some kind of **global governance**, they exist within a context in which notions of **sovereignty** and **non-intervention** are taken for granted and are only to be overridden with great reluctance. For example, abolishing the slave trade, which involves international transactions, was much easier than abolishing slavery, which concerns what states do to their own people—indeed, pockets of slavery survive to this day in parts of Africa and the Middle East.

All the while sovereignty remains a **norm** of the system, humanitarian impulses can only take the form of exhortation and standard-setting. In nineteenth-century England, Manchester School radical liberals such as John Bright and Richard Cobden were bitterly critical of traditional diplomacy, but supported the norm of non-intervention on the grounds that their opponents used moral arguments in support of interventions which were really engaged in for reasons of power-politics and general mischief-making. This is, of course, a familiar line of argument most likely in the twenty-first century to be directed at the American heirs of Britain's position in the world.

Cobden was a consistent anti-interventionist and anti-imperialist—other liberals were more selective. Gladstone's 1870s campaign to throw the Ottoman Empire out of Europe bag and baggage was based on the more common view that different standards applied as between 'civilized' and 'uncivilized' peoples. In Gladstone's view, the Ottoman Empire—although, since 1856, a full member of **international society**—could not claim the rights of a sovereign

---

Box 29.3 Sovereignty and the standards of civilization

When nineteenth-century Europeans travelled to China, Japan, and other non-European countries in pursuit of trade, they were reluctant to put themselves (and their property) under the jurisdiction of local legal systems, which often violated what Europeans regarded as basic principles of justice—for example, by allowing the aristocracy and military elite to dispense summary justice. However, a basic principle of international society is the sovereignty of states, which required respect towards, and non-interference with, the institutions of the states which were its members. Where they had the power to do so,

Europeans solved this problem by requiring that the countries concerned respected European legal conventions (the 'standards of civilization') before they were allowed full membership of international society. In the meantime, special courts would be established by and for Europeans and those who dealt with them. These restrictions were bitterly resented as implying inferior status, and removing the regime of 'Capitulations'—as it was called—was a key nationalist demand everywhere in which they were set in place.

state because its institutions did not come up to the requisite standards. Indeed, this latter position was briefly established in international law in the notion of **standards of civilization**. In the late twentieth century, this notion disturbs and unsettles, yet current conventional wisdom on human rights is based on quite similar ideas.

The willingness of liberals to extend their thinking on human rights in a more interventionist direction was characteristic of the second half of the twentieth century. The horrors of the 1914–18 war stimulated attempts to create a peace-system based on a form of international government, and although the **League of Nations** of 1919 had no explicit human rights provision, the underlying assumption was that its members would be states governed by the rule of law and respecting individual rights. The **Charter of the United Nations** of 1945, in the wake of the Second World War, does have some explicit reference to human rights—a tribute to the impact on the general climate of thought of the horrors of that war and, in particular, of the murder of millions of Jews, Gypsies, and Slavs in the extermination camps of National Socialist Germany. In this context, the need to assert a universal position was deeply felt, and the scene was set for the burst of international human rights legislation of the post-war era.

Key Points

- From out of medieval theory and practice a synthesis emerged, the liberal position on human rights, which combines universal and particularist thinking—universal rights established by a contract between rulers and ruled.
- This position is conceptually suspect, but politically and rhetorically powerful.

- Nineteenth-century Liberalism supported international humanitarian reform but within the limits of the norms of sovereignty and non-intervention.
- For some liberals, these latter norms did not apply when the standards of civilization were in question. Twentieth-century thinking on human rights has been less restrictive, largely because of the horrors of the world wars and the Holocaust.

1948 and the modern agenda

The post-1945 humanitarian impulse identified above led to the burst of law-making and standard-setting described in the introduction to this chapter. Although the 1966 covenants now have the status of international law, and although the **European Convention** of 1950 has the most effective enforcement machinery, nonetheless, for all its declamatory status and lack of teeth, the **Universal Declaration of Human Rights** by the UN General Assembly in 1948 is, symbolically, central. This was the first time in history that the international community had attempted to define a comprehensive code for the internal government of its members. During the late 1940s the United Nations was dominated by the West, and the contents of the Declaration represented this fact, with its emphasis on political freedom. The voting was 48 for and none against. Eight states abstained, for interestingly different reasons.

South Africa abstained. The white-dominated regime in South Africa denied political rights to the majority of its people and clearly could not accept that 'all are born free and equal in dignity and rights' (Article 1), claiming it violated the protection of the domestic jurisdiction of states guaranteed by Article 2(7) of the United Nations Charter. This is a clear and uncomplicated case of a first-generation (political) rights issue.

The Soviet Union and five Soviet bloc countries abstained. Although Stalin's Russia was clearly a tyranny, the Soviet government did not officially object to the political freedoms set forth in the Declaration. Instead, the Soviet objection was to the absence of sufficient attention to social and economic rights by comparison to the detailed elaboration of 'bourgeois' freedoms and property rights. The Soviets saw the Declaration as a cold war document, designed to stigmatize socialist regimes—a not wholly inaccurate description of the motives of its promulgators.

Saudi Arabia abstained. Saudi Arabia was one of the few non-Western members of the United Nations in 1948 and just about the only one whose system of government was not, in principle, based on some Western model. Saudi Arabia objected to the Declaration on religious grounds, specifically objecting to Article 18, which specifies the freedom to change and practise the

religion of one's choice. These provisions did not simply contravene specific Saudi laws which, for example, forbade (and still forbid) the practice of the Christian religion in Saudi Arabia, they contravened the tenets of Islam, which does not recognize a right of apostasy. Here, to complete the picture, we have an assertion of

third-generation rights and a denial of the universalism of the Declaration.

Thus, the opening moment of the **universal human rights regime** sees the emergence of the themes which will make up the politics of human rights over the subsequent fifty years.

Key Points

- The politics of the Universal Declaration of 1948 allow us to identify the three major human rights issues of the post-1945 era.
- First, there is the contest between the old norm of sovereignty and the new norm of universal domestic standards.

- Second, there is the contest between political and liberal and social and economic formulations of human rights.
- Finally, there is the assertion of the rights of peoples to be different.

Political and economic rights

'No one shall be subjected to torture or to cruel, inhuman or degrading treatment or punishment' (UN Declaration Article 5, Covenant on Civil and Political Rights Article 7, Convention on Torture, etc.). This is an **immunity** that is now well established but what in practice does this mean for someone faced with the prospect of such treatment? If fortunate enough to live in a country governed by the rule of law, its domestic courts may well uphold an individual's immunity, and the international side of things will come into play only on the margins. Thus, a European who is dissatisfied with his or her treatment at home may be able to continue a legal dispute over a particular practice beyond his or her national courts to the **European Commission on Human Rights and European Court of Human Rights**. In non-European countries governed by the rule of law, no such direct remedy is available but the notion of universal rights at least reinforces the rhetorical case for rights which are established elsewhere, that is in the domestic political order.

The more interesting case emerges if potential victims do not live in such a law-governed society, if, that is, 'their' government and courts are the problem and not the source of a possible solution. What assistance have they the right to expect from the international community? What consequences will flow from their government's failure to live up to its obligations? The problem is that even in cases where violations are quite blatant, it may be difficult to see what other states are able to actually do, even supposing they are willing to act, which, since states

rarely if ever act simply in terms of human rights considerations, cannot be taken for granted.

Thus, during the cold war, the West regularly issued verbal condemnations of human rights violations by the Soviet Union and its associates, but rarely acted on these condemnations—the power of the Soviet Union made direct intervention imprudent, while even relatively minor sanctions would only be adopted if the general state of East–West relations suggested this would be appropriate (see Ch. 4). Similar considerations apply today to relations between Western countries and China. Conversely, violations by countries associated with the West were routinely overlooked or, in some cases, even justified—the global war on terror provides contemporary examples. With the ending of the cold war it seemed possible that a more even-handed approach to human rights violations might emerge, and, indeed, more active policies have been pursued in some cases, but expectations of major changes in attitude have not been met. In 1997, for example, the incoming Labour government in Britain declared its determination to place human rights at the heart of its foreign policy. Perhaps predictably, the actual policy of the government has frequently been seen to be as determined by political and commercial considerations as in the past, and this was true even before the impact of 9/11 and the war on terror is taken into consideration (Smith and Light 2001).

All told, it seems unlikely that individuals ill-treated by non-constitutional regimes will find any real support from

the international community unless their persecutors are weak, of no strategic significance, and commercially unimportant—and even then it is unlikely that effective action will be taken unless one further factor is present, namely the force of public opinion. This is the one positive factor that may goad states into action—the growth of humanitarian non-governmental organizations has produced a context in which sometimes the force of public opinion can make itself felt, not necessarily in the oppressing regime, but in the policy-formation processes of the potential providers of succour.

The situation with respect to second-generation rights is more complicated. Consider, for example, 'the right of everyone to an adequate standard of living for himself and his family, including adequate food, clothing and housing, and to the continuous improvement of living conditions' (Covenant on Economic, Social and Cultural Rights, Article 11.1), or the 'right of everyone to be free from hunger' (Article 11.2). It has been argued by numerous cosmopolitan writers that such rights are, or should be, central. For example, Henry Shue (1996) argues that only if such basic rights are met can any other rights be claimed, and Thomas Pogge (2002) sees the relief of world **poverty** as a central task for the human rights regime.

The Covenant makes the realization of these rights an obligation on its signatories, but, arguably, this is a different kind of obligation from the obligation to refrain from, for example, 'cruel or degrading' punishments. In the latter case, as with other basically political rights, the remedy is clearly in the hands of national governments. The way to end torture is for states to stop torturing. The right not to be tortured is associated with a duty not to torture. The right to be free from hunger, on the other hand, is not simply a matter of a duty on the part of one's own and other states not to pursue policies that lead to starvation. It also involves a duty to act to 'ensure an equitable distribution of world food supplies in relation to need' (Covenant on Economic, Social and Cultural Rights, Article 11.2(b)). The distinction here is sometimes seen as that between 'negative' and 'positive' rights, although this is not entirely satisfactory, since negative (political) rights often require positive action if they are to be protected effectively. In any event, there are problems with the notion of economic rights.

First, it is by no means clear that, even assuming goodwill, these social and economic goals could always be met, and to think in terms of having a right to

something that could not be achieved is to misuse language. In such circumstances a right simply means 'a generally desirable state of affairs', and this weakening of the concept may have the effect of undermining more precise claims to rights which, one must hope, can be achieved (such as the right not to be tortured). Second, some states may seek to use economic and social rights more directly to undermine political rights. Thus, dictatorial regimes in poor countries quite frequently justify the curtailment of political rights in the alleged name of promoting economic growth, or economic equality. In fact, there is no reason to accept the general validity of this argument—Amartya Sen argues cogently that **development** and freedom go together (Sen 1999)—but it will still be made, and not always in bad faith. Finally, if it is accepted that all states have a positive duty to promote economic well-being and freedom from hunger everywhere, then the consequences go beyond the requirement of the rich to share with the poor, revolutionary though such a requirement would be. Virtually all national social and economic policies become a matter for international regulation. Clearly rich states would have a duty to make economic and social policy with a view to its consequences on the poor, but so would poor states. The poor's right to assistance creates a duty on the rich to assist, but this in turn creates a right of the rich to insist that the poor have a duty not to worsen their plight—for example, by failing to restrict population growth or by inappropriate economic policies. Aid programmes promoted by the Commonwealth and World Bank, and the structural adjustment programmes of the International Monetary Fund regularly include conditions of this kind. They are, however, widely resented because they contradict another widely supported economic and social right that 'All peoples have the right of **self-determination**. By virtue of that right they freely determine their political status and freely pursue their economic, social and cultural development' (Covenant on Economic, Social and Cultural Rights, Article 1.1). Even when applied in a well-meaning and consistent way, external pressures to change policy are rarely popular, even with those they are intended to benefit.

As against these points, it is certainly true that people suffering from brutal poverty and severe malnourishment are unlikely to be able to exercise any rights at all unless their condition is attended to, and it may be true, as Pogge argues, that the transfers actually required to raise

living standards to an acceptable level across the world are sufficiently modest that they would not actually raise the problems outlined above. Still, most economic and social 'rights' are best seen as collectively agreed upon aspirations rather than as rights as the term has conventionally been used.

Key Points

- The politics of rights varies according to whether constitutional or non-constitutional regimes are involved.
- In any event, the international community rarely acts on human rights cases unless public opinion is engaged.

- Economic and social rights are conceptually different from political rights, and present a more basic challenge to existing norms of sovereignty and non-intervention.

Universalism challenged

The very idea of human rights implies limits to the range of variation in domestic political regimes that is acceptable internationally. Post-1945 human rights law, if taken seriously and at face value, would create a situation where all states would be obliged to conform to a quite rigid template which dictated most aspects of their political, social, and economic structures and policies.

Conventional defenders of human rights argue that this would be a Good Thing—the universal spread of best practice in human rights matters is in the interest of all people. Others disagree. Does post-1945 law actually constitute best practice? The feminist critique of universal human rights is particularly apposite here. The universal documents all, in varying degrees, privilege a patriarchal view of the family as the basic unit of society. Even such documents as the **Convention on Elimination of Discrimination against Women** (CEDAW) of 1979 do no more than extend to women the standard liberal package of rights, and modern feminists debate whether this constitutes a genuine advance (Peters and Wolper 1995).

More fundamentally, is the very idea of best practice sound? We have already met one objection to the idea in the Saudi abstention of 1948. The argument is simple: universalism is destructive not just of undesirable differences between societies but of desirable and desired differences. The human rights movement stresses the common humanity of the peoples of the world, but for many, the things that distinguish us from one another are as important as the things that unify us. For example, the **Declaration of Principles of Indigenous Rights** adopted in Panama in 1984 by a non-governmental group, the **World Council of Indigenous Peoples**, lays out positions which are designed to preserve the traditions, customs, institutions, and practices of indigenous peoples (many of which, it need hardly be said, contradict contemporary liberal norms). As with feminist critiques, the argument here is that the present international human rights regime rests too heavily on the experiences of one part of humanity, in this case the Wes—of course, in practice, the cultural critique and the feminist critique may lead in different directions (see Case Study 2).

Box 29.4 The feminist critique of human rights

Until recently, it has been conventional for human rights treaties to be cast in language that assumes that the rights-bearer is a man and the head of a household. Many feminists argue that this reflects more than an old-fashioned linguistic convention. The classic political and civil rights (freedom of speech, association, from arbitrary arrest, and so on) assume that the rights-bearer will be living, or would wish to live, a life of active citizenship, but, until very recently, such a life was denied to nearly all women in nearly all cultures. Instead of this public life, women were limited to the private sphere and subjected to the arbitrary and capricious power of the male head of the household. It is only very recently in the Western liberal democracies that women have been able to vote, to stand for office, or to own property in their own name, and such issues as the criminalization of rape in marriage and effective measures to prevent domestic violence against women are still controversial. The situation is, if anything, rather worse in non-Western polities—see Case Study 2 on 'Islam, gender and human rights'. It may be that a genuinely gender-neutral account of human rights is possible, but some radical feminists argue that a different kind of thinking altogether is required (see Catherine Mackinnon 1993).

Both cultural critics and feminists argue, convincingly, that the model of a rights-bearer inherent in the contemporary international human rights regime is based on the experiences of Western men. Agreement collapses, however, when the implications of this common position are explored. Liberal feminists wish to see the rights of men extended to women, while radical feminists wish to promote a new model of what it is to be human that privileges neither men nor women. Most cultural critics, on the other hand, wish to preserve inherited status and power differences based on gender. The contradictions here are sharpest when it comes to relations between the world of Islam and the human rights regime, largely because relations between Islam and

the West are so fraught on other grounds that all differences are magnified. Radical or traditional Islamists argue for conventional gender roles, support quite severe restrictions on the freedom of women, and promote the compulsory wearing of restrictive clothing such as the *niqab* or the *burqa*. Many of these petty restrictions have no basis in the Koran or the Sayings of the Prophet, and can simply be understood as methods of preserving male dominance—although, it should be said that they are often accepted by Muslim women as ways of asserting their identity. More serious for the human rights regime are those verses of the Koran that unambiguously deny gender equality. It is often, and truly, said that the Koran's attitude to the status of women was in advance of much contemporary seventh-century CE thought—including Christian and Jewish thought of the age—but it remains the case that, for example, in a shariah court the evidence of a woman is worth less than that of a man, and sexual intercourse outside marriage is punishable for a woman even in the case of rape. The other Abrahamic religions continue to preserve misogynist vestiges, but mainstream Christian and Jewish theologians have re-interpreted those aspects of their traditions that radically disadvantage women. Given the importance attached to the literal text of the Koran, this will prove more difficult for Muslims. The role of women under Islam will be a continuing problem for the international human rights regime as it attempts to divest itself of its Western Judaeo-Christian heritage and adopt a more inclusive framework, as well, of course, as being an even bigger problem for those women who live in oppressive Muslim regimes.

This philosophical point took on a political form in the 1990s. In the immediate post-cold war world, and especially after the election of US President Bill Clinton in 1992, there was some talk of the USA adopting active policies of democracy promotion, and a number of East Asian governments and intellectuals asserted in response the notion that there were specifically 'Asian values' that required defending from this development. The argument was that human rights boil down to no more that a set of particular social choices which need not to be considered binding by those whose values (and hence social choices) are differently formed, for example, by Islam or Confucianism rather than by an increasingly secularized Christianity. The wording of the **Vienna Declaration on Human Rights** of 1993, which refers to the need to bear in mind 'the significance of national and regional particularities and various historical, cultural and religious backgrounds' when considering human rights, partially reflects this viewpoint—and has been criticized for this by some human rights activists.

Returning to the history of rights, it is here that the distinction between rights grounded in natural law and

rights grounded in a contract becomes crucial. As was noted above, it is only if rights are grounded in some account of human flourishing and reason that they are genuinely universal in scope. But is this position, as its adherents insist, free of cultural bias, a set of ideas that all rational beings must accept? It seems not, at least in so far as many apparently rational Muslims, Hindus, Buddhists, Atheists, Utilitarians, and so on clearly do not accept its doctrines! It seems that either the standards derived from natural law, or some similar doctrine, are cast in such general terms that virtually any continuing social system will exemplify them, or, if cast more specifically, the standards described are not in fact universally desired.

Of course, we are under no obligation to accept all critiques of universalism at face value. Human rights may have first emerged in the West, but this does not in itself make rights thinking 'Western'. It may be that an apparently principled rejection of universalism is, in fact, no more than a rationalization of tyranny. How do we know that the inhabitants of Saudi Arabia, say, actually prefer not to live in a democratic system with Western liberal rights, as their government asserts? There is an obvious

Box 29.5 Asian values

That Western states, intergovernmental organizations and NGOs have sometimes taken it upon themselves to promote human rights has always been resented as hypocritical in the nonWestern world, where the imperialist record of the West over the last four centuries has not been forgotten. In the 1990s, this resentment led a number of the leaders of the quasiauthoritarian newly industrializing nations of SouthEast Asia to assert the existence of Asian values that could be counterpoised to the (allegedly) Western values associated with the international human rights regime—in this they seemed to confirm the forthcoming `Clash of Civilizations' forecast by Huntington (1996). Such thinking was partially reflected in the **Bangkok Declaration** of 1993, made by Asian ministers in the runup to the **Vienna Conference** of that year (for texts see Tang 1994). Western notions of human rights were seen as excessively individualistic, as opposed to the stress on the family of Asian societies, and insufficiently supportive of (if not downright hostile to) religion. Further,

some regarded the West as morally decadent because of the growth of gay rights and the relative success of the women's movement in combating gender discrimination. Some have argued that such positions are simply intended to legitimate authoritarian rule, although it should be noted that `Asian Values' can only perform this task if the argument strikes a chord with ordinary people. More to the point, it may be doubted whether the conservative positions expressed by proponents of Asian values are in any genuine sense 'Asian'; many Western conservatives and fundamentalists share their critique of the West, while progressive Asian human rights activists are critical. Notions such as `the West' or `Asia' are unacceptably `essentialist'—all cultures and civilizations contain different and often conflicting tendencies; the world of Islam, or of `Confucian capitalism', is no more monolithic than is Christianity or Western secularism. The Asian values argument petered out at the end of the 1990s, but the problems it illustrated remain.

---

dilemma here: if we insist that we will only accept democratically validated regimes, we will be imposing an alien test of legitimacy on these societies—yet what other form of validation is available?

In any event, does not the body of legal acts for the protection of universal human rights outlined in Box 29.1 apply even if rights are, in effect, convenient fictions? Again, defenders of difference will argue that international law is itself a Western, universalist, notion and, in any event, they rightly note that the Western record of adherence to universal norms is not such as to justify any claim to moral superiority, pointing to the many crimes of the age of **imperialism** as well as to contemporary issues such as the treatment of asylum seekers and refugees, and, of course, the by-products of the global war on terror.

The general point is that there is no neutral language with which to discuss human rights. Whatever way the question is posed reflects a particular viewpoint, and this is no accident. It is built into the nature of the discourse. Is there any way in which the notion of universal rights can be saved from its critics? Two modern approaches seem fruitful. Even if we find it difficult to specify human rights, it may still be possible to talk of human wrongs—similarly, some have argued that it is easier to specify what is *unjust* than what is *just* (see Booth 1999). To use Michael Walzer's terminology (1994), there may be no thick moral code that is universally acceptable, to which

all local codes conform, but there may be a thin code which at least can be used to delegitimize some actions. Thus, for example, the **Genocide Convention** of 1948 seems a plausible example of a piece of international legislation that outlaws an obvious wrong, and, similarly, while some local variations in the rights associated with gender may be unavoidable, it is still possible to say that practices which severely restrict human capabilities, such as **female genital mutilation**, are simply wrong. Any code which did not condemn such suffering would be unworthy of respect.

This may not take us as far as some would wish—essential to this approach is the notion that there are going to be some practices which many would condemn but which will have to be tolerated—but it may be the most appropriate response to contemporary **Pluralism.** An alternative approach is more supportive of universal ideas but on a non-foundationalist basis. This involves recognizing that human rights are based on a particular culture—Richard Rorty (1993) calls this the 'human rights culture'—and defending them in these terms rather than by reference to some cross-cultural code. This approach would involve abandoning the idea that human rights exist. Instead, it involves proselytizing on behalf of the sort of culture in which rights are deemed to exist. The basic point is that human life is safer, pleasanter, and more dignified when rights are acknowledged than when they are not.

Key Points

- The human rights template severely limits the degree of acceptable variation in social practices.
- This universalism can be challenged on feminist grounds as privileging patriarchy.
- More generally, the liberal position on rights privileges a particular account of human dignity.

- Cultural critics of universal rights, such as proponents of Asian values, can be seen as self-serving, but no neutral criteria for assessing this criticism can exist.
- But a set of basic rights may be defensible, likewise the idea of a human rights culture.

Conclusion

The last decade has seen the elaboration of the notion of humanitarian intervention and the emergence of international legal doctrines which support 'universal jurisdiction' in respect of severe human rights violations, along with the establishment of an **International Criminal Court** (ICC) in 2002 (see Ch.16 and Ch.30). Each of these developments suggests that human rights will be taken more seriously in the future, although each also assumes a degree of global consensus which, as suggested above, may not actually exist. It is striking, for example, that three of the five 'veto powers' in the UN have not signed up to the ICC (China, Russia, and the USA), and even more striking that no major Asian power has joined, or intends to join. Still, setting aside these innovations, the most significant recent development in the area of human rights has been the fallout from the terrorist attacks on New York and Washington on 9/11.

This awful event has had consequences in two different directions. On the one hand, the political exigencies of the 'global war on terror' that followed 9/11 have meant that many of the worst habits of the cold war have come back in fashion—on this see Case Study 1. On the other hand, it may be that the need to address the root causes of **terrorism** will actually focus attention more clearly on human rights. It was certainly the intention of the 'Neo-Conservative' movement that US power should be used in the Middle

East to promote democratic forms of government and the observance of human rights, but the failure of the Iraq War of 2003 to produce a stable democracy in that country has put such ideas on the back-burner. Cosmopolitan liberals have always challenged the Neo-Conservative lack of interest in social and economic rights, but, more seriously, it is possible that greater democracy in the region might actually make things worse in some areas of human rights, especially those connected to gender. The triumph of Islamic over secular political parties in Iraq and Palestine point in that direction. Still, the possibility that, in the long run, 9/11 will revitalize the international human rights regime should not be completely discounted.

In any event, whatever politicians and philosophers of right and left may say or do, it is on the strength of popular support for universal human rights that the idea will flourish or die in the twenty-first century. If the idea of human rights captures the imagination of the peoples of the world, then the shortcomings of Western leaders and the opposition of authoritarian rulers elsewhere will be of little long-run significance. If, on the other hand, people insist on defining themselves in terms which deny the existence of universal rights, whether those terms are religious, ethnic, or national, then the work of human rights activists will be equally fruitless. There is no predetermined outcome to this contest.

❓ Questions

1 Do you agree that the only true rights are political rights?

2 What is the relationship between rights and duties?

3 Is there a useful distinction between 'negative' and 'positive' rights?

4 Why is the promotion of human rights so rarely seen as an appropriate foreign policy goal of states?

5 In what sense can one speak of a right to be free from hunger?

6 What are the problems involved in assigning rights to peoples as opposed to individuals?

7 Are human rights the new 'standards of civilization'?

8 In what ways can gender bias be identified in the modern human rights regime?

9 What is the relationship between democracy and human rights? Is it always the case that democracies are more likely to respect human rights than authoritarian regimes?

10 Do you agree that the 'Asian values' debate was generated by the desire of authoritarian regimes in the region to protect themselves from criticism?

11 Can the compromising of human rights in the face of the threat of terrorism ever be justified as the lesser of two evils?

12 Do you agree that the global war on terror can only be won if the West promotes human rights more vigourously?

➡ Guide to further reading

Brownlie, I., and Goodwin-Gill, G. (eds) (2006), *Basic Instruments on Human Rights*, 5th revised edn (Oxford: Clarendon Press). Contains the texts of all the most important treaties and declarations.

Finnis, J. (1980), *Natural Law and Natural Rights* (Oxford: Clarendon Press). The best introduction to modern natural law thinking.

Freeman, M. (2002), *Human Rights: A Multidisciplinary Approach* (Cambridge: Polity Press). This book also discusses the philosophical problems posed by the idea of rights.

Jones, P. (1994), *Rights* (Basingstoke: Macmillan). Discusses the philosophical problems posed by the idea of rights.

Steiner, H. J., and Alston, P. (2000), *International Human Rights in Context: Law, Politics, Morals: Texts and Materials*, 2nd edn (Oxford: Clarendon Press). Contains abbreviated texts and a great deal of useful commentary in its 1,500 + pages! It is the single most useful book for the study of international human rights. A third edition is due in 2007.

International human rights

Donnelly, J. (2002), *Universal Human Rights in Theory and Practice*, 2nd edn (Ithaca, NY: Cornell University Press). Another valuable introduction to international human rights.

Dunne, T., and Wheeler, N. J. (eds) (1999), *Human Rights in Global Politics* (Cambridge: Cambridge University Press). This is the best introductory collection on international human rights.

Smith, K. E., and Light, M. (eds) (2001), *Ethics and Foreign Policy* (Cambridge: Cambridge University Press). Examines the problems involved in making human rights central to foreign policy.

Vincent R. J. (1986), *Human Rights and International Relations* (Cambridge: Cambridge University Press). An older but still useful text which links human rights protection to the theory of International Society.

Second-generation rights

Pogge, T. (2002), *World Poverty and Human Rights: Cosmopolitan Responsibilities and Reforms* (Cambridge: Polity Press). The most important and influential modern statement in this area.

—— (ed.) (2007) *Freedom from Poverty as a Human Right: Who Owes What to the Very Poor* (Oxford: Clarendon Press). Further elaborates the position of second-generation rights.

Shue, H. (1996), *Basic Rights: Subsistence, Affluence and US Foreign Policy,* 2nd rev. edn (Princeton, NJ: Princeton University Press). A very influential defence of second-generation rights as genuine rights.

Third-generation rights and the so-called Asian values

Bauer, J., and Bell, D. A. (eds) (1999), *The East Asian Challenge for Human Rights* (Cambridge: Cambridge University Press). The best collection of writings on the Asian value debate, covering a wide range of perspectives.

Crawford, J. (ed.) (1988), *The Rights of Peoples* (Oxford: Clarendon Press). A collection on the rights of indigenous peoples, edited by a leading international lawyer.

Sen, A. (1999), *Development as Freedom* (Oxford: Oxford University Press). Persuasively disposes of the argument that development requires the curtailment of human rights.

Tang, J. H. (ed.) (1994), *Human Rights and International Relations in the Asia-Pacific Region* (London: Pinter Press). Extracts some key documents.

On the wider, very controversial, context for these arguments

Huntington, S. (1996), *The Clash of Civilizations and the Remaking of World Order* (New York: Simon & Schuster). A key contribution, much criticized by academics, but which has entered the public consciousness, especially since 9/11.

Peters, J. S., and Wolper, A. (eds) (1995), *Women's Rights, Human Rights: International Feminist Perspectives* (New York: Routledge,). A good collection of feminist views.

Shute, S., and Hurley, S. (eds) (1993), *On Human Rights* (New York: Basic Books). An excellent collection of papers on the philosophy of human rights, including essays by John Rawls, Richard Rorty, and Catherine Mackinnon.

Walzer, M. (1994), *Thick and Thin: Moral Argument at Home and Abroad* (Notre Dame, Ind.: University of Notre Dame Press). Argues for a 'thin' cross-cultural moral code.

Human rights, the war on terror, and the 'torture debate'

Dershowitz, A. M. (2003), *Why Terrorism Works: Responding to the Challenge* (New Haven, Conn.: Yale University Press). An elaboration of the views of a key exponent on this subject.

Greenberg, K. (ed.) (2006), *The Torture Debate in America* (New York: Cambridge University Press). A collection of essays, mostly by lawyers, focusing on Guantanamo and Abu Graib, as opposed to the more philosophically oriented papers collected in Levinson (ed.) (2004).

Ignatieff, M. (2005), *The Lesser Evil: Political Ethics in an Age of Terror* (Princeton, NJ: Princeton University Press) and

—— (2005), *American Exceptionalism and Human Rights* (Princeton, NJ: Princeton University Press). Both texts offer a more nuanced approach to the problem of the appropriate means to combat terrorism.

Levinson, A. (ed.) (2004), Torture: A Collection (New York: Oxford University Press). Contains essays by Michael Walzer, Jean Bethke Elshtain, and Alan Dershowitz.

The most useful journals in the field are: *Human Rights Quarterly: a Comparative and International Journal of the Social Sciences, Philosophy and Law* (Baltimore, Md.: Johns Hopkins University Press), *Ethics and International Affairs* (New York: Carnegie Institute), and *The International Journal of Human Rights* (London: Frank Cass).

 Visit the Online Resource Centre that accompanies this book to access more learning resources on this chapter topic at www.oxfordtextbooks.co.uk/uk/orc/baylis_smith4e/

Chapter 30

Humanitarian intervention in world politics

ALEX J. BELLAMY · NICHOLAS J. WHEELER

- Introduction ··· 524
- The case for humanitarian intervention ··· 524
- The case against humanitarian intervention ··· 526
- The 1990s: a golden era of humanitarian activism? ··· 528
- Humanitarian intervention and the war on terror ··· 531
- The responsibility to protect ··· 535
- Conclusion ··· 538

Reader's Guide

Non-intervention is commonly understood as the norm in international society, but should military intervention be permissible when governments massively violate the human rights of their citizens, are unable to prevent such violations, or if states have collapsed into civil war and anarchy? This is the guiding question addressed in this chapter. International law forbids the use of force except for purposes of self-defence and collective enforcement action authorized by the UN Security Council (UNSC). The challenge posed by humanitarian intervention is whether it also should be exempted from the general ban on the use of force. This chapter examines arguments for and against forcible humanitarian intervention. The theoretical analysis is explored in relation to humanitarian intervention during the 1990s and the war on terror. The final section focuses on the responsibility to protect, an important attempt to address this challenge.

Introduction

Humanitarian intervention poses a hard test for an international society built on principles of **sovereignty, non-intervention**, and the non-use of force. Immediately after the **Holocaust**, the **society of states** established laws prohibiting genocide, forbidding the mistreatment of civilians, and recognizing basic human rights. These humanitarian principles often conflict with principles of sovereignty and non-intervention. Sovereign **states** are expected to act as guardians of their citizens' **security**, but what happens if states behave as criminals towards their own people, treating sovereignty as a licence to kill? Should **tyrannical states** (Hoffmann 1995–6: 31) be recognized as legitimate members of **international society** and accorded the protection afforded by the non-intervention principle? Or, should states forfeit their sovereign rights and be exposed to legitimate intervention if they actively abuse or fail to protect their citizens? Related to this, what responsibilities do other states or **institutions** have to enforce human rights **norms** against governments that massively violate them?

Armed humanitarian intervention was not a legitimate practice during the **cold war** because states placed more value on sovereignty and **order** than on the enforcement of human rights. There was a significant shift of attitudes during the 1990s, especially among liberal democratic states, which led the way in pressing new humanitarian claims within international society. The UN Secretary-General noted the extent of this change in a speech to the Gen-eral Assembly in September 1999. Kofi Annan declared that there was a 'developing international norm' to forcibly protect civilians who were at risk from genocide and mass killing. The new norm was a weak one, however. At no time did the UN Security Council (UNSC) authorize forcible intervention against a fully-functioning sovereign state, and intervention without UNSC authority remained controversial. States in the **global South** especially continued to worry that humanitarian intervention was a 'Trojan horse': rhetoric designed to legitimate the interference of the strong in the affairs of the weak. At the same time, however, a group of liberal democratic states and **non-governmental organizations** (NGOs) attempted to build a consensus around the principle of the **responsibility to protect**. The responsibility to protect insists that states have primary responsibility for protecting their own citizens. However, if they are unwilling or unable to do so, the responsibility to end atrocities and mass killing is transferred to the wider 'international community'. The responsibility to protect was adopted by the UN General Assembly in a formal declaration at the **2005 UN World Summit**. Its advocates argue that it will play an important role in building consensus about humanitarian action while making it harder for states to **abuse** humanitarian justifications.

This chapter is divided into five sections. The first sets out the arguments for both a legal right and a moral duty of humanitarian intervention. The second section outlines objections to humanitarian intervention, including **Realist**, legal and moral objections. Next we consider the evolution of state practice during the 1990s, and in the post-**9/11** era. The final section focuses on the responsibility to protect.

The case for humanitarian intervention

In the first part, we explore the **legal** case for a right of humanitarian intervention, commonly labelled **counter-restrictionist**, and in the second part we discuss the **moral justification for it.**

The legal argument

The 'counter-restrictionist' case for a legal right of individual and collective humanitarian intervention rests on two claims: first, the **UN Charter** (1945) commits states to protecting fundamental human rights, and second, there is a right of humanitarian intervention in customary **international law**.

Counter-restrictionists argue that human rights are just as important as peace and security in the UN Charter. The Charter's preamble and Articles 1(3), 55, and 56 all highlight the importance of human rights. Indeed, Article 1(3) identifies the protection of human rights as one of the principal purposes of the UN system. This has led counter-restrictionists to read a humanitarian exception to the ban on the use of force in the UN

Charter. Michael Reisman (1985: 279–80) argued that given the human rights principles in the Charter, the UNSC should have taken armed action during the cold war against states that committed genocide and mass murder. The ongoing failure of the UNSC to fulfil this legal responsibility led him to assert that a legal exception to the ban on the use of force in Article 2(4) of the Charter should be created that would permit individual states to use force on humanitarian grounds. Likewise, some international lawyers (e.g. Damrosch 1991: 219)

Box 30.1 *The Responsibility to Protect:* principles for military intervention

(1) The Just Cause Threshold

Military intervention for human protection purposes is an exceptional and extraordinary measure. To be warranted, there must be serious and irreparable harm occurring to human beings, or imminently likely to occur, of the following kind:

A. **large-scale loss of life**, actual or apprehended, with genocidal intent or not, which is the product either of deliberate state action, or state neglect or inability to act, or a failed state situation; or

B. **large-scale ethnic cleansing**, actual or apprehended, whether carried out by killing, forced expulsion, acts of terror or rape.

(2) The Precautionary Principles

A. **Right intention:** The primary purpose of the intervention, whatever other motives intervening states may have, must be to halt or avert human suffering. Right intention is better assured with multilateral operations, clearly supported by regional opinion and the victims concerned.

B. **Last resort:** Military intervention can only be justified when every non-military option for the prevention or peaceful resolution of the crisis has been explored, with reasonable grounds for believing lesser measures would not have succeeded.

C. **Proportional means:** The scale, duration and intensity of the planned military intervention should be the minimum necessary to secure the defined human protection objective.

D. **Reasonable prospects:** There must be a reasonable chance of success in halting or averting the suffering which has justified the intervention, with the consequences of action not likely to be worse than the consequences of inaction.

(3) Right Authority

A. There is no better or more appropriate body than the United Nations Security Council to authorize military intervention for human protection purposes. The task is not to find alternatives to the Security Council as a source of authority, but to make the Security Council work better than it has.

B. Security Council authorization should in all cases be sought prior to any military intervention action being carried out. Those calling for an intervention should formally request such authorization, or have the Council raise the matter on its own initiative, or have the Secretary-General raise it under Article 99 of the UN Charter.

C. The Security Council should deal promptly with any request for authority to intervene where there are allegations of large-scale loss of human life or ethnic cleansing. It should in this context seek adequate verification of facts or conditions on the ground that might support a military intervention.

D. The Permanent Five members of the Security Council should agree not to apply their veto power, in matters where their vital state interests are not involved, to obstruct the passage of resolutions authorizing military intervention for human protection purposes for which there is otherwise majority support.

E. If the Security Council rejects a proposal or fails to deal with it in a reasonable time, alternative options are:

  I. consideration of the matter by the General Assembly in Emergency Special Session under the 'Uniting for Peace' procedure; and

  II. action within area of jurisdiction by regional or subregional organizations under Chapter VIII of the Charter, subject to their seeking subsequent authorization from the Security Council.

F. The Security Council should take into account in all its deliberations that, if it fails to discharge its responsibility to protect in conscience-shocking situations crying out for action, concerned states may not rule out other means to meet the gravity and urgency of that situation—and that the stature and credibility of the United Nations may suffer thereby.

(4) Operational Principles

A. Clear objectives; clear and unambiguous mandate at all times; and resources to match.

B. Common military approach among involved partners; unity of command; clear and unequivocal communications and chain of command.

C. Acceptance of limitations, incrementalism and gradualism in the application of force, the objective being protection of a population, not defeat of a state.

D. Rules of engagement which fit the operational concept; are precise; reflect the principle of proportionality; and involve total adherence to international humanitarian law.

E. Acceptance that force protection cannot become the principal objective.

F. Maximum possible coordination with humanitarian organizations.

(International Commission on Intervention and State Sovereighty (2001: xii—xiii))

argued that humanitarian intervention did not breach Article 2(4) because the article only prohibits the use of force against the 'political independence' and 'territorial integrity' of states and humanitarian intervention does neither of these things.

Other counter-restrictionists admitted that there is no legal basis for **unilateral humanitarian intervention** in the UN Charter, but argued that it is permitted by customary international law. For a **rule** to count as customary international law, states must actually engage in the practice that is claimed to have the status of law, and they must do so because they believe that the law permits this. International lawyers describe this as *opinio juris*. Counter-restrictionists contend that the customary right to humanitarian intervention preceded the UN Charter, evidenced by the legal arguments offered to justify the British, French, and Russian intervention in Greece (1827) and American intervention in Cuba (1898). They also point to British and French references to customary international law to justify the creation of safe havens in Iraq (1991) and Kofi Annan's insistence that even unilateral intervention to halt the 1994 genocide in Rwanda would have been legitimate.

There are, however, a number of problems with both elements of the counter-restrictionist case. They exaggerate the extent of consensus about the rules governing the use of force and their reading of the textual provisions of the UN Charter runs contrary to both majority international legal opinion (e.g. Brownlie; 1974, Chesterman 2001) and the opinions expressed by its architects at the end of the Second World War.

The moral case

Many writers argue that irrespective of what the law says, there is a moral duty to intervene to protect civilians from genocide and mass killing. They argue that **sovereignty** derives from a state's responsibility to protect its citizens, and when a state fails in its duty, it loses its sovereign rights (Tesón 2003: 93). There are a number of different ways of arriving at this argument. Some point to the idea of **common humanity** to argue that all individuals have basic human rights and duties to uphold the rights of others (Caney 1997: 34). Others argue that today's globalized world is so integrated that massive human rights violations in one part of the world have an effect on every other part, creating moral obligations (Blair 1999). Some advocates of **just war theory** argue that the duty to offer charity to those in need is universal (Ramsey 2002: 35–6). A further variety of this argument insists that there is moral agreement between the world's major religions and ethical systems that genocide and mass killing are grave wrongs and that others have a duty to prevent them and punish the perpetrators (Lepard 2002).

There are problems with this perspective too. Granting states a moral permit to intervene opens the door to potential abuse: the use of humanitarian arguments to justify wars that are anything but. Furthermore, those who advance moral justifications for intervention run up against the problem of how bad a humanitarian crisis has to have become before force can be used, and there is also the thorny issue of whether force should be used to prevent a humanitarian emergency from developing in the first place.

Key Points

- Counter-restrictionists argue in favour of a legal right of humanitarian intervention based on interpretations of the UN Charter and customary international law.
- The claims for a moral duty of humanitarian intervention stem from the basic proposition that all individuals are entitled to a minimum level of protection from harm by virtue of their common humanity.

The case against humanitarian intervention

Seven key objections to humanitarian intervention have been advanced at various times by scholars, international lawyers, and policy-makers. These objections are not mutually exclusive and can be found in the writings of Realists, Liberals, Feminists, Post-colonial theorists and others, though these different theories afford different weight to each of the objections.

No basis for humanitarian intervention in international law

Restrictionist international lawyers insist that the common good is best preserved by maintaining a ban on any use of force not authorized by the UNSC. They argue that aside from the right of individual and collective self-defence enshrined in Article 51 of the UN Charter, there are no other exceptions to Article 2(4). They also point to the fact that during the cold war, when states acting unilaterally could have plausibly invoked humanitarian claims (the key cases are India's intervention in East Pakistan in 1971, Vietnam's intervention in Cambodia in December 1978, and Tanzania's intervention in Uganda in January 1979), they had chosen not to do so. Interveners have typically either claimed to be acting in self-defence (during the cold war especially), have pointed to the 'implied authorization' of UNSC resolutions, or have refrained from making legal arguments at all.

States do not intervene for primarily humanitarian reasons

States almost always have mixed motives for intervening and are rarely prepared to sacrifice their own soldiers overseas unless they have self-interested reasons for doing so. For **Realists** this means that genuine humanitarian intervention is imprudent because it does not serve the **national interest**. For other critics, it points to the idea that the powerful only intervene when it suits them to do so and that strategies of **intervention** are more likely to be guided by calculations of national interest than by what is best for the victims in whose name the intervention is ostensibly being carried out.

States are not allowed to risk the lives of their soldiers to save strangers

Realists not only argue that states do not intervene for humanitarian purposes; their **statist** paradigm also asserts that states should not behave in this way. Political leaders do not have the moral right to shed the blood of their own citizens on behalf of suffering foreigners. Bhikhu Parekh (1997: 56) encapsulates this position: 'citizens are the exclusive responsibility of their state, and their state is entirely their own business'. Thus, if a civil

authority has broken down or is behaving in an appalling way towards its citizens, this is the responsibility of that state's citizens, and crucially its political leaders.

The problem of abuse

In the absence of an impartial mechanism for deciding when humanitarian intervention is permissible, states might espouse humanitarian motives as a pretext to cover the pursuit of national self-interest (Franck and Rodley 1973). The classic case of **abuse** was Hitler's argument that it was necessary to invade Czechoslovakia to protect the 'life and liberty' of that country's German population. Creating a right of humanitarian intervention would only make it easier for the powerful to justify interfering in the affairs of the weak. Critics argue that a right to intervention would not create more 'genuine' humanitarian action because self-interest not sovereignty has traditionally been the main barrier to intervention. However, it would make the world a more dangerous place by giving states more ways of justifying force (Chesterman 2001).

Selectivity of response

States always apply principles of humanitarian intervention selectively, resulting in an inconsistency in policy. Because state behaviour is governed by what governments judge to be in their interest, they are selective about when they choose to intervene. The problem of selectivity arises when an agreed moral principle is at stake in more than one situation, but national interest dictates a divergence of responses. A good example of the **selectivity** of response is the argument that **NATO's** intervention in Kosovo could not have been driven by humanitarian concerns because it has done nothing to address the very much larger humanitarian catastrophe in Darfur. Selectivity of response is the problem of failing to treat like cases alike.

Disagreement about moral principles

Pluralist international society theory identifies an additional objection to humanitarian intervention, the problem of how to reach a consensus on what moral principles

should underpin it. **Pluralism** is sensitive to human rights concerns but argues that humanitarian intervention should not be permitted in the face of disagreement about what constitutes extreme human rights violations. The concern is that in the absence of consensus on what principles should govern a right of humanitarian intervention, the most powerful states would be free to impose their own culturally determined moral values on weaker members of international society.

Intervention does not work

A final set of criticisms suggests that humanitarian intervention should be avoided because it is impossible for outsiders to impose human rights. **Liberals** argue that states are established by the informed consent of their citizens. Thus, one of the foremost nineteenth-century liberal thinkers, John Stuart Mill (1973: 377–8), argued that **democracy** could only be established by a domestic struggle for liberty. Human rights cannot take root if they are imposed or enforced by outsiders. Interveners will therefore find either that they become embroiled in an unending commitment or that human rights abuses re-ignite after they depart. Mill argued that oppressed peoples should themselves overthrow tyrannical government.

Key Points

- States will not intervene for primarily humanitarian purposes.
- States should not place their citizens in harm's way in order to protect foreigners.
- A legal right of humanitarian intervention would be vulnerable to abuse as states employ humanitarian claims to cloak the pursuit of self-interest.
- States will apply principles of humanitarian intervention selectively.
- In the absence of consensus about what principles should guide humanitarian intervention, a right of humanitarian intervention would undermine international order.
- Humanitarian intervention will always be based on the cultural preferences of the powerful.

The 1990s: a golden era of humanitarian activism?

It has become common to describe the immediate post-cold war period as something of a 'golden era' for humanitarian activism. Thomas Weiss (2004: 136) argues that 'the notion that human beings matter more than sovereignty radiated brightly, albeit briefly, across the international political horizon of the 1990s'. There is no doubt that during the 1990s, states began to contemplate intervention to protect imperilled strangers in distant lands. This was symbolized for many by NATO's intervention to halt Serb atrocities in Kosovo in March 1999 and the Australian-led intervention to end mass killing in East Timor. But the 1990s also saw the world stand aside during the genocides in Rwanda and Srebrenica. This section tries to make sense of these developments by focusing on international interventions in northern Iraq, Somalia, Rwanda, and Kosovo. It is divided into three parts: the place of humanitarian impulses in decisions to intervene; the legality and legitimacy of the interventions; and the effectiveness of these military interventions.

The role of humanitarian sentiments in decisions to intervene

In the case of northern Iraq in April 1991, but also Somalia in December 1992, domestic public opinion played an important role in pressurizing policy-makers into using force for humanitarian purposes. In the face of a massive refugee crisis caused by Saddam Hussein's oppression of the Kurds in the aftermath of the 1991 Gulf War, US, British, French, and Dutch military forces intervened to create protected 'safe havens' for the Kurdish people. Similarly, the US military intervention in Somalia in December 1992 was a response to sentiments of compassion on the part of US citizens. However, this sense of solidarity disappeared once the United States began sustaining casualties. The fact that the White House pulled the plug on its Somali intervention after the loss of eighteen US Rangers in a firefight in October 1993 indicates how capricious public

opinion is. Television pictures of starving and dying Somalis had persuaded the outgoing Bush administration to launch a humanitarian rescue mission, but once the US public saw dead Americans dragged through the streets of Mogadishu, the Clinton administration announced a timetable for withdrawal. What this case demonstrates is that the 'CNN effect' is a double-edged sword: it can pressurize governments into humanitarian intervention, yet with equal rapidity produce public disillusionment and calls for withdrawal. However, these cases suggest that even if there are no vital national interests at stake, liberal states might launch humanitarian rescue missions if sufficient public pressure is mobilized. Certainly, there is no evidence in either of these cases to support the realist claim that states cloak power political motives behind the guise of humanitarianism.

By contrast, the French intervention in Rwanda in July 1994 seems to be an example of **abuse**. The French government emphasized the strictly humanitarian character of the operation, but this interpretation lacks credibility given the evidence that they were covertly pursuing national self-interest. France had propped up the one-party Hutu state for twenty years, even providing troops when the Rwandan Patriotic Front (RPF), operating out of neighbouring Uganda, threatened to overrun the country in 1990 and 1993. The French President, François Mitterrand, was reportedly anxious to restore waning French influence in Africa, and was fearful that an RPF victory in French-speaking Rwanda would bring the country under the influence of Anglophones. France therefore did not intervene until the latter stages of the genocide, which was ended primarily by the RPF's military victory. It seems, therefore, that French behaviour accords with the realist premise that states will only risk their soldiers in defence of the national interest. French leaders may have been partly motivated by humanitarian sentiments but this seems to be a case of a state abusing the concept of humanitarian intervention since the primary purpose of the intervention was to protect French national interests.

The moral question raised by French intervention is why international society failed to intervene when the genocide began in early April 1994. French intervention might have saved some lives but it came far too late to halt the genocide. Some 800,000 people were killed in a mere hundred days. The failure of international society to stop

the genocide indicates that state leaders remain gripped by the mind-set of **statism**. There was no intervention for the simple reason that those with the military capability to stop the genocide were unwilling to sacrifice troops and treasure to protect Rwandans. International solidarity in the face of genocide was limited to moral outrage and the provision of humanitarian aid.

If the French intervention in Rwanda can be criticized for being too little, too late, NATO's intervention in Kosovo in 1999 was criticized for being too much, too soon. At the beginning of the war, NATO said it was intervening to prevent a humanitarian catastrophe. To do this, NATO aircraft were given two objectives, reduce Serbia's military capacity and coerce Milošević into accepting the Rambouillet settlement, with the emphasis initially placed on the former. Three arguments were adduced to support NATO's claim that the resort to force was justifiable. First, it was argued that Serbian actions in Kosovo had created a humanitarian emergency and breached a whole range of international legal commitments. Second, NATO governments argued that the Serbs were committing crimes against humanity, possibly including genocide. Third, it was contended that the Milošević regime's use of force against the Kosovar Albanians challenged global norms of **common humanity.**

Closer analysis of the justifications articulated by Western leaders suggests that while humanitarianism may have provided the primary impulse for action, it was by no means the exclusive impulse, and the complexity of the motives of the interveners coloured the character of the intervention. Indeed, NATO was propelled into action by a mixture of humanitarian concern and self-interest gathered around three sets of issues. The first might be called the 'Srebrenica syndrome'—a fear that left unchecked Milošević's henchmen would replicate the carnage of Bosnia. The second is related directly to self-interest and was a concern that protracted conflict in the southern Balkans would create a massive refugee crisis in Europe. Finally, NATO governments were worried that if they failed to contain the crisis, it would spread and engulf several neighbouring states, especially Macedonia, Albania, and Bulgaria (Bellamy 2002: 3). This suggests that humanitarian intervention might be prompted by mixed motives. This only becomes a problem if the non-humanitarian motives undermine the chances of achieving the humanitarian purposes.

How legal and legitimate were the interventions?

In contrast with state practice during the cold war, the interventions in northern Iraq, Somalia, Rwanda, and Kosovo were all justified in humanitarian terms by the intervening states. Justifying the use of force on humanitarian grounds remained hotly contested, with China, Russia, and members of the Non-Aligned Movement (NAM) defending a traditional interpretation of **state sovereignty**. However, this position became less tenable as the 1990s progressed, and by the end of the decade most states were prepared to accept that the UNSC was entitled to authorize armed humanitarian intervention. Thus, almost every **peacekeeping** mandate passed by the UNSC since 2000 contains an instruction for international soldiers to protect endangered civilians, using force if necessary and prudent. **Chapter VII** of the Charter enables the UNSC to authorize military enforcement action only in cases where it finds a threat to 'international peace and security'. Since the early 1990s, the UNSC has expanded its list of what counts as a threat to the peace to include human suffering, the overthrow of democratic government, state failure, refugee movements, and ethnic cleansing. This attempt to justify humanitarian intervention on the grounds that human suffering constitutes a threat to international security was first controversially employed in the cases of northern Iraq and Somalia (Wheeler 2000, 2003: 32–41).

NATO's intervention in Kosovo raised the fundamental question of how international society should treat intervention where a state, or in this case a group of states, decide to use force to alleviate human suffering without the explicit authorization of the Security Council. Although the UN did not expressly sanction NATO's use of force, the UNSC also chose not to condemn it. Russia tabled a draft UNSC resolution on 26 March 1999 condemning NATO's use of force and demanding an immediate halt to the bombing. Surprisingly, only Russia, China, and Namibia voted in favour, leading to a resounding defeat of the resolution. The UNSC's response to NATO's breach of the UN Charter's rules governing the use of force suggested that while it was not prepared to endorse unilateral humanitarian intervention, it was not necessarily going to condemn it either.

What emerges from post-cold war state practice is that Western states took the lead in advancing a new norm of armed humanitarian intervention. Although some states, notably Russia, China, India, and some members of the NAM remained very uneasy with this development, they reluctantly came to accept that military intervention authorized by the UNSC was justifiable in cases of genocide and mass killing. The best illustration of this is the fact that no member of the UNSC tried to oppose intervention in Rwanda to end the genocide on the grounds that this violated its sovereignty. Instead, the barrier to intervention was the lack of political will on the part of states to incur the costs and risks of armed intervention to save Rwandans. There were also important limits to the emerging norm: intervention outside the UN remained very controversial; the UNSC refrained from authorizing intervention against fully functioning states; and although it is inconceivable that any state would have complained about intervention in Rwanda, this was a uniquely horrible case with a rate of killing higher than that of the Holocaust.

Were the interventions successful?

Does the record of post-cold war interventions lend support to the proposition that the use of force can promote humanitarian values? Humanitarian outcomes might usefully be divided into short- and long-term ones. The former would refer to the immediate alleviation of human suffering through the termination of genocide or mass murder and/or the delivery of humanitarian aid to civilians trapped in war zones. Long-term humanitarian outcomes focus on how far intervention addresses the underlying causes of human suffering by facilitating conflict resolution and the construction of viable polities.

'Operation Safe Haven' in Iraq enjoyed initial success in dealing with the refugee problem in northern Iraq and clearly saved lives. However, as the media spotlight began to shift elsewhere and public interest waned, so did the commitment of Western governments to protect the Kurds. While Western air forces continued to police a 'no-fly zone' over northern Iraq, the intervening states quickly handed over the running of the safe havens to what they knew was an ill-equipped and badly supported UN relief operation. This faced enormous problems owing to Iraqi hostility towards its Kurdish minority. Nevertheless, the Kurds were able to fashion a significant degree of autonomy in the 1990s, which has persisted since the 2003 US-led invasion.

Some commentators identify the initial US intervention in Somalia in the period between December 1992 and May 1993 as a successful humanitarian intervention. In terms of short-term success, the US claims that it saved thousands of Somalis from starvation, though this is disputed (Weiss 1999: 82–7). What is not disputed is that the mission ended in disaster. This can be traced to the attempt by UNOSOM II (this UN force took over from the United States in May 1993 but its military missions were principally controlled by US commanders) to go beyond the initial US mission of famine relief to the disarmament of the warring factions and the provision of law and order. Suffering always has political causes, and the rationale behind the expanded mandate of UNOSOM II was to try to put in place a framework of political civility that would prevent a return to civil war and famine. However, this attempt to convert a short-term humanitarian outcome (famine relief) into the longer-term one of conflict resolution and reconstruction proved a failure. Once the UNSC had sanctioned the arrest of General Aidid after his forces killed 23 UN peacekeepers in June 1993, UNOSOM II acted like an imperial power, relying on high-tech American weaponry to police the streets of southern Mogadishu.

The jury remains out on whether the international community can succeed in building a new multi-ethnic state in Kosovo. On the one hand, an improved security situation has enabled a marked decrease in the number of international soldiers and police deployed there and there have been a number of successful elections and transitions of power. On the other hand, ethnic violence remains a feature of life in province, there is high unemployment, and Kosovo has become a haven for organized crime. Looking back, the NATO-led force that entered Kosovo at the end of Operation Allied Force succeeded in returning Kosovar Albanian refugees to their homes but failed to protect the Serbian community from reprisal attacks.

The conclusion that emerges from this brief overview is that forcible intervention in humanitarian crises is most likely to be a short-term palliative that does little to address the underlying political causes of the violence and suffering. It is for this reason that the International Commission on Intervention and State Sovereignty (ICISS) insisted that intervention was only one of three international responsibilities, the other two involving long-term commitments to building the political, social, economic, military, and legal conditions necessary for the promotion and protection of human rights.

Key Points

- The 1990s were described as a golden era of humanitarian activism because of a dramatic increase in the number of humanitarian interventions.
- Although some interventions were motivated by humanitarian concerns, others were not. Most interventions were prompted by mixed motives.
- The legality and legitimacy of humanitarian intervention remains hotly contested but a norm of intervention authorized by the Security Council emerged in the 1990s.
- Interventions tended to be more successful in stopping immediate killing and less successful in building long-term peace.

Humanitarian intervention and the war on terror

What effect did the terrorist attacks on **11 September 2001** have on humanitarian intervention? Has the war on terror made it less likely that powerful states will use their militaries to save strangers? Is there a danger that US administrations will return to their cold war policy of prioritizing strategic advantage over human rights? There are two prominent perspectives on these questions.

The first is a sceptical position. It holds that since the 'war on terror' began, the United States has placed its own strategic interests ahead of concern for human rights, both overseas and at home. It has become more willing to align itself with repressive governments, such as Tajikistan and Sudan, that support its anti-terror strategy (Ignatieff 2002). According to this view, where it might have been difficult to marshal Western commitment to humanitarian intervention in the 1990s, it has become virtually impossible after 9/11. Since 2001, the Western contribution to peace operations has markedly declined. Just as worrying for the sceptics is the fear that the USA and its allies are actually undermining the consensus on humanitarian intervention by **abusing** humanitarian principles in justifying their use of force.

The second perspective is more optimistic. It springs from the core premise that Western states will only militarily intervene in humanitarian emergencies if they believe that vital security interests are at stake. For the optimists, Afghanistan seemed to show that there is often a critical linkage between **failed states** and **terrorism**. Therefore, they predicted that the war on terror could provide the necessary strategic interests to motivate intervention that is defensible on grounds of both human rights and national security (Chesterman 2004). The Afghanistan experience might be seen as supporting the optimistic viewpoint, though important question marks can be raised over whether military means have been properly calibrated to humanitarian ends since the intervention in October 2001 (Wheeler and Morris 2006). However, the more recent experiences in relation to Iraq and Darfur suggests not only that the war on terror has fractured the fragile consensus over humanitarian intervention, but also that the problem of political will continues to bedevil effective humanitarian intervention as it did over Rwanda. Indeed, the Darfur case suggests that the West's commitment to the war on terror is making it less likely to intervene to save strangers in strategically unimportant regions.

Afghanistan

Although the US-led intervention in Afghanistan was a war of self-defence, the US President nevertheless felt the need to make a humanitarian argument to support his case. He told Afghans that, 'the oppressed people of Afghanistan will know the generosity of America and its allies. As we strike military targets, we'll also drop food, medicine and supplies to the starving and suffering men and women and children of Afghanistan' (Bush 2001). The United States took steps to minimize noncombatant suffering in Afghanistan but at least two operational choices undermined the humanitarian credentials of the war. The first was the decision to rely heavily on intelligence provided by different Afghan factions for the identification of military targets. This reflected the US determination to reduce the risks to its own armed forces. But this decision left US forces open to manipulation by Afghans eager to settle scores with their rivals, resulting in a number of attacks where innocent civilians were killed. The second failure was Washington's

refusal to contribute ground troops to the UN-mandated International Security Assistance Force (ISAF) and make a sustained contribution to rebuilding Afghanistan. The ISAF was initially confined to operating in Kabul and even though it was later expanded, only relatively small 'reconstruction teams' were dispatched to other regional centres. In 2005, ISAF became primarily engaged with combating a resurgent Taliban. The relative neglect of post-intervention Afghanistan can be measured by the amount of resources committed to it. In 2004, the United States committed $18.4 billion of development spending to Iraq and a mere $1.77 billion to Afghanistan.

The fact that the United States and its allies felt it necessary to employ humanitarian arguments in this case highlights the extent to which this justification has become a legitimating basis for military intervention in the post-cold war world. However, the use of humanitarian language did not presage a new Western commitment to protecting civilians in need. In Afghanistan, the humanitarian impulse has been less important than political and strategic considerations, the protection of allied soldiers has been prioritized over the security of Afghans, and there has been insufficient commitment to post-conflict reconstruction (Wheeler 2004*a*; Wheeler and Morris 2006). This lends credence to the sceptical view about humanitarian intervention in a post-9/11 world.

Iraq

The use of humanitarian arguments by the United States, United Kingdom, and Australia to justify the invasion and occupation of Iraq posed a crucial challenge to the legitimacy of humanitarian intervention in international society. The Iraq War was primarily justified as one necessitated by the danger posed by Saddam Hussein's **weapons of mass destruction** (WMD). However, as the offending weapons became more elusive, those justifying the use of force to remove Saddam Hussein relied increasingly on humanitarian rationales. As criticism of the war mounted, President Bush and British Prime Minister Tony Blair frequently retorted that regardless of WMD, the war was justifiable because 'Iraq is a better place' without Saddam (see Cushman 2005). There are two important issues that stem from this. First, was

Case Study Iraq—a humanitarian intervention?

The case for

The case for seeing Iraq as a legitimate humanitarian intervention came from a variety of sources, including liberals, neo-conservatives, and the left. We will focus only on the **liberal** case, as put forward by Fernando Tesón (2005: 1–20; see also Cushman 2005). Tesón's case was predicated on four claims. First, the invasion of Iraq had as its purpose the ending of tyranny. According to Tesón, humanitarian intervention requires humanitarian intent, not humanitarian motive (like **Realists**, Tesón believes that states will never act out of purely humanitarian motives). Even though the US-led coalition was not motivated by humanitarian impulses, it still had humanitarian intentions because only by removing tyranny and installing democracy would the threat posed by Iraq be removed. Second, Tesón insisted that the abuse of civilians by the Iraqi government was severe enough to warrant intervention, saying that it makes no sense to argue that intervention should be reserved for ongoing mass-killing because that rule would have prohibited the removal of Hitler after the

Holocaust. Third, Tesón pointed to the fact that the overwhelming majority of Iraqis welcomed the intervention as providing an important source of legitimacy. Finally, he argued that although UN authorization is preferable, the doctrine of humanitarian intervention permits unauthorized intervention, as in the case of Kosovo.

The case against

Opposition to this case came from an equally diverse range of people. Even some people who defend an expansive right to humanitarian intervention rejected the humanitarian case for invading Iraq. We will focus on Terry Nardin's response to Tesón's argument (Nardin 2005: 21; see also Evans 2004; Wheeler and Morris 2006). Nardin argued that Tesón's case involved 'significant revision' of the traditional doctrine of humanitarian intervention. First, according to the traditional doctrine, intervention is permitted only by the commission of particular crimes (genocide, mass killing) not by the 'character' of the regime. As Nardin put it, 'humanitarian intervention aims to rescue the potential victims of massacre or some other crime against humanity by thwarting the violence against them' (2005: 22). Second, Nardin argued that Tesón's position overlooked international society's strong predisposition towards non-intervention. Third, he claimed that humanitarian intervention could only be justified if it was calculated to cause more good than harm. Iraq's current woes were foreseen. Finally, Nardin argues that Tesón's account misunderstood the place of humanitarian intervention in international society. Nardin argued that international society is based on rules of **coexistence** and that humanitarian intervention is a carefully calibrated exception to those rules. Tesón understands world politics as being based 'not on rules of coexistence but solely and directly on universal principles of morality and human rights'. *(2005: 23)*

---

the war in Iraq a legitimate humanitarian intervention? We cover the arguments for and against this proposition in the Case Study. Second, how was Iraq perceived by the **society of states**, and what effect has this case had on the emerging norm of humanitarian intervention?

Many commentators and politicians believe that the use of humanitarian justifications in relation to Iraq damaged the emerging norm of humanitarian intervention by highlighting the potential for the norm to be **abused** by the powerful to justify interfering in the affairs of the weak. Of course, many states were deeply sceptical about humanitarian intervention before Iraq, but there is evidence that some states that were initially supportive of humanitarian intervention have become less so as a result of the perceived misuse of humanitarian rationales over Iraq. For example, in 2003 Germany—a strong sup-

porter of the Kosovo intervention—refused to endorse a British statement on the responsibility to protect because it feared that any doctrine of humanitarian intervention outside the UNSC might be used by the United States and the United Kingdom to justify the invasion of Iraq (Bellamy 2005: 39). A more subtle variant on this argument holds that while Iraq may not have damaged the norm itself, it has damaged the status of the United States and the United Kingdom as **norm carriers**, weakening the extent to which they are able to persuade others to agree to action in humanitarian crises (Bellamy 2005; Wheeler and Morris 2006). As Kenneth Roth of Human Rights Watch grimly predicted, as a consequence of the use of humanitarian justifications in relation to Iraq, 'it will be more difficult next time for us to call on military action when we need it to save potentially hundreds of thousands of lives'

(Roth 2004*a*: 2–3). Sadly, Roth's prediction was proved correct by the world's response to the humanitarian catastrophe in Darfur.

Darfur

Since 2003, the Sudanese government and its 'janjaweed' militia have embarked on what the UN has described as a 'reign of terror' in Darfur. At least 250,000 people have died and over two million people have been forced from their homes. Despite this toll of human suffering, at the time of writing the world's response had been limited to the deployment of an understaffed and under-funded African Union (AU) mission that has proved utterly incapable of protecting civilians from harm.

Why has the world's response been so tepid? Three sets of factors are at work. The first, emphasized by the British and American governments especially, are prudential concerns. The Sudanese government has steadfastly refused to contemplate any non-African deployments in Darfur, so any armed intervention might be strongly resisted. In addition, intervention might make the Sudanese government close its ports to aid agencies, making it difficult to get life-saving assistance to the refugees. There are also worries that firm action in Darfur might ruin a peace settlement for Sudan's other civil war, which claimed two million lives over more than a decade. The second set of factors relate more directly to the war on terror. The idea of forcible Western intervention in Darfur is strongly opposed by Russia, China, the AU, and the NAM. Since the invasion of Iraq, many states have been keen to reaffirm the principle of state sovereignty and are less willing than before to contemplate actions that violate this. Finally, the reluctance to act in Darfur demonstrates the continuing relevance of **statism**. Just as in Rwanda, Western governments do not want to sacrifice troops and treasure to stop one group of Africans killing another group. Furthermore, several of the great powers have self-interested reasons for not upsetting the Sudanese government: China has significant

interests in Sudanese oil; Russia has a smaller oil interest but also sells arms to Sudan; and the United States sees Sudan as a vital regional ally in the war on terror. The enduring logic of statism means that these powers afford more weight to their interests than they do to the lives of Darfurians.

Overall, the sceptical position has proven more accurate than the optimistic one in relation to humanitarian intervention after 9/11. Humanitarian justifications are being used with greater frequency to justify a wide range of military operations, but the developing consensus on a new norm charted in the previous section has been set back by the perceived **abuse** of humanitarian claims in relation to Afghanistan and especially Iraq. Many governments, especially in the NAM, have reacted to this by reaffirming state sovereignty. This worrying development was manifested in international society's failure to prevent or end the humanitarian catastrophe in Darfur. Yet at the same time, the inroads that humanitarian concerns have made into the sovereign prerogatives of states can be seen in the agreement at the 2005 UN **World Summit** to the idea of the 'responsibility to protect'. The next section will explore how far this offers the basis for a new global consensus on the use of force to protect endangered peoples.

Key Points

- Optimists argued that 9/11 injected self-interest into humanitarian endeavours, making states more likely to intervene to halt human suffering.
- Sceptics worried that the war on terror would 'crowd out' humanitarianism and encourage powerful states to cloak self-interest in the veneer of humanitarian concern.
- There was a major debate about whether or not the war in Iraq could be justified as a legitimate humanitarian intervention.
- Iraq has made many states more wary of embracing a humanitarian exception to the rule of non-intervention.
- A combination of prudence and statism has contributed towards inactivity in the face of the humanitarian catastrophe in Darfur.

The responsibility to protect

The Responsibility to Protect, the 2001 report of the International Commission on Intervention and State Sovereignty (ICISS), attempted to resolve the tension between the competing claims of sovereignty and human rights by building a new consensus around the principles that should govern the protection of endangered peoples. The principle of responsibility to protect was adopted by the UN General Assembly at the 2005 World Summit, a move described as a 'revolution ... in international affairs' by one commentator (Lindberg 2005). But what is the 'responsibility to protect', how was it adopted, and what does it mean for the future of humanitarian intervention?

The Commission argued that states have the primary responsibility to protect their citizens. When they are unable or unwilling to do so, or when they deliberately terrorize their citizens, the 'the principle of non-intervention yields to the international responsibility to protect' (ICISS 2001: xi). The report broadens this responsibility to encompass not only the responsibility to react to humanitarian crises but also the responsibility to prevent such crises and the 'responsibility to rebuild' failed and tyrannical states. This reframing of the debate away from the question of whether states have a right of intervention towards the question of where responsibility rests for protecting endangered peoples formed the basis of an attempt to generate a new international political consensus supporting what the ICISS report calls 'intervention for human protection purposes' (ICISS 2001: xiii).

Two crucial motivating factors behind the setting up of ICISS were the aspiration to avoid future situations like Kosovo, where the UNSC was paralyzed by division among the five permanent members of the UNSC (P–5), and future situations like Rwanda, where the world stood aside as genocide unfolded.

There are two competing accounts of the causes of deadlock in the UNSC over Kosovo. On the one hand, there are those like British Prime Minister Tony Blair, who argued that it was caused by 'unreasonable' threats of veto on the part of Russia and China (Bellamy 2006: 148; see also Wheeler and Dunne 2004). This position was endorsed by the two co-chairs of the ICISS when they described the UNSC's failure to authorize armed

intervention in Kosovo as a failure 'to discharge its own responsibility to protect in a conscience-shocking situation crying out for action' (Evans and Sahnoun 2002: 108). The alternative position holds that Russia and China had genuine concerns about the use of force, based on their view that the level of killing and ethnic cleansing was not bad enough to warrant intervention. To build an international consensus that would help prevent future Kosovos, therefore, the ICISS needed to make it more difficult for members of the UNSC to use the veto capriciously, but also to make it harder for states to **abuse** humanitarian justifications. The principal device for achieving this goal was a set of criteria that governments and other observers could use to evaluate whether military intervention would be legitimate on humanitarian grounds (see Box 30.1). The ICISS argued that if states committed to these principles, it would make it easier to build consensus on how to respond to humanitarian emergencies. On the one hand, it would be harder for states like China and Russia to oppose genuine humanitarian intervention because they would have committed themselves to the responsibility to protect in cases of genocide, mass killing, and large-scale ethnic cleansing (the **thresholds established** by the ICISS that justify military intervention). On the other hand, it would be harder for states to abuse humanitarian justifications because it would be very difficult to satisfy these criteria in cases where there was not a compelling humanitarian rationale to act.

Preventing future Rwandas can be boiled down to overcoming a single obstacle: how to persuade states, particularly powerful states, to risk troops and treasure to save strangers in distant lands where few strategic interests at stake. Overcoming this obstacle requires that two fundamental problems be addressed: first, identifying precisely which actors should assume the responsibility to protect, and second, persuading those actors to accept the obligation to use force for 'human protection purposes'.

According to the ICISS, the UNSC has the primary responsibility to act. The report argued that if it failed to live up to this responsibility, there was a danger that other states might choose to take the law into their own hands with negative consequences for both order and justice. The Commissioners warned that:

Box 30.2 Paragraphs 138 and 139 of the 2005 World Summit Outcome Document

138. Each individual state has the responsibility to protect its populations from genocide, war crimes, ethnic cleansing and crimes against humanity. This responsibility entails the prevention of such crimes, including their incitement, through appropriate and necessary means. We accept that responsibility and will act in accordance with it. The international community should, as appropriate, encourage and help States to exercise this responsibility and support the United Nations in establishing an early warning capability.

139. The international community, through the United Nations, also has the responsibility to use appropriate diplomatic, humanitarian and other peaceful means, in accordance with Chapters VI and VIII of the Charter of the United Nations, to help protect populations from war crimes, ethnic cleansing and crimes against humanity. In this context, we are prepared to take collective action, in a timely and decisive manner, through the Security Council, in accordance with the Charter, including Chapter VII, on a case-by-case basis and in **cooperation** with relevant regional organizations as appropriate, should peaceful means be inadequate and national authorities are manifestly failing to protect their populations from genocide, war crimes, ethnic cleansing and crimes against humanity.

if the Security Council fails to discharge its responsibility in conscience-shocking situations crying out for action, then it is unrealistic to expect that concerned states will rule out other means and forms of action to meet the gravity and urgency of these situations. If collective organizations will not authorize collection intervention against regimes that flout the most elemental forms of legitimate governmental behaviour, then the pressures for intervention by *ad hoc* coalitions or individual states will surely intensify. And there is a risk then that such interventions, without the discipline and constraints of UN authorization, will not be conducted for the right reasons or with the right commitment to the necessary precautionary principles.

(ICISS 2001: 71)

In cases where there is majority support for intervention in the UNSC (a resolution supporting intervention for humanitarian purposes has secured nine votes or more), but collective action is blocked by a veto, the ICISS suggested that states seek political support from the General Assembly. If it was not possible to secure a two-thirds majority in that body recommending military action (the legal basis of which would be highly dubious), the report even more tentatively suggested that intervention might still be justifiable if authorized by a relevant regional organizations (ICISS 2001: 75). This suggests a hierarchy of where responsibility lies, starting with the host state, then the UNSC, the General Assembly, regional organizations, coalitions of the willing, and finally individual states.

How, though, are we to persuade governments to abandon the statism that caused the world to stand aside in Rwanda and, more recently, Darfur? The ICISS had an answer to this, too. A commitment to the **just cause thresholds** would create expectations among domestic publics about when their governments ought to act to save imperilled people. Thus, in cases of mass killing and ethnic cleansing, governments would be put under pressure to act because they had already committed in principle to doing so.

Although the ICISS marked a bold and important step towards building consensus, there are at least three important problems with the logic that it employed.

Agreement on criteria does not guarantee agreement on action in real cases

States might agree on what criteria to use in making judgements about humanitarian intervention, but the application of the criteria to real cases is always open to interpretation. Skilled lawyers and diplomats will use the criteria to make convincing arguments both for and against particular interventions, as they did in the recent case of Darfur (Bellamy 2005). In 2005, UNSC members argued about whether or not the Sudanese government had indeed proven itself 'unable and unwilling' to protect its people. Without an authoritative judge to determine such matters, the criteria can only provide a language for argument and discussion. They cannot resolve differences of opinion.

The criteria are open to manipulation by powerful actors

Although criteria reduces the dangers of abuse by establishing the parameters within which justifying arguments have to be framed, the way the facts are interpreted and the arguments presented are inevitably shaped by power politics. Moreover, the interpretations of powerful states with the capacity to reward and punish others are likely to carry

---

Box 30.3 Recommendations of the High-Level Panel on Measures to Prevent War

1 The Security Council should be prepared to refer matters to the International Criminal Court.

2 The UN and other agencies should work towards cooperative agreements about the management of natural resources.

3 The UN should develop frameworks for minority rights and the protection of democratic governments from unconstitutional overthrow.

4 The UN should expedite negotiations on the marking and tracing of small arms.

5 Member states should give accurate reports to the UN Register on Conventional Arms.

6 A training facility should be created for Special-Representatives to

the Secretary-General.

7 The UN's Department for Political Affairs should be given additional resources for preventive **diplomacy**.

8 The UN should create a mediation support capacity, develop its competence on thematic issues, increase its interaction with other agencies and consult with **civil society** during peace processes.

9 Parties to conflicts should make constructive use of preventive peacekeepers.

(United Nations High Level-Panel on Threats, Challenges and Change 2004: 90–104)

---

more weight in the deliberations of governments than the arguments of those who lack such sticks and carrots.

Assumes that governments can be persuaded to act

Translating the responsibility to protect from the ideal into reality rests on the notion that governments can be shamed into acting to end genocide, mass killing, and large-scale ethnic cleansing by moral pressure from other governments, their own citizens, and wider world public opinion. There are reasons to doubt that these pressures can really be so effective. Imagine if there had been an ICISS report in early 1994. Would New Zealand, as President of the UNSC for April (the presidency rotates each month between the members of the UNSC), have been able to 'shame' the Clinton administration into intervening in Rwanda? If this logic holds, why were major public campaigns such as the Save Darfur Coalition unable to persuade their governments to act more effectively? Public opinion can only galvanize action when governments themselves are already predisposed towards taking it. Sadly, few citizens change the way they vote because their government chooses not to intervene to save foreigners.

The 2005 World Summit

In 2005, the UN World Summit adopted a declaration committing all 191 member states to the principle of the responsibility to protect. Some lauded it as a major breakthrough, while others argued that the ICISS report's findings had been watered down to such an extent that it

would not, in practice, afford new protections to imperiled peoples. There are some notable differences between the ICISS report and the World Summit text. What are those differences and how did they come about?

The 2001 ICISS report was received most favourably by states such as Canada (the progenitor of the idea of the ICISS and the political custodian of the process), Germany, and the United Kingdom (since the 1999 Kosovo intervention, the British, led by the Secretary of State for Foreign Affairs, Robin Cook, had been exploring the potential to develop criteria to guide global decision-making about humanitarian intervention). Other supporters of the ICISS report included Argentina, Australia, Colombia, Croatia, Ireland, South Korea, New Zealand, Norway, Peru, Rwanda, Sweden, and Tanzania. The great powers were much more sceptical from the outset. The United States rejected the idea of criteria on the grounds that it could not offer pre-commitments to engage its military forces where it had no national interests at stake, and that it would not bind itself to criteria that would constrain its right to decide when and where to use force (Welsh 2004: 180). China insisted that all questions relating to the use of force should be dealt with by the UNSC, a position supported by Russia. Both of these countries argued that the UN was already equipped to deal with humanitarian crises, and that by countenancing unauthorized intervention, the *Responsibility to Protect* risked undermining the UN Charter.

Opinion outside the UNSC was also generally cautious. The NAM rejected the concept. India, for example, argued that the UNSC was already sufficiently empowered to act in humanitarian emergencies and observed that the failure to act in the past was caused by a lack of political will not a lack of authority. Speaking on behalf

of the NAM, the Malaysian government argued that the *Responsibility to Protect* represented a reincarnation of humanitarian intervention for which there was no basis in international law.

As a result of these doubts, significant changes had to be made to persuade states to adopt the principle of the responsibility to protect. In particular, the proposal to include criteria governing the use of force was dropped during the negotiations leading up to the agreement at the World Summit. Moreover, and significantly watering down the recommendations in the ICISS report, it was agreed that **responsibility to protect intervention** required express UNSC authorization. This closed down the possibility of appealing to other bodies even if the will of a majority of Council members was blocked by one or more of the P–5 exercising the veto. Although momentous in that this was the first time that the society of states had formally declared that sovereignty might sometimes give way to concerns about human rights, it is perhaps best understood as a codification of the humanitarian intervention norm that had developed in the 1990s.

Key Points

- The 'responsibility to protect' switches the focus from a debate about sovereignty versus human rights to a discussion of how best to protect endangered peoples.
- The ICISS report attempted to move the norm of humanitarian intervention forward by forging a new consensus around the criteria for judging when armed intervention for humanitarian purposes was justifiable.
- There are good reasons to think that criteria alone will not galvanize action or consensus in difficult cases.
- The responsibility to protect was adopted by states at the 2005 World Summit, but in a significantly revised form.

Conclusion

Globalization is bringing nearer Kant's vision of moral interconnectedness, but as the Rwandan genocide and global inaction over Darfur so brutally demonstrate, this growth in cosmopolitan sensibilities has not yet been translated into a global consensus on **forcible humanitarian intervention**. Western publics are increasingly sensitized to the human suffering of others, but this media-nurtured sense of compassion is very selective in its response to human suffering. The media spotlight ensured that governments directed their humanitarian energies to the crises in northern Iraq, Somalia, and Bosnia, but during the same period millions perished in the brutal civil wars in Angola, Liberia, and the Democratic Republic of Congo.

Each case has to be judged on its merits, but as the examples of Somalia and perhaps Kosovo demonstrate, interventions which begin with humanitarian credentials can all too easily degenerate into 'a range of policies and activities which go beyond, or even conflict with, the label "humanitarian"' (Roberts 1993: 448). A further fundamental problem with a strategy of forcible humanitarian intervention concerns the so-called 'body-bag' factor. Is domestic public opinion, especially in Western states, prepared to see their military personnel die in the cause of humanitarian intervention? A striking feature of all post-cold war humanitarian interventions is that no Western government has yet chosen to risk its military personnel in defence of human rights where there was a significant risk of casualties from the outset.

Since 9/11, Western states have expressed humanitarian sentiments in relation to many different types of war. While this indicates the growing power of humanitarianism, the downside of this is that states might abuse humanitarian rationales in justifying their use of force, while only **selectively** responding to humanitarian crises in strategically important areas. For many in the developing world, this is precisely what the United States and the United Kingdom have done in Iraq, damaging rather than furthering the humanitarian agenda.

The chapter ended by considering the responsibility to protect, which has sought to reshape the terms of the debate between supporters and opponents of humanitarian intervention. The concept has certainly helped change the political language used to describe and debate humanitarian intervention, and its adoption at the UN World Summit was an important milestone. The real test, however, is whether it will generate a new political will on the part of the major states to incur the costs and risks of saving strangers. The evidence from Darfur is not encouraging in this regard.

? Questions

1 How far is the use of force the defining characteristic of a humanitarian intervention?

2 How important are motives, intentions, means, and outcomes in judging the humanitarian credentials of an intervention?

3 How persuasive is the counter-restrictionist case for a legal right of humanitarian intervention?

4 Should considerations of international order always be privileged over concerns of individual justice in the society of states?

5 Why has the society of states failed to arrive at a collective consensus on what moral principles should underpin a right of humanitarian intervention?

6 Is there a new norm of legitimate humanitarian intervention?

7 Has the 'war on terror' made it less likely that powerful states will use their armed forces to 'save strangers'?

8 Was the 2003 invasion of Iraq a legitimate humanitarian intervention?

9 To what extent does the 'responsibility to protect' principle resolve some of the political problems association with humanitarian intervention?

10 How far is military force an effective instrument for the promotion of humanitarian values?

⤳ Guide to further reading

Bellamy, A. (2006), *Just Wars: From Cicero to Iraq* (Cambridge: Polity Press). This book charts the development of the 'just war' tradition and its relationship with international law. It contains a chapter on humanitarian intervention addressed from a 'just war' perspective.

Chesterman, S. (2001), *Just War or Just Peace: Humanitarian Intervention in International Law* (Oxford: Oxford University Press). An excellent analysis of the legality of humanitarian intervention which strongly supports the 'restrictionist' view.

Holzgrefe, J. F., and Keohane R. (eds) (2002), *Humanitarian Intervention: Ethical, Legal and Political Dilemmas* (Cambridge: Cambridge University Press). A superb edited collection that explores the practice of humanitarian intervention from the perspectives of moral philosophy, international law, and political practice.

Weiss, T. G. (2007), *Humanitarian Intervention: Ideas in Action* (Cambridge: Polity Press). Provides a compelling introduction to the theory and practice of humanitarian intervention and covers the responsibility to protect.

Welsh, J. (ed.) (2004), *Humanitarian Intervention and International Relations* (Oxford: Oxford University Press). Another first-rate edited volume which brings together International Relations theorists and practitioners who have been involved in intervention in the past decade. It includes a chapter by Wheeler that analyzes the development of the humanitarian intervention norm into the twenty–first century.

Wheeler, N. J. (2000), *Saving Strangers: Humanitarian Intervention in International Society* (Oxford: Oxford University Press). Offers a new way of evaluating humanitarian interventions and considers a wide range of interventions in the cold war and post-cold war eras.

Online Resource Centre

 Visit the Online Resource Centre that accompanies this book to access more learning resources on this chapter topic at www.oxfordtextbooks.co.uk/uk/orc/baylis_smith4e/

Part Five
Globalization in the future

In this final part of the book we want to offer you some reflections on the impact of globalization for world politics in the new millennium. We thought long and hard about whether the editors should write a conclusion to the previous editions of this book given that some readers wrote to us to suggest that there should be a concluding section to the book. We eventually decided that it was impossible to do this given all the very different perspectives on globalization found in the preceding chapters. This is an approach we have continued in this edition. Our intention all along has been to show you that there are very distinct ways of looking at globalization, and writing a conclusion would have meant taking sides on which of these we preferred: we think that this is something that you should do. Therefore we asked two scholars to contribute chapters in this part, and, although neither of them is intended as a conclusion, together they outline the main questions concerning the nature of world politics in the current world. Andrew Linklater's chapter examines the forms of political community that are emerging under globalization, while Ian Clark's chapter looks at the question of what kind of order exists in the post-cold war period. We have two main aims for this part of the book: **first**, we want to end the book by returning to world politics, rather than international politics, by asking about the relationship between political community and globalization; **second**, we want to summarize the main arguments about the nature of world politics since the cold war, to bring the historical story up to date, so to speak. Each of these chapters problematizes the traditional international politics notion of hermetically sealed states acting within a states-system. Above all, we want to leave you with a series of deep questions about the effect of globalization both on the state and on world politics. Is the form of political community found in the globalized world different from that found before? Is the state still the unit for political community or does globalization make cosmopolitan politics more possible? Is there order in the post-cold war world? Is there much difference between the form of order found in the contemporary period and that found in the cold war? Does globalization help or hinder the creation of a more just, or a more equal, world order? We hope that these two chapters will raise a series of questions that will allow you to come to judgements about the overall impact of globalization on politics in the world.

Chapter 31

Globalization and the transformation of political community

ANDREW LINKLATER

- Introduction: what is a political community? ·· 544
- Nationalism and political community ·· 545
- Community and citizenship ··· 547
- The changing nature of political community ··· 549
- Beyond Realism? ·· 553
- Conclusion··· 556

Reader's Guide

Realist approaches to international relations focus on competition and conflict between independent political communities. They argue that the condition of anarchy involves permanent struggles for security and power. In the main, Realists believe that separate states will survive well into the future. Many of their critics maintain that important challenges to traditional ideas about political community have developed in recent times. Globalization has led scholars and activists to question the nation-state's capacity to solve global problems such as accelerating environmental devastation. It has led many to defend cosmopolitan responses to those problems in addition to increased sympathy for the suffering of distant communities. Many nation-states are challenged on a second front by national or ethnic movements which believe they possess little more than 'second-class citizenship'. Some of these groups have pursued the politics of secession, their aim being to establish their own sovereign institutions. Others have sought to alter national political institutions as part of the struggle for the recognition of group rights. This chapter explains how the nation-state became the dominant form of political community in the modern world. It analyzes approaches to new forms of community and citizenship which have appeared over the last two decades, and it asks how far the nation-state seems likely to endure as the main object of political loyalty.

Introduction: what is a political community?

Many different types of **community** exist in the modern world. They include local communities such as neighbourhood groups, political associations such as sovereign states, transnational movements such as scientific associations or **international non-governmental organizations** (INGO's), and 'virtual communities' made possible by instant forms of global communication. Each of these communities has its particular kind of human solidarity and distinctive pattern of **cooperation**. Each depends on a powerful sense of emotional identification with the group and on the willingness to make some personal sacrifices for a more general good.

Politics exist in all such communities because members do not have identical views about the goals of society or about how to realize them. In modern states there are sharp divisions between those who think that governments should redistribute wealth and those who believe that unfettered markets should allocate resources. Like **states**, religious communities have their politics, but they may not be political communities according to the definition used in this chapter. The desire to worship with others is central to a religious community but it is the aspiration for **self-rule**—the ambition to be free from the dominion of others—which turns religious and other associations into **political communities** (see Ch.23).

The **loyalty** and trust which bind together the members of a political community determine the outer limits of close cooperation. Members much prefer to cooperate with each other and to avoid sharing political power and material resources with 'outsiders'. References to a shared past, which often includes the shared experience of suffering in warfare, are frequently central elements of social and political **integration**. Annual commemorations of **9/11** are a recent example of how death, threat, and sacrifice feature in national histories. National memories of, for example, the struggle against fascism during the Second World War commemorate the loss of those who died for the community. Some religious communities have expected their members to be martyrs for the cause. However, the expectation that members will sacrifice their lives in war for the sake of the larger group is a recurrent feature of the history of independent political communities.

Most people belong to several communities at the same time—to professional or religious groups which may be transnational as well as to the **nation-state**. Some **regimes**, such as Nazi Germany, tried to compel their members to forsake loyalties that clash with the state. Totalitarian states such as Stalin's Russia demanded the same from their citizens but they failed in part because many citizens attached more importance to their religious or ethnic affiliation than to the state. Liberal-democratic forms of political community recognize that their citizens value many different loyalties, some directed towards local communities, others connected with membership of international non-governmental associations such as Greenpeace and Amnesty International. Most of these states also believe they have moral duties to peoples elsewhere. Most believe that they should obey **international law** and promote respect for human rights in other parts of the world. Whether **globalization** corrodes national loyalties and encourages closer identification with distant peoples is one of the most interesting questions of the modern age.

We return to this question later. Whatever the future may hold, there is no doubt that war has had a massive impact on the evolution of political communities since the earliest times. Modern states are no different from the predecessors in seeking to ensure that they can count on their citizens' loyalty when national **survival** is at stake (see Ch.13). The importance of this demand on citizens is no longer as great in those political communities which have been spared the ordeal of war in recent decades. The period since the end of the Second World War has been described as the longest period of peace between the great powers since the Peace of Westphalia in 1648. This has been the era in which liberals began to argue that globalization—the condition in which social, cultural, economic, and political developments affect all places more or less simultaneously, thereby marking a new stage in the long history of the interconnectedness of the species—started to overtake great power conflict as the primary determinant of the course of world politics (on globalization, see the introduction to Mazlish and Iriye 2005). Realists argue that globalization does not have radical political consequences. The use of force to oust the Taliban in Afghanistan and to remove Saddam Hussein as part of the so-called **war on terror** have provided a sharp reminder of the centrality of power politics. The proliferation of **weapons of mass destruction** may

result in a new era of inter-state rivalries. On this account, there is no reason to suppose that **cosmopolitanism** will be the main beneficiary of globalization—and there are no grounds for thinking that the current era stands at the threshold of a new era in the history of political community (see also Ch. 23).

Box 31.1 Some political theorists on political community

'The primary good that we distribute to one another is membership in some human community.'

(Michael Walzer)

'Clearly then, as all associations aim at some good, that association which is most sovereign among them all and embraces all others will aim highest, that is at the most sovereign of all goods. This is the association which we call the state, the association which is "political".'

(Aristotle)

'What makes a man a citizen [is] the mutual obligation between subject and sovereign.'

(Jean Bodin)

'Individuals are so constituted that they could accomplish but little by themselves and could scarcely get on without the assistance of civil society and its laws. But as soon as a sufficient number have united under a government, they are able to provide for most of their needs, and they find the help of other political societies not so necessary to them as the State is itself to individuals.'

(Emmerich de Vattel)

'Do we want peoples to be virtuous? If so, let us begin by making them love their homeland. But how will they come to love it, if their homeland means nothing more to them than it does to foreigners, and if it grants to them only what it cannot refuse to anyone?'

(Jean-Jacques Rousseau)

'should we have been so slow to see that . . . each one of us being in the civil state as regards our fellow citizens, but in the state of nature as regards the rest of the world, we have taken all kinds of precautions against private wars only to kindle national wars a thousand times more terrible? And that in joining a particular group of men, we have really declared ourselves to be enemies of the whole race?'

(Jean-Jacques Rousseau)

'both routine and extraordinary decisions taken by representatives of nations and nation-states profoundly affect citizens of other nation-states—who in all probability have had no opportunity to signal consent or lack of it—but . . . the international order is structured by agencies and forces over which citizens have minimum, if any, control, and in regard to which they have little basis to signal their [disagreement].'

(David Held)

'I am a citizen of the world.'

(Diogenes)

'I am not a citizen of the world . . . I am not even aware that there is a world such that one could be a citizen of it. No one has ever offered me citizenship, or described the naturalisation process, or enlisted me in the world's institutional structures, or given me an account of its decision procedures . . . or provided me with a list of the benefits and obligations of citizenship, or shown me the world's calendar and the common celebrations and commemorations of its citizens.'

(Michael Walzer)

Key Points

- The members of a political community are usually committed to self-government.
- Because of expectations of war, states have tried to persuade their citizens to place obligations to the 'national community' ahead of duties to other associations.
- Totalitarian states attempted to make the political community absolute. Liberal-democratic states recognize that their citizens value their membership of many communities alongside the nation-state.

- Some liberals have argued that globalization promises a new era of peace between the great powers. This is a condition in which more cosmopolitan political communities may develop.
- Many realists have argued that the war on terror and the renewed risk of nuclear proliferation indicate that globalization will not alter the basic features of world politics.

Nationalism and political community

The nation-state has been the dominant form of political community since the French Revolution but very different kinds of political community existed in earlier times. The first city-states of Mesopotamia and ancient Greece, the early **empires** of Assyria, Persia, and Rome, and the Ottoman and Chinese Empires were all political communities but they were radically different from nation-states. Ancient Greek city-states, for example, cherished their independence but, compared with modern democracies, they had highly exclusionary conceptions of community. Rights of political participation were restricted to adult male citizens in the *polis*. Women, resident aliens, and slaves were not full members of the community because they were denied citizenship. Most forms of

political community in human history have been hostile to popular rule. Empires, for example, have been governed by military elites, not by the people at large. Ruling elites did not believe that states should represent **nations** or think that each nation should have its own state. These are recent ideas which have dominated political life for about two centuries. However 'natural' these ideas may seem, they are exceptional features of political life. The historical record advises against assuming that they will last forever.

If we look at European states in the seventeenth century we will see that they were not nation-states in the modern sense, but **territorial states** which were governed by absolutist monarchs engaged in a struggle for economic and political power. It is important to explain how territorial states differed from earlier states, how they were replaced by nation-states, and how pressures on these relatively new forms of community have arisen in the recent phase of globalization.

Territorial states

As Max Weber argued, all states aim to monopolize control of the instruments of violence. But they differ greatly in what they can do with coercive power. Pre-modern states had a limited ability to direct the lives of their subjects, whereas modern territorial states have the capacity to regulate (if not control) most aspects of society, including the economy and life within the family. Regarding this difference, Michael Mann (1986: 7–10) argues that modern states have acquired high levels of 'intensive power': **power** that can be projected deep into society. In addition, pre-modern states had poorly defined frontiers and a limited ability to control frontier populations. Viable modern states have clearly demarcated borders and the ability to project power across and often beyond national **territories**. Commenting on this second difference, Mann (1986) argues that modern territorial states have acquired a high level of 'extensive power': power that can be projected across space. The vast colonial empires which encompassed the Americas, Asia-Pacific, and Africa were evidence of the modern state's exceptional 'global reach'. This is crucial for understanding the history of globalization. When the Spanish and Portuguese colonized Central and South America in the sixteenth century, and when **Europe** embarked on

second wave of imperial expansion in the nineteenth century, it was states that created new levels and forms of global interconnectedness (Held *et al.* 1999).

From territorial states to nation-states

The territorial states which established the first overseas empires gradually turned into nation-states. As Norbert Elias (2000) argued, the modern state's monopoly control of the instruments of violence led to the pacification of society. In this context, closer emotional ties between citizens gradually developed. There were at least two reasons for this second **development**: the rise of **capitalism** and **endemic warfare**. Benedict Anderson (1991) has argued that 'print capitalism' made national consciousness possible. Books, pamphlets, and the more recent mass media disseminated national symbols along with shared narratives about the past and the sense of a common destiny. Print capitalism meant that strangers who would never meet could identify with what Anderson calls the 'imagined community' of the nation. Ernest Gellner (1983) argued that industrialization was a primary reason for the rise of national languages and cultures. The sheer number of commercial exchanges which typify modern industrial societies simply could not occur unless strangers could communicate in the same language. The crucial point is that the human race is not divided naturally into nations. States played a central role in creating national **identities** not least by building education systems that promoted shared values.

Modern territorial states emerged in the cauldron of war; indeed, they were largely instruments for waging war. It has been said that the successful European states in the sixteenth century were small enough to be governed from a central administrative point and large enough to withstand external threats (Mattingly 1955; see also Tilly 1992). Warfare was crucial for the **transition** from territorial states to national states. Warring states promoted national solidarity to ensure that citizens would stay loyal in times of military conflict. The turning point in modern history was the **French Revolution**, which created the idea of the 'nation in arms' along with national conscription. From that period, **nationalism** has been the ideology which has had the greatest **influence** on the evolution of political communities.

It is important to remember then that warfare and industrialization created modern peoples with a strong sense of national consciousness. By claiming to represent the nation, states increased their ability to mobilize populations for war and for building overseas empires. At the close of the nineteenth century, European nation-states expanded their worldwide empires by drawing non-European peoples into new chains of global interconnectedness. The nation-state has played a central role in the economic and political integration of the human race, while at the same time intensifying national differences.

Nationalism was a European invention which spread to the rest of the world. **Third World** nationalist movements used European ideas to replace alien government with self-rule. Their success meant that the number of sovereign states more than tripled in the three decades following the Second World War, but many of these new political units failed to become viable nation-states. Frequently, ethnic rivalries meant that a sense of identification with the state did not develop. In many regions, such as the Indian subcontinent, divided peoples dismembered the former colonial territories in order to establish their own nation-states. The separation of India and Pakistan in 1947, and of East Pakistan (Bangladesh) from West Pakistan in 1971, are two examples. However, because of decolonization, the modern state which is not indigenous to non-European societies became the principal form of political community across the world. The globalization of the modern state is one of the main features of increased global interconnectedness.

Key Points

- Most forms of political community in human history have not represented the nation or the people.
- The idea that the state should represent the nation is a European development which has dominated politics for just over two hundred years.
- War and capitalism are two reasons why the nation-state became the dominant form of political community.
- The extraordinary power of modern states—the growth of their 'intensive' and 'extensive' power—made global empires possible.
- States have been the principal architects of global interconnectedness over the last five centuries.
- The global spread of the state and nationalism are key examples of global interconnectedness.

Community and citizenship

We have seen that modern political communities accumulated extraordinary powers. The vast overseas empires they once commanded illustrate the point. It may appear odd that these political communities have been the site for unusual experiments in liberal-democratic forms of governance, but there is no paradox here. Modern states created national peoples which they mobilized for war. The peoples which were formed in this way resisted the state's increased power over their lives. They organized politically to extract **citizenship** rights from the state. Demands for citizenship were first heard within the major European states but they are now a powerful theme in political communities in all regions of the world. Along with the spread of the language of universal human rights, these demands reveal that the outlines of a global political culture have appeared alongside the increased interconnectedness of peoples in recent decades (see Ch.29).

Citizenship and rights

Territorial states in early modern Europe were governed by absolute monarchs who saw the state as their private domain. During the eighteenth and nineteenth centuries, the rising commercial and industrial classes challenged monarchical power; they argued for **political rights** which were commensurate with their increasing economic importance. The middle classes sought to destroy royal privileges and promote constitutional government. They demanded the **rule of law** and **representation** in politics. They succeeded in winning democratic rightss but they refused to grant the same rights to subordinate groups such as women and the working classes. The struggle to extend the suffrage to all adult men and women was a dominant theme in all modern industrial societies during the latter part of the nineteenth century and the first part of the twentieth century. Demands for welfare rights soon followed.

The main point to note is that labour movements and political parties on the Left argued that inequalities of power and wealth had increased under capitalism with the result that the poor were denied the benefits of full membership of the community. The contention was that legal and political rights mean very little unless individuals have the power to exercise them. Pressures mounted to deepen the meaning of citizenship by adding **social or welfare rights** to the legal and political rights which had been won earlier. In the first part of the twentieth century, many Western states introduced national health services, welfare provision for the poor, and more open educational systems in response to struggles to create more inclusive communities.

The most influential account of the evolution of citizenship, at least as far as Britain is concerned, can be found in the writings of **T. H. Marshall,** who maintained that political communities acquired greater legitimacy by becoming more inclusive, and by giving all citizens the legal, political, and social rights which had previously been monopolized by dominant groups. Certainly, many governments in the industrialized West supported this package of citizenship to defuse social tensions. It may seem extraordinary now, but many writers in the 1950s and 1960s believed that 'the end of ideology' had arrived in societies such as the United States. What they meant was that Western liberal democracies had solved—or would shortly solve—the social conflicts which have long threatened political stability.

In the 1950s and 1960s, many believed that Europe's former colonies would follow Western patterns of economic and political development. Modernization theorists, as they were called, spoke about the impending 'modernization' or 'development' of 'traditional' societies. They thought that new states would undergo the nation-building process which had occurred earlier in the West. New states would undergo democratization and imitate Western models of capitalist development. In other words, increased global connectedness would lead to a general consensus about the most desirable systems of government.

Modernization theory and the end of ideology thesis were seriously flawed doctrines. Civil rights movements, the student revolt, opposition to the Vietnam War, **feminism**, and environmental movements revealed the errors of the 'end of ideology' thesis. Ethnic and religious conflict in new states, the rise of military government as opposed to democratization, and economic stagnation rather than capitalist development, demonstrated that modernization theorists had underestimated the challenges facing post-colonial societies. What was striking about modernization theory, though, was its belief that most societies would gravitate to the Western path of economic and political development. Echoes of the approach are evident in the claim at the end of the bipolar world that liberal-democratic capitalist forms of political organization are spreading to most parts of the globe, just as nationalism and the idea of the modern state had spread across the world in an earlier epoch. The spread of liberal democracy was championed on the grounds that liberal states belong to a unique realm of peace (Fukuyama 1989). The belief in an expanding global consensus was famously rejected by the notion of an approaching **Clash of Civilizations** (Huntington 1993). More recent emphases on the religious revolt against Western secular modernity which have flourished since '9/11' have argued that globalization may produce new cultural cleavages and ideological conflicts rather than shared moral and political beliefs.

Key Points

- Citizenship rights developed by way of reaction to the growing power of modern states.
- The demand to be recognized as a free and equal citizen began with struggles for legal and political rights to which welfare rights were added in the nineteenth and early twentieth centuries.
- The stability of modern forms of political community has owed a great deal to the fact that citizens won these rights. Indeed, some modernization theorists in the 1960s believed that liberal democracies had largely solved the social conflicts of earlier centuries.
- Modernization theory also assumed that non-Western societies would emulate Western paths of development. This thesis resurfaced in the West at the end of the bipolar era. It was linked with the belief that liberal democracies belong to a unique sphere of peace.
- Huntington's notion of the Clash of Civilizations challenged the idea that globalization will lead to a world moral and political consensus.

The changing nature of political community

One paradox of the modern world is that the globalization of economic and political life has increased in recent years with the result that the global influence of Western capitalist democracies is greater than ever, and yet the national fragmentation of political communities has not declined. The processes of **globalization** and **fragmentation** are two major influences on political communities at the present time.

As noted earlier, the fragmentation of societies has been pronounced in many Third World regions. The division of India and Pakistan in 1947, the civil war in Nigeria in the late 1960s, and the creation of the separate state of Bangladesh in 1971 were part of a larger trend which has included civil war in Ethiopia and the establishment of the new state of Eritrea in 1993. Novel approaches to precarious Third World states appeared in the early 1990s. The concept of the **quasi-state** described states which enjoy international recognition as sovereign communities but are unable to protect the basic needs of their populations (Jackson 1990). The notion of the **failed state** has been used to describe states which are unable to govern their societies without significant external support (Helman and Ratner 1992/3).

Many thinkers have asked whether liberal-democratic societies have moral responsibilities to the peoples of failed states which include intervening when serious violations of human rights occur (see Ch.30). But in an extraordinary and largely unforeseen development, the failed state is no longer a problem limited to the Third World. The disintegration of the former Yugoslavia was a striking example of a failed state in what was regarded as one of the most liberal and affluent socialist societies in Eastern Europe. Although there were major public disagreements, **NATO** had substantial public backing for its military intervention in Kosovo in 1999 and for sponsoring the prosecution of human rights violators under international criminal law.

In the Yugoslav case, violent nationalism destroyed a multicultural political community which seemed to have succeeded in creating harmony between different cultural groups. Developments in societies such as Canada, Belgium, Italy, and the United Kingdom illustrate the more general point that needs to be made. It is that collective demands for respect for national or ethnic differences exist in virtually all nation-states. These demands are part of a global movement in which minority nations and indigenous peoples seek respect for their languages and cultures. Nationalist reactions to the influx of Western values are widespread in India and throughout the Muslim world, but they are rarely a challenge to globalization in itself (see Ch.24). Al Qaeda, which is an unusually violent example of this trend, has relied on globalization in the form of the global banking and communications system to promote its objectives and to rally support for a transnational cause. There is no more dramatic example of the rejection of Western forms of political community (and Western political influence) in the modern world.

The politics of cultural difference

Another way of expressing the last few points is to suggest that traditional ideas about citizenship are being reconsidered across the world in the current phase of globalization. To understand what is changing we need to return to the relationship between war and the evolution of modern political communities. In the course of creating national cultures in modern Europe, ruling groups invariably imposed a dominant language and customs on subordinate groups. Success in war went to states which succeeded in creating an overarching idea of the nation with its sense of a shared history and common symbols defined by national flags and anthems, annual commemorations, and so forth. But as British politics reveal, the sense of Scottish, Welsh, or Irish identity survived alongside efforts to create more encompassing national identities. Similar patterns are evident in most modern states.

The desire to preserve local cultures and to achieve some degree of autonomy if not outright independence can be found in all modern nation-states but success was limited when political communities faced the permanent threat of war. The 'long peace' between the great powers has given national movements new opportunities to assert cultural and political rights. Core industrial states no longer need to mobilize their citizens for war, and they

may be less able to use national symbols persuasively, especially in multicultural societies which are subject to the forces of globalization and fragmentation. Of course, the war on terror and the 2003 invasion of Iraq have shown that states can harness popular support for war if they can convince citizens of immediate threats to personal and **national security**. On the other hand, public opposition to the Iraq War in the Western democracies indicated the extent to which large sections of the population make loyalty to the state conditional on **compliance** with international law and respect for the United Nations system. The increasingly conditional nature of loyalties may be one of the most important characteristics of political communities in the modern age (Waller and Linklater 2003). However, the ethnic revolt has long indicated that many minority nations and indigenous peoples give qualified or begrudging support to their respective nation-states.

Group rights

Claims for **group rights** have produced global changes in attitudes to citizenship (Young 1990). Earlier struggles for legal, political, and social rights usually assumed there were no significant cultural differences between citizens. Feminists have argued that the advancement of citizenship was **gender** blind since no account was taken of the special needs of women. Exponents of new conceptions of citizenship have maintained that the differences between citizens—differences of culture and gender—must be reflected in public policy. Minority nations throughout the world and indigenous peoples in societies such as Australia, Canada, and New Zealand have spearheaded the claim that group rights should be respected by the wider polity, for example by assisting self-government and recognizing 'land rights'. These are not simply important developments within nation-states; the political representatives of these movements belong to transnational alliances which work to create a global political culture which affirms group rights.

The mass movement of peoples is one consequence of globalization that feeds into this process. Here too an important argument is that traditional conceptions of citizenship should be adapted to fit the multicultural nature of modern societies. Recent discussions about the wearing of 'the veil' in Britain and elsewhere have led many to argue that multiculturalism encourages the development of parallel societies and the corrosion of national bonds. Claims that migrant and other groups should integrate

into the wider community have been pressed in Britain, especially since '7/7' following terrorist attacks committed by British citizens.

No discussion of the continuing struggle over the nature of political community and national citizenship would be complete without noting how feminist movements have influenced definitions of community. Many have challenged gendered ideas of the national culture which have been shaped by the male experience of war. Many protest against what they regard as the patriarchal assumptions which underpin the wearing of the veil by Muslim women, although many Muslim women reject this claim on the grounds that the veil gives expression to their religious identity. Discontent with 'traditional' structures and values often exists alongside efforts to preserve them from the encroaching influence of Western modernity. Various forms of religious **fundamentalism**— Christian, Hindu, Islamic, etc.—demonstrate that global interconnections facilitate the spread of modern Western values as well as cultural and religious resistance to these values at both the national and international levels.

Cosmopolitan democracy and transnational citizenship

One of the most intriguing dimensions of political communities is how they deal with internal differences of class, gender, sexual identity, religion, race, and ethnicity. No less important is how they understand differences between citizens and aliens. Resistance to doctrines which claim that one race, nation, or gender has the right to dominate another is evident in most parts of the world. Modern nation-states have been transformed by egalitarian ideas which have challenged 'natural' hierarchies between persons. One of the central questions to ask about globalization is whether it will change one of the core assumptions of political communities over many millennia—the belief that members of the in-group have special duties to each other and few, and possibly no, obligations towards outgroups. One must ask whether, over the decades and centuries to come, increased connections between human groups will encourage a greater sense of solidarity between the members of different communities or generate new conflicts over how human beings are bound together.

Globalization has invited many to question the idea that political communities are primarily responsible for promoting the interests of their citizens. Various global

problems which states cannot hope to solve on their own—climate change, for example—have encouraged the development of **non-governmental organizations** (NGOs) which are concerned with the fate of the Earth. Affluent populations are often disturbed by images of human suffering caused by state terror, civil conflict, natural disaster, and famine. Public support for humanitarian intervention in Somalia and Kosovo, and assistance for the victims of the Asian Tsunami in 2004, developed in the wake of images of suffering disseminated by the global media. Many think that global **civil society** reveals the dawn of a new era of human cooperation. Sceptics are quick to stress the continuing appeal of nationalism, the tenacity of the state, and the weakness of cosmopolitan loyalties (see Ch.23). For them, interventions in Somalia in 1993 and in Kosovo in 1999—and inaction with respect to the Rwandan genocide in 1994—reveal that national populations are unwilling to sacrifice the lives of significant numbers of co-nationals for 'distant strangers' (see Ch.30).

Cosmopolitan democracy

Cosmopolitan approaches to political community have enjoyed a renaissance in recent years. The idea of world citizenship is a concept which international non-governmental organizations have used to promote a stronger sense of

responsibility for the global environment and for the human species. Proponents of **cosmopolitan democracy** have argued that national democracies have little control over global markets, and a limited ability to influence decisions taken by **transnational corporations** which influence currency values, employment prospects, and so forth (see Held 1995). They maintain that democracy may not survive if it remains tied to the nation-state. They argue for democratizing international organizations such as the **World Trade Organization**, and for ensuring that transnational corporations are held accountable for decisions that may harm vulnerable persons in different parts of the world. One response to globalization, then, argues for new forms of **cosmopolitan political community**, in which the members of different societies come together as **cosmopolitan citizens** to influence decisions that have global influence. Critics argue that the vision of cosmopolitan democracy is utopian. They maintain that democracy is unlikely to flourish at the global level because there is no counterpart to the nation which engages the emotions of millions of people. Democracy requires a level of trust and a commitment to the public good which only exists—at least at this stage in human history—between those who share a common nationality (Miller 1999). Better then to improve existing nation-states than to squander resources pursuing a utopian ideal of global cooperation.

Box 31.2 Contrasting views about the scope of human sympathy

'Whether we can conceive of a way to think of morality that extends some form of sympathy further than our own group remains perhaps the fundamental moral question for contemporary life.'

(Jean Tronto)

'We should all agree that each of us is bound to show kindness to his parents and spouse and children, and to other kinsmen in a less degree: and to those who have rendered services to him, and any others whom he may have admitted into his intimacy and called friends: and to neighbours and to fellow-countrymen more than others: and perhaps we may say to those of our own race more than to black or yellow men, and generally to human beings in proportion to their affinity to ourselves.'

(Henry Sidgwick)

'If he was to lose his little finger to-morrow, he would not sleep tonight; but provided he never saw them, he will snore with the most profound security over the ruin of a hundred millions of his brethren, and the destruction of that immense multitude seems plainly an object less interesting to him, than this paltry misfortune of his own.'

(Adam Smith)

'[O]ur sense of solidarity is strongest when those with whom solidarity is expressed are thought of as "one of us", where "us" means

something smaller and more local than the human race.'

(Richard Rorty)

'The fact that a person is physically near to us. . . . may make it more likely that we shall assist him, but this does not show that we ought to help him rather than another who happens to be further away.'

(Peter Singer)

'Those closer to us will tend to be more vulnerable to our actions and choices than those distant from us, and thus we are not obliged to weigh everyone's interests exactly equally. Yet in so far as those distant from us are particularly vulnerable to our actions and choices, we have special obligations to care for them.'

(Grace Clement)

'We are nowadays more strongly than ever aware that an enormously large part of humanity live their entire lives on the verge of starvation, that in fact there are always and in many places people dying of hunger. . . . Many members of richer communities feel it to be almost a duty to do something about the misery of other human groups. To avoid misunderstanding on the issue, let it be said that relatively little is done.'

(Norbert Elias)

Do the 'oceans make a community of nations impossible?'

(Immanuel Kant)

Box 31.3 Visions of new forms of community and citizenship

'The bourgeoisie has through its exploitation of the world-market given a cosmopolitan character to production and consumption in every country.... All old-fashioned national industries have been destroyed or are daily being destroyed.... In place of the old wants, satisfied by the productions of the country, we find new wants, requiring for their satisfaction the products of different lands and climes. In place of the old local and national seclusion and self-sufficiency, we have intercourse in every direction, universal interdependence of nations.... The bourgeoisie, by the rapid improvement of all instruments of production, by the immensely facilitated means of communication, draws all, even the most barbarian nations, into civilisation. It compels all nations, on pain of extinction, to adopt the bourgeois mode of production... .that is to become bourgeois themselves. In one word, it creates a world after its own image.'

(Karl Marx)

'We have a system of national citizenship in a social context which requires a new theory of internationalism and universalistic citizenship.'

(Bryan Turner)

'Every person holding the nationality of a Member State shall be a citizen of the Union.'

(The Maastricht Treaty)

It is 'time to go higher in our search for citizenship, but also lower and wider. Higher to the world, lower to the locality.... The citizen has been too puffed and too compressed.'

(Andrew Wright)

'We may envisage a situation in which, say, a Scottish authority in Edinburgh, a British authority in London, and a European authority in Brussels were all actors in world politics and all enjoyed representations in world political organisations, together with rights and duties of various kinds in world law, but in which none of them claimed sovereignty or supremacy over the others, and a person living in Glasgow had no exclusive or overriding loyalty to any one of them. Such an outcome would take us truly "beyond the sovereign state" and is by no means implausible.'

(Hedley Bull)

'The preference of Western powers, especially the United States, for air strikes, despite the physical and psychological damage caused even with highly accurate munitions, arises from [the] privileging of nationals or Westerners. This type of national or statist thinking has not yet come to terms with the concept of a common human community... . Whereas the soldier, as the traditional bearer of arms, had to be prepared to die for his country, the international soldier/policeman [would] risk] his or her life for humanity.'

(Mary Kaldor)

'Europeans have stepped out of the Hobbesian world of anarchy into the Kantian world of perpetual peace.'

(Robert Kagan)

Neo-medievalist approaches

Neo-medievalism is a related vision of new form of political community which has attracted attention in recent years. Neo-medievalism refers to an ideal political **order** in which individuals are governed by several overlapping authorities—which is roughly how political community was organized in Europe in the Middle Ages prior to the rise of the modern state. The forces of globalization and fragmentation have renewed interest in a neo-medieval **world order** in which states transfer some powers to international **institutions** which will deal with global problems while other powers are transferred to domestic regions where the sense of cultural difference remains strong (Linklater 1998; Falk 2000). According to this vision, national governments should retain many powers, and citizens should remain loyal to the state, which would be only one tier of government however. Loyalty to the state would exist alongside emotional attachments to sub-state and transnational authorities. None of those authorities or loyalties would dominate the others.

The best prospects for neo-medievalism are to be found in those parts of Europe (such as the European Union) where some erosion of sovereign powers has taken place and where traditional conceptions of national interests have reduced importance (see Ch.25). It is no small achievement that the neo-medieval vision commands some support in a region which was frequently embroiled in major wars. Whether this normative vision will ever appeal beyond Europe is a moot point. No less important is how organizations such as the EU support a global 'civilizing process' through efforts to maintain respect for global **norms**, including the one that prohibits torture.

Key Points

- Globalization and fragmentation are two phenomena that challenge traditional conceptions of community and citizenship.
- Ethnic fragmentation is one reason for the failed state in Europe as well as in the Third World, but demands for the recognition of cultural differences exist in all political communities.
- Globalization theorists have defended cosmopolitan democracy on the grounds that national democracies are unable to influence the global forces which affect them.

Case Study Torture and the War against Terror

The modern civilizing process, as Elias (2000) called it, has involved changing sensibilities to violence. The abolition of the death penalty and public execution, and the eradication of judicial torture are examples of the civilizing process. The international community declared its opposition to torture in the 1984 **Convention against Torture and Other Cruel, Inhuman or Degrading Treatment or Punishment**. In reality, great powers such as the United States have often ignored human rights violations committed by allies in Third World regions. Nevertheless, the belief that torture is unacceptable acquired the status of a sacrosanct norm after 1945. It was a key element in the distinction between 'progressive' liberal and 'backward' authoritarian regimes. It was evidence of a global civilizing process.

The war on terror led the USA and its allies to cooperate with various states such as Uzbekistan (deemed guilty of serious human rights violations by the UN Special Rapporteur on Torture in 2002). Security needs were placed above human rights. One consequence of this development is that many non-Western governments claimed they are equally entitled to violate human rights in their struggle against domestic opponents. Western liberal democracies also debated whether certain forms of torture can be used to extract information from terrorist suspects. 'Extraordinary rendition' refers to the alleged practice of transferring suspects to authoritarian regimes such as Uzbekistan which allegedly use forms of torture which are deemed illegitimate or excessive in the West. Western powers have been accused of being complicit in tolerating acts of violence which are contrary to international law.

The relaxation of the global norm prohibiting torture raises profound questions about the extent to which liberal restrictions on violence will influence the course of world politics. Prior to 9/11, there was a global consensus that torture is illegitimate. At least regimes that used torture rarely did so openly. Many observers have assumed that the onus is on liberal states and organizations such as the European Union to protest against torture across the world. Whether the war on terror involves only a temporary setback to the torture norm is unclear. Realists may argue that recent pressures on that norm have demonstrated that states will disregard legal conventions when they clash with vital security interests. The fact that these 'moral compromises' do not go unchallenged may provide hope to those who believe that the ideal of eradicating torture and other forms of human suffering may yet prevail in world politics (see Foot 2006).

Beyond Realism?

In recent years, globalization and fragmentation have weakened or destroyed centralized nation-states as different as Indonesia, Yugoslavia, the USSR and Czechoslovakia. Perhaps new forms of political community, which are more respectful of cultural differences and more cosmopolitan than their predecessors, will emerge in future.

As far as the great powers are concerned, the apex of violent nationalism was reached in the first half of the twentieth century (see Ch.3). In 1914, European governments led their populations into the most destructive war in human history. Two decades later, an even more devastating international conflict took place. The desire not to return to major war was the main reason for the creation of the European Community after the Second World War and for the development of the universal human rights culture. War no longer seems likely to engulf the European continent, and it is improbable that it will be waged between the core industrial powers in the foreseeable future. This may be a revolution in world politics although the Realist approach to international relations insists there is no warranty that peace between the great powers will survive indefinitely. It is impossible to say that the kind of nationalism which characterized international politics in the first half of the twentieth century has run its course. Certainly, the war on terror has made security politics more central than they were in the 1990s. The level of public support which Bush and Blair commanded during the war against Iraq demonstrated that the state matters more than the United Nations when fears

for personal and national security run high (although public concerns about needless civilian suffering in war are significant). Since 9/11 we have witnessed the revival of an old theme which is that the state remains the only political association which can take effective measures to protect the **security** of its citizens. From this perspective, any expectation of new forms of community ignores the most basic fact of political life. A related point is that violent nationalism can be the main beneficiary of the weakening of the nation-state, as occurred in Yugoslavia.

Realists will argue that the points which were made about security in the last paragraph hold the key to the future of political community. They argue that it is almost certain that human beings will continue to look to the state to guarantee their security—or to local warlords when state power disintegrates. Even so, there have been several efforts to develop visions of alternative forms of community and citizenship in recent years, not least because of the belief that globalization and fragmentation pose new challenges to states and create new possibilities for transforming world politics (Linklater 1998). These are important developments in a discipline that has been powerfully influenced by **Realism** and **neo-realism**, with their focus on continuities rather than change in world politics—that is on war, the balance of power, the rise and fall of great powers, and so forth. Three broad theoretical approaches to the study of community merit consideration because they cast great light on whether globalization and fragmentation have the capacity to transform political community. They are **communitarianism**, post-structuralism, and cosmopolitanism, (see Ch.10).

Communitarianism

Communitarianism (which is a strand of argument rather than a monolithic doctrine) maintains that cosmopolitans underestimate the role that separate communities play in the moral lives of human beings. Its proponents contend that individuals acquire their most fundamental rights and responsibilities as members of particular communities, and not as members of the human race (Walzer 1995a). Communitarians do not deny that societies have obligations to one another, but they insist that it is appropriate that most human beings are moved more by attachments to their community than by appeals to

common humanity. On this view, it is wrong to suppose that globalization will so weaken particular communities that human beings will replace national ties with cosmopolitan loyalties. To act on the assumption that this is likely to occur is to endanger existing viable political communities.

Walzer's position on the idea of world citizenship is a good example of this critique of cosmopolitanism (Walzer 1994). He argues that citizenship refers to a web of political rights and duties which only exist when there is a strong sense of identification with the nation-state. In his view, it is highly unlikely that any meaningful sense of citizenship (which includes the right to participate in politics and a willingness to make personal sacrifices for the larger society) will develop beyond the nation-state. For example, according to the Maastricht Treaty, the citizens of member states of the European Union are European citizens, but this is a pale imitation of the forms of citizenship which exist within nation-states. In short, citizenship is a national achievement; cosmopolitan citizenship is illusory. As the idea of 'communitarian realism' indicates, these sentiments can be connected with Realism to argue that the struggle for power and security in the context of **anarchy** will ensure the survival of strong attachments to independent political communities.

Post-structuralism

Post-structuralism has challenged visions of more cosmopolitan political communities on the grounds that all standpoints that claim to represent humanity contain the risk of domination. Foucault's claim that all forms of knowledge are potentially dangerous, including those that are designed to promote progress, informs this critique (see Ch.10). This is a telling criticism of Marxism, which set out to liberate the human race but became an instrument of totalitarian rule (see Ch.8). Richard Ashley and R. B. J. Walker (1990) have argued that all perspectives that claim to have uncovered universal moral and political truths contain this danger. Intrinsic to such worldviews are distinctions between those who possess the truth and those who live in ignorance. Therein lies the danger of domination. In the case of cosmopolitanism, the distinction between those who think globally and those who remain wedded to particular communities may lead to

forms of power and exclusion which are established in the name of humanity.

This argument resonates with claims that cosmopolitan perspectives, which include the universal human rights culture, may form the basis for new forms of Western power over 'backward' societies. The idea of **humanitarian intervention** has been criticized because it elevates 'civilized' Western liberal societies and because it increases the danger of force which may cause great suffering to those it is designed to assist (as in Iraq at the present time). Similar fears inform discussions about the possible consequences of efforts to create a new international community in Europe. Jacques Derrida (1992) argued that a Europe which reduces the monopoly powers of the nation-state and gives expression to new forms of citizenship is desirable. But movement in this direction is not risk-free since it may be that pernicious distinctions between, for example, Europe and the Islamic world are created in the attempt to promote close cooperation within Europe. There is no guarantee, then, that efforts to create 'post-national' communities will dispense with the exclusionary practices which have been central to the history of modern states.

Post-structuralists have not confined their criticisms to the advocates of cosmopolitan perspectives. They have argued that communitarian arguments often fail to appreciate the extent to which the dominant constructions of community exclude marginal groups. Members of minority nations and indigenous peoples have advanced similar claims. Many feminist movements have argued that large numbers of women suffer exclusion at the hands of 'their' community. The main lesson to draw is that all communities include some human beings as full members but exclude others in the process. The important warning is that this danger will remain whether peoples remain loyal to sovereign states or try to build new forms of political community at the regional and global levels.

Cosmopolitanism

Globalization may seem to create new opportunities for promoting the cosmopolitan idea that all human beings are equal. The greater interconnectedness of human beings has increased popular awareness of common threats, such as global environmental degradation, which affect all human beings (but not in identical ways). The global media convey images of distant suffering into the living rooms of affluent populations across the world. They invite the affluent to reflect on whether there are personal and collective responsibilities to alleviate misery on a worldwide scale. The poor are not only connected with the affluent as images in the global media. Affluent societies have become increasingly aware of how the global trading system, agricultural subsidies, and so forth disadvantage vulnerable producers in Third World societies. There is perhaps a growing awareness of how global affluence and poverty are interconnected.

Concerns about human rights violations, global **poverty** and inequality, and environmental degradation form the triad of moral themes on which contemporary cosmopolitan ideas have come to rest. How political communities and individuals should respond to the problems of global interconnectedness is one of the great moral challenges of the age. Some stress the importance of institutional innovations such as the establishment of the International Criminal Court in the effort to promote what Mary Kaldor (1999: 124ff.) has called 'cosmopolitan law enforcement'. Others stress the need to reform global organizations such as the World Trade Organization (Pogge 2002). Some draw the conclusion that greater global interconnectedness requires lifestyle changes in the form of global environmental citizenship, support for fair trade and socially responsible investment, ethical tourism, and so forth. Such claims reflect the fact that individuals are linked with 'distant strangers' in unprecedented ways and cannot easily avoid difficult questions about the moral **principles** which should bind them together.

It is impossible to know whether globalization will lead to greater identification with all peoples in more cosmopolitan forms of political community. It may be unwise to expect one trend to dominate. Some people respond to global problems by supporting non-governmental organizations; some experience 'compassion fatigue'; some stress the dangers inherent in global projects to alleviate suffering; and some doubt that the global measures will progress far in a world of self-interested states. Whether human sympathy will develop beyond the nation-state—and whether more cosmopolitan political communities will emerge as a result—are two of the most fundamental questions raised by globalization.

Key Points

- The apex of nationalism in relations between the great powers occurred in the first half of the twentieth century.
- Nationalism remains a powerful force in the modern world but globalization and fragmentation have led to discussions about the possibility of new forms of political community.
- Cosmopolitan approaches which envisage an international system in which all individuals are respected as equal have flourished in the contemporary phase of globalization.

- Communitarians argue that most people value their membership of a particular political community; they are unlikely to shift their loyalty from the nation-state to the human race.
- Post-structuralists argue that all forms of political community contain the danger of domination or exclusion.

Conclusion

The study of international politics has been largely concerned with understanding the relations between separate political communities, and particularly relations between the great powers. Realists and neo-realists argue that all states are forced to compete for security and survival in the context of anarchy. They contend that separate states look to their own interests first and foremost. They maintain that the sense of community which exists between the citizens of particular states is unlikely to develop within the world at large. Realists and neo-realists do not expect this condition to change while international anarchy survives.

There is no reason to think that sovereign states are about to be replaced by new forms of political association but there can be little doubt that globalization and fragmentation pose novel challenges for political communities across the world. The most recent phase in the development of globalization invites a discussion of how far the forms of cooperation which exist within viable nation-states can develop globally. While it is difficult

to be optimistic about the immediate future, it must be remembered that the modern condition of globalization is a very recent development in the history of the human race, one to which the species is still learning to adapt (McNeill and McNeill 2003).

A large number of perspectives are relevant to that discussion. They include the more optimistic standpoints that regard the rise of global civil society as evidence that cooperation between the members of different political communities is flourishing. They include the belief that political communities may yet evolve together in the direction of neo-medievalism or cosmopolitan democracy. They include pessimistic standpoints which maintain that the US response to 9/11, along with growing concerns about the proliferation of weapons of mass destruction, reveal the continuing centrality of geopolitics. What is at stake in this discussion is whether globalization has a unique capacity to disrupt the forms of competition and conflict which have shaped independent political communities for centuries.

? Questions

1 What is community, and what makes a community a political community?

2 Why has the modern state been the dominant form of political community?

3 What is the relationship between nationalism, citizenship, and political community?

4 What is the relationship between war and political community?

5 To what extent are globalization and fragmentation transforming political communities?

6 Can one be a citizen of the world?

7 What are the arguments for and against cosmopolitan democracy?

8 What are the main differences between the cosmopolitan, communitarian, and post-structuralist approaches to political community?

9 How far has the 'war against terror' revealed the precariousness of the global norm against torture when national and personal security are threatened?

10 What evidence is there that globalization is engendering cosmopolitan sympathies for the suffering?

Guide to further reading

General

Linklater, A. (1998), *The Transformation of Political Community: Ethical Foundations of the Post-Westphalian Era* (Cambridge: Polity Press). Provides a more detailed analysis of many of the themes considered in this chapter.

Waller, M., and Linklater, A. (eds) (2003), *Political Loyalty and the Nation-State* (London: Routledge). A collection of papers on whether the European nation-state continues to command the loyalty of its citizens.

Communitarianism and cosmopolitanism

Nussbaum, M. (2002), *In Defence of Country* (Boston: Beacon Press). An excellent collection of essays on patriotism and cosmopolitanism.

The modern state

Elias, N. (2000), *The Civilizing Process: Sociogenetic and Psychogenetic Investigations* (Oxford: Basil Blackwell). A landmark study of the rise of the modern state.

Mann, M. (1986; 1993), *Sources of Social Power, Vol. 1: A History of Power from the Beginning to AD 1760* and *Vol. 2: The Rise of Classes and Nation-States, 1760–1914* (Cambridge: Cambridge University Press). This two-volume work contains a wealth of information about city-states and ancient empires as well as the modern state.

Tilly, C. (1992), *Coercion, Capital and European States: AD 990–1992* (Oxford: Blackwell). An outstanding account of how the modern state eclipsed other forms of political organization.

Nationalism and group rights

Anderson, B. (1983; revised 1991), *Imagined Communities: Reflections on the Origin and Spread of Nationalism* (London: Verso). A key reference point in discussions about modern nationalism.

Gellner, E. (1983), *Nations and Nationalism* (Oxford: Basil Blackwell). A classic study of the relationship between industrialization and nationalism.

Kymlicka, W. (1989), *Liberalism, Community and Culture* (Oxford: Oxford University Press). A pathbreaking study of the significance of the struggle for 'indigenous' rights for liberal-democratic communities.

National and world citizenship

Dower, N., and Williams, J. (eds) (2002), *Global Citizenship* (Edinburgh: Edinburgh University Press). A comprehensive collection of essays on world citizenship.

Hutchings, K., and Danreuther, R. (eds) (1999), *Cosmopolitan Citizenship* (London: Macmillan). A useful set of debates about the idea of cosmopolitan citizenship.

Marshall, T. H. (1973), *Class, Citizenship and Social Development* (Westport, Conn.: Greenwood Press). A central study of the development of legal, political, and social rights.

Emotional responses to suffering in other societies
Cohen, S. (2001), *States of Denial: Knowing about Atrocities and Suffering* (Cambridge: Polity Press). An excellent sociological study of attitudes to human suffering.
Sontag, S. (2003), *Regarding the Pain of Others* (London: Hamish Hamilton). An excellent work on photographic images of suffering in other societies.

Alternatives to the nation-state
Held, D. (1995), *Democracy and the Global Order: From the Modern State to Global Governance* (Cambridge: Polity Press). An influential defence of cosmopolitan democracy.

Globalization and world history
McNeill, J. R., and McNeill, W. H. (2003), *The Human Web: A Bird's Eye View of World History* (New York: W. W. Norton). A highly accessible overview of how the human race has become interconnected over several millennia.
Mazlish, B., and Iriye, A. (eds) (2005), *The Global History Reader* (Abingdon: Routledge). A comprehensive guide to the history of globalization.

Online Resource Centre

 Visit the Online Resource Centre that accompanies this book to access more learning resources on this chapter topic at www.oxfordtextbooks.co.uk/uk/orc/baylis_smith4e/

Chapter 32

Globalization and the post-cold war order

IAN CLARK

- Introduction ··· 562
- A typology of order ··· 563
- The elements of contemporary order ························ 564
- Globalization and the post-Westphalian order? ········· 567
- Globalization and legitimacy ······························· 569
- An international order of globalized states? ············· 571
- Conclusion ·· 573

Reader's Guide

This chapter explores the nature of the order that has developed across the period since the end of the cold war. It asks whether that order is distinctive. It asks also whether globalization is its defining feature. After distinguishing between various types of order—international, world, and global—the chapter sketches out the main ingredients of the contemporary order. These extend well beyond the traditional domain of international military security. The argument then addresses globalization as one of the forces that helped to bring the cold war to an end, and investigates the associated trend towards a post-Westphalian order. It explores also the ways in which globalization now causes problems and tensions in the present order, especially with regard to its legitimacy. The chapter ends by suggesting that globalization reflects changes within states, not just between them: what is distinctive about the present order is not the imminent demise of the states-system, but the continuation of an international order, the constituent units of which are globalized states.

Introduction

Box 32.1 Elements of discontinuity and continuity between cold war and post-cold war orders

Cold war

Discontinuity

Post-cold war

Soviet power in Eastern Europe

Bipolar competition

Rival ideologies

Global security integration

Military security as high politics

Dissolution of the Soviet Union

Unipolar peacemaking

Supremacy of liberal capitalism

Greater regional autonomy

National identity as high politics

Continuity

Some security structures, e.g. NATO

Economic globalization

Human rights

Reaction against secular state

Multiple identities

Environmental agendas

Poverty in the South

This chapter is concerned with two key questions. The first is whether there is now a distinctive pattern of **order** in the post-**cold war** world and, if so, what are its principal elements. The second is whether this order should be defined in terms of **globalization.**

Is there now a pattern of international politics sufficiently distinctive to mark it off from the dominant traits during the cold war? What we need to devise is a description of the present order that tells us something substantive about how it functions. Fully to understand our present period, we need to know more than that it was the phase that came after the cold war.

The second question directs attention to whether contemporary order can be captured by the imagery of globalization. There is, of course, intense debate as to the precise meaning, novelty, and extent of globalization. That some kind of transformation is underway is scarcely in doubt, even if commentators are unable to agree on its significance, or on whether the changes are to be welcomed or not. Is globalization simply one feature among many others of the post-cold war order? Or is it so central to its nature that we can define the order in relation to it? Is the contemporary order above all a **globalized order**, and what might this mean in practice?

Study of the overall character of the post-cold war order remains problematic, as we are still too immersed in it to have any proper sense of perspective. While there have been studies aplenty of individual aspects of this present order (ethnicity, **identity**, religion, **peacekeeping**, **humanitarian intervention**, globalization, regionalism, economic transition, democratization, **integration**, financial instability, **terrorism** and the war against it, **weapons of mass destruction**, **regime** change, etc.), we still lack any grand synthesis of its essential nature.

In analyzing the contemporary order, we need to be mindful of how much greater are the demands upon,

Key Points

- The principal characteristics of the contemporary order that give it its distinctive quality are difficult to discern.
- As we live in its midst, it is hard to get any sense of historical perspective.
- Our understanding of, say, the inter-war period (1919–39) is informed by how it ended, but we do not yet know how our present period will 'end'.
- The international order now delivers a range of international 'goods', but also a wide range of 'bads'

and the expectations about, the **international order** today than previously. In earlier periods, the interest in the international order was largely 'negative', and lay in prevention of any threats that might emerge from it. The interest is now 'positive' as well, as the international order is a much greater source than hitherto of a range of social goods. It can deliver information, economic resources, human rights, intervention, access to global **social movements** and **international non-governmental organizations** (INGOs), and an abundance of cultural artifacts. Many of these 'goods' may be regarded as unwelcome intrusions, but they remain highly sought after by some governments, and/or sectors of society, around the world.

A typology of order

At the present moment, our ideas about order are being pulled in a number of competing directions. At the one end, they continue to be largely state-centred and retain traditional concerns with the structure of the **balance of power,** the polarity of the **international system**, and the current forms of **collective security**. At the other is a widening agenda that encompasses the relationship between economic and political dimensions, new thinking about **human security** (see Ch.28), debates about the distributive consequences of globalization, the role of human rights, the impact of environmentalism, and strategies for human emancipation. Clearly, a number of differing, and potentially competing, conceptions of order are at work.

This was nicely illustrated at the end of the cold war when then US President George Bush spoke about his vision of a New World Order. In an address to Congress on 11 September 1990, Bush outlined

> A new era—freer from the threat of terror, stronger in pursuit of justice and more secure in the quest for peace, an era in which nations of the world . . . can prosper—a world where rule of law supplants the rule of the jungle, a world in which nations recognize the shared responsibility for freedom and justice, a world where the strong respect the rights of the weak.

Individually, these goals might all have been highly desirable, but the troublesome question was how they would fit together into a consistent whole and, given the tensions among them, what priority should be assigned to each respectively. Underlying the separate elements of this vision, we can distinguish competing frameworks of order. Some derive from traditional state-centric models and emphasize stability and peace among states. Others take the individual human being as the unit of account and construct models of order in terms of rights, justice, and prosperity.

These draw our attention to a number of important distinctions. Are we to judge the effectiveness of order solely as an aspect of the inter-state system, and thus speak of international order? Or are we to widen the discussion and consider order in terms of its impact on individual human lives and aspirations, and thus talk of a **world order**? Such a distinction is widely noted in the literature, and is replicated in the similar distinction between **international society** and world society (Clark 2007). However, how does the introduction of the concept of globalization impact upon the analysis? Does globalized order signify the same as world order or something different? An attempt will be made to answer that question in the final section of this chapter.

The search for the definitive elements of the contemporary order proceeds within quite separate theoretical frameworks (see Introduction). The first is the broadly realist. This concentrates upon the structure of the post-cold war system, especially upon the number of great power actors and the distribution of **capabilities** among them. It defines order largely in terms of the security **structure**. It spawned a debate in the early 1990s about the polarity of the post-cold war system, about the possibility of a renewed **concert**, and about the worrisome eventuality that a return to **multipolarity** could herald the erosion of the stability generated by the cold war's **bipolarity**.

The second is broadly liberal in derivation and focuses upon regimes and **institutions**, and their associated **norms** and **values**. Its central claim is that patterns of **integration** and **interdependence** had become so deeply embedded in the cold war period, albeit for strategic and geopolitical reasons, that they had by then created a self-sustaining momentum. Since complex systems of **global governance** had been spawned in the interim, these regimes would survive the collapse of the 'realist' conditions that had given rise to them in the first place.

	Units	Characteristics
Globalized	Global system	End of national polities, societies, and economies
International	States	Concern with agenda of sovereignty and stability
World	Humanity	Concern with agenda of rights, needs, and justice
Globalized international	Globalized states	Agenda of managing relations between states penetrated by global system but still distinguishable within it

Table 32.1 Typologies of order

A third line is the one that assesses order in terms of its achievement of individual human emancipation. The mere fact of stability among the major powers, or the **institutionalization** of relations among the dominant groups of states, tells us little about the quality of life for most inhabitants of the globe. If it is true, as writers like Ken Booth (1999) argue, that governments are the main source of the **abuse** of human rights, we need to do more than study the international human rights' agreements that these very governments enter into, but look also at what is really happening to people on the ground.

A fourth line of exploration is directly via the literature on globalization. This chapter asks simply whether or not globalization may be thought tantamount to a form of order. Must we speak of globalization as an ongoing process without any end-state, or can we instead speak of a globalized order as a distinctive political form? The latter view is clearly set forth in the suggestion that the contemporary Western state conglomerate, collectively, constitutes an 'emergent *global state*' (Shaw 1997: 503–4;

2000). Globalization, on this view, represents an incipient political order in its own right.

Key Points

- When we speak of order, we need to specify order for whom—states, peoples, groups, or individuals.
- International order focuses on stable and peaceful relations between states, often related to the balance of power. It is primarily about military security.
- World order is concerned with other values, such as justice, development, rights, and emancipation.
- A pattern of order may advance some values at the expense of others. There is often a tension, for example, between state-centred concepts of order and those that promote individual values. For instance, policies based on the balance of power might lead to support for regimes with bad human rights' records.
- A key question about globalization is whether it supercedes other ideas of international order, or whether it can be incorporated into more traditional ideas.

The elements of contemporary order

The 'social-state' system

Initially, there is the basic nature of the contemporary **state system** itself. The state system is 'social', first, in the sense that **states** over the past century have performed a range of social functions that distinguish them from earlier phases. The great revival in the political viability of states, from the nadir of the Second World War, is

attributable to the largely successful undertaking of this task. While not all states are equal in their ability to deliver these functions, most would now list responsibility for **development** and economic management, health, welfare, and social planning as essential tasks for the state.

It is 'social' also in the second sense that pressures for emulation tend to reinforce common patterns of behaviour, and similar forms of state institutional structure.

Historically, states have emulated each other in developing the social and economic infrastructures of military power. Now this task has broadened as states seek to adopt 'best practice' in terms of economic competitiveness and efficiency. They face also the social pressure to conform to certain standards of human rights, and this has permitted a measure of dilution and delegation of the state's exclusive jurisdiction over its own domestic affairs. In consequence, some of the key **rules** of the states-system (**sovereignty, non-intervention**) are undergoing considerable adaptation, and this gives the contemporary order many of its complex and ambivalent qualities.

Identity and the nation-state

A second feature is the multiplicity of issues about identity that have become prevalent since the 1990s. Some of these revolve around contemporary forms of **nationalism**, and are subject to contested assessments as to whether they represent a 'new' nationalism, or a reversion to a pre-existing **primordialism**. The state is both challenged and reinforced by a welter of additional crises of identity—tendencies towards apparently new forms of political community driven by ethnic separatism, regional identities, new transnational projects, new social movements, and the return to **culture**/religion. The key question here is the extent to which these are wholly new tendencies, or represent some kind of historical atavism. The politics of identity at the beginning of the new millennium impacts on the social nature of the state, as it raises explicit questions about **citizenship**—who is to count as a citizen, and what is the nature of the contract between state and citizen (see Ch.31).

It must not, however, be imagined that all such issues of identity have emerged only in the aftermath of the cold war. For example, it could be said that there has been a widespread reaction throughout much of the developing world against what has been seen as the imposition of a modernizing, Westernizing, and secular form of state. The revolution in Iran in 1979 is a case in point, and cautions us not to assume that 'identity politics' were invented simply with the end of the cold war. This is particularly so with regard to the resurgence of religion as a factor in international relations. While it may seem that religion has suddenly been rediscovered, the more plausible account is that it had never gone away, but simply had been less visible under the alternative distractions of the cold war.

Polarity and the collectivization of security

A key area of concern remains the traditional security order. This addresses the present distribution of power, and whether that distribution should be described as **unipolarity**, or as bipolar, multipolar, or some kind of hybrid. This debate has shifted considerably since the early 1990s. At that point, expectations of a resumption of multipolarity were widespread, and a US-centred unipolarity thought likely to last for a 'moment', at most. Since then, US predominance has become much more clearly established, so that analysts now routinely refer to American **hegemony**, or some kind of American **empire** (see Ch.4). This trend results from US economic successes during the 1990s, coupled with the ongoing difficulties of its other competitors. Japan's economy stagnated over the same period. Russia became embroiled in protracted and deep-seated domestic political and economic transformation. The European Union, although it has both widened and deepened, continues to have difficulty in acting decisively on its own in international crises. China's power remains a long-term prospect, although its economy has certainly grown prodigiously in the early years of the new millennium. In consequence, a key determinant of the present security order remains the role of the United States, and its willingness to become involved in general order-maintenance. This element has been highly variable, with the prominent US role in Kosovo in 1999 and in Iraq in 2003 standing in marked contrast to its unwillingness to become engaged in Rwanda in 1994 or Sudan in 2005–6. Without doubt, there was a marked shift in US policy in the early 2000s under the administration of President George W. Bush. This crystallized after the terrorist attacks of **11 September 2001**: these did not change the facts of US power so much as they intensified the political will of US policy-makers to deploy that power in a direct fashion. This has been demonstrated in the open-ended **war on terror** that was declared shortly after 11 September. Whether or not such a commitment will prove sustainable in the longer term may be shaped largely by the political fall-out from the war in Iraq.

The organization of production and exchange

Another prominent dimension is the political economy of the present order. Central to it is the degree of stability within the international trading and financial systems. The former remains beset by disputes between the world's three great trading groups or **triads**, and their trading relationship with the developing world; the latter shows periodic signs of undergoing meltdown, as during the financial turmoil that afflicted the East Asian economies towards the late 1990s. This economic order is partially managed by those elements of governance institutionalized in bodies such as the **International Monetary Fund** (IMF), World Bank, and the **World Trade Organization** (WTO). The resulting economic order penetrates deeply: such bodies do not determine just the rules for international trade and borrowing, nor shape exchange rates alone. The full effects of this **internationalization** of production include its impact on those many other things that determine the quality of human lives: production of military equipment, the condition of the environment, social welfare, human (and specifically child) rights in the area of labour, and **gender** inequalities within the economy and in processes of development.

Multilateral management and governance

One remarkable aspect of the order is the highly dense **network** of contemporary forms of international governance (regimes, **international organizations**, and INGOs). These cover most aspects of life, including developments in legal (human rights, war crimes, the International Criminal Court), environmental (Kyoto Protocol), and economic regimes, as well as in the core peacekeeping activities of universal organizations like the United Nations. To what extent can we sensibly refer to globalization as giving rise, in turn, to a system of global governance? What is its potential for further development? Are current **international regimes** dependent on the underlying power structure of Western dominance and reflective of Western preferences, and how sustainable are they given the cultural diversity of the present world? These issues link the discussion directly to the next element of order, since much of this regime infrastructure is to be found at a regional level.

Box 32.2 Elements of order

Structural elements	Purposive elements
Polarity	Social-state
Multilateralism	Identity
Regionalism	Economic order
Two worlds	Liberal rights

Regionalism

The development of contemporary **regionalism** is yet another key to understanding the emerging order. This takes various forms, including economic (trading regions), security (such as **NATO**), and cultural activities. The intensification of regionalism is occasionally viewed as a denial of globalization, but is more plausibly regarded as one aspect of it, rather than as evidence to the contrary. The fact that a number of regions feel the need to develop regional institutions is itself a manifestation of globalization, in the same way that the universal spread of the **nation-state**, as the principal political form, was an earlier product of globalization. Nonetheless, there are interesting questions about the significance of regionalism for the post-cold war order, such as the seemingly greater degree of autonomy 'enjoyed' by regions since the end of the cold war, and the role of regions in constituting new forms of identity. There is perhaps a paradox that, with the loss of cold war constraints, regions now appear to have greater autonomy—while, at the same time, levels of interpenetration and globalization indicate diminished possibilities for regional insulation.

The liberal rights order

Arguably, this is the feature with the most striking continuities to the cold war period. Human rights had become a conspicuous feature of post-1945 international politics, largely in reaction to the catastrophic experiences of the period before 1945 (see Ch.29). This theme was a paramount aspect of the cold war period itself and was again highlighted with the collapse of the Soviet bloc, since that event was portrayed as a major step forward in extending the liberal order. In this respect, the focus on **liberal rights** is another element of continuity between the two periods.

Indeed, it is often argued that it was the growth of concern with rights in the former Eastern Europe that had a corrosive effect on the maintenance of authoritarian political systems within the region. However, the post-cold war order is paradoxically under pressure precisely because of its seemingly greater promotion of a type of universalism, thought to be evoking forms of religious and cultural resistance.

This relates directly to wider questions about the future of democratization. How this develops is of momentous import for the future stability of the international order and touches on a series of interrelated issues: about the status of **democracy** as a universal norm; the current variable experience with democratization; the pressures upon democracy arising from globalization (and hence the appeals for cosmopolitan forms of democracy); and the future of democracy as a source of inter-state peace and stability (see Ch.13).

North–South and the two world orders

Any examination of the contemporary order must give a high profile to the apparent gulf within it, separating the experience of the industrialized North from the increasingly marginalized South. Some see the tensions to which this gives rise as undermining the prospects for longer-term stability (see Ch.27). Are North–South relations more stable now than in the previous eras, or do they remain precariously rooted in inequalities of power, massive gaps in quality of life, and incompatibilities of cultural values? It is also a very moot point, and a key area of disagreement, whether globalization is aggravating these inequalities, or, as its supporters believe, whether it remains the best available means of rectifying them in the longer term. Otherwise expressed,

are the problems of the South due to the processes of globalization, or to the South's relative exclusion from them? In any case, does this divide threaten the durability of the post-cold war order, or must we simply recognize it as a key component of that order, and for that reason understand it as an element of structural continuity with its predecessors?

As against this image of two monolithic blocs of North and South, other analysts insist that such a conception is now out of date. The impacts of globalization cut across states and not just between them, yielding complex patterns of stratification that defy easy classification into North and South. There are enormous variations and inequalities within states, and regions, and not just between them. For this reason, it may be too artificial to speak of two such orders, as there is much more diversity than such crude dichotomies tend to imply.

Key Points

- Order is shaped by the changed nature of states and of the tasks they perform.
- There are complex questions about whether the end of the cold war has released a new agenda of nationalism and national identity, or whether these issues have been present all along.
- Security is increasingly dealt with on a multilateral basis even when this does not conform to classical 'collective security' models.
- The global economy is primarily shaped by relations between the three key groupings (North America, Western Europe, and East Asia) and is managed by a panoply of Western-dominated institutions.
- There are dense patterns of international institutions in all functional areas.
- There are strong trends towards regionalism, but they take different forms in various regions.
- Human rights have a much higher profile than in earlier historical periods.
- Are there two separate orders in the North and South, or a more complex diversity of orders?

Globalization and the post-Westphalian order

There is a tendency to regard the current high degree of globalization as simply a consequence of the end of the cold war. This is especially so with regard to the geographical extent of globalization. Areas of the world that were formerly excluded from the full force of global **capi-**

talism, global communications, and global cultural intrusions are now much more integrated into these networks than at any previous time. In that sense, the main effect of the end of the cold war has been precisely to break down the barriers that previously held globalization at bay, at

least in so far as the 'second' or 'socialist' world had been concerned. This view has become coupled to a more general argument about the end of the Westphalian order.

Not surprisingly, many commentators see the post-cold war period as characterized by the intensification of the processes of globalization, particularly with regard to financial integration. The global financial order is now virtually universal in its reach, as is the influence of its principal institutions, such as the World Bank and the International Monetary Fund.

On this reasoning, it is the ending of the cold war that has allowed the further spread of globalization to occur, and we can therefore regard the scope of globalization as a point of difference between the cold war and post-cold war worlds. Unfortunately, there is a danger in such an analysis. The problem is that to regard globalization as simply the consequence of the end of the cold war is to neglect the extent to which globalization also served as a cause of its end. In other words, globalization marks a point of continuity, not simply discontinuity, between the two periods.

In a wider sense, the danger with such a procedure is that it neglects other dimensions of continuity, such as in the construction of a liberal capitalist order (Ikenberry 2001). What is the historical evidence for this type of argument? Its principal element is the view that globalization developed out of the core of Western capitalist states that formed during the cold war. This became such a powerful force that it finally both weakened the other cold war protagonist, namely the Soviet Union, and also made the point of the cold war increasingly irrelevant. As regards the Soviet Union, what damaged and eroded its capacity as a military power was precisely the fact that it had not become integrated into the financial and technological sinews of global capitalism. As regards the logic of the cold war as a whole, the existence of a hostile Soviet bloc was crucial in the initial integration of the Western system. By the 1980s, however, this system was effectively self-sustaining, and no longer required any external enemy to provide its dynamic for growth. In this sense, the Soviet Union had become redundant as far as the needs of the dominant Western system were concerned.

If globalization was both an element of the pre-existing cold war system and also stands out sharply as an element of the contemporary order, it needs to be seen as a point of continuity between the two periods. This logic, in turn, requires us to concede that the present order is not *sui generis*, as it contains within it elements previously present during the cold war. This suggests that the contemporary order should be understood as not wholly distinct from that which preceded it. But if globalization is the element that binds both together, can it be also the key to understanding the present order? Is it the defining quality of today's world?

The claim that globalization defines the essential quality of the present order has been denied for a number of reasons. Most generally, if globalization is seen as a long-term historical trend—with various waves—then to interpret the present order in terms of globalization does not say enough about what is specific to the current situation in particular.

Beyond this, globalization has been described as the dystopic absence of order: negative qualities appear in abundance but without any seeming coherence. The clearest example is provided in the description of globalization as 'a constellation of market, technological, ideological and civilizational developments that have

---

Box 32.3 Interpretations of globalization and the end of the cold war

'The end of the Cold War division into competing world orders marks a crucial substantive and symbolic transition to single-world economic, cultural and political orders.'

(Shaw 1999: 194)

'America has ceased to be a superpower, because it has met its match: globalization—a globalization which, moreover, it helps to promote despite not managing to master totally its meaning.'

(Laidi 1998: 170)

'Globalization is the most significant development and theme in contemporary life and social theory to emerge since the collapse of Marxist systems.'

(Albrow 1996: 89)

'Globalists continue to maintain that there are big, *fin-de-siècle* transformations under way in the world at large, which can be laid at the door of something called globalization. This new era—popularized as "a world without borders" and symbolized by the dismantling of the Berlin Wall—ostensibly came into its own where the cold war left off.'

(Weiss 1999: 59)

'To talk of 1989 as the beginning of globalisation is very misleading. . . . [G]lobalisation . . . was happening during the Cold War and has continued since. If the Cold War system dominated international politics from 1945 to 1989, then its successor is American hegemony, not globalisation.'

(Legrain 2002: 11)

nothing in common' (Falk 1997: 125). The general claim is that 'no one seems now to be in control' (Bauman 1998: 58). Even at the most basic level, globalization seems not to constitute a **minimum order** of the kind that has traditionally underpinned international society (Bull 1977). It has no common institutions fulfilling minimally agreed societal functions.

It is for this reason that globalization has come to be associated with a more general thesis about the demise of the Westphalian order. This system had typified the order since 1648, and its hallmarks were clearly defined states, with hard borders, each enjoying full **sovereignty** and jurisdiction within its own **territory**. The rules of the game dictated that states would not intervene in the domestic affairs of each other. Globalization, in contrast, is thought to question the efficacy of borders. This is very much so in the case of the global economy, where it is suggested that borders no longer mean as much as they once did. It applies also to other aspects of political life, such as human rights and **humanitarian intervention**, where the norms of the Westphalian order have come under increasing pressure.

All of these arguments suggest that globalization may be inadequate as the exclusive conceptual basis for understanding the contemporary order because of what globalization *does*. It is too varied in its effects, and so lacking in purpose and goals, that we cannot visualize a single order constructed on that basis alone. Indeed, the main theme of

these writings is just how disorderly is the process of globalization. But a different form of argument can be made on the basis of what globalization *is*, not just what it does. We need to be more precise about its nature, and not look only at its effects. This will be set out in the final section, after we have reviewed some of the political problems that appear to be attached to globalization today. These arise exactly from that sense of purposelessness and lack of control.

Key Points

- Globalization is often portrayed as an effect of the end of the cold war because this led to its further geographical spread.
- At the same time, globalization needs to be understood as one of the factors that contributed to the end of the cold war. It was the Soviet Union's marginalization from processes of globalization that revealed, and intensified, its weaknesses.
- Accordingly, globalization should be regarded as an element of continuity between the cold war and post-cold war orders, and the latter should not be regarded as wholly distinct.
- There is reason for scepticism that globalization is the exclusive hallmark of contemporary order.
- One of the reasons is that, as a long-term historical trend, globalization is not specific to the late twentieth or the early twenty-first century.
- Globalization is often associated with a 'borderless world' in which the old Westphalian order no longer applies.
- Globalization embodies a range of often competing values.
- Globalization is too much outside our control to form an order on its own. We are its objects rather than its subjects.

Globalization and legitimacy

On the face of it, globalization potentially creates several problems for the political stability of the current order. Not least is this so with regard to its legitimacy. There is a widely shared view that the emergence of a diffuse protest movement against globalization is symptomatic of a new wave of resistance to it. This creates tensions at several levels. The central problem is understood to be one of the limited effectiveness of democratic practice in present world conditions. At a time when so much emphasis is placed on the virtues of democracy, many question its viability when organized on a purely national basis, given the context of globalization. There are two facets to this issue: representation and accountability. It is all very well for citizens to be represented in national electoral institutions, but what voice does this

give them in controlling those very economic, social, and cultural forces that cut across national borders, if their own governments do not have the capacity to deal with these? Conversely, this creates an issue of accountability. There may be little point in holding national and local politicians accountable through elections if these politicians remain relatively powerless to exercise influence over global corporations, global technology, global environmental changes, or the global financial system. These concerns apply specifically to just how democratic are bodies such as the World Bank and the International Monetary Fund, as well as international organizations such as the United Nations. On a regional level, there has been recurrent anxiety about the so-called legitimacy deficits that afflict the institutions of

the European Union (see Ch.25). The general issue is the lack of congruence between the geographical organization of our various political systems, and the 'deterritorialized' nature of our current economic, social, and political activities.

In the face of these concerns, there has been much debate about the role of an emerging global **civil society** (Keane 2003). This embraces a variety of cross-national social movements, including anti-globalization activists, as well as a multitude of international non-governmental organizations, such as Greenpeace and Amnesty International. Their proponents see these movements as the only feasible way of directly influencing global policies on such matters as development, environment, human rights, and international security, and hence as the best way of democratizing global governance. Others, however, remain sceptical. There is nothing inherently democratic about global civil society as such, as there is no legitimate basis of representation or accountability to many of these movements (Van Rooy 2003). They may simply represent sectional interests, and make policy hostage to those that are better organized, have greater resources, and are more vocal.

Indeed, from the perspective of many governments in the South, global civil society may aggravate the inequalities between rich and poor. Civil society is resented as an extension of the power of the North, for the reason that such movements have a much more solid basis in the developed world, and are more likely to speak for its interests. This is illustrated, for example, in the tension between the economic development objectives of many governments in the South, and the preferred policies of many environmental movements in the North. The possible objection is that this perpetuates the sense of two contrasting global orders, one for the North (represented both by strong governments and strong civil society movements), as against the South (led by weak governments, and weakly organized civil society). This may contribute to a perceived crisis of legitimacy for the state in the developing world.

Key Points

- There is evidence of resistance to globalization.
- Some of this is generated by the feeling that traditional democracy does not offer effective representation in the global order.
- National elections may not make politicians accountable if they cannot control wider global forces.
- There is a heated debate about whether global civil society can help democratize international institutions, or whether they themselves are largely undemocratic.
- Some governments in the South remain suspicious of social movements that may be better organized in developed countries.

Box 32.4 The debate about globalization and legitimacy

'The process of globalization has had a mixed impact on the legitimacy of international organizations. The demand for international co-ordination and common action has obviously increased. But at the same time, the effectiveness of IOs has diminished.'

(Junne 2001: 218–19)

'Global structures violate commitments to the politics of consent: there is a global democratic deficit that must be reduced if worldwide arrangements are to be legitimate.'

(Linklater 1999: 477)

'It will be argued that the rising need for enlarged and deepened international cooperation in the age of globalization led to the establishment of new international institutions with specific features. As a result, the intrusiveness of those new international institutions into national societies has increased dramatically.'

(Zurn 2004: 261–2)

'The democratic project is to globalize democracy as we have globalized the economy.'

(Barber 2002a: 255)

'Some theorists have pointed to the activity of social movements working beyond state borders as a method of increasing democratic practice. They see a contradiction between the fact that the structures of power . . . are firmly rooted in the global context, but participation, representation and legitimacy are fixed at the state level.'

(O'Brien et al. 2000: 21–2)

'However much individual INGOs and global social movements may have contributed to the extension of democratic politics across the world, they do not currently possess the requisite degree of legitimacy and accountability to be considered as democratic representatives in a globalized political community.'

(Colas 2002: 163)

'Rather than reform, these critics insist that what is required is an alternative system of global governance, privileging people over profits, and the local over the global.'

(Held and McGrew 2002: 64)

Case Study The crisis of developing state legitimacy

The idea of the two world orders—one applying to the rich and stable North and the other to the poor and unstable South—reinforces the image of a crisis of state legitimacy in the South. Many of these have, since decolonization, been depicted as **quasi-states** (Jackson 1990), not enjoying the full capacities of strong states. The period since the end of the cold war has reinforced this tendency. It has become commonplace to refer to a number of **failed states** (e.g. Lebanon, Cambodia, Afghanistan, Somalia, Rwanda, Zaïre, Zimbabwe), indicating their inability to maintain central order within the state, or to produce at least minimal conditions of social welfare and economic subsistence. In some cases, law and order has broken down into civil war, creating fiefdoms organized by rival warlords.

The deployment by the international community of a number of peacebuilding missions has been implicitly justified on the grounds of the 'failure' of these national authorities to maintain order on their own, especially in the aftermath of international or civil conflict. This has been associated with the revival of doctrines of trusteeship in the international community, charging the strong with some responsibility for protecting the welfare of the weak.

However, there is considerable resentment against this notion of failed states, and it is often suggested that the failures are exactly the outcome of the structural conditions that the Northern powers have themselves created by their economic and political actions. This resentment leads to charges that the instruments of the international community are being used to erode the political legitimacy of Southern governments, thereby making Southern societies more vulnerable to intervention, and more adaptable to the preferences of the rich states. This is further compounded when the most powerful states themselves question the legitimacy of some governments, by designating them as rogue states, or sponsors of terrorism, and questioning their full entitlement to be represented within international negotiations, or to enjoy equal rights with other states. The objection raised is that state failures, and the resulting diminished legitimacy of developing states, are not 'objective' conditions but the products of Northern policies.

An international order of globalized states?

Finally, the chapter returns to whether globalization can be regarded as the defining element in contemporary order. Globalization could be taken to represent the mainstay of today's order only if it superseded all traditional elements of the international order. But if globalization is an addition to, not a substitute for, the existing international order, then it is not wholly adequate to the task of providing us with the single key to the post-cold war order.

If it can be convincingly held that globalization is not some process over and above the activities of states, but is instead an element within state transformation, we can develop on this basis a conception of the **globalized state**. Globalization does not make the state disappear, but is a way of thinking about its present form. By extension, globalization does not make redundant the notion of an international order, but instead requires us to think about a **globalized international order**. In short, what is required is a notion of international order composed of globalized states.

Much of the confusion results from the tendency to see globalization as exclusively pertaining to the environment in which states find themselves: globalization is a force wholly external to the individual states, and demands an outside-in perspective on the resulting outcomes. On this view, globalization is a claim about the degree of interconnectedness between states, such that the significance of borders, and the reality of separate national actors, is called seriously into question. There is no denying that this is part of what globalization signifies. But what such a one-sided interpretation leaves out is the extent to which globalization refers also to a 'domestic' process of change within states. Regarded in this alternative way, globalization can be understood as an expression of the profound transformations in the nature of the state, and in state–society relations, that have developed in recent decades. This requires an inside-out view of globalization as well. This leads us to think not of the demise or retreat of the

state, but about its changing functionality: states still exist but do different things, do some things less well than they used to, and also have taken on new responsibilities in exchange.

Even in an age of globalization, there remain both states and a states-system. While, as noted above, the idea of international order is more limited than that of world or global order, the suggestion that globalization refers (at least in part) to a condition within states invites us to develop a theory about the nature of international order appropriate for globalized states. We need to face the seeming paradox that there can indeed be an international order of globalized states. The mistake then is to imagine that globalization signifies the end of all projects for international order, when what in fact is underway is the reconfiguration of the **principles** of international order to reflect the new realities of globalized states.

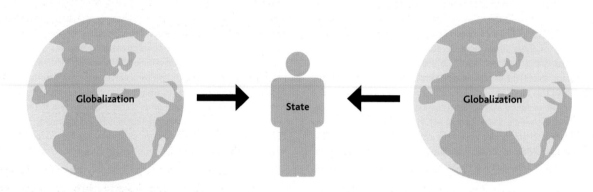

Figure 32.1 Outside-in view of globalization

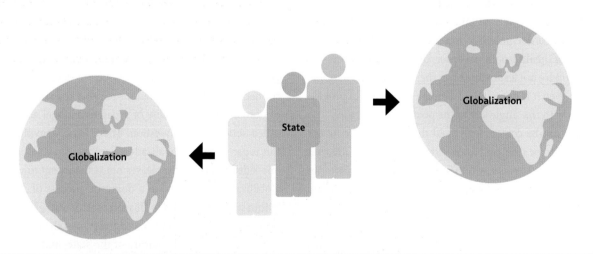

Figure 32.2 Inside-out view of globalization

Key Points

- Globalization is often thought of as an extreme form of interdependence. This sees it exclusively as an outside-in development.
- The implication of such analyses is that states are now much weaker as actors. Consequently, they are in retreat or becoming obsolete.
- If this were the case, ideas of international order would be much less relevant to our concept of order.
- But if globalization is considered as a transformation in the nature of states themselves, it suggests that states are still central to the discussion of order: they are different but not obsolete. This leads to the idea of a globalized state as a state form, and introduces an inside-out element.
- In this case, there is no contradiction between the norms and rules of a state system operating alongside globalized states.
- This international order will nonetheless have different norms and rules in recognition of the new nature of states and their transformed functions. Rules of sovereignty and non-intervention are undergoing change as symptoms of this adaptation.

Conclusion

In short, we now face a hybrid situation in which states share a host of responsibilities with both intergovernmental organizations and a multiplicity of non-governmental and **transnational actors**. Formerly, the function of the international order was largely to cushion and protect the states so that they might go about their business as the principal providers of social goods to their citizens. This situation is now vastly more complex. Much of that provision (economic goods, monitoring of human rights, access to information, security, and so on) originates beyond the individual state itself, and indeed in non-state components that fall outside the jurisdiction of the international order narrowly conceived.

This does not, however, mean that the international order has become redundant. It means simply that it needs to be redesigned to take account of the new division of labour between states, **global networks**, and the rudimentary forms of global governance. As long as states persist as important sources of political agency, they will construct a states-system with its own rules and norms. It is this that we regard as the essential basis of the international order. Currently, the identity of states is undergoing considerable change, to the extent that we can describe them as globalized states. But these globalized states still coexist within an international order, albeit one that now differs from its recent historical forms. This order is currently seeking to develop a set of principles to reflect that transformation. The quest for a post-cold war order is the expression of this uneasy search. There is no reason to assume that recent trends are irreversible, as the revival of the security state after 11 September would seem to indicate. The globalized state of the late twentieth century is evidently not the only model of likely state development in the future.

? Questions

1 Is the post-cold war order still an international order?

2 How important an element in the contemporary order is the condition of globalization?

3 How would you distinguish between an international and a world order, and which is the more important framework for assessing the contemporary situation?

4 In which respects are the 'identities' of states undergoing change?

5 How would you define the polarity of the contemporary international system?

6 Is global governance a significant element of today's order?

7 Is regionalism a contradiction of globalization?

8 Is the prominence of democracy and liberal rights convincing evidence of the impact of globalization? If so, why is globalization so problematic for democracy?

9 In which ways is globalization creating problems of political legitimacy?

10 Is the idea of an international order of globalized states contradictory?

⮕ Guide to further reading

International order

Bull, H. (1977), *The Anarchical Society: A Study of Order in World Politics* (London: Macmillan), especially Part 1. Provides the standard introduction to this issue from an international society perspective.

Cox, R. (1996), 'Social Forces, States, and World Orders: Beyond International Relations Theory', in R. Cox with T. J. Sinclair, *Approaches to World Order* (Cambridge: Cambridge University Press). An alternative to the 'English School' approach and steps outside the state-centric framework.

Vincent, R. J. (1990), 'Order in International Politics', in J. D. B. Miller and R. J. Vincent (eds), *Order and Violence* (Oxford: Oxford University Press). Gives a useful commentary on Bull's position.

New world orders and the post-cold war world

Clark, I. (2001), *The Post-Cold War Order: The Spoils of Peace* (Oxford: Oxford University Press). Presents a guide to the debates about the post-cold war period, viewing the order as the equivalent of a historical peace settlement.

Ikenberry, G. John (2001), *After Victory: Institutions, Strategic Restraint, and the Rebuilding of Order after Major Wars* (Princeton, NJ: Princeton University Press). Also sets post-cold war developments in their historical context and argues for the emergence of an increasingly 'constitutional' international order after 1945.

Williams, A. (1998), *Failed Imagination? New World Orders of the Twentieth Century* (Manchester: Manchester University Press). Discusses the historical precedents for new orders during the twentieth century.

Globalization in the present order

Clark, I. (1999), *Globalization and International Relations Theory* (Oxford: Oxford University Press). Develops a theoretical account of globalization in terms of state transformation.

—— (1997), *Globalization and Fragmentation: International Relations in the Twentieth Century* (Oxford: Oxford University Press). Places the contemporary debates about globalization in historical perspective.

Held, D., and McGrew, A. (eds) (2003), *The Global Transformations Reader: An Introduction to the Globalization Debate*, 2nd edn (Cambridge: Polity Press). A detailed selection of readings about contemporary globalization and its implications.

Scholte, J. A. (2004), *Globalization: A Critical Introduction*, 2nd edn (Basingstoke: Palgrave). Provides a substantial theoretical overview of globalization.

Wolf, M. (2004), *Why Globalization Works: The Case for the Global Market Economy* (New Haven, Conn.: Yale University Press). Offers a defence of the economic benefits of globalization.

International legitimacy

Clark, I. (2005), *Legitimacy in World Society* (Oxford: Oxford University Press). Explores the nature of legitimacy within the states system.

—— (2007), *International Legitimacy and World Society* (Oxford: Oxford University Press). Tries to explain how world-society norms are adopted by international society.

Online Resource Centre

 Visit the Online Resource Centre that accompanies this book to access more learning resources on this chapter topic at www.oxfordtextbooks.co.uk/uk/orc/baylis_smith4e/

Glossary

Absolute gains: all states seek to gain more power and influence in the system to secure their national interests. This is absolute gain. Offensive neo-realists are also concerned with increasing power relative to other states. One must have enough power to secure interests and more power than any other state in the system—friend or foe.

Abuse: states justify self-interested wars by reference to humanitarian principles.

Agent-structure problem: the problem is how to think about the relationship between agents and structures. One view is that agents are born with already formed identities and interests and then treat other actors and the broad structure that their interactions produce as a constraint on their interests. But this suggests that actors are pre-social to the extent that there is little interest in their identities or possibility that they might change their interests through their interactions with others. Another view is to treat the structure not as a constraint but rather as constituting the actors themselves. Yet this might treat agents as cultural dupes because they are nothing more than artefacts of that structure. The proposed solution to the agent-structure problem is to try and find a way to understand how agents and structures constitute each other.

Anarchic system: the 'ordering principle' of international politics according to Realism, and that which defines its structure.

Anarchy: a system operating in the absence of any central government. Does not imply chaos, but in Realist theory the absence of political authority.

Anti-foundationalist: positions argue that there are never neutral grounds for asserting what is true in any given time or space. Our theories of world define what counts as the facts and so there is no neutral position available to determine between rival claims.

Apartheid: system of racial segregation introduced in South Africa in 1948, designed to ensure white minority domination.

Appeasement: a policy of making concessions to a revanchist (or otherwise territorially acquisitive) state in the hope that settlement of more modest claims will assuage that state's expansionist appetites. Appeasement remains most (in)famously associated with British Prime Minister Neville Chamberlain's acquiescence to Hitler's incursions into Austria and then Czechoslovakia, culminating in the Munich Agreement of September 1938. Since then, appeasement has generally been seen as synonymous with a craven collapse before the demands of dictators—encouraging, not disarming, their aggressive designs.

ASEAN: a geopolitical and economic organization of several countries located in South-East Asia. Initially formed as a display of solidarity against Communism, its aims now have been redefined and broadened to include the acceleration of economic growth and the promotion of regional peace. By 2005 the ASEAN countries had a combined GDP of about $884 billion.

Asymmetrical globalization: describes the way in which contemporary globalization is unequally experienced across the world and among different social groups in such a way that it produces a distinctive geography of inclusion in, and exclusion from, the global system.

Axis of evil: phrase deliberately used by George W. Bush in January 2001 to characterize Iran, North Korea, and Iraq.

Balance of power: in Realist theory, refers to an equilibrium between states; historical Realists regard it as the product of diplomacy (contrived balance) whereas structural Realists regard the system as having a tendency towards a natural equilibrium (fortuitous balance). It is a doctrine and an arrangement whereby the power of one state (or group of states) is checked by the countervailing power of other states.

Bank for International Settlements: established in 1930 with headquarters in Basle. Membership (2004) of 55 shareholding central banks, although many other public financial institutions also use BIS facilities. Promotes cooperation among central banks and provides various services for global financial operations. For example, the Basle Committee on Banking Supervision, formed through the BIS in 1974, has spearheaded efforts at multilateral regulation of global banking. See further www.bis.org.

Battle of the sexes: a scenario in game theory illustrating the need for a coordination strategy.

Battlespace: in the era of aircraft and satellites, the traditional 'battlefield' has given way to the three-dimensional battlespace.

Bipolarity: term employed by scholars of International Relations to describe the post-war order before the USSR fell apart in 1991, leaving the United States as the sole superpower.

Bond: a contractual obligation of a corporation, association, or governance agency to make payments of interest and repayments of principal on borrowed funds at certain fixed times.

Breadwinner: a traditionally masculine role of working in the public sphere for wages and providing for the economic needs of the family.

Brezhnev doctrine: declaration by Soviet premier Leonid Brezhnev in November 1968 that members of the Warsaw Pact would enjoy only 'limited sovereignty' in their political development. It was associated with the idea of 'limited sovereignty' for Soviet bloc nations, which was used to justify the crushing of the reform movement in Czechoslovakia in 1968.

Capabilities: the resources that are under an actor's direct control such as population and size of territory, resources, economic strength, military capability, and competence (Waltz 1979: 131).

Capacity building: providing the funds and technical training to allow developing countries to participate in global environmental governance.

Capitalism: a system of production in which human labour and its products are commodities that are bought and sold in the market-place. In Marxist analysis, the capitalist mode of production involved a specific set of social relations that were particular to a specific historical period. For Marx there were three main characteristics of capitalism: (1) Everything involved in production (e.g. raw materials, machines, labour involved in the creation of commodities, and the commodities themselves) is given an exchange value, and all can be exchanged, one for the other. In essence, under capitalism everything has its price, including people's working time. (2) Everything that is needed to undertake production (i.e. the factories, and the raw materials) is owned by one class—the capitalists. (3) Workers are 'free', but in order to survive must sell their labour to the capitalist class in order to survive, and because the capitalist class own the *means of production*, and control the *relations of production*, they also control the profit that results from the labour of workers.

Citizenship: the status of having the right to participate in and to be represented in politics.

Civic nationalism: a nationalism which claims the nation is based on commitment to a common set of political values and institutions.

Civil society: (1) the totality of all individuals and groups in a society who are not acting as participants in any government institutions, or (2) all individuals and groups who are neither participants in government nor acting in the interests of commercial companies. The two meanings

are incompatible and contested. There is a third meaning: the network of social institutions and practices (economic relationships, family and kinship groups, religious, and other social affiliations) which underlie strictly political institutions. For democratic theorists the voluntary character of these associations is taken to be essential to the workings of democratic politics.

Civilization: is the broadest construction of cultural identity to which individuals may subscribe. A number of broad cultures have emerged from world history, including the Western, Islamic, and Chinese civilizations. However, the definition of civilization has sometimes been conflated with a particular standard of good or achievement. At one time or other, for instance, people from the Western, Islamic, and Chinese civilizations have claimed that their civilization represented the ultimate standard of good.

Claim-rights: the most basic rights—the only true rights, the American jurist Wesley Hofeld believed (see Jones 1994 for a modern version); the classic example of a claim-right is a right generated by a contract and accompanied by correlative duties.

Clash of civilizations: controversial idea first used by Samuel Huntington in 1993 to describe the main cultural fault-line of international conflict in a world without communism; the notion has become more popular still since 9/11.

Coexistence: the doctrine of live and let live between political communities, or states.

Cold war: extended worldwide conflict between communism and capitalism that is normally taken to have begun in 1947 and concluded in 1989 with the collapse of Soviet power in Europe.

Collaboration: a form of cooperation requiring parties not to defect from a mutually desirable strategy for an individually preferable strategy.

Collective security: refers to an arrangement where 'each state in the system accepts that the security of one is the concern of all, and agrees to join in a collective response to aggression' (Roberts and Kingsbury 1993: 30). It is also the foundational principle of the League of Nations: namely, that member states would take a threat or attack on one member as an assault on them all (and on international norms more generally). The League would accordingly respond in unison to such violations of international law. Appreciating that such concerted action would ensue, putative violators—the League's framers hoped—would be duly deterred from launching aggressive strikes in the first place. As the 1920s and 1930s showed, however, theory and practice diverged wildly, with League members failing to take concerted action against Japanese imperialism in Asia, and German and Italian expansionism in Europe and Africa.

Collectivization of security: the tendency for security to be organized on a multilateral basis, but without the institutional formality of a fully fledged collective security system.

Combating terrorism: Combating terrorism is comprised of anti-terrorism efforts (measures to protect against or mitigate future terrorist attacks) and counter-terrorism efforts (proactive actions designed to retaliate against or forestall terrorist actions).

Common humanity: we all have human rights by virtue of our common humanity, and these rights generate correlative moral duties for individuals and states.

Common security: to accept 'as the organizing principle for efforts to reduce the risk of war, limit arms, and move towards disarmament, means, in principle, that co-operation will replace confrontation in resolving conflicts of interest. This is not to say that differences among nations should be expected to disappear ... The task is only to ensure that these conflicts do not come to be expressed in acts of war, or in preparations for war. It means that nations must come to understand that the maintenance of world peace must be given a higher priority than the assertion of their own ideological or political positions.' (Palme Report 1992).

Communitarianism: the ultimate source of meaning and value in human life resides in the community, whether ethnic, national, or perhaps even 'virtual'. In terms of human rights, communitarians will look to, at best, a basic minimum of universal standards with emphasis on the community setting its own standards for most purposes.

Community: a human association in which members share common symbols and wish to cooperate to realize common objectives.

Community-based organization (CBO): any group of people organized in a local village, small town, or local district of a city. Logically, a CBO is a local NGO. However, in political debate, CBOs are sometimes contrasted with NGOs and seen as being more radical.

Compliance: if a state is in compliance it is living up to its obligations under a treaty. Many MEAs have some form of 'monitoring and compliance procedures' to help ensure that this happens.

Concert: the directorial role played by a number of Great Powers, based on norms of mutual consent.

Consequentialist: for consequentialists, it is the likely consequences of an action that should guide decisions. In international ethics, realism and utilitarianism are the most prominent consequentialist ethics.

Constitutive theories: theories that assume that our theories of the social world help to construct the social world and what we see as the external world. Thus the very concepts we use to think about the world help to make that world what it is.

Constructivism: an approach to international politics that concerns itself with the centrality of ideas and human consciousness and stresses a holistic and Idealist view of structures. As Constructivists have examined world politics they have been broadly interested in how the structure constructs the actors' identities and interests, how their interactions are organized and constrained by that structure, and how their very interaction serves to either reproduce or transform that structure.

Containment: American political strategy for resisting perceived Soviet expansion, first publicly espoused by an American diplomat, George Kennan, in 1947. Containment became a powerful factor in American policy towards the Soviet Union for the next forty years, and a self-image of Western policy-makers.

Convention: a type of general treaty between states, often the result of an international conference. A framework convention sets out goals, organizations, scientific research, and review procedures with a view to developing future action to establish and solve environmental problems—in terms of a 'framework convention—adjustable protocol' model.

Conventional warfare: the use of regular, uniformed, national military units to achieve military or political objectives. Conventional warfare can be distinguished from nuclear warfare, and from 'unconventional warfare' involving guerrilla or terrorist techniques.

Cooperation: is required in any situation where parties must act together in order to achieve a mutually acceptable outcome.

Coordination: a form of cooperation requiring parties to pursue a common strategy in order to avoid the mutually undesirable outcome arising from the pursuit of divergent strategies.

CoP: Conference of the Parties to a convention, usually held annually.

Cosmopolitan democracy: a condition in which international organizations, transnational corporations, global markets, and so forth are accountable to the peoples of the world. Associated with David Held, Daniele Archibugi, Mary Kaldor, and others, a cosmopolitan model of democracy requires the following: the creation of regional parliaments and the extension of the authority of such regional bodies (like the European Union) which are already in existence; human rights conventions

must be entrenched in national parliaments and monitored by a new International Court of Human Rights; the UN must be replaced with a genuinely democratic and accountable global parliament.

Cosmopolitanism: the ultimate source of meaning and value in human life resides with the individual (or perhaps with God). Cosmopolitans are disposed to favour very extensive accounts of universal human rights.

Counter-restrictionists: international lawyers who argue that there is a legal right of humanitarian intervention in both UN Charter law and customary international law.

Customary international law: this comprises a wide range of rules that are binding upon all states, regardless of their explicit consent. Two things are considered necessary before a rule can be considered customary law: evidence of general state practice (that is, states habitually acting in a manner consistent with the rule); and evidence that states accepted such practice as law (*opinio juris*).

D **Decision-making procedures:** there identify specific prescriptions for behaviour, the system of voting, for example, which will regularly change as a regime is consolidated and extended. The rules and procedures governing the GATT, for example, underwent substantial modification during its history. Indeed, the purpose of the successive conferences was to change the rules and decisionmaking procedures (Krasner 1985: 4–5).

Defensive realism: a structural theory of Realism that views states as security maximizers.

Democracy promotion: the strategy adopted by leading Western states and institutions—particularly the USA—to use instruments of foreign and economic policy to spread liberal values. Advocates make an explicit linkage between the mutually reinforcing effects of democratization and open markets.

Democratic peace: a central plank of liberal internationalist thought, the democratic peace thesis makes two claims: first, liberal polities exhibit restraint in their relations with other liberal polities (the so-called separate peace) but are imprudent in relations with authoritarian states. The validity of the democratic peace thesis has been fiercely debated in the IR literature.

Deontological: theories are concerned with the nature of human duty or obligation. They prioritize questions of the 'right' over those of the good. They focus on rules that are always right for everyone to follow, in contrast to rules that might produce a good outcome for an individual, or their society.

Deregulation: the removal of all regulation so that market forces, not government policy, control economic developments.

Derivative: a financial contract that 'derives' its value from an underlying asset, exchange rate, interest level, or market index.

Détente: relaxation of tension between East and West; Soviet–American détente lasted from the late 1960s to the late 1970s, and was characterized by negotiations and nuclear arms control agreements.

Deterrence: the threat or use of force to prevent an actor from doing something they would otherwise do.

Deterritorialization: a process in which the organization of social activities is increasingly less constrained by geographical proximity and national territorial boundaries. Accelerated by the technological revolution and refers to the diminution of influence of territorial places, distances, and boundaries over the way people collectively identify themselves or seek political recognition. This permits an expansion of global civil society but equally an expansion of global criminal or terrorist networks.

Development, core ideas, and assumptions: in the orthodox view, the possibility of unlimited economic growth in a free-market system. Economies would reach a 'take-off' point and thereafter wealth would trickle down to those at the bottom. Superiority of the 'Western' model and knowledge. Belief that the process would ultimately benefit everyone. Domination, exploitation of nature. In the alternative view, sufficiency. The inherent value of nature, cultural diversity, and the community-controlled commons (water, land, air, forest). Human activity in balance with nature. Self-reliance. Democratic inclusion, participation, for example, voice for marginalized groups, e.g. women, indigenous groups. Local control.

Development, measurement of: in the orthodox view, economic growth; Gross Domestic Product (GDP) per capita: industrialization, including of agriculture. In the alternative view, fulfilment of basic material and non-material human needs of everyone; condition of the natural environment. Political empowerment of marginalized.

Development, process of: in the orthodox view, top-down; reliance on 'expert knowledge', usually Western and definitely external; large capital investments in large projects; advanced technology; expansion of the private sphere. In the alternative view, bottom-up; participatory; reliance on appropriate (often local) knowledge and technology; small investments in small-scale projects; protection of the commons.

Development, purpose of: in the orthodox view, transformation of traditional subsistence economies defined as 'backward' into industrial, commodified economies defined as 'modern'. Production of surplus. Individuals sell their labour for money, rather than producing to meet their family's needs. In the alternative view, the creation of human well-being through sustainable societies in social, cultural, political, and economic terms.

Diplomacy: in foreign policy it refers to the use of diplomacy as a policy instrument possibly in association with other instruments such as economic or military force to enable an international actor to achieve its policy objectives. Diplomacy in world politics refers to a communications process between international actors that seeks through negotiation to resolve conflict short of war. This process has been refined, institutionalized, and professionalized over many centuries.

Disaggregated state: the tendency for states to become increasingly fragmented actors in global politics as every part of the government machine becomes entangled with its foreign counterparts and others in dealing with global issues through proliferating transgovernmental and global policy networks.

Double burden: when women enter the public workforce working for wages, they usually remain responsible for most of the reproductive and caring labour in the private sphere, thus creating a double workload.

Dual moral standards: in Realist theory, the idea that there are two principles or standards of right and wrong: one for the individual citizen and a different one for the state.

E **Ecological footprint:** used to demonstrate the load placed upon the Earth's carrying capacity by individuals or nations. It does this by estimating the area of productive land or aqua-system required to sustain a population at its specified standard of living.

Emancipatory knowledge: much feminist scholarship is openly committed to gender equality as a normative ideal, and is dedicated to producing knowledge that furthers this goal. Knowledge that is produced with such normative ideals is called emancipatory knowledge.

Empire: a distinct type of political entity, which may or may not be a state, possessing both a home territory and foreign territories. It is a disputed concept that some have tried to apply to the United States to describe its international reach, huge capabilities, and vital global role of underwriting world order.

End of history: famous phrase employed by Francis Fukuyama in 1989; this argued that one phase of history shaped by the antagonism between collectivism and individualism had (two hundred years after the French Revolution) come to an end, leaving Liberalism triumphant.

Endemic warfare: the condition in which warfare is a recurrent feature of the relations between states not least because they regard it as inevitable.

Enlightenment: associated with rationalist thinkers of the eighteenth century. Key ideas (which some would argue remain mottoes for our age) include: secularism, progress, reason, science, knowledge, and freedom. The motto of the Enlightenment is: *'Sapere aude!* Have courage to use your own understanding' (Kant 1991: 54).

Epistemic community: knowledge-based transnational communities of experts and policy activists.

Epistemology: the study of how we can claim to know something. It is about our theories of knowledge.

Equality of states: the principle that sovereign states enjoy legal equality in their international relations, so that, for example, all have the same voting power in the United Nations.

Equity: also called stock or share; a number of equal portions in the nominal capital of a company; the shareholder thereby owns part of the enterprise.

Ethic of responsibility: for historical Realists, an ethic of responsibility is the limits of ethics in international politics; it involves the weighing up of consequences and the realization that positive outcomes may result from amoral actions.

Ethnic nationalism: a nationalism which claims the nation is based on common descent, descent which may be indicated through such characteristics as language, history, way of life, or physical appearance.

Ethno-symbolism: the theory that nations are grounded upon ethnicity, understood as shared myths and memories which are transmitted from generation to generation. It is different from primordialism because it does not claim that nations (as opposed to ethnies) are pre-modern, tending to see nations as modern formations that have economic, political, and other features in addition to that of ethnic identity.

Eurobond: a bond denominated in a currency that is alien to a substantial proportion of the underwriters through whom it is distributed and investors to whom it is sold; the borrower, the syndicate of managers, the investors, and the securities exchange on which the bond is listed are spread over a number of countries.

Eurocurrency: national money in the hands of persons and institutions domiciled outside the currency's territorial 'home': hence 'eurodollar', 'eurozloty', etc.

Euroequity: a share issue that is offered simultaneously in different stock-markets, usually across several time zones; also called global equity.

Europe: a geographical expression that during the course of the cold war came to be identified with Western Europe, but since 1989 has once again come to be associated with the whole of the European continent.

European Union (EU): the EU was formally created in 1992 following the signing of the Maastricht Treaty. However, the origins of the EU can be traced back to 1951 and the creation of the European Coal and Steel Community, followed in 1957 with a broader customs union (The Treaty of Rome 1958). Originally a grouping of six countries in 1957, 'Europe' grew by adding new members in 1973, 1981, and 1986. Since the fall of the planned economies in Eastern Europe in 1989, Europe has grown and now includes 27 members states.

Explanatory theories: theories that see the social world as something external to our theories of the social world. On this view, the task of theory is to report on a world that exists independent from the observer and his or her theoretical position.

Exponential growth: a situation where the rate of growth is not constant or linear but increases over time.

Extraterritoriality: occurs when one government attempts to exercise its legal authority in the territory of another state. It mainly arises when the US federal government deliberately tries to use domestic law to control the global activities of TNCs.

F **Failed state:** this is a state that has collapsed and cannot provide for its citizens without substantial external support and where the government of the state has ceased to exist inside the territorial borders of the state.

Femininity: defined in opposition to the qualities of masculinity, femininity is the set of characteristics associated with being a woman. Typical associations are weakness, dependence/connection, emotionality, and the private sphere.

Feminization of labour: recognizing the increasing global demand for women as 'cheap labour', on the global assembly line, and in the provision of paid as well as unpaid reproductive labour and care.

Feminism: a political project to understand so as to change women's inequality, liberation, or oppression. For some, aiming to move beyond gender, so that it no longer matters; for others, to validate women's interests, experiences, and choices; for others, to work for more equal and inclusive social relations overall.

Flexible labour: refers to workers who lack job security, benefits, or the right to unionize. It gives companies more flexibility in hiring and firing their workforce.

Forcible humanitarian intervention: military intervention which breaches the principle of state sovereignty where the primary purpose is to alleviate the human suffering of some or all within a state's borders.

Foundationalist: positions assume that all truth claims (about some feature of the world) can be judged objectively true or false.

Fourteen Points: President Woodrow Wilson's vision of international society, first articulated in January 1918, included the principle of self-determination, the conduct of diplomacy on an open (not secret) basis, and the establishment of an association of nations to provide guarantees of independence and territorial integrity. Wilson's ideas exerted an important influence on the Paris Peace Conference, though the principle of self-determination was only selectively pursued when it came to American colonial interests.

Fundamentalism: a strict interpretation of a religious-cultural form drawn from particular understandings—often literal—of basic/fundamental scripture, doctrines, and practices. Fundamentalists typically seek to convert or exclude non-believers from their community.

G **G8 (Group of Eight):** established in 1975 as the G5 (France, Germany, Japan, the UK, and the USA); subsequently expanded as the G7 to include Canada and Italy and since 1998 the G8 to include the Russian Federation. The G8 conducts semi-formal collaboration on world economic problems. Government leaders meet in annual G8 Summits, while finance ministers and/or their leading officials periodically hold other consultations. See further www.g8online.org.

Game theory: a branch of mathematics which explores strategic interaction.

Gender: what it means to be male or female in a particular place or time; the social construction of sexual difference.

Gender relations: power relations: the relational construction of masculinity and femininity, in which the masculine is usually privileged; and which are contested, and changing.

Gendered division of labour (GDL): the notion of 'women's work', which everywhere includes women's primary responsibility for child-care and housework, and which designates many public and paid forms of work as 'women's' or 'men's', too.

Gendering globalization: applying a 'gender lens' to globalization, to reveal that women are differently positioned in relation to globalization processes and differently impacted upon by them; and that women become global players in response to these gendered effects.

General Agreement on Tariffs and Trade (GATT): established in 1947 with offices in Geneva. Membership had reached 122 states when it was absorbed into the World Trade Organization (WTO) in 1995. The GATT coordinated eight 'rounds' of multilateral negotiations to reduce state restrictions on cross-border merchandise trade.

Glasnost: policy of greater openness pursued by Soviet premier Mikhail Gorbachev from 1985, involving greater toleration of internal dissent and criticism.

Global covenant: the rules, values, and norms which govern the global society of states.

Global environmental governance: governance is the performance of regulative functions often in the absence of a central government authority. Global environmental governance usually refers to the structure of international agreements and organizations but can also involve governance by the private sector or NGOs.

Global governance: the evolving system of (formal and informal) political coordination—across multiple levels from the local to the global—among public authorities (states and intergovernmental organizations) and private agencies (NGOs and corporate actors) seeking to realize common purposes or resolve collective problems through the making and implementing of global or transnational norms, rules, programmes, and policies. The loose framework of global regulation, both institutional and normative, that constrains conduct. It has many elements: international organizations and law; transnational organizations and frameworks; elements of global civil society; and shared normative principles.

Global network: digital networks that span the globe allowing instant voice and data communication worldwide—the global information highway.

Global policy networks: complexes which bring together the representatives of governments, international organizations, NGOs, and the corporate sector for the formulation and implementation of global public policy.

Global politics: the politics of global social relations in which the pursuit of power, interests, order, and justice transcends regions and continents.

Global polity: the collective structures and processes by which 'interests are articulated and aggregated, decisions are made, values allocated and policies conducted through international or transnational political processes' (Ougaard 2004: 5).

Globalism: the condition of globalization at any point in time usually gauged by its thickness or thinness.

Globalization: a historical process involving a fundamental shift or transformation in the spatial scale of human social organization that links distant communities and expands the reach of power relations across regions and continents. It is also something of a catch-all phrase often used to describe a single world-economy after the collapse of communism, though sometimes employed to define the growing integration of the international capitalist system in the post-war period.

Globalized state: the notion of a particular kind of state that helps sustain globalization, as well as responding to its pressures. The distinctive feature of this concept is that the state is not 'in retreat' but simply behaving differently.

Great Depression: a byword for the global economic collapse that ensued following the US Wall Street stock-market crash in October 1929. Economic shockwaves soon rippled around a world already densely interconnected by webs of trade and foreign direct investment with the result that the events of October 1929 were felt in countries as distant as Brazil and Japan.

Group rights: rights that are said to belong to groups such as minority nations or indigenous peoples rather than to individuals.

Harmony of interests: common among nineteenth-century Liberals was the idea of a natural order between peoples which had been corrupted by undemocratic state leaders and outdated policies such as the balance of power. If these distortions could be swept away, they believed, we would find that there were no *real* conflicts between peoples.

Hegemonic stability theory: a Realist-based explanation for cooperation that argues that a dominant state is required to ensure a liberal, free-trade, international political economy.

Hegemony: a system regulated by a dominant leader, or political (and/or economic) domination of a region, usually by a superpower. In Realist theory, the influence a Great Power is able to establish on other states in the system; extent of influence ranges from leadership to dominance. It is also power and control exercised by a leading state over other states.

Holism: the view that structures cannot be decomposed to the individual units and their interactions because structures are more than the sum of their parts and are irreducibly social. The effects of structures, moreover, go beyond merely constraining the actors but also construct them. Constructivism holds that the international structure shapes the identities and interests of the actors.

Holocaust: the term used to describe the attempts by the Nazis to murder the Jewish population of Europe. Some 6 million Jewish people were killed in concentration camps, along with a further million, including Soviet prisoners, gypsies, Poles, communists, gay people, and physically or mentally disabled.

Horizontal proliferation: means an increase in the number of actors who possess nuclear weapons.

Housewife: a traditionally feminine role of working in the private domestic sphere without pay.

Human development: a capability-oriented approach to development which, in the word of Mahabub ul Haq, seeks to expands the 'the range of things that people can do, and what they can be . . . . The most basic capabilities for human development are leading a long and healthy life, being educated and having adequate resources for a decent standard of living . . . [and] social and political participation in society.'

Human security: the security of people, including their physical safety, their economic and social well-being, respect for their dignity, and the protection of their human rights.

Humanitarian intervention: the principle that the international community has a right to intervene in states which have suffered large-scale loss of life or genocide whether due to deliberate action by its government or because of the collapse of governance.

Hybrid international non-governmental organization (INGO): a third type of international organization, in which governments and NGOs form joint organizations in which they are each allowed to be members. Logically they should be hybrid international organizations, but in diplomatic practice they are identified among the international NGOs and so hybrid INGOs is perhaps a more appropriate term.

Idealism: holds that ideas have important causal effect on events in international politics, and that ideas can change. Referred to by Realists as utopianism since it underestimates the logic of power

politics and the constraints this imposes upon political action. Idealism as a substantive theory of international relations is generally associated with the claim that it is possible to create a world of peace. But Idealism as a social theory refers to the claim that the most fundamental feature of society is social consciousness. Ideas shape how we see ourselves and our interests, the knowledge that we use to categorize and understand the world, the beliefs we have of others, and the possible and impossible solutions to challenges and threats. The emphasis on ideas does not mean a neglect of material forces such as technology and geography. Instead it is to suggest that the meanings and consequences of these material forces are not given by nature but rather driven by human interpretations and understandings. Idealists seek to apply liberal thinking in domestic politics to international relations, in other words, institutionalize the rule of law. This reasoning is known as the domestic analogy. According to Idealists in the early twentieth century, there were two principal requirements for a new world order. First: state leaders, intellectuals, and public opinion had to believe that progress was possible. Second: an international organization had to be created to facilitate peaceful change, disarmament, arbitration, and (where necessary) enforcement. The League of Nations was founded in 1920 but its collective security system failed to prevent the descent into world war in the 1930s.

Identity: the understanding of the self in relationship to an 'other'. Identities are social and thus are always formed in relationship to others. Constructivists generally hold that identities shape interests; we cannot know what we want unless we know who we are. But because identities are social and are produced through interactions, identities can change.

Immunity rights: the essence of this is that others are disbarred from making claims under certain circumstances, for example, to be legally insane, or under age, is to be *immune* from criminal prosecution.

Imperialism: the practice of foreign conquest and rule in the context of global relations of hierarchy and subordination. It can lead to the establishment of an empire.

Individualism: the view that structures can be reduced to the aggregation of individuals and their interactions. International relations theories that ascribe to individualism begin with some assumption of the nature of the units and their interests, usually states and the pursuit of power or wealth, and then examine how the broad structure, usually the distribution of power, constrains how states can act and generates certain patterns in international politics. Individualism stands in contrast to holism.

Influence: the ability of one actor to change the values or the behaviour of another actor.

Institutionalization: the degree to which networks or patterns of social interaction are formally constituted as organizations with specific purposes.

Institutions: persistent and having connected sets of rules and practices that prescribe roles, constrain activity, and shape the expectations of actors. Institutions may include organizations, bureaucratic agencies, treaties and agreements, and informal practices that states accept as binding. The balance of power in the international system is an example of an institution. (Adapted from Haas, Keohane, and Levy 1993: 4–5.)

Integration: a process of ever closer union between states, in a regional or international context. The process often begins with cooperation to solve technical problems, referred to by Mitrany (1943) as ramification.

Intellectual property rights: rules that protect the owners of content through copyright, patents, trade marks and trade secrets.

Interdependence: a condition where states (or peoples) are affected by decisions taken by others; for example, a decision to raise interest rates in the USA automatically exerts upward pressure on interest rates in other states. Interdependence can be symmetric, i.e. both sets of actors are affected equally, or it can be asymmetric, where the impact varies between actors. A condition where the actions of one state impact upon other states (can be strategic interdependence or economic). Realists equate interdependence with vulnerability.

Intergovernmental organization (IGO): an international organization in which full legal membership is officially solely open to states and the decisionmaking authority lies with representatives from governments.

International hierarchy: a structure of authority in which states and other international actors are ranked according to their relative power.

International law: the formal rules of conduct that states acknowledge or contract between themselves.

International Monetary Fund: Established in 1945 with headquarters in Washington, DC. Membership (2004) of 184 states. The IMF monitors short-term cross-border payments and foreign exchange positions. When a country develops chronic imbalances in its external accounts, the IMF supports corrective policy reforms, often called 'structural adjustment programmes'. Since 1978 the IMF has undertaken comprehensive surveillance both of the economic performance of individual member states and of the world-economy as a whole. The IMF also provides extensive technical assistance. In recent years the Fund has pursued various initiatives to promote efficiency and stability in global financial markets. See further www.imf.org.

International non-governmental organization (INGOs): an international organization in which membership is open to transnational actors. There are many different types, with membership from 'national' NGOs, local NGOs, companies, political parties, or individual people. A few have other INGOs as members and some have mixed membership structures.

International order: the normative and the institutional pattern in the relationship between states. The elements of this might be thought to include such things as sovereignty, the forms of diplomacy, international law, the role of the Great Powers, and the codes circumscribing the use of force. It is a shared value and condition of stability and predictability in the relations of states.

International organization: any institution with formal procedures and formal membership from three or more countries. The minimum number of countries is set at three rather than two, because multilateral relationships have significantly greater complexity than bilateral relationships.

International regime: a concept developed by neo-realists to analyse the paradox—for them—that international cooperation occurs in some issue-areas, despite the struggle for power between states. They assume regimes are created and maintained by a dominant state and/or participation in a regime is the result of a rational cost–benefit calculation by each state. In contrast, Pluralists would also stress the independent impact of institutions, the importance of leadership, the involvement of transnational NGOs and companies, and processes of cognitive change, such as growing concern about human rights or the environment.

International society: the structure formed when different political communities accept common rules and institutions to govern their relations with each other.

International system: a set of interrelated parts connected to form a whole. In Realist theory, systems have defining principles such as hierarchy (in domestic politics) and anarchy (in international politics).

Internationalization: growing interactions between national states. This term is used to denote high levels of international interaction and interdependence, most commonly with regard to the world-economy. In this context it refers to the volume of international trade and investment and to the organization of production. The term is often used to

distinguish this condition from globalization as the latter implies that there are no longer distinct national economies in a position to interact. It also describes the increase in transactions among states reflected in flows of trade, investment, and capital (cf. the argument that these flows have not increased as much as is claimed: UNDP 1997). The processes of internationalization have been facilitated and are shaped by inter-state agreements on trade, investment, and capital, as well as by domestic policies permitting the private sector to transact abroad.

Intervention: when there is direct involvement within a state by an outside actor to achieve an outcome preferred by the intervening agency without the consent of the host state.

Intra-firm trade: international trade from one branch of a TNC to an affiliate of the same company in a different country.

Islam: a religious faith developed by the Prophet Muhammaed which in the contemporary period functions as a form of political identity for millions and the inspiration of what some at least now regard as the most important ideological opposition to Western modern values.

Issue, an: consists of a set of political questions that are seen as being related, because they all invoke the same value conflicts, e.g. the issue of human rights concerns questions that invoke freedom versus order.

J *Jihad:* in Arabic *jihad* simply means struggle. *Jihad* can refer to a purely internal struggle to be a better Muslim, or a struggle to make society more closely align with the teachings of the Koran. There is also the *jihad* of the 'hand' or 'sword'. The only time that individuals are enjoined to undertake *jihad* on their own volition is as a response to direct external aggression or invasion of Islamic territories. For instance, the Palestinian group Hamas defend their actions against Israel in terms of recovering and restoring lost Islamic territory.

Jus ad bellum: The laws of war governing when it is legally permitted to use force or wage war. Chapter 7 of the United Nations Charter, for example, restricts the legitimate use of force to two areas: international peace-enforcement actions authorized by the Security Council, and individual or collective self-defence in response to an armed attack.

Jus cogens: the term used to describe peremptory norms of international law. These are norms that are considered so fundamental that states are not permitted to contract out of them. Commonly cited examples of peremptory norms are the norm against aggression and the norm governing the inviolability of diplomatic agents.

Jus in bello: The laws of war governing the conduct of war once launched. These laws cover, among other things, the proportionate use of force, the targeting of civilians, the treatment of political prisoners. The principal legal instruments in this area are the Geneva Conventions of 1949, and the Additional Protocols to the Conventions of 1977.

Justice: fair or morally defensible treatment for individuals, in the light of human rights standards or standards of economic or social well-being.

L **Liberal rights:** the agenda of human rights that is driven largely from a Western perspective and derived from classical Liberal positions.

Liberalism: according to Doyle (1997: 207), Liberalism includes the following four claims. First, all citizens are juridically equal and have equal rights to education, access to a free press, and religious toleration. Second, the legislative assembly of the state possesses only the authority invested in it by the people, whose basic rights it is not permitted to abuse. Third, a key dimension of the liberty of the individual is the right to own property including productive forces. Fourth, Liberalism contends that the most effective system of economic exchange is one that is largely market driven and not one that is subordinate to bureaucratic regulation and control either domestically or internationally.

Liberalization: describes government policies which reduce the role of the state in the economy such as through the dismantling of trade tariffs and barriers, the deregulation and opening of the financial sector to foreign investors, and the privatization of state enterprises.

Liberty-rights occur when an individual has the right to do something in the sense that he or she has no obligation *not* to do it—for example, to dress as he or she pleases. Here there is no correlative duty, except perhaps the duty to let the individual do as he or she chooses. Sometimes a right involves the exercise of a power. For example, to have the *right* to vote means to be *empowered* to vote, to be enfranchised.

Light industry: industry that requires less capital investment to fund and operate. It is performed with light, rather than heavy, machinery.

Loyalty: an emotional disposition in which people give institutions (or each other) some degree of unconditional support.

M **Market failure:** results from the inability of the market to produce goods which require collaborative strategies.

Masculinity: customarily defined as manliness, the characteristics of masculinity are conventionally associated with power, autonomy, rationality and the public sphere, as well as the male sex. Masculinity is defined in opposition to femininity.

Materialism: the view that the most fundamental feature of society is the organization of material forces. Material forces include natural resources, geography, military power, and technology. To understand how the world works, therefore, requires taking these fundamentals into account. For international relations scholars, this leads to forms of technological determinism or the distribution of military power for understanding the state's foreign policy and patterns of international politics.

Means (or forces) of production: in Marxist theory, these are the elements that combine in the production process. They include labour as well as the tools and technology available during any given historical period.

Microeconomics: the branch of economics studying the behaviour of the firm in a market setting.

Millennium Development Goals: target-based, time-limited commitments in the UN Millennium Declaration 2000 to improve eight areas: poverty and hunger, primary education, gender equality, child mortality, maternal health, tackling diseases such as HIV/AIDS and malaria, environmental sustainability, and partnership working.

Minimum order: a view of international order that is concerned with peace and stability, rather than with the attainment of other values, such as justice.

Modernism: has a variety of meanings but in the nationalism literature it is the view that nations and nationalism are modern constructs and that the idea of a long pre-modern basis for nations (whether primordialist or ethno-symbolist) is best understood as one element in modern nationalist myth-making. However, modernists differ very much among themselves as to how modernity has led to the construction of nations and nationalism.

MoP: Meeting of the Parties to a protocol.

Multilateralism: the tendency for functional aspects of international relations (such as security, trade, or environmental management) to be organized around large numbers of states, or universally, rather than by unilateral state action.

Multipolarity: a distribution of power among a number (at least three) of major powers or 'poles'.

Mutually assured destruction (MAD): condition in which both superpowers possessed the capacity to destroy their adversary even after being attacked first with nuclear weapons.

N **Nation:** a group of people who recognize each other as sharing a common identity, with a focus on a homeland.

National interest: invoked by Realists and state leaders to signify that which is most important to the state—survival being at the top of the list.

National security: a fundamental value in the foreign policy of states.

National self-determination: the right of distinct national groups to become states.

Nationalism: the *idea* that the world is divided into nations which provide the overriding focus of political identity and loyalty which in turn demands national self-determination. Nationalism also can refer to this idea in the form of a strong sense of identity (*sentiment*) or organizations and movements seeking to realize this idea (*politics*).

Nation-state: a political community in which the state claims legitimacy on the grounds that it represents the nation. The nation-state would exist if nearly all the members of a single nation were organized in a single state, without any other national communities being present. Although the term is widely used, no such entities exist.

Natural: a word used to describe socially appropriate gender-role behaviour. When behaviour is seen as natural it is hard to change.

Natural law: the origin of natural law thinking can be traced to the classical Greeks and early Christians, but in its modern form it is based on medieval Catholic theology. The central idea is that human beings have an essential nature which dictates that certain kinds of human goods are always and everywhere desired; because of this there are common moral standards that govern all human relations and these common standards can be discerned by the application of reason to human affairs.

Neoclassical realism: a version of Realism that combines both structural factors such as the distribution of power and unit-level factors such as the interests of states (status quo or revisionist).

Neo-medievalism: a condition in which political power is dispersed between local, national, and supranational institutions none of which commands supreme loyalty.

Neo-realism: modification of the Realist approach, by recognizing economic resources—in addition to military capabilities—are a basis for exercising influence. Also, the concept of a single international system is abandoned in favour of analysing issue-specific systems, each characterized by their own power structure. Thus Saudi Arabia may be the most powerful state in the politics of oil, while Brazil is the most powerful in the politics of rainforests.

Network: any structure of communication for individuals and/or organizations to exchange information, share experiences, or discuss political goals and tactics. There is no clear boundary between a network and an NGO. A network is less likely than an NGO to become permanent, to have formal membership, to have identifiable leaders or to engage in collective action.

9/11: refers specifically to the morning of 11 September 2001 when 19 men highjacked four domestic flights *en route* to California which were subsequently flown into the World Trade Center and the Pentagon. The fourth plane crashed in Pennsylvania. There were 2,974 fatalities, not including the 19 highjackers, 15 of whom were from Saudi Arabia. The planning and organization for the attack was coordinated in Afghanistan by Osama bin Laden, the leader of Al Qaeda. Approximately a month after the attack the United States and its allies launched an attack against Afghanistan to remove the Taliban from power.

Non-discrimination: a doctrine of equal treatment between states.

Non-forcible/non-violent intervention: pacific intervention which can be either consensual (Red Cross) or non-consensual (Médecins Sans Frontières) and which is practised by states, international organizations, and INGOs (international non-governmental organizations). It can be short term (delivery of humanitarian aid) or long term (conflict resolution and reconstruction of political life within failed states).

Non-governmental organization (NGO): an organization, usually a grassroots one, with policy goals, but neither governmental nor corporate in make-up. Examples include Amnesty International and the Internati-onal Campaign to Ban Landmines. An NGO is any group of people relating to each other regularly in some formal manner and engaging in collective action, provided that the activities are non-commercial and non-violent, and are not on behalf of a government. People are often baffled by the dry, bland term, 'non-governmental organization'. Nevertheless, some of the international NGOs, such as Amnesty International, Greenpeace, or the Red Cross are better known than some smaller countries.

Non-intervention: the principle that external powers should not intervene in the domestic affairs of sovereign states.

Non-nuclear weapons state: refers to a state that is party to the Treaty on the Non-Proliferation of Nuclear Weapons, meaning it does not possess nuclear weapons.

Non-state actor: a term widely used to mean any actor that is not a government. Often it is not clear whether the term is being used to cover bodies such as the United Nations. Ambiguity is best avoided by referring separately to two categories, transnational actors and international organizations.

Normative structure: international relations theory traditionally defines structure in material terms, such as the distribution of power, and then treats structure as a constraint on actors. By identifying a normative structure, Constructivists are noting how structures also are defined by collectively held ideas such as knowledge, rules, beliefs, and norms that not only constrain actors, but also construct categories of meaning, constitute their identities and interests, and define standards of appropriate conduct. Critical here is the concept of a norm, a standard of appropriate behaviour for actors with a given identity. Actors adhere to norms not only because of benefits and costs for doing so but also because they are related to a sense of self.

Normative theory: systematic analyses of the ethical, moral, and political principles which either govern or ought to govern the organization or conduct of global politics. The belief that theories should be concerned with what ought to be, rather than merely diagnosing what is. Norm creation refers to the setting of standards in international relations which governments (and other actors) ought to meet.

Norms: specify general standards of behaviour, and identify the rights and obligations of states. So, in the case of the GATT, the basic norm is that tariffs and non-tariff barriers should be reduced and eventually eliminated. Together, norms and principles define the essential character of a regime and these cannot be changed without transforming the nature of the regime.

North Atlantic Treaty Organization (NATO): organization established by treaty in April 1949 comprising 12 (later 16) countries from Western Europe and North America. The most important aspect of the NATO alliance was the American commitment to the defence of Western Europe.

Nuclear weapon state: refers to a state that is party to the Non-Proliferation Treaty which has tested a nuclear weapon or other nuclear explosive device before 1 January 1967.

Nuclear Weapons Free Zone: these are agreements which establish specific environments or geographic regions as nuclear weapons free, although there may be varying requirements between zones.

O **Offensive realism:** a structural theory of Realism that views states as security maximizers.

Offshore finance centre: a site for financial business offering inducements such as tax reductions, regulation waivers, subsidies and rebates, secrecy guarantees, and so on; most are located in island and other mini-states, though offshore provisions also cover arrangements like International Banking Facilities in New York (since 1981), the Tokyo-based Japan Offshore Market (since 1986), and the Bangkok International Banking Facility (since 1993).

Ontology: the study of what is. It is about the nature of being.

Opinio juris: the conviction on the part of states that a certain form of action is required or permitted by international law.

Order: this may denote any regular or discernible pattern of relationships that are stable over time, or may additionally refer to a condition that allows certain goals to be achieved.

Organization of Economic Co-operation and Development: founded in 1962 with headquarters in Paris. Membership (2004) of 30 states with advanced industrial economies and other relationships with 70 states. Provides a forum for multilateral intergovernmental consultations on a wide range of economic and social issues. OECD measures have especially addressed environmental questions, taxation, and transborder corporations. At regular intervals the OECD Secretariat produces an assessment of the macroeconomic performance of each member, including suggestions for policy changes. See further www.oecd.org.

Ostpolitik: the West German government's 'Eastern Policy' of the mid- to late 1960s, designed to develop relations between West Germany and members of the Warsaw Pact.

P **Patriarchy:** a persistent society-wide structure within which gender relations are defined by male dominance and female subordination.

Pax Americana: Latin phrase (literally American peace, adapted from Pax Romana) implying a global peace dictated by American power.

Peace enforcement: designed to bring hostile parties to agreement, which may occur without the consent of the parties.

Peace Treaty of Versailles, 1919: the Treaty of Versailles formally ended the First World War (1914–18). The Treaty established the League of Nations, specified the rights and obligations of the victorious and defeated powers (including the notorious regime of reparations on Germany), and created the 'Mandatories' system under which 'advanced nations' were given legal tutelage over colonial peoples.

Peacekeeping: the deployment of a UN presence in the field with the consent of all parties (this refers to classical peacekeeping).

Peacemaking: designed to bring hostile parties to agreement, essentially through peaceful means. However, when all peaceful means have failed peace enforcement authorized under Chapter VII of the Charter may be necessary.

Perennialism: the historical claim that there have been cases of nations and even nationalism before the modern period. It is different from primordialism and ethno-symbolism because this is presented as an empirical historical claim rather than a theory about primary descent or culture or the centrality of ethnic myths and memories.

Perestroika: policy of restructuring, pursued by former Soviet premier, Mikhail Gorbachev in tandem with *glasnost,* and intended to modernize the Soviet political and economic system.

Petrodollars: earnings from oil exports deposited outside the USA; they provided the largest single spur to growth in the euromarkets in the 1970s.

Pluralism: an umbrella term, borrowed from American political science, used to signify international relations theorists who rejected the Realist view of the primacy of the state, the priority of national security,

and the assumption that states are unitary actors. It is the theoretical approach that considers all organized groups as being potential political actors and analyses the processes by which actors mobilize support to achieve policy goals. Pluralists can accept that transnational actors and international organizations may influence governments. Equated by some writers with Liberalism, but Pluralists reject any such link, denying that theory necessarily has a normative component, and holding that Liberals are still highly state-centric.

Pluralist international society theory: states are conscious of sharing common interests and common values, but these are limited to norms of sovereignty and non-intervention.

Polarity: a structural feature of balance-of-power systems determined by the overall nature of the balance. Bipolar systems consist of *two* dominant powers, multipolar systems of *several,* and unipolar systems of just one.

Policy domain: consists of a set of political questions that have to be decided together because they are linked by the political processes in an international organization, e.g. financial policy is resolved in the IMF. A policy domain may cover several issues: financial policy includes development, the environment, and gender issues.

Political community: a community that wishes to govern itself and to be free from alien rule.

Post-conflict peacebuilding: to develop the social, political, and economic infrastructure to prevent further violence and to consolidate peace.

Post-Washington Consensus: a slightly modified version of the Washington Consensus, promoting economic growth through trade liberalization coupled with pro-poor growth and poverty reduction policies.

Poverty: in the orthodox view, a situation suffered by people who do not have the *money to buy food* and satisfy other basic *material needs.* In the alternative view, a situation suffered by people who are not able to meet their *material and non-material needs* through their own effort.

Power: in the most general sense, the ability of a political actor to achieve its goals. In the Realist approach, it is assumed that possession of capabilities will result in influence, so the single word, power, is often used ambiguously to cover both. In the Pluralist approach, it is assumed that political interactions can modify the translation of capabilities into influence and therefore it is important to distinguish between the two. Power is defined by most Realists in terms of the important resources such as size of armed forces, gross national product, and population that a state possesses. There is the implicit belief that material resources translate into influence.

Primordialism: the belief that certain human or social characteristics, such as ethnicity, are deeply embedded in historical conditions.

Principles: in regime theory, they are represented by coherent bodies of theoretical statements about how the world works. The GATT operated on the basis of liberal principles which assert that global welfare will be maximized by free trade.

Prisoners' dilemma: a scenario in game theory illustrating the need for a collaboration strategy.

Programmes and Funds: institutions which are subject to the supervision of the General Assembly and which depend upon voluntary funding by states and other donors.

Protection myth: a popular assumption that male heroes fight wars to protect the vulnerable, primarily women and children. It is used as a justification for states' national security policies, particularly in times of war.

Protocol: a legal instrument that is added to a convention, usually containing detailed rules and undertakings, so that environmental problems can be controlled. There can be many protocols to one convention or treaty.

Public bads: the negative consequences which can arise when actors fail to collaborate.

Public goods: goods which can only be produced by a collective decision, and which cannot, therefore, be produced in the market-place.

Quasi-state: a state which has 'negative sovereignty' because other states respect its sovereign independence but lacks 'positive sovereignty' because it does not have the resources or the will to satisfy the needs of its people.

Rapprochement: re-establishment of more friendly relations between the People's Republic of China and the United States in the early 1970s.

Ratification: the procedure by which a state approves a convention or protocol that it has signed. There will be rules in the treaty concerning the number of ratifications required before it can enter into force.

Rational choice: an approach that emphasizes how actors attempt to maximize their interests, how they attempt to select the most efficient means to achieve those interests, and attempts to explain collective outcomes by virtue of the attempt by actors to maximize their preferences under a set of constraints. Deriving largely from economic theorizing, the rational choice to politics and international politics has been immensely influential and applied to a range of issues.

Rationality: reflected in the ability of individuals to place their preferences in rank order and choose the best available preference.

Realism: the theoretical approach that analyzes all international relations as the relation of states engaged in the pursuit of power. Realism cannot accommodate non-state actors within its analysis

Reason of state: the practical application of the doctrine of Realism and virtually synonymous with it.

Reciprocity: reflects a 'tit for tat' strategy, only cooperating if others do likewise.

Regimes: these are sets of implicit or explicit principles, norms, rules, and decisionmaking procedures around which actors' expectations converge in a given area of international relations. They are social institutions that are based on agreed rules, norms, principles, and decisionmaking procedures. These govern the interactions of various state and non-state actors in issue-areas such as the environment or human rights. The global market in coffee, for example, is governed by a variety of treaties, trade agreements, scientific and research protocols, market protocols, and the interests of producers, consumers, and distributors. States organize these interests and consider the practices, rules, and procedures to create a governing arrangement or regime that controls the production of coffee, monitors its distribution, and ultimately determines the price for consumers. (Adapted from Young 1997: 6.)

Regionalism: development of institutionalized cooperation among states and other actors on the basis of regional contiguity as a feature of the international system.

Regionalization: growing interdependence between geographically contiguous states, as in the European Union.

Regulatory arbitrage: in the world of banking, the process of moving funds or business activity from one country to another, in order to increase profits by escaping the constraints imposed by government regulations. By analogy the term can be applied to any transfer of economic activity by any company in response to government policy.

Relations of production: in Marxist theory, relations of production link and organize the means of production in the production process. They involve both the technical and institutional relationships necessary to allow the production process to proceed, as well as the broader structures that govern the control of the means of production, and control of the end product(s) of that process. Private property

and wage labour are two of the key features of the relations of production in capitalist society.

Relative gains: one of the factors that Realists argue constrain the willingness of states to cooperate. States are less concerned about whether everyone benefits (absolute gains) and more concerned about whether someone may benefit more than someone else.

Responsibility to protect: states have a responsibility to protect their own citizens, but when they are unable or unwilling to do so this responsibility is transferred to the society of states.

Restrictionists: international lawyers who argue that humanitarian intervention violates Article 2(4) of the UN Charter and is illegal under both UN Charter law and customary international law.

Revolution in military affairs: describes a radical change in the conduct of warfare. This may be driven by technology, but may also result from organizational, doctrinal, or other developments. When the change is of several orders of magnitude, and impacts deeply on wider society, the term 'military revolution' is used to describe it.

Right of self-defence: a state's right to wage war in its own defence.

Rules: operate at a lower level of generality to principles and norms, and they are often designed to reconcile conflicts which may exist between the principles and norms. Third World states, for example, wanted rules which differentiated between developed and underdeveloped countries.

Sanctions: penalties incurred by states which violate agreed international norms.

Security community: 'A group of people which has become "integrated". By integration we mean the attainment, within a territory, of a "sense of community" and of institutions and practices strong enough and widespread enough to assure ... dependable expectations of "peaceful change" among its population. By a "sense of community" we mean a belief ... that common social problems must and can be resolved by processes of "peaceful change"' (Karl Deutsch *et al.* 1957).

Security complex: involves 'a group of states whose primary security concerns link together sufficiently closely that their national securities cannot realistically be considered apart from one another' (Barry Buzan 1983).

Security regimes: these occur 'when a group of states cooperate to manage their disputes and avoid war by seeking to mute the security dilemma both by their own actions and by their assumptions about the behaviour of others' (Robert Jervis 1983*b*).

Security: in finance, a contract with a claim to future payments in which (in contrast to bank credits) there is a direct and formally identified relationship between the investor and the borrower; also unlike bank loans, securities are traded in markets.

Selectivity: an agreed moral principle is at stake in more than one situation, but national interest dictates a divergence of response.

Self-determination: a principle ardently, but selectively, espoused by US President Woodrow Wilson in the peacemaking that followed the First World War: namely that each 'people' should enjoy self-government over its own sovereign nation-state. Wilson pressed for application of this principle to East/Central Europe, but did not believe that other nationalities (in colonized Asia, Africa, the Pacific and Caribbean) were fit for self-rule.

Self-help: in Realist theory, in an anarchical environment, states cannot assume other states will come to their defence even if they are allies. *Each state must take care of itself.*

11 September 2001: the day when four aircraft were hijacked by Islamic terrorists in the United States—two of which destroyed the World Trade Center in New York, one which partially destroyed the Pentagon, and a fourth which crash-landed in a field in Pennsylvania (see also 9/11).

Sex: biological difference, born male or female; the sex act; sexual difference.

Sexuality: including normalized heterosexuality, and other, often stigmatized sexualities: homosexuality, minority masculinities, shifting or multiple sexualities.

Shadow of the future: a metaphor indicating that decisionmakers are conscious of the future when making decisions.

Sinatra doctrine: statement by the Soviet foreign ministry in October 1989 that countries of Eastern Europe were 'doing it their way' (a reference to Frank Sinatra's song 'I did it my way') and which marked the end of the Brezhnev doctrine and Soviet hegemony in Eastern Europe.

Social movement: people with a diffuse sense of collective identity, solidarity, and common purpose that usually leads to collective political behaviour. The concept covers all the different NGOs and networks, plus all their members and all the other individuals who share the common value(s). Thus, the women's movement and the environmental movement are much more than the specific NGOs that provide leadership and focus the desire for social change.

Society of states: an association of sovereign states based on their common interests, values, and norms.

Sovereignty: the condition of a state being free from any higher legal authority. It is related to, but distinct from, the condition of a government being free from any external political constraints. It is the rightful entitlement to exclusive, unqualified, and supreme rule within a delimited territory. The state has supreme authority domestically and independence internationally.

Specialized Agencies: international institutions which have a special relationship with the central system of the United Nations but which are constitutionally independent, having their own assessed budgets, executive heads and committees, and assemblies of the representatives of all state members.

State autonomy: in a more interdependent world, simply to achieve domestic objectives national governments are forced to engage in extensive multilateral collaboration and cooperation. But in becoming more embedded in frameworks of global and regional governance states confront a real dilemma: in return for more effective public policy and meeting their citizens' demands, whether in relation to the drugs trade or employment, their capacity for self-governance—that is state autonomy—is compromised.

State of war: the conditions (often described by classical Realists) where there is no actual conflict, but a permanent cold war that could become a 'hot' war at any time.

State sovereignty: in any post Westphalian order the sovereign power and authority of national government—the entitlement of states to rule within their own territorial space—is being transformed but not necessarily eroded. Sovereignty today is increasingly understood as the shared exercise of public power and authority between national, regional, and global authorities.

State-sponsored terrorism: including providing funding, training, and resources to terrorist groups to avoid direct confrontation with an adversary. States go to great lengths to ensure that their involvement is as clandestine as possible so that their leaders have a degree of plausible deniability when the respond to such charges. Often confused with 'state terror' (the use of violence by the state to keep its own citizenry fearful, or the original connotation of terrorism).

State system: the regular patterns of interaction between states, but without implying any shared values between them. This is distinguished from the view of a 'society' of states.

State: a legal territorial entity composed of a stable population and a government; it possesses a monopoly over the legitimate use of force; its sovereignty is recognized by other states in the international system. This one word is used to refer to three distinct concepts: 1. In international law, a state is an entity that is recognized to exist when a government is in control of a community of people within a defined territory. It is comparable to the idea in domestic law of a company being a legal person. 2. In the study of international politics, each state is a country. It is a community of people who interact in the same political system and who have some common values. 3. In philosophy and sociology, the state consists of the apparatus of government, in its broadest sense, covering the executive, the legislature, the administration, the judiciary, the armed forces, and the police.

Statism: in Realist theory, the ideology that supports the organization of humankind into particular communities; the values and beliefs of that community are protected and sustained by the state.

Structure: in the philosophy of the social sciences a structure is something that exists independently of the actor (e.g. social class) but is an important determinant in the nature of the action (e.g. revolution). For contemporary structural Realists, the number of Great Powers in the international system constitutes the structure.

Subsistence production: refers to goods produced to meet immediate family needs rather than goods produced for sale in the market economy. Subsistence producers do not receive wages.

Summit diplomacy: refers to a direct meeting between heads of government (of the superpowers in particular) to resolve major problems. The 'summit' became a regular mode of contact during the cold war.

Superpower: term used to describe the United States and the Soviet Union after 1945, denoting their global political involvements and military capabilities, including in particular their nuclear arsenals.

Supranationalism: concept in integration theory that implies the creation of common institutions having independent decision-making authority and thus the ability to impose certain decisions and rules on member states.

Supraterritoriality: a quality whereby certain global social relations substanially transcend the geographical framework of territorial places, distances, and borders. Such circumstances can (like a satellite television broadcast or global warming) extend anywhere across the planet at the same time and/or can (like e-mail or electronic bank transfers) move anywhere on the planet in no time.

Survival: the first priority for state leaders, emphasized by historical Realists such as Machiavelli, Meinecke, and Weber.

Sustainable development: this has been defined as development that meets the needs of the present without compromising the ability of future generations to meet their own needs.

T **Tactics:** the conduct and management of military capabilities in or near the battle area.

Technological revolution: refers to the way modern communications (the Internet, satellite communications, high-tech computers) made possible by technological advances have made distance and location less important factors not just for government (including at local and regional levels) but equally in the calculations of other actors such as firms' investment decisions or in the activities of social movements.

Territorial state: a state that has power over the population which resides on its territory but which does not seek to represent the nation or the people as a whole.

Territoriality: borders and territory still remain important, not least for administrative purposes. Under conditions of globalization, however, a new geography of political organization and political power is emerging which transcends territories and borders.

Territory: a portion of the earth's surface appropriated by a political community, or state.

Terrorism: the use of illegitimate violence by sub-state groups to inspire fear, by attacking civilians and/or symbolic targets. This is done for

purposes such as drawing widespread attention to a grievance, provoking a severe response, or wearing down their opponent's moral resolve, to affect political change. Determining when the use of violence is legitimate, which is based on contextual morality of the act as opposed to its effects, is the source for disagreement over what constitutes acts of terrorism.

Theocracy: a state based on religion.

Third World: a notion that was first used in the late 1950s to define both the underdeveloped world and the political and economic project that would help overcome underdevelopment: employed less in the post-cold war era.

Time–space compression: the technologically induced erosion of distance and time giving the appearance of a world that is in communication terms shrinking.

Total war: a term given to the twentieth century's two world wars to denote not only their global scale but also the combatants' pursuit of their opponents' 'unconditional surrender' (a phrase particularly associated with the Western allies in the Second World War). Total war also signifies the mobilization of whole populations—including women into factory work, auxiliary civil defence units, and as paramilitaries and paramedics—as part of the total call-up of all able-bodied citizens in pursuit of victory.

Transfer price: the price set by a TNC for intra-firm trade of goods or services. For accounting purposes, a price must be set for exports, but it need not be related to any market price.

Transition: usually taken to mean the lengthy period between the end of communist planning in the Soviet bloc and the final emergence of a fully functioning democratic capitalist system.

Transnational actor: any civil society actor from one country that has relations with any actor from another country or with an international organization.

Transnational civil society: a political arena in which citizens and private interests collaborate across borders to advance their mutual goals or to bring governments and the formal institutions of global governance to account for their activities.

Transnational company/corporation (TNC): a company that has affiliates in a foreign country. The affiliates may be branches of the parent company, separately incorporated subsidiaries, or associates, with large minority shareholdings.

Transnational feminism: a sustained cross-border response to globalization, especially in its negative impacts on women, taking advantage of new opportunities for women's organizing through UN and other international conferences and global communications technology.

Treaties of Utrecht 1713: the Treaties of Utrecht, which brought an end to the Wars of Spanish Succession, consolidated the move to territorial sovereignty in Europe. The Treaties of Westphalia 1648 did little to define the territorial scope of sovereign rights, the geographical domain over which such rights could extend. By establishing that fixed territorial boundaries, rather than the reach of family ties, should define the reach of sovereign authority, the Treaties of Utrecht were crucial in establishing the present link between sovereign authority and territorial boundaries.

Treaties of Westphalia 1648: the Treaties of Osnabruck and Munster, which together form the 'Peace of Westphalia', ended the Thirty Years War and were crucial in delimiting the political rights and authority of European monarchs. Among other things, the Treaties granted monarchs rights to maintain standing armies, build fortifications, and levy taxes.

Treaty: a formal written agreement between distinct political communities.

Triads: the three economic groupings (North America, Europe, and East Asia).

Triangulation: occurs when trade between two countries is routed indirectly via a third country. For example, in the early 1980s, neither the Argentine Government nor the British Government permitted trade between the two countries, but companies simply sent their exports via Brazil or Western Europe.

Truman doctrine: statement made by US President Harry Truman in March 1947 that it 'must be the policy of the United States to support free people who are resisting attempted subjugation by armed minorities or by outside pressures'. Intended to persuade Congress to support limited aid to Turkey and Greece, the doctrine came to underpin the policy of containment and American economic and political support for its allies.

Tyrannical states: states where the sovereign government is massively abusing the human rights of its citizens, engaging in acts of mass killing, ethnic cleansing, and/or genocide.

Unilateral humanitarian intervention: Military intervention for humanitarian purposes which is undertaken without the express authorization of the United Nations Security Council.

Unipolarity: theoretical notion that takes as its working assumption the fact that the United States has now become and is likely to remain the only major power in the world. It is a distribution of power internationally in which there is clearly only one dominant power or 'pole'. Some analysts argue that the international system became unipolar in the 1990s since there was no longer any rival to American power.

United Nations Charter (1945): the Charter of the United Nations is the legal regime that created the United Nations as the world's only 'supranational' organization. The Charter defines the structure of the United Nations, the powers of its constitutive agencies, and the rights and obligations of sovereign states party to the Charter. Among other things, the Charter is the key legal document limiting the use of force to instances of self-defence and collective peace enforcement endorsed by the United Nations Security Council.

United Nations Conference on Trade and Development: established in 1964 with offices in Geneva. Membership (2004) of 192 states. UNCTAD monitors the effects of world trade and investment on economic development, especially in the South. It provided a key forum in the 1970s for discussions of a New International Economic Order. See further www.unctad.org.

Utilitarianism: utilitarians follow Jeremy Bentham's claim that action should be directed towards producing the 'greatest happiness of the greatest number'. In more recent years, the emphasis has been not on happiness, but on welfare or general benefit (happiness being too difficult to achieve). There are also differences between act and rule utilitarians. Act utilitarianism focuses on the impact of actions, whereas rule utilitarianism refers to the utility maximization following from universal conformity with a rule or set of rules.

Versailles Treaty: see Peace Treaty of Versailles.

Vertical proliferation: refers to the increase in the number of nuclear weapons by those states already in possession of such weapons.

War on terror: an umbrella term coined by the Bush administration and refers to the various military, political, and legal actions taken by the USA and its allies after the attacks on 11 September 2001 to curb the spread of terrorism in general but Islamic-inspired terrorism in particular.

Warsaw Pact: the Warsaw Pact was created in May 1955 in response to West Germany's rearmament and entry into NATO. It comprised the USSR and seven communist states (though Albania withdrew support in 1961). The organization was officially dissolved in July 1991.

Washington Consensus: the belief of key opinion-formers in Washington that global welfare would be maximized by the universal application of neoclassical economic policies which favour a minimalist state and an enhanced role for the market.

Weapons of mass destruction: a category defined by the United Nations in 1948 to include 'atomic explosive weapons, radioactive material

weapons, lethal chemical and biological weapons, and any weapons developed in the future which have characteristics comparable in destructive effects to those of the atomic bomb or other weapons mentioned above'.

World Bank Group: a collection of five agencies, the first established in 1945, with head offices in Washington, DC. The WBG promotes development in medium- and low-income countries with project loans, structural adjustment programmes, and various advisory services. See further www.worldbank.org.

World government: associated in particular with those Idealists who believe that peace can never be achieved in a world divided into separate sovereign states. Just as governments abolished the state of nature in civil society, the establishment of a world government must end the state of war in international society.

World order: this is a wider category of order than the 'international'. It takes as its units of order, not states, but individual human beings, and assesses the degree of order on the basis of the delivery of certain kinds of goods (be it security, human rights, basic needs, or justice) for humanity as a whole.

World society: the society produced by globalization.

World Trade Organization (WTO): established in 1995 with headquarters in Geneva. Membership (2004) of 146 states. The WTO is a permanent institution to replace the provisional GATT. It has a wider agenda, covering services, intellectual property, and investment issues as well as merchandise trade. The WTO also has greater powers of enforcement through its dispute-settlement mechanism. The organization's Trade Policy Review Body conducts surveillance of members' commercial measures.

References

A Abbott, K., Keohane, R. O., Moravcsik, A., Slaughter, A.-M., and Snidal, D. (2000), 'The Concept of Legalization', *International Organization*, 54(3): 401–20.

Abu-Lughod, J. L. (1989), *Before European Hegemony: The World System AD 1250–1350* (Oxford: Oxford University Press).

Adams, N. B. (1993), *Worlds Apart: The North–South Divide and the International System* (London: Zed).

Acharya, A. (1993), *Third World Conflicts and International Order after the Cold War*, Working Paper No. 134 (Canberra: Australian National University, Peace Research Centre).

——(1997) 'Beyond Anarchy: Third World Instability and International Order after the Cold War', in S. Neumann (ed), *International Relations Theory and the Third World* (New York: St Martins Press): 159–211.

——(2004), 'A Holistic Paradigm', *Security Dialogue* 35 (September): 355–6.

——(2007), *Promoting Human Security: Ethical, Normative and Educational Frameworks in South East Asia* (Paris: United Nations Scientific, Cultural and Educational Organization).

Adler, E. (1992), 'The Emergence of Cooperation: National Epistemic Communities and the International Evolution of the Idea of Nuclear Arms Control', *International Organization*, 46 (Winter): 101–45.

——and Haas, P. (1992), 'Conclusion: Epistemic Communities, World Order, and the Creation of a Reflective Research Program', *International Organization*, 46(1): 367–90.

——and Barnett, M. (eds) (1998a), *Security Communities* (Cambridge: Cambridge University Press).

—— ——(1998b) 'A Framework for the Study of Security Communities', in E. Adler and M. Barnett (eds), *Security Communities* (Cambridge: Cambridge University Press): 29-65.

Agnew, J., and Corbridge, S. (1995), *Mastering Space: Hegemony, Territory, and International Political-Economy* (London: Routledge).

Albrow, M. (1996), *The Global Age* (Cambridge: Polity Press).

Allison, G. (2000), 'The Impact of Globalization on National and International Security', in J. S. Nye and J. D. Donahue (eds), *Governance in a Globalizing World* (Washington, DC: Brookings Institution): 72–85.

——(2004), 'How to Stop Nuclear Terror', *Foreign Affairs*, 83(1) (Jan./Feb.): 64–74.

Alperovitz, G. (1965), *Atomic Diplomacy: Hiroshima and Potsdam: The Use of the Atomic Bomb and the American Confrontation with Soviet Power* (New York: Simon & Schuster).

Anderson, B. (1983; revised 1991), *Imagined Communities: Reflections on the Origin and Spread of Nationalism* (London: Verso). www.nationalismproject.org/books/a_b.htm# Anchor-Anderson-23526

Anderson, P. (1974a), *Passages from Antiquity to Feudalism* (London: New Left Books).

Anghie, A. (1996), 'Francisco de Vitoria and the Colonial Origins of International Law', *Social and Legal Studies* 5(3): 321-36.

Annan, K. (2001), 'Towards a Culture of Peace', http://www.unesco. org/opi2/lettres/TextAnglais/AnnanE.html, symbol last accessed 25 June 2007.

Armstrong, D. (1993), *Revolution and World Order: The Revolutionary State in International Society* (Oxford: Clarendon Press).

Armstrong, K. (1997), 'Fundamentalism', *Demos*, 11: 15–17.

Aron, R. (1954), *The Century of Total War* (New York: Garden City)

Ashley, R. K. (1987), 'The Geopolitics of Geopolitical Space: Toward a Critical Social Theory of International Politics', *Alternatives*, 12(4): 403–34.

——(1988), 'Untying the Sovereign State: A Double Reading of the Anarchy Problematique', *Millennium*, 17(2): 227–62.

——and Walker, R. B. J. (1990), 'Reading Dissidence/Writing the Discipline: Crisis and the Question of Sovereignty in International Studies', *International Studies Quarterly*, 34: 367–416.

Association of South-East Asian Nations (2007), Declaration on the Acceleration of the Establishment of an ASEAN Community by 2015 (12th ASEAN Summit, Cebu, Phillipines, 13 January). Available online at http://www.12thaseansummit.org.ph/innertemplate3.asp?category=docs&docid=21, last accessed 7 September 2007.

Austin, J. (1996), *Lectures in Jurisprudence*, Vol. 1 (Bristol: Thoemmes Press).

Axford, B. (1995), *The Global System: Economics, Politics, and Culture* (Cambridge: Polity Press).

Ayson, R. (2001), 'Management, Abolition, and Nullification: Nuclear Nonproliferation Strategies in the 21st Century', *The Nonproliferation Review*, 8(3) (Fall/Winter): 67–81.

B Bakker, E. (2006), *Jihadi Terrorists in Europe, Their Characteristics and the Circumstances in Which They Joined the Jihad: An Exploratory Study* (Clingendael: Netherlands Institute of International Relations).

Baldwin, D. (ed.) (1993), *Neo-realism and Neo-liberalism: The Contemporary Debate* (New York: Columbia University Press).

Barber, B. (1996), *Jihad vs McWorld* (New York: Ballantine Books).

——(2002a), *Fear's Empire: War, Terrorism, and Democracy* (New York: W. W. Norton).

——(2002b), 'Democracy and Terror in the Era of Jihad vs. McWorld', in K. Booth and T. Dunne (eds), *Worlds in Collision: Terror and the Future of Global Order* (Basingstoke: Palgrave Macmillan): 245–62.

Barkawi, T. (2004), 'On the Pedagogy of Small Wars', *International Affairs*, 80(1): 19–38.

——(2006) *Globalization and Warfare* (London: Rowman & Littlefield).

——and Laffey, M. (2006) 'The Postcolonial Moment in Security Studies', *Review of International Studies*, 32(2): 329-52.

Barker, D., and Mander, J. (1999), *Invisible Government: The World Trade Organization: Global Government for the Millennium?* (San Francisco, Cal.: International Forum on Globalization).

Barraclough, G. (ed.) (1984), *The Times Atlas of World History* (London: Times Books).

Bartelson, J. (1995), *A Genealogy of Sovereignty* (Cambridge: Cambridge University Press).

Bauman, Z. (1998), *Globalization: The Human Consequences* (Cambridge: Polity Press).

Baylis, J., and O'Neill, R. (eds) (2000), *Alternative Nuclear Futures* (Oxford: Oxford University Press).

Beitz, C. (1979), *Political Theory and International Relations* (Princeton, NJ: Princeton University Press).

——(1992), 'Cosmopolitanism and Sovereignty', *Ethics*, 103: 48–75.

Bellamy, A. J. (2002), *Kosovo and International Society* (Basingstoke: Palgrave).

——(2005), 'Responsibility to Protect or Trojan Horse? The Crisis in Darfur and Humanitarian Intervention after Iraq', *Ethics and International Affairs*, 19(2): 31-54.

——(2006), 'Whither the Responsibility to Protect? Humanitarian Intervention and the 2005 World Summit', *Ethics and International Affairs*, 20(2): 143-70.

Bello, W. (1994), *Dark Victory: The United States, Structural Adjustment and Global Poverty* (London: Pluto Press).

Bennett, J., and George, S. (1987), *The Hunger Machine* (Cambridge: Polity Press).

Bergsten, C. F. (1997), 'Open Regionalism', *The World Economy*, 20: 545–65.

Best, E. (2006), 'Regional Integration and (Good) Regional Governance: Are Common Standards and Indicators Possible?', in P. De Lombaerde (ed.), *Assessment and Measurement of Regional Integration* (London and New York: Routledge): 183–214.

Bethell, L. (1970), *The Abolition of the Brazilian Slave Trade: Britain, Brazil and the Slave Trade Question 1807–1869* (Cambridge: Cambridge University Press).

Bhabha, H. K. (1994), *The Location of Culture* (London: Routledge).

—— (ed.) (1990), *Nation and Narration* (London: Routledge).

Bhagwati, J. (1991), *The World Trading System at Risk* (Princeton, NJ: Princeton University Press).

Bigelow, R. (1969), *The Dawn Warriors* (London: Scientific Book Club).

BIS (1996), *International Banking and Financial Market Developments* (Basle: Bank for International Settlements).

—— (2006) 'Semiannual OTC Derivatives Statistics at End-June 2006', at www.bis.org/statistics, last accessed 25 June 2007.

Blair, T. (1999), 'Speech by the Prime Minister, Tony Blair, to the Economic Club of Chicago', The Hilton Hotel, Chicago, USA, 22 April 1999 at www.globalpolicy.org/globaliz/politics/blair.htm.

Bloom, M. (2005), *Dying to Win: The Allure of Suicide Terror* (New York: Columbia University Press).

Bodin, J. (1967), *Six Books of the Commonwealth* (Oxford: Basil Blackwell).

Bohlen, A. (2003), 'The Rise and Fall of Arms Control', *Survival* (Autumn): 7–34.

Booth, K. (1991), 'Security Emancipation', *Review of International Studies*, 17(4): 313–26.

—— (1999), 'Three Tyrannies', in T. Dunne and N. J. Wheeler (eds), *Human Rights in Global Politics* (Cambridge: Cambridge University Press).

—— (ed.) (2004), *Critical Security Studies in World Politics* (Boulder, Col.: Lynne Rienner).

—— and Dunne, T. (1999), 'Learning beyond Frontiers', in T. Dunne and N. J. Wheeler (eds), *Human Rights in Global Politics* (Cambridge: Cambridge University Press): 303–28.

—— —— (eds) (2002), *Worlds in Collision: Terror and the Future of Global Order* (London: Palgrave Macmillan).

Bosch, O., and Van Ham, P. (eds) (2007), *Global Non-Proliferation and Counter-Terrorism* (Washington, DC: Brookings Institute Press).

Boutros-Ghali, B. (1992), *An Agenda for Peace* (New York: United Nations).

Bracken, P. (2003), 'The Structure of the Second Nuclear Age', *Orbis*, 47(3) (Summer): 399–413.

—— (2004), 'Thinking (Again) about Arms Control', *Orbis*, 48(1) (Winter): 149–59.

Brass, P. (1991), *Ethnicity and Nationalism* (Sage: London).

Braun, L. (1987), *Selected Writings on Feminism and Socialism* (Bloomington: Indiana University Press).

Breman, J. G. (2001), 'The Ears of the Hippopotamus: Manifestations, Determinants, and Estimates of the Malaria Burden', *American Journal of Tropical Medicine and Hygiene*, 64(1/2): 1–11. Available online at: http://www.ajtmh.org/cgi/reprint/64/1_suppl/1-c, last accessed 25 June 2007.

Bretherton, C., and Ponton, G. (eds) (1996), *Global Politics: An Introduction* (Oxford: Blackwell).

Brewer, A. (1990), *Marxist Theories of Imperialism: A Critical Survey*, 2nd edn (London: Routledge).

Brittan, A. (1989), *Masculinity and Power* (Oxford: Basil Blackwell).

Brocklehurst, H. (2007), 'Children and War', in A. Collins (ed.), *Contemporary Security Studies* (Oxford: Oxford University Press): 367–82.

Brodie, B. (ed.) (1946), *The Absolute Weapon: Atomic Power and World Order* (New York: Harcourt Brace).

Brown, C. (1988), 'Ethics of Coexistence: The International Theory of Terry Nardin', *Review of International Studies*, 14: 213-22.

—— (1992), *International Relations Theory: New Normative Approaches* (Hemel Hempstead: Harvester Wheatsheaf).

—— (1999), 'History Ends, Worlds Collide', in M. Cox, K. Booth, and T. Dunne (eds), *The Interregnum: Controversies in World Politics 1989–1999* (Cambridge: Cambridge University Press): 41–57.

Brown, D. (2006) 'Study Claims Iraq's "Excess" Death Toll has Reached 655,000', *Washington Post*, 11 October: A12.

Brown, L. R., and Kane, H. (1995), *Full House: Reassessing the Earth's Population Carrying Capacity* (London: Earthscan).

Brown, S., *et al.* (1977), *Regimes for the Ocean, Outer Space and the Weather* (Washington, DC: Brookings Institution).

Brownlie, I. (1974), 'Humanitarian Intervention', in J. N. Moore (ed.), *Law and Civil War in the Modern World* (Baltimore, Md.: Johns Hopkins University Press).

Brundtland, G. H., *et al.* (1987), *Our Common Future: Report of the World Commission on Environment and Development* (The Brundtland Report) (Oxford: Oxford University Press).

Bull, H. (1977), *The Anarchical Society: A Study of Order in World Politics* (London: Macmillan).

Burchill, S., and Linklater, A., *et al.* (1996), *Theories of International Relations* (Basingstoke: Macmillan).

Burke, A. (2004), 'Just War or Ethical Peace? Moral Discourses of Strategic Violence after 9/11', *International Affairs*, 80(2): 329–53.

Burnham, P. (1991), 'Neo-Gramscian Hegemony and International Order', *Capital & Class*, 45: 73–93.

Burtless, G., *et al.* (1998), *Globalphobia: Confronting Fears about Open Trade* (Washington, DC: Brookings Institution).

Burton, J. (1972), *World Society* (Cambridge: Cambridge University Press).

Bush, G. W. (2001), 'Bush Announces Military Strikes in Afghanistan', 9 October, available online at: www.usinfo.state.gov, last accessed 25 June 2004.

—— (2003), 'Remarks by President George W. Bush', Press Conference, Camp David, 27 March, available online at: www.acronym.org.uk/docs/0303/doc29.htm, last accessed 25 June 2007.

Butler, J. (1990), *Gender Trouble: Feminism and the Subversion of Identity* (London: Routledge).

Buvinic, M. (1997), 'Women in Poverty: A New Global Underclass', *Foreign Policy* (Fall): 38–53.

Buzan, B. (1983), *People, States and Fear* (London: Harvester Wheatsheaf).

—— (2001), 'Human Security in International Perspective', in M. C. Anthony and M. J. Hassan (eds), *The Asia Pacific in the New Millennium: Political and Security Challenges* (Kuala Lumpur: Institute of Strategic and International Studies): 583-96.

—— and Herring, E. (1998), *The Arms Dynamic in World Politics* (London: Lynne Rienner).

—— and Little, R. (2000), *International Systems in World History* (Oxford: Oxford University Press).

Byers, M. (1999), *Custom, Power, and the Power of Rules: International Relations and Customary International Law* (Cambridge: Cambridge University Press).

C **Camdessus, M.** (2000), 'Address to the Tenth UNCTAD', Bangkok, February, *World Bank Development News* (Washington, DC: World Bank).

Cammack, P. (2002), 'The Mother of All Governments: The World Bank's Matrix for Global Governance', in R. Wilkinson and S. Hughes (eds), *Global Governance: Critical Perspectives* (London: Routledge).

Campbell, D. (1992), *Writing Security: United States Foreign Policy and the Politics of Identity* (Manchester: Manchester University Press).

—— (1993), *Politics Without Principle: Sovereignty, Ethics and the Narratives of the Gulf War* (Boulder, Col.: Lynne Rienner).

—— (1998), *National Deconstruction: Violence, Identity, and Justice in Bosnia* (Minneapolis: University of Minnesota Press).

Campbell, K. M., Einhorn, R. J., and Reiss, M. B. (2004), *The Nuclear Tipping Point: Why States Reconsider their Nuclear Choices* (Washington, DC: Brookings Institute Press).

Caney, S. (1997), 'Human Rights and the Rights of States: Terry Nardin on Non-Intervention', *International Political Science Review*, 18(1).

Carpenter, C. (2003), ' "Women and Children First": Gender, Norms and Humanitarian Evacuation in the Balkans 1991–1995', *International Organization*, 57(4) (Fall): 66–94.

Carr, E. H. (1939; 2nd edn, 1946), *The Twenty Years' Crisis 1919–1939: An Introduction to the Study of International Relations* (London: Macmillan).

Carson, R. (1962), *Silent Spring* (Harmondsworth: Penguin).

Carver, T. (1996), *Gender Is Not a Synonym for Women* (Boulder, Col.: Lynne Rienner).

Castells, M. (2000), *The Rise of the Network Society* (Oxford: Blackwell).

Castles, S. (2000), 'The Racisms of Globalization', in *Ethnicity and Globalization: From Migrant Worker to Transnational Citizen* (London: Sage).

Center for Disease Control (2005), 'Fact Sheet: Tuberculosis in the United States', 17 March 2005, available online at: http://www.cdc.gov/tb/pubs/TBfactsheets.htm, last accessed 25 June 2007.

Chalk, P. (1996), *West European Terrorism and Counter-Terrorism: The Evolving Dynamic* (New York: St Martin's Press).

Chase-Dunn, C. (1994), 'Technology and the Logic of World-Systems', in R. Palan and B. K. Gills (eds), *Transcending the State–Global Divide: A Neostructuralist Agenda in International Relations* (Boulder, Col.: Lynne Rienner): 84–105.

—— (1998), *Global Formation: Structures of the World-Economy*, updated edition (London: Rowman & Littlefield).

Chesterman, S. (2001), *Just War or Just Peace? Humanitarian Intervention and International Law* (Oxford: Oxford University Press).

—— (2004), 'Humanitarian Intervention and Afghanistan', in J. Welsh (ed.), *Humanitarian Intervention in International Relations Theory* (Oxford: Oxford University Press).

Ching, F. (1999); 'Social Impact of the Regional Financial Crisis', in Linda Y. C. Lim, F. Ching, and Bernardo M. Villegas, *The Asian Economic Crisis: Policy Choices, Social Consequences and the Phillipine Case* (New York: Asia Society), available online at: http://www.asiasociety.org/publications/update_crisis_ching.html, last accessed 25 June 2007.

Chowdhry, G., and Nair, S. (eds) (2002), *Power, Post-colonialism and International Relations: Reading Race, Gender and Class* (London: Routledge).

Christensen, T. (1996), *Useful Adversaries: Grand Strategy, Domestic Mobilization and Sino-American Conflict, 1947–1958* (Princeton, NJ: Princeton University Press).

—— Jørgensen, K. E., and Wiener, A. (eds) (2001), *The Social Construction of Europe* (London: Sage).

Clark, I. (1980), *Reform and Resistance in the International Order* (Cambridge: Cambridge University Press).

—— (1989), *The Hierarchy of States: Reform and Resistance in the International Order* (Cambridge: Cambridge University Press).

—— (1999), *Globalization and International Relations Theory* (Oxford: Oxford University Press).

—— (2007), *International Legitimacy and World Society* (Oxford: Oxford University Press)

Coates, A. (1997), *The Ethics of War* (Manchester: Manchester University Press).

Cobban, A. and Hunt, J. W. (1969) translation of A. Sorel (1888), *Europe and the French Revolution* (London: Fontana).

Cohn, C. (1993), 'Wars, Wimps and Women', in M. Cooke and A. Woollacott (eds), *Gendering War Talk* (Princeton, NJ: Princeton University Press): 227–46.

Colas, A. (2002), *International Civil Society: Social Movements in World Politics* (Cambridge: Polity Press).

Connell, R. W. (1995), *Masculinities* (London: Routledge).

Connor, W. (1994), *Ethno-Nationalism: The Quest for Understanding* (Princeton, NJ: Princeton University Press).

Cooper, R. (1968), *The Economics of Interdependence* (New York: McGraw-Hill).

Cox, R. (1981), 'Social Forces, States and World Orders: Beyond International Relations Theory', *Millennium Journal of International Studies*, 10(2): 126–55.

Crawford, N. (2002), *Argument and Change in World Politics: Ethics, Decolonization and Humanitarian Intervention* (Cambridge: Cambridge University Press).

Crenshaw, M. (ed.) (1983), *Terrorism, Legitimacy, and Power* (Middletown, Conn.: Wesleyan University Press).

Cronin, A. K. (2002/3), 'Behind the Curve: Globalization and International Terrorism', *International Security*, 27(3) (Winter/Spring): 30–58.

Cronin, B. (2003), *Institutions for the Common Good: International Protection Regimes in International Society* (Cambridge: Cambridge University Press).

Cushman, T. (ed.) (2005), *A Matter of Principle: Humanitarian Arguments for War in Iraq* (Berkeley: University of California Press).

Cusimano, M. K. (ed.) (2000), *Beyond Sovereignty* (New York: St Martins Press).

D **Dag Hammarskjöld Foundation** (1975), *What Now? Another Development?* (Uppsala: DHF).

Damrosch, L. F. (1991), 'Commentary on collective military intervention to enforce human rights', in L. F. Damrosch and D. J. Scheffer (eds), *Law and Force in the New International Order* (Boulder, Col: Westview).

—— (ed.) (1993), *Enforcing Restraint: Collective Intervention in Internal Conflicts* (New York: Council on Foreign Relations).

Davis, Z. S., and Frankel, B. (eds) (1993), *The Proliferation Puzzle: Why Nuclear Weapons Spread and What Results* (London: Frank Cass).

Dean, M. (1994), *Critical and Effective Histories: Foucault's Methods and Historical Sociology* (London: Routledge).

Declaration of Jihad Against the Country's Tyrants: Military Series (n.d.), US Government Exhibit 1677-T; UK translation, pp. BM-8-BM.9.

Denemark, R. A., Freidman, J., Gills, B. K., and Modelski, G. (eds) (2000), *World System History* (London: Routledge).

Department for International Development (2005), *Fighting Poverty to Build a Safer World* (London: HMSO). Available online at: http://www.dfid.gov.uk/pubs/files/securityforall.pdf, last accessed on 25 June 2007.

—— (2006), *Eliminating World Poverty: Making Governance Work for the Poor,* Cm 6876 (London: HMSO). Available online at: http://www.dfid.gov.uk/pubs/files/whitepaper2006/wp2006section3.pdf, last accessed on 25 June 2007.

Department of Foreign Affairs and International Trade (Canada) (DFAIT) (1999), *Human Security: Safety for People in a Changing World* (Ottawa: DFAIT).

——(2000), *Freedom from Fear: Canada's Foreign Policy for Human Security* (Ottawa: DFAIT), available online at: http://pubx.dfait-maeci. gc.ca/00_global/Pubs_(at).nsf/4d5c1b5e541f152485256cbb006bb5ff/ 56153893ff8dfda285256bc700653b9f? Open Document, last accessed 25 June 2007.

Der Derian, J. (1987), *On Diplomacy: A Genealogy of Western Estrangement* (Oxford: Blackwell).

Derrida, J. (1976), *Of Grammatology* (Baltimore, Md.: Johns Hopkins University Press).

——(1992), *The Other Heading: Reflections on Today's Europe* (Bloomington: Indiana University Press).

Dershowitz, A. M. (2003), *Why Terrorism Works: Responding to the Challenge* (New Haven, Conn.: Yale University Press).

Desch, M. (2003), 'The Humanity of American Realism', *Review of International Studies*, 29(3) (July): 415–26.

Deutsch, K. W. (1968), *The Analysis of International Relations* (Englewood Cliffs, NJ: Prentice-Hall).

Director-General of the Foreign Ministry of Japan, Statement at the International Conference on Human Security in a Globalized World, Ulan Bator, 8 May 2000, posted on UNDP Mongolia website at: www. un-mongolia.mn/undp, last accessed 25 June 2007.

Doty, R. L. (1993), 'The Bounds of "Race" in International Relations', *Millennium*, 22(3): 443–61.

——(1996), *Imperial Encounters: The Politics of Representation in North–South Relations* (Minneapolis: University of Minnesota Press).

Doyle, M. W. (1983a), 'Kant, Liberal Legacies, and Foreign Affairs, part 1', *Philosophy and Public Affairs*, 12(3).

——(1983b), 'Kant, Liberal Legacies, and Foreign Affairs, part 2', *Philosophy and Public Affairs*, 12(4).

——(1986), 'Liberalism and World Politics', *American Political Science Review*, 80(4): 1151–69.

——(1995a), 'On the Democratic Peace', *International Security*, 19(4): 164–84.

——(1995b), 'Liberalism and World Politics Revisited', in Charles W. Kegley (ed.), *Controversies in International Relations Theory: Realism and the Neoliberal Challenge* (New York: St Martins Press): 83–105.

——(1997), *Ways of War and Peace: Realism, Liberalism, and Socialism* (New York: W. W. Norton).

——(1999), 'A Liberal View: Preserving and Expanding the Liberal Pacific Union', in T. V. Paul and John A. Hall (eds), *International Order and the Future of World Politics* (Oxford: Oxford University Press): 41–66.

Drake, M. (2001), *Problematics of Military Power: Government, Discipline and the Subject of Violence* (London: Frank Cass).

DuBois, W. E. B. (1993), *The Souls of Black Folk* (New York: Knopf).

Duffield, M. (1998), 'Post-modern Conflict: Warlords, Post-adjustment States and Private Protection', *Civil Wars*, 1: 65–102.

——(2001), *Global Governance and the New Wars* (London: Zed).

Dunne, T. (1995), 'The Social Construction of International Society', *European Journal of International Relations*, 1(3).

——(1998), *Inventing International Society* (London: Macmillan).

E **Easterly, W.** (2002), 'How Did Heavily Indebted Poor Countries Become Heavily Indebted? Reviewing Two Decades of Debt Relief', *World Development*, 30(10): 1677–96.

EC (2003), *A Secure Europe in a Better World: The European Security Strategy* (Brussels: European Council).

Economic Commission for Africa (ECA) and African Union (AU) (2006), *Assessing Regional Integration in Africa II: Rationalizing Regional Economic Communities* (Addis Abbaba: ECA).

Edkins, J., Persram, N., and Pin-Fat, V. (1999), *Sovereignty and Subjectivity* (Boulder, Col.: Lynne Rienner).

Edwards, P. (1996), *The Closed World: Computers and the Politics of Discourse in Cold War America* (Cambridge, Mass.: MIT Press).

Ekins, P. (1992), *A New World Order: Grassroots Movements for Global Change* (London: Routledge).

Elias, N. (2000), *The Civilizing Process: Sociogenetic and Psychogenetic Investigations* (Oxford: Basil Blackwell).

Elshtain, J. B. (1987), *Women and War* (New York: Basic Books).

——**and Tobias, S.** (eds) (1990), *Women, Militarism, and War: Essays in History, Politics, and Social Theory* (Totowa, NJ: Rowman & Littlefield).

Enloe, C. (1989), *Bananas, Beaches and Bases: Making Feminist Sense of International Politics* (London: Pandora Books).

——(1993), *The Morning After: Sexual Politics at the End of the Cold War* (Berkeley: University of California Press).

——(2000), *Maneuvers: The International Politics of Militarizing Women's Lives* (Berkeley: University of California Press).

——(2004), *The Curious Feminist: Searching for Women in a New Age of Empire* (Berkeley: University of California Press).

Environmental Degradation and Conflict in Darfur: A Workshop Organized by the University of Peace of the United Nations and the Peace Research Institute, University of Khartoum, Khartoum, 15/16 December 2004.

Erksine, T. (2003), *Can Institutions Have Responsibilities? Collective Moral Agency and International Relations* (London: Palgrave).

Evans, G. (2004), 'When Is It Right to Fight?', *Survival*, 46(3): 59–82.

——**and M. Sahnoun** (2002), 'The Responsibility to Protect', *Foreign Affairs*, 81(6): 99–110.

F **Falk, R.** (1975), *A Study of Future Worlds* (New York: Free Press).

——(1993), 'Global Apartheid: The Structure of the World-Economy', *Third World Resurgence*, 37 (Nov.).

——(1995a), 'Liberalism at the Global Level: The Last of the Independent Commissions', *Millennium Special Issue: The Globalization of Liberalism?*, 24(3): 563–76.

——(1995b), *On Humane Governance: Toward a New Global Politics* (Cambridge: Polity Press).

——(1997), 'State of Siege: Will Globalization Win Out?', *International Affairs*, 73(1).

——(2000), 'A "New Medievalism"', in G. Fry and J. O'Hagan (eds), *Contending Images of World Politics* (Basingstoke: Macmillan).

Fanon, F. (1967a), *Black Skin, White Masks* (New York: Grove Press).

——(1967b; reissued 1990), *The Wretched of the Earth* (Harmondsworth: Penguin).

Fausto-Sterling, A. (1992), *Myths of Gender: Biological Theories about Women and Men* (New York: Basic Books).

——(2000), *Sexing the Body: Gender Politics and the Construction of Sexuality* (New York: Basic Books).

Fawcett, L., and Hurrell, A. (1995), *Regionalism in World Politics* (Oxford: Oxford University Press).

Feinstein, L., and Slaughter, A.-M. (2004), 'A Duty to Prevent', *Foreign Affairs*, 83(1) (Jan./Feb.): 136–50.

Feldstein, M. (1998), 'Refocusing the IMF', *Foreign Affairs*, 77: 24.

Finnemore, M. (1996a), 'Norms, Culture, and World Politics: Insights from Sociology's Institutionalism', *International Organization*, 50(2): 325–47.

—— (1996*b*), *National Interests in International Society* (Ithaca, NY: Cornell University Press).

—— (2000), 'Are Legal Norms Distinctive?', *International Law and Politics*, 32.

—— **and Sikkink, K.** (1998), 'International Norm Dynamics and Political Change', *International Organization*, 52 (Oct.): 887–918.

Finnis, J. (1980), *Natural Law and Natural Rights* (Oxford: Clarendon Press).

Fischer, F. (1967), *Germany's Aims in the First World War* (New York: W. W. Norton).

Foot, R. (2006), 'Torture: The Struggle over a Peremptory Norm in a Counter-Terrorist Era', *International Relations*, 20: 131-51.

Forsythe, D. P. (1988), 'The United Nations and Human Rights', in L. S. Finkelstein (ed.), *Politics in the United Nations System* (Durham, NC, and London: Duke University Press).

Foucault, M. (1977), *Discipline and Punish: The Birth of the Prison* (New York: Vintage Books).

—— (1978/1990), *The History of Sexuality* (London/Penguin).

—— (1984), *The Foucault Reader* (New York: Pantheon Books).

—— (1994), *Power* (New York: New Press).

—— (1996), 'What Our Present Is', in M. Foucault, *Foucault Live: Collected Interviews 1961–1984* (New York: Semiotent).

Fox-Keller, E. (1985), *Reflections on Gender and Science* (New Haven, Conn.: Yale University Press).

Francis, D. (2004), *Rethinking War and Peace* (London: Pluto Press).

Franck, T., and Rodley, N. (1973), 'After Bangladesh: The Law of Humanitarian Intervention by Force', *American Journal of International Law*, 67: 275–305.

Frank, A. G. (1967), *Capitalism and Underdevelopment in Latin America* (New York: Monthly Review Press).

—— (1998), *ReORIENT: Global Economy in the Asian Age* (Berkeley: University of California Press).

—— **and Gills, B.** (eds) (1996), *The World System: Five Hundred Years or Five Thousand?* (London: Routledge).

Frankel, B. (ed.) (1991), *Opaque Nuclear Proliferation* (London: Frank Cass).

Freedman, L. (1998), *The Revolution in Strategic Affairs*, Adelphi Paper 318 (Oxford: Oxford University Press).

—— (ed.) (1994), *War* (Oxford: Oxford University Press).

Friedberg, A. L. (1993), 'Ripe for Rivalry: Prospects for Peace in a Multipolar Asia', *International Security*, 18(3): 3–33.

Friedman, J. (ed.) (2003), *Globalization, the State and Violence* (Oxford: AltaMira Press).

—— (2005), *The World is Flat: A Brief History of the Twenty-first Century* (New York: Farrar, Straus and Giroux).

Fukuyama, F. (1989), 'The End of History', *The National Interest*, 16.

—— (1992), *The End of History and the Last Man* (London: Hamish Hamilton).

G **Gardner, G. T.** (1994), *Nuclear Nonproliferation: A Primer* (London and Boulder, Col.: Lynne Rienner).

Gates Jr., H. L. (ed.) (1987), *Classic Slave Narratives* (New York: Mentor).

Gellner, E. (1983), *Nations and Nationalism* (Oxford: Blackwell).

—— (2006), *Nations and Nationalism,* 2nd edn (Oxford: Blackwell).

Gendering Human Security: From Marginalisation to the Integration of Women in Peace-Building (Oslo: Norwegian Institute of International Affairs and Fafo Forum on Gender Relations in Post-Conflict Transitions, 2001). Available online at: http://www.fafo.no/pub/rapp/352/352.pdf, last accessed on 25 June 2007.

Germain, R., and Kenny, M. (1998), 'Engaging Gramsci: International Relations Theory and the New Gramscians', *Review of International Studies*, 24(1): 3–21.

Giddens, A. (1990), *The Consequences of Modernity: Self and Society in the Late Modern Age* (Cambridge: Polity Press, and Stanford, Cal.: Stanford University Press).

Gilmore, R. W. (1989/9), 'Globalisation and US Prison Growth: From Military Keynesianism to Post-Keynesian Militarism', *Race and Class*, 40(2–3): 171–88.

Gilpin, R. (2001), *Global Political Economy* (Princeton, NJ: Princeton University Press).

—— (2002), *The Challenge of Global Capitalism* (Princeton, NJ: Princeton University Press).

Gioseffi, D. (ed.) (2003), *Women on War: An International Anthology of Women's Writings from Antiquity to the Present*, 2nd edn (New York: Feminist Press at the City University of New York).

Glendon, M. A. (2002), *A World Made New: Eleanor Roosevelt and the Universal Declaration of Human Rights* (New York: Random House).

Goldblat, J. (2002), *Arms Control: A New Guide to Negotiations and Agreements* (London: Sage).

Goldstein, J., Kahler, M., Keohane, R. O., and Slaughter, A. (2000), 'Legalization in World Politics', *International Organization*, 54(3).

Gong, G. W. (1984), *The Standard of 'Civilization' in International Society* (Oxford: Clarendon Press).

Goodin, R. E. (1988), 'What Is So Special about Our Fellow Countrymen?', *Ethics*, 98(4) (July): 663–86.

Goodman, D., and Redclift, M. (1991), *Refashioning Nature: Food, Ecology and Culture* (London: Routledge).

Gottlieb, R. S. (ed.) (1989), *An Anthology of Western Marxism: From Lukacs and Gramsci to Socialist-Feminism* (Oxford: Oxford University Press).

Gowa, J. (1983), *Closing the Cold Window: Domestic Politics and the End of Bretton Woods* (Ithaca, NY: Cornell University Press).

Grace, C. S. (1994), *Nuclear Weapons: Principles, Effects and Survivability* (London: Brassey's).

Gramsci, A. (1971), *Selections from the Prison Notebooks*, ed. and trans. Q. Hoare and G. Nowell Smith (London: Lawrence & Wishart).

Gray, C. S. (1996), 'The Second Nuclear Age: Insecurity, Proliferation, and the Control of Arms', in W. Murrey (ed.), *The Brassey's Mershon American Defense Annual, 1995–1996: The United States and the Emerging Strategic Environment* (Washington, DC: Brassey's): 135–54.

—— (1999*a*), *The Second Nuclear Age* (Boulder, Col. and London: Lynne Rienner).

—— (1999*b*), 'Clausewitz Rules, OK? The Future Is the Past—with GPS', *Review of International Studies*, 25: 161–82.

—— (2002), *Strategy for Chaos: Revolutions in Military Affairs and the Evidence of History* (London: Frank Cass).

Gray, J. (1995), *Enlightenment's Wake: Politics and Culture at the Close of the Modern Age* (London: Routledge).

Green, D. (1995), *Silent Revolution: The Rise of Market Economics in Latin America* (London: Latin America Bureau).

Greenwood, B. M., Bojang, K., Whitty, C. J., and Targett, G. A. (2005), 'Malaria', The *Lancet*, 365 (9469): 1487–98.

Greenwood, C. (1993), 'Is there a Right of Humanitarian Intervention?', *The World Today*, 49.

Grieco, J. (1988*a*), 'Anarchy and the Limits of Cooperation: A Realist Critique of the Newest Liberal Institution', *International Organization*, 42 (Aug.): 485–507.

Grieco, J. (1988b), 'Realist Theory and the Problem of International Cooperation', *Journal of Politics*, 50 (Summer): 600–24.

Grotius, H. (1925), *The Law of War and Peace: De Jure Belli ac Pacis Libri Trea* (New York: Bobbs-Merrill). First published 1625.

Grovogui, S. N. (1996), *Sovereigns and Quasi Sovereigns, and Africans: Race and Self-Determination in International Law* (Minneapolis: University of Minnesota Press).

Gunaratna, R. (2002), *Inside Al Qaeda: Global Network of Terror* (New York: Columbia University Press).

Haas, P. M., Keohane, R. O., and Levy, M. (eds) (1993), *Institutions for the Earth: Sources of Effective International Environmental Action* (London: MIT Press).

Hall, C. (1992), *White, Male, and Middle Class: Explorations in Feminism and History* (Cambridge: Polity Press).

——(2002), *Civilising Subjects: Metropole and Colony in the English Imagination 1830–1867* (Cambridge: Polity Press).

Hall, J. A. (1985), *Powers and Liberties: The Causes and Consequences of the Rise of the West* (Oxford: Blackwell).

——(1994), *Coercion and Consent: Studies on the Modern State* (Cambridge: Polity Press).

Halliday, F. (1986), *The Making of the Second Cold War,* 2nd edn (London: Verso).

Hansen, L. (2006), *Security as Practice: Discourse Analysis and the Bosnian War* (London: Routledge).

Haq, M. (1995), *Reflections on Human Development* (Oxford: Oxford University Press).

Haraway, D. (1989), *Primate Visions: Gender, Race, and Nature in the World of Modern Science* (New York: Routledge).

——(1991), *Symians, Cyborgs and Women: The Re-Invention of Nature* (New York: Routledge).

Hardin, G. (1968), 'The Tragedy of the Commons', *Science*, 162: 1243–8.

Hardt, M., and Negri, A. (2000), *Empire* (Cambridge, Mass.: Harvard University Press).

Hart, H. L. A. (1994), *The Concept of Law*, 2nd edn (Oxford: Oxford University Press).

Hartsock, N. (1998), *The Feminist Standpoint Revisited and Other Essays* (Boulder, Col.: Westview Press).

Harvey, D. (1989), *The Condition of Postmodernity: An Enquiry into the Conditions of Cultural Change* (Oxford: Blackwell).

Hasenclever, A. (2000), 'Integrating Theories of Regimes', *Review of International Studies*, 26: 3–33.

——Mayer, P., and Rittberger, V. (1997), *Theories of International Regimes* (Cambridge: Cambridge University Press).

Hashemi, S. (1996), 'International Society and its Islamic Malcontents', *The Fletcher Forum of World Affairs*, 20(2).

Hastings, A. (1997), *The Construction of Nationhood: Ethnicity, Religion and Nationalism* (Cambridge: Cambridge University Press).

Hay, C. (2000), 'Contemporary Capitalism, Globalization, Regionalization and the Persistence of National Variation', *Review of International Studies*, 26(4): 509–32.

Heazle, M. (2006), *Scientific Uncertainty and the Politics of Whaling* (Washington, DC: University of Washington Press).

Heeren, A. H. L. (1971), *A Manual of the History of the Political System of Europe and Its Colonies,* 2 vols (Oxford: Oxford University Press, 1833; repr. New York: Books for Libraries Press).

Held, D. (1993), 'Democracy: From City-states to a Cosmopolitan Order?', in D. Held (ed.), *Prospects for Democracy: North, South, East, West* (Cambridge: Polity Press): 13–52.

——(1995), *Democracy and the Global Order: From the Modern State to Cosmopolitan Governance* (Cambridge: Polity Press).

——(2002), 'Cosmopolitanism: Ideas, Realities, Deficits', in D. Held and A. McGrew (eds), *Governing Globalization* (Cambridge: Polity Press): 305–24.

——and McGrew, A. (2002, 2007), *Globalization/Anti-Globalization* (Cambridge: Polity Press; 2nd edn, 2007).

—— ——Goldblatt, D., and Perraton, J. (1999), *Global Transformations: Politics, Economics and Culture* (Cambridge: Polity Press).

Helman, G. B., and Ratner, S. R. (1992/3), 'Saving Failed States', *Foreign Policy*, 89: 3–20.

Henkin, L. (1995), *International Law: Politics and Values* (Dordrecht: Martinus Nijhoff).

Hennessy, R., and Ingraham, C. (eds) (1997), *Materialist Feminism: A Reader in Class, Difference, and Women's Lives* (London: Routledge).

Hettne, B. (1999), 'Globalization and the New Regionalism: The Second Great Transformation', in B. Hettne, A. Intoai, and O. Sunkel (eds), *Globalism and the New Regionalism* (Basingstoke: Macmillan).

Higgins, R. (1994), *Problems and Process: International Law and How We Use It* (Oxford: Oxford University Press).

Higgott, R. (1995), 'Economic Co-operation in the Asia Pacific: A Theoretical Comparison with the European Union', *Journal of European Public Policy,* 2(3): 361–83.

Hirst, P., and Thompson, G. (1996; 2nd edn, 1999), *Globalization in Question: The International Economy and the Possibilities of Governance* (Cambridge: Polity Press).

—— ——(2003), 'Globalization—a necessary myth?', in D. Held and A. McGrew (eds), *The Global Transformations Reader*, 2nd edn (Cambridge: Polity Press): 98–106.

Hobden, S. (1998), *International Relations and Historical Sociology: Breaking Down Boundaries* (London: Routledge).

——and Hobson, J. M. (2002), *Historical Sociology of International Relations* (Cambridge: Cambridge University Press).

Hobsbawm, E. (1990), *Nations and Nationalism since 1780: Programme, Myth, Reality* (Cambridge: Cambridge University Press). www.nationalismproject.org/books/g-h.htm#Anchor-Hobsbawm-46430

Hoffmann, S. (1987), *Janus and Minerva: Essays on the Theory and Practice of International Politics* (Boulder, Col.: Westview Press).

——(1995–6), 'The Politics and Ethics of Military Intervention', *Survival*, 37(4): 29–51.

Holden, P. and Ruppel, R. J. (eds) (2003), *Imperial Desire: Dissident Sexualities and Colonial Literature* (Minneapolis: University of Minnesota Press).

Homer-Dixon, T. (1991), 'On the Threshold: Environmental Changes as Causes of Acute Conflict', *International Security,* 16: 76–116.

——(1994), 'Environmental Scarcities and Violent Conflict: Evidence from Cases', *International Security* 19(1): 5–40.

Hoogvelt, A. (2001), *Globalization and the Post-Colonial World* (Basingstoke: Palgrave).

Hooper, C. (2001), *Manly States* (New York: Columbia University Press).

Hroch, M. (1996), `From National Movement to the Fully-formed Nation: The Nation-building Process in Europe', in G. Balakrishnan (ed.), *Mapping the Nation* (London: Verso).

Hubert, D. (2004), 'An Idea that Works in Practice', *Security Dialogue*, 35 (September): 351–2.

Humphreys, M., and Varshney, A. (2004), *Violent Conflict and the Millennium Development: Goals: Diagnosis and Recommendations,* CGSD Working Paper No. 19 (New York: Center on Globalization and Sustainable Development, The Earth Institute at Columbia University). Available online at: http://www.earthinstitute.columbia.edu/cgsd/documents/humphreys_conflict_and_MDG.pdf, last accessed on 25 June 2007.

Huntington, S. (1993), 'The Clash of Civilizations', *Foreign Affairs*, 72(3): 22–169.

—— (1996), *The Clash of Civilizations and the Remaking of the World Order* (New York: Simon & Schuster).

Hurrell, A. (1995), 'Regionalism in Theoretical Perspective', in L. Fawcett and A. Hurrell (eds), *Regionalism in World Politics: Regional Organization and International Order* (Oxford: Oxford University Press): 37–73.

—— (2006), 'The State of International Society', in R. Little and J. Williams (eds), *The Anarchical Society in a Globalized World* (Basingstoke: Palgrave).

—— and Kingsbury, B. (eds) (1992), *The International Politics of the Environment: Actors, Interests and Institutions* (Oxford: Clarendon Press).

—— and Woods, N. (1995), 'Globalization and Inequality', *Millennium*, 24(3): 447–70.

Hymans, J. E. (2006), *The Psychology of Nucleas Proliferation* (Cambridge: Cambridge University Press).

ICPF (International Commission on Peace and Food) (1994), *Uncommon Opportunities: An Agenda for Peace and Equitable Development* (London: Zed).

Ignatieff, M. (2002), 'Is the Human Rights Era Ending?', *New York Times*, 5 February.

—— (2005), *The Lesser Evil: Political Ethics in an Age of Terror* (Princeton, NJ: Princeton University Press).

Ikenberry, G. J. (1999), 'Liberal Hegemony and the Future of American Post-war Order', in T. V. Paul and J. A. Hall (eds), *International Order and the Future of World Politics* (Cambridge: Cambridge University Press): 123–45.

—— (2001), *After Victory: Institutions, Strategic Restraint, and the Rebuilding of Order after Major Wars* (Princeton, NJ: Princeton University Press).

Independent Commission on International Development Issues (Chairman: Willy Brandt) (1980), *North–South: A Programme for Survival: Report of the Independent Commission on International Development Issues* (London: Pan).

Intergovernmental Panel on Climate Change (IPCC) (2007), *Climate Change 2007: The Physical Science BASIS*. Contribution of Working Group 1 to the Fourth Assessment Report of the Intergovernmental Panel on Climate Change, www.ipcc.ch.

International Affairs (2000), *Europe: Where Does It Begin and Where Does It End?* Special Issue, 76(3): 437–574.

International Commission on Intervention and State Sovereignty (2001), *The Responsibility to Protect* (Ottawa: ICISS).

International Parliamentary Union, *IPU PARLINE database*, available online at: http://www.ipu.org/english/home.htm, last accessed on 25 June 2007.

Jackson, R. H. (1990), *Quasi-States: Sovereignty, International Relations and the Third World* (Cambridge: Cambridge University Press).

—— (2000), *The Global Covenant: Human Conduct in a World of States* (Oxford: Oxford University Press).

—— and Owens, P. (2001), 'The Evolution of International Society', in J. Baylis, and S. Smith (eds), *The Globalization of World Politics*, 3rd edn (Oxford: Oxford University Press): 45–62.

Jaquette, J. (2003), 'Feminism and the Challenges of the "Post-Cold War" World', *International Feminist Journal of Politics*, 5(3): 331–54.

Jervis, R. (1983), 'Security Regimes', in S. D. Krasner (ed.), *International Regimes* (Ithaca, NY: Cornell University Press).

—— (1999), 'Realism, Neo-liberalism, and Cooperation: Understanding the Debate', *International Security*, 24 (Summer): 42–63.

John, I. M. W., and Garnett, J. (1972), 'International Politics at Aberystwyth 1919–1969', in B. Porter (ed.), *The Aberystwyth Papers: International Politics 1919–1969* (London: Oxford University Press): 86–102.

Jolly, R., and Ray, D. B. (2006), *National Human Development Reports and the Human Security Framework: A Review of Analysis and Experience* (Brighton: Institute of Development Studies).

Jones, P. (1994), *Rights* (Basingstoke: Macmillan).

Jones, R. W. (1995), ' "Message in a Bottle"—Theory and Praxis in Critical Security Studies', *Contemporary Security Policy*, 16(3).

—— (1999), *Security, Strategy and Critical Theory* (Boulder, Col.: Lynne Rienner).

—— (ed.) (2000), *Critical Theory and World Politics* (Boulder, Col.: Lynne Rienner).

Junaid, S. (2005), *Terrorism and Global Power Systems* (Oxford: Oxford University Press).

Junne, G. C. A. (2001), 'International Organizations in a Period of Globalization: New (Problems of) Legitimacy', in J.-M. Coicaud and V. Heiskanen (eds), *The Legitimacy of International Organizations* (Tokyo: United Nations University Press).

Kaldor, M. (1999), *New and Old Wars: Organized Violence in a Global Era* (Cambridge: Polity Press).

Kant, I. (1991), *Political Writings*, ed. Hans Reiss (Cambridge: Cambridge University Press).

Karp, A. (1995), *Ballistic Missile Proliferation: The Politics and Technics* (Oxford: Oxford University Press for Stockholm International Peace Research Institute).

Katzenstein, P. (ed.) (1996), *The Culture of National Security: Norms and Identity in World Politics* (New York: Columbia University Press).

Keal, P. (2003), *European Conquest and the Rights of Indigenous Peoples: The Moral Backwardness of International Society* (Cambridge: Cambridge University Press).

Keane, J. (2003), *Global Civil Society?* (Cambridge: Cambridge University Press).

Keck, M., and Sikkink, K. (1998), *Activists beyond Borders: Transnational Advocacy Networks in International Politics* (Ithaca, NY: Cornell University Press).

Kedourie, E. (1960), *Nationalism* (London: Hutchinson).

Kendall, G., and Wickham, G. (1999), *Using Foucault's Methods* (London: Sage).

Kennan, G. F. (1996), 'Diplomacy in the Modern World', in R. J. Beck, A. Clark Arend, and R. D. Vanger Lugt (eds), *International Rules: Approaches from International Law and International Relations* (Oxford: Oxford University Press): 99–106.

Keohane, R. (1984), *After Hegemony: Cooperation and Discord in the World Political Economy* (Princeton, NJ: Princeton University Press).

—— (ed.) (1989a), *International Institutions and State Power: Essays in International Relations Theory* (Boulder, Col.: Westview Press).

—— (1989b), 'Theory of World Politics: Structural Realism and Beyond', in R. Keohane (ed.), *International Institutions and State Power: Essays in International Relations Theory* (Boulder, Col.: Westview Press).

—— (2002a), 'The Globalization of Informal Violence, Theories of World Politics, and the "Liberalism of Fear"', in R. Keohane (ed.), *Power and Governance in a Partially Globalized World* (London: Routledge): 272–87.

—— (2002b), 'The Public Delegitimation of Terrorism and Coalitional Politics', in K. Booth and T. Dunne (eds), *Worlds in Collision: Terror and the Future of Global Order* (London: Palgrave Macmillan): 141–51.

Keohane, R. and Martin, L. (1995), 'The Promise of Institutionalist Theory', *International Security*, 20(1): 39–51.

—— —— (1999). *Institutional Theory, Endogeneity and Delegation* (Cambridge, mass: Weatherhead Centre for International Affairs, Harvard University).

—— **and Nye, J.** (eds) (1972), *Transnational Relations and World Politics* (Cambridge, Mass.: Harvard University Press).

—— —— (1977), *Power and Interdependence: World Politics in Transition* (Boston: Little, Brown).

—— —— (2003), 'Globalization: What's New? What's Not? (And So What?)', in D. Held and A. McGrew (eds), *The Global Transformations Reader* (Cambridge: Polity Press): 75–84.

—— —— **and Hoffmann, S.** (eds) (1993), *After the Cold War: International Institutions and State Strategies in Europe 1989–1991* (London: Harvard University Press).

Khong, Y. F. (2001), 'Human Security: A Shotgun Approach to Alleviating Human Misery', *Global Governance*, 7: 231–37.

Kinsella, H. M. (2003), 'For a Careful Reading: The Conservativism of Gender Constructivism', *International Studies Review*, 5: 294–7.

—— (2005a), 'Discourses of Difference: Civilians, Combatants, and Compliance with the Laws of War,' *Review of International Studies*, Special Issue,163–85.

—— (2005b), 'Securing the Civilian: Sex and Gender and Laws of War', in M. Barnett and R. Duvall (eds), *Power in Global Governance* (Cambridge: Cambridge University Press): 249–72.

—— (2006) 'Gendering Grotius: Sex and Sex Difference in the Laws of War', *Political Theory*, 34(2): 161-91.

Kirkpatrick, J. (1979), 'Dictatorships and Double Standards', *Commentary*, 68.

Kissinger, H. A. (1977), *American Foreign Policy*, 3rd edn (New York: W. W. Norton).

Koehler, S. (2007), 'Professor Explains Continuous Threat from Land Mines', Ozarks Local News, 7 February, available online at: http://www.banminesusa.org., last accessed 25 June 2007.

Koskenniemi, M. (1989), *From Apology to Utopia: The Structure of International Legal Argument* (Helsinki: Finnish Lawyers Publishing Co.).

Krasner, S. D. (1983), 'Structural Causes and Regime Consequences: Regimes as Intervening Variables', in S. D. Krasner (ed.), *International Regimes* (Ithaca, NY: Cornell University Press): 1–22.

—— (1985), *Structural Conflict: The Third World Against Global Liberalism* (Berkeley: University of California Press).

—— (1991), 'Global Communications and National Power: Life on the Pareto Frontier', *World Politics*, 43: 336–66.

—— (1993), 'Sovereignty, Regimes and Human Rights', in V. Rittberger (ed.), *Regime Theory and International Relations* (Oxford: Clarendon Press).

—— (1999), *Sovereignty: Organized Hypocrisy* (Princeton, NJ: Princeton University Press).

Kratochwil, F. (1989), *Rules, Norms, and Decisions* (Cambridge: Cambridge University Press).

Krause, K., and Williams, M. C. (eds) (1997), *Critical Security Studies: Concepts and Cases* (London: UCL Press).

Laidi, Z. (1998), *A World Without Meaning: The Crisis of Meaning in International Politics* (London: Routledge).

Lapid, Y. (1989), 'The Third Debate: On the Prospects of International Theory in a Post-Positivist Era', *International Studies Quarterly*, 33(3): 225–35.

Laqueur, W. (1996), 'Post-modern Terrorism', *Foreign Affairs*, 75(5): 24–37.

Lavoy, P. (1995), 'The Strategic Consequences of Nuclear Proliferation. A Review Essay', *Security Studies*, 4(4): 695–753.

Lawler, L. (1995), 'The Core Assumptions and Presumptions of "Cooperative Security" ', in S. Lawson (ed.), *The New Agenda for Global Security: Cooperating for Peace and Beyond* (St Leonards: Allen & Unwin).

Legrain, P. (2002), *Open World: The Truth about Globalisation* (London: Abacus).

Lenin, V. I. ([1917] 1966), *Imperialism, the Highest Stage of Capitalism: A Popular Outline*, 13th edn (Moscow: Progress Publishers).

Lepard, B. (2002), *Rethinking Humanitarian Intervention: A Fresh Approach based on Fundamental Ethical Principles in International Law and World Religions* (University Park: Pennsylvania State University).

Leventhal, P., and Alexander, Y. (eds) (1987), *Preventing Nuclear Terrorism* (Lexington, Mass., and Toronto: Lexington Books).

Levy, M. A., Young, O. R., and Zurn, M. (1995), 'The Study of International Regimes', *European Journal of International Relations*, 1(3): 267–330.

Lieven, A., and Hulsman, J. (2006), *Ethical Realism: A Vision for America's Role in the World* (New York: Pantheon Books).

Lindberg, T. (2005), 'Protect the People', *Washington Times*, 27 September.

Linklater, A. (1990a), *Men and Citizens in the Theory of International Relations*, 2nd edn (London: Macmillan; 1st edn 1982).

—— (1998), *The Transformation of Political Community: Ethical Foundations of the Post-Westphalian Era* (Cambridge: Polity).

—— (1999), 'The Evolving Spheres of International Justice', *International Affairs*, 75(3).

—— (2002), 'Cosmopolitan Political Communities in International Relations', *International Relations*, 16(1): 135–50.

—— (2005), 'The Harm Principle and Global Ethics', *Global Society*, 20(3) (July): 20.

Little, R. (1996), 'The Growing Relevance of Pluralism?', in S. Smith, K. Booth, and M. Zalewski (eds), *International Theory: Positivism and Beyond* (Cambridge: Cambridge University Press): 66–86.

Lodgaard, S. (2000), 'Human Security: Concept and Operationalization', Paper presented to the Expert Seminar on Human Rights and Peace 2000, Palais Wilson, Geneva, 8–9 December.

Longino, H. E. (1990), *Science as Social Knowledge: Values and Objectivity in Scientific Inquiry* (Princeton, NJ: Princeton University Press).

Luard, E. (ed.) (1992), *Basic Texts in International Relations* (London: Macmillan).

Luttwak, E. (1998), *Turbo Capitalism: Winners and Losers in the Global Economy* (London: Weidenfield & Nicolson).

Lyotard, J.-F. (1984), *The Post-modern Condition: A Report on Knowledge* (Manchester: Manchester University Press).

MacFarlane, N., and Khong Yuen Foong (2006), *Human Security and the UN: A Critical History* (Bloomington: Indiana University Press).

Machiavelli, N. (1988), *The Prince*, ed. Q. Skinner (Cambridge: Cambridge University Press).

Mack, A. (2004), 'A Signifier of Shared Values', *Security Dialogue*, 35(3): 366–7.

—— **Lewis, P., et al.** (1992), *Global Politics* (Cambridge: Polity Press).

Mackinnon, C. (1993), 'Crimes of War, Crimes of Peace', in S. Shute and S. Hurley (eds), *On Human Rights* (New York: Basic Books).

McLuhan, M. (1964), *Understanding Media* (London: Routledge).

McNeill, D. (2006), 'Japan and the Whaling Ban: Siege Mentality Fuels "Sustainability" Claims', http://www.japanfocus.org/products/details/2353, last accessed on 25 June 2007.

McNeill, J. R., and McNeill, W. H. (2003), *The Human Web: A Bird's Eye View of World History* (New York: W. W. Norton).

McNeill, W. H. (1982), *The Pursuit of Power: Armed Force, Technology and Society* (Oxford: Blackwell).

Mann, M. (1986), *The Sources of Social Power*, Vol. 1. *A History of Power from the Beginning to AD 1760* (Cambridge: Cambridge University Press).

—— (1993), *The Sources of Social Power*, Vol. 2. *The Rise of Classes and Nation States, 1760–1914* (Cambridge: Cambridge University Press).

Mansbach, R., Ferguson, Y., and Lampert, D. (1976), *The Web of World Politics* (Englewood Cliffs, NJ: Prentice-Hall).

Marx, K. (1992), *Capital: Student Edition*, ed. C. J. Arthur (London: Lawrence & Wishart). First published 1867.

—— and Engels, F. (1967), *The Communist Manifesto*, with an Introduction by A. J. P. Taylor (Harmondsworth: Penguin): 83–4.

Mattingly, G. (1955), *Renaissance Diplomacy* (Harmondsworth: Penguin).

Mattli, W. (1999), *The Logic of Regional Integration: Europe and Beyond* (Cambridge: Cambridge University Press).

—— and Slaughter, A. (1995), 'Law and Politics in the European Union: A Reply to Garrett', *International Organization*, 49(1): 183–90.

—— —— (1998), 'Revisiting the European Court of Justice', *International Organization*, 52(1): 177–210.

Mazlish, B., and Iriye, A. (eds) (2005), *The Global History Reader* (Abingdon: Routledge).

Meadows, D. H., Meadows, D. L., and Randers, J. (1972), *The Limits to Growth* (London: Earth Island).

Mearsheimer, J. (1990), 'Back to the Future: Instability after the Cold War', *International Security*, 15(1): 5–56.

—— (1994/5), 'The False Promise of International Institutions', *International Security* 19(3): 5–49.

—— (2001), *The Tragedy of Great Power Politics* (New York: W. W. Norton).

—— and Walt, S. (2003), 'An Unnecessary War', *Foreign Policy* (Jan.–Feb.): 51–9.

Médecins Sans Frontières (2000), *Notes from the Field: The Work of Médecins Sans Frontières* (London: Médecins Sans Frontières).

Meinecke, F. (1957), *Machiavellism: The Doctrine of 'Raison d'Etat' and Its Place in Modern History*, trans. D. Scott (London: Routledge).

Mendlovitz, S. (1975), *On the Creation of a Just World Order* (New York: Free Press).

Metcalf, T. (1997), *Ideologies of the Raj* (Cambridge: Cambridge University Press).

Meyer, S. M. (1984), *The Dynamics of Nuclear Proliferation* (Chicago: University of Chicago Press).

Mill, J. S. (1973), 'A Few Words on Non-Intervention', in G. Himmelfarb (ed.), *Essays on Politics and Culture* (Gloucester, Mass.: Peter Smith).

Miller, D. (1999), 'Bounded Citizenship', in K. Hutchings and R. Danreuther (eds), *Cosmopolitan Citizenship* (London: Macmillan).

—— (2000), 'Justice and Inequality', in N. Woods and A. Hurrell (eds), *Inequality, Globalisation and World Politics* (Oxford: Oxford University Press); 187–210.

—— (2002), 'Caney's International Distributive Justice: A Response', *Political Studies*, 50: 974–7.

—— (2004), 'National Responsibility and International Justice', in D. K. Chatterjee (ed.), *The Ethics of Assistance* (Cambridge: Cambridge University Press): 23–143.

Miller, P. (1998), *Transformations of Patriarchy in the West, 1500–1900* (Bloomington: Indiana University Press).

Milner, H. V. (1988), *Resisting Protectionism: Global Industries and the Politics of International Trade* (Princeton, NJ: Princeton University Press).

Minear, L., and Weiss, T. G. (1995), *Mercy under Fire: War and the Global Humanitarian Community* (Boulder, Col.: Westview Press).

Mingst, K. (2004), *Essentials of International Relations* (New York: W. W. Norton).

Mitrany, D. (1943), *A Working Peace System* (London: RIIA).

Modelski, G. (1972), *Principles of World Politics* (New York: Free Press).

Moellendorf, D. (2002), *Cosmopolitan Justice* (Boulder, Col.: Westview Press).

Mohanty, C. (1988), 'Under Western Eyes: Feminist Scholarship and Colonial Discourses', *Feminist Review*, 30: 61-88.

Moon, K. (1997), *Sex Among Allies: Military Prostitution in US–Korea Relations* (New York: Columbia University Press).

Moravcsik, A. (1997), 'Taking Preferences Seriously: A Liberal Theory of International Politics', *International Organization*, 51(4): 513–53.

—— (1998), *The Choice for Europe: Social Purpose and State Power from Messina to Maastricht* (Ithaca, NY: Cornell University Press).

Morgenthau, H. J. ([1948] 1955, 1962, 1978), *Politics among Nations: The Struggle for Power and Peace*, 2nd edn (New York: Knopf).

—— (1952), *American Foreign Policy: A Critical Examination* (London: Methuen) (also published as *In Defence of the National Interest*).

—— (1985), *Politics among Nations*, 6th edn (New York: McGraw-Hill).

Morse, E. (1976), *Modernization and the Transformation of International Relations* (New York: Free Press).

Mousseau, F., and Mittal, A. (2006), 'Free Market Famine', Foreign Policy in Focus Commentary, 26 October, www.fpif.org/pdf/gac/0610famine.pdf, last accessed on 25 June 2007.

Murden, S. (1999), 'Review Article: Huntington and His Critics', *Political Geography*, 18: 1017–22.

Murray, A. J. H. (1997), *Reconstructing Realism: Between Power Politics and Cosmopolitan Ethics* (Edinburgh: Keele University Press).

N Naím, M. (2002), 'Post-terror Surprises', *Foreign Policy*, September–October.

Naisbitt, J. (1994), *Global Paradox: The Bigger the World-Economy, the More Powerful its Smallest Players* (London: Brealey).

Nardin, T. (1983), *Law, Morality and the Relations of States* (Princeton, NJ: Princeton University Press).

—— (2005), 'Humanitarian Imperialism: Response to "Ending Tyranny in Iraq"', *Ethics and International Affairs*, 19(2): 21–6.

National Counter Terrorism Center (2005), *NCTC Fact Sheet and Observations Related to 2005 Terrorist Incidents*, available online at: www.NCTC.Gov, last accessed on 25 June 2007.

Nef, J. (1999), *Human Security and Mutual Vulnerability*, 2nd edn (Ottawa: IDRC).

NSS (2001, 2002), *National Security Strategy of the United States of America* (Washington, DC: US Government Printing Office).

Nussbaum, M. (1996), *For Love of Country: Debating the Limits of Patriotism* (Boston: Beacon Press).

O O'Brien, R. (1992), *Global Financial Integration: The End of Geography* (London: Pinter).

—— Goetz, A. M., Scholte, J. A., and Williams, M. (2000), *Contesting Global Governance: Multilateral Economic Institutions and Global Social Movements* (Cambridge: Cambridge University Press).

Office of the Director of National Intelligence (2005), 'Letter from Al-Zawahiri to Al-Zarqawi', 11 October.

Ogilvie-White, T. (1996), 'Is there a Theory of Nuclear Proliferation?', *The Nonproliferation Review*, 4(1): 43–60.

—— and Simpson, J. (2003), 'The NPT and Its PrepCom Session: A Regime in Need of Intensive Care', *The Nonproliferation Review*, 10(1) (Spring): 40–58.

Ohmae, K. (1990), *The Borderless World: Power and Strategy in the Interlinked Economy* (London: Fontana).

—— (1995), *The End of the Nation State: The Rise of Regional Economies* (New York: Free Press).

Olson, J. S. (ed.) (1988), *Dictionary of the Vietnam War* (New York: Greenwood Press).

Olson, M. (1965), *The Logic of Collective Action* (Cambridge, Mass.: Harvard University Press).

Onwudiwe, I. D. (2001), *The Globalization of Terror* (Burlington, VT: Ashgate).

Ougaard, M. (2004), *Political Globalization—State, Power and Social Forces* (London: Palgrave).

Owens, P. (2007), *Between War and Politics: International Relations and the Thought of Hannah Arendt* (Oxford: Oxford University Press).

Oxfam (2003), 'Boxing Match in Agricultural Trade', Briefing Paper No. 32, available online at: www.oxfam.org, last accessed on 25 June 2007.

—— (2006), 'Grounds for Change: Creating a Voice for Small Farmers and Farm Workers with Next International Coffee Agreement', available online at: http://www.oxfam.org/en/policy/briefingnotes/bn0604_coffee_groundsforchange, last accessed on 25 June 2007.

Palme Commission (1982), *Common Security: A Programme for Disarmament*. The Report of the Palme Commission (London: Pan Books).

Panofsky, W. K. H. (1998), 'Dismantling The Concept of "Weapons of Mass Destruction"', *Arms Control Today*, 28(3) (April): 3–8.

Pape, R. (2005), *Dying to Win: The Strategic Logic of Suicide Terrorism* (New York: Random House).

Parekh, B. (1997a), 'When Religion Meets Politics', *Demos*, 11: 5–7.

—— (1997b), 'Rethinking Humanitarian Intervention', *International Political Science Review*, 18(1): 49–70.

Paris, R. (2001), 'Human Security: Paradigm Shift or Hot Air', *International Security* 26(2) (Fall): 87-102.

Pearson, R. (2000), 'Rethinking Gender Matters in Development', in T. Allen and A. Thomas (eds), *Poverty and Development into the Twenty-first Century* (Oxford: Oxford University Press): 383–402.

Pendergrast, M. (1993), *For God, Country and Coca-Cola: The Unauthorized History of the Great American Soft Drink and the Company that Makes It* (London: Weidenfeld & Nicolson).

Persaud, R. B. (2002), 'Situating Race in International Relations: The Dialectics of Civilizational Security in American Immigration', in G. Chowdhry and S. Nair (eds), *Power, Post-colonialism and International Relations: Reading Race, Gender and Class* (London: Routledge).

Peters, J. S., and Wolper, A. (eds) (1995), *Women's Rights, Human Rights: International Feminist Perspectives* (New York: Routledge).

Peterson, V. S. (2003), *A Critical Rewriting of Global Political Economy: Reproductive, Productive and Virtual Economies* (London and New York: Routledge).

—— and Runyan, A. S. (1999), *Global Gender Issues*, 2nd edn (Boulder, Col.: Westview Press).

Pettman, J. J. (1996), *Worlding Women: A Feminist International Politics* (St Leonards: Allen & Unwin).

Petzold-Bradley, E., Carius, A., and Vincze, A. (eds) (2001), *Responding to Environmental Conflicts: Implications for Theory and Practice* (Dordrecht: Kluwer Academic).

Pogge, T. (1989), *Realizing Rawls* (Ithaca, NY: Cornell University Press).

—— (1994), 'Cosmopolitarism and sovereignty', in C. Brown (ed.), *Political Restructuring in Europe: Ethical Perspectives* (London: Routledge).

—— (2001a), 'Priorities of Global Justice', *Metaphilosophy*, 32(1-2).

—— (2001b), 'Moral Universalism and Global Economic Justice', *Politics Philosophy and Economics*, 1(1): 29–58.

—— (2002), *World Poverty and Human Rights: Cosmopolitan Responsibilities and Reforms* (Cambridge: Polity Press).

Porter, B. D. (1994), *War and the Rise of the State* (New York: Free Press).

Posen, B. (1993), 'The Security Dilemma and Ethnic Conflict', *Survival*, 35(1): 27–47.

Power and Interest News Report (2006), 'Asia's Coming Water Wars' (22 August), http://www.pinr.com, last accessed 25 June 2007.

PR Newswire Europe (2002), 'London tuberculosis rates now at Third World proportions', *PR Newswire Europe Ltd.*, 4 December, available online at: http://www.prnewswire.co.uk/cgi/news/release?id=95088, last accessed on 25 June 2007.

Price, R. (1998), 'Reversing the Gun Sights: Transnational Civil Society Targets Land Mines', *International Organization*, 52(3).

—— (2004), 'Emerging Customary Norms and Anti-Personnel Landmines', in C. Reus-Smit (ed.), *The Politics of International Law* (Cambridge: Cambridge University Press): 106–30.

—— and Reus-Smit, C. (1998), 'Dangerous Liaisons? Critical International Relations Theory and Constructivism', *European Journal of International Relations*, 4(2): 259–94.

—— and Tannenwald, N. (1996), 'Norms and Deterrence: The Nuclear and Chemical Weapons Taboos', in P. J. Katzenstein (ed.), *The Culture of National Security: Norms and Identity in World Politics* (New York: Columbia University Press): 114–52.

Prügl, E. (1999), *The Global Construction of Gender* (New York: Columbia University Press).

Pugh, M. (2001), 'Peacekeeping and Humanitarian Intervention', in B. White, R. Little, and M. Smith (eds), *Issues in World Politics*, 2nd edn (London: Palgrave).

Purvis, N. (1991), 'Critical Legal Studies in Public International Law', *Harvard International Law Journal*, 32(1): 81–127.

Rabasa, A., Chalk, P., *et al.* (2006), *Beyond al-Qaeda: Part 2, The Outer Rings of the Terrorist Universe* (Santa Monica, Cal.: RAND).

Ramsey, P. (2002), *The Just War: Force and Political Responsibility* (Lanham, Md.: Rowman & Littlefield).

Rapley, J. (1996), *Understanding Development* (Boulder, Col.: Lynne Rienner).

Rawls, J. (1971), *A Theory of Justice* (Oxford: Oxford University Press).

—— (1999), *The Law of Peoples* (Cambridge, Mass.: Harvard University Press).

Rehn, E., and Sirleaf, E. J. (2002), *Women, War, Peace: The Independent Experts' Assessment on the Impact of Armed Conflict on Women and Women's Role in Peace-Building,* available online at: http://www.unifem.org/resources/item_detail.php?ProductID=17, last accessed on 25 June 2007.

Reisman, W. M. (1985), 'Criteria for the Lawful use of Force in International Law', *Yale Journal of International Law* 10: 279–85.

Resolution adopted by the General Assembly, 24 October 2005: 60/1. 2005 World Summit Outcome, available online at: http://www.un.org/summit2005/documents.htm, last assessed on 25 June 2007.

Reus-Smit, C. (1999), *The Moral Purpose of the State* (Princeton, NJ: Princeton University Press).

—— (2001a), 'The Strange Death of Liberal International Theory', *European Journal of International Law*, 12(3): 573–93.

——(2001*b*), 'Human Rights and the Social Construction of Sovereignty', *Review of International Studies*, 27(4): 519–38.

——(2003), 'Politics and International Legal Obligation', *European Journal of International Relations*, 9(4): 591–625.

——(ed.) (2004), *The Politics of International Law* (Cambridge: Cambridge University Press).

Rhodes, E. (2003), 'The Imperial Logic of Bush's Liberal Agenda', *Survival*, 45: 131–54.

Rice, S. (2006), 'The Threat of Global Poverty', *The National Interest* (Spring): 76–82.

Richardson, J. l. (1997), 'Contending Liberalisms: Past and Present', *European Journal of International Relations*, 3(1): 5–33.

Roberts, A. (1993), 'Humanitarian War: Military Intervention and Human Rights', *International Affairs*, 69.

——(1996), 'The United Nations: Variants of Collective Security', in N. Woods (ed.), *Explaining International Relations since 1945* (Oxford: Oxford University Press): 309–36.

——and Kingsbury, B. (1993), 'Introduction: The UN's Roles in International Society since 1945', in A. Roberts and B. Kingsbury (eds), *United Nations, Divided World* (Oxford: Clarendon Press).

Roberts, G. (1984), *Questioning Development* (London: Returned Volunteer Action).

Roberts, S. (1994), 'Fictitious Capital, Fictitious Spaces: The Geography of Offshore Financial Flows', in S. Corbridge *et al.* (eds), *Money, Power and Space* (Oxford: Blackwell).

Robinson, W. I. (1996), *Promoting Polyarchy: Globalization, US Intervention, and Hegemony* (Cambridge: Cambridge University Press).

——(2004), *A Theory of Global Capitalism: Production, Class, and State in a Transnational World* (Baltimore, Md.: Johns Hopkins University Press).

Roche, D. (1986), 'Balance Out of Kilter in Arms/Society Needs', *The Financial Post* (Toronto), 18 January, p.8.

Rodrik, D. (1997), *Has Globalization Gone Too Far?* (Washington, DC: Institute for International Economics).

——(1999), *The New Global Economy and Developing Countries: Making Openness Work* (Washington, DC: Overseas Development Council): 148.

Rorty, R. (1993), 'Sentimentality and Human Rights', in S. Shute and S. Hurley (eds), *On Human Rights* (New York: Basic Books).

Rosamond, B. (2000), *Theories of European Integration* (Basingstoke: Macmillan).

Rose, G. (1998), 'Neoclassical Realism and Theories of Foreign Policy' *World Politics*, 51(1): 144–72.

Rosenau, J. N. (1997), 'The Dynamics of Globalization: Toward an Operational Formula', *Security Dialogue*, 27(3): 247–62.

Rosenberg, J. (1994), *The Empire of Civil Society: A Critique of the Realist Theory of International Relations* (London: Verso).

——(2000), *The Follies of Globalisation Theory: Polemical Essays* (London: Verso).

——(2006), 'Globalization Theory: A Postmortem', *International Politics*, 42(1): 2–74.

Rostow, W. (1960), *The Stages of Economic Growth: A Non-Communist Manifesto* (London: Cambridge University Press).

Roth, K. (2004*a*), 'The War in Iraq: Justified as Humanitarian Intervention?', Kroc Institute Occasional Paper No. 25 (Notre Dame, Ind.: The Joan B. Kroc Institute).

——(2004*b*), 'War in Iraq: Not a Humanitarian Intervention', *Human Rights Watch World Report*. Available online at: www.hrw.org/wr2k4/3.htm, last assessed on 25 June 2007.

Rousseau, J.-J. (1987), *The Basic Political Writings*, trans. Donald A. Cress (Cambridge: Hackett).

——(1991), 'The State of War', in S. Hoffmann and D. P. Fidler (eds), *Rousseau on International Relations* (Oxford: Clarendon Press).

Ruggie, J. G. (1993), 'Multilateralism: The Anatomy of an Institution', in J. G. Ruggie (ed.), *Multilateralism Matters* (New York: Columbia University Press): 3–50.

——(1998), *Constructing the World Polity: Essays on International Institutionalization* (London: Routledge).

Rupert, M. (1995), *Producing Hegemony: The Politics of Mass Production and American Global Power* (Cambridge: Cambridge University Press).

——(2000), *Ideologies of Globalization: Contending Vision of a New World Order* (London: Routledge).

——and Solomon, M. S. (2005), *Globalization and International Political Economy: The Politics of Alternative Futures* (Lanhan, Md.: Rowman & Littlefield).

Russett, B. (1993), *Grasping the Democratic Peace: Principles for a Post-Cold War World* (Princeton, NJ: Princeton University Press).

——(1995), 'The Democratic Peace', *International Security*, 19(4): 164–84.

Sagan, S. D., and Waltz, K. N. (1995, 2003), *The Spread of Nuclear Weapons: A Debate* (New York and London: W. W. Norton; 2nd edn, 2003).

Sageman, M. (2004), *Understanding Terror Networks* (Philadelphia: University of Pennsylvania Press).

Said, E. (1979), *Orientalism: Western Conceptions of the Orient* (London: Penguin).

——(1993), *Culture and Imperialism* (New York: Vintage Books).

Sargent, L. (ed.) (1981), *Women and Revolution: A Discussion of the Unhappy Marriage of Marxism and Feminism* (Boston, Mass.: South End).

Saurin, J. (1996), 'Globalisation, Poverty and the Promises of Modernity', *Millennium: Journal of International Studies*, 25(3): 657–80.

Schelling, T. C. (1960), *The Strategy of Conflict* (Oxford: Oxford University Press).

Scholte, J. A. (2000, 2005), *Globalization: A Critical Introduction* (Basingstoke: Macmillan; 2nd edn, 2005).

Schumacher, E. F. (1973), *Small is Beautiful: Economics as if People Mattered* (New York: Harper & Row).

Schwarz, A. (1999), *A Nation in Waiting: Indonesia's Search for Stability* (Sydney, NSW: Allen & Unwin).

Schweller, R. L. (1996), 'Neo-realism's Status-quo Bias: What Security Dilemma?', *Security Studies*, 5: 90–121.

——(1998), *Deadly Imbalances: Tripolarity and Hitler's Strategy of World Conquest* (New York: Columbia University Press).

Scruton, R. (2002), *The West and the Rest: Globalization and the Terrorist Threat* (London: Continuum).

Seidler, V. (1989), *Rediscovering Masculinity: Reason, Language and Sexuality* (London: Routledge).

Sen, A. (1981), *Poverty and Famines* (Oxford: Clarendon Press).

——(1983), 'The Food Problem: Theory and Policy', in A. Gauhar (ed.), *South–South Strategy* (London: Zed).

——(1999), *Development as Freedom* (Oxford: Oxford University Press).

Shaker, M. I. (1980), *The Nuclear Non-Proliferation Treaty*, Vols 1–2 (London: Oceana).

Shaw, M. (1997), 'The State of Globalization: Towards a Theory of State Transformation', *Review of International Political Economy*, 4(3).

Shaw, M. (1999), 'The Global Revolution and the Twenty-first Century: From International Relations to Global Politics', in S. Chan and J. Wiener (eds), *Twentieth Century International History* (London: I. B. Tauris).

—— (2000), *Theory of the Global State: Globality as an Unfinished Revolution* (Cambridge: Cambridge University Press).

—— (2003), *War and Genocide: Organized Killing in Modern Society* (Cambridge: Polity Press).

—— (ed.) (1984), *War, State, and Society* (New York: St Martins Press).

Shue, H. (1996), *Basic Rights*, 2nd edn (Princeton, NJ: Princeton University Press).

Simon, J. (1998), 'Refugees in a Carceral Age: The Rebirth of Immigration Prisons in the United States', *Public Culture*, 10(3): 577–607.

Singer, P. (1985), 'Famine, Affluence, Morality', in C. Beitz (ed.), *International Ethics* (Princeton, NJ: Princeton University Press).

—— (1999), 'The Singer Solution to World Poverty', *New York Times*, 5 July.

—— (2002), *One World: The Ethics of Globalisation* (Melbourne: Text Publishing).

—— and Gregg, T. (2004), *How Ethical is Australia: An Examination of Australia's Record as a Global Citizen* (Melbourne: The Australian Collaboration in conjunction with Black Inc.).

Singer, P. and Small, M. (1976), 'The war proneness of democratic regimes', *Jerusalem Journal of International Relations*, 11(4): 50–69.

Skoepol, T. (1979), *States and Social Revolutions: A Comparative Analysis of France, Russia, and China* (Cambridge: Cambridge University Press).

—— (1992), *Protecting Soldiers and Mothers* (Cambridge, Mass.: Harvard University Press).

—— (ed.) (1984), *Vision and Method in Historical Sociology* (Cambridge: Cambridge University Press).

Slaughter, A. (1995), 'International Law in a World of Liberal States', *European Journal of International Law*, 6.

—— (2000), 'A Liberal Theory of International Law' (unpublished manuscript).

—— (2004), *A New World Order* (Princeton, NJ: Princeton University Press).

Smith, A. D. (1986), *The Ethnic Origins of Nations* (Oxford: Blackwell).

Smith, D. (1991), *The Rise of Historical Sociology* (Cambridge: Polity Press).

Smith, K. E., and Light, M. (eds) (2001), *Ethics and Foreign Policy* (Cambridge: Cambridge University Press).

Smith, M. (1986), *Realist Thought from Weber to Kissinger* (Baton Rouge, La.: Louisiana State University Press).

—— (2002), 'On Thin Ice: First Steps for the Ballistic Missile Code of Conduct', *Arms Control Today*, 32(6) (July): 9–13.

Smith, S. (1999), 'The Increasing Insecurity of Security Studies: Conceptualising Security in the Last Twenty Years', *Contemporary Security Policy*, 20(3) (Dec.).

—— (2000), 'Wendt's World', *Review of International Studies*, 26(1): 151–63.

Snyder, J. (1991), *Myths of Empire: Domestic Politics and International Ambition* (Ithaca, NY: Cornell University Press).

Spivak, G. C. (1987), *In Other Worlds: Essays in Cultural Politics* (London: Routledge).

—— (1988), 'Can the Subaltern Speak?', in C. Nelson and L. Grossberg (eds), *Marxism and the Interpretation of Culture* (Basingstoke: Macmillan).

—— (1998), 'Cultural Talks on the Hot Peace: Revisiting the "Global Village" ', in P. Cheah and B. Robbins (eds), *Cosmopolitics: Thinking and Feeling Beyond the Nation* (Minneapolis: University of Minnesota Press).

Stanlis, P. J. (1953) 'Edmund Burke and the Law of Nations', *American Journal of International Law*, 47(3): 404–5.

Steans, J. (1998), *Gender and International Relations: An Introduction* (Cambridge: Polity Press).

Stein, A. (1983), 'Coordination and Collaboration in an Anarchic World', in S. D. Krasner (ed.), *International Regimes* (Ithaca, NY: Cornell University Press): 115–40.

Stiglitz, J. (1998), 'Towards a New Paradigm for Development: Strategies, Policies and Processes', The Prebisch Lecture (Geneva, UNCTAD, 19 October). Available online at: http:siteresources.worldbank.org/CDF/Resources/prebisch98.pdf, last assessed on 25 June 2007.

Stubbs, R. (2002), 'Review of "The Many Faces of Asian Security"' (ed. Sheldon W. Simon), *Contemporary South-East Asia*, 24: 1.

Suganami, H. (1989), *The Domestic Analogy and World Order Proposals* (Cambridge: Cambridge University Press).

Suhrke, A. (2004), 'A Stalled Initiative', *Security Dialogue*, 35(3): 365.

T   Tang, J. H. (ed.) (1994), *Human Rights and International Relations in the Asia-Pacific Region* (London: Pinter).

Tannenwald, N. (1999), 'The Nuclear Taboo: The United States and the Normative Basis of Nuclear Non-Use', *International Organization*, 53(3): 433–68.

Taylor, A. J. P. (1961), *The Origins of the Second World War* (Harmondsworth: Penguin).

Terriff, T., Croft, S., James, L., and Morgan, P. (1999), *Security Studies Today* (Cambridge: Polity Press).

Teschke, B. (2003), *The Myth of 1648: Class, Geopolitics and the Making of Modern International Relations* (London: Verso).

Tesón, F. (2003), 'The Liberal Case for Humanitarian Intervention', in J. L. Holzgrefe and R. O. Keohane (eds), *Humanitarian Intervention: Ethical, Legal and Political Dilemmas* (Cambridge: Cambridge University Press): 93–129.

—— (2005), 'Ending Tyranny in Iraq', *Ethics and International Affairs*, 19(2): 1–20.

The Ottawa Citizen (1998), 'Canada, Norway change their ways: New approach bases foreign policy on human issues', *The Ottawa Citizen*, 28 May, p. A18.

Thomas, A., *et al.* (1994), *Third World Atlas*, 2nd edn (Milton Keynes: Open University Press).

Thomas, C. (1985), *New States, Sovereignty and Intervention* (Aldershot: Gower).

—— (1993), 'The Pragmatic Case against Intervention', in I. Forbes and M. Hoffmann (eds), *Political Theory, International Relations and the Ethics of Intervention* (Basingstoke: St Martins Press).

—— (1999), 'Where is the Third World Now?', *Review of International Studies*, December, special millennium edition.

—— (2000), *Global Governance, Development and Human Security* (London: Pluto).

—— and Wilkin, P. (2004), 'Still Waiting after All These Years: The Third World on the Periphery of International Relations', *British Journal of Politics and International Relations*, 6: 223–40.

Thucydides ([1954] 1972), *The Peloponnesian War*, trans. R. Warner (London: Penguin).

Tickner, J. A. (1988), 'Hans Morgenthau's Principles of Political Realism: A Feminist Reformulation', *Millennium*, 17(3): 429–40.

—— (1992), *Gender in International Relations: Feminist Perspectives on Achieving Global Security* (New York: Columbia University Press).

—— (2002), 'Feminist Perspectives on 9/11', *International Studies Perspectives*, 3(4): 333–50.

Tilly, C. (1975), 'Reflections on the history of European state-making', in C. Tilly (ed.), *The Formation of National States in Western Europe* (Princeton, NJ: Princeton University Press).

—— (1981), *As Sociology Meets History* (New York: Academic Press).

—— (1990), *Coercion, Capital, and European States, AD 990–1990* (Oxford: Blackwell).

—— (1992), *Coercion, Capital and European States, AD 900–1992* (Cambridge, Mass.: Blackwell).

—— (1995), 'States and Nationalism in Europe, 1492–1992', in J. M. Comaroff and P. C. Stern (eds), *Perspectives on Nationalism* (Amsterdam: Gordon and Breach Science Publishers).

Toffler, A., and Toffler, H. (1993), *War and Anti-War* (Boston: Little, Brown).

Tow, W. T., and Trood, R. (2000), 'Linkages between Traditional Security and Human Security', in W. T. Tow, R. Thakur, and In-Taek Hyun (eds), *Asia's Emerging Regional Order* (New York: United Nations University Press): 14.

True, J. (2003), 'Mainstreaming Gender in Global Public Policy', *International Feminist Journal of Politics*, 5(3): 368–96.

Tucker, R. W. (1977), *The Inequality of Nations* (New York: Basic Books).

U **UN** (1999), *1999 World Survey on the Role of Women in Development: Globalization, Gender and Work* (New York: United Nations).

—— (2002), *Women, Peace and Security: Study Submitted by the Secretary-General Pursuant to Security Council Resolution 1325 (2000)* (New York: United Nations). Available online at: http://www.un.org/womenwatch/feature/wps/, last accessed on 25 June 2007.

—— (2005) *In Larger Freedom: Towards Development, Security and Human Rights for All: Report of the Secretary-General*, March.

—— (2006) *The Millennium Development Goals Report: Statistical Annex 2006* (New York: United Nations): 10.

—— (n.d.), Peacekeeping, http://www.un.org/Depts/dpko/dpko, last accessed 25 June 2007.

UN Commission on Human Security (2003), *Human Security Now: Protecting and Empowering People* (New York: United Nations): 4. Available online: http://www.humansecurity-chs.org, Date accessed 8 April 2007.

UNCTAD, Division on Transnational Corporations and Investment (1995), *World Investment Report 1995* (New York: United Nations Conference on Trade and Development).

—— (1996), *Transnational Corporations and World Development* (London: International Thomson Business Press).

—— (1999), *World Investment Report 1999: Foreign Direct Investment and the Challenge of Development* (Geneva: United Nations Conference on Trade and Development).

—— (2006a), *Trade and Development Report* (Geneva: United Nations Conference on Trade and Development).

—— (2006b), *World Investment Report 2006* (Geneva: United Nations Conference on Trade and Development).

UNDP (1994), *United Nations Human Development Report* (New York: Oxford University Press).

—— (1995), *United Nations Human Development Report 1994,* as cited in the Report of the Commission on Global Governance, *Our Global Neighbourhood* (Oxford: Oxford University Press).

—— (1997) *United Nations Human Development Report 1997* (New York: United Nations Development Programme).

—— (1998) *United Nations Human Development Report 1998* (Oxford: Oxford University Press).

—— (2003), *United Nations Human Development Report* (New York: United Nations Development Programme).

—— (2005), *Human Development Report 2005: International Co-operation at a Crossroads* (New York: United Nations Development Programme).

—— (2006a), *Human Development Report 2006: Beyond Scarcity: Power, Poverty and the Global Water Crisis* (New York: United Nations Development Programme).

—— (2006b), *Global Partnership for Development: United Nations Development Program Annual Report* (New York: United Nations Development Programme).

United Nations High-Level Panel on Threats, Challenges and Change (2004), *A More Secure World: Our Shared Responsibility*, A/59/565, December (New York: United Nations).

United Nations Human Development Commission (2003), *United Nations Human Development Report,* available online at: http://hdr.undp.org/reports/global/2003/, last accessed 25 June 2007.

United Nations Inter-Agency Committee on Women and Gender Equality (1999), *Final Communiqué, Women's Empowerment in the Context of Human Security* (7–8 December 1999, ESCAP, Bangkok, Thailand). Available online at: http://www.un.org/womenwatch/ianwge/collaboration/finalcomm1999.htm, last accessed 25 June 2007.

University of British Columbia, Human Security Center (2005), *Human Security Report 2005: War and Peace in the 21st Century* (New York: Oxford University Press).

—— (2006), *The Human Security Brief 2006*, available online at: http://www.humansecuritybrief.info/, last accessed on 25 June 2007.

US Department of State (2003), *Country Reports on Human Rights Practices, Burma,* 31 March 2003, available online at: http://www.state.gov/g/drl/rls/hrrpt/2002/18237.htm, last accessed on 25 June 2007.

V **Van Rooy, A.** (2003), *The Global Legitimacy Game: Civil Society, Globalization, and Protest* (Basingstoke: Palgrave).

Vincent, R. J. (1974), *Nonintervention and International Order* (Princeton, NJ: Princeton University Press).

—— (1986), *Human Rights and International Relations* (Cambridge: Cambridge University Press).

Viotti, P. R., and Kauppi, M. V. (eds) (1999), *International Relations Theory: Realism, Pluralism, Globalism and Beyond* (Boston: Allyn and Bacon).

Vitalis, R. (2000), 'The Graceful and Generous Liberal Gesture: Making Racism Invisible in American International Relations', *Millennium*, 29(2): 331–56.

Von Martens, G. F. (1795), *Summary of the Law of Nations Founded on the Treaties and Customs of Modern Nations* (Philadelphia: Thomas Bradford).

W **Waever, O., Buzan, B., Kelstrup, M., and Lemaitre, P.** (1993), *Identity, Migration and the New Security Agenda in Europe* (London: Pinter).

Walker, R. B. J. (1993), *Inside/Outside: International Relations as Political Theory* (Cambridge: Cambridge University Press).

Waller, M., and Linklater, A. (eds) (2003), *Political Loyalty and the Nation-State* (London: Routledge).

Wallerstein, I. (1974), *The Modern World-System.* Vol. 1, *Capitalist Agriculture and the Origins of the European World-Economy in the Sixteenth Century* (San Diego, Cal.: Academic Press).

—— (1979), *The Capitalist World-Economy* (Cambridge: Cambridge University Press).

Wallerstein, I. (1984), *The Politics of the World-Economy: The States, the Movements, and the Civilisations* (Cambridge: Cambridge University Press).

—— (1991), *Unthinking Social Science: The Limits of Nineteenth-Century Paradigms* (Cambridge: Polity Press).

—— (1995), *After Liberalism* (New York: New Press).

—— (1998), *Utopistics: Or Historical Choices of the Twenty-First Century* (New York: New Press).

—— (1999), *The End of the World as We Know it: Social Science for the Twenty-first Century* (Minneapolis: University of Minnesota Press).

—— (2003), *The Decline of American Power: The US in a Chaotic World* (New York: New Press).

—— (2004), *Alternatives: The United States Confronts the World* (London: Paradigm).

—— (2006), *European Universalism: The Rhetoric of Power* (New York: New Press).

Waltz, K. (1954), *Man, the State and War* (New York: Columbia University Press).

—— (1959), *Man, the State and War* (New York: Columbia University Press).

—— (1979), *Theory of International Politics* (Reading, Mass.: Addison-Wesley).

—— (1989), 'The Origins of War in Neorealist Theory', in R. I. Rotberg and T. K. Rabb (eds), *The Origin and Prevention of Major Wars* (Cambridge: Cambridge University Press): 39–52.

—— (2000), 'Globalization and American Power', *The National Interest*, 59 (Spring): 46–56.

—— (2002), 'The Continuity of International Politics', in K. Booth and T. Dunne (eds), *Worlds in Collision: Terror and the Future of Global Order* (London: Palgrave Macmillan).

Walzer, M. (1977), *Just and Unjust Wars: A Moral Argument with Historical Illustration* (Harmondsworth: Penguin, and New York: Basic Books).

—— (1983, 1995a), *The Spheres of Justice: A Defence of Pluralism and Equality* (Oxford: Blackwell).

—— (1994), *Thick and Thin: Moral Argument at Home and Abroad* (Notre Dame, Ind.: University of Notre Dame Press).

—— (1995b), 'The Politics of Rescue', *Dissent* (Winter).

Weber, C. (1995), *Simulating Sovereignty: Intervention, the State and Symbolic Exchange* (Cambridge: Cambridge University Press).

Weber, H. (2001), *The Politics of Microcredit: Global Governance and Poverty Reduction* (London: Pluto).

—— (2002), 'Global Governance and Poverty Reduction', in S. Hughes and R. Wilkinson (eds), *Global Governance: Critical Perspectives* (London: Palgrave): ch. 8.

Weber, M. (1949), *The Methodology of the Social Sciences*, ed. E. Shils and H. Finch (New York: Free Press).

Webster (1961), *Webster's Third New International Dictionary of the English Language Unabridged* (Springfield, Mass.: Merriam).

Weismann, D. (2006), *Global Hunger Index 2006: A Basis for Cross-country Comparisons*, Issue Brief 47 (Washington, DC: International Food Policy Research Institute). Available online at: http://www.ifpri.org/pubs/ib/ib47.pdf, last accessed on 25 June 2007.

Weiss, L. (1998), *The Myth of the Powerless State* (Ithaca, NY: Cornell University Press).

—— (1999), 'Globalization and Governance', *Review of International Studies*, 25 (Special Issue).

Weiss, T. G. (1999), *Military–Civil Interactions: Intervening in Humanitarian Crises* (Lanham, Md.: Rowman & Littlefield).

—— (2004), 'The Sunset of Humanitarian Intervention? The Responsibility to Protect in a Unipolar Era', *Security Dialogue*, 35(2):135–53.

—— *et al.* (1994), *The United Nations and Changing World Politics* (Boulder, Col.: Westview Press).

Welsh, J. (ed.) (2003), *Humanitarian Intervention and International Relations* (Oxford: Oxford University Press).

Weltman, J. J. (1995), *World Politics and the Evolution of War* (Baltimore, Md. and London: Johns Hopkins University Press).

Wendt, A. (1992), 'Anarchy is What States Make of It: The Social Construction of Power Politics', *International Organisation*, 46(2): 391–425.

—— (1995), 'Constructing International Politics', *International Security*, 20(1).

—— (1999), *Social Theory of International Politics* (Cambridge: Cambridge University Press).

Wessel, I., and Wimhofer, G. (eds) (2001), *Violence in Indonesia* (Hamburg: Abera-Verl).

Weston, B. H., Falk, R., and D'Amato, A. (1990), *Basic Documents in International Law*, 2nd edn (St Paul, Minn.: West Publishing).

Wheeler, N. J. (2000), *Saving Strangers: Humanitarian Intervention in International Society* (Oxford: Oxford University Press).

—— (2003), 'The Humanitarian Responsibilities of Sovereignty', in J. Welsh, *Humanitarian Intervention and International Relations* (Oxford: Oxford University Press).

—— (2004a), 'Humanitarian Intervention after September 11', in A. Lang (ed.), *Just Intervention* (Georgetown: Georgetown University Press).

—— (2004b), 'The Kosovo Bombing Campaign', in C. Reus-Smit (ed.), *The Politics of International Law* (Cambridge: Cambridge University Press): 189–216.

—— and Booth, K. (1992), 'The Security Dilemma', in J. Baylis and N. J. Rengger (eds), *Dilemmas of World Politics: International Issues in a Changing World* (Oxford: Oxford University Press).

—— —— and Dunne, T. (2004), 'Moral Britannia: Evaluating the Ethical Dimension in Britain's Foreign Policy', *Foreign Policy Centre*, 26 April.

—— and Morris, J. (2006), 'Justifying Iraq as a Humanitarian Intervention: The Cure is Worse than the Disease', in R. Thakur and W. P. S. Sidhu (eds), *The Iraq Crisis and World Order: Structural, Institutional and Normative Challenges* (Tokyo: United Nations University Press).

Whitworth, S. (1994), *Feminism and International Relations: Towards a Political Economy of Gender in Inter-state and Non-Governmental Institutions* (Basingstoke: Macmillan).

Whyte, A. F. (1919), *The Practice of Diplomacy*, trans. of François de Callière's *De la manière de négocier avec les souverains* (London: Constable & Co).

Wiener, A., and Diez, T. (eds) (2004), *European Integration Theory* (Oxford: Oxford University Press).

Wight, M. (1977), *Systems of States* (Leicester: Leicester University Press).

Wilkinson, P. (2003), 'Implications of the Attacks of 9/11 for the Future of Terrorism', in M. Buckley and R. Fawn (eds), *Global Responses to Terrorism* (London: Routledge).

Williams, M. C. (2005), *The Realist Tradition and the Limits of International Relations* (Cambridge: Cambridge University Press).

—— (ed.) (2007) *Realism Reconsidered: The Legacy of Hans Morgenthau in International Relations* (Oxford: Oxford University Press)

Wippman, D. (2004), 'The International Criminal Court', in C. Reus-Smit (ed.), *The Politics of International Law* (Cambridge: Cambridge University Press): 151–88.

Wohlforth, W. (1993), *The Elusive Balance: Power and Perceptions during the Cold War* ((Ithaca, NY: Cornell University Press).

Wolfensohn, J. (1995), 'President Wolfensohn's speech at the 1995 Beijing Conference', available online at: www.worldbank.org/gender/how/policy.htm, last accessed on 25 June 2007.

——and Bourguignon, F. (2004), 'Development and Poverty Reduction: Looking Back, Looking Ahead', May 2004, prepared for the 2004 Annual Meetings of the World Bank and IMF, available online at: http://www.worldbank.org/ambc/lookingbacklookingahead.pdf, last accessed on 25 June 2007.

World Bank (2000), *Addressing Gender Equity: World Bank Action since Beijing* (Washington, DC: World Bank).

——(2005), *Global Economic Prospects 2005: Trade, Regionalism and Development* (Washington, DC: World Bank).

——(2006) *World Development Indicators, 2006* (Washington, DC: World Bank).

World Commission on the Social Dimensions of Globalization (2004), *A Fair Globalization: Creating Opportunities for All* (Geneva: International Labour Organization).

World Health Organization (n.d.), *Roll Back Malaria: The Economic Costs of Malaria* (Geneva: WHO). Available online at: http://www.rbm.who.int/cmc_upload/0/000/015/363/RBMInfosheet_10.htm, last accessed on 25 June 2007.

——(2006), *Avian Influenza ('Bird Flu')—Fact Sheet* (February 2006), www.who.int/mediacentre/factsheets/avian_influenza/en/. Last accessed 25 June 2007.

World Trade Organization (1995), *International Trade: Trends and Statistics* (Geneva: WTO).

Worsley, P. (1980), 'One World or Three? A Critique of the World-System Theory of Immanuel Wallerstein', *Socialist Register* (London: Merlin Press).

Wright, Q. (1965), *A Study of War* (Chicago: Chicago University Press).

Wright, R. (1986), *Sacred Rage: The Wrath of Militant Islam* (New York: Simon & Schuster).

Y Yale University Cambodian Genocide Program website, http://www.yale.edu/cgp, last accessed 25 June 2007.

Young, I. M. (1990), *Justice and the Politics of Difference* (Princeton, NJ: Princeton University Press).

Z Zacher, M. W., with Sutton, B. A. (1996), *Governing Global Networks: International Regimes for Transportation and Communications* (Cambridge: Cambridge University Press).

Zakaria, F. (1998), *From Wealth to Power: The Unusual Origins of America's World Role* (Princeton, NJ: Princeton University Press).

Zalewski, M. (1993a), 'Feminist Standpoint Theory Meets International Relations Theory: A Feminist Version of David and Goliath', *Fletcher Forum of World Affairs*, 17(2).

——and Parpart, J. (eds) (1998), *The 'Man' Question in International Relations* (Boulder, Col.: Westview Press).

Zevin, R. (1992), 'Are World Financial Markets More Open? If So, Why and With What Effects?', in T. Banuri and J. B. Schor (eds), *Financial Openness and National Autonomy: Opportunities and Constraints* (Oxford: Clarendon Press).

Zurn, M. (2004), 'Global Governance and Legitimacy Problems', *Government and Opposition*, 39(2).

INDEX

Numbers in bold denote major section devoted to the subject.

A

Aarhus Convention on Access to Information in Environmental Matters ···········354
Abbott, K. ···290, 437
Abu-Lughold, Janet ·····························149
Abuja Treaty ···442
accountability ·························11, 31, 569–70
Acharya, Amitav ·····························494, 501
acid rain ··354, 356
Adams, N.B. ··476
Adler, E. ···392
  and Barnett, M. ·······························437
Adorno, Theodor ···································153
advocacy networks ···············135, 136, 341
Afghanistan ··571
  and Islamic terrorism ·······················429
  Soviet Union action (1979) ··············64
  US action (2001) ·········217, 269, 323, 532
Africa
  conflict management ·······················442
  GDP ··476, 477
  regional integration ·······················441–2
  sub-Saharan ···········472, 476, 477, 487
  see also South Africa
Africa Emerging Markets Fund ···········461
African Charter on Human and Peoples'
  Rights ··508
African Economic
  Community ····································442
African Union (AU) ···········26, 442, 534
Age of Absolutism ·························283, 285
Agnew, John ··422
agriculture ·····························17, 272, 486
Ahmadinejad, Mahmoud ·····················430
aid see humanitarian aid
Aidid, General Mohammed
  Farah ··531
AIDS ·························25, 478, 499, 501, 503
air pollution ·····················352, 354, 356, 501
air travel ·······································374, 381
Albania ···444, 529
Albrow, M. ···568
Alexander, Y. with Levanthal, P. ·········394
Alexandrowicz, C.H. ·····························45
Algeria ·····································59, 60, 424
Alliance of Small Island States ···········363
Allison, Graham ·····················132, 389
Alperovitz, Gar ······································58
Amazon forest ·······································479
American International Group ·············458
American War of Independence ···········40
Amnesty International ·······26, 50, 345, 503
Amsterdam Treaty (1997) ····················445
Amstutz, Dan ···486

anarchy
  and collaboration ················297, 303–4
  and constructivism ···························165
  double reading ································187
  and neo-neo debate ···········127, 129, 134
  realist concept of ·····························93
Ancient Greece ·····················41, 96–8, 545
ancient world ·································39–42
Andean Community
  of Nations (CAN) ···························441
Anderson, Benedict ·····························405
Angola ···························59, 64, 220, 538
Annan, Kofi
  and genocide ··························524, 526
  and human security ·························493
  threats to global peace ·····················321
  and UN reform ·······························327
  and women ·····································500
Antarctica ·························354, 358, 359
Anti-Apartheid Movement ····················345
appeasement ··57
Apple ··19
Arab Maghreb Union ·····························442
Arab nationalism ·························167, 426
Arab–Israeli war ····································64
Archibugi, Danielle ······························119
Arendt, Hannah ·····································181
Argentina ·························440, 459, 537
Aristotle ···545
Armenia ··443, 444
arms control ·····················66, 301, 305, 493
arms race ···62
  see also nuclear weapons
arms trade ······································213, 224
Armstrong, K. ·································49, 424
Aron, Raymond ·····································221
ASEAN (Association of South-East Asian
  Nations) ·····················26, 80, 442–3
Ashley, Richard ·············185, 186, 187, 554
Asia ···442–3
  financial crisis
  (1997–8) ·······254, 255, 256, 459, 501
  see also Eurasia; South-East Asia
Asia Pacific Cooperation (APEC) ·········443
Asian values ··························510, 517, 518
Assyrian Empire ···································545
Atta, Mohammed ··································381
Augsburg Treaty ···································282
Australia ···364, 537
autonomy ····································23–4, 28
avian influenza ·····························499, 501
Axford, B. ···421
axis of evil ··429
Axworthy, Lloyd ···································495
Ayson, R. ···389
Azerbaijan ···444

B

baby milks ··343
Bakker, E. ···377
balance of power
  and constructivism ···························163
  definition ····································5, 94
  and international society ···············44–8
  and stability ·······························102, 128
  Third World ·······························305, 307
Baldwin, David ·····························126, 131
Bali bombing ··17
Ban, Ki-Moon ·······································317
Bangkok Declaration ·····························518
Bangladesh ···········272, 483, 484, 547, 549
Banjul Charter ································508–9
Bank for International
  Settlements (BIS) ·····························452
banking ·······························455–6, 460
  Basle Committee rules ·······336, 452, 465
Barber, Benjamin ·············422, 429–30, 570
Barings Bank ···462
Barkawi, Tarak and Laffey, M. ·············188
Barker, D. and Mander, J. ····················136
Barnett, M. with Adler, E. ····················437
Barraclough, G. ·····································454
Bartelson, Jens ·····································185
Basel Action Network ····························129
Basle Committee on Banking
  Supervision ·····················336, 452, 465
Basle Convention on hazardous waste ······302
Battle of the Sexes game theory ·········306–7
Bauman, Z. ···569
Baylis, John and O'Neill, R. ··················398
Beitz, Charles ·················196, 203, 204, 320
Belarus ···443, 444
Bellamy, A.J. ···············529, 533, 535, 536
Bello, W. ···472
Benetton ···458
Benin ···441
Bennett, J. and George, S. ····················485
Bentham, Jeremy ···········112, 113, 511–12
Berger, Thomas ······································81
Bergsten, C.F. ··438
Berlin ···61, 63
Best, E. ···437
Bethell, L. ···322
Bhabha, Homi K. ···································188
Bhopal chemical disaster ·····················354
Bin Laden, Osama ·········83–4, 376, 377, 428
biological diversity ············302, 325, 354, 357
biological weapons ················66, 375, 382, 390
biotechnology ······································357
bipolarity ···72, 562
  see also cold war
Black Sea Economic Cooperation (BSEC) ····444
Blair, Tony ·····················74, 85, 526, 532, 535
Bloom, M. ···378

Bodin, Jean ·· 282, 545
Body Shop ·· 458
Bohlen, A. ·· 389
Bolívar, Simon ··· 438
Bolivia ·· 136, 441
Bollywood ··· 423
Booth, Ken ························· 154, 518, 564
 with Dunne, T. ·············· 104, 118, 240
 with Wheeler, N.J. ·············· 102, 229
Borneo ·· 442
Bosch, O. and Van Ham, P. ············· 391
Bosnia ················· 223, 235, 237, 268, 324
Bosnia and Herzegovina ·················· 268
Botswana ·· 441
Boutros-Ghali, Boutros ············· 320, 321
Bracken, P. ·· 389
branded goods ··· 422
Brandt Report ·· 247
Brandt, Willy ··· 63
Brass, Paul ··· 405
Braun, L. ··· 182
Brazil ······················ 438, 440, 459, 476, 483
Breman, J.G. ·· 499
Bretherton, C. and Ponton, G. ········· 238
Bretton Woods Campaign ················· 481
Bretton Woods system ·········· 244, 245, 246
Brewer, A. ··· 147
Brezhnev doctrine ····································· 65
bribery ·· 336
Bright, John ·· 512
Bristol-Meyers ·· 343
Britain ·················· 59, 304, 406–7, 407
Brittan, A. ·· 181
Brocklehurst, Helen ································ 222
Brodie, Bernard ·· 392
Brown, Chris ··· 24
Brown, D. ·· 497
Brown, L.R. and Kane, H. ···················· 478
Brown, S. ·· 306
Brownlie, I. ··· 526
Brundtland Commission ·········· 354, 355, 493
Brunei ·· 501
Buddhism ··· 420
Bulgaria ·· 529
Bull, Hedley ··················· 9, 38, 200, 214,
 280, 552, 569
Burke, Edmund ·· 46
Burkina Faso ·· 441
Burma (Myanmar) ·················· 59, 443, 501
Burnham, P. ·· 150
Burtles, G. ·· 137
Burton, John ··· 9
Burundi ·· 321, 442
Bush, President George
 (senior) ····························· 66, 115, 563
Bush, President George W. ·········· 117–18,
 218, 270, 299, 364, 532, 565
Butterfield, Herbert ·························· 98, 239
Buvinic, M. ·· 470

Buzan, Barry ·················· 229, 230, 393, 494
 with Little, R. ··································· 39–40
Byers, M. ··· 283
Byzantine Empire ······································· 42
Callière, François de ···················· 46
Cambodia ········· 64, 443, 501, 527, 571
Camdessus, Michael ······························ 487
Cameroon ··· 59
Cammack, P. ··· 476
Campbell, David ···································· 185–6
Campbell, K.M., Einhorn, R.J.,
 and Reiss, M.B. ································ 393
Campbell Soup ··· 458
Canada ···················· 320, 493, 495, 503, 537
Caney, S. ··· 526
Cape Verde ··· 59, 64
capital flows see financial flows
capitalism ··························· 82, 115, 144–5,
 147, 155, 422, 546
carbon emissions ···································· 352
Cardoso, Henrique Fernando ············· 147
Caribbean ··· 472
Carius, A. with Petzold-Bradley, E. ····· 499
Carlos the Jackal ···································· 375
Carpenter, Charli ····································· 166
Carr, E.H. ······························· 92, 98, 199
Carson, Rachel, Silent Spring ············· 355
Cartagena Protocol ································· 357
Carter, President Jimmy ··························· 64
Carver, T. ·· 181
Castells, M. ··· 22
Castles, S. ··· 189
Castro, Fidel ······································· 63, 67
categorical imperative ···························· 197
Catholic Church ···································· 43, 45
Cayman Islands ······································· 460
Central Africa ··· 441
Central African Republic ························· 59
Central America ································ 438, 440
Central Asian Commonwealth ············ 444
Chad ·· 59
Chalk, P. ··· 383
 with Rabasa, A. ································ 377
Chase-Dunn, Christopher ············· 149, 157
Chavez, Hugo ··· 136
Chechnya ····················· 79, 224, 429, 503
chemical industry ······························ 354, 360
chemical weapons ············· 66, 289, 382, 390
Chernobyl nuclear accident ··········· 68, 388
Chesterman, S. ····················· 526, 527, 532
Chetley, A. ·· 343
children
 employment ·· 26
 mortality ······························· 2, 146, 478
 refugees ·· 277
 in war ··················· 222, 235, 268, 497–8
China
 and climate change ···························· 363
 cultural influence ······························· 423

China—Cont.
 economy ··············· 19, 81, 82, 105, 248,
  476, 477, 565
 and EU ··· 78
 Falun Gong cult ·································· 420
 history ························· 42, 57, 58, 61
 and human rights ························· 509, 514
 and humanitarian intervention ··· 530, 537
 and Kosovo ··· 535
 nuclear weapons ···················· 391, 397, 399
 outsourcing ·································· 19, 272
 population growth ······························ 483
 poverty ··· 472
 and regional integration ············· 443, 444
 and Soviet Union ································· 63
 and Sudan ·· 534
 and Taiwan ··· 80
 and US ··· 63, 509
Ching, F. ··· 501
Chipko movement ··································· 479
Chirac, President Jacques ····················· 105
chlorofluorocarbons (CFCs) ················· 360
 see also greenhouse gases
Chowdhry, G. and Nair, S. ··················· 189
Christensen, Thomas ······························ 231
 Jørgensen, K.E. and Wiener, A. ········ 446
Christianity ··· 42–3, 420
cinema ··· 422, 423
citizenship ············· 547–8, 550, 554, 565
civil aviation ·································· 306–7, 383
 see also hijacking
civil society
 achievements ······································ 119
 dispersal of values ······························ 150
 global ································· 26–7, 556, 570
 as source of change ···························· 344
 and the state ······································· 333
civil war ····················· 222–3, 237, 497, 538
 UN peacekeeping ······················· 319–20, 321
civilization ··········· 376, 421, 424, 430, 512, 513
 clash of civilizations ··········· 50, 85, 376, 422,
  424–6, 548
claim rights ··· 511
Clark, Ian ··· 47, 237
classical realism ·································· 95–8
Clausewitz, Carl von ················· 213, 214, 216
Clearstream/Cedel ·································· 461
Clement, Grace ·· 551
Climate Action Network ·························· 17
climate change ························· 198, **361–4**
 UN Framework Convention
  (UNFCCC) ········· 299, 325, 354, 362–4
Clinton, President Bill ·········· 24, 233, 269, 299
Cobban, A. and Hunt, J.W. ···················· 46
Cobden, Richard ······················· 111, 113, 512
cobweb model of world politics ············· 9
Coca-Cola ··· 422, 458
coffee sector ·· 474
Cohen, William ·· 217

Colas, A. — 570
cold war — **60–8**
  in Asia — 61
  crises — 63, 65, 67, 68
  deaths — 72
  and decolonisation — 67
  failure to predict end of — 73
  and globalization — 74–5, 567–9
  and human rights — 566–7
  independence movements — 60
  link to post-cold war — 562–3, 566–7
  in Middle East — 61–2
  military build-up — 62
  and nation-states — 410–12
  and nuclear weapons — 56, 62–3, 65–8, 73, 410–11
  origins — 60–1, 67
  permanent character — 72–3
  and religion — 565
  'second' cold war — 65
  and Third World — 410–11, 475
  and UN — 48
Collective Security Treaty Organization (CSTO) — 443
Colombia — 381, 537
colonialism — 188, 408, 410, 546
  see also decolonization; post-colonialism
Commonwealth of Independent States (CIS) — 443, 472
communication
  and language — 306–7
  regimes — 298, 302, 307
  skills — 342–3
  technological advances in — 9, 10, 17, 252, 380
communism — 74, 80, 144, 345, 409, 410
communitarianism — 195, 554, 556
community — 544
  see also political community
Concert of Europe — 47, 301
Conference on Security and Cooperation in Europe (CSCE) — 493, 503
Confucius — 40
Congo, Democratic Republic — 223, 238, 497, 498, 538
Connell, R.W. — 181
Connor, Walker — 405
constitutive theory — 176–7
constructivism — 6, **161–72**
  and anarchy — 165
  and balance of power — 163
  and causality — 166
  cold war confrontation — 73
  feminist constructivism — 267
  and global change — 168–71
  and globalization — 7
  and holism — 162–3
  and idealism — 162–3
  and international law — 290–1

constructivism—Cont.
  international political economy — 257–8
  logic of appropriateness — 163
  logic of consequences — 163
  and neo-liberal institutionalism — 161, 162
  and neo-realism — 161, 162
  and rational choice — 162, 163, 167
  and security — 234–5
  as social theory — 162, 171
consumerism — 422–3
containment policy — 61
Convention against Torture and Other Cruel, Inhuman or Degrading Treatment or Punishment — 508, 553
Convention on Biological Diversity — 302, 325, 354, 357
Convention on the Elimination of Discrimination against Women (CEDAW) — 274, 508, 516
Convention on International Trade in Endangered Species (CITES) — 354, 356
Convention on Long-Range Transboundary Air Pollution (LRTAP) — 354, 356
Convention on the Prevention and Punishment of the Crime of Genocide — 508, 518
Cooper, Richard — 9
Corbridge, Stewart — 422
cosmopolitan democracy — 30–1, 119, 550–1
cosmopolitanism — **194–9**, 554–5
Costa Rica — 440
Côte d'Ivoire — 441, 442
Council of Constance — 40, 45
Council of Europe — 345, 514
Council of Ministers — 446
Court of Auditors — 446
Coventry — 58
Cox, Michael — 73, 240
Cox, Robert W. — 150–1, 235
Crawford, N. — 188
credit cards — 459, 462
Crenshaw, Martha — 373
crime — 223, 337–9
Crimean War — 40
critical security studies — 154, 235
critical theory — 151, 153–4, 235
Croatia — 220, 537
Cronin, Audrey Kurth — 372, 378
Cronin, B. — 299
CSCE (Conference on Security and Cooperation in Europe) — 493, 503
Cuba — 62, 63, 76, 400, 526
Cuban missile crisis (1962) — 62, 63
culture — **419–32**
  global products — 19, 422–3, 465–6
  in human affairs — 17, 21, 420–1
  Islamic — 426–7
  multiculturalism — 423, 429, 550

currency see global finance; money
Cushman, T. — 532, 533
Cusimano, M.K. — 24
Cyprus — 319
Czechoslovakia — 527
D Dag Hammarskjöld Foundation — 479
  Darfur conflict — 323, 497, 499, 534
Davies, David — 4
Davis, F.Z. and Frankel, B. — 392
de Klerk, President F.W. — 394
Dean, M. — 181
debt — 464, 475
  Heavily Indebted Poor Countries (HIPCs) — 464, 480, 481
Debt Crisis Network — 464
decolonization — 48, 58–60, 67, 411, 412
  UN Declaration — 282, 320
deconstruction — 186–7
democracy
  cosmopolitan model — 30–1, 119, 550–1
  democratic deficit — 29–31, 119, 569–70
  democratic peace theory — 112–13, 118, 233
  liberal democracy — 9, 544
  promotion of — 233, 510, 517, 519, 567
  radical democracy — 154
Denmark, R.A. — 149
Deobandi Muslim groups — 429
deontology — 194, 196
dependency theory — 247
derivatives — 461–2, 463
Derrida, Jacques — 183, 186–7, 555
Dershowitz, A.M. — 509
Desch, M. — 93
détente — 63–4
Deutsch, Karl W. — 230, 304
developing countries
  and civil society — 570
  and climate change — 362, 363, 364
  economic growth — 476, 477
  New International Economic Order (NIEO) — 247
  TNCs in — 335
  see also debt; inequality; poverty; Third World
development — **473–81**
  Human Development Index — 274, 480
Development Alternatives with Women for a New Era (DAWN) — 274
devolution — 413, 414
diasporas — 187–8, 414
dictatorships — 320
Diez, T. with Wiener, A. — 445
diffusion — 168–71
Diogenes — 196, 545
diplomacy — 5, 44, 47
disarmament see arms control
disasters — 354, 355, 499, 501
diseases — 146, 478, 498, 499

Disney····················· 422, 423
displaced persons··············· 277, 496
Doty, R.L.······················ 188, 189
double reading·················· 186–7
Doyle, Michael ··········9, 95, 111, 112–13, 118, 233
Drake, M.·························· 181
Dresden··························· 58
drugs trade······················ 17, 337
Dubai Ports World················ 335
Dublin Group······················ 17
DuBois, W.E.B.·················· 187, 189
Duffield, Mark··················· 188, 222
Dunne, T.
    with Booth, K.·········· 104, 118, 240
    with Wheeler, N.J.··········50, 535
e-commerce··············· 458, 462
e-mail communication··········· 380
Earth Summit··········· 325, 354–5, 357–8, 362
East Africa····················· 441, 442
East Timor····················· 501, 528
Easterly, W.······················ 477
Eastern Europe················· 65, 77, 79
ecological globalization·············21, 157
Economic Community of West African States (ECOWAS)····················· 441, 442
Economic Cooperation Organization (ECO)···························· 444
economic globalization
    cross-border transactions········· 157, 453–4
    governance ············ 302, 452–3, 566
    history·····················453–4
    open-border transactions···········454–6
    sceptical views ········ 10, 20–1, 137, 453–4
    statistical indicators··············· 454
    transborder transactions ············456–7
    see also global economy; world economy
economic integration················16
economic interdependence ···········9, 10
economic order····················· 566
economic sanctions··············· 114, 115, 315, 335, 394, 395
economic shocks···················· 250
The Economist ····················· 267
Ecuador························· 136, 441
Edkins, Jenny····················· 185
education······················· 146, 478
Edwards, P.······················· 185
Egypt············62, 64, 424, 426, 428
Ehrlich, Paul····················· 483
Einhorn, R.J. with Campbell, K.M. ··········· 393
Eisenhower, President Dwight D.·········62, 396
Ekins, P.························· 479
El Salvador······················· 440
Elias, Norbert··············· 546, 551, 553
Elshtain, J.B.······················ 182
    with Tobias, S.···················· 182
emancipation ················· 146, 154
    emancipatory knowledge········264, 273–5
emissions trading················· 362, 364

empires·················59–60, 67, 545–6
    see also imperialism
employment···················271–3, 276
Engels, Friedrich··············· 146, 157
English School of International Relations ······················ 38, 50
Enlightenment ················· 112, 116
Enloe, Cynthia ··········· 182, 238, 266, 272
environment················· **351–68**
    Aarhus Convention·················· 358
    Agenda 21 ···················355, 357–8
    chronology······················ 354
    and developing countries ··········· 355, 358
    disasters ·············· 354, 355, 499, 501
    environmental degradation···· 352–3, 354
    Global Environmental Facility (GEF)··· 358
    governance ···················352–3
    international cooperation ··········· 356–60
    multilateral agreements ·· 354, 356–7, 359
    NGOs ····················308–9, 355
    political actors ···················· 345
    precautionary principle ·············· 357
    regimes ·········· 301–2, 359, 365, 366
    and scientific information··· 358, 365, 366
    and security issues················365–6
    tragedy of the commons···········358–9
    and transboundary trade···········356–7
    war damage·················· 498
    see also climate change; Earth Summit; pollution; sustainable development; United Nations
epistemology·················· 177, 178
Eritrea ····················· 500, 549
ethics······················ **193–206**
    categorical imperative················ 197
    and communitarianism··············· 195
    cosmopolitanism··············194–9, 205
    definition ························ 194
    deontology ················ 194, 196
    and globalization··················201–5
    and pluralism ········ 195, 200–1, 205
    positive and negative duties ··········· 198–9
    and realism·············92, 195, 199–200, 205, 231
    see also moral duty
Ethiopia ·····················64, 220
    see also Eritrea
ethnic cleansing ··· 59, 221, 268, 322, 412, 525
ethnic nationalism ·················· 404, 408, 411, 412–13, 501
Eurasia ························443–4
Euroclear························· 461
European Atomic Energy Community (EURATOM) ·········· 398, 399, 444, 445
European Central Bank················ 446
European Coal and Steel Community (ECSC)······················ 444, 445
European Commission··············· 446
European Commission on Human Rights································ 514

European Convention on Human Rights ················ 508, 513, 514
European Council···················· 446
European Court of Human Rights ············· 514
European Court of Justice············· 446
European Network on Debt and Development···················· 464
European Parliament················· 446
European Union (EU)
    and China·······················78
    citizenship ······················ 554
    Constitutional Treaty ········· 445, 447
    emissions trading ············ 362, 364
    enlargement ········· 77, 78, 233, 446–7
    future················78, 105, 446–7
    institutions ··············· 445, 446
    and international crises ············· 565
    regional integration ············444–7
    regions ················· 413, 414
    Schengen Agreement·············· 381
    security and defence policy··········· 233
    Treaty reforms ············ 445, 447
Evans, G.························· 533
Evans, M. and Sahnoun, M.············· 535
exchange rates ············ 254, 454, 455
explanatory theory ················176–7
export processing zones (EPZs) ········457–8
extraordinary rendition·············· 509, 553
failed states················ 238, 239, 412, 501, 549, 571
Falk, Richard···········9, 118, 119, 552, 569
Falun Gong cult··················· 420
family planning··············· 345, 483
famine························· 484
Fanon, Franz··················· 189, 377
fascism······················ 408, 410
Feinstein, L. and Slaughter, A. ······· 592
Feldstein, M.····················· 254
femininity······················· 265
feminism
    emancipatory knowledge········264, 273–5
    and human rights············· 516, 517
    and political community··············· 550
    and security············· 235–6, 268–71
    see also gender; women
feminist theory
    feminist constructivism················· 267
    feminist critical theory················ 267, 268
    feminist post-modernism ········· 267, 268
    liberal feminism················181–2, 264–5, 266–7, 268
    post-colonial feminism··· 182, 184, 267–8
    post-modern feminism ······· 183, 267, 268
    socialist/Marxist feminism ············· 182
    standpoint feminism··············182–3
    types················· 181, 264
Ferguson, R. with Mansbach, R.··········· 9, 16
Fifty Years is Enough campaign ············· 481
film industry ·················· 422, 423
Financial Action Task Force ············· 17, 26

financial flows
  liberalization ·········· 455–6
  scale ·········· 23, 254, 454
  and sovereignty ·········· 335, 465
  variety of business ·········· 459–60, 462
  see also global finance; money
Financial Times ·········· 458
Finnemore, M. ·········· 291
  and Sikkink, K. ·········· 167, 170
Finnis, John ·········· 510
First World War ·········· 56–7, 113, 408, 497
Fischer, Fritz ·········· 56
fisheries ·········· 359
Fissile Material Cut-off Treaty
    (FMCT) ·········· 398
food ·········· 423, 483–4, 485
Food and Agriculture Organization (FAO) ·········· 483
Foot, R. ·········· 553
Ford, Henry ·········· 458
Foucault, Michel
  concept of genealogy ·········· 181, 185, 186
  and constructivism ·········· 162
  power and knowledge ·········· 185, 187, 554
  on war ·········· 215, 221
foundational/anti-foundational
    theories ·········· 177–8
Fox-Keller, E. ·········· 183
France
  empire ·········· 59–60
  and EU ·········· 447
  French Revolution ·········· 40, 46–7,
    406, 512, 546
  intervention in Rwanda ·········· 529
  and Iraq War ·········· 323
  nuclear weapons ·········· 391, 399
Francis, D. ·········· 215
Franck, T. and Rodley, N. ·········· 527
Frank, André Gunder ·········· 147, 149, 478
  with Gills, B. ·········· 149
Frankfurt School ·········· 153–4
Freedman, L. ·········· 213, 218
French Revolution ·········· 40, 46–7, 406,
    512, 546
Friedberg, Aaron ·········· 80
Friedman, Jonathan ·········· 230
Friedman, Milton ·········· 452
Friedman, Thomas ·········· 131
Friends of the Earth ·········· 26, 345, 355
Fukuyama, Francis ·········· 9, 74, 113, 422, 429
fundamentalism ·········· 222, 424, 427–8
G G7 (Group of Seven) ·········· 246, 452,
    475, 476
G8 (Group of Eight) ·········· 26, 256, 452,
    464, 476, 480
G77 (developing countries) ·········· 26
Gabon ·········· 59
game theories ·········· 303–5, 306–7
Gardner, G.T. ·········· 390
Gates, Bill ·········· 269
Gates, Jr., H.L. ·········· 187

GATT (General Agreement on Tariffs
    and Trade) ·········· 245, 246, 300, 357, 452
  Uruguay Round ·········· 455
GDP (gross domestic product) ·········· 470, 476, 477
Gellner, Ernest ·········· 405, 546
gender ·········· **264–77**
  definition ·········· 265
  division of labour ·········· 271–3, 276
  Gender Development Index ·········· 274, 275
  gender-sensitive lenses ·········· 266, 273
  and Islam ·········· 517
  and laws of war ·········· 165, 166
  mainstreaming ·········· 274, 275
  masculinist assumptions ·········· 510
  sex and gender ·········· 183
  see also feminist theory; women
genealogical approach ·········· 181, 185, 186
General Electric ·········· 335
genetically modified organisms (GMOs) ·········· 357
Geneva Conventions ·········· 40, 202, 205,
    287, 289, 512
genocide ·········· 496, 508, 518, 524, 526
  see also civil war
George, Susan ·········· 484–5
Georgia ·········· 443, 444
Germain, R. and Kenny, M. ·········· 150
German Red Army Faction ·········· 377
Germany
  Berlin ·········· 61, 63
  emergence of nationalism ·········· 408, 409
  history ·········· 57, 408, 409
  and humanitarian intervention ·········· 537
  and Iraq War ·········· 533
  nuclear weapons ·········· 391
  rearmament ·········· 62
  reunification ·········· 65, 409
  rise of Nazism ·········· 57, 67, 409
  and World Wars ·········· 57
Ghana ·········· 59
Giddens, A. ·········· 17
Gilbert, Christopher and Vines, D. ·········· 254
Gills, B. with Frank, A.G. ·········· 149
Gilmore, R.W. ·········· 189
Gilpin, R. ·········· 16, 17, 21
Gioseffi, D. ·········· 183
Gladstone, William Ewart ·········· 512
Glendon, M.A. ·········· 286
global change ·········· 168–71
global commons ·········· 358
Global Compact ·········· 337
global economy ·········· 253, 341, 453–7, 567
Global Environmental Facility (GEF) ·········· 358
global finance
  Clearstream/Cedel ·········· 461
  credit cards ·········· 459, 462
  crises ·········· 254, 255, 256, 459, 463
  currency exchanges ·········· 254, 454, 455
  derivatives ·········· 461–2, 463
  Euroclear ·········· 461
  governance ·········· 254, 452

global finance—*Cont.*
  instantaneity ·········· 456, 460
  key events ·········· 463
  loss of sovereignty ·········· 335
  money ·········· 459–60, 462
  offshore finance ·········· 462–3, 463, 464, 465
  securities ·········· 460–1, 463, 465
  Special Drawing Rights (SDRs) ·········· 459
  stability of ·········· 566
  territoriality ·········· 464–5
  uneven distribution ·········· 462–4
  universality of ·········· 568
  see also banking; financial flows; money
global goods ·········· 19, 458
global governance ·········· 11, 24–7, 31,
    323, 452, 566
global politics ·········· 28–9, 332, 342, 412–13, 414
global polity ·········· 10
global society ·········· 204, 219–20, 229, 236–7
Global System for Mobile
    Communications (GSM) ·········· 380
global trade
  cross-border ·········· 454
  and environmental protection ·········· 356–7
  export processing zones (EPZs) ·········· 457–8
  global goods ·········· 19, 458
  governance ·········· 355–6, 452
  intra-firm ·········· 335
  key events ·········· 463
  regulation ·········· 335
  sanctions ·········· 114, 115, 315, 335, 394, 395
  stability of ·········· 566
  territorial production ·········· 464–5
  transborder production ·········· 457–9
  triangulation ·········· 335, 337
  uneven distribution ·········· 462–4
  see also transnational companies
global war on terror (GWOT) *see* war on
    terror
global warming *see* climate change
globalization
  asymmetrical ·········· 22
  concept ·········· 18–20
  definition ·········· 8, 17, 19, 74, 75
  deterritorialization ·········· 252–3
  history ·········· 22
  hyperglobalist approach ·········· 16
  nature and impact ·········· 252–3
  precursors ·········· 8–10
  sceptical views ·········· 10–11, 16, 20–1, 569
  technological revolution ·········· 252–3
  thick ·········· 23
  transformationalist perspective ·········· 16
  see also economic globalization
globalphobia ·········· 136
Globo television ·········· 458
glocal (global and local) politics ·········· 135
Goldblat, J. ·········· 396
Goldblatt, D. with Held, D. ·········· 546
Goldstein, J. ·········· 290

Gong, G.W. ⋯⋯⋯⋯⋯⋯⋯⋯⋯⋯ 286
Goodman, David ⋯⋯⋯⋯⋯⋯⋯⋯ 485
Gorbachev, Mikhail ⋯⋯⋯⋯⋯ 65–6, 73
Gottlieb, R.S. ⋯⋯⋯⋯⋯⋯⋯⋯⋯ 182
governance
   economic ⋯⋯⋯⋯⋯ 302, 452–3, 566
   environmental ⋯⋯⋯⋯⋯⋯⋯ 352–3
   NGO networks ⋯⋯⋯⋯⋯⋯⋯ 341
   self-governance ⋯⋯⋯⋯⋯⋯⋯ 28
   trade and finance ⋯⋯⋯ 254, 355–6, 452
   see also global governance
Gowa, J. ⋯⋯⋯⋯⋯⋯⋯⋯⋯⋯⋯ 245
Grace, C.S. ⋯⋯⋯⋯⋯⋯⋯⋯⋯⋯ 390
Grameen Bank ⋯⋯⋯⋯⋯⋯⋯⋯ 272–3
Gramsci, Antonio ⋯⋯⋯⋯⋯⋯ 149–50
Gramscianism ⋯⋯⋯ 15, 149–53, 188, 189
grassroots movements ⋯⋯⋯⋯⋯ 479
Gray, Colin S. ⋯⋯⋯⋯ 216, 217, 392, 398
Gray, John ⋯⋯⋯⋯⋯⋯⋯⋯⋯ 20, 104
Greece ⋯⋯⋯⋯⋯⋯⋯⋯⋯⋯⋯⋯ **526**
Green, Duncan ⋯⋯⋯⋯⋯⋯⋯⋯ 152
greenhouse gases ⋯⋯⋯⋯⋯⋯⋯ 361–4
Greenpeace ⋯⋯⋯ 17, 50, 308, 345, 354, 355
Greenwood, B.M. ⋯⋯⋯⋯⋯⋯⋯ 499
Gregg, T. with Singer, P. ⋯⋯⋯ 198, 203
Grenada ⋯⋯⋯⋯⋯⋯⋯⋯⋯⋯⋯ 64, 65
Grieco, Joseph ⋯⋯⋯⋯⋯ 127, 129, 131
Grotius, Hugo ⋯⋯⋯ 40, 45, 282, 283, 288, 511
Grovogui, S.N. ⋯⋯⋯⋯⋯⋯⋯⋯ 188
GUAM Organization for Democracy and
   Economic Development ⋯⋯⋯ 444
Guantanamo Bay ⋯⋯⋯⋯⋯⋯ 383, 509
Guatemala ⋯⋯⋯⋯⋯⋯⋯⋯⋯⋯ 440
guerrilla movements ⋯⋯⋯⋯⋯ 337–9, 345
Guinea-Bissau ⋯⋯⋯⋯⋯ 59, 64, 441, 442
Gulf States ⋯⋯⋯⋯⋯⋯⋯⋯⋯⋯ 430
Gulf War ⋯⋯⋯⋯⋯⋯ 115, 217, 324

H   Haas, P., Keohane, R.,
     and Levy, M.A. ⋯⋯⋯⋯⋯ 134
Habermas, Jürgen ⋯⋯⋯⋯ 153, 154, 155
Hague Convention for the Suppression of
   Unlawful Seizure of Aircraft
   (1970) ⋯⋯⋯⋯⋯⋯⋯⋯⋯ 383
Hague Convention on War (1907) ⋯⋯⋯ 512
Haiti ⋯⋯⋯⋯⋯⋯⋯⋯⋯⋯ 321, 486
Hall, C. ⋯⋯⋯⋯⋯⋯⋯⋯⋯ 179, 188
Hall, John A. ⋯⋯⋯⋯⋯⋯⋯⋯⋯ 179
Halliday, F. ⋯⋯⋯⋯⋯⋯⋯⋯⋯⋯ 64
Hansen, Lene ⋯⋯⋯⋯⋯⋯⋯⋯⋯ 187
Haq, Mahabub ul ⋯⋯⋯⋯ 492, 493, 495
Haraway, D. ⋯⋯⋯⋯⋯⋯⋯⋯⋯ 183
Hardin, Garrett ⋯⋯⋯⋯⋯⋯⋯⋯ 359
Hart, H.L.A. ⋯⋯⋯⋯⋯⋯⋯⋯⋯ 284
Hartsock, N. ⋯⋯⋯⋯⋯⋯⋯⋯⋯ 182
Hasenclever, A., Mayer, P.,
   and Rittberger, V. ⋯⋯⋯⋯⋯ 298
Hashemi, Sohail ⋯⋯⋯⋯⋯⋯⋯⋯ 427
Hastings, Adrian ⋯⋯⋯⋯⋯⋯⋯⋯ 405
Hay, C. ⋯⋯⋯⋯⋯⋯⋯⋯⋯⋯⋯⋯ 21
hazardous waste ⋯⋯⋯⋯⋯ 128–9, 302, 356

health ⋯⋯⋯⋯⋯⋯⋯⋯⋯⋯⋯⋯ 478
   see also AIDS; diseases
Heazle, M. ⋯⋯⋯⋯⋯⋯⋯⋯⋯⋯ 308
Heeren, A.H.L. ⋯⋯⋯⋯⋯⋯⋯⋯⋯ 46
Hegel, G.W.F. ⋯⋯⋯⋯⋯⋯⋯⋯⋯ 511
hegemony
   Gramsci's concept ⋯⋯⋯ 150–1, 188, 189
     Cox's view ⋯⋯⋯⋯⋯⋯⋯ 150–1
   Great Britain ⋯⋯⋯⋯⋯⋯ 304, 407
   superpowers ⋯⋯⋯⋯⋯⋯⋯⋯ 60
   US ⋯⋯⋯⋯ 50, 75–6, 152, 299, 305, 565
     declining ⋯⋯⋯⋯⋯⋯ 86, 149, 245
Heineken beer ⋯⋯⋯⋯⋯⋯⋯⋯⋯ 458
Heinlein, Robert A. ⋯⋯⋯⋯⋯⋯⋯ 215
Heinz ⋯⋯⋯⋯⋯⋯⋯⋯⋯⋯⋯⋯ 458
Held, David ⋯⋯⋯⋯⋯⋯ 23, 30, 119, 545
   Goldblatt, D. and Perraton, J. ⋯⋯⋯ 546
   with McGrew, A. ⋯⋯⋯⋯ 22, 119, 570
Helman, G.B. and Ratner, S.R. ⋯⋯⋯⋯ 549
Henkin, Louis ⋯⋯⋯⋯⋯⋯⋯⋯⋯ 283
Hennessy, R. and Ingraham, C. ⋯⋯⋯ 182
Herring, Eric ⋯⋯⋯⋯⋯⋯⋯⋯⋯ 393
Hettne, B. ⋯⋯⋯⋯⋯⋯⋯⋯⋯⋯ 438
Higgins, R. ⋯⋯⋯⋯⋯⋯⋯⋯ 286, 287
Higgott, R. ⋯⋯⋯⋯⋯⋯⋯⋯⋯⋯ 443
hijacking ⋯⋯⋯⋯⋯⋯⋯⋯ 374–5, 383
Hikma Pharmaceuticals ⋯⋯⋯⋯⋯ 335
Hinduism ⋯⋯⋯⋯⋯⋯⋯⋯⋯ 40, 420
Hiroshima ⋯⋯⋯⋯⋯⋯⋯⋯⋯ 58, 388
Hirst, Paul and Thompson, G. ⋯⋯⋯ 10–11,
   20, 21, 454
historic bloc ⋯⋯⋯⋯⋯⋯⋯⋯⋯ 150
historical materialism ⋯⋯⋯⋯⋯⋯ 145
   see also Marxism
historical sociology ⋯⋯⋯⋯⋯⋯ 178–81
Hitler, Adolf ⋯⋯⋯⋯⋯⋯⋯ 57, 58, 527
HIV/AIDS ⋯⋯⋯⋯⋯ 25, 478, 499, 501, 503
Ho Chi Minh ⋯⋯⋯⋯⋯⋯⋯⋯⋯ 67
Hobbes, Thomas ⋯⋯⋯⋯ 92, 165, 230, 511
Hobden, S. ⋯⋯⋯⋯⋯⋯⋯⋯⋯⋯ 179
   and Hobson, J.M. ⋯⋯⋯⋯⋯⋯ 179
Hobsbawm, Eric ⋯⋯⋯⋯⋯⋯⋯⋯ 405
Hobson, J.A. ⋯⋯⋯⋯⋯⋯⋯⋯⋯ 111
Hobson, J.M. with Hobden, S. ⋯⋯⋯⋯ 179
Hofeld, Wesley ⋯⋯⋯⋯⋯⋯⋯⋯ 511
Hoffmann, Stanley ⋯⋯⋯⋯⋯ 110, 524
Holden, P., and Ruppel, R.J. ⋯⋯⋯⋯ 188
holism ⋯⋯⋯⋯⋯⋯⋯⋯⋯⋯⋯ 162–3
Hollis, M., and Smith, S. ⋯⋯⋯⋯⋯ 177
holocaust ⋯⋯⋯⋯⋯⋯⋯⋯⋯ 57, 513
Holroyd, F. ⋯⋯⋯⋯⋯⋯⋯⋯⋯⋯ 66
home-based work ⋯⋯⋯⋯ 271–2, 274, 275
HomeNet Organization ⋯⋯⋯⋯⋯ 275
Homer-Dixon, T. ⋯⋯⋯⋯⋯⋯⋯ 498
Homework Convention (ILO) ⋯⋯⋯ 267, 275
Honduras ⋯⋯⋯⋯⋯⋯⋯⋯⋯⋯ 440
Hoogevelt, A. ⋯⋯⋯⋯⋯⋯⋯⋯⋯ 21
Hooper, Charlotte ⋯⋯⋯⋯⋯⋯⋯ 267
Horkheimer, Max ⋯⋯⋯⋯⋯⋯⋯ 153
Hroch, Miroslav ⋯⋯⋯⋯⋯⋯⋯⋯ 405

Hulsman, J. with Lieven, A. ⋯⋯⋯⋯⋯ 231
human rights ⋯⋯⋯⋯⋯⋯⋯⋯⋯ **507–21**
   Asian values ⋯⋯⋯⋯⋯ 510, 517, 518
   Bangkok Declaration ⋯⋯⋯⋯⋯ 518
   civil and political ⋯⋯⋯ 286, 508, 513, 515
   codes ⋯⋯⋯⋯⋯ 119, 286, 508, 518
   in cold war ⋯⋯⋯⋯⋯⋯⋯⋯ 566–7
   and democracy promotion ⋯ 510, 517, 519
   economic, social, and cultural ⋯⋯⋯ 508, 515
   European Convention ⋯⋯⋯ 508, 513, 514
   and feminism ⋯⋯⋯⋯⋯⋯⋯ 516, 517
   and foreign relations ⋯⋯⋯⋯⋯ 509, 514
   government abuse ⋯⋯⋯⋯⋯⋯ 564
   and international community ⋯⋯⋯ 514–15
   law ⋯⋯⋯⋯⋯⋯⋯⋯⋯⋯⋯ 286
   origins ⋯⋯⋯⋯⋯⋯⋯⋯⋯⋯ 508
   political actors ⋯⋯⋯⋯⋯ 119, 345, 514–15
   UN Charter ⋯⋯⋯⋯⋯⋯⋯ 513, 524–5
   Universal Declaration (1948) ⋯⋯⋯ 24, 205,
     286, 513
   universality ⋯⋯⋯⋯⋯⋯⋯⋯ 516–18
   Vienna Declaration (1993) ⋯⋯⋯⋯ 517
   Vienna global conference ⋯⋯⋯⋯ 325
   violations ⋯⋯⋯⋯ 169, 287, 510, 514
   see also International Criminal Court
Human Rights Watch ⋯⋯⋯⋯⋯ 383, 533
human security ⋯⋯⋯⋯⋯⋯⋯⋯ **491–505**
   conception of ⋯⋯⋯⋯⋯⋯⋯ 492–5
   and disease ⋯⋯⋯⋯⋯⋯⋯⋯ 499
   freedom from fear/want ⋯⋯⋯⋯ 495, 501
   government violations ⋯⋯⋯⋯⋯ 503
   Human Development Report ⋯⋯⋯ 492, 503
   Human Security Report ⋯⋯⋯ 495, 497, 498
   and NGOs ⋯⋯⋯⋯⋯⋯⋯⋯ 502–3
   scope ⋯⋯⋯⋯⋯⋯⋯⋯⋯⋯ 492
   South-East Asia ⋯⋯⋯⋯⋯⋯⋯ 501
   and the state ⋯⋯⋯⋯⋯ 494, 553–4
   and the UN ⋯⋯⋯⋯⋯⋯⋯⋯ 502
human sympathy ⋯⋯⋯⋯⋯⋯⋯⋯ 551
humanitarian aid ⋯⋯⋯⋯⋯⋯⋯ 509, 515
humanitarian intervention ⋯⋯⋯⋯ **523–39**
   counter-restrictionist case ⋯⋯⋯⋯ 524–6
   criteria for ⋯⋯⋯⋯⋯⋯⋯⋯ 536–7
   growing acceptance of ⋯⋯⋯ 170, 412–13
   just cause thresholds ⋯⋯⋯ 525, 535, 536
   mixed motives ⋯⋯⋯⋯⋯⋯⋯ 527, 529
   as moral duty ⋯⋯⋯⋯⋯ 198, 526–8
   objections ⋯⋯⋯⋯⋯⋯⋯⋯⋯ 526–8
   outcomes ⋯⋯⋯⋯⋯⋯⋯⋯⋯ 530–1
   precautionary principles ⋯⋯⋯⋯ 525
   and public opinion ⋯⋯⋯⋯ 528–9, 538
   Responsibility to Protect ⋯⋯ 170, 197, 322,
     338, 524, 535–8
   and self-interest ⋯⋯⋯⋯⋯⋯ 527, 529
   and sovereignty ⋯⋯ 237, 322, 524, 525, 530
   and UN ⋯⋯⋯ 287, 322–4, 502, 524–6, 530,
     535–6
   and war on terror ⋯⋯⋯⋯⋯⋯ 531–4
   and Western powers ⋯⋯⋯⋯⋯ 286
Humphreys, M. and Varshney, A. ⋯⋯⋯ 498

Hungary······62
hunger······482–6
Hunt, J.W. with Cobban, A.······46
Huntington, Samuel
　civilizations······376
　clash of civilizations······50, 85, 422, 424–6, 548
Hurd, Douglas······233
Hurrell, Andrew······50–1, 436
　with Woods, N.······118
Hussein, Saddam······115, 323, 503
Hymans, Jacques E.······392

I IBFAN (International Baby Food Action Network)······343
IBRD (International Bank for Reconstruction and Development)······245
　see also World Bank
Iceland······308
idealism······4, 92, 114, 116, 162–3, 228
identity
　and multiculturism······423
　and nation-states······549–50, 565
　and post-modernism······185–6
　and war······222
Ignatieff, Michael······509
IKEA······458
Ikenberry, G. John······116, 117, 568
illiteracy······146
IMF (International Monetary Fund)······152, 245, 248, 452, 475
　Asian financial crisis (1997)······254, 255
　protests against······258, 479
immigration policies······189, 456
immunity rights······511
imperialism······11, 22, 38, 45, 118, 407
　see also empires
India
　agriculture······486
　cultural influence······423
　and East Pakistan (1971)······527
　economy······82, 476, 477
　fundamental extremism······424
　grassroots movements······479
　history······41–2, 59, 409–10, 547, 549
　and humanitarian intervention······537
　nuclear weapons······391, 396, 398, 400
　outsourcing······19
　and Pakistan······219
　politics······420
　population growth······483
　poverty······472
　and regional integration······444
　self-employed women······275
Indian Ocean tsunami······499, 501
indigenous peoples······289, 479, 516, 550
Indo-China······59, 60
Indonesia······59, 272, 442, 483, 499, 501
　Asian financial crisis (1997)······254, 255

inequality
　indicators of······117, 146, 463–4, 470, 476–7
　as moral problem······203–5
　security challenges from······82–3
Infant Formula Action Coalition······343
Ingraham, C. with Hennessy, R.······182
intelligence organizations······62
Inter-American Court of Human Rights······438
Inter-American Development Bank······438
intergovernmental organizations······332
Intergovernmental Panel on Climate Change (IPCC)······358, 361
Intermediate Nuclear Forces (INF) Treaty···66
International Convention for the Prevention of Pollution from Ships (MARPOL)······354
International Atomic Energy Authority (IAEA)···390, 395, 396, 399
International Civil Aviation Organization (ICAO)······17, 306, 383
International Commission on Intervention and State Sovereignty (ICISS)······322, 525, 531, 535
International Committee of the Red Cross······502–3
International Convention on the Elimination of All Forms of Racial Discrimination······508
International Convention on the Elimination of Child Labour (ICECL)······26
International Council for the Exploration of the Seas (ICES)······358
International Court of Justice······318
International Covenant on Civil and Political Rights······286, 508
International Covenant on Economic, Social and Cultural Rights······508, 515
International Criminal Court······205, 289, 290, 502, 519, 537
international criminal tribunals······287, 289, 338
International Development Association (IDA)······245
International Energy Agency······364
International Finance Corporation (IFC)···245
international institutions······280–1
　vs. international organizations······280
International Labour Organization (ILO)···267, 275, 512
international law······**279–94**
　consent and legal obligation···283–4, 285
　and constructivism······290–1
　critical legal studies······293
　customary······526
　discourse of institutional autonomy······284–5
　language and practice of justification······284, 285
　and liberalism······292, 293

international law—*Cont.*
　multilateralism······283, 285
　and neo-liberal institutionalism······290
　and new liberalism······291–2
　opinio juris······284, 526
　origins and history··45–6, 47, 281–3, 285
　paradox of······280, 293
　and realism······289–90, 293
　and states······286–7, 288
　supranationality······286–8, 289
　Western bias······286
International Monetary Fund *see* IMF
international non-governmental organizations (INGOs)······332, 341, 342, 345, 508, 566, 570
international order······562, 563, 571–3
International Organization of Securities Commissions (IOSCO)······452, 465
international organizations··· 17, 25–6, 341–2
　and international institutions······280
　protests against······137, 256–7, 258, 479, 569
International Planned Parenthood Federation······267, 345
international political economy (IPE)······**242–58**
　constructivist approach······257–8
　globalization debate······253–9
　Gramscian influence······149–53
　institutional approach······250–1, 256, 257, 258
　Italian School······149
　liberal tradition······249, 250
　Marxian tradition······249–50
　mercantilist tradition······249, 250
　neo-Gramscian approach······251
　political economy approach······250, 251
　rational choice/neo-utilitarian approach······250, 252
　realist approach······257, 258
　scope of······244
　social constructivist approach······251, 252
International Relations
　English School······38, 50
　inter-paradigm debate······6–8, 176, 178
　and religion······565
　state-centric approach······332
　theories······177–8, 190
international society······9, 37–9, 44–51
International Union for the Conservation of Nature (IUCN)······358
International Whaling Commission······308–9, 353
Interpol······383
intervention
　Brezhnev doctrine······322
　cause of conflict······111
　definition······321–2
　increase in······412
　justification for······322, 413

intervention—*Cont.*
   non-intervention ············ 44, 100, 287, 565
   and UN ·· 322–4
   see also humanitarian intervention
investment ···························· 253, 455–6, 461
iPod ···19
IRA (Irish Republican Army) ····················381
Iran ································· 76, 430, 444
   Iranian Revolution···48, 49, 375, 428, 430
   and Iraq ····································84, 382
   nuclear programme ······················ 169, 395
   and popular culture ···························424
Iraq ··························· 76, 429, 497, 519
   safe havens ······················ 526, 528, 530
   weapons of mass destruction ······ 394, 400
   see also Gulf War
Iraq War
   case study ···································218
   consequences ·································84
   criticism of·············· 17, 104, 130, 132,
    256, 533, 538
   fatalities····································497
   and globalization······························19
   legitimacy of···················· 132, 163, 533
   origins ···························· 5, 84, 394
   and Privatized Military Firms ···········220
   and UN ······················· 285, 322–3,
    324, 327
   US technology··················· 217, 218
Ireland ·····································537
Iriye, A. with Mazlish, B. ·····················544
Islam
   in Afghan–Pakistan milieu················429
   culture································426–7
   in cyberspace ····················· 380, 430–1
   doctrines ···················· 43, 49, 427
   fundamentalism ············· 222, 424, 427–8
   and gender equality ·························517
   and Iranian Revolution ······················49
   Islamic law ···················· 427, 428
   jihad·································43, 377
   just war tradition ···························202
   mainstream vs. extremists················428
   origins·····································43–4
   revival ····················· 420, 426–7, 428
   shura (consultation) ·······················430
   wearing of the veil ··········· 424, 517, 550
   and the West··················· 375–6, 426,
    429, 431
Islamic terrorism···········76, 84–5, 375, 376,
   377–8, 379
   jihad···················85, 377–8, 379, 427
   see also Al Qaeda
Israel ·························· 61–2, 64, 67, 426
Italian Red Brigades ·····························377
Ivory Coast·························· 59, 128–9
J   Jackson, Robert H. ··············· 200,
    201, 571
   with Owens, P. ·························49–50
Jacquette, J.···································274

Japan
   foreign policy·································80
   and human security ············ 493, 503, 595
   invasion of China ························ 57, 58
   Minimata mercury poisoning ···············355
   nuclear weapons·····························391
   and regional integration ···················443
   and Second World War········· 58, 388, 390
   Tokyo underground attack··········· 394, 424
   and UN ·······································320
   and whaling·······························308–9
Japanese Red Army ······························378
Jervis, Robert·············· 130, 133–4, 230, 301
Jolly, R. and Ray, D.B. ·························493
Jordan·······································430
Jørgensen, K.E. with Christensen, T.
   and Wiener, A. ····························446
Joseph, C. ·····································19
Jubilee 2000 ···························· 464, 481
Jubilee Research ·······························146
Judaism···420
Junaid, S.·······································376
Junne, G.C.A.···································570
jus ad bellum···························201–2, 288
jus in bello·····················201–2, 288–9
just war tradition·················201–2, 373, 526
K   Kabila, Joseph························238
   Kabila, Laurent-Desiré ·····················238
Kagan, Robert ·································552
Kaldor, Mary················· 119, 221–2, 237,
   552, 555
Kane, H. with Brown, L.R. ·····················478
Kant, Immanuel··········9, 112, 165, 196–7,
   233, 551
Karp, A. ·······································397
Katzenstein, P.·································291
Kautilya, *Arthasastra* ···················40, 41–2
Kazakhstan ·························· 443, 444
Keane, J.·······································570
Keck, M. and Sikkink, K.·······················135
Kedourie, Elie··································405
Kemal, Mustafa··································426
Kendall, G. and Wickham, G.····················181
Kennan, George F.····················· 199, 289
Kennedy, President John F.······················63
Kenny, M. with Germain, R.·····················150
Kentucky Fried Chicken·························423
Kenya ······························ 59, 76, 441
Keohane, Robert
   and free trade ·······························116
   with Haas, P.·································134
   international relations
    theory ··················· 126, 132, 190
   with Martin, L.··················· 134, 233
   with Nye, J.·············· 9, 23, 115, 132
   and US hegemony ···························245
   and violence ···································28
Kerry, John ·····································270
Keynesianism ···································247
Khatami, Mohammad ···························430

Khomeini, Grand Ayatollah
   Ruhollah················ 49, 427, 428, 430
Khong, Yuen Foong·····························494
   with MacFarlane, N. ························502
Khrushchev, Nikita ························ 62, 63
Kingsbury, Benedict with Roberts, A. ···114
Kinsella, Helen M.·······························183
Kirkpatrick, Jean ································320
Kissinger, Henry·······················64, 102, 199
Kiwi shoe polish·································458
knowledge
   and power ···················· 185, 187, 554
   scientific ···················· 358, 365, 366
Koehler, S.·····································498
Korea *see* North Korea; South Korea
Korean War·······················61, 319
Koskenniemi, M. ································292
Kosovo
   civil war····························· 220, 237
   and NATO···············322, 527, 528, 529,
    530, 531, 549
   and UN ······················ 322, 324, 535
Krasner, Stephen D.···16, 24, 46, 300, 305, 307
Kratochwil, Friedrich ·················· 284, 291
Krause, Keith·························· 154, 235
   and Williams, M.C. ················· 154, 392
Kristensen, H. with Norris, R.S.·················66
Kuhn, Thomas ···································6
Kurds ······················· 429, 528, 530
Kuwait ···························· 115, 217
Kyoto Protocol ·············· 299, 354, 362–4
Kyrgystan ·························· 443, 444
L   Laffey, Mark with Barkawi, T.·········188
   Laidi, Z.·····································568
Lambeth, Benjamin S.···························219
Lampert, D. with Mansbach, R.·············9, 16
landmines ···················· 287, 498, 502
language··························· 306–7, 546
Laos ·························· 64, 443, 501
Lapid, Yosef···································178
Laqueur, W.····································377
Latin America
   financial crisis ·······························459
   GDP ···························· 476, 477
   nuclear weapons·····························399
   poverty·······································472
   regional integration ··············· 438, 440–1
Lavoy, P.·······································392
Lawler, L.·······································238
Layne, Christopher································76
League of Nations·······47–8, 57, 114, 314–15,
   408, 513
Lebanon·························· 239, 571
Leeson, Nick····································462
legal globalization································21
legal regimes ···································566
legitimacy
   constraining power of·························165
   deficit in global system········· 29–31, 119,
    569–70

legitimacy—*Cont.*
  of Iraq War ·········· 132, 163, 533
  of nation-states ·· 168–9, 170–1, 415, 571
  terrorist ············· 373, 374, 384
Legrain, P. ························· 568
Lenin, Vladimir Ilich ·············· 147
Leningrad ························· 58
Lenovo ··························· 335
Lepard, B. ······················· 526
Lesotho ·························· 441
Leventhal, P. and Alexander, Y. ···· 394
Levy, M.A.
  with Haas, P. ··················· 134
  Young, O.R. and Zurn, M. ······· 298,
    300
liberal democracy ············· 9, 544
liberal feminism ········· 181–2, 264–5, 266–7
liberal institutionalism ·········· 232–4, 298–9,
    302–5, 307–8, 365
liberal peace theory ············· 9–10
liberalism ···················· 5, **109–22**
  causes of war ················· 110–11
  commercial ················· 131, 133
  conflicting principles ············ 111
  core ideas ···················· 112
  definition ················· 110, 111
  democratic peace theory ······· 112–13,
    118, 233
  and globalization ········· 7, 544, 545
  and humanitarian intervention ···· 528
  idealism ··················· 114, 116
  and imperialism ················ 118
  and international law ········ 292, 293
  and Islam ···················· 427
  liberal feminism ······· 181–2, 264–5, 266–7
  neo-liberal *see* neo-liberalism
  radical ····················· 118–21
  republican ················· 131, 133
  sociological ···················· 131
  and sovereignty ················· 5
  transnationalism ············· 114–15
liberalization ················· 252, 437
Liberia ················· 220, 321, 442, 538
liberty rights ···················· 511
Libya ··············· 76, 373, 400, 441
Liddell Hart, Basil ················ 212
Lieven, A. and Hulsman, J. ········· 231
life expectancy ··················· 146
Light, M. with Smith, K.E. ········· 514
Lindberg, T. ····················· 535
Linklater, Andrew
  cosmopolitanism ··········· 195, 198
  and critical theory ········ 153, 154, 155
  democratic deficit ··············· 570
  Kant's categorical imperative ····· 196–7
  and political community ······· 550, 554
  world order ···················· 552
Lippman, Walter ·················· 229
Little, R. ························ 115
  with Buzan, B. ················ 39–40

Locke, John ·············· 111, 165, 511
Lodgaard, Sverre ················· 493
logic of appropriateness ··········· 163
logic of consequences ············· 163
Longino, H.E. ···················· 183
Luard, E. ························ 113
Luttwak, Edward ·················· 220
Luxembourg ······················ 461
Lyotard, Jean-François ········· 185, 187
Maastricht Treaty ············· 445, 552
McDonald's ················ 422, 423, 462
Macedonia ···················· 444, 529
MacFarlane, N., and Khong, Y.F. ······ 502
McGrew, A. with Held, D. ···· 22, 119, 570
Machiavelli, Niccolo ·········· 92, 93, 96, 98,
    101, 118, 230
Mack, Andrew ················ 494, 495
Mackinnon, Catherine ·············· 516
McLuhan, Marshall ·················· 9
Macmillan, Harold ················· 59
McNeill, D. ······················ 309
McNeill, J. R. ···················· 556
McNeill, W.H. ················ 180, 556
McWorld ·························· 422
Madagascar ···················· 59, 441
Magna Carta ····················· 510
Mahathir, Dr Mohammed ············ 443
Make Poverty History ·············· 481
malaria ·················· 25, 478, 499
Malaya ···················· 59, 60, 442
Malaysia ····· 254, 255, 424, 442, 443, 501, 538
Mali ························· 59, 441
Malthus, Thomas Robert ············ 482
Manchuria ······················· 57
Mander, J. with Barker, D. ·········· 136
Mann, Michael ············ 179, 180, 546
Mansbach, R., Ferguson, R.,
    and Lampert, D. ·············· 9, 16
March, James ···················· 162
Marcopolo ······················ 335
Marcuse, Herbert ················· 153
marine pollution ········· 353, 354, 358, 359
Marlboro Country ················· 458
Marshall Plan ················· 61, 246
Marshall, T.H. ··················· 548
Martin, Liza with Keohane, R. ···· 134, 233
Marx, Karl
  and bourgeoisie ················ 552
  Capital ····················· 147
  and capitalism ················· 145
  Communist Manifesto ········ 146, 157
  means of production ········· 146, 155
  on rights ····················· 512
Marxism ····················· 5–6, **143–58**
  base-superstructure model ········ 146
  and capitalism ············· 144–5, 147
  collapse of Soviet Union ·········· 144
  diverging trends ················· 67
  and globalization ····· 7, 155–6, 157–8
  international political economy ·· 249–50

Marxism—*Cont.*
  materialist conception of history ······· 145
  socialist/Marxist feminism ········ 182
  Third World liberation
    movements ·················· 67
  see also capitalism; critical theory;
    Gramscianism
Marxism-Leninism ············· 144, 375
masculinity ············· 265, 267, 276
materialist conception of history ······· 145
Mattingly, G. ···················· 546
Mattli, W. ······················· 437
  and Slaughter, A. ··············· 291
Mauritania ······················· 59
al-Mawdudi, Abu al-Ala ············· 427
Mayer, P. with Hasenclever, A. ······· 298
Mazlish, B. and Iriye, A. ··········· 544
Meadows, Denis ··················· 483
Meadows, Donella ················· 483
Mearsheimer, John
  and China ···················· 105
  conflict and instability ·········· 231–2
  and Iraq War ················ 104, 130
  post-cold war ··················· 74
  and power ················· 101, 130
  and states ····················· 99
  Tragedy of Great Power Politics ······ 96
  and US ··············· 104, 130, 200
measles ························· 478
media ················ 215, 220, 374–5, 380
Médicins sans Frontières ········ 26, 503
Meinecke, Friedrich ················ 92
Melian dialogue ············ 41, 96–8, 553
Mendlovitz, S. ····················· 9
MERCOSUR (Common Market
    of the South) ············· 26, 440, 441
Mesopotamia ···················· 545
Metcalf, T. ······················ 189
Metz, Steven ····················· 223
Mexico ············ 248, 458, 464, 475, 476, 479
Meyer, John ····················· 162
Meyer, S.M. ····················· 392
microcredit ················· 272–3, 275
migration ················· 17, 21, 83
military globalization ············ 21, 408
military technology ······· 213, 217–18, 219
Mill, John Stuart ················· 528
Millennium Development
    Goals ··············· 325, 470, 472
  progress ··················· 478, 487
Miller, David ············· 195, 201, 551
Miller, P. ························ 180
Milner, H.V. ····················· 458
Milošević, Slobodan ··········· 502, 529
Mingst, K. ······················ 212
Missile Technology Control Regime ······· 397
Mitrany, David ··················· 114
Mittal, A. with Mousseau, F. ······· 486
Mitterand, President François ········ 529
Modelski, G. ······················· 8

modernity·················215
see also post-modernism
modernization theory·············8, 548
Moellendorf, Darrel·········30, 203, 204
Mohanty, Chandra·············268
Moldova···············224, 444
money
laundering··········25, 223, 337
lending···········272–3, 275
see also financial flows; global finance
Mongolia·················444
Montenegro···············444
Montevideo Convention on the Rights
and Duties of States·······286–7
Montreal Protocol·······360, 362, 363
Moon, Katharine·············269
moral conflicts·············51
moral duty
in humanitarian
intervention······198, 526–8
in international politics······92–3, 102
poverty alleviation········202–5
Moravcsik, A.···········291–2, 437
Morgenthau, Hans J.
and cold war·············73
and ethics··········195, 199
and globalization············75
interactions of states·········127
and international law·········289
male values·············183
and natural environment·······353
Politics among Nations·········96
and power··········92, 100–1
and realism········93, 95–6, 97–8
on Vietnam War············104
on war·············280
Morocco·············430
Morris, J. with Wheeler, N.J.····532, 533
Morse, E.·············8
Mousseau, F. and Mittal, A.·······486
Mozambique·········59, 64
Muhammad·············40
multiculturalism·······423, 429, 550
Multifiber Arrangement··········247
Multilateral Guarantee Agency
(MIGA)············245
multilateralism
environmental agreements········356
international law··········283
multinational companies see transnational
companies
multipolarity············5, 565
Munich Olympics············375
Muntada al-Ansar al-Islami·······380
Murden, S.·············425
Murdoch, Rupert············465
Murray, Alastair J.H.··········231
Muslim Brotherhood········427–8, 429
see also Islam; Islamic terrorism
Myanmar (Burma)········59, 443, 501

Nagasaki············58, 388
Naim, M.·············20
Nair, S. with Chowdhry, S.·······189
Naisbitt, J.·············452
Namibia·············441
Napoleonic Wars············48
Nardin, Terry·········320–1, 533
Nasar, Mustafa Setmariam········379
Nasdaq (National Association of Securities
Dealers Automated Quotation)····461
Nasser, Gamal Abdel·········62, 428
nation-states
and capitalism············546
and cold war·········410–12
definition········4–5, 404, 405
demise of·············16
formation of······411, 412, 415, 547
and identity·········546, 549–50
legitimacy······168–9, 170–1, 415, 571
loyalty·············334
and nationalism····411, 412, 415, 547
numbers·············404
power·············413
social function············564
and sovereignty············565
and war·········546–7, 549–50
see also state/s
national liberation movements·····337–9
National Rifle Association········340
nationalism·············404–17
Arab···········167, 426
civic··········404, 411
and colonialism·······408, 410
definition·············404
diaspora·············414
ethnic········404, 408, 411, 412–13
and global politics·······412–13
historical evolution·······405–11
in modern world············556
and nation-state formation·····411, 412, 415, 547
and political community····545–7, 556
and religion·········407, 415
and state strengthening······404, 412, 413, 415
and state subversion·····404, 408, 412, 413, 415
typologies·········404, 405
NATO··········61, 77, 233, 527
Able Archer training exercise·····63, 65
importance of············233
and Kosovo·······322, 527, 528, 529, 530, 531, 549
natural law theory·······510, 511, 517
naturalist theories············177
nature conservation········357, 358
Nazism···········57, 67, 409
neo-conservatism············519
neo-liberal institutionalism·····131–3, 137–8, 161, 162, 290

neo-liberalism········121, 125, 131–3
and developing countries········152, 475–6, 477
and globalization········136–7
and neo-realism········115–16
and US foreign policy······138, 152
see also neo-neo debate; Washington
Consensus
neo-medievalism············552
neo-neo debate·······125, 127, 130, 133–5
and anarchy········127, 129, 134
neo-realism········5, 125, 127–31
and constructivism······161, 162
critique of·············151
and globalization········136–8
and neo-liberalism·······115–16
offensive and defensive······126, 130
relative and absolute gains······129
and security·······129–31, 137, 138, 231–2
see also neo-neo debate
neo-realist/neo-liberal debate see neo-neo
debate
neoclassical realism·······95, 99, 231
Nescafé·············458
Nestlé·············343
Netherlands·············447
New International Economic Order
(NIEO)············247
new liberalism·············291–2
New Marxism·············155–6
new medievalism·············9
new world order········115, 563
NGOs
advocacy networks······135, 136, 341
at the UN··········339–40
caucus networks············341
and development········479, 481
environmental········308–9, 355
governance networks·········341
and human security·········502–3
number and range········332, 333
significance of·········332, 344–5
transnational cooperation········340–1
and women··········273–5
Nicaragua·········64, 65, 440
Nice Treaty·············445
Niebuhr, Reinhold············92
Niger··········59, 441, 486
Nigeria··········59, 483, 549
Nike·············422
Nixon, President Richard··········64
Nokia mobile phones············458
Non-Aligned Movement (NAM)····530, 537–8
non-intervention see humanitarian
intervention; intervention
Non-Proliferation Treaty········62–3, 66, 281, 396, 399, 400
Review and Extension
Conferences·········397, 398, 400
non-state actors see transnational actors

normative theory·····························2, 4
norms······································169–70
Norris, R.S. and Kristensen, H. ··········66
North American Free Trade Agreement
    (NAFTA) ·································440
North Korea (DPRK)··············76, 429
    nuclear programme·········80, 394,
    395, 398, 400
North–South dialogue···· 485, 486, 567, 570
Norway····································537
nuclear energy··························396
nuclear proliferation ················**387–401**
    agreements·················66, 399–400
    Anti-Ballistic Missile Treaty (ABM) ·······66,
    391–2, 400
    capabilities and motivations··········393–4
    Comprehensive Test Ban Treaty
        (CTBT)···················396, 397
    conceptual issues··············392–3
    export guidelines··········396, 399
    Fissile Material Cut-off Treaty (FMCT)·· 398
    and global security ···········388–9
    Intermediate Nuclear Forces (INF)
        Treaty·····························66
    Missile Technology Control Regime·····397
    non-proliferation regime·······396–9
    Nuclear Weapons Free Zones
        (NWFZ)··················388, 396
    Partial Test Ban Treaty (PTBT)·······66, 301,
    396
    Proliferation Security Initiative (PSI)·····398
    Strategic Arms Limitation Talks
        (SALT)··············64, 66, 301
    Strategic Arms Reduction
        Treaty (START)········66, 388, 392
    Strategic Defense Initiative (SDI)··········65
    Strategic Offensive Reductions Treaty
        (SORT) ·······················391–2
    treaty obligations···············394–5
    Zangger Committee·········396, 399
    see also Non-Proliferation Treaty
nuclear safety··················68, 388
nuclear suppliers ···················396
nuclear weapons
    1945 Japanese bombings······58, 388, 390
    in cold war ········ 56, 62–3, 65–6, 67–8, 73
    defence systems···············391–2
    destructive effects of···········68, 388, 390
    as deterrent··················68, 388
    diffusion of nuclear technology···········391
    Hague Code of Conduct ············397
    India ···········391, 396, 398, 400
    and military governments············389
    non-use·······················392–3
    North Korea ···········80, 394, 395, 398, 400
    Pakistan···················391, 398
    Soviet Union ··············391, 399
    states with capability ··············391
    technology···················389–90
    and terrorism···············393–4

Nussbaum, Martha·················195
Nye, Joseph with
    Keohane, R. ········9, 23, 115, 132
    O'Brien, R. ·······················570
    offshore finance ··········462–3, 463,
    464, 465
Ogilvie-White, T. ···················392
    and Simpson, J. ·················389
Ohmae, Kenichi ···············16, 253
Olson, J.S. ·························501
Olson, M. ··························304
O'Neill, R. with Baylis, J. ···········398
Onwudiwe, I.D. ····················377
order
    economic order ···············566
    international order···········562, 563, 571–3
    New International Economic Order
        (NIEO) ·······················247
    realist approach ·················563
    typology ······················563–4
    world order ···········9, 114, 552, 563
Organization of African Unity
    (OAU) ·····················345, 442
Organization of American States (OAS) ··· 438
Organization for Economic Co-operation and
    Development (OECD) ········336, 452
Organization of Petroleum Exporting
    Countries (OPEC) ·················375
Organization for Security and Co-operation
    in Europe (OSCE)···············233
orientalism ·····················188, 189
Ottawa Convention on Landmines ··········287
Ottoman Empire······ 40, 43, 44, 426, 512, 545
Ougaard, M. ·························25
outsourcing ·····················19, 272
Owens, P. ··························181
    with Jackson, R.H.···············49–50
Oxfam······················474, 486
ozone layer·········359–60, 360, 362, 363
Pakistan·············59, 444, 483,
    484, 547
    and India·····················219, 527
    and Islam·····················410, 429
    nuclear weapons··········391, 398, 400
Palestine················316, 338, 427, 519
Palestine Liberation Organization ···········338
Palme Commission ··········230, 493
Panofsky, W.K.H.···················390
Pape, R. ··························378
Paraguay ···························440
Parekh, Bhikhu················420, 527
Pareto optimal outcomes·········304, 306–7
Pareto, Vilfredo ·····················304
Paris Peace Conference (1919) ··········57, 58
Paris, Roland ······················494
Paris Treaties
    1814 ··························282
    1951 ··························445
Parpart, J. with Zalewski, M.···········181
Partial Test Ban Treaty (PTBT) ······66, 301, 396

peace
    democratic peace theory ···········112–13,
    118, 233
    liberal peace theory·················9–10
    role of women in ·················500
    and UN···········315, 319–21, 324,
    500, 502, 537
Pearson, R. ·························472
Pelosi, Nancy ·······················270
Pendergrast, M. ····················458
Perraton, J. with Held, D. ···········546
Persaud, R.B. ·······················189
Persian Empire ·····················545
Peru ·····························537
pesticides ·························355
Peters, J.S. and Wolper, A.···········516
Peterson, V. Spike ···············184, 266
Pettman, J.J.·······················268
Petzold-Bradley, E., Carius, A.,
    and Vincze, A.·····················499
Philippines···········254, 429, 442, 501
Pinochet, Augusto ···················287
pluralism ············195, 200–1, 205, 527–8
    see also liberalism
Pogge, Thomas··········195, 204, 515–16, 555
political community ·················**543–58**
    and citizenship··················547–8
    communitarianism ··············554
    and cosmopolitanism ··········550–1, 555
    and feminism ···················550
    and liberal democracy ············544
    and nationalism ···········545–7, 556
    and neo-medievalism ·············552
    and post-structuralism··········554–5
    and realism ····················553–4
political rights··················547–8
politicide ·························496
pollution
    air··············352, 354, 356, 501
    emissions trading ·········362, 364
    marine ············353, 354, 358, 359
    toxic waste ············128–9, 302, 356
population·········267, 325, 345, 482–4, 498
PortalPlayer··························19
Porter, B.D. ·······················215
Portugal·························59, 64
positivism ·························178
post-cold war era
    expectations······················72
    and globalization···········74–5, 567–8
    links with cold war era ·······562–3, 566–7
    and Russia ···················78–9, 565
    security threats ·········212, 213, 239
    see also United States; hegemony
post-colonial feminism··········182, 184, 267–8
post-colonialism ················187–9, 188–9,
    286, 411, 548
post-modern feminism ·········183, 267, 268
post-modernism ···········**185–7**, 215, 236
post-modernity ·····················215

post-structuralism········554–5
poverty
    alleviation as moral duty········202–5
    conceptions of········471–3
    eradication········50, 355
    and women········271, 472
    see also inequality
power
    and communication skills········342–3
    balance of *see* balance of power
    definition········101–2
    IEMP model········180
    and knowledge········185, 187, 554
    and neo-realism········128
    power politics········234
    and realism········93, 98–9
    and rights········511
Prahalad, C.K.········75
Prebisch, Raul········147
Price, R.········284, 287
    and Tannenwald, N.········392
primary education········146, 478
print capitalism········546
Prisoners' Dilemma game theory········303–5
problem-solving theories········151, 235
Proliferation Security Initiative (PSI)········398
prostitution········269
protectionism········455, 458
protests
    anti-globalization········17, 137, 256–7, 258, 479, 569
    Iraq War········17, 256
Prügl, Elisabeth········267, 273
public policy networks········26
Pugh, M.········319
Purvis, Nigel········292
Putin, Vladimir········79
Al Qaeda
    decentralization········380–1
    and globalization········2, 338, 380, 549
    goals········104, 202, 338
    networks········429
    origins········428
    weapons of mass destruction········382
Al Qaeda Associated Movement (AQAM)··376
Qutb, Sayyid········427, 428
Qutbist Muslim Brotherhood········429
    Rabasa, A. with Chalk, P.········377
    race········188–9, 485
racism········508
Rafsanjani, Hashemi········430
Rainforest Action Network········26
raison d'état········92–3
Ramsey, P.········526
Randers, J. with Meadows, D.H.········483
rape, in war········268, 289, 500
Rapley, J.········474
rational choice········162, 163, 167, 250
Ratner, S.R. with Helman, G.B.········549
Rawls, John, *The Law of Peoples*·····200, 203–4

Ray, D.B. with Jolly, R.········493
Reagan, President Ronald········64, 65, 66, 73
realism········4–5, **91–106**
    and anarchy········93
    and balance of power········94
    classical········95–8
    critique of········155
    and end of cold war········73, 94–5
    and ethics········92, 195, 199–200, 205, 231
    and globalization········7, 544, 545
    and humanitarian intervention········527
    and idealism········92
    and international law········289–90, 293
    international political economy···257, 258
    modern········95
    moral standards········92–3, 102
    neo-realism *see* neo-realism
    neoclassical········95, 99, 231
    and political community········553–4
    and power········93, 98–9
    and regime formation········298–9, 305–8
    and security········236
    self-help principle········93, 102–3
    and sovereignty········5, 7
    and statism········93, 100–1, 103, 527
    structural *see* structural realism
    survival principle········101–2, 103
    and war········94, 103–4
realpolitik········234
recessions········458
Redclift, Michael········485
refugees········83, 164, 268, 277, 496, 500
regimes········**297–310**
    classification········300–2
    collaboration········303–5
    communication regimes·····298, 302, 307
    coordination········306–7
    dead-letter········301
    definition········300
    economic········302, 452–3, 566
    environmental········301–2, 359, 365, 366
    formation of········298, 299, 303–7
    full-blown········301
    and liberal institutionalism········298–9, 302–5, 307–8
    and realism········298–9, 305–8
    security········301
    shadow of the future········305, 308
    tacit········301
    US support for········299, 302, 363, 364
regional integration········436–8
regionalism········20, **435–49**
    in Africa········439, 441–2
    in the Americas········438–41
    in Asia········439, 442–3
    in Eurasia and post-Soviet states········439, 443–4
    and globalization········447, 566
Rehn, E. and Sirleaf, E.········500
Reisman, Michael········525

Reiss, M.B. with Campbell, K.M.········393
religion
    and culture········420
    fundamentalism········424, 431, 550
    and international relations········565
    and nationalism········407, 415
    religious communities········544
    revivalism········424
    and values········423–4
Responsibility to Protect········170, 197, 322, 338, 524, 535–8
retail chains········458
Reus-Smit, C.········281, 284, 286, 291–2
revolution in military affairs (RMA)····217–19
Rhodes, E.········117
Rice, Condoleezza········265
rice market········486
Rice, S.········498, 499
Richardson, J.L.········116
rights········**510–13**, 517, 547–8, 550, 556–7
    see also human rights
Rio Summit *see* Earth Summit
risk culture········10
Rittberger, V.········298
Roberts, Adam········114, 398, 538
    and Kingsbury, B.········114
Roberts, Glyn········473, 478
Robinson, W.I.········151–2
Roche, D.········493
Rodley, N. with Franck, T.········527
Rodrik, Dani········136, 255
rogue states········76
Roman Empire········40, 42, 545
Rome Treaties (1957)········445
Roosevelt, President Franklin D.········58
Rorty, Richard········518, 551
Rosamond, B.········445
Rose, Gideon········99
Rosenau, J.N.········16, 18
Rosenberg, Justin········155–6
Rostow, Walt········8–9
Roth, Kenneth········533–4
Rotterdam Convention on Hazardous Chemicals and Pesticides········354
Rousseau, Jean-Jacques·····92, 103, 230, 545
Royal Society for the Protection of Birds··355
Ruggie, J.G.········162, 166, 283
Runyan, Anne Sisson········266
Ruppel, R.J. with Holden, P.········188
Rupert, Mark········151
    with Solomon, M.S.········151
Rush-Bagot agreement········301
Russett, Bruce········9, 233
Russia
    and arms control········392
    and Chechnya········79, 503
    and climate change········363
    and Eastern Europe········79
    economic reform········79
    financial crisis········459

Russia—*Cont.*
and humanitarian intervention··· 530, 537
and Iraq War················· 323
and Kosovo················· 535
in post-cold war era ············ 78–9, 565
and regional integration ·········· 443, 444
and Sudan················· 534
Rwanda·················· 59, 571
conflict··········· 220, 238, 500, 528, 529, 530, 537
international criminal tribunal ···· 287, 289

Sabah·················· 442
Sachs, Jeffrey D.············· 82
Sadat, Anwar··············· 167
Sagan, Scott D.············· 388–9
Sageman, M.·············· 377
Sahnoun, M. with Evans, M.······· 535
Said, Edward·············· 188, 189
sanctions········· 114, 115, 315, 335, 394, 395
Sao Tome··············· 59, 64
Sargent, L.··············· 182
SARS (Severe Acute Respiratory Syndrome)············ 501
satellite surveillance··········· 305–6
Saudi Arabia··· 2, 363, 424, 428, 513–14
Save the Children············ 503
Schelling, T.C.············· 306
Schengen Agreement·········· 381
Scholte, Jan Aart·········· 16, 17, 119
Schumacher, E.F.············ 472
Schwarz, A.··············· 501
Schweller, Randall··········· 99, 231
scientific information········ 358, 365, 366
Scruton, Roger············· 430
Second World War
bombings········· 202, 220, 388, 390
casualties··········· 28, 58, 497
causes············· 57, 409, 527
consequences············· 56
extermination camps·········· 513
and nationalism············ 408
securities markets······· 460–1, 463, 465
security·············· **227–41**
collective·········· 47, 111, 114, 115
critical security studies········· 154, 235
definition··············· 229–30
and environment··········· 365–6
European Union············· 78
and feminism········· 235–6, 270
and globalization········ 132, 236–9
and liberal institutionalism······· 232–4
national·················· 230–1
and neo-realism····· 129–31, 137, 138, 231–2
post-cold war threats ········· 212, 213, 219
post-modernism············· 236
and realism··············· 236
security dilemma············ 102
and social constructivism········· 234–5

security—*Cont.*
US policy················ 565
see also human security
Seidler, V.··············· 181
self-determination ········· 23, 222, 287, 408
Self-Employed Women's Association·········· 274–5
self-governance *see* autonomy
self-help·············· 93, 102–3
Sen, Amartya········ 484, 495, 515
Senegal·············· 59, 441
separation of powers·········· 285
separatist movements ········· 414
September 11 terrorist attacks
consequences······ 83–4, 85, 429, 509, 519
coordination··········· 12, 380
and global security·········· 240
and globalization········· 2, 12, 20
and masculinity············ 269
motives·················· 2
realist view············· 104–5
Serbia··············· 217, 444
7-Eleven··············· 458
sex discrimination············ 516
see also gender; women
Shaker, M.I.·············· 396
Shanghai Cooperation Organization (SCO)·········· 444
sharia··············· 427, 428
Shaw, Martin········· 179, 221, 564, 568
shopping malls············· 422
Shue, Henry··············· 515
Sidgwick, Henry············· 551
Sierra Club··············· 355
Sierra Leone ········ 59, 220, 222, 321, 442
Sikhism·················· 420
Sikkink, K.
with Finnemore, M.······· 167, 170
with Keck, M.············· 135
Simes, Dimitri K.············ 85
Simpson, J. with Ogilvie-White, T. ····· 389
Singapore········· 424, 442, 501
Singer, Peter·········· 214, 551
with Gregg, T.··········· 198, 203
Single European Act··········· 445
Sirleaf, E. with Rehn, E.········· 500
Skocpol, Theda············· 179
Slaughter, Anne-Marie·········· 291–2
with Feinstein, L.·········· 389
with Mattli, W.············ 291
slavery·············· 304, 322, 512
Small, M. with Singer, P.········· 214
Smith, K.E. and Light, M.········· 514
Smith, Adam··············· 551
Smith, Anthony············· 405
Smith, Dennis··············· 179
Smith, M.········ 95, 100, 102, 104, 397
Smith, S.··············· 236
with Hollis, M.············ 177
Snyder, Jack··············· 130

social constructivism *see* constructivism
social facts·············· 163
social movements ········ 273–5, 479, 570
social property relations ········· 156
social relations·············· 155
social security············· 484–5
Solomon, M.S. with Rupert, M.······· 151
Somalia·················· 571
civil war············· 237, 319
and UN ······· 321, 323, 324, 531
and US······· 76, 528–9, 531
Sony·················· 422
Sorel, Albert·············· 46
South Africa········· 59, 345, 394, 400, 513
South Korea
Asian financial crisis········ 254, 255
humanitarian intervention········ 537
international institutions········· 248
KAL 007 airliner·········· 65, 298
and women············ 269, 272
South-East Asia····· 80–1, 442–3, 476, 477, 498–9, 501
sovereignty
and decolonization··········· 48
and financial flows········· 335, 465
and human rights··········· 538
and intervention····· 237, 322–3, 524, 525, 530
and liberalism············· 5
and Marxism··············· 6
and nation-states··········· 565
organized hypocrisy·········· 46
and post-modernism·········· 185
and realism·············· 5, 7
and standards of civilization········· 512
of states·········· 24, 28, 322
and TNCs·············· 335–6
see also self-determination; Westphalian system
Soviet Union
and Afghanistan············· 64
and China··············· 63
collapse of········ 48, 65, 144, 412
and human rights············ 514
and Hungary··············· 62
Korean airliner affair········ 65, 298
and Marxism··············· 144
nuclear weapons········ 391, 399
and Third World········· 410–11, 475
Universal Declaration of Human Rights············· 513
weakness·············· 568, 569
see also cold war; post-cold war era; Russia
space·················· 358
Spain················ 373, 380
Spivak, Gayatri········· 184, 188
sports stadiums············· 422
Sri Lanka············· 59, 499, 500
Stanlis, P.J.··············· 46

state/s
  ambiguity of meaning················333
  autonomy ·················23–4, 28
  and civil society·······················333
  collaboration·······················303–4
  core (industrialized)··················249
  failed········238, 239, 412, 501, 549, 571
  financial influence··············335, 465
  fragmentation of·······················237
  and globalization··················571–3
  historical sociological view··········179–80
  and international law·········286–7, 288
  origins······················215
  periphery (developing)··················249
  as provider of security·········494, 553–4
  quasi-states·················549, 571
  rights and duties of················286–7
  survival·················101–2, 103
  territorial·················546
  three tiers·················223
  tyrannical·················524
  weak/strong·················255
  see also nation-states; sovereignty
statism·················93, 100–1, 103, 527
  Rwanda and Darfur···········534, 536
Steans, Jill·················181, 236
Stein, A.·················308
Stiglitz, Joseph·················254
stock exchanges·················461
Strange, Susan·················75
Strategic Arms Limitation Talks
  (SALT)·················64, 66, 301
Strategic Arms Reduction Treaty
  (START)·················66, 388, 392
Strategic Defense Initiative
  (SDI)·················65
Strategic Offensive Reductions Treaty
  (SORT)·················391–2
structural realism·················90–100, 95, 96,
  127, 131, 231
structuralism·················5
  see also Marxism
Stubbs, R.·················240
sub-Saharan Africa···········472, 476, 477, 487
subaltern peoples·················188
Sudan·················442, 534
  see also Darfur conflict
Suez crisis·················319
Suganami, H.·················113
Suhrke, A.·················503
al-Suri, Abu Musab·················379
sustainable development·················325, 354,
  355, 358, 366, 480
Sutton, B.A. with Zacher, M.W.··············302
Swaziland·················441
Sweden·················537
SWIFT (Society for Worldwide
  Interbank Financial
  Telecommunications)·················460
sympathy·················551

Taiwan·················19, 80, 272
Tajikistan·················443, 444, 531
Taliban·················104, 429
Tang, J.H.·················518
Tanganyika·················59, 441
Tannenwald, Nina·················393
  with Price, R.·················392
Tanzania·················76, 146, 441, 527, 537
Tata·················335
Taylor, A.J.P.·················57
Taylor, Charles·················502
technics·················22
technology
  military·················213, 217–18, 219
  nuclear weapons·················389–90
  technological change·················22
  technological revolution·················252–3
  and terrorism····372, 374, 378–81, 383–4
  see also communication
Terriff, T.·················236
territoriality·················18–19, 23–4, 28, 45, 252–3,
  464–5
terrorism·················337–9, **371–85**
  counter-terrorism·················382–4
  definition·················372, 374
  Islamic see Islamic terrorism
  legitimacy of·················373, 374, 384
  Marxist-Leninist·················375
  and the media·················2, 12, 374–5, 380
  mobility·················374, 381
  motives·················373, 376–7
  'new'·················377
  and nuclear weapons·················393–4
  and religion·················377–8, 384
  and religious fundamentalism·················426
  suicide attacks·················17, 373, 375, 380,
    384, 424, 428
  and technological advances·················372, 374,
    378–81, 383–4
  threshold of violence·················375
  transnational terrorism·················374–5
  and weapons of mass
    destruction·················375, 382
  see also Al Qaeda; September 11 terrorist
    attacks
Teschke, Benno·················156
Tesón, Fernando·················526, 533
textile industry·················271–2
textual strategies·················186
Thailand·················254, 255, 272, 442, 501
Thatcher, Margaret·················66, 233, 265
Third World·················64, 82, 152, 305, 307
  superpower involvement·················410–11, 475
  see also debt; developing countries
Third World Action Group (AgDW)·················343
Thirty Years War·················46, 215
Thomas, C.·················472, 474, 479
Thomas Cook·················458
Thompson, Grahame
  with Hirst, P.·················10–11, 20, 21, 454

Thorsson, Inga·················493
Thucydides·················41, 92, 93, 96–8, 214
Tickner, J. Ann·················183, 235, 269
Tilly, Charles·················179, 215, 405, 546
Tlatelolco Treaty·················396
Tobias, S. with Elshtain, J.B.·················182
Toffler, A. and Toffler, H.·················219
Togo·················441
Torrey Canyon·················355
torture 508, 509, 514, 515, 553
totalitarianism·················544
Tow, W.T. with Trood, R.·················494
toxic waste·················128–9, 302, 356
Toys 'Я' Us·················458
trade see global trade
transnational actors·················287, 332, 333, 343–5
  see also civil society; NGOs
transnational companies (TNCs)·················**334–7**
  definition·················10, 334
  and developing countries·················335
  economic importance·················16–17, 335–6
  numbers·················332, 334–5, 455
  regulation·················335–7
transnational organizations·················25–6
transnational social movements·················136
transnationalism·················114–15
Trenin, Dmitri·················79
Tronto, Jean·················551
Trood, R. with Tow, W.T.·················494
Trotsky, Leon·················212
True, J.·················274
Truman doctrine·················61
Truman, President Harry S.·················58
Tsouli, Younis·················379
tsunami (2004)·················499, 501
tuberculosis·················478, 499
Tucker, R.W.·················305
Tupac Amaru Revolutionary Movement·················379
Turkey·················78, 248, 426, 444
Turner, Bryan·················552
Uganda·················59, 238, 527
Ukraine·················444
Unger, Peter·················203
unipolarity·················50, 85, 565
United Kingdom
  Clean Air Act·················354
  Department for International
    Development·················498
  and human rights·················514
  and humanitarian intervention·················537
  and Iraq War·················323
  London bombings·················380
  nuclear weapons·················391, 399
United Nations (UN)·················**313–28**
  Atomic Energy Commission·················396, 399
  Charter·················24, 119, 282, 288, 314, 315
    and human rights·················513, 524–5
  Children's Fund (UNICEF)·················502
  Commission on Human
    Security·················493, 494

United Nations (UN)—*Cont.*
 Commission on Population and
  Development·······················345
 Commission on Sustainable
  Development·············· 325, 345, 355
 Committee Against Apartheid···········345
 Conference on Environment and
  Development (UNCED) (Earth
  Summit)········ 325, 354–5, 357–8, 480
 Conference on the Human Environment
  (UNCHE)·····················353, 354
 Conference on Trade and Development
  (UNCTAD)·········· 335, 452, 476, 477
 Decade for Women·····················274
 Department for Political Affairs·········537
 Development Fund for Women
  (UNIFEM)·····························502
 Development Programme (UNDP)····· 146,
  345, 472, 476, 480, 493, 502
  *Human Development
  Report*························492, 503
 Economic and Social Council
  (ECOSOC)······· 318, 324, 326–7, 340
 Environment Programme (UNEP)······· 345,
  353, 354, 356
 Framework Convention on Climate
  Change (UNFCCC)······· 299, 325, 354,
  362–4
 Functional Commissions··········316, 326–7
 General Assembly················247, 316, 317
 Global Conferences····················325
 and government status··········320, 327
 and Gulf War·····················115, 342
 High Commissioner for Refugees
  (UNHCR)·······················164, 502
 High Level Panel on Threats, Challenges
  and Change·····················502, 537
 history···························314–15
 human rights *see* human rights
 Human Rights Council···········345
 humanitarian intervention *see*
  humanitarian intervention
 International Conference on the
  Relationship between Disarmament
  and Development·······················493
 International Court of Justice···········318
 and Iraq (Special Committee
  (UNSCOM))····················394, 400
 and Iraq War··········· 285, 322–3, 324, 327
 membership·····························404
 Millennium Summit····················325
 Monterrey Conference on Financing for
  Development·····························480
 and NGOs·······················339–40
 Peacebuilding Commission··········321, 502
 peacekeeping activities··········315,
  319–21, 324, 500, 502, 537
 Population Fund·····················345
 Programmes and Funds··········316, 318
 reforms···························326–7

United Nations (UN)—*Cont.*
 relevance and effectiveness···············314
 Responsibility to Protect···········535–8
 Secretariat····················316, 317
 Secretary-General·············317–18
 Security Council········ 119, 315, 316,
  317, 319, 327
 in Somalia (UNOSOM II)···········531
 Special Session on Disarmament····396–7
 Specialised Agencies······· 314, 316, 502
 Trusteeship Council····················318
 World Summit (2005)··········535, 537–8
United States
 and Afghanistan·················269, 323
 and Bretton Woods system·········245, 246
 and China····················63, 509
 and climate change···· 299, 362, 363, 364
 and cold war *see* cold war
 and developing country TNCs·········335
 First World War····················56–7
 foreign policy········· 84, 104, 116–18, 138,
  199–200
 fundamental extremism··········424
 Guantanamo Bay·············383, 509
 hegemony····50, 75–6, 152, 299, 305, 565
  declining··········86, 149, 245
 and humanitarian
  intervention···············531–2, 537
 and India·······················397
 and Iraq War *see* Iraq War
 military superiority··········217–18, 219
 nuclear weapons·················391–2
 and regime support···· 299, 302, 363, 364
 and regional integration·········438, 440
 revivalist Christians···········424
 and Saudi Arabia·············428
 security policy·················565
 and Somalia·········76, 528–9, 531
 and Sudan·······················534
 and Third World··········410–11, 475
 USS Cole bombing···········76
 Vietnam War···········60, 104, 501
 whaling·······················308–9
 World Trade Center bombing
  (1993)·······················76, 394
 see also September 11 terrorist attacks
University of British Columbia, Human
  Security Center·········· 495, 497, 498
Upper Volta·······················59
Uppsala Conflict Data Project··········497
Uruguay·······················440
Uruguay Round·······················455
USSR (Union of Soviet Socialist Republics)
  see Soviet Union
Utrecht, Treaties of············· 40, 46, 282
Uzbekistan·······················444, 553
Uzbeks, and Al Qaeda··········429
 Van Ham, P. with Bosch, O.··········391
 Van Rooy, A.·······················570
Varshney, A. with Humphreys, M.···········498

Vattel, Emerich de··········45, 282, 545
Vedrine, Hubert·······················75
Venezuela·············· 136, 248, 441
Versailles Treaty·······················57, 282
videos·······················380
Vienna Convention for the Protection of the
  Ozone Layer·········· 360, 362, 363
Vienna Declaration on Human
  Rights (1993)·····················517
Vietnam·············· 443, 501, 527
Vietnam War···········60, 104, 501
Vincent, R.J.·······················200
Vincze, A. with Petzold-Bradley, E.··········499
Vines, David with Gilbert, C.··········254
violence·····················27–8, 214, 375
virtual community·····················544
Vitalis, R.·······················189
Vitoria, Francisco de·······················45
Von Martens, G.F.·······················283
 Walker, R.B.J.·········· 187, 554
 Waller, M. and Linklater, A.··········550
Wallerstein, Immanuel·········· 147–9, 179
Walt, Stephen·····················99, 104
 with Meersheimer, J.·········· 104, 130
Waltz, Kenneth
 and 9/11·······················104
 causes of conflict··········111, 228
 and globalization·······················75
 interdependence·····················115
 international system·····················179
 metaphor of the stag··········103
 and neo-realism·········· 126, 127, 131, 136
 and nuclear weapons··········388
 and power·········· 38, 98–9, 101, 128
 and self-help·····················102
 Theory of International Politics·······95, 115
Walzer, Michael·········· 195, 201, 320–1,
  518, 545, 554
war on terror
 and gender·····················269–70
 and human rights·········· 383, 509, 519
 and humanitarian intervention·······531–4
 and Iraq·······················104
 nature of·····················223, 376
 origins·······················83–5
 trial of Saddam Hussein··········503
 use of torture·····················509, 553
War on Want·······················343
wars·······················**211–25**
 agent of historical change··········216
 asymmetric conflicts··········217–18
 battlespace·······················213
 casualties···········212, 220, 224, 268,
  496, 497
 causes·········· 110–11, 228
 children in············ 222, 235, 268, 497–8
 combatants·······················222
 definition·····················213–14
 and disease·······················498
 effects of·······················498

wars—*Cont.*

Geneva Conventions·············40, 202, 205, 287, 289, 512

globalization of·······················27–8

Hague Convention·······················512

hyberbolic wars·························221

improbability of, in Europe···········553

information·····························219

inter-state wars *see* civil war

intra-state war·············94, 238, 497

laws of·····························288–9

   see also just war tradition

and the media·················215, 220

nature and character of···········213–16

new wars·····················221–4, 237

non-combatants·················289, 497

obsolescence·························212

outsourcing·························220

post-cold war···············212, 213

post-modern war·········219–21, 222

Privatized Military Firms
   (PMFs)·························220

protection myth···········268–9, 270

rape in war···········268, 289, 500

and realism·····················103–4

revolution in military affairs
   (RMA)·························217–19

total war·············56–7, 67, 220–1

trends·············212, 496–7, 498

virtual war·················220, 221

war criminals·········287, 289, 338, 502

   see also International Criminal Court

women in·········165, 166, 222, 235, 268–9, 270, 500

see also individual wars

Washington Consensus·········136, 152, 248, 470, 475

water resources·················146, 498–9

Waterloo·····························40

wealth distribution·················202–3

   see also inequality

weapons

biological···········66, 375, 382, 390

chemical···········66, 289, 382, 390

chemical, biological, radiological and
   nuclear (CBRN)·················390

weapons of mass destruction
   (WMD)·········68, 83, 375, 382, 390

see also military technology; nuclear
   weapons

Weather Underground···········378, 382

Weber, Cynthia·······················185

Weber, H.·····························472

Weber, Max···········100, 164, 166, 546

Weismann, D.·························482

Weiss, Thomas···········528, 531, 568

welfare rights·························548

Wendt, Alexander·········6, 113, 162, 164, 165, 185–6, 258

Wessel, I. and Wimhofer, G.···········501

West Africa·····························441

Western European Union (WEU)···········233

Westphalia Treaties···········156, 282

Westphalian system·········23–4, 47, 119, 218, 222–3, 569

whaling···················308–9, 353

Wheeler, N.J.·················290, 532

and Booth, K.·················102, 229

and Dunne, T.·················50, 535

and Morris, J.·················532, 533

Whitworth, Sandra·················267

WHO *see* World Health Organization

Wiener, A.

and Diez, T.·····················445

with Jørgensen, K.E.
   and Christensen, T.·············446

Wight, Martin·························43

Wilkinson, P.·························394

Williams, Michael C.·········73, 154, 187, 235

with Krause, K.·················154, 392

Wilson, President Woodrow·········47, 111

Fourteen Points·········57, 113–14, 408

Wimhofer, G. with Wessel, I.···········501

Wippman, D.·························290

Wohlforth, William·················231

Wolfensohn, James·················472

Wolfers, Arnold·················98, 229

Wolper, A. with Peters, J.S.···········516

women

Beijing conference···········274, 325, 481

CEDAW Convention···········274, 508, 516

childbirth·························146

double burden·················272, 273

and education·····················478

employment···········271–2, 274, 275, 478

genital mutilation·················518

and health·························478

as housewives·····················271

and Islam···········424, 517, 550

leaders·················266, 270

and microcredit···········272–3, 275

military prostitution·················269

and peacekeeping·················500

in politics···········266, 270, 478

and poverty···········271, 472

refugees·················277, 500

and social movements···········273–5

socio-economic status···········271–3

third world·····················268

and United Nations···········274, 502

in war·········165, 166, 222, 235, 268–9, 270, 500

wearing of the veil···········424, 517, 550

Woods, N. with Hurrell, A.···········118

Woolf, Leonard·····················113

World Bank

establishment of·················481

and gender·················480, 481

and poverty···········146, 472, 481

protests against·················258, 479

structural adjustment advice·········475

World Development Indicators·········470

World Bank Group·················316, 452

World Commission on Environment and
   Development
   (Brundtland)···········354, 355, 493

World Conservation Union·················345

world economy·················75, 157

World Health Organization
   (WHO)···········343, 499, 502

World Meteorological Organization
   (WMO)·························358

world order···········9, 114, 552, 563

world politics·········3, 6–8, 9, 176, 178

see also global governance

World Trade Organization
   (WTO)·········246, 248, 280, 357, 452

Doha Round·····················205

protests against·········256, 258, 479

World Wildlife Fund (WWF)···········345, 355

world-economy·····················147–8

world-system theory···········5, 147–9

see also Marxism

Wright, Andrew·····················552

Wright, Quincy···········213, 214, 215–16

Wright, R.·····························377

WTO *see* World Trade Organization

Wyn Jones, Richard·················154

Yeltsin, Boris·························79

Yemen·····························237

Young, I.M.·························550

Young, O.R. with Levy, M.A.·········298, 300

Yugoslavia·························61, 77

international criminal
   tribunal···········287, 289

nationalism·····················549

war·················220, 319

Yumus, Muhammad·················272–3

Zacher, M.W. with Sutton, B.A.·········302

Zaïre·························59, 571

Zakaria, Fareed···········96, 99, 231

Zalewski, M.·················181, 182

with Parpart, J.·················181

Zambia·····························146

Zangger Committee···········396, 399

al-Zarqawi, Abu Musab·················376

al-Zawahiri, Ayman·················377

Zevin, R.·····························454

Zimbabwe·················59, 571

Zurn, M.·····························570

with Levy, M.A.·················298, 300